OPERATIONS MANAGEMENT

OPERATIONS MANAGEMENT

SOUTHERN AFRICA EDITION

MIKE PYCRAFT

HEMMANTH SINGH

KHOMOTSO PHIHLELA

NIGEL SLACK

STUART CHAMBERS

CHRISTINE HARLAND

ALAN HARRISON

ROBERT JOHNSTON

London · Hong Kong · Johannesburg · Melbourne · Singapore · Washington DC

PITMAN PUBLISHING
128 Long Acre, London WC2E 9AN
Tel: +44(0)171 447 2000
Fax: +44(0)171 240 5771

A Division of Pearson Professional Limited

First published in Great Britain in 1995
Southern Africa edition published in 1997

© Mike Pycraft, Hemmanth Singh, Khomotso Phihlela,
Nigel Slack, Stuart Chambers, Christine Harland,
Alan Harrison, Robert Johnston 1997

ISBN 0 273 62676 0

British Library Cataloguing in Publication Data
A CIP catalogue record for this book can be obtained from the British Library

1 3 5 7 9 10 8 6 4 2

Typeset by Pantek Arts, Maidstone, Kent.
Printed and bound in South Africa.

The Publishers' policy is to use paper manufactured from sustainable forests.

CONTENTS

About the authors   viii
Foreword   xi
Preface   xiii
Acknowledgements   xvi
How to use this book   xvii
Plan of the book   xviii

PART ONE
INTRODUCTION

1 Operations management   30
Effective operations management •
Operations in the organization • The
transformation model • Types of operations •
The activities of operations management •
The model of operations management •
Personal profile: Alan Phillips, Colgate
Palmolive • Case exercise: A business trip to
Brussels

**2 The strategic role and objectives
   of operations**   41
The role of the operations function •
Judging the operation's contribution •
The five performance objectives • Personal
profile: Tony Gainsford, Molex SA • Case
exercise: Operations objectives at the
Penang Mutiara

3 Operations strategy   70
What is strategy? • Operations strategy •
The content and process of operations
strategy • Priority of performance
objectives • Operations strategy decision
areas • Personal profile: Mary Reeks,
GM Aerotek • Case exercise: Birmingham
Amusement Machines

PART TWO
DESIGN

4 Design in operations management   105
What is design? • Simulation in design •
The four Cs of design • Environmentally
sensitive design • The volume–variety effect
on design • Process types in manufacturing
and services • Design – the structure of Part
Two • Personal profile: Raj Siriram, Electric
Motor Component Manufacturing • Case
exercise: OKP (Pty) Ltd

**5 The design of products and
   services**   138
The competitive advantage of good
design • What is designed in a product or
service? • The stages of design – from
concept to specification • Concept
generation • Concept screening •
Preliminary design • Design evaluation
and improvement • Prototyping and final
design • The benefits of interactive design •
Personal profile: Debbie Lundberg,
Design Executive • Case exercise: The
Royal Mint

6 Design of the operations network   176
The network perspective • The vertical
integration of capacity • The location of
capacity • Long-term capacity management•
Personal profile: Colin Carmichael, Pleasure
Foods • Case exercise: Delta Synthetic Fibres

7 Layout and flow   213
The layout procedure • The basic layout
types • Detailed design of the layout •
Personal profile: Bob Malcomess, Green
Valley • Case exercise: Weldon Hand Tools

8 Process technology 260
What is process technology? • Materials processing technology • Information processing technology • Customer processing technology • The dimensions of technology • Personal profile: Mark Kneen, Consol Glass • Case exercise: Rochem Ltd

9 Job design and work organization 303
The design of jobs • Division of labour • Scientific management • Ergonomics • Behavioural approaches to job design • Empowerment • Control versus commitment • Personal profile: Neil Cumming, Nampak Polyfoil • Case exercise: Secret plans at Penn Savings Bank

**PART THREE
PLANNING AND CONTROL**

10 The nature of planning and control 342
What is planning and control? • Nature of demand and supply • The planning and control task • The volume–variety effect on planning and control • Personal profile: Paola Petré, Brussels Airport Terminal Company SA • Case exercise: Rosslyn Safaris – service with a difference

11 Capacity planning and control 376
What is capacity? • Planning and controlling capacity • Measuring demand and capacity • The alternative capacity plans • Choosing a capacity planning and control approach • Personal profile: Chief Inspector Brian Paddick, London Metropolitan Police • Case exercise: Fine Country Fruit Cakes

12 Inventory planning and control 418
What is inventory? • The volume decision – how much to order • The timing decision – when to place an order • Inventory analysis and control systems • Personal profile: Gerrit Kruger,
ADTrans • Case exercise: Plastix (Pty) Ltd

13 Supply chain planning and control 457
What is supply chain planning and control? • Purchasing and supplier development • Physical distribution management • Integrated concepts • Types of relationships in supply chains • Personal profile: Julia Dawson, Rover Group. • Case exercise: Laura Ashley's strategic alliance with Federal Express

14 MRP 494
What is MRP? • What is required to run MRP I? • MRP calculations • Optimized production technology (OPT) • Personal profile: Andreas Tabane, Mokoena Lighting (Pty) Ltd • Case exercise: Psycho Sports Ltd

15 Just-in-time planning and control 528
What is just-in-time? • The philosophy of just-in-time • JIT techniques • Just-in-time planning and control • JIT in service operations • JIT and MRP • Personal profile: Graham Kirkland, Suncorp • Case exercise: Just-in-time at Jimmy's

16 Project planning and control 566
What is a project? • Successful project management • The project planning and control process • Network planning • Personal profile: Gerry Moolman, Sentech (Pty) Ltd • Case exercise: Bushveld Television

17 Quality planning and control 611
What is quality and why is it so important? • Conformance to specification • Statistical process control (SPC) • Acceptance sampling • Personal profile: Zak Limbada, Pretoria Portland Cement Company • Case exercise: Handles and Hinges Ltd (CH & H)

PART FOUR
IMPROVEMENT

18 Operations improvement   651
Measuring and improving performance •
Improvement priorities • Approaches to
improvement • The techniques of
improvement • Personal profile: Charles
Wilkins, Lever Pond's, Durban • Case
exercise: Chamdor Brewery, South
African Breweries

19 Failure prevention and recovery   693
System failure • Failure detection and
analysis • Improving the operation's
reliability • Recovery • Personal profile:
Sifiso Dabengwa, Eskom • Case exercise 1:
Better late and happy than just late
Case exercise 2: The Chernobyl failure

20 Total quality management   731
The origins of TQM • What is TQM? •
Implementing TQM improvement
programmes • Quality awards • Personal

profile: Cyril Gamede, Umgeni Water •
Case exercise: The Waterlander Hotel

PART FIVE
THE OPERATIONS CHALLENGE

21 The operations challenge   765
The strategy challenge • Strategies must
be ethical • Strategies must be
international • Strategies must be
creative • Strategies must be implemented •
Personal profile: Jeff Max Bloch,
Nando's International • Case exercise:
Banco Evora do Sul

Appendix 1   800
Forecasting the volume of demand

Appendix 2   806
Time estimation – work measurement

Appendix 3   815
The recording techniques of method study

Index   821

ABOUT THE AUTHORS

Mike Pycraft is Senior Lecturer in Operations Management and Technology at the Wits Business School in Johannesburg.

While studying for his Mechanical Engineering degree at the University of Manchester (1973 to 1976), he was selected for the ICI vacation scholarship scheme. After university, he completed his training with Amalgamated Power Engineering (APE), part of the NEI group, in Bedford, England. APE manufactures steam turbines, diesel engines, pumps and gearboxes. His first post was handling large multi-disciplinary projects in the Middle East. He then came to South Africa on further project work in 1980. He also holds a Master's degree in Business Leadership from the University of South Africa.

Mike moved back into manufacturing as the Engineering Manager of a turbomachinery manufacturing company in Johannesburg. He joined Sulzer Brothers SA in 1988 and was responsible for the formulation of strategy and the implementation of plans for a high-tech turbomachinery service centre. In 1991, he joined the University of the Witwatersrand within the Faculty of Management at Wits Business School. His research interests are in the direction of measurement systems and Operations Strategy. He has published in the *South African Mechanical Engineer* and has presented papers at a number of conferences in Europe and South Africa. He has carried out consulting assignments for some leading South African organizations.

Hemmanth Singh held the position of general manager and director at ELMAC Laminations for five years. ELMAC part of the Reunert Group and a joint venture with Siemens and GEC-Alsthom, manufacturing electric motors. He has had hands-on experience with CIM, MRP and JIT within both jobbing and repetitive manufacturing environments.

He has worked as a strategy consultant with the Monitor group. He was a General Manager for four low voltage equipment manufacturing companies within the AEG group. He currently held the position of Managing Director within the Siemens group. He also holds the position of Managing Director of Suncorp Manufacturing, the first black-owned photovoltaic module assembler in SA, which he was responsible for setting up.

He has a BSc in Mechanical Engineering supported by a postgraduate GDE qualification in Industrial Engineering, both from The University of the Witwatersrand. He obtained his MBA with distinction from Wits Business School in 1990. He received the MBA Graduate of the Year award from that school in the same year. He has also presented and published papers at various conferences and in national journals respectively. Hemmanth has been lecturing on the Wits Business School Management Advancement Programme in the field of Operations Management for five years.

Khomotso Phihlela is a divisional director of Printpak Ltd within the Nampak Group. He is responsible for continuous improvement and is involved in promoting world-class manufacturing techniques with a specific focus on total productive maintenance (TPM). He trains and educates plant managers, facilitators, coordinators and plant operators. He leads pilot projects at various factory sites within the Nampak group. He has also been the engineering manager at an oil mill in the Unilever Group and a project engineer with South African Breweries.

Khomotso has a BSc from the University of Cape Town, specializing in mechanical and industrial engineering. After working briefly with Shell SA, he was selected for an overseas scholarship scheme by the Confederation of British Industries, and worked with Bass Brewing plc's Burton-upon-Trent brewery.

Khomotso completed his MBA part-time, through Wits Business School in the years 1991 to 1994, completing with a research report in the field of Total Productive Maintenance. He lectures to the part-time postgraduate diploma classes at Wits Business School.

Nigel Slack is the A E Higgs Professor of Manufacturing Policy and Strategy at Warwick Business School. Previously he was Professor of Manufacturing Strategy and Lucas Professor of Manufacturing Systems Engineering at Brunel University, University Lecturer in Management Studies at Oxford University and Fellow in Operations Management at Templeton College, Oxford.

He worked initially as an industrial apprentice in the hand-tool industry and then as a production engineer and production manager in light engineering. He holds a Bachelor's degree in Engineering and Master's and Doctor's degrees in Management. He is also a chartered engineer. He is the author of several publications in the Operations Management area, including *The Manufacturing Advantage*, published by Mercury Business Books, 1991, and *Making Management Decisions* (with Steve Cooke) now in its second edition, 1991, published by Prentice Hall, *Service Superiority* (with Robert Johnston), published in 1993 and *Cases in Operations Management* (with Robert Johnston, Alan Harrison, Stuart Chambers and Christine Harland) (second edition) published by Pitman Publishing in 1997. He has lectured on manufacturing strategy in Europe, the USA, South Africa, Latin America and Australia and has carried out consultancy work for several large companies. His research is in the Operations and Manufacturing Flexibility and Operations Strategy areas.

Stuart Chambers is Lecturer in Operations Management at Warwick Business School. He began his career as an undergraduate apprentice at Rolls Royce Aerospace, graduating in mechanical engineering, and then worked in production and general management with companies including Tube Investments and the Marley Tile Company. In his mid-thirties and seeking a career change, he studied for an MBA, and then took up a three-year contract as a researcher in the rapidly-evolving fields of manufacturing strategy. This work took him into 15 diverse businesses, where he worked with the executives to help develop the analyses, concepts and practical solutions required for them to develop manufacturing strategies that best met the need of their chosen markets. Several of the case studies prepared from this work have been published in an American textbook on manufacturing strategy.

In addition to lecturing on a range of operations courses at the Business School and in industry, Stuart is continuing his research in the manufacturing strategy field, with particular interest in cellular production. He is also developing a research interest in service quality management in leisure and catering businesses. He undertakes consultancy in a diverse range of industries, and is co-author of several operations management books.

Christine Harland is Senior Research Fellow in Strategic Purchasing and Supply at the School of Management, University of Bath. Her specialist area is Supply Chain Management which includes interest in Purchasing and Supply Management, Logistics, Materials Management and Operations Planning and Control.

Qualified in Purchasing and Supply, Production and Inventory Control and with a first degree in business, Christine worked in industry as a buyer, production planner, inventory manager and materials manager for manufacturing companies including the Dowty Group and GEC Telecommunications.

Her research and consultancy is in Operations Strategy and Supply Chain Management and has taken place in various industries including automotive, aerospace, electronics, textiles, food, paper, utilities and public sector administration.

Alan Harrison, MA, MSc, CEng, MIEE, is currently Exel Fellow in Automotive Logistics at Cranfield School of Management. Prior to joining Cranfield, he taught at Warwick Business School; prior to this he was with Procter & Gamble, BL and GEC – where he was head of manufacturing of two product companies. His research interests focus on the application of

Japanese methods and he is working with Exel Logistics on the flow of materials in different operations environments. Alan has written two books – *How to Make Japanese Management Methods Work in the West* (with Kazuo Murata) and *Just-in-Time Manufacturing in Perspective* – and numerous papers and articles. He also lectures and consults with a number of companies both in the UK and internationally.

Robert Johnston is Reader in Operations Management at Warwick Business School and a specialist in service operations. Before moving to academia in 1980, he held several line management and senior management posts in a number of service organizations in both the public and private sectors. He continues to maintain close and active links with many large and small organizations through his research, training and consultancy activities. His main research interests are performance measurement, service quality and operations strategy. He is the author or co-author of six books, more than ten chapters in other texts, about twenty papers and case studies and three computer-based simulations. He is the director of the Modular MBA programme and editor of the *International Journal of Service Industry Management*.

FOREWORD

TO THE SOUTHERN AFRICA EDITION

by Alec Erwin

Minister of Trade and Industry, South Africa

It gives me great pleasure to introduce this Southern Africa edition of one of the highest quality operations management textbooks available. Rupert Gasser, the executive vice president of Nestlé SA, in his foreword to the international version, highlighted just how beneficial this type of text is to private sector organizations. He commended Nigel Slack and his team on producing a text with a fine selection of up-to-date thinking in this area.

Mike Pycraft, Hemmanth Singh and Khomotso Phihlela, a team based at the Wits Business School, are to be congratulated on their Southern Africa edition of this text. The 'New South Africa' is emerging into a global business world and South African business leaders are having to adjust to the levels of competition that exist today. At the heart of competitive organizations lie empowered people. What better way to empower people than to give them a true understanding of the concepts explained throughout this text. Here in South Africa, our managers, both in the private and the public sectors, will have to become highly proficient in operations management and its language. In addition those in government, business and labour will have to be able to communicate and deal with these matters with a high degree of common understanding as we restructure our economy to achieve high and sustainable growth rates.

Though there are many Southern African companies that are achieving world-class status, we need more such companies. We have to increase our overall level of competitiveness if we are to become a successful economy. To do this, we have to have people who understand and can implement the techniques explained in this text, techniques such as quality, technological innovation, optimal use of resources, distribution and supply chain management, global operations and a common-sense approach to the enabling and the motivation of the people that work with us. In the South African Department of Trade and Industry we are also setting ourselves high standards of efficiency because we see other governments doing it as we interact with them. These pressures are a reality, and in both the public and private sectors, Southern Africa needs to link into the best of global practices that are available.

This text ties best practice into a strategic framework that will encourage creative thinking at all levels within the organization. To be a learning organization is no longer really a choice, it is essential. This text forms a great reference for people who wish to learn. It is also a text which would be suitable for both the academic environment and for business or government organizations. It does not dwell on philosophical points but explores many practical tools for people who wish to improve their operation's performance. What Mike Pycraft and his team have accomplished in the Southern Africa edition is to take this collection of world-class practices and illustrate their use and application in Southern Africa. They have done this by weaving in some wonderful stories from the real world of business in Southern Africa. Real live cases, profiles of individuals and stories make it clear to any reader that there is no excuse for not using the best techniques available. Just as South Africa is fast becoming an example to the world in terms of cross-cultural co-operation, we need to listen to the rest of the world with regard to best operating practice. The text also picks up on the crucial but simple aspects of world-class manufacturing, such as good housekeeping and safety, both of which are fundamental to other aspects of quality and general business performance.

In any enterprise differences can arise between management and labour and good industrial relations practice will solve these as soon after they arise as possible. Over time, however, an enterprise – both management and labour – are competing with the rest of the world. The sections of the text that deal with quality, operations improvement and the future challenges for operations management highlight these issues and include an explicit coverage of the ethical issues that underlie many operational decisions. These more rounded views on operations management supplement the slightly more technical sections dealing with straightforward and implementable techniques.

Mike Pycraft and his team have taken this lively and interesting text, founded on operations management theory, and, by great attention to detail throughout the text, have converted it to be easily readable in the Southern African context. The examples given in chapters and the questions at the end of chapters are also relevant to those who are studying in this region. In addition, even though the text is now much more accessible for the Southern African user, it has not lost its basic international orientation. I am sure that this text will bring the subject of operations management to the forefront of business for both the managers and workforces of tomorrow.

ALEC ERWIN
MINISTER OF TRADE AND INDUSTRY
SOUTH AFRICA

PREFACE

Introduction

Operations management gets as close as we can in business life to the act of creation. It is concerned with *creating* the products and services upon which we all depend. Since the creation of products and services is the very reason for any organization's existence, operations management should be at the heart of its affairs. No student of organizational or business life should therefore be without, at the very least, an understanding of the role, objectives and activities of operations management. It is, after all, operations managers who hold the key to either satisfying or disappointing the customers upon whom the whole organization depends, a fact which is well understood by most senior managers. For example, one survey of Chief Executive Officers[1] shows 43 per cent of them citing operations as the most important area of employee know-how (followed by sales and marketing at 29 per cent, technology at 17 per cent and finance at 6 per cent). But, as those who read this book shall see, the principles of operations management are central to all managers irrespective of their job title. They all create products and services for (often internal) customers. In that sense, *all managers are operations managers*. In the Southern Africa region, it is often in the operational area that organizations fail to meet expectations. The ideas may be good. The customers and the funds may both be available. But can we deliver? Operations management skills are essential for delivery in all areas – education, health, food, water, housing and products or services of all types.

[1] Hall, R. (1992) 'The Strategic Analysis of Intangible Resources', *The Strategic Management Journal*, Vol 13, p 142.

The aim of this book

The aim of this book is to provide a clear, well structured and interesting treatment of operations management as it applies to a variety of businesses and organizations. The text is intended to provide both a logical path through the activities of operations management and an understanding of the strategic context in which operations managers work. This book has been produced as a Southern Africa edition in order to allow readers from this region to associate more clearly with what is now normal global business practice.

More specifically this text aims to be:

● *Strategic* in its perspective of operations management's contribution to the organization's long-term success. We are unambiguous in treating the operations function as being at the centre of most organizations' drive to improve their competitiveness.

● *Conceptual* in the way it explains the reasons why operations managers need to take decisions in each activity area. Although some quantitative techniques are included, their primary aim is to illustrate the underlying principles of operations decisions.

● *Comprehensive* in its coverage of the significant ideas and issues which are relevant to most types of operation.

● *Practical* in the sense that the issues and difficulties in making operations management decisions in practice are discussed, and generally the treatment of topics reflects actual operations practice. This book is practical also in that Case Exercises illustrating the approaches taken by actual companies are used to illustrate operations issues.

- *Southern African and international* in its use of examples, cases, personal profiles and stories. Though this entire edition has been produced to read well from a Southern Africa perspective, it maintains an international flavour through the use of examples from Europe, North America and other countries.
- *Balanced* in its treatment of the various types of organizations which create products and services. This means we treat service operations with the same level of seriousness as we do manufacturing operations. It also means that, where possible, we have included both a service and a manufacturing example to illustrate a point.

Who should use this book?

This book is intended to provide an introduction to operations management for all students who wish to understand the nature and activities of operations management.

- *Undergraduates* on Business Studies, technical or joint degrees should find it sufficiently structured to provide an understandable route through the subject (no prior knowledge of the area is assumed).
- *MBA students* should find that its practical discussions of operations management activities enhance their own experience.
- *Postgraduate students* on other specialist masters degrees should find that it provides them with a well-grounded and, at times, critical approach to the subject.
- *Practising managers* in both the private and the public sectors will find this book a wonderful reference on the latest thinking in the area of operations management.

Distinctive features

- *Clear structure*

There are several models which operations management teachers can use to structure their courses. We have chosen to base the structure of this book on the most common of these – the design, planning and control distinction. But we have supported the modern view of operations which sees the separation of planning activities from control activities as inappropriate. Most significantly we have separated out the improvement activities of operations to reflect the emerging view of operations managers as being responsible for continually improving the performance of their operations. Furthermore we both start and finish the book by treating the strategic aspects of the subject.

- *Illustration based*

Operations management is a subject which should be based on practice, it cannot be taught satisfactorily in a purely theoretical manner. For this reason we frequently have used abstracted examples to illustrate points of theory. The words 'for example' occur often and we make no apology for this. In addition there are over 70 boxes, all of which explain the issues faced by real operations managers in real companies.

- *Personal profiles*

Again reflecting the practical orientation of our treatment of the subject, we include at the end of each chapter a personal profile. These are verbatim comments (together with some background information) from interviews with practising operations managers in a variety of operations. They comment on their own experiences in applying some of the ideas discussed in each chapter and sometimes their reactions to their own jobs. We hope these will provide students with a more personal 'way in' to the issues discussed in each chapter.

- *Chapter summaries*

We have summarized each chapter in the form of a list of bullet points. These extract the essential points from each chapter which can act as a revision list for students.

- *Case exercises*

Every chapter includes a case exercise which is a short case study suitable for class discussion. The cases, all of which are based on real companies (even if their identities have sometimes been disguised), are usually short enough to serve as illustrations which can be referred to in class, but have sufficient content to serve as the basis for seminar-style case sessions.

● *Selected further readings*
Every chapter ends with a list of further readings which either take the topics covered in the chapter further, or treat some important issues related to those treated in the chapter. These are intended to enable any student who wishes to take their exploration of the subject beyond the introductory stage.

● *Instructor's Manual*
An Instructor's Manual is available to lecturers or course facilitators adopting this textbook. The Manual follows the same structure as the chapters in this text and provides the following:

– chapter summaries which can be used as hand-outs;
– OHP masters (which are also available as an MS PowerPoint file);
– key points for each OHP;
– discussion points and/or solutions for the cases and discussion questions in the text.

The Instructor's Manual is produced specifically for the Southern Africa edition.

● *Computerized material*
A set of slides produced using Microsoft PowerPoint is available for lecturers who adopt this text.

ACKNOWLEDGEMENTS
FOR THE SOUTHERN AFRICA EDITION

Mike Pycraft, Hemmanth Singh and Khomotso Phihlela acknowledge the assistance given by many individuals in the preparation of this Southern Africa edition of *Operations Management*. In particular, we would like to mention the following people: Dr L.P. Krüger of the Department of Business Management at UNISA; E.R. Mentoor of the Department of Management at the University of the Western Cape; and R Huckle of the Business Studies Department at Peninsula Technikon, for all their constructive comments and advice.

We also thank and acknowledge those people who gave input as students through their work with different organizations throughout Southern Africa.

We thank the initial team of Nigel Slack, Stuart Chambers, Christine Harland, Alan Harrison and Robert Johnston who produced the first European edition of the book. They have structured an operations management text in a form that allows students to gain a full and thorough grasp of this subject area.

Finally, we would like to thank the team at Pitman Publishing: Penelope Woolf and Sharlene Tilley for really getting this project moving, and Annette McFadyen for making sure the book was completed 'just-in-time'!

HOW TO USE THIS BOOK

All academic textbooks in business management are, to some extent, simplifications of the messy reality which is actual organizational life. Any book has to separate topics, in order to study them, which in reality are closely related. For example, technology choice impacts on job design which in turn impacts on quality control; yet we have treated these topics individually. The first hint therefore in using this book effectively is to *look out for all the links between the individual topics*. Similarly with the sequence of topics, although the chapters follow a logical structure, they need not be studied in this order. With the exceptions of Chapters 1, 4, 10 and 18 which form introductions to each part of the book, every chapter is, more or less, self-contained. Therefore study the chapters in whatever sequence is appropriate to your course or your individual interests. But because each part has an introductory chapter, those students who wish to start with a brief 'overview' of the subject may wish first to study Chapters 1, 4, 10 and 18 and the chapter summaries of selected chapters. The same applies to revision – *study the introductory chapters and chapter summaries*.

The book makes full use of the many practical examples and illustrations which can be found in all operations. Many of these were provided by our contacts in companies, but many also come from journals, magazines and newspapers. So if you want to understand the importance of opera-

tions management in everyday business life *look for examples and illustrations of operations management decisions and activities in newspapers and magazines*. There are also examples which you can observe every day. Whenever you use a shop, eat a meal in a restaurant, borrow a book from the library or ride on public transport, *consider the operations management issues of all the operations for which you are a customer*.

The case exercises and discussion questions are there to provide an opportunity for you to think further about the ideas discussed in the chapters. Discussion questions should be used to test out your understanding of the specific points and issues discussed in the chapter. *If you cannot answer these you should revisit the relevant parts of the chapter*. The case exercises at the end of each chapter will require some more thought. *Use the questions at the end of each case exercise to guide you through the logic of analysing the issue treated in the case*. When you have done this individually *try to discuss your analysis with other course members*. Most important of all, every time you analyse one of the case exercises (or any other case or example in operations management) start off your analysis with the two fundamental questions:

● how is this organization trying to compete (or satisfy its strategic objectives if a not-for-profit organization)?, and,
● what can the operation do to help the organization compete more effectively?

PLAN OF THE BOOK

PART ONE – INTRODUCTION

Chapter 1 Operations management	Chapter 2 The strategic role and objectives of operations	Chapter 3 Operations strategy

PART TWO – DESIGN

Chapter 4 Design in operations management	Chapter 5 The design of products and services	Chapter 6 Design of the operations network
Chapter 7 Layout and flow	Chapter 8 Process technology	Chapter 9 Job design and work organization

PART THREE – PLANNING AND CONTROL

Chapter 10 The nature of planning and control	Chapter 11 Capacity planning and control	Chapter 12 Inventory planning and control
Chapter 13 Supply chain planning and control	Chapter 14 MRP	Chapter 15 Just-in-time planning and control

Chapter 16 Project planning and control	Chapter 17 Quality planning and control

PART FOUR – IMPROVEMENT

Chapter 18 Operations improvement	Chapter 19 Failure prevention and recovery	Chapter 20 Total quality management

PART FIVE – THE OPERATIONS CHALLENGE

Chapter 21 The operations challenge

INTRODUCTION

This part of the book introduces the idea of the operations function in different types of organization. It identifies the common set of objectives to which operations managers aspire in order to serve their customers, and it explains how operations strategy influences the activities of operations managers.

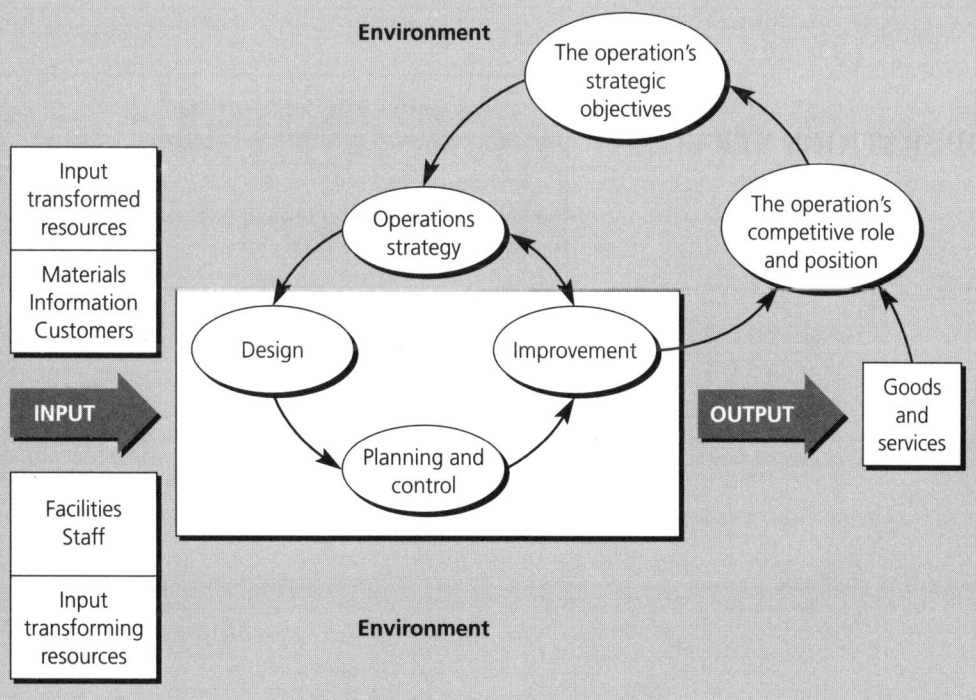

Chapter 1
OPERATIONS MANAGEMENT

- *What is operations management and how does it fit within the other functional areas of the organization?*
- *How do the operations functions of organizations differ?*
- *What do operations managers do?*

Chapter 2
THE STRATEGIC ROLE AND OBJECTIVES OF OPERATIONS

- *How can operations managers help the organization to be competitive?*
- *What are the 'performance objectives' of an operations function?*

Chapter 3
OPERATIONS STRATEGY

- *What is an operations strategy?*
- *How does an operations strategy fit into a company's overall strategy?*
- *How do we know which performance objectives are the most important?*

CHAPTER 1

OPERATIONS MANAGEMENT

INTRODUCTION

Operations management is about the way organizations produce goods and services. Everything you wear, eat, sit on, use, read or knock about on the sports field comes to you courtesy of the operations managers who organized its production. Every book you borrow from the library, every treatment you receive at the hospital, every service you expect in the shops and every lecture you attend at university – all have been produced. While the people who supervised their 'production' may not always be called operations managers, that is what they really are. And that is what this book is concerned with – the tasks, issues and decisions of those operations managers who have made the services and products on which we all depend. In this introductory chapter we will examine the overall nature of operations management and the activities of operations managers. The model which is developed to explain the subject is shown in Fig. 1.1.

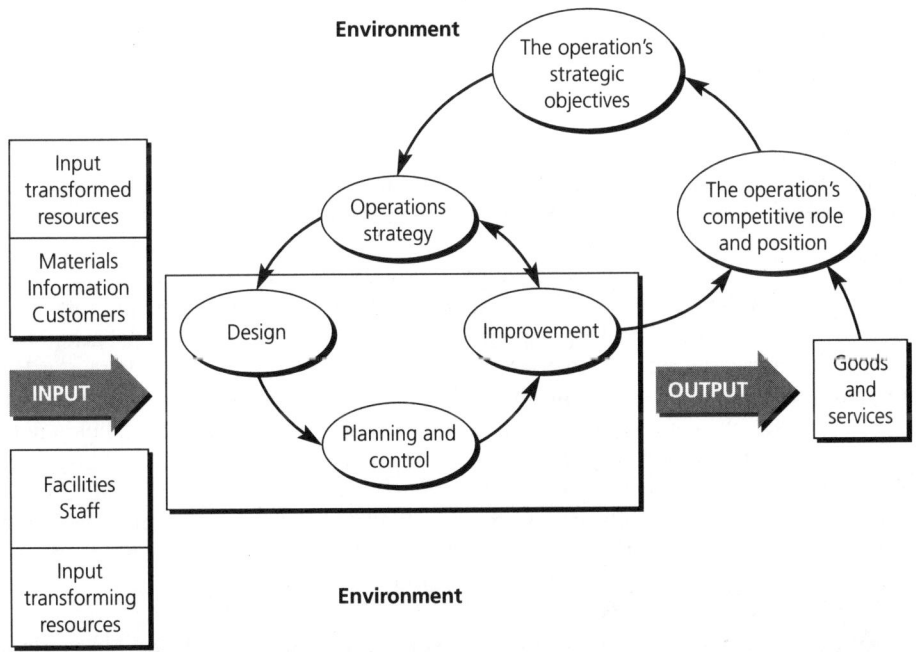

Figure 1.1 A general model of operations management

OBJECTIVES

This chapter will examine:

- the part which operations management plays in organizations;

- the position of the operations function in the structure of an organization;

- how the input–transformation–output model can be used to describe all types of operation no matter what they produce;

- the concepts of macro and micro operations and internal customer–supplier relationships;

- the many different types of operation and how they can be categorized using four dimensions;

- the activities of operations managers.

EFFECTIVE OPERATIONS MANAGEMENT

Operations management is, above all else, a practical subject which deals with real issues. So let us start our examination of the subject with a practical example of an organization which is known for the originality of its operations.

IKEA[1]

IKEA is a furniture retailer with a difference. With around a 100 giant stores operating in over 15 countries world-wide it has managed to develop its own special way of selling furniture which seems to impress customers of all nationalities. IKEA customers typically spend between one and a half and two hours in the store – far longer than in rival furniture retailers. An important reason for this is the effectiveness of the way it organizes its stores – all of which are the same in most important respects all around the world. The design and philosophy of its store operations go back to the original business which was started in southern Sweden by Ingvar Kamprad in the 1950s. At that time Mr Kamprad was successfully selling furniture, through a catalogue operation. In response to customer requests to be able to see some of his furniture, he built a showroom in Stockholm, not in the centre of the city where land was expensive, but on the outskirts of town. Instead of buying expensive display stands, he simply set the furniture out more or less as it would be in a domestic setting. Also, instead of moving the furniture from the warehouse to the showroom area, he asked customers to pick the furniture up themselves from the warehouse. This 'anti-service' approach to service, as it has been described, is the foundation of IKEA's stores today.

IKEA's furniture is 'value for money' with a wide range of choice. It is usually designed to be stored and sold as a 'flat pack' but is capable of easy assembly by the customer. The stores are all designed around the same self-service concept – that finding the store, parking, moving through the store itself, and ordering and picking up goods should be simple, smooth and problem-free.

At the entrance to each store are large notice-boards which proclaim IKEA's philosophy and provide advice to shoppers who have not used the store before. Catalogues are also available at this point showing illustrations, dimensions and the available range of the store's products. Perhaps most significantly for shoppers with young children, there is also a supervised children's play area, a small cinema, a parent and baby room and toilets. Parents can leave their children in the supervised play area for a limited period of time. Each child is attired in a yellow, numbered top while he or she is in this area and parents are recalled via the loudspeaker system if the child has any problems. Customers may also borrow pushchairs to keep their children with them as they move round the store.

Some parts of the showroom are set out in 'room settings', while others show, for example, all beds together, so that customers can make comparisons. Customers are not approached by staff offering help or advice. The IKEA philosophy is not to 'hassle' customers in this way but rather to let them make up their minds in their own time. If a customer does want advice, there are information points around the showroom where staff, in their bright red uniforms, can help and guide customers, provide measuring rules, paper for sketching and so on. Every piece of furniture carries a ticket which indicates its dimensions, price, materials used, country of origin and the other colours in which it is available. It also has a code number which indicates the location in the warehouse from where it can be collected. The tickets on larger items ask customers to go to the information desks for assistance. After viewing the showroom, customers pass into the 'free-service' area where smaller items are displayed on shelves. These can be picked directly off the display shelves by customers and put into yellow shoulder bags or trolleys. Customers then pass through the self-service warehouse where they can pick up the items they viewed in the showroom. Finally, the customers pay at the check-outs, each of which is constructed with a ramped conveyor belt which moves the customer's purchases up to the check-out staff member and along to the exit area. At the exit area there are information and service points, and often a 'Swedish Shop' with Swedish food-stuffs. A large loading area allows customers to bring their cars from the car park and load their purchases. That is not the end of IKEA's service, however. Any customers who have bought more than their car can carry, can rent or buy a roof rack.

Nor is IKEA's innovative approach to its business confined only to the physical layout and design of its stores; it also extends to its management style and philosophy. All employees in the store wear either red or grey sweatshirts which distinguish customer-contact and non-contact staff. The staff themselves are well grounded in the various elements of the IKEA philosophy. For example, in the company's words:

● *The product range – our identity*. We shall offer a wide range of home furnishing items of good design and function at prices so low the majority of people can afford to buy them. We must not compromise on function or technical quality.

● *The IKEA spirit – strong and living reality*. The true IKEA is founded on our enthusiasm, our constant will to renew, our cost-consciousness, our willingness to assume responsibility, the simplicity in our behaviour.

● *Profit gives us resources*. Forcing ourselves to develop products in a more economic way, to purchase better, to save on costs; this is our secret and reason for success.

● *To reach good results with small means*. Expensive solutions are often a sign of mediocrity.

● *Simplicity is a virtue*. Complicated rules paralyse. Exaggerated planning can be fatal. Simplification is an honoured tradition.

● *The different way*. By daring to be different, we find new ways. 'Why?' remains an important keyword.

● *To assume responsibility – a privilege*. The more responsible people, the less red tape. The fear of making mistakes is the root of bureaucracy and the enemy of evaluation. ■

So why is IKEA able to survive and succeed? It certainly keeps a very tight control of its costs, and it also understands its market and how it can serve the needs of its customers. Furthermore, the products it designs and sells must be regarded by its customers as representing outstanding value for money. At least as important as all these, however, is the way it organizes the delivery of its services within its stores. This is the responsibility of the company's operations management. The staff in the store, the staff who liaise with suppliers, the staff who store and transport goods to the stores and the staff who design, plan, control and constantly improve the way things are done, the buildings, the computers and check-outs, the warehouses and the transportation system – all are engaged in *operations management*. IKEA owes its success, in no small measure, to the effectiveness of its operations management, who provide:

- a smooth customer flow;
- a clean, well designed environment;
- sufficient goods to satisfy demand;
- sufficient staff to serve customers and stock the warehouse;
- an appropriate quality of service;
- a continuous stream of ideas to improve its, already impressive, operations performance.

Without these, the company, no matter how well it marketed and financed its activities, would not be the success it is.

Now is the point to establish some definitions.

- The *operations function* of the organization is the arrangement of resources which is devoted to the production of its goods and services. Every organization has an operations function because every organization produces some type of goods and/or services. However, not all types of organization will necessarily call the operations function by this name, as we will discuss later.

    Note that we also use the shorter terms 'the operation' or 'operations' and, at times, the 'operations system' interchangeably with the 'operations function'.
- *Operations managers* are the staff of the organization who have particular responsibility for managing some, or all, of the resources which comprise the operations function. Again in some organizations the operations manager could be called by some other name. For example, he or she might be called the 'fleet manager' in a distribution company, or the 'administrative manager' in a hospital, or the 'store manager' in a supermarket.
- *Operations management* is the term which is used for the activities, decisions and responsibilities of operations managers.

    As we have seen in the case of IKEA, if the operations function is to be effective it must use its resources efficiently and produce goods and services in a way that satisfies its customers. In addition it must be creative, innovative and energetic in introducing novel and improved ways of producing goods and services (*see* the box on Swatch, for example). If the operation can do these things it will provide the organization with the means to survive in the long term because it gives the organization a competitive advantage over its commercial rivals. An alternative way of putting this in a not-for-profit organization, is that an effective operation gives the means to fulfil the organization's long-term strategic goals.

SWATCH REVOLUTIONIZES WATCH MANUFACTURE[2]

In the early 1980s the Swiss watch industry was nearly dead. Competition from cheap but often high-quality products from Far Eastern manufacturers such as Seiko and Casio had almost obliterated the traditional Swiss industry. Trying to protect their investments, the Swiss banks organized a merger of the two largest companies on the advice of Nicolas Hayek, now Chairman and Chief Executive of Swatch's parent company SMH formed from the merger. He saw the potential of a new plastic-cased watch which was already being developed inside one of the companies. One of its major advantages was that it could be made in high volume at very low cost. The quartz mechanism was built directly into the all-plastic case and the number of components in the watch had been cut to just 51; this was less than half the number in most other watches. Fewer components also meant that the manufacture of the watch could be fully automated. This made Swatches cheap to produce even in Switzerland which has one of the highest labour costs in the world.

The innovative design, some creative marketing, but above all else the operation's success at producing the watch cheaper than anyone else brought the company significant rewards. In the early 1980s the total market share for all Swiss watches was around 25 per cent; ten years later it had more than doubled. The ability to offer a good watch at a low price had released the potential of the watch to become a fashion accessory – a trend which meant that the company's operations reaped the benefits of high volume but had to cope with an ever-increasing variety of product designs. Through automation and rigid standardization of the internal mechanism of the watch, the company managed this increase in variety without it crippling its costs. It is the success of the company's operations managers in keeping their costs low (direct labour cost is now less than 7 per cent of the total cost of production) that has allowed Swatch to succeed. Not that everything the company has done has been successful. Some designs never caught the public imagination and some distribution and marketing mistakes were made, especially in the United States. However, continuing innovation, high quality and low cost makes it much easier to overcome such problems. ■

OPERATIONS IN THE ORGANIZATION

The operations function is central to the organization because it produces the goods and services which are its reason for existing, but it is neither the only, nor necessarily even the most important, function. All organizations have other functions with their own particular responsibilities. These other functions, although having their own part to play in the organization's activities, are (or should be) bound together, along with operations, by common organizational goals.

In practice, different organizations will adopt different organizational structures and define different functions. For our purposes here, in addition to the operations function, we divide the organization into three other *major functions* (in terms of the fundamental roles they play in the organization):

● the marketing function
● the accounting and finance function
● the product/service development function

and *support functions*, which supply and support the operations function, including:

- the human resources function
- the purchasing function
- the engineering/technical function.

Table 1.1 shows the activities of these functions for a sample of operations.

It is important to stress, however, that functional names, boundaries and responsibilities vary between organizations – a complication which is particularly true of the operations function. This leads to some confusion over the practical boundaries of the operations function. For example, a narrow organizational definition of the operations function's boundaries would exclude all activities shared with any other functions. Defined in this way, operations personnel would not be directly involved in such activities as developing products and services, choosing process technology, devising delivery schedules, buying materials or services, devising budgets, recruiting or training staff, and so on. They would accept the resources which they were given, and do as they were told. At the other extreme a very broad definition of operations would include all activities which had any connection with the production of goods and services – in practice every activity with the exception of the core marketing/selling and accounting/finance activities. Figure 1.2 illustrates the function boundary of operations management implied by both narrow and broad definitions.

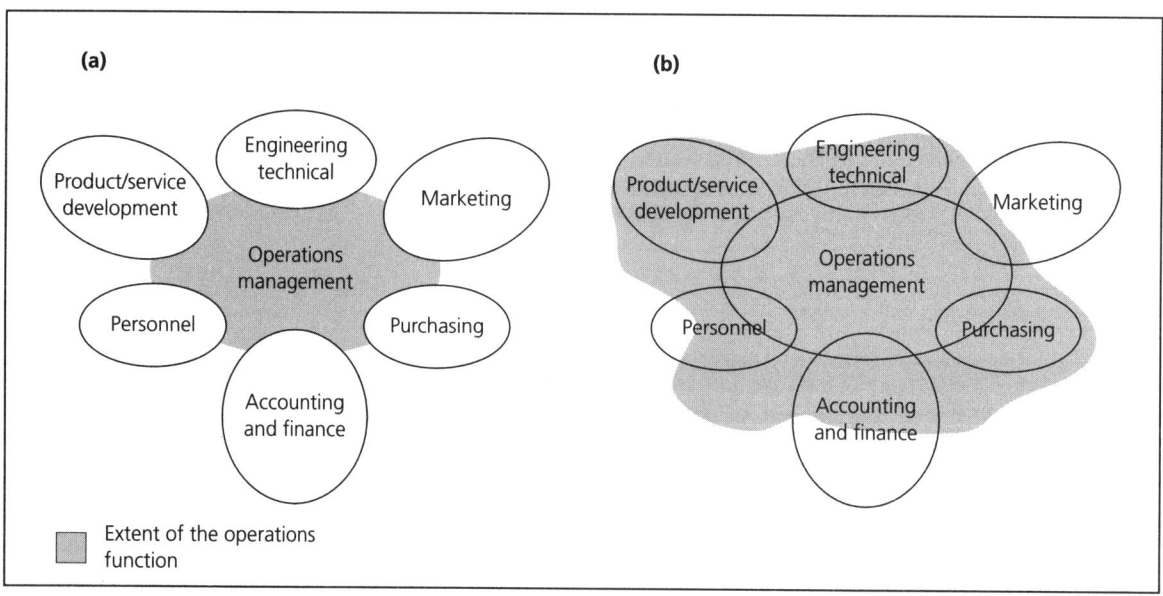

Figure 1.2 The boundaries of the operations function: (a) a narrow definition, (b) a broad definition

In this book we incline towards a relatively broad definition of operations. We treat much of product/service development activities, most of the engineering/technical and purchasing activities and some of the personnel, marketing and accounting and finance activities as coming within the sphere of operations management. However, in covering these areas we do not set out to take the place of more detailed texts in these areas. We do not address the technical core of these other functions. For example, we

Table 1.1 The activities of functions in some organizations

Typical functional activities	Church	Fast food chain	University	Furniture manufacturer
Marketing	Call on newcomers Proselytize	Advertise in TV Devise promotional materials	Develop brochures Mail out brochures Attend shows	Advertise in magazines Determine pricing policy Sell to stores
Accounting and finance	Count contributions Manage appeals Pay rents Pay bills	Pay suppliers Collect takings Pay staff	Pay faculty and support staff Monitor expenditure Collect fees	Pay staff Pay suppliers Prepare budgets Manage cash
Product/service development	Search for meaning of existence Retranslate scriptures	Design hamburgers, pizzas, etc. Design decor for restaurants	Develop new courses Design research programmes	Design new furniture Coordinate with fashionable colours
Operations	Conduct weddings Conduct funerals Conduct services Save souls	Make burgers, pizzas, etc. Serve customers Clear away Maintain equipment	Communicate knowledge Conduct research Administer courses	Make components Assemble furniture
Personnel	Train priests Appraise priestly performance	Train staff Devise remuneration schemes	Train staff Manage contracts Appraise performance	Recruit staff Train staff
Purchasing	Buy consumables Develop vestment supplies	Buy foodstuff Buy plates, cartons, napkins, etc.	Buy equipment Buy consumables	By raw materials, wood, etc. Buy fabric
Engineering/technical	Maintain church buildings, etc.	Develop or purchase equipment, ovens, etc. Install equipment, ovens, etc.	Purchase audiovisual equipment Maintain equipment and facilities	Develop or purchase woodworking machines Maintain machines

Adapted from Heizer and Render[3]

do not discuss the science behind product or service development, or the engineering behind the technical development of process technologies, or the legislation of employment contracts, or the technicalities of financial reporting. Rather we have included topics and issues which have direct implications for our central concern – the production of goods and services.

THE TRANSFORMATION MODEL

All operations produce goods or services or a mixture of the two, and they do this by a *process of transformation*. By transformation we mean that they use their *resources* to change the state or condition of something to produce *outputs*. Figure 1.3 shows this general *transformation model* which is used to describe the nature of operations. Put simply, operations take in a set of input resources and use them either to transform something, or to be transformed themselves, into outputs of goods and services.

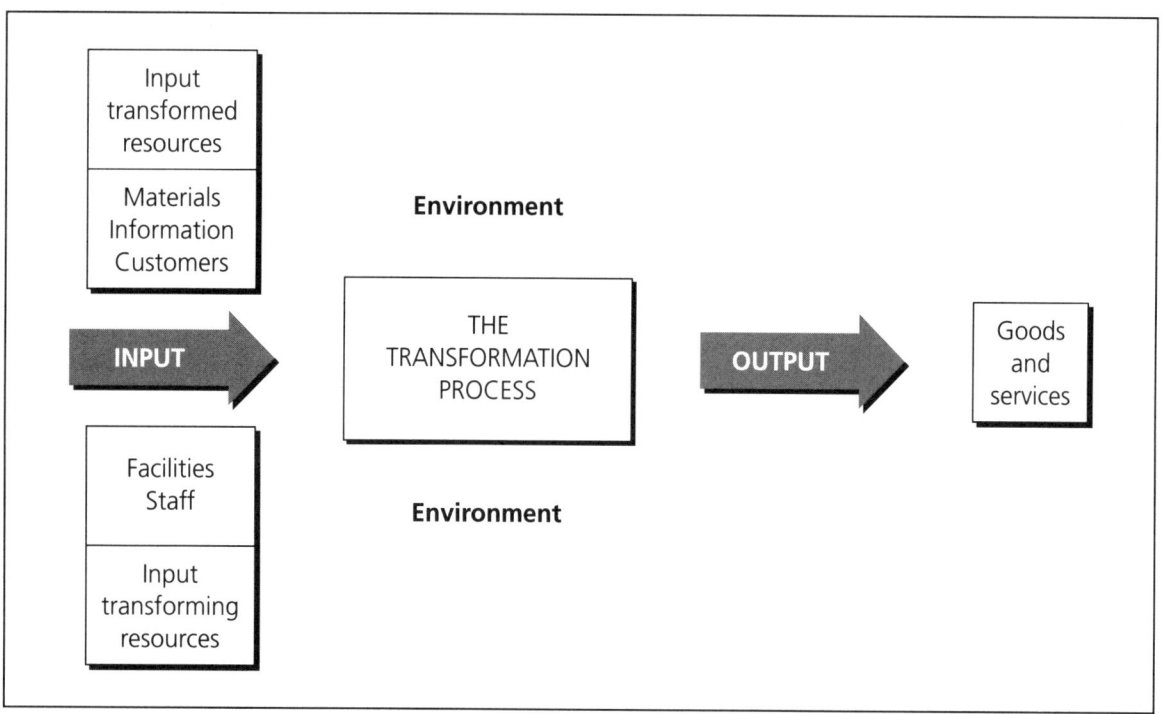

Figure 1.3 All operations are input–transformation–output processes

All operations conform to this general input–transformation–output model. For example, hospitals have inputs of doctors, nurses and other medical staff, administrators, cleaning staff, beds, medical equipment, pharmaceuticals, blood, dressings and so on. Their purpose is to transform sick patients into healthy patients. The outputs from the operation are treated patients, medical test results, medical research and 'best practice' medical procedures. Table 1.2 shows that one can describe a wide range of operations in this way. There are differences between different operations, however. If you stand far enough away from, say, a hospital or a motor vehicle plant, they might look the same. Each is likely to be a large building into which staff enter and deliveries take place. But move closer to these two operations and clear differences do start to emerge. For a start, one is a manufacturing operation producing largely physical goods and one is a service operation which produces changes in the physiological condition, feelings and behaviour of patients. The nature of the processes which each building contains will also be different. The motor vehicle plant contains metal cutting and forming machinery and assembly processes – while the hospital contains diagnostic, care and therapeutic processes – separate sets of facilities (machines, buildings, etc.) which employ very different process technologies. Perhaps the most important difference between the two operations, however, is the nature of their inputs. Both have 'staff' and 'facilities' as inputs to the operation but they act upon very different things. The motor vehicle plant uses its staff and facilities to *transform steel, plastic, cloth, tyres and other materials*. They make them into vehicles which eventually are delivered to customers. The staff and technology in the hospital, on the other hand, *transform the customers themselves*. The patients form part of the input to the operation – it is they who are being 'processed'. This has important implications for how the operation needs to be managed. It will be explored later in this chapter. The main point here is that we need to examine the nature of inputs, transformation and outputs in a little more detail.

Inputs to the transformation process

The inputs to operation can be conveniently classified as either

● *transformed resources* – the resources that are treated, transformed or converted in some way;
● *transforming resources* – the resources that act upon the transformed resources.

Transformed resources

The transformed resources which operations take in are usually a mixture of

● materials,
● information, and
● customers.

Often one of these is dominant in an operation. For example, a bank devotes part of its energies to producing printed statements of accounts for its customers. In doing so, it is processing materials and acting as a printer but no one would claim that a bank and a printer are the same type of operation. The bank also processes customers. It gives them advice regarding their financial affairs, cashes their cheques, deposits their cash, and has direct contact with them. However, most of the bank's activities are concerned probably with processing information about its customers' financial affairs. As customers, we may be unhappy with badly printed statements and we may be more unhappy if we are not treated appropriately in the bank. If the bank makes errors in our financial transactions, however, we suffer in a far more funda-

Table 1.2 Some operations described in terms of input–transformation–output processes

Operation	Input resources	Transformation process	Outputs

Airline	Aircraft
	Pilots and aircrew
	Groundcrew
	Passengers and freight
		Move passengers and
		  freight around the world
			Transported passengers
			  and freight

Department store	Goods for sale Staff sales Computerized registers Customers	Display goods Give sales advice Sell goods	Customers and goods assembled together
Dentist	Dental surgeons Dental equipment Nurses Patients	Check and treat teeth Give preventative advice	Patients with healthy teeth and gums
Zoo	Zoo keepers Animals Simulated environments Customers	Display animals Educate customers Breed animals	Entertained customers Informed customers Non-extinct species
Printer	Printers and designers Printing presses Paper, ink, etc.	Design Print Bind	Designed and printed material

Container port	Ships and cargo
	Staff
	Container handling
	  equipment
		Move cargo from ship
		  to shore and *vice versa*
			Empty or full ships

Police	Police officers
	Computer systems
	Information
	Public (law-abiding
	  and criminals)
		Prevent crime
		Solve crime
		Apprehend criminals
			Lawful society
			Public with feeling of
			  security

Accountant	Accounting staff Information Computer systems	Prepare accounts Give advice	Certified and published accounts
Frozen food manufacturer	Fresh food Operators Food processing equipment Freezers	Food preparation Freeze	Frozen food

mental way. This is not to say that materials processing or customer processing is unimportant to the bank. On the contrary, it must be good at these things to keep its customers happy. Error-free, fast and efficient *information processing* though is the central objective of the bank.

It is the same with other types of operation. Take, for example, a company which manufactures the high-speed machinery used for packaging food products. Some of the company's operation will be devoted to taking information regarding the exact technical requirements of its customers, and processing it into 'applications engineering' designs. The operation will also need to 'process' the customers by visiting their factories to collect the information in the first place, bringing the customers to the factory to see the progress being made on the equipment, working with the customers during the installation of the equipment and finally educating the customers in the use of the equipment. Yet although the operation will process both information and people, its main task is *materials processing* to make the equipment itself.

Finally, a hospital will process information, in the form of patients' medical records, pharmaceuticals inventory information and so on. It will also devote some of its resources to processing materials, for example in the way it produces meals for patients. The main operations task of a hospital, however, is to process customers in a way which satisfies its patients, maximizes their health care and minimizes its costs. It is predominantly a *customer processing* operation.

Table 1.3 gives examples of operations with their dominant transformed resources.

Table 1.3 Dominant transformed materials on various operations

Predominantly materials processors	Predominantly information processors	Predominantly customer processors
All manufacturing operations	Accountants	Hairdresser
Mining and extraction companies	Bank headquarters	Hotels
Retail operations	Market research company	Hospital
Warehouses	Financial analysts	Mass rapid transport
Postal services	News service	Theatre
Container shipping line	University research unit	Theme park
Trucking companies	Archives	Dentist
	Telecoms company	

Transforming resources

There is less difference between operations transforming resources. In fact there are two types of transforming resource which form the 'building blocks' of all operations:

- *facilities* – the buildings, equipment, plant and process technology of the operation;
- *staff* – those who operate, maintain, plan and manage the operation. (Note we use the term 'staff' to describe all the people in the operation, at any level.)

Of course the exact nature of both facilities and staff will differ between operations. To an international, five-star hotel, its facilities consist mainly of buildings, furniture and fittings. To a nuclear-powered aircraft carrier its facilities are the nuclear generator, turbines, sophisticated electronic detection equipment and so on. One operation has relatively 'low-technology' facilities and one 'high-technology' facilities – seemingly very different from each other but both important to the operation concerned. A five-star hotel would be just as ineffective with worn and broken furniture as an aircraft carrier would be with inoperative electronics.

The nature of staff will also differ between operations. The majority of staff employed in a factory assembling domestic refrigerators do not need a particularly high level of technical skill. In contrast, the majority of staff employed by an accounting company which sells audit services are likely to be highly skilled in their own particular 'technical' skill (accounting). Although the extent and nature of the skills needed by staff will vary, however, they all have a contribution to make to the effectiveness of their operation. An assembly worker who consistently misassembles refrigerators will dissatisfy customers and cause cost to the operation just as surely as an accountant who cannot add up. Table 1.4 shows the transforming resources to be found in some operations.

Table 1.4 The facilities and staff transforming resources of three operations

	Ferry company	*Paper manufacturer*	*Radio station*

Types of facilities	Ships
	On-board navigation
	  equipment
	Dry docks
	Materials handling
	  equipment
	On-shore buildings
	Computerized reservation
	  systems
	Warehouses
		Pulp-making vats
		Paper-making machines
		Reeling equipment
		Slitting equipment
		Packing machinery
		Steam-generating boilers
		Warehouses
			Broadcasting
			  equipment
			Studios and
			  studio equipment
			Transmitters
			Outside broadcast
			  vehicles

Types of staff	Sailors
	Engineers
	Catering staff
	On-board shop assistants
	Cleaners
	Maintenance staff
	Ticketing staff
		Operators
		Chemists and chemical
		  engineers
		Process plant
		  engineers
			Disc jockeys
			Announcers
			Technicians

The transformation process

The purpose of the transformation process in operations is closely connected with the nature of its transformed input resources.

Materials processing

Operations which process materials could do so to transform their *physical properties* (such as physical shape, or composition or characteristics). Most manufacturing operations are like this. Other operations which process materials do so to change their *location* (parcel delivery companies, for example). Some, like retail operations, do so to change the *possession* or ownership of the materials. Finally some material-processing operations do so primarily to *store* or *accommodate* them, such as a warehouse.

Information processing

Operations which process information could do so to transform their *informational properties* (that is the shape or form of the information); accountants do this. Some change the *possession* of the information, for example market research companies. Some *store* or *accommodate* the information, for example archives and libraries. Finally some operations change the *location* of the information, such as telecommunication companies.

Customer processing

Operations which process customers might also transform them in a variety of ways. Some change their *physical properties* in a similar way to material processors: for example, hairdressers or even cosmetic surgeons. Some customer-processing operations *store* or (more politely) *accommodate* them: hotels, for example. Airlines, mass rapid transport systems and bus companies transform the *location* of their customers. Some are concerned with transforming the *physiological state* of their customers, such as hospitals. Finally some customer-processing operations are concerned with transforming the *psychological state* of their customers, for example most entertainment services such as music, theatre, television, radio and theme parks. Table 1.5 summarizes these various types of transformation process.

Outputs from the transformation process

The outputs from (and purpose of) the transformation process are goods and services, which are generally seen as being different.

Tangibility

Goods are usually *tangible,* for example you can physically touch a television set or a newspaper. Services are usually *intangible.* You cannot touch consultancy advice or a haircut (although you can often see or feel the results of these services).

Storability

Partly because of their tangibility, goods can also be *stored,* at least for a short time after their production. Services, on the other hand, are usually *non-storable:* for example, the service of 'accommodation in an hotel room for tonight' will perish if it is not sold before tonight – accommodation in the same room tomorrow is a different output from the service.

Transportability

Another consequence of tangibility is the ability to *transport* goods. Automobiles, machine tools and video cameras can all be moved. However, if services are intangible they are *untransportable.* Health services, for example, cannot be exported as such (though the means of producing health services can).

15

Table 1.5 Different types of transformation processes

	Physical properties	Informational properties	Possession	Location	Storage/ Accommodation	Physiological state	Psychological state
Materials processors	All manufacturing operations Mining and extraction		Retail operations	Postal services Freight distribution Port operations	Warehouses		
Information processors		Bank HQs Accountants Architects	Financial analysts Market research companies Universities Consultants News services	Telecoms company	Library Archives		
Customer processors	Hairdressers Plastic surgeons			Public transport Taxis	Hotels	Hospitals Other health care	Education Psychoanalysts Theatres Theme parks

Simultaneity

The other main distinction between goods and services concerns the timing of their production. Goods are nearly always *produced prior* to the customer receiving (or even seeing) them. For example the CD you just bought was produced well before you bought it. Services, however, are often *produced simultaneously* with their consumption. The service which the shop provided in selling you the CD happened at the same time as you 'consumed' the service by buying it.

Customer contact

The implication of this is that customers have a *low contact* level with the operations which produce goods. Although you probably will have bought and consumed bread for most of your life, you have probably never seen the inside of a bakery. Whereas in services, because they are produced and consumed simultaneously, they must have *high contact* between the customer and the operation.

Quality

Finally, because generally customers do not see the production of goods, they will judge the quality of the operation which produced them on the evidence of the goods themselves. The quality of goods is reasonably *evident*. Even if we disagree as to the quality of our new personal computer, for example, we can measure its capabilities and record its reliability in a reasonably objective manner. But, in services, the customer, who is probably inside the operation, judges not only the outcome of the service, but also the aspects of the way in which it was produced. For example, in purchasing a new pair of shoes you might be perfectly satisfied that the shoes were in stock and that you were promptly served. If the shop assistant was discourteous, abrupt or threatening, however, you would not consider the service to be of a high quality. Other customers, on the other hand, might be less sensitive than you are in consuming and judging the service. How then should the operation judge its quality of service? (Chapter 17 deals with this point.)

Some operations produce just goods and some produce just services, but most operations produce a mixture of the two. Figure 1.4 shows a number of operations positioned in a spectrum from 'pure' goods producers to 'pure' service producers.

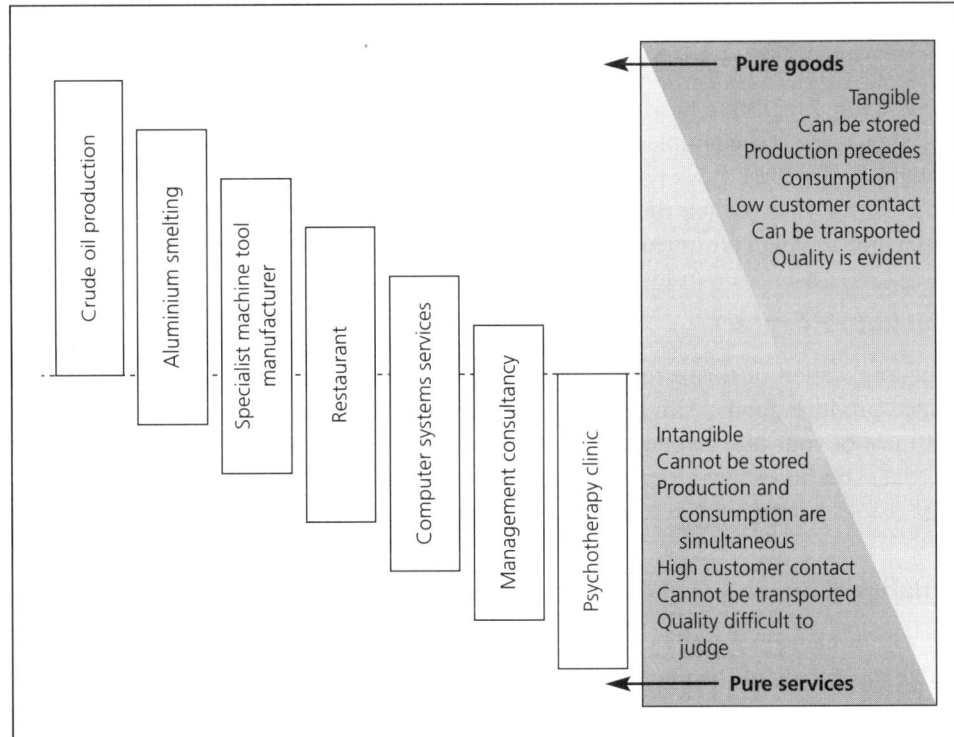

Figure 1.4
The output from most types of operation is a mixture of goods and services

The operations system hierarchy

The input–transformation–output model can also be used within operations. Look inside most operations and they will be made up of several units or departments, which themselves act as smaller versions of the whole operation of which they form a part.

For example, the operations function of a large television broadcasting company has inputs of programme and technical staff, cameras, recording and transmission equipment, news and programme information, video tape, and so on. It transforms these into finished programmes which it broadcasts on the network. Within this overall operation, however, there are many smaller operations. For example, there will be:

● workshops which manufacture the scenery and properties for the productions;
● costume departments which make costumes for current productions and store costumes from previous productions;
● researchers who test out programme ideas on potential audiences and give information and advice to programme makers;
● a maintenance department which maintains, cares for and repairs the programme-making and broadcasting equipment;
● outside broadcast units which transport broadcasting facilities to locations away from the main sites,

and many more.

The whole television broadcasting operation could be termed a *macro operation*, while its departments could be termed *micro operations* (*see* Fig. 1.5). These micro operations have inputs, some of which will come from outside the macro operation but many of which will be supplied from other internal micro operations. Each micro operation will also produce outputs of goods and services for the benefit of customers. Again though, some of each micro operation's customers will be other micro operations. This concept of macro and micro operations can be extended further. Within each micro operation

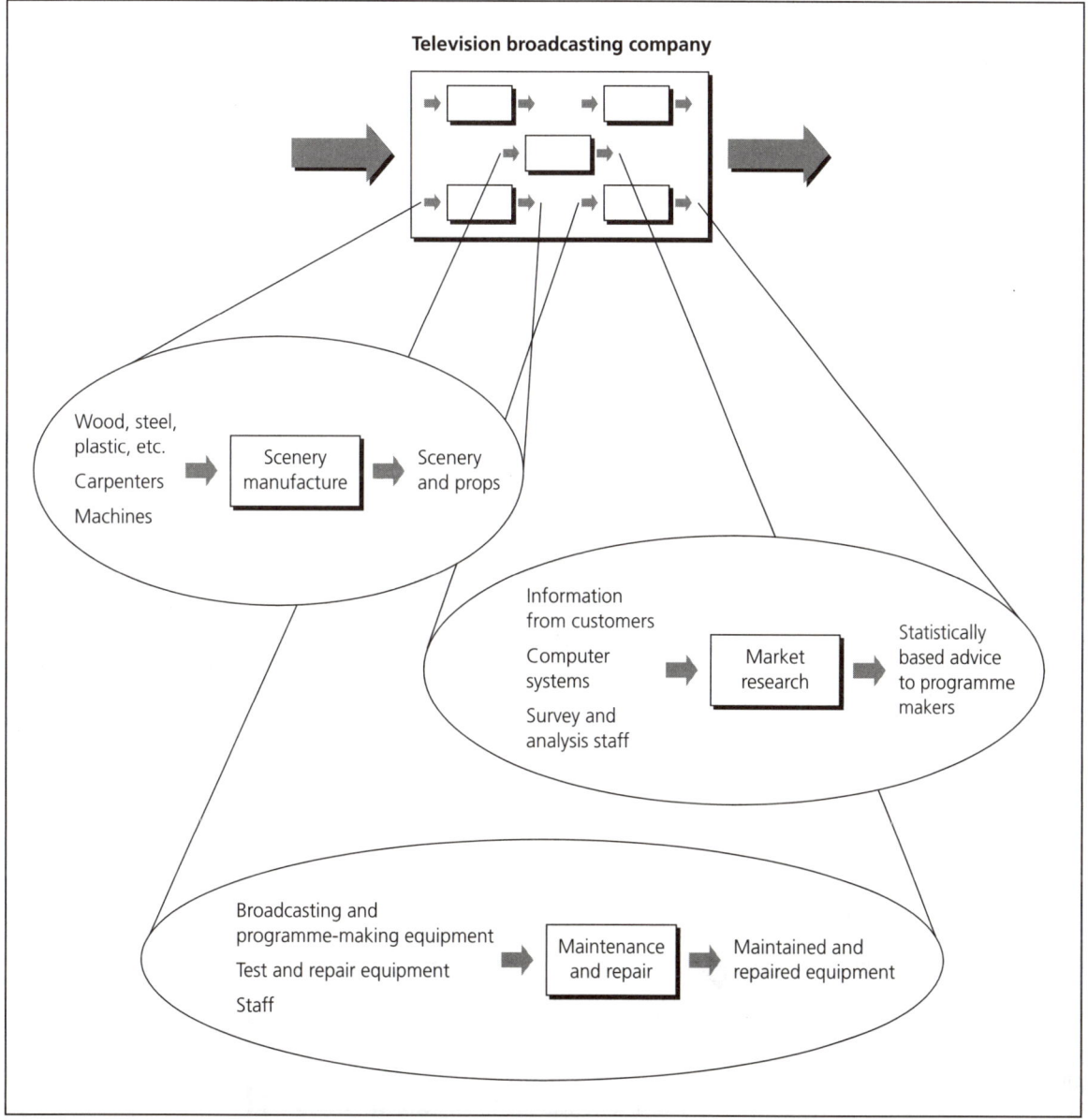

Figure 1.5 All macro operations are made up of many micro operations

there might be sections or groups which also can be considered as operations in their own right. These sections or groups might also take much of their input from, and give much of their output to, other sections or groups, both within their own micro operation and outside it. In this way any operations function can be considered as a *hierarchy of operations* – perhaps extending down even as far as the individual staff member taking inputs, carrying out a transforming process and producing outputs.

This concept of a hierarchy of operations has two particularly important implications. One concerns the linkage of micro operations to form internal customer– internal supplier relationships. The other concerns the way we can view all parts of the organization as operations, requiring operations management.

Internal customer–internal supplier relationships

The terms *internal customer* and *internal supplier* can be used to describe those who take outputs from, and give inputs to, any micro operations. These internal customers and internal suppliers are, of course, other micro operations. Thus we could model any operations function as a network of micro operations which are engaged in transforming materials, information, or customers (that is staff) for each other, each micro operation being at the same time both an internal supplier of goods and services and an internal customer for the other micro operation's goods and services (*see* Fig. 1.6).

We cannot treat *internal* customers and suppliers in exactly the same way as we do *external* customers and suppliers, however. External customers and suppliers usually operate in a free market. If an organization believes that in the long run it can get a better deal by purchasing goods and services from another supplier, it will do so. Similarly, the organization would not expect its customers to purchase its own goods and services unless it could in some way offer a better deal than its competitors. Internal customers and suppliers, however, cannot operate like this. They are not in a 'free market' and they usually cannot look outside either to purchase input resources or to sell their output goods and services (although some organizations are moving this way (*see* Chapter 13)).

Provided we remember that there are differences between internal and external customers, the concept is a very useful one. First, it provides us with a model to analyse the internal activities of an operation. If the macro operation is not working as

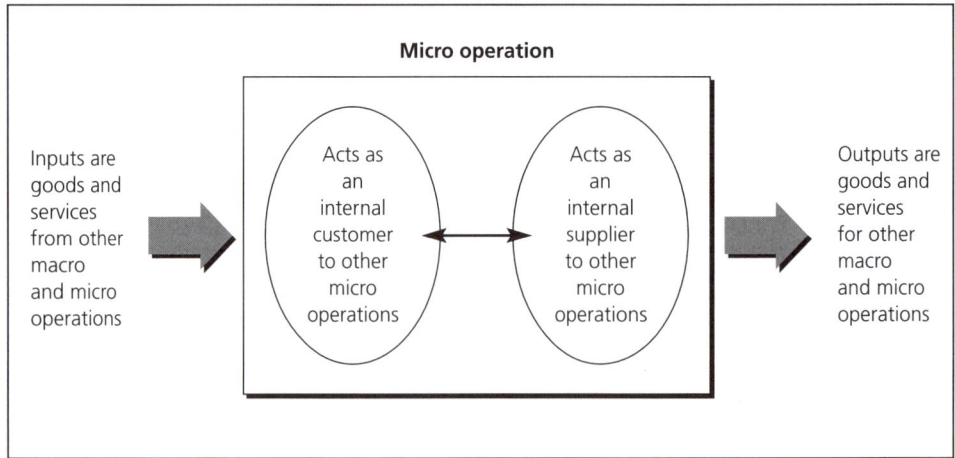

**Figure 1.6
All macro and micro operations are both customers and suppliers**

it should, we can trace the problem back along the internal network of customers and suppliers. Second, it is a useful reminder to all parts of the operation that, by treating their internal customers with the same degree of care that they exercise on their external customers, the effectiveness of the whole operation can be improved. This idea is one of the foundations of total quality management, which we cover in Chapter 20.

Buffering the operation

The turbulent environment in which most organizations do business means that the operations function is having to adjust continually to changing circumstances. Operations are vulnerable to 'environmental' uncertainty in both supply and demand. A food-processing operation might not be able to predict exactly when some foods will be harvested. In extreme cases very bad weather might totally disrupt the supply to a factory for weeks. Demand could also be prone to disruption. Unpredictable changes in the weather, a 'health scare' story in the press, and so on, can all introduce turbulence. One way in which operations managers try to minimize 'environmental' disruption is by *buffering* the operation in some way. This means insulating the operations function from the external environment. It can be done in two ways:[4]

● *physical buffering* – designing an inventory or stock of resources either at the input side of the transformation process, or at the output side;
● *organizational buffering* – allocating the responsibilities of the various functions in the organization so that the operations function is protected from the external environment by other functions.

The disadvantages of buffering the operation

The whole concept of buffering the operations function is not without its critics, especially in recent years, and partly due to the influence of Japanese operations practice.[5]
A number of objections to buffering can be made:

● The time lag of communicating between the insulating function and the operations function makes change difficult. By the time the insulating function has responded, operations has 'moved on to the next problem'.
● Operations never develops the understanding of the environment (e.g. labour or technological markets) which would help it exploit new developments (not true for companies such as Body Shop (*see* the box)).
● Operations is never required to take responsibility for its actions. There is always another function to blame and unhelpful conflict may arise between functions.
● Physical buffering often involves tolerating large stocks of input or output resources. These are both expensive (*see* Chapter 12, Inventory planning and control) and prevent the operation improving (*see* Chapter 15, Just-in-time planning and control).
● Physical buffering in customer-processing operations means making the customer wait for service, which in turn could lead to customer dissatisfaction.

For of all these reasons, there has been, in general and in most types of operation, a move towards exposing the operations function to its environment. Operations, in order to cope with this, has needed to develop the necessary flexibility to respond to, and understand, what is really happening with its customers and suppliers. The relationship between the operation's functions and the other functions is also changing. Some functions are now seeing their role as one of *facilitating* rather than *replacing* contact between the operation and the environment.

GREEN OPERATIONS AT BODY SHOP[6]

The Body Shop formulates and manufactures skin- and hair-care products, but perhaps it is best known for its unique and highly successful shops which brim with brightly coloured lotions, soaps, shampoos and oils. It is also renowned for its positive approach to environmentally conscious operations. The company has led the field in green operations by using only minimal and simple packaging, encouraging the recycling and refilling of containers, by not testing products on animals, by using natural materials wherever possible, and by having strong and explicit social policies. Although not without its critics, Body Shop argues that it wanted to prove that it is possible to develop a profitable business and at the same time maintain a respect for the environment, the communities where its operations have an impact, its employees, and its customers. This philosophy affects its operations management policies in a number of ways.

- *Socially responsible purchasing*. At one time wooden foot rollers were purchased from a company in Frankfurt. The company now sources them from a workshop which it set up in an Indian village to provide employment and training for the older children in an orphanage. Ignoring the lower costs, the company paid the same price to the workshop, the revenue being used to help the village to improve its education, health and nutritional standards. Six similar workshops have now been established in India.
- *Using renewable sources*. The company took a lead in encouraging a Nepalese paper factory to switch from clearing the local forest for its raw materials to using renewable sources such as banana skins.
- *Social location*. The company bought an abandoned factory in a deprived area of Glasgow and converted it into a soap factory which now makes over 25 million bars sold throughout the world. As well as bringing much needed employment to the area, a quarter of the profit is returned for community projects.
- *Re-using*. The company provides a refill service in all its shops where empty plastic bottles can be refilled in return for a reduction on the purchase price. Over two million bottles are refilled every year in the UK alone.
- *Recycling waste*. Most synthetic polymers which can be recycled need to be sorted prior to recycling. The company has a standard labelling scheme which identifies the type of plastic used on each of its packages. This makes the sorting process, and therefore recycling, easier. ■

TYPES OF OPERATIONS

We have already noted that operations are all similar to each other in the way they all transform input resources into output goods and services. We now examine some of the differences between operations. More importantly we identify the implications of these differences.

There are four particularly important measures which can be used to distinguish between different operations:

- the *volume* of their output;
- the *variety* of their output;
- the *variation* in the demand for their output;
- the *degree of customer contact* which is involved in producing the output.

The volume dimension

Let us take a familiar example – the production and sale of the internationally ubiquitous hamburger. The epitome of high-volume hamburger production is McDonald's which serves approximately 23 million burgers around the world every day! This is high volume, even when it is divided by its around 13 000 branches world-wide. The volume of burgers produced and served by McDonald's has important implications for the way its operations are organized. Look behind the counter in a high-volume burger bar and the first thing you notice is the *repeatability* of the tasks people are doing. Because tasks are repeated frequently it makes sense to *specialize* the tasks: one person assigned to cooking the burgers, another assembling the buns, another serving, and so on. And when tasks are divided in this way it also allows the *systemization* of the work. In fact large fast food chains nearly always have standard procedures, set down in a manual, with instructions on how each part of the job should be carried out. Systemization can also lead to higher *capital intensity* of the operation, for example the development of specialized fryers and ovens. The most important implication of high volume, though, is that it gives *low unit costs*; the fixed costs of the operation, such as heating and rent, are spread over a large number of products or services.

Compare a small local cafeteria serving a few 'short order' dishes with the multinational burger chain. The range of items on the menu is likely to be similar to the larger operation, but the volume will be far lower. Here the degree of repetition will be far lower because of the lower volume. Furthermore the number of staff will be lower (possibly only one person) and, therefore, the amount of the whole job of making and serving the food which each staff member performs will be greater. This may be more rewarding for the staff, but less open to systemization. Fewer burgers cooked also makes it less feasible to invest in specialized equipment. For all of these reasons it follows that the cost per burger served is likely to be higher (even if the price is comparable).

Table 1.6 lists examples of operations which are either high or low volume. It is advisable to take care, however, when applying the conventional generalization regarding high- and low-volume operations. For example, aircraft manufacture is relatively low volume compared with television manufacture. Yet much of our comments on high-volume operations still apply to aircraft production. It is highly systemized, with

Table 1.6 High- and low-volume operations

High-volume operations	Low-volume operations
Television manufacture	Aircraft manufacture
Fast food restaurant	Small high-class restaurant
Routine surgery	Pioneering surgery
Mass rapid transport system	Taxi service
Theme park	Studio theatre

specialized jobs, performed by staff who only undertake a small part of the total job. Aircraft are even made on an assembly line basis (albeit a very slow one) like televisions. This seeming anomaly is partly due to the care taken in the construction of

THE HENRY FORD OF OPHTHALMOLOGY[7]

High-volume operations can be found in some surprising places – even surgery. Not all surgery conforms to our preconceptions of the individual 'super-craftsperson', aided by his or her back-up team, performing the whole operation from first incision to final stitch. Many surgical procedures are, in fact, fairly routine. There can be few examples, however, of surgery being made quite as routine as in the Russian clinics of eye surgeon, Svyatoslav Fyodorov.

He has been called the 'Henry Ford of Ophthalmology', and his methods are indeed closer to the automobile assembly plant than the conventional operating theatre. The surgical procedure in which he specializes is a revolutionary treatment for myopia (short sightedness) called radial keratotomy. In the treatment the curvature of the cornea is corrected surgically – still a controversial procedure among some in the profession, but very successful for Fyodorov. From his Moscow headquarters he controls nine clinics throughout Russia.

The source of his fame is not the treatment as such – other eye surgeons around the world perform similar procedures – but the way he organizes the business of the surgery itself. Eight patients lie on moving tables arranged like the spokes of a wheel around its central axis, only their eyes uncovered. Six surgeons, each with his or her 'station', are positioned around the rim of the wheel so that they can access the patients' eyes. After the surgeons have completed their own particular portion of the whole procedure, the wheel indexes round to take patients to the next stage of their treatment. The surgeons check to make sure that the previous stage of the operation was performed correctly and then go on to perform their own task. Each surgeon's activity is monitored on TV screens overhead and the surgeons talk with each other through miniature microphones and headsets.

The result of this mass production approach to surgery according to Fyodorov is not only far cheaper unit costs (he and his staff are paid for each patient treated so they are all exceptionally wealthy as a result) but also a better success rate than that obtained in conventional surgery. ■

aircraft because of safety considerations. It is mainly due, however, to the amount of work which goes into each aircraft. The number of products made may be relatively low, but the number of staff hours which are devoted to a day's production is very high, as is the number of times a rivet is inserted and a cable is joined each day.

The variety dimension

A taxi company offers a high variety service. It may confine its services to the transportation of people and their luggage, but it is prepared to pick you up from almost anywhere and drop you almost anywhere. It may even (at a price) take you by a route of your choice. In order to do this it must be relatively *flexible*. It must make sure that its drivers have a good knowledge of the area and that the communication between its base and the taxis is effective. The task of keeping track of all its customers' requests and the status of all its taxis can be complex, partly because of the variety of pick-up and drop-off points and routes 'live' at any one time. However, the variety on offer by the service does allow it to match its services closely to its customers' needs. Flexibility, however, does come at a price. The cost per kilometre travelled will be higher for a taxi than for a lower variety, less customized form of transport such as a bus service.

There are similarities between a bus service and a taxi service. Both serve, more or less, the same customers with the same needs by providing transport over relatively short distances (say less than 20 km). Yet in some ways their operations are very dissimilar. This is largely due to the difference in the variety or services they offer. Whereas the taxi service has in theory an infinite number of routes to offer its customers, the bus service has a few, well defined routes. The buses travel these routes according to a set schedule, published well in advance and adhered to in a routine manner. If all goes to schedule, little, if any, flexibility is required from the operation. All is *standardized* and *regular*. More significantly, the lack of change and disruption in the day-to-day running of the operation results in relatively low costs compared with using a taxi for the same journey. Table 1.7 illustrates some high- and low-variety operations.

Table 1.7 High- and low-variety operations

High-variety operations	Low-variety operations
Customized birthday cake decoration shop	Mass production of birthday cakes
Made-to-measure suit manufacture	Off-the-peg suit manufacture
Tutorials at university	Lectures at university
Tax consultancy advice by accounting company	Financial audits by accounting company
Department store	Jeans shop
Corporate banking	Credit card transaction processing

The variation dimension

Consider the demand pattern for a successful summer holiday resort hotel. Not surprisingly more customers want to stay in summer vacation times than in the middle of winter. At the height of 'the season' the hotel could possibly accommodate twice its capacity if it had the space. Off-season demand, however, could be a small fraction of its capacity; it might even consider closing down in very quiet periods. The implication of such a marked variation in demand levels is that the operation *must change its capacity* in some way. It might, for example, hire extra staff for the summer period only. There are other options which an operation might adopt so as to minimize the extent to which it has to change its capacity: for example, if its outputs are storable (as in manufacturing) it could store them in anticipation of future demand. Nevertheless, some kind of *flexibility* either in its output level or the amount of goods it stores will be necessary. But in flexing its activities the hotel must try to predict the level of demand it is likely to receive. If it gets this wrong and adjusts its capacity below the actual demand level, it will lose business. All of these factors have the effect of increasing the hotel's costs. Recruitment costs, overtime costs, and underutilization of its rooms all make for a relatively high cost per guest operation compared with an hotel of a similar standard with level demand.

Conversely, an hotel which is close to both a major road network and a tourist attraction might be patronized by business travellers during the week and by tourists at weekends and holiday periods. Its demand is therefore relatively level. Under these circumstances the hotel can plan its activities well in advance. Staff can be scheduled, food can be bought and rooms can be cleaned in a *routine* and *predictable* manner. This results in a *high utilization* of resources. Not surprisingly the unit costs of this hotel are likely to be lower than the comparable hotel with a highly variable demand pattern. Table 1.8 shows different operations with either high or low demand variations. This whole issue of how operations cope with demand fluctuation is treated in Chapter 11.

Table 1.8 High and low 'variation in demand' operations

High-variation operations	*Low-variation operations*
Electricity utility	Bread bakery
Firework manufacturer	Consultancy advice by accounting companies
Financial audits by accounting companies	Shopping mall security operation
Police and emergency services	Frozen food transport distribution
Underground metro network	Cosmetic surgery unit
Maternity unit	

The customer contact dimension

Earlier it was noted that for some operations the primary transformed resource is their customers. The decision of whether to accept customers into the operation, or keep them away, is a fundamental one, and is very much related to the nature of the service or product itself. This means it is unusual to find a pure high-contact and a pure low-contact version of the same category of operation. Nevertheless, within limits, some organizations do have a choice as to how they wish to develop their operations. For example in clothes retailing, an organization could decide to operate as a chain of conventional boutique-type shops. Alternatively, it could decide not to have any shops at all but rather to run a catalogue-based operation.

The shop operation would be a high-contact operation insomuch as the majority of its 'value-adding' activities take place with the customer present. Customers in this type of operation have a relatively *short waiting tolerance*. They will walk out if not served in a reasonable time (unless they are desperate). They might also judge the operation by their perceptions of it rather than always by objective criteria. If they perceive that a member of the operation's staff is discourteous to them, they are likely to be dissatisfied (even if the staff member meant no discourtesy). Given this, high-contact operations require staff with good customer contact skills. Customers could also request goods which clearly would not be sold in such a shop, but because the customers are actually in the operation they can ask what they like! This is called *high received variety*, and will occur even if the variety of service for which the operation is designed is low. This does not make it easy for high-contact operations to achieve high productivity of resources, with the consequence that they tend to be relatively high-cost operations.

Contrast the clothes shop with the catalogue-based operation. The latter is not a pure low-contact operation; it still has to communicate with its customers if it wishes to receive their orders. It will do this either by telephone or (lower contact still) through the mail. For the part of the process which involves the customer talking by telephone with the customer service staff, all the characteristics of the shop will apply. The customers will not want to be kept waiting for the telephone to be answered, the perceptions of different customers can vary even if the service is the same, good customer contact skills (though slightly different) are needed and received variety is high.

However the remainder of the process is more 'factory like'. The *time lag* between the order being placed and the items ordered by the customer being retrieved and dispatched does not have to be minutes as in the shop, but can be hours or even days. This allows the tasks of finding the items, packing and dispatching them to be *standardized* by organizing staff, who need *no customer contact skills*, so as to achieve *high staff utilization*. The catalogue-based organization can also centralize its operation on one site, whereas the shop chain, because of its high-contact nature, necessarily needs many sites close to centres of demand. For all these reasons the catalogue operation will have lower costs than the shop chain. Table 1.9 shows some examples of high-, low-, and mixed-contact operations and Fig. 1.7 summarizes the implications of all four dimensions.

Table 1.9 High-, low- and mixed-customer contact operations

High-contact operations	Mixed-, high- and low-contact operations	Low-contact operations
Health care service	Computer field servicing	Most manufacturing
Home improvement builders	Bank branches	Bank back office operations
Cook at your table restaurant	Bistro-style restaurant	Prepackaged sandwich maker
Dentist	Estate agent	Dental technicians
Music teacher	University	Distance-learning college

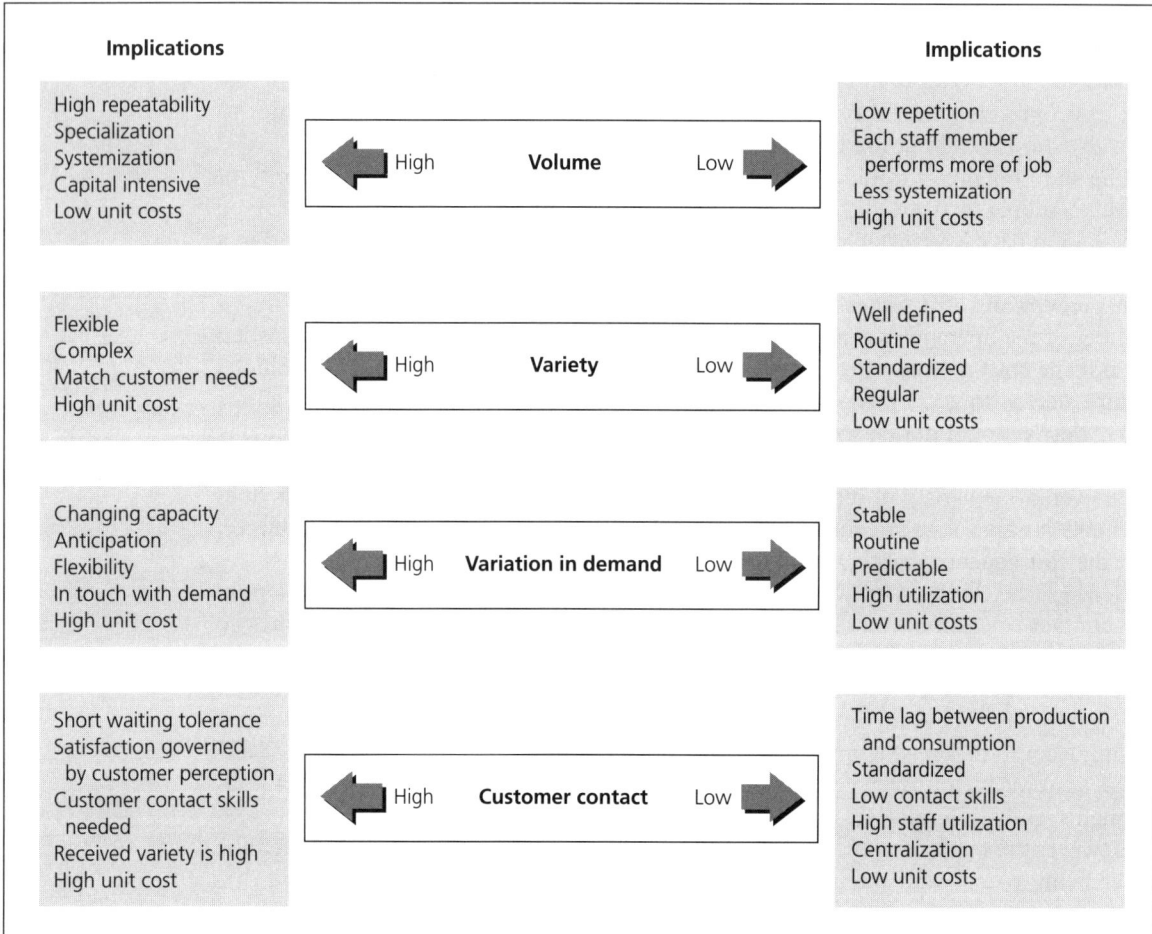

Implications

High repeatability
Specialization
Systemization
Capital intensive
Low unit costs

High **Volume** Low

Low repetition
Each staff member
  performs more of job
Less systemization
High unit costs

Implications

Flexible
Complex
Match customer needs
High unit cost

High **Variety** Low

Well defined
Routine
Standardized
Regular
Low unit costs

Changing capacity
Anticipation
Flexibility
In touch with demand
High unit cost

High **Variation in demand** Low

Stable
Routine
Predictable
High utilization
Low unit costs

Short waiting tolerance
Satisfaction governed
  by customer perception
Customer contact skills
  needed
Received variety is high
High unit cost

High **Customer contact** Low

Time lag between production
  and consumption
Standardized
Low contact skills
High staff utilization
Centralization
Low unit costs

Figure 1.7 A typology of operations

Mixed high- and low-contact operations

The clothes catalogue retail operation described above had both high-contact and low-contact micro operations within the same macro operation. This is typical of many operations and it serves to emphasize the difference which the degree of customer contact makes. Take an airport as an example: some of its activities involve high contact with its customers (ticketing staff dealing with the queues of travellers; the information desk answering people's queries; caterers serving meals and drinks; and passport control and security staff checking documentation and baggage). These staff operate in what is termed a *front-office* environment. That is, they are in the high customer contact micro operations. Other parts of the airport have relatively little if any direct contact with the customers (the baggage handlers; the overnight freight operations staff; the ground crew putting meals on board and refreshing the aircraft; the cleaners preparing them for their next flight; the cooks and the administrators). We rarely see these staff: they perform all the vital low customer contact tasks, and they do so in what is termed the *back-office* part of the operation.

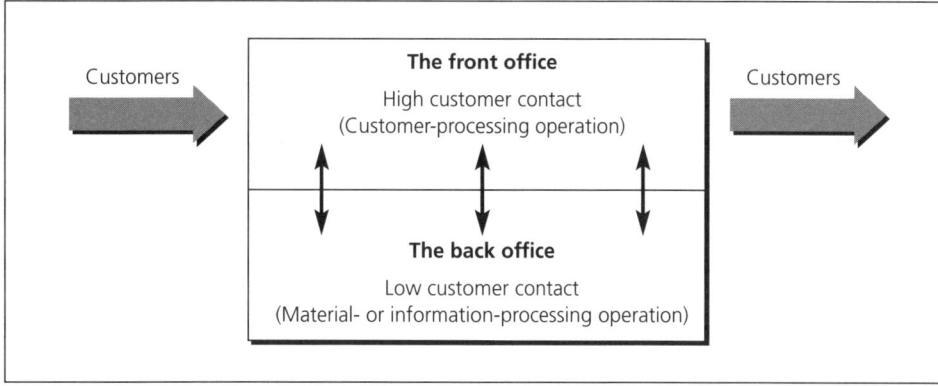

Figure 1.8
When an operation has mixed high and low customer contact, it is often separated into back and front offices

Operations such as airports find it convenient to separate the front-office, high-contact, from back-office, low-contact parts of the operation. They do so because they require different skills from their staff, different ways of organizing work, and different operational objectives. Figure 1.8 illustrates this separation.

FORMULE 1 – THE MOST AFFORDABLE HOTEL CHAIN[8]

Providing budget-priced hotel accommodation which is also modern, comfortable, hygienic and of consistent quality seems to be almost a contradiction. Hotels, after all, are outstanding examples of high-contact services – they are both staff intensive and have to cope with the variety demanded by customers, each with a variety of needs and expectations. Is it then impossible to run a highly successful chain of affordable hotels without the crippling costs of high customer contact? Not for Formule 1, a subsidiary of the French Accor group, whose chain of budget hotels stretches throughout Europe and South Africa. They manage to offer outstanding value by adopting two principles not always associated with hotel operations – standardization and an innovative use of technology.

Formule 1 hotels are usually located close to industrial trading estates by trunk roads, junctions and close to cities, in order to be visible and accessible for prospective customers. The hotels themselves, which are instantly recognizable and made from state-of-the-art volumetric prefabrications, come in five sizes – 50, 64, 73, 80 and 98 rooms. The prefabricated units are arranged in various configurations to suit the characteristics of each individual site. All rooms are nine square metres in area, and are designed to be attractive, functional, comfortable and soundproof. Most important, they are designed to be easy to clean and maintain. All have the same fittings including a double bed, an additional bunk-type bed, a wash basin, a storage area, a working table with seat, a wardrobe and a television set.

The reception of a Formule 1 hotel is staffed only from 6.30 am to 10.00 am and from 5.00 pm to 10.00 pm. Outside these times an automatic machine sells rooms to credit card users, providing access to the hotel, dispensing a security code for the room and even printing out a receipt. Technology is also evident in the washrooms. Showers and toilets are automatically cleaned after each use by using nozzles and heating elements to spray the room with a disinfectant solution and dry it before it is used again.

To keep things even simpler, Formule 1 hotels do not include a restaurant, as they are usually located near existing restaurants. However, a continental breakfast is available, usually between 6.30 am and 10.00 am, and of course on a 'self-service' basis! ■

THE ACTIVITIES OF OPERATIONS MANAGEMENT

Operations managers have some responsibility for all the activities in the organization which contribute to the effective production of goods and services. This area of responsibility is probably considerably wider than the operations function itself, no matter how wide is the organization's definition of what constitutes 'operations'. It is the term 'responsibility' which needs further explanation. Operations managers have:

- *indirect responsibility* for some activities, and
- *direct responsibility* for other activities.

The indirect responsibilities of operations managers

Many of the activities which take place in organizations fall well outside the conventional boundaries of the operations function yet do have an effect on the way it produces its goods and services. For example, the way in which organizations produce their advertising plans is almost always a direct responsibility of the marketing function. Does this mean that operations managers should bear no responsibility for the organization's advertising plans? While the activity is quite clearly in the marketing domain, the effect of the activity could have a significant impact on the operation. It will affect overall demand levels and the exact mix of products and services which customers will want.

In these circumstances the responsibility of operations management is to explore the possible consequences of the advertising plans with the marketing function. It should understand their impact on the operation, make clear to marketing what the operation can and cannot do in response to any change in demand, and work together with marketing to find ways of allowing them to meet, or manage, market needs while also allowing the operation to run efficiently and effectively.

Generally the indirect responsibilities of operations management can be summarized as:

- to inform other functions of the opportunities and constraints provided by the operation's capabilities;
- to discuss with other functions how both operations' plans and their own plans might be modified for the benefit of both functions;
- to encourage other functions to suggest ways in which the operations function can improve its 'service' to the rest of the organization.

This approach *of mutual responsibility* for other functions' activities is one effect of the *internal customer–internal supplier* concept discussed earlier. To those with experience of organizational life it might also seem somewhat idealistic. It is an idealistic approach in the sense that it points the way to what undoubtedly should be good practice in any organization, but it is not a 'hopeless' aspiration. Many organizations are feeling the benefits of breaking down some of their traditional organizational barriers.

The direct responsibilities of operations management

The exact nature of the operations function's direct responsibilities will, to some extent, depend on the way the organization has chosen to define its operation function. This was discussed previously (*see* Fig. 1.2). There are some general classes of activities, however, which apply to all types of operation no matter how functional boundaries have been drawn. These activities include:

- understanding the operation's strategic objectives;
- developing an operations strategy for the organization;
- designing the operation's products, services and processes;
- planning and controlling the operation;
- improving the performance of the operation.

Understanding the operation's strategic objectives

The first responsibility of any operations management team is to understand what it is trying to achieve. This involves two sets of decisions. The first is to develop a clear vision of what *role* the operation is to play in the organization: that is broadly how should the operation contribute to the organization achieving its long-term goals. The second is to translate the organization's goals into their implications for the operations *performance objectives*. We include in operations performance objectives the *quality* of its goods and services, the *speed* with which they are delivered to customers, the *dependability* with which the operation keeps its delivery promises, the *flexibility* of the operation to change what it does, and the *cost* of producing its goods and services. All these issues are discussed in Chapter 2.

Developing an operations strategy for the organization

Operations management is a very immediate occupation. It involves hundreds of minute-by-minute decisions through the working week. Because of this it is vital that operations managers have a set of general principles which can guide decision-making towards the organization's longer-term goals. This is an *operations strategy*. It involves being able to place operations strategy in the general strategy hierarchy of the organization, which connects functional and business strategies together. It also involves prioritizing the operations performance objectives in a way which links them to customer needs and competitor behaviour. Chapter 3 deals with operations strategy.

Designing the operation's products, services and processes

Design, in our terms, is the activity of determining the physical form, shape and composition of products, services and processes. In operations management it is the set of activities which literally sets the scene for all its other activities.

Direct responsibility for the design of the products and services of the organization might not be part of the operations function in some organizations. However, it is so crucial to the operation's other activities that we consider the design process in general in Chapter 4 and the design of products and services in particular in Chapter 5. But the design activity is also crucial to an area which is always under the direct responsibility of the operations function – the transformation process itself. At the most strategic level, process design means designing the whole network of operations which provide inputs to the operations function and deliver its output to customers. This activity involves consideration of the boundaries of ownership for the operation. These issues are dealt with in Chapter 6. At a more immediate level, operations managers need to design their process layouts and flows of transformed resources through the operation, an issue treated in Chapter 7. The design issues involving the two main 'ingredients' which make up the operation, process technology and staff, are treated in Chapter 8 and Chapter 9 respectively.

Planning and controlling the operation

The design activities should have put all the operation's resources in place, but to work effectively they need to be planned and controlled.

Planning and control is the activity of deciding what the operations resources should be doing, then making sure that they really are doing it. Chapter 10 explains the nature of planning and control activities. At its most aggregated level, planning and control involves managing the capacity of the operation so as to meet fluctuating demand levels, an issue treated in Chapter 11. The planning and control of the flow of the transformed resources through the operation is treated in two parts. Chapter 12 deals with inventory management. Chapter 13 deals with the 'supply chain' management – the flow of goods and services from suppliers to customers. Managing the planning and control of the transformation process itself depends partly on the nature of the operation. Some particular approaches have been developed which are appropriate under different circumstances. For example, Material Requirements Planning (MRP) controls the timing and quantity of processing in complex operations, and is treated in Chapter 14. The just-in-time (JIT) approach to planning and control is described in Chapter 15, although it is worth noting that many of the philosophies of just-in-time management have influenced several other parts of this book. Chapter 16 treats planning and control in project operations. Finally, Chapter 17 treats the management of the quality of products and services.

Improving the performance of the operation

The strategy of the operation is set, its products, services and processes are designed, and its work is being planned and controlled on an ongoing basis. Yet this is not the end of operations management's direct responsibilities. The continuing responsibility of all operations managers is to improve the performance of their operation. Failure to improve at least as fast as competitors (in for-profit organizations) or at the rate of customers' rising expectations (in all organizations) is to condemn the operations function always to fall short of what the organization should expect from it. Chapter 18 describes how the process of improvement can be organized within the operation. The other side of making operations better is stopping them going wrong in the first place. Chapter 19 deals with how failures are prevented in operations, and how the operation can recover when failure does occur. Finally in this area there is what is probably the most powerful of all the improvement ideas to influence operations world-wide – Total Quality Management (TQM). This is covered in Chapter 20.

WHAT OPERATIONS MANAGERS ACTUALLY DO[9]

In all of operations management's direct and indirect activities there is a need to communicate both with internal staff and with external customers, suppliers and the broader community. One survey carried out by Professor Arnoud De Meyer shows how much of a factory manager's time is spent on different activities, and how the importance of each is changing (*see* Table 1.10).

Table 1.10 Breakdown of factory manager's work

Activity	% of time	Degree of change (1 = spending less time, 7 = spending more time)
Direct supervision and support	22	3.5
Consulting with plant staff	16	3.9
Consulting with upper management	12	4.0
Consulting with sales and marketing	10	4.8
Communicating with customers	7	4.8
Communicating with suppliers	7	4.4
Consulting with Research and Development	5	4.7
Dealing with the community	5	4.5
Training (as trainer)	4	4.6
Training (as trainee)	4	4.6

Consulting and communicating with operations staff clearly takes up a large amount of these operations managers' time. But the proportion of their time spent communicating with people outside the operations function and even outside the organization appears to be gaining in importance. This means, says Professor De Meyer, that operations managers are evolving to be more '*.... managers of interfaces, as opposed to a caretaker of an isolated manufacturing function*'. ■

THE MODEL OF OPERATIONS MANAGEMENT

We can now combine two of the ideas we have described, to develop the model of operations management which will be used throughout this book. The first idea is the input–transformation–output model and the second is the categorization of operations management's activity areas. Figure 1.9 shows how these two ideas go together. The fundamental purpose of operations management, the transformation of input resources into goods and services, is illustrated by the input–transformation–output diagram. Within the transformation process are the three activity areas which select, locate and organize the transforming resources and which determine the nature and timing of the flow of transformed resources. These are the *design*, *planning and control* and *improvement* activities. They are shown as being connected in, more or less, the chronological order in which they would happen if a totally new operation was being developed. It would first be designed, it would then be operated through planning and control activities and over time would be continually improved.

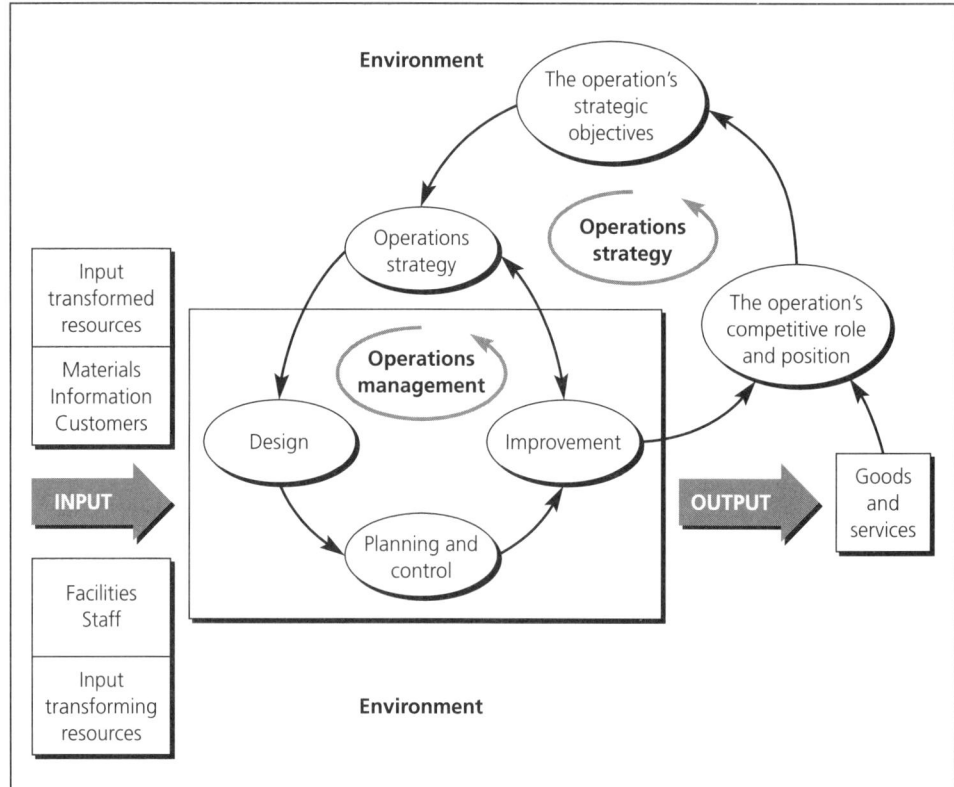

**Figure 1.9
A general model
of operations
management
and operations
strategy**

The market's reaction to the output of the operation's goods and services into the environment will determine whether the operation is being well managed. If the way goods and services are produced satisfies the organization's customers, the role of the operations function in contributing to competitive or strategic objectives will be confirmed. If it does not, the strategic objectives of the operations function will need to be reviewed. These objectives are refined and 'operationalized' in the operations strategy of the organization. 'Operationalized' in this sense means that the organization's strategic objectives and its operations activities are brought together. This is shown as a connection between operations strategy and the design activity primarily, but in reality operations strategy will also influence the planning and control and improvement activities. Of course, as the improvement activity gradually enhances the performance of the operation it can affect the operation's strategy by providing new opportunities for the operation to contribute to competitiveness. It can also change the role of the operation in the organization, moving it towards a central role in the organization's future.

The model now shows two interconnected loops of activities. The bottom one more or less corresponds to what is usually seen as *operations management*, and the top one to what is seen as *operations strategy*. This book concentrates on the former but tries to cover enough of the latter to allow the reader to make strategic sense of the operations manager's job.

Alan Phillips, Colgate Palmolive

Alan Phillips has been a factory manager at Colgate Palmolive, Dunswart factory, for the last 15 months. His key tasks include planning, budgeting, maintaining discipline and, most importantly, developing a continuous improvement programme. The factory provides employment to approximately 430 workers who work three shifts of eight and a quarter hours each. When he joined the company, its Dunswart factory had been running at a loss for three consecutive years. However, this year it has shown a profit again. To handle this type of change and then to maintain continuous improvement is a challenge.

'It was apparent that it would be possible to attain the same level of output if the staff were reduced by 35 per cent and if resources were applied differently. Also, it had previously taken two days to count raw material and packaging stocks. If a thick layer of dust has settled on inventory, it is a clear sign that unnecessary stocks are being kept. Some stocks were obsolete. Inventories were drastically reduced and it now takes five hours to do a stock count. The company insists on a customer service level of 98 per cent. This is measured in terms of deliveries being made in full and on time. Because it is essential to maintain a high customer service level, we keep buffer stock. Four weeks' supplies of finished goods are stocked in the warehouse and a two weeks' supply is stocked at a central depot.

'There is no doubt about it, working in the manufacturing operations area can be tough, but it is very rewarding. All the other functions of the business have to work with us, and, in a way, support us in our efforts to become more competitive. It is a great responsibility to lead this team of workers and the greatest challenge is to communicate well, both with the workforce and with the different disciplines in the business.

'For us, continuous improvement hinges on staff performance, the improvement of product formulations and the improvement of processes. It was discouraging for the workers who stayed behind when we had to let 35 per cent of the workforce go. They felt insecure about their jobs. Workers also perform monotonous, repetitive tasks. In order to maintain loyalty and stimulate their interest in the work, much time is invested in education and training. We distinguish between core, core + 1 and core + 2 workers. Core workers, which include forklift drivers, are low skilled. They are taught English and basic arithmetic. Machine operators are Core + 1 workers and are also taught artisan skills. They can change machine settings and perform minor maintenance tasks. Core + 2 workers function as team leaders and supervisors and are taught leadership and basic business skills. Workers are encouraged to seek promotion and acquire as many skills as possible.

'Although they are supposed to work an eight-hour shift, workers arrive a quarter of an hour before their shift starts. They meet in a designated 'green' area and discuss the work that has to be completed in the shift. At these meetings they are also encouraged to make suggestions on how the production process can be improved.' ■

Source: By kind permission of Colgate Palmolive

SUMMARY

■ All organizations have an operations function which produces their goods and services, and all organizations have operations managers who are responsible for running the operations function.

■ The operations function (or 'operation', or 'operations system') is important to the organization because it directly affects how well the organization satisfies its customers. The exact boundaries and terminology used to define the operations function vary between different operations, however. This book takes a relatively broad definition of operations management and includes some topics which, although they may be located in other functions in some organizations, have an impact on the production of goods and services.

■ The most useful method of modelling operations is as an input–transformation–output system. All operations can be described using this model. Input resources can be classified as transforming resources (the staff and facilities) which act upon the transformed resources (materials, information and customers) which are in some way transformed by the operation.

■ Outputs from the operation are usually a mixture of goods and services although some operations are pure goods producers or pure service producers.

■ This model of operations can also be used to model the units and departments within an operation to form an operations hierarchy. The total operation of the organization is termed the macro operation while its constituent departments and units are termed micro operations. Micro operations form a network of internal customer–internal supplier relationships within the operation.

■ Macro operations can be disrupted by the environment acting upon its inputs and outputs. Organizations sometimes seek to buffer their operations, either physically by using inventory, or organizationally by their organization structures. However, excessive buffering of the operation function can be seen as allowing it to become unresponsive to its suppliers and customers.

■ Operations can be classified along four dimensions which indicate their level of volume, variety, variation and customer contact. An organization's position on each of these dimensions will determine many of the characteristics of its operation such as its systemization, standardization, repetitions, the degree of the processing task undertaken by each member of the operation's staff, flexibility, and above all, the unit cost of producing goods and services.

■ The direct activities of operations management can be divided into various classes of activity. These are, understanding the strategic objectives of the operation, defining an operations strategy, designing the products, services and processes of the operation, planning and controlling its work, and improving its performance.

■ The input–transformation–output model of operations can be combined with the approximate chronological sequence of its activities to form a general model of operations management.

CASE EXERCISE

A business trip to Brussels

My flight to Stockholm would be late landing. The pilot told us that we were in a 'stack' of planes circling above the snow clouds that were giving Brussels its first taste of winter. Air traffic control had closed the runways for a short period at dawn, and the early morning flights from all around Europe were now being allocated new landing slots along with the long-haul jumbos from the Far East and the US. After a twenty-minute delay, we descended bumpily through the clouds, and landed on a recently cleared runway. Even then there was a further 'hold' on a taxiway; we were told that the de-icing of the apron was being completed so that planes could proceed to their allocated stands and airbridges. All around the airport I could see the scurrying flashing beacons of the snow-clearing vehicles, the catering suppliers' vans, the aviation fuel trucks, the baggage trailers, buses transporting crews and passengers, security police cars, and an assortment of other vehicles all going purposefully about their work. Brussels airport always looks busy, with over 10 million passengers a year, but this morning the complexity and scale of the operations were particularly evident.

Finally, about an hour late, we pulled up to the gate, the engines were turned off, and we disembarked into an icy-cold airbridge, leaving behind a particularly untidy plane strewn with the litter left behind by a full cabin of restless passengers. We passed the team of cleaners and maintenance staff waiting just outside. 'They will have a hard time this morning; more mess to clear and probably less time than usual to do it, as the airline will want a quick turnaround to get back on to schedule,' I commented to my colleagues. We could just hear the sounds of frantic activities going on below the plane: baggage and cargo being unloaded, catering vehicles arriving, fuel being loaded, and technicians checking over the engines and control surfaces – everyone trying to get their work completed quickly and correctly, not least so that they could get back indoors out of the biting cold wind!

From the airbridge we walked past the crowded seating areas, where plane-sized groups were gathering anxiously awaiting the signal from the gate staff to board their much delayed flights. Then on to the moving walkways, conveyed leisurely past other departure lounges, equally overfilled with passengers. Anxious to get ahead of the crowd, we took to a running pace past the rows of cafés, bars and shops, hoping to avoid the usual morning queue for Passport Control. I should have remembered the old saying 'more haste, less speed' because my next journey was to the First Aid room! I had apparently slipped on some spilt coffee that had not been cleaned up in the haste of the morning, and had fallen awkwardly, straining my ankle, and breaking my duty-free brandy. 'At least they would clean the floor after that', I thought, sadly.

Suitably patched up, I hobbled with my colleagues and joined the long queue for Passport Control, and eventually through to Baggage Reclaim. Even with the excellent new baggage handling systems in Brussels, the passengers usually get there first, but the accident had changed all that! Scanning the video screens, we found no reference to our flight arrival; the remaining bags from our flight had apparently already been removed from the carousel and stored in an adjacent office. After a simple signing ceremony, we were reunited with our belongings, and hastened (slowly in my case) to the taxi rank. Our hopes of a quick ride to the city were dispelled when we saw the long queue in the icy wind, so we made our way to the station below, where a dedicated 'City Express' train departs every 20 minutes for the Gare de Nord and Gare Centrale. We just missed one!

After a busy and successful day at our Brussels office, a taxi was called, and we were back at the airport in the thick of the evening rush hour. The departures check-in area is the upper floor of a vast new terminal extension, and very orderly and well equipped. Facing you on entry from the taxi drop-off point is a huge electronic display which lists all departures scheduled for the next few hours, and showing the appropriate check-in desk number for each flight. The speed of the check-in systems has been improved dramatically, so there was no queue at our desk, and the three of us were issued with boarding passes in only a couple of minutes. Our baggage sped away on conveyors down to the new sorting hall two storeys below. Brochures explain that the new terminal extension was designed to make it possible to go from check-in to final boarding in only 20 minutes, which has involved investment in a state-of-the-art automated baggage handling system. On my last visit, following traffic delays on the way to the airport, I found that this system works, but I doubt that it would if *everyone* arrived only 20 minutes before departure! It is no wonder that they advise checking in one hour before: it also gives passengers much more time to spend money in the duty-free shops, restaurants and bars! ▶

By this time, my injured leg had swollen up and was throbbing painfully. This seemed to be a routine situation for the check-in staff, who arranged for a wheelchair and attendant to take me through Border Control and security checks. While my colleagues travelled down to the departures hall by escalator, I took the slower route by lift, arriving together just outside the duty-free shops where the attendant left them to take care of me. We had some time to spare, so we replenished the brandy, bought some Belgian chocolates, and headed for a café-bar. While Brussels is renowned for its excellent cuisine, we didn't expect to find high standards of food in the quick-service environment of an airport, but we were wrong! The delicious aromas of freshly prepared food attracted our custom, and we weren't disappointed. After a welcome glass of speciality raspberry-flavoured beer to round off the meal, we headed for the airline's executive lounge.

The view across the airfield was not promising! After a bright, crisp day, more snow-laden clouds had arrived, and a chill wind cut across the tarmac. De-icing crews were working on the parked aircraft, and others were treating the runways, taking quick action between the aircraft movements. Concerned that we might be delayed and miss our connection at Oslo, we checked with the staff at the airline's flight information desk. After some phoning, they confirmed that, although there could be some delays, Oslo had arranged to hold connecting flights, as many passengers originated from Brussels. Their professional and friendly advice made us feel much more at ease, and they even offered to allow us to send fax or phone messages to our destination. They couldn't have been more helpful!

Announcements of the minor delays were made over the speaker system, but it wasn't long before we were directed to the departure lounge and were preparing to board. Outside, around the aircraft in the gloom, the baggage trucks were pulling away, and the giant push-off tractor was being connected up to the nose-wheel. Ten minutes later, we were at the end of the runway, ready for take-off.

'Today must have been a very busy one for everyone involved in keeping the airport open,' I thought, 'but perhaps every day has its own challenges in such a complex operation.' ∎

Questions

1 Identify all the micro operations and their activities which are mentioned.

2 Classify them in accordance with the structure in Table 1.5.

3 Which of these micro operations were most affected by the severe weather?

4 Approximately how many different organizations are involved in delivering the goods and services described in this report? What are the implications of this?

DISCUSSION QUESTIONS

(All chapters have discussion questions. Some of them can be answered by reading the chapter. Others will require some general knowledge of business activity and some might require an element of investigation.)

1 The port of Cape Town is one of the largest ports in South Africa. It provides a vital link between sea-based transportation of cargo and inland transport into Southern Africa such as rail, road and inland waterways. List the transformation processes which you think the port's operations managers have to run, and identify their inputs and outputs.

2 Describe the operations of the following organizations using the transformation model. Carefully identify the transforming resources, transformed resources, the type of transformation process and the outputs from the transformation process:
> an international airport
> a supermarket
> a high-volume car plant.

3 What mixture of goods and services are produced by the following operations:
> Bell Equipment
> Lesotho Highlands Hydro Scheme
> Woolworths
> DHL Express Delivery Service
> Volkswagen Uitenhage
> Holiday Inn hotels?

4 Why is operations management relevant to managers in other organization functions?

5 Explain the difference between micro and macro operations. Describe some of the micro operations in a university and discuss the relationships between their internal customers and suppliers.

6 Talk with an operations manager from a local organization and find out what they say they do and how they work with the organization's marketing, financial, personnel and purchasing functions.

7 Draw the hierarchy of operations for a small manufacturing company.

8 What are the main differences between internal and external customers?

9 Discuss the advantages and disadvantages of buffering an operation from the environment. Illustrate your answer with an organization of your choice.

10 How do you think a blood transfusion service operation buffers itself against environmental uncertainty?

11 Describe the relative volume, variety, variation and customer contact for the following organizations:
> Sun City
> a bread bakery
> a dentist.

12 Explain the advantages and disadvantages to an operation of reducing its volume, variety and customer contact. How could a university change volume, variety and customer contact in order to reduce its costs?

13 What do you think would be the main design, planning and control, and improvement activities in a large airport such as Johannesburg International airport?

14 Over recent years there has been a resurgence of interest in operations management, in universities but especially in business. Why do you think this is?

NOTES ON CHAPTER

1 Sources: Thornhill, J. (1992) 'Hard Sell on the High Street', the *Financial Times*, May 16. Horovitz, J. and Jurgens Panak, M. (1992) *Total Customer Satisfaction*, Pitman Publishing. Walley, P. and Hart, K. (1993) IKEA (UK) Ltd, Loughborough University Business School.

2 Source: 'Hayek's Watch Works', *World Link*, July 1994.

3 Heizer, J.H. and Render, B. (1988) *Production and Operations Management* (3rd edn), Allyn and Bacon, p 5.

4 A number of authors have commented on the way the operations function is protected from the environment. For example, Thompson, J.D. (1967) *Organizations in Action*, McGraw-Hill, originally commented on organization buffering, while Wild, R. (1977) *Concepts for Operations Management*, John Wiley, extended the ideas to physical buffering.

5 One of the most articulate proponents of how an organization can be more responsive to environment influence is Richard Schonburger. *See*, for example, *Building a Chain of Customers*, Hutchinson Business Books, 1990.

6 Sources: Franssen, M. (1993) 'Beyond Profits', *Business Quarterly*, Autumn. Hopfenbeck, W. (1992) *The Green Management Revolution*, Prentice Hall.

7 Sources: Pean, P. (1989) 'How to Get Rich on Perestroika', *Fortune*, 8 May, pp 95–6, and 'Vision Factory', *National Geographic*, Nov 1993.

8 Sources: Groupe Accor published accounts 1992, *Formule 1, The Most Affordable Hotel Chain*, company information brochure. Sharon Dannelley (1993) 'Groupe Accor', *Warwick Business School Report*.

9 Source: De Meyer, A. (1993) *Creating the Virtual Factor*, the EFME Conference, London Business School.

SELECTED FURTHER READINGS

Adams, E.E. and Ebert, R.J. (1992) *Production and Operations Management* (5th edn), Prentice Hall.

Albrecht, K. and Bradford, L.J. (1990) *The Service Advantage*, Dow Jones Irwin.

Andrews, C.G. (1982) 'The Critical Importance of Production and Operations Management', *Academy of Management Review*, Vol 7, Jan.

Bowen, D.E., Chase, R.B., Cummings, T.G. and Associates (1990) *Service Management Effectiveness*, Jossey-Bass.

Collier, D.A. (1987) *Service Management: Operating Decisions*, Prentice Hall.

Gaither, N. (1994) *Production and Operations Management*, Dryden Press.

Gronroos, C. (1990) *Service Management and Marketing*, Lexington Books.

Harris, N.D. (1989) *Service Operations Management*, Cassell.

Hill, T. (1991) *Production/Operations Management* (2nd edn), Prentice Hall.

Joffe, A. (1995) *Improving Manufacturing Performance in South Africa: The Report of the Industrial Strategy Project*, University of Cape Town/Industrial Strategy Project, UCT Press.

Johnston, R., Chambers, S., Harland, C., Harrison, A. and Slack, N. (1997) *Cases in Operations Management* (2nd edn), Pitman Publishing.

Krajewski, L.J. and Ritzman, I.P. (1987) *Operations Management* (3rd edn), Addison-Wesley.

Schonberger, R. (1990) *Building a Chain of Customers*, Hutchinson Business Books.

Wild, R. (1989) *Production and Operations Management* (4th edn), Cassell.

THE STRATEGIC ROLE AND OBJECTIVES OF OPERATIONS

INTRODUCTION

In Chapter 1 we looked at the activities in which operations managers are involved, as well as the many different types of operation which they are managing. But examining what operations managers do does not answer a far more fundamental question: 'What should any company or organization expect from its operation?' Or, to put it another way, 'How does the operations function contribute to the organization's competitiveness or strategic direction?'

If any operation wants to understand its contribution to the organization of which it is a part, it must answer two questions. First, what is the *role* of the operations function – that is, what part is it expected to play within the business? Second, what are the

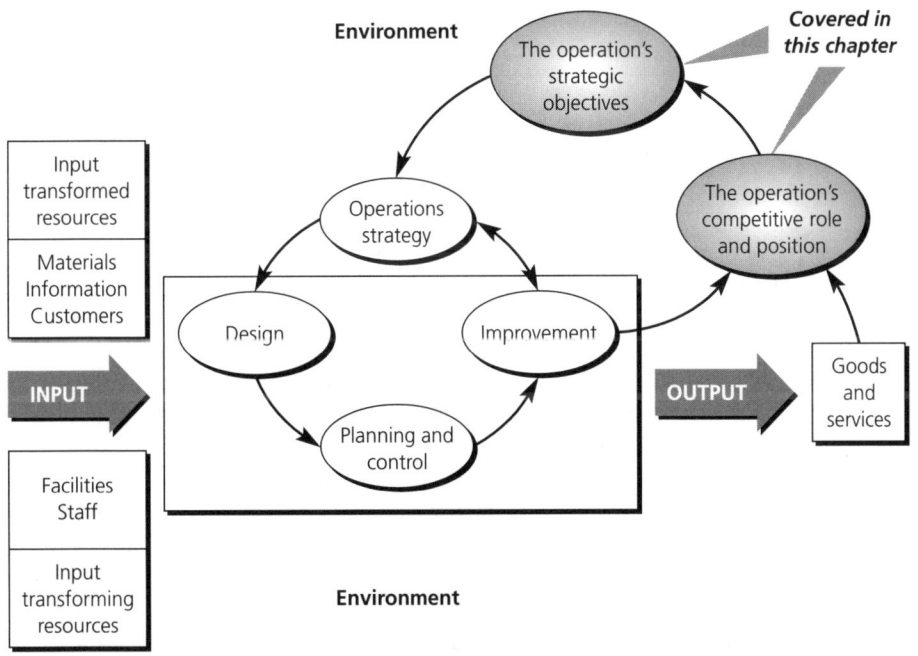

Figure 2.1 This chapter covers the role and strategic objectives of operations management

specific *performance objectives* against which the business can assess the contribution of the operation to its strategic aspirations? Both these issues are vitally important to any operation. Without an appreciation of its role within the business, the people who manage the operation can never be sure that they really are contributing to the long-term success of the business. At a more practical level, it is impossible to know whether an operation is succeeding or not if the specific performance objectives against which its success is measured are not clearly spelt out. This chapter deals with both these issues. On our general model of operations management they are represented by the shaded areas of Fig. 2.1.

OBJECTIVES

This chapter will examine:

- the *role* of the operations function in the organization's strategic plans;

- how the *contribution* of the operations function to the organization's competitiveness can be assessed;

- the meaning of the operations function's five *performance objectives* – quality, speed, dependability, flexibility and cost;

- the *internal* and *external* benefits which an operation can derive from excelling in each of its performance objectives.

THE ROLE OF THE OPERATIONS FUNCTION

All parts of any business have their own role to play in achieving its success. At the simplest level the role of each function is reflected in its name. The marketing function positions the company's products or services in the market place. The finance function monitors and controls the company's financial resources. The operations function produces the services and goods demanded by the company's customers. Here we use the role of the operations function to mean something beyond its obvious responsibilities and tasks in the company, however. We use it to mean the underlying rationale of the function – the very reason that the function exists.

Why should any business go to the bother of having an operations function? Most companies and organizations have the option of contracting out the production of their services and goods. They could simply pay some other business to provide what their operations function currently does for them. This then prompts the further question 'What does the operations function have to do in order to justify its continued existence within the business?' This is what we mean by its role. Three roles seem to be particularly important for the operations function:

- as a *support* to business strategy;
- as the *implementer* of business strategy;
- as the *driver* of business strategy.

Supporting business strategy

One role of the operations part of the business is to support strategy.[1] That is, it must develop its resources to provide the capabilities which are needed to allow the organization to achieve its strategic goals. For example, if a manufacturer of personal computers has decided to compete by being the first in the market with every available new product innovation, then its operations function needs to be capable of coping with the changes which constant innovation will bring. It must develop or purchase processes which are flexible enough to manufacture novel parts and products. It must organize and train its staff to understand the way products are changing and put in place the necessary changes to the operation. It must develop relationships with its suppliers which help them respond quickly when supplying new parts. Everything about the operation, its technology, staff, and its systems and procedures, must be appropriate for the company's competitive strategy. The better the operation is at doing these things, the more support it is giving to the company's strategy. If the company had adopted a different business strategy, its operations function would have needed to adopt different objectives. This idea is developed further in the next chapter.

Implementing business strategy

The second role of the operations part of the business is to implement strategy. Most companies will have some kind of strategy but it is the operation which puts it into practice. You cannot after all touch a strategy; you cannot even see it; all you can see is how the operation behaves in practice. For example, if an airline has a strategy of attracting a higher proportion of business class travellers, it is the operations part of each function which has the task of 'operationalizing' the strategy. Its marketing 'operation' must organize appropriate promotions and pricing activities. The personnel 'operation' needs to train its cabin and ground staff to achieve higher levels of customer service. Most significantly, its operations function will have to supervise the refitting of the aircraft, organize express ticketing, baggage handling and waiting facilities, and design special food, beverages and entertainment for the cabin service. The strategy of the airline is only a statement of intent – operations management makes it happen. The implication of this role for the operations function is very significant. It means that even the most original and brilliant strategy can be rendered totally ineffective by an inept operations function.

Driving business strategy

The third role of the operations part of the business is to drive strategy by giving it a long-term competitive edge. Different parts of the business have different effects on a company's ability to prosper. If the finance function does not control cash flow accurately, the business could run out of cash and go out of business almost immediately.

Poor financial management can have a serious short-term effect on the business. If the marketing department fails to understand the nature of the company's markets, and how it should set its promotion policies, product positioning, distribution channels and pricing policies, the company will find it difficult to thrive in its markets. Poor marketing management will hamper the company in the medium term. No amount of excellent financial management or clever market positioning, however, can compensate for poor operations performance. Badly made products, sloppy service, slow delivery, broken promises, too little choice of products or services or an operations cost base which is too high will sink any company in the long term. Conversely, any business which makes its products and/or services better, faster, on-time, in greater variety and less expensively than its competition has the best long-term advantage any company could desire. The important point here is that all the things which promote long-term success come directly or indirectly from the operations function. It is the operations part of the business which is the ultimate custodian of competitiveness. Its role is to 'do things better'; that is, 'make products better' and 'deliver services better' than other similar operations.

Figure 2.2 summarizes the three roles of the operations function.

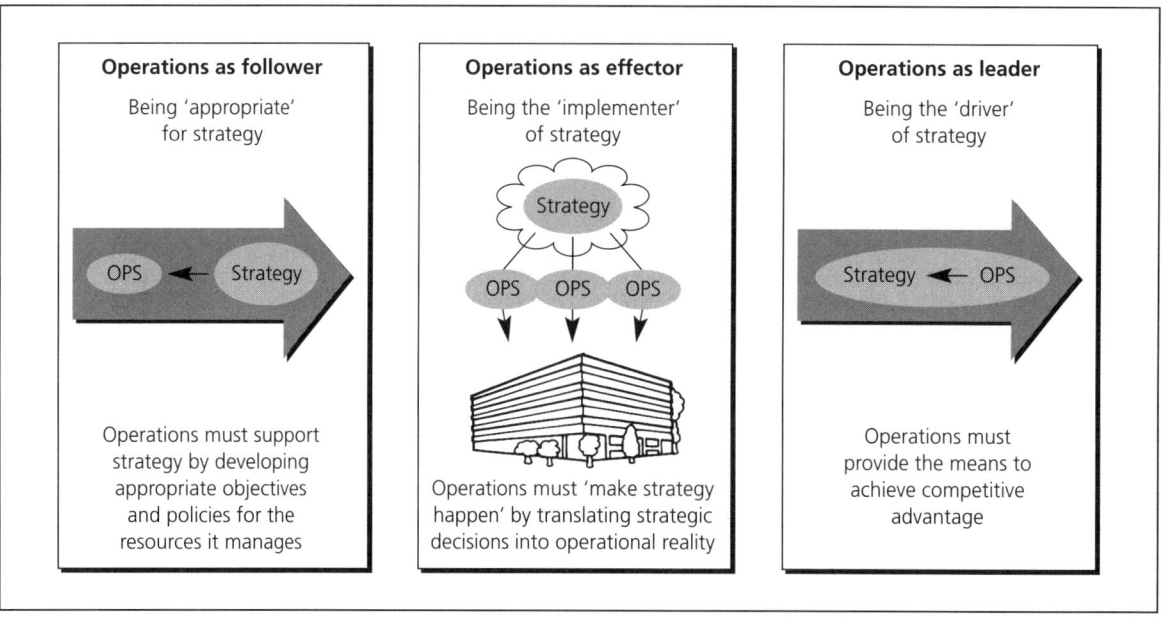

Figure 2.2 The three roles of the operations function

JUDGING THE OPERATION'S CONTRIBUTION

The ability of any operation to play these roles within the organization can be judged by considering the organizational aims or aspirations of the operations function. Professors Hayes and Wheelwright of Harvard University,[2] with later contributions from Professor Chase of the University of Southern California,[3] have developed what they call the '*Four-Stage Model*' which can be used to evaluate the competitive role and contribution of the operations function of any type of company. The model traces the progression of the operations function, from what is the largely negative role of Stage 1 operations to it becoming the central element of competitive strategy in excellent Stage 4 operations.

Stage 1 Internal neutrality

This is the very poorest level of contribution by the operations function. In a Stage 1 organization the operation is considered a 'necessary evil'. The other functions, if they have anything to say at all about operations, regard it as holding them back from competing effectively. The operations function, they would say, is inward looking and at best reactive. It certainly has very little positive to contribute towards competitive success. It is unlikely even to have developed its resources so as to be appropriate for the company's competitive position. The best that the function can hope for is to be ignored. At least when operations is being ignored it isn't holding the company back in any way. Certainly the rest of the organization would not look to operations as the source of any originality, flair or competitive drive. In effect the operations function is aspiring only to reach the minimum acceptable standards implied by the rest of the organization. It is trying to be 'internally neutral', a position it attempts to achieve not by anything positive but by avoiding the bigger mistakes. Certainly even when good organizations are let down by their operations function the resulting publicity can be damaging (*see* Fig. 2.3).

Stage 2 External neutrality

Hayes and Wheelwright's idea of the first step of breaking out of Stage 1 is for the operations function to begin comparing itself with similar companies or organizations in the outside market. This may not immediately take it to the 'first division' of companies in the market, but at least it is aspiring to reach that position and is measuring itself against its competitors' performance. The operations function is certainly not holding the company back. It may not yet be particularly creative in the way it manages its operations but it is trying to be 'appropriate', by adopting 'best practice' from its competitors. By taking the best ideas and norms of performance from the rest of its industry it is trying to be 'externally neutral'.

Stage 3 Internally supportive

Stage 3 operations have probably reached the 'first division' in their market. They may not be better than their competitors on every aspect of operations performance but they are broadly up with the best. Nevertheless, good as they may be, Stage 3 operations aspire to be clearly and unambiguously the very best in the market. They try to achieve this by gaining a clear view of the company's competitive or strategic goals and then they organize and develop the operations resources to excel in the things in which the company needs to compete effectively. Not only are they

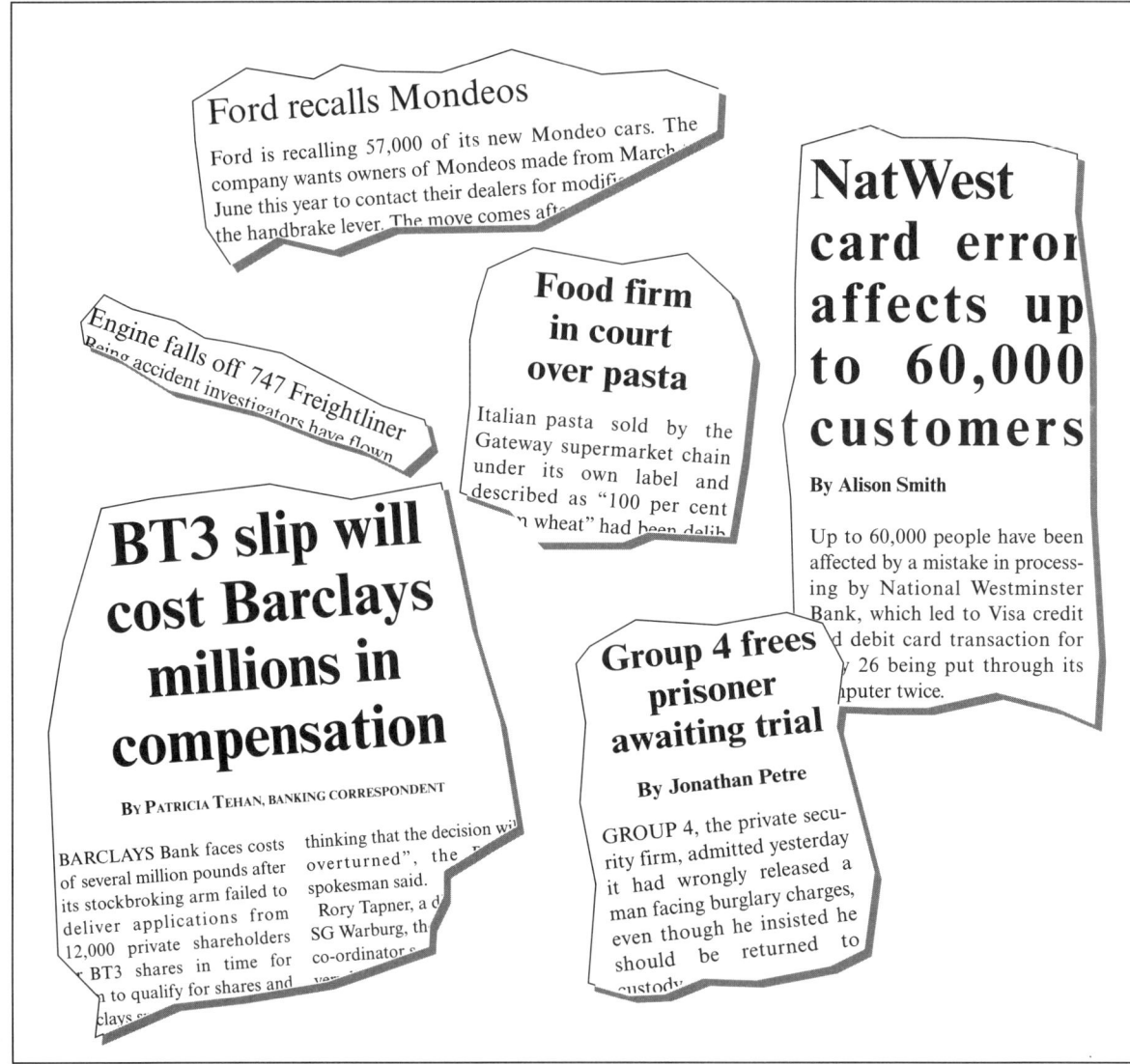

Figure 2.3 Even the best organizations can be let down by their operations
(*Sources:* (left to right) *The Sunday Times, Flight International, The Times,* the *Daily Telegraph,* the *Financial Times*)

developing 'appropriate' resources, they are taking on the role of the 'implementers' of strategy. The operation is trying to be 'internally supportive' by providing a credible operations strategy.

Stage 4 Externally supportive

Until the last few years Stage 3 was taken as the limit of the operations function's contribution. Yet Hayes and Wheelwright capture the emerging sense of the growing importance of operations management by suggesting a further stage – Stage 4.

The difference between Stage 3 and Stage 4 is admitted by Hayes and Wheelwright to be subtle, but nevertheless it is very important. In essence, a Stage 4 company is one which sees the operations function as providing the foundation for its future competitive success. Operations looks to the long term. It forecasts likely changes in markets and supply, and it develops operations-based strategies which provide the company with the performance which will be required to compete in future market conditions. In effect the operations function is becoming central to strategy making (though Hayes and Wheelwright stress that they are not 'playing games' between the functions or claiming that therefore operations is in some way more important than other functions). Stage 4 operations are creative and proactive. They are likely to organize their resources in ways which are innovative and capable of adaptation as markets change. Essentially they are trying to be 'one step ahead' of competitors in the way that they create products and services and organize their operations – what Hayes and Wheelwright call being 'externally supportive'. At Stage 4, operations are not only developing 'appropriate' resources and 'implementing' competitive strategy, they are also the long-term driver of strategy.

The Hayes and Wheelwright model is illustrated in Fig. 2.4. The Four-Stage Model may be a simplification, but two points are worth considering.

● It assesses the performance of operations by the function's aspirations. In other words, it asks the operations function how it would like to be seen and the rest of the organization how they actually see the contribution of the operations function.
● As companies move from Stage 1 to Stage 4 there is a progressive shift from operations' contribution being negative and operational through to its contribution being positive (indeed in some ways leading) and strategic. The company is relying on an 'operations-based' advantage in its competitive strategy.

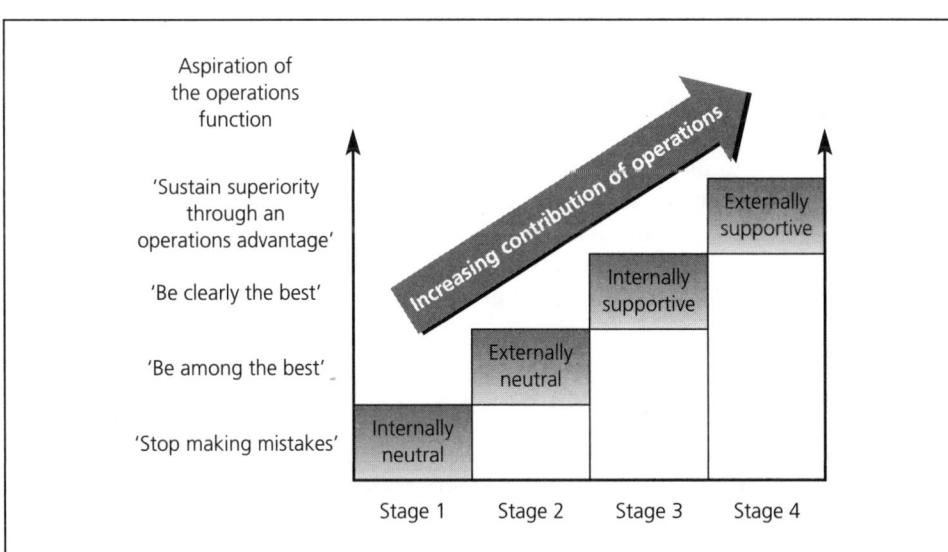

Figure 2.4 Hayes and Wheelwright's Four-Stage Model holds that the strategic contribution of an operations function can be judged by its aspirations

THE FIVE PERFORMANCE OBJECTIVES[4]

For any organization which wants to succeed in the long term the contribution of its operations function is vital. It gives the organization an 'operations-based advantage'. But precisely how does the operations function contribute to achieving this idea of an operations-based advantage?

It does so through five basic 'performance objectives'. These can be derived from first principles. Imagine that you are an operations manager in any kind of business – a hospital administrator, for example, or a production manager at a car plant, the operations manager for a city bus company or the manager of a large supermarket. What kind of things are you likely to want to do in order to contribute to competitiveness? Or, to be slightly more ambitious, what would you want to be good at if you really did want to achieve an 'operations-based' advantage?

- You would want to '*do things right*': that is you would not want to make mistakes. You would want to satisfy your customers by providing error-free goods and services which are 'fit for their purpose'. If the operation succeeds in achieving all this it is giving a *quality advantage* to the company.
- You would want to *do things fast*: that is you would want to minimize the time between a customer asking for goods or services and the customer receiving them in full. In doing this you would be increasing the availability of your goods and services to customers and you would be giving the company a *speed advantage*.
- You would want to *do things on time*, so as to keep the delivery promises which you have given to your customers. This might mean being able to estimate a delivery date accurately (or perhaps even accept the customer's required delivery date), communicate this clearly to the customer, and then deliver exactly on time. If the operation can do this, it is giving a *dependability advantage* to its customers.
- You would want to be able to *change what you do*: that is being able to vary or adapt the operation's activities, either because you have to cope with some unexpected circumstances (an individual customer changing his or her mind, or more customers than you expected demanding your services perhaps) or because customers require individual treatment, so the range of goods and services which you produce has to be wide enough to deal with all customer possibilities. Either way, being able to change far enough and fast enough to meet customer requirements gives a *flexibility advantage* to your customers.
- You would want to *do things cheaply*: that is produce goods and services at a cost which enables them to be priced appropriately for the market while still allowing for a return to the organization. Alternatively, if the organization is a not-for-profit organization, doing things cheaply means giving good value to the tax payers or whoever is funding the operation. When the organization is managing to do this, it is giving a *cost advantage* to its customers.

Figure 2.5 illustrates these five performance objectives.

The next part of this chapter examines these five performance objectives in more detail by looking at what they mean for the four different operations previously mentioned: a general hospital, an automobile factory, a city bus company and a supermarket chain.

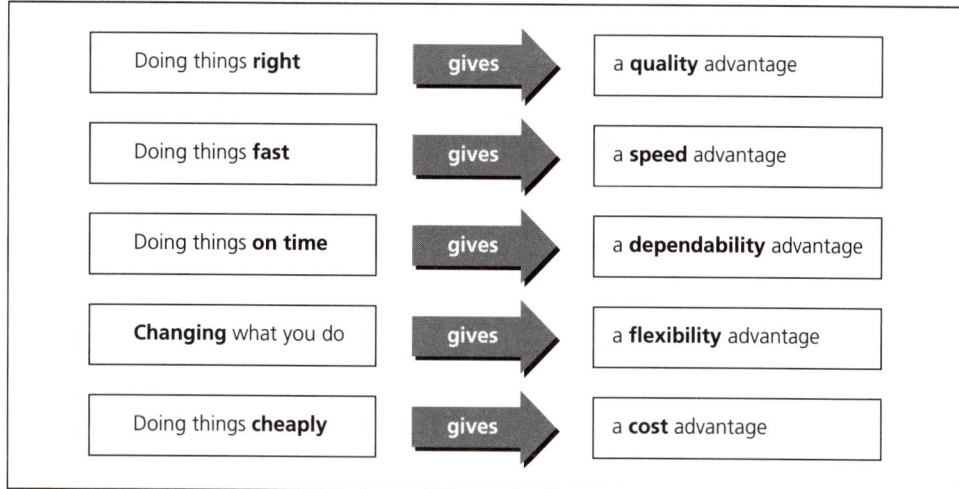

**Figure 2.5
An operation contributes to business strategy by achieving five 'performance objectives'**

The quality objective

Quality means 'doing things right', but the things which the operation needs to do right will vary according to the kind of operation (*see* Fig. 2.6). For example, in the hospital, quality could mean making sure that patients get the most appropriate treatment, that the treatment is carried out in a medically correct manner, that patients are kept clearly informed as to what is happening and also are consulted if there are alternative forms of treatment. It would also include such things as ensuring that the hospital is clean, hygienic and tidy and that the staff are well informed and courteous towards patients. In the automobile factory quality means that the car is made to its specifications and is reliable. All parts are assembled correctly and all extras and documents are present and in the right place. Visually the car should look attractive and be blemish- and scratch-free. In a city bus company quality means that the buses are clean, quiet and do not put out unpleasant fumes. It also means that timetables and other published information relating to the bus service are accurate and usable. Finally, it means that the bus staff are courteous and helpful to passengers. For the manager of the supermarket, quality means that the goods it sells are in good condition, that the store is clean and tidy, that the decor is attractive and that the staff are helpful and courteous.

Put this way it is not surprising that all operations regard quality as a particularly important objective. Some even advertise themselves on the basis of their quality performance or quality systems. In some ways quality is the most visible part of what an operation does. Furthermore, it is something that a customer finds relatively easy to judge about the operation. Is the product or service as it is supposed to be? Is it right or is it wrong? There is something fundamental about quality. Because of this, it is clearly a major influence on customer satisfaction or dissatisfaction. Good quality products and services mean high customer satisfaction and therefore the likelihood that the customer will return. Conversely, poor quality reduces the chances of a customer coming back for more.

Quality inside the operation

Good quality performance in an operation not only leads to external customer satisfaction. It makes life easier inside the operation as well. Satisfying internal customers can be as important as satisfying external customers.

Quality reduces costs

The fewer mistakes each micro operation or unit makes in the operation, the less time it will need to spend correcting these mistakes and the less confusion and irritation will be spread. For example, if a supermarket's regional warehouse sends the wrong goods to the supermarket, it will mean staff time, and therefore cost, being used to sort out the problem.

Quality increases dependability

Increased costs are not the only consequence of poor quality, however. At the supermarket it could also mean that goods run out on the supermarket shelves with a resulting loss of revenue to the operation and irritation to the external customers. Sorting the problem out could also distract the supermarket management from giving its attention to the other parts of the supermarket operation. This in turn could result in further mistakes being made. On the other hand, if the supermarket rarely if ever makes any errors, internal customers do not have to spend time putting mistakes right or checking that the rest of the operation is doing its job correctly. It can spend its time concentrating on being good at its own tasks.

The important point here is that the performance objective of quality (like the other performance objectives, as we shall see) has both an external aspect to it which leads to customer satisfaction, and an internal aspect to it which leads to a stable and efficient organization.

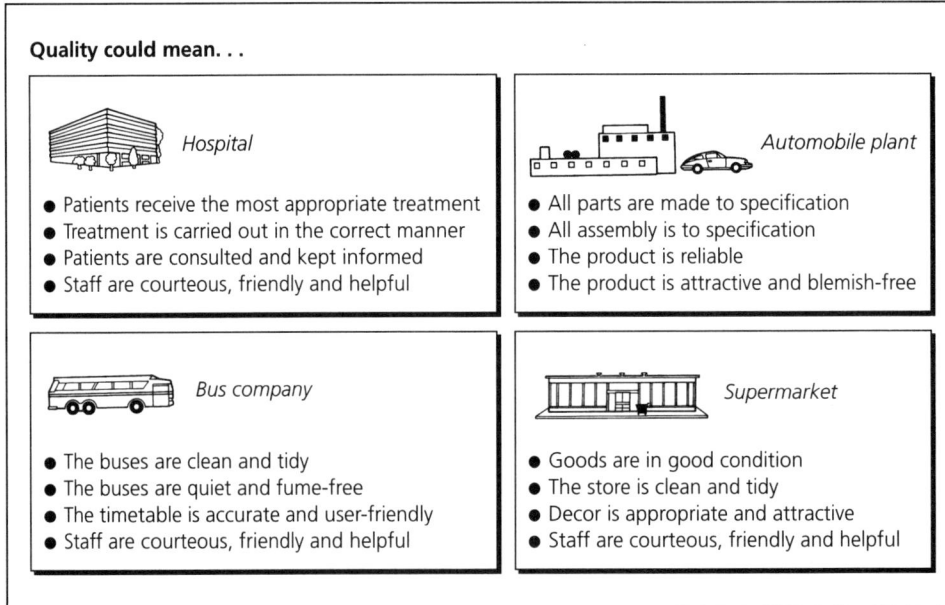

Figure 2.6 Quality means different things in different operations

Quality could mean. . .

Hospital
- Patients receive the most appropriate treatment
- Treatment is carried out in the correct manner
- Patients are consulted and kept informed
- Staff are courteous, friendly and helpful

Automobile plant
- All parts are made to specification
- All assembly is to specification
- The product is reliable
- The product is attractive and blemish-free

Bus company
- The buses are clean and tidy
- The buses are quiet and fume-free
- The timetable is accurate and user-friendly
- Staff are courteous, friendly and helpful

Supermarket
- Goods are in good condition
- The store is clean and tidy
- Decor is appropriate and attractive
- Staff are courteous, friendly and helpful

The speed objective

Speed is concerned with how long customers have to wait to receive their products or services (*see* Fig. 2.7). For example, in the hospital it means that patients in the Accident and Emergency Department are seen and treated quickly before they suffer any further distress. It also means that the patients with less urgent needs do not have to suffer a long waiting list. For the automobile factory, speed means that the time between a dealer ordering a particular car for one of its customers and the car being delivered from the factory is as short as possible. For the city bus company, speed literally means how fast the operation can get customers from A to B. For the supermarket manager, speed means how fast customers can get to the store, park their cars, select their purchases, get through the check-out, return to their cars, and arrive back home. In operations like this, speed is also about the availability of goods. If the goods which a customer wants are on the shelf, the customer can have them immediately (that is very fast, in fact instant, service). If the goods are not on the shelf, the likelihood is that the customer will either forego the purchase or alternatively go elsewhere and not buy the particular good from that supermarket (that is very slow, in fact infinitely delayed, service).

The main benefit to the operation's (external) customers of speedy delivery of goods and services lies in the way it enhances the operation's offering to the customer. Quite simply, for most goods and services, the faster a customer can have the product or service, the more likely he or she is to buy it. To some operations speed is particularly important and would, again, be reflected in their advertising.

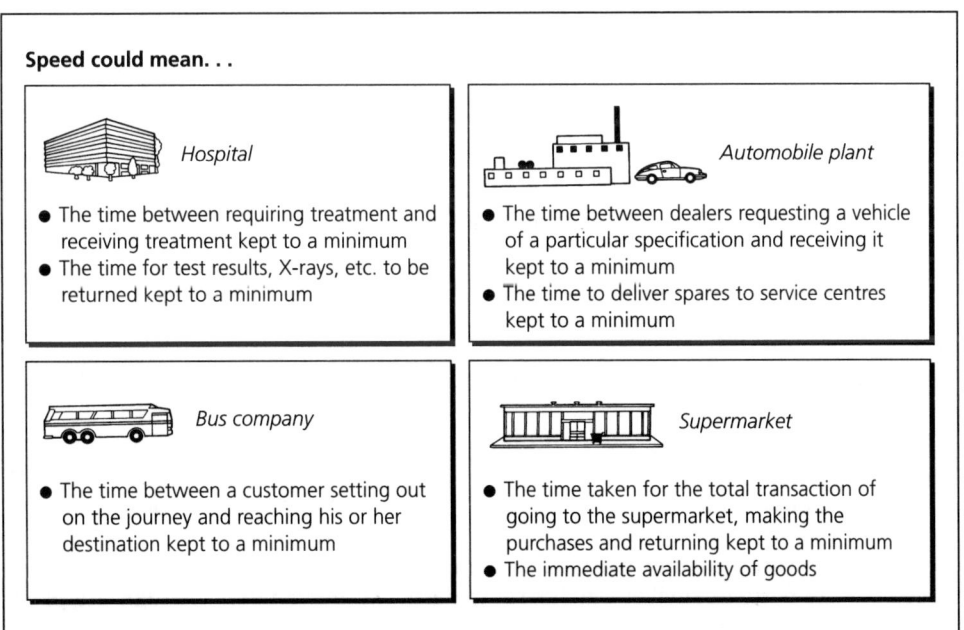

Speed could mean. . .

Hospital
- The time between requiring treatment and receiving treatment kept to a minimum
- The time for test results, X-rays, etc. to be returned kept to a minimum

Automobile plant
- The time between dealers requesting a vehicle of a particular specification and receiving it kept to a minimum
- The time to deliver spares to service centres kept to a minimum

Bus company
- The time between a customer setting out on the journey and reaching his or her destination kept to a minimum

Supermarket
- The time taken for the total transaction of going to the supermarket, making the purchases and returning kept to a minimum
- The immediate availability of goods

Figure 2.7 Speed means different things in different operations

NORTHERN TELECOM COMPETES ON SPEED[5]

Northern Telecom, a Canadian company which makes telecommunications products and services, appreciates the importance of speed to its internal operations.

'... Everything we wanted to do to improve operations had something to do with squeezing time out of our process ... it became clear that what we really needed to satisfy customer needs was the ability to do things faster than ever before. We needed to reorientate ... to a whole new operations strategy in which the number one priority was time ...'

Within a three-year period from the start of its speed initiative, one part of Northern Telecom reduced the elapsed time it took to manufacture some products down to about half of its original level. This doubling of 'throughput velocity' had a dramatic effect on operations performance. For example, customer satisfaction scores increased by 25 per cent over the same period and inventory levels reduced by about 30 per cent, as did operations overhead costs (the cost of supporting the direct operations activities). ■

Speed inside the operation

Inside the operation speed is also important. Fast response to external customers is greatly helped by speedy decision making and speedy movement of materials and information inside the operation. Internal speed can have further benefits, however.[6]

Speed reduces inventories

Take, for example, the automobile plant. The steel which is used to make the vehicle's door panels is first delivered to the press shop where it is pressed out into shape. It is then transported to the painting area where it is coated for colour and protection. After this it is moved to the assembly line where it is fitted to the automobile. This is a simple three-stage manufacturing process, but in practice each door panel does not flow smoothly from one stage to the next. If you follow one product through the process, its journey can take a surprisingly long time. First, the steel is delivered as part of a far larger batch, containing enough steel to make possibly several hundred products. It might be inspected and then waits to be used. Eventually it is taken to the press area where it is pressed into shape and again waits, along with many other door panels, until transportation to the paint area. It again waits until it can be painted, only to wait once more until it is transported to the assembly line. Yet again it waits by the trackside until it is eventually fitted to the automobile. A relatively short journey along the assembly line then takes it to the end of its journey where it leaves the factory as part of the finished product.

The door panel's journey through the factory was both far longer than the time needed to actually make and fit the product, and was also composed mainly of waiting time. When hundreds of products are moving through the plant every day, this waiting time results in large stocks (or inventories) of parts and products hanging around in the plant. If, on the other hand, the waiting can be reduced (say by moving and processing the parts in smaller batches), the parts will move faster through the plant and as a result the amount of inventories between each stage of the process will be reduced. This idea has some very important implications which will be explored in Chapter 15 on just-in-time.

Speed reduces risks

No one really knows what will happen in the future. Yet forecasting tomorrow's events is far less of a risky business than forecasting next year's. For this reason, most companies will have a greater confidence in their forecasts for sales one period (day, week, month or year depending on the industry) ahead than they have in their forecasts two or three periods ahead. The further ahead they forecast, the more likely they are to get it wrong. This has important implications for the throughput speed of any operation. Consider the automobile plant again. If the total time for the door panel to complete its journey through the plant is six weeks, door panels are being processed through their first operation six weeks before they reach their final destination. The quantity of door panels being processed will be determined by the forecasts for demand six weeks ahead. Almost certainly the plant at any time will be making the wrong number of door panels because the forecast for six weeks ahead will be wrong.

Alternatively, consider the risk of making the wrong number of door panels if, instead of six weeks, they take only one week to move through the plant. Now the door panels being processed through their first stage are intended to meet demand only one week ahead. Under these circumstances it is far more likely that the number and type of door panels being processed are the number and type which eventually will be needed. Thus the faster material moves through the operation, the more likely the operation is to be making what will really be required by its customers.

The dependability objective

Dependability means doing things in time for customers to receive their goods or services when they were promised (*see* Fig. 2.8). A hospital with a high standard of dependability would not cancel operations or any other appointments made with its patients. It would always, for example, deliver the results of tests and X-ray

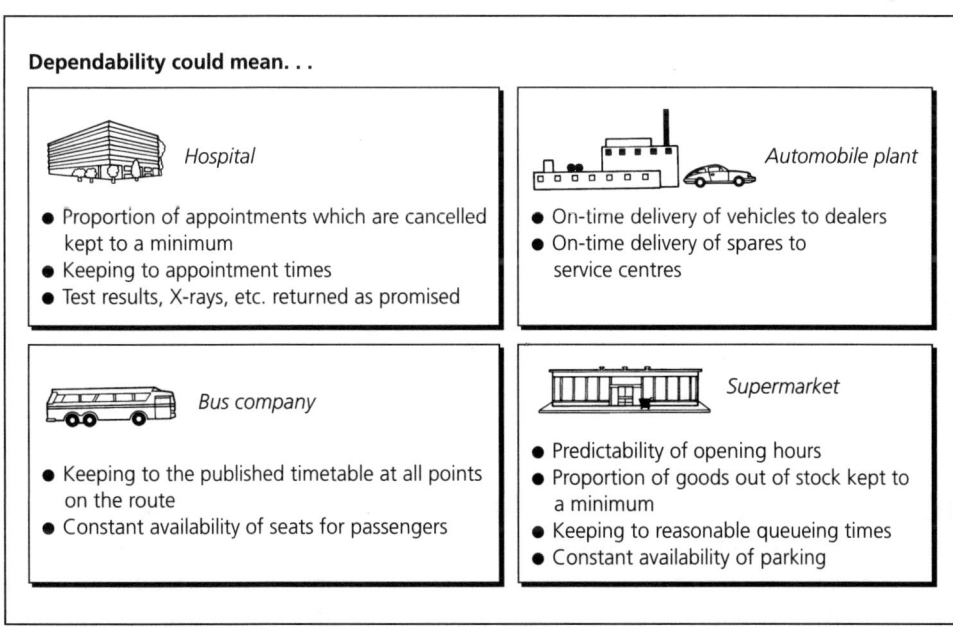

Figure 2.8
Dependability
means different
things in different
operations

investigations on time and keep to schedule on its immunization programmes. A dependable automobile plant will deliver cars and spare parts to the car dealers and service centres exactly as promised. A dependable city bus company will always keep to its published timetable, picking up passengers at every point on the journey precisely on schedule. Furthermore, there will be seats available for the passengers who are there to catch the bus. Each season the company will also publish its revised timetables on the day promised. A dependable supermarket chain has predictable opening hours. It will never run out of stock of any of the items which it has led its customers to expect to be in stock (by advertising or past practice).

Customers might only judge the dependability of an operation after the product or service has been delivered. For example, a customer would probably decide to take a bus across town initially on the criteria of speed and cost. After taking the journey the customer will have some view about the dependability of the service. Initially this will not affect the likelihood that customers will select the service – they have already 'consumed' it. It will affect the chances of them buying the service again, however. In that sense dependability is not something which will affect the customer's desire to purchase products or services immediately. Over time, however, dependability can override all other criteria. No matter how cheap a bus service is, or how fast it is advertised as being, if the service is always late (or unpredictably early) or the buses are always full, then potential passengers will be better off calling a taxi. Some operations compete directly on their ability to deliver on time (*see* Fig. 2.9).

Dependability inside the operation

Inside the operation dependability has a similar effect. Internal customers will judge each other's performance partly by how reliable the other micro operations are in delivering material or information on time. Operations where internal dependability is high are more effective than those which are not for a number of reasons.

Dependability saves time

Take, for example, the maintenance and repair centre for the city bus company. The manager will always have a plan of the centre's activities each day for a period ahead. Probably this plan has been drawn up to keep the centre's facilities as fully utilized as possible while ensuring that the bus fleet always has enough clean and serviced vehicles to match demand at any time. If, one day, the centre runs out of some crucial spare parts which are needed to repair two of the buses which are booked in for servicing that day, the manager of the centre will need to spend time trying to arrange a special delivery of the required parts within the next few days. It is unlikely that the resources which had been reserved to service the buses can be used as productively as they would have been without this disruption. More seriously, the fleet will be short of two buses until they can be repaired. The fleet operations manager will have to spend time rescheduling the services so as to minimize the disruption to customers. On this particular day (and entirely due to the one failure of dependability of supply) a significant part of the operation's time will have been occupied trying to cope with the disruption rather than doing anything directly productive.

Dependability saves money

Most of this ineffective use of time will translate into extra cost in the operation. The spare parts might cost more to be delivered at short notice than by regular delivery, for example. The maintenance staff will expect to be paid even when there is not a

Figure 2.9
Some organizations promote their products or service through the dependability of their operations

bus to work on. Similarly, the fixed costs of the operation such as heating and rent will not reduce because the two buses are not being serviced. Out on the road the disruption will also have financial consequences. The rescheduling of buses to routes will probably mean that some routes have inappropriately sized buses and some services could have to be cancelled. This will result in empty bus seats (if too large a bus has to be used) or a loss of revenue (if potential passengers are not transported).

Dependability gives stability

The disruption caused to operations by a lack of dependability goes beyond time and cost. It affects the 'quality' of the operation. If everything in an operation is perfectly dependable, and has been for some time, a level of trust will build up between the different parts of the operation. There will be no 'surprises' and everything will be predictable. Under such circumstances each part of the operation can concentrate on improving its own part of the operation without having its attention continually diverted by the lack of dependable service from the other parts of the operation.

The flexibility objective[7]

Flexibility means being able to change the operation in some way. This may mean changing what the operation does, how it is doing it, or when it is doing it, but change is the key idea.

Most operations need to be able to change in order to satisfy their customers' requirements. Specifically customers will need the operation to change so that it can provide four types of requirement:

- *product/service flexibility* – different products and services;
- *mix flexibility* – a wide range or mix of products and services;
- *volume flexibility* – different quantities or volumes of products and services;
- *delivery flexibility* – different delivery times.

Figure 2.10 gives examples of what these different types of flexibility mean to the four operations.

Flexibility could mean. . .

Hospital
- Product/Service flexibility – the introduction of new types of treatment
- Mix flexibility – a wide range of available treatments
- Volume flexibility – the ability to adjust the number of patients treated
- Delivery flexibility – the ability to reschedule appointments

Automobile plant
- Product/Service flexibility – the introduction of new models
- Mix flexibility – a wide range of options available
- Volume flexibility – the ability to adjust the number of vehicles manufactured
- Delivery flexibility – the ability to reschedule manufacturing priorities

Bus company
- Product/Service flexibility – the introduction of new routes or excursions
- Mix flexibility – a large number of locations served
- Volume flexibility – the ability to adjust the frequency of services
- Delivery flexibility – the ability to reschedule trips

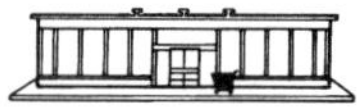

Supermarket
- Product/Service flexibility – the introduction of new goods or promotions
- Mix flexibility – a wide range of goods stocked
- Volume flexibility – the ability to adjust the number of customers served
- Delivery flexibility – the ability to obtain out of stock items (very occasionally)

Figure 2.10 Flexibility means different things in different operations

THE *NINE O'CLOCK NEWS* CANNOT BE LATE[8]

Some businesses rely on their operations to be on time, all the time, and every time. The news business is like this. A daily newspaper delivered one day late is practically worthless. The news operation where dependability is perhaps at its most critical, however, is television news. The BBC's *Nine O'Clock News* is expected to start on the second of nine o'clock and last exactly 30 minutes (unless a programming decision is taken to delay it for a sporting event or other exceptional circumstances). The BBC's ability to achieve this level of dependability is made possible by the technology employed in news gathering and editing. For example, until recently a news editor would have scheduled a video-taped report to start its countdown five seconds prior to its broadcast time. The screen would show the numbers as the count-down proceeded and the team would anxiously wait for the visuals to appear to make sure that the correct tape had indeed been loaded. With new technology the tape can be started from a freeze-frame and will roll the instant the command to play is given. The team has faith in the dependability of the process. In addition, technology allows them the flexibility to achieve dependability even when news stories break just before transmission. In the hours before scheduled transmission journalists and editors prepare an 'inventory' of news items stored electronically. The presenter will prepare his or her commentary on the autocue and each item will be timed to the second. (From experience the team can estimate exactly how long it will take to read any number of words.) If the team needs to make short-term adjustments to the planned schedule of items the news studio's technology allows the editors to take broadcasts live from journalists at their locations on satellite 'takes', directly into the programme. Editors can even type news reports directly on to the autocue for the presenter to read as they are typed. Nerve-racking, but it keeps the programme on time. ∎

Product/Service flexibility

Product/Service flexibility is the operation's ability to introduce new products and services. In the hospital this could mean introducing new surgical techniques or new medical record information. In the automobile plant it means the ability to adapt its manufacturing resources so that it can launch new models. To the city bus company it means that it could introduce new routes or special excursion services, while to the supermarket it means introducing new lines on its shelves, novel promotions or new payment services.

Mix flexibility

Mix flexibility means being able to provide a wide range or mix of products and services. Most operations produce more than one product or service. In addition most operations do not make their products or services in high enough volumes to dedicate all parts of their activities exclusively to a single product or service. This means that most parts of any operation will have to process more than one type of product or service and so will at times need to change from doing one activity to doing another. For example, some parts of a hospital need to provide a relatively wide range of services. The Accident and Emergency department has to provide immediate treatment for the wide range of complaints from which its patients suffer. The General Surgery department also has a similarly wide range of complaints to treat. The staff, technology and organization of these departments need to be flexible enough to cope with this variety. Other departments in the hospital will require less flexibility because they provide a comparatively narrow range of services. The X-ray department, for example, is expected only to provide radiographic services. In the automobile plant, flexibility is needed to provide all the range of options which customers are able to choose when buying their cars. The city bus company needs to provide a wide enough variety of routes to satisfy demand between its more popular areas of the city. It will probably do this by carefully designing its routes to pass through popular pick-up points and destinations and by making sure that its mix of vehicles allows it to provide adequate coverage of its routes, at any one time. To the supermarket, mix flexibility means being able to stock a wide range of products on its shelves. This will require its purchasing staff to be flexible enough to deal with a large number of suppliers, and its warehouses to receive and ship a wide variety of items.

Volume flexibility

Volume flexibility is the ability of the operation to change its level of output or activity. All operations will need to change their level of activity because all operations to some extent have to cope with fluctuating demand for their products and services. Of course all operations could theoretically ignore these fluctuations in demand, dispense with all volume flexibility and keep their activity level constant. However this totally 'inflexible' option can have serious consequences on customer service, operating costs or both. (Chapter 11 on capacity management will deal with this.)

In the hospital the demand for its various services will vary depending on the type of area it serves. For example, a hospital Accident and Emergency unit in a city area which takes in a large number of commuting workers will have to cope with heavy demand during the working and travelling hours of the day but will have relatively quiet evenings, weekends and summer vacation periods. The hospital will need to be flexible enough to provide an appropriate level of service as demand varies throughout the day, as well as over the week and the year. In addition it will need to cope with the occasional unpredictable demand for its services such as a major road accident. In a similar way, the demand for automobiles will vary through the year and the automobile factory will need to adjust its output accordingly. The city bus company will also need to change its activity levels throughout the day as demand levels vary. It might also need to change the relative balance of the frequency of its services among its various routes throughout the day: more buses for its commuter routes in the morning and evening peaks perhaps, and more buses to local shopping areas in the middle of the day. In the supermarket, flexibility again means coping with a variety of activity levels as demand varies throughout the day.

Delivery flexibility

Delivery flexibility is the ability to change the timing of the delivery of the service. Usually this means the operation providing goods or services earlier than anticipated, although it may mean delaying delivery. Usually the latter is the easier task.

In the hospital, delivery flexibility means rescheduling a patient's treatment. A maternity ward, for example, needs to have high delivery flexibility (in both senses!) to deal with a patient's premature labour. The automobile plant might occasionally have to rush a particular product through the plant to meet the special needs of a customer (although this might cause expensive disruption to the plant's schedules). The city bus company would be even more unlikely to reschedule its regular services so as to change their delivery times, but might have to do this for its excursion services. For example if the company accepted a contract to transport pupils on a school trip, the date of which was changed, it would itself need to change the delivery of its service. Similarly the supermarket might not generally want to change the regular delivery schedules to its stores but, in exceptional circumstances, to placate a dissatisfied customer, for example, it might bring forward the delivery of an out-of-stock item.

Some operations compete quite explicitly on their ability to be flexible and, again, advertise this strength.

Flexibility inside the operation

Developing a flexible operation can also have advantages to the internal customers within the operation.

Flexibility speeds up response

Being able to give fast service often depends on the operation being flexible. For example, if the hospital has to cope with a sudden influx of patients from a road accident, it clearly needs to deal with injuries quickly. Under such circumstances a flexible hospital which can speedily transfer extra skilled staff and equipment to the Accident and Emergency department will provide the fast service which the patients need.

FLEXIBILITY AT GODIVA CHOCOLATIER[9]

The world-famous chocolate maker, Godiva Chocolatier, is situated right in the heart of Brussels, Europe's centre of quality chocolate manufacturing. Inside its four-storey factory, highly skilled staff transform selected natural ingredients into a delicious range of products which are distributed world-wide. Demand for these premium chocolates has been rising fast, typically in excess of 10 per cent per year, which has forced the operations department to examine ways of expanding capacity. At the same time, the competitive need to continue to introduce new, improved flavours, shapes, and types of packaging has created an ever-widening range of products for operations to produce, pack, store and distribute. With an output of only about 1500 tonnes per year, Godiva is a relatively small producer who makes more than 100 different chocolates and packs them in a vast range of cartons and bulk packs to suit its different niche markets. Over the last ten years, the company has invested carefully to achieve improvements in productivity through automation, but at the same time to ensure that maximum flexibility is built in at every stage of production. There are two basic methods of production used at Godiva: *enrobing* and *moulding*.

Enrobed products begin as extruded strips of relatively hard fillings such as marzipan, which are cut into short pieces and passed through a machine which coats them in the appropriate liquid chocolate. Decorative finishes such as crystal sugar, nuts, or applied patterns, if required, can then be added by skilled hand-work or specialized machinery. The enrobing department operates by linking together the various pieces of equipment (extruders, guillotines, depositors, enrobers, decorators, etc.) in different sequences and combinations to suit the individual product designs. Sometimes, where the volumes justify the effort involved in ▶

repositioning them, this is done by using moveable conveyors to make the link between the machines. Otherwise, the products are transferred around as required in plastic trays, allowing the equipment (and the skilled staff) to be decoupled and thereby to work at different speeds and times. Only small tanks of liquid chocolate (dark, milk and white) are used at the enrobing machines so that change-overs can be fast. Typically it takes only 20 minutes to disconnect the tank and clean out the enrobing machine prior to starting another colour. Because of the wide variety of products made this way, planning is complex, with the sequence of products being critical to productivity, utilization and quality. Normally, it is considered uneconomic and impractical to produce less than 300 kg of a particular colour, but where possible, longer runs of different products with the same chocolate coating are planned, so that the colour change can be carried out at the end of the day's production. Short runs can be made entirely by traditional hand-made methods, but the cost is prohibitive except for special premium products and for prototypes.

Most *moulded products* are produced on a new and complicated 80 metre long production line, which was designed to handle almost the full range of moulded products. It can mould all three colours with a 20 minute change-over of the liquid chocolate. These are normally done only at the end of a day's production, so as not to waste productive capacity. Moulds can be changed without stopping the line using a simple operator-assisted mould changing device. Filling the shells with creams, fondants, etc. is carried out using computer-controlled depositing machines, which give tight control of volume and speed to take account of the physical properties of the fillings. Three of these depositors are available, allowing one or two to be in use while the third is moved aside for cleaning, programming, and setting-up with the next batch of filling. It is possible, therefore, to change product in under one minute, and to use two depositors simultaneously for products where nuts or cherries are to be incorporated in the middle of creams. This operation is carried out by a special automated depositor which has taken the place of 16 people (although two have been retained to put in the few that are missed by the machine). After demoulding, the chocolates can be routed to an automatic individual wrapping machine, but most are conveyed directly to a new packing robot which picks and places the products on blister packs for bulk sales to shops, or on flat plastic trays for transfer to the assortment packing lines.

The most flexible part of the operation is the *assortment packing* section. Here, the wide range of finished chocolates is carefully packed according to the appropriate mix and positions in the various retail cartons. These pass along a conveyor where each type of chocolate is added by hand. Although it is technically possible for this to be done by a robot, Godiva engineers have found that people are less expensive and can also continuously inspect the quality of every chocolate packed. Many of the staff are also very adept at adding sophisticated and complicated value-added features to the packaging, such as ribbons, bows and labels.

Godiva's production system has been developed to support the company's strategy of providing a wide range of high quality, well presented products. Flexibility which was initially provided by skilled labour has been supplemented and enhanced by automated lines which allow both quick change-overs and alternative routings. Innovative products can be developed and brought quickly into production because of the inherent flexibility which was designed into the lines. ■

Source: By kind permission of Godiva SA

Flexibility saves time

In many parts of the hospital staff have to treat a wide variety of complaints. Fractures, cuts or drug overdoses do not come in batches. Each patient is an individual with individual needs. The hospital staff cannot take time to 'get into the routine' of treating a particular complaint; they must have the flexibility to adapt quickly. They must also have sufficiently flexible facilities and equipment so that time is not wasted waiting for equipment to be brought to the patient. The time of the hospital's resources is being saved because they are flexible in 'changing over' from one task to the next. (*See* also box on Godiva Chocolatier for an example of how flexibility can save time.)

Flexibility maintains dependability

Internal flexibility can also help to keep the operation on schedule when unexpected events disrupt the operation's plans. For example, if the sudden influx of patients to the hospital also results in emergency surgery being performed, the emergency patients will almost certainly displace other routine operations. The patients who were expecting to undergo their routine operations will have been admitted and probably prepared for their operations. Cancelling their operations is likely to cause them distress and probably considerable inconvenience. A flexible hospital might be able to minimize the disruption by possibly having reserved operating theatres for such an emergency, and being able to bring in medical staff quickly who are 'on call'.

The cost objective

Cost is the last objective to be covered. Last not because it is the least important but because it is the most important. To the companies which compete directly on price, cost will be clearly their major operations objective. The lower the cost of producing their goods and services, the lower can be the price to their customers. Even those companies which compete on things other than price, however, will be interested in keeping their costs low. Every rand, dollar or guilder removed from an operation's cost base is a further rand, dollar or guilder added to its profits. Not surprisingly, low cost is a universally attractive objective.

The way in which operations management can influence cost on the operation will depend largely on where the operation costs are incurred. Put simply, the operation will spend its money on

- *staff costs* (the money spent on employing people);
- *facilities, technology and equipment costs* (the money spent on buying, caring for, operating and replacing the operation's 'hardware';
- *material costs* (the money spent on the materials consumed or transformed in the operation).

Figure 2.11 shows typical cost breakdowns for the hospital, car plant, supermarket, and bus company.

Although comparing the cost structure of different operations is not always straightforward, and depends on how costs are categorized, some general points can be made.

Many of the hospital's costs are fixed and will change little for small changes in the number of patients it treats. Its facilities such as beds, operating theatres and laboratories are expensive, as are some of its highly skilled staff. This means that it must be

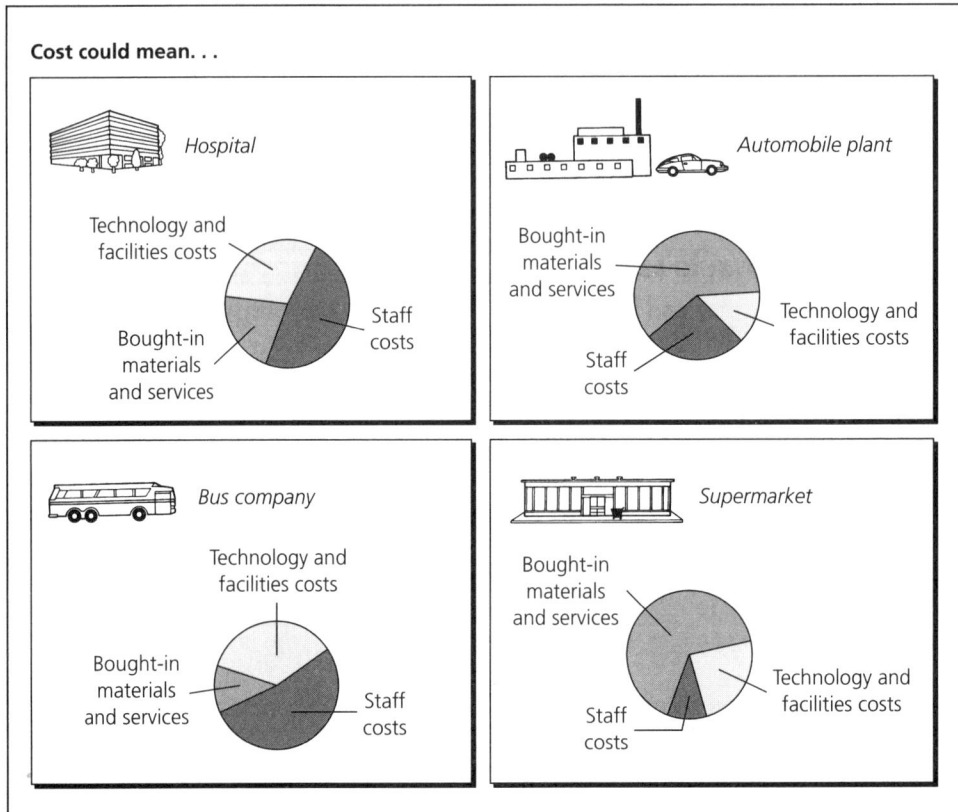

**Figure 2.11
Cost means
different things
in different
operations**

very careful to concentrate its expensive resources where they will do the most good and then make sure that they are fully utilized. Some of the hospital's costs will be payments to outside suppliers of drugs, medical supplies and externally sourced services such as cleaning, but probably not as high a proportion as in the car factory. The car factory's payment for materials and other supplies will by far outweigh all its other costs put together. Because of this it will put considerable effort into developing its suppliers to provide responsive and low-cost supply. It will also try to move its products quickly through the operation to minimize the delay between paying for the materials and getting the revenue from selling its products. Conversely, the city bus company will pay very little for its supplies, fuel being one of its main bought-in items. The utilization of its equipment and facilities (buses) and its labour, however, will have a significant effect on its costs per passenger mile. At the other extreme, the supermarket's costs are dominated by the cost of buying its supplies. In spite of its high 'material' costs, however, an individual supermarket can do little if anything to affect the cost of goods it sells. All purchasing decisions probably will be made at company headquarters. The individual supermarket will be more concerned with the utilization of its main asset, the building itself, and its staff. For this reason 'sales value per square metre' will be one of its main measures of its operating productivity, and staff scheduling to maximize their utilization will be one of its main operating tasks.

Cost is affected by the other performance objectives

So far we have described the meaning and effects of quality, speed, dependability and flexibility for the operations function. In doing so, we have distinguished between the value of each performance objective to external customers and, inside the operation, to internal customers. Each of the various performance objectives has several internal effects, but all of them affect cost.

● High-quality operations do not waste time or effort having to re-do things nor are their internal customers inconvenienced by flawed service. In other words, high quality can mean low costs.
● Fast operations reduce the level of in-process inventory between micro operations as well as reducing administrative overheads. Both these effects can reduce the overall cost of the operation.

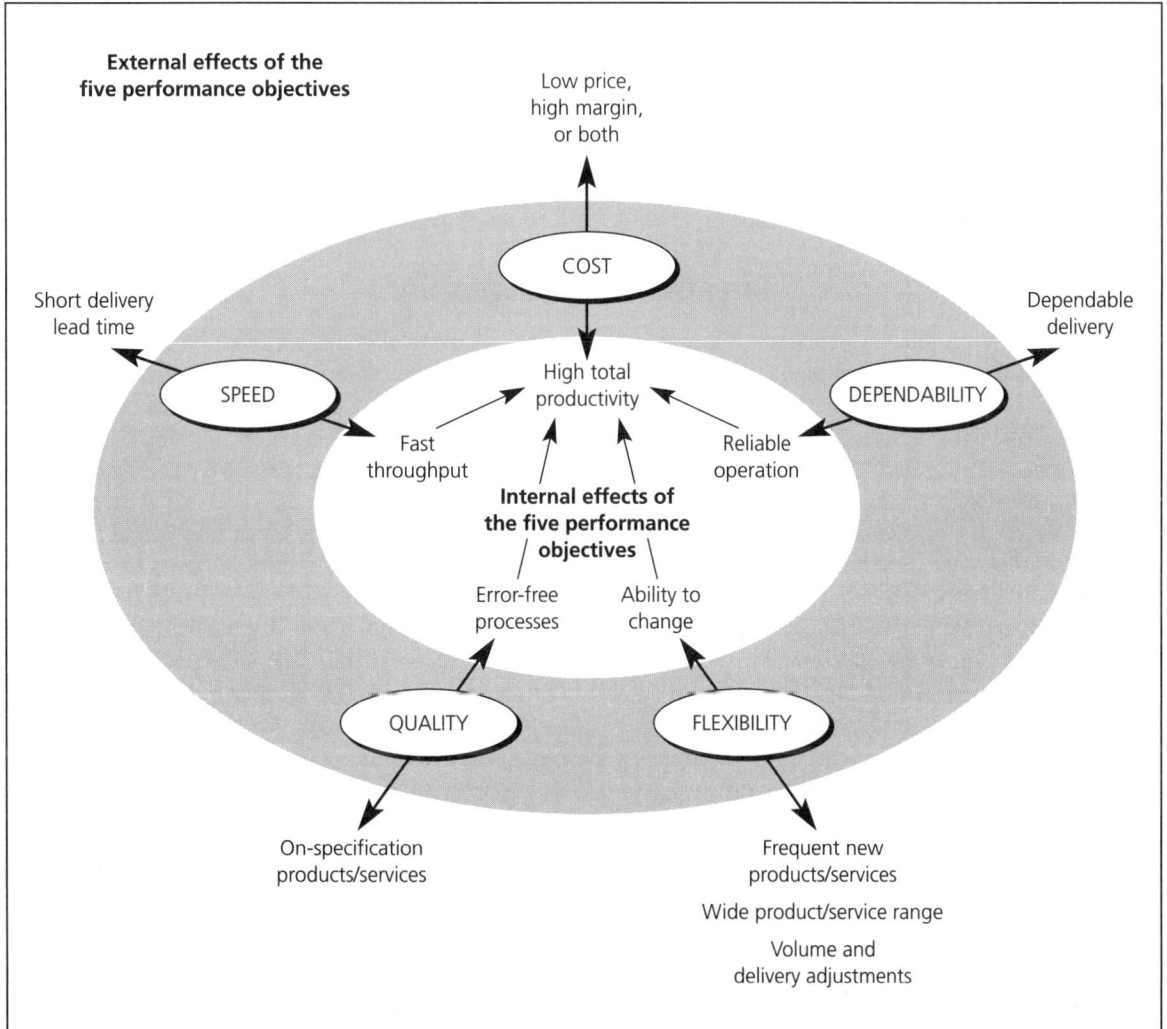

Figure 2.12 Performance objectives have both external and internal effects. Internally cost is influenced by the other performance objectives

● Dependable operations do not spring any unwelcome surprises on their internal customers. They can be relied on to deliver exactly as planned. This eliminates wasteful disruption and allows the other micro operations to operate efficiently.

● Flexible operations adapt to changing circumstances quickly and without disrupting the rest of the operation. Flexible micro operations can also change over between tasks quickly and without wasting time and capacity, again saving costs.

Inside the operation, therefore, one important way to improve cost performance is to improve the performance of the other operations objectives (*see* Fig. 2.12). The implication of this is very important because it tells us about the relationship between the external and internal aspects of operations performance. All organizations are interested in reducing the cost of their operations. Lower cost allows the organization to reduce its prices or increase its profits or a combination of the two. So if all organizations are interested in the cost of their operations to their external customers, they must also be interested in their internal quality, speed, dependability and flexibility.

Tony Gainsford, Molex SA

Molex is an international company that supplies electrical connectors to the automotive, white goods, brown goods and telecommunications industries. Molex offers 50 000 different products, 4000 of which are sold in South Africa.

Tony Gainsford is the operations manager at Molex SA. His responsibilities include heading up the manufacturing team, organizing the warehousing and managing the entire facility, including the telephones and fax facilities. He also has an interest in the use of computers in his company.

Tony's education included an apprenticeship in the aircraft industry, an engineering diploma, a BA degree in Psychology, a Management Advancement Programme and a Production Management course. He has worked at Atlas engineering, a small coal-mining company, and is now working at Molex.

'What motivates my work in operations is a desire to see things done well. At Molex, the operations function links into the strategy of the organization. In order to put together a strategy, we need to understand our own capabilities. Product spread, design capabilities and throughput all impact on our future plans. The operations function needs to work more closely with marketing than we are doing at the moment, to ensure that we are meeting the needs of our customer. This is something we are trying to improve.

'Molex is involved in a variety of markets, so that even though specific industries have large variations in demand, these balance each other out and our total demand is reasonably constant. Our customers do not have a good understanding of how our business operates and often expect us to have inventory on hand for them. However, the head office in the United States has strict inventory holding requirements. We have to balance this with the needs of our clients so that we can minimize our own costs and make a profit.

'The situation of each department in the factory is purposeful. Let's look at one particular product, the splice, and its transformation process. Reels of material are delivered to the entrance of the plating department. The material undergoes a process of electrolysis which results in plating. Thereafter, the *plated material is delivered to the press shop, where it is stamped into terminals. Simultaneously, plastic supplies are delivered to the moulding department, where the plastic component is manufactured. These processes are planned so that the different components arrive at assembly at the same time and can be assembled to meet delivery schedules. From assembly, the terminals are taken to stores. This is where customers collect their orders. It is also used as a display room for prospective customers. The toolroom and quality department are support functions. The tool-room makes and repairs the dyes for stamping and moulding, and repairs the plating equipment. The quality department ensures that Molex's products meet the specifications which customers require.*

'My work involves a lot of careful planning, and communication with different work stations. I have to take the chosen goals of the organization and translate them back into operational priorities that can guide and assist daily activity on the shop floor. These goals and priorities should be understood and agreed at all levels of the organization.' ■

Source: By kind permission of Molex SA

SUMMARY

■ The operations function has three main roles to play within any organization:

- *As a supporter of the organization's overall strategy*. It does this by developing the operation's resources in such a way as to make them appropriate for whatever strategy the operation chooses to adopt.

- *As an implementer of the organization's strategies*. The operation must make sure that the company's strategy really does happen in practice.

- *As a leader of strategy*. This means that the operations function should provide the organization with all the aspects of performance which it needs to achieve its long-term (competitive) aims.

■ The extent to which the operations function fulfils these roles together with its aspirations can be used to judge the operations function's contribution to the organization. Hayes and Wheelwright provide a four-stage model for doing this. Stage 1 operations do not provide any contribution to the organization; they hold it back by making mistakes. Stage 2 operations are looking to have a performance level which is up to the standard of the better organizations in their industry. Stage 3 operations are already good but want to be clearly the best in their industry. Stage 4 operations not only want to be the best in their industry, they want to establish a clear lead by relying on their operations function to outperform any rival organization.

■ Assessing the contribution of an operation can be done through a number of performance objectives. These are:

- the quality of goods and services provided by the operation;

- the speed with which it delivers its goods and services;

- the dependability with which it keeps its delivery promises;

- the flexibility of the operation to change;

- the cost of producing its goods and services.

■ All these performance objectives have both external and internal effects. The internal effects of high quality, speed, dependability and flexibility are generally to reduce costs within the operation.

Operations objectives at the Penang Mutiara[10]

There are many luxurious hotels in the South-East Asia region but few can compare with the Penang Mutiara, a 440 room top-of-the-market hotel which nestles in the lush greenery of Malaysia's Indian Ocean Coast. Owned by Pernas–OUE of Malaysia and managed by Singapore Mandarin International Hotels, the hotel's General Manager is Wernie Eisen, a Swiss hotelier who has managed luxury hotels all over the world.

He is under no illusions about the importance of running an effective operation.

'Managing a hotel of this size is an immensely complicated task', he says. *'Our customers have every right to be demanding. They expect first-class service and that's what we have to give them. If we have any problems with managing this operation, the customer sees them immediately and that's the biggest incentive for us to take operations performance seriously.*

'Our quality of service just has to be impeccable. First of all this means dealing with the basics. For example, our staff must be courteous at all times and yet also friendly towards our guests. And of course they must have the knowledge to be able to answer guests' questions. The building and equipment, in fact all the hardware of the operation, must support the luxury atmosphere which we have created in the hotel. Stylish design and top-class materials not only create the right impression but, if we choose them carefully, they are also durable so the hotel still looks good over the years. Most of all though, quality is about anticipating our guests' needs, thinking ahead so you can identify what will delight or irritate a guest.'

The hotel tries to anticipate guests' needs in a number of ways. For example, if guests have been to the hotel before, staff avoid their having to repeat the information which they gave on the previous visit. Reception staff simply check to see if guests have stayed before, retrieve the information and take them straight to their room without irritating delays. Quality of service also means helping guests sort out their own problems. If the airline loses a guest's luggage *en route* to the hotel, for example, he or she will arrive at the hotel understandably irritated.

'The fact that it is not us who have irritated them is not really the issue. It is our job to make them feel better.'

Speed, in terms of fast response to customers' requests is something else that is important.

'A guest just should not be kept waiting. If a guest has a request he or she has that request now *so it needs to be sorted out* now. *This is not always easy but we do our best. For example, if every guest in the hotel tonight decided to call room service and request a meal instead of going to the restaurants, our room service department would obviously be grossly overloaded and customers would have to wait an unacceptably long time before the meals were brought up to their rooms. We cope with this by keeping a close watch on how demand for room service is building up. If we think it's going to get above the level where response time to customers would become unacceptably long, we will call in staff from other restaurants in the hotel. Of course, to do this we have to make sure that our staff are multi-skilled. In fact we have a policy of making sure that restaurant staff can always do more than one job. It's this kind of flexibility which allows us to maintain fast response to the customer.'*

Likewise, Wernie regards dependability as a fundamental principle of a well managed hotel.

'We must always keep our promises. For example, rooms must be ready on time and accounts must be ready for presentation when a guest departs; the guests expect a dependable service and anything less than full dependability is a legitimate cause for dissatisfaction.'

It is on the grand occasions, however, when dependability is particularly important in the hotel. When staging a banquet, for example, everything has to be on time. Drinks, food, entertainment have to be available exactly as planned. Any deviation from plan will very soon be noticed by customers.

'It is largely a matter of planning the details and anticipating what could go wrong,' says Wernie. *'Once we've done the planning we can anticipate possible problems and plan how to cope with them, or better still, prevent them from occurring in the first place.'*

Flexibility means a number of things to the hotel. First of all it means that they should be able to meet a guest's requests.

'We never like to say NO!' says Wernie. *'For example, if a guest asks for some Camembert cheese and we don't have it in stock, we will make sure that someone goes to the supermarket and tries to get it. If, in spite of our best efforts, we can't get any, we will negotiate an alternative solution with the guest. This has an important side effect – it greatly helps*

us to maintain the motivation of our staff. We are constantly being asked to do the seemingly impossible – yet we do it, and our staff think it's great. We all like to be part of an organization which is capable of achieving the very difficult if not the impossible.'

Flexibility in the hotel also means the ability to cope with the seasonal fluctuations in demand. They achieve this partly by using temporary part-time staff. In the back office parts of the hotel this isn't a major problem. In the laundry, for example, it is relatively easy to put on an extra shift in busy periods by increasing staffing levels. However, this is more of a problem in the parts of the hotel that have direct contact with the customer.

'New temporary staff can't be expected to have the same customer contact skills as our more regular staff. Our solution to this is to keep the temporary staff as far in the background as we possibly can and make sure that our skilled, well trained staff are the ones who usually interact with the customer. So, for example, a waiter who would normally take orders, service the food, and take away the dirty plates would in peak times restrict his or her activities to taking orders and serving the food. The less skilled part of the job, taking away the plates, could be left to temporary staff.'

As far as cost is concerned, around 60 per cent of the hotel's total operating expenses go on food and beverages, so one obvious way of keeping costs down is by making sure that food is not wasted. Energy costs at 6 per cent of total operating costs are also a potential source of saving. However, although cost savings are welcome, the hotel is very careful never to compromise the quality of its service in order to cut costs. Wernie's view is quite clear.

'It is impeccable customer service which gives us our competitive advantage, not price. Good service means that our guests return again and again. At times, around half our guests are people who have been before. The more guests we have, the higher is our utilization of rooms and restaurants, and this is what really keeps cost per guest down and profitability reasonable. So in the end we've come full circle: it's the quality of our service which keeps our volumes high and our costs low.' ∎

Questions

1 Describe how you think Wernie will
(a) make sure that the way he manages the hotel is *appropriate* to the way it competes for business;
(b) *implement* any change in strategy;
(c) develop his operation so that *it drives* the long-term strategy of the hotel.

2 What questions might Wernie ask to judge whether his operation is a Stage 1, Stage 2, Stage 3, or Stage 4 operation on Hayes and Wheelwright's scale of excellence?

3 The case describes how quality, speed, dependability, flexibility and cost impact on the hotel's external customers. Explain how each of these performance objectives might have internal benefits.

DISCUSSION QUESTIONS

1 For the following organizations explain how their operations functions can support business strategy, implement business strategy and drive business strategy:
> a fast food restaurant
> a film processing service
> an oil refinery.

2 Explain the seeming paradox of the operations function, which is concerned with day-to-day operational decisions, while having a central role to play in achieving long-term strategic success.

3 Describe how the operations function of a car hire company might perform as it progressed from being a Stage 1 to a Stage 4 operation (using Hayes and Wheelwright's terms).

4 Illustrate the concept of a Stage 4 company by explaining how a Stage 4 operations function within the following organizations could contribute to their long-term competitive success:
> a salted snack manufacturer
> an airline
> a parcel delivery service
> an hotel.

5 Discuss what constitutes quality, speed, dependability and flexibility in the following operations:

> a university library
> a university sports centre
> a university restaurant
> an operations management course.
(Try asking the managers of these operations!)

6 Describe the different types of flexibility that might be found in each of the following operations:
> a university
> a factory making tennis racquets
> a rail network.

7 For each of the following organizations explain what is meant by, and discuss the relative importance of, quality, speed, dependability and flexibility:
> a high-volume car producer
> a hairdresser
> a package collection and distribution service (e.g. UPS or Federal Express).

8 Many organizations see the role of operations as getting on with the job of making products or serving customers. Discuss the implications of this view of the operations function.

9 Using an example of your own choice, describe how the cost of the operation might be affected by changing the levels of performance of quality, speed, dependability and flexibility.

NOTES ON CHAPTER

1 This idea was first popularized by Wickham Skinner at Harvard University. *See* Skinner, W. (1985) *Manufacturing: the Formidable Competitive Weapon*, John Wiley.

2 Hayes, R.H. and Wheelwright, S.C. (1984) *Restoring our Competitive Edge*, John Wiley.

3 Chase, R. and Hayes, R.H. (1991) 'Beefing up Service Firms', *Sloan Management Review*, Fall.

4 The five performance objectives are discussed in far more detail in Slack, N. (1991) *The Manufacturing Advantage*, Mercury Books.

5 Source: Merrill, R. (1989) 'How Northern Telecom Competes on Time', *Harvard Business Review*, Vol 67, No 4.

6 For a much more detailed discussion of the speed objective, *see* Stalk, G. and Hout, T.M. (1990) *Competing Against Time*, Free Press.

7 For a further discussion of the flexibility objective, *see* Slack, N. (1989) 'Focus on Flexibility' *in* Wild, R. (ed) *International Handbook of Production/Operations Management*, Cassell.

8 Source: discussions with the News Team at the BBC.

9 Source: Benjamin, M. (1994) 'Chocolate Secrets Unwrapped', *The European*, 1–7 April, and the management of Godiva Chocolatier.

10 We are grateful to Wernie Eisen and the management of the Penang Mutiara for permission to use this example.

SELECTED FURTHER READINGS

Azzone, G., Bertelé, U. and Masella, C. (1991) 'The Design of Performance Measures for Time Based Companies', *International Journal of Operations and Production Management*, Vol 11, No 3.

Blenkinsop, A. and Burns, N. (1992) 'Performance Measurement Revisited', *International Journal of Operations and Production Management*, Vol 12, No 10.

Chase, R. and Hayes, R.H. (1991) 'Beefing up Operations in Service Firms', *Sloan Management Review*, Fall, pp 15–26.

De Meyer, A. and Fedows, K. (1990) 'The Influence of Manufacturing Improvement Programmes on Performance', *International Journal of Operations and Production Management*, Vol 10, No 2.

Gupta, Y.P., Lonial, S.C. and Mangold, W.G. (1991) 'An Examination of the Relationship between Manufacturing Strategy and Marketing Objectives', *International Journal of Operations and Production Management*, Vol 11, No 10.

Hayes, R.H. and Wheelwright, S.C. (1984) *Restoring Our Competitive Edge*, John Wiley, Chap 14.

Hill, T. (1993) *Manufacturing Strategy* (2nd edn), Macmillan.

New, C. (1992) 'World-Class Manufacturing versus Strategic Trade-offs', *International Journal of Operations and Production Management*, Vol 12, No 4.

Pine, B.J. (1993) *Mass Customization*, Harvard Business School Press.

Shaw, W.N., Clarkson, A.H. and Stone, M.A. (1992) 'The Competitive Characteristics of Scottish Manufacturing Companies', *International Journal of Operations and Production Management*, Vol 12, No 6.

Slack, N. (1991) *The Manufacturing Advantage*, Mercury Business Books.

Snaddon, D.R. (1993) 'The Goals of Manufacturing Strategy, POM Techniques and Perceptions: A Pilot Study', *South African Journal of Business Management*, Vol 24, No 4.

Stalk, G. (1988) 'Time – The Next Source of Competitive Advantage', *Harvard Business Review*, Vol 66, No 4.

OPERATIONS STRATEGY

INTRODUCTION

No organization can plan in detail every aspect of its current or future actions, but all organizations can benefit from some idea of where they are heading and how they could get there. Put another way, all organizations need some strategic direction. It is just the same with the operations function. Once the operations function has understood its role in the business and after it has articulated the performance objectives which define its contribution to strategy, it needs to formulate a set of general principles which will guide its decision making. This is the *operations strategy* of the company. This chapter establishes the concept of 'strategy' and fits operations strategy within the overall strategic decision making in the organization. It also indicates the type of decisions which an operation will have to take in order to establish the content of its operations strategy. Figure 3.1 shows the position of the ideas described in this chapter on the general model of operations management.

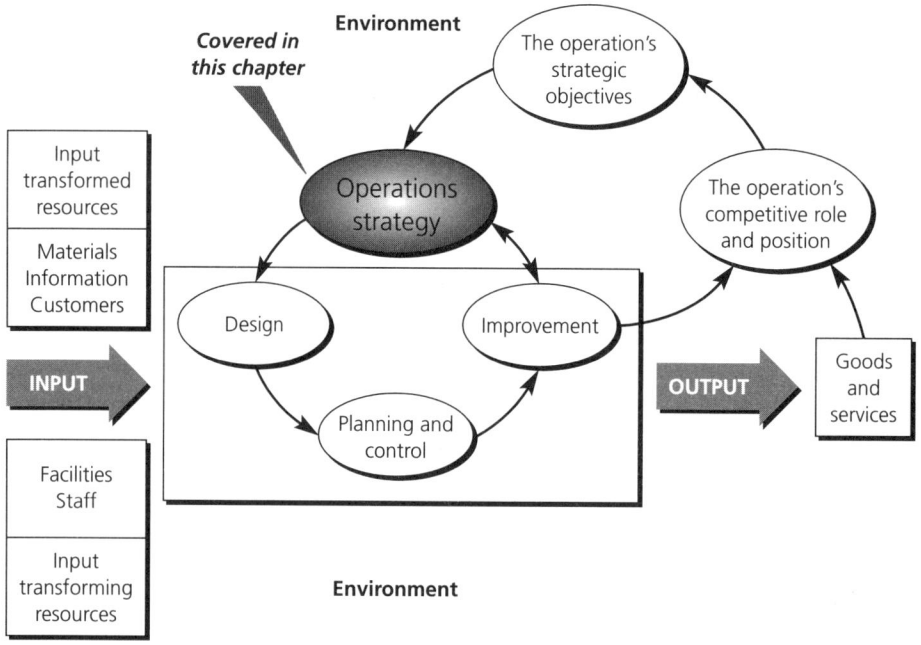

Figure 3.1 This chapter examines operations strategy

OBJECTIVES

This chapter will examine:

- the *strategy hierarchy* of which operations strategy is a part;

- the *nature and content* of operations strategy;

- how performance objectives will have different *priorities* depending on the organization's *customers, competitors* and the position of its products and services in their *life cycle*;

- the operations strategy *decision areas*;

- the impact of the operations strategy decision areas on *performance objectives*.

WHAT IS STRATEGY?

Before dealing with operations strategy it is necessary to consider what we mean by the term 'strategy'. One thing we assume when an organization articulates its 'strategy' is that it is going to do one set of things rather than another – that it has made decisions which commit the organization to a particular set of actions. The first thing about strategy, therefore, is that it is a commitment to action. Managers make decisions all the time, however, which presumably will commit them to do something, but not all of these are strategic decisions.

By the term strategic we usually mean those decisions which:

- are widespread in their effect and so are significant in the part of the organization to which the strategy refers;
- define the position of the organization relative to its environment;
- move the organization closer to its long-term goals.

A 'strategy' then is the total pattern of the decisions and actions which position the organization in its environment and are intended to achieve its long-term goals.[1]

The strategy hierarchy

The term 'strategy', as we have defined it above, depends partly on what we mean by 'the organization'. If 'the organization' is a large diversified corporation, its strategy will position it in its global, economic, political and social environment and will consist of decisions about what types of business the group wants to be in, in what parts of the world it wants to operate, what businesses to acquire and what to divest, how to allocate its cash between its various businesses and so on. Decisions such as these form the *corporate strategy* of the corporation – they guide and manoeuvre the corporation in its global, economic, social and political environment. Each business unit within the corporate group will also need to put together its own *business strategy* which sets out its individual mission and objectives as well as defining how it intends to compete in its markets. This business strategy guides the business in an environment which consists of its customers, markets and competitors, but also includes the corporate group of which it is a part. Similarly, within the business, each function will need to consider what part it should play in contributing to the strategic and/or competitive objectives of the business. The operations, marketing, finance, research and development, and other functions will all need to translate the objectives of the business into terms which have meaning for them and consider how best they should organize their resources to support them. In other words, each function of the business needs a *functional strategy* which guides its actions within the business. This time the 'environment' of the function includes the business itself.

These three levels of strategy – corporate, business and functional – form a hierarchy with business strategy being an important part of the environment into which functional strategies operate, and corporate strategy being an important element of the environment into which business strategies fit. Figure 3.2 illustrates this strategic hierarchy, with some of the decisions at each level and the main influences on the strategic decisions.

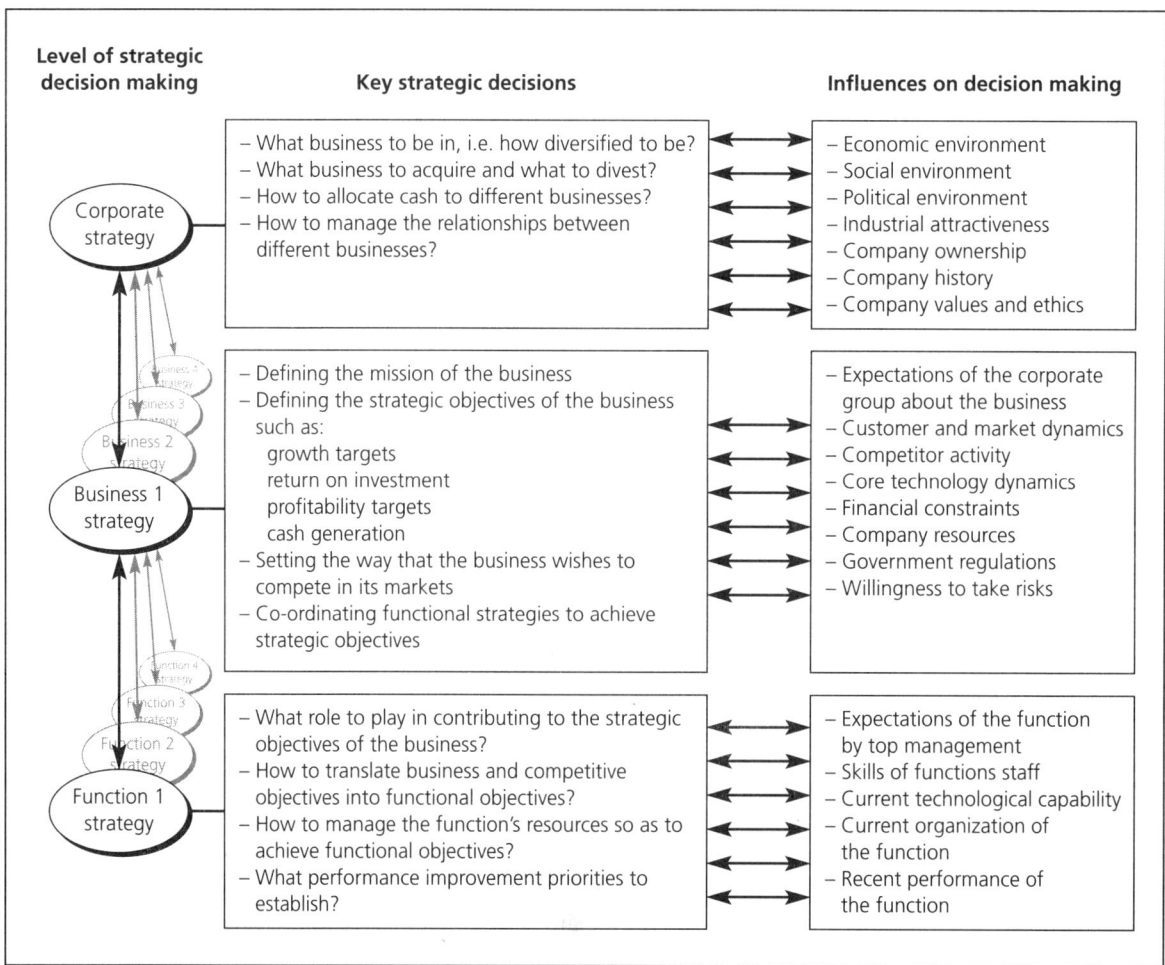

Figure 3.2 Decisions and influences at different levels in the strategy hierarchy

In fact the relationship between the levels in the strategy hierarchy is more complex than this. The hierarchy model is a convenient way of thinking about strategy but is not intended to represent the way strategies really are formulated. At the simplest level the connection between the three levels of strategy might be taken to indicate a 'top-down' relationship. That is, business strategy is devised only within the context of a well defined corporate strategy, and functional strategies only within a well defined business strategy. This is neither what does, or should, happen in reality. When any group is reviewing its corporate strategy, it will of course be influenced by environmental factors such as market conditions. It will also take into account, however, the circumstances, preferences, and capabilities of the various businesses which form the group. Similarly, the individual businesses, when reviewing their strategies, will consult the individual functions within the business about their constraints and capabilities. The three levels of strategy, in reality, both overlap and influence each other.

OPERATIONS STRATEGY

Accepting the simplifications of the hierarchical model, we can take the hierarchical nature of strategic linkage further into the operation itself. As we discussed in Chapter 1, all an organization's 'macro' operations are made up of a hierarchy of 'micro' operations. Each micro operation might need to develop its own unit or departmental plans which, in the context of the micro operation, might be termed strategic in that they will guide its decision making within the total (macro) operation.

At the level of the macro operation, operations strategy can be defined as follows:

Operations strategy is the total pattern of decisions and actions which set the role, objectives and activities of the operation so that they contribute to and support the organization's business strategy.[2]

At the level of the micro operation, an operation's plan or strategy can be defined as follows:

(Micro) operations strategy is the total pattern of decisions and actions which set the role, objectives and activities of each part of the operation so that they contribute to and support the operations strategy of the business.

So each unit's operations strategy contributes to the strategic objectives of the next level up. But as well as helping the next level up in the hierarchy to achieve its strategic objectives, operations strategy must take into account the needs of its internal customers and suppliers, as we discussed in Chapter 1. No function within an organization, and no part of any function can contribute to strategic objectives if it is not helped by the other parts of the organization which are its internal suppliers. Nor is any part of the organization contributing fully to strategic objectives if it is not itself helping its own internal customers.

This means that an operations strategy always has two purposes:

● to contribute directly to the strategic objectives of the next level up in the hierarchy, and
● to help other parts of the business make their own contribution to strategy.

Figure 3.3 illustrates this idea.

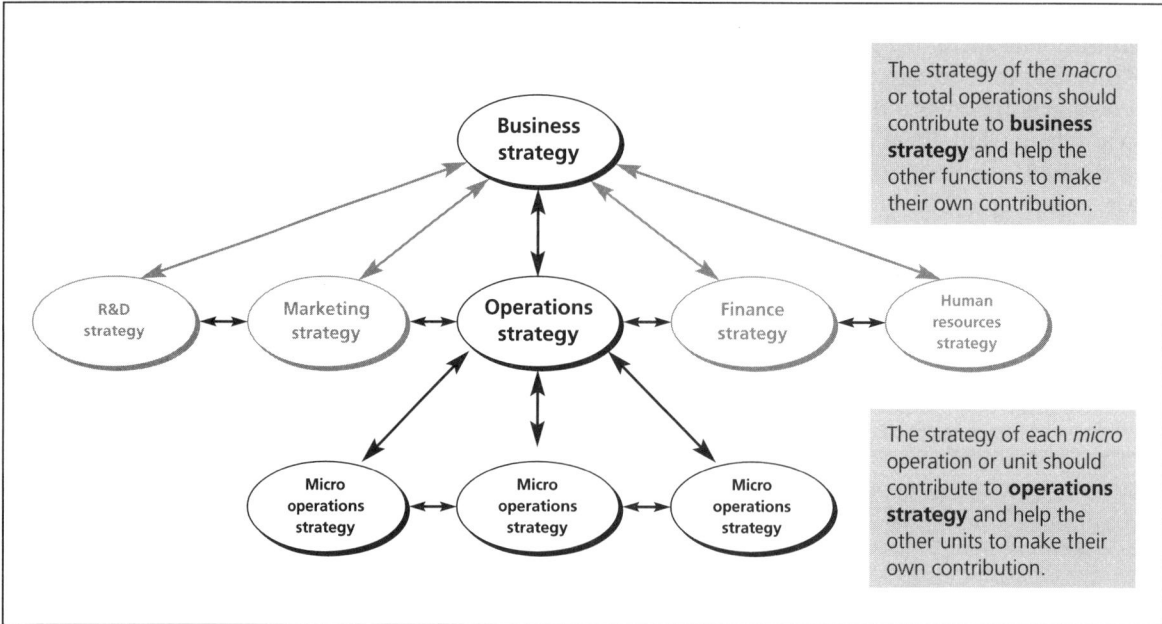

Figure 3.3 The contribution of operations strategy

THE CONTENT AND PROCESS OF OPERATIONS STRATEGY

When operations at any point in the hierarchy develop their operations strategies they must consider two separate, but overlapping, sets of questions. Some questions will be concerned with what is known as the *content* of the operations strategy. These are questions which will determine the specific strategies which govern the day-to-day decision making in the operation. The other set of questions will be concerned with the *process* of how these strategies are actually determined in the organization. The best way of illustrating the difference between the content and process of operations strategy is through an example.

Example: Synchro Signals and Control

Synchro Signals and Control (SSC) is a fast growing company which develops, manufactures, installs and maintains control systems for many types of processes. One of its divisions develops, manufactures and services traffic management systems. These are the electronic devices which control the operation of traffic lights, hazard warning signs and other road signals. The company decided that it needed to develop an operations strategy. As a first step the senior management team of the division listed the questions which the operations strategy should address. Some of these questions concerned the *content* of their operations strategy. They were:

● What are the most important aspects of the products and services we provide (quality of products and services, speed of delivery, dependability of delivery, flexibility of service or cost of the operation)?

- How many factories and service branches should we have, how large should they be, and where should they be located?
- How should we change and develop the products and services which we offer to our customers?
- How should we lay out the various departments and facilities within the operation?
- What type of machines and process technology should we be purchasing?
- What human resource strategies regarding working responsibilities and practices should we adopt for our staff?
- How should we adjust our capacity as demand fluctuates?
- How should we develop systems which manage the activities which produce services and products for our customers?
- How should we monitor the performance of the operation?
- How should we plan to improve the performance of the operation?

Some of the questions which the company needed to address related to the way in which it would make all the content decisions. These questions define the *process* of the company's operations strategy:

- Why are we reviewing our operations strategy at this point?
- Who should take overall responsibility for formulating our operations strategy?
- Is the formulation process to consider all aspects of all parts of our operation, or is it to be more focused?
- Who should be involved in the process of formulating the operations strategy?
- How should we organize ourselves to formulate the operations strategy?
- What should we do first, second, third, and so on?
- What 'action plans' or specific projects should we initiate to achieve our new strategy?
- How should we manage the implementation of our strategic plans?

The content of operations strategy

Operations strategy *content* is the collection of policies, plans and behaviours which the operation chooses to pursue. In this chapter we deal exclusively with the content of operations strategy. The process of operations strategy requires some considerable understanding of operations management generally, and so we treat that as one of the final issues in this book in Chapter 21.

In order to examine the content of operations strategy further, return to the list of operations strategy content questions which the Synchro Signals company (described in the previous example) has set itself. The first question requires the company to determine the *priority of its performance objectives*, that is which performance objectives are particularly important to it. Should it concentrate on being particularly good at quality or speed or dependability or flexibility or cost or perhaps some combination of two or more of them? All the other questions relate to the specific decision areas of the company. Those questions concerning the number, size and location of plants relate to *design decisions*, as do the questions concerning the product/service design, layout, technology and human resources. The questions concerning capacity adjustment and the systems which manage the delivery of products both relate to *planning and control decisions*. The questions which concern the monitoring and improvement of the operation's performance clearly relate to *improvement decisions*.

PRIORITY OF PERFORMANCE OBJECTIVES

Chapter 2 described and illustrated the five performance objectives as they apply to several different kinds of operation. But in our discussion nothing was implied about under what circumstances some of the performance objectives might become particularly important to an organization. The relative importance of performance objectives for this, or any other, operation will depend on a number of different influences. Three things are particularly important in determining which performance objectives are stressed (*see* Fig. 3.4):

● the specific needs of the company's *customer groups*;
● the activities of the company's *competitors*;
● the stage of the *product life cycle* at which the product or service stands.

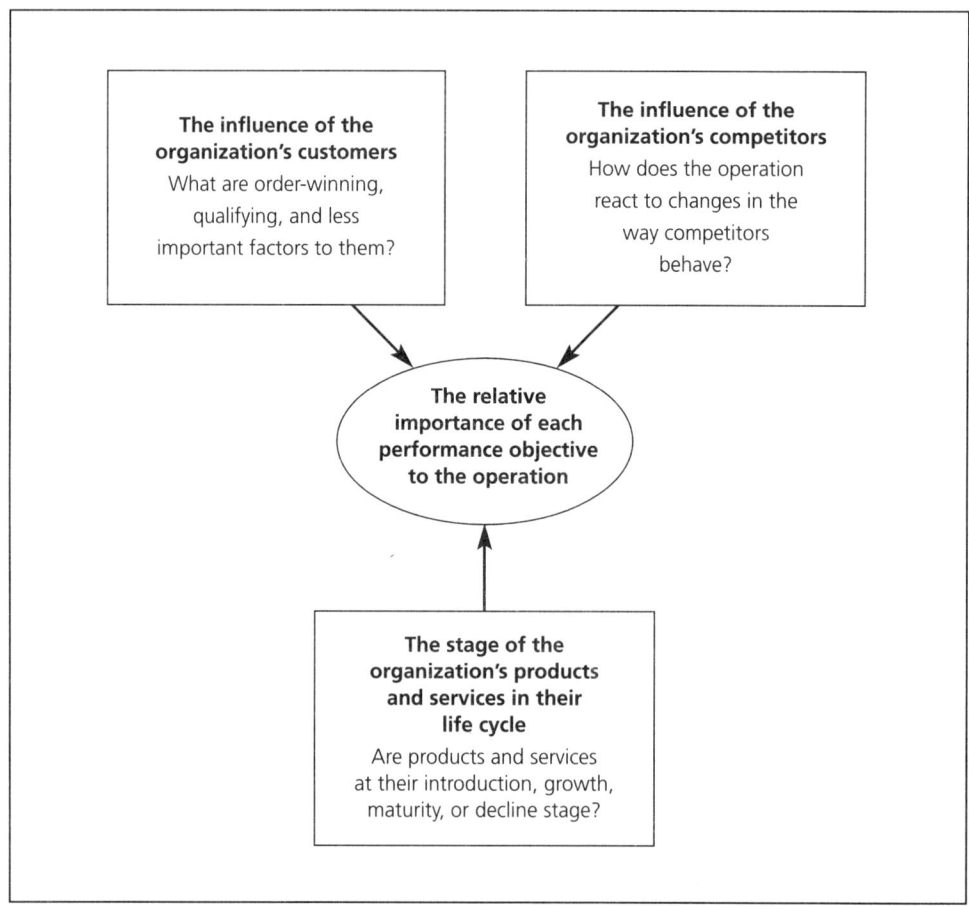

**Figure 3.4
The influences
on the relative
importance of
performance
objectives**

Customer influence on performance objectives

Of all the influences on the priority an organization gives to its performance objectives the most immediate are the organization's customers. Operations seek to satisfy customers through developing their five performance objectives. For example, if customers particularly value low-priced products or services, the operation will put emphasis on its cost performance. If customers insist on error-free products or services, the operation will concentrate on its quality performance. A customer emphasis on fast delivery will make speed important with the operation, while a customer emphasis on reliable delivery will make dependability important. If customers expect very innovative products and services, the operation must provide a high degree of flexibility in order to get its innovations to its customers before its rivals. Similarly, if a wide range of products and services are demanded by customers, the operation will need to be flexible enough to provide the necessary variety without excessive cost.

These factors which define the customer's requirements are called *competitive factors*.[3] How well an organization meets its customers' requirements is determined by how well its operations function excels at the performance objectives which influence the competitive factors. Figure 3.5 shows the relationship between some of the more common competitive factors and the operation's performance objectives. This list of competitive factors is not supposed to be exhaustive. In any particular set of circumstances many other factors could be important, from the location of an hotel to the willingness of company executives to play golf with customers. The important point is that the relative priority of each performance objective is influenced by how the organization translates the needs (and potential needs) of its customers into terms which are meaningful to the operation. Customers are the prime arbiters of what performance objectives an operation should regard as important.

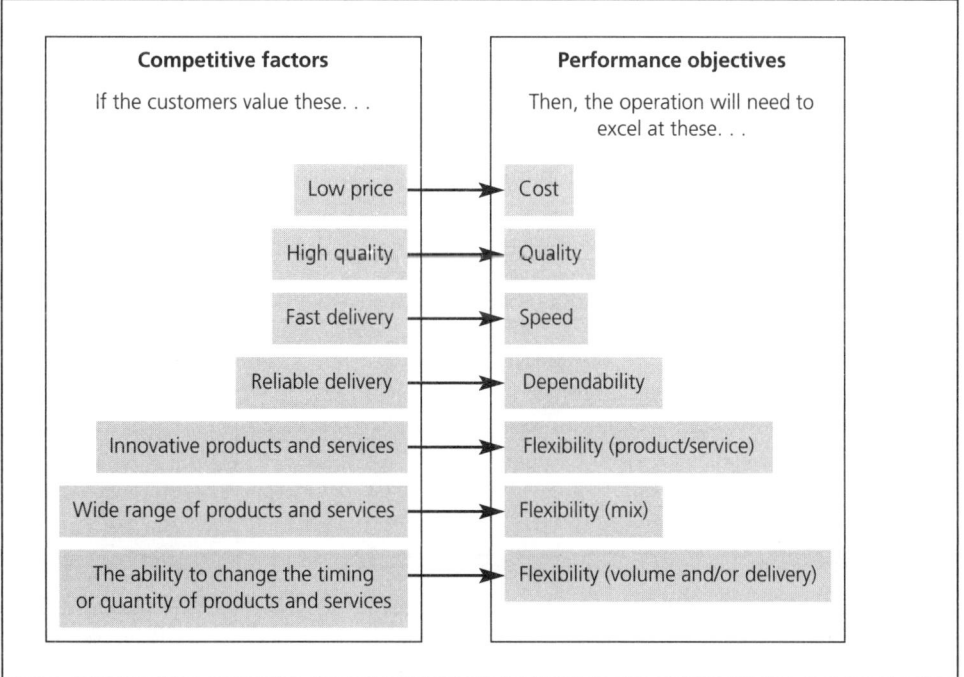

Figure 3.5 Different competitive factors imply different performance objectives

Translating customer needs involves, for example, deciding whether price is more important to customers than delivery time, or the range of products and services, or delivery dependability, or anything else. If customers do regard price as the most important competitive factor, then by how much? Which is their second most important factor? In other words, organizations must decide how customers value the competitive factors. The relative importance of the competitive factors to customers will then influence the relative importance of the operation's performance objectives. A common response to this idea among some managers is to claim that all competitive factors are important to customers. While it may be true that many things are important to customers, however, some must have a greater significance than others.

Order-winning and qualifying objectives

A particularly useful way of determining the relative importance of competitive factors is to distinguish between what Professor Terry Hill of London Business School calls 'order-winning' and 'qualifying' factors.[4]

Order-winning factors are those things which directly and significantly contribute to winning business. They are regarded by customers as key reasons for purchasing the product or service. They are, therefore, the most important aspects of the way a company defines its competitive stance. Raising performance in an order-winning factor will either result in more business or improve the chances of gaining more business.

Qualifying factors may not be the major competitive determinants of success, but are important in another way. They are those aspects of competitiveness where the operation's performance has to be above a particular level just to be considered by the customer. Below this 'qualifying' level of performance the company probably won't even be considered by many customers. Above the 'qualifying' level, it will be considered, but mainly in terms of its performance in the order-winning factors. Any further improvement in qualifying factors above the qualifying level is unlikely to gain much competitive benefit.

To order-winning and qualifying factors can be added *less important factors* which are those factors which are neither order-winning nor qualifying. They do not influence customers in any significant way. They are worth mentioning here only because they may be of importance in other parts of the operation's activities.

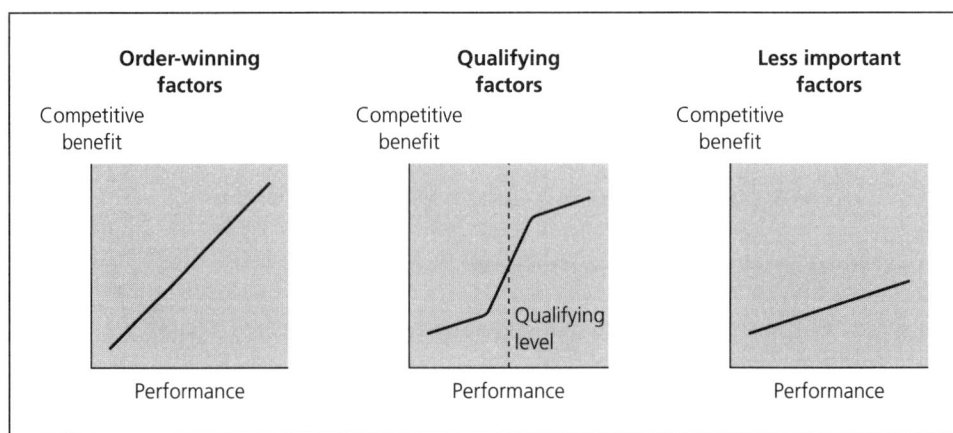

Figure 3.6
Order-winning, qualifying and less important competitive factors

Figure 3.6 shows the difference between order-winning, qualifying and less important factors in terms of their utility or worth to the competitiveness of the organization. The curves illustrate the relative amount of competitiveness (or attractiveness to customers) as the operation's performance at the factor varies. Order-winning factors show a steady and significant increase in their contribution to competitiveness as the operation gets better at providing them. Qualifying objectives only start to make much of a contribution to competitiveness when the operation manages to raise its performance to the qualifying level. Less important objectives have little impact on customers no matter how well the operation performs in them.

Different customers often mean different objectives

If, as is likely, an operation produces goods or services for more than one customer group, it will need to determine the order-winning, qualifying and less important competitive factors for each group. For example, Table 3.1 shows how two product groups manufactured by one instrument manufacturer differ in their manufacturing requirements. The first product group is a range of standard electronic medical equipment which is sold 'off the shelf' direct to hospitals and clinics. The second product group is a wider range of electronic measuring devices which are sold to original equipment manufacturers who incorporate them in their own products. These electronic measuring devices often have to be customized to individual customer requirements.[5]

The analysis of the two product groups shown in Table 3.1 shows that they have very different competitive factors. Therefore different performance objectives are required from the manufacturing operation. Product group 1 needs to concentrate on cost and quality; product group 2 needs the flexibility to cope with a wide product range and with considerable design turbulence. Such very different competitive needs could possibly require two separate operations – one for each product group – each focused on its own objectives and devoted to providing the things which are important in its particular markets.

Table 3.2 shows a similar analysis but this time in the banking industry.[6] Here the distinction is drawn between the customers who are looking for banking services for their private and domestic needs (current accounts, overdraft facilities, savings accounts, mortgage loans, etc.) and those corporate customers who need banking services for their, often large, organizations. These latter services would include such things as letters of credit, cash transfer services and commercial loans.

Underlying this type of analysis is the pre-eminence of customers' needs as a guide to operations objectives. Customers needs are rarely static, however. They will change with customers' own circumstances and they will respond to whatever products and services are available. What is regarded as acceptable performance at one point in time can be rendered inadequate by a competitor raising its own, and possibly the whole industry's, standards.

Competitor influence on performance objectives

Customers are clearly an important influence on the priority of performance objectives within an operation, but they are not the only one. At any point in time, operations are also influenced by what competitors are doing. If, for example, a home delivery pizza operation competes by guaranteeing a fast delivery to customers in its area, it is concentrating on delivery speed because that is what it believes its customers want. However if a rival pizza shop offers equally fast delivery together with an extended range of pizza toppings, the operation could become concerned with extending its own range. Its priorities might shift from speed towards developing the flexibility to offer a sufficiently wide range of products to match its competitor.

Table 3.1 Different product groups require different performance objectives

	Product Group 1	*Product Group 2*
Products	Standard electronic medical equipment	Electronic measuring devices
Customers	Hospitals/clinics	Other medical equipment companies
Product specification	Not high tech, but periodic updates	Most types, high performance
Product range	Narrow – four variants	Very wide, some customization
Design changes	Infrequent	Continual
Delivery	Fast – from stock	On-time delivery important
Quality	Means reliability	Means performance
Demand	Predictable	Unpredictable
Volume per product type	High	Medium to low
Profit margins	Low to medium	Medium to very high

Competitive factors		
Order winners	Price Product reliability	Product specification Product range
Qualifiers	Delivery speed Product performance Quality	On-time delivery Delivery speed Price
Less important	Product range	

Internal performance objectives	Cost Quality	Product/service flexibility Mix flexibility Dependability

Table 3.2 Different banking services require different performance objectives

	Retail banking	*Corporate banking*
Products	Personal financial services such as loans and credit cards	Special services for corporate customers
Customers	Individuals	Businesses
Product range	Medium but standardized, little need for special terms	Very wide range, many needs to be customized
Design changes	Occasional	Continual
Delivery	Fast decisions	Dependable service
Quality	Means error-free transactions	Means close relationships
Volume per service type	Most services are high volume	Most services are low volume
Profit margins	Most are low to medium, some high	Medium to high

Competitive factors		
Order winners	Price Accessibility Speed	Customization Quality of service Reliability
Qualifiers	Quality Range	Speed Price
Less important		Accessibility

Internal performance objectives		
	Cost Speed Quality	Flexibility Quality Dependability

Not that an organization will always match its competitors' moves. The pizza operation could have responded to its competitor's extended product range by shifting its priorities to some totally different competitive factor. For example, instead of extending its own range it could have chosen to shorten its delivery times even more, so as to capitalize on its experience of fast delivery. Alternatively, it could have chosen an entirely new competitive direction such as cutting its prices. Figure 3.7 illustrates how this organization could respond to competitor activity and therefore how its performance objectives might change.

The main point here is that even without any direct change in the preferences of its customers, an organization could have to change the way it competes and therefore change the priority of the performance objectives it expects from its operation. Alternatively, an organization might choose to compete in a different way to its rivals in order to distinguish itself from their competitive stance (*see* the box on Imperial Car Rental).

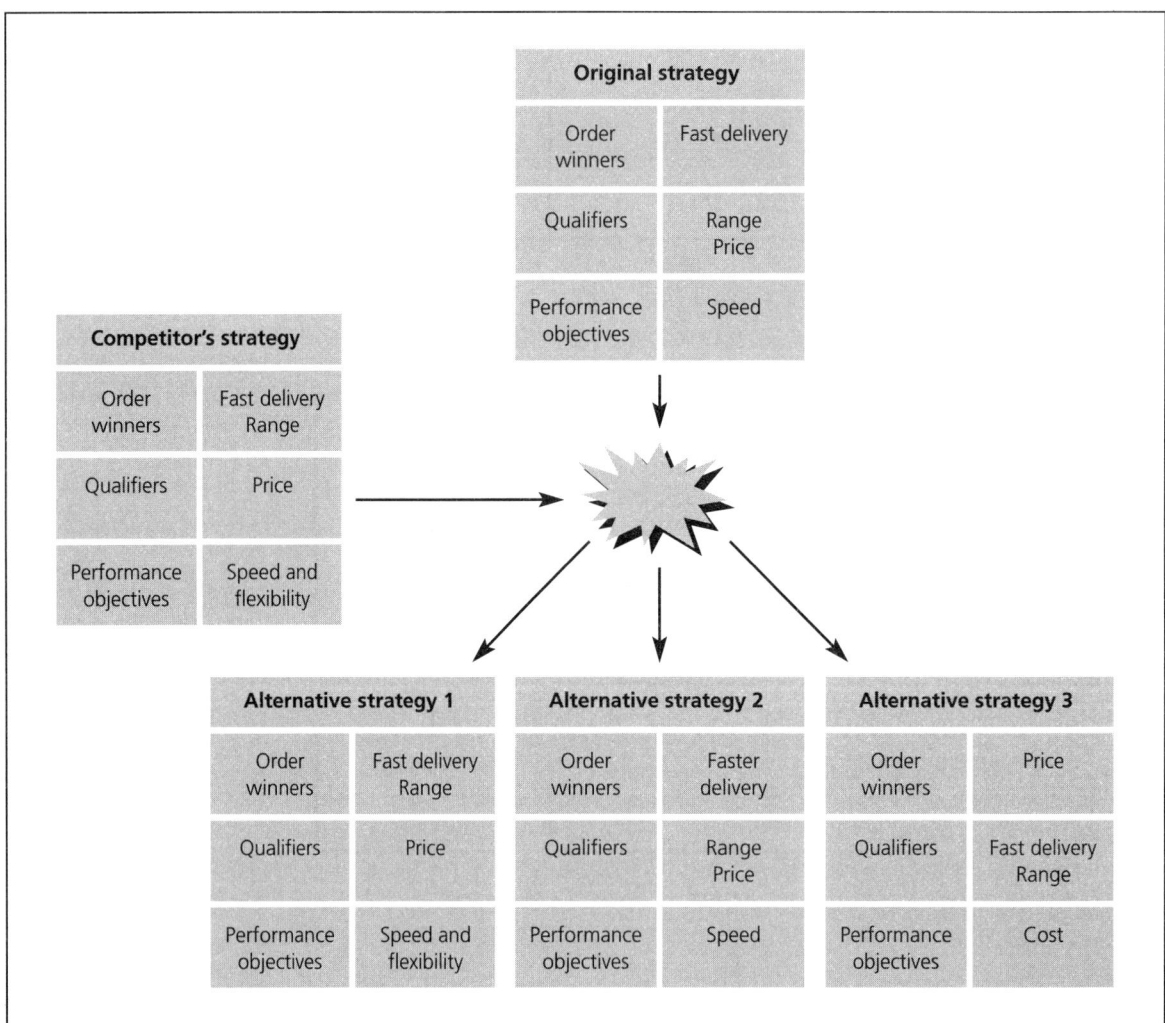

Figure 3.7 Competitor activity can affect the relative importance of performance objectives

IMPERIAL CAR RENTAL – 'YOURS PERSONALLY'[7]

Imperial Car Rental has benefited greatly from the recent political and economic changes experienced in South Africa. These have led to an upswing in the car rental industry. In fact, Imperial has experienced high growth in the number of rentals, and the company remains optimistic about sustaining this growth over the next few years. This growth is illustrated by Imperial's fleet of over 7000 cars, larger than any other car rental company in South Africa, which it intends to increase to 10 000 cars. Imperial has a motto of 'Yours Personally'. This entails a very personal attitude towards clients. The staff at Imperial believe that the best way of achieving results is to give customers exactly what they want and also to treat each and every customer as an individual. Thus Imperial can be seen as a very customer-oriented organization.

Imperial aims to maintain and enhance a world-class service, and it has realized that to achieve this there is the need for a large amount of technological investment. There is a very efficient support infrastructure and a high level of technology present, which enables Imperial staff to deliver the highest levels of service. This in turn has led to improved productivity, higher vehicle utilization and increased long-term profitability. Imperial has approached its processes in a very simple way. Basically, if the process does not add value to the customer, then it must be abolished. If a process adds value to the staff only, it must be automated so that it does not add cost.

Imperial has developed many products to serve the needs of customers. Some of these are developed even if the customer has not realized a need for the service. It was this approach which led to the creation of Imperial's 24-hour Emergency Service. By dialling a 24-hour toll-free number, Imperial customers can have a car delivered to them at any place, at any time. Another product is 'leisure wheels', whereby customers get a special rate for renting a car for longer than five days. Another service introduced by Imperial in 1990 was Speedline. This ensured that cars would be ready for customers as soon as they get off the plane. The customer just walks up to the counter, hands over a Speedline voucher and is immediately given the car keys. This saves the customer the hassles of having to sign forms and show identification.

Imperial's policy is to under-promise and over-deliver rather than disappoint a customer. The aim is to exceed customer expectations. Even though Imperial is the market leader, it has still maintained a small company mentality with great attention to detail. The staff are part of the company culture, and service must be a necessity that they promote of their own accord, by making Imperial service more customer friendly. The company believes in treating staff as it would like staff to treat its customers. During staff training, the emphasis is on developing better interpersonal skills. This ensures that staff are better able to communicate with customers.

As for cars, they must be there for the customer in the right condition. This means that each car must be fully maintained, cleaned and quality checked on a regular basis. Imperial has recently built a huge distribution centre close to Johannesburg International Airport, where the greatest demand is. This new distribution centre currently handles over 20 000 car movements per month. The facility is around 8 acres in area, and can park 3000 cars at one time. The facility also has one of the most sophisticated car cleaning systems in the world. When operating at full capacity, it employs over 200 people.

This is an example of the continuous effort required to differentiate a service company from its rivals at the same time as maintaining cost competitiveness. ■

The product/service life cycle[8] influence on performance objectives

One way of generalizing the behaviour of both customers and competitors is to link it to the life cycle of the products or services which the operation is producing. From the time it is introduced by a company to the point at which customers are no longer interested in purchasing it, a product or service passes through several distinct stages. At each stage the company will experience different challenges both in selling the product or service and in producing it. The exact form of product/service life cycles will vary, but generally are shown as the sales volume passing through four stages – *introduction, growth, maturity* and *decline*. Figure 3.8 shows this general form of the product/service life cycle.

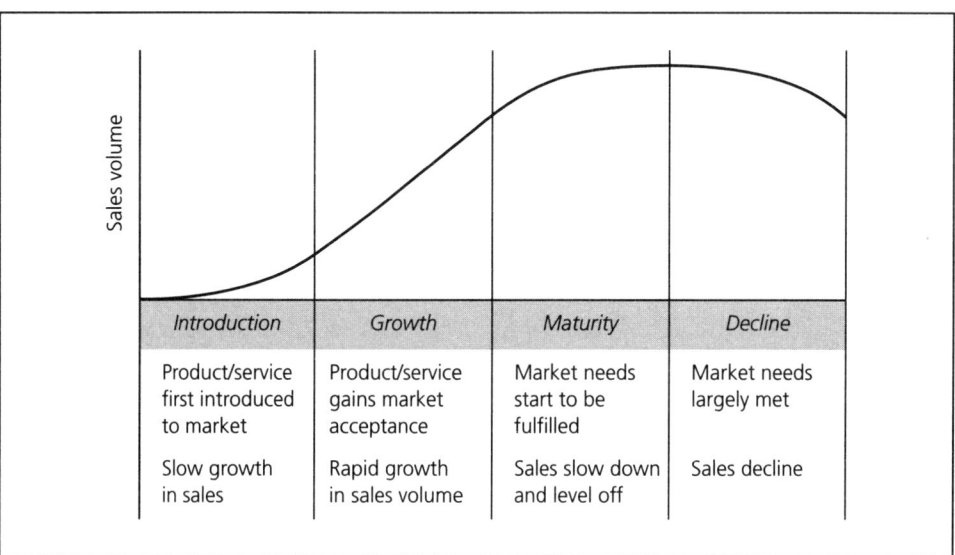

**Figure 3.8
The product/
service life cycle**

Professor Philip Kotler, the well-known marketing authority, derives four implications from the product life cycle.[9]

1 Products (or services) have a limited life.
2 Sales of the product (or service) pass through distinct stages, each posing different challenges to the seller (and producer).
3 Profits rise and fall at different stages of the product life cycle.
4 Products (and services) require different marketing, financial, manufacturing (or operations), purchasing and personnel strategies, in each stage of their life cycle.

It is the last point that is particularly important for all operations managers. It implies that the way in which operations should be managed and the objectives they should set themselves will change as the product or service ages in its market. Figure 3.9 shows how product/service and industry characteristics are likely to vary through different stages of the product/service life cycle.

Introduction stage

When a product or service is first introduced, it is likely to be presented to the market on the basis that it is offering something new in terms of its design or performance. If the product or service is really novel, few if any competitors will be offering the same product or service and, because the number of customers is also relatively low and because their needs are possibly not perfectly understood, the design of the product or service could be subject to frequent change. Given the relatively high uncertainty inherent in these market conditions, the operations management of the company can best contribute to competitiveness by developing the flexibility to cope with changes in the specification of the product or service and possibly also in its output volume. At the same time they will also need to maintain quality levels so as not to undermine the performance of the product/service which is the main basis of competitiveness.

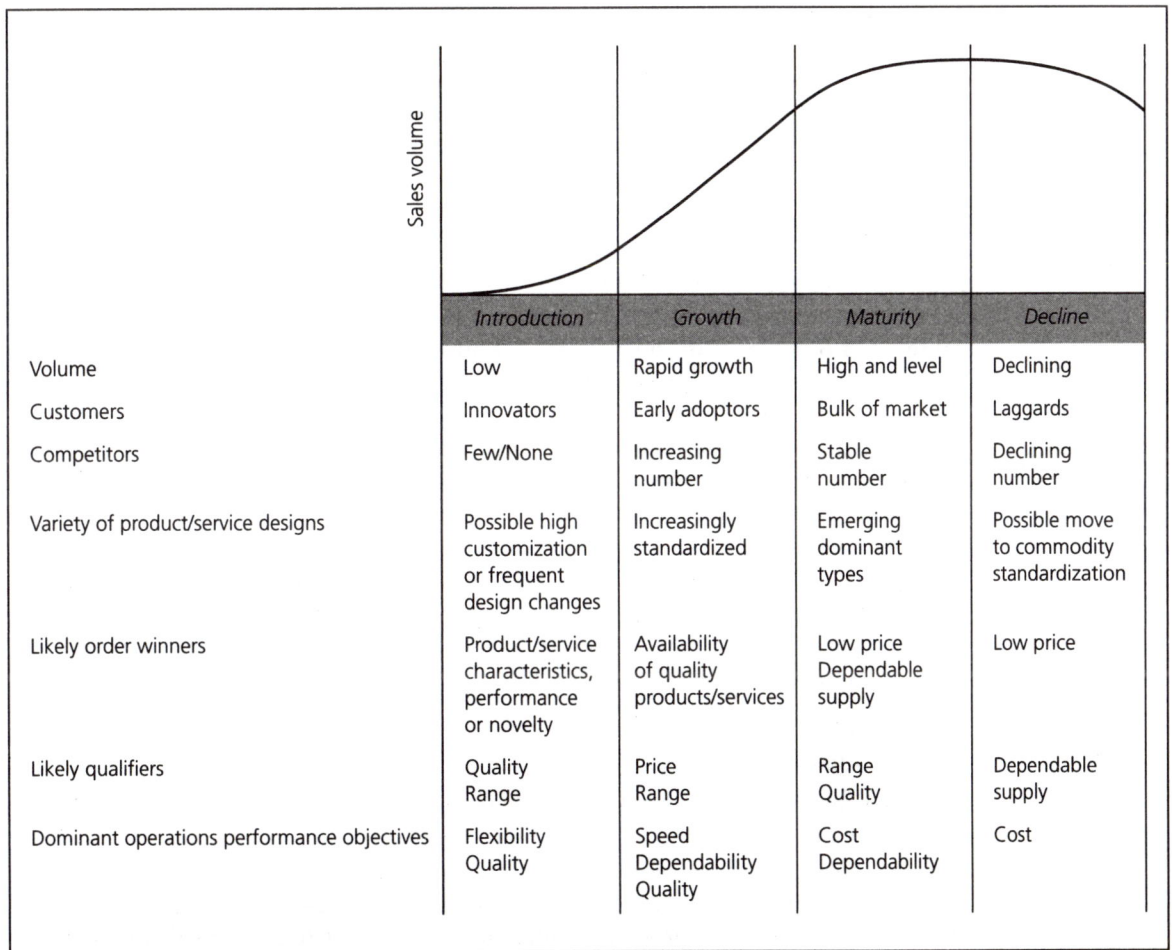

	Introduction	Growth	Maturity	Decline
Volume	Low	Rapid growth	High and level	Declining
Customers	Innovators	Early adoptors	Bulk of market	Laggards
Competitors	Few/None	Increasing number	Stable number	Declining number
Variety of product/service designs	Possible high customization or frequent design changes	Increasingly standardized	Emerging dominant types	Possible move to commodity standardization
Likely order winners	Product/service characteristics, performance or novelty	Availability of quality products/services	Low price Dependable supply	Low price
Likely qualifiers	Quality Range	Price Range	Range Quality	Dependable supply
Dominant operations performance objectives	Flexibility Quality	Speed Dependability Quality	Cost Dependability	Cost

Figure 3.9 The effects of the product/service life cycle on the organization

Example: Synchro Signals and Control (cont.)

For example, suppose Synchro Signals and Control (from the earlier example) as part of its product development effort develops an intelligent traffic signal controller system which can sense traffic build-up along major urban routes by using sensors in the road surface. The system can manipulate the operation of a whole network of traffic signals in the area in order to maximize the flow of vehicles along different routes at different times of day. Although based on existing technology, the system is totally new. Products are on the market which control individual sets of lights according to the immediate traffic build-up, but this is the first product which controls a whole area of several interlinked lights.

When the company first introduces this product to the market, its customers (local road authorities) will need convincing that such a novel product really can achieve the performance claimed for it. The early adoptors of the system will need convincing that it can be made to fit their individual needs. The company will need to customize, or at least adapt, the system according to customer requirements. In fact the company will have as much interest as its customers in seeing how the product can be made to work in practice. In this early stage the company will certainly need to be flexible in how it adapts the design of the system to the requirements of these early adoptors, as well as needing to be flexible in the manufacture of different systems for different customers. Nor can the company afford to let the performance of its products (which is the main basis of its competitive stance) be compromised by poor manufacturing or installation quality.

Growth stage

If products or services survive the rigours of their introduction to the market, they will begin to be more widely adopted. Increasing numbers of customers accept the value of the product or service and volume starts to grow – perhaps rapidly. Competitors, seeing the attractiveness of the product or service, start to develop their own versions, both to keep up with the market and to protect their own position within it. In the growing market different customer groups will probably start to emerge and the design of the product or service could start to standardize. Standardization is actually quite helpful in that it allows the operation to supply the rapidly growing market. Keeping up with demand could prove to be the main preoccupation of organizations which have products or services in this part of the life cycle. Rapid and dependable response to demand will help to keep demand buoyant while ensuring that the company keeps its share of the market as competition starts to increase. The increasing competition also means that the company cannot afford to let its quality levels drop as it ramps up its level of activity.

Example: Synchro Signals (cont.)

Back at Synchro Signals, by the time demand for the intelligent traffic signal controller starts to take off the company will already have smoothed out any technical problems in its design by working closely with its early customers. Different groups within the company's now increasing number of customers start to demand different characteristics from the product. Some customers want relatively small systems to control only two sets of traffic lights; some want systems to control large but simple linear routes; some want large systems which are also complex with different routes

ENVIRONMENTAL INFLUENCES ON OPERATIONS – A LOOK AT DOUGLASDALE DAIRY[10]

Douglasdale Dairy is situated in Bryanston, Johannesburg. It is a dairy that has grown in stature from the delivery of milk in mule carts, to the acquisition of its own workshop to service its 75 trucks. These trucks deliver milk throughout the northern suburbs of Johannesburg.

Although customers and competitors are the main drivers of strategic change, strategies can be changed as a response to other factors. Sometimes there are significant changes in the environment that require due attention. South Africa has been through a time of rapid political change and this has brought many improvements to the situation regarding human rights. The 'New South Africa' has brought a great sense of opportunity but there is a learning curve for this young democracy. Crime has been on the rise and many are trying to find solutions to the problem. However, individual organizations also have to adapt.

Douglasdale Dairy's biggest threat does not lie with its direct competition. The primary problem Douglasdale Dairy has is theft and fraud. This problem, which is quite widespread in the society, has shaped and moulded Douglasdale's operations management function and made inventory and the control thereof a time-consuming and costly affair. The three-day cycle of loading, treating and packaging that milk goes through requires many extra checkpoints to prevent the theft that has been prevalent.

What is frustrating to management is that none of these controls and checks serve to improve the product in any way whatsoever. The processes of pasteurizing and homogenizing the milk, packaging and delivery are so routine that there hardly needs to be any monitoring of these processes. The drivers who deliver the milk know the quantities used so well that they stock the shops to the required amount and tell the shop managers what they need.

The problem of theft is so great that when a new plant was built in Centurion, the plant was designed so as to make inventory checks and control easier and more time efficient. The older plant at Douglasdale was built before these problems arose, so the checks were not built into the process. The importance of this illustration is to demonstrate that inventory control, job design, throughput time and quality of the product (because with the perishability of milk the shorter the throughput time, the higher the quality) can all be influenced by factors outside management's direct control. These types of strategies would be unique to a particular environment or social circumstance. ∎

in the control area taking priority at different times of day. In response to this segmentation of demand the company develops three different products within the original general product class, each targeted at a different set of customers. This also helps the company to reorganize its manufacturing operation and ramp up production levels. During this time, keeping up with demand through fast and dependable delivery and keeping quality levels high, while also expanding capacity, is operations management's main task.

Maturity stage

After a period of rapid growth, products and services are no longer the novel or even the 'up-and-coming' forces in the market. They become the 'norm', the 'standard' – they 'mature'. Demand starts to level off because many customers have already been supplied. Some early competitors might even have left the market and the industry has probably settled down to a few larger companies, perhaps with some smaller companies occupying small niches in the market. The designs of the products or services have probably also stabilized to a few standard types. Competition will almost certainly move to emphasize price or value for money, although individual companies might try to prevent this by attempting to differentiate themselves in some way. This increasingly competitive and price-conscious environment means that operations will be expected to get its costs down, either to maintain profits or to allow price cutting, or both. Because of this shift to price competition, cost and productivity issues together with dependable supply are likely to be the operation's main concerns.

Example: Synchro Signals (cont.)

In the traffic signal market Synchro's product is now well established. It is no longer alone in the market, and some smaller companies have captured the 'small systems' end of the market, but the company's experience as the first into the market has allowed it to maintain its position as a leader in the field. Synchro now only manufactures the larger systems where it has a technical superiority, but its competitors who survived the growth period are also capable of making near-equivalent systems. Opportunities still exist for growth (for example, in export markets) but volumes are levelling off and customers, knowing that they could be supplied from the company's competitors, are demanding price discounts. The relatively high volumes and standardized narrower range of products are helping Synchro's manufacturing operation, not only to keep its costs down but also progressively to improve its cost performance in the future. This is fortunate because a low operations cost base is the most effective way that manufacturing operations can help the company to stay competitive.

Decline stage

When the product or service has been in the market for some time, the need which it was filling will eventually be largely met. Sales will decline. Competitors are likely to start dropping out of the market, the rate of their drop-out governing, to some extent, the speed of decline of whatever business is left for the remaining companies. The products or services serving the market could possibly fragment. To the companies left with the old products or services there might be a residual market but, if capacity in the industry lags demand, the market will continue to be dominated by price competition. Operations objectives will therefore still be dominated by cost.

Example: Synchro Signals (cont.)

Eventually most of the business at Synchro will be 'replacement business', that is replacing or upgrading systems which it, or one of its competitors, supplied previously. Volumes will inevitably decline and probably price competition will become even fiercer. It is hoped that the company will have already developed new replacement products which will now need to be introduced to the market – products which, if successful, will themselves progress through the same stages of their own life cycle.

AIR TRAVEL TAKES OFF[11]

Air travel has grown substantially over the last thirty years. Once the prerogative of the relatively wealthy, it is now an accepted part of leisure and business travel. Although, like any industry, it has had its ups and downs – world politics, wars and economic cycles all affect our tendency to travel – growth in passenger miles travelled is forecast to continue for some years yet. Increasing volume prompted changes in airline operations process technology, such as the introduction of wide bodied aircraft. This reduced airline costs even further and this has been translated into lower prices. In addition, changes in the industry, most especially deregulation of the market in some parts of the world and the privatization of some airlines, have also kept costs down.

The increasing importance of price-based competition is reflected in Fig. 3.10 which shows the growth in volume (and forecast volume) in the industry and the fall in yields. Yields are the revenue which the airlines make for every mile they carry a passenger. At around 22 (US) cents per passenger mile in 1970, they have fallen to around 13 cents per passenger mile and are expected to continue to fall away. Because costs have also been declining, this fall in yield reflects an even more significant fall in real prices.

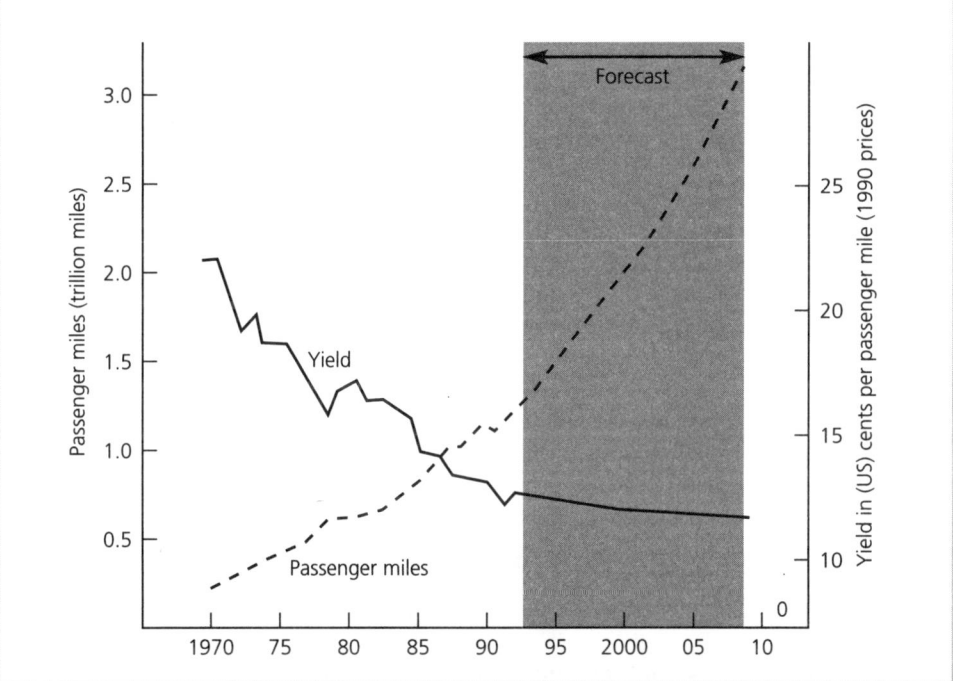

Figure 3.10 Yield (one indicator of price) decreases as air travel (volume) increases

Increasing volumes and increasing price competition have also resulted in a change in the way airlines organize their operations. Especially in the US, airlines have moved to a 'hub-and-spoke' arrangement of routes. This involves aircraft flying between 'hub' airports where passengers connect with flights to other hubs. It is the same principle which is used in mail sorting offices. Although the system is not always convenient for some passengers, the airlines see it as the only way to 'standardize' their routes, and keep costs down. ■

The polar representation of performance objectives

The relative importance of each performance objective is influenced by customers' preferences, competitor actions and the stage of the product or service in its life cycle. A useful way of representing the 'pattern' of performance objectives for a product or service is shown in Fig. 3.11. This is called the *polar representation* because the scales which represent the importance of each performance objective have the same origin. A line describes the importance of each performance objective. The closer the line is to the common origin, the less important is the performance objective. Figure 3.11 illustrates how the two services of corporate and retail banking, described earlier in Table 3.2, might look on a polar representation. The differences between the two services is clearly shown by the diagram.

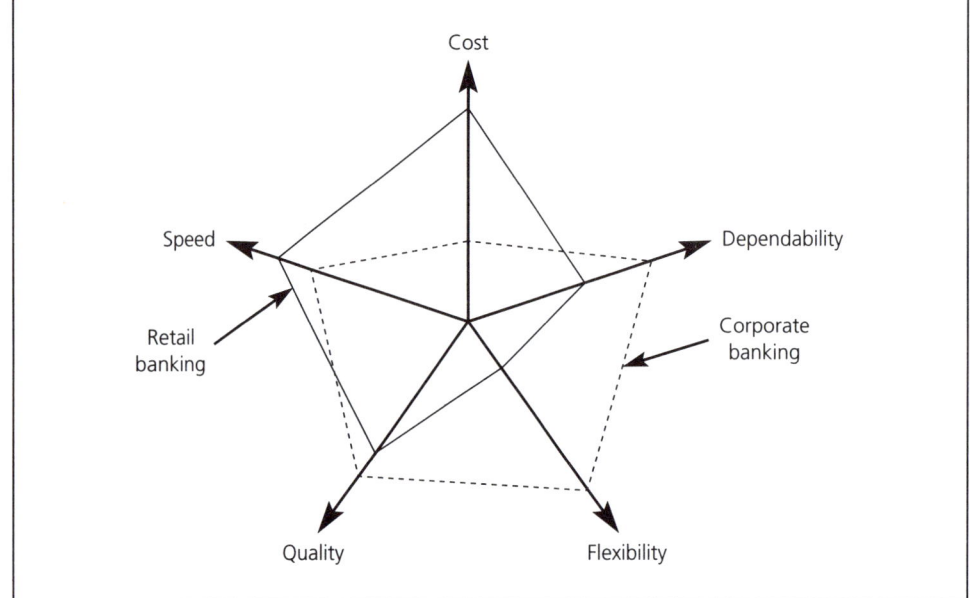

**Figure 3.11
A polar representation of a banking operation's performance objectives for its corporate and retail banking services**

OPERATIONS STRATEGY DECISION AREAS

As well as determining which are the most significant performance objectives, the other requirement of an operations strategy is that it sets the general direction for each of the operation's major decision areas.[12]

Structural and infrastructural strategies

A common distinction in operations strategy is that which is drawn between the strategic decisions which determine an operation's structure, and those which determine its infrastructure. An operation's structural strategy areas are those which we have classed as primarily influencing design activities, while infrastructural strategy areas are those which influence the planning and control and improvement activities. This distinction in operations strategy has been compared to that between 'hardware' and 'software' in a computer system.[13] The hardware of a computer sets limits to what it can do. Some computers, because of their technology and their architecture, are capable of higher performance than others, although those computers with high performance are often more expensive. In a similar way, investing in advanced technology and building more or better facilities can raise the potential capability of any type of operation. Within the capabilities which are imposed by the hardware of a computer, the software governs how effective the computer actually is in practice. The most powerful computer can only work to its full potential if its software is capable of exploiting the potential embedded in its hardware. The same principle applies with operations. The best and most costly facilities and technology will only be effective if the operation also has an appropriate infrastructure which governs the way it will work on a day-to-day basis.

Strategies which influence design

Design activities are those which define the physical form of the operation and its products and services. They shape the 'architecture' of the operation – the parts of the operation of which it is composed, and the way in which they relate to each other. The strategies which influence the design decision area are:

● *New product/service development strategy*. Influences the role and organization of the resources which update and originate product and service designs.
● *Vertical integration strategy*. Influences the direction and extent of the operation's ownership of its supplier and customer network.
● *Facilities strategy*. Influences the size, location and activities of each part of the operation.
● *Technology strategy*. Influences the type of plant, equipment, or other process technologies which are used in the operation.
● *Workforce and organization strategy*. Influences how the operation's human resources are organized, developed and contribute to the management of the operation.

Table 3.3 illustrates each of these strategy areas by showing typical questions which they should be addressing. Note how many of these questions are 'what' questions. Design-related strategies often determine what physical and human resources the operation will ultimately possess.

Strategies which influence planning and control

The planning and control activities define the systems, procedures and policies which determine the way the operation will actually work in practice. They deal with how resource allocation and timing decisions are made and how the operation copes with the circumstances in which it operates. The strategies within the planning and control

Table 3.3 Strategies which influence the design activity

Design strategy areas	Typical questions which the strategy should help to answer
New product/service development strategy	Should the operation be developing its own novel product or service ideas or following the lead of others? How should the operation decide which products or services to develop and how to manage the development process?
Vertical integration strategy	Should the operation expand by acquiring its suppliers or its customers? If so, what suppliers should it acquire? And if so, what customers should it acquire? What balance of capabilities should it develop along its network of operations?
Facilities strategy	What number of geographically separate sites should the operation have? Where should the operations facilities be located? What activities and capacity should be allocated to each plant?
Technology strategy	What broad types of technology should the operation be using? Should it be at the leading edge of technology or wait until the technology is established? What technology should the operation be developing internally and what should it be buying in?
Workforce and organization strategy	What role should the people who staff the operation play in its management? How should responsibility for the activities of the operations function be allocated between different groups in the operation? What skills should be developed in the staff of the operation?

Table 3.4 Strategies which influence the planning and control activity

Planning and control strategy areas	Typical questions which the strategy should help to answer
Capacity adjustment strategy	How should the operation forecast and monitor the demand for its products and services? How should the operation adjust its activity levels in response to demand fluctuations?
Supplier development strategy	How should the operation choose its suppliers? How should it develop its relationship with its suppliers? How should it monitor its suppliers' performance?
Inventory strategy	How should the operation decide how much inventory to have and where it is to be located? How should the operation control the size and composition of its inventories?
Planning and control systems strategy	Using what system should the operation plan its future activities? How should the operation decide the resources to be allocated to its various activities?

decision area can be categorized as follows:

- *Capacity adjustment strategy.* Influences the way the operation adjusts its capacity in response to changes, or forecast changes, in the demand for its products and services.
- *Supplier development strategy.* Influences how the operation chooses, develops and works with its suppliers.
- *Inventory strategy.* Influences how the operation plans, monitors and controls the flow of materials through its processes.
- *Planning and control systems strategy.* Influences the philosophy and practice of how the operation organizes its planning and control activities.

Table 3.4 again illustrates each of these planning and control strategy areas by showing some typical questions for each. Note how many of these planning and control strategy questions start with 'how'. The design policies determine the physical resources of the operations but it is the planning and control strategies (together with improvement strategies) which influence how they are used.

Strategies which influence improvement

Improvement decisions are those which, by measuring and improving the performance of the operation, bring it closer to fulfilling the organization's strategic goals. The strategies within the improvement area are categorized as follows:

- *Improvement process strategy.* Influences the way the operation organizes its improvement activities.
- *Failure prevention and recovery strategy.* Influences the way the operation seeks to prevent failure and disruption to its activities and the way it reacts when operations failure does occur.

Table 3.5 illustrates each of these improvement strategy areas by again showing some typical questions for each. Once more the questions are often 'how'-type questions.

Table 3.5 Strategies which influence the improvement activities

Improvement strategy areas	Typical questions which the strategy should help to answer
Improvement process strategy	How should the operations performance be measured?
	How should the operation decide whether its performance is satisfactory?
	How should the operation ensure that its performance is reflected in its improvement priorities?
	Who should be involved in the improvement process?
	How fast should the operation expect improvement in performance to be?
	How should the improvement process be managed?
Failure prevention and recovery strategy	How should the operation maintain its resources so as to prevent failure?
	How should the operation plan to cope with a failure if one occurs?

Operations strategy influences the activities of operations management

This is not a book about operations strategy as such. Rather it is a book about operations management in all its forms, though it does try to take a 'strategic perspective' of the subject. We will therefore not be treating the strategy areas we have just identified in any detail. It is important, however, to understand the purpose of these strategy areas in operations management. A strategy is there to provide the overall direction for decision making in the operation but it does not (usually) answer the more detailed or specific questions.

For example a strategy which states 'the operation should possess its own unique process technology which will enable us to provide our customers with customized products' does provide clear guidance to operations management as to what kind of processes to develop. It does not say, however, whether the processes should embody totally new technology or developments of existing technology, nor whether the company should develop its own processes or contract out the development, nor does it say exactly how the process should be managed, located, staffed or supported. All these decisions are still to be made. The decisions taken in the design, planning and control, and improvement areas just start off the business of putting strategy into practice. Furthermore, the influence of each strategy is not confined to its own decision area. The strategy which guides the operation towards owning unique process technologies will clearly affect the design decisions in the operation. But it will also have implications for planning and control decisions (for example, by facilitating frequent product changes) and improvement decisions (for example, by encouraging certain maintenance skills). This idea is illustrated in Fig. 3.12.

IMPROVEMENT STRATEGIES AT ROVER[14]

During the 1960s and '70s large parts of the British motor industry came together in a vast conglomerate. The resulting (nationalized) company's structure was messy, its factories relatively inefficient, and its products were failing to compete against Japanese imports to Europe. By 1994 the company, now known as The Rover Group, had been turned round to become a successful and respected company within BMW, the up-market German automobile manufacturer.

Rover's improvement strategy had been responsible for this change. It started with what the company called *Roverization* – meaning that it moved its products to occupy the top of each product class. Between 1989 and 1993 Rover also embarked on what was to become the most intensive new model introduction programme in its history. But, most important, underpinning the development of attractive new products was a revolution in the company's manufacturing operations. This improvement strategy had a number of elements.

These included a *quality strategy* which formed part of the foundations of all the company's activities. It involved training the entire workforce of more than 30 000 people in the philosophies and tools of total quality management (discussed in Chapter 20). Not only did the strategy emphasize the use of improvement tools (described in Chapter 18), it helped to create an appropriate environment for a 'step change' in quality and working practices within the company. Fundamental to its quality strategy was a concept of how the company wanted its customers to react. It summarized this in the phrase *extraordinary customer satisfaction* – a phrase which Rover's Chief Executive described as the three most important words in the company.

Competitor benchmarking (discussed in Chapter 18) was also an important element in Rover's improvement strategy – what some in the company called 'knowing your enemy'. In looking outside the company it was influenced by the experiences of North American manufacturers in their own home market. For every Japanese-owned factory which had opened, an American manufacturer's plant had closed. By studying the performance and methods of Japanese motor manufacturers, Rover knew just how good it had to be in order to compete. Its long association with Honda, recognized as a world-class company, was a considerable help in understanding how Japanese 'lean' operations practices could be adapted to a Western environment (these are discussed fully in Chapter 15).

Perhaps though, the most significant element of Rover's improvement strategy was the revolution in how it approached its *human resources*. A reorientation towards seeing the workforce (or associates as Rover calls them) as the most important resource in the company and the driver of continuous improvement was supported by a belief that people needed to work not just harder but smarter as well. The *Rover Tomorrow* programme involved briefing all employees about the company's plans for the future. People policies also included:

- total flexibility in working practices and between jobs;
- single status for all associates no matter what their job within the company.

The reason why improvement strategies were so central to Rover was very simple – the company might not have survived without them. ■

Operations strategy influences performance objectives

To some extent all the decisions made in all strategy areas will exert some influence on all the performance objectives of the operation. Some strategies however are particularly influential on certain objectives. Table 3.6 highlights those objectives which will be particularly influenced by each strategy (though remember that the important links between strategies and objectives will to some extent depend on the type of operation and the circumstances in which it finds itself).

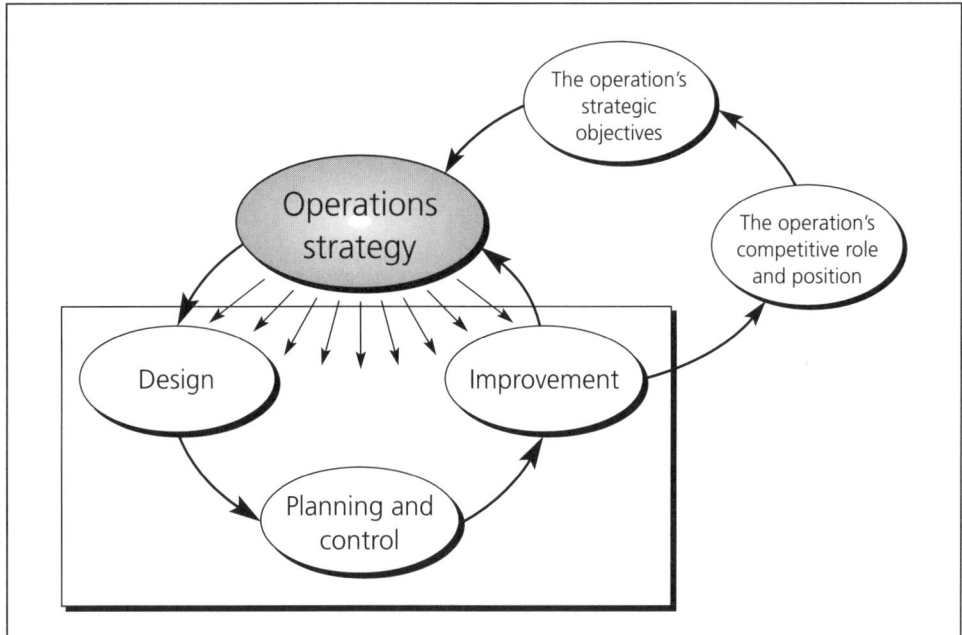

**Figure 3.12
Each aspect of
operations strategy
influences all
operations
activities**

Table 3.6 Strategies with a particularly significant effect on particular performance objectives

	Quality	Speed	Dependability	Flexibility	Cost
New product/service development strategy	✔				✔
Vertical integration strategy		✔	✔		✔
Facilities strategy		✔	✔	✔	✔
Technology strategy	✔			✔	✔
Workforce and organization strategy	✔			✔	✔
Capacity adjustment strategy		✔		✔	✔
Supplier development strategy	✔		✔		✔
Inventory strategy		✔	✔		✔
Planning and control systems strategy		✔	✔		✔
Improvement process strategy	✔	✔	✔	✔	✔
Failure prevention and recovery strategy	✔		✔		✔

Mary Reeks, Aerotech

Mary Reeks is the Managing Director of Aerotech South Africa, a local South African manufacturer that has recently landed a R22 million contract to supply right-hand drive components to BMW, Germany, for a new model that begins European production in April 1998.

'Some 350 000 components a year will be manufactured and exported over a nine-year period', says Mary. 'The company is about to clinch another export deal with a German vehicle manufacturer and is at present also exporting air-conditioning assemblies to BMW Germany.'

Aerotech South Africa has a licenced technology and distribution agreement with the US multinational Aeroquip, and forms part of that company's global sourcing programme.

'One of our key focus areas for the next two years is to pursue and develop, together with local raw material and component manufacturers, the opportunity to export these components worldwide, specifically aluminium tubes and componentry, as well as steel and rubber components.

'The Automotive Division, which was established in 1986 and already holds about 27% of the local market, claims to be one of the fastest-growing manufacturers and suppliers of air-conditioning and power-steering assemblies to the local original equipment manufacture (OEM) sector.

'In November 1995 the company moved to new premises in Spartan, which enabled a change in the manufacturing process from job lots to cell-type flow lines. State-of-the-art machinery includes computer numerically-controlled tube forming and manipulation and bending machines that operate up to a 20mm diameter. Other procedures include tube rolling, assembly and hose crimping and pressure testing, while extensive quality testing equipment is used throughout the process.

'Product quality is of vital importance in a global market, and thus the company's accreditation includes ISO 9002 awarded in 1992, a VDA 6AB rating awarded in 1994 and Q101 in 1996', explains Mary.

'The philosophy of continuous improvement is synonymous with Aerotech, and higher quality standards form part of the company's objectives, which include a QS9000 and Ford Q1 rating next year. Each manufacturing or assembly cell has a team leader reporting to the manufacturing director, who in turn is directly responsible to the MD. This four-tier structure minimizes middle management and empowers the factory floor with responsibility, self-motivation and a strong role in decision making. The aim is to devolve responsibility to the point where each cell becomes a business unit responsible for its own budgeting and logistics.

'Teams are responsible for reporting their own productivity and have weekly targets to comply with, while monthly quality reports are being compiled to monitor progress. Statistical process control highlights key production characteristics and daily production meetings ensure that problems leading to material being rejected are promptly ironed out.

'In 1996 3% of the payroll was allocated for training, which increased to 4% in 1997, while a share trust fund with 17% employee participation was established. The company runs two shifts with a staff complement of 15 and 60 employees on the shopfloor. Material and service subsupplier sourcing is based on cost, delivery and quality, with a formal quality agreement signed by a subsupplier.'

Mary comments that the company is committed to adding value to raw materials by exporting aluminium tubes and components for global OEM requirements and, through its successful empowerment strategies, is developing local labour into a crucial resource.

Mary rose from the position of Administration Manager in the accounting department to become the leader of a management buyout in 1995. Her philosophies on management are based on people development, high expectations for performance and straight-talking. To have achieved such export success is evidence of a natural ability to implement sound operating strategies. Mary leads a small but highly competent and motivated management team. The team is now planning to move to larger premises, in order to meet the future predicted growth of the company. ■

SUMMARY

■ The strategy of any organization or part of an organization is the total pattern of decisions and actions which position the organization in its environment. Within this definition of strategy we can identify different levels which make up the strategy hierarchy.

■ Corporate strategy sets the objectives for its different businesses. Business strategy sets the objectives for its various functions or parts. Functional strategy sets the objectives for the functions' contribution to the business strategy.

■ In the operations function there may also be several units or micro operations. Each of these could have a micro operations strategy which identifies how the micro operation is going to contribute to the operations strategy (macro) of the business.

■ At the level of the (macro) operations strategy, decisions can be divided into those which define the content of the strategy and those which indicate the process of how it is to be formulated.

■ The content of an operations strategy deals with the relative importance of performance objectives to the operation. This is influenced by the organization's specific customer groups, the activities of the organization's competitors, and the stage of its products and services in their life cycle.

■ The content of an operations strategy is also concerned with giving general guidance to the decision-making activities in the operation. It does this by formulating a number of strategies dealing with design, planning and control and improvement.

Birmingham Amusement Machines[15]

Birmingham Amusement Machines was a company which manufactured gaming and video-amusement machines. The company sold its products to an operating company which distributed them to bars, country clubs, casinos and pubs. Both companies were started by Bob Greenwood, an engineer who was fascinated by the design of the early mechanical gaming machines. Largely through innovative design, the company had grown to be one of the four largest in the market with 30 per cent market share.

Four years ago Bob Greenwood sold out to a large industrial group, but he was retained as Chief Executive of the manufacturing company. The new owners were happy to let Bob indulge his talent for design, especially since the company had entered the video-amusement market. Video-amusement machines did not pay out cash prizes like gaming machines, but allowed the player time on the machine to play a game, usually with a theme drawn from the 'Wild West' or 'Interplanetary Space Warfare'. The company manufactured all parts for the gaming machines and assembled them in its factory. However, many of the components for the video-amusement machines were imported and only assembled into the outer casings in the factories.

Recently, the owners became dissatisfied with the company's performance. The market for its goods was still growing, but the company's profitability had failed to match expectations. The owners decided to install a new chief executive and to fire Bob, who was predictably upset at being replaced:

'It's always been the combination of high technology and fashion that's fascinated me about this industry. You have to be first in the field with every advance in technology, especially now video amusements are a big part of our business, but you also have to keep an eye out for the fashionable trends. On average, we've brought out a new product every four months, for the last five years. You can't run a company like this by putting an accountant as its boss – you need an innovator.'

In fact the owners had installed an accountant to be the head of the company. On his first day, the new boss made a tour of the plant, after which he called the manufacturing manager into his office and began to criticize what he had seen of the production set-up:

'It seems to me that the whole plant is totally disorganized. There's part-finished goods everywhere, and no one seems to know exactly what they're going to do next. I found some parts of the plant clearly overworked, and other parts with nothing to do. I am sure, with a bit of tighter management, you could get your unit production costs down dramatically.'

The production manager was defensive.

'Of course I'd like to get my unit costs down, and of course I could rearrange the whole plant to make it more efficient. The trouble is, the design department are getting me to change products every few months, so I never really have time to let the production system settle down. At the same time, marketing are wanting me to give them instant delivery on new products, almost as soon as I have the drawings from the design office, and they insist on quality being of the highest standard at all times.'

The new boss called in the marketing manager to explain these demands placed on the production system. The marketing manager was equally forthright.

'I couldn't care less about his unit costs. It's not low cost which sells these machines. Look at it this way: in a heavy gambling club one of these machines can pay for itself in less than three months. Under those circumstances, nobody in this industry is competing on price. It's not totally unimportant, but plus or minus 10 per cent isn't going to make much difference to our sales. What sells machines is a new product on the books every few months or so and almost instant delivery – many of the club owners buy on impulse – and an unimpeachable reputation for the highest product reliability.'

After listening to the testimony of both his managers, the new boss was a lot less certain on how he should proceed to reshape the business. ■

Questions

1 What do you think were Bob Greenwood's objectives when he ran the company?

2 List what you think might now be the priority objectives of:

(a) the production manager
(b) the marketing manager
(c) the new boss.

DISCUSSION QUESTIONS

1 Explain the difference between corporate strategy, business strategy and functional strategy.

2 Describe what you think is the business strategy for your university (you might like to have this confirmed). Describe what you think might be the strategies of some of the micro operations, such as library, catering, student union and grounds maintenance. You might like to compare your views with those of the managers of some of these operations.

3 Illustrate how the strategy hierarchy would operate in a 'not-for-profit' organization such as a charity which provides hostel accommodation and other welfare services to vagrants.

4 Explain how an individual branch of a large supermarket chain can:
(a) contribute directly to the strategic aims of the whole company;
(b) help other parts of the company to contribute.

5 Take the example of a prison and describe the specific needs of the different groups of customers (prisoners, society and the victims). For each customer, identify what you think will be the key operations performance objectives and discuss any conflicts between them.

6 Identify what you think might be the order-winning, qualifying and less important objectives for a music store selling records, tapes and compact discs. Discuss how the organization might go about changing its operation by focusing on the less important objectives to give itself an advantage in the market place.

7 Assuming that video cassette recorders (VCRs) are in the maturity stage of their life cycle, how might the main performance objectives of a VCR manufacturer have changed over the life of the product type so far.

8 For organizations providing the following products or services, what do you think would be their order-winning factors and qualifying factors?
Estate agency services
School textbooks
Basic aluminium extrusions
Accountancy services
Industrial washing machines.

9 'When a company is introducing a totally novel product or service, it is competing exclusively on the technical specification of the product or service. The operations function therefore has no significant role to play.' Discuss.

10 Many Japanese manufacturers have based their success on products which were regarded as well into their 'mature' stage, such as automobiles and televisions. How did they manage to revitalize the markets for these products and what part did operations management play in this?

11 'A Rolls Royce motor car will always cost more than a Skoda.' Discuss this statement with reference to the trade-off theory of operations objectives.

12 Draw up a list of design, planning and control, and improvement strategies for the following operations:
a TV rental company
a ship repair facility
Kruger National Park
a national train network.

NOTES ON CHAPTER

1   There are many good books on strategy. For example, *see* Johnson, G. and Scholes, K. (1992) *Exploring Business Strategy* (3rd edn), Prentice Hall.
2   For a thorough review of the literature relating to operations strategy, *see* Anderson, J.C., Cleveland, G. and Schroeder, R. (1989) 'Operations Strategy – a Literature Review', *Journal of Operations Management*, Vol 8, No 2. There are also many definitions of operations (or more usually, manufacturing) strategy: for example, Hayes and Wheelwright (*see* Note 14) define it as

'. . . *a sequence of decisions that, over time, enables a business to achieve a desired manufacturing structure, infrastructure and set of specific capabilities'.*

An interesting slant on the topic is given by Professor Abby Ghobadian who defines it as

'. . . *the manner and extent by which the management put the company's manufacturing resources at risk in order to support and achieve its chosen overall objective'.*

3 Also called critical success factors by some authors.

4 Hill, T. (1993) *Manufacturing Strategy* (2nd edn), Macmillan.

5 Adapted from an example in Slack, N. (1991) *The Manufacturing Advantage*, Mercury Business Books.

6 Adapted from Lim, B.K. (1993) 'Gaining Competitive Advantage from Operations in a Bank', Internal document, University of Warwick.

7 Source: By kind permission of Imperial Car Rental.

8 There are many treatments of the product life cycle. *See,* for example, Doyle, P. (1976) 'The Realities of the Product Life Cycle', *Quarterly Review of Marketing*, Summer.

9 Kotler, P. (1991) *Marketing Management*, Prentice Hall International.

10 Source: By kind permission of Douglasdale Dairy.

11 Source: 'Wrong altitude', *The Economist*, 6 Mar 1993.

12 Skinner, W. (1985) *Manufacturing: The Formidable Competitive Weapon*, John Wiley.

13 Hayes, R.H. and Wheelwright, S.C. (1984) *Restoring our Competitive Edge*, John Wiley.

14 Source: Towers, J. (1994) 'Driving ahead', *Manufacturing Engineer*, Aug.

15 Adapted from Cooke, S. and Slack, N. (1991) *Making Management Decisions* (2nd edn), Prentice Hall.

SELECTED FURTHER READINGS

Berry, W.L. and Hill, T. (1992) 'Linking Systems to Strategy', *International Journal of Operations and Production Management*, Vol 12, No 10.

Croom-Morgan, S. (1994) 'Managing External Resources: Strategic Positioning and Organizational Capability' *in* Platts, K.W., Gregory, M.J. and Neely, A.D. (eds) *Operations Strategy and Performance*, European Operations Management Association, Cambridge University.

Davidow, W.H. and Uttal, B. (1989) 'Service Companies: Focus or Falter', *Harvard Business Review*, Vol 67, No 4.

Hayes, R.H. and Wheelwright, S.C. (1984) *Restoring our Competitive Edge*, John Wiley, Chap 2.

Hayes, R.H., Wheelwright, S.C. and Clarke, K.B. (1988) *Dynamic Manufacturing*, Free Press, Chaps 1 and 2.

Hill, T. (1993) *Manufacturing Strategy* (2nd edn), Macmillan, Chaps 2 and 3.

Kinnie, N.J., Staughton, R.V.W. and Davies, E.H. (1992) 'Changing Manufacturing Strategy: Some Approaches and Experiences', *International Journal of Operations and Production Management*, Vol 12, No 7/8.

Lindberg, P. (1990) 'Strategic Manufacturing Management: A Proactive Approach', *International Journal of Operations and Production Management*, Vol 10, No 2.

Lindberg, P. and Trygg, L. (1991) 'Manufacturing Strategy in the Value System', *International Journal of Operations and Production Management*, Vol 11, No 3.

New, C. (1992) 'World Class Manufacturing Versus Strategic Trade-offs', *International Journal of Operations and Production Management*, Vol 12, No 4.

Nicholson, T.A.J. (1991) 'Strategy and the Shop Floor: A One-Way Initiative?', *International Journal of Operations and Production Management*, Vol 11, No 3.

Roth, A.V. (1994) 'Global Manufacturing Strategies' *in* Platts, K.W., Gregory, M.J. and Neely, A.D. (eds) *Operations Strategy and Performance*, European Operations Management Association, Cambridge University.

Samson, D. (1991) *Manufacturing and Operations Strategy*, Prentice Hall, Chap 1.

Slack, N. (1991) *The Manufacturing Advantage*, Mercury Business Books.

Stobaugh, R. and Telesio, P. (1983) 'Match Manufacturing Policies and Products Strategies', *Harvard Business Review*, Vol 61, No 2.

Sweeney, M.T. (1991) 'Towards a Unified Theory of Strategic Manufacturing Management', *International Journal of Operations and Production Management*, Vol 11, No 8.

Voss, C.A. (1992) *Manufacturing Strategy*, Chapman and Hall, Part 4.

Woodcock, D.J. (1989) 'Measuring Strategic Control and Improvement in Manufacturing', *International Journal of Operations and Production Management*, Vol 9, No 5.

PART TWO

DESIGN

This part of the book looks at the design of products and services as well as the design of the processes which produce them. At the most strategic level process design means designing the network of operations which get products and services to the customer. At a more operational level process design means the physical arrangement of the operation's facilities, technology and people.

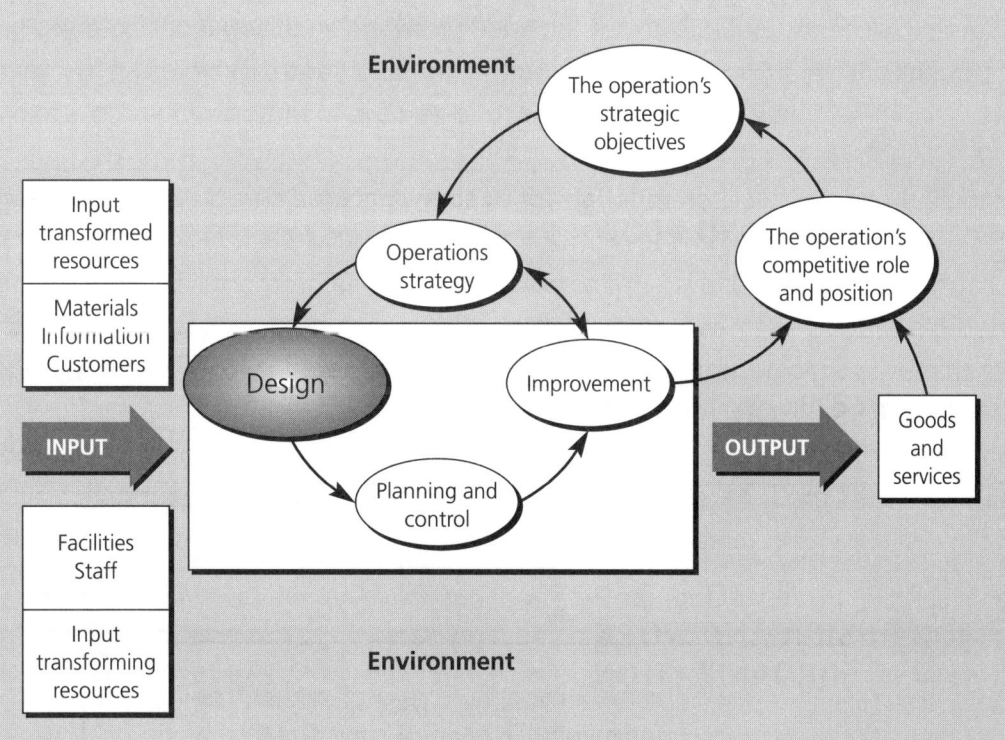

Chapter 4
DESIGN IN OPERATIONS MANAGEMENT

- *How is the design activity organized?*
- *How do we choose between alternative designs?*
- *How do volume and variety affect the design activity?*

Chapter 5
THE DESIGN OF PRODUCTS AND SERVICES

- *What decisions need to be made at each stage in the design of products and services?*
- *How can product or service design and process design be brought together to speed up time-to-market?*

Chapter 6
DESIGN OF THE OPERATIONS NETWORK

- *Should an organization take a total supply network perspective?*
- *How much of a network should an operation own?*
- *Where should an operation be located?*
- *How much capacity should an operation plan to have?*

Chapter 7
LAYOUT AND FLOW

- *What type of layout should an operation choose?*
- *How should the details of a layout be designed?*

Chapter 8
PROCESS TECHNOLOGY

- *What types of technology are available?*
- *How does volume and variety influence the choice of process technology?*

Chapter 9
JOB DESIGN AND WORK ORGANIZATION

- *What should operations managers take into account when they design jobs?*
- *Which approach to job design should operations managers take?*

DESIGN IN OPERATIONS MANAGEMENT

INTRODUCTION

All operations managers are designers since many of their day-to-day decisions shape the design of the *processes* they manage, and in so doing they influence the products and services which they produce. The purchase of every machine or piece of equipment which is bought is a design decision because it affects the physical shape and nature of the operation. Similarly, every time a machine or piece of equipment is moved or a method improved, or a member of staff's responsibility changed, the

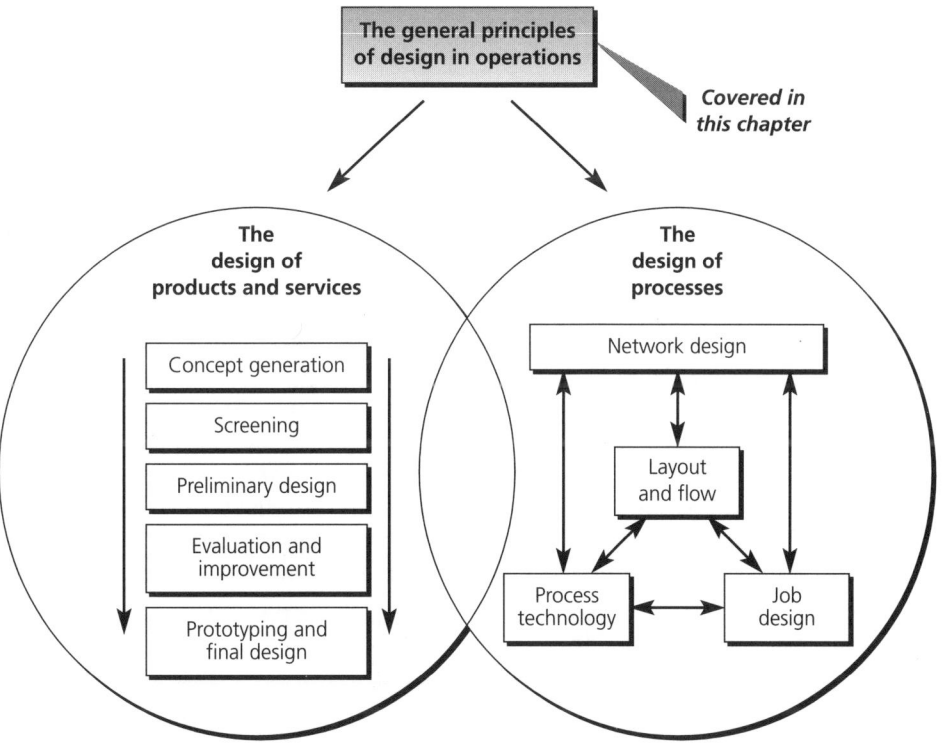

Figure 4.1 The design activities in operations management covered in this chapter

105

design of the operation is changed. Operations managers also have an important influence on the 'technical' design of the *products and services* they produce, by providing much of the information necessary for their design, as well as providing the systems which produce them. This chapter serves as an introduction to Part Two of this book, which treats all the main issues concerned with the design activity in operations management. This includes *both* the design of products and services and the design of the processes which create them. Figure 4.1 shows the issues covered in Part Two and how they relate to each other.

OBJECTIVES

This chapter will examine:

- the nature and purpose of the design activity in operations;
- the way in which the purpose of the design activity must always be to satisfy customers;
- the management of the design activity;
- the way in which the range of design options narrows during the design activity;
- how design can be considered to be a decision-making process;
- the effects of volume and variety on design.

WHAT IS DESIGN?

Our view of the meaning of design is neatly captured by this quotation:

'In my definition, design is the conceptual process by which some functional requirement of people, individually or en masse, is satisfied through the use of a product or of a system which derives from the physical translation of the concept. As examples of individual products which satisfy a public or a market need there is the motor car, the television set and the radio, the fridge and the dishwasher, shoes and socks and baby nappies but also the painting, the sculpture, the musical score and the other manifold realized expressionism of the artist, etc.; and as to systems there is the telephone and the railway, the motorway and the supermarket, the orchestra, the provision of utilities (gas, water and electricity), and so on.'

(Sir Monty Finneston: Address to the Department of Education and Science Conference, Loughborough University, 1987.)[1]

The important points which can be extracted from this description of design are as follows.

● The purpose of the design activity is to *satisfy the needs of customers.*
● The design activity applies both to *products* (or *services*) and *systems* (what we would call *processes*).
● The design activity is itself a *transformation process.*
● Design starts with a *concept* and ends in the translation of that concept into a *specification* of something which can be created.

Each of these aspects of design is worth considering further.

Design means satisfying the needs of customers

The design activity in operations has one over-riding objective: to provide the type of products, services and processes which will satisfy the operation's customers (*see* box on the design of the Boeing 777, p. 109). Product designers will try to achieve aesthetically pleasing designs which meet or exceed customers' expectations. They will also try to design a product which performs well and is reliable during its lifetime. Further, they should design the product so that it can be manufactured easily and quickly, so that errors during manufacture are unlikely and manufacturing costs are minimized. Similarly, service designers try to put together a service which customers will see as at least meeting their expectations. Yet at the same time the service must be within the capabilities of the operation and be delivered at reasonable cost.

Of more direct concern to operations managers is the design of the transformation processes which they manage, though the same argument still holds. The way in which the process which creates the product or service is designed will have a significant impact on the ability of the operation to meet its customers' needs. A process which has been located in the wrong place, or with insufficient capacity, or arranged in a jumbled and confused layout, or given inappropriate technology, or staffed with unskilled people, cannot satisfy customers because it cannot perform efficiently or effectively. Design then, both of products and services, and of processes, will affect all of the operation's performance objectives which we introduced in Chapter 2. Table 4.1 illustrates how each performance objective of an operation is affected by the design of products and services and the design of the process which creates them.

Table 4.1 The impact of product/service and process design on performance objectives

Performance objective	Influence of good product/service design	Influence of good process design
Quality	Can eliminate potential fail points and 'error-prone' aspects of the product or service	Can provide the appropriate resources which are capable of producing the product or service to its design specifications
Speed	Can specify products which can be made quickly (for example, using modular design principles) or services which avoid unnecessary delays	Can move materials, information or customers through each stage of the process without delays
Dependability	Can help to make each stage of the process predictable by requiring standardized, predictable processes	Can provide technology and staff who are themselves dependable
Flexibility	Can allow for variations which allow a range of products or services to be offered to customers	Can provide resources which can be changed quickly so as to create a range of products or services
Cost	Can reduce the costs of each component part which goes into the product or service and also can reduce the cost of putting them together	Can ensure high utilization of resources and therefore efficient and low-cost processes

Products, services and processes are all designed

In our terms the design activity extends also to the processes which create products and services.

Product/service design and process design are interrelated

Often we will treat the design of products and services on the one hand, and the design of the processes which make them on the other, as though they were separate activities. Yet in practice they are (or should be) clearly interrelated. It would be foolish to commit an organization to the detailed design of any product or service without some consideration of how it is to be produced. Small changes in the design of products and services can have profound and expensive implications for the way the operation eventually has to produce them. Similarly the design of a process can constrain the freedom of product and service designers to operate as they would wish (*see* Fig. 4.2).

BOEING BRINGS ITS CUSTOMERS ON BOARD[2]

Arguably the most innovative new passenger aircraft to enter service over the last few years was the Boeing 777. The 777 design project was launched in October 1990, with the objective of creating a new twin-engined aircraft, in the 300-plus seats category, to compete with established models from McDonnell and Airbus. The existence of established competitor products is important. When Boeing developed the 747 'Jumbo' jet aircraft, it had had no direct competitors. The company's customers either wanted the product or they didn't. Not so for the 777: Boeing knew that it must consider its customers' requirements. The company had to take a new course – to understand its customers' needs and then to transform these into an aircraft that could best meet those needs. Furthermore, Boeing needed to understand as well as the airlines how the aircraft would operate in practice.

Boeing has always maintained close involvement with its customers, but this project called for a new depth of listening and understanding. Initially, eight large potential customers (including British Airways, Japan Airlines and Qantas) were invited to participate in creating the design concepts: effectively to start with a blank sheet of paper, and to finish with a fully specified configuration. It soon became clear that the customers did have important requirements, the most vital of which was that the aircraft should be around 25 per cent wider than the 767. In fact Boeing had originally hoped to lengthen the 767 fuselage to give the extra capacity, so avoiding some of the costs involved in a completely new fuselage. The customers also wanted much more flexibility in the configuration of the passenger space. Conventionally cabin space had been divided up into sections, separated by fixed galleys and toilets at predetermined positions. This arrangement had effectively fixed the ratio of passenger capacities of each class. However, the airlines all indicated that they wanted to be able to configure the cabin to their daily requirements. If they could do this, they would never have to turn away valuable business class revenue. Finally, the airlines insisted that the new design should be free of the usual level of minor, but irritating, faults which had bugged the early operations of some of the other aircraft.

Boeing did meet its customers' requirements and even improved upon them in some ways. (For example, the lavatories and galleys can be physically moved to change the ratio of first-, business- and economy-class seats.) They achieved this by using design/build teams (a concept similar to the interactive design principle described in Chapter 5), and by a particularly powerful computer-aided design (CAD) system (CAD is also described in Chapter 5). Just as important, however, was the close involvement of customers right from the start of the design. They even came up with some good suggestions. For example, one airline suggested a new layout for the rear galley which allowed an extra twelve seats to be included in the aircraft. ■

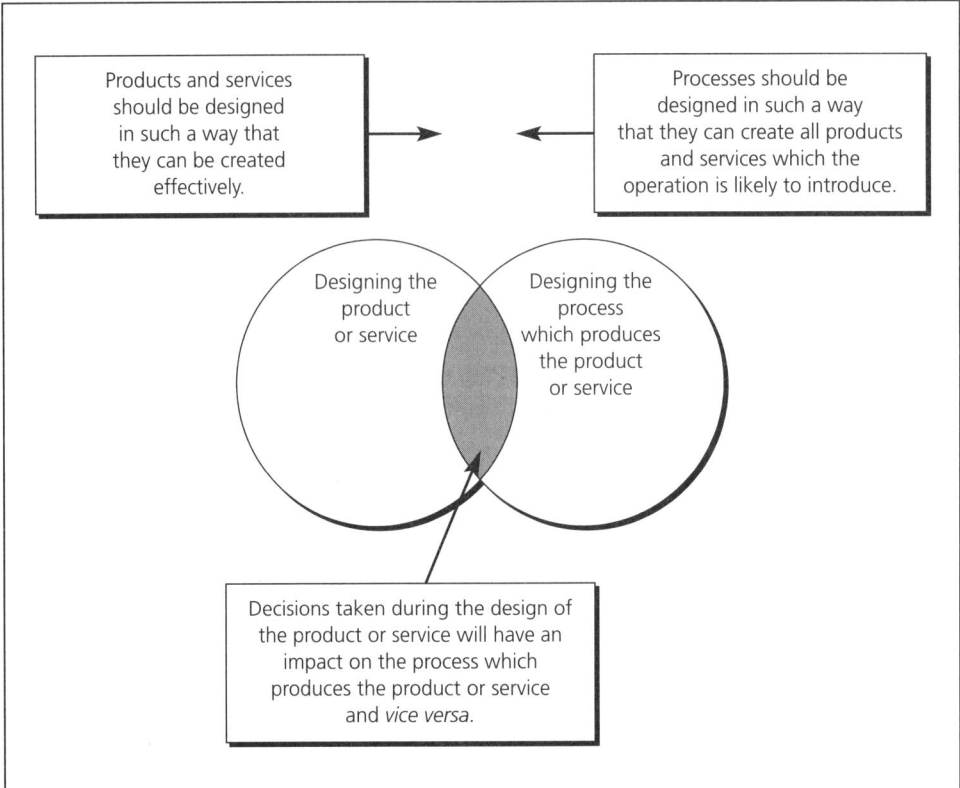

**Figure 4.2
The design of products/services and processes are interrelated and should be treated together**

The overlap has become important in manufacturing operations

This interrelationship means that the design of products and services and the design of processes should be considered as overlapping activities. In manufacturing especially, considerable effort has recently been put into examining this overlap. There are probably two reasons for this. First is a growing recognition that the design of products has a major effect on the cost of making them. Many of the decisions taken during the design of products (for example, choosing the material from which the product is going to be made, or the way in which the various components are fastened together, or the overall shape of the product and the tolerances to which it is to be made) will all define much of the cost of making it. It makes sense therefore to evaluate the various choices which the designer faces in terms of their effect on manufacturing cost as well as the functionality of the product itself. Second, the way overlap between product or service design and process design is managed has a significant effect on the time between having the initial concept for the product and service and eventually getting it to market. An effective and smooth transition between product/service design and process design helps to reduce its 'time-to-market' and therefore allows products and services to be introduced to customers ahead of the competition. This will be discussed further in Chapter 5.

The overlap is greater in services

The benefits of pushing together the activities of 'product' design and process design hold good whether the operation is producing products or services. However, the overlap between the two activities is generally greater in operations which produce services. After all, many services involve the customer in being part of the transformation process. The nature and form of the service, as far as the customer sees it, cannot be separated from the process to which the customer is subjected. Of course not all the processes in a service operation will involve the customer. The back-office part of the operation (*see* Chapter 1) will have processes which can be designed, to some extent, separately from the design of the service itself. However, for the most part, the design of a service is difficult to separate from the process which produces it.

The design activity is itself a transformation process

Producing designs for products, services or the processes which create them is itself a transformation process which conforms to the input–transformation–output model which was described in Chapter 1 and therefore has to be managed. Figure 4.3 illustrates the design activity as an input–transformation–output diagram. The inputs, as usual, include transformed resources and transforming resources. The transformed resources will consist mainly of information in the form of market forecasts, market preferences, technical data and so on. However, transformed resources might also at times include materials, or parts, which need to be tested for the suitability of their performance, and perhaps people to act as test customers. Transforming resources in the design activity include administrative, clerical and technical staff, design equipment such as computer-aided design (CAD) systems (*see* Chapter 5) and perhaps development and testing equipment.

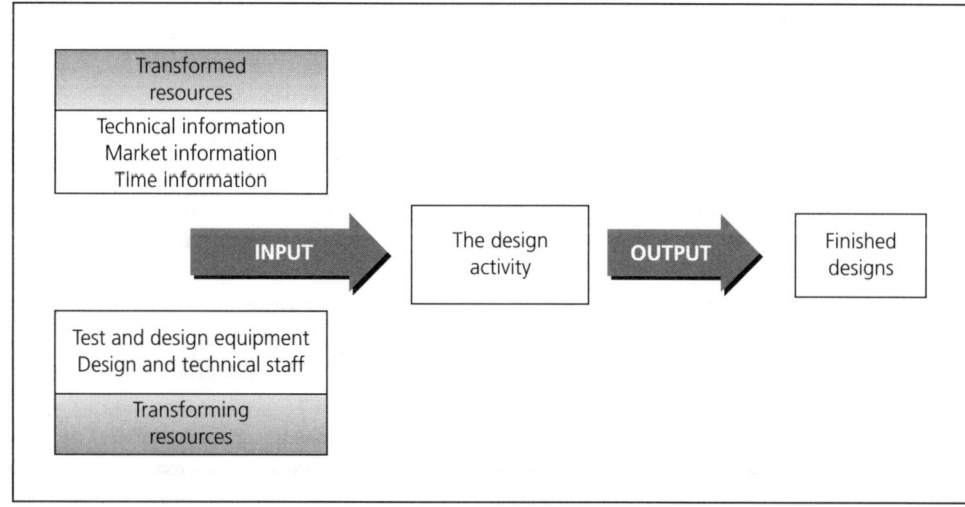

Figure 4.3 Design as a transformation process

The design transformation process is usually concerned with changing what in Chapter 1 we called the 'informational properties' of the inputs, but it might also include changing physical properties (for example, when making prototype models).

In addition to any technical information, which will vary depending on what is being designed, two types of information are particularly important in all types of design activity. They are:

● the *volume* in which the product or service will need to be produced; and
● the *time,* or duration, associated with each part of the product, service or process.

The *volume* of output of a product or service affects all aspects, not only of its design but also of the process which creates it. For example, a craftsperson who designs and makes furniture to order will have a totally different approach to all aspects of design than a large multinational furniture manufacturer. The influence of volume on the design activity is discussed later in the chapter. Appendix 1 at the end of the book outlines some of the approaches to forecasting the volumes which an operation will have to produce.

The *time* 'content' of products and services is also an important input to the design process. Unless designers know how long it takes to put together parts of a product, treat a customer, or process a piece of material, it is difficult to develop an effective design. For example, a designer of mass-produced clothing will need to understand the effect of every extra seam and button designed into each garment. In order to do this the designer needs to know how much extra time will have to be devoted to the manufacture of the garments. Extra time means extra cost, and cost is an important criterion for all designers. Similarly, the time to create each stage of a product or service is a prerequisite to the process designer who allocates tasks to each part of the transformation process. Appendix 2 at the end of the book discusses some of the more common approaches to measuring the time aspects of work in operations.

Performance objectives of the design activity

If we can use the input–transformation–output model to describe the design activity, we can also describe the objectives of the design activity in the same way as we do any transformation process.

Therefore, designers should try to produce designs which are:

● *high quality* – which means producing error-free designs of products, services or processes which fulfil their purpose in an effective and creative manner;
● *produced in a speedy manner* – which means producing designs of products, services or processes which have been moved from concept to detailed specification in as short a time as possible;
● *produced on a dependable basis* – which means producing designs which meet their quoted and planned delivery date;
● *produced flexibly* – which means producing designs which have changed to incorporate new and emerging ideas or requirements;
● *produced at low cost* – which means producing designs in such a way that the design activity has not consumed excessive resources during the creation process.

The design activity moves from concept to a specification

Fully specified designs, which totally define every part or activity, do not spring fully formed from the designer's imagination. A design starts as a more general, ill-defined, even vague idea of what might be an appropriate solution to a felt need. Over time this original idea, or 'concept', is refined and made progressively more detailed until it contains sufficient information to be turned into an actual product, service or process. The transition from concept to detailed specification can be divided into stages (Chapter 5 divides the process into six stages). This has two important implications.

The first is that at each stage, when a decision is made about the design, the decision cuts down the number of options which will be available further along in the design activity. For example, if a designer decides to make the outside casing of a camera case in aluminium rather than plastic, the cost of making that decision might be relatively small. Because the decision has been made in favour of aluminium, however, this limits decisions which have yet to be made, such as the overall size and shape of the case, the way the body is jointed together and the way in which the outer layer is bonded on to the case. The decision to make the case of aluminium has therefore committed the designer to particular options later on in the process by 'screening out' the other designs. This means that the uncertainty surrounding the design reduces as the number of alternative designs being considered by the designer decreases. In fact the design activity can be considered as one of progressively reducing the uncertainty regarding a product, service or process (*see* Fig. 4.4).

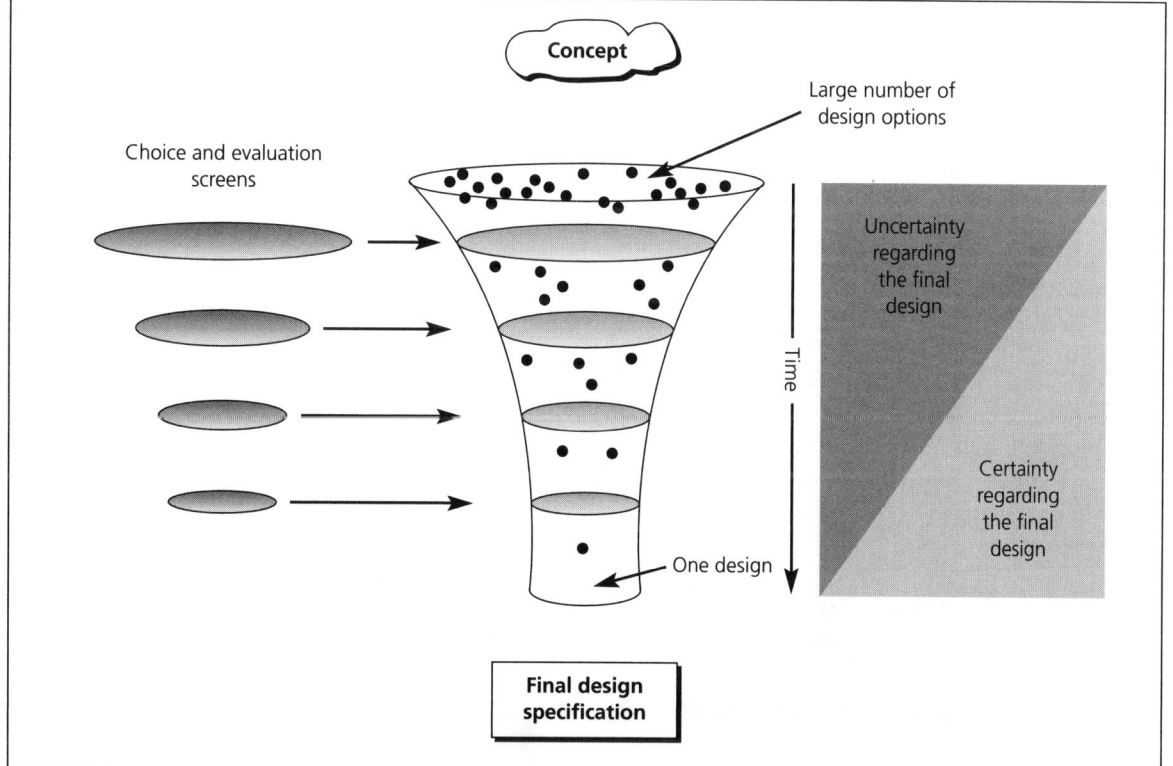

Figure 4.4 Design involves progressively reducing the number of possibilities until the final design is reached

The second consequence of the progression from concept to detailed specification concerns the cost of the designers changing their minds on some detail of the design. In most stages of design the cost of changing a decision is bound to incur some sort of rethinking and recalculation of costs. Close to the start of the design activity, before too many fundamental decisions have been made, the costs of change are relatively low. Relatively quickly, however, as the design progresses, the interrelated and cumulative decisions which are made become increasingly expensive to change. Figure 4.5 shows the relative costs of changing the design through the design process for a typical project. The cost of changes later on in the process is clearly much higher than earlier in the process.

Design involves identifying options

At each stage in the design of products, services or processes, until the final stage, designers are faced with *options*. Sometimes the range of options is narrow. It could be yes or no. For example, 'Should we go ahead with redesigning the hotel or not?' At other times the range of options is almost infinite: for example, 'How thick should we make the shielding of a nuclear reactor?' Any thickness between zero to very thick indeed is possible, with different consequences for safety and cost. The box on banking system design identifies some of the options available in home-banking service design, for example.

Design involves evaluating options

Evaluation in design means assessing the worth or value of each design option, so that a choice can be made between them. This involves assessing each option against a number of *design criteria*. While the criteria used in any particular design exercise will depend on the nature and circumstances of the exercise, it is useful to think in terms of three broad categories of design criteria.[4]

BANKING SYSTEM DESIGN OPTIONS[3]

The way in which banks deliver financial services to the home or office involves choice between a number of 'component technologies'. These can be assembled in a number of different configurations which result in the design of different types of service. First, the technical infrastructure (the medium of communication) has to be selected. Second, the delivery system itself (the particular 'technology' used) needs to be chosen. Finally, the package of services which will be provided to the customer can be chosen. This hierarchy of design options is shown in Fig. 4.6 which also includes the UK financial service companies which have chosen a particular set of options. Note, however, that an 'option tree' such as this one is not a decision tree. No bank would take decisions in this order. If anything, it would work backwards from the types of service which it wants to offer its customers, towards the technology choices which could provide them. ■

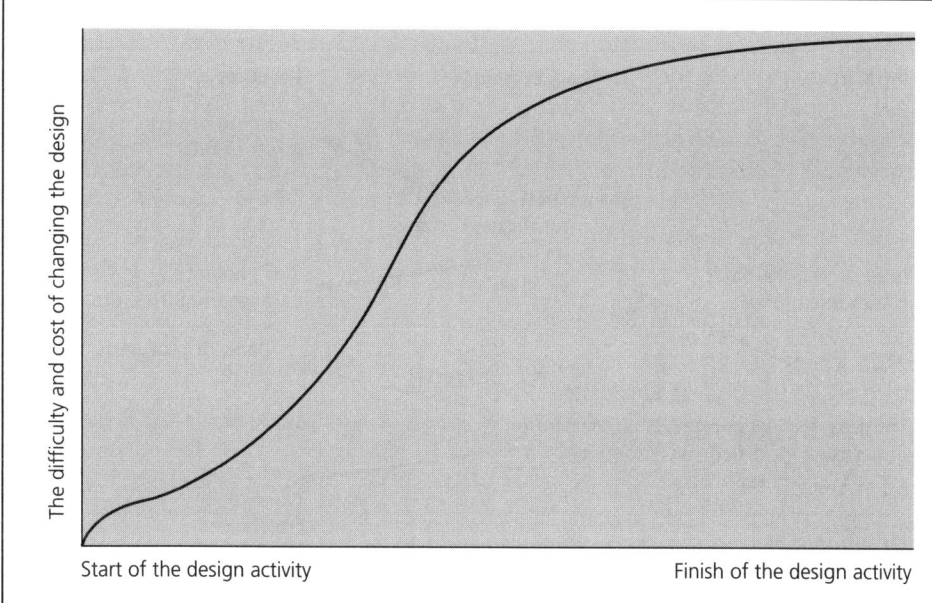

Figure 4.5 Changing design decisions becomes progressively more expensive as the design process continues

- The *feasibility* of the design option – can we do it?
- The *acceptability* of the design option – do we want to do it?
- The *vulnerability* of each design option – do we want to take the risk?

The feasibility of a design option indicates the degree of difficulty in adopting it and should assess the *investment* in time, effort and money which will be needed. The acceptability of a design option assesses how well it takes the design towards its objectives. It is the *return* or benefit the design gets from choosing the option. The vulnerability of a design option is the extent to which things could go wrong if it is chosen. It is the *risk* which is incurred by the designers in choosing an option.

Key questions to assess the feasibility of a design option include:

- Do we have the skills (quality of resources) to cope with this option?
- Do we have the organizational capacity (quantity of resources) to cope with this option?
- Do we have the financial resources to cope with this option?

Key questions to assess the acceptability of a design option are:

- Does the option satisfy the performance criteria which the design is trying to achieve? (These will differ for different designs.)
- Does the option give a satisfactory financial return?

Key questions to assess the vulnerability of a design option include:

- Do we understand the full consequences of adopting the option?
- Being pessimistic, what could go wrong if we adopt the option? What would be the consequences of everything going wrong? (This is called the 'downside risk' of an option.)

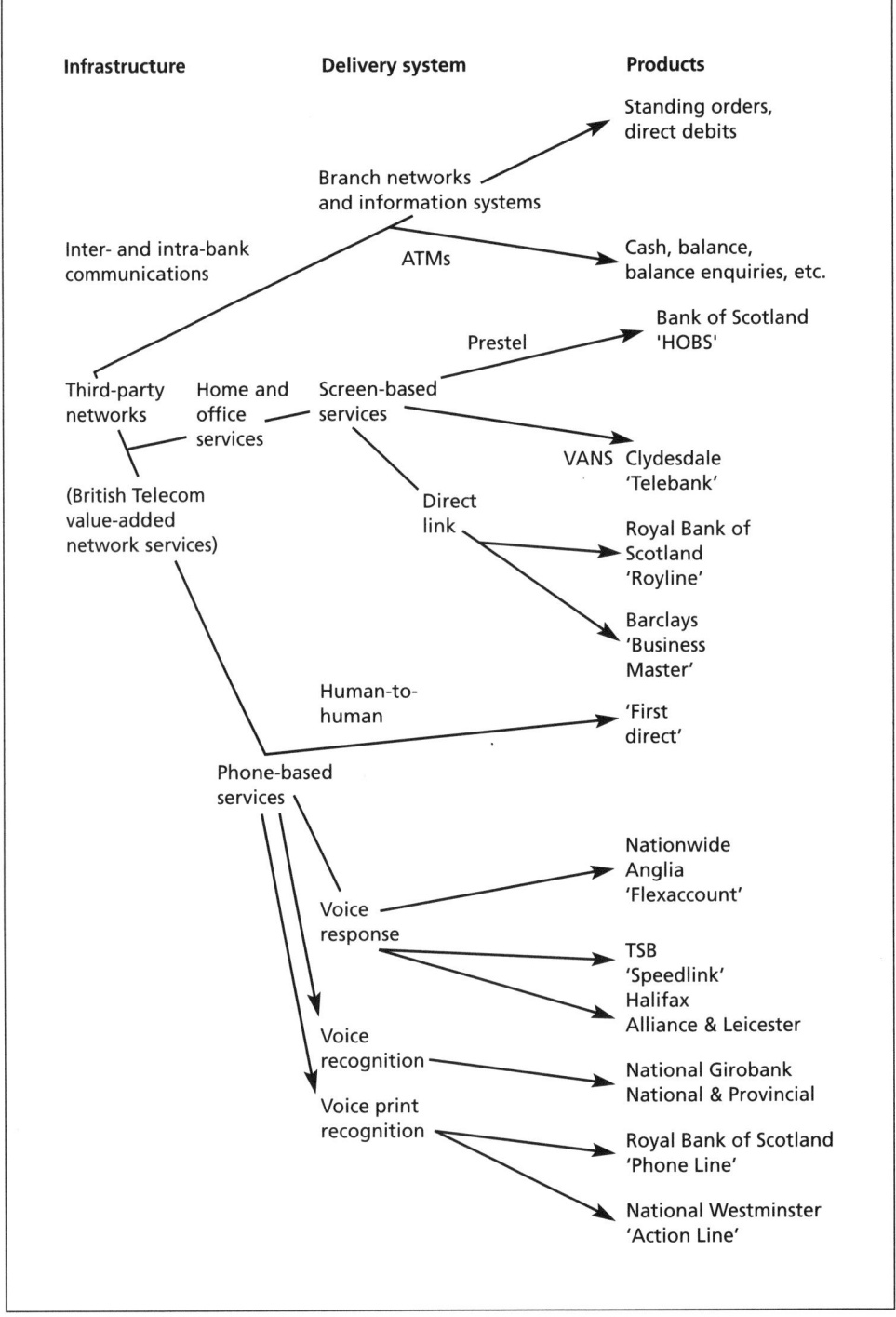

Figure 4.6 Design options in home-banking services
Source: Reproduced with permission from Scarborough, H. and Corbett, H.M. (1992) *Technology in Organizations*, Routledge

Example: Materials selection for LPG containers

A company which manufactures containers for transporting liquid petroleum gas (LPG), used mainly for the domestic heating and cooking market, is reviewing the design of its containers. Recently several advances have been made in materials and manufacturing technology, which means that alternatives to the present mild steel gas cylinder are worth considering. The alternative materials such as aluminium, stainless steel and glass-reinforced plastic would all be lighter than the present container, and opportunities would therefore exist for LPG to be marketed in areas where previously the weight of the product had discouraged sales, such as in multistorey housing.

The container material would affect the weight and therefore market factors such as:

● the total potential market
● the market growth rate
● the market share
● the selling price.

The container material would also influence:

● the amount of investment needed in a new manufacturing plant
● the unit cost of manufacturing.

All these factors were unknowns at the stage when the design evaluation was being carried out. The designers in the company could only guess at the relationship between weight and the potential market, or the price premium a product could command. Similarly, since the technology involved would, for the most part, be totally new, the operations managers could not perfectly predict the capital investment needed or the manufacturing costs.

Table 4.2 shows how the company evaluated three alternative materials in terms of their feasibility, acceptability and vulnerability. The ROI estimate made by the company refers to the 'return on investment' of each option. This is one of several common measures of financial acceptability. In this case the company decided to adopt aluminium as the material for its containers. The acceptability criteria were viewed as offering sufficient advantages to outweigh any feasibility and vulnerability disadvantages.

Table 4.2 Using the feasibility, acceptability and vulnerability criteria to evaluate design options

Criteria	Mild steel	Aluminium	Glass-reinforced plastic
Feasibility			
Skills in working with material	Good	Some in-house	None
Capability to cope with change	No change	Yes	Yes with difficulty
Financial resources	None required	Yes	Yes
Acceptability			
Weight	Poor	Good	Very good
Impact strength	Very good	Good	Poor
Durability	Very good	Good	Poor
Appearance	OK	Good	OK
Ease of manufacture	Good	OK	OK
Unit cost	100	160	145
Price premium	0	80%	50%
Sales increase potential	0	30%	25%
ROI	–	19%	11%
Vulnerability			
Risk of manufacturing problems	None – current	Medium	Medium
Risk of poor market reaction	High	Low	Medium
Downside risk assessment	Medium in short term	Medium in short term	High in short term
	High in long term	Low in long term	Medium in long term

SIMULATION IN DESIGN

The essence of design is that the designer is making decisions in advance of the real product, service or process being created. This means that the designer is often not totally sure of the consequences of his or her decision. For example, a running shoe designer might make a decision about the construction of the shoe, or an architect about the layout of a public building, based on previous experience and basic theories. To increase their own confidence in their design decision, however, they will probably try to *simulate* how the product and the layout would work in practice. Simulation explores the consequences of decision making rather than directly advising on the decision itself – it is a *predictive* rather than an *optimizing* technique.

Simulation of some sort or other is one of the most useful tools which a designer can use to explore the consequences of a design decision without having to construct the product, service or process. If some 'model' of the design is made, the designer can experiment and test the 'model' and then use the results to either confirm the original design or adjust it based on the simulated behaviour. The simulation 'model' itself can take many forms. In the case of the running shoe design, the 'model' might be almost identical to the intended product, except that a 'one-off' prototype shoe would have been made rather than one produced on the actual manufacturing system which would be used for the eventual product. The prototype shoe would then be flexed many millions of times to simulate prolonged wear. In the case of the public building, the architect could devise a computer-based 'model' which would simulate the movement of people through the building according to the probability distribution which describes their random arrival and movement. This could then be used to predict where the layout might become overcrowded or where extra space might be reduced.

Simulation is especially useful in the design of very complex operations processes. For example, a typical use was a computer simulation which was used to redesign a North African shipping port. The model helped the designers to gain an understanding of how the detailed design of the docks and berths for the ships would affect the utilization and turn-round time of the ships depositing and picking up their cargoes at the port. The simulation led to a design which resulted in substantial savings to the World Bank who were involved in the funding of the project.[5] On a more accessible scale, Fig. 4.7 illustrates the screen of a computer-based simulation of a manufacturing operations. This model was used to redesign the process so as to reduce bottle-necks.[6]

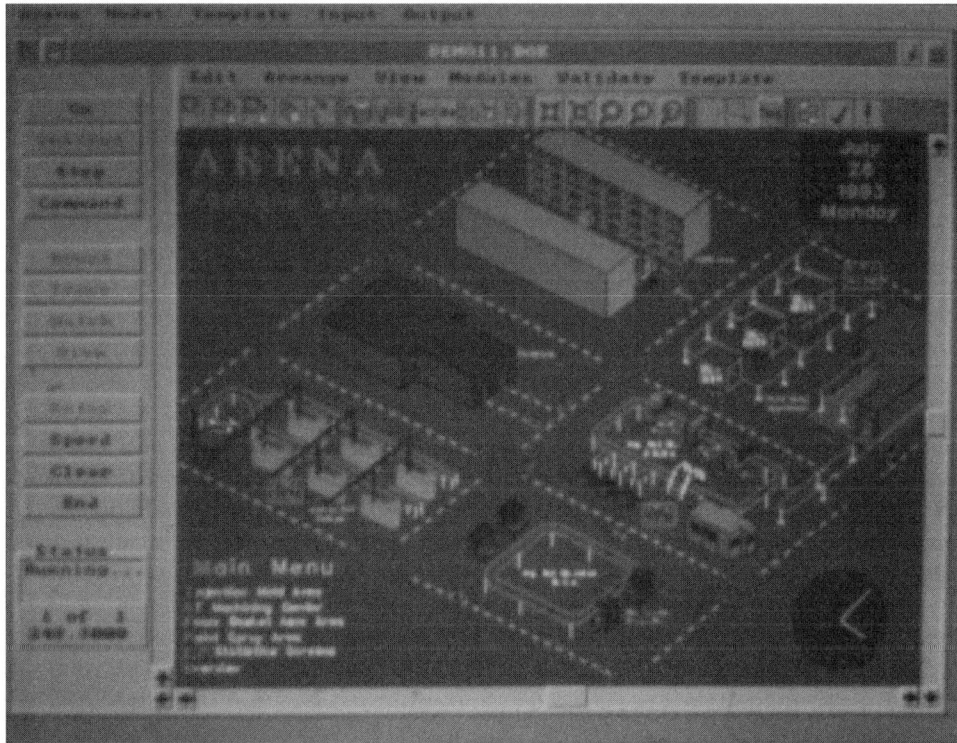

Figure 4.7 Computer simulation used for capacity planning, factory operational design and layout
Source: Courtesy of the CIMulation Centre

THE FOUR Cs OF DESIGN[7]

In the next five chapters we will deal with many different aspects of design, but it should already be clear that design is both important and central to operations management. As to the nature of design activity, it can be characterized by the *four Cs of design*. They were originally intended to describe product design, but in fact they succinctly summarize the nature of design in all aspects of operations management.

● *Creativity*. Design requires the creation of something that has not existed before (ranging from a variation on an existing design to a completely new concept).
● *Complexity*. Design involves decisions on a large number of parameters and variables (ranging from overall configuration and performance to components, materials, appearance and method of manufacture).
● *Compromise*. Design requires balancing multiple and sometimes conflicting requirements (such as performance and cost; appearance and ease of use; materials and durability).
● *Choice*. Design requires making choices between many possible solutions to a problem at all levels from basic concept to the smallest detail of colour or form.

THE VIRTUAL REALITY OF DESIGN[8]

The safety of passengers is a key design consideration for motor vehicle manufacturers. Predicting how the vehicle and passengers will react in a crash is a necessary piece of information for the vehicle designer.

The Swedish car manufacturer, Volvo, which has an enviable reputation for the safety of its products, uses a virtual-reality system to improve further its Side Impact Protection System (SIPS). A passenger gets into a mock-up of a Volvo 850, and wears a virtual-reality helmet which gives the impression of being in the driving position, including a 40 kph side impact with a truck. Recordings of the virtual incident can then be played back at slow speed to review the action of the seat belts, driver's airbag system, and the deformation of the bodyshell components, enabling the design team to make detailed improvements. The system is also expected to be a good marketing tool in the showrooms.

In fact, virtual reality, sometimes seen solely as a high technology arcade entertainment medium, is quietly establishing itself as a powerful, three-dimensional professional design tool, with applications including architecture, car design, and the planning of delicate surgical operations. It gives the expert designer a much clearer concept of the relative positions of the individual detailed parts than is possible with static two-dimensional representations. Perhaps even more importantly, it also allows others, in particular the non-technically trained customer or user, to visualize and suggest modifications to the design before any work is done on physical entity concerned. Thus the architect can allow the client to roam around the virtual building, walking along corridors and entering rooms at will, with any required changes being quickly and effectively incorporated. The car designer can allow others to visualize the internal layout and visibility from a driver's point of view, and simulated tests can be conducted without the expense and time involved with preparing real cars. In hospitals the surgeon can familiarize all members of the team with the preferred method of surgery, any uncertainties or confusion being resolved before the patient is on the operating table. Machinery designers can check to see whether maintenance engineers can access each part of the machine in the event of a breakdown. The range of applications of virtual reality in design seems only to be limited by the relatively high, but reducing, capital cost of the technology. The benefits of using virtual reality can be significant. Product development lead times can be reduced, as the need for extensive cross-checking and for various prototypes is eliminated. Costs can be reduced because designer productivity is enhanced, and costly mistakes can be eliminated. ■

ENVIRONMENTALLY SENSITIVE DESIGN

With the issues of environmental protection becoming more important, designers are increasingly having to take account of 'green' issues in their work. In many developed countries legislation has already provided some basic standards which restrict the use of toxic materials, limit discharges to air and water, and protect employees and the public from immediate and long-term harm. Most of these constraints affect both the design and operation of *processes* and the design of the products themselves.

Interest has focused on some fundamental issues:

● *The sources of materials* used in a product. (Will it damage rain forests? Will it use up scarce minerals? Will it exploit the poor, or use child labour?)

● *Quantities and sources of energy* consumed in the process. (Do plastic beverage bottles use more energy than glass ones? Should waste heat be recovered and used in fish farming?)

● *The amounts and type of waste material* that is created in the manufacturing processes. (Can this waste be recycled efficiently, or must it be burnt or buried in landfill sites? Will the waste have a long-term impact on the environment as it decomposes and escapes?)

● *The life of the product itself.* It is argued that if a product has a useful life of, say, twenty years, it will consume less resources than one that only lasts five years, which must, therefore, be replaced four times in the same period. However, the long-life product may require more initial inputs, and may prove to be inefficient in the latter part of its use, when the latest products use less energy or maintenance to run.

● *The end-of-life of the product.* (Will the redundant product be difficult to dispose of in an environmentally friendly way? Could it be recycled or used as a source of energy? Could it still be useful in third world conditions? Could it be used to benefit the environment, such as old cars being used to make artificial reefs for sea life?)

Designers are faced with complex trade-offs between these factors, although it is not always easy to obtain all the information that is needed to make the 'best' choices. For example, it is relatively straightforward to design a long-life product, using strong material, over-designed components, ample corrosion protection and so on. But its production might use more materials and energy and it could create more waste on disposal. To help make more rational decisions in the design process, some industries are experimenting with *Life Cycle Analysis*. This technique analyses all the production inputs, the life-cycle use of the product and its final disposal, in terms of total energy used (and more recently, of all the emitted wastes such as carbon dioxide, sulphurous and nitrous gases, organic solvents, solid waste, etc.). The inputs and wastes are evaluated at *every* stage in its creation, beginning with the extraction or farming of the basic raw materials.

THE VOLUME–VARIETY EFFECT ON DESIGN

Although, so far, we have discussed those aspects of design which apply to all types of operations, there are differences between the design activity in, say, an architects' practice and that in an electricity utility. The most significant factor is the differences between their volume and variety characteristics.

In Chapter 1 we saw how operations can range from producing a very high volume of products or services (for example, a food canning factory) to very low volume (for example, major project consulting engineers). We also saw how operations can range from producing a very low variety of products or services (for example, in an electricity utility) to very high variety (as, for example, in an architects' practice). Usually the two dimensions of volume and variety go together. Low-volume operations often have a high variety of products and services, and high-volume operations often have a narrow variety of products and services. Thus there is a continuum from low volume–high variety through to high volume–low variety, on which we can position operations.

Different operations, perhaps within the same industry, have adopted different approaches to the design of their products, services and processes.[9] Even within a single operation, different approaches to designing products, services and processes can be found. Many manufacturing plants will have a large area, organized on a 'mass-production' basis, in which it makes its high-volume 'best selling' products. In another part of the plant it may also have an area where it makes a wide variety of products in much smaller volumes. Both the design of each set of products and the design of the process which makes them are likely to be different. Similarly in a medical service, compare the approach taken during mass medical treatments such as large-scale immunization programmes with a transplant operation where the treatment is designed specifically to meet the needs of one person. These differences are explained by the fact that no one way of arranging resources is best for all types of operation in all circumstances. The differences are explained largely by the different *volume–variety positions* of the operations.

Volume and variety influence performance objectives

The volume and variety of an operation's activities are particularly influential in determining the way it thinks about its performance objectives, and therefore the objectives it sets for all aspects of its design activity. Figure 4.8 illustrates how the definitions of quality, speed, dependability, flexibility and cost are influenced by the volume–variety position of the operation.

Quality

Quality in a low volume–high variety process, such as an architects' practice, for example, is largely concerned with the final aesthetic appearance of the building and the appropriateness of its detailed design. In a fast-food outlet, where volume is higher and variety lower, quality concerns the actual taste of the food, but equally important is the conformity of the product or service to its designed specification. The food must be 'as advertised' in content and quantity, the eating area must be clean, etc. In an exception-

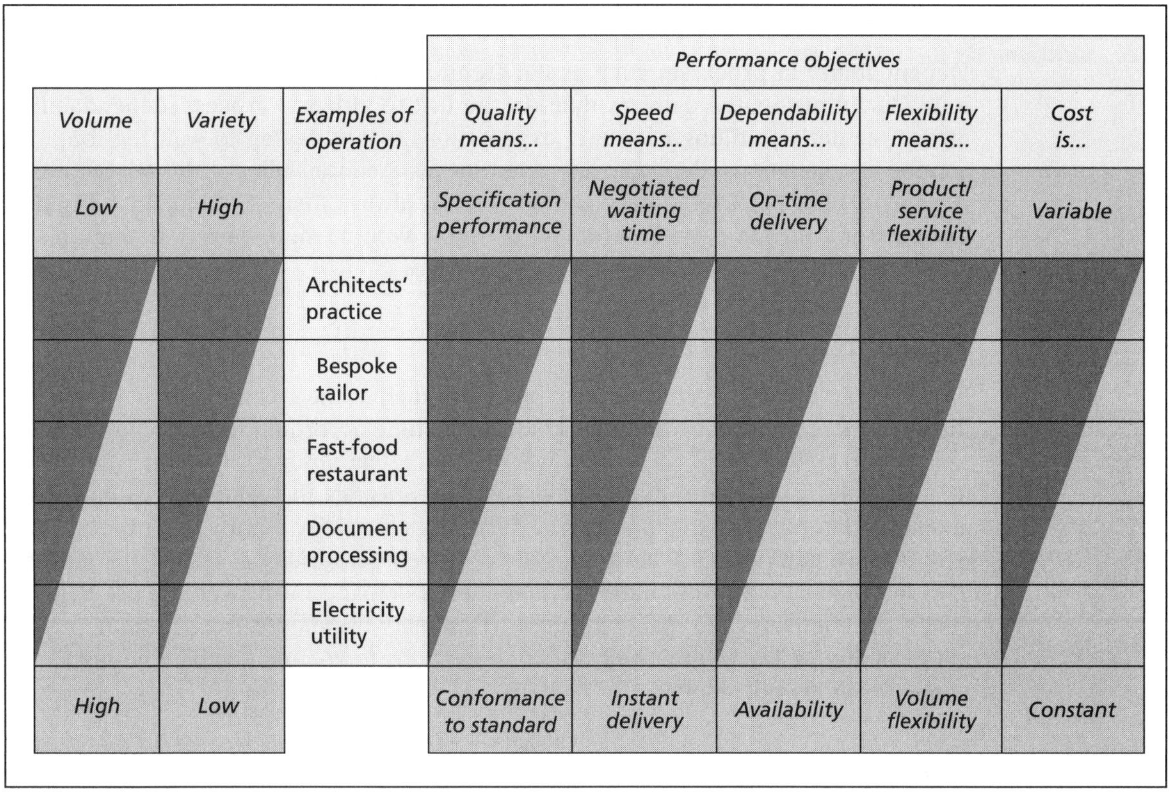

Volume	Variety	Examples of operation	Performance objectives				
			Quality means...	Speed means...	Dependability means...	Flexibility means...	Cost is...
Low	High		Specification performance	Negotiated waiting time	On-time delivery	Product/ service flexibility	Variable
		Architects' practice					
		Bespoke tailor					
		Fast-food restaurant					
		Document processing					
		Electricity utility					
High	Low		Conformance to standard	Instant delivery	Availability	Volume flexibility	Constant

Figure 4.8 An operation's position on the volume–variety continuum influences the meaning of the operation's performance objectives

ally high-volume and low-variety process such as an electricity supply company, quality is exclusively concerned with error-free service – electricity must be constantly available in the correct form (in terms of voltage, hertz, etc.). The meaning of quality has shifted from being concerned primarily with the performance and specification of the product or service towards conformity to a predefined standard as we move from low volume–high variety operations through to high volume–low variety operations.

Speed

Speed for the architects' projects means negotiating a completion date with each client, based on the client's needs and the architects' estimates of how much work is involved in each project. The fast-food restaurant can again ask its customers to wait for service – but not for a long time. Here, although there is some customer tolerance of waiting time, service must be available within that time. Speed is taken to its extreme in the electricity utility where speed means literally instant delivery. No electricity company could ask its customers to wait for their 'delivery' of electricity. Speed therefore means an individually negotiated delivery time in low volume–high variety operations but moves towards meaning 'instant' delivery in some high volume–low variety operations.

Dependability

Dependability in processes such as the architects' practice means keeping to each individually negotiated delivery date. In the fast food batch process, dependability means regularly fulfilling customer expectations of not having to wait too long. In continuous operations, dependability often means the availability of the service itself. A dependable electricity supply is one which is always there. So dependability has moved from meaning 'on-time delivery' in low volume–high variety operations to 'availability' in high volume–low variety operations.

Flexibility

Flexibility in low volume–high variety processes such as the architects' practice means the ability to design many different kinds of building according to its clients' various requirements. The fast food process will need a certain amount of product flexibility to cope with its several products but will also need to flex the volume of its output to accommodate varying demand levels. With the electricity company's process, the need for product flexibility has disappeared entirely (electricity is electricity, more or less) but the ability to meet almost instantaneous demand means volume flexibility is vital if the company is to maintain supply. Flexibility has moved from meaning product flexibility in low volume–high variety operations to volume flexibility in high volume–low variety operations.

Cost

Cost, in terms of the unit cost per product or service, varies with both the volume of output of the operation and the variety of products or services it produces. The variety of products or services in low-volume operations is relatively high which means that running the operation will be expensive because of the flexible and high skill levels employed. Further, because the volume of output is relatively low, a few products or services are bearing the operation's high cost base. Also, and more significantly for the operation, the cost of each product or service is different. At the other end of the scale, high-volume operations usually produce similar products or services, output is high, so that whatever the base cost of the operation, it is shared among a high number of products or services. Cost per unit of output is therefore usually low for operations such as the electricity utility but, more significantly, the cost of producing one second of electricity is the same as the next second. Cost is relatively constant.

Volume and variety affect the design activity

The volume–variety position of an operation will also influence almost every aspect of the operation's design activities. Table 4.3 illustrates just how some aspects of the design activity will vary with volume and variety.

Take again the two operations discussed previously at the extremes of the volume–variety spectrum – the architects' practice and the electricity utility. The architects' high variety means that its services have little standardization. Some elements of the service will be common – all new designs will need a proposal to put before the client, an internal schedule of activities, plans, and so on – but the details of

Table 4.3 The impact of the volume–variety position of an operation on different aspects of its design activities

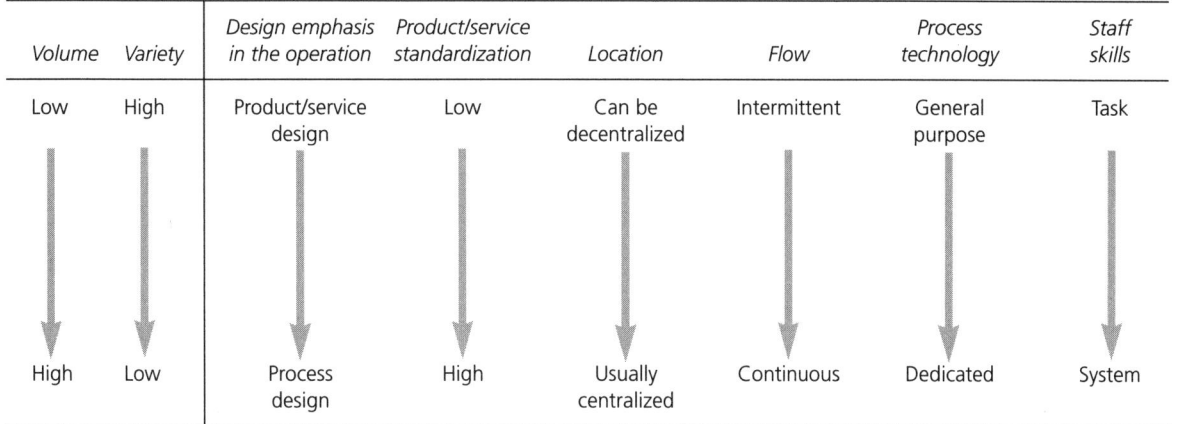

Volume	Variety	Design emphasis in the operation	Product/service standardization	Location	Flow	Process technology	Staff skills
Low	High	Product/service design	Low	Can be decentralized	Intermittent	General purpose	Task
High	Low	Process design	High	Usually centralized	Continuous	Dedicated	System

these will vary from job to job. This variety of activities also means that whatever technology the operation possesses (for example, computer-aided design systems) will need to be sufficiently general purpose to cope with all types of job. The flow of information within the operation will depend on the state of the projects being designed, the circumstances of clients and the overall level of activity in the operation. It will certainly not be regular, rather it will flow in an intermittent manner. The individual task skills of the architects themselves are likely to be more valued by the practice than the skill involved in running the operation itself.

The electricity utility on the other hand exhibits almost the mirror image characteristics of the architects' practice. Volume is high, variety is virtually non-existent, since electricity is almost a totally standardized product. The generators – its process technology – cannot be used to do much else but make electricity, which it does more or less continuously. No individual craft skills are needed directly to make electricity (although they will be needed to maintain the generators) but the skills of managing the 'electricity generating system', so as to provide continuous supply at the lowest feasible cost, are considerable.

PROCESS TYPES IN MANUFACTURING AND SERVICES

The position of an operation on the volume–variety continuum, by influencing the nature of its performance objectives and its design activities, also shapes the general approach it takes to managing the transformation process. These 'general approaches' to managing the transformation process are called *process types*. Different terms are used to identify process types in manufacturing and service industries.

In manufacturing, these process types are (in order of increasing volume and decreasing variety):

- Project processes
- Jobbing processes
- Batch processes

- Mass processes
- Continuous processes.

In service operations there is less consensus on the terms of the process type. The terms we use here are (again in order of increasing volume and decreasing variety):[10]

- Professional services
- Service shops
- Mass services.

Process types in manufacturing

Each process type in manufacturing implies a different way of organizing operations' activities with different volume and variety characteristics (*see* Fig. 4.9).

Project processes

Project processes are those which deal with discrete, usually highly customized products. Often the timescale of making the product or service is relatively long, as is the interval between the completion of each product or service. So low volume and high variety are characteristics of project processes. The activities involved in making the product can be ill defined and uncertain, sometimes changing during the production process itself. Examples of project processes include shipbuilding, most construction companies, movie production companies, building the Channel

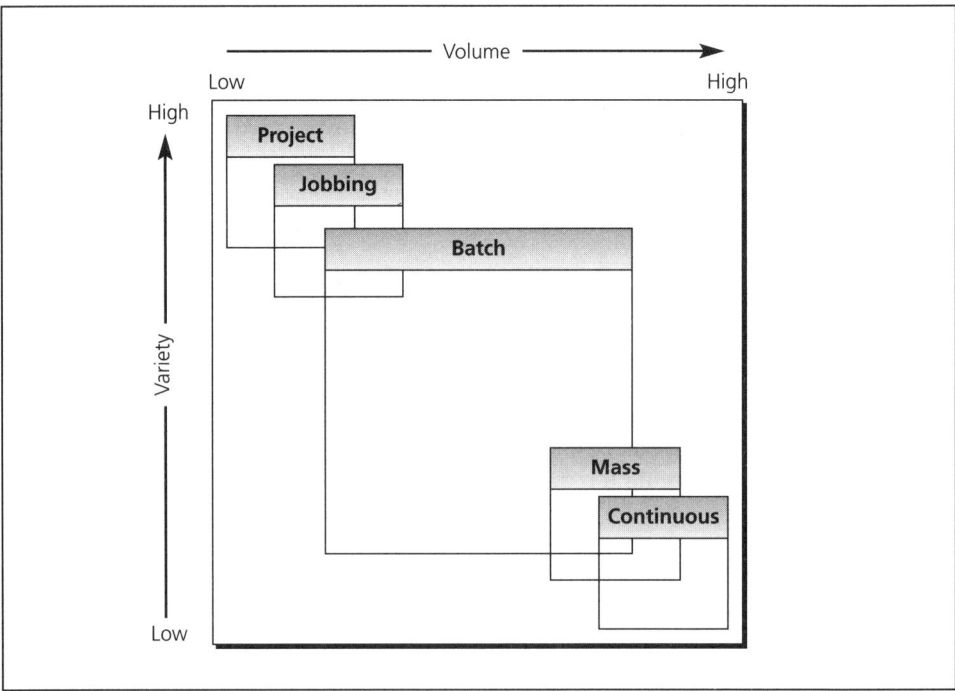

**Figure 4.9
Process types in
manufacturing
operations**

Tunnel, large fabrication operations such as those manufacturing turbo generators, drilling oil wells, and installing a computer system. The essence of project processes is that each job has a well defined start and finish, the time interval between starting different jobs is relatively long and the transforming resources which make the product will probably have been organized especially for each product.

Jobbing processes

Jobbing processes also deal with very high variety and low volumes. Whereas in project processes each product has resources devoted more or less exclusively to it, however, in jobbing processes each product has to share the operation's resources with many others. The resources of the operation will process a series of products but, although all the products will require the same kind of attention, each will differ in its exact needs. Examples of jobbing processes include many precision engineers such as specialist toolmakers, furniture restorers, bespoke tailors, and the printer who produces tickets for the local social event. Jobbing processes produce more and usually smaller items than project processes but, like project processes, the degree of repetition is low. Most jobs will probably be 'one-offs'.

Batch processes

Batch processes can often look like jobbing processes, but batch does not have quite the degree of variety associated with jobbing. As the name implies, each time batch processes produce a product they produce more than one. So each part of the operation has periods when it is repeating itself, at least while the 'batch' is being processed. The size of the batch could be just two or three, in which case the batch process would differ little from jobbing, especially if each batch is a totally novel product. Conversely, if the batches are large, and especially if the products are familiar to the operation, batch processes can be fairly repetitive. Because of this, the batch type of process can be found over a wider range of volume and variety levels than other process types. Examples of batch processes include machine tool manufacturing, the production of some special gourmet frozen foods, the manufacture of most of the component parts which go into mass-produced assemblies such as automobiles, and the production of most clothing.

Mass processes

Mass processes are those which produce goods in high volume and relatively narrow variety – narrow, that is, in terms of the fundamentals of the product design. An automobile plant, for example, might produce several thousand variants of car if every option of engine size, colour, extra equipment, etc. is taken into account. Yet essentially it is a mass operation because the different variants of its product do not affect the basic process of production. The activities in the automobile plant, like all mass operations, are essentially repetitive and largely predictable. Examples of mass processes include the automobile plant, most consumer durable manufacturers such as a television plant, most food processes such as a frozen pizza manufacturer, a beer bottling plant and CD production.

Continuous processes

Continuous processes are one step beyond mass processes insomuch as they operate at even higher volume and often have even lower variety. They also usually operate for far longer periods of time. Sometimes they are literally continuous in that their products are inseparable, being produced in an endless flow. They may even be continuous in that the operation must supply the products without a break. Continuous processes are often associated with relatively inflexible, capital-intensive technologies with highly predictable flow. Examples of continuous processes include petrochemical refineries, electricity utilities, steel making, and some paper making.

Process types in service operations

As with manufacturing operations, each process type in service operations implies a different way of organizing the operation to cope with different volume–variety characteristics (*see* Fig. 4.10).

Professional services

Professional services are defined as high-contact organizations where customers spend a considerable time in the service process. Such services provide high levels of customization, the service process being highly adaptable in order to meet individual customer needs. A great deal of staff time is spent in the front office and contact staff are given considerable discretion in servicing customers. The amount of time and attention provided for each customer probably means that the ratio of staff to customers is high. Professional services tend to be people-based rather than equipment-based, with emphasis placed on the process (how the service is delivered) rather than the 'product' (what is delivered). Professional services include management consultants, e.g. Andersen Consulting, lawyers' practices, architects, doctors' surgeries, auditors, health and safety inspectors and some computer field service operations.

At the other extreme are mass services.

Mass services

Mass services have many customer transactions, involving limited contact time and little customization. Such services are often predominantly equipment-based and 'product'-oriented, with most value added in the back office and relatively little judgement applied by front-office staff. The mainly non-professional staff are likely to have a closely defined division of labour and to follow set procedures. Mass services include supermarkets, a national rail network, e.g. Transnet, an airport, telecommunications service, library, television station, the police service, and the enquiry desk at a utility.

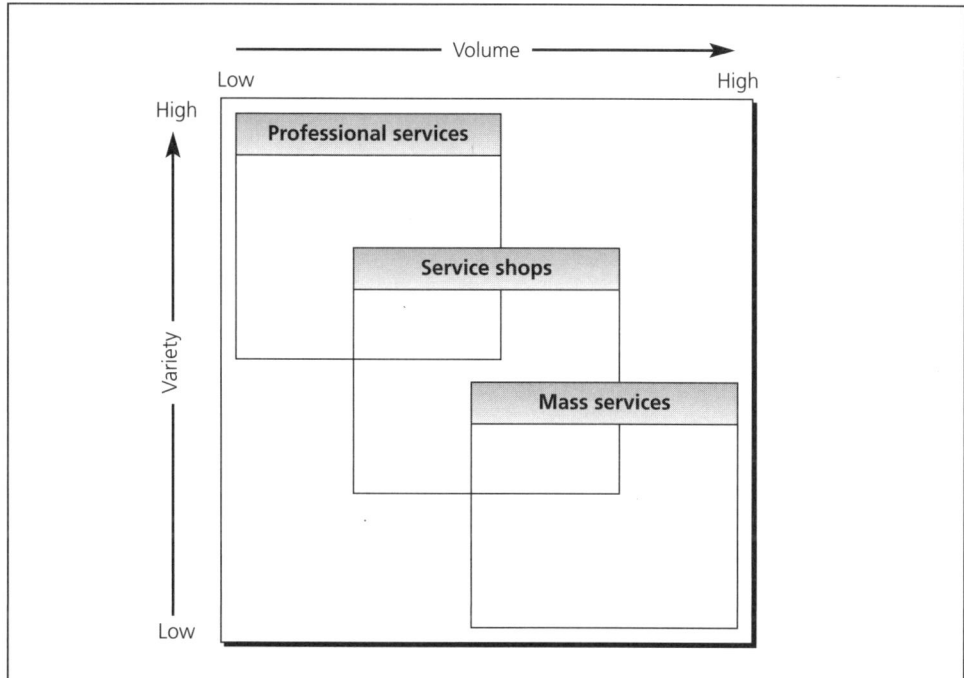

Figure 4.10
Process types in
service operations

Service shops

Service shops are characterized by levels of customer contact, customization, volumes of customers and staff discretion which position them between the extremes of professional and mass services. Service is provided by means of mixes of front- and back-office activities, people and equipment, and of product/process emphasis. Service shops include banks, high street shops, holiday tour operators, car rental companies, schools, most restaurants, hotels and travel agents.

The product–process matrix

In both manufacturing and service operations, because the different process types overlap, organizations often have a choice of what type of process to employ. This choice will have consequences to the operation, especially in terms of its cost and flexibility.

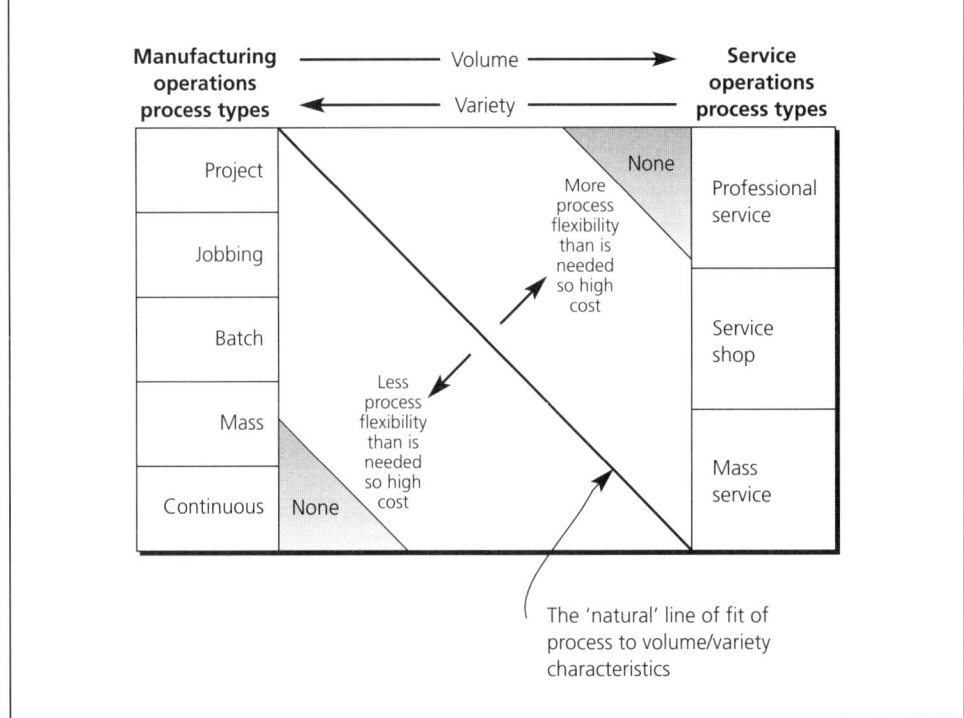

Figure 4.11
Deviating from the
natural diagonal
on the
product–process
matrix has
consequences for
cost and flexibility
Source: Adapted from
Hayes and Wheelwright

The classic representation of how cost and flexibility vary with process choice comes from Professors Hayes and Wheelwright of Harvard University.[11] They represent process choices on a matrix, with the volume–variety as one dimension, and what we have called process types as the other. Figure 4.11 shows their matrix adapted to fit with the terminology used here. Most operations stick to the 'natural' diagonal of the matrix, and few, if any, operations are found in the extreme corners of the matrix. However, because there is some overlap between the various process types, operations might be positioned slightly off the diagonal.

The diagonal of the matrix shown in Fig. 4.11 represents a 'natural' lowest cost position for an operation. Operations which are on the right of the 'natural' diagonal have processes which would normally be associated with lower volumes and higher variety. This means that their processes are likely to be more flexible than seems to be warranted by their actual volume–variety position. Because of this, their costs are likely to be higher than they would be with a process which was closer to the diagonal. Conversely, operations who are on the left of the diagonal have adopted processes which would normally be used in a higher volume and lower variety situation. Their processes will therefore be 'over-standardized' and probably too inflexible for their volume–variety position. This lack of flexibility can also lead to high costs because the process will not be able to change from one activity to another as efficiently as a more flexible process.

DESIGN – THE STRUCTURE OF PART TWO

The various aspects of the design activity in operations management, some of which were illustrated in Fig. 4.8, are treated in the remaining five chapters of Part Two. All these aspects are shown in Fig. 4.1 at the beginning of this chapter.

The design of products and services is a prerequisite (Chapter 5)

Notwithstanding our emphasis on the desirability of overlapping the design of products and services and the design of the processes which create them, some understanding of the product or service must be the starting point for all design considerations in operations management. This is why we begin our detailed examination of design with the *design of products and services* in Chapter 5. It will look at some of the basic design principles which we have covered in this chapter and apply them to the various stages which form the product/service design activity. These stages take the designer from the original concept for the product or service through to its final detailed specification.

Process design starts with the whole network (Chapter 6)

With an outline of what the products and services should look like, an operation can start to design the processes which will have to create them. At its most strategic level this means considering the whole network of operations which together produce and deliver products and services to the customers. From the perspective of a single operation within the network, design decisions will include how much of the network the operation wants to own (its vertical integration), where to place its sites (its location), and how large to make each site (its capacity). Chapter 6, *Design of the operations network*, covers all these design decisions.

Designing the operations layout defines its flow (Chapter 7)

The location decision is also significant within each individual site in the total operations network. At this level the decisions concerning where to locate machines, equipment, facilities, and people relative to each other, is usually termed the operations layout. Layout decisions are particularly important because they determine the pattern of flow through the operation. Chapter 7, *Process layout and flow*, deals with these decisions.

Technology plays a key role (Chapter 8)

Location of the machines and equipment within the operation will determine the pattern of its flow, but the nature of its technology will determine its capability. Although operations managers do not always need to know all the detailed science which lies behind the technologies they use, it is necessary to understand the implications of using alternative technologies. Chapter 8, *Process technology*, describes some of the more significant technologies which process materials, information and customers.

People make the processes work (Chapter 9)

Even after the products and services have been designed, the network configured, each site's layout determined and the process technology chosen, the operation cannot work until it is staffed. The people in any operation are the catalyst which makes the whole operation come alive. While the subject of this text is not human resources management as such, it is important to understand how the staff in the operation interact with its physical design. Chapter 9, *Job design and work organization*, examines how different approaches to designing people's jobs in operations influences the performance of the operation as a whole.

PERSONAL PROFILE

Raj Siriram, Electric Motor Component Manufacturing

Raj Siriram is the Manufacturing Manager at Africa's largest motor manufacturing plant located on Gauteng's East Rand. He is responsible for the division that produces the laminations, which are precision steel pressings, used in the manufacture of the magnetic core of a motor.

His Laminations Division services the needs of a range of different motor manufacturing operations, ranging from custom producers of low-volume High Voltage motors to producers of very high volumes of standard domestic appliance motors, as well as a range of clients in between. He talks about the difficulties associated with the design of manufacturing processes that would adequately cater for the needs of their fragmented market.

'The first reality that we recognized in our process redesign endeavour was that it would be impossible for one process design to simultaneously cater for the needs of the entire market that we served. We therefore looked at each market segment separately by analysing its volume and variety characteristics.

'A fundamental truth in this industry is that, being a press shop intensive industry, it is mainly driven by the cost and design of tooling. To be an excellent producer of laminations one has to first become an excellent designer and manufacturer of press tooling. This led to the establishment of an in-house tooling facility. The extremely low volume and customized nature of this tooling business makes it a project-type operation and led us to implement a project management system with highly flexible CADAM systems, operated by highly skilled designers and toolmakers.

'There was a recognition that we would have to build in process flexibility to cater for the needs of our 'custom markets' for laminations. These included the High Voltage market, the repair markets and the speciality markets. These markets require a process that is capable of catering for short run, unique design pressings. This is a classic jobbing environment. The flexibility required needs an ability to cope with varying manufacturing sequences, short life tooling and the ability to fit an extremely wide range of tools into a limited range of presses. We therefore designed a labour-intensive process which needs simple, low cost tools and semi-skilled operators but which employs highly skilled setters who can cater for the continuous routing changes that are occurring. The presses were modified to handle the full range of tools with simple set-up requirements. Both the tooling facility and the custom press shop feature function-oriented layouts in line with the jobbing nature of their operations.

'At the other extreme, the laminations business has to cope with volumes of up to ten million units per year of a single design of component for the appliance or motor vehicle industries. The process design approach adopted here was to set up a number of continuous flow lines which are highly automated. Each line is restricted to a limited range of product; in other words they have a product-oriented layout. The follow-on or progression tooling used is highly product specific and expensive but results in remarkably low costs per unit. The setters are highly skilled but only on their specific flow line which they are required to both set and operate.

'The intermediate part of our laminations market is made up of repetitive demand on a larger range of components. The runs here are about 50 times higher than those in the custom section but, more importantly, an order is received for the same item about eight to ten times a year. This market is batch oriented and we adopted a group layout concept in the process design. The tooling used is more expensive and features higher levels of automation than those in the custom area, but not as much automation as for the follow-on tooling. These tool / press combinations can also be changed over in less than ten minutes due to the tool design. The setters in this area are accordingly of a lower skill level than those in the customized product area.

'Ultimately, we ended up with four differently configured plants-within-a-plant. This allows each business within the Laminations Division to cater, in an optimized manner, for the market that it is seeking to serve. It also makes the overall business a lot more manageable and optimizes the relative cost position of the Division in each of its market segments. The business has grown to become the largest producer in South Africa within its industry and has developed a thriving export business.' ■

Source: By kind permission of Electric Motor Component Manufacturing

SUMMARY

■ The overall purpose of the design activity is to meet the needs of customers, whether through the design of the products or services themselves, or through the design of the processes which will produce them. All the performance objectives of the operation (quality, speed, dependability, flexibility, cost) will be influenced by the design activity.

■ The design activity, therefore, is equally applicable to both product and service design and to process design.

■ The two activities of product/service design and process design are interrelated. One should not be done independently of the other. Bringing them together has many benefits including better designs and fast time-to-market. In fact in services it is impossible to separate out the service from the process which produces it.

■ The design activity is itself a transformation process which needs to be managed in order to achieve its own performance objectives. As a transformation process, it transforms information into finished designs to appropriate levels of quality, speed, dependability, flexibility and cost.

■ Design is a multi-stage process which moves from concept through to a detailed specification. It does so by evaluating and choosing between options at each stage of the process. This progressively reduces the uncertainty concerning the design but also makes it difficult to change previous decisions.

■ Design is a process which is characterized by Creativity, Complexity, Compromise, and Choice. These are known as the four Cs of design.

■ An operation's position on the volume–variety continuum will determine the way in which its performance objectives are defined.

■ An operation's position on the volume–variety continuum influences many aspects of its design activity, including the emphasis which is placed on either product/service design or process design, the location policy it chooses, the standardization of its products and services, its choice of process technology, the nature of its layout and flow, the staff skills which it will require, and its robustness to disruption.

OKP (Pty) Ltd

OKP (Oosthuizen, Khumalo & Peterson) Pty Ltd is a firm of consulting engineers, based in Gauteng with offices in Durban and Cape Town. It specializes in the design of chemical process plants. Although a relatively small company, it has already established itself as an innovator in the process design field. The company was particularly excited by a new design technique recently developed by one of its young engineers. She claimed that by using this new technique, significant construction cost savings could be achieved on almost any type of plant. The technique had been reviewed by the company's senior engineers and seemed to be theoretically sound, but, as yet, no actual plant had been designed using the technique, and no experimental pilot rig had been constructed for verification tests.

While the senior engineers were deciding whether to sanction the expense of a pilot rig to test the new technique, the company won an order to design a chemical plant in China. Immediately, two design teams started to produce preliminary designs, one using conventional design techniques and the other using the new technique. These designs became known as Design 1 and Design 2, respectively. At the same time, cost estimates were collected to establish the total cost of setting up an experimental pilot rig to test some of the assumptions involved in the new design, Design 2, before final plans would have to be submitted. In fact, the Design 2 team produced two designs – one using the new technique, and one which was a modification of the new design, which could be used if the design did not prove successful.

When all this information had been brought together, the senior engineers were presented with the following financial summary:

Cost of pilot rig test	=	R800 000
Design 1 (conventional design) Profit to the company	=	R2 000 000
Design 2 (experimental design) Profit to the company if the design is successful	=	R4 000 000
Profit to the company if modification is necessary	=	R500 000

Both designs were relatively straightforward to build, although Design 2 would involve more of the company's engineers to be allocated to the project during its construction. This might limit the company's ability to take on any other major projects. The performance of the plant, whether constructed to Design 1 or Design 2, would almost certainly be identical, but Design 2, if successful, would be finished in about 80 per cent of the time which would be necessary to construct the conventional plant built to Design 1. This could give the company a considerable advantage in winning further orders. However, if the Design 2 was attempted, but needed subsequent modification, the company's reputation might suffer, temporarily.

The senior engineers then discussed the chances of the designs being successful. They were agreed that Design 1, using tried and tested conventional theories, was sure to be successful. They were less sure, however, of the experimental design. The theory looked good, but it hadn't been tried before, so without further information they assessed the chances of the design being successful at around 60 per cent.

Discussion then turned to considering the advisability of building a pilot rig to test the new design. They had built similar rigs before, and knew that they were extremely reliable in indicating whether a design was feasible or not. If they decided to build the test rig, they would still have plenty of time to decide between Design 1 and Design 2. ∎

Questions

1 What specific criteria do you think the company should use to evaluate the two designs? (Use the general headings of feasibility, acceptability and vulnerability.)

2 Within the limits of the information you have available, draw up a table of the relative merits of the two designs.

3 Where do you think the company would be positioned on the volume–variety continuum, and what does that indicate about the nature of all aspects of design (not just product design) in the company?

DISCUSSION QUESTIONS

1 Explain how the good design of the products or services and processes of the following operations can support the five performance objectives:

a washing-machine manufacturer

a computer-software house specializing in accountancy packages

a rock concert.

2 Why do you think product design and process design have been separate activities in many manufacturing organizations? Explain why this is changing.

3 Describe the activity of designing a new product or service of your choice in terms of the transformed and transforming resources, the activity and the outputs.

4 Discuss with someone who is involved in designing new products or services the problems involved.

5 The university catering manager is contemplating adding a take-away burger bar to its portfolio of outlets. Explain how the idea can be assessed.

6 Consider the design decision summarized in Table 4.2. Why do you think the company decided to adopt aluminium? What further questions would you ask if you had to make the decision?

7 Explain how the 'four Cs' of design might apply to the design of a 'home-banking' service.

8 Explain the importance of the volume–variety dimension as a way of understanding operations and their approach to design.

9 Describe how the five performance objectives vary between:

a burger bar and a high-class restaurant

a high-volume car producer and a classic car restorer

a corner grocery store and a supermarket.

10 What do you think would be the key design issues to be faced when setting up a hairdressing salon?

11 Explain the relationship between variety and volume and describe why you are unlikely to find many high-volume/high-variety and low-volume/low-variety operations.

NOTES ON CHAPTER

1 Sir Monty Finneston (1987) Address to the Department of Education and Science Conference, Loughborough University, UK, quoted *in* Norman, E., Riley J., Urry, S. and Whitacker, M. (1990) *Advanced Design and Technology*, Longman.

2 Sources: Wheatley, M. (1993/94) 'Boeing, Boeing', *Business Life*, Dec/Jan.

3 Source: Scarborough, H. and Corbett, H.M. (1992) *Technology in Organizations*, Routledge.

4 Cooke, S. and Slack, N. (1991) *Making Management Decisions* (2nd edn), Prentice Hall.

5 Most textbooks on financial analysis will describe the return on investment (ROI) criterion. For example, *see* Cooke, S. and Slack, N., *op. cit.*

6 Source: The CIMulation Centre.

7 Walsh, V., Roy, R., Bruce, M. and Potter, S. (1992) *Winning By Design, Technology, Product Design and International Competitiveness*, Blackwell.

8 Source: Lloyd, C. (1994) 'Business Drives into Virtual Reality', *The Sunday Times*, 6 Feb.

9 Source: Walley, P. and Slack, N. (1994) 'The Management of Operations', Course Notes, Warwick University MBA.

10 Fitzgerald, L., Johnston, R., Brignall, S., Silvestro, R. and Voss, C. (1991) *Performance Measurement in Service Industries*, CIMA.

11 Hayes, R.H. and Wheelwright, S.C. (1984) *Restoring our Competitive Edge*, John Wiley.

SELECTED FURTHER READINGS

Abernathy, W.J. (1976) 'Production Process Structure and Technological Change', *Design Sciences*, Vol 7, No 4.

Chaharbaghi, K. (1990) 'Using Simulation to Solve Design and Operational Problems', *International Journal of Operations and Production Management*, Vol 10, No 9.

Cooke, S. and Slack, N. (1991) *Making Management Decisions* (2nd edn), Prentice Hall.

Cross, N. (1984) *Developments in Design Methodology*, John Wiley.

de Bono, E. (1970) *Lateral Thinking – A Textbook of Creativity*, Ward Lock Educational.

Fox, J. (1993) *Quality Through Design: The Key to Successful Product Delivery*, McGraw-Hill.

Lorenz, C. (1990) *The Design Dimension*, Blackwell.

Shostack, G.L. (1982) 'How to Design a Service', *European Journal of Marketing*, Vol 16, No 1.

Sparke, P. (1986) *An Introduction to Design and Culture in the Twentieth Century*, Allan and Unwin.

Walker, D. and Cross, N. (1983) *An Introduction to Design*, Open University Press.

Walsh, V., Roy, R., Bruce, M. and Potter, S. (1992) *Winning By Design, Technology, Product Design and International Competitiveness*, Blackwell.

Webb, A. (1994) *Managing Innovative Projects*, Chapman and Hall.

THE DESIGN OF PRODUCTS AND SERVICES

INTRODUCTION

Products and services are usually the first thing which customers see of a company. This is why it is important that they are designed to meet customers' needs and expectations. Customers might also expect that designs are updated at frequent intervals to reflect fashion, technological advances or their changing needs. So in addition to the intrinsic merit of its product and service designs, for many organizations, it is also the continual development of designs and the creation of totally new designs which help to shape their competitive position.

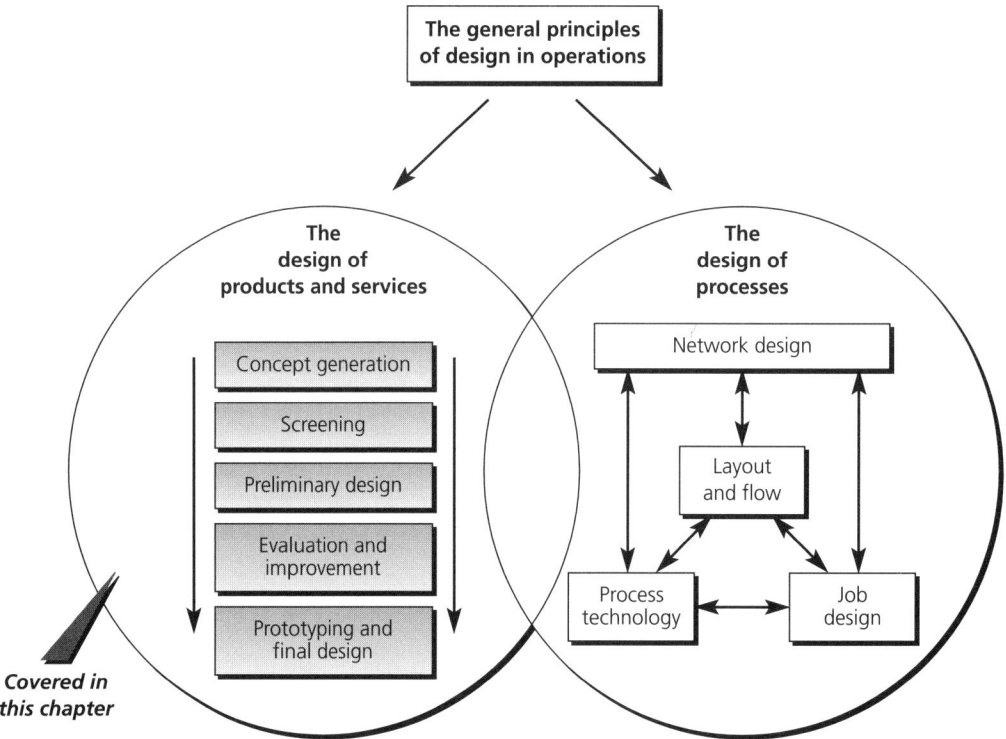

Figure 5.1 The design activities in operations management covered in this chapter

Figure 5.1 shows where this chapter fits into the overall operations design model. Remember though that there is an overlap between product/service design and process design, especially in the design of services. For this reason it is important to include consideration of the process which makes and delivers products and (especially) services.

OBJECTIVES

This chapter will examine:

- the aspects of products and services which need designing (more specifically, how design affects the concept, the package, and the process which comprise the product or service);

- the outputs from the product and service design activity;

- the stages which are involved in designing any product or service:
  - product/service concept generation
  - screening of the concept
  - the preliminary design of the product or service
  - the evaluation and improvement of the preliminary design
  - prototyping and the final design;
- the recent 'interactive' approaches to concurrent and multi-disciplinary design which encourage fast and efficient time-to-market.

THE COMPETITIVE ADVANTAGE OF GOOD DESIGN

The objective of designing products and services is to satisfy customers by meeting their actual or anticipated needs and expectations. This, in turn, enhances the competitiveness of the organization. Product and service design, therefore, can be seen as starting and ending with the customer. First, the task of marketing is to gather information from customers (and sometimes non-customers) in order to understand and identify their needs and expectations, and also to look for possible market opportunities. Following this, the task of the product and service designers is to take those needs and expectations, as interpreted by marketing, and create a specification for the product or service. This is a complex task which involves bringing together many different aspects of a company's objectives (*see* box on Braun). The specification is then used as the input to the operation itself which creates and delivers the product or service to its customers (*see* Fig. 5.2).

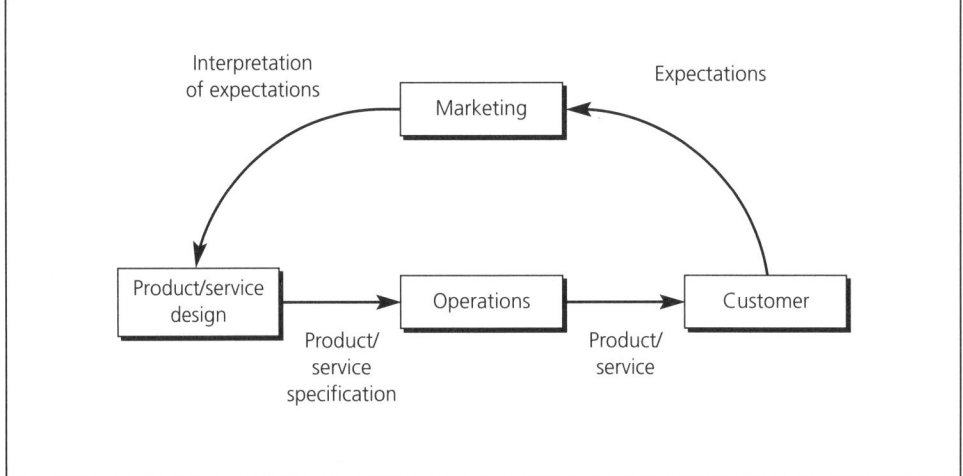

**Figure 5.2
The customer–
marketing–design
feedback loop**

DESIGN PRINCIPLES AT BRAUN AG AND THE NEW BRAUN MULTIMIX[1]

Braun, the leading European manufacturer of small appliances, is renowned for the innovative and functional designs of its products. Its range of around 200 different Braun-branded products is constantly being updated (over 60 per cent of the company's sales are of products which were launched within the last five years). Braun's corporate strategy focuses on a conviction that 'superior performance, achieved through technical and design innovation, must be the primary objective of product development'. Following its convictions, the company has 150 of its products in the permanent collection of Europe's most renowned contemporary art collection in the Centre Pompidou in Paris and has 40 products on permanent exhibition at the New York Museum of Modern Art.

But Braun's design principles go beyond the aesthetic. Its designers follow their 'Ten principles of good design'. As an example of the applications of these, we will describe the design of the Braun Multimix. The design brief was 'to combine three specialist kitchen appliances (blender, food processor, kitchen machine) in such a way that the new single product performs at least as well in each of the applications as the best equivalent specialized product'.

Braun's ten industrial design principles applied to the Multimix

1 *Usefulness.* To Braun engineers, the functionality of a product is the central reason for its existence. They decided to align the motor, gearing and attachments in a single vertical direction (competitive products have horizontal motor and vertical attachments, requiring a complex gearbox). The 'form' of the product then follows its 'function'.

2 *Quality.* Braun designers emphasize four aspects of quality which they believe differentiate the Multimix in the market place. First, its *versatility* provides a full range of tasks required in

cooking; mixing, blending, kneading and chopping – no comparable mixer offers a chopping facility. Second, the high mechanical efficiency of the appliance and the seven speed settings provide *high performance* across the range of tasks from slow kneading to high-speed whipping of cream. Third, many unique *safety features* have been included to prevent contact with moving parts and to prevent accidents. Fourth, the application of *advanced process technology* has enabled many integrated elements to be incorporated in a single moulding. The most complex production moulding tool ever used at Braun was developed to produce two entire housings in one injection moulding step, and to do so without any shrinkage marks which can easily impair a quality finish. This replaces between five and ten individual injection moulding operations that are used by competitors, saving moulding and assembly costs and giving great precision and excellent surface finish.

3 *Ease of use.* Great emphasis was placed on 'human engineering' to ensure that the Multimix is convenient, comfortable to use and easy to clean. Emphasis on small details, such as the central location of the pivoting cord outlet and a soft, plastic non-slip standing ring were developed from user trials.

4 *Simplicity.* Braun engineers believe in achieving maximum results with minimum means: what is relevant is stressed, what is superfluous is omitted. Some of the 'simple features', such as the cord outlet locking device, create a challenge of complex shapes for the company's engineers to overcome.

5 *Clarity.* Particular emphasis is placed on eliminating the need for complex instructions: the Multimix controls 'speak for themselves'. For example, insertion of the attachments automatically sets the appropriate speed range of the drive, and the switch system clearly differentiates between the different speeds, pulse setting and eject button.

6 *Order.* All details of a product such as Multimix have a logical, meaningful place; nothing is arbitrary or coincidental. Order leads to an impression of balance and total harmony, which Braun says is typical of its design philosophy.

7 *Naturalness.* Braun designers, although using simple and even austere designs, strive to avoid any forced, contrived, or artificial decorative elements or finishes. Braun refer to a principle of 'understatement and modesty'.

8 *Aesthetics.* Although aesthetic quality is not a primary objective of the Braun designers during the development process, it is achieved through attention to detail and the quest for order and naturalness.

9 *Innovation.* Braun is committed to achieving long-lasting appeal in its designs, so innovations are carefully developed and brought together for new appliances such as the Multimix.

10 *Truthfulness.* A pervading principle followed by Braun designers is that 'only honest design can be good design', so any attempt to play on people's emotions and weaknesses is avoided. ■

WHAT IS DESIGNED IN A PRODUCT OR SERVICE?

In our broad definition, a product or service is anything that can be offered to customers in order to satisfy their needs and expectations. All products and services can be considered as having three aspects:

● *a concept*, which is the set of expected benefits that the customer is buying;
● *a package* of 'component' products and services that provide those benefits defined in the concept;
● *the process* by which the operation produces the package of 'component' products and services.

Customers buy 'concepts'

When customers make a purchase, they are not simply buying a product or service. They are buying a set of expected benefits to meet their needs and expectations. This is known as the concept of the product or service. For example, when customers buy a washing machine, they are purchasing a set of expected benefits which might include:

● an attractive metal box
● that will fit in a conventional kitchen space
● and will provide the means of cleaning clothes
● over a long period of time
● in the comfort of the customer's own home.

The set of expected benefits is referred to as the *product* or *service concept* – that is, the overall intention of the product or service as seen from the customer's perspective. The concept is not a statement of the physical bits and pieces that we buy, the box, pumps or drum of the washing machine; rather it is the way the customers, and hopefully also the organization, its staff and shareholders, perceive the benefits of the product or service. It follows that, in order to design products or services, operations managers must understand exactly what it is that the customers are buying from them. That is, they must thoroughly understand the concept.

Concepts comprise a package of products and services

Normally the word product implies a tangible physical object, such as a washing machine or a watch, and a service implies a more intangible experience, such as an evening at a restaurant or a night club. In fact, as we discussed in Chapter 1, most, if not all, things that we buy comprise a combination of products *and* services. The purchase of the washing machine includes:

● the product, that is 'the washing machine itself';
● services such as 'warranties', 'after-sales services' and 'the services of the person selling the machine'.

This means that whatever is being designed, whether it is nominally a 'product' or a 'service', it will usually involve designing a collection of component products and services. This collection of products and services is usually referred to as the *package* that customers buy. Some of the products or services in the package are *core*, that is they are fundamental to the purchase and could not be removed without destroying the nature of the package. Other parts will serve to enhance the core. These are *supporting* goods and services. In the case of the washing machine, the attractive box and guarantees are supporting goods and services. The core good is the machine itself.

By changing the core, or adding or subtracting supporting goods and services, organizations can provide different packages, and in so doing design quite different product or service concepts. For instance, a washing machine could be built to a smaller size supporting a concept of a machine for the 'smaller kitchen'. Alternatively, it could be provided without after-sales support and guarantees as an 'economical purchase'. It is defining the package of goods and services which starts the design activity of translating the concept into reality.

Products and services have to be created – the process

This chapter, though primarily focusing on the design of products and services, includes some discussion of process design because of the interrelationships between product or service design and process design. As it was explained in Chapter 4, it is quite possible, particularly in the case of manufactured products, to design the product and the process independently of each other. This is more difficult in services where the process by which the service is delivered is an integral part of the service itself. For example, it is difficult to distinguish between a service that includes food served at the table and the process of bringing the food to the table. The 'process' is the part of the operation that creates the goods and services, puts them together into the package and delivers them to the customer to fulfil the concept.

The provision of most goods and services requires many different types of processes. For example, the washing machine includes three main types of processes:

- the manufacture and assembly of components;
- the retailing of the machine;
- after-sales support and servicing.

Each process can be broken down further into many sub-processes. The manufacture and assembly of components, for example, will include such sub-processes as body pressing, wiring and stock control.

THE STAGES OF DESIGN – FROM CONCEPT TO SPECIFICATION

The outcome of the activity of design is a fully detailed specification of the product or service. The specification will require the collection of information which fully defines the product or service, namely:

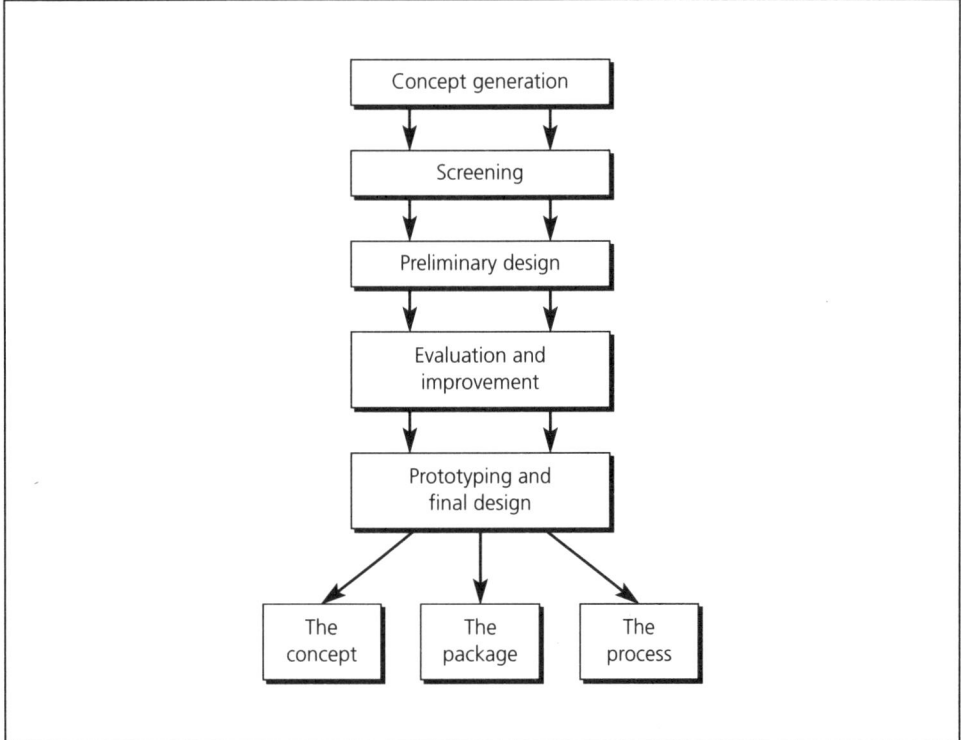

**Figure 5.3
The stages of
product/service
design**

- its overall concept (specifying the form, function and overall purpose of the design and the benefits it will provide);
- its package (specifying all the collection of individual products and services which are required to provide and support the concept);
- the process by which the package will be created (specifying how the various individual products and services in the package are to be produced).

To get to this point, the design activity must pass through several stages. These form an approximate sequence, although in practice designers will occasionally recycle or backtrack through the stages. We will describe them in the order in which they usually occur, as shown in Fig. 5.3.

The *concept generation* stage starts with an idea for a product or service. This may emanate from customers or be required to counter the activities of competitors. These ideas need to be formalized by translating them into a product or service concept. The concepts are then *screened* by different parts of the organization to try to ensure that, in broad terms, they will be a sensible addition to its product/service portfolio. The outcome of these first two stages is an agreed and acceptable product/service concept. The agreed concept has then to be turned into a *preliminary design* of the package and the process. This preliminary design then goes through a stage of *evaluation and improvement* to see if the concept can be served better, more cheaply or more easily. An agreed design can then be subjected to *prototyping and final design*. The outcome of this stage is a fully developed specification of the product or service.

CONCEPT GENERATION

The ideas for new product or service concepts can come from sources, both outside the organization, such as customers or competitors, and from sources within the organization, such as staff (for example, from sales staff and front-of-house staff) or from the R&D department (*see* Fig. 5.4).

Ideas from customers

Marketing is responsible for keeping an eye and ear on the market place in order to identify new opportunities and possible products or services that might be appropriate. There are many market research tools for gathering data in a formal and structured way from customers, including questionnaires and interviews. These techniques, however, usually tend to be structured in such a way as only to test out ideas or check products or services against predetermined criteria. Listening to the customer, in a less structured way, is sometimes seen as a better means of generating new ideas.[2]

Focus groups

One formal but unstructured way of collecting ideas and suggestions from customers is through focus group discussions. A focus group typically comprises seven to ten participants who are unfamiliar with each other but who have been selected because they have certain characteristics in common that relate to the particular topic of the focus group.[3] Participants in focus groups are invited to 'discuss' or 'share ideas with others'. The concept researcher tries to create a permissive environment in the focus

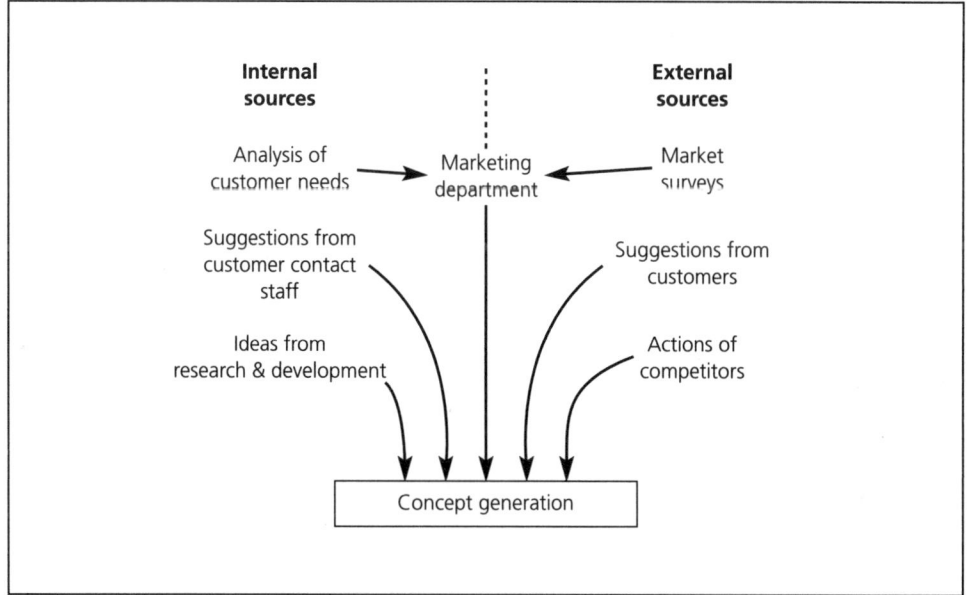

Figure 5.4
Ideas can originate from both inside and outside the organization

145

group that nurtures different perceptions and points of view, without pressurizing participants to vote, plan or reach a consensus. The group discussion is conducted several times with similar types of participants in order to identify trends and patterns in perceptions.

Listening to customers

Many suggestions and ideas may come from customers on a day-to-day basis. Customers may write to complain about a particular product or service, or make suggestions for its improvement or replacement. Ideas may also come in the form of suggestions to staff during the purchase of the product or delivery of the service.

Ideas from competitor activity

Many organizations keep a sharp eye on the activities of their competitors. A new idea translated into a saleable concept, package and process may give a competitor an edge in the market place, even if it is only a temporary one. Competing organizations will then have to decide whether to follow the actions of the competitor with a similar product or service, or alternatively to come up with a somewhat different idea that may minimize or even reverse the competitor's lead.

Ideas from staff

Just one step away from the customers are the people who have to deal directly with them. The contact worker in a service organization or the sales person in a product-oriented organization could meet customers every day. These staff may have good ideas about what customers like and do not like. They may have gathered suggestions from customers or have ideas of their own as to how products or services could be developed to meet the needs of their customers more effectively, or how a gap could be filled in the product or service range.

Ideas from research and development

One formal function found in many product-based organizations (but as yet few service-based organizations) is Research & Development. As its name implies, its role is twofold. Research usually means attempting to develop new knowledge and ideas in order to solve a particular problem or opportunity. Development is the attempt to try to utilize and operationalize the ideas that come from research. In this chapter we are mainly concerned with the 'development' part of R&D – for example, exploiting new ideas that might be afforded by new materials such as thermoplastics or new technologies such as satellite communications.

Reverse engineering

'Reverse engineering' is taking apart a product, to understand how a competing organization has made it. Closely analysing exactly what constitutes a competitor's design

THE PRICE OF NEW PRODUCT FAILURE IN PHARMACEUTICALS[4]

The role of research and development on the product design process can be particularly important in some industries. Pharmaceuticals, for example, is an industry with relatively few major product breakthroughs, but when one does come it can transform a company's prospects. Conversely, if a company fails to come up with a new product, the slide can be equally dramatic. Take Hoffmann-la-Roche, the Swiss pharmaceutical and health care company. Founded over 100 years ago in Basle, it employs over 55 000 staff in over 100 countries world-wide. In 1963 the company's R&D scored a major success with the introduction of its new drug Valium, a tranquillizer. When it became a major seller it made Hoffmann-la-Roche the largest drug company in the world, as well as being one of the most profitable. However, the company failed to continue its pace of development, and had not developed a replacement product by the time its patent on the tranquillizer ran out. Although, now healthy once more, only a few years from the peak of its success, the company came close to bankruptcy. ∎

and how the product has been produced can help to isolate the key features of the design which are worth emulating. As a result a company may amend and incorporate the key features in some way. Alternatively, it might apply to use, under licence, the part of the product that seems to be providing the difference.

Some aspects of services may be more difficult to reverse engineer (especially back-office services) as they are less transparent to competitors. However, by consumer testing a service, it may be possible to make educated guesses about how it has been created. Many service organizations employ 'testers' to check out the services provided by competitors. Just as supermarkets regularly check the prices displayed by rival supermarkets, so too do they investigate new services, such as delivery services, cash-back options, telephone ordering and packing services, to see if they might be suitable for developing or reproducing. Even if particular aspects of a competitor's product or service are not reproducible, they can still provide the stimulus for creativity.

From idea to concept

Ideas are not the same as concepts. In fact ideas need to be transformed into concepts so that they can be evaluated and then 'operationalized' by the organization. Concepts are different to ideas in that they are clear statements that both encapsulate the idea and also indicate the overall form, function, purpose and benefits of the idea (*see* Fig. 5.5). The concept should be simple to communicate so that everyone in the organization can understand it, make it, and sell it.

Example: Adventure holiday

An adventure holiday company may see an opportunity to expand its coverage of holidays into a younger age group than it currently serves. The 'idea', therefore, is to

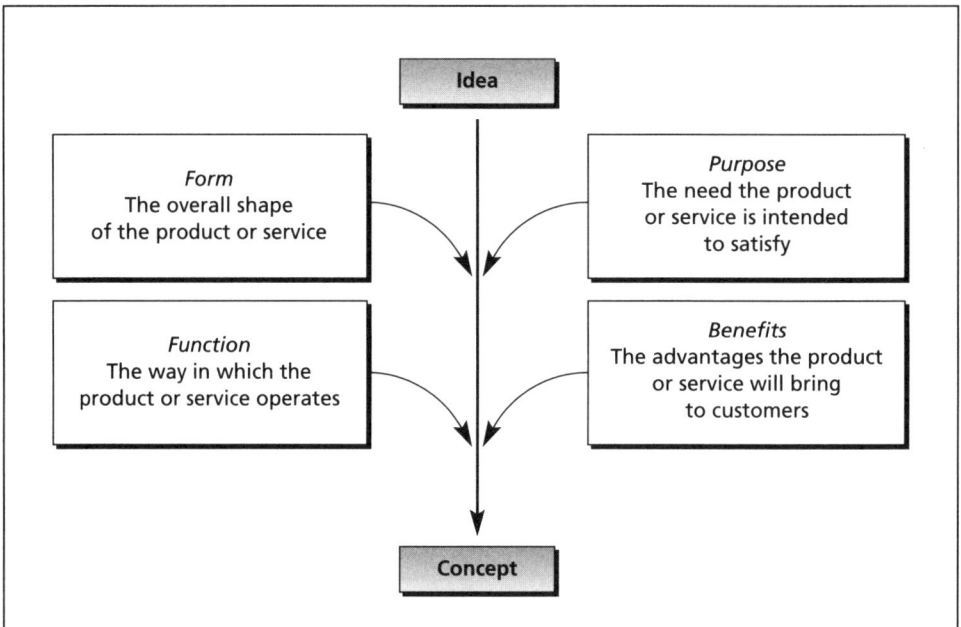

**Figure 5.5
Transforming an
idea into a concept**

provide adventure holidays for 10 to 12 year olds. To 'operationalize' the idea – that is, to know what you are selling to customers – the form, function, purpose and benefits of the idea need to be encapsulated into a statement of concept. This is done in Fig. 5.6.

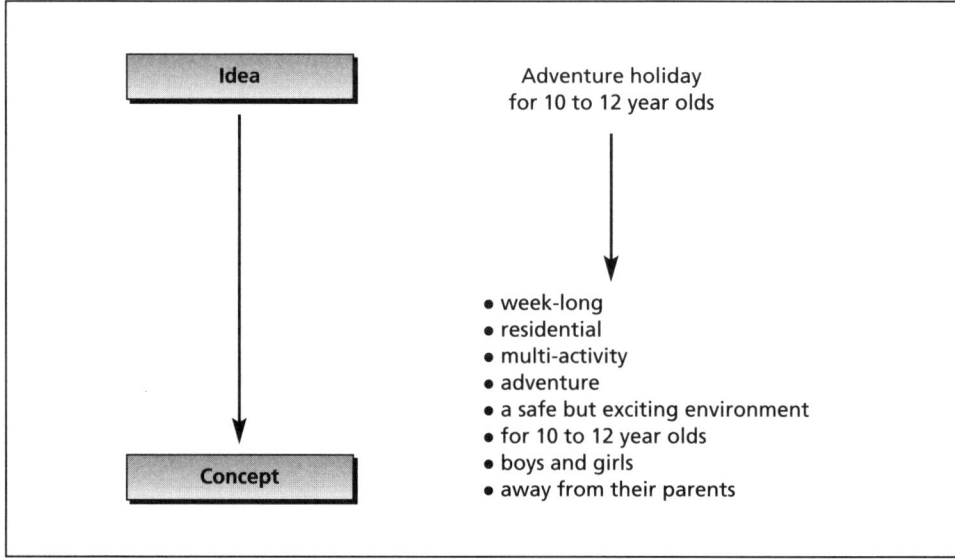

**Figure 5.6
Transforming an
idea into a concept
for an adventure
holiday**

148

CONCEPT SCREENING

Not all concepts which are generated will necessarily be capable of further development into products and services. Designers need to be selective as to which concepts they progress to the point of designing the preliminary aspects of their package and processes. The purpose of the concept screening stage is to take the flow of concepts emerging from the organization and evaluate them for their feasibility, acceptability and 'vulnerability' or risk (*see* Chapter 4). Concepts may have to pass through many different screens, and several functions might be involved (for example, marketing, operations and finance), though they may each use different criteria to screen the proposals (*see* Fig. 5.7).

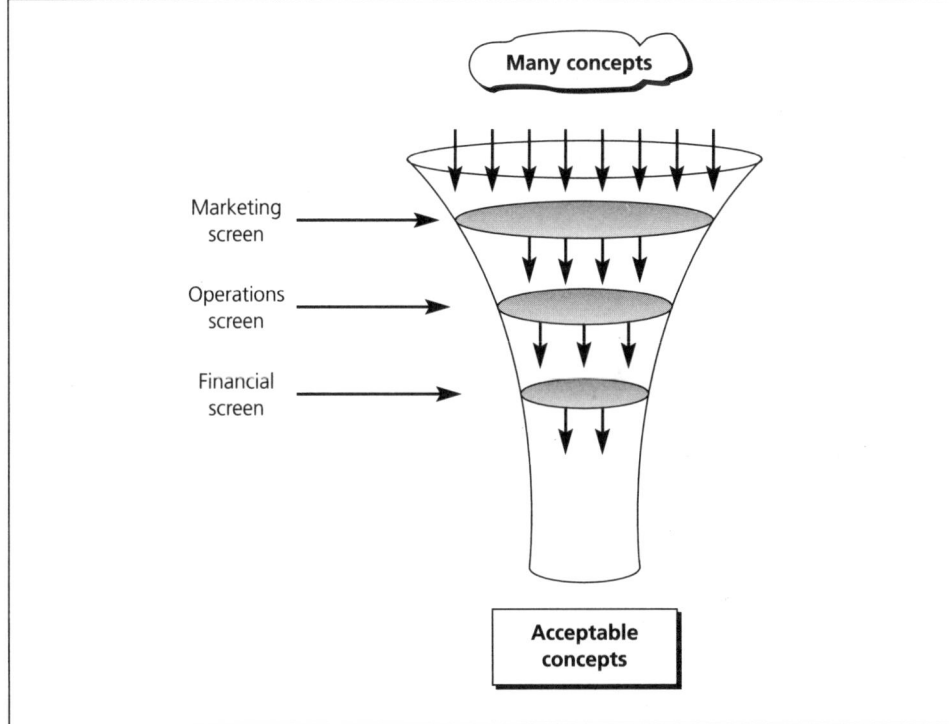

Figure 5.7
Concept screening involves progressively filtering concepts

The marketing screen

From its close relationship with customers and knowledge of the market place, marketing may be concerned to screen out concepts that it feels:

● will not work in the markets;
● are too similar to, or even too different from, competing products or services;
● would not be able to generate sufficient demand to make it worthwhile;
● will not fit with existing marketing policy.

The operations screen

At this stage the operations function is primarily concerned with the feasibility of the new product/service concepts. It needs to judge whether it can produce the product or provide the service. In particular, it needs to decide whether it has available, or could make available, the following resources:

- the capacity within the operation;
- the skills in its human resources;
- the technology which would be necessary.

In addition, the operations function will need to provide the information which can be used to estimate the likely cost of creating the product or service.

Finance screen

The finance department will need to calculate the financial implications of any new product or service such as:

- capital and investment requirements;
- operating costs;
- profit margins;
- likely pay-back rate.

PRELIMINARY DESIGN

Having generated a product or service concept that is acceptable to the various parts of an organization, an organization tackles the next stage, which is to create a preliminary design. The objective of this stage is to have a first attempt at:

- specifying the component products and services in the *package*;
- defining the *processes* to create the package.

Specify the components of the package

The first task in this stage of design is to define exactly what will go into the product or service, that is, specifying the components of the package. This will require the collection of information about such things as the *constituent component parts* which make up the product or service package, *the product/service structure*, that is the order in which the component parts of the package have to be put together, and the *bill of materials* (BOM), that is the quantities of each component part required to make up the total package. The BOM, in particular, is a method of defining products or services which is used widely in other areas of operations management's activity (*see* for example Chapter 14).

Example: Adventure holiday

Each activity on the adventure holiday can be broken down in this way. For example, the materials and equipment needed for each child to undertake the rifle-shooting activity might include:

- a .22 air rifle
- some shot
- a backboard
- a target holder
- some card targets
- some model targets.

The product/service structure is shown in Fig. 5.8. The bill of materials which incorporates the product/service structure and also includes the quantities which will be required is shown in Table 5.1.

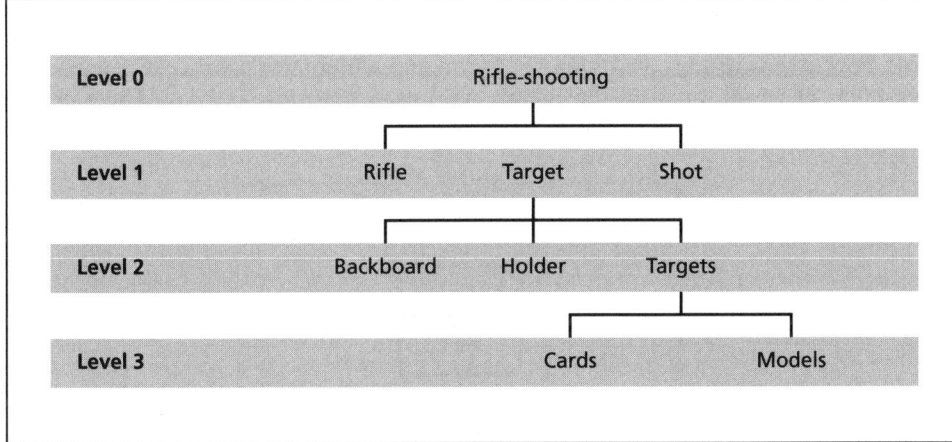

**Figure 5.8
The product/
activity structure
for rifle-shooting**

Table 5.1 Bill of materials for the rifle-shooting activity

Level 0	Level 1	Level 2	Level 3	Quantity
Rifle-shooting activity				
	Rifle			1
	Shot			50
	Target			
		Backboard		1
		Holder		1
		Targets		
			Cards	10
			Models	5

Define the processes to create the package

The product/service structure and bill of materials specify *what* has to be put together; the next stage is to specify *how* the processes will put together the various components to create the final product or service. There are many techniques which can be used for documenting processes (or *blueprinting,* as it is sometimes called). However, all the techniques have two main features:[5]

- they show the *flow* of materials or people or information through the operation;
- they identify the different *activities* that take place during the process.

We shall examine four common types of blueprinting techniques here. These are:

- simple flow charts
- routing sheets
- process flow charts
- the customer-processing framework.

Simple flow charts

Simple flow charts are used to identify the main elements of a process. Figure 5.9 shows a flow chart for a person during one day on an adventure holiday. These charts can also be used for flows of materials or information.

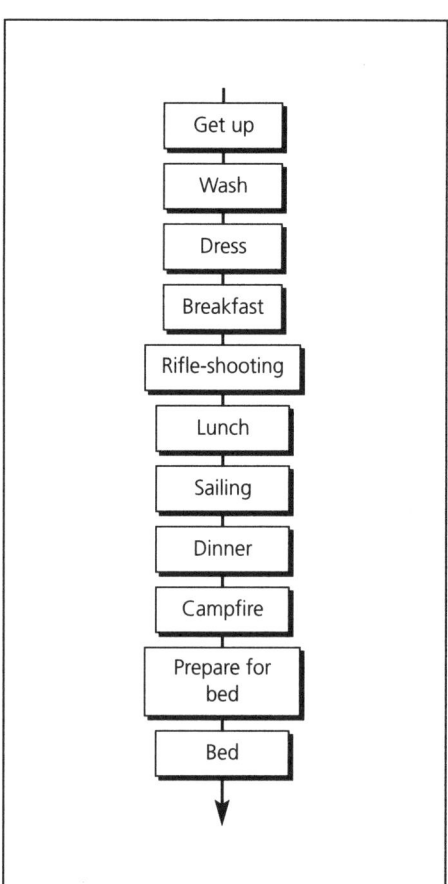

**Figure 5.9
Simple flow chart
of one day's
activity on the
adventure holiday**

Flow charts showing flows of information can be enhanced by the addition of computer charting symbols identifying the key decisions in the process and the implications of each decision. Figure 5.10 shows a flow chart which indicates the flow of information in the customer enquiries bureau of an electricity utility company.

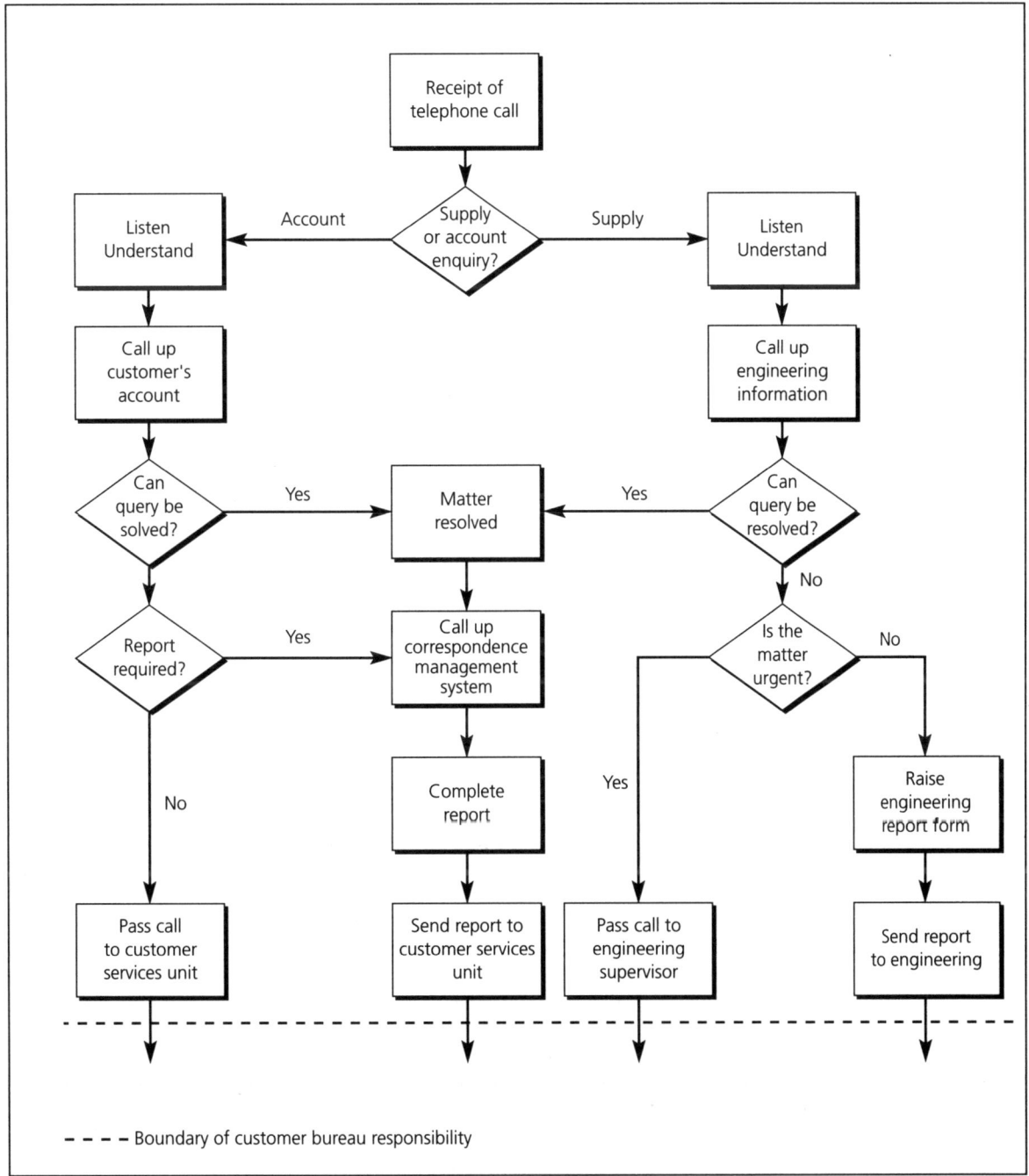

Figure 5.10 Information flow chart for a customer enquiry bureau of a utility company

Routing sheets

Routing sheets (also known as operations process charts) provide more information about the activities involved in the process, including a description of the activity and the tools or equipment needed. Part of a route sheet for the assembly of a telephone is shown in Fig. 5.11.

Route sheet

Item	Telephone h1209	**Date**	1 / 5 / 95
Item No.	# 1209 (h)	**Issued by**	

Operation number	Operation description	Equipment
1	Assemble earpiece and mouthpiece	Jig #24/35A
2	Fix to lower casing	Jig #24/122
3	Insert and fix cord	Wire stripper (type #22)
		and screwholder/driver
4	Assemble upper casing	-- --
5	Align and seal	Jig #24/490 and polysege
6	Light and vibration test	Qualitest 12 (main #488)
		and vibration board

**Figure 5.11
Routing sheet
for a telephone**

Process flow chart

The most commonly used chart for documenting processes in operations management is the process flow chart. This type of chart, as well as documenting the flow and the various activities, uses a number of different symbols to identify the different types of activities (*see* Fig. 5.12).

Process flow charts permit a more detailed evaluation of a design. Figure 5.13 shows a process flow chart for one day on an adventure holiday. This charting method is covered in greater detail in Appendix 3 at the end of this book.

Customer-processing framework

The customer-processing framework[6] is a charting method devised specifically for customer flows. It identifies some of the key activities that may occur in 'processing' customers through an operation, including:

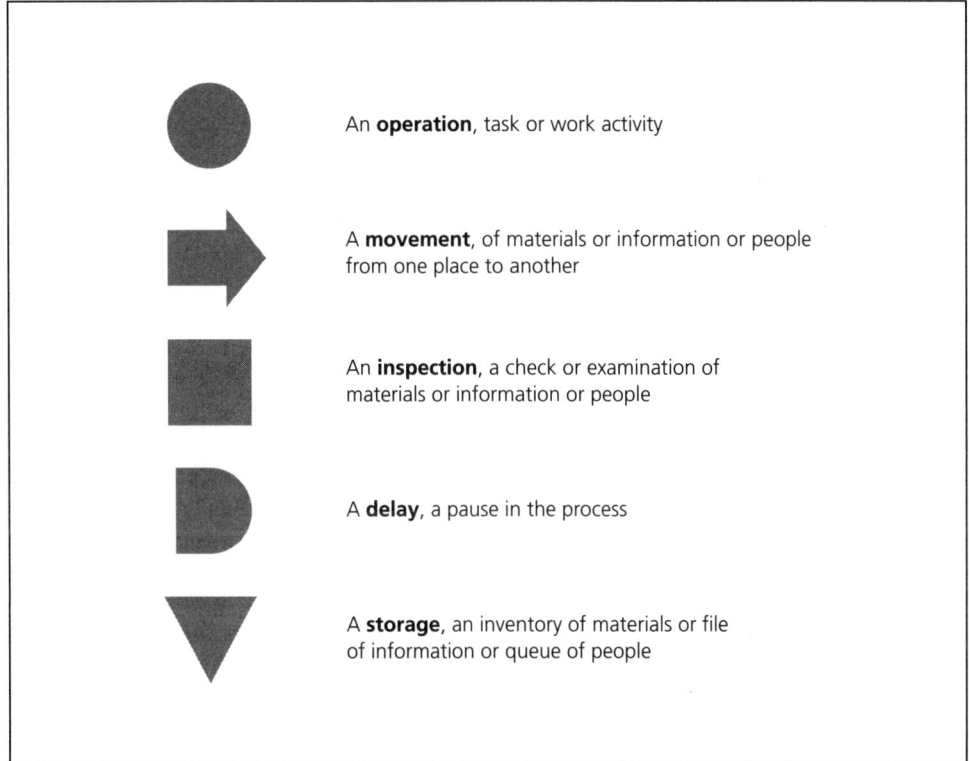

Figure 5.12
Process flow chart symbols

- the *selection* – the decision by the customer to choose one of several possible service operations;
- the *point of entry* – the point at which the customer first makes contact with the chosen operation, either physically by entering the system, or remotely by telephone, for example;
- the *response time* – the time a customer has to wait for the system to respond;
- the *point of impact* – the moment at which the service worker starts to deal with the customer;
- the *delivery* – the part of the process which delivers the core service to the customer;
- the *point of departure* – the point at which the customer leaves the service process;
- the *follow up* – the activities of the service staff to check on the customer after the completion of the service.

Figure 5.14 illustrates these key stages in the design of a hospital's Accident and Emergency Department. However, when examined in more detail, most service operations comprise several customer-processing sequences which may be in series and/or in parallel with each other. The number of processes and the interrelationships between them are indications of the scale and complexity of the operations task.

Flow process chart

	Activity	A day on the adventure holiday	Location	Perinong				

	Description of element	●	➡	D	■	▼
1	Get up					
2	Go to wash room					
3	Wash, brush teeth					
4	Return to bedroom					
5	Dress					
6	Go to dining room					
7	Await serving					
8	Eat					
9	Go to rifle range					
10	Await instructor and equipment					
11	Check equipment					
12	Rifle-shooting					
13	Go to dining room					
14	Eat lunch					
15	Go to bedroom					
16	Prepare for sailing					
17	Go to lake					
18	Await instructor					
19	Check equipment					
20	Sailing					
21	Go to bedroom					
22	Change					
23	Go to dining room					
24	Eat					
25	Wait for camp fire					
26	Camp fire					
27	Go to bedroom					
28	Prepare for bed					
29	Go to wash room					
30	Go to bed					
31	Go to toilet					
32	Go to bed again					
33	Sleep					

Figure 5.13 Process flow chart for one day on an adventure holiday

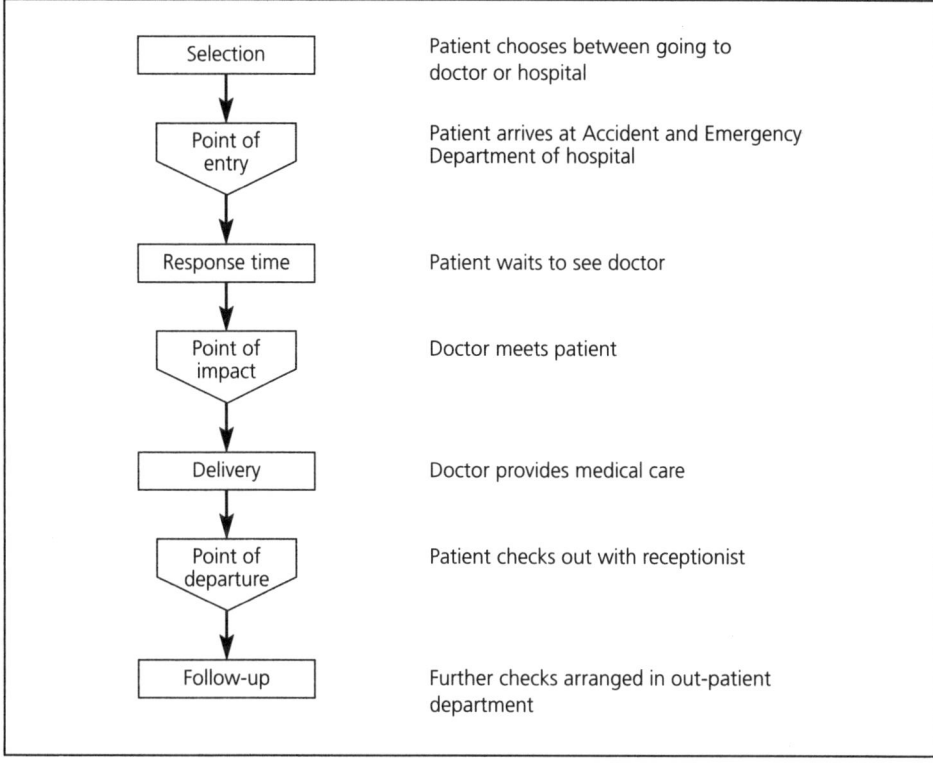

Figure 5.14
Key stages as shown on a customer-processing framework diagram for a patient receiving treatment in an Accident and Emergency Department

DESIGN EVALUATION AND IMPROVEMENT

The purpose of this stage in the design activity is to take the preliminary design and see if it can be improved before the product or service is tested in the market. There are a number of techniques that can be employed at this stage to evaluate and improve the preliminary design. Here we treat three which have proved particularly useful. They are:

- Quality function deployment (QFD)
- Value engineering (VE)
- Taguchi methods.

Quality function deployment

The key purpose of quality function deployment is to try to ensure that the eventual design of a product or service actually meets the needs of its customers. Customers may not have been considered explicitly since the concept generation stage, and therefore it is appropriate to check that what is being proposed for the design of the product or service will meet those needs.

Quality function deployment (QFD) is a technique that was developed in Japan at Mitsubishi's Kobe shipyard and used extensively by Toyota, the motor vehicle

HOW ICL USES QFD[8]

In ICL, the computer company, a small team is formed to work on a new product opportunity or enhancement. A typical team consists of two customers, one marketing professional, two engineers, and one manufacturing or service representative. The team, which is kept small, is assisted by a facilitator who provides training in the priority and matrix techniques as required. The team will translate the needs into solutions, using the information to concentrate their efforts on the features which provide most value to customers.

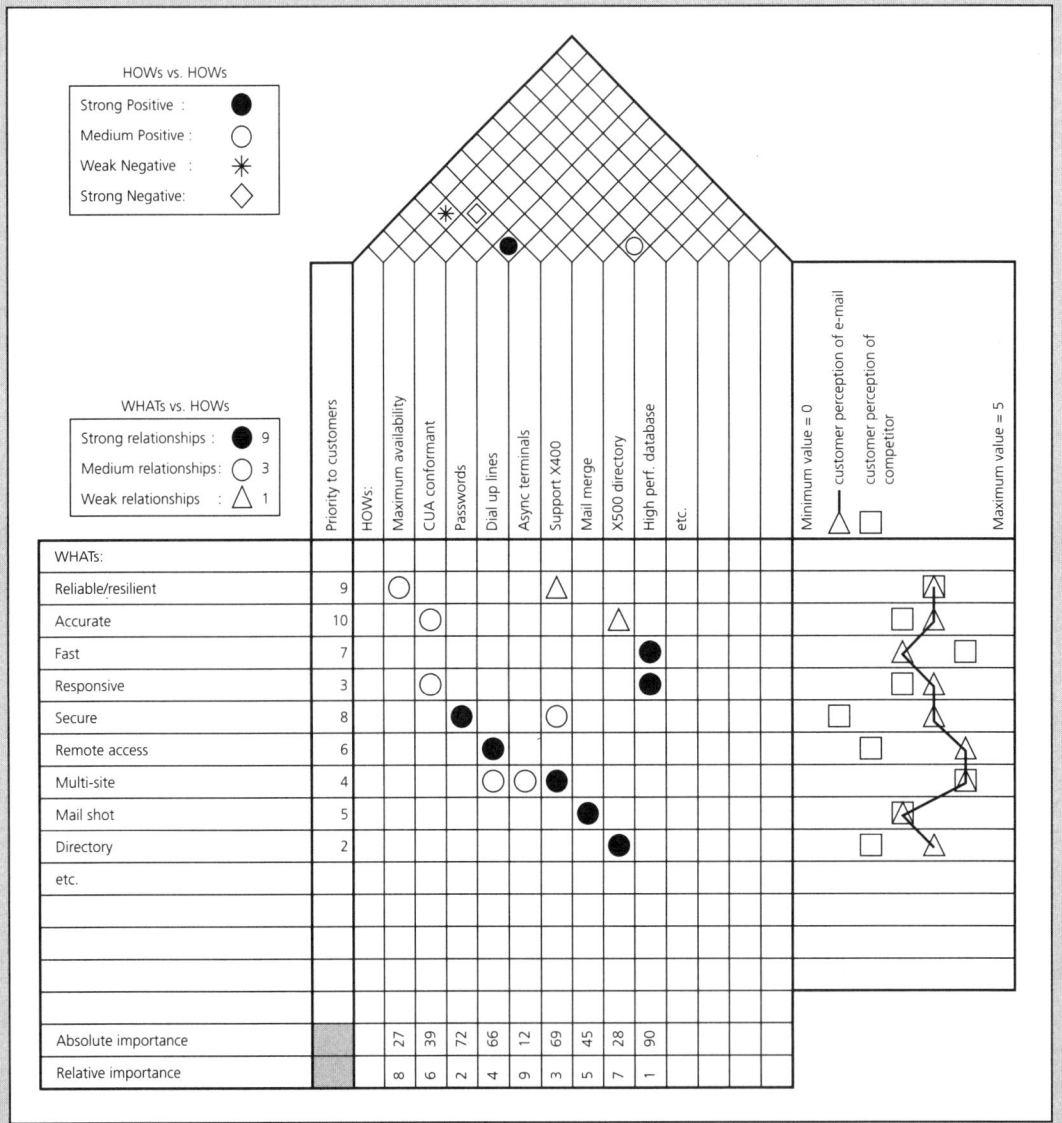

Figure 5.15 Quality function deployment used to investigate the design of an electronic mail product
Source: Courtesy of ICL Training

158

The example shown in Fig. 5.15 is an extract from a typical study about a product requirement – in this case electronic mail. The customers' needs are shown, and their opinions about a similar product from a competitor. The various sections of the matrix are explained in the order they are used.

A The *whats* are verbatim customer perceived needs, and the *relative priority* of these is recorded (with *accurate* being the highest priority in this case).
B The customers' perception of how a competitor's mail system might perform is recorded on the right. The triangle is the assessment of ICL's system, and the square of the competitor's. They are better than the competitor for remote access, but worse for fast.
C The team then uses brain-storming techniques to work out *how* the needs can best be met.
D The central matrix represents the team's view of the interrelationship between the *whats* and *hows*, based on a value judgement of whether the contribution made by each how towards meeting a particular need is strong, medium, weak or none. (For example, the relationship between passwords and secure is strong.) All the relationships are studied, but in many cases there is none.

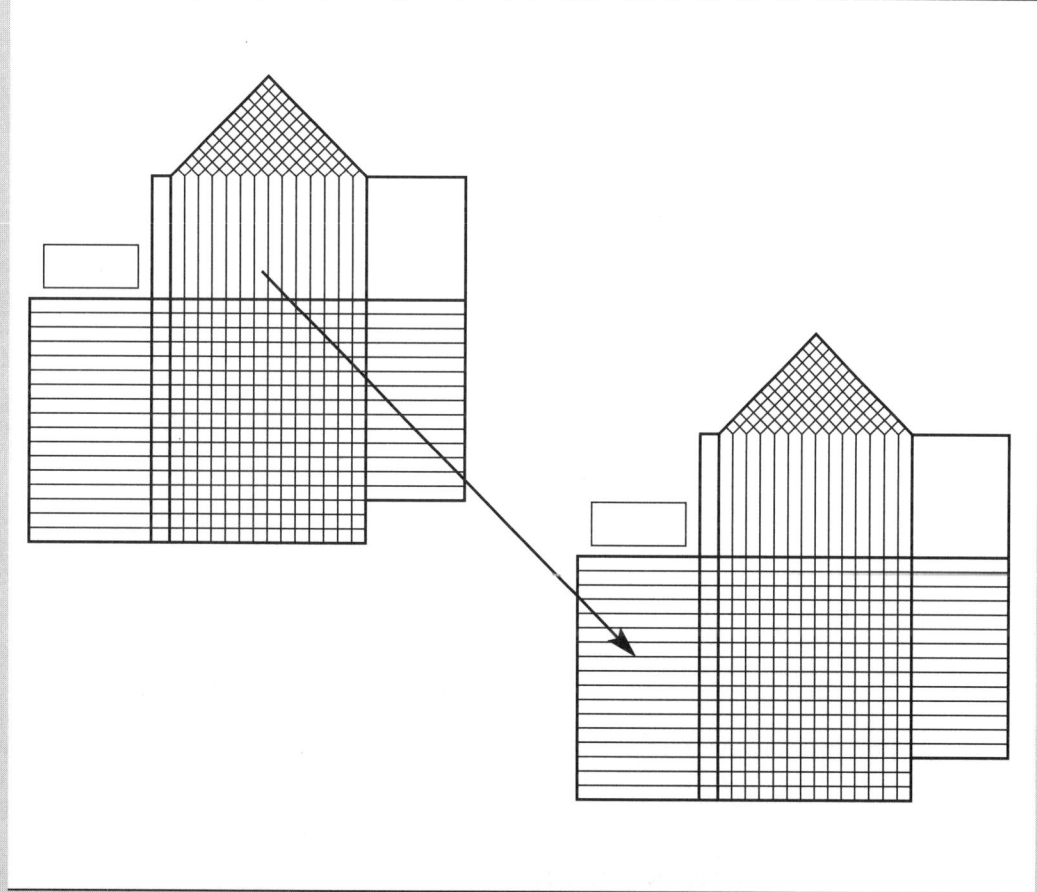

Figure 5.16 Quality function deployment matrices can be linked with the 'hows' of the upper matrix forming the 'whats' of the lower

▶

E A calculation which combines the customer priority and the interrelationships gives the *absolute importance*. (For example, dial up lines has an importance of 6×9 + 4×3 = 66.) The ranking of the *hows* is given by numerical calculation and gives the *relative importance*. In this case high performance database is the most important.

F The roof of the House captures any information the team have about the correlations (positive) or conflicts (negative) between the *hows*.

Next the *hows*, with target values, are listed in priority order, and are taken forward for future evaluation. In particular, if there is inadequate time or resources to provide all the elements of the solution, a subset can be selected which maximizes customer satisfaction.

The continuing work can also be represented by a House of Quality, where the *hows* from the previous stage become the *whats* of the next (*see* Fig. 5.16). Some experienced users of QFD have up to four houses. If engineering or process trade-offs need to be made at a later stage, the interrelated Houses enable the effect on customer perception to be determined. ∎

manufacturer, and its suppliers. It is also known as the 'House of Quality' (because of its shape) and the 'Voice of the Customer' (because of its purpose). The technique tries to capture *what* the customer needs and *how* it might be achieved.[7]

Value engineering

The purpose of value engineering is to try to reduce costs, and prevent any unnecessary costs, before producing the product or service. Simply put, it tries to eliminate any costs that do not contribute to the value and performance of the product or service. (Value analysis is the name given to the same process when it is concerned with cost reduction after the product or service has been introduced.)

Value engineering programmes are usually conducted by project teams consisting of designers, purchasing specialists, operations managers and financial analysts. Pareto analysis (*see* Chapters 12 and 18) is often used to identify the parts of the package that are worthy of most attention. The team analyses the function and cost of those elements and tries to find any similar components that could do the same job at lower cost. More specifically, the team would attempt to:

● reduce the number of components;
● use cheaper materials;
● simplify the processes.

For example, Motorola, the electronics manufacturer, used value engineering to reduce the production cost of its cellular phone. Initially its cellular phone had about 3200 parts. Three years later, after value engineering its new models, the number of parts had been reduced to 400. In so doing, the time to make the phone had been reduced from 40 hours to less than two.

Value engineering requires innovative and critical thinking but it is also carried out using a formal procedure. The procedure examines the purpose of the product or service, its basic functions and its secondary functions. Taking an example of a telephone:

- The *purpose* of the telephone is to communicate with another person.
- The *basic functions* are to hear and speak to the other person.
- The *secondary functions* are to connect with the other person's equipment, to key other numbers and to store other people's telephone numbers.

Team members would then propose ways to improve the secondary functions by combining, revising or eliminating them. For example, the earpiece and mouthpiece could be incorporated into the base casing, eliminating the need for a handset, or the circuitry and dial pad could be incorporated into the handset, eliminating the need for a base. All ideas would then be checked for feasibility, acceptability and vulnerability and their contribution to the value and purpose of the product or service.

Cost-to-function analyses

A revealing analysis of any product or service can be gained by examining how much of its cost is spent on its primary and secondary functions. Components of the product or service which seem to be taking up a disproportionate share of the total cost when related to their function would warrant special attention. For example, Table 5.2 shows the breakdown of the washing machine's functions and the percentage of the total cost of the product which is devoted to achieving each function. In this case 77.09 per cent of its cost is associated with achieving its basic function.[9] As the machine is an automatic model, much of the cost is devoted to controlling the sequence of its activities. After the functions which provide the washing and controlling function, the remainder of the cost is spent on the functions which make the machine practical in operation and marketable to customers.

Table 5.2 The functional breakdown of a washing machine

Function	% of cost	Cumulative % of costs
Control operations	24.41	24.41
Provide or restrain motion	28.48	52.82
Distribute water	11.09	63.91
Retain water	8.89	72.80
Heat water	4.29	77.09
Provide protection	10.07	87.16
Position parts	6.67	93.82
Look attractive	6.18	100.00

The washing function / A practical machine / A marketable product

Taguchi methods

The main purpose of Taguchi methods, as advocated by Genichi Taguchi,[10] is to test the robustness of a design. The basis of the idea is that the product or service should still perform in extreme conditions. A telephone, for example, should still work even when it has been knocked on to the floor. Although one does not expect customers to knock a telephone to the floor, this does happen and so the need to build strength into the casing should be considered in its design.

Likewise a pizza parlour should be able to cope with a sudden rush of customers and an hotel should be able to cope with early arrivals. Product and service designers therefore need to brain-storm to try to identify all the possible situations that might occur and check that the product or service is capable of dealing with those that are deemed to be necessary and cost effective.

In the case of the adventure holiday, for example, the designers need to plan for such contingencies as:

- foul weather – the need for bad weather alternatives;
- equipment failure – the provision of enough equipment to cover for maintenance;
- staff shortages – flexible working to allow cover from one area to another;
- accidents – the ability to deal with an accident without jeopardizing the other children in the group, with easily accessible first-aid equipment, and using facilities and equipment that are easy to clean and unlikely to cause damage to children;
- illnesses – the ability to deal with ill children who are unable to take part in an activity.

The job of the product or service designer is to achieve a design which can cope with all these uncertainties. The major problem designers face is that the number of design factors which they could vary to try to cope with the uncertainties, when taken together, is very large. For example, in designing the telephone casing there could be many thousands of combinations of casing size, casing shape, casing thickness, materials, jointing methods, etc. Performing all the investigations (or experiments as they are called in the Taguchi technique) to try to find a combination of design factors which gives an optimum design can be a lengthy process. The Taguchi procedure is a statistical procedure for carrying out relatively few experiments and yet still being able to determine the best combination of design factors. Here 'best' means the lowest cost and the highest degree of uniformity.

PROTOTYPING AND FINAL DESIGN

The next stage in the design activity is to turn the improved design into a prototype so that it can be tested. It may be too risky to go into full production of the holiday, before testing it out, so it is usually more appropriate to create a prototype.

Product prototypes may include card or clay models and computer simulations, for example. Service prototypes may also include computer simulations but also the actual implementation of the service on a pilot basis. Many retailing organizations pilot new products and services in a small number of stores in order to test customers' reaction to them.

Computer-aided design (CAD)

The construction of physical prototypes has been eased as a result of the use of new technologies such as computer-aided design (CAD). CAD entails the use of computer simulations of products where the performance of the product can be tested to a high degree of accuracy without physical testing. Similar computer simulations are also used in the simulation of many services, such as the scheduling of aircraft to landing slots and the training of aircraft pilots. It should be stressed, however, that CAD is not only used in the prototyping stage of design. It is now extensively used in all stages.

CAD systems provide the computer-aided ability to create and modify product drawings. These systems allow conventionally used shapes (called entities) such as points, lines, arcs, circles, and text, to be added to a computer-based representation of the product. Once incorporated into the design, these entities can be copied, moved about, rotated through angles, magnified, or deleted. The designs thus created can be saved in the memory of the system and retrieved for later use. This enables a library of standardized drawings of parts and components to be built up. Not only can this dramatically increase the productivity of the process but it also aids the standardization of parts in the design activity.

CAD hardware

CAD systems can be configured in various ways. These range from using large mainframe computers down to single PC-based systems. Most configurations follow the pattern as shown in Fig. 5.17, however, CAD systems first of all need some kind of input device – these include such things as joysticks, light pens, electronic tablets, a mouse, or even the keyboard itself. The processing unit includes the central processing unit (CPU) and the software. The data storage part of the system usually includes either disk storage or magnetic tape storage. The display unit is usually a graphic terminal while the output device can either be a printer or a plotter.

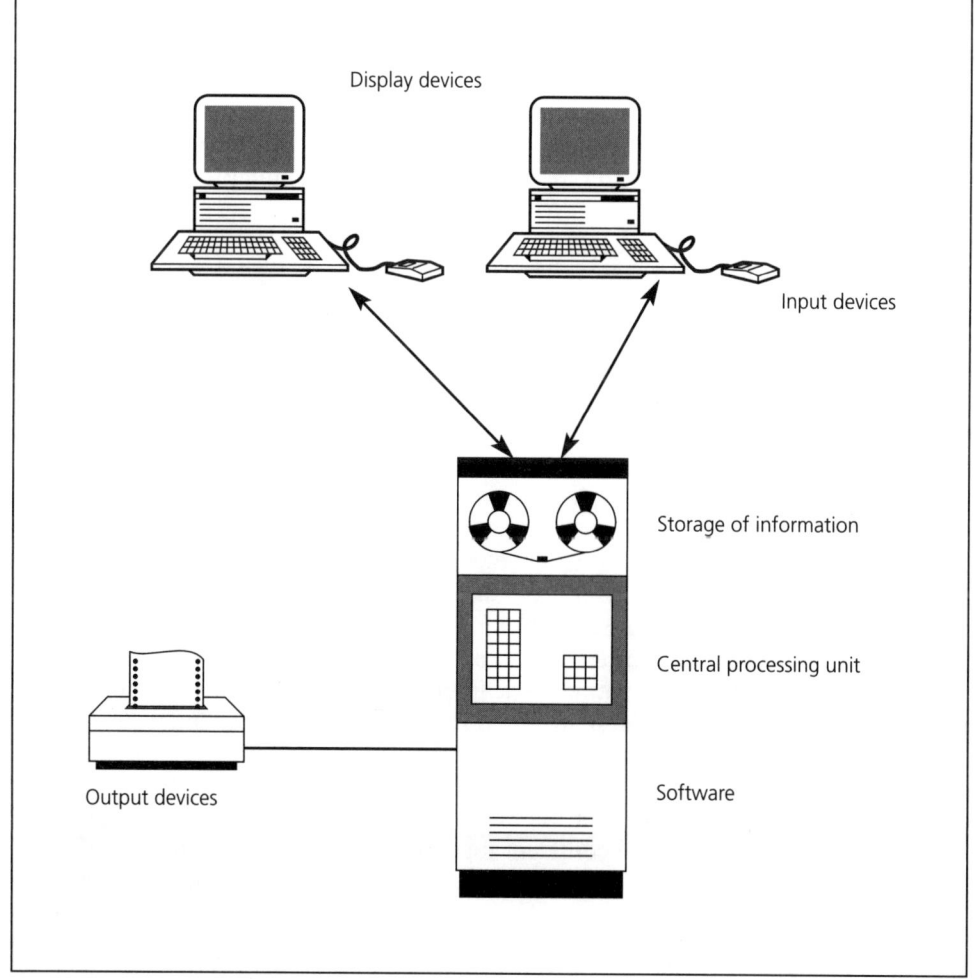

Figure 5.17
The general configuration of a CAD system

CAD software

The software used in CAD systems varies in its degree of sophistication and modelling ability. The simplest type models only on two dimensions. This produces plans and elevations of the design in a similar way to a conventional engineering 'blueprint'. More sophisticated systems can model products in three dimensions. This can be done in very basic form by 'extruding' the two-dimensional image to give thickness to different parts of the two-dimensional shape. However, this approach is not capable of modelling complex products. It is often known as the two-and-a-half dimension approach. True three-dimensional software is capable of presenting an object accurately in full three-dimensional form. It may do this either by representing the edges and corners of the shape (known as a wire-frame model) or as a full solid model. The advantage of wire-frame modelling is that it demands considerably less computer power because an object is represented only by its outline. However, for complex objects wire-frame models can be confusing.

The advantages of CAD

The most obvious advantage of CAD systems is that their ability to store and retrieve design data quickly, as well as their ability to manipulate design details, can considerably increase the productivity of the design activity. In addition to this, however, because changes can be made rapidly to designs, CAD systems can considerably enhance the flexibility of the design activity, enabling modifications to be made much more rapidly. Further, the use of standardized libraries of shapes and entities can reduce the possibility of errors in the design. Perhaps most significantly, though, CAD can be seen as a prototyping device as well as a drafting device. In effect the deigner is modelling the design in order to assess its suitability prior to full production.

SIEMENS – THE DEVELOPMENT OF THE 'EURO-SCOUT' PROJECT[11]

Testing out a prototype design in practice is particularly important when the consequences of design flaws could kill the project. The rapidly emerging technologies of traffic management are one such example. The technology, which attempts to reduce or relieve traffic congestion, is based on the idea of a driver being able to receive 'on-line' traffic information, details of parking facilities, public transport timetables, and recommended or preferred routes for a particular journey. The information can be displayed in the vehicle on a screen and by a synthesized voice.

Siemens, the German electronics and communications company, is one of the leaders in this field, and has been promoting the idea of a 'Pan European Intelligent Vehicle Highway System'. Their own project is named Euro-Scout and is formed from a network of linking inner-city and out-of-town management centres. To test out their prototypes the Berlin-based project was trialled with 700 vehicles participating. During the introductory stages of the project, designers were concerned that such a system would distract the drivers' attention from the road, but the commissioning (prototyping) trials have shown that, by presenting the information in the form of a pictogram and by using a precise synthesized speech output, the driver is not distracted to any significant extent. As the project progressed, new and better features were incorporated. Siemens became confident that the idea would help reduce vehicle emission, enhance fuel economy, and save time, by balancing traffic flow in built-up areas. ■

THE BENEFITS OF INTERACTIVE DESIGN

Operations managers should have some involvement, from the initial evaluation of the concept right through to the production of the product or service and its introduction to the market. Merging the design of products/services and the processes which create them is sometimes called *interactive design*.

The benefits of interactive design are best described in terms of the elapsed time taken for the whole design activity, from concept through to market introduction. This is often called the design's *time-to-market* (TTM). The argument in favour of reducing time-to-market is quite simply that doing so gives increased competitive advantage. For example, if it takes a company five years to develop a product from concept to market, with a given set of resources, it can introduce a new product only once every five years. If its rival can develop products in three years it can introduce its new product, together with its (presumably) improved performance, once every three years. This means that the rival company does not have to make such radical improvements in performance each time it introduces a new product because it is introducing its new products more frequently. In other words, shorter TTM means that companies get more opportunities to improve the performance of their products or services.

In addition, if a company is late in getting its products and services to market compared to its competitors, the effects will be felt on its costs, its revenue and therefore its overall profitability. If the development process takes longer than expected (or even worse, longer than its competitors) two effects are likely to show. The first is that the costs of development will increase. Perhaps more seriously, the late introduction of the product or service will delay the revenue from its sale (and possibly reduce the total revenue substantially if competitors have already got to the market with their own products or services). The net effect of this could be not only a considerable reduction in sales but also reduced profitability – an outcome which could considerably extend the time before the company breaks even on its investment in the new product or service. This is illustrated in Fig. 5.18.

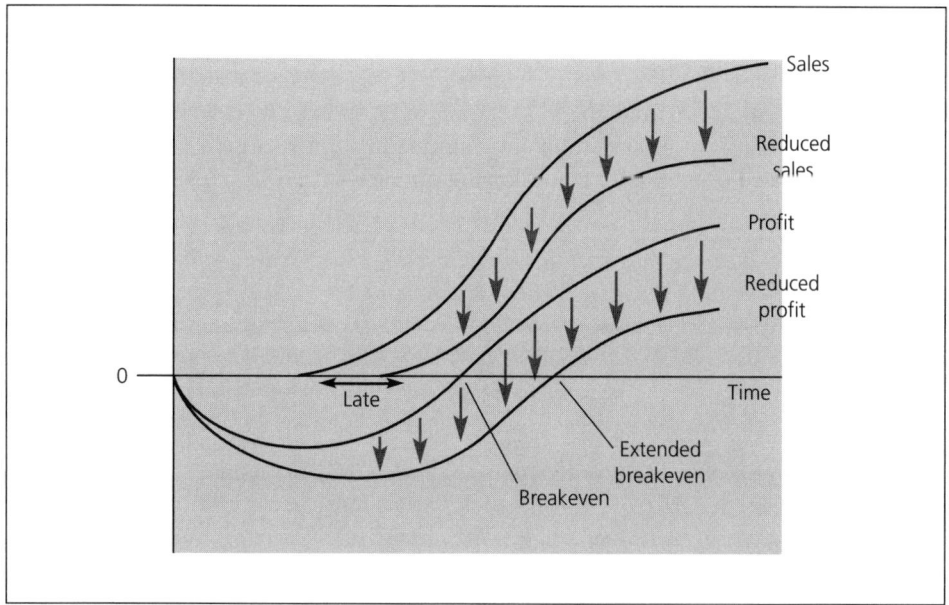

**Figure 5.18
Late design and development increases costs and reduces sales and profits**

A number of factors have been suggested which can significantly reduce time-to-market for a product or services, including the following:

- simultaneous development of the various stages in the overall process;
- an early resolution of design conflict and uncertainty;
- an organizational structure which reflects the development project.

Simultaneous development

Earlier in the chapter we described the design process as essentially a set of individual, predetermined stages. Sometimes one stage is completed before the next one commences. This step-by-step, or *sequential*, approach has traditionally been the typical form of product/service development. The main problem of the sequential approach is that it is both time consuming and costly. When each stage is separate, with a clearly defined set of tasks, any difficulties encountered during the design at one stage might necessitate the design being halted while responsibility moves back to the previous stage. This sequential approach is shown in Fig. 5.19(a).

Often there is really little need to wait until the absolute finalization of one stage, however, before starting the next. For example, perhaps while generating the concept, the evaluation activity of screening and selection could be started. It would have to be a crude evaluation maybe, but nevertheless it is likely that some concepts could be judged as 'non-starters' relatively early on in the process of idea generation. Similarly, during the screening stage, it is likely that some aspects of the design will become obvious before the phase is finally complete. Therefore the preliminary work on these parts of the design could be commenced before the end of the final screening and selection process. This principle can be taken right through all the stages of design. In other words, one stage commences before the previous one has finished, so there is *simultaneous* or *concurrent* work on the stages (*see* Fig. 5.19(b)).

Simultaneous engineering

What we have called simultaneous development is often called simultaneous (or concurrent) engineering in manufacturing operations. Although there is no single universally accepted definition of simultaneous engineering, most organizations' views are reasonably similar. For example, the following quotations give an idea of how the term is understood.

'Simultaneous engineering means that people who design or manufacture products work under the same targets and the same sense of values to tackle the same problems enthusiastically from the early phases. The targets here are the reduction of lead time, design for manufacturing, product development and development of advanced production technologies. The common measure of value is the satisfaction of customers, which is one of the corporate philosophies of the entire company.'[12]

'Simultaneous engineering attempts to optimize the design of the product and manufacturing process to achieve reduced lead times and improve quality and cost by the integration of design and manufacturing activities and by maximizing parallelism in working practices.'[13]

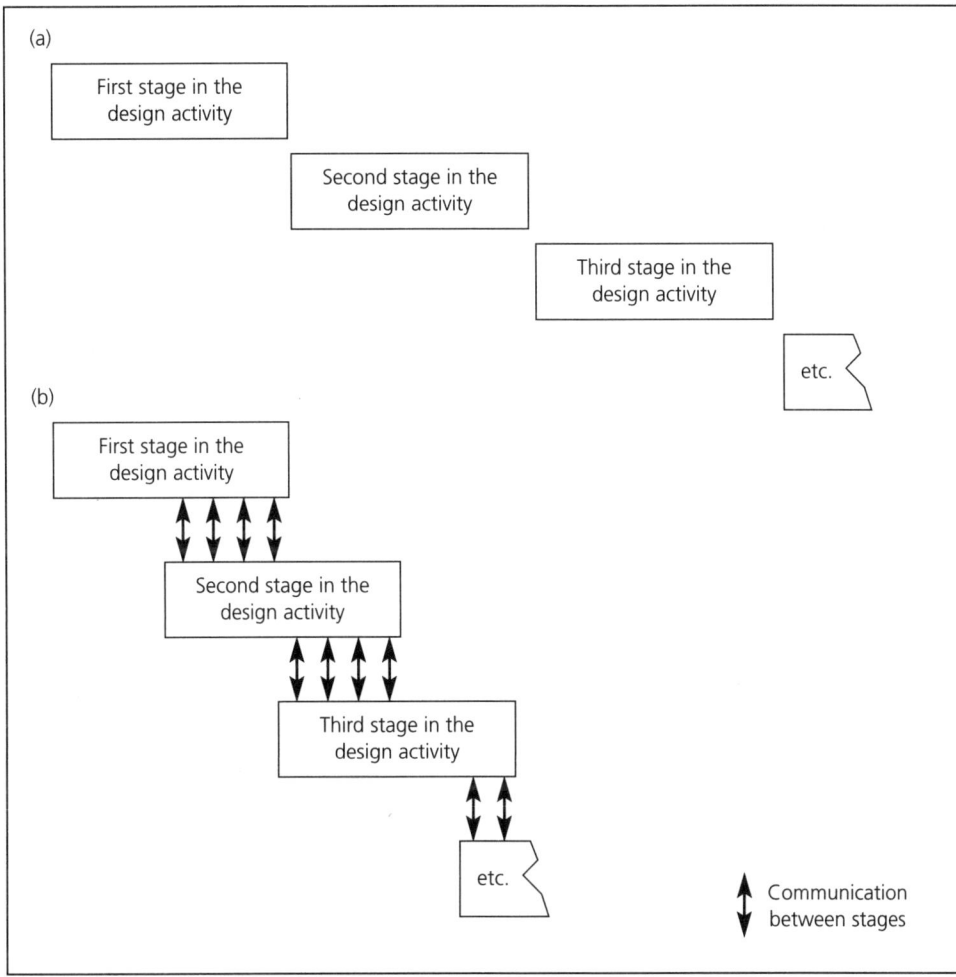

**Figure 5.19
(a) Sequential
arrangement of the
stages in the
design activity,
(b) simultaneous
arrangement of the
stages in the
design activity**

Early conflict resolution

Characterizing the design activity as a whole series of decisions is a useful way of thinking about design. However, a decision, once made, need not totally and utterly commit the organization. For example, if a design team is designing a new vacuum cleaner, the decision to adopt a particular style and type of electric motor might have seemed sensible at the time the decision was made but might have to be changed later, in the light of new information. It could be that a new electric motor becomes available which is clearly superior to the one initially selected. Under those circumstances the designers might very well want to change their decision.

There are other, more avoidable, reasons for designers changing their minds during the design activity, however. Perhaps one of the initial design decisions was made without sufficient discussion among those in the organization who have a valid contribution to make. It may even be that when the decision was made there was insufficient

THE MANIFOLD FOR THE FORD ZETA ENGINE[14]

The development of the 1.6 Zeta engine by Ford was one of its most important design projects for years. Like any engine design, it was a huge and complex task. Indeed each part of the engine needed to go through all the stages of the 'concept through to market' design activity. Take, for example, the air intake manifold. This plays a particularly important part in the engine because it recirculates exhaust gases from the engine, reburning some of them and therefore reducing the overall emission levels from the engine.

In the Zeta engine the manifold (unusually) is made not from metal but from a glass-reinforced nylon resin. The advantages of using this material include its strength, impact resistance, heat resistance and ease of processing. However, there were many design problems to sort out including noise and vibration, the dimensional stability of the product and the ability of the material to stand up to the very high temperatures involved.

The design of the engine manifold took almost three years and was organized using all the interactive design principles. First of all, the various stages in the design were compressed and run in parallel (what Ford calls 'concurrent engineering'). Second, the various fundamental design problems were sorted out right at the beginning of the process. Third, a design team was put together involving not only various personnel from the Ford Motor Company but also the more significant suppliers. Those involved included design representatives from the Du Pont chemical company who were supplying the material, Dunlop who were to perform the moulding operation, and several specialist suppliers including Dowty who were designing the seals, Elring who were involved in gasket design, Elm Steel who were involved with supplying tubing, and so on.

Design technology also played a large part in the development of this product. For example, Du Pont used computer-aided design (CAD) techniques to study the effects of engine vibration on the manifold. By simulating engine conditions the various stress levels in the manifold could be estimated. This allowed the team to explore different design solutions without having to devote time and cost to manufacturing too many alternative prototypes – particularly important because the design of the manifold had to fit in with the overall design of the engine itself. Prototype manifolds were needed to supply the main engine design team who were wanting to start engine testing several months before the end of the manifold design process.

By involving its suppliers, by using them to resolve the considerable technical problems early on in the project, and by solving the technical problems in an interactive and simultaneous manner, the team managed to get a highly complex and very novel product designed to fit into the overall engine project more quickly, more cheaply and more dependably than it could otherwise have done. ∎

agreement to formalize it, and the design team decided to carry on without formally making the decision. Yet subsequent decisions might be made as though the decision had been formalized. For example, suppose the company could not agree on the correct size of electric motor to put in its vacuum cleaner. It might well carry on with the rest of the design work while further discussions and investigations take place on what kind of electric motor to incorporate in the design. Yet much of the rest of the design of the product is likely to depend on the choice of the electric motor. The plastic housings, the bearings, the sizes of various apertures and so on could all be affected by this decision. Failure to resolve these conflicts and/or decisions early on in the process can prolong the degree of uncertainty in the total design activity. In addition, if a decision is made (even implicitly) and then changed later on in the process, the costs of that change can be very large. In fact the costs of changing aspects of the design tend to become high relatively early in the design period (as was discussed in Chapter 4).

However, if the design team manage to resolve conflict early in the design activity this will reduce the degree of uncertainty within the project and reduce the extra cost and, most significantly, time associated with either managing this uncertainty or changing decisions already made. Figure 5.20 illustrates two patterns of design changes through the life of the total design, which imply different time-to-market performances.

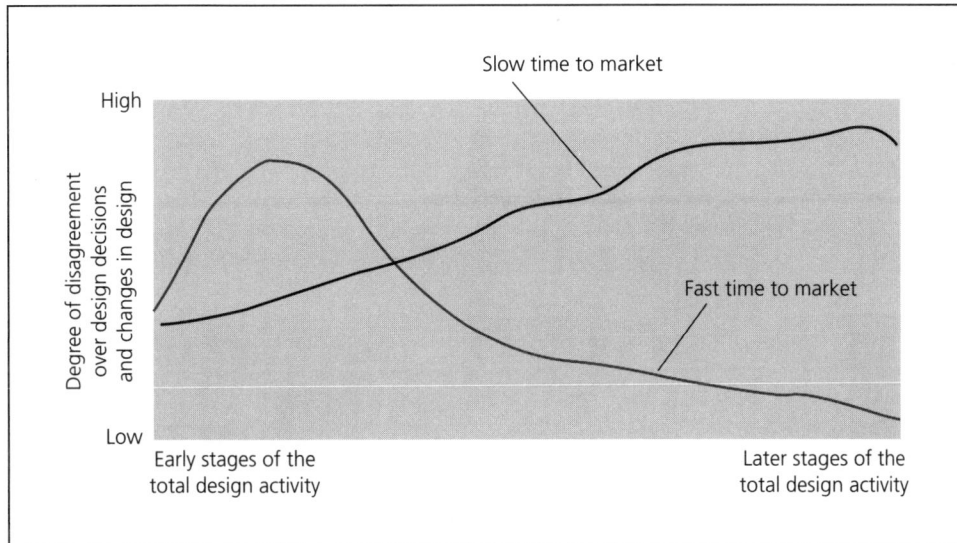

Figure 5.20
Sorting out problems early saves greater disruption later in the design activity

Project-based organization structures

The total process of developing concepts through to market will almost certainly involve personnel from several different areas of the organization. To continue the vacuum cleaner example, it is likely that the vacuum cleaner company would involve staff from its research and development department, engineering, production management, marketing, and finance. All these different functions will have some part to play in making the decisions which will shape the final design. Yet any design project will also have an existence of its own. It will have a project name, an individual manager or group of staff who are championing the project, a budget and, hopefully, a clear strategic purpose in the organization. The organizational question is which of these two ideas – the various organizational functions which contribute to the design or the design project itself – should dominate the way in which the design activity is managed?

Before answering this it is useful to look at the range of organizational structures which are available – from pure functional to pure project forms. In a pure functional organization all staff associated with the design project are based unambiguously in their functional groups. There is no project-based group at all. They may be working full-time on the project but all communication and liaison is carried out through their functional manager. The project exists because of agreement between these functional managers.

At the other extreme, all the individual members of staff from each function who are involved in the project could be moved out of their functions and perhaps even physically relocated to a 'task force' dedicated solely to the project. The task force could be led by a project manager who might hold all the budget allocated to the design project. Not all members of the task force necessarily have to stay in the team throughout the development period, but a substantial core might see the project through from start to finish. Some members of a design team may even be from other companies, as in the team which developed the inlet manifold for the Ford Zeta engine (*see* box on page 168).

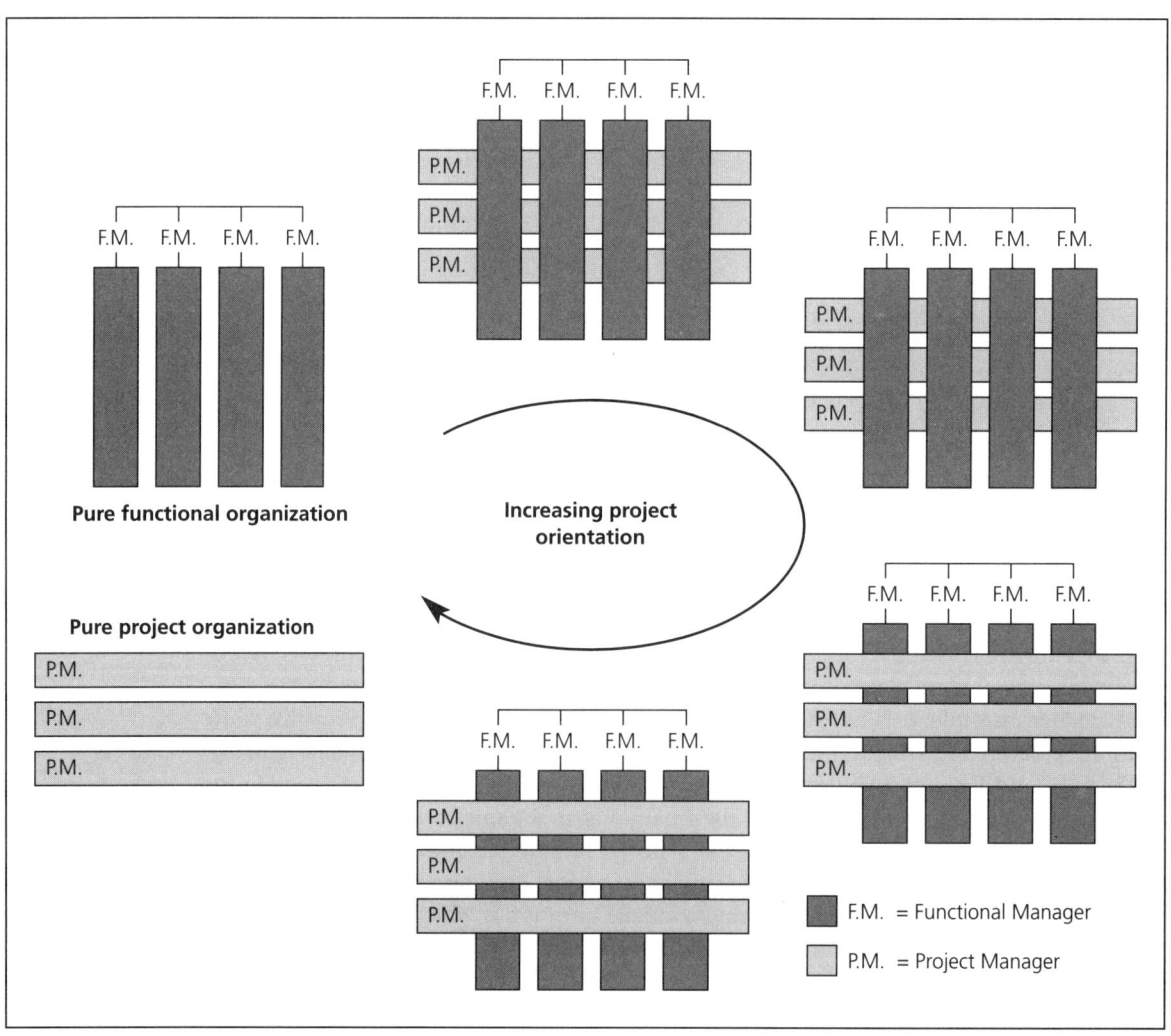

Figure 5.21 Organization structures for the design activity

reduce the possibility of errors in the design. Perhaps most significantly, though, CAD can be seen as a prototyping device as well as a drafting device. In effect the designer is modelling the design in order to assess its suitability prior to full production.

In between these two extremes there are various types of 'matrix' organization with varying emphasis on these two aspects of the organization (*see* Fig. 5.21).

Although the 'task force' type of organization, especially for small projects, can sometimes be a little cumbersome, it seems to be generally agreed that, for substantial projects at least, it is more effective at reducing overall time-to-market.[15]

PERSONAL PROFILE

Debbie Lundberg, Design Executive

Debbie is responsible for a team of over 20 designers who use the latest computer-aided design (CAD) to create the concepts and detailed patterns for new garments.

'Because most of our design work is ultimately prepared for the retailers Marks and Spencer (M&S), yet is contracted by clothing manufacturers, I have to ensure that we work effectively as a three-way partnership, which is a major challenge.

'We used to have specialist designers employed to work on particular types of clothing, such as ladies' wear or children's wear, with a similar separation in the prototype production areas; so machinists specialized as well. Now we have moved to project teams, to share ideas and develop new ranges of products. All our employees are more multi-skilled, which gives us greater flexibility to respond to changes in the mix of work, and it also stimulates the generation of new ideas.'

Debbie's work involves some market research, in conjunction with major customers, but above all she has to keep the team up to date with trends in the fashion industry, fabric technologies, new sources and types of fabric, and ways of illustrating concepts and specific designs prior to manufacturing.

'In the past, perhaps only eight out of 400 designs would be chosen for full-scale production, meaning that vast amounts of design effort and costing were wasted. Nowadays, development times are much shorter than in the past – the customers demand it. But CAD has speeded things up considerably, and gives us the opportunity to come very much closer to what the customer wants first time. Now we would expect only to prepare 50 designs for a show, of which perhaps ten would be chosen.

'The CAD system is being improved all the time, and we are exploring new ways of using it. For example, three-dimensional modelling allows us to show clothes on a 3D body, giving clients a much more realistic impression of the appearance of the garment before we obtain materials and produce a prototype. We can fine-tune any feature as we discuss the design, so finalizing the proposals is quicker than ever before. Although CAD systems started in engineering and graphic design, they are now much more tailored to the specific needs of the textile and garments industry. Not only do they help us conceptualize a product, but they allow us to communicate quickly and effectively with our clients and with the factories. It is also possible to link effectively the CAD system to CAM (computer-aided manufacturing) systems which produce patterns and cut cloth. The business opportunities afforded by this technology are almost beyond belief.' ■

SUMMARY

■ Product and service design involves turning ideas for new products or services into a detailed specification. The ideas for new products and services may emanate from within the organization, the R&D department or from staff, or from outside the organization from customers or as a result of the action of competitors.

■ Ideas need to be transformed into a product or service concept, indicating the form, function, purpose and benefits of the idea. Not all the concepts may be acceptable and so they are screened, in broad terms, to try to ensure that they are sensible additions to the product/service portfolio, that they will be feasible, acceptable and within the bounds of acceptable risk.

■ The agreed concept is then turned into a preliminary package and process design. This involves the identification of all the component parts of the product or service, the way they fit together, and the quantities required. Process design is aided by documentation, or blueprinting, techniques which include process flow charts, routing sheets and the customer-processing framework.

■ The resulting preliminary design is then evaluated to see if it can be done in a better way, more cheaply, or more easily – for example, using techniques such as quality function deployment, value engineering and Taguchi methods.

■ The agreed design is then tested, using computer simulations such as CAD or by market tests or trials using a prototype. As a result of this activity the design may be amended and then finally fixed ready for the operation to produce and provide to customers. The outcome of this stage is a fully developed specification for the products and services and the processes that will make and deliver them to customers.

■ During the last few years many organizations have been moving away from the sequential approach to product and service design and have been applying interactive design methods. This approach undertakes part of each design stage concurrently using multi-disciplinary teams. The key advantages of this approach are that it shortens the time-to-market, reduces the number of production problems, particularly quality problems, reduces development costs and provides an earlier return on investment.

■ The key determinants of speedy time-to-market are simultaneous development, early conflict resolution and the project-based organization of design activities.

The Royal Mint

A unique manufacturing operation in the UK is the Royal Mint at Llantrisant in South Wales. The Royal Mint is designated as an Executive Agency responsible to the Treasury of HM Government. The Chancellor of the Exchequer is appointed (*ex officio*) as Master of the Mint. Its objective is to provide the Government with coinage at a competitive price. The Royal Mint has the capacity to handle all of the UK business and still be able to bid for contracts from those countries who do not have their own minting operation. It serves over 60 countries in any one year and produces in excess of three billion coins annually. Its manufacturing requirement ranges from high volumes of standard coinage to individual service medals or commemorative coins.

In the UK, the Treasury contracts with the Royal Mint on an annual basis for the likely requirements for coin in the following 12 months, and the Treasury is also responsible for decisions on any changes to the coinage. The Mint recently completed the introduction of the new, smaller 10p coin; this involved an issue of over one billion new coins and the withdrawal of all the old coins from circulation. This represents one of the largest single projects they have undertaken and a massive logistics exercise to co-ordinate the movement of the coins. The Mint meets every three months with executives from the UK clearing banks to discuss their requirements for currency in the shorter term. These estimates are then updated at weekly planning meetings. The Mint would like to work to a 'just-in-time' schedule, but because of the nature of the product and the implications of the money not being available, they are obliged to keep a predetermined safety stock to cover any shortfalls.

As in any manufacturing operation, the unit cost of the product is a critical factor in measuring performance, and in the case of the Royal Mint, there is a unique cost ceiling, in that their cost base must always be less than the face value of the coins being produced. Therefore this mass manufacturing process must focus on monitoring their operating costs. The issue of payment for the product is an interesting concept within the 'minting' industry and in the UK. The clearing banks pay the face value of the coins to the Treasury, and the annual contract agreement with the Royal Mint is based on the Treasury agreeing to cover a fixed percentage of their fixed costs and the variable cost of each unit then purchased over the year. The Royal Mint can then invoice the Treasury for the currency produced.

The coins are costed in terms of pounds per thousand pieces and, of that cost, approximately 40 to 50 per cent comprise the raw material cost, with the next 20 to 40 per cent coming from the production process which transforms that raw metal into a blank coin. The actual stamping of the die on to the coin and the simultaneous milling of the edges are an almost insignificant part of the overall process cost, mainly due to the vast economies of scale at this stage. The efficiency of the stamping process is nominally determined by the life expectancy of the die and the research at the Mint is involved in initiatives to improve the materials being used in both the coins and dies to extend this period of use. The coining machines used in the manufacturing process are flexible in that they can run to produce any of the UK and most overseas coins without long changeover periods, and orders vary from 1000 million coins for a large country to an order of 5000 for a small island. The machines are able to operate at speeds up to 750 coins per minute and therefore the nature of a 5000 coin run is very costly, but all the same still viable.

One issue has been the threat of the intrinsic raw metal cost exceeding the face value of the coin, something which has been most prevalent in those countries facing high inflation, and this leads to coinage being withdrawn from circulation by those wishing to capitalize on the returns available from the base material. In the UK, the smaller denominations were reaching that point and the Mint had to change the composition of the 2p and 1p coins to a steel core with an electroplated copper outer layer. This reduced the unit cost of the coin and also added to its expected lifetime because it used a less expensive base metal. This new format of coin represents the biggest change in the manufacturing process of coins to occur over the past few years and the pioneering of the electroplating technique, whereby a mild steel core is electroplated with copper, nickel or brass, resulted in a process which will aid the conservation of materials. The reduction in costs is also being achieved without a noticeable reduction in the recognized value of the coin. Another consequence of the electroplating procedure is that the coins have magnetic properties due to the presence of a mild steel core and this has caused initial problems for vending machine manufacturers. ■

Source: Reproduced by kind permission of the Royal Mint

Questions

1 What is the 'concept' of the Mint's products?

2 Explain the criteria which the Mint will need to take into account when it designs new coinage.

3 How might the concept of simultaneous design be applied in the design of coinage?

DISCUSSION QUESTIONS

1 Describe what you think might be the concept, package and the main processes involved in creating or providing the following:

a high performance car

an airline flight

a visit to the dentist

an operations management textbook.

2 Using your knowledge as a customer of a university library, try to generate three new ways in which library services could be provided to you. Discuss the acceptability, feasibility and viability of each.

3 Take apart a simple product, such as a pen or an old cassette. Explain how it might have been put together (reverse engineering) and see if you can improve on its design.

4 Explain the difference between an idea and a concept. A hairdresser is considering opening up on campus. Develop this idea into what you think might be an acceptable, feasible and viable concept.

5 Look carefully at an item of furniture you have and create a product structure and bill of materials for it. Don't forget the nails, different types of screws and glue.

6 Draw an information flow chart describing the decision processes involved in a decision you frequently have to make, such as what to do in an evening. Evaluate the complexity and completeness of the chart.

7 Draw a process flow chart describing your last visit to see the doctor. How do you think the process could be improved?

8 Blueprinting, in one form or another, is a key tool for analysing, designing and developing products and services. Why do you think this is so?

9 Apply quality function deployment to a product or service of your choice and assess how well it appears to meet your perceived needs.

10 Explain what is meant by 'interactive design' and discuss the benefits for those organizations that employ it.

11 Why is it difficult or inappropriate to separate out the design of a product or service from the process of creating it?

12 Read the box on Braun's Multimix design at the beginning of this chapter and answer the following questions:

(a) To what extent do the 'Braun Design Principles' appear to incorporate elements of:

design for manufacture

standardization

simultaneous engineering

quality function deployment.

(b) Which performance objectives are the most important for Braun?

(c) Braun has chosen to undertake most of its manufacturing operations in Europe, and much of it in Germany. What are the implications of this policy for the design of the company's products?

NOTES ON CHAPTER

1 Source: Presentation speech by Hartmut Stroth, Director of Communication at Braun AG, Mar 1994.

2 Peters, T. and Waterman, R. (1982) *In Search of Excellence*, Harper & Row, New York.

3 For more information on focus groups, *see*, for example, Krueger, K.A. (1988) *Focus Groups*, Sage Publications.

4 Source: *The Economist*, 28 Sept 1991, and company records.

5 Quinn, J.B. and Gagnon, C.E. (1986) 'Will Services Follow Manufacturing into Decline?', *Harvard Business Review*, Vol 64, No 6, pp 95–103.

6 Johnston, R. (1987) 'A Framework for Developing a Quality Strategy in a Customer Processing Operation', *International Journal of Quality and Reliability Management*, Vol 4, No 4, pp 35–44.

7 For more information on QFD for products and services, *see*, for example:

Behara, R.S. and Chase, R.B. (1993) 'Service Quality Deployment: Quality Service by Design' *in* Sarin, R.V. (ed) *Perspectives in Operations Management: Essays in Honor of Elwood S. Buffa*, Kluwer Academic Publisher.

Evans, J.R. and Lindsay, W.M. (1993) *The Management and Control of Quality* (2nd edn), West.

Fitzsimmons, J.A. and Fitzsimmons, M.J. (1994) *Service Management for Competitive Advantage*, McGraw-Hill.

Harrison, A. (1992) *Just-in-Time Manufacturing in Perspective*, Prentice Hall.

Hauser, J.R. and Clausing, D. (1988) 'The House of Quality', *Harvard Business Review*, Vol 66, No 3, pp 63–73.

Meredith, J.R. (1992) *The Management of Operations* (4th edn), John Wiley.

8 Cambridge, M. (1992) 'Quality Function Deployment', *Quality and Corporate Affairs Business Improvement Series*, 92/03 ICL, Dec.

9 This example is used by kind permission of Allan Webb, from Webb, A. (1994) *Managing Innovative Projects*, Chapman and Hall.

10 Taguchi, G. and Clausing, D. (1990) 'Robust Quality', *Harvard Business Review*, Vol 68, No 1, pp 65–75.

11 Source: *Siemens World*, June 1994.

12 Yamazoe, T. (1990) 'Simultaneous Engineering: A Nissan Perspective' *in The Proceedings of the First International Conference on Simultaneous Engineering*, London, pp 73–80.

13 Broughton, T. (1990) 'Simultaneous Engineering in Aero Gas Turbine Design and Manufacture' *in The Proceedings of the First International Conference on Simultaneous Engineering*, London, pp 25–36.

14 Costanzo, L. (1992) 'Working as One', *Engineering*, Nov.

15 Hayes, R.H., Wheelwright, S.C. and Clarke, K.B. (1988) *Dynamic Manufacturing*, Free Press.

SELECTED FURTHER READINGS

Albrecht, K. and Bradford, L.J. (1990) *The Service Advantage*, Dow Jones/Irwin.

Bitner, M.J. (1992) 'Servicescapes: The Impact of Physical Surroundings on Customers and Employees', *Journal of Marketing*, Vol 56, April, pp 57–71.

Chase, R.B. (1991) 'The Service Factory: A Future Vision', *International Journal of Service Industry Management*, Vol 2, No 3, pp 60–70.

Dean, J.H. and Susman, G.I. (1984) 'Organizing for Manufacturable Design', *Harvard Business Review*, Vol 62, No 1, pp 28–36.

Groover, M.P. and Zimmers, E.W. (1984) *CAD/CAM Computer-Aided Design and Manufacturing*, Prentice Hall.

Heskett, J.L., Sasser, W.E. and Hart, C.W.L. (1990) *Service Breakthroughs: Changing the Rules of the Game*, The Free Press.

Kingman-Brundage, J. (1989) 'The ABCs of Service System Blueprinting' *in* Bitner, M.J. and Crosby, L. (eds) *Designing a Winning Service Strategy*, American Marketing Association. Also to be found *in* Lovelock, C.H. (1992) *Managing Services* (2nd edn), Prentice Hall International.

Shostack, G.L. (1984) 'Designing Services that Deliver', *Harvard Business Review*, Vol 62, No 1, pp 133–9.

Shostack, G.L. (1987) 'Service Positioning Through Structural Change', *Journal of Marketing*, Vol 51, Jan, pp 34–43.

Whitney, D.E. (1988) 'Manufacturing by Design', *Harvard Business Review*, Vol 66, No 1, Jan–Feb, pp 83–91.

DESIGN OF THE OPERATIONS NETWORK

INTRODUCTION

Every operation is part of a larger and interconnected network of other operations. This network will include suppliers and customers. It will also include suppliers' suppliers and customers' customers, and so on. At a strategic level, operations managers are involved in 'designing' the shape and form of the network in which their operation is set. These network design decisions start with setting the strategic objectives for an operation's position in its network. This helps to determine the extent to which an operation chooses to be 'vertically integrated' into the network, the location of each operation within the network, and the capacity of each part of the network. This chapter treats all these strategic design decisions in the context of operations networks (*see* Fig. 6.1).

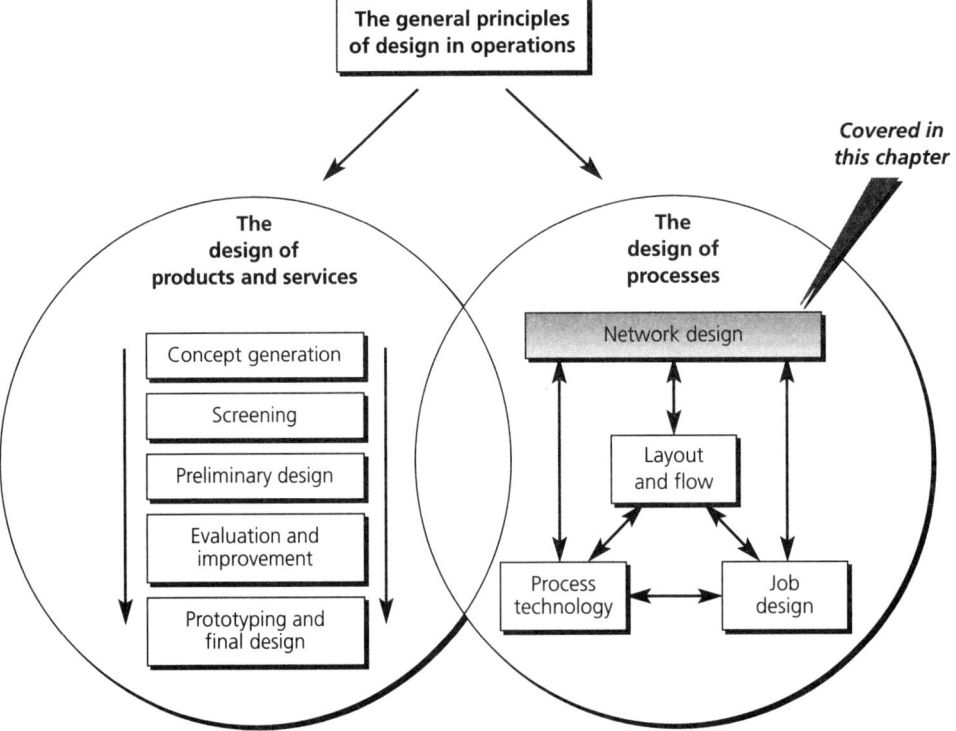

Figure 6.1 The design activities in operations management covered in this chapter

OBJECTIVES

This chapter will examine:

- the nature of operations networks and the concept of the 'supply side' and the 'demand side' parts of the network;

- the advantages of taking a network perspective in making these strategic design decisions;

- the direction, extent and balance of the operation's vertical integration and how these factors can affect the performance of the operation;

- the location of operations, and how supply-side and demand-side influences determine location decisions;

- how the capacity of an operation is determined, and how long-term capacity levels are changed as demand changes over time.

THE NETWORK PERSPECTIVE

Materials, parts, assemblies, information, ideas and sometimes people, all flow through the network of customer–supplier relationships formed by all these operations. On its *supply side* an operation has its suppliers of parts, or information, or services. These suppliers themselves have their own suppliers who in turn could also have suppliers, and so on. On the *demand side* the operation has customers. These customers might not be the final consumers of the operation's products or services; they might have their own set of customers.

Figure 6.2 illustrates one such network. On its supply side is a group of operations which directly supply the operation; these are often called 'first-tier' suppliers. They are supplied by 'second-tier' suppliers. However, some operations which are primarily second-tier suppliers in an industry may also supply an operation directly, thus missing out a link in the network. Similarly, on the demand side of the network, 'first-tier' customers are the main customer group for the operation. These in turn supply 'second-tier' customers, although again the operation may at times supply second-tier customers directly. The suppliers and customers who have direct contact with an operation are called its *immediate supply network*, whereas all the operations which form the network of supplier's suppliers and customer's customers, etc., are called the *total supply network*.

Figure 6.3 illustrates the total supply network for a plastic homewares (for example, kitchen bowls, food containers, etc.) manufacturer. The company is supplied with plastic granules which feed its injection moulding machines. These granules come from a stockist who keeps a wide range of similar products. The stockist is in turn supplied by chemical companies who manufacture the plastic. Similarly the company

177

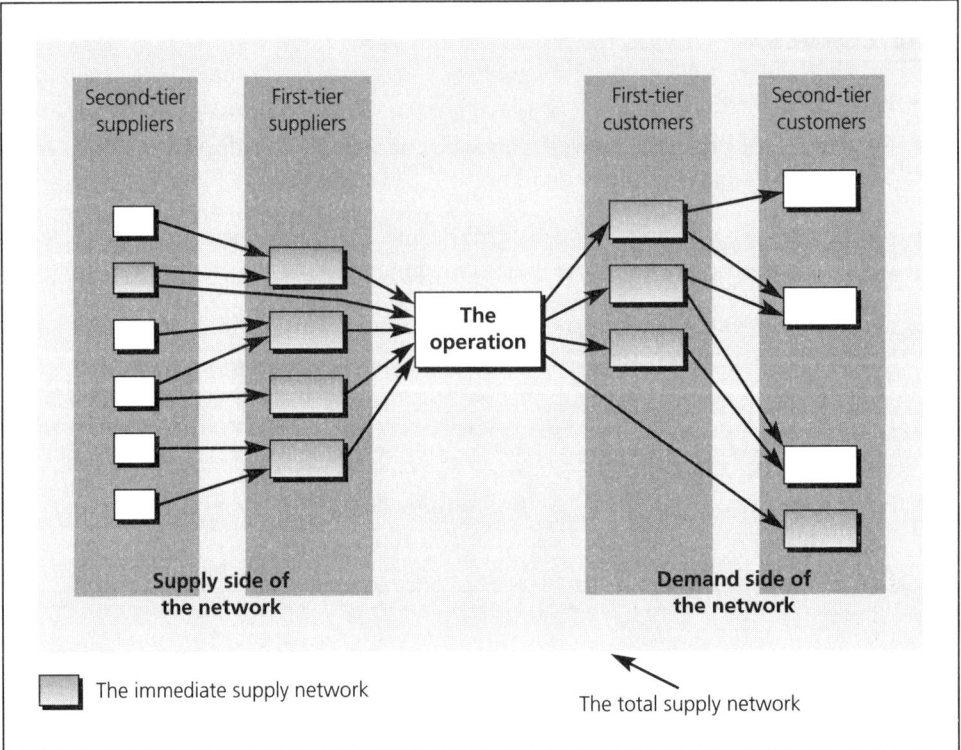

**Figure 6.2
Total and
immediate supply
networks**

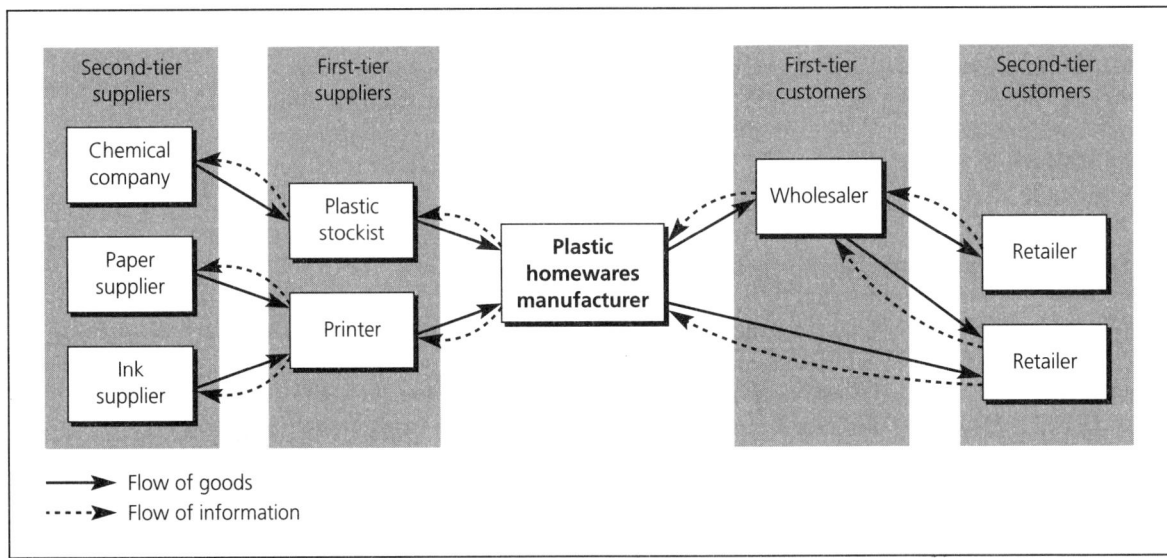

Figure 6.3 Operations network for a plastic homewares manufacturer

is also supplied with packaging materials by a printing company which is itself supplied by paper and ink producers. On the supply side the homeware manufacturer supplies some of its basic products to wholesalers who supply retail outlets. However it also supplies some retailers directly with 'made-to-order' products.

178

Along with the flow of goods in the network from suppliers to customers, each link in the network will feed back orders and information to its suppliers. When stocks run low, the retailers will place orders with the wholesaler or directly with the manufacturer. The wholesaler will likewise place orders with the manufacturer who will in turn place orders with its suppliers, who will replenish their own stocks from their suppliers. It is a two-way process with goods flowing one way and information flowing the other.

Why consider the whole network?

At its most strategic level, the design activity of operations management must include the whole of the network of which an operation is a part. There are three important reasons for this.[1]

- It helps a company to understand how it can compete effectively.
- It helps to identify particularly significant links in the network.
- It helps the company to focus on its long-term position in the network.

Understanding competitiveness

Immediate customers and immediate suppliers, quite understandably, are the main concern to competitively minded companies. Any operation has only two options if it wants to understand its ultimate customers at the end of the network. First, it can rely on all the intermediate customers and customers' customers, etc., which form the links in the network between the company and its end customers, to transmit the end-customer needs efficiently back up the network. Second, it can take the responsibility on itself for understanding how customer–supplier relationships transmit competitive requirements through the network. Increasingly, organizations are taking the latter course. Relying on one's immediate network is seen as putting too much faith in someone else's judgement of things which are central to an organization's own competitive health. Supply networks might become obsolete no matter how good some of the individual parts of the network may be.

Identifying significant links in the network

The key to understanding supply networks lies in identifying the parts of the network which contribute to those performance objectives valued by end customers. Any analysis of networks must start therefore with an understanding of the elements of competitiveness at the 'downstream' end of the network. After this, the parts of the network which contribute most to end customer service will need to be identified. This analysis will probably show that links in the network will contribute something; but not all contributions will be equally significant.

For example, the important end customers for some types of domestic plumbing parts and appliances are the installers and service companies who deal directly with domestic consumers. They are supplied by 'stock holders' whose competitive success relies on a combination of price, range and above all a high availability of supply. That means having all parts in stock and delivering them fast. Suppliers of parts to the stock holders can best contribute to their customers' competitiveness partly by offering a short delivery lead time but mainly through dependable delivery. The key players in this example are the stock holders. Without effective service levels and competitive prices from them, the end customers will not be as likely to buy the products of the parts manufacturer. The best way of winning end-customer business is by helping the key players in the network, in this case by giving them prompt delivery which helps keep costs down while providing high availability of parts.[2]

Focus on long-term issues

There are times when circumstances render parts of a supply network weaker than its adjacent links. A major machine breakdown, for example, or a labour dispute, might disrupt an operation. How then should its immediate customers and suppliers react? Should they exploit the weakness as a legitimate move to enhance their own competitive position or should they ignore the opportunity, tolerate the problems, and hope the customer or supplier will eventually recover?[3] Sometimes short-term adversarial opportunities seem too good to miss, and short-term issues too pressing to give thought to how the total supply network is being affected. However, a longer-term view would be to weigh the relative advantages to be gained from assisting or replacing the weak link.

Design decisions in the network

It is useful to consider organizations as forming part of a network of customers and suppliers because doing so prompts three particularly important design decisions:
The three decisions are:

1 How much of the network should the operation own? Should it own any of its suppliers or customers? If it does this, it is in effect taking over part of a link in the network. This decision is called the *vertical integration* decision of the organization.
2 Where should each part of the network owned by the company be located? If the homewares company builds a new factory, should it be close to its suppliers or close to its customers, or somewhere in between? These decisions are called *operations location* decisions.
3 What physical capacity should each part of the network owned by the company have at any point in time? How large should the homewares factory be? If it expands, should it do so in large capacity steps or small ones? These decisions are called *long-term capacity management* decisions.

THE VERTICAL INTEGRATION OF CAPACITY

Vertical integration is the extent to which an organization owns the network of which it is a part. In its strategic sense it involves an organization assessing the wisdom of acquiring suppliers or customers. At the level of individual products or services it means the operation deciding whether to make a particular individual component or to perform a particular service itself, or alternatively buy it in from a supplier.

Professors Hayes and Wheelwright of Harvard Business School[4] define an organization's vertical integration strategy in terms of:

- the *direction* of any expansion
- the *extent* of the process span required
- the *balance* among the resulting vertically integrated stages.

The direction of vertical integration

The first vertical integration decision an organization must take concerns the *direction* of any ownership in the network. If the plastic homewares manufacturer illustrated in Fig. 6.3 decides that it should control more of its network, should it expand by buying one of its suppliers (becoming its own plastic materials stockist, for instance) or should it expand by buying one of its customers (a wholesaler or a retailer)? The strategy of expanding on the supply side of the network is sometimes called *backward* or *'upstream' vertical integration* and expanding on the demand side is sometimes called *forward* or *'downstream' vertical integration*.

Backward vertical integration, by allowing an organization to take control of its suppliers, is often used either to gain cost advantages or to prevent competitors gaining control of important suppliers. This is why backward vertical integration is sometimes considered a strategically *defensive* move. Forward vertical integration, on the other hand, takes an organization closer to its markets and allows more freedom for an organization to make contact directly with its customers. For this reason forward vertical integration is sometimes considered an *offensive* strategic move. Figure 6.4 illustrates backward and forward vertical integration.

The extent of vertical integration

Having established its direction of expansion, an organization must then decide how far it wishes to take the extent of its vertical integration. Some organizations deliberately choose not to integrate far, if at all, from their original part of the network.

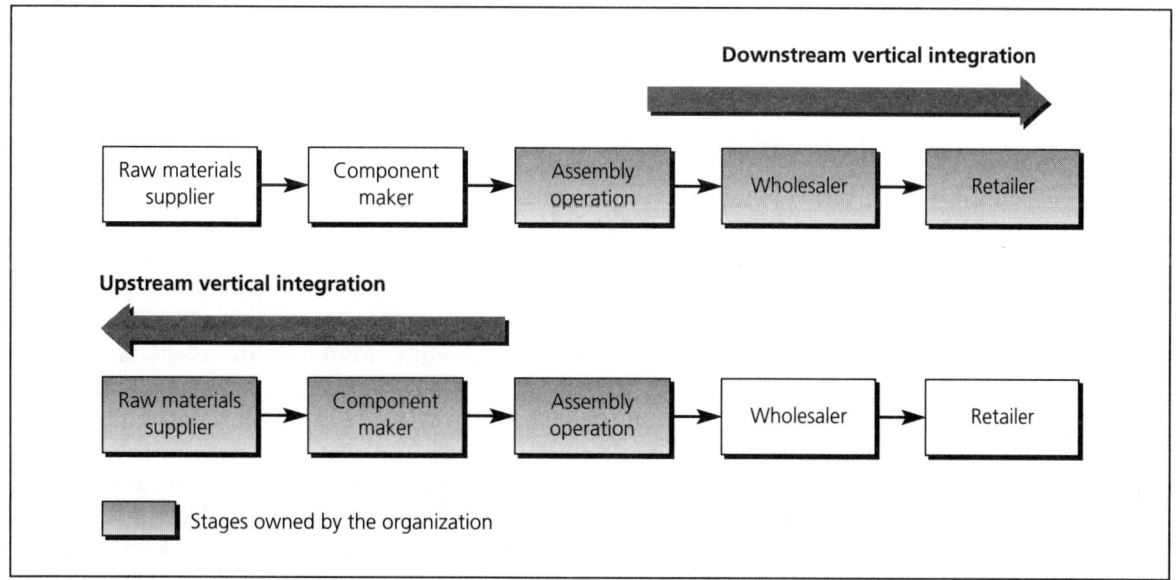

Figure 6.4 The direction of vertical integration for an assembly operation

Alternatively, some organizations choose to become very vertically integrated. Take a large international aluminium company, such as Alcan, for example. Alcan is involved with smelting the minerals which produce aluminium (as well as recycling used aluminium products) to produce its basic ingots of aluminium. It also has operations which take the ingots and roll them into sheet form. Separate Alcan operations then roll the sheet further to produce aluminium foil which can then be made into aluminium containers (for take-away food or home freezing) at yet another Alcan operation. This path (one of several for its different products) has moved the material through the total network of processes, all of which are owned (wholly or partly) by the one company. Figure 6.5 illustrates two organizations, one with a narrow 'extent' of vertical integration and one with a wide 'extent' of vertical integration.

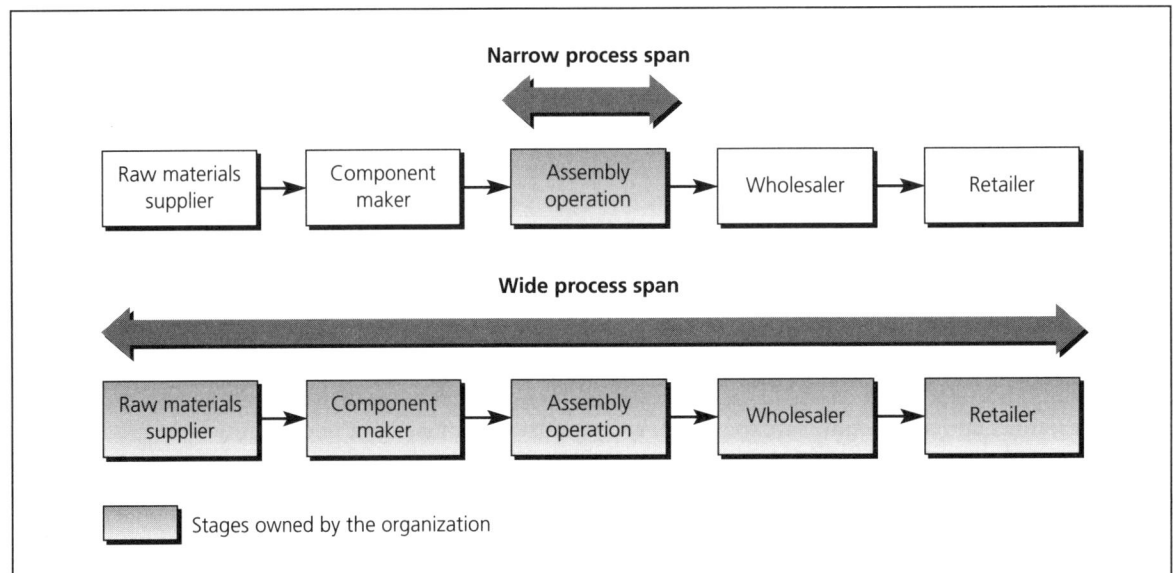

Figure 6.5 The extent of process span of vertical integration for an assembly operation

The balance among stages

The final vertical integration decision is not strictly about the ownership of the network; it concerns the capacity and, to some extent, the operating behaviour of each stage in the network which is owned by the organization. The *balance* of the part of the network owned by an organization is the amount of the capacity at each stage in the network which is devoted to supplying the next stage. So a totally balanced network relationship is one where one stage produces only for the next stage in the network and totally satisfies its requirements. Less than full balance in the stages allows each stage to sell its output to other companies or to buy in some of its supplies from other companies.

Fully balanced networks have the virtue of simplicity and also allow each stage to focus on the requirements of the next stage along in the network. Having to supply other organizations, perhaps with slightly different requirements, might serve to distract from what is needed by its (owned) primary customer. However a totally self-sufficient network is sometimes not feasible. For example, within the network of

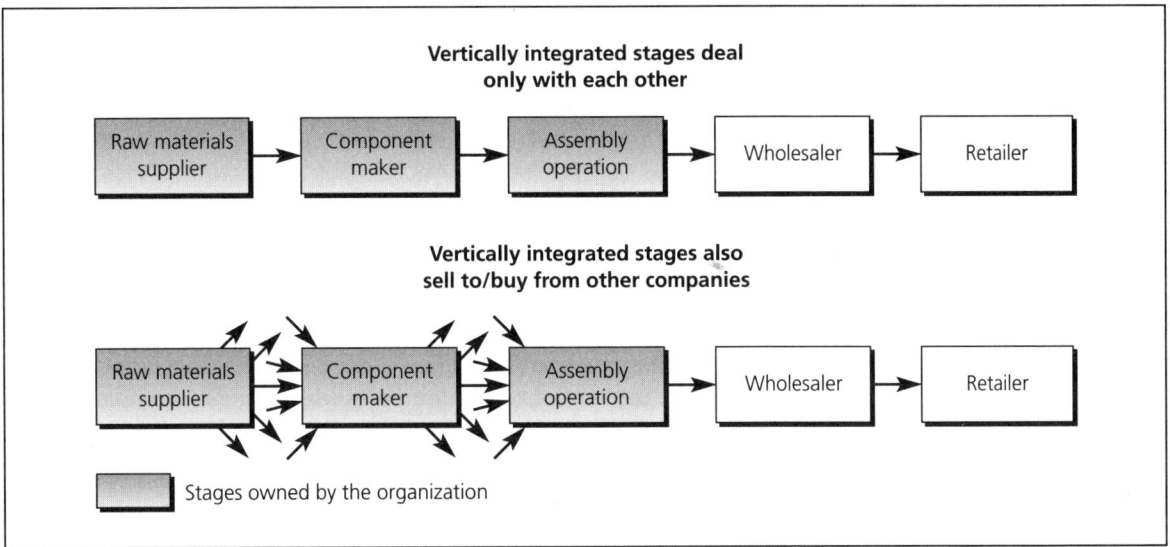

Figure 6.6 The balance of internal/external trade in a vertically integrated assembly operation

operations which are owned by Alcan are some 'stock-holding' operations; these are the companies which hold stocks of metals in semi-finished form, such as aluminium sheets and extruded bars. They sell partly to the small and medium-sized customers who do not warrant direct deliveries from Alcan's factories. These stock-holding operations could be limited to stocking only Alcan manufactured products. In fact they are not so limited. A stock-holding company which held the products from only one company would not offer as effective a service to its customers as one which is free to supply a full range of products, including those which Alcan does not manufacture. Figure 6.6 illustrates this.

The effects of vertical integration

The vertical integration question which all organizations must answer is relatively simple, even if the decision itself is not: 'Do the advantages which vertical integration gives in an organization's particular set of circumstances match the performance objectives which it requires in order to compete more effectively in its markets?' For example, if the main performance objectives for an operation are dependable delivery and meeting short-term changes in customers' delivery requirements, the key question should be 'How does vertical integration enhance dependability and delivery flexibility?'

Answering these questions means judging two sets of opposing factors – those which give the *potential to improve performance*, and those which *work against this potential being realized*.

Vertical integration affects quality

As far as *quality* is concerned, the potential benefits of vertical integration derive from the closeness of the operation to its customers and its suppliers. The origins of any quality problems are usually easier to trace through 'in-house' operations than through outside suppliers and the subsequent quality problem-solving activity can be concentrated at the most appropriate point in the network. Acting against this is the danger that in-house operations, which are freed from the discipline of a true commercial relationship, will have less incentive to co-operate in quality improvement if there is no real possibility of their losing the business of their captive customers.

Vertical integration affects speed

As far as *delivery speed* is concerned, vertically integrated operations can mean a closer synchronization of schedules which speeds up the throughput of materials and information along the network. In addition, being close to suppliers and customers can help forecasting. Again these potential advantages can be eroded if guaranteed 'in-house' demand means that the 'in-house' customers get low priority compared with 'proper' outside customers who can take their business elsewhere.

Vertical integration affects dependability

As far as *dependability* is concerned, improved communications along a vertically integrated network which can give better forecasts can also result in more realistic delivery promises. All of which again assumes that the relationship between vertically integrated links in the network will indeed receive a high priority rather than being overlooked in favour of customers who can trade with competitors if they are not satisfied with the service they receive.

Vertical integration affects flexibility

As far as *new product flexibility* is concerned, vertical integration gives the potential to guide technological developments as well as deny them to competitors. Forward vertical integration gives the potential for products and services to be developed specifically and more precisely to customer needs. As far as *volume and delivery flexibility* are concerned, the ownership of suppliers can give the potential to dictate volume changes to match downstream fluctuations, as well as helping to expedite specific orders through the network. Against this there can be a reluctance to inflict volume changes on in-house suppliers and customers.

Vertical integration affects costs

As far as *cost* is concerned, vertically integrated operations can provide the potential for sharing some costs, research and development or logistics, for example. Over the longer term, vertical integration can also allow capacity, and therefore capacity utilization, to be balanced. Perhaps more significantly, if margins are high in supplier operations, it allows integrated companies to capture the profits which would otherwise be lost, and reduce the costs of bought-in parts or services. This assumes that other customers of a newly acquired supplier will be content to continue doing business with it. If they are not, demand could fall and therefore unit costs increase. Even if demand does keep at the same level, there is the question of whether a management now concerned with more separate businesses will be as concerned with keeping costs low as one which is concentrating on keeping its customers.

THE LOCATION OF CAPACITY

After deciding on the overall shape of its operations network through vertical integration decisions, an organization must choose the location of each operation. Location is the geographical positioning of an operation relative to the resources, other operations or customers with which it interacts.

The importance of location

It was reputedly Lord Sieff, the boss of Marks and Spencer, the UK-based retail organization, who said,

> *'There are three important things in retailing – location, location and location.'*

Any retailing operation knows exactly what he meant. Get the location wrong, put a store on the wrong street, or even the wrong side of the street, for example, and it can have a significant impact on profits. In retailing a difference in location of a few metres can make the difference between profit and loss.

The impact of location in retailing may be particularly significant, but the location decision is also important in other types of operation. For example, mislocating a fire service station can slow down the average journey time of the fire crews in getting to the fires; locating a factory where there is difficulty attracting labour who have the appropriate skills will affect the effectiveness of the factory's operations, and so on. In other words, location decisions will usually have an effect on an operation's costs as well as its ability to serve its customers (and therefore its revenues). The other reason why location decisions are important is that, once taken, they are difficult to undo. The costs of moving an operation from one site to another can be hugely expensive and the risks of inconveniencing customers very high.

Reasons for location decisions

There are two categories of stimuli which cause organizations to make location decisions:

- changes in *demand* for goods and services;
- changes in *supply* of inputs to the operation.

Location decisions prompted by demand changes are often due to increases or decreases in the aggregated volume of demand. For example, increasing demand for a clothing manufacturer's products may necessitate more capacity. The company could either expand its existing site or, alternatively, if the site could not accommodate a larger facility, it could choose a larger site in another location. A third option would be to keep its existing plant and find a second location for an additional plant. Two of these options will involve a location decision.

High-contact, customer-processing operations often do not have the choice of expanding on the same site to meet rising demand. For example, if a company which offers a one-hour photo-processing service is so successful that it wants to expand its activities, enlarging its existing site would only bring in marginally more business. The company offers a local, and therefore convenient, service. Finding a new location for an additional operation is probably its only option for expansion.

Changes in the cost, or availability, of the supply of inputs to the operation is the other reason for making the location decision. For example, a mining or oil company will need to relocate as the minerals it is extracting become depleted. A manufacturing company might choose to relocate its operations to a part of the world where labour costs are low, because the equivalent resources (people) in its original location have become relatively expensive.

The objectives of the location decision

The aim of the location decision is to achieve an appropriate balance between three related objectives:

● the *spatially variable costs* of the operation (spatially variable means that something changes with geographical location);
● the *service* the operation is able to provide to its customers;
● the *revenue* potential of the operation.

In for-profit organizations the last two objectives are related. The assumption is that the better the service the operation can provide to its customers, the better will be its potential to attract custom and therefore generate revenue. In not-for-profit organizations, revenue potential might not be a relevant objective and so cost and customer service are often taken as the twin objectives of location.

In making decisions about where to locate an operation, operations managers are concerned with minimizing spatially variable costs and maximizing revenue/customer service. Location affects both of these but not equally for all types of operation. For example, when we buy products we do not usually care where they were made. Moving the operation which made them is unlikely to affect the operation's revenues significantly. On the other hand, the costs of the operation will probably be very greatly affected by location.

The location decision for any operation is determined by the relative strength of supply-side and demand-side factors. Figure 6.7 illustrates some supply-side and demand-side factors. Not all will apply to every location decision made by all operations, but they give an indication of the factors which usually need to be taken into account when making location decisions.

Supply-side influences

Labour costs

The wage and other costs of employing people with particular skills can vary between different areas in any country, but is likely to be a far more significant factor when international comparisons are made. For example, Fig. 6.8 shows the wage and non-wage cost of employment for a number of countries.[5] Wage costs are fairly self-explanatory; they are the costs to the organization of paying wages directly to individual employees. Non-wage costs are the employment taxes, social security costs, holiday payments and any welfare provision which the organization has to make in order to employ people.

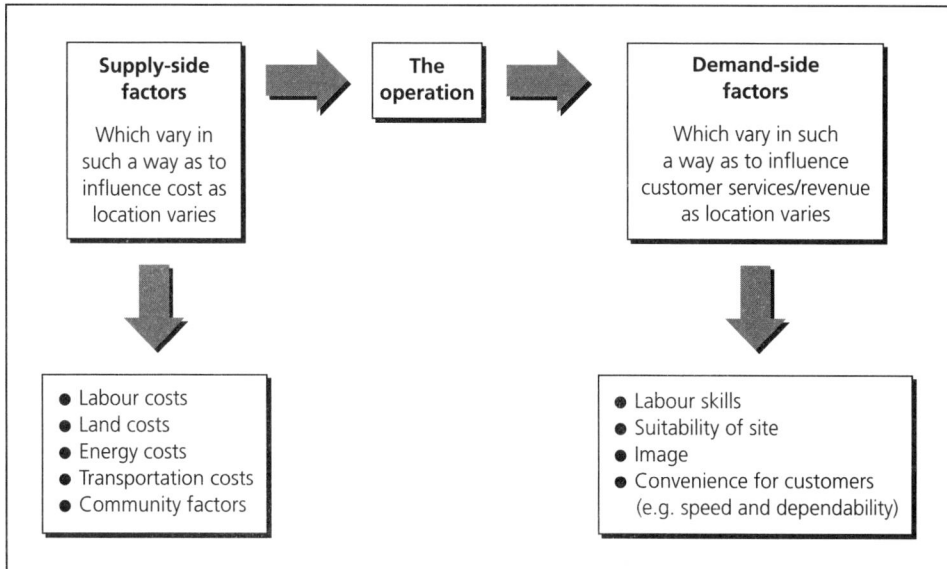

**Figure 6.7
Supply-side and demand-side factors in location decisions**

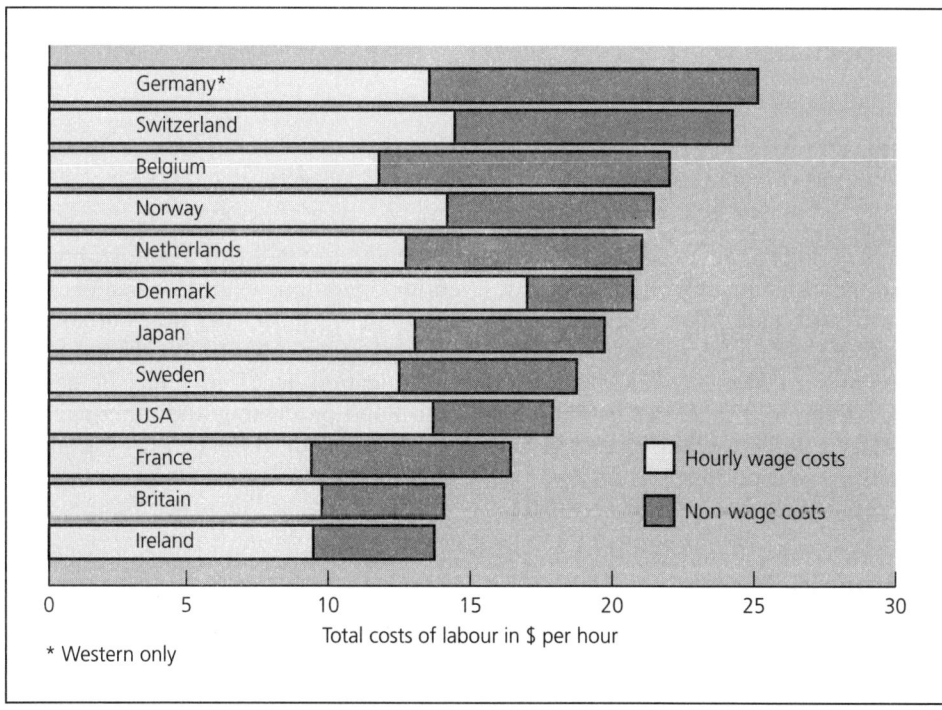

**Figure 6.8
The total costs of labour in manufacturing for selected countries (1993)**

The labour costs illustrated in Fig. 6.8 should be read with some caution, however. Two factors can influence them. The first is the productivity of labour. On an international level, this tends to be inversely related to labour costs. That means that generally each person can produce more in a given unit of time in the countries with higher labour costs. This effect goes some way to offset the large international variations in labour costs. The second factor is the rate of exchange of the countries' currencies. Although all costs are quoted in the same currency, exchange rates can swing considerably over time. This in turn changes relative labour costs. Yet in spite of any minor adjustments to the actual value of relative labour costs, they exert a major influence on the location decision, especially in some industries such as clothing where labour costs as a proportion of total costs are relatively high.

Land costs

The cost of acquiring the site itself is sometimes a relevant factor in choosing a location. Land and rental costs vary between countries and cities. At a more local level land costs are also important. A retail operation, when choosing 'high street' sites, will pay a particular level of rent only if it believes it can generate a certain level of revenue from the site.

Energy costs

Operations which use large amounts of energy, such as aluminium smelters, can be influenced in their location decisions by the availability of relatively inexpensive energy. This may be direct, as in the availability of hydro-electric generation in an area, for example, or indirect, such as low-cost coal which can be used to generate inexpensive electricity.

Transportation costs

Transportation costs can be considered in two parts:

(a) the costs of transporting inputs from their source to the site of the operation;
(b) the cost of transporting goods from the site to customers.

Whereas almost all operations are concerned to some extent with (a), not all operations transport goods to customers, rather customers come to them (for example, hotels), and so they are not concerned with (b). Even for operations who do transport their goods to customers (most manufacturers, for example), we consider transportation as a supply-side factor because as location changes transportation costs also change.

Proximity to sources of *supply* dominates the location decision where the cost of transporting input materials is high or difficult. Food processing and other agricultural-based activities, for example, are often carried out close to growing areas. Conversely, transportation to *customers* dominates location decisions where transportation to customers is expensive or difficult.

Community factors

Community factors are those influences on an operation's costs which derive from the social, political and economic environment of its site. These include:

● local tax rates
● capital movement restrictions
● government financial assistance
● government planning assistance
● political stability
● local attitudes to 'inwards investment'

MOVING INTO CHINA?[6]

Intensive competition in their domestic market has driven some European garment manufacturers to look for cheaper sourcing sites and new markets. China is attracting a high level of new investment, and its government is keen to encourage foreign enterprise. It can offer the availability of a large, low-cost labour pool, and is also rich in textile raw material resources, making it a natural target for garment companies searching for long-term competitiveness. This example shows the alternatives faced by a French garment manufacturing company which was considering investment in China, but had yet to decide where to locate, whether to look initially at contract manufacture, or to set up its own manufacturing facility on a greenfield site, or to enter into a joint venture with a local agent. The executives had agreed that their initial priorities were to minimize the risks involved and to keep costs low, while developing a presence in the Chinese market to facilitate longer-term growth in an enormous new market.

The company initially identified four suitable areas for investment: Dalian, Shanghai, Jiangsu province and Guangdong province. Each satisfied the company's selection criteria of convenient sea and land access, good raw materials availability, a basic infrastructure, an established industrial base, and proximity to potential markets. Although there was no standard authoritative single source of comparisons of the sites, the executives managed to gather together a diverse set of information (summarized in Table 6.1) to help put their decision into perspective.

Table 6.1 Some factors affecting location decision of French garment manufacturer

Aspect	Shanghai	Jiangsu	Guangdong	Dalian
Local government incentives	Established special zones in the City	Some special incentive zones	The first to establish special economic zones	Some deals for foreign joint ventures
Local government authority to be able to permit new ventures	Unlimited	Up to US$10 million	Up to US$1.5 million	Up to US$5 million
Major sources of raw materials supplies	Mostly from Shanghai	From within the province	From Hong Kong	From throughout China
Approximate labour costs/month in local currency	350	230	350–800	220
Skills and availability	2% educated to higher level. Productivity very high, quality high	Productivity above national average, skilled labour	Skilled labour available in the City, unskilled in rural areas	No details, but believed adequate
Foreign exchange controls	Not convertable, SWAP centre available	SWAPs from Shanghai	Hong Kong dollar available	Remote, details unclear

▶

Table 6.1 (cont.)

Aspect	Shanghai	Jiangsu	Guangdong	Dalian
Electricity	Linked to major grid, although not always reliable	Charged at domestic rates	6 days/week only, nuclear plant being built	Supports heavy industry
Telecommunications	Under pressure	–	Good system	–
Transport	Largest port – very congested. Rail and air services excellent	Reliant on nearby Shanghai	Very close to Hong Kong. Transport links being developed rapidly	Remote from main cities – but good rail links
Textiles history	Largest in China with 1000+ factories	Largest cloth producer, largest wool manufacturer	Textiles are a low priority, but still has 1700 textile mills	1800+ factories; a large garment manufacturing centre
Knowledge of foreign dealing	Very experienced	Many foreign companies	International community	Over 500 foreign invested enterprises
Regional industry development	Second leading exporter	Agriculture very important	Top exporting region	Heavy industry

The company finally decided on a two-stage entry strategy. Initially it would use contract manufacturing, to give the flexibility of being able to order variable batch sizes, and to test out the quality and reliability of various suppliers. In this way, the company will have enough time and experience to enable it to identify a future joint venture partner. The area selected was Shanghai, primarily because of the good availability of skilled labour and its experience in the textiles industry. The company felt that Shanghai's familiarity in dealing with foreign investments would help to limit the bureaucracy involved in the early contract negotiations.

For this company, many factors came into play when trying to select a new overseas site for strategic development; and in this case, the solution that gave the most flexibility in the short term, with a view to building up solid relationships for the longer term, was seen as the most appropriate. In a different economic climate, or in another industry perhaps, the decision could have been very different. The choice is never routine. ■

- language
- local amenities (schools, theatres, shops, etc.)
- availability of support services
- history of labour relations
- labour absenteeism and turnover rates
- environmental restrictions and waste disposal
- planning procedures and restrictions.

Community factors can have a direct impact on the profitability of an organization. Local tax rates, for example, not surprisingly, play an important part in the location decisions of international companies. Others, such as the language spoken in the area, may not seem to have many cost consequences but can in practice prove very important. (*See* box on Japanese UK investment.)

WHY JAPAN INVESTED IN THE UK[7]

There are over 700 Japanese companies who have manufacturing operations located in Europe, of which there are around 200 in the UK, 120 in France, 110 in Germany and 60 in Spain. Large Japanese companies have recognized the importance of developing a manufacturing foothold in the huge European market, particularly to avoid having to add import duties to the costs of their products.

The UK is a popular location for a combination of reasons each of which has been weighted differently by each company. Some large early arrivals, such as Nissan, were attracted to the UK by generous government-funded financial support and tax concessions in regional development areas, most of which were in areas of high unemployment, yet with a tradition of industrial activity. They recognized that although potential employees did not necessarily have the skills needed to make their products, they were willing to be trained, and did not come with any 'bad habits' picked up from similar employment. Later arrivals had much fewer direct financial incentives to come to the UK, but saw the other advantages gained by the early arrivals. In some areas, such as Telford and Milton Keynes, a critical mass of Japanese companies developed, creating a flow of good publicity back to Japan, and encouraging further interest in these locations. This success was reinforced by a growth in support infrastructure such as Japanese schools, social activities, and even food retailing to help the expatriate families feel at home.

Another important factor was language. Many Japanese manufacturing companies are accustomed to trading and producing in the US, and so the English language is the first foreign language of most business people. Drawings of products and processes, instruction sheets and computer programs were often immediately available for use without further translation for the UK. This meant a lower risk of misunderstandings and mistranslation, smoothing communications between the new plant and head office in Japan.

As Japanese corporations became aware of some of the early successes in the UK, it became apparent that both the quality and cost of labour was an important reason to locate in the UK. While many large indigenous manufacturing companies had been criticizing the educational standard of the work-force, Japanese companies took great care to select employees who were keen to learn, adaptable, willing to work hard, and able to create improvements. Some companies were able to quote exceptionally high levels of productivity and quality performance in the UK, as an example to their Japanese work-force. Others began to export ▶

products from the UK to Japan. At the same time, the total cost of labour in the UK was relatively low, both due to hourly wage rates significantly below those typically paid in some other European Union countries, but also because of low costs directly associated with labour, such as state insurance and sickness benefit. Other significant reasons for a choice of the UK have been the relatively low rate of corporation tax, good communication links with most parts of the world, and a stable political and social system that doesn't create too many surprises. The development planning process is (as in most advanced economies) cumbersome, but at least they are transparent and difficulties of bribery and protection do not usually arise.

There are also other underlying factors which cannot be discounted. The UK is renowned for its excellent golf courses; spacious housing is available in countryside near industrial development areas; and London is known for its excellent shopping and leisure facilities. The climate, although not the kindest in Europe, is temperate and the rainfall is not unlike that in Japan. ■

Demand-side influences

Labour skills

The abilities of a local labour force can have an effect on customer reaction to the products or services which the operation produces. For example, 'science parks' are usually located close to universities because they hope to attract companies who are interested in using the skills available at the university. The companies who move to the science park hope that the quality of expertise locally available will reflect on the way in which their own customers view their own services or products.

The suitability of the site itself

Different sites are likely to have different intrinsic characteristics which can affect an operation's ability to serve customers and generate revenue. For example, the location of a luxury resort hotel which offers up-market holiday accommodation is very largely dependent on the intrinsic characteristics of the site. Located next to the beach surrounded by swaying palm trees and overlooking a picturesque bay, the hotel is very attractive to its customers. Move it a few kilometres away into the centre of an industrial estate, and it rapidly loses its attraction.

Image of the location

Some locations are firmly associated in customers' minds with a particular image. Suits from Savile Row (the centre of the up-market bespoke tailoring district in London) may be no better than high-quality suits made elsewhere but by locating its operation there, a tailor has probably enhanced its reputation and therefore its revenue. The product and fashion design houses of Milan and the financial services in the City of London's 'square mile' also enjoy a reputation shaped partly by that of their location.

Convenience for customers

Of all the demand-side factors this is, for many operations, the most important. Locating a general hospital, for instance, in the middle of the countryside may have many advantages for its staff and even maybe for its costs, but it clearly would be very inconvenient to its customers. Those visiting the hospital would need to travel long distances. Those being attended to in an emergency would have to wait longer than necessary to be brought in for admission. Because of this, general hospitals are located close to centres of demand. Similarly with other public services, location has a significant effect on the ability of the operation to serve its customers effectively. Likewise with restaurants, stores, banks, petrol filling stations and many other high customer contact operations, location determines the extent to which customers have to go in order to use the operation and therefore its revenue.

Levels of the location decision

The location decision is usually presented at three levels:

- choosing the region/country in which to locate the operation;
- choosing the area of the country or region;
- choosing the specific site within the area.

Choosing the region or country

Companies choosing in which part of the world to locate their operations have a wide range of options. While it has always been possible to manufacture in one part of the world in order to sell in another, until recently non-manufacturing operations were assumed to be confined to their home market. But no longer; the operational skills (as well as the brand image) of many service operations are transferable across national boundaries. Companies, such as Novotel hotels, McDonald's restaurants, Benetton clothing shops and Price Waterhouse the accountants, make location decisions on an international stage. Similarly, information processing operations can now locate outside their immediate home base, thanks to sophisticated telecommunications networks. If a bank sees a cost advantage in locating part of its back-office operation in a part of the world where the 'cost per transaction' is lower, it can do so. The keyboard operators, computer service managers and computer programmers of Stockholm, Frankfurt and London are now often competing directly with those in Delhi, Kuala Lumpur and Seoul.

Choosing an area within the country or region

Once an organization has decided in which country it wishes to locate, it will then need to choose an area of the country. Many of the factors which went into deciding the country will also play a part in deciding the area. Political stability and language might be less of an issue. Land prices, the local labour force, infrastructural development and community factors can play an important part, however.

Choosing a site

The choice of a site within an area is a different type of decision to those taken at the two 'higher' levels. In choosing a country or an area, an organization is selecting one of a relatively large number of options. For example, if a company is to build a new plant in Germany, it has several hundred towns and cities to choose from. However, the choice of a specific site is far more opportunistic. Usually the number of alternatives is far smaller. At any time there may be just one available site, and the decision is whether to take it or not.

The factors used to accept or reject a site are usually concerned with the characteristics of the specific site and its immediate surroundings. For example, the shape of the site and its soil composition can limit the nature of any buildings erected on the site. More difficult to judge can be the capability of the site to fit in with future developments in the operation. Room for expansion, for example, might be an issue, so the ability to lease or buy land close by or adjacent to the site could be important.

Location techniques

Although operations managers must exercise considerable judgement in the choice of alternative locations, there are some systematic and quantitative techniques which can help the decision process. We describe two here – the weighted-scoring method and the centre-of-gravity method.

Weighted scoring

The procedure involves, first of all, identifying the criteria which will be used to evaluate the various locations. Second, it involves establishing the relative importance of each criterion and giving weighting factors to them. Third, it means rating each location according to each criterion. The scale of the score is arbitrary. In our example we shall use 0 to 100, where 0 represents the worst possible score and 100 the best.

Example

An Irish company which prints and makes specialist packaging materials for the pharmaceutical industry has decided to build a new factory somewhere in Gauteng so as to provide a speedy service for its customers in Southern Africa. In order to choose a site it has decided to evaluate all options against a number of criteria. These criteria are:

- the cost of the site;
- the rate of local property taxation;
- the availability of suitable skills in the local labour force;
- the site's access to the motorway network;
- the potential of the site for future expansion.

After consultation with its property agents the company identifies three sites which seem to be broadly acceptable. These are known as sites A, B and C. The company also investigates each site and draws up the weighted score table shown in Table 6.2. It is important to remember that the scores shown in Table 6.2 are those which the manager has given as an indication of how each site meets the company's needs specifically. Nothing is necessarily being implied regarding any intrinsic worth of the locations.

Likewise, the weightings are an indication of how important the company finds each criterion in the circumstances in which it finds itself. The 'value' of a site for each criterion is then calculated by multiplying its score by the weightings for each criterion.

Table 6.2 Weighted score method for the three sites

Criteria	Importance weighting	Scores Sites		
		A	B	C
Cost of the site	4	80	65	60
Local taxes	2	20	50	80
Skills availability	1	80	60	40
Access to motorways	1	50	60	40
Access to airport	1	20	60	70
Potential for expansion	1	75	40	55
Total weighted scores		585	580	605[*]

[*]Preferred option

For location A, its score for the 'cost-of-site' criterion is 80 and the weighting of this criterion is 4, so its value is 80 × 4 = 320. All these values are then summed for each site to obtain its total weighted score.

Table 6.2 indicates that location C has the highest total weighted score and therefore would be the preferred choice. It is interesting to note, however, that location C has the lowest score on what is, by the company's own choice, the most important criterion – cost of the site. The high total weighted score which location C achieves in other criteria, however, outweighs this deficiency. If, on examination of this table, a company cannot accept what appears to be an inconsistency, then either the weights which have been given to each criterion, or the scores that have been allocated, do not truly reflect the company's preference.

The centre-of-gravity method

The centre of gravity method is used to find a location which minimizes transportation costs. It is based on the idea that all possible locations have a 'value' which is the sum of all transportation costs to and from that location. The best location, the one which minimizes costs, is represented by what in a physical analogy would be the weighted centre of gravity of all points to and from which goods are transported. So, for example, in Fig. 6.9 two suppliers, each sending 20 tonnes of parts per month to a factory, are located at points A and B. The factory must then assemble these parts and send them to one customer located at point C. Since point C receives twice as many tonnes as points A and B (transportation cost is assumed to be directly related to the tonnes of goods shipped) then it has twice the weighting of points A or B. The lowest transportation cost location for the factory is at the centre of gravity of a (weightless) board where the two suppliers' and one customer's locations are represented to scale and have weights equivalent to the weightings of the number of tonnes they send or receive.

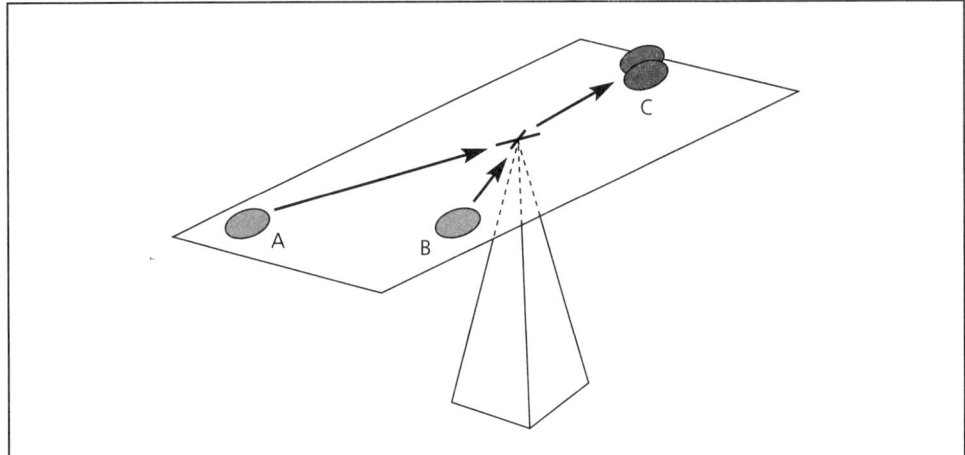

Figure 6.9
The centre-of-gravity method

Example

A company which operates four out-of-town garden centres has decided to keep all its stocks of products in a single warehouse. Each garden centre, instead of keeping large stocks of products, will fax its orders to the warehouse staff who will then deliver replenishment stocks to each garden centre as necessary.

The location of each garden centre is shown in the map in Fig. 6.10. A reference grid is superimposed over the map. The centre-of-gravity coordinates of the lowest cost location for the warehouse, $\bar{x}$ and $\bar{y}$, are given by the formulae:

$$\bar{x} = \frac{\sum x_i V_i}{\sum V_i}$$

and

$$\bar{y} = \frac{\sum y_i V_i}{\sum V_i}$$

where

x_i = the x coordinate of source or destination i

y_i = the y coordinate of source or destination i

V_i = the amount to be shipped to or from source or destination i.

Each of the garden centres is of a different size and has different sales volumes. In terms of the number of truck loads of products sold each week, Table 6.3 shows the sales of the four centres.

In this case

$$\bar{x} = \frac{(1 \times 5) + (5 \times 10) + (5 \times 12) + (9 \times 8)}{35}$$
$$= 5.34$$

and

$$\bar{y} = \frac{(2 \times 5) + (3 \times 10) + (1 \times 12) + (4 \times 8)}{35}$$

$$= 1.14$$

Table 6.3 The weekly demand levels (in truck loads) at each of the four garden centres

	Sales per week (truck loads)
Garden centre A	5
Garden centre B	10
Garden centre C	12
Garden centre D	8
Total	35

So the minimum cost location for the warehouse is at point (5.34, 1.14) as shown in Fig. 6.10. That is at least theoretically. In practice, the optimum location might also be influenced by other factors such as the transportation network. So if the optimum location was at a point with poor access to a suitable road or at some other unsuitable location (in a residential area, or the middle of a lake, for example) then the chosen location will need to be adjusted. The technique does go some way, however, towards providing an indication of the area in which the company should be looking for sites for its warehouse.

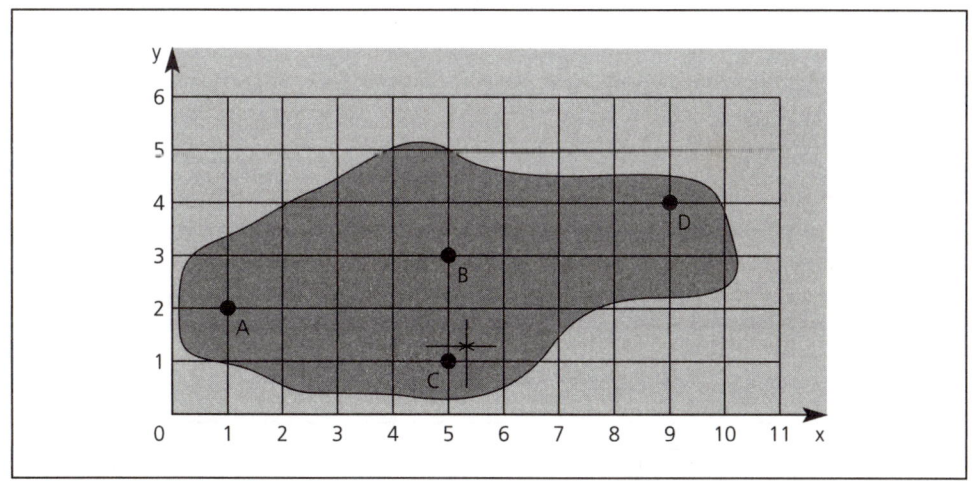

Figure 6.10 Centre-of-gravity location for the garden centre warehouse

LONG-TERM CAPACITY MANAGEMENT

After the vertical integration of the operation's network and the location of its various operations have been decided, the next set of decisions concerns the size or capacity of each part of the network. Here we shall treat capacity in a general long-term sense. The specific issues involved in measuring and adjusting capacity in the medium and short terms are examined in Chapter 11.

The optimum capacity level

Most organizations need to decide on the size (in terms of capacity) of each of their facilities. An air conditioning unit company, for example, might operate plants each of which has a capacity (at normal product mix) of 800 units per week. At activity levels below this, the average cost of producing each unit will increase because the fixed costs of the factory are being covered by fewer units produced. Figure 6.11 illustrates the theoretical cost curve for the factory. The total production costs of the factory have some elements which are fixed – they will be incurred irrespective of how much, or little, the factory produces. The slope of the total cost line in Fig. 6.11 represents the variable cost per unit produced – that is, the costs incurred by the factory for each unit it produces. Dividing the total cost at any output level by the output level itself gives the average cost of producing units at that output rate.

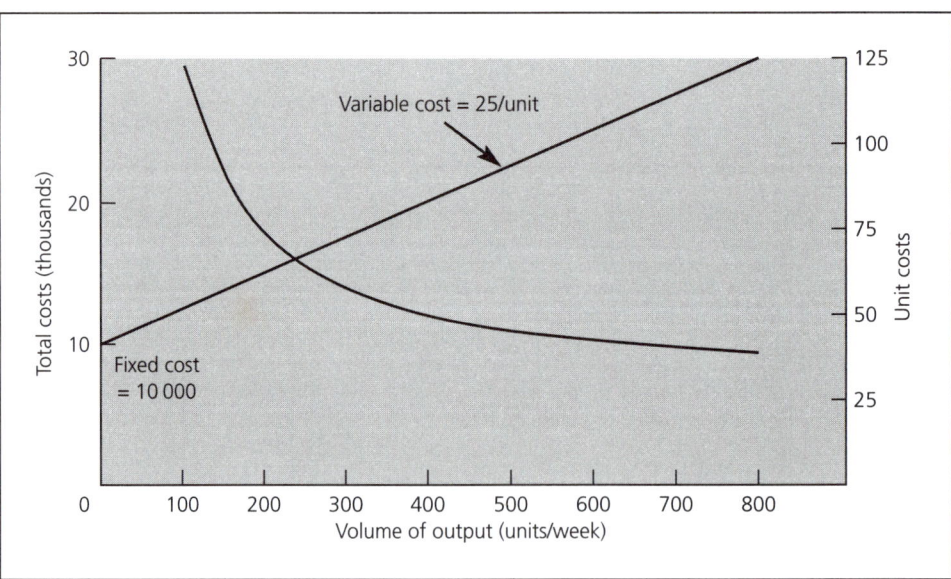

**Figure 6.11
Unit cost of output
varies as volume of
output varies**

The average cost of producing the units seems to reach its lowest point at maximum capacity. However, the actual average cost curve may be different from that shown in Fig. 6.11 for a number of reasons.

● All fixed costs are not incurred at one time as the factory starts to operate. Rather they occur at many points (called fixed cost 'breaks') as volume increases. This makes the theoretically smooth average cost curve more discontinuous.

● Production levels may be increased above the theoretical capacity of the plant, by using prolonged overtime, for example, or temporarily sub-contracting some parts of the work.

● There may be less obvious cost penalties of operating the plant at levels close to or above its nominal capacity. For example, long periods of overtime may reduce productivity levels as well as costing more in extra payments to staff; operating plant for long periods with reduced maintenance time may increase the chances of breakdown, and so on. This usually means that average costs start to increase after a point which will often be lower than the theoretical capacity of the plant.

Figure 6.12 illustrates how the actual (smoothed) average cost curve might look for the 800-unit-a-week plant.

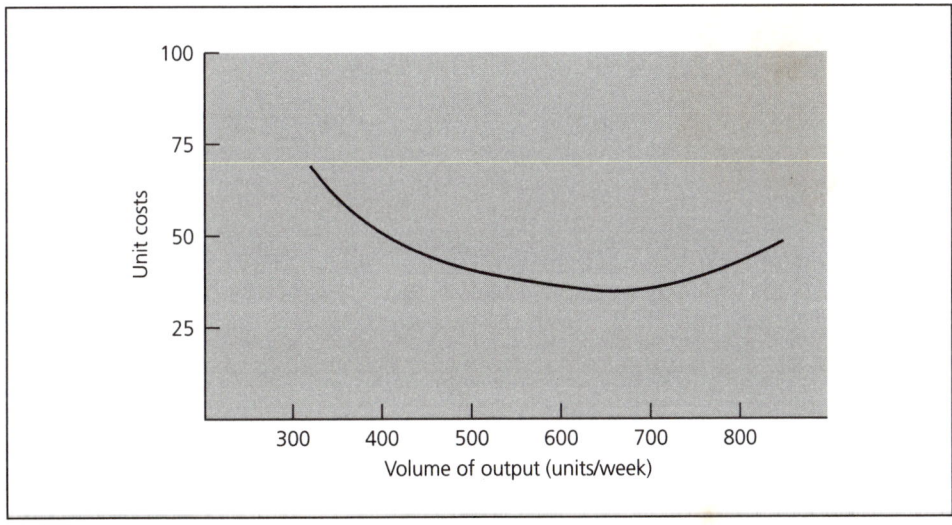

Figure 6.12
Unit costs of output allowing for diseconomies of scale

A similar relationship occurs between the average cost curves for plants of increasing size. Figure 6.13 illustrates a series of average cost curves. At first, as the nominal capacity of the plants increases, the lowest cost points reduce. There are two main reasons for this.

● The fixed costs of an operation do not increase proportionately as its capacity increases. An 800-unit plant has less than twice the fixed costs of a 400-unit plant.

● The capital costs of building the plant do not increase proportionately to its capacity. An 800-unit plant costs less to build than twice the cost of a 400-unit plant.

These two factors, taken together, are often referred to as *economies of scale*. However, above a certain size, the lowest cost point may increase. In the illustration in Fig. 6.13 this happens with plants above 800 units capacity. This occurs because of what are called the *diseconomies of scale*, two of which are particularly important.

● Transportation costs can be high for large operations. For example, if a manufacturer supplies the whole of its European market from one major plant in Denmark, all supplies may have to be brought from several countries to the single plant and all products shipped from there throughout Europe. Conversely, if the company has three smaller plants located closer to their relevant markets and suppliers, transportation costs will be lower.

● Complexity costs increase as size increases. The communications and coordination effort necessary to manage an operation tends to increase faster than capacity.

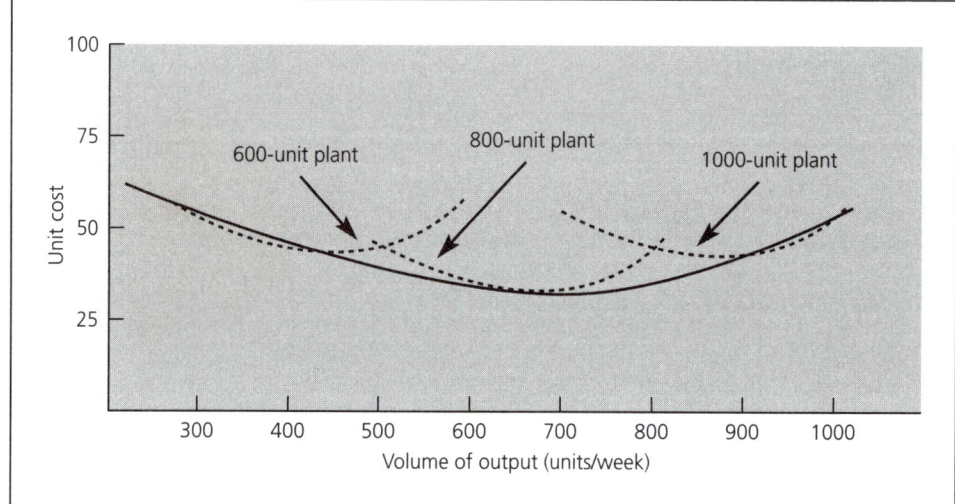

**Figure 6.13
Unit cost of
output curves for
plants of varying
capacities**

Scale of capacity and the demand–capacity balance

Large units of capacity also have some disadvantages when the capacity of the operation is being changed to match changing demand. For example, suppose that the air conditioning unit manufacturer forecasts demand increase over the next three years as shown in Fig. 6.14, to level off at around 2400 units a week. If the company seeks to satisfy all demand by building three plants, each of 800 units capacity, the company will have substantial amounts of over-capacity for much of the period when demand is increasing. Over-capacity means low capacity utilization which in turn means higher unit costs (from the average cost curve in Fig. 6.11). If the company builds smaller plants, say 400-unit plants, there will still be over-capacity but to a lesser extent, which means higher capacity utilization and possibly lower costs.

The inherent risks of changing capacity using large increments can also be high. For example, if demand does not reach 2400 units a week but levels off at 2000 units a week, the final 800-unit plant will only be 50 per cent utilized. However, if 400-unit plants are used the likelihood is that the over-optimistic forecast would have been detected in time to delay or cancel the final plant, leaving demand and capacity in balance (*see* Fig. 6.15).

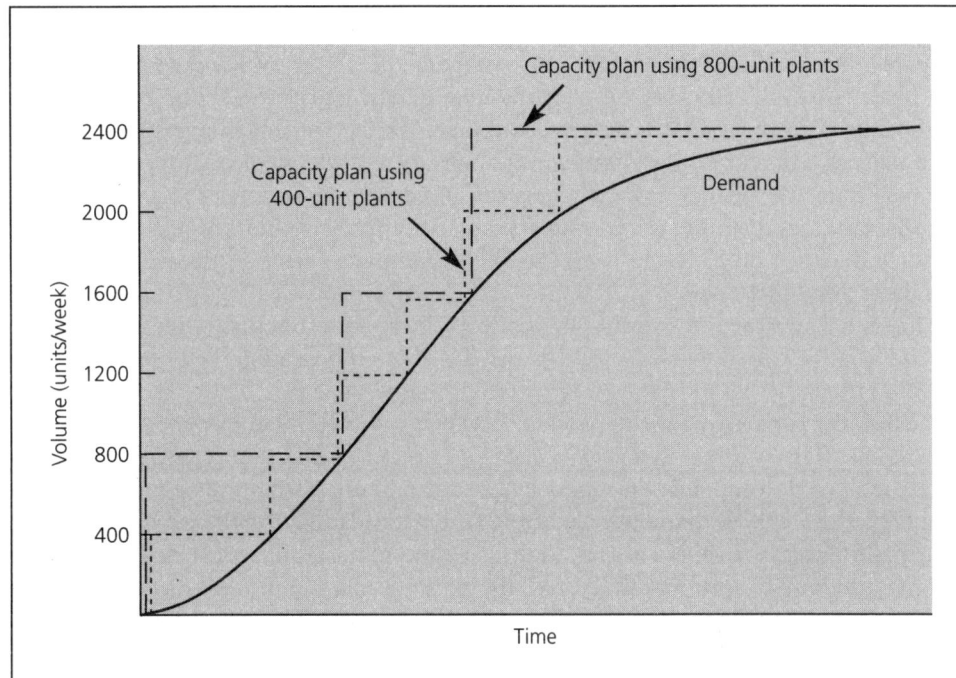

Figure 6.14
The scale of capacity increments affects the utilization of capacity

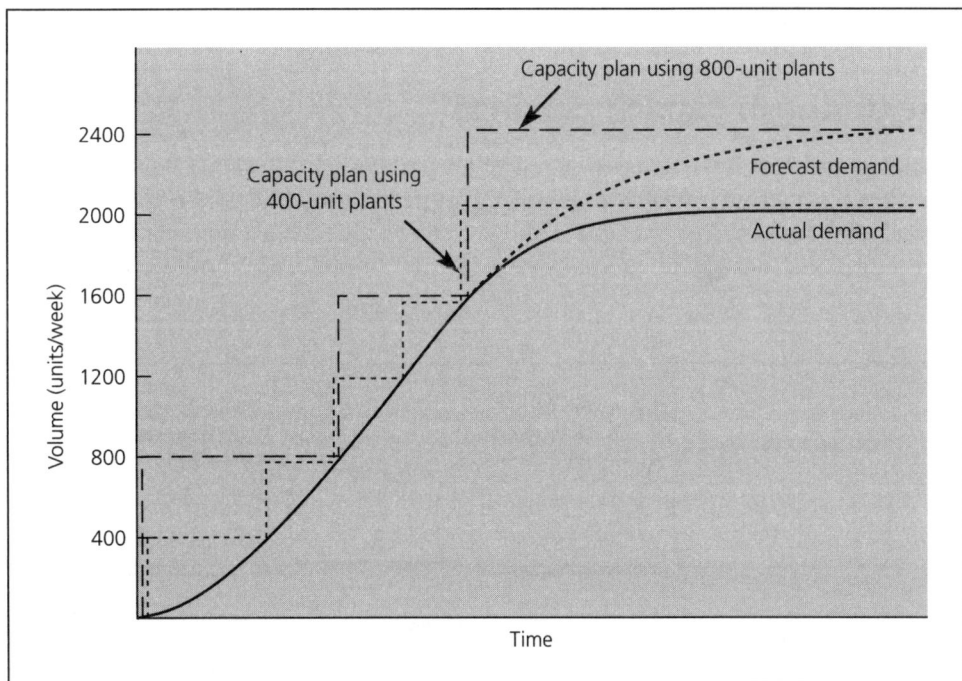

Figure 6.15
Smaller scale capacity increments allow the capacity plan to be adjusted to accommodate changes in demand

Balancing capacity

So far we have confined our discussion of capacity to the assumption that a single operation is internally homogeneous. Yet, as we discussed in Chapter 1, all operations are made up of micro operations, and each micro operation will itself have its own capacity. So, for example, the 800-unit capacity air conditioning unit factory not only assembles the products but probably also manufactures most of the parts from which it is made. If so, the capacity of the parts manufacturing section of the factory must be capable of producing parts at a rate sufficient for the assembly department to produce units at a rate of 800 per week, if the output from the whole factory is not to be reduced. Similarly further down the network of internal operations, the air conditioning units are moved to the warehouse after assembly, where they are packed in cases, stored and loaded on to trucks as needed. The company's fleet of trucks then distributes them to its customers.

This is a four-stage network of operations. Parts manufacturing feeds assembly which feeds the warehouse which feeds the distribution operation. For the network to operate efficiently, all its stages must have the same capacity. If they have different capacities, the capacity of the network as a whole will be limited to the capacity of its slowest link. This can be visualized as a series of pipes of different diameters, through which liquid is flowing. The throughput rate of the whole system will be limited by the pipe with the smallest diameter. Figure 6.16 illustrates this for the air conditioning unit manufacturer. In this case the output of the plant is not constrained by parts manufacturing, but once manufactured, the products cannot move through the warehouse at a rate sufficient to keep pace with the factory. The warehouse is what is called the *bottle-neck* in the supply network.

The concept of the bottle-neck is an important one because it is the ultimate constraint on the capacity of any system of operations. In different forms the concept will occur at several points in this book.

The timing of capacity change

Changing the capacity of an operation is not just a matter of deciding on the best size of a capacity increment. The operation also needs to decide when to bring 'on-stream' new capacity. For example, Fig. 6.17 shows the forecast demand for the new air conditioning unit. The company has decided to build 400-unit/week plants in

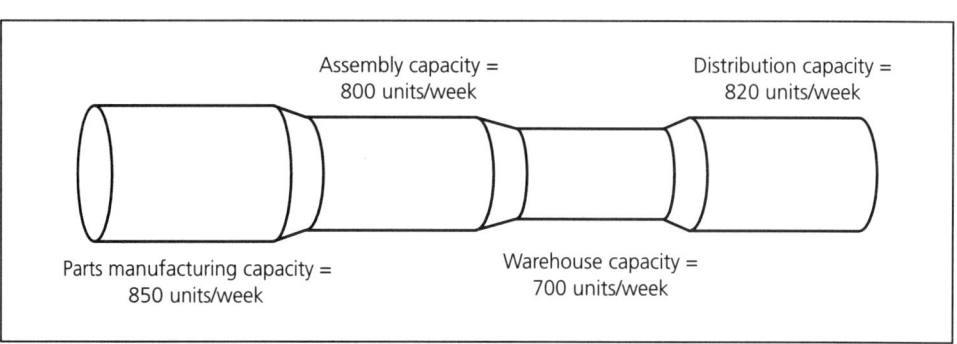

Figure 6.16 When capacity at each stage is not balanced, the capacity of the total system is limited by that of the bottle-neck stage

Assembly capacity = 800 units/week

Distribution capacity = 820 units/week

Parts manufacturing capacity = 850 units/week

Warehouse capacity = 700 units/week

order to meet the growth in demand for its new product. In deciding *when* the new plants are to be introduced the company must choose a position somewhere between two extreme strategies.

● *Capacity leads demand* – timing the introduction of capacity in such a way that there is always sufficient capacity to meet forecast demand;
● *Capacity lags demand* – timing the introduction of capacity so that demand is always equal to or greater than capacity.

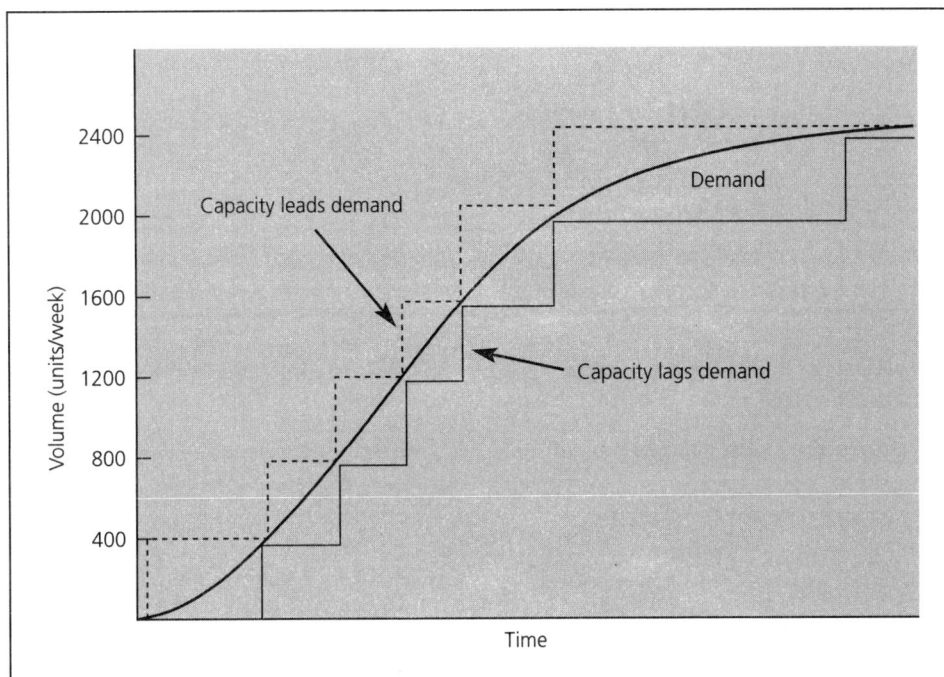

Figure 6.17
Capacity-leading and capacity-lagging strategies

Figure 6.17 shows these two extreme strategies, though in practice the company is likely to choose a position somewhere between the two extremes. Each strategy has its own advantages and disadvantages. These are shown in Table 6.4. The actual approach taken by any company will depend on how it views these advantages and disadvantages. For example, if the company's access to funds for capital expenditure is limited, it is likely to find the delayed capital expenditure requirement of the capacity-lagging strategy relatively attractive.

'Smoothing' with inventory

The strategy on the continuum between pure leading and lagging strategies can be implemented so that no inventories are accumulated. All demand in one period is satisfied (or not) by the activity of the operation in the same period. Indeed, for customer-processing operations there is no alternative to this. An hotel cannot satisfy demand in one year by using rooms which were vacant the previous year. For some materials- and information-processing operations, however, the output from the

Table 6.4 The arguments for and against pure leading and pure lagging strategies of capacity timing

Advantages	Disadvantages
Capacity-leading strategies	
Always sufficient capacity to meet demand, therefore revenue is maximized and customers satisfied.	Utilization of the plants is always relatively low, therefore costs will be high.
Most of the time there is a 'capacity cushion' which can absorb extra demand if forecasts are pessimistic.	Risks of even greater (or even permanent) over-capacity if demand does not reach forecast levels.
Any critical start-up problems with new plants are less likely to affect supply to customers.	Capital spending on plant early.
Capacity-lagging strategies	
Always sufficient demand to keep the plants working at full capacity, therefore unit costs are minimized.	Insufficient capacity to meet demand fully, therefore reduced revenue and dissatisfied customers.
Over-capacity problems are minimized if forecasts are optimistic.	No ability to exploit short-term increases in demand.
Capital spending on the plants is delayed.	Under-supply position even worse if there are start-up problems with the new plants.

operation which is not required in one period can be stored for use in the next period. The economies of using inventories are fully explored in Chapter 12. Here we confine ourselves to noting that inventories can be used to obtain both the advantages of capacity leading and lagging.

Figure 6.18 shows how this can be done. Here the plants have been introduced such that over-capacity in one period is used to make air conditioning units for the following or subsequent periods. Capacity is introduced such that demand can always be met by a combination of production and inventories, and capacity is, with the occasional exception, fully utilized.

This may seem like an ideal state. Demand is always met and so revenue is maximized. Capacity is usually fully utilized and so costs are minimized. The profitability of the operation is therefore likely to be high. There is a price to pay, however, and that is the cost of carrying the inventories. Not only will these have to be funded (*see* Chapter 12) but the risks of obsolescence and deterioration of stock are introduced.

Possible life-cycle effects

Whether operations choose predominantly leading, predominantly lagging, or, if they can, a smoothing-with-inventories strategy, will depend on their own circumstances. These will vary greatly, but some generalization can be made, especially concerning how a company's position on the product/service life cycle can affect the choice of strategy.

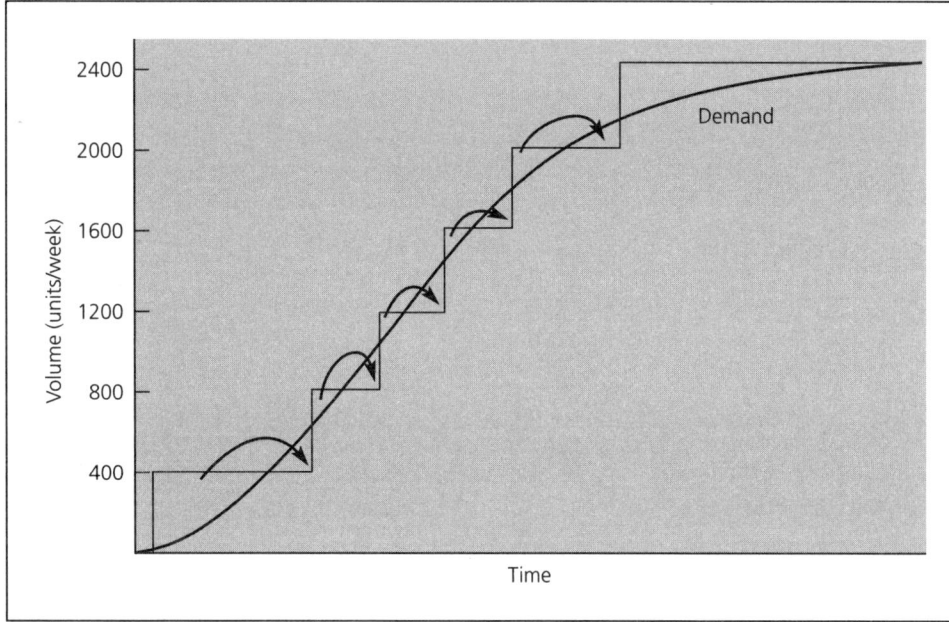

Figure 6.18
Smoothing with inventory means using the excess capacity of one period to produce inventory which can be used to supply the under-capacity period

At the product/service *introduction* stage of the life cycle it is difficult to adapt any other than a *capacity-leading strategy*. Capacity must be available to produce the goods or deliver the services, otherwise customers will not have the ability to sample them and make a judgement of their acceptability. Furthermore the main disadvantages of capacity-leading strategies, namely low utilization and therefore high costs, is more likely to be tolerated at the introduction stage where competition might not be based on low prices.

During the *growth* phase of the life cycle, demand forecasting is particularly difficult because small changes in growth rates can result in very different levels of demand. With uncertain demand the existence of high inventories might not seem as much of a disadvantage as when they are seen purely as a cost. Therefore *smoothing with inventory* might be preferred as a strategy where this is possible.

On reaching *maturity* the nature of competition usually emphasizes low price more than in earlier stages. When price competition is tough, most companies will be more concerned with keeping their costs low. This will make the full utilization of *capacity-lagging* strategies seem attractive. Figure 6.19 illustrates this.

Break-even analysis of capacity expansion

An alternative view of capacity expansion can be gained by examining the cost implications of adding increments of capacity on a break-even basis. Figure 6.20 shows how increasing capacity can move an operation from profitability to loss. Each additional unit of capacity results in a *fixed-cost break*, that is a further lump of expenditure which will have to be incurred before any further activity can be undertaken in the operation. The operation is therefore unlikely to be profitable at very low

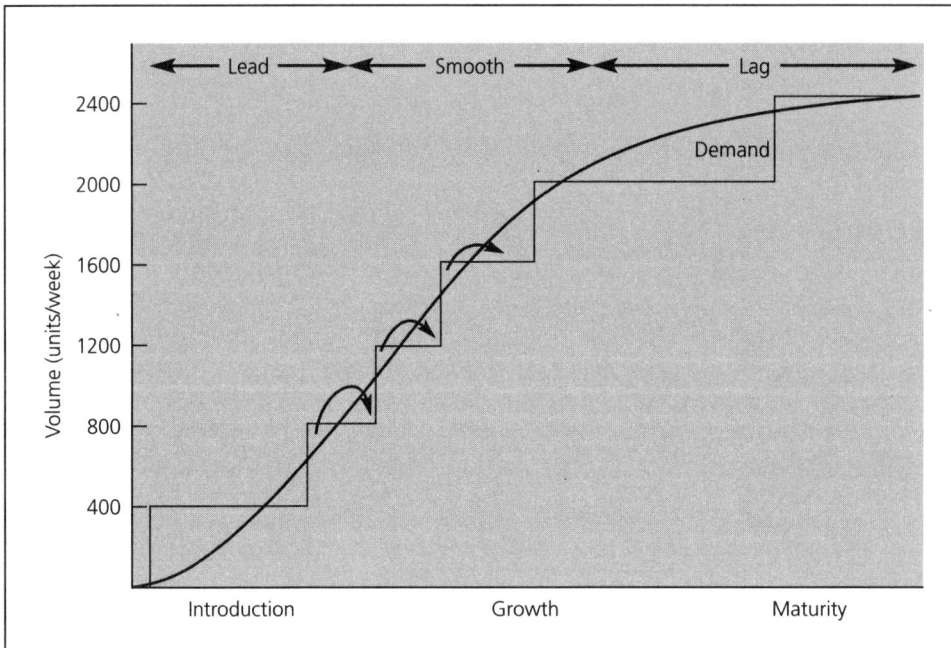

**Figure 6.19
The life-cycle effect
on capacity
strategies**

levels of output. Eventually, assuming that prices are greater than marginal costs, revenue will exceed total costs. However, the level of profitability at the point where the output level is equal to the capacity of the operation may not be sufficient to absorb all the extra fixed costs of a further increment in capacity. This could make the operation unprofitable in some stages of its expansion.

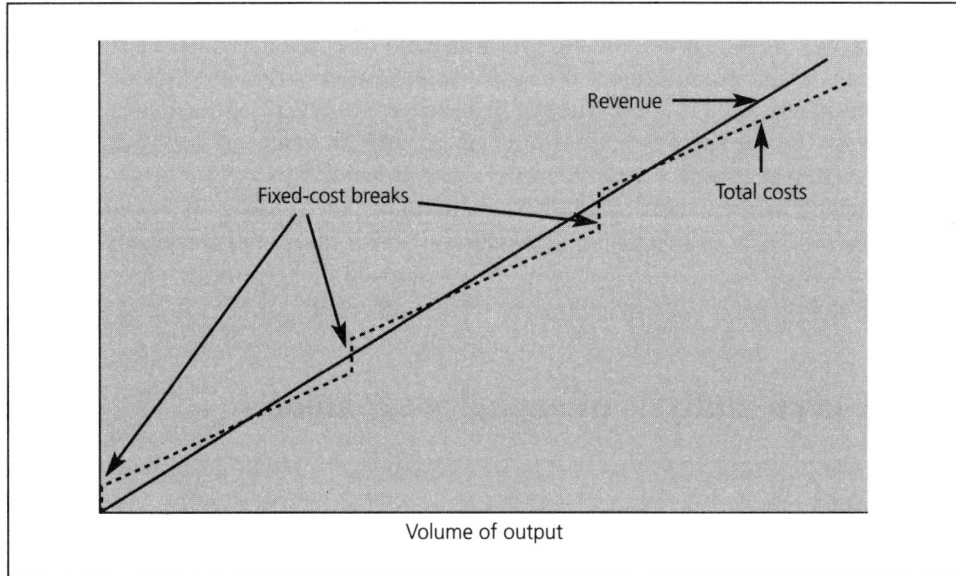

**Figure 6.20
Repeated incurring
of fixed costs can
raise total costs
above revenue**

Colin Carmichael, Pleasure Foods

Colin Carmichael is the general manager of the Juicy Lucy brand at Pleasure Foods. This organization is part of the Anglovaal Group and is the holding company for a range of franchise brands including Wimpy and Milky Lane. The Juicy Lucy franchise received the 1996 award for the fastest growing brand in the group in terms of sales, outlets and profitability. Colin discusses his approach towards growing the market share of the Juicy Lucy brand.

'The Juicy Lucy brand has been on the market now for over 15 years and has carved out its own special niche in the over-traded fast-food market in South Africa. The brand appeals to a particular segment of this market, namely the health conscious individual. This encompasses the entire range of age groups from retired but active individuals to diet-aware teenagers, as well as the fitness-conscious executive. The target market typically includes the A and B income groups and in certain establishments extends to the super As.

'Our first priority is obviously to grow sales through existing outlets because this benefits our existing franchisees and maximizes returns on capacity that has already been installed. A further growth opportunity is to open up new stores, although this places a particular strain on the resources of the franchiser organization. The process of identifying potentially viable store locations, negotiating leases, screening and selecting franchisees and physically opening stores is quite a complex one. This is, however, aided by the fact that the Juicy Lucy concept is quite well packaged and easily replicated.

'We started out with a theme and developed that theme into a service package that we could easily install into a new building. We would experiment with store layouts and menu designs until we had everything as we wanted it. We then documented all of our standard practises into a training manual. We also attempt to work on a standard menu across all outlets although we review choices together on a regular basis. The standardization of operations extends even to choices of ingredient, packaging and crockery suppliers, as well as equipment and service providers.

'The choice of every new site that we opened was always a matter of assessing the potential market that we thought would exist in an area and at the same time considering the structural constraints of any potential properties. Present target establishments for new stores are in health clubs, malls and entertainment centres: anywhere, in fact, that our target market enjoy hanging out. We therefore spend lots of time with developers and operators of this sort of establishment to ensure that attractive sites are brought into the chain.

'The concept is also being adapted to widen the range of establishments that the chain could expand into. This could involve either scaling the concept up or down or even altering it in more fundamental ways. The Juicy Lucy Express concept was initiated to break into the convenience store markets in service stations. This scaled down version was less successful than we would have hoped and a new version which is scaled down even further is being used to relaunch the brand in this particular niche.

'Our learning curve was quite rapid and we are now in a position where we can recognize more quickly whether or not a site will be appropriate, and have got the period from moving in to opening up down to less than two weeks. The restaurant staff and franchisees are trained in other outlets in the country and the furniture and fittings are all standardized and ordered in advance, so it is really just a matter of adding the finishing touches and commissioning the equipment, and we're in and running.

'We also had to ensure that we could keep up with the rapid pace of expansion. Opening a new site needs both management and specialist resources. We put a lot of effort into working out the workload implications of each step in our expansion. The roll-out programme on new stores occurs in parallel with concept innovations and with new marketing campaigns and product promotions. ▶

The opening of new stores is therefore carefully scheduled to avoid overloading our limited resources at head office.

'We recognize that the staff and franchisees are our most valuable asset. The planning and preparation for each step in our expansion programme will bring no success if we cannot get the people side right. Training starts weeks before the store has opened and continues after opening. The franchise strives for excellence in all things, including its people. For this reason the organization has a policy of ongoing training and people development, including an annual "excellence recognition" conference.' ■

Source: By kind permission of Pleasure Foods

SUMMARY

■ All operations are part of a larger network of customers and suppliers. Taking a broad perspective, the operations network can be traced back to the original sources of goods and services and forward to the final end customers. All of the operations on the supply side and the demand side of an operation, taken together, are called the total supply network for the operation. The customers and suppliers with which an operation has immediate contact are known as the immediate supply network.

■ There are a number of advantages of considering the whole network in which an operation is set. These are first that it helps any operation to understand how it can compete more effectively within the network. Second, it helps to identify particularly significant links within the network. Third, it helps a company to focus on its long-term strategic position within a network.

■ The design decisions at this strategic network level are concerned with the vertical integration of the network, the location of the various operations of the network, and the capacity of each part of the network.

■ Vertical integration means the extent to which an organization owns the network of which it is a part. It is defined by three decisions. The direction of ownership can be either backwards towards suppliers or forwards towards customers. The extent of ownership can be narrowly focused on the original operation or, at the other extreme, widely spread throughout the network. The balance among the stages in the network can either involve exclusive relationships in which each stage serves only its own in-house customers, or alternatively, where each stage is free to trade with parts of the network which are not owned by the organization.

■ Vertical integration affects all performance objectives but carries both benefits and risks for each one.

■ The location decision can have effects on the cost base of an operation, the degree to which it serves its customers, and the revenue-earning potential of the operation.

■ The stimulus for changing location and the costs which organizations take into account when choosing a new location can be divided into supply-side and demand-side influences. Supply-side influences are the factors such as labour, land, and utility costs which change as location changes. Demand-side influences include such things as the image of the location, its convenience for customers, and the suitability of the site itself.

■ All these factors can be applied (to different degrees) at three levels: the choice of a country or region, the choice of an area within a country or region, the choice of the specific site itself.

■ The capacity decisions which need to be taken in a network include choosing the optimum capacity for each site, balancing the various capacity levels of the operations in the network, and timing the changes in their capacity of each part of the network.

Delta Synthetic Fibres[8]

DSF is a small but technically successful company in the man-made fibre industry. The company was heavily dependent on the sales of Britlene, a product it had developed itself, which accounted in 1994 for some 95 per cent of total sales.

Britlene was used mainly in heavy-duty clothing, although small quantities were used to produce industrial goods such as tyre cord and industrial belting. Its main properties were very high wear resistance, thermal and electrical insulation.

In 1994 the company had developed a new product, Britlon. Britlon had all the properties of Britlene but was superior in its heat resistant qualities. It was hoped that this additional property would open up new clothing uses (e.g. a substitute for mineral wool clothing, added to night-wear to improve its inflammability), and new industrial uses in thermal and electrical insulation.

By late 1994 the major technical and engineering problems associated with bulk production of Britlon seemed to have been solved and the company had set up a working party to put forward proposals on how the new product should be phased into the company's activities.

The basic production method of Britlene and Britlon was similar to that of most man-made fibres. To make a man-made fibre, an oil-based organic chemical is polymerized (a process of joining several molecules into a long chain) in conditions of intense pressure and heat, often by the addition of a suitable catalyst. This polymerization takes place in large autoclaves (an industrial pressure cooker). The polymer is then extruded (forced through a nozzle like the rose of a garden watering can), rapidly cooled and then either spun on to cones or collected in bales.

The raw materials for Britlene and Britlon were produced at Teeside in the UK.

Britlene facilities

Britlene was produced at three factories in the UK: Teeside, Bradford and Dumfries. The largest site was Teeside with three plants. There was one plant at each of the other two sites.

All five production plants had a design capacity of 5.5 million kg per year of Britlene. However, after allowing for maintenance and an annual shutdown, expected output was 5 million kg per year. Each plant operated on a 24-hours-per-day, 7-days-per-week basis.

Proposed Britlon facilities

Britlon's production process was very similar to that used for Britlene but a totally new type of polymerization unit was needed prior to the extrusion stage.

DSF had approached Alpen Engineering Company, an international chemical plant construction company, for help on a large-scale plant design of the new unit. Together they had produced and tested an acceptable design.

Acquiring Britlon capacity

There were two ways of acquiring Britlon capacity. DSF could convert a Britlene plant, or they could construct an entirely new plant.

For a conversion, the new polymer unit would need to be constructed first. When complete it would be connected to the extrusion unit which would require minor conversion. At least two years would be needed either to build a new Britlon plant or to convert an old Britlene plant to Britlon production.

The company Chief Executive Officer had been quoted as saying:

'*The creation of an entirely new site would increase the complexities of multi-site operation to an unacceptable level. Conversely, the complete closure of one of the three existing sites is, I consider, a waste of the manpower and physical resources that we have invested in that location. I believe expansion could take place at one, two or all of the existing sites.*'

Table 6.5 Forecast sales for Britlene and Britlon (millions of kg per year)

Potential sales	Britlene	Britlon
1994 (actual)	24.7	–
1995	22	–
1996	20	–
1997	17	3 (assuming availability)
1998	13	16
1999	11	27
2000	10	29

Only on Teeside was there higher than average general unemployment, but the unemployment rate for skilled and semi-skilled workers was quite low at all sites. Demand for skilled labour on Teeside was from two giant companies, ▶

both of whom were expanding in that area; at Dumfries and Bradford there was little or no competition.

Demand

Demand forecasts for the two products are shown in Table 6.5. They show that, although Britlene sales will probably fall rapidly once Britlon is introduced, there is likely to be a residual level of sales of the older product. ■

Questions

1 What order schedule would you propose for conversions and new plant?
2 In which locations would you make these capacity changes?
3 What criteria have you used to make your recommendations?
4 What do you see as the main dangers facing DSF as it changes its capacity over the next five or six years?

DISCUSSION QUESTIONS

1 Talk to an operations manager and then construct a diagram depicting the organization's supply network. How is the performance of suppliers monitored?

2 Why should operations managers be concerned with the whole network? Illustrate your answer using an organization of your own choice.

3 Explain what is meant by vertical integration. Explain how and why upstream and downstream integration might be used by a Mediterranean-based sailing holiday company.

4 Most organizations could, if they wished, choose to reduce the extent of their vertical integration. For the following operations, which activities do you think the organization could subcontract out if it wished to focus more on its primary activity of serving customers:
  a public library
  a sports complex
  a fast-food restaurant
  a bank?

5 Oil companies are some of the most integrated companies in the world. For a large oil company, such as BP or Shell, draw the supply network from raw materials through to the end customers. Which of the activities you have drawn in the network do you think a company like Shell are involved in? Why do you think such companies are so vertically integrated?

6 An aluminium extrusion company, part of a large integrated aluminium company, has traditionally been engaged in extruding aluminium sections for use in the construction of double-glazed windows. However, the fashion in double-glazed windows has recently moved from aluminium towards a combination of aluminium and UPVC (a polymer). Currently all the aluminium which the extrusion company buys in comes from other parts of the integrated company. Do you think the extrusion company should continue to extrude aluminium sections and provide demand for the other parts of the company, in spite of the changes in its own markets? Alternatively, should the company pursue its own interests and begin extruding aluminium/UPVC combined sections, which it would appear the market wants?

7 A research company has decided to set up a new laboratory in Australia to provide analysis services for mineral extraction companies. Table 6.6 shows the three locations it is considering and the criteria which it is using to make the decision. If the first two factors are twice as important as the rest, which location do you think is most suitable for the new laboratory?

8 A Hong Kong company specializing in the manufacture of garden furniture has decided to establish a distribution centre in Europe. The possible locations are Birmingham, Amsterdam and Belgrade. Several criteria have been scored out of 100 (*see* Table 6.7).

Table 6.6 Scoring for three locations (scores out of 100)

Factor	Perth	Sydney	Darwin
Closeness to customers	80	50	90
Closeness to universities	70	90	20
Attractiveness of city	70	90	50
Climate	60	80	60
Schools	70	80	60
Housing costs	60	20	100
Availability of sites	70	50	100

Table 6.7 Scoring for three locations

Factor	Birmingham	Amsterdam	Belgrade
Cost of land	60	50	80
Distribution costs	15	70	60
Expected annual labour turnover	30	30	70
Housing availability	60	20	75
Market access	50	60	55
Expansion possibilities	70	20	80

The Managing Director considers the cost of land and the distribution costs to be three times as important as labour turnover and housing availability and twice as important as the market access and expansion possibilities. Which location should the company adopt?

9 Join with a colleague and assess the location of two or three competing services, for example, supermarkets, dentists or car repair garages. Undertake your assessment individually then compare your results and identify and try to reconcile the differences in ratings and criteria. Are there any other performance criteria that compensate for any organization's poor location?

10 The Vegocream Corporation has decided to extend its operations from North America to Europe. The company retails its extensive range of vegetable-flavoured ice-creams through its high street outlets, where it caters for sit-down customers as well as take-away business. What decisions do you think the Vegocream company will have to take in planning its locations

strategy? Draw up a series of questions which you think might be useful to the company when it decides whether to take up the lease on a particular site when it is offered it.

11 Location is always considered of particular importance in retail operations. Why do you think this is so?

12 A company which assembles garden furniture obtains its components from three suppliers. Supplier A provides all the boxes and packaging material; supplier B provides all metal components; supplier C provides all plastic components. Supplier A sends one truck load of the materials per week to the factory and is located at the position (1,1) on a grid reference which covers the local area. Supplier B sends four truck loads of components per week to the factory and is located at point (2,3) on the grid. Supplier C sends three truck loads of components per week to the factory and is located at point (4,3) on the grid. After assembly all the products are sent to a warehouse which is located at point (5,1) on the grid. Assuming there is little or no waste generated in the process, where should the company locate its factory so as to minimize transportation costs? Assume that transportation costs are directly proportional to the number of truck loads of parts, or finished goods, transported per week.

13 What is meant by capacity? What input and output measures of capacity might be used for the following operations and explain which one is more likely to be used:
  car plant
  bus company
  water company
  chiropodist?

14 The forecast demand for a new product over the next seven periods is as shown in Table 6.8 (overleaf). The company is deciding the timing of its capacity expansion and contraction strategy. If the company has decided to build plants with a capacity of 15 000 units per period, when would you recommend the company commissions, or takes out of commission, its plants, assuming that:
(a) it adopts a capacity-leading strategy; or
(b) it adopts a capacity-lagging strategy.

Table 6.8 Forecast demand

Period	Demand
1	10 000
2	30 000
3	50 000
4	60 000
5	64 000
6	62 000
7	55 000

15 A solicitor, although not as yet working as much as he would like, wishes to treble the size of his practice over the next five years. Explain how this might be achieved and the advantages and disadvantages of leading or lagging demand.

16 Why should the timing of capacity expansion affect the profitability of a company and its cash flow? Do you think the strategy which maximizes profitability also gives the best cash flow performance?

NOTES ON CHAPTER

1 Jones, C. (1990) 'Cross-boundary Supply Chain Management', *Professional Engineer*, Vol 3, No 5.
2 Slack, N. (1991) *The Manufacturing Advantage*, Mercury Books.
3 Jones, C. (1990), *op. cit.*
4 Hayes, R.H. and Wheelwright, S.C. (1994) *Restoring our Competitive Edge*, John Wiley.
5 Source: the Swedish Employers Confederation.
6 Based on a real location decision – company disguised.
7 Sources: Pitman, J. (1994) 'Land of the Rising Sun Casts a Long Shadow', *The Times*, 7 Sept 1994, and Garner, R. (1990) 'Why Toyota Chose Derby', the *Financial Times*, 5 June 1990.
8 This case is based on an original case 'Doman Synthetic Fibres' by Peter Jones of Sheffield Hallam University, UK.

SELECTED FURTHER READINGS

Bartlett, C. and Ghoshal, S. (1989) *Managing Across Borders*, Harvard Business School Press.
Blackstone, W.H. Jnr (1989) *Capacity Management*, South Western.
Bulow, J.J. (1985) 'Holding Idle Capacity to Deter Entry', *Economic Journal*, Vol 95, Mar.
Craig, C.S. *et al.* (1984) 'Models of the Retail Location Process', *Journal of Retailing*, Vol 60, No 1.
Freidenfelds, J. (1981) *Capacity Expansion*, Elsevier-North Holland.
Ghosh, A. and Craig, C.S. (1983) 'Formulating Retail Location Strategy in a Changing Environment', *Journal of Marketing*, Vol 47, Summer.
Goldhar, J.D. and Jelenek, M. (1983) 'Plan for Economies of Scope', *Harvard Business Review*, Vol 61, No 6.
Hammesfahr, R.D.J., Hope, J.A. and Ardalan, A. (1993) 'Strategic Planning for Production Capacity', *International Journal of Operations and Production Management*, Vol 13, No 5.

Hayes, R.H. and Wheelwright, S.C. (1984) *Restoring our Competitive Edge*, John Wiley.
Kanter, R.M. (1991) 'Transcending Business Boundaries, 12,000 World Managers You Change', *Harvard Business Review*, Vol 69, No 3.
Lamming, R. (1993) *Beyond Partnership: Strategies for Innovation and Lean Supply*, Prentice Hall.
Manne, A.S. (1967) *Investments for Capacity Expansion*, George Allen and Unwin.
Sasser, W.E. (1976) 'Match Supply and Demand in Service Industries', *Harvard Business Review*, Vol 54, No 6.
Schmenner, R.W. (1976) 'Before You Build a Big Factory', *Harvard Business Review*, Vol 54, No 4.
Schmenner, R.W. (1982) *Making Business Location Decisions*, Prentice Hall.
Sugiura, H. (1990) 'How Honda Localises its Global Strategy', *Sloan Management Review*, Fall.
Voss, C.A. (1989) 'The Managerial Challenges of Integrated Manufacturing', *International Journal of Operations and Production Management*, Vol 9, No 5.

CHAPTER 7

LAYOUT AND FLOW

INTRODUCTION

The layout of an operation is concerned with the physical location of its transforming resources. Put simply, layout is deciding where to put all the facilities, machines, equipment and staff in the operation. Layout is one of the most obvious characteristics of an operation. It is the thing most of us would first notice on entering an operation for the first time, because it determines its 'shape' and appearance. It also determines the way in which the transformed resources – the materials, information and customers – flow through the operation. Relatively small changes in the position of a machine in a factory, or goods in a supermarket, or changing rooms in a sports centre can affect the flow of materials or people through the operation. This, in turn, can affect the costs and general effectiveness of the operation. Figure 7.1 shows the facilities layout activity in the overall model of design in operations.

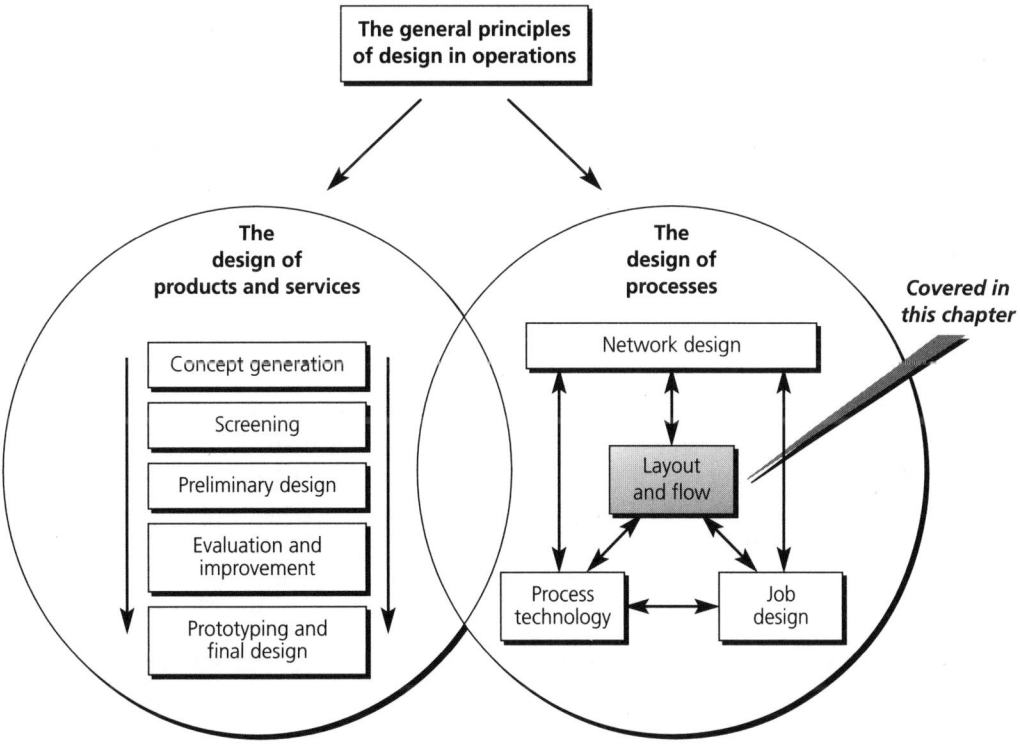

Figure 7.1 The design activities in operations management covered in this chapter

OBJECTIVES

This chapter will examine:

- the procedure by which operations finalize the detailed design of their layouts;

- the nature of the basic layout types:
  - fixed position layout
  - process layout
  - cell layout, and
  - product layout;

- the volume–variety characteristics of the basic layout types;

- the advantages and disadvantages of each basic layout type and the fixed and variable cost characteristics of each;

- the detailed design techniques which can be used to design each basic layout type.

THE LAYOUT PROCEDURE

There are some practical reasons why the layout decision is an important one in most operations.

- Layout is often a lengthy and difficult task because of the physical size of the transforming resources being moved.
- The re-layout of an existing operation can disrupt its smooth running, leading to customer dissatisfaction or lost production.
- If the layout (with hindsight) is wrong, it can lead to over-long or confused flow patterns, inventory of materials, customer queues building up in the operation, customers being inconvenienced, long process times, inflexible operations, unpredictable flow and high cost.

In effect there is a double pressure on the layout decision. Changing a layout can be difficult and expensive to execute so operations managers are reluctant to do it too often. At the same time they have to get it right. The consequences of any misjudgements in an operation's layout will have a considerable, and usually long-term, effect on the operation.

Understanding the operation's strategic objectives, however, is only the starting point of what is a multi-stage process which leads to the final physical layout of the operation (*see* Fig. 7.2).

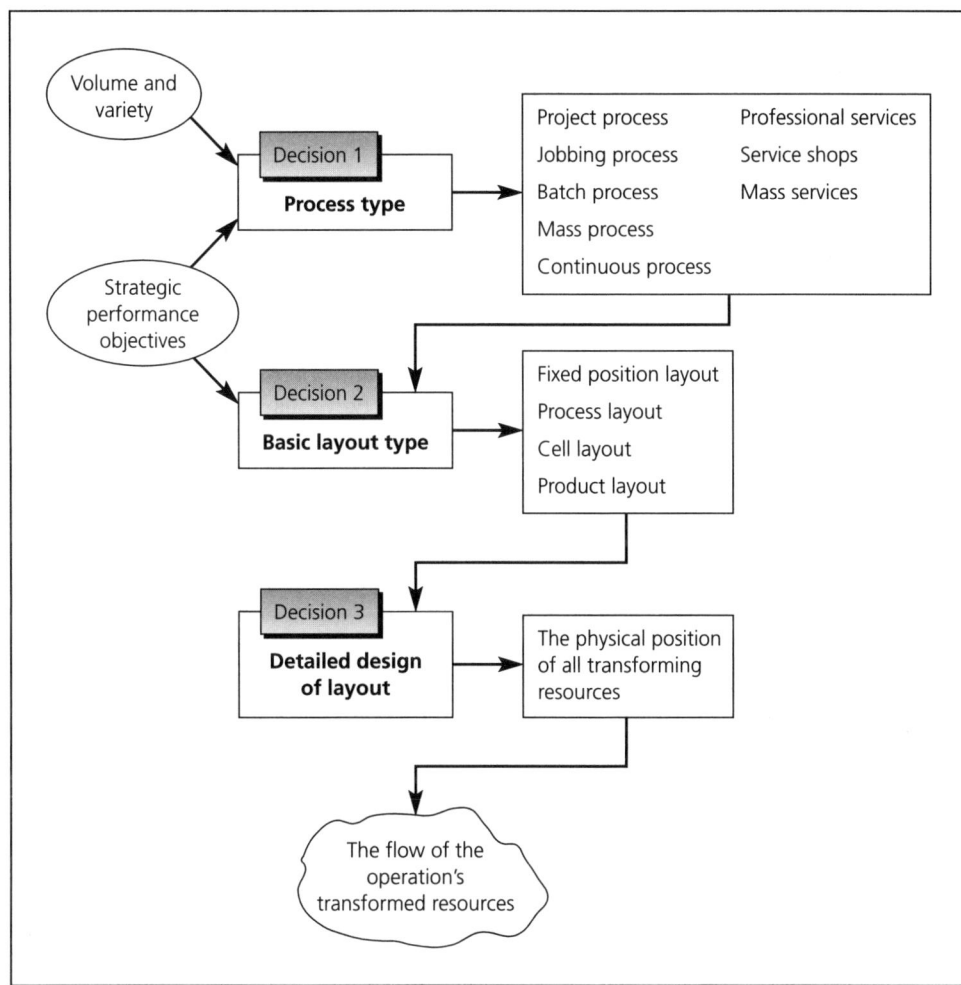

Figure 7.2
The facilities
layout decision

Select the process type

The first decision which will need to be made was described in Chapter 4, namely the choice of *process type*. Largely it is the volume–variety characteristics of the operation which dictate its process type. There is often some overlap, however, between the process types which can be used for a given volume–variety position. In cases where more than one process type is possible, the relative importance of the operation's performance objectives can influence the decision.

Select the basic layout

After the process type is selected, the *basic layout* type needs to be selected. The basic layout type is the general form of the arrangement of the facilities in the operation.

There are many different ways of arranging transforming resources. Furthermore the variety of layouts will seem even larger than it is because some of the transforming resources will look very dissimilar. Under these circumstances it is difficult to detect the similarities which lie underneath such seemingly diverse layouts.

In spite of this, most practical layouts are derived from only four *basic layout types*. They are:

● fixed position layout
● process layout
● cell layout
● product layout.

The relationship between process type and basic layout type is not totally deterministic. One process type does not necessarily imply one particular basic layout. As Table 7.1 indicates, each process types could adopt different basic layout types.

Table 7.1 The relationship between process types and basic layout types

Manufacturing process types	Basic layout types	Service process types
Project processes	Fixed position layout	Professional services
Jobbing processes		
	Process layout	
Batch processes		Service shops
	Cell layout	
Mass processes		
	Product layout	Mass services
Continuous processes		

Selecting the detailed design of the layout

Although the choice of a basic layout type governs the general way in which facilities are arranged relative to each other, it does not precisely define the exact position of each individual part of the operation. The final stage in the layout activity is to move towards this fully specified design of the layout. There are many techniques which help to do this, some of which are described later in the chapter.

THE BASIC LAYOUT TYPES

Fixed position layout

Fixed position layout is in some ways a contradiction in terms since the transformed resources do not move between the transforming resources, but the other way round. Instead of materials, information or customers flowing through an operation, the recipient of the processing is stationary and the equipment, machinery, plant and people who do the processing move to and from the scene of the processing as necessary. The reasons for this could be either that the product or the recipient of the service is too large to be moved conveniently, or it might be too delicate to move, or perhaps it could object to being moved.

For example:

- *Motorway construction* – The product is too large to move.
- *Open-heart surgery* – Patients are too delicate to move.
- *High-class service restaurant* – Customers would object to being moved to where food is prepared.
- *Shipbuilding* – The product is too large to move.
- *Mainframe computer maintenance* – The product is too big and probably also too delicate to move, and the customer might object to bringing it in for repair.

A construction site is typical of a fixed position layout in that there is a limited amount of space which must be allocated to the various transforming resources – in this case the contractors who will be constructing the building, their storage areas and the general resources such as the site management's offices. The main problem in designing this layout will be to allocate areas of the site to the various contractors so that:

- they have adequate space for their needs;
- they can receive and store their deliveries of materials;
- all contractors can have access to the part of the project on which they are working without interfering with each other's movements;
- the total movement of contractors and their vehicles and materials is minimized as far as possible.

Process layout

Process layout is so called because the needs and convenience of the transforming resources which constitute the processes in the operation dominate the layout decision. In process layout, similar processes (or processes with similar needs) are located together. The reason can be that it is convenient for the operation to group them together, or that the utilization of transforming resources is improved. This means that when products, information or customers flow through the operation they will take a route from process to process according to their needs. Different products or customers will have different needs and therefore take different routes through the operation. For this reason the flow pattern in the operation will be very complex.

Examples of process layouts include:

- *Hospital* – Some processes (e.g. X-ray machines and laboratories) are required by several types of patient; some processes (e.g. general wards) can achieve high staff and bed utilization.
- *Machining the parts which go into aircraft engines* – Some processes (e.g. heat treatment) need specialist support (heat and fume extraction); some processes (e.g. machining centres) require the same technical support from specialist setter–operators; some processes (e.g. grinding machines) achieve high machine utilization as all parts which need grinding pass through a single grinding section.

FIXED POSITION LAYOUT AT GEC ALSTHOM COMBINED-CYCLE GENERATORS[1]

GEC Alsthom, an Anglo-French joint venture company, is one of the world's largest manufacturers of power generation and traction machinery. A growing area of its business is in the project management, manufacturing and construction of combined-cycle gas-turbine electricity generation stations. These have become a popular option for many electricity utilities, because of their exceptionally high thermal efficiencies (around 55 per cent compared to conventional generation at around 40 per cent), relatively low capital cost, and their 'green' credentials of low levels of waste energy, of greenhouse gases, and of gases that create acid rain. A typical project, illustrated in Fig. 7.3, is an enormous undertaking, extending over at least three years. Most of the equipment is made-to-order, very large and heavy, and manufactured to very high specification and conformance.

Almost all aspects of the site construction of a power station involve fixed position layouts. To begin with, most of the activities are all the types of civil engineering involved in the building of roadways, foundations, floors, and structure, along with service ducting, site electricity supply, and so on. Components and raw materials, such as concrete and steel, are brought to the point of use and are progressively incorporated into the work. Cranes, building machinery and all the specialist equipment needed for the tasks are brought to site, along with the skilled employees and contractors who each undertake specific tasks on the project.

**Combined-Cycle Power Plant
VEGA 109F Single Shaft – 350 MW**

Figure 7.3 Products like this one are manufactured in a fixed position layout
Source: Courtesy of GEC Alsthom Gas Turbines and Diesels

Once most of this work is completed, the mechanical and electrical items are delivered to the site, according to a carefully prepared schedule. Some of these arrive as complete units, others as modules or kits of parts to be built up on site in their fixed positions. For example, one part of the steam turbine (which uses steam raised in the heat-recovery steam generators at the exhaust side of the gas turbine) is the 'H.P. cylinder' which is a complete high-pressure turbine module, about three metres in diameter, and weighing around 250 tonnes. This is made and assembled at the factory, again using a fixed position layout, and then transported in one piece to site. A similar approach is used for the generator stator assembly which is built up on a frame in the factory.

At one time it was normal for the whole turbine/generator to be fully assembled in a fixed position in the factory; it was then dismantled and taken to site for re-assembly. This was because many of the parts had to be adjusted to fit together perfectly, and so pre-assembly was used to ensure that everything was correct before delivery. Now, however, improvements in design and manufacturing technologies have enabled the company to make these large components much more accurately, so that much more assembly can be done once only at the exact position required on site. This has also helped the company respond to market pressures which require much shorter lead times and lower prices. ∎

● *Supermarket* – Some processes, such as the area holding tinned vegetables, are convenient to re-stock if grouped together. Some, such as the area holding frozen vegetables, need the common technology of freezer cabinets. Others, such as the areas holding fresh vegetables, might be together because together they can be made to look attractive to customers (vegetables on market stalls, for example).

Figure 7.4 shows a process layout in a library. The various 'processes' – reference books, enquiry desk, journals, and so on – are located in different parts of the operation. The customer is free to move between the processes depending on his or her requirements. The figure also shows the route taken by one customer on one visit to the library. If the routes taken by all the customers who visited the library, over a period of time when demand for the library's services was typical, were superimposed on the plan, the pattern of the traffic between the various parts of the operation would be revealed. The density of this traffic flow is an important piece of information in the detailed design of this type of layout, as we shall see later in this chapter. The main point to understand at this point is that changing the location of the various processes in the library will change the pattern of flow for the library as a whole and therefore the convenience of each individual customer.

Cell layout

A cell layout is one where the transformed resources entering the operation are preselected (or preselect themselves) to move to one part of the operation (or cell) in which all the transforming resources to meet their immediate processing needs are located. The cell itself may be arranged in either a process or product (*see* next section) layout. After being processed in the cell, the transformed resources may go on to another cell.

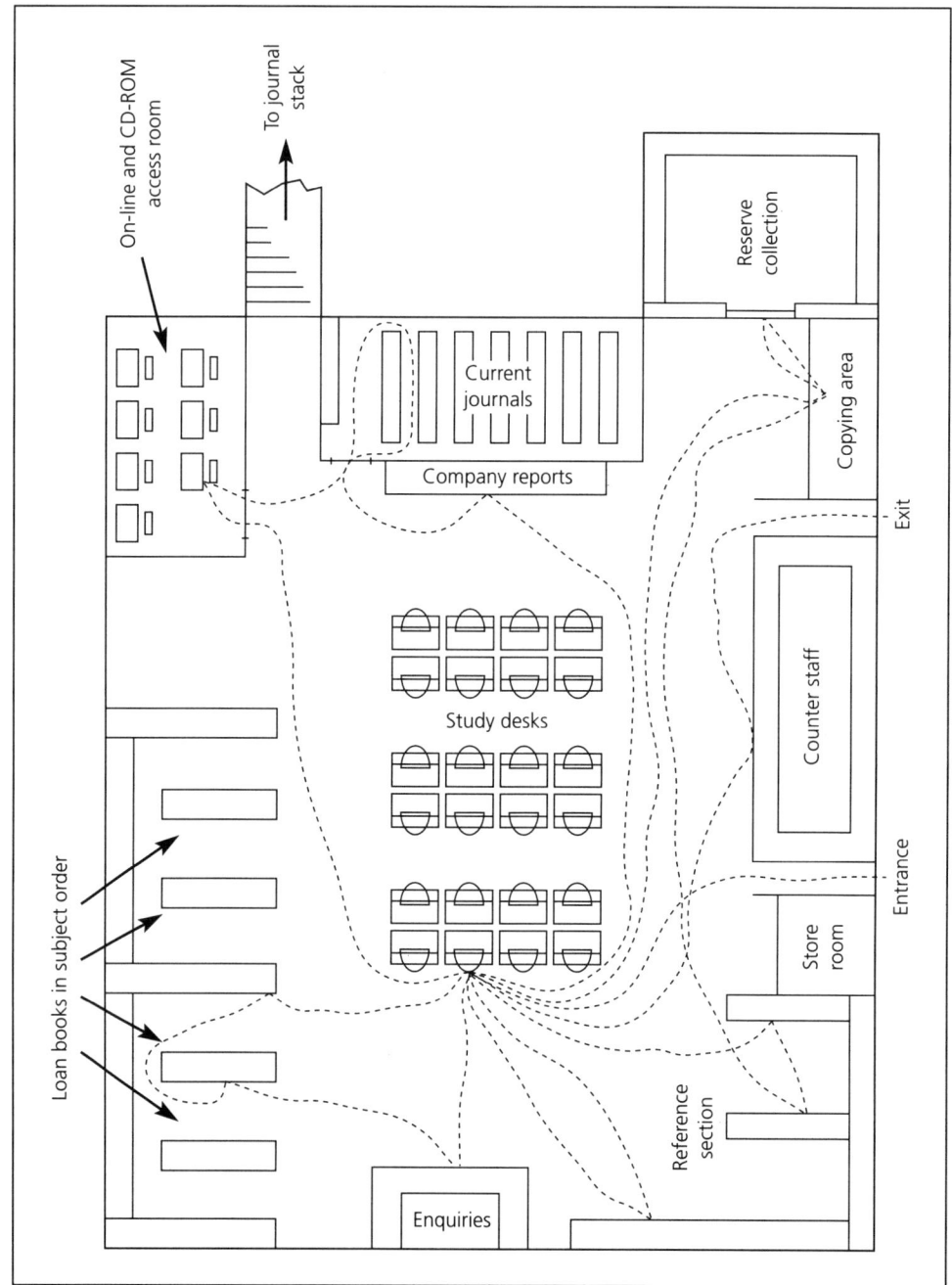

Figure 7.4
An example of a process layout in a library showing the path of just one customer

In effect cell layout is an attempt to bring some order to the complexity of flow which characterizes process layout.

Examples of cell layouts include:

● *Some computer component manufacture* – The processing and assembly of some types of computer parts may need a special area dedicated to the manufacturing of parts for one particular customer who has special requirements such as particularly high-quality levels.

LAYOUT OF SPAR SUPERMARKET IN VORNA VALLEY, GAUTENG[2]

The Spar Group operates supermarkets in South Africa. Spar supermarkets compete by choices of location, which are convenient for basic necessities and daily small supplies. To remain profitable, every Spar manager must maximize the revenue and contribution per square metre but also minimize the costs of operating the store, in terms of items stocked.

A typical Spar supermarket has an unusual layout. In common with most supermarket designs, the check-outs are positioned near the exit, but during most of the day only a few are used. Cigarettes, billtong and sweets are sold at the check-outs. Daily newspapers are placed near the exit door. Cashiers face into the store, towards the queue. The store has four to five check-outs – a very large number for the size of the stores. This is because there is a large peak of sales in the early evening, when people return from work, and long queues at the check-out would be totally unacceptable to regular (tired) customers.

Spar has chosen to use relatively wide aisles between the shelves, to ensure good flows of trolleys, but this has been at the expense of reduced shelf space, which would allow a wider range of stocked products. Having established a basic layout of the fixed equipment, the actual location of all products is a critical management decision, directly affecting the convenience for the customer, their level of spontaneous purchase, the costs of filling the shelves and the variety of product range. The overall layout of the supermarket is a typical process layout, with separate, clearly marked self-service areas for packaged food, drinks, fruit and vegetables. Customer flows are random, because of the frequent but relatively small purchases made by regular customers. In contrast, shoppers at many large hypermarkets are encouraged to flow past most of the displays in a logical and uniform route. The served delicatessen (which sells products with above-average margins) is located between the bakery and the butchery/dairy areas so that most shoppers must pass it – to be tempted by attractive displays and to make spontaneous purchases. The displays of fruit and vegetables are located adjacent to the main entrance, as a signal of freshness and wholesomeness, providing an attractive and welcoming point of entry to the store.

At a more detailed level, the actual position selected for each product must be decided. High turnover, 'essential', known value items (KVIs), such as rice, pasta, sugar and oil, are positioned centrally and visibly, so that they are easy to find. Profitable, fast-moving items are displayed at eye level, both to help the customer and to make restocking easier for employees. Conversely, low-margin and low-turnover items are placed low down. Bulky or heavy products are located at the end of aisles, near the storage area, to facilitate restocking. Frozen foods are located at the end of the aisles, near the check-outs, so that they can be purchased last. In some supermarkets, these positions are only used for promotion, as customers move more slowly around the end of the aisles and the goods on display can be seen from most directions. ■

● *'Lunch' products area in a supermarket* – Some customers use the supermarket just to purchase sandwiches, savoury snacks, cool drinks, yoghurt, etc. for their lunch. These are often located close together so that customers who are just buying lunch do not have to search round the store.

● *Maternity unit in a hospital* – Customers needing maternity attention are a well defined group who can be treated together and who are unlikely to need the other facilities of the hospital at the same time that they need the maternity unit.

Figure 7.5 shows one type of cell layout in a retail operation. Although the idea of cell layout is often associated with manufacturing operations, the same principle can, and is, used in services. In Fig. 7.5 the ground floor of a department store is shown comprising displays of various types of goods in different parts of the store. In this sense the predominant layout of the store is a process layout. Each display area can be considered a separate process devoted to selling a particular class of good – shoes, clothes, books and so on. The exception is the sports shop. This area is a shop-within-a-shop area which is devoted to many types of goods which have a common sporting theme. For example, it will stock sports clothes, sports shoes, sports bags, sports magazines, sports books and videos, sports equipment and gifts and sports energy drinks. Within the 'cell' there are all the 'processes' which are also located elsewhere in the store. They have been located in the 'cell' not because they are similar goods (shoes, books and drinks would not usually be located together) but because they are needed to

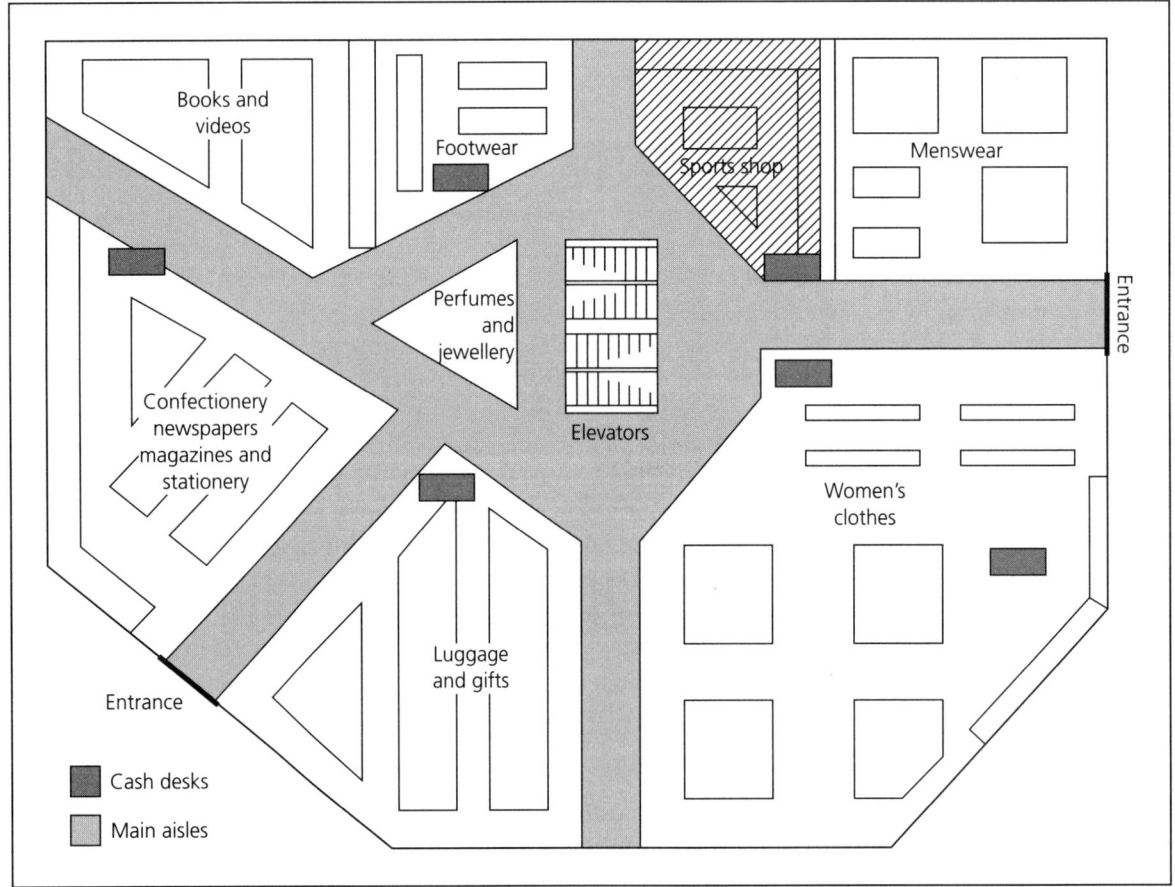

Figure 7.5 The ground floor plan of a department store showing the sports goods shop-within-a-shop retail 'cell'

satisfy the needs of a particular type of customer. The store management calculates that enough customers come to the store to buy 'sports goods', rather than shoes, clothes, books, etc. separately, to devote an area specifically for them. The store is also aware that someone coming to the store with the intention of purchasing some sports shoes might also be persuaded to buy other sports goods if they are placed in the same area.

Product layout

Product layout involves locating the transforming resources entirely for the convenience of the transformed resources. Each product, piece of information or customer follows a pre-arranged route in which the sequence of activities which are required matches the sequence in which the processes have been located. The transformed resources 'flow' along a 'line' of processes. This is why this type of layout is sometimes called 'flow' or 'line' layout. The flow of products, information or customers in product layout is clear, predictable and therefore relatively easy to control. In fact in some customer-processing service operations a product layout is adopted partly to help control the flow of customers through the operation. Predominantly though it is the standardized requirements of the product or service which·lead to operations choosing product layouts.

Examples of product layout include:

- *Automobile assembly* – Almost all variants of the same model require the same sequence of processes.
- *Mass-immunization programme* – All customers require the same sequence of clerical, medical and counselling activities.
- *Self-service cafeteria* – Generally the sequence of customer requirements (starter, main course, dessert, drinks) is common to all customers, but layout also helps control customer flow.

Figure 7.6 shows the sequence of processes in a paper-making operation. Such an operation would use product layout. The flow of materials through the operation is both evident and regular. Gone are the complexities of flow which characterized processes, and to a lesser extent cell layout, and although different types of paper are produced in this operation, all types have the same processing requirements. First, the wood chips are combined with chemicals, water and steam in the 'cooking' process to form the 'pulp'. The pulp is then put through a cleaning process before being refined to help the fibres lock together. The mixing process combines the refined pulp with more water, fillers, chemicals and dyes, after which it is spread on a fine flexible wire or plastic mesh. This is shaken from side to side as it moves along to lock the fibres into the sheet of paper and to drain away the water. The press rollers squeeze more water out of the paper and press the fibres closer together. The drying process continues to reduce the water level in the paper before, finally, it is wound on to large reels.[4]

It makes sense then to locate these processes in the order that they are required by the product and let materials flow along in a predictable manner. In fact this particular example of product layout is an extreme one in some ways because for the first part of its manufacture the paper is in a semi-liquid form. It would be physically difficult to handle the product in any way other than causing it to 'flow' between processes. Nevertheless, other products which have a common sequence of processes such as televisions, freezers, air conditioning units and so on, are also manufactured using product layouts.

SHANDON SCIENTIFIC LIMITED[3]

Shandon Scientific Ltd is a subsidiary of Life Sciences International, a world-wide manufacturer of automated pathological testing machines used in medical laboratories. These 'high-tech' work-top machines are complex designs of mechanical, electrical and electronic parts which are assembled into plastic and sheet metal cases.

Shandon's products competed largely on the technical excellence of their designs and product quality. Then price competition began to be significant as competitors began to offer technically similar products. Increasingly, also, some customers demanded delivery in less than Shandon's normal lead time of 12 weeks. The company's initial response was to hold higher levels of finished product inventory, based on sales forecasts (which were often quite unreliable). The result was that the average level of inventory increased significantly.

Up to this time the company had adopted a process layout. Batches of components and sub-assemblies were made in the appropriate section (e.g. Wiring Assembly) and then taken to a warehouse area. Later these would be drawn from the warehouse and further operations would be performed on them. At various stages, components, sub-assemblies, and finished products were inspected and tested in a separate department. Packing was carried out in the warehouse prior to despatch. The Planning and Control Department coordinated all these activities, keeping track of the location and sequencing of tens of thousands of material movements per year.

In response to the new competitive environment, the company reorganized production around 11 'cells'. One assembly cell was devoted to each of its eight products. In addition there was a sheet metal work cell, a painting cell, and a mechanical components cell. Each cell was made responsible for all detailed planning, for purchasing of components and services, for all inventory, for quality control, as well as for packing finished products where appropriate. Where one cell provided components or services to another, this was arranged formally as a supplier–customer relationship, with performance measured in terms of dependability and quality.

The new cell arrangement was a great success. Lead times were reduced to less than four weeks, allowing all products to be made to order. Inventory was halved, and quality levels improved dramatically. The warehouse now only needed to be small since it only stored finished products for a short time (and no longer needed raw materials and sub-assemblies). There was also an overall saving of about 20 staff, mainly in the warehouse and in production planning, which helped the company keep costs down. Most important, customer satisfaction levels, which are monitored regularly, soared to their highest level ever. ∎

Mixed layouts

Many operations either design themselves hybrid layouts which combine elements of some or all of the basic layout types, or alternatively use the 'pure' basic layout types in different parts of the operation. For example, a hospital would normally be arranged on process-layout principles – each department representing a particular type of process (the X-ray department, the surgical theatres, the blood processing laboratory and so on). Yet within each department quite different layouts are used. The X-ray department is probably arranged in a process layout, the surgical theatres in a fixed-position layout, and the blood processing laboratory in a product layout.

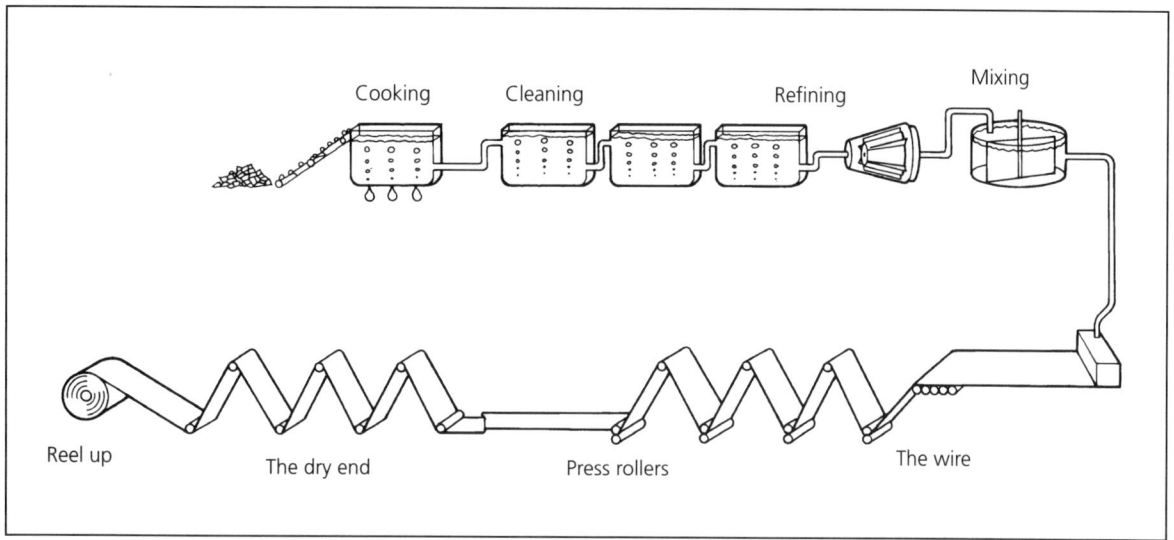

Figure 7.6 The sequence of processes in papermaking; each process will be laid out in the same sequence

Another example is shown in Fig. 7.7. Here a restaurant complex is shown with three different types of restaurant and the kitchen which serves them all. The kitchen is arranged in a process layout with the various processes (food storage, food preparation, cooking processes, etc.) grouped together. Different foods will take different routes between the processes depending on their processing requirements. The traditional service restaurant is arranged in a fixed-position layout. The customers stay at their tables while the food is brought to (and sometimes cooked at) the tables. The buffet restaurant is arranged in a cell-type layout with each buffet area having all the processes (dishes) necessary to serve customers with either their starter, main course or dessert. In this case customers who intend to partake of all three courses will need to be processed through all three cells before the completion of the service. Finally, in the cafeteria restaurant all customers take the same route when being served with their meal. They may not take the opportunity to be served with every dish but they move through the same sequence of processes.

Volume–variety and layout type

The previous examples of the four basic layout types show that the flow of materials, information or customers will very much depend on the layout chosen. The importance of flow to an operation will depend on its volume and variety characteristics. When volume is very low and variety is relatively high, 'flow' is not a major issue. For example, in telecommunications satellite manufacture, a fixed position layout is likely to be appropriate because each product is different and because products 'flow' through the operation very infrequently. Under these conditions it is just not worth arranging facilities to minimize the flow of parts through the operation.

With somewhat higher volume and lower variety, the flow of the transformed resources becomes an issue which any layout must address. If the variety is still high, however, an entirely flow-dominated arrangement is difficult because products or

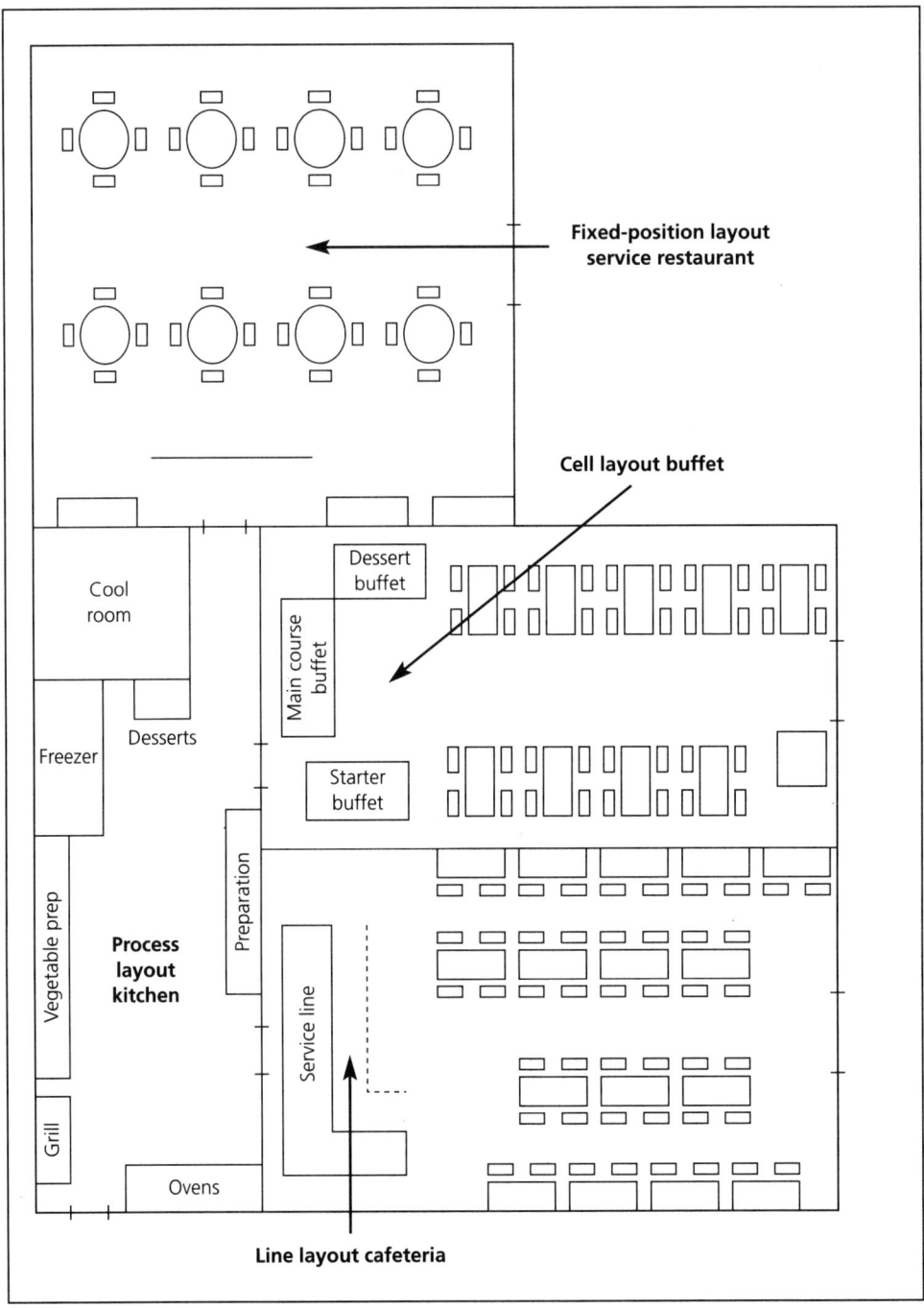

**Figure 7.7
A restaurant
complex with all
four basic layout
types**

customers will have different flow patterns. For example, the library in Fig. 7.4 will arrange its different categories of books and its other services partly to minimize the average distance its customers have to 'flow' through the operation. Because its customers' needs vary, however, the library at best will arrange its layout to satisfy a majority of its customers but perhaps inconvenience a minority. When the variety of products or services reduces to the point where a distinct 'category' with similar requirements becomes evident but variety is still not small, cell layout could become appropriate, as in the sports goods cell in Fig. 7.5. When the variety of products or services is relatively small and volume high, the flow of materials, information or customers can become regularized and a product-based layout is likely to be appropriate, as in an assembly plant.

Examining these examples of the different basic layout types, we can see the different effects of volume and variety (*see* Fig. 7.8). As volume increases the importance of getting flow right increases. As variety reduces it becomes increasingly possible to arrange transforming resources according to the needs of the product or service. The variety of different satellite designs, or needs of customers in the library, effectively eliminates the possibility of regular predictable flow. The narrow variety of the television plant, however, presents little or no barrier to a layout designed around the product's needs. Therefore, increasing volume increases the *importance* of flow, whereas reducing variety increases the *feasibility* of a layout based on evident and regular flow.

Selecting a layout type

The decision of which layout type to adopt rarely, if ever, involves choosing between all four basic types. The volume–variety characteristics of the operation will, to a large extent, narrow the choice down to one or two options. Yet, as is implied in Fig. 7.8, the spans of volumes and varieties encompassed by each layout type do overlap. The decision as to which layout type to adopt will be influenced by an understanding of their relative advantages and disadvantages.

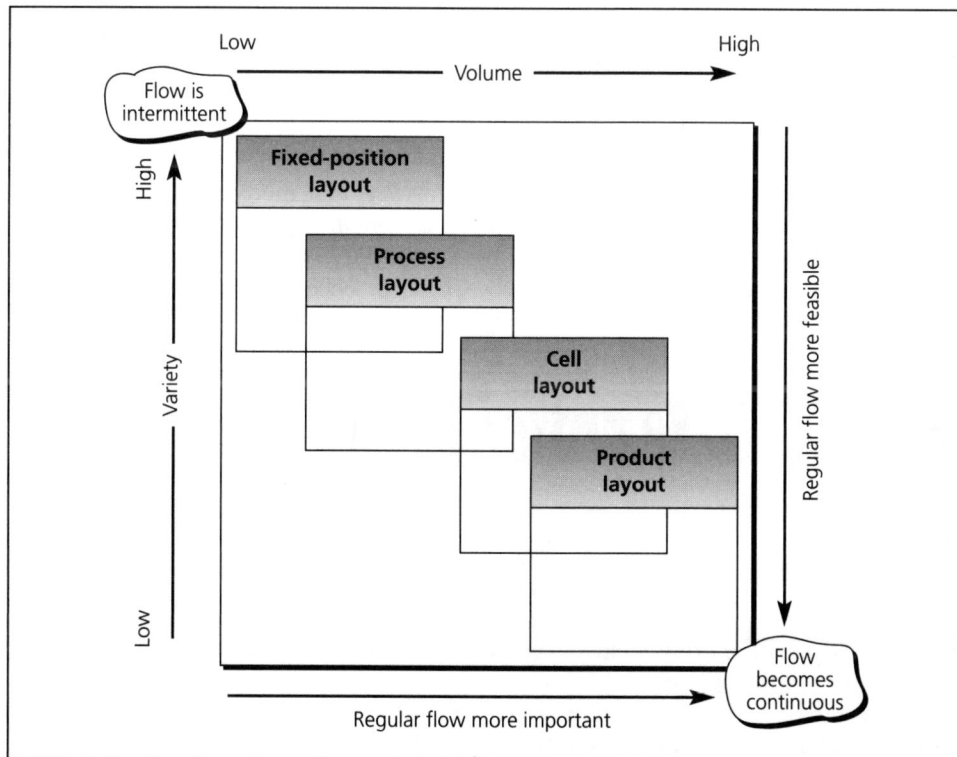

Figure 7.8 The volume–variety process position of an operation influences its layout and in turn the flow of transformed resources

THE PASSENGER TERMINAL AT JOHANNESBURG INTERNATIONAL AIRPORT[5]

The newly upgraded Johannesburg International Airport is the biggest in South Africa and is still growing. The airport, which is managed by the Airports Company, handles eight million domestic and international passengers with more than 100 000 aircraft landing and taking off per year.

Like many regional airports, aircraft movement, and therefore passenger flows, are programmed in waves. Each day, there is an initial burst of outgoing flights and then, after a short break, the morning incoming flights from all over the world start to arrive, all more or less together. Then, throughout the day passenger 'waves' flow through the terminal, finishing up with the final evening international departures and arrivals from other Southern African cities. In all, the terminal has to cope with eight waves per day. This presents an intriguing layout problem: a mass of passenger flow in a predictable manner eight times a day, but each alternate wave in the opposite direction. This problem has been somewhat minimized by permanently segregating international from domestic terminals and domestic arrivals from departures (necessary so that passengers don't stray).

The complex routing of passengers through the airport is done by using door locks on the apron-tunnels and multi-level walkways. This enables them to designate aprons as either disembark or embark for a period, effectively controlling the flow of people throughout the building. It also facilitates short aircraft turnaround times. When the planes arrive and the passengers are ready to disembark, the doors are opened to allow passengers to walk on the lower walkways only, and the route to the upper walkway is closed. Once the plane is ready to take off again for its next journey, the door is switched so that the entry door from the upper walkway is opened and the exit route downstairs to the arrivals hall is closed off. ■

Table 7.2 shows some of the more significant advantages and disadvantages associated with each layout type. It should be stressed, however, that the type of operation will influence their relative importance. For example a high-volume television manufacturer may find the low-cost characteristics of a product layout attractive but an amusement theme park may adopt the same layout type primarily because of the way it 'controls' customer flow.

DETAILED DESIGN OF THE LAYOUT

Once the basic layout type has been decided the next step is to decide the detailed design of the layout. Detailed design is the act of operationalizing the broad principles which were implicit in the choice of the basic layout type.

The output from the detailed design stage of layout is:

● the precise location of all facilities, plant, equipment and staff which constitute the 'work centres' of the operation;
● the space to be devoted to each work centre;
● the tasks which will be undertaken by each work centre.

Table 7.2 The advantages and disadvantages of the basic layout types

	Advantages	Disadvantages
Fixed Position	Very high mix and product flexibility Product or customer not moved or disturbed High variety of tasks for staff	Very high unit costs Scheduling of space and activities can be difficult Can mean much movement of plant and staff
Process	High mix and product flexibility Relatively robust in the case of disruptions Relatively easy supervision of equipment or plant	Low facilities utilization Can have very high work-in-progress or customer queueing Complex flow can be difficult to control
Cell	Can give a good compromise between cost and flexibility for relatively high-variety operations Fast throughput Group work can result in good motivation	Can be costly to rearrange existing layout Can need more plant and equipment Can give lower plant utilization
Product	Low unit costs for high volume Gives opportunities for specialization of equipment Materials or customer movement is convenient	Can have low mix flexibility Not very robust if disruption Work can be very repetitive

What makes a good layout?

Before considering the various methods used in the detailed design of layouts, it is useful to consider the objectives of the activity. To a certain extent the objectives will depend on circumstances, but there are some general objectives which are relevant to all operations.[6]

● *Inherent safety* – All processes which might constitute a danger to either staff or customers should not be accessible to the unauthorized. Fire exits should be clearly marked with uninhibited access. Pathways should be clearly defined and not cluttered.
● *Length of flow* – The flow of materials, information or customers should be channelled by the layout so as to be appropriate for the objectives of the operation. In many operations this means minimizing the distance travelled by transformed resources. Although not always, supermarkets, for example, might wish to make sure that customers pass particular goods on their way round the store.

- *Clarity of flow* – All flow of materials and customers should be well signposted, clear and evident to staff and customers alike. For example, manufacturing operations usually have clearly marked gangways. Service operations often rely on signposted routes, such as in hospitals which often have different coloured lines painted on the floor to indicate the routes to various departments.
- *Staff comfort* – Staff should be located away from noisy or unpleasant parts of the operation. The layout should provide for a well ventilated, well lit and, where possible, pleasant working environment.
- *Management coordination* – Supervision and communication should be assisted by the location of staff and communication devices.
- *Accessibility* – All machines, plant or equipment should be accessible to a degree which is sufficient for proper cleaning and maintenance.
- *Use of space* – All layouts should achieve an appropriate use of the total space available in the operation (including height as well as floor space). This usually means minimizing the space used for a particular purpose, but sometimes can mean achieving an impression of spacious luxury, as in the entrance lobby of a high-class hotel.
- *Long-term flexibility* – Layouts need to be changed periodically as the needs of the operation change. A good layout will have been devised with the possible future needs of the operation in mind. For example, if demand is likely to increase for a product or service, has the layout been designed to accommodate any future expansion?

Detailed design in fixed-position layout

In fixed-position arrangements, the detailed design of the layout is concerned with the physical location of transforming resources, as it is for all other basic layout types. Here though the location of resources will be determined not on the basis of the flow of transformed resources but on the convenience of transforming resources themselves. The objective of the detailed design of fixed-position layouts is to achieve a layout for the operation which allows all the transforming resources to maximize their contribution to the transformation process by allowing them to provide an effective 'service' to the transformed resources. The detailed layout of some fixed-position layouts, such as building sites, can become very complicated and fluid over the period of construction, especially if the planned schedule of activities is changed frequently. The poor layout of a fixed-position arrangement can reduce its effectiveness considerably. Imagine the chaos on a construction site if heavy trucks continually (and noisily) drove past the site office, delivery trucks for one contractor had to cross other contractors' areas to get to where they were storing their own materials, and the staff who spent most time at the building itself were located furthest away from it.

Resource location analysis

Resource location analysis is a systematic approach to allocating work centres to locations in stable, fixed-position arrangements. It involves evaluating the effects of locating the various transforming resources (known as resource centres) at all available locations on the site by using criteria associated with the site itself (site criteria) and criteria associated with the interaction of the resources (relative-location criteria).

The procedure in resource location analysis is as follows:

Step 1 Define the site and its available locations.

Step 2 Define the resource centres to be located and their requirements.

Step 3 Formalize the evaluation criteria by considering the site characteristics and the requirements of the resource centres, and by doing so define (a) the site criteria and (b) the relative location criteria.

Step 4 Calculate the degree of fit between resource centres and available locations using the site criteria.

Step 5 Devise a preliminary allocation of resource centres to locations based on site criteria.

Step 6 Adjust the allocation of resource centres to locations based on the relative location criteria.

As an example of resource location analysis, we can consider a manufacturer of specialist marine exploration equipment which has devoted part of its plant to the assembly of underwater exploration vehicles using a fixed-position layout. These vehicles are small submarine-like vessels, used by oil exploration and mineral extraction companies. All the vehicles are made to order and all individual vehicles are different in some way from each other.

Step 1 – Define the site

The assembly area for this product is shown in Fig. 7.9. Two assembly bays have already been located in the centre of the area and a 'free-access' zone has been designated around the bays to avoid the assembly bays becoming cluttered. There are two access points: one to the outside of the plant, the second to the other parts of the plant. The remaining available area is shown divided into 14 locations of approximately equal size. It is these locations which need to be allocated to the resource centres.

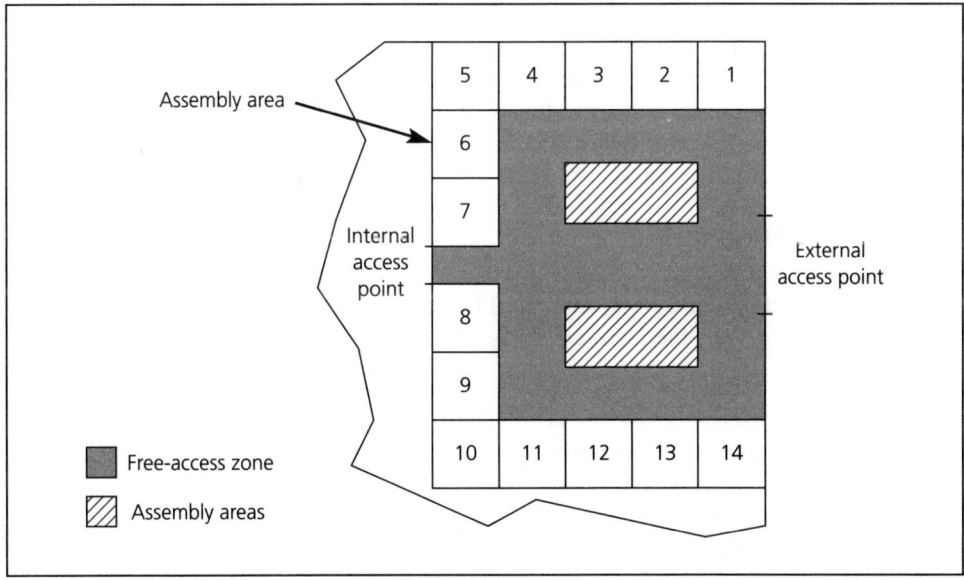

**Figure 7.9
The assembly area of a specialist underwater exploration vehicle**

231

Step 2 – Define the needs of resource centres

Many different types of staff together with their equipment and materials will need access to the assembly bays. Six resource centres were judged to need permanent space in the assembly area, however. The locations allocated to the resources should also be together if possible.

● *Structural fabricators.* This group need four locations to store their materials and set up their own work areas. They receive most of the heavy materials which go into the product, and pre-cut and weld sections prior to their forming the structure and shell of the vehicle. It is important that they are located close to the external access point so that they can receive deliveries of material. It is also necessary to extract the fumes from their welding and painting operations so a location on an external wall would be convenient.

● *Mechanical fitters.* This group need three location areas: they perform much of the installation of the engines and drive mechanisms in the product. They receive some material delivered directly to the assembly area but most comes into the area after being pre-processed elsewhere in the factory.

● *Electricians.* This group need two location areas: they pre-form the wiring harnesses and install the electrical equipment and the wiring harnesses. They also test electrical equipment. Because of the sensitivity of their testing operations it is advisable that they are located away from the structural fabrication area where noise, fumes and vibration could interfere with the tests.

● *Control engineers.* This group require two location areas: they test and install the engine management and other control systems. They need to be relatively close to the access point for the other areas in the plant and, again, should not be close to the structural fabricators.

● *Communication engineers.* This group need two location areas: they design and tailor the hardware and software of the vehicle's communications systems. Because of customer-driven changes in the communication systems during assembly, this group would like to be close to the planning office to make sure that there is effective communication. They also need to be away from their structural fabrication colleagues.

● *The planning office.* This group needs only one location area and houses the operations manager, project managers and a meeting area. It needs to be in a location which affords it good access to the rest of the area and, especially, a good view of the direct delivery of materials to the assembly area. It also needs to be away from any noisy processes.

Step 3 – Formalize evaluation criteria

From Step 2 it would seem that there are five obvious criteria on which the location of the resource centres could be evaluated. Three of these criteria are site criteria since they are associated with the characteristics of the particular site, and two are relative-location criteria.

● *Site criteria*
(a) Closeness to external access point
(b) Closeness to internal access point
(c) Closeness to external wall
● *Relative location criteria*
(a) Closeness to planning office
(b) Distance from structural fabricators

Step 4 – Calculate the degree of fit

This step is carried out in three stages. The first stage is to allocate a 'location score' for how well each of the locations satisfies the site criteria. The simplest way of doing this is to score each location as follows.

Location is ideal   = 3
Location is acceptable = 2
Location is poor   = 1

In this example, the operations management team scored the locations as shown in Table 7.3.

The next stage is to allocate a weighting factor to each of the site criteria which corresponds to the perceived importance of the criteria to each of the resources. Table 7.4 shows how the criteria were scored in this example, using the scale as follows:

Very important criterion   = 3
Important criterion   = 2
Fairly important criterion   = 1
Not at all important criterion = 0

Table 7.3 Individual location scores for underwater vehicle assembly area

Site criteria	Location													
	1	2	3	4	5	6	7	8	9	10	11	12	13	14
External access	3	3	2	2	1	1	1	1	1	1	2	2	3	3
Internal access	1	1	2	2	3	3	3	3	3	3	2	2	1	1
External wall	3	3	3	3	3	2	2	1	1	1	1	1	1	1

Table 7.4 Weightings for importance of each site criterion to the resource centres

Site criteria	Structural fabricators	Mechanical fitters	Electricians	Control engineers	Communications engineers	Planning office
External access	3	1	0	0	0	2
Internal access	1	3	1	1	1	1
External wall	3	0	0	0	0	0

Now the final stage of calculating a 'degree-of-fit' score for each resource being allocated to each location can be carried out. This is done by simply summing the weighting multiplied by the location score for each criterion.

So, for example, the degree of fit allocating the structural fabricators to location 1 is as follows.

external access weight × location score for location 1's external access
plus internal access weight × location score for location 1's internal access
plus external wall weight × location score for location 1's external wall

This equals

$(3 \times 3) + (1 \times 1) + (3 \times 3) = 19$

233

Table 7.5 shows the degree-of-fit resource location scores for each of the resources in all the locations.

Table 7.5 Resource location scores for the underwater vehicle assembly area

Resource centre	Location 1	2	3	4	5	6	7	8	9	10	11	12	13	14
Structural fabricators	19	19	17	17	15	12	12	9	9	9	11	11	13	13
Mechanical fitters	6	6	8	8	10	10	10	10	10	10	8	8	6	6
Electricians	1	1	2	2	3	3	3	3	3	3	2	2	1	1
Control engineers	1	1	2	2	3	3	3	3	3	3	2	2	1	1
Communications engineers	1	1	2	2	3	3	3	3	3	3	2	2	1	1
Planning office	7	7	6	6	5	5	5	5	5	5	6	6	7	7

Step 5 – Devise preliminary layout

The resource location scores shown in Table 7.5 give an indication not only of the degree of fit between a resource centre and a location (the higher the score, the better the fit) but also of how important its location is to each resource centre. The structural fabricators, for example, have high resource location scores which shows that they are particularly sensitive to their location. The resource centres with the higher scores should therefore be allocated locations first. In this example the structural fabricators should be located first, initially to the four locations which give them their highest location scores – locations 1, 2, 3 and 4. After this the mechanical fitters are allocated location, and so on. Figure 7.10 shows the preliminary location which results from this process.

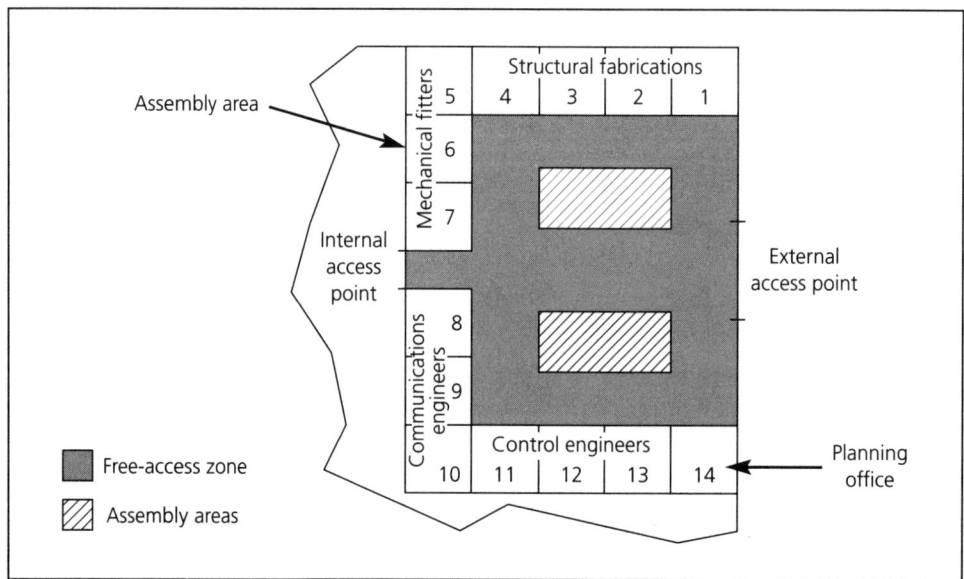

Figure 7.10 Preliminary layout for the assembly area

Step 6 – Adjust the layout

The final step is to check the preliminary layout against the relative location criteria. In this example all the resources which needed to avoid the structural fabricators have done so in the preliminary layout. The communications engineers are not adjacent to the planning office, however. Reference to the resource location scores in Table 7.5 shows that the control engineers and the communications engineers could exchange their respective locations without any loss of score. The final layout is shown in Fig. 7.11.

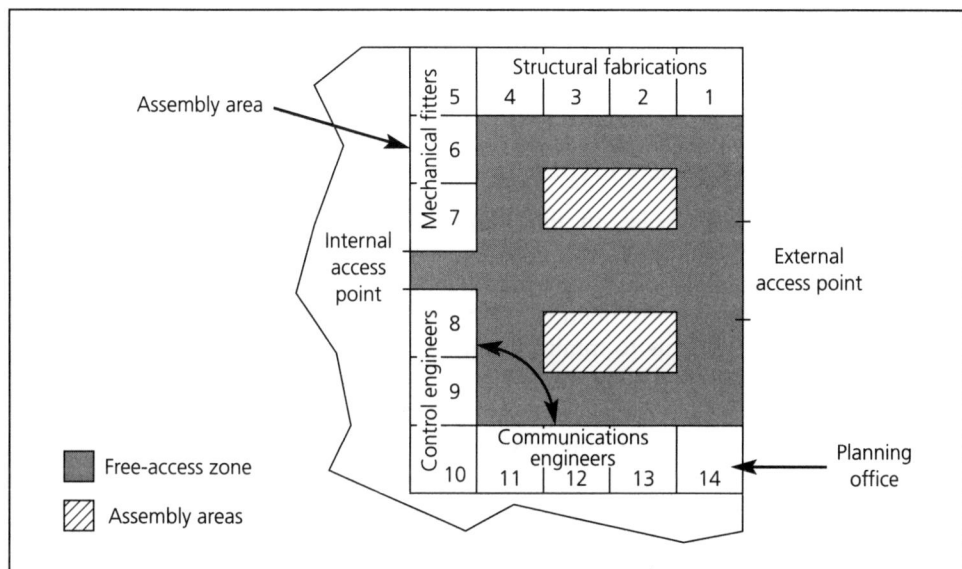

**Figure 7.11
Final layout of the assembly area**

Detailed design in process layout

The detailed design of process layouts is marked by the complexity which is also the main flow characteristic of this type of layout. Chief among the factors which lead to this complexity is the very large number of different options. For example, in the very simplest case of just two work centres, there are only two ways of arranging these *relative to each other*. But there are six ways of arranging four centres and 120 ways of arranging five centres.

The relationship is a factorial one. For N centres there are factorial N (written $N!$) different ways of arranging the centres, where

$$N! = N \times (N-1) \times (N-2) \times \ldots (1)$$

So for a relatively simple process layout with, say, 20 work centres there are

$$20! = 2.433 \times 10^{18}$$

ways of arranging the operation.

It is partly because of this *combinatorial complexity* of process layouts that optimal solutions are difficult to achieve in practice. Most process layouts are designed by a combination of intuition, common sense, and systematic trial and error.

The information for process layout

Before starting the process of detailed design in process layouts there are some essential pieces of information which the designer needs:

● the area required by each work centre;
● the constraints on the shape of the area allocated to each work centre;
● the degree and direction of flow between each work centre (for example, number of journeys, number of loads, or cost of flow per distance travelled);
● the desirability of work centres being close together or close to some fixed point in the layout.

The last two pieces of information are particularly important because both influence directly the consequences of locating work centres relative to each other.

The objectives of process layout

In most examples of process layout, the prime objective is to minimize the costs to the operation which are associated with the flow of transformed resources through the operation. So, for example, a furniture manufacturer would locate work centres in the factory so as to minimize the need to transport components. Similarly, a hospital would locate its departments to minimize the movement of its patients (and perhaps staff). In some operations the emphasis is shifted to maximizing the revenue associated with flow rather than minimizing its cost. Retail operations especially might lay out their operations to this objective (*see*, for example, box on the Spar supermarket). Some entertainment operations such as theme parks may also have this objective. Cost minimization is by far the most common objective, however.

At the simplest level an operation might judge the effectiveness of its layout solely on the total distance travelled in the operation. For example, Fig. 7.12(a) shows a simple six-centre process layout with the total number of journeys between centres each day. The effectiveness of the layout, at this simple level, can be calculated from:

Effectiveness of layout $= \sum F_{ij} D_{ij}$ for all i not $= j$.

where $F_{ij} = $ the flow in loads or journeys per period of time from work centre i to work centre j

$D_{ij} = $ the distance between work centre i and work centre j.

The lower the effectiveness score, the better the layout.

In this example the total of the number of journeys multiplied by the distance for each pair of departments where there is some flow is 4450 metres. This measure will indicate whether changes to the layout improve its effectiveness (at least in the narrow terms defined here). For example if centres C and E are exchanged as in Fig. 7.12(b) the effectiveness measure becomes 3750 showing that the layout now has reduced the total distance travelled in the operation.

The calculations above assume that all journeys are the same in that their cost to the operation is the same. In some operations this is not so, however. For example some journeys in the furniture manufacture industry might be relatively low-effort trips which simply transport a light load of components from one centre to another. Other journeys might involve heavy and inconvenient loads which require more staff and time to execute them. Similarly, in the hospital, some journeys involving healthy

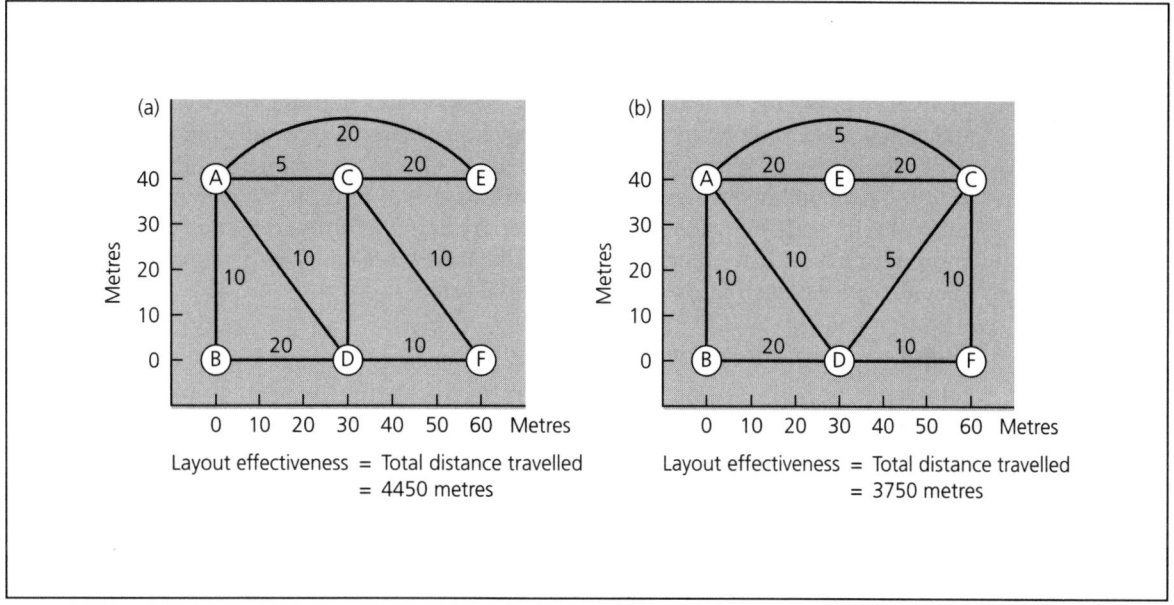

Figure 7.12 (a) and (b) The objective of most process layouts is to minimize the cost associated with movement in the operation, sometimes simplified to minimizing the total distance travelled

staff and relatively fit patients would have little importance compared with other journeys where very sick patients need to be moved from the operating theatres to intensive-care wards.

In these cases it might be worthwhile to incorporate a cost (or difficulty) element into the measure of layout effectiveness which is being minimized.

Effectiveness of layout $= \sum F_{ij} D_{ij} C_{ij}$ for all i not $= j$

where C_{ij} = the cost per distance travelled of making a journey between departments i and j.

The general process layout design method

The general approach to determining the location of work centres in process layout is as follows.

Step 1 Collect information relating to the work centres and the flow between them.

Step 2 Draw up a schematic layout showing the work centres and the flow between them, putting the work centres with the greatest flow closest to each other.

Step 3 Adjust the schematic layout to take into account the constraints of the area into which the layout must fit.

Step 4 Draw the layout showing the actual work centre areas and distances which materials or customers must travel. Calculate the effectiveness measure of the layout either as total distance travelled or as the cost of movement.

Step 5 Check to see if exchanging any two work centres will reduce the total distance travelled or the cost of movement. If so, make the exchange and return to Step 4. If not, make this the final layout.

237

Example: Rotterdam Educational Group

As an example of a process layout, we can consider Rotterdam Educational Group (REG), a company which commissions, designs and manufactures education packs for distance-learning courses and training. It has leased a new building with an area of 1800 square metres, into which it needs to fit eleven 'departments'. Prior to moving into the new building it has conducted an exercise to find the average number of trips taken by its staff between the eleven departments. Although some trips are a little more significant than others (because of the loads carried by staff) it has been decided that all trips will be treated as being of equal value.

Step 1 – Collect information

The areas required by each department together with the average daily number of trips between departments are shown in the flow chart in Fig. 7.13. In this example the direction of flow is not relevant and very low flow rates (less than five trips per day) have not been included.

Step 2 – Draw schematic layout

Figure 7.14 shows the first schematic arrangement of departments. The thickest lines represent high flow rates of between 70 and 120 trips per day, the medium lines are used for flow rates of between 20 and 69 trips a day, and the thinnest lines for flow

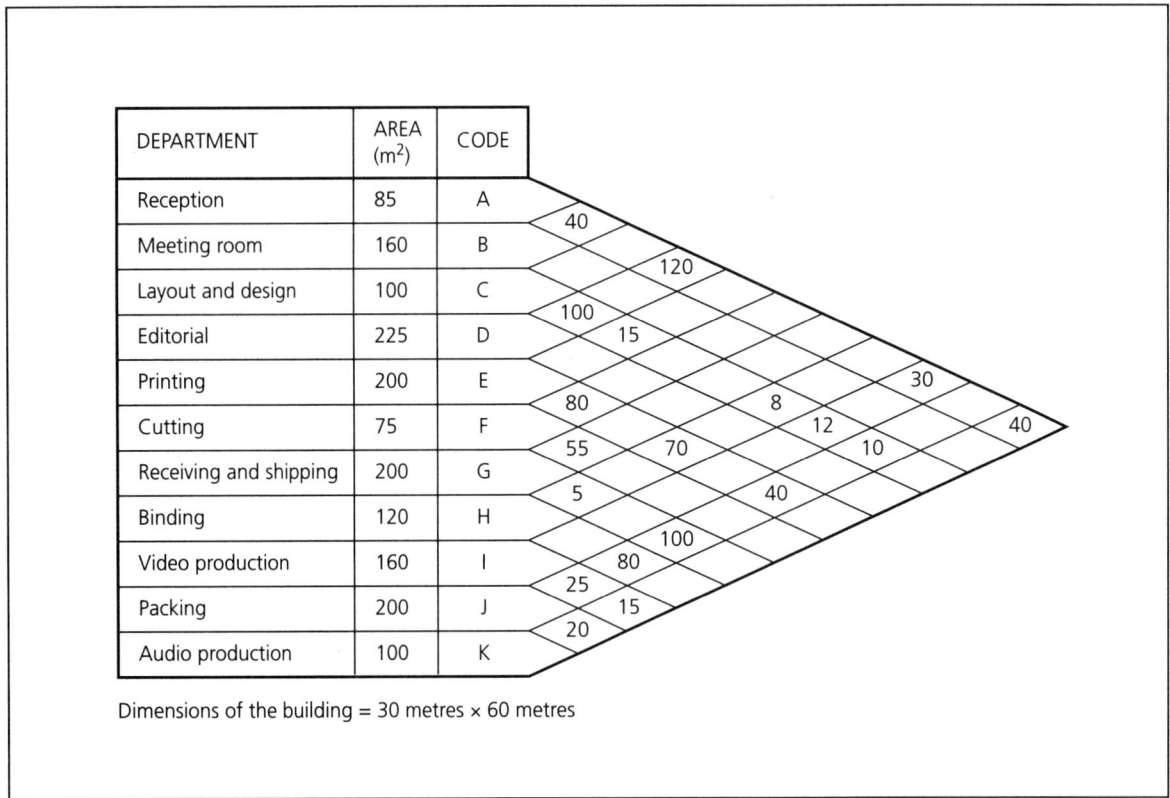

DEPARTMENT	AREA (m²)	CODE
Reception	85	A
Meeting room	160	B
Layout and design	100	C
Editorial	225	D
Printing	200	E
Cutting	75	F
Receiving and shipping	200	G
Binding	120	H
Video production	160	I
Packing	200	J
Audio production	100	K

Dimensions of the building = 30 metres × 60 metres

Figure 7.13 Flow information for Rotterdam Educational

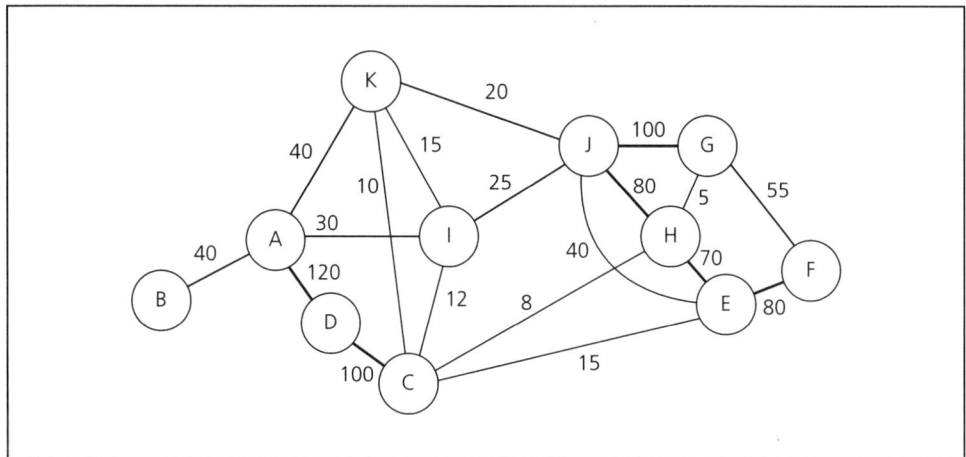

Figure 7.14
Schematic layout placing centres with high traffic levels close to each other

rates between 5 and 19 trips a day. The objective here is to arrange the work centres so that those with the thick lines are closest together. The higher the flow rate, the shorter the line should be.

Step 3 – Adjust the schematic layout

If departments were arranged exactly as shown in Fig. 7.14 the building which housed them would be of an irregular, and therefore high-cost, shape. The layout needs adjusting to take into account the shape of the building. Figure 7.15 shows the departments arranged in a more ordered fashion which corresponds to the dimensions of the building.

Step 4 – Draw the layout

Figure 7.16 shows the departments arranged with the actual dimensions of the building and occupying areas which approximate to their required areas. Although the distances between the centroids of departments have changed from Fig. 7.15 to accommodate their physical shape, their relative positions are the same. It is at this stage when a quantitative expression of the cost of movement associated with this relative layout can be calculated.

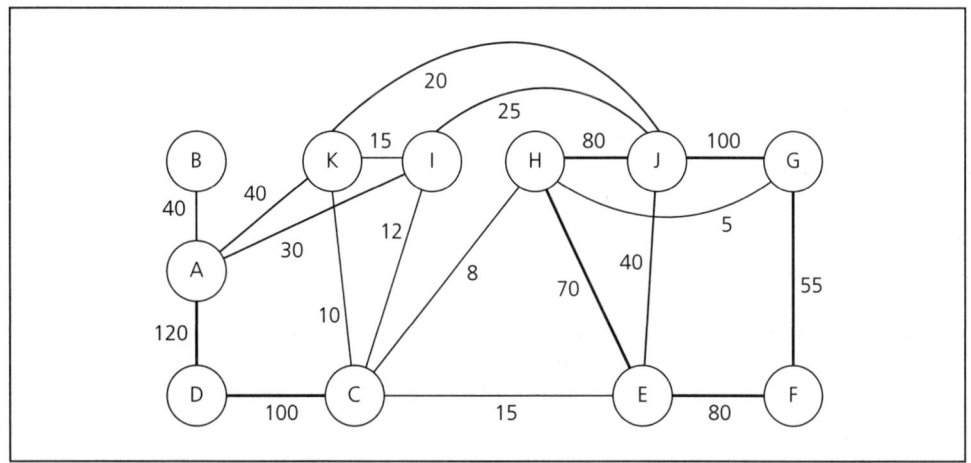

Figure 7.15
Schematic layout adjusted to fit building geometry

239

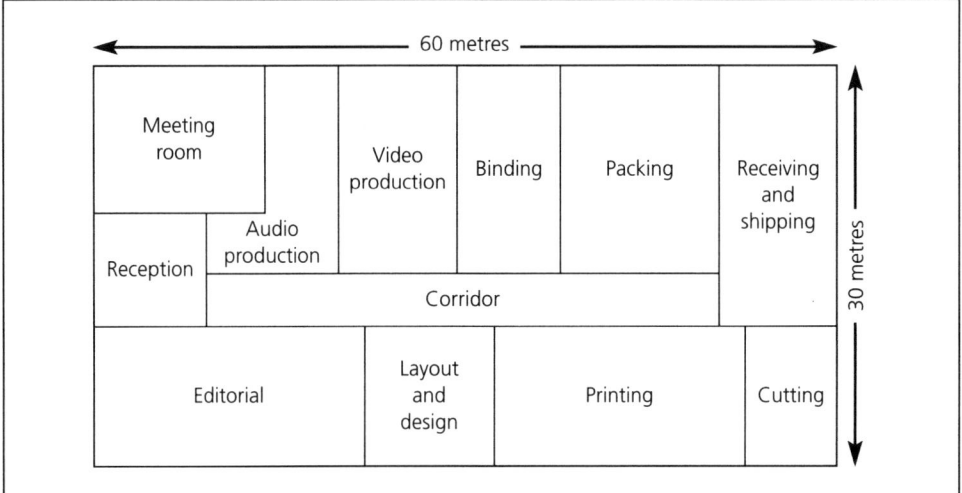

**Figure 7.16
Final layout of
building**

Step 5 – Check by exchanging

The layout in Fig. 7.16 seems to be reasonably effective but it is usually worthwhile to check for improvement by exchanging pairs of departments to see if any reduction in total flow can be obtained. For example, departments H and J might be exchanged, and the total distance travelled calculated again to see if any reduction has been achieved.

Detailed design in cell layout

Cells are a compromise between the flexibility of process layout and the simplicity of product layout (treated next). For example, Fig. 7.17 shows how a process layout has been divided into four cells each of which has the resources to process a 'family' of parts. In doing this the operations management has implicitly taken two interrelated decisions regarding:

● the extent and nature of the cells it has chosen to adopt, and
● which resources to allocate to which cells.

The extent and nature of cells

The extended nature of cells can best be described by examining the amount of the direct and indirect resources which are located within the cell. Direct resources are those which directly transform material, information or customers. Indirect resources are there to support the direct resources in their transformation activities. Figure 7.18 shows a two-way classification of cells based on the degree of direct and indirect resources included in the cell.

In the bottom-right quadrant are what might be called 'pure' cells in that most operations managers would probably define a cell in this way. Its activities are focused on completing the whole of the transformation, and all the direct resources needed to do this are included in the cell. The top-right quadrant represents the logical extension of the cell concept to include all the support and administrative indirect

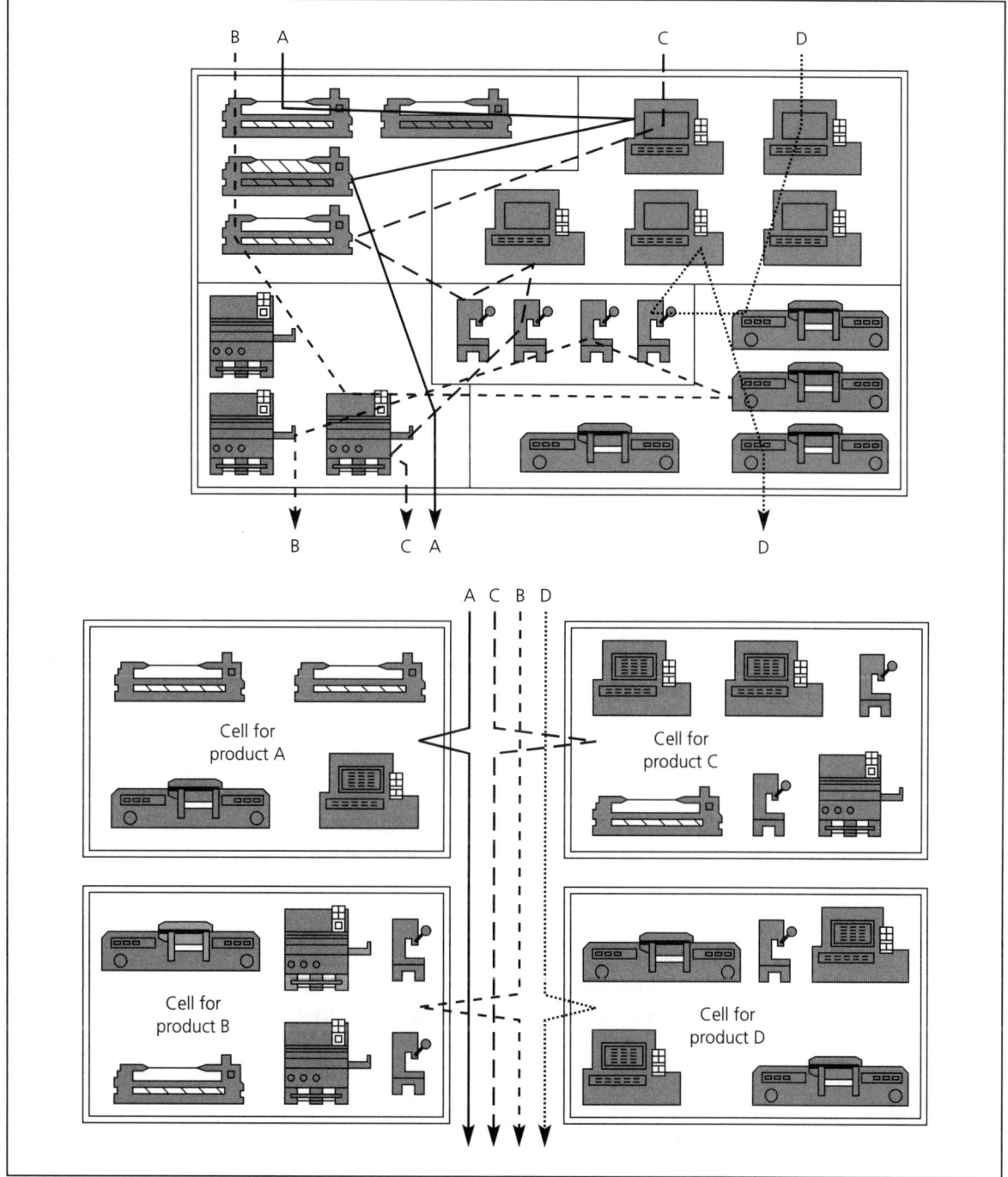

Figure 7.17 Cell layout groups processes together which are necessary for a family of products

resources needed for the cell to 'stand alone'. These large 'cells' are sometimes referred to as the plant-within-a-plant concept: in effect, the division of a manufacturing plant into several mini-plants on the same site. Similarly, a maternity unit

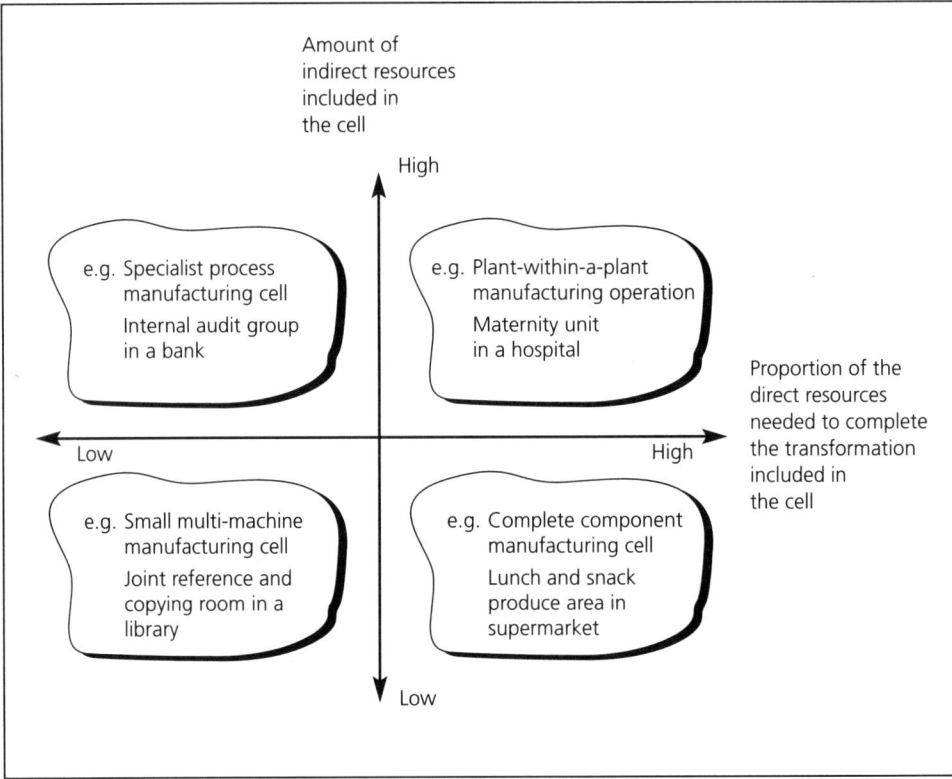

**Figure 7.18
Types of cell**

could, if it contains all its support resources, also stand alone. The bottom-left quadrant represents the type of cell where resources are placed together because they are frequently needed in the same part of total transformation. For example, two machines which are always used one after the other could be put together. Similarly a large library, although it probably has a copy machine area, could also locate a copy machine in the reference area for users to make copies if required. Finally the top-left quadrant represents cells which some would dispute deserve the name. They only have the direct resources to apply to part of the total process, and in this way they might seem to be little different from a conventional work centre or department in a process layout. The difference is that they include all or most of the indirect resources they need. Again they might theoretically be capable of 'standing alone' outside the rest of the operation. The internal audit section of a bank might need to contain its own technical and administrative support – perhaps to maintain its independence from the rest of the operation which it is auditing.

Allocating resources to cells

The detailed design of cellular layouts is difficult partly because the idea of a cell is itself a compromise between process and product layout. With process layout we focus on the location of the various processes in the operation. With product layout (treated next) we focus on the requirements of the 'product' – cell layout needs to consider the needs of both.

Sometimes, in order to simplify the task, it is useful to concentrate on either the process or product aspects of cell layout. If cell designers choose to concentrate on processes they could use *cluster analysis* to find which processes group naturally together. This involves examining each type of process and asking which other types of processes a product or part using that process is also likely to need. For example, in furniture manufacture, if all the parts which need holes drilling in them also need countersinking, then whatever the cell arrangement which is finally decided, drilling and countersink machines will need to go together in the same cells. Alternatively, if the operation chooses to concentrate on its products to design its cell formation they would probably use one of the *parts family coding and classification systems*. These systems use multi-digit codes for each part or product. The codes indicate the characteristics of the product such as shape, size, material and any other factors which define its processing requirements.

Production flow analysis (PFA)[7]

Perhaps the most popular approach to allocating tasks and machines to cells is production flow analysis (PFA), which examines both product requirements and process grouping simultaneously. In Fig. 7.19(a) a manufacturing operation has grouped the components it makes into eight families – for example, the components in family 1 require machines 2 and 5. In this state the matrix does not seem to exhibit any natural groupings. If the order of the rows and columns is changed, however, to move the crosses as close as possible to the diagonal of the matrix which goes from top left to bottom right, then a clearer pattern emerges. This is shown in Fig. 7.19(b) and shows that the machines could conveniently be grouped together in three cells, indicated on the diagram as cells A, B and C. Although this procedure is a particularly useful way to allocate machines to cells, the analysis is rarely totally clean. This is the case here where component family 8 needs processing by machine 3 which has been allocated to cell B.

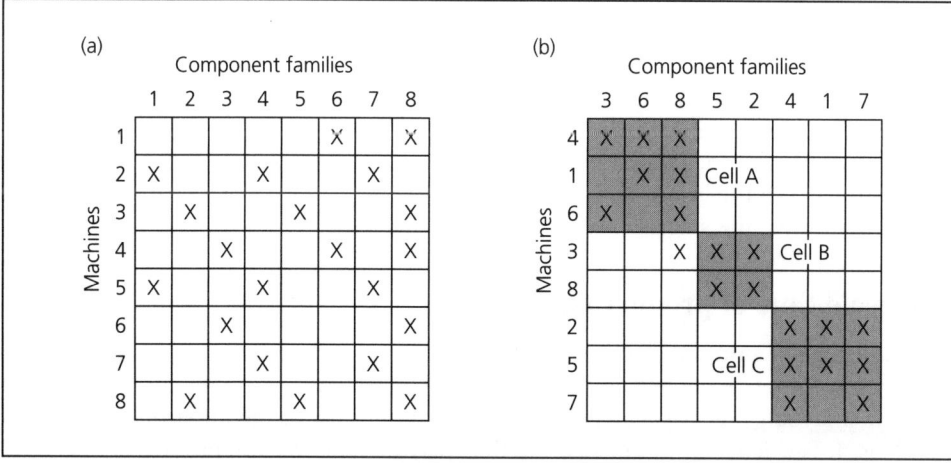

Figure 7.19 (a) and (b) Using production flow analysis to allocate machines to cells

Generally there are three ways of dealing with this, none of them totally satisfactory.

● Another machine the same as machine 3 could be purchased and put in cell A. This would clearly solve the problem but requires investing capital in a new machine which might be under-utilized.

● Send components in family 8 to cell B after they have been processed in cell A (or even in the middle of their processing route if necessary). This solution avoids the need to purchase another machine but it conflicts partly with the basic idea of cell layout – to achieve a simplification of a previously complex flow.

● If there are several components which have this problem it might be necessary to devise a special cell for them (usually called a *remainder cell*) which will almost be like a mini-process layout. Again this does not conform strictly to the simplicity of pure cell layout and also can involve extra capital expenditure. The remainder cell does remove the 'inconvenient' components from the rest of the operation, however, leaving it with a more ordered and predictable flow.

Detailed design in product layout

The detailed design of any type of layout is largely concerned with where to locate resources. It may seem therefore that there is little detailed design necessary in product layout because it involves arranging the transforming resources of the operation to fit the sequence required by the product or service. However, although the requirements of the product or service do indeed dominate product layout design, there are still many detailed design decisions to be taken. The nature of the design decision also changes a little. In other types of layout the decision is 'where to place what'. In product layout it is concerned more with 'what to place where', insomuch as locations are frequently decided upon and then work tasks are allocated to the location. For example, it may have been decided that four stations are needed to make briefcases on an assembly-line basis. The decision is then which of the tasks that go into making the briefcase should be allocated to which of the four stations.

This design decision is called the '*line-balancing*' decision and is only one (although sometimes the most difficult) of the decisions involved in the detailed design of product layouts. These decisions are as follows:

● What cycle time is needed?
● How many stages are needed?
● How to cope with the task-time variation?
● How to balance the layout?
● How to arrange the stages?

The cycle time of product layouts

The cycle time of a product layout is the time for completed products, pieces of information or customers to emerge from the operation. Cycle time is a vital factor in the design of product layouts and has a significant influence on most of the other detailed design decisions. It is calculated by considering the likely demand for the products or services over a period and the amount of production time available in that period.

For example, suppose the regional back-office operation of a large bank is designing an operation which will process its mortgage applications. The number of applications to be processed is 160 per week and the time available to process the applications is 40 hours per week.

$$\text{The cycle time for the layout} = \frac{\text{Time available}}{\text{Number to be processed}}$$

$$\text{In this case cycle time} = \frac{40}{160} = \frac{1}{4} \text{ hours}$$

$$= 15 \text{ minutes}$$

So the bank's layout must be capable of processing a completed application once every 15 minutes.

The number of stages

The next decision on the detailed design of a product layout concerns the number of stages in the layout. In practice this can be anything between one and several hundred, depending partly on the cycle time required and the total quantity of work involved in producing the product or service. This latter piece of information is called the *total work content* of the product or service. The larger the total work content and the smaller the required cycle time, the more stages will be necessary.

For example, suppose the bank calculated that the average total work content of processing a mortgage application is 60 minutes. The number of stages needed to produce a processed application every 15 minutes can be calculated as follows:

$$\text{Number of stages} = \frac{\text{Total work content}}{\text{Required cycle time}}$$

$$= \frac{60 \text{ minutes}}{15 \text{ minutes}}$$

$$= 4 \text{ stages}$$

The mortgage-processing layout therefore will need four stages. If this figure had not emerged as a whole number it would have been necessary to round it up to the next largest whole number. It is difficult (although not always impossible) to hire fractions of people to staff the stages.

Task-time variation

Thus far we could imagine a line of four stages each contributing a quarter of the total work content of processing the mortgage, and passing the documentation on to the next stage every 15 minutes. In practice, of course, the flow would not be so regular. Each station's allocation of work might on average take fifteen minutes, but almost certainly the time will vary each time a mortgage application is processed. This is a general characteristic of all repetitive processing (and indeed of all work performed by humans – *see* Appendix 2 at the end of the book) and can be caused by a number of different factors.

● Each product or service being processed along the line might be different – for example different models of automobile going down the same line.

● Products or services, although essentially the same, might require slightly different treatment. For example, in the mortgage processing example, the time some tasks require will vary depending on the personal circumstances of the person applying for the loan.

● There are usually slight variations in the physical coordination and effort on the part of the person performing the task.

This variation can introduce irregularity into the flow along the line, which in turn can lead to both periodic queues at the stages and lost processing time. It may even prove necessary to introduce more resources into the operation to compensate for the loss of efficiency resulting from worktime variation.

Balancing worktime allocation

Perhaps the most problematic of all the detailed design decisions in product layout is that of ensuring the equal allocation of tasks to each stage in the line. This process is called *line balancing*. In the mortgage-processing example we have assumed that the 15 minutes of work content has been allocated equally to the four stations as in Figure 7.20(a). This is nearly always impossible to achieve in practice and some imbalance in the work allocation between stages results, as illustrated in Fig. 7.20(b). Inevitably this will raise the effective cycle time of the line. If it becomes greater than the required cycle time it may be necessary to devote extra resources, in the shape of a further stage, to compensate for the imbalance.

Measuring balancing loss

The effectiveness of the line balancing activity is measured by what is called *balancing loss*. This is the time wasted through the unequal allocation of work as a percentage of the total time invested in processing the product or service. In Fig. 7.21 the work allocations in a four-stage line are illustrated. The total amount of time invested in producing each product or service is four times the cycle time because for every unit produced all four stages have been working for the cycle time. In this case the total time invested is 4 × 3.0 = 12 minutes. Three of the stages have worktime allocations of 2.8, 2.6 and 2.7 minutes respectively, however. Between them they are wasting 0.19 minutes in idle time. The balancing loss of this layout is therefore calculated as 7.5%.

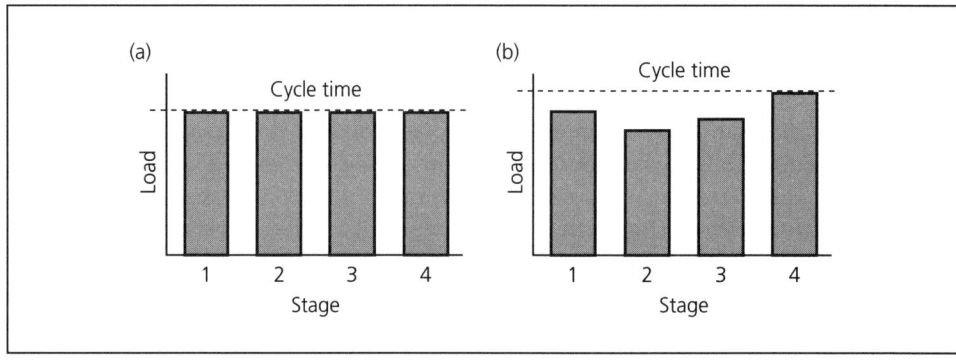

Figure 7.20 Unequal allocation of work between stages reduces efficiency: (a) ideal balance, (b) less than ideal balance

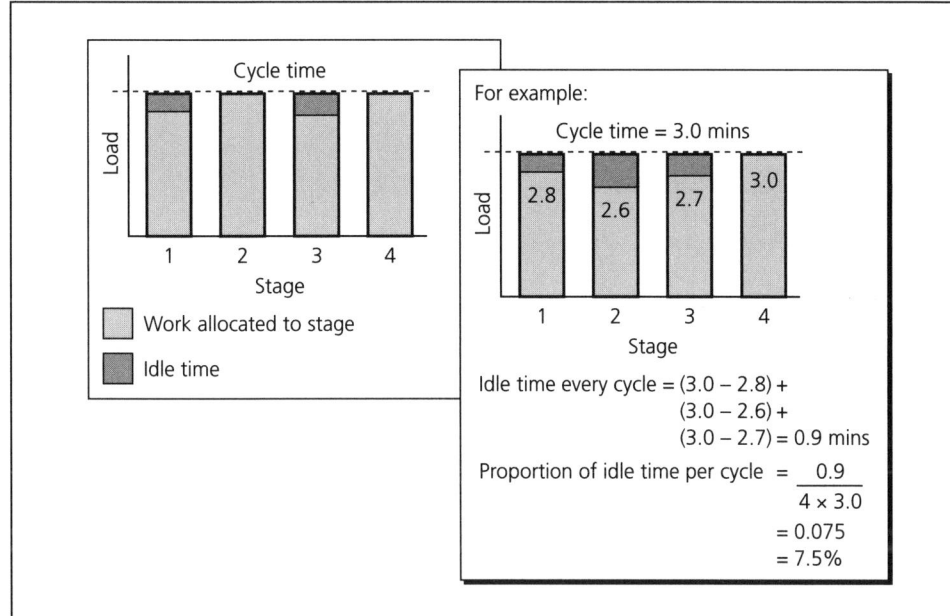

Figure 7.21
Balancing loss is the percentage of time not used productively

Balancing techniques[8]

As in the other basic layout types, there are a number of techniques available to help in the line balancing task. Again, in practice, the most useful and most used 'techniques' are the simple heuristic approaches. Foremost among the latter is the *precedence diagram*.

The precedence diagram is a representation of the ordering of the elements which comprise the total work content of the product or service. Each element is represented by a circle. The circles are connected by arrows which signify the ordering of the elements. For example, Fig. 7.22 shows the precedence diagram for processing mortgage applications. Two rules apply when constructing the diagram:

● the circles which represent the elements are drawn as far to the left as possible; and
● none of the arrows which show the precedence of the elements should be vertical.

In the case of the mortgage processing example, Fig. 7.22 shows that element a must be carried out before element b, after which elements c or d can be carried out, and so on. The precedence diagram, either using circles and arrows or transposed into tabular form, is the most common starting point for most balancing techniques. We do not treat the more complex of these techniques here but it is useful to describe the general approach to balancing product layouts.

This general approach is to allocate elements from the precedence diagram to the first stage, starting from the left, in order of the columns, until the work allocated to the stage is as close to, but less than, the cycle time. When that stage is as full of work as is possible without exceeding the cycle time, move on to the next stage and so on until all the work elements are allocated. The key issue is how to select an element to be allocated to a stage when more than one element could be chosen. Two heuristic rules have been found to be particularly useful in deciding this.

● Simply choose the largest which will 'fit' into the time remaining at the stage.
● Choose the element with the most 'followers', that is the highest number of elements which can only be allocated when that element has been allocated.

247

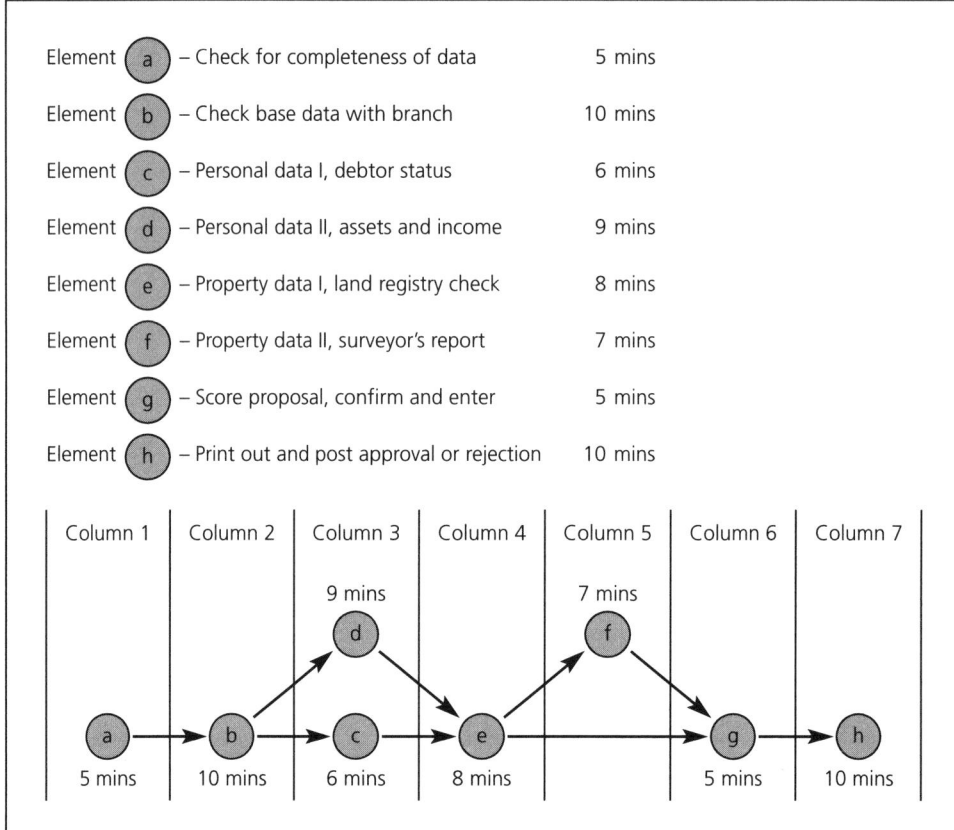

Figure 7.22
Element listing and precedence diagram for the mortgage processing operation

The use of both these heuristics can usually result in a reasonable, if not an optimal, solution. In the mortgage-processing example, the allocation is both straightforward and exceptionally convenient!

Stage 1 would contain elements a and b.
Stage 2 would contain elements c and d.
Stage 3 would contain elements e and f.
Stage 4 would contain elements g and h.

Resulting in a perfectly balanced four-stage layout with a cycle time of the required 15 minutes.

Example: Ouma's Koeksisters

As an example of balancing a product layout, we can consider Ouma's Koeksisters (OK), a manufacturer of specialityconfectionary, which has recently obtained a contract to supply a major supermarket chain with a product in the shape of a twisted ribbon. It has been decided that the volumes required by the supermarket warrant a special production line to perform the frying, finishing and packing of the product. This line would have to carry out the elements shown in Fig. 7.23 which also shows the precedence diagram for the total job. The initial order from the supermarket is for 500 Koeksisters a week and the number of hours worked by the factory is 40 per week. From this:

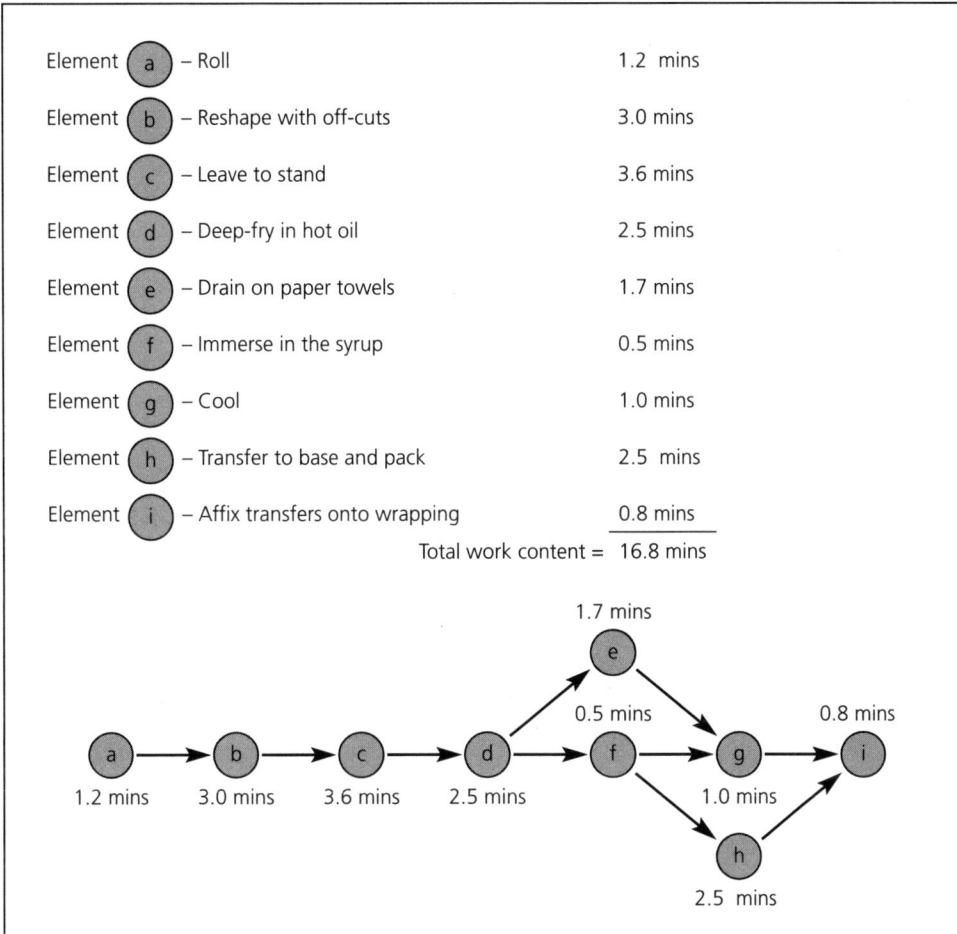

Element (a) – Roll   1.2 mins

Element (b) – Reshape with off-cuts   3.0 mins

Element (c) – Leave to stand   3.6 mins

Element (d) – Deep-fry in hot oil   2.5 mins

Element (e) – Drain on paper towels   1.7 mins

Element (f) – Immerse in the syrup   0.5 mins

Element (g) – Cool   1.0 mins

Element (h) – Transfer to base and pack   2.5 mins

Element (i) – Affix transfers onto wrapping   0.8 mins

Total work content = 16.8 mins

Figure 7.23 Element listing and precedence diagram for Ouma's Koeksisters

$$\text{The required cycle time} = \frac{40 \text{ hrs} \times 60 \text{ mins}}{500}$$

$$= 4.8 \text{ mins}$$

$$\text{The required number of stages} = \frac{16.8 \text{ mins (the total work content)}}{4.8 \text{ mins (the required cycle time)}}$$

$$= 3.5 \text{ stages}$$

This means four stages.

Working from the left on the precedence diagram, elements a and b can be allocated to stage 1. Allocating element c to stage 1 would exceed the cycle time. In fact only element c can be allocated to stage 2 because including element d would again exceed the cycle time. Element d can be allocated to stage 3. Either element e or element f can also be allocated to stage 3, but not both or the cycle time would be exceeded. Following the 'largest element' heuristic rule, element e is chosen. The remaining elements then are allocated to stage 4. Figure 7.24 shows the final allocation and the balancing loss of the line.

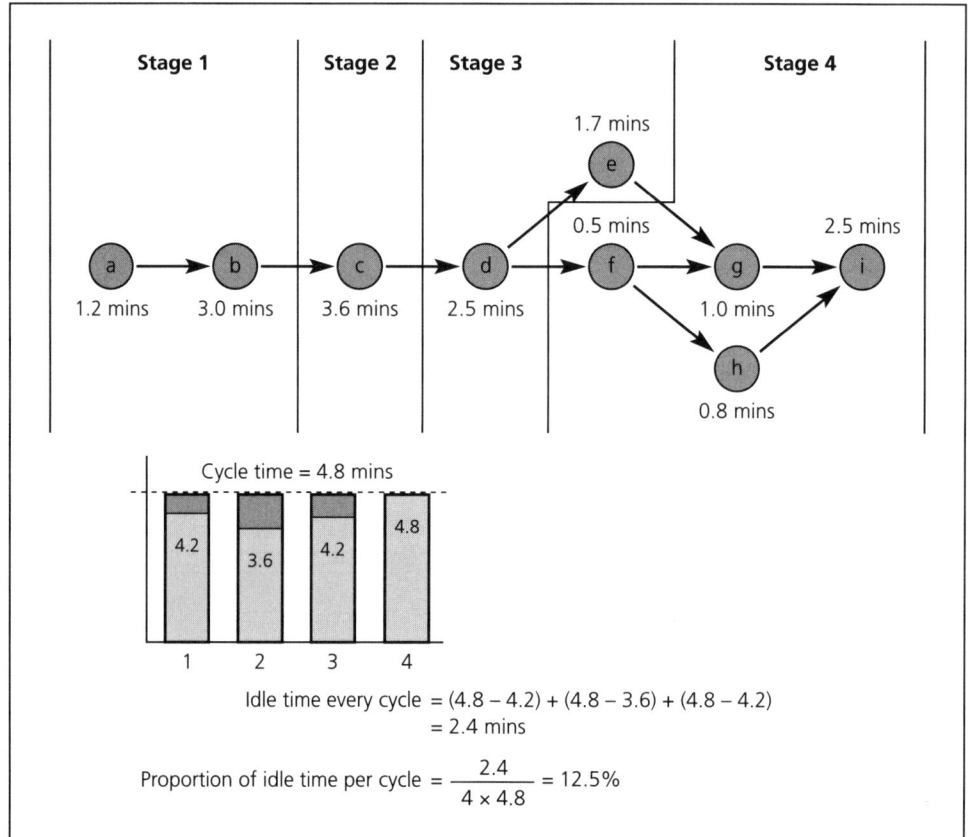

Figure 7.24
Allocation of
elements to stages
and balancing loss
for Ouma's
Koeksisters

Arranging the stages

Our assumption so far has been that all the stages necessary to fulfil the requirements of the layout will be arranged in a sequential 'single line'. Yet this need not necessarily be so. Return to the mortgage-processing example which requires four stages working on the task to maintain a cycle time of one processed application every 15 minutes. The conventional arrangement of the four stages would be to lay them out in one line, each stage having 15 minutes' worth of work. However, nominally, the same output rate could also be achieved by arranging the four stages as two shorter lines, each of two stages with 30 minutes' worth of work each. Alternatively, following this logic to its ultimate conclusion, the stages could be arranged as four parallel stages, each responsible for the whole work content. Figure 7.25 shows these options.

This may be a simplified example, but it represents a genuine issue. Should the layout be arranged as a single 'long-thin' line, as several 'short-fat' parallel lines, or somewhere in between? (Note that 'long' means the number of stages and 'fat' means the amount of work allocated to each stage.) In any particular situation there are usually technical constraints which limit either how 'long and thin' or 'short and fat' the layout can be, but there is usually a range of possible options within which a choice needs to be made. The advantages of each extreme of the long-thin to short-fat spectrum are very different and help to explain why different arrangements are adopted. If the supermarket chain pushes up the order to 5000 per week, then Ouma's Koeksisters could possibly put batches of ten through the same process.

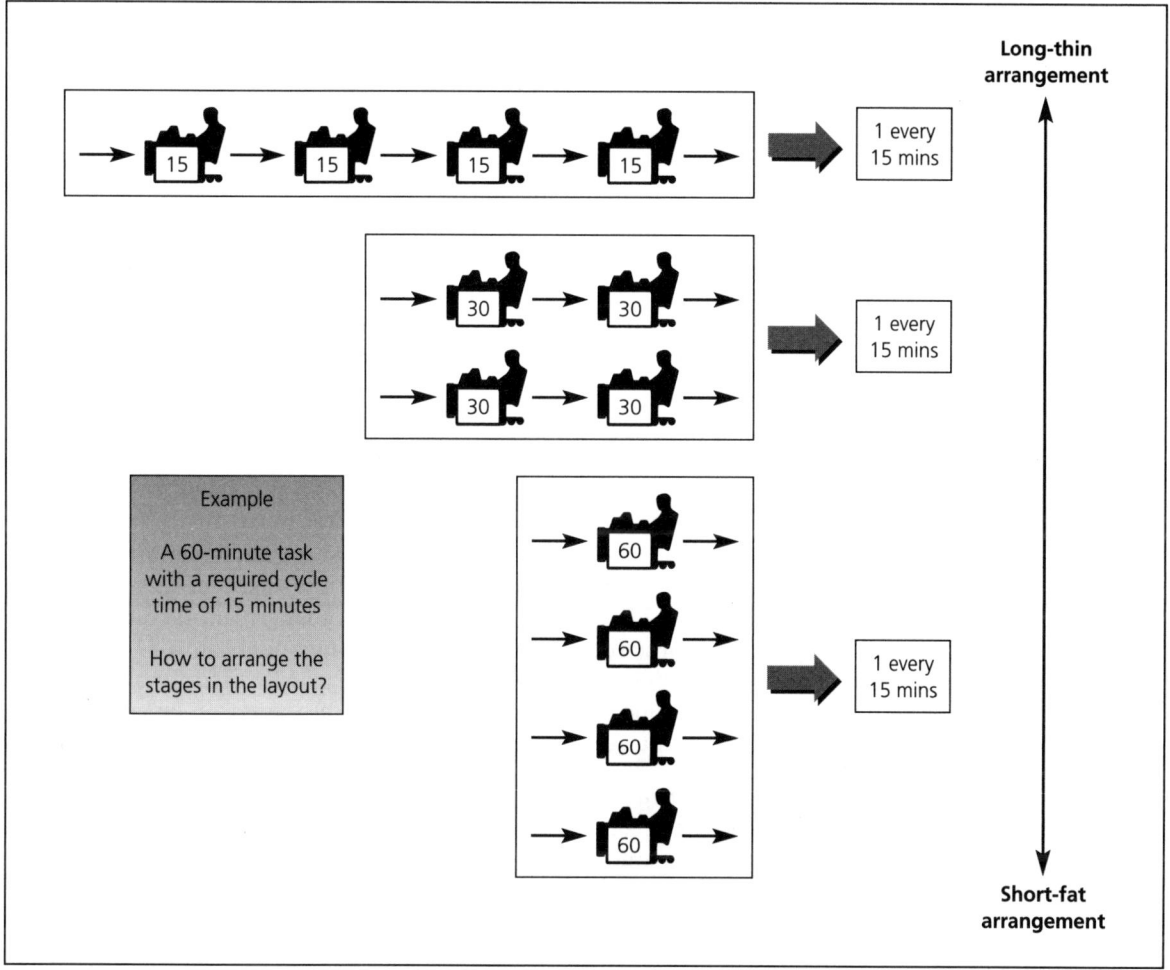

Figure 7.25 The arrangement of stages in product layout can be described on a spectrum from 'long-thin' to 'short-fat'

The advantages of the long-thin arrangement

These include:

- *Controlled flow of materials or customers* – which is easy to manage.
- *Simple materials handling* – especially if a product being manufactured is heavy, large or difficult to move.
- *Lower capital requirements*. If a specialist piece of equipment is needed for one element in the job, only one piece of equipment would need to be purchased; on short-fat arrangements every stage would need one.
- *More efficient operation*. If each stage is only performing a small part of the total job, the person at the stage will have a higher proportion of direct productive work as opposed to the non-productive parts of the job, such as picking up tools and materials.

This last point is particularly important and is fully explained in Chapter 9 when we discuss job design.

The advantages of the short-fat arrangement

These include:

- *Higher mix flexibility.* If the layout needs to process several types of product or service, each stage or line could specialize in different types.
- *Higher volume flexibility.* As volume varies stages can simply be closed down or started up as required; long-thin arrangements would need rebalancing each time the cycle time changed.
- *Higher robustness.* If one stage breaks down or ceases operation in some way the other parallel stages are unaffected; a long-thin arrangement would cease operating completely.
- *Less monotonous work.* In the mortgage example the staff in the short-fat arrangement are repeating their tasks only every hour; in the long-thin arrangement it is every fifteen minutes.

Again, this last point is particularly important and is treated further in Chapter 9.

The shape of the line

If it is decided to adopt an arrangement which involves some sequential flow between stages arranged in series, a further decision concerns the shape of the line. Partly inspired by the experience of Japanese manufacturers, many manufacturing operations are adopting the practice of curving line arrangements into U-shaped or 'serpentine' arrangements (*see* Fig. 7.26). U-shapes are usually used for shorter lines and serpentines for longer lines. Richard Schonberger, the expert on Japanese manufacturing, sees several advantages in this.[9]

- *Staffing flexibility and balance.* The U-shape enables one person to tend several work-stations – adjacent or across the U – without much walking. This opens up options for balancing work among the people: when demand grows, more labour can be added until every station has an operator.
- *Rework.* When the line bends around itself, it is easy to return bad work to an earlier station for rework without either fuss or much distance travelled.

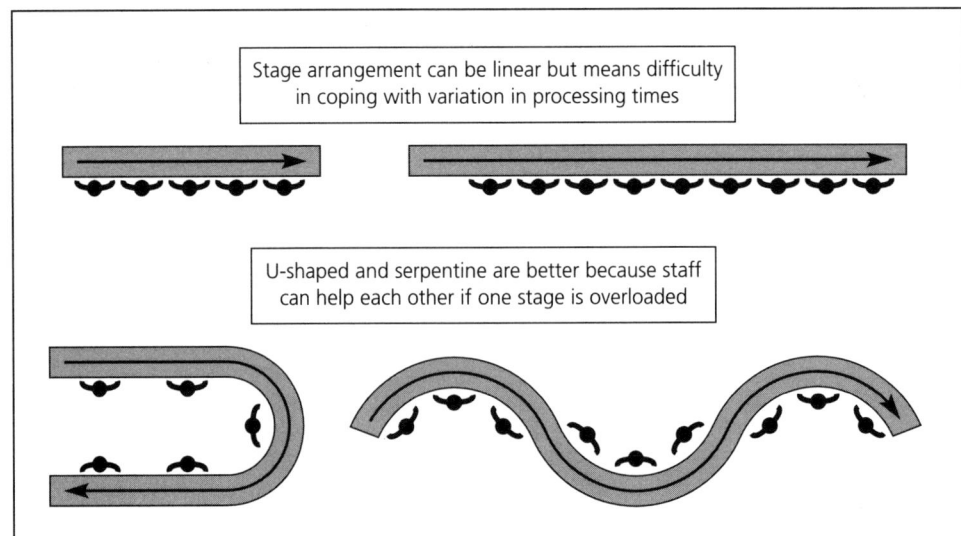

**Figure 7.26
The arrangement
of stages –
U-shaped
arrangements**

- *Handling.* From a centre position within the U, a handler (human, vehicle, crane, or robot) can deliver materials and handle tools conveniently.
- *Passage.* Long straight lines interfere with cross travel in the rest of the operation. It is annoying when shelving in a supermarket is too long. People protest when a super-highway cuts a neighbourhood in half. It is the same with flow lines.
- *Teamwork.* A semicircle even looks like a team.

Bob Malcomess, Green Valley

Bob is the manufacturing director of Green Valley, situated in Selby south of Johannesburg. Green Valley is a factory which produces value-added frozen food dishes. Green Valley is a very impressive factory in terms of its factory layout, cleanliness and its reputation as a producer of high quality frozen convenience food dishes. Bob is an ex-supply manager for a motor car assembly plant. At Green Valley, he was integrally involved in setting the business strategy, and had a hand in deciding on the location and process flow of the new facility. He says factors affecting the location decision were power supply, public transport, communications infrastructure and labour availability, efficiency and productivity. Bob says:

'Some products are "factory-friendly" and others are "factory-unfriendly". For example, the lasagne dish is classified as "factory-unfriendly" as it has 12 layers of pasta, meat sauce and cheese, and therefore requires high labour input. South African production managers have to balance the productivity imperative against that of social responsibility. It is not always desirable to eradicate jobs. The day-to-day running of the factory is about the efficient utilization of resources. The overall flow of product needs to be balanced against estimated demand as determined by marketing and sales. Ideally the work has to be planned so that at no time are any of the resources underutilized – no equipment on the line should be idle. Operations managers know the capacities of the different machines and make an effort to balance them.

'The layout of the factory is a single line flow with batch processing: from Delivery to Kitchen preparation to Cooking to Dishing area to Packaging to Freezing to Dispatch.

'Once the raw foodstuffs have been checked for quality, they proceed along one of two routes: to the holding refrigerators or to the freezers. Vegetables, meats, cheese and milk products are stored separately by means of partitions. Ideally they should be in separate rooms, but cost considerations prevented this. Dry foodstuffs such as pasta are stored in another room, and there is a room dedicated to spices and herbs. When they are to be used, frozen foods move to the thawing room, where liquids drain out and are washed away. The entire factory has a non-slip floor built up nine inches above the original floor height, with drainage channels covered by stainless steel grids for sluicing. Cooked foods are all weighed, tagged and signed off, and then sent to the 4°C room before being moved to the packaging room where the inner packaging is done. Dishes are then transferred to the blast freezer, which operates at a temperature of between −15°C and −30°C. Once frozen, they go to the outer packaging room, onto the conveyor belt to dispatch. All products come in and leave on a conveyor belt through a hatch. In this way constant temperature is maintained throughout the process.' ∎

Source: By kind permission of Green Valley

SUMMARY

■ The layout decision is a particularly important one because changing a layout is often a lengthy and difficult task, which is both expensive and disruptive to the smooth running of the operation. For this reason it is not taken frequently. However, if the layout turns out to be inappropriate the flow of materials and people through the operation can turn out to be confusing and often high cost.

■ The layout decision procedure starts with a decision on process type, which will be influenced by the volume–variety characteristics of the operation and its strategic performance objectives. The process type goes some way to determining which of the four basic layout types are likely to be appropriate for the operation. Once the basic layout is chosen, the detailed design of the layout can be approached.

■ There are four basic layout types. They are:
fixed-position layout
process layout
cell layout
product layout.

■ Fixed-position layout is usually used when the materials or people being transformed are either too large, or too delicate, or would object to being moved.

■ Process layout groups all similar transforming resources together within the operation. The different types of transformed resources will then make their own way through the operation according to their processing needs. Process layout is usually used where variety is relatively high.

■ Cell layout is where the resources needed for a particular class of product are grouped together in some way. 'Shop-within-a-shop' layouts in retail operations and a maternity unit in a hospital are both examples of cell layout.

■ Product layout is where the transforming resources are located in sequence specifically for the convenience of product or product types.

■ The flow of people, or information, or materials through an operation is determined by the type of layout chosen. At one extreme in fixed position layout flow is intermittent. At the other extreme in product layout flow becomes more continuous.

■ In the detailed design of fixed-position layouts resource location analysis (RLA) can be used to allocate areas within a site to particular resources.

■ In the detailed design of process layouts the objective is usually (although not always) to minimize the distance travelled by the transformed resources moving through the operation. Either manual or computer-based methods can be used to devise the detailed design in process layout.

■ There are many different types of cell layout which can be classified by the amount of indirect resources included in the cell and the proportion of direct resources needed to complete the transformation which are included in the cell. Production flow analysis (PFA) can be used to allocate products to cells.

■ In the detailed design of product layouts there are a number of individual decisions to be made. These include the cycle time to which the design must conform, the number of stages in the operation, the way tasks are allocated to the stages in the line, and the arrangement of the stages in the line.

254

Weldon Hand Tools

Weldon Hand Tools, successful the African hand tool manufacturer, decided to move into the 'woodworking' tools market. Previously its products had been confined to car maintenance, home decorating, and general hand tools. One of the first products which it decided to manufacture was a general-purpose 'smoothing plane', a tool which smooths and shapes wood. Their product designers devised a suitable design and the company's work measurement engineers estimated the time it would take (in standard minutes – see Appendix 2 at the end of the book) to perform each element in the assembly process. The marketing department also estimated the likely demand (export and local) for the new product. Their sales forecast is shown in Table 7.6.

Table 7.6 Sales forecast for smoothing plane

Time period	Volume
Year 1	
1st Quarter	98 000 units
2nd Quarter	140 000 units
3rd Quarter	140 000 units
4th Quarter	170 000 units
Year 2	
1st Quarter	140 000 units
2nd Quarter	170 000 units
3rd Quarter	200 000 units
4th Quarter	230 000 units

The marketing department was not totally confident of its forecast, however.

'A substantial proportion of demand is likely to be export sales, which we find difficult to predict. But whatever demand does turn out to be, we will have to react quickly to meet it. The more we enter these parts of the market, the more we are into impulse buying and the more sales we lose if we don't supply.'

This plane was likely to be the first of several similar planes. A further model had already been approved for launch about one year after this, and two or three further models were in the planning stage. All the planes were similar, merely varying in length and width.

Table 7.7 Standard times for each element of assembly task

Fly-press operations

Assemble poke S/A	0.12 S.M.
(LH poke, RH poke, poke bush)	(standard minutes)
Fit poke S/A to frog	0.10 S.M.
(poke, S/A, poke pin, frog)	
Rivet adjusting lever to frog	0.15 S.M.
(adjust lever, rivet, frog)	
Press adjusting nut screw to frog	0.08 S.M.
(frog, adjusting nut screw)	
TOTAL PRESS OPERATIONS	0.45 S.M.

Bench operations

Fit adjusting nut to frog	0.15 S.M.
Fit frog screw to frog	0.05 S.M.

FROG S/A COMPLETE

Fit knob to base	0.15 S.M.
Fit handle to base	0.17 S.M.
Fit frog S/A to base	0.15 S.M.
Assemble blade S/A	0.08 S.M.
Assemble blade S/A, clamp and	
label to base and adjust	0.20 S.M.

PLANE COMPLETE

TOTAL FOR PRESS AND ASSEMBLY OPERATIONS	1.40 S.M.
Make up box, wrap plane, pack and stock	0.20 S.M.
TOTAL WORK TIME FOR ASSEMBLY AREA	1.60 S.M.

▶

Designing the manufacturing operation

It was decided to assemble all planes at one of the company's smaller factory sites where a whole workshop was unused. Within the workshop there was plenty of room for expansion if demand proved higher than forecast. All machining and finishing of parts would be performed at the main factory and the parts shipped to the smaller site where they would be assembled at the available workshop.

An idea of the assembly task can be gained from the partially exploded view of the product (*see*

Fig. 7.27). Table 7.7 gives the 'standard time' for each element of the assembly task. Some of the tasks are described as 'fly-press' operations. A fly press is a relatively simple tool, about a metre high, which has two weights mounted on to a screw thread. When the two weights are rotated they give momentum to the downward action of the screw thread which applies a downward force. This force is used for simple bending, riveting or force-fitting operations. A fly press is not an expensive or sophisticated technology.

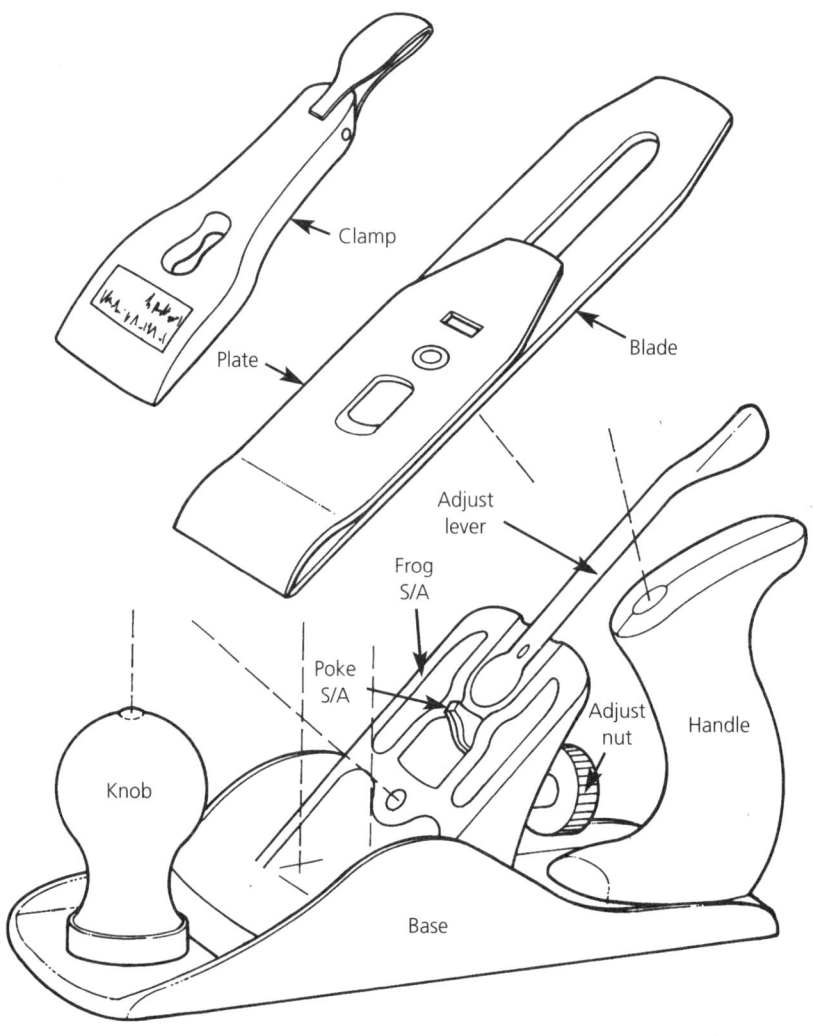

Figure 7.27 Partially exploded view of the new plane

Costs and pricing

The standard costing system at the company involved adding a 150 per cent overhead charge to the direct labour cost of manufacturing the product, and the product would retail for the equivalent of around R170 in Europe where most retailers will sell this type of product for about 70–120 per cent more than they buy it from the manufacturer. ■

Questions

1 How many staff should the company employ?
2 What type of facilities and technology will the company need to buy in order to assemble this product?
3 Design a layout for the assembly operation (to include the fly-press work) including the tasks to be performed at each part of the system.
4 How would the layout need to be adjusted as demand for this and similar products builds up?

DISCUSSION QUESTIONS

1 Identify the type of layout that might be adopted by the following organizations, explaining the reasoning for your choice:
  a holiday resort
  a dairy farm
  a tree surgeon
  a bakery
  a bank.
Discuss the implications of variety and volume on flow.

2 Sketch the layout of your local shop, coffee bar or sports hall reception area. Observe the area and draw on to your sketch the movements of people through the area over a sufficient period of time to get over 20 observations. Assess the flow in terms of volume, variety and type of layout.

3 A tractor manufacturer, making a wide range of tractors to customer specification, is considering changing its layout from product to process. Discuss the implications of so doing.

4 Identify the main stages in the construction of a house from laying services and foundations to plastering and decorating. If each of these tasks were to be carried out by different subcontractors, describe the potential layout problems.

5 (a) Visit a supermarket in your area. Try to get an appointment to talk with the manager to discuss the layout design issues.

(b) Compare the design of your supermarket with that of the Spar store described in the box. List and tabulate the main similarities and differences, and try to understand the reasons for these differences.

(c) What do you think, therefore, are the main criteria considered in the design of a supermarket layout?

(d) What competitive or environmental changes may result in the need to change store layouts in the future? Will these apply to all supermarkets, or only certain ones, such as town-centre stores?

6 The flow of materials through eight departments is shown in Table 7.8.

Table 7.8

	D1	D2	D3	D4	D5	D6	D7	D8
D1	\	30						
D2	10	\	15	20				
D3		5	\	12	2		15	
D4		6		\	10	20		
D5				8	\	8	10	12
D6	3			2		\	30	
D7	3					13	\	2
D8				10	6		15	\

Assuming that the direction of the flow of materials is not important, construct a relationship chart, a schematic layout and a suggested layout, given that each department is the same size and the eight departments should be arranged four along each side of a corridor.

7 The university's students' union is going to rearrange the layout of its lounge. It has been noticed that different groups of students use the two bars and four machines in the room in different ways, as shown in Table 7.9. The Union would like to group the facilities in twos. Which groupings would you suggest, given that the sandwich bar and drinks bars are at opposite ends of the room and cannot be moved.

Table 7.9 Students' use of Union facilities

Facility	Student type					
	1	2	3	4	5	6
Cola machine			X	X		X
Drinks bar		X	X			
Hot-drink machine	X		X		X	
Cigarette machine		X	X			
Sandwich bar	X				X	
Chocolate machine				X		X

8 Table 7.10 shows 12 work elements that constitute the total work content of an assembly task. Using the information about duration times and

precedences in the table, draw a precedence diagram and design an assembly line to produce as near as possible, but no less than, three items per hour. Calculate the balancing loss for the line.

9 Visit an assembly factory and look at the shape of the line. Find out why the line is the shape that it is.

10 A bicycle plant currently has a straight 20-stage assembly line with raw materials coming in at one side of the factory and the finished bikes going out at the other. Assess the implications of moving to a U-shaped line.

Table 7.10

Element number	Duration (mins)	Preceding element(s)
1	4	–
2	7	–
3	5	1
4	6	1,2
5	4	2
6	3	2
7	4	3
8	6	4,5
9	5	5,6
10	4	9
11	6	8,10
12	6	7,11

NOTES ON CHAPTER

1 Source: Discussions with GEC staff.
2 Source: By kind permission of Spar Supermarkets.
3 Source: Interviews with company staff.
4 Source: (1991) *Paper and the Environment*, Arjo Wiggins Fine Papers, used with permission.
5 Source: Interviews with Johannesburg International staff.
6 This list kindly supplied by Paul Walley of Loughborough University Business School, UK.
7 Burbidge, J.L. (1978) *The Principles of Production Control* (4th edn), Macdonald and Evans.
8 There are many different methods of balancing. *See*, for example, Kilbridge, K. and Wester, L. (1961) 'A Heuristic Method of Assembly Line Balancing', *Journal of Industrial Engineering*, Vol 57, No 4, or Steyn, P.G. (1977) 'Scheduling Multi-Model Production Lines', *Business Management*, Vol 8, No 1.
9 Schonberger, R. (1990) *Building a Chain of Customers*, Hutchinson Business Books.

SELECTED FURTHER READINGS

Apple, J.M. (1977) *Plant Layout and Materials Handling*, John Wiley.

Francis, R.L. and White, J.A. (1987) *Facility Layout and Location: An Analytical Approach*, Prentice Hall.

Gaither, N., Frazier, B.V. and Wei, J.C. (1990) 'From Job Shops to Manufacturing Cells', *Production and Inventory Management Journal*, Vol 31, No 4.

Green, T.J. and Sadowski, R.P. (1984) 'A Review of Cellular Manufacturing Assumptions and Advantages and Design Techniques', *Journal of Operations Management*, Vol 4, No 2.

Gunther, R.E., Johnson, G.D. and Peterson, R.S. (1983) 'Currently Practiced Formulations of The Assembly Line Balance Problem', *Journal of Operations Management*, Vol 3, No 3.

Hyer, N.L. and Wemmerlov, U. (1984) 'Group Technology and Productivity', *Harvard Business Review*, Vol 62, No 4.

Malas, G.H. (1990) 'Assembly Line Balancing – Let's Remove the Mystery', *Journal of Industrial Engineering*, May.

Miller, J. G. and Vollmann, T.E. (1985) 'The Hidden Factory', *Harvard Business Review*, Vol 63, No 5.

Moore, J.M. (1980) 'Computer Methods in Facilities Layout', *Industrial Engineering*, Sept.

Schuler, R.S., Writzman, L.P. and Davis, V.L. (1981) 'Merging Prescriptive and Behavioural Approaches for Office Layout', *Journal of Operations Management*, Vol 1, No 3.

Shafer, S.M. and Meredith, J.R. (1993) 'An Empirically Based Simulation Study of Functional Versus Cellular Layouts with Operations Overlapping', *International Journal of Operations and Production Management*, Vol 13, No 2.

Sule, V.E. (1988) *Manufacturing Facilities – Location Planning and Design*, PWS-Kent.

CHAPTER 8

PROCESS TECHNOLOGY

INTRODUCTION

All operations use some kind of process technology. Whether its process technology is a humble word processor or the most complex and sophisticated of automated factories, the operation will have chosen to use the technology because it hopes to get some kind of advantage from it. All operations managers need to understand what emerging technologies can do, in broad terms how they do it, what advantages the technology can give and what constraints it might impose on the operation. This is the purpose of this chapter. Figure 8.1 shows how the issues which it covers relate to the overall model of design of operations.

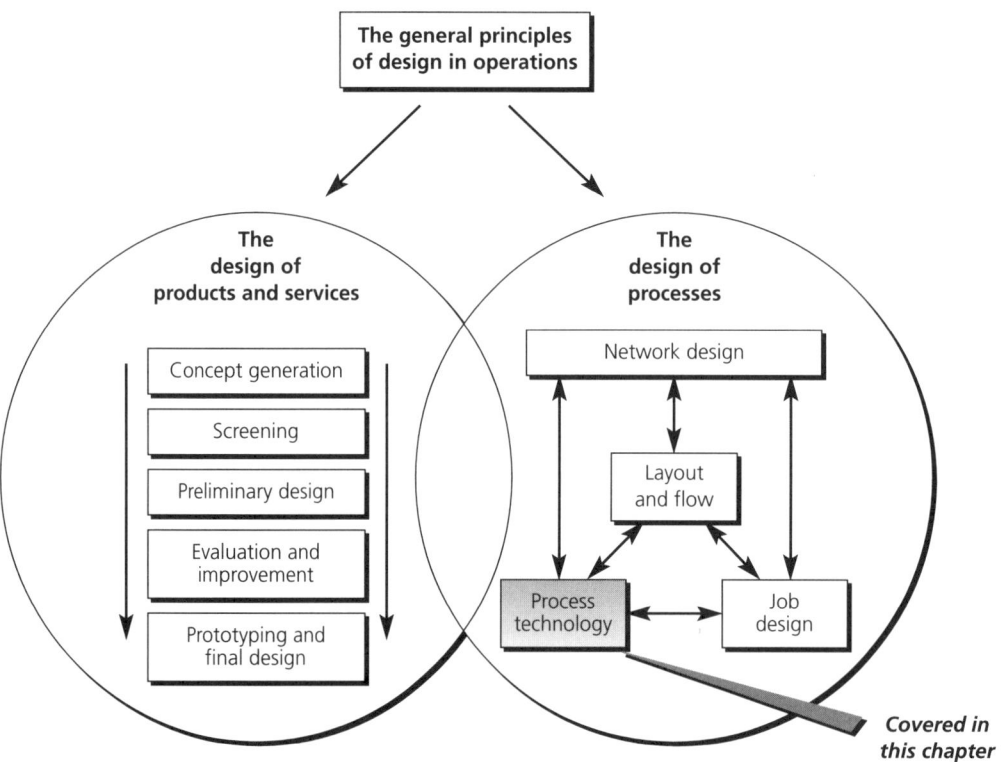

Figure 8.1 The design activities in operations management covered in this chapter

OBJECTIVES

This chapter will examine:

- the relationship between product and process technology;

- process technology developments in materials processing operations;

- process technology developments in information processing operations;

- process technology developments in customer processing operations;

- the three general 'dimensions' which are used to define all types of process technology
  - its degree of automation
  - its scale of operation
  - its degree of integration.

WHAT IS PROCESS TECHNOLOGY?

Process technologies are the machines, equipment and devices which help the operation to transform materials and information and customers in order to add value and fulfil the operation's strategic objectives. Fax machines, computers, mobile telephones, mechanical milking machines, robots, body scanners, combine harvesters, aircraft, overhead projectors, optical character recognition scanners, machine tools, and car wash machines are all examples of process technology. All operations use process technologies, even the most labour intensive.

Product/service and process technology

It is necessary, although sometimes difficult, to distinguish between product or service technology on the one hand and process technology on the other. In manufacturing operations it is a relatively simple matter to separate product from process technology. For example, the technology of a video cassette recorder (VCR) is the way it converts TV signals into a form which can be transferred on to video tape, the way it controls the movement of the tape and the way it reads the information recorded on the tape and converts it into television pictures. On the other hand, the technology of the process which made the VCR is nothing like that. The process technology consists of the machine tools which made the metal components, the machines which mounted the electronic components on to printed circuit boards, the machines which shaped and bent the sheet metal for the casing and the robots which assembled the components.

In some service operations it is far more difficult to distinguish process from product/service technology. For example, large theme park entertainment complexes such as Disney World use flight simulator type technologies in some of their rides. These are large rooms mounted on moveable hydraulic struts which can move the whole room. A combination of wide screen projection and movement can give a realistic

261

experience of, say, space flight. Yet is it product/service or process technology? It clearly processes Disney's customers. They literally go in at one side and emerge (the happier for their experience) at the other. It also helps Disney World add value for its customers which is the purpose of process technology. But the technology is also part of the product. In fact customers go there especially to 'experience' the technology. In cases like this product/service and process technology are, in effect, the same thing.

Life-cycle effects on product/service and process technology

If product/service and process technologies can sensibly be separated in an operation, they will not always receive equal attention. Sometimes developing product technology will be seen as more important than developing process technology and sometimes *vice versa*. One factor which influences this is the stage of the product or service in its life cycle, that is the *maturity* of the product. Figure 8.2 illustrates how the relative rates of product/service and process technology innovation vary as a product matures.[1]

For example, examine how the relative emphasis on product and process technology of personal computers (PCs) has changed since their introduction in the late 1970s. For the first few years after their introduction the product technologies of PCs were their main feature. The fact that a product which was capable of being so conveniently transported could also be so powerful was a major innovation in product technology. These early PCs were often assembled using the most basic production methods. Apple Computer, for example, built their first machines in a garage. That did not matter to customers who were concerned more with what their products could do. As the rate of change in product technology slowed, a little more thought was put into how PCs were to be produced. Increasing volumes made continued use

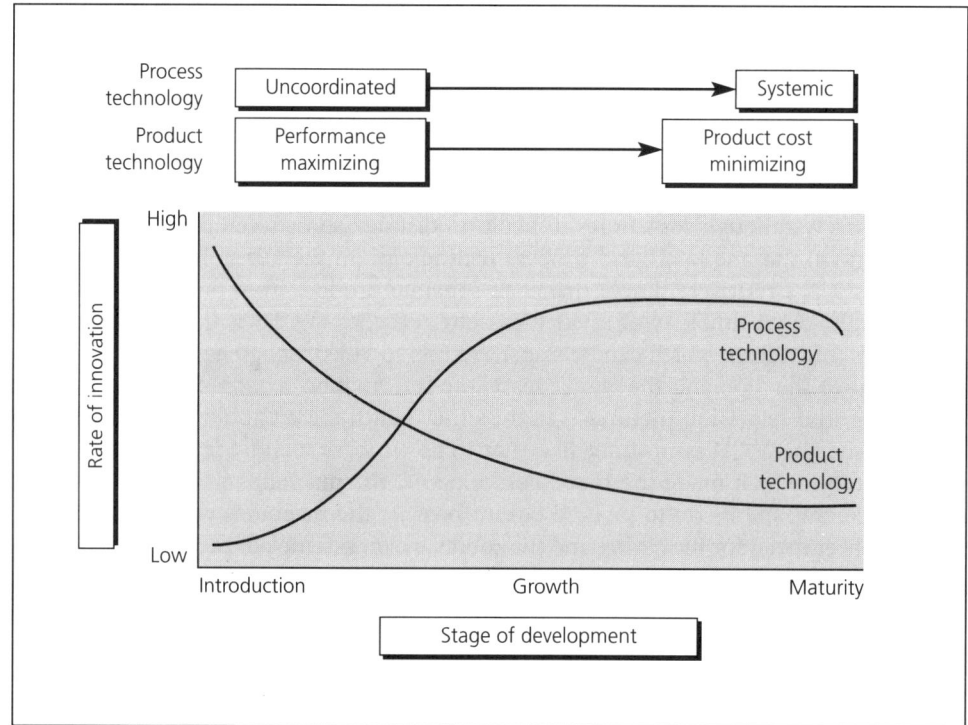

Figure 8.2 Relative rates of innovation for product and process technology as products progress through their life cycle
Source: Adapted from Abernathy and Utterback (1975)

of a 'garage' approach to production technology both infeasible and uneconomic. Some PC manufacturers, most notably Apple again, had come to the conclusion that further market success would depend not only on their consolidating their product technology but also by investing in automated production technology. The process technology used to manufacture the Apple Macintosh computer, for example, was more sophisticated than the company's previous models.

Operations management and process technology

Operations managers are continually involved in the management of process technology. To do so effectively they should be able to:

- articulate how technology could improve the operation's effectiveness;
- be involved in the choice of the technology itself;
- manage the installation and adoption of the technology so that it does not interfere with ongoing operations activities;
- integrate the technology into the rest of the operation;
- monitor continually its performance; and
- upgrade or replace the technology when necessary.

There are some fundamental questions which any operations manager must be able to answer when managing any type of technology.

- What does the technology do which is different to other similar technologies?
- How does it do it? That is, what particular characteristics of the technology are used to perform its function?
- What benefits does using the technology give to the operation?
- What constraints does using the technology place on the operation?

Technology in materials, information and customer processing

The rates of innovation in product/service and process technology shown in Fig. 8.2 are relative only to each other. Taken historically, process technology changes more in some periods than others. Since the 1980s, most types of operation have, arguably, seen a noticeable increase in the rate of innovation in their process technology. Radical changes in telecommunications technologies such as information 'super-highways', the totally automated 'factory of the future', and large and/or faster aircraft, are just some of the process technologies which will have a dramatic impact on operations management. Behind almost all of these technological advances is one dominant factor: the availability of commercially available low-cost microprocessing.

In the next section of this chapter we examine some of the process technologies which have particular significance for operations managers. These have been categorized as either materials processing (as in manufacturing operations), information processing (as in financial services, for example), and customer processing (as in retail, medical, hotel, transport operations, etc.). This distinction is for convenience only, however. In practice most of the newer technologies are different from what they have replaced because of their information processing capabilities (*see* Fig. 8.3).

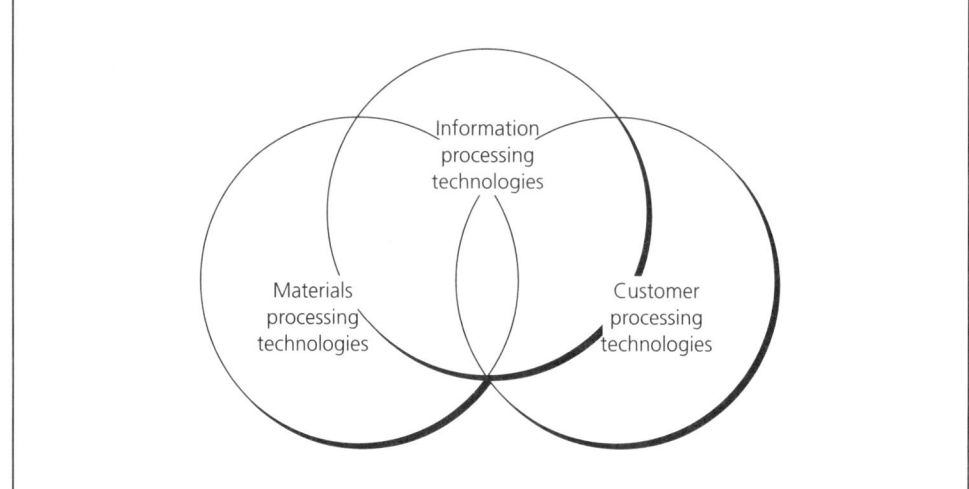

Figure 8.3 Information processing technologies dominate other developments in processing technology

MATERIALS PROCESSING TECHNOLOGY

The way in which metals, plastics, fabric and other materials are processed has generally improved over time. New shaping, forming, cutting, moulding and bending techniques using harder cutting tools, spark erosion and lasers have impacted on many industries. It is not the specific materials forming technologies with which we are concerned here, however. Rather it is the immediate technological context in which they are used. This includes such issues as the way forming technologies are controlled, how materials are physically moved and how the manufacturing systems which include the technology are organized.

Numerically controlled machine tools

It was in the 1950s when an American company developed a method of controlling the machine tools which it used to machine helicopter blades. The method involved storing the information which instructed the machine, a numerically controlled (NC) machine, in the form of a punched paper tape. The machine could then read the paper tape which controlled the movements of its tools and the speed of the machine throughout the processing operation. Although most technology of this type is now controlled through its own computer, with instructions stored on disk, the principles are the same. Machines with their own computer are sometimes called computer numerically controlled (CNC) machines. The set of coded instructions and the computers attached to the machine have taken the place of the operator who would previously have controlled the machine by hand. This replacement gives more accuracy, precision and repeatability to the process. It can also give better productivity, partly through the elimination of possible operator error, partly because computer control can work to optimum cutting patterns and partly because of the substitution of expensive, skilled labour.

NC machining centres

Most early NC machine tools did not actually do much more than the conventional machine tools which they replaced. They did do it better or cheaper, or both, however. The later technologies developed in two ways. First they increased the degrees of freedom with which their cutting heads moved. Very simple machine tools such as a drilling machine might have only one degree of freedom – up and down. Others such as a lathe, which turns cylindrical shapes, have two – in and out and along the piece being shaped. Machining centres usually have three or more (where the cutting head tilts) degrees of freedom which allow them to shape more complex parts. The second development was the ability of most machining centres to change their own tools. Magazines of different cutting tools are stored within the machine, and when the programme calls for a change of tool the old tool is replaced in the magazine and the new tool put into the cutting head. Together, these two developments greatly increased the variety of different parts which machines could produce, as well as allowing more complex parts to be machined.

Robotics

Robots were first introduced for industrial applications in the early 1960s, since which time their number and versatility have increased steadily. A robot can be defined as:

'...an automatic position-controlled reprogrammable multi-function manipulator having several degrees of freedom capable of handling materials, parts, tools or specialized devices through variable programmed motions for the performance of a variety of tasks... It often has the appearance of one or several arms ending in a wrist. Its control unit uses a memorizing device and sometimes it can use sensing and adaptation appliances that take account of the environment and circumstances. These multi-purpose machines are generally designed to carry out repetitive functions and can be adapted to other functions without permanent alternation of the equipment.' [2]

The movement of robots is controlled in a similar manner to NC machine tools but most robots have many degrees of freedom. Figure 8.4 shows the six standard movements of a robot arm.[3] In terms of their application robots can be classified as follows:[4]

- *Handling robots*. The work piece is handled by the robot, for example, for material handling, loading and unloading of work pieces for machine tools, casting, pressing, injection moulding, forging, fitting, etc.
- *Process robots*. The tool is gripped by the robot, for example, in various types of metal-working operations (cutting, drilling, grinding, chipping), joining of materials (welding, gluing, wiring), surface treatment (paint spraying, surface coating, polishing), etc.
- *Assembly robots*. Robots are used in the assembly of parts into components and complete products.

More recent robots can also include some limited sensory feedback through vision control and touch control. However, although the sophistication of robotic movement is increasing, their abilities are still more limited than popular images of robot-driven factories suggest. In fact most robots are, in practice, used for mundane operations such as:

- welding
- paint spraying

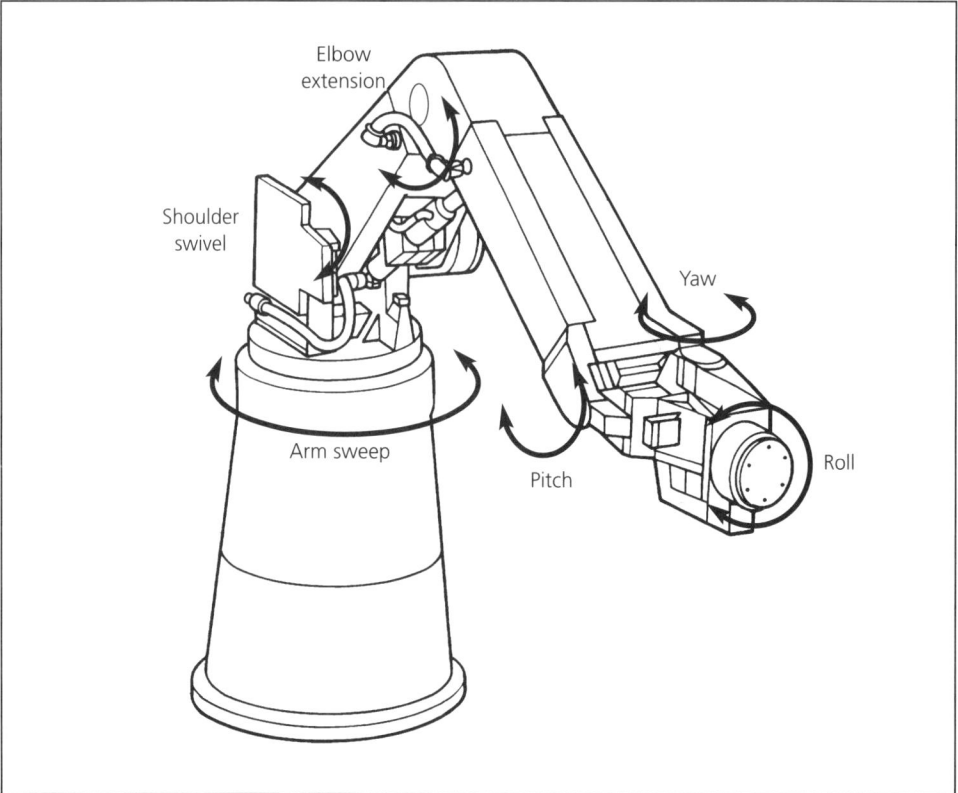

Figure 8.4
Robot with six standard movements

- stacking pallets
- grinding/deburring
- packing
- loading and unloading machines.

In these tasks the attribute of the robots which is being exploited is their ability to perform repetitive, monotonous and sometimes hazardous tasks for long periods, without variation and without complaining. (*See* box on ABB's robots.)

Automated guided vehicles (AGVs)

For every activity in a manufacturing process which adds value to the product by physically transferring it, there is usually one which moves or stores the material. Although they are often unavoidable, such activities add no value to the material. Not surprising then that operations managers seek ways of automating them. Automatic guided vehicles (AGVs) are one class of technology which does this. They are small, independently powered vehicles which move materials to and from value-adding operations. They are usually guided by cables buried in the floor of the operation and receive instructions from a central computer.

In some industries they are also used as mobile work stations to replace the more traditional conveyor systems. For example, truck engines can be assembled on AGVs, with the AGV moving between assembly stations. The ability to move independently

ABB ROBOTS TAKE OVER SOME OF THE REPETITIVE WORK AT ECCO SHOES AND AT SCANIA TRUCKS[5]

Asea Brown Boveri (ABB) Robotics is a leading manufacturer of industrial robots, whose machines are used in a wide variety of applications, including packing army meal rations, assembling washing machines, and unloading plastic moulding machines. Two very different examples of the application of ABB robots are the final assembly of shoes in Denmark, and the painting of truck axles in Sweden.

Ecco, a Danish shoe company, produces over seven million shoes each year, and has invested in extensive robot facilities in the manufacturing operation, primarily to improve its quality consistency. It has installed over 20 robots since 1984, which work in its factories in Portugal, Denmark and Japan. Initial manufacturing stages are still processed by hand. The soft leather upper is cut and sewn together in the Indian and Indonesian factories before being shipped to the more automated plants for completion. A robot is used to cut a five millimetre track around

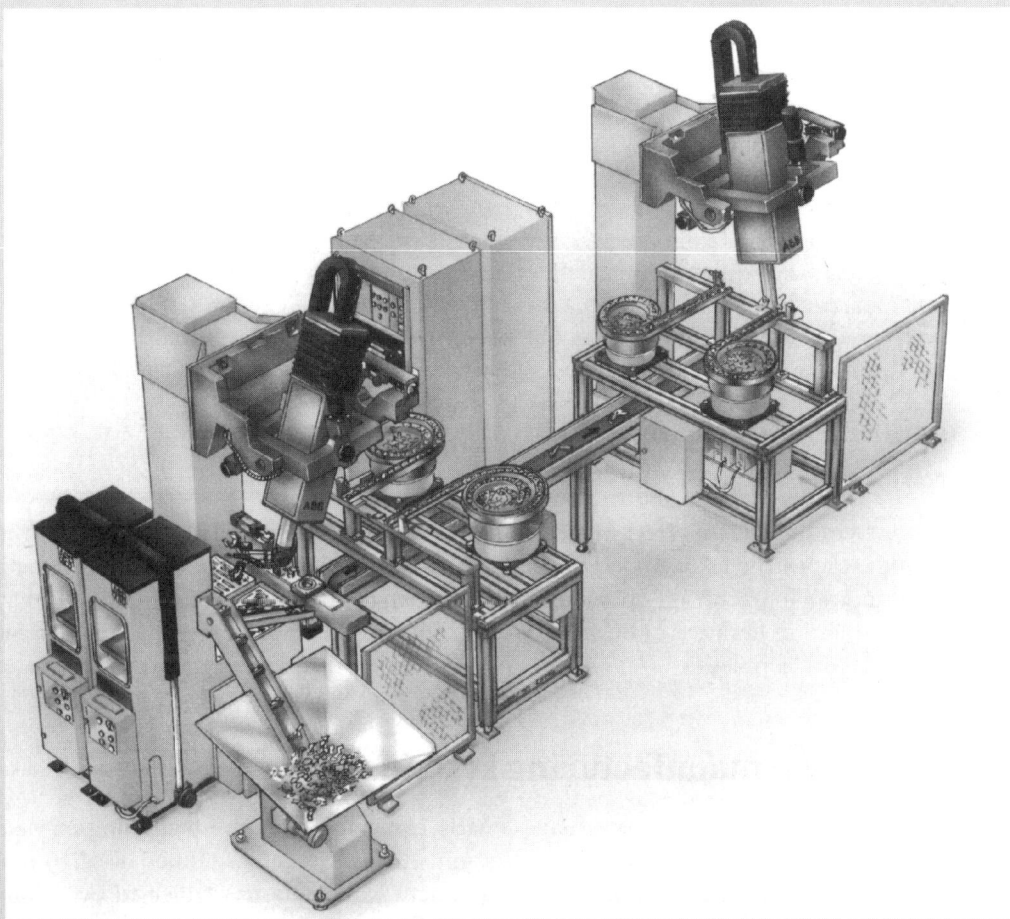

Figure 8.5 Robots used in small parts assembly
Source: Courtesy of ABB Robotics

the leather upper which is then transferred by a second robot to the sole-forming machine where the leather upper is moulded on to a flexible sole. A third robot is employed to cut away any excess material from the sole, without damaging the upper. Each robot is programmed to operate according to the recognized size and model of shoe being processed. Finally, in order to prevent the completed shoe curling up as it cools, it is passed through a controlled cooling tunnel, visually inspected, laced, waterproofed, and given a final polish. Ecco operations managers believe that the working environment is much improved by using robots for the more physically demanding or boring tasks, as well as giving increased productivity and enhancing quality.

The Swedish truck group Scania decided to build a new painting facility for its axles factory at Falun. Scania wanted the new plant to be flexible and operator friendly, and so the company opted to invest in the latest robotics technology to cope with its wide range of different axles. The decision to use robotics in the paint shop was based on their ability to meet precise customer requirements for paint type, colour, and specification. The robots are simple to use, easily and quickly changed over and adaptable to new products. It only takes two minutes to paint a typical axle. Two operators can run the whole system from a control room, where computer screens depict the movements and settings for each of the robots. The robot first prepares and cleans the parts, then dries off the moisture by blowing compressed air into the cavities and remaining holes, then the parts are primed and finally painted, again all by robots. The axle parts on Scania trucks are shaped differently, which means that the spray guns on the painting system need to be adjusted continually during the process. There is an integrated computer control system which coordinates all of these adjustments, controlling the amount of paint being sprayed and thus reducing spillage (both an environmental and cost benefit). The movement of the spray head can be adjusted in only milliseconds and there are flow sensors on the robot arm which feed information back to the control system to maximize the effective usage of the paint. Essentially, the main feature of the robots is their flexibility. Scania is confident that it can adapt the systems as necessary to suit its precise needs in the future. The use of robots has also improved the working conditions of the employees, and has assisted in reducing waste and solvent emissions. ■

reduces the pacing effect on each stage in the process and allows for variation in the time each stage takes to perform its task. AGVs are sometimes used to move materials in non-manufacturing operations. Warehousing is the obvious example, but they are used also in libraries to move books, in offices to move mail and even in hospitals to transport samples.

Flexible manufacturing systems

Flexible manufacturing systems (FMS) bring together the technologies we have already described into a coherent system. An FMS can be defined as 'a computer-controlled configuration of semi-independent work stations connected by automated material handling and machine loading'.[7] This definition gives an indication of the component parts of an FMS:

AGVs AT NEWS INTERNATIONAL, WAPPING[6]

The News International plant at Wapping, in London, produces three daily newspapers and two Sunday papers. Together these have a weekly circulation of around 25 million papers. The facilities at the plant include 16 printing presses, which run through the evening and into the night at full speed, to ensure the completion of the run before the early morning delivery deadlines. To the production staff at News International it is vital to achieve high levels of dependability and reliability. Their major objective during the print run each night is to minimize downtime which could have repercussions on their achieving their production volumes and times.

Each of the 16 printing presses uses one roll of paper every 20 minutes during the seven-hour production period. These rolls of paper each weigh about one tonne. The paper is delivered from the nearby warehouse daily, and once checked, is stored for collection at the plant entrance. The process of delivering the paper reel to the press and loading the new reel into position has been automated by the use of AGVs. These AGVs are basically cradles designed to carry one roll of paper. They are guided by a predetermined metal strip in the floor and controlled by an information system which links the vehicles to the presses. A sensor on each press will request a new reel once the previous spare has been loaded for use. An AGV arrives at the press and loads the reel into an initial position which is checked for alignment by the operator before the final loading is started. Once the roll reaches a lower limit, the new reel can be brought up to speed, ready for automatic change-over. ■

Source: By kind permission of News International plc

● NC 'workstations', either machine tools or more sophisticated work centres, which perform the 'machining' operations;
● Loading/unloading facilities, often robots which move parts to and from the workstations;
● Transport/materials-handling facilities which move the parts between workstations (These may be AGVs or conveyor systems or, if distances are short, robots.);
● A central computer control system which controls and coordinates the activities in the system. This coordination could include not only the control of the individual facilities (workstations, robots, AGVs) but also the production-planning sequencing and routing of the parts through the system.

An FMS is more than a single technology as such. It has integrated the single technologies into a system which has the potential to be greater than the sum of its parts. In effect an FMS is a self-contained 'micro operation' which is capable of manufacturing a whole component from start to finish. Furthermore, the flexibility of each of the individual technologies combine to make an FMS (at least in theory) a supremely versatile manufacturing technology. A sequence of products, each different but within the capability 'envelope' of the system, could be processed in the system in any order and without change-over delays between each product. The 'envelope of capability' concept is important here. Any collection of machines within an FMS must have some finite limits on the size and shape of the materials it can process. The implication of this is that an FMS is best suited to manufacturing applications where the design of parts are basically similar yet whose batch sizes can be small (perhaps as small as one).

Are FMS really flexible?

The 'flexibility' characteristics of FMS seem to be their main advantage. However, their flexibility advantage may not be what it seems. It is certainly true that, when compared to any previous attempts to automate manufacturing processes, FMS are extremely flexible. Previous, so-called 'hard' automation required the instructions to the machine to be fixed in its hardware. Any change in how the machine was to operate required the machine itself to be physically reconfigured (changing cams, gears and slides, for example). The new manufacturing technologies such as FMS hold their instructions in the form of software which can be changed very easily.

Perhaps this is not the real point, however. FMS may be more flexible than any previous automated manufacturing technologies, but they may not be more flexible than the manufacturing systems which they aim to replace. The fairly high-variety, fairly low-volume operations where FMS seem to be most appropriate would previously have used stand-alone machine tools arranged either in a process or cell layout (*see* Chapter 7 for a description of these layouts). Such a manufacturing system is extremely flexible in terms of the variety of components it can process, certainly more flexible than any FMS. Perhaps this is why most FMS are used for applications where the range of parts is not particularly wide.

FMS AT YAMAZAKI MAZAK

When the Japanese tool manufacturers, Yamazaki, opened their new European factory at Worcester in the UK, it represented a £35 million investment, and was seen as the company's gateway into the European Union. They had already established successful bases in Japan and the United States. Fifteen million pounds of the initial costs was taken up by the installation of four fully computer-integrated FMS, making the factory one of the most advanced machine tool manufacturing operations in Europe.

The complete FMS which Yamazaki developed allow overnight unmanned production and thereby make the most of its investment in the technology. Of course, the Yamazaki products are built by an entirely Yamazaki FMS (*see* Fig. 8.6).

Behind the decision to invest in this system was the need to compete directly with European manufacturers. With a wide range of over 60 products, individual volumes are small. Because of this the company wanted an operation that would be so flexible it would not matter in which order items were processed. High utilization would be maintained by having very fast set-ups, which would also reduce the need for large batches. The operation can make individual pieces to suit its tight production schedules. This enables the company to offer typical order lead times of only four weeks, in comparison to competitors' lead times of eight or more for similar products.

All component workpieces are loaded into fixtures mounted on special pallets. The operators prepare enough work to enable the system to run overnight unsupervised. At the centre of the FMS is a host computer which schedules and controls the activity of each machining centre and the materials handling devices. The computer predetermines the pallet locations and, as the machining centres become free, an automatic pick/load device will select the next workpiece from the waiting queue and will place it into the available machine. Each machine is capable of handling almost any of the components, so that bottle-necks do not develop at

Figure 8.6 The FMS installation at Yamazaki Mazak

any point in the system. Spare tools used for the machining centres are stored in a central tool bank at the ends of the area and are transported to the required machine when requested by the system. The tools are delivered by a holding device on a highway which runs above the machining centres. At the end of the shift, the incoming operator can consult the computer for a printout of the tools that have been used and which may subsequently need to be replaced in the tool bank. Many of the materials are delivered from the warehouse to the factory by AGVs, which pick up the items on request from the central scheduling system and travel along a sunken wire track around the factory. This again allows unmanned production during the night.

The factory has won the *Management Today* 'Best Factory Award' in its category and the Queen's Award for Export Achievement, with around 85 per cent of its output shipped overseas, a third of which goes to Germany. It has also been labelled as 'Best in the World' by the Royal Swedish Academy of Engineering Sciences. ∎

Source: By kind permission of Yamazaki Machinery UK Ltd

The advantages of FMS

One kind of flexibility at which FMS do excel is what we called in Chapter 2 *product flexibility*, that is the ability to introduce changes to product designs. The integrated control and programmable flexibility of FMS make this a relatively straightforward task, especially when compared with the hard automation which was used previously. However, in spite of its flexibility image, most of the benefits reported by companies who have adopted this type of technology come in terms of the other performance objectives.

A survey of 31 firms who have adopted FMS, reported by Professor John Bessant of Brighton University, identifies the following benefits:[8]

1 *Lead time and throughput (factory door-to-door) time reduction.* Here the general experience is that substantial savings can be made in throughput (factory door-to-door) time. Savings of between 60 per cent and 70 per cent were reported.

2 *Inventory savings (especially of work-in-progress).* Another expected consequence of reducing set-up times and integrating process elements is that there is smoother flow of material through the factory with less queueing and build-up of material waiting for machining. For the firms which provided a percentage estimate, the average saving was over 70 per cent.

3 *Increased utilization.* One major problem in batch manufacturing is the relatively low level of utilization of equipment, since so much time is spent waiting for products to be put on machines which are stopped for resetting, maintenance, and so on. The extent of reported improvement over previous methods ranged from 200 per cent to 400 per cent.

4 *Reduced set-up times.* Closely linked to improved utilization is the reduction in set-up times between different batches. Twelve firms reported improvements over previous methods of between 50 per cent and 90 per cent.

5 *Reduced number of machines or operations.* Part of the reduction in set-up times and in throughput times is derived from the physical integration of operations into fewer, more complex machines. In this sample ten firms provided estimates of the extent of reduction of number of machines, ranging from 45 per cent to 90 per cent.

6 *Increased quality.* Quality improvements cannot be wholly attributed to that technology, since in many firms there is considerable effort being spent to improve quality performance. However, 20 firms reported improved quality as an outcome of their investments, with several others which involved new plant also commenting on the high levels which they were able to achieve. Estimates of this improvement ranged from 20 per cent to 90 per cent.

In addition to the above benefits, a number of others were reported, often on a firm-specific basis. These included:

- space savings
- reduced dependence on subcontractors
- skill saving
- increased responsiveness to customers (speed and quality of service)
- facilitated more rapid production innovation cycles
- improved prototyping capability.

Comparisons of advanced manufacturing technologies

The progression from conventional machine tools to FMS involves a gradual replacement of manual operations with automated operations. Table 8.1 shows how Professor Chris Voss, of London Business School,[9] characterizes the relationship between the degree of possible automation and some of the technologies we have described. Note how the steps at the core of the process, involving the shaping or cutting activities, are the first to be automated, after which the more peripheral activities at either end of the whole process are gradually included within the capabilities of the technology.

Table 8.1 The spectrum of automation in manufacturing

Step	Conventional	Stand-alone		Integrated	
		Stand-alone NC	Machining centre	FMC	FMS
1 Move workpiece to machine	Manual	Manual	Manual	Automated	Automated
2 Load and affix workpiece on machine	Manual	Manual	Manual	Automated	Automated
3 Select and insert tool	Manual	Manual	Automated	Automated	Automated
4 Establish and insert speeds	Manual	Automated	Automated	Automated	Automated
5 Control cutting	Manual	Automated	Automated	Automated	Automated
6 Sequence tools and motions	Manual	Manual	Automated	Automated	Automated
7 Unload part from machine	Manual	Manual	Manual	Automated	Automated
8 Movement between machines	Manual	Manual	Manual	Manual	Automated

(Manual) = Manual (Automated) = Automated

Volume and variety characteristics

These technologies differ in their flexibility capabilities and economics and will therefore each be appropriate for different parts of the volume–variety continuum.

Figure 8.7 positions the technologies on the volume–variety matrix which we introduced in Chapter 4. Stand-alone NC machine tools can cope with very high varieties but become uneconomic at anything but low volumes. NC machining centres extend the volumes which can be manufactured slightly. Simple FMS which do not include automated transfer between the machines, sometimes called *flexible manufacturing cells* (FMC), can cope with higher volumes economically but constrain the variety of parts and shapes which can be made. FMS occupy the middle ground of the matrix, while *flexible transfer lines* (FTLs) are intended for narrow product ranges but higher volumes. At very high volumes, with little or no variety, totally dedicated technology, specifically designed for the particular sequence of activities required, is likely to be most appropriate.

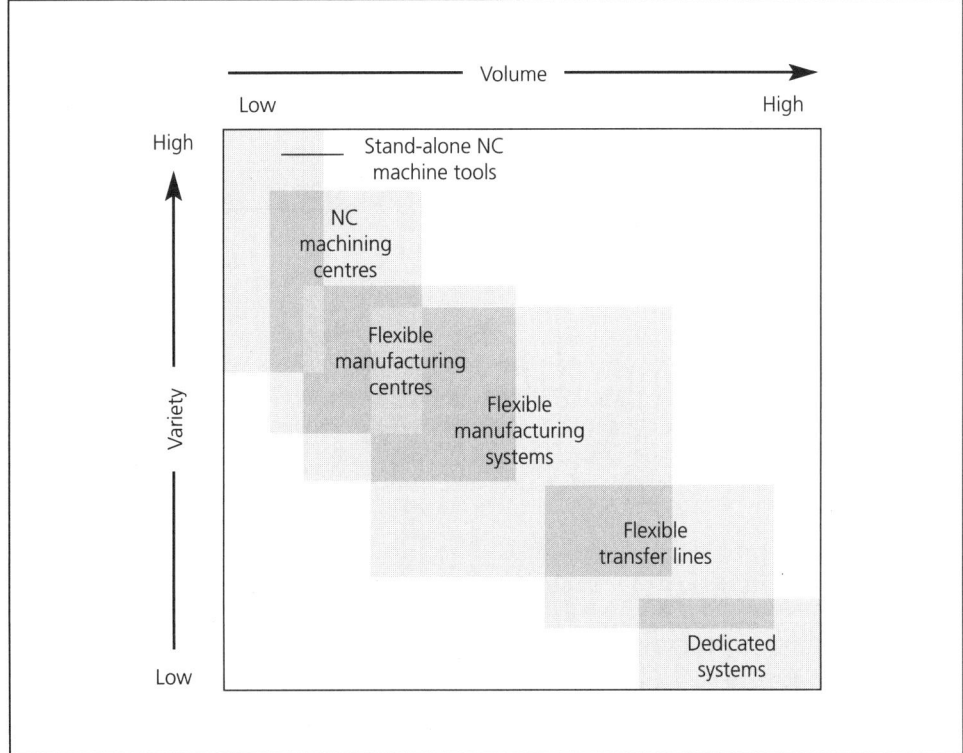

Figure 8.7
The volume–variety characteristics of manufacturing technologies

Computer-integrated manufacturing (CIM)

The integration of the separate developments in manufacturing technology exemplified by FMS can be taken further. FMS integrates those activities which are concerned directly with the transformation process but need not necessarily include the other activities which must have happened prior to the transformation. The products must have been designed, for example, quite possibly using the computer-aided design (CAD) technology described in Chapter 5. Similarly, the production-planning activity must have occurred, otherwise the manufacturing system would not know what to make or when to make it. Behind these activities other systems in the organization which forecast sales, take orders, set quality standards, plan maintenance, and so on will also be happening. The actual manufacturing system which directly transforms materials is at the centre of many other procedures, activities and systems.

Most of these 'surrounding' systems will themselves be computer based, using information technology which processes data and uses instructions in more or less the same way as the computer systems which link the elements in the FMS. It follows then that the potential must exist for these 'surrounding' systems to be integrated with the direct materials-processing technologies such as FMS. This wider integration is known as *computer-integrated manufacturing* (CIM). It can be defined as 'the integration of computer-based monitoring and control of all aspects of the manufacturing process, drawing on a common database and communicating via some form of computer network', although the term CIM is now frequently used to indicate far less ambitious forms of integrated manufacturing.[10]

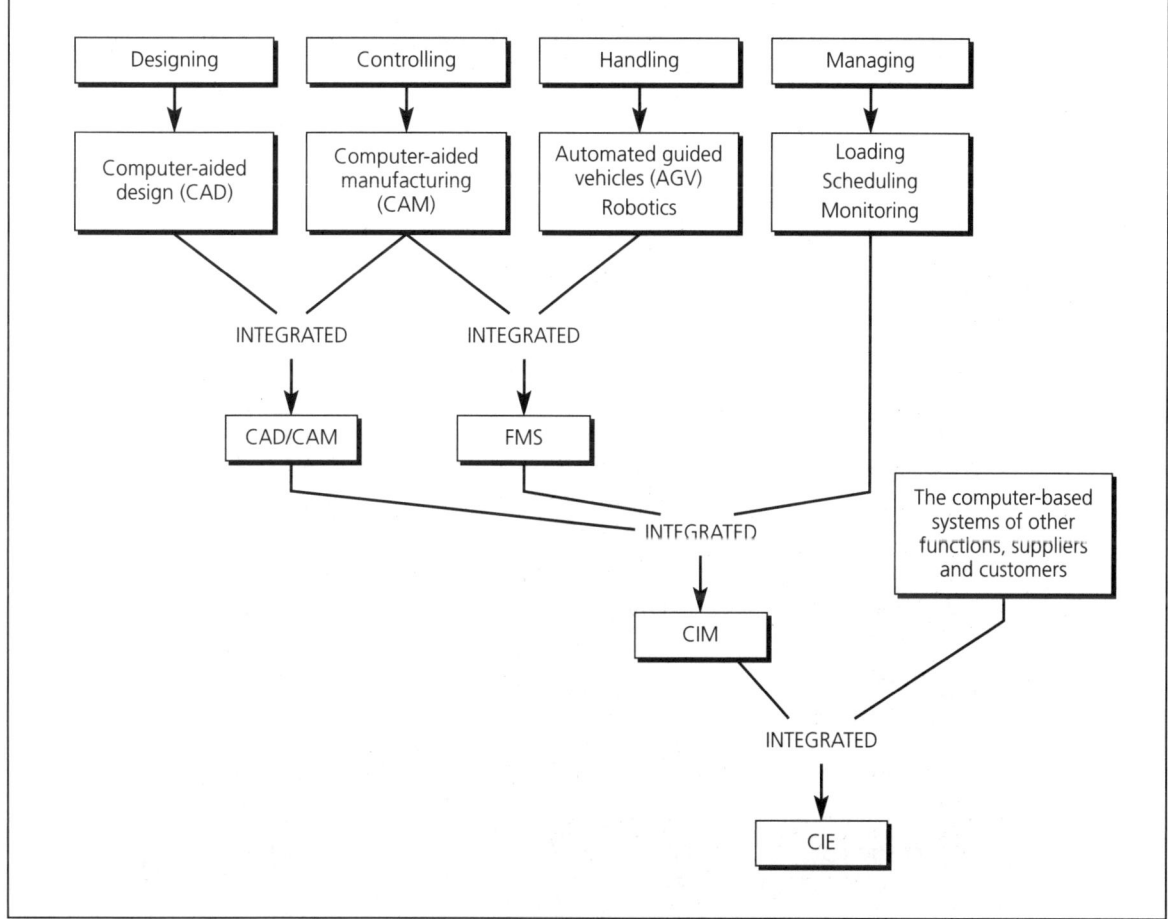

Figure 8.8 Increasing integration of manufacturing technologies

The hierarchy of integration

No matter how we define the concept of CIM, the integration of technologies and systems which could (and often do) themselves stand alone in the operation is its central theme. Figure 8.8 illustrates how manufacturing technologies can be described as being progressively more integrated states of more basic technologies. The basic technologies which help to design products, control the tools which form materials, transport materials and manage some of the operational aspects of the manufacturing process can come together in stages. The first stage is the integration *between* areas of activity to produce such combined technologies as CAD/CAM and FMS. Second, the integration of all the internal activities produces the broad definition of CIM. Finally, integration of the organization's CIM activity with other functions and perhaps even suppliers and customers, approaches what has been termed the *computer-integrated enterprise* (CIE).

Human-centred CIM

The desirability of the seemingly inexorable progress towards increasing automation of manufacturing has not gone unchallenged. Some argue that, by taking a purely technical perspective on developing integrated manufacturing systems, process technologies are neglecting the skills of the people who staff them. Rather than design CIM systems to technical criteria and then consider how people are to fit into them, it

Table 8.2 A comparison of technology-centred and human-centred AMT systems design

Design choice point	Technology-centred systems	Human-centred systems
Allocation of function	Operator carries out only those functions that cannot be automated	Operator allocates functions depending upon particular circumstances and judgement during production
Systems architecture	Centralized control system, with production machines controlled at highest possible level	Decentralized control system, with machines controlled at lowest possible level
Control characteristics of human-machine interface	User actions paced and regulated by directives stored in machine	User discretion and control maximized, the technology does not dictate work methods
Information characteristics	System status data presented only to management; restricted access for shop-floor users	System status data available at all machines; facilitation of cross-functional communication
Allocation of responsibilities	Work controlled by functional specialists	Work controlled by multi-skilled shop-floor users

Source: Adapted from Corbett, J.M. (1992) 'Working at the Interface' *in* Adler, P.S. and Winograd, T.A. *Usability*, Oxford University Press.

is argued that a 'parallel design' approach should be adopted. This would allow users of a CIM system to shape their design before the format of the system is finally fixed. This encourages users to integrate their skills and contribution with the technological elements of the system. Table 8.2 illustrates how 'pure' human-centred systems might differ from purely technology-centred systems.

INFORMATION PROCESSING TECHNOLOGY

Information processing technologies include any devices which collect, manipulate, store or distribute information. Most of these we class under the general heading of 'computer-based technologies', although it should also include those associated with telecommunications operations. Taken together these technologies include:

- computers: mainframe, mini and personal;
- peripheral devices: storage, printers, readers, etc;
- transmission/receiving devices: satellite dishes, modems, optical cable networks, faxes, telephones;
- software and systems and applications.

Centralized information processing

All computers used for management purposes (as opposed to process control) were, at one time, large. It was simply the most economical way of buying processing power. With such clear economies of scale it made sense for organizations to buy a single large computer for all its information processing requirements. The different parts of the organization originally accessed the computer in *batch mode*: that is, each of the separate transactions associated with a particular activity would not be processed as they were originated. Instead they would be collected together or 'batched' until there were sufficient transactions to process together as a batch. Alternatively (and more usually) a particular processing activity would be performed at regular intervals. For example, suppose the back office of a bank used a batch access system to process its loan applications. Each time a loan application was received it would be kept until the time allocated to processing loans, and then processed along with all the other loan applications received since the last batch was run. All the documentation and file updating was done at this time. Figure 8.9(a) illustrates the batch mode of using centralized information processing.

More recently the increasing sophistication and power of processors and storage devices has allowed what is known as *teleprocessing* access to central computers. This mode of access locates input devices, such as keyboards, and perhaps also output devices, such as screens or printers, at the point where the transaction originated. When staff wish to process a transaction they can input the data directly to the computer which processes it as soon as it has the capacity to do so. So for the loan-application processing operation, each time an application is received its details are entered into the computer which carries out the transaction as soon as it has the capacity to do so. File updates and documents are produced immediately. Figure 8.9 (b) illustrates the teleprocessing mode of access to centralized information processing.

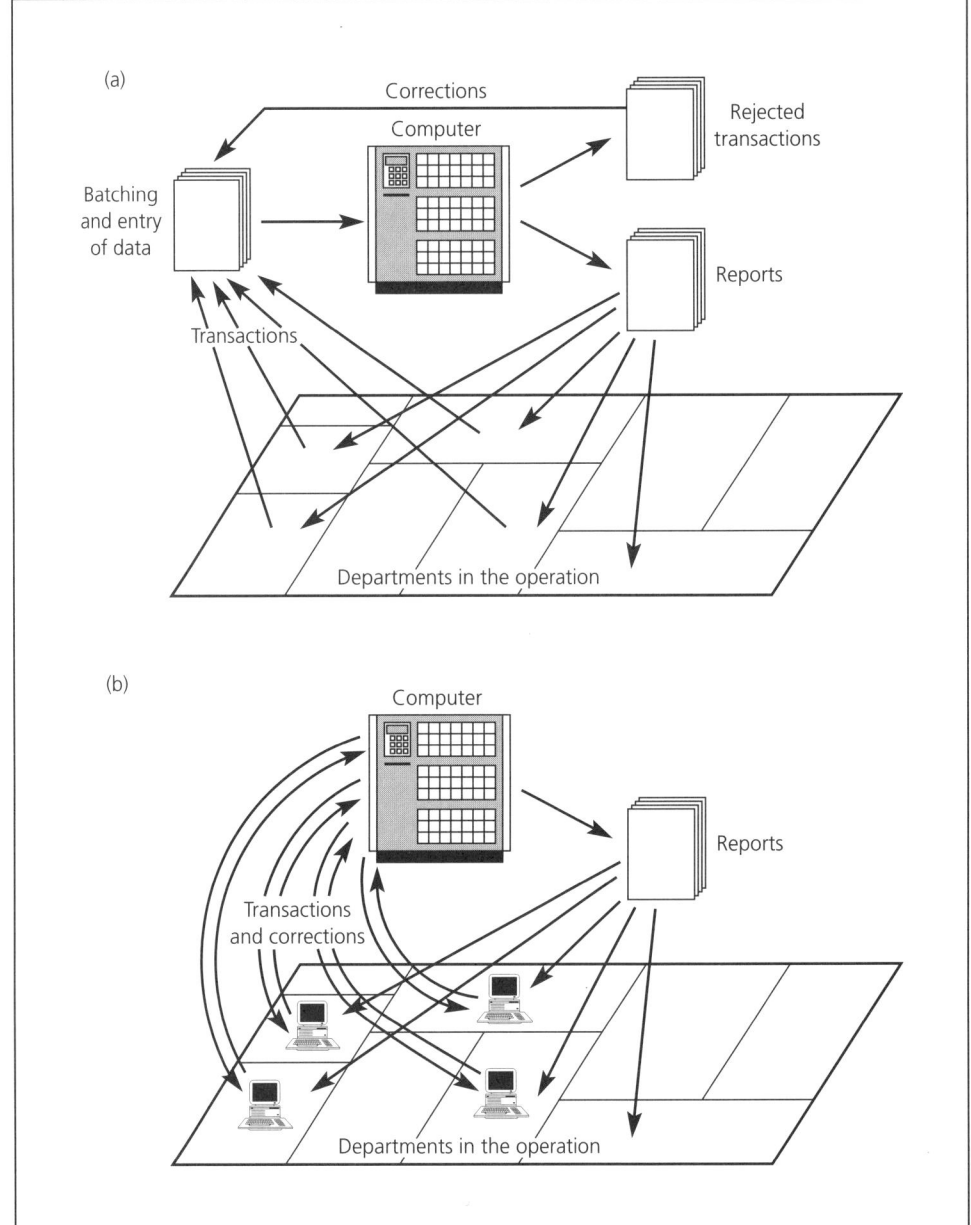

**Figure 8.9
(a) Batch
processing
in centralized
information
processing,
(b) teleprocessing
in centralized
information
processing**

Decentralized information processing

With the increasing use of computer-based technology and the development of more
specifically tailored applications software, centralized computers became viewed as
cumbersome for some applications. At the same time the cost and power of
mid-range computers reached the point where it was economically feasible for
different parts of the operation to have their own dedicated computer. Those

'minicomputers' could be under the direct control of the staff who would use them. Applications software could be designed specifically for their needs and transactions processed when and how they thought appropriate. This is the *distributed processing* concept. The obvious problem with such an arrangement is that, in bringing computing power closer to its users, coordinating all the various processing activities is more complex. The obvious answer to the problem is for the distributed minicomputers to exchange information. The technical problems of achieving total compatibility between essentially stand-alone minicomputer-based systems is sufficiently great to cause considerable operating problems.

Local area networks (LANs)

The need to retain the clear advantages of distributed processing while retaining the control and communication benefits of centralized computing, focused attention on the mechanism of communications itself – that is the *network* which connects the distributed processing power. Combine the concept of the network with smaller and cheaper personal computers (PCs), and the concept of the *local area network* (LAN) emerges.

A LAN is a communications network which operates over a limited distance, usually within an operation. Connected to the network are devices such as personal computers, display screens, printers, interfaces and minicomputers. The most common type of LAN connects the PCs in a work group or several departments and allows all staff to share common access to data files, other devices such as printers, and links to outside networks such as telephone lines. Figure 8.10 illustrates a LAN.

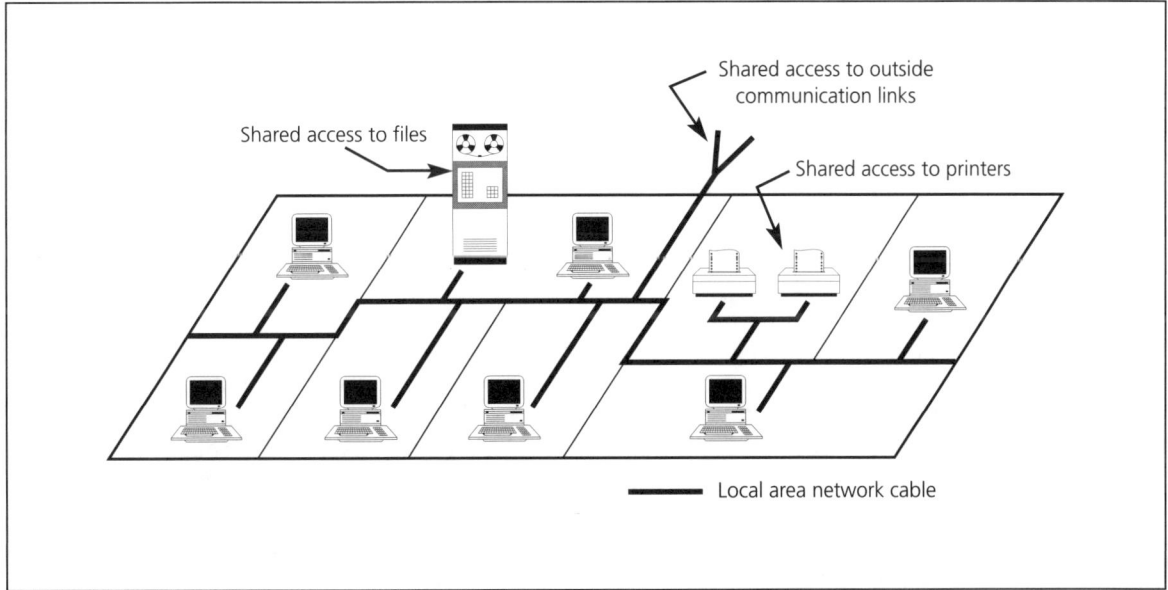

Figure 8.10 A local area network (LAN)

The great advantage of LANs is their greater flexibility when compared with other more cumbersome forms of distributed processing. In particular, advantages include the following:[11]

- *Incremental growth*. New devices can be added to the network as they are required or become available.
- *Redundancy*. Robustness can be built into the system by keeping spare machines and duplicate files.
- *Location flexibility*. Workstations and peripherals can be located where needed and relocated with relatively little disruption when necessary.
- *Operational autonomy*. Both the control and the administration of hardware and software can be assigned to those staff who use them.

Telecommunications and information technology

Computer-based technologies in business use have always been based on digital principles, that is converting information into a *binary* form, using 0s and 1s. Telecommunications, on the other hand, were originally based on analogue technology. The digitization of telecommunications transmissions (including digital compression techniques, which allows information to be squeezed into a smaller 'space' so that more can be sent using a given amount of transmission capacity), together with the use of high-capacity optical fibre networks, brings new possibilities, however. The technologies of computing and telecommunications have, in effect, merged. One implication of this is to add even more pressure toward the distribution of processing power closer to its users, the limitations of geography being no longer an obstacle to access. Digital telecommunication lines can carry both voice and non-voice (text, data, etc.) traffic at the same time, so separate sites of the same organization, or separate operations, could lease lines for their exclusive use. Alternatively, separate operations could use one of the public *integrated services digital networks* (ISDN). The capacity of these networks also means that two-way communication, interactive information exchange is possible.

The effect on telecommunications companies of these developments has been far reaching. Figure 8.11 shows the increase in the new types of services they can offer, most of which are the result of digital technologies.

Electronic data interchange

Data exchange networks have probably had their greatest impact in the way information relating to inter-operations trade can be processed. Details of orders placed with suppliers, orders received from customers, payments made to suppliers and payments received from customers, can all be transmitted through information networks. If suppliers, customers and the banks involved in the financial arrangements have themselves adopted compatible technology, the information can remain in its digital form. This eliminates the need to read paper-based information and key it into their own computers. The use of networks for trading in this

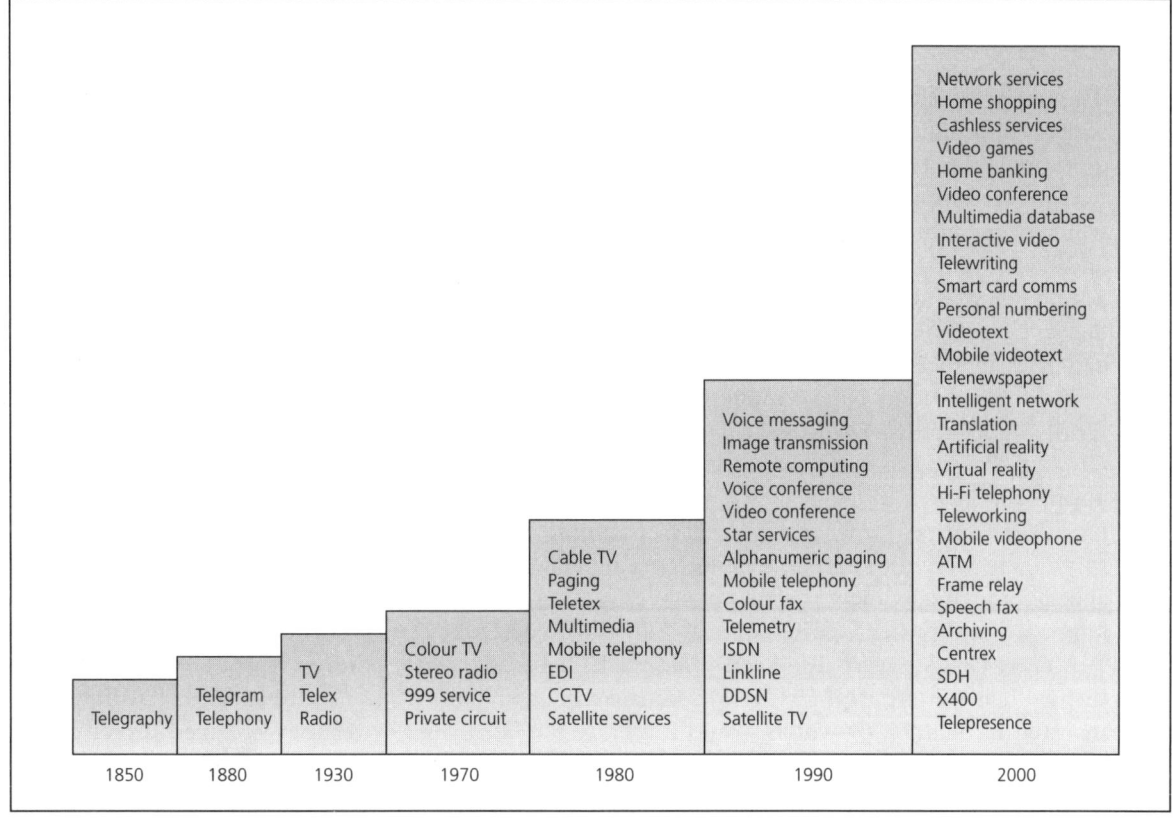

Figure 8.11 The growth in telecommunications services

way is called *electronic data interchange* (EDI), one of the fastest growing areas of business information processing.

Management information systems (MIS)

Most of our discussion so far has concerned the arrangement of information processing technologies – what computers and similar devices can do, and how they are connected to each other. Within the configuration of the physical system, however, what is important is the way in which information moves, is changed, is manipulated and presented so it can be used in managing an organization. These systems are *management information systems* (MIS). Operations managers make considerable use of MIS, especially in their planning and control activities. Systems which are concerned with inventory management, the timing and scheduling of activities, demand forecasting, order processing, quality management, and many other activities are an integral part of many operations managers' working lives, and are referred to in the planning and control chapters of Part 3.

EDI IN RETAILING OPERATIONS[12]

The use of EDI has revolutionized the way the large retail operations in Europe do business with their suppliers. One of the biggest users of EDI is the UK supermarket chain, Tesco. Tesco uses the Tradanet network to link its ordering systems with the order processing systems of its suppliers. Tesco sees EDI as a vital part of its streamlined distribution chain which has reduced the need to hold large inventories, speeded up delivery from its suppliers, and helped improve profits. EDI's potential for sales-based forecasting is also a significant advantage. Trends in sales can be quickly interpreted and forecasts adjusted, and with short delivery lead times (helped by EDI) short-term surges in demand for a particular product can be easily met the next day.

Tesco has around 1000 suppliers linked via EDI, including Unilever, the Anglo-Dutch food manufacturer, Pedigree, the pet food part of the Mars corporation and Colgate–Palmolive. Colgate's experience is typical of many suppliers. In 1988 Tesco approached them to suggest that they stop receiving Tesco's orders by post but instead receive the orders direct from Tesco's computer over the telephone line. The advantages to Colgate were presented as being connected with the speed of order processing, the speed with which Colgate could invoice Tesco for goods dispatched and the elimination of keyboard errors because Colgate would not need to key in data received in this way. However, Colgate were also keen to adopt EDI because they believed it would be attractive to their other customers. It was because of their faith in the future of EDI that they invested in technology which would integrate the electronic order they received directly into their order processing system. An expensive exercise but, once done, it allowed Colgate to connect with any of their other customers who wanted to trade in the same way. After a company has committed to EDI, the more business it does, the faster is the payback on its investment.

The electronic trading networks which link customers and suppliers in EDI can also be used *within* a company. In yet another manifestation of the internal customer concept, some companies are using the value-added networks (VANs) not only to communicate with other organizations but also for intra-company communications. For example, Sears, the retail group, uses a commercial network (Edinet) to handle messages and data between its sites. Even so, the problems of compatibility between company, local, national and international networks are formidable. ■

VERENIGDE BLOEMENVEILINGEN AALSMEER (VBA) – (UNITED FLOWER AUCTIONS, AALSMEER, HOLLAND)[13]

VBA is the largest flower auction in the world. Its auction centre, in one of the largest commercial buildings in Europe, covers more than 630 000 square metres. The operation comprises two main parts. The first is the sellers' area known as the 'Auction Section' where flowers are received, held in cooled storage areas and auctioned. The second is the 'Buyers' Section' where around 350 buyers, exporters and wholesalers rent space to prepare flowers for shipment. From this section over 2000 trucks leave Aalsmeer every working day to destinations (including airports) throughout Europe. On a typical day there are about 10 000 people working at the centre (of which only 1700 work directly for VBA), together handling 15 million cut flowers and 1.5 million plants. By any standards, this is a very large and complex operation and it is held together by its information processing technology.

Flowers are extremely perishable, so dealing with them in such large quantities makes the speed, accuracy and dependability of the operation critical. During the evening and night flowers are brought in to the operation in standard containers which are subsequently handled in standard wheeled cages (there are over 100 000 of these 'trolleys' in circulation). Each lot of flowers is assigned a reference number, a quality inspection is made by VBA staff, and a description is entered in the 'delivery forms' attached to each trolley. The trolleys are then held in cold storage until they are collected for the auctioning process the following morning. Details from the delivery forms are then entered into the central auction computers.

The auctions take place on every week day in five separate halls, specialized by category of flower or plant. The largest flower auction hall has tiered desks for up to 500 buyers, each linked to the auction computers, and each with an uninterrupted view of the flowers (which are automatically conveyed through the auction halls in their trolleys), and three auction price 'clocks' behind the auctioneers. Each registered buyer is given a punched identity card which is inserted into a card reader in the desk, so allowing access to the bidding process. Buyers can then choose the clock of their choice at any time using a selection switch. The auctioneer in charge of each clock may give brief information on the quality of a particular lot, relayed to the appropriate bidders' desk speakers, but most important information about the flowers is shown automatically on the clocks' displays (see Fig. 8.12). Flowers are sold by 'Dutch auction', whereby the clock, scaled 100 to 1 at its rim, is started by the auctioneer and moves rapidly downwards. The first bidder to press his other desk button stops the clock and becomes the buyer of that lot. This type of bidding is particularly suitable for automation because only one bid needs to be recorded for each transaction. All the details are recorded by the computer and printed out on a 'distribution voucher' which is attached to the appropriate trolley when it leaves the auction hall on the conveyor system. The whole bidding process, including the processing of the information, takes only a few seconds. The bidders' identity numbers are used to sort the lots which are then distributed on the trolleys to the appropriate packing or loading areas. For each buyer, the VBA computer prints an invoice for all the purchases made, which must be settled daily by bank letter of credit or by cash drawn at one of the four banks adjacent to the cashier's office. In this way the sellers are certain to receive their payments quickly, as no credit is allowed.

▶

Figure 8.12 The auction room at VBA

The high levels of computerization and automation of material flow at Aalsmeer allows VBA to operate with very low costs (about 5 per cent of turnover), at high speed and dependability. Each clock handles about 1000 transactions per hour, that is one every three and a half seconds. Almost all business takes place between 7.00 am and 10.00 am so that fresh flowers can be in the shops as early as possible: by lunchtime in Holland, by early afternoon in London, Paris and Berlin and by early morning the next day in New York. ∎

CUSTOMER PROCESSING TECHNOLOGY

Traditionally, customer processing operations have been seen as 'low-technology' when compared with materials processing operations. The assumption is that manufacturing needs machines while services rely on people. To some extent this is understandable: visit most factories and their technology is often very evident. For example, there is no mistaking the significance of a steel producer's process technology to its business. On the other hand, an office or a bank or even a hospital does not seem to be as dominated by process technology. In these types of operations it is the people one would notice before the technology.

This is missing the point, however. Even if customer processing operations, on average, do invest less in process technology than their manufacturing counterparts, their competitiveness can be affected just as critically by good or bad process technology decisions. A bank whose automatic teller machines (ATMs) do not work effectively is prevented from competing just as effectively as a steel producer with unreliable rolling mills. An airline whose aircraft are unreliable is failing its customers in an even more direct and serious way than, say, an electronics manufacturer whose machines cannot assemble electronic components as they should.

Back- and front-office technology

In Chapter 1 we distinguished between the front-office part of customer processing operations, which has direct contact with customers, and the back-office part, with which the customers have little or no direct contact. Technology is often present in both the front and back office. Much of back-office technology is concerned with information processing and is of the type previously described. Front-office technology has some kind of contact (direct or indirect) with customers. In some cases, ATMs for example, the technology is there to link customers in the front-office with the information processing power of the back-office (*see* Fig. 8.13).

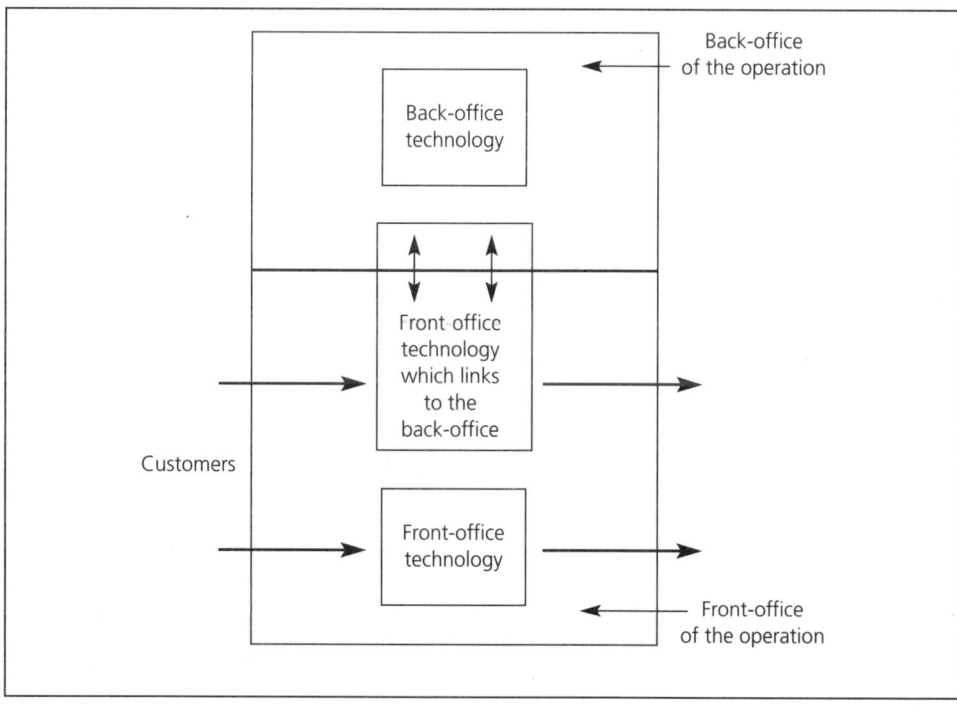

Figure 8.13 Customer processing technology can either operate in the front-office or enable customers to interact with the back-office

The customer–staff–technology interaction

In material or information processing, operations managers are concerned with the interaction between staff and technology. In customer processing operations, however, there is a three-way set of interactions between customers, staff and technology (*see* Fig. 8.14). It is the nature of this interaction which can be used to categorize the various types of customer processing technology.

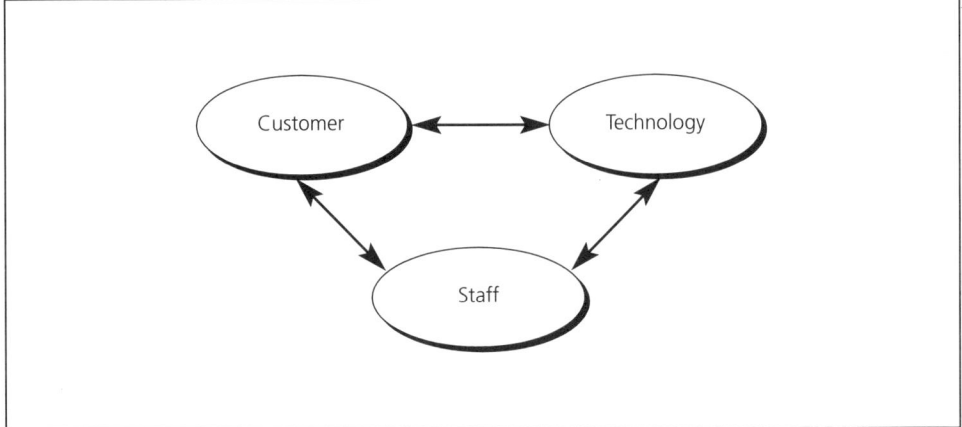

Figure 8.14 Customer processing technology can interact both with customers and the staff of the operation

Here we distinguish between three types of interaction. The distinction between the categories is not always clear, but they do represent broad approaches to the use of customer processing technology. They are:

● where there is *no direct interaction* between customers and the technology;
● where there is *passive interaction* between customers and the technology;
● where there is *active interaction* between customers and the technology.

Technology with no direct customer interaction

When the customers of an airline check in at the airport, they choose their seats, give any special requests and receive their boarding passes. To do this the airline staff operate a computer terminal which links into the airline's systems and a printer which prints boarding passes and baggage tickets. This process technology is vital to the smooth running of the check-in operation. Using it benefits both the airline and the customer. The customer does not directly use the technology, however; the staff member does that on behalf of the customer. The customer may 'navigate'[14] or guide the process but does not 'drive' it. The technology may even be arranged to help customers navigate the process. For example, some airlines have a screen with the seat layout of the aircraft facing the customer, showing which seats are still available. This is an aid to the customer, who has no direct contact as such, however (*see* Fig. 8.15).

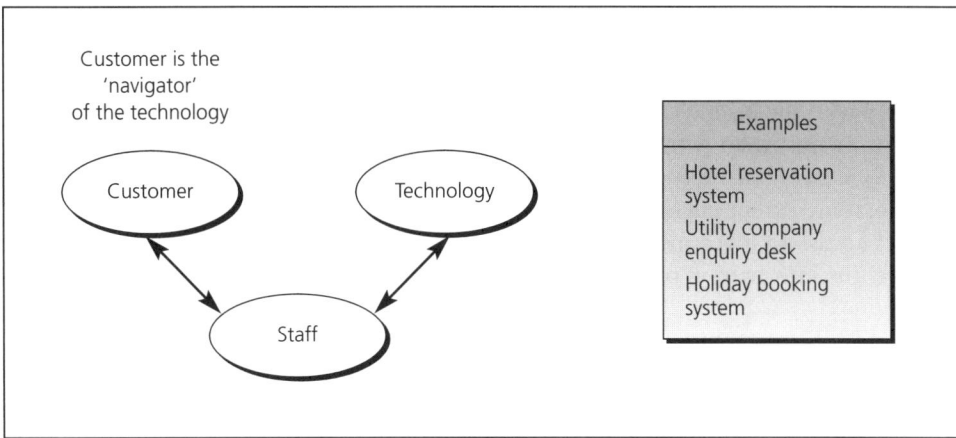

Customer is the
'navigator'
of the technology

Customer

Technology

Staff

Examples

Hotel reservation
system

Utility company
enquiry desk

Holiday booking
system

**Figure 8.15
Technology with
no direct customer
interaction**

TECHNOLOGY AT THE ROBECO GROUP[15]

The Robeco Group, a Netherlands-based financial services group, sells investments and offers its customers financial advice by telephone. With three central offices in Rotterdam, Paris and Geneva, the company deals with over 350 000 calls every year at each office. With almost half a million customers, Robeco relies on technology to give a prompt and efficient service each time one of them phones to seek advice, enquire on his or her account status, or to conduct a transaction (buying or selling shares in mutual funds). In addition, customers can obtain leaflets on particula r financial products.

To transact their business, customers call investment advisers in the company. Each adviser is linked through the company's computer system to various sources of information and advice covering such issues as interest-rate movements, stock markets around the world, economic forecasts, business news and political developments which could affect investments. When a customer phones, the investment adviser can access all information regarding the customer's account: for example, the financial return the customer has been getting for his or her investment (by month or by year), the transactions associated with the account and a full record of advice given and literature sent to the customer. Access to this shared information enables any investment adviser to respond to any customer (although very large customers have their own assigned account adviser). The computer system includes expert systems and models which help the adviser respond to sometimes very general enquiries. For example, if a customer asks about the impact on his investments of a change in the London housing market, the system might include a list of factors which impact the customer's investments, the proportion of the funds invested in London and so on.

Robeco staffs its lines from 8.00 am to 9.00 pm and attempts to answer all calls in the shortest possible time. All responses made by advisers to customers' specific enquiries are noted in the customers' account files and any brochures sent out by the adviser (through another department which stocks the brochures) are dispatched on the same day the enquiry was received. ∎

The reason for using this type of technology is usually to produce some combination of better or faster or cheaper services. The hotel or theatre reservation system, for example, facilitates fast response to customers and high utilization of reservation staff. Similarly with the airline check-in technology, customers receive a faster service, with fewer problems, than if the technology were not used. The technology used by the Robeco advisers (*see* box) gives both these advantages and also produces a better service. To some extent customers use the company because the technology gives them indirect access to investment information. The advisers' role is partly to access and interpret the information provided by the technology.

Hidden technology

In most examples of this type of technology, even when the technology is not obvious to customers, it is not actually hidden from them. Some technologies are invisible or transparent to customers, however. The technology is 'aware' of customers but not the other way round: for example, security monitoring technologies in shopping malls or at national frontier customs areas. The objective of these technologies is for staff to track customers' movements or transactions in an unobtrusive way. Supermarkets, for example, can use bar-code scanner technologies to track the movement of customers around the store and indicate the relationship between customers' propensity to buy particular products. Suppose a retailer wanted to sell soft toys by displaying them next to children's clothes. Bar-code data scanners at the check-out could indicate that these two types of product were purchased by the same customers more often when they were placed next to each other. This would confirm the store's display decision. The same technology could, for example, issue a customer with a discount voucher for a product only if the customer had bought a rival brand. Figure 8.16 illustrates the nature of the relationship in this type of technology.[16]

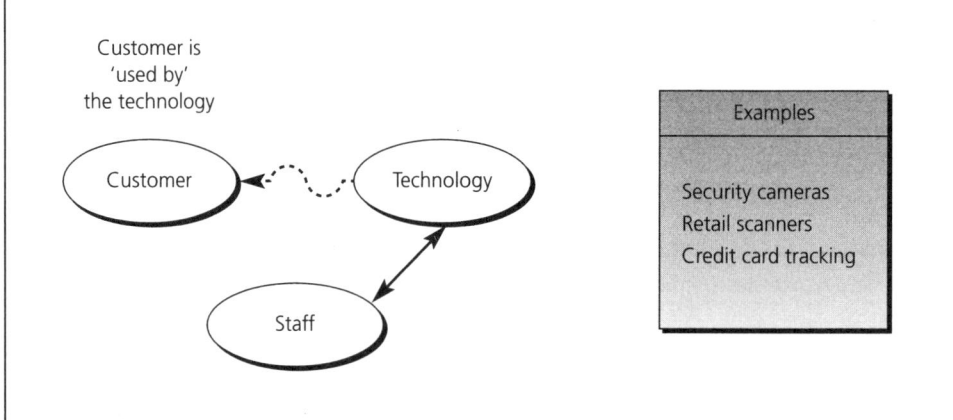

Figure 8.16 Technology with passive and hidden customer interaction

Technology with passive customer interaction

A passenger taking a flight is interacting with technology – the aircraft. The technology is neither hidden from the customer nor is it merely a mechanism for helping the airline's staff to serve its customers – customers are in direct physical contact with it. In this case, however, they do not have much influence over the technology. The customer's role is a predominantly passive one. The technology guides customers rather than the other way round. Customers are 'passengers' of the technology; in the case of transportation operations such as the airline, literally passengers. In addition to aircraft, other transport technologies such as buses, mass rapid transport systems, even moving walkways, also fall into this category. In all these cases the technology 'processes' customers and also *controls* them by constraining their actions in some way. The technology helps to reduce the variety in the operation. Figure 8.17 illustrates this class of technology in terms of customers, staff and technology.

Some medical technologies are also of this type. Body-scanning equipment, X-ray technology, and conventional renal dialysis, all process customers, but the customer, although a necessary part of the activity, has only a passive role. Even surgery has become 'high-tech'; robot technology is becoming more common in surgical procedures. While the hand of the most experienced and skilled surgeon trembles slightly, the robot arm is totally steady. The precision of robotic technology gives significant advantages where manual manipulation would be risky and where the parts of the body being operated on do not move when cut (such as in orthopaedic surgery). Less radically, robots are also used to move instruments around inside the patient under the direction of the surgeon.[17]

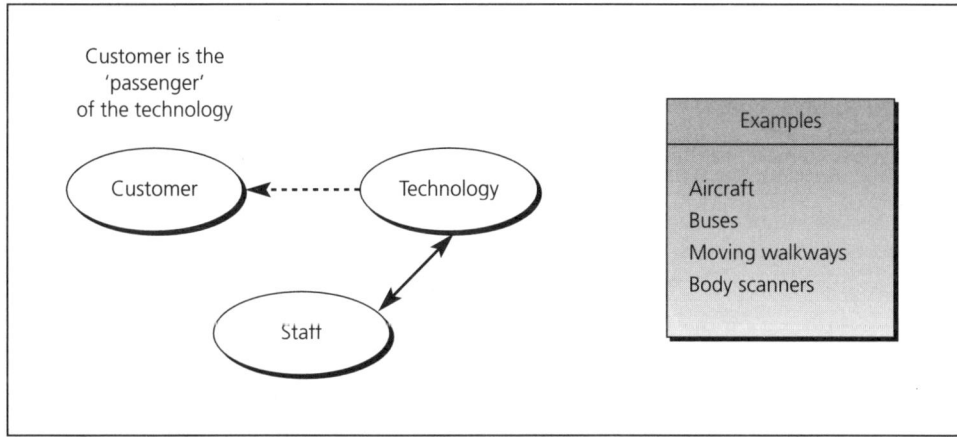

Figure 8.17 Technology with passive customer interaction

The main concern in the development of these types of technology, whether aircraft or medical robots, is the safety of the customer. This is why aircraft, and most other transport technologies, are governed by strict governmental regulations. Similarly with medical technologies, the pace of progress in robot surgery, for example, is relatively slow, not because of technological constraints, but because surgeons cannot take risks with their patients' lives.

Technology with active customer interaction

Having been checked in to his or her flight by staff who were aided by technology, and having been transported by technology in which he or she was a passive user, the airline passenger may choose to use the aircraft's entertainment facilities. This is likely to be an individual screen and headphones which can be used to view movies or listen to audio entertainment. The passenger might even make use of telecommunications-based technology to book hotels or car rental. The type of technology the passenger is using here is of the third type – where customers are actively involved in using, or 'driving', the technology. Figure 8.18 illustrates this type of technology. The main interaction is between the customer and the technology, although staff may also occasionally interact with the technology. For example, banking staff occasionally will need to fill an ATM with cash, and vending machine companies need to replenish goods and empty cash from their machines.

In complex variants of this category of technology there may be interaction on all three dimensions: customer–technology, technology–staff and staff–customers. Some types of medical technology, for example renal dialysis, are used in this way. Similarly some on-line software packages may be primarily intended for customers to use (customer–technology interaction) but customers may also require advice from a 'help-line' (customer–staff interaction) and staff may even be able to intervene in the use of the software itself (staff–technology interaction).

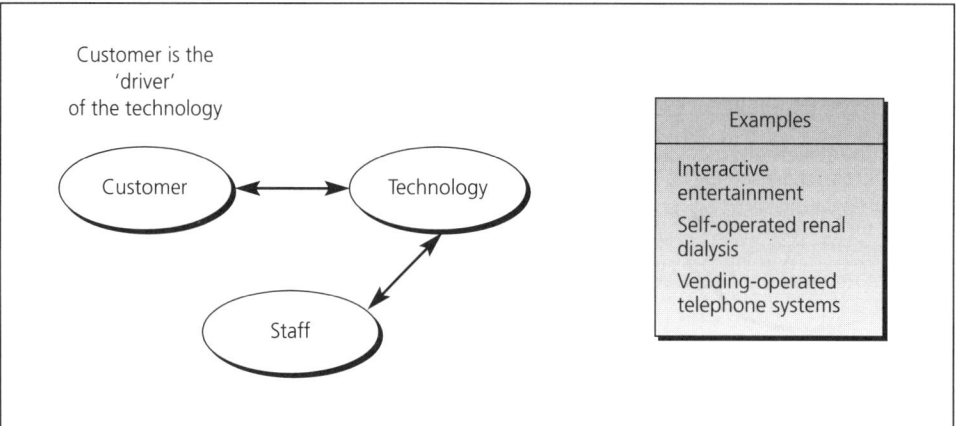

**Figure 8.18
Technology with
active customer
interaction**

Customer training

If customers are to have direct contact with technology, they must have some idea as to how to operate it. Where customers have an active interaction with technology the limitations of customers' understanding of the technology can be the main constraint on its use. For example, even some domestic technology such as video recorders cannot be used to their full potential by most owners. Other 'customer-driven' technologies can face the same problem, with the important addition that if customers cannot use technologies such as ATMs there are serious commercial consequences for a bank's customer service.

QUASAR CREATES A NEW MARKET[18]

Especially in customer processing operations, the emergence of a new technology can create the possibility of an entirely new service. One such example is Quasar, a laser-gun role-playing game. Although noisy, fast and at times furious, Quasar is a non-contact fighting game, like a high-technology version of 'Cowboys and Indians', and has a wide appeal, from teenager to adults of all ages, making it popular with families, and even suitable for corporate entertainment. Few businesses in the leisure industry grew as fast as 'Quasar', which successfully developed a new market. From a modest start at the Trocadero in London, the company quickly opened more sites in the UK, and expanded into continental Europe, initially with sites in Spain, and then France, Greece, Germany, and The Netherlands. The Quasar technology captured the imagination of a fun-seeking and eager public (and an equally excited set of leisure-sector investors) by capitalizing on the public's growing interest in participative, active recreation and entertainment.

The Quasar game is a package of facilities and technology, including the scenery and fitments needed to convert existing buildings into a complex setting ('alien world') of darkened passages, rooms, and landscapes. One core technology is the hand guns which shoot harmless low-powered red or green laser light beams, and the computerized coloured vests for each player which record hits. The other core technology of Quasar is the information system which keeps the score of each player's hits. Customers can play without having to worry about the state of play. The computerized information system also helps to manage bookings and the cash management of the operation. ■

Walley and Amin[19] suggest that the ability of the operation to train its customers in the use of its technology depends on a number of factors.

The complexity of the service

If services are complex to operate, higher levels of training will be needed to ensure correct use of the technology. Alternatively, the need for customer training can be reduced, if operational complexity is minimized. In some cases the training is delivered by potential customers watching experienced customers performing the task correctly. For example, the technology in theme parks and fast-food outlets relies on customers copying the behaviour of others. This may be analogous to on-the-job training. Complexity is also a relative factor. Many technologies such as vending machines, ticket dispensers and ATMs are generally more complex than when they were first introduced. Their customers, often becoming 'trained' on simple versions of the technology, can have their skills upgraded incrementally.

Repetition of the service

The frequency with which a technology is used is an important factor in two ways. First, if a service has to invest in customer training for the technology, then the payback for this investment will be greater if the customer uses the technology frequently. The greater the repetition, the more worthwhile the investment becomes. Second, customers may, over time, forget how to use the technology. Regular repetition will reinforce the training. Conversely, if customers do not use the technology for a long period they may require retraining. For example, customers' use of technologies such as continuous ski lifts becomes noticeably more efficient as they become more practised. Mistakes are more likely to occur at the start of a customer's holiday, after a period of non-use.

Low variety of focus

Training will be easier if the customer is presented with a low variety of tasks. This will help to minimize confusion. For example, vending machines tend to concentrate on one category of product, so that the sequence of tasks to operate the technology properly remains consistent.

THE DIMENSIONS OF TECHNOLOGY

So far, at least one thing should be clear – process technology comes in many different forms. This makes it difficult to generalize across technologies which are used for such a wide variety of purposes. All operations make choices regarding their technology, however, and there are always alternative ways of configuring any technology. Exploring these alternatives involves thinking on three dimensions:

- the degree of *automation* of the technology;
- the *scale* of the technology;
- the degree of *integration* of the technology.

The degree of automation of the technology

No technology operates totally without human intervention. To some extent they all need human intervention some of the time. It may be minimal – for example, the periodic maintenance interventions in a petrochemical refinery, or occasional re-programming of a computer control system. Conversely, the staff member who operates the technology may be the entire 'brains' of the process – for example, the operator working a precision lathe or the surgeon using keyhole surgery techniques.

The benefits of automation

Two benefits of increasing the degree of automation in a process technology are usually cited.

- It saves direct labour costs.
- It reduces variability in the operation.

Automation is usually justified on the former, but it is sometimes the latter which is more significant. Nevertheless it is worth examining what type of labour can be saved through automation in any particular case. Direct labour can often be saved, but that does not mean that the net effect is an overall cost saving. Operations managers need to consider the following points before automating for cost savings alone:[20]

● Can the technology perform the task better or safer than a human? Not just faster (although this can obviously be important), but better in a broader sense. Can the technology make fewer mistakes, change over from one task to the next faster and more reliably, or respond to breakdowns effectively?

● What support activities, such as maintenance or programming, does the technology need in order to function effectively? What will be the effect on indirect costs? Not just the extra people and skills which might be necessary, but also the effect of increased complexity of support activities.

● Can the technology cope with new product or service possibilities as effectively as less automated alternatives? This is a difficult question because no one will know exactly what the operation will need to produce in the future. Nevertheless, it is an important question; automation represents a risk as well as an opportunity.

● What is the potential for human creativity and problem solving to improve the machines' performance? Is it worth getting rid of human potential along with its cost?

Methodology before technology

Automated technologies in many operations have provided the potential for improved performance, but there is a danger. Technology can be seen as a panacea for all the operation's ills, a 'technology fix' which avoids more fundamental problems. If the methods and processes are themselves flawed, technology will just speed up the problems, not solve them. Those companies which have attempted the difficult task of separating the benefits which come directly from investment in automated technology from the benefits which come from improved methodology have reported some surprising results. Paradoxically, capital investment often makes it necessary to consider the organization of the operation as a whole, which in turn prompts improvements which are independent of the technology for which it is preparing the way. For example, the following are extracts from surveys of companies which have installed Flexible Manufacturing Systems (FMS):

'... on average 40 per cent of the benefits predicted for an FMS are in fact achievable, or have been achieved, before the FMS is delivered. This is because the planning process itself has highlighted existing custom and practice which ... can be put right without major investment.'[21]

'(We) frequently receive estimates that approximately half of the benefits of FMS were derived from managerial and work-based organisational change.'[22]

'... companies who operate FMS, and who have presumably undergone some formal evaluation process, tend to concentrate their efforts more than other manufacturing firms on improving product quality, shortening lead times and set-up times and integrating information and control systems.'[23]

This does not mean that investing in capital-intensive automated equipment is a waste of time; rather that there are considerable benefits to be gained from rethinking the overall 'methodology' of the operation whether or not the investment in technology is subsequently made. Perhaps the right order should be first to improve the methods of the operation and only then to put in automated technology where it is needed.

The scale of the technology

Operations often need to decide between acquiring one large-scale unit of technology or several smaller ones. For example, the duplicating department of a large office complex may decide to invest in a single, very large, fast copier, or alternatively several smaller, slower copiers. An airline may purchase one or two wide-bodied aircraft or a larger number of smaller aircraft. A manufacturer may design its operation around a single large-capacity machine or several smaller machines. No matter what the technology, there is usually some discretion as to how large a piece of plant it is wise to acquire. The economies of the technology itself will influence the decision. Some process technologies, such as intercontinental aircraft, petrochemical refineries, or steel making plants benefit from scale, and so tend to come in large capacity increments. Others, like personal computers or ATMs for example, are efficient when operating on a small scale.

The advantages of large-scale technologies are similar to the advantages of large-capacity increments discussed in Chapter 6 and are summarized in Table 8.3.

Table 8.3 Advantages of large-scale and small-scale technologies

Advantages of large-scale technology	Advantages of small-scale technology
Economies of scale can lead to lower cost per product or service delivered	Good mix flexibility – each unit of technology can be engaged on different activities
Lower capital costs per unit of capacity	High robustness against failure
Can incorporate support and control elements in the technology (e.g. 'rest room' facilities in larger buses)	Lower obsolescence risk
Can pool work for better utilization (e.g. batch processing in centralized computer systems)	Can be located closer to where the technology is needed

Many of the advantages of large-scale technologies are connected with the cost advantages they can bring. Capital and operating cost per unit of capacity are generally lower. If cost factors are a strength of large units of technology, however, nimbleness and flexibility can be virtues of smaller-scale technology. Mix flexibility (*see* Chapter 2) especially is enhanced. For example, four small machines can between them produce four different products simultaneously (albeit slowly), whereas a single large machine with four times the output can produce one product four times faster. Small-scale technologies are also more robust. Suppose the choice is between three small machines and two larger ones. In the first case, if one machine breaks down, a third of the capacity is lost, but in the second, capacity is halved. It is also easier to take advantage of technology improvement with small-scale technology. Buying a small machine just equal to current needs allows the operation to buy the latest technology when demand increases.

The degree of integration of the technology

Integration means the linking together of previously separated activities within a single piece of technology or system. This issue has arisen at points earlier in this chapter. For example, the technological development represented by local area networks (LANs) is largely that of integration. Similarly, the development of advanced manufacturing technologies is the result of microprocessor-based integration.

Integration, synchronization and speed

The benefits of integration come directly from the effects of combining several separate technology units into one simple synchronized whole. First, there is fast throughput of information or of materials. For example, in an FMS there is no inter-machine decision making over which job has priority. Second, and as a consequence of throughput speed, inventory of materials or information will be lower – it can't accumulate when there are no 'gaps' between activities. Third, flow is simple and predictable. It is easier to keep track of parts when they pass through fewer stages, or information when it is automatically distributed to all parts of an information network.

Integrated technology can be more expensive, however. For example, in manufacturing, even simple material handling linkages are costly. Furthermore, the more integrated the technology, the higher the skills can be which are needed to maintain it. When failures do occur, the whole integrated system is likely to go down. In one sense this makes integrated plant more vulnerable. If integration involves linking several production stages which would otherwise be loosely connected in series, this 'disadvantage' of integration can be a useful discipline. If one link in a chain stops then the other should do so anyway. To do otherwise would mean producing for work-in-progress, not for the end customer.

Mark Kneen, Consol Glass

Mark Kneen is the Chief Engineer at Consol Glass and has supervised the acquisition of new capital plant, the upgrade of existing plant and the integration of control systems in the pursuit of CIM. His experiences demonstrate some of the main issues associated with this rapidly expanding area of technology.

'Consol Glass finds itself in a remarkably competitive environment in SA today. The entry of new competitors, the accelerating use of alternative packaging media and the low barriers to entry to some segments of the packaging market have combined to make trading conditions more difficult than in the past. This difficulty is epitomized by the small businessman who purchases a plastic injection moulding machine and operates it out of his garage. He clearly has a cost advantage due to his much lower overhead structure compared to the more established and conventional producer of glass packaging.

'Our approach towards countering these threats is to focus on the process technology in use in our many plants and to use it as a competitive weapon. This will provide us with cost, quality, lead time and flexibility advantages. We clearly cannot reveal details of this strategy, given its competitive thrust, but a broad overview of our approach will illustrate the salient points without excessive disclosure. One example of our approach is that used in the enhancement of our glass manufacturing processes. We scoured the world to locate the top producer of plant in this category and have now standardized our processes around their well proven American equipment. A key factor in our decision was the level of expertise that the supplier had in the glass making process and the extent to which that knowledge had been encapsulated into the equipment design.

'This approach on the hardware side was extended to the information and automation side of the plant. We performed a detailed evaluation of the products and services available from various equipment providers before standardizing our entire multi-plant organization on one German supplier who also maintained a presence both in the USA and in this country. A key factor in the decision was the extent to which the CIM system would allow us to optimize the processes using a programmed knowledge base. The final system design allowed us to reduce manual control over the process and to automate the process in order to allow it to run at optimum operating conditions on a continuous basis. The spin-off benefits from this were substantial.

'The hardware supplier was made responsible for ensuring full integration of all aspects of the system, although Consol would create the final hierarchical control system. Problems occurred due to the use of state-of-the-art and unfamiliar technology and the long, trans-continental lines of communication. The access to local support and the solid integration capabilities of the hardware supplier were important factors in our subsequent success.

'It must be emphasized that the final process technology implemented was in fact custom designed with our assistance for our specific application. This proves the truth in the statement that "You cannot buy a competitive edge, you have to develop it". Competitors are not going to be able to buy a solution off the shelf; this is a typical benefit of competing on the basis of process technology. Consol is well on its way to becoming a world class competitor due to its innovative approach to the enhancement of its process technology.' ∎

Source: By kind permission of Consol Glass

SUMMARY

■ Process technology is any device, machine or equipment which helps to transform materials, information or customers. In manufacturing operations it is usually relatively easy to separate product from process technology. In service operations it can be difficult to distinguish between them.

■ Operations managers need not be specialists in the technology which they are managing but they should be able to understand enough about the technology to define its purpose, the way in which it performs its function, the benefits of using the technology in their operation, and the constraints which using the technology might place upon the operation.

■ Both process technology and product/service technology exhibit a life-cycle effect. In the introduction stage of a product or service life cycle it is the technology of the product or service itself which is likely to dominate. As the product or service moves through its life cycle the rate of innovation of its technology is likely to decrease progressively, while the rate of innovation associated with its process technology is likely to increase.

■ The basis of many recently developed technologies is the availability of cheap and powerful microprocessing. For this reason many technologies in different operations are partly information processing technologies. However, a convenient way of classifying all technologies is according to their primary transformed resource: this can be materials, information or customers.

■ Developments in materials processing technology include such things as numerically controlled machine tools and machining centres, robotics, automated guided vehicles, and flexible manufacturing systems. The degree to which these technologies are utilized is a function partly of an operation's position on the volume–variety continuum.

■ The increasing integration of manufacturing technologies has led to the concept of computer-integrated manufacturing (CIM).

■ Information processing technology can be organized on a centralized basis, where a central processing unit serves many different users, or on a decentralized basis, where information processing is distributed around an organization to place it closer to its users. Local area networks may be used to integrate computing power distributed in such a way.

■ Increasingly the information technologies are merging with telecommunications technologies. Electronic data interchange (EDI) is one example of this.

■ Customer processing technologies can be categorized according to the relationship between the technology itself, the staff of the operation, and the customers of the operation.

■ Some customer processing technology in fact does not have any direct interaction with the customer but is used by the staff of an operation to help the customer. The customer 'navigates' the technology but does not operate it.

■ Some customer processing technology has a direct interaction with the customer, even though the customer does not directly control the technology. Many transportation and medical technologies are of this type.

■ Some customer processing technology requires the customer to 'drive' the technology directly, for example, automatic teller machines (ATMs), vending machines, etc. Any such technology, which requires customers to control it, must take into account the need to train the customer in the appropriate skills.

■ All technologies can be conceptualized on three dimensions:
– the degree of automation of the technology (that is how much it substitutes technology for labour);
– the scale of the technology (that is how large the capacity of the technology is);
– the degree of integration of the technology (that is how much the different parts of the technology are connected with each other).

Rochem Ltd

Dr Rhodes was losing his temper.

'It should be a simple enough decision. There are only two alternatives. You are only being asked to choose a machine!'

The Management Committee looked abashed.

Rochem Ltd by 1995 was one of the largest independent companies supplying the food-processing industry. Its initial success had come in the late 1980s with a food preservative, used mainly for meat-based products, and marketed under the name of 'Lerentyl'. Other products were subsequently developed in the food colouring and food container coating fields, so that now Lerentyl accounted for only 25 per cent of total company sales, which in 1995 were slightly under R50 million.

The decision

The problem over which there was such controversy related to the replacement of one of the process units used to manufacture Lerentyl. Only two such units were used, both were 'Chemling' machines. It was the older of the two Chemling units which was giving trouble. High breakdown figures, with erratic quality levels, meant that output level requirements were only just being reached. The problem was: should the company replace the ageing Chemling with a new Chemling, or should it buy the only other plant on the market capable of the required process, the 'AFU' unit? The Chief Chemist's staff had drawn up a comparison of the two units, shown in Table 8.4.

The body considering the problem was the newly formed Management Committee. The committee consisted of the four senior managers in the firm: the Chief Chemist and the Marketing Manager, who had been with the firm since its beginning, together with the Production Manager and the Accountant, both of whom had joined the company only six months before.

What follows is a condensed version of the information presented by each manager to the committee, together with their attitudes to the decision.

The Marketing Manager

By 1995 the market for this type of preservative had reached a size of some R25 million of which Rochem Ltd supplied approximately 48 per cent. There had, of late, been significant changes in the market – in particular many of the users of preservatives were now able to buy products similar to Lerentyl. The result had been the evo-

Table 8.4 A comparison of the two alternative machines

	CHEMLING	AFU
Capital cost	R590 000	R880 000
Processing costs	Fixed: R15 000/mth Variable: R750/kg	Fixed: R40 000/mth Variable: R600/kg
Design capacity	105 kg/mth	140 kg/mth
Quality	98%±0.7% purity Manual testing	99.5%±0.2% purity Automatic testing
Maintenance	Adequate but needs servicing	Not known – probably good
After-sales services	Very good	Not known – unlikely to be good
Delivery	Three months	Immediate

lution of a much more price-sensitive market than had previously been the case. Further market projections were somewhat uncertain. It was clear that the total market would not shrink (in volume terms) and best estimates suggested a market of perhaps R30 million by 1999 (at current prices). However, there were some people in the industry who believed that the present market only represented the tip of the iceberg.

Although the food preservative market had advanced by a series of technical innovations, 'real' changes in the basic product were now few and far between. Lerentyl was sold in either solid powder or liquid form, depending on the particular needs of the customer. Prices tended to be related to the weight of chemical used, however. Thus, for example, in 1995 the average market price was approximately R5250 per kg. There were, of course, wide variations depending on order size, etc.

'At the moment I am mainly interested in getting the right quantity and quality of Lerentyl each month and although Production have never let me down yet, I'm worried that unless we get a reliable new unit quickly, they soon will. The AFU machine could be on line in a few weeks, giving better quality too. Furthermore, if demand does increase (but I'm not saying it will), the AFU will give us the extra capacity. I will admit that we are not trying to increase our share of the preservative market as yet. We see our priority as establishing our other products first. When that's

achieved, we will go back to concentrating on the preservative side of things.'

The Chief Chemist

The Chief Chemist was an old friend of John Rhodes and together they had been largely responsible for every product innovation. At the moment, the major part of his budget was devoted to modifying basic Lerentyl so that it could be used for more acidic food products such as fruit. This was not proving easy and as yet nothing had come of the research, although the Chief Chemist remained optimistic.

'If we succeed in modifying Lerentyl, the market opportunities will be doubled overnight and we will need the extra capacity. I know we would be taking a risk by going for the AFU machine, but our company has grown by gambling on our research findings, and we must continue to show faith.'

The Production Manager

The Lerentyl Department was virtually self-contained as a production unit. In fact it was physically separate, being in a building a few yards detached from the rest of the plant. Production requirements for Lerentyl were currently at a steady rate of 190 kg per month. The six technicians who staffed the machines were the only technicians in Rochem who did all their own minor repairs and full quality control. The reason for this was largely historical, since when the firm started, the product was experimental and qualified technicians were needed to operate the plant. Four of the six had been with the firm almost from its beginning.

'It's all right for Dave and Eric (Marketing Manager and Chief Chemist) to talk about a big expansion of Lerentyl sales; they don't have to cope with all the problems if it doesn't happen. The fixed costs of the AFU unit are nearly three times those of the Chemling. Just think what that will do to my budget at low volumes of output. As I understand it, there is absolutely no evidence to show a large upswing

in Lerentyl. No, the whole idea (of the AFU plant) is just too risky. Not only is there the risk. I don't think it is generally understood what the consequences of the AFU would mean. We would need twice the variety of spares for a start. But what really worries me is the staff's reaction. As fully qualified technicians they regard themselves as the elite of the firm; so they should, they are paid practically the same as I am! If we get the AFU plant all their most interesting work, like the testing and the maintenance, will disappear or be greatly reduced. They will finish up as highly paid process workers.'

The Accountant

The company had financed nearly all its recent capital investment from its own retained profits, but would be taking out short-term loans in 1995 for the first time for several years.

'At the moment, I don't think it wise to invest extra capital we can't afford in an attempt to give us extra capacity we don't need at the moment. This year will be an expensive one for the company. We are already committed to considerably increased expenditure on promotion of our other products and capital investment in other parts of the firm, and Dr Rhodes is not in favour of excessive funding from outside the firm. I accept that there might eventually be an upsurge in Lerentyl demand but, if it does come, it probably won't be this year and it will be far bigger than the AFU can cope with anyway, so we might as well have three Chemling plants at that time.' ■

Questions

1 How do the two alternative process technologies (Chemling and AFU) differ in terms of their scale and automation? What are the implications of this for Rochem?

2 Remind yourself of the distinction between feasibility, acceptability, and vulnerability, discussed in Chapter 4. Evaluate both technologies using these criteria.

3 What would you recommend the company should do?

DISCUSSION QUESTIONS

1 Identify as many applications of automation as you can in the following operations:
- a hospital
- an airline
- a university
- a chain of hotels
- retail banking
- farming and agriculture.

2 Many universities and colleges around the world are under increasing pressure to reduce the cost per student of their activities. How do you think technology could help operations such as universities to keep their costs down but their quality of education high?

3 In the popular press there have been many stories about the 'fully automated factory', sometimes known as the 'dark factory' because it does not need any human intervention (who would switch the lights on!). What do you think might be some of the major problems in trying to achieve this goal of the fully automated factory? In what kind of manufacturing do you think we are first likely to see the extensive use of full automation?

4 Identify some technologies you use in day-to-day life. Assess the value of them by thinking what it would be like to be without them. Can you identify which ones are product/service technologies and which are process technologies?

5 Assess the differences between a fax machine and a telephone in terms of their operational capabilities.

6 Discuss the relationship between product/service and process technology for a product or service of which you are familiar.

7 Talk to the manager of a plant that has an FMS. Assess the relative volume and variety of products that are produced by the FMS. Does the manager believe that the advantages of FMS (identified by John Bessant) have been attained?

8 'The real advantage of flexible manufacturing systems (FMS) is not in their flexibility at all. Rather it is in the fact that they can process materials cheaper than any previous technology. They really should have been called "low-cost manufacturing systems" rather than "flexible manufacturing systems".' Do you think this statement is right? If so, why do you think that flexible manufacturing systems have been called by that name?

9 The human-centred CIM philosophy aims to retain the advantages of computer-integrated manufacturing while also allowing humans to interact with such systems, so as to fulfil their own job aspirations and needs. Do you think this is just idealism or, alternatively, the only way to achieve the best of the mechanized and human worlds?

10 Explain the differences and relationships between CIE, CIM, FMS and CAD/CAM.

11 Discuss the advantages and disadvantages between centralized and decentralized information processing for air traffic controllers.

12 What benefits could EDI bring to a university?

13 Describe the following technologies that might be found at an airport in terms of the customer–staff–technology interactions:
- X-ray machines for customers at an airport
- airbridges connecting walkways to the aircraft
- air traffic control system
- scanners that check the destination bar codes on luggage
- automatic ticket machines.

14 The vast majority of services offered by retail banks could be provided entirely automatically. Automatic teller machines, automated depositing facilities, interactive screen information links in the branches, and the full range of voice activated and person-to-person home banking services all raise the possibility of a bank where customers never have face-to-face communication with the staff of the bank. What factors do you think influence retail banks when they are deciding how far to automate their various services?

15 Robot-type technology is starting to play a part in some medical surgical procedures. What would it take before you were willing to subject yourself to a robot doctor?

16 Visit your local or university library and write a report on how technology could be applied to enhance the efficiency and effectiveness of the operation. What do you think might be the biggest problems if the library attempted to operate on an entirely automated basis?

17 Airlines are already discussing with aircraft manufacturers the possibility of the development of an aircraft carrying 600 to 700 passengers. The desire for such large aircraft comes from the increased demand for air travel, especially on some routes. Generally it is cheaper and faster to run one large aircraft than two half the size. In principle, current technology could allow the development of aircraft which could carry around 1000 passengers. What do you think might limit the use of technology to develop such large aircraft?

18 A high street bank is considering providing a home banking service using modems and customers' own home-based PCs. What do you think are the main issues that the bank will have to consider in terms of getting customers to use this service?

19 Some Japanese manufacturers prefer to employ simple and unsophisticated technologies rather than large-scale fully integrated technologies. Why do you think this is so?

20 One problem with technology which is open to all members of the public to use, for example cash machines (ATMs), is that they could be open to fraud or misinterpretation. For example, some bank customers have complained that they did not make the transactions at cash machines which have shown up on their accounts. How do you think the technology might be developed to overcome this problem?

NOTES ON CHAPTER

1 Abernathy, W.J. and Utterback, J. (1975) 'A Dynamic Model of Process and Product Innovation', *Omega*, Vol 3, No 6, pp 639–57.

2 Economic Commission for Europe (1985) *Production and Use of Industrial Robots*, UN Economic Commission for Europe, ENC/ENG.ATV/15.

3 From Voss, C.A. (1986) *Managing New Manufacturing Technologies*, Operations Management Association, Monograph 1.

4 Edquist, C. and Jacobsson, S. (1988) *Flexible Automation*, Blackwell.

5 Source: *ABB Robotics Review*, No 2, 1993 and company literature, kindly supplied by ABB.

6 Source: Discussion with company staff.

7 Voss, C.A., *op. cit.*

8 Bessant, J. (1991) *Managing Advanced Manufacturing Technology*, Blackwell.

9 Voss, C.A., *op. cit.*

10 Boaden, R. and Dale, B. (1986) 'What is computer integrated manufacturing?', *International Journal of Operations and Production Management*, Vol 6, No 3.

11 Gunton, T. (1990) *Inside Information Technology*, Prentice Hall.

12 Sources: Sarson, R.M (1993) 'Companies Adopt a New Way of Talking', *The Times*, 24 Sept. Harris, D. (1991) 'Fast Orders Help Trades Net Profits',

Accounting, Nov.

13 Sources: Company information and discussions with company staff.

14 Walley, P. and Amin, V. (1994) 'Automation in a Customer Contact Environment', *International Journal of Operations and Production Management*, Vol 14, No 5, pp 86–100.

15 Source: Horovitz, J. and Jurgens Panak, M. (1992) *Total Customer Satisfaction*, FT/Pitman Publishing.

16 Tansik, D.A. and Smith, W.L. (1993) 'Technology Issues in Services: a Typology and Implications' *in* Johnston, R. and Slack, N. (eds) *Service Superiority*, OMA.

17 Cookson, C. (1993) 'Calling Dr Dalek – Your Patient is Waiting', the *Financial Times*, 26 June.

18 Source: *British Airways Business Life*, Feb 1994.

19 Walley, P. and Amin, V., *op. cit.*

20 Slack, N. (1991) *The Manufacturing Advantage*, Mercury Business Books.

21 Bessant, J., *op. cit.*

22 Dempsey, P. (1983) 'New Corporate Perspectives on FMS', *FMS Conference Proceedings*, IFS.

23 Tombak, M. and De Meyer, A. (1986) 'How the Managerial Attitudes of Firms with FMS Differ from Other Manufacturing Firms', *INSEAD Working Paper*, No 86/15.

SELECTED FURTHER READINGS

Abernathy, W.J. (1976) 'Production Process Structure and Technological Change', *Decision Sciences*, Vol 7, No 4.

Adler, T.S. and Winograd, T.A. (1992) *Usability, Turning Technology in Tools*, Oxford University Press.

Avishai, B. (1989) 'A CEO's Common Sense of CIM: An Interview with J.Tracy O'Rourke', *Harvard Business Review*, Vol 67, No 1.

Bennett, D., Forrester, P. and Hassard, J. (1992) 'Market-driven Strategies and the Design of Flexible Production Systems: Evidence from the Electronics Industry', *International Journal of Operations and Production Management*, Vol 12, No 2.

Bessant, J. (1991) *Managing Advanced Manufacturing Technology, The Challenge of the Fifth Wave*, NCC, Blackwell.

Collier, D.A. (1985) *Service Management: The Automation of Services*, Reston Publishing.

Delene, L.M. and Lyte, D.M. (1989) 'Interactive Service Operations: The Relationships Among Information, Technology and Exchange Transactions on the Quality of the Customer-Contact Interface', *International Journal of Operations and Production Management*, Vol 9. No 5.

Gerwin, D. (1982) 'Dos and Don'ts of Computerised Manufacturing', *Harvard Business Review*, Vol 60, No 2.

Goldhar, J.D. and Jelinek, M. (1983) 'Plan for Economies of Scope', *Harvard Business Review*, Vol 61, No 6.

Gunton, T. (1990) *Inside Information Technology, A Practical Guide to Management Issues*, Prentice Hall.

Harrison, M. (1990) *Advanced Manufacturing Technology Management*, Pitman Publishing.

Jaikumar, R. (1986) 'Postindustrial Manufacturing', *Harvard Business Review*, Vol 64, No 6.

Kaplan, R.S. (1986) 'Must CIM be Justified by Faith Alone?' *Harvard Business Review*, Vol 64, No 2.

Karlsson, C. (1992) 'Knowledge and Material Flow in Future Industrial Networks', *International Journal of Operations and Production Management*, Vol 12, No 7/8.

Lindburg, P. (1992) 'The Management of Uncertainty in AMT Implementation: The Case of FMS', *International Journal of Operations and Production Management*, Vol 12, No 7/8.

McCutchon, D.M. and Wood, A.R. (1989) 'The Effects of Technical Experience on Robot Implementations', *International Journal of Operations and Production Management*, Vol 9, No 7.

Monroe, J. (1989) 'Strategic Use of Technology', *California Management Review*, Summer.

Rhodes, D. (1989) 'CIM and the Integration of Users, Vendors and Educators', *International Journal of Operations and Production Management*, Vol 9, No 2.

Skinner, W. (1984) 'Operations Technology: Blind Spot in Strategic Management', *Interfaces*, Vol 14, No 1.

Zorkoczy, P. (1993) *Information Technology: An Introduction* (3rd edn), Pitman Publishing.

CHAPTER 9

JOB DESIGN AND WORK ORGANIZATION

INTRODUCTION

Operations management is often presented as a subject whose main focus is on technology, systems, procedures and facilities – in other words the non-human parts of the organization. This is not true of course. On the contrary, the manner in which an organization's human resources are managed has a profound impact on the effectiveness of its operations function. In this chapter we look especially at the elements of human resource management which are traditionally seen as being directly within the sphere of operations management. These are the activities which influence the relationship between people, the technology they use, and the work methods employed by the operation. This is usually called job design. Figure 9.1 shows how job design fits into the overall model of design.

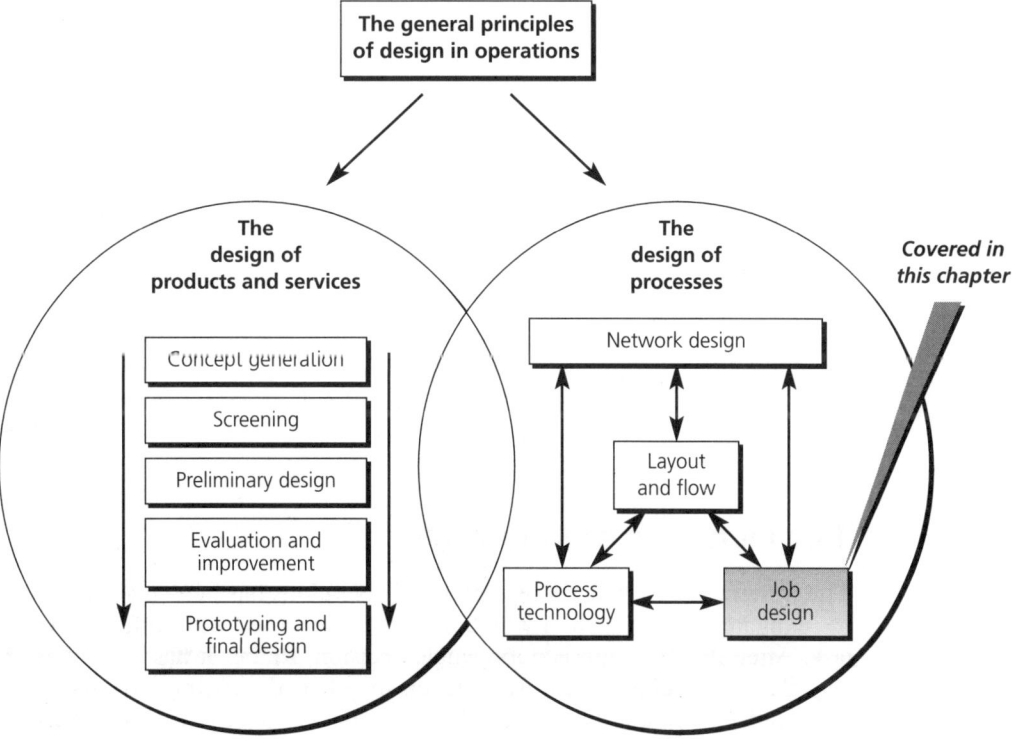

Figure 9.1 The design activities in operations management covered in this chapter

THE DESIGN OF JOBS

To say that an organization's human resources are its greatest asset is at best axiomatic and at worst a cliché. Yet for all that it is true, and it is worth reminding ourselves of the importance of human resources, especially in the operations function. In most organizations it is in the operations function where the bulk of its human resources are to be found. It follows that it is operations managers who are most involved in the leadership, development and organization of human resources. In fact the influence of operations management on the organization's staff is not limited to how their jobs are designed. (Nor is the coverage of this book: Chapters 18 and 20, for example, are concerned largely with how the contribution of the operation's staff can be harnessed.) Job design has a particularly pivotal role. Job design defines the way in which people go about their working lives. It positions their expectations of what is required of them, and it influences their perceptions of how they contribute to the organization. It positions their activities in relation to their work colleagues and it channels the flows of communication between different parts of the operation. But of most importance, it helps to develop the culture of the organization – its shared values, beliefs and assumptions. It is for this reason that job design is seen by some as the central aspect of the design of any transformation process.

The elements of job design

The activity of designing people's jobs in operations has been modified over the years by many influences, each of which has been concerned with different elements of the task. After all job design is not a single decision. Rather it has a number of separate, yet related elements which, when taken together, define the jobs of the people who work in the operation. Figure 9.2 illustrates some of the elements of job design.

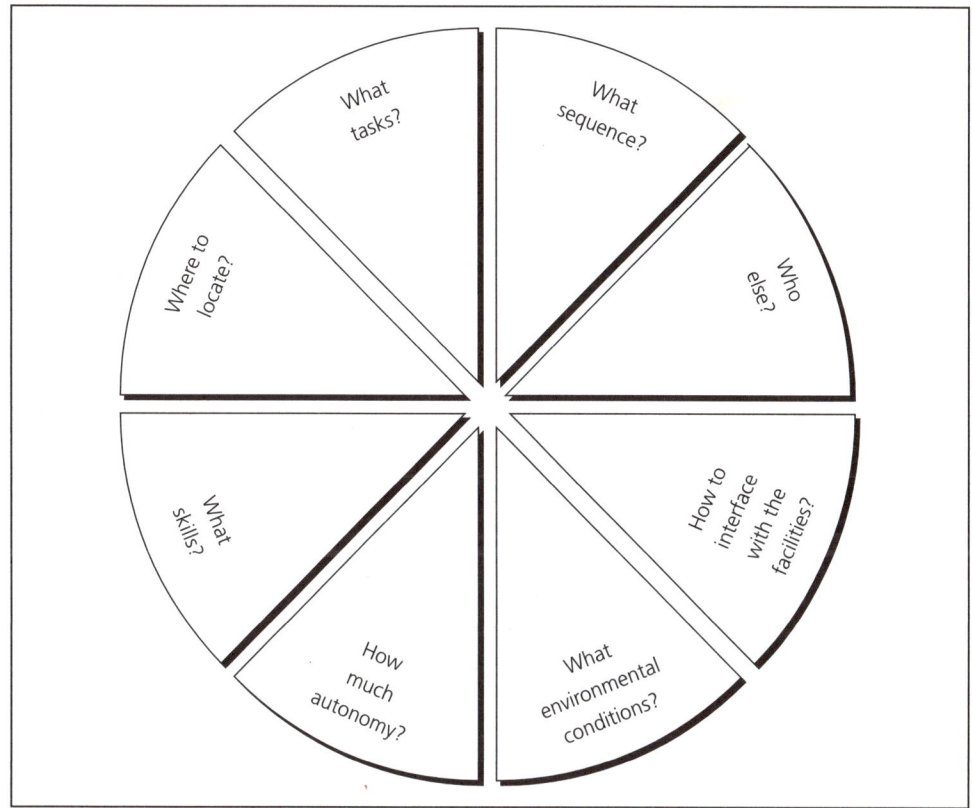

Figure 9.2
The elements of job design

What tasks are to be allocated to each person in the operation?

Producing goods and services on a continuing basis involves a whole range of different tasks which need to be divided between all the people who staff the operation. Different approaches to job design will lead to different task allocations. For example, one operation might choose to confine each staff member to repeating the same type of task, so as to encourage simplicity and efficiency. Another operation might choose to allocate a wide variety of tasks to each staff member so as to reduce the monotony of his or her job.

What sequence of tasks is to be established as the approved manner to do the job?

Sometimes the sequence of tasks is dictated by the design of the product or service. For example, an operator working on an automobile assembly line must put the wheels in place before putting on the wheel nuts. No other sequence would result in a satisfactory product. Sometimes sequence is determined by the desire to avoid mistakes. Next time you pay for goods at a supermarket check-out, note the sequence of taking your cash or card, asking you to sign the authorization form, returning your card, receipt and payment slip and so on. This standardized sequence of tasks is designed largely to prevent errors in the process.

Where is the job to be located within the operation?

Some jobs can be performed quite satisfactorily in more than one place. For example, a maintenance worker in a large hospital could be located centrally along with all other maintenance jobs. Alternatively, he or she could be assigned responsibility for just one part of the hospital and located in that part. Different locations could also mean different task allocations. For example, the maintenance worker located away from the central workshops would probably have to be made responsible for deciding whether to repair or replace failed equipment.

Who else should be involved in the job?

It may be that instead of allocating a well defined set of tasks to each person in the operation, a larger set of tasks is allocated to a group of people. The group then might choose, or be guided to, a flexible task-sharing, or a task-rotation, pattern of working. If so, the size of the group and its interactions with other groups and individuals must be decided.

How are the facilities and equipment used in the job to be interfaced with?

Very few jobs do not involve some interaction with tools, equipment, machines or facilities. Inappropriately positioned computer screens, badly designed controls and ill fitting desks are all failures to consider the interfaces between people and the 'hardware' of their job. Decisions here involve such things as the dimensions and settings of physical equipment, the positioning of each part of the workplace and the design of controls.

What environmental conditions should be established in the workplace?

The conditions under which jobs are performed can have just as significant an impact on people's effectiveness, comfort and safety as the intrinsic details of the tasks themselves. Decisions include determining an appropriate temperature range, lighting intensity, noise control and air quality.

How much autonomy is to be included in the job?

There is a difference between allocating tasks to an individual and encouraging autonomy for the way the job is performed. For example, a retail operation might decide that the staff in a section of the shop should be allocated the tasks of re-ordering stock when it runs low, displaying the goods, organizing their own meal breaks and so on. This allocation of tasks places a large part of the running of that section of the shop in the hands of its staff. Yet allocating the responsibility for the effectiveness of the section to the staff has implied something further. It implies that the staff can also modify the way the section is run. They are being given the autonomy to affect how the tasks are performed.

What skills are to be developed in staff?

Different decisions in the elements of job design described here all have implications for the skills and capabilities which people will need to perform their jobs effectively. The skills which may be necessary might include simple manual skills, equipment manipulation skills, equipment adjustment and maintenance skills, monitoring and measurement skills, scheduling skills or even problem-solving skills for improving the job itself.

The objectives of job design

Jobs can be designed by adopting any of the many options in each of the eight areas in Fig. 9.2. There are clearly many alternative designs for any given job. For this reason, an understanding of what the job design is supposed to achieve is particularly important. As before, the five performance objectives of quality, speed, dependability, flexibility and cost give us a guide to what is relevant in job design decisions. In addition, job design will influence two other particularly important objectives:

Health and safety

Whatever else a job design achieves, it must not endanger the well-being of the person who does the job, other staff of the operation, the customers who might be present in the operation, or those who use any products made by the operation.

Quality of working life

The design of any job should take into account its effect on job security, intrinsic interest, variety, opportunities for development, stress level and attitude of the person performing the job.

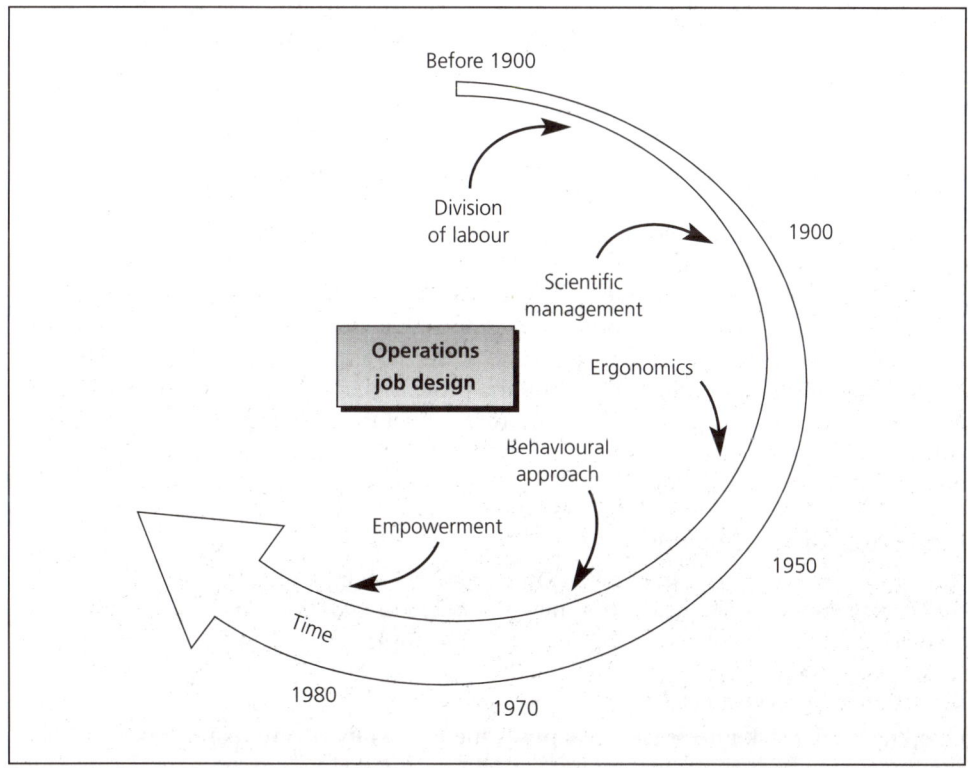

**Figure 9.3
The chronology of
the different
approaches to job
design**

Approaches to job design practice

There are several approaches which can be taken to job design. Over the years different approaches have been particularly influential at different times. None of these approaches are mutually exclusive as such, but they do represent different philosophies or, at least, emphasize different aspects of job design. This is mainly because they were advanced at different points in the history of operations management. Chronologically, the approaches are as shown in Fig. 9.3, and it is in this order that we will treat them here. It should be stressed, however, that these approaches did not replace each other. The influence of all of them is still evident in the way jobs are designed today. Rather each added a new 'layer' or perspective to the job design activity.

DIVISION OF LABOUR

The division of labour becomes an issue in job design as soon as the operation is large enough to warrant the employment of more than one person. In very small operations with just a single person providing the goods or services, there is obviously no potential for dividing the work between separate individuals. For example, a single tailor will measure clients, select the cloth, cut the cloth, sew the pieces together, fit the clothes to the customer, try to elicit further business and so on. As soon as business increases such that two or more people are needed to staff the business, the possibility of specialization arises. For example, if volume warrants three people, they could divide the total set of tasks so that one person serves in the shop and measures customers, the second person cuts out the material and the third person sews the clothes.

This idea is called the division of labour – dividing the total task down into smaller parts, each of which is accomplished by a single person. It is an idea which has been evident in job design from the earliest times of organizational activity (arguably back to Greece in the fourth century BC), though it was first formalized as a concept by the economist Adam Smith in his *Wealth of Nations* in 1746.[1] Perhaps the epitome of the division of labour is the assembly line, where products move along a single path and are built up by operators continually repeating a single task. The assembly line is an image of industrial life which many would see as either old-fashioned or demeaning to its operators, or both. Yet it is still the predominant model of job design in most mass-produced products, and in some mass-produced services (fast food, for example). This is because, in spite of its drawbacks, there are some real advantages in division-of-labour principles.

It promotes faster learning

It is obviously easier to learn how to do a relatively short and simple task than a long and complex one. This means that new members of staff can be quickly trained and assigned to their tasks when tasks are short and simple.

Automation becomes easier

Dividing a total task into small parts raises the possibility of automating some of those small tasks. Substituting technology for labour is considerably easier for short and simple tasks than for long and complex ones.

Reduced non-productive work

This is probably the most important benefit of division of labour and goes a long way to explaining why so many highly divided jobs still exist. In large complex tasks the proportion of time spent picking up tools and materials, putting them down again, and generally finding, positioning and searching can be very high indeed. Consider, for example, the unlikely event of one person assembling a whole motor car engine. The task would probably take two or three hours and would involve much bending, searching for parts, positioning and so on. None of these activities actually contributes directly to making the product. They are there because of the way the job has been designed (one person making the whole product). In a complex product like this it could be that around half the person's time is spent on these reaching, positioning, finding types of tasks (called non-productive elements of work) rather than directly making the product. Now consider how a motor car engine is actually made in practice. The total job is probably divided into 20 or 30 separate stages. Each stage will be staffed by a person who carries out only a proportion of the total job. Because the individual operatives are concentrating only on one piece of the job, specialist equipment and materials-handling devices can be devised to help them carry out their job more efficiently. Furthermore, there is relatively little 'finding', 'positioning' and 'reaching' involved in this simplified task. Non-productive work can be considerably reduced perhaps to under 10 per cent. Such improvements in labour efficiency are, or can be, very significant in the costs of the operation.

All these benefits contributed to the wide adoption of division-of-labour principles as industrialization took hold in the developed economies of the early twentieth century. Henry Ford described his use of the principles for the manufacture of the flywheel magneto of the 'Model T' in 1913.

'We had previously assembled the flywheel magneto in the usual method. With one workman doing a complete job he could turn out from 35 to 40 pieces in a nine-hour day, or about 20 minutes to an assembly. What he did alone was then spread into 29 operations; that cut down the assembly time to 13 minutes 10 seconds. Then we raised the height of the line eight inches – this was in 1914 – and cut the time to seven minutes. Further experimenting with the speed that the work should move at cut the time down to five minutes. In short, the result is this; by aid of scientific study one man is now able to do somewhat more than four did only a comparatively few years ago. That line established the efficiency of the method and we now use it everywhere.'[2]

However, it soon became evident that there are also serious drawbacks to highly divided jobs.

1 Monotony

The shorter the task, the more often operators will need to repeat the task. Repeating the same task, for example every thirty seconds, eight hours a day and five days a week, can hardly be called a fulfilling job. As well as any ethical objections to deliberately designing jobs which are unremittingly monotonous, there are other, more obviously practical objections to jobs which induce such boredom. These include the increased likelihood of absenteeism, staff turnover, the increased likelihood of error and even the deliberate sabotage of the job.

2 Physical injury

The continued repetition of a very narrow range of movements, as well as being monotonous, in extreme cases leads to physical injury. The over-use of some parts of the body (especially the arms, hands and wrists) can result in pain and a reduction in physical capability. This is sometimes called repetitive strain injury (RSI), and although the extent of physical injury through repetitive work is a cause of some controversy, the fact that repeated work can, under some conditions, cause injury is largely accepted.

3 Low flexibility

Dividing a task up into many small parts often gives the job design a rigidity which is difficult to change under changing circumstances. For example, if an assembly line has been designed to make one particular product but then has to change to manufacturing a quite different product, the whole line will need redesigning. This will probably involve changing every operator's set of tasks, which can be a long and difficult procedure. Compare this with a situation, for example, where each operator manufactures the whole product. Under these circumstances, changing from making one product to another one would be a relatively straightforward matter.

4 Poor robustness

Highly divided jobs imply materials (or people, or information) passing between several stages. If one of these stages is not working correctly, for example because some equipment is faulty, the whole operation is affected. On the other hand, if each person is performing the whole of the job, any problems will only affect that one person's output. The rest of the operation will carry on producing as normal.

SCIENTIFIC MANAGEMENT

In the last ten years of the nineteenth century and the first twenty years of the twentieth century, a number of (mainly American) management thinkers developed ideas and principles of job and work design which collectively became known as 'scientific management'. The term 'scientific management' became established in 1911 with the publication of the book of the same name by Fredrick Winslow Taylor (in fact this whole approach to job design is sometimes referred to, pejoratively, as 'Taylorism'). In this work he identified what he saw as the basic tenets of scientific management.[3]

● All aspects of work should be investigated on a scientific basis to establish the laws, rules and formulae governing the best methods of working.
● Such an investigative approach to the study of work is necessary to establish what constitutes a 'fair day's work'.
● Workers should be selected, trained and developed methodically to perform their tasks.
● Managers should act as the planners of the work (analysing jobs and standardizing the best method of doing the job) while workers should be responsible for carrying out the jobs to the standards laid down.

- Co-operation should be achieved between management and workers based on the 'maximum prosperity' of both.

Other contributors to the scientific management movement included Gilbreth, Gantt and Bedaux, all working in the United States. From them all, two separate, but related, fields of study emerged. One, *method study*, concentrates on determining the methods and activities which should be included in jobs. The other, *work measurement*, is concerned with measuring the time which should be taken for performing jobs. Together these two fields are often referred to as *work study* (*see* Fig. 9.4). Work measurement is treated in Appendix 2 at the end of the book. Method study is discussed later in this chapter.

The important thing to remember about scientific management is that it is not particularly 'scientific' as such, although it certainly does take an 'investigative' approach to improving operations. Perhaps a better term for it would be 'systematic management'. The various people who were the leaders of the so-called scientific management movement (two of whom, Taylor and Gilbreth, are the best known) were among the first people to investigate systematically how products should be made.

For example, a tale is told of Frank Gilbreth (the founder of method study) addressing a scientific conference with a paper entitled 'The Best Way To Get Dressed in A Morning'. In his presentation he rather bemused the scientific audience by analysing the 'best' way of buttoning up one's waistcoat in a morning. Among his conclusions was that waistcoats should always be buttoned from the bottom upwards, rather than from the top button downwards. This would enable the man getting dressed to straighten his tie in the same motion. Buttoning from the top downwards would mean that the hands would have to be raised again (a wasted motion) in order to straighten the tie. What his scientific audience felt about these conclusions is not on record, but think of this example if you want to understand scientific management and method study in particular. First of all he is quite right. Method study and the other techniques of scientific management may often be without any intellectual or scientific validation, but by and large they do seem to work. At least they provide results within the limited objectives which they wish to address. Second, Gilbreth reached his conclusion by a systematic and critical analysis of what motions were necessary to do the job. Again these are characteristics of scientific management – detailed analysis and painstakingly systematic examination. Third (and possibly most important), the results are relatively trivial. A great deal of effort was put into reaching a conclusion that was unlikely to have any earth-shattering consequences. Indeed, one of the criticisms of scientific management, as developed in the early part of the twentieth century, is that it concentrated on relatively limited, and sometimes trivial, objectives. It certainly is not a strategic approach to operations; nor is this the only criticism of scientific management.

Criticisms of scientific management

As early as 1915 criticisms of the scientific management approach were being voiced.[4] In a submission to the United States Commission on Industrial Relations, scientific management is described as:

- being in 'spirit and essence a cunningly devised speeding up and sweating system';
- intensifying the 'modern tendency towards specialization of the work and the task';

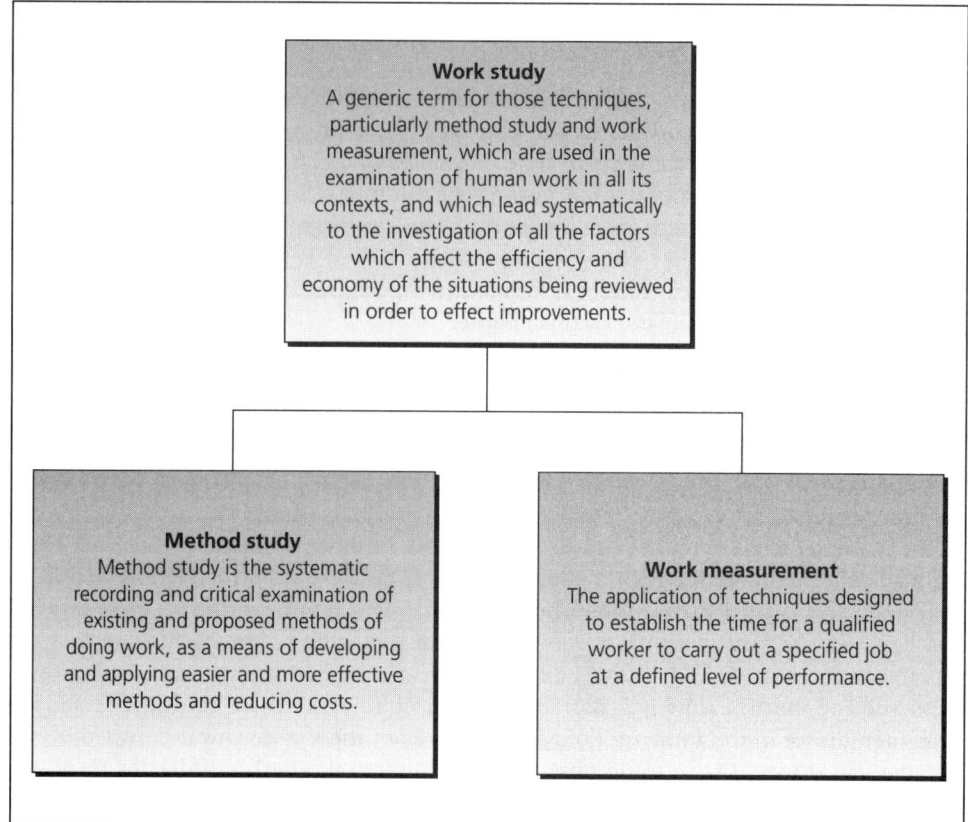

**Figure 9.4
Work study
comprises method
study and work
measurement**

- condemning 'the worker to a monotonous routine';
- putting 'into the hands of employers an immense mass of information and methods that may be used unscrupulously to the detriment of workers';
- tending to 'transfer to the management all the traditional knowledge, the judgement and skills of workers';
- greatly intensifying 'unnecessary managerial dictation and discipline';
- tending to 'emphasize quantity of product at the expense of quality'.

Some of this criticism could perhaps be seen in terms of the 'management *versus* organized labour' organizational power struggle which was prevalent at the time. The two themes evident in this early criticism do warrant closer attention, however. The first is that scientific management inevitably results in standardization of highly divided jobs and thus reinforces the negative effects of excessive division of labour previously mentioned. Second, that scientific management formalizes the separation of the judgemental, planning and skilled tasks, which are done by 'management', from the routine, standardized and low-skill tasks, which are left for 'operators'. Such a separation, at the very least, deprives the majority of staff of an opportunity to contribute in a meaningful way to their jobs (and incidentally deprives the organization of their contribution). Both of these themes in the criticisms of scientific management lead to the same point, that the jobs designed under strict scientific-management principles lead to low motivation among staff, frustration at the lack of control over their work, and alienation from the job.

But before dismissing the whole of the work done by the followers of scientific management it is worth making two points.

● More recent applications of *some* of the principles of scientific management claim to have overcome, at least partly, the objections to it by moving responsibility for the use of its methods and procedures from 'management' to the staff who are being studied. (The box on how scientific management principles were used at the NUMMI plant illustrates this.)

● Some of the methods and techniques of scientific management, as opposed to its philosophy (especially those which come under the general heading of 'method study') can, in practice, prove useful in critically re-examining job designs. It is the practicality of these techniques which possibly explains why they have survived to be influential still in job design almost a century after their inception.

For both these reasons we believe it is important for students of operations management to understand the method study approach to job design.

Method study

Method study is the part of scientific management which makes the most direct contribution to job design. It is more of a systematic approach to job design than a set of techniques. It is defined in Fig. 9.4.

The method study approach involves systematically following six steps.

1 Select the work to be studied.
2 Record all the relevant facts of the present method.
3 Examine those facts critically and in sequence.
4 Develop the most practical, economic and effective method.
5 Install the new method.
6 Maintain the method by periodically checking it in use.

Step 1 – Selecting the work to be studied

Most operations have many hundreds and possibly thousands of discrete jobs and activities which could be subjected to study. The first stage in method study is to select those jobs to be studied which will give the most return on the investment of the time spent studying them. This means it is unlikely that it will be worth studying activities which, for example, may soon be discontinued or are only performed occasionally. On the other hand, the type of jobs which should be studied as a matter of priority are those which, for example, seem to offer the greatest scope for improvement, or which are causing bottle-necks, delays, or problems in the operation.

NUMMI – NEW UNITED MOTOR MANUFACTURING[5]

In practically all parts of the world, Japanese motor manufacturers are producing their cars to rigorously high standards of quality and cost by using production methods similar to those developed in Japan. One of the most remarkable of these Japanese 'implants' is the Toyota plant in Freemont, California. The plant is in fact a joint venture between General Motors (GM) and Toyota using a plant which GM had previously closed in 1982. The reasons for GM closing this particular plant were not difficult to understand. Through the '70s and early '80s the quality of products produced in the Freemont plant was extremely poor, even by the relatively low standards of the time. Productivity was among the lowest of any GM plant in the United States, absenteeism was running at around 20 per cent of the workforce, labour relations in the plant were such that it had earned a national reputation for militancy and wild-cat strikes, and alcohol and drug abuse was a problem both inside the plant and out.

Soon after GM had closed the plant, it began discussions with Toyota about the possibility of a joint venture. Agreement was reached in 1983 to produce a Japanese-designed car, sold under the GM name but manufactured using Toyota's methods of production. The NUMMI plant, as it was now called, was formally opened in 1984. Over the next two years the plant built up production levels, progressively hiring more workers, about 85 per cent of whom had worked in the plant before GM had closed it; several came from the old union hierarchy. The first to be recruited were the team leaders, 450 of whom, together with the entire NUMMI management team, took part in a three-week training programme in Japan. Those trained then played a part in organizing and training the new workers.

The performance of the NUMMI plant could hardly have contrasted more with that of the old GM-run factory. Even though the workforce was largely the same, by the end of 1986 the plant's productivity was more than twice as high as when it was run by GM, and higher than any other GM factory. Indeed productivity was almost as high as Toyota's Takoaka plant in Japan, in spite of the fact that NUMMI's workforce was new to Toyota's production methods and, on average, ten years older. Quality also improved dramatically. Audits showed that quality levels were almost as high as Takoaka's and certainly higher than any other GM plant. Absenteeism had dropped from over 20 per cent in the old GM-run plant to between 3 and 4 per cent. Industrial relations had also improved very significantly. Such improved levels of performance attracted increased investment, both in new manufacturing technology and new products.

Many reasons for the success of the NUMMI plant have been put forward. These include clearer organizational goals, a selective approach to recruiting those employees who had been employed previously in the plant, the move towards single status and dress codes for everyone in the factory, even the pride of working on an intrinsically better designed product. However, what is notable is that the new plant and its management did not abandon the techniques of scientific management which the previous plant's regime had supposedly used. The philosophy of job standardization was still rigorously applied, if anything more rigorously than in the past. Every job in the plant is carefully analysed using method study principles to achieve maximum efficiency and quality. Jobs are timed, using stop watches, and the detail of jobs questioned critically.

Yet there is a major difference between the way the old GM-run plant approached scientific management job design and the way it happens under the NUMMI philosophy. Whereas before, the company's industrial engineers were in charge of applying method study techniques, now it is the operators (or team members as they are called) themselves who perform the analysis of their own jobs. Team members time each other, using stop watches, and analyse the sequence of tasks in each job. They look for alternative ways of doing the job which improve safety and efficiency and can be sustained at a reasonable pace throughout the day. Each team will then take its improved job proposals and compare them with those developed by the comparable team doing the same job on a different shift. The resulting new job specification is then recorded and becomes the standard work definition for all staff performing that job.

NUMMI's claim is that the standardization of tasks results in less variability in task performance, which has in turn led to several further benefits:

● Safety and work-related stress injuries improve because potentially dangerous or harmful elements have been removed from the job.
● Productivity improves because wasted elements of the job have been eliminated.
● Quality standards improve because potential 'fail points' in the job have been analysed out.
● Flexibility improves and job rotation is easier because standards are clearer and all staff understand the intrinsic structure of their jobs.

One team leader compared the way in which the industrial engineers in the old plant had designed jobs with the way it was done under the NUMMI regime:

'I don't think the industrial engineers were dumb. They were just ignorant. Anyone can watch someone else doing a job and come up with improvement suggestions ... and it's even easier to come up with the ideal procedure if you don't even bother to watch the worker at work, but just do it from your office ... almost anything can look good that way. Even when we do our own analysis in our teams some of the silliest ideas can slip through before we actually try them out. ... there's a lot of things that enter into a good job design ... the person actually doing the job is the only one who can see all factors.' ■

Step 2 – Recording the present method

There are many different recording techniques used in method study. Most of them:

● record the sequence of activities in the job;
● record the time interrelationship of the activities in the job; or,
● record the path of movement of some part of the job.

Perhaps the most commonly used recording technique in method study is the flow process chart which was discussed in Chapter 5 and is extended in Appendix 3 at the end of the book.

Note that we are here recording the present method of doing the job. It may seem strange to devote so much time and effort to recording what is currently happening when, after all, the objective of method study is to devise a better method. The rationale for this is first of all that recording the present method can give a far greater insight into the job itself, and this can lead to new ways of doing it. Second, recording the present method is a good starting point from which to evaluate critically and therefore improve the method. In this last point the assumption is that it is easier to improve the method by starting from the current method and then criticizing it in detail rather than starting with a 'blank sheet of paper'.

There are other types of process chart which can be used to record the sequence of activities in a job. There are also many other recording techniques used in method study. Appendix 3 at the end of the book describes the more important of these in a little more detail.

Step 3 – Examining the facts

This is probably the most important stage in method study and the idea here is to examine the current method thoroughly and critically. This is often done by using the so-called 'questioning technique'. This technique attempts to expose the reasons behind existing methods in order to detect weaknesses in their rationale and therefore develop alternative methods.

Questions are asked regarding:

● *the purpose of each element.*
   What is done?
   Why is it done?
   What else could be done?
   What should be done?
● *the place in which each element is done.*
   Where is it done?
   Why is it done there?
   Where else could it be done?
   Where should it be done?

This may suggest a combination of certain activities or operations.

● *the sequence in which the elements are done.*
   When is it done?
   Why is it done then?
   When should it be done?

This may suggest a change in the sequence of the operation.

● *the person who does the element.*
   Who does it?
   Why does that person do it?
   Who else could do it?
   Who should do it?

This may suggest a combination and/or change in sequence.

- *the means by which each element is done.*
    How is it done?
    Why is it done in that way?
    How else could it be done?
    How should it be done?

Following this approach may appear somewhat detailed and tedious, yet it is fundamental to the method study philosophy – everything must be critically examined. Understanding the natural tendency to be less than rigorous at this stage, some organizations use pro forma questionnaires, asking each of these questions and leaving space for formal replies and/or justifications, which the job designer is required to complete.

Step 4 – Developing a new method

The previous critical examination of current methods has by this stage probably indicated some changes and improvements. This stage involves taking these ideas further in an attempt to:

- eliminate parts of the activity altogether;
- combine elements together;
- change the sequence of events so as to improve the efficiency of the job; or
- simplify the activity to reduce the work content.

A useful aid during this process is a checklist such as the 'Revised Principles of Motion Economy'. Table 9.1 illustrates these.

Steps 5 and 6 – Install the new method and regularly maintain it

The method study approach to the installation of new work practices is, by modern standards, rather naïve. It concentrates largely on 'project managing' the installation process (*see* Chapter 16 for a full description of project management) rather than examining the reactions of the staff whose jobs and methods are being affected. The method study approach also emphasizes the need to monitor regularly the effectiveness of job designs after they have been installed. However, although this was not intended as some kind of 'continuous improvement' philosophy (rather it was to make sure that conditions had not changed to make the method anything less than optimal for its purpose), it can be used as an opportunity to rethink and improve methods on a continuous basis.

Table 9.1 The principles of motion economy

Using the human body the way it works best	1	Work should be arranged so that a natural rhythm can become automatic.
	2	Consider the symmetry of the body, for example the motions of the arms should be: ● simultaneous, and ● opposite and symmetrical.
	3	The full capabilities of the human body should be employed. For example: ● Neither hand should ever be idle. ● Work should be distributed to parts of the body in line with their ability. ● The safe 'design limits' of the body should be observed.
	4	Arms and hands as weights are subject to the physical laws, and energy should be conserved. For example: ● Momentum should work for the body and not against it. ● The smooth, continuous arc of ballistic motions is most efficient. ● The distance of movements should be minimized.
	5	Tasks should be simplified. For example: ● Eye contacts should be few and grouped together. ● Unnecessary actions, delays, and idle time should be eliminated. ● The degree of required precision and control should be minimized. ● The number of individual motions should be minimized along with the number of muscle groups involved.
Arranging the workplace to assist performance	1	There should be a defined place for all tools and materials.
	2	Tools, materials, and controls should be located close to the point of use.
	3	Tools, materials, and controls should be located to permit the best sequence and path of motions.
	4	The workplace should be fitted both to the tasks and to human capabilities.
Using mechanical devices to reduce human effort	1	Vices and clamps should hold the work precisely where needed.
	2	Guides should assist in positioning the work without close operator attention.
	3	Controls and foot-operated devices can relieve the hands of work.
	4	Mechanical devices can multiply human abilities.
	5	Mechanical systems should be fitted to human use.

Source: Adapted from Barnes, Frank C. (1938) 'Principles of Motion Economy: Revisited, Reviewed, and Restored', *Proceedings of the Southern Management Association Annual Meeting* (Atlanta, GA 1983), p 298.

METHOD STUDY AT INTEL

Although dating from the scientific management period, method study has undergone something of a revival in the last few years. In non-manufacturing operations especially, the method study approach of systematically challenging methods of work is proving an effective approach to improvement. For example, Fig. 9.5 shows the flow process chart which Intel Corporation, the computer chip company, drew to describe its method of processing expense reports (claims forms).

Flow process chart

Activity	Processing expense reports	Location	Accounts Dept

	Description of element	●	➡	D	■	▼
1	Report arrives at accounts payable desk					
2	Wait for processing					
3	Check expenses report					
4	Stamp and date report					
5	Send cash to receipt desk					
6	Wait for processing					
7	Check to see if advance payment has been made					
8	Send to accounts receivable desk					
9	Wait for processing					
10	Check employee's past account					
11	Send to accounts payable desk					
12	Attach payment voucher to report					
13	Log report					
14	Check items against company guidelines					
15	Wait for batching					
16	Collect reports into batch					
17	Batch goes to audit desk					
18	Wait for processing					
19	Batch of reports logged					
20	Check payment vouchers					
21	Reports go to batch control					
22	Control number applied to batch					
23	Copies of reports to filing					
24	Reports filed					
25	Copies of payment voucher to keyboard					
26	Cheque					

Symbol	Element	No.
●	Operation	7
➡	Transport	8
D	Delay	5
■	Inspection	5
▼	Storage	1

Figure 9.5 The flow process chart for processing expense reports at Intel

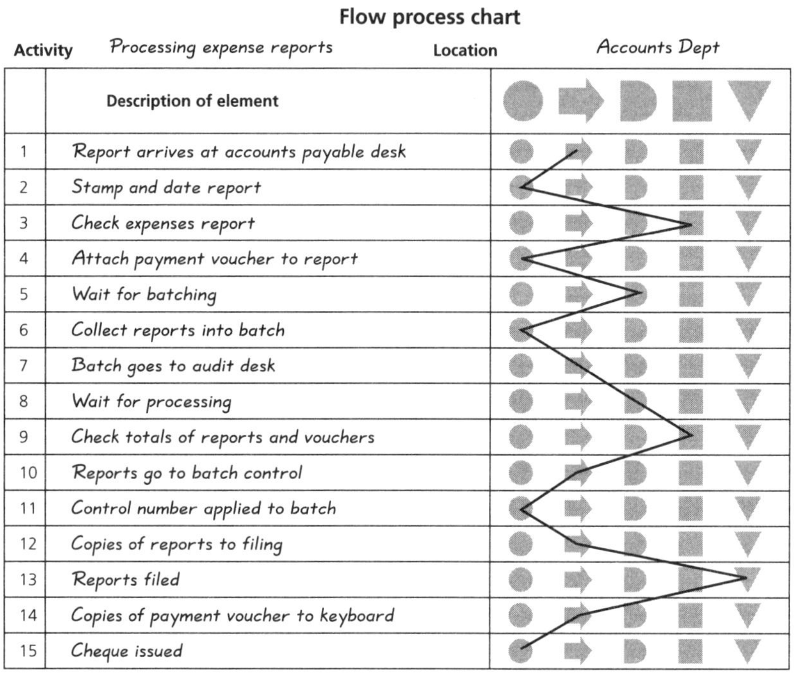

Flow process chart

Activity	Processing expense reports		Location	Accounts Dept				
	Description of element			●	➡	◗	■	▼
1	Report arrives at accounts payable desk			●	➡	◗	■	▼
2	Stamp and date report			●	➡	◗	■	▼
3	Check expenses report			●	➡	◗	■	▼
4	Attach payment voucher to report			●	➡	◗	■	▼
5	Wait for batching			●	➡	◗	■	▼
6	Collect reports into batch			●	➡	◗	■	▼
7	Batch goes to audit desk			●	➡	◗	■	▼
8	Wait for processing			●	➡	◗	■	▼
9	Check totals of reports and vouchers			●	➡	◗	■	▼
10	Reports go to batch control			●	➡	◗	■	▼
11	Control number applied to batch			●	➡	◗	■	▼
12	Copies of reports to filing			●	➡	◗	■	▼
13	Reports filed			●	➡	◗	■	▼
14	Copies of payment voucher to keyboard			●	➡	◗	■	▼
15	Cheque issued			●	➡	◗	■	▼

Symbol	Element	No.	Total time
●	Operation	5	
➡	Transport	5	
◗	Delay	2	
■	Inspection	2	
▼	Storage	1	

Figure 9.6 The flow process chart for processing expense reports at Intel after critical analysis

After critically examining its existing method of processing these reports the company developed a new method which cut the number of elements from 26 down to 15 (*see* Fig. 9.6). The accounts payable desk's activities were combined with the cash-receipt's activities of checking employees' past expense accounts (elements 8, 10 and 11) which also eliminated elements 5 and 7. After consideration, it was decided to eliminate the activity of checking items against company guidelines, because it seemed '... *more trouble than it was worth*'. Also logging the batches was deemed unnecessary. All this combination and elimination of activities has the effect of removing several 'delays' from the process. The end result was a much simplified process which reduced the staff time needed to do the job by 28 per cent and considerably speeded up the whole process. ∎

ERGONOMICS

Ergonomics is concerned primarily with the physiological aspects of job design: that is, with the human body and how it fits into its surroundings. This involves two aspects which are illustrated in Fig. 9.7. First of all ergonomics is concerned with how the person interfaces with the physical aspect of his or her workplace, where the 'workplace' includes tables, chairs, desks, machines, computers and so on. Second, it involves how a person interfaces with the environmental conditions prevalent in his or her immediate working area. By this we mean the ambient conditions in which the person works, for example the temperature, lighting, noise environment and so on. Ergonomics is the term usually adopted in most parts of the world; however, it is sometimes referred to as 'human factors engineering' or just 'human factors'.

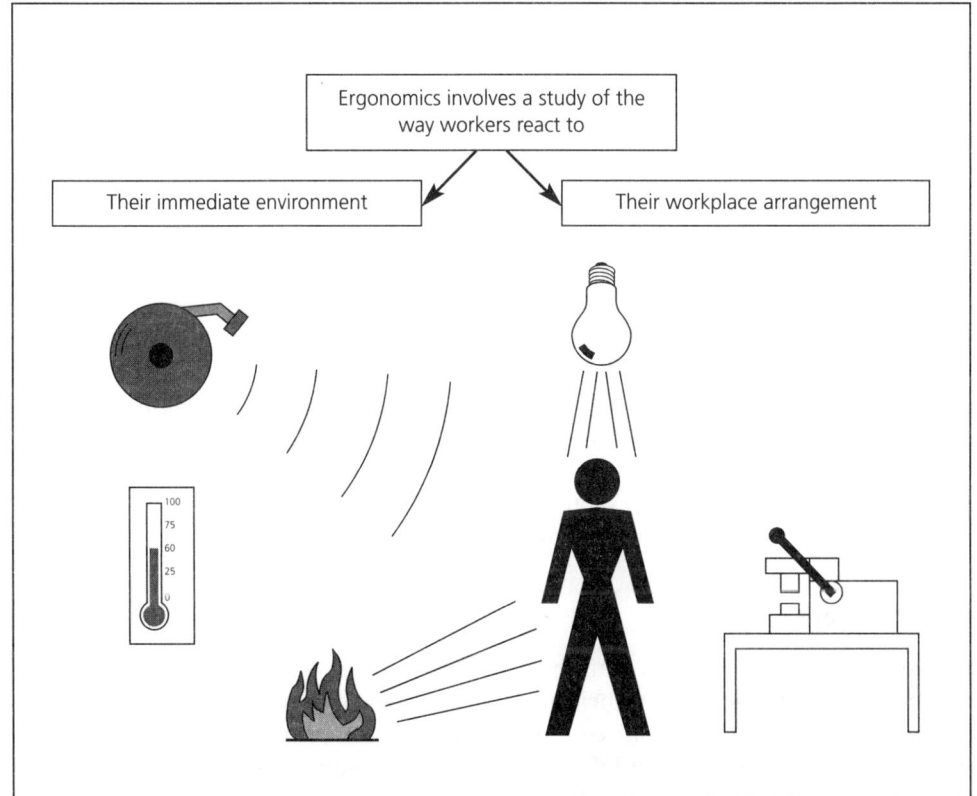

Figure 9.7
Ergonomics treats the physiological aspects of the way people fit their jobs

Both of these aspects are linked by two common ideas which permeate the ergonomics approach to job design.

● The first idea is that there must be a fit between people and the jobs they do. To achieve this fit there are only two alternatives. Either the job can be made to fit the people who are doing it, or, alternatively, the people can be made (or perhaps less radically, recruited) to fit the job. Ergonomics addresses the former alternative.

● The second theme which runs through ergonomics is that of data collection. We said earlier that scientific management was to some extent a misnomer, but the same criticism cannot be made of ergonomics. It really does attempt to take a 'scientific' approach to job design insomuch as it collects data to indicate how people react under different job design conditions and tries to find the best set of conditions for comfort and performance.

Ergonomic workplace design

Within the workplaces of a wide variety of operations, new demands, technologies and work methods have refocused attention on the need to consider the way people interface with the physical parts of their jobs. This is especially noticeable in office and information-related work because of the predominance of computer, keyboard and screen-based 'interfaces'.

Understanding how workplaces affect performance, fatigue, physical strain and injury are all part of the ergonomics approach to job design.

It is important to understand that, as individuals, we all vary in our size and capabilities. It is therefore not the average capability of people in which ergonomists are particularly interested but the range of capabilities – usually expressed in percentile terms. Figure 9.8 illustrates this idea. This shows the idea of size (in this case height) variation. Only 5 per cent of the population are smaller than the person on the extreme left (5th percentile), whereas 95 per cent of the population are smaller than the person on the extreme right (95th percentile). When this principle is applied to other dimensions of the body, for example arm length, it can be used to design work areas. Figure 9.8 shows the normal and maximum work areas derived from anthropometric data. It would be inadvisable, for example, to place frequently used components or tools outside the maximum work area derived from the 5th percentile dimensions of human reach.

Neurological aspects

Ergonomics is also concerned with the way in which people's sensory capabilities are engaged when interfacing with their workplaces. These so-called neurological aspects of job design include the sight, feel, sound and perhaps even smell, which the workplace displays in order to give information to an operator, and the way in which an operator can transmit instructions back to the workplace. The part of the 'workplace' in which we are interested is usually some type of process technology or machine, and the interface between the operator and machine involves *displays* of information from the machine to operator and the manipulation of *controls* by the operator in communicating to the machine. Figure 9.9 illustrates this 'person–machine loop'.

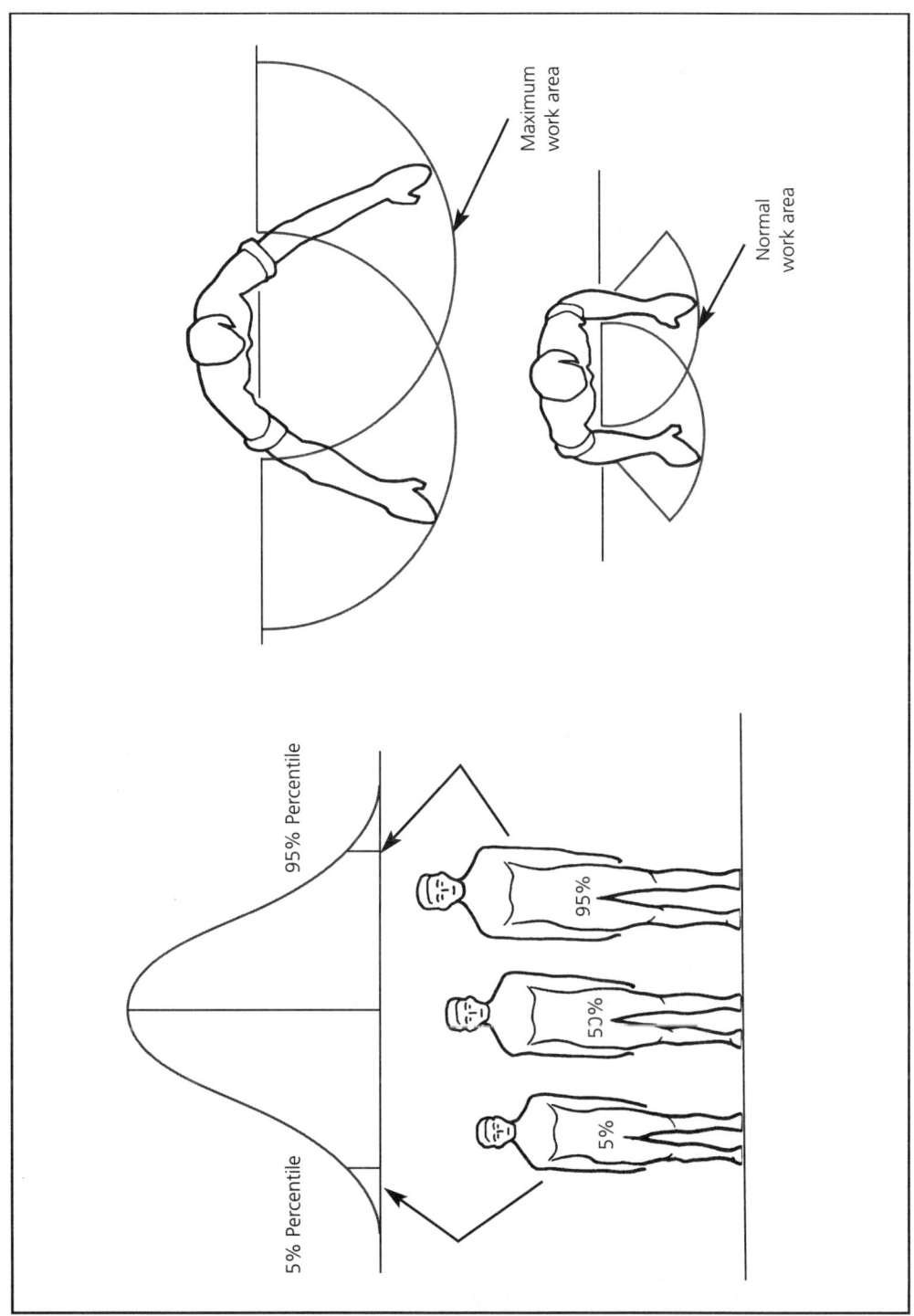

Figure 9.8 The use of anthropometric data in job design

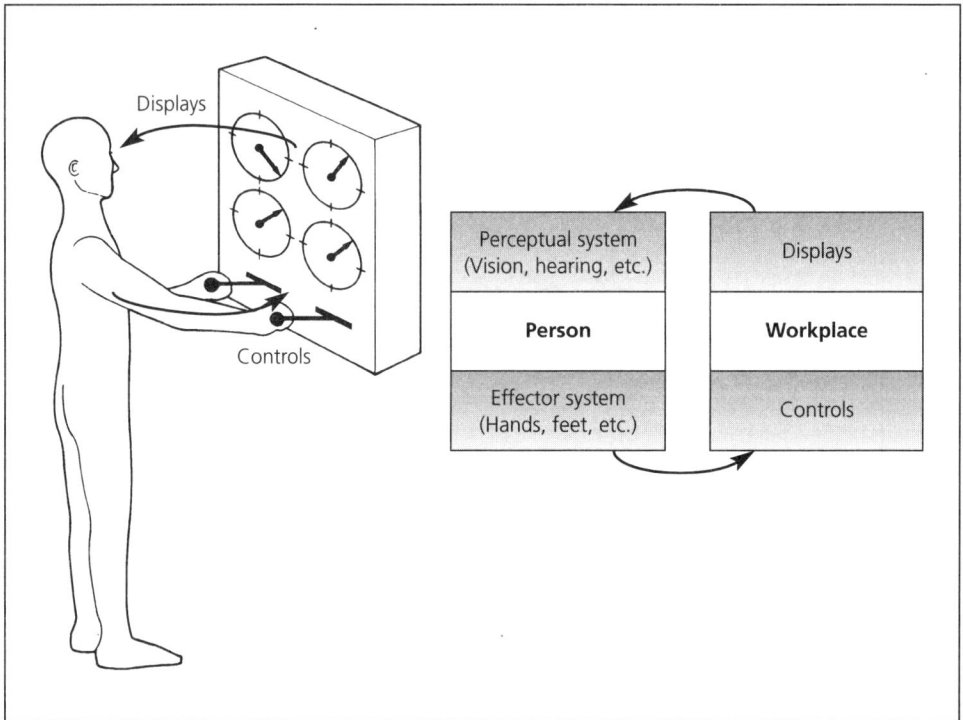

**Figure 9.9
The 'person–
workplace' loop**

Ergonomic environmental design

The immediate environment in which jobs take place can influence the way they are performed. Working conditions which are too hot or too cold, insufficiently illuminated or glaringly bright, excessively noisy or irritatingly silent, will all influence the way jobs are carried out. Ergonomics is also concerned with this aspect of job design. Perhaps one point to note is the boost which this aspect of ergonomics received from the introduction of occupational health and safety legislation. The Occupational Health and Safety Act in South Africa is an example of a piece of legislation which controls environmental conditions in workplaces. A thorough understanding of this aspect of ergonomics is necessary to work within the guidelines of this legislation.

Working temperature

Predicting the reactions of individuals to working temperature is not straightforward. Individuals vary in the way their performance and comfort vary with temperature. Furthermore, most of us judging 'temperature' will also be influenced by other factors such as humidity and air movement. Nevertheless, some general points regarding working temperatures provide guidance to job designers.[6]

● Comfortable temperature range will depend on the type of work being carried out – lighter work requiring higher temperatures than heavier work.

● The effectiveness of people at performing vigilance tasks reduces at temperatures above about 29°C; the equivalent temperature for people performing light manual tasks is a little lower.

● The chances of accidents occurring increase at temperatures which are above or below the comfortable range for the work involved.

Illumination levels

The intensity of lighting required to perform any job satisfactorily will depend on the nature of the job. Some jobs which involve extremely delicate and precise movement, surgery for example, require very high levels of illumination. Other, less delicate, jobs do not require such high levels. Table 9.2 shows the recommended illumination levels (measured in lux) for a range of activities.

Table 9.2 Examples of recommended lighting levels for various activities[7]

Activity	Illuminance (lx)
Normal activities in the home, general lighting	50
Furnace rooms in glass factory	150
General office work	500
Motor vehicle assembly	500
Proofreading	750
Colour matching in paint factory	1 000
Electronic assembly	1 000
Close inspection of knitwear	1 500
Engineering testing inspection using small instruments	3 000
Watchmaking and fine jewellery manufacture	3 000
Surgery, local lighting	10 000–50 000

Noise levels

The damaging effects of excessive noise levels are perhaps easier to understand than some other environmental factors. Noise-induced hearing loss is a well documented consequence of working environments where noise is not kept below safe limits. The noise levels of various activities are shown in Table 9.3. When reading this list bear in mind that the recommended (and often legal) maximum noise level to which people can be subjected over the working day is 90 decibels (dB) in South Africa (although in some parts of the world the legal level is lower than this). Also bear in mind that the decibels unit of noise is based on a logarithmic scale, which means that noise intensity doubles about every 3 dB.

In addition to the damaging effects of high levels of noise, it can also affect work performance at far lower levels – for example on tasks requiring attention and judgement:[8]

● Intermittent and unpredictable noises are more disruptive than steady-state noise at the same level.

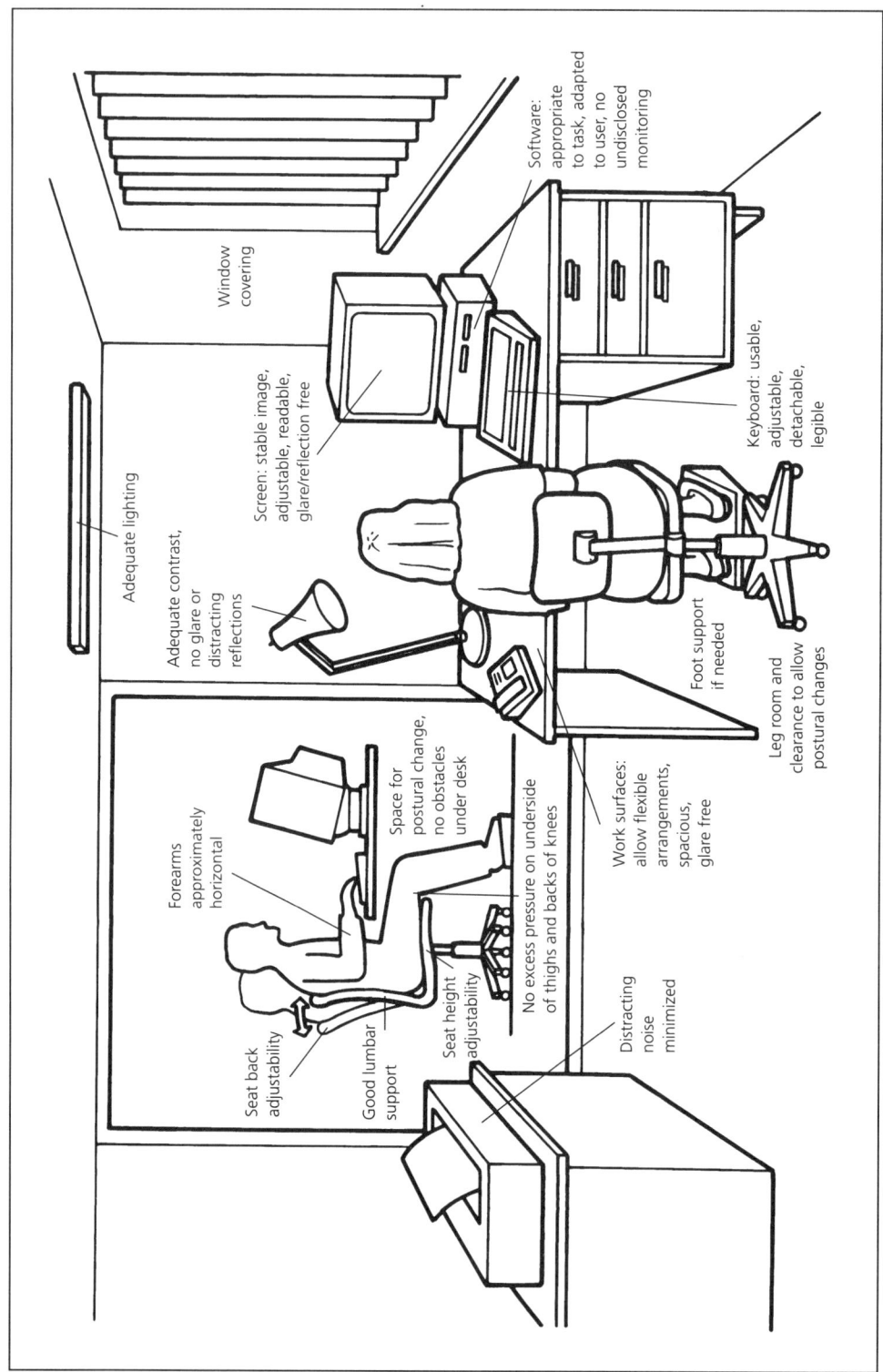

Figure 9.10 Ergonomics in the office environment

- High-frequency noise (above about 2000 Hz) usually produces more interference with performance than low-frequency noise.
- Noise is more likely to affect the error rate (quality) of work rather than the rate of working.

Table 9.3 Noise levels for various activities

Noise	Decibels (dB)
Quiet speech	40
Light traffic at 25 metres	50
Large busy office	60
Busy street heavy traffic	70
Pneumatic drill at 20 metres	80
Textile factory	90
Circular saw – close work	100
Riveting machine – close work	110
Jet aircraft taking off at 100 metres	120

Ergonomics in the office

As the number of people working in offices (or office-like workplaces) has increased, ergonomic principles have been applied increasingly to this type of work. At the same time, legislation has been moving to cover office technology such as computer screens and keyboards. For example, European Union directives on working with display screen equipment require organizations to:[9]

- assess all workstations to reduce the risks inherent in their use;
- make sure that all workstations meet specific requirements;
- plan work times to include breaks and changes in activity;
- provide information and training for users;
- test the eyesight of users if they request it.

Figure 9.10 illustrates some of the ergonomic factors which should be taken in account when designing office jobs.

BEHAVIOURAL APPROACHES TO JOB DESIGN

Chronologically, the next major influence on job design practice came in the 1960s and 1970s, although its roots precede that time. This was what one might call (for the want of a better term) the 'behavioural' approach to job design. The ideas and concepts concerning motivation theory contributed to the behavioural approach to job design. It was argued that the jobs which were designed purely on division of labour, scientific management, or even purely ergonomic principles, often alienated the people performing the jobs. What was needed was an approach to job design which took into account the need for people to gain something positive out of their work. Jobs designed to fulfil people's needs for self-esteem and personal development would therefore not only be more satisfying but also more motivating in the sense of encouraging people to contribute more of their skills and talents. This would achieve two important objectives of job design. First, it provides jobs which have an intrinsically higher quality of working life – an ethically desirable end in itself. Second, because of the higher levels of motivation it engenders, it is instrumental in achieving better performance for the operation, both in terms of the quality and the quantity of output.[10]

In fact the behavioural approach does represent a major shift in how job design was seen as a process. *See* Fig. 9.11.

Whereas previous approaches to job design assumed a more or less direct connection between the characteristics of the job and people's performance at that job, the behavioural approach to job design implicitly adopted a different model. This assumed an intervening variable of the person's motivation for performing the job. Now the approach to job design would involve two stages: first, exploring how the various characteristics of the job affect people's motivation; second, exploring how individuals' motivation towards the job affect their performance at that job. Generally, it was held that, to reduce alienation and increase personal motivation and commitment, the job should:

● allow people to feel personally responsible for an identifiable and meaningful portion of the work;
● provide a set of tasks which are intrinsically meaningful or worthwhile;
● provide feedback about performance effectiveness.

Typical of the models which underlie this approach to job design is that by Hackman and Oldham shown in Fig. 9.12.[11] Here a number of 'techniques' of job design are recommended in order to affect particular core 'characteristics' of the job. These core characteristics of the job are held to influence various positive 'mental states' towards the job. In turn these are assumed to give certain performance outcomes.

In Fig. 9.12 some of the 'techniques' (which Hackman and Oldham originally called 'implementing concepts') need a little further explanation.

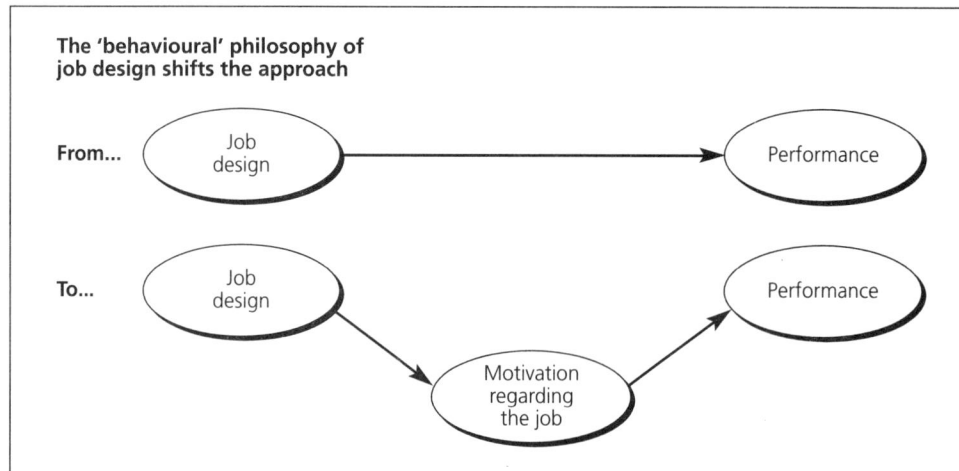

Figure 9.11
The concept of the individual's attitude to the job as an intervening variable

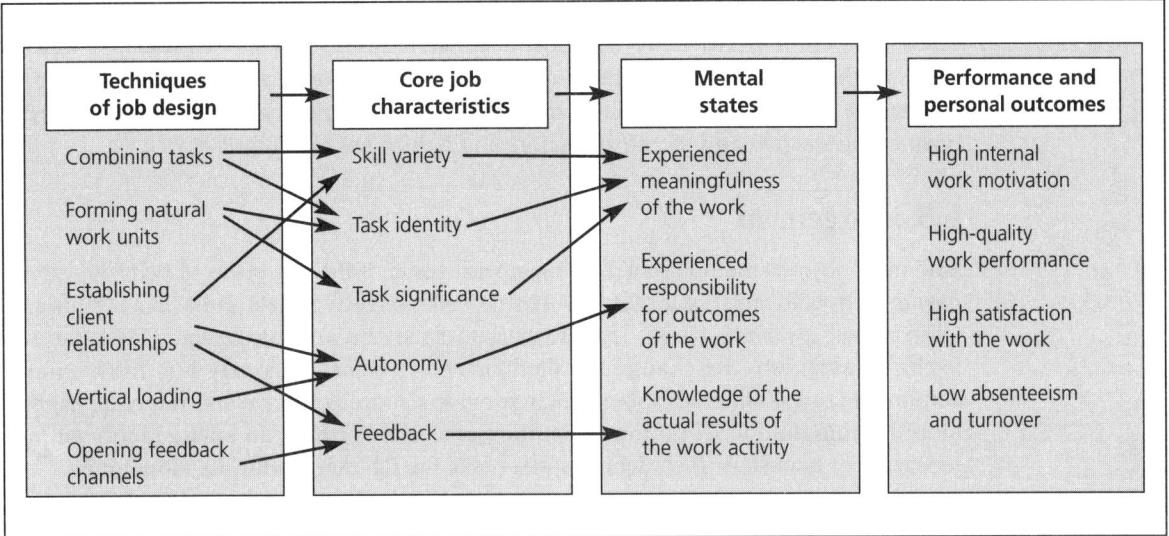

Figure 9.12 A typical 'behaviour' job design model

● Combining tasks means increasing the number of separate elements or activities allocated to individuals.
● Forming natural work units means putting together activities which make a coherent (preferably also a continuing) whole.
● Establishing client relationships means that staff make contact with their internal customers (*see* Chapter 1) directly rather than exclusively through their supervisors.
● Vertical loading means including 'indirect' activities (such as the maintenance, scheduling and general management of the job) in the tasks allocated to the individual.
● Opening feedback channels means ensuring that not only internal customers feedack perceptions of performance directly to staff, but also that they are provided with information regarding their overall performance.

Hackman and Oldham also indicate how these techniques of job design shape the core characteristics of the resulting job, and further, how the core characteristics influence the 'mental states' of the person doing the job. By 'mental states' they mean the attitude of individuals towards their jobs – specifically, how meaningful they find the job, how much responsibility and control they feel they have over the way the job is done, and how much they understand about the results of their efforts. High levels of all these mental states, it is held, positively influence people's performance at their job in terms of their motivation, quality of work, satisfaction with their work, turnover and absenteeism.

Job rotation

If increasing the number of related tasks in the job is constrained in some way, for example by the technology of the process, one approach may be to rotate jobs. This means moving individuals periodically between different sets of tasks to provide some variety in their activities. When successful, job rotation can increase skill flexibility and make a small contribution to reducing monotony. However, it is not viewed as universally beneficial either by management, because it can disrupt the smooth flow of work, or by the people performing the jobs, because it can interfere with their rhythm of work. In the assembly line example the original ten-station line could be retained and a schedule of job rotation agreed which involved each person moving to a different position on the line and therefore performing a different set of tasks.

Job enlargement

The most obvious method of achieving at least some of the objectives of behavioural job design is by allocating a larger number of tasks to individuals (what Hackman and Oldham call *combining* tasks). If these extra tasks are broadly of the same type as those in the original job, the change is called *job enlargement*. This may not involve more demanding or fulfilling tasks, but it may provide a more complete and therefore slightly more meaningful job. If nothing else, the person performing an enlarged job will not repeat his or herself as often, which could make the job marginally less monotonous.

Job enrichment

Job enrichment, like job enlargement, increases the number of tasks which are allocated to jobs. However, it means allocating extra tasks which involve more decision making, greater autonomy and therefore greater control over the job.

EMPOWERMENT

The last phase in any sequence of developments is always likely to be controversial. We do not have the clarity of hindsight to judge whether a popular idea was either a temporary 'blip' or a genuine trend. With this in mind the latest trend is (arguably) the move towards the *empowerment* of people in their jobs. Empowerment is an extension of the *autonomy* job characteristic prominent in the behavioural approach to job design.

Empowerment, however, is usually taken to mean more than autonomy. Whereas autonomy means giving staff the *ability* to change how they do their jobs, empowerment means giving staff the *authority* to make changes to the job itself as well as how it is performed. This can be designed into jobs to different degrees: 'suggestion involvement', 'job involvement', or 'high involvement'.[12]

● *Suggestion involvement* is not really empowerment in its true form but does 'empower' staff to contribute their suggestions for how the operation might be improved. However, staff do not have the autonomy to implement changes to their jobs. High-volume operations, such as fast-food restaurants or the NUMMI car plant in the earlier box, may choose not to dilute their highly standardized task methods, yet they do want staff to be involved in how these methods are implemented. 'Empowerment' in such cases may be limited to 'suggestion involvement'.
● *Job involvement* goes much further and empowers staff to redesign their jobs. However, again there must be some limits on the way each individual makes changes which could impact on other staff and on the performance of the operations as a

"I arrived at Hong Kong airport without my case. Thanks to the foresight of the Marriott concierge, it managed to arrive without me. It was just as my flight was about to depart that I realised I'd left my briefcase by the reception desk when I checked out. I would have been lost without it and rang the hotel in the vain hope that they could help. To my delight, the concierge informed me that my case had been noticed and sent after me in another cab. His initiative saved the day. I understand that this kind of conscientiousness on behalf of their guests is typical of all Marriott staff. They call it Empowerment. I call it remarkable.

ALWAYS IN THE RIGHT PLACE AT THE RIGHT TIME. **Marriott.**

HOTELS · RESORTS · SUITES

Over 240 locations worldwide for reservations call on 0800 - 22 12 22 or contact your travel agent

Figure 9.13 Marriott sees empowerment as providing a competitive advantage.

whole. Staff are often formed into design teams to make sure that redesigned jobs fit together in a way which meets operational objectives, while at the operational level staff are empowered to make decisions which they believe will be in the interests of the organization. Figure 9.13 shows how one company promoted its services by stressing the way its staff are empowered to solve problems and how that can benefit its customers. The implication of this is that the managerial mechanisms which control and support the job must be adapted to reflect empowered staff. For example, training and development must give the problem-solving skills necessary for staff to improve their operations. Perhaps more importantly, managers need to take on *facilitating* rather than *controlling* roles.

● *High involvement* means including all staff in the strategic direction and performance of the whole organization. Clearly this is the most radical type of empowerment and there are few examples. However, the degree to which individual staff of an operation contribute towards, and take responsibility for, overall strategy can be seen as a variable of job design which, for some operations, could be beneficial. For example, a professional service such as a group of consulting engineers (who design large engineering projects) might very well move in this direction. It may be partly to motivate all their staff. It may be partly to ensure that the operation can capture everyone's potentially useful ideas.

CONTROL VERSUS COMMITMENT

This chapter has reviewed the main influences on job design as it is practised in operations. It is important to stress again that, although we have presented them in the chronological order of their emergence, the various approaches have not replaced each other. The principles of division of labour are still influential today and take their place along with ideas concerning empowerment and all the other approaches. However, there are clear differences between the approaches, both in the methods and 'techniques' which they adopt to design jobs and, more importantly, in their underlying aims and philosophies. The most obvious difference between approaches is the relative emphasis they place on the need for management to *control* the job, and the desire to engage the *commitment* of the staff performing the job.

Figure 9.14 shows how the balance between control and commitment has moved with the emergence of each approach to job design. Division of labour is totally concerned with controlling the work done by staff. Management control over the job allows it to be reduced, routinized and thereby made more efficient. Scientific management in its original form might also be regarded as concerned exclusively with controlling the way the job is performed. Again, it is argued that control is necessary to find the 'best' method of doing the job. However, the recent developments in method study could be seen as moving the use of scientific management techniques more into the hands of staff, and thereby increasing its concern with staff commitment. Ergonomics, by being concerned with the way staff respond to physical and environmental conditions, can be considered to be, at least partly, attempting to influence their commitment. However, ergonomics is concerned more with staff's physiological responses as much as, if not more than, their psychological responses. Behavioural approaches to job design focus far more on the commitment of staff to their jobs, and indeed place staff engagement and motivation as the central theme of job design. Finally, empowerment not only highlights the commitment of staff but also transfers to them at least part of the control of their jobs. Paradoxically, this moves the emphasis back to control, but now it is individual or group control rather than 'managerial' control.

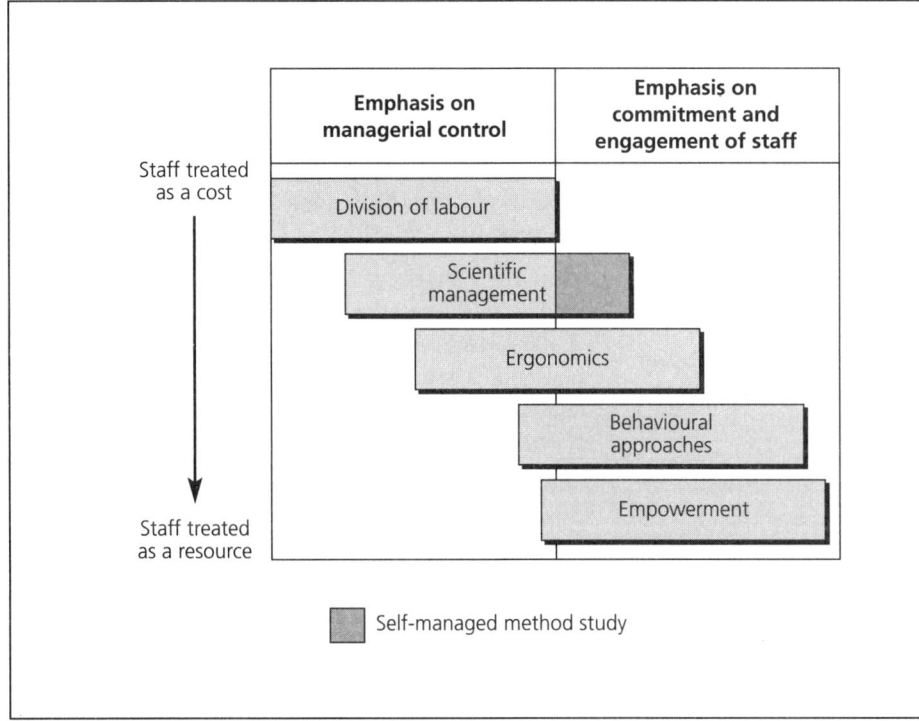

**Figure 9.14
The different approaches to job design: each implies a different balance between control and commitment**

Neil Cumming, Nampak Polyfoil

Nampak – one of the largest packaging companies in the world, with the distinction of being among the most diversified – has designed a management system for its specific needs.

'When you have a business like ours, with over 120 operations around the country and 18 different operating divisions, then you need to have a management structure and a workplace organization that will specifically accommodate it,' says Polyfoil's Chief Executive Officer, Neil Cumming.

Polyfoil, a division of Nampak, is the largest manufacturer in South Africa of plastic counter bags and check-out bags for retailers. One bright spot for Polyfoil is the export market, where, says Neil, the company has done 'excellent work' in penetrating overseas markets – primarily in the UK, Europe and the Middle East. However, Neil notes that the company is facing strong competition, especially on price, from converters in the Far East. As Neil says:

'To remain a competitive concern and become a "world beater" we realized the urgent necessity to obtain and develop people who are motivated, skilled and feel part of the organization. Employers inevitably have to sit down and ask themselves what the new South Africa will mean to them in terms of the structures, styles, and cultures of the people engaged in the workplace. You then have to consider what you must do internally to align yourself to this new reality. We started building "democratic" structures in the workplace which ▶

333

embrace the training and development of people. The objective is the ultimate restructuring of the factory so employees can deliver a better result, an example of which is the formation of production cells or natural work teams.

'These work teams were given training and a business agenda (failure to do this would have caused burn out, as happens with many "green areas" or "quality circle" type arrangements). An extremely useful business agenda for the first work team was autonomous maintenance (the process of stripping, cleaning, tagging and repairing their machine). The "new" machine was launched with all the rituals of African ceremony (prayers, speeches, toyi-toying, slaughtering of cows, etc.). Thereafter the next teams were set up, following a similar process, until the entire factory, including administration and service departments, had been through this mass mobilization approach. Teams are now responsible for their own performance, the maintenance of their machines, quality, and work scheduling. Foremen, or middle managers, become part of the multidisciplinary teams, examining more complex problems and assisting with coaching, training and troubleshooting. The teams elect their own leaders and effectively the structure is "de-layered". Worker empowerment has been taken a significant step forward.'

This process 'shifts' the factory culture and significantly increases its overall efficiency. In short what has happened is the introduction of a new shop-floor system and a new workplace organization, built on the best of African and international experiences. Neil adds:

'Change management is sometimes like watching a swimming pool being filled with a hosepipe – you know something is happening, but you cannot see it. Essentially what we did was to create a difference. Making visible change happen quickly in a small area of the factory is another work reorganization learning point.' ■

Source: By kind permission of Nampak Polyfoil

SUMMARY

■ Job design involves deciding what tasks to allocate to each person in the organization, and in what sequence to perform them, where to locate the job, who else should be involved in it, how people should interact with their workplace and their immediate work environment, what autonomy to give to staff and what skills to develop in staff.

■ The decisions taken in each of the above areas should attempt to define jobs which have high interest, safety, give a reasonable quality of working life, high productivity, quality and flexibility.

■ There are many influences on job design. Historically, the first of these was the concept of the division of labour. The division of labour involves taking a total task and dividing it into separate parts, each of which can be allocated to a different individual to perform. The advantages of highly divided jobs are largely concerned with reducing costs, especially through the reduction of non-productive work. However, highly divided jobs are monotonous and, in their extreme form, contribute to physical injury.

■ Scientific management took some of the ideas of the division of labour but applied them more systematically across a wide range of industrial activities. The area of work study is that most often associated with the scientific management principles. Work study is conventionally divided up into method study (the way in which methods and activities within jobs are determined) and work measurement (concerned with measuring the time which should be taken for performing jobs). Although scientific management in its extreme form has fallen from favour, newer forms in which staff within an operation themselves perform method study analyses have been successfully applied more recently.

■ The scientific management approach which is perhaps most widespread is that of method study. Method study is a systematic approach to examining the way jobs are currently performed. It follows a set procedure which consists of selecting a job to be studied, recording the present method of doing a job, examining that method systematically, developing a new method based on a critique of the current method, installing the new method, and regularly maintaining it.

■ Ergonomics is concerned primarily with the physiological aspects of job design. This can be divided into two areas. First is the study of how the human body fits within its workplace. The second is a study of how humans react to the immediate environment, especially its heating, lighting and noise characteristics.

■ Behavioural models of job design are more concerned with individuals' reactions to and attitudes to their jobs. It is argued that jobs which are designed to fulfil people's needs for self-esteem and personal development are more likely to result in satisfactory work performance. Ways of achieving this include job enlargement, job rotation, job enrichment and team working.

■ The empowerment principle of job design concentrates on increasing the autonomy which individuals have to shape the nature of their own jobs. It involves moving the decision-making process down to the people who are doing a job about which the decision is being made.

CASE EXERCISE

Secret plans at Penn Savings Bank[13]

During the last few years, almost every retail bank has launched into some sort of major 'customer-care' or 'service-improvement' programme, in an attempt to win or retain business in their intensively competitive market places. Regrettably, a great many of these initiatives have failed to create sustained changes, and have even been known to discredit the judgement of the senior managers.

At Penn Savings Bank in the US, the directors realized that they first had to make customer service part of their philosophy and a key part of their corporate culture, influencing the everyday attitudes and behaviour of all employees. Their initiative developed into an unusual and large-scale project. Customer and employee surveys had indicated that they shared a common view of what was meant by high-quality service; and this included such things as promptness, accuracy, knowledge and basic courtesy. The bank decided that it wanted its service programme to be memorable and fun and they developed the Penn Savings SECRET formula – with each letter in SECRET denoting what was seen as a key behavioural requirement when dealing with the customers – Smiles, Enthusiasm, Caring, Response, Ensured satisfaction and Thanks. The SECRET formula was launched at the Employees' Awards Dinner, and subsequently all staff attended customer-service programmes, covering material relevant to the different areas of their jobs, but always focusing on how better to service the customer, even the internal ones.

After months of preparation, the launch date for the programme arrived and each staff member wore a T-shirt proclaiming 'Customers are Number 1 at Penn Savings Bank' and everyone entering the building was greeted with a polite 'I'm glad that you are here!' The bank management were involved too, at every branch, ensuring that employees gained motivation and encouragement through seeing the commitment to the programme from the top levels of the organization. Throughout the day, branches of the bank received deliveries of mementos such as pens and balloons, all containing messages of commitment to customers and all adding to the feeling of involvement and sincerity. The initiative continued with the production of business cards for all employees, giving their title as purely 'Customer Service' – the idea being that a business card always states what an individual is responsible for in the organization, and the bank wanted everyone to be aware of their basic responsibility for customer service.

Another unusual enhancement to the programme involved a monthly draw in which two lucky customers from each branch were sent a five dollar note, along with an explanatory letter. This asked them to please bring in the money on their next visit to the branch, and if they received good service, to give the five dollars to their cashier; if the service was unacceptable in any way, to keep it and have lunch on the bank. Within only two weeks, nine employees had received five dollar notes from satisfied customers! The issue of empowerment became more prominent with the management decision to allow any employee in the bank the autonomy to spend up to $50 on the spot to recover a potentially damaging situation with a customer. This added a higher level of responsiveness to the service delivery and also helped to sustain staff morale, by encouraging them to take ownership of a problem as it arose and to use their initiative to ensure that their customers left the bank feeling comfortable with the final situation. ■

Questions

1 List the key characteristics of Penn Savings Bank's approach to designing the jobs of its staff, as they are portrayed in the case exercise.

2 To what extent are each of these characteristics concerned with control and to what extent with commitment?

3 How generally applicable are the characteristics to other high customer contact operations?

4 How could 'empowerment' be taken further at Penn Savings Bank?

DISCUSSION QUESTIONS

1 Imagine that you and four friends have to prepare and serve a five-course meal for 20 people. Identify and describe the main elements that will be involved in designing the jobs involved.

2 Explain how the design of a job making overhead transparencies for university lecturers might affect the performance of the lecturers.

3 Explain the difference between division of labour and scientific management.

4 Get together with a few colleagues and undertake a method study of an operation, for example, the loading and unloading of a local train, a small catering operation or a gardening task. What improvements could you make and how acceptable might they be to the operators involved?

5 Draw a process chart for the following tasks:
loading paper into a printer
changing the tyre on a car
making a cup of coffee.

6 Assess the workplace design of your lecture theatre.

7 Explain why some operations managers might be concerned about implementing job rotation, enrichment and enlargement.

8 Explain how empowerment differs from the behavioural approaches.

9 How might empowerment differ between professional and mass-service organizations? Illustrate your answer with references to organizations of your choice.

NOTES ON CHAPTER

1 For a discussion of the origins of the division of labour, *see* Wild, R. (1972) *Mass Production Management*, John Wiley.

2 Ford, H. with Crowther, S. (1924) *My Life and Works* (rev. edn), Heinemann.

3 Taylor, F.W. (1947) *Scientific Management* (edn published by Harper & Row), New York.

4 Hoxie, R.F. (1915) *Scientific Management and Labour*, D. Appleton.

5 Source: Adler, P.S. (1933) 'Time and Motion Regained', *Harvard Business Review*, Vol 11, No 1.

6 Kobrick, J.L. and Fine, B.J. (1983) 'Climate and Human Performance' *in* Osborne, D.J. and Gruneberg, M.M. (eds) *The Physical Environment and Work*, John Wiley.

7 *Illuminating Engineering Society*, IES Code for Interior Lighting, 1977.

8 Environmental Protection Agency (US)(1974), 'Information on Levels of Environmental Noise Requisite to Protect Public Health and Welfare with Adequate Margin of Safety', EPA.

9 There are other recommendations similar to those published in the European Union Directive; they broadly agree on what is good practice.

10 Hackman, J.R. and Lawler, E.E. (1971) 'Employee Reaction to Job Characteristics', *Journal of Applied Psychology*, Vol 55, pp 259–86.

11 Hackman, J.R. and Oldham, G. (1975) 'A New Strategy for Job Enrichment', *California Management Review*, Vol 17.

12 Bowen, D. and Lawler, E. (1992) 'Empowerment', *Sloan Management Review*, Apr.

13 Source: Nangle, J.S. (1990) 'How Penn Savings Keeps the Focus on Service', *Bank Marketing Journal*, Vol 22, No 1.

SELECTED FURTHER READINGS

Bailey, J. (1983) *Job Design and Work Organisation*, Prentice Hall.

Berggren, C. (1992) *The Volvo Experience, Alternatives to Lean Production in the Swedish Auto Industry*, Macmillan.

Carlisle, B. (1983) 'Job Design Implications for Operations Managers', *International Journal of Operations and Production Management*, Vol 3, No 2.

Clegg, C.W. and Corbett, J.M. (1987) 'Research and Development in "Humanising" Advanced Manufacturing Technology' *in* Wall, T.D., Clegg, C.W. and Kemp, N.J. (eds) *The Human Side of Advanced Manufacturing Technology*, John Wiley.

Corlett, N., Wilson, J. and Manencia, F. (eds) (1986) *Ergonomics of Working Posture*, Taylor and Francis.

Cunningham, J.B. and Eberle, T. (1990) 'A Guide to Job Enrichment and Redesign', *Personnel*, Feb.

Fourie, J. (1996) 'Workplace Forums: Make them Work', *Productivity SA*, Vol 22, No 3, pp 36–7.

Hackman, R.J. and Oldham, G. (1980) *Work Redesign*, Addison-Wesley.

Herzberg, F. (1987) 'One More Time: How Do You Motivate Employees?' (with retrospective commentary), *Harvard Business Review*, Vol 65, No 5.

Knights, D., Willmott, H. and Collison, D. (1985) (eds) *Job Redesign*, Gower.

Main, J. (1982) 'Battling your own Bureaucracy' *in Working Smarter*, by the Editors of *Fortune*, New York, Viking Press, Prentice Hall, pp 88–9.

Maisela, T. (1995) 'Participative Management Facilitates a Productive Work Place', *Human Resource Management*, Vol 11, No 5, pp 20–2.

Rubenowitz, S. (1992) 'The Role of Management in Production Units with Autonomous Work Groups', *International Journal of Operations and Production Management*, Vol 12, No 7/8.

Scarborough, H. and Corbet, M. (1992) *Technology and Organisation*, Routledge.

Wild, R. (1975) *Work Organisation*, John Wiley.

PLANNING AND CONTROL

The physical design of an operation should have provided the resources which are capable of satisfying customers' demands. Planning and control is concerned with operating those resources on a day-to-day level in order to supply the goods and services which fulfil customers' demands. This part of the book will look at several different aspects of planning and control, including some of the specialist approaches which are used in particular types of operations.

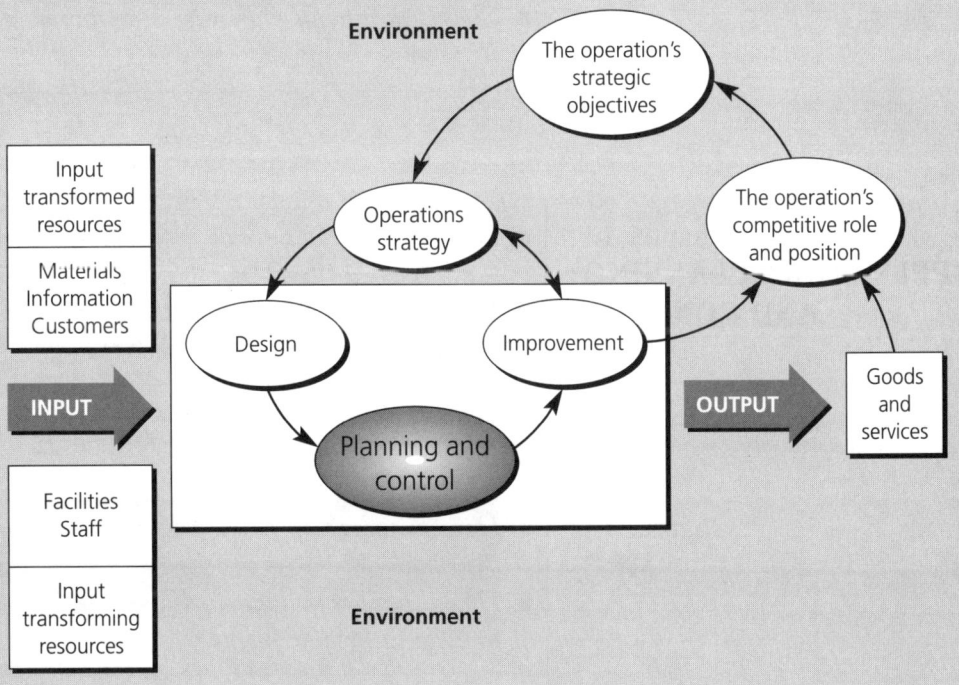

Chapter 10
THE NATURE OF PLANNING AND CONTROL

- *Why do operations managers need to plan and control their activities?*
- *How do operations managers decide what, where and when activities should be happening?*

Chapter 11
CAPACITY PLANNING AND CONTROL

- *How do operations know how much they can produce?*
- *How should operations cope with fluctuating demand?*

Chapter 12
INVENTORY PLANNING AND CONTROL

- *Why does inventory exist?*
- *How do operations managers decide how much inventory they need and when to order it?*
- *Should operations managers control some stocked items more closely than others?*

Chapter 13
SUPPLY CHAIN PLANNING AND CONTROL

- *How do operations decide from whom to buy their input goods and services?*
- *How do operations organize the distribution of their goods or services through to their customers?*

Chapter 14
MRP

- *How do operations decide when and how much of their material inputs to order?*
- *How can other manufacturing resources be linked to materials requirements?*

Chapter 15
JUST-IN-TIME PLANNING AND CONTROL

- *Is just-in-time a set of manufacturing techniques or an overall philosophy?*
- *How do JIT principles control material flow in operations?*
- *Should JIT and MRP be merged together?*

Chapter 16
PROJECT PLANNING AND CONTROL

- *What are the stages of project management?*
- *How can network techniques be used to help us plan and control projects?*

Chapter 17
QUALITY PLANNING AND CONTROL

- *What is quality?*
- *Why is quality so important?*
- *How can we use statistical techniques to help us control quality?*

THE NATURE OF PLANNING AND CONTROL

INTRODUCTION

The previous part of this book was concerned with the design of the operation. Design sets the physical form and structure of the operation. Within the constraints imposed by its design an operation then has to be run on an ongoing basis. This is what 'planning and control' is concerned with – managing the ongoing activities of the operation so as to satisfy customer demand. All operations require plans and require controlling, though the formality and detail of the plans and the control may vary. Some operations are more difficult to plan than others. Those where there is a high level of unpredictability can be particularly difficult to plan. Some operations are more difficult to control than others. Those which have high customer contact may be difficult to control because of the immediate nature of their operations. This chapter introduces and provides an overview of some of the principles and methods of planning and control, which will be treated in more detail in the rest of this part of the book. In all cases, however, the different aspects of planning and control can be viewed as representing the reconciliation of supply with demand (*see* Fig. 10.1).

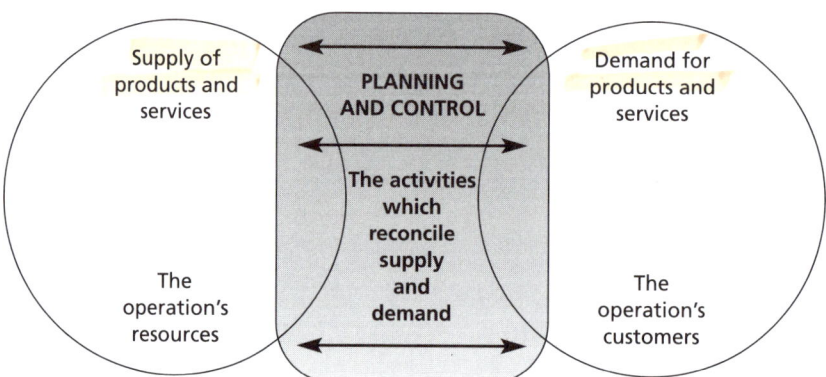

Figure 10.1 Planning and control reconciles the supply of an operation's products and services with the demand for them

OBJECTIVES

This chapter will examine:

- what is planning and control, what is the difference between planning and control and how does the balance of planning and control vary over time?

- nature of demand and supply;

- loading – finite and infinite loading;

- sequencing – sequencing rules and their effect on operational performance;

- scheduling – forward and backward scheduling, push and pull scheduling, constraint scheduling;

- the volume–variety influences on planning and control.

WHAT IS PLANNING AND CONTROL?

In Chapter 1 we introduced the model of input–transformation–output to represent an 'operation'. The previous part of this book examined the design activities which operations managers must perform on the input–transformation–output system. These design activities determine the form and nature of the system and the resources it contains, but they are not concerned with the day-to-day running of the system. That is the purpose of planning and control – to ensure that the operation runs effectively and produces products and services as it should do. This requires that the resources of the operation are available

- in the appropriate *quantity*
- at the appropriate *time*, and
- at the appropriate level of *quality*.

Consider, for example, the organization of a rock concert. Ticket holders turn up on the night, take their seats and enjoy the performance. What they don't see is the months, sometimes years, of planning and preparation that went on before the night. One of the first details that requires planning is an agreed date and venue for the concert. This is then the date that all other plans are geared up to. There will need to be a plan that informs every electrician of the work which is required and when to supply the lighting and sound systems. Even before this, someone must plan how many electricians will be required. Someone also has to predict how many people will attend; this determines the amount of support services required such as food facilities. Someone must understand the sequence in which jobs must be done – in flexible layout concert halls the size and position of the stage set may determine where spectator seating can and cannot be positioned. Some locations may have an obscured view. Every floor covering that needs tacking down, every burger bun that needs slicing, every T-shirt display that needs arranging – hundreds of people using millions of pounds' worth of buildings, equipment and technology all need to know what they are to do and when they are to do it. Just as important, however, in the run-up to the concert and during the performance, adjustments to the plans will have to be made to keep the event on track. All this is the planning and control task.

Reconciling supply with demand

The design activities which we described in the previous chapters were concerned with setting the nature of the resources within the operation. The sum of the design activities set the capabilities of the staff and facilities within the operation. In making these decisions operations managers try to meet the broad competitive and strategic objectives of quality, speed, dependability, flexibility and cost. In effect design sets the potential of the operation's performance – the broad limits within which the operation can work. Customers, when considered, are treated *en masse*, as a group creating a demand which must be met in general terms. They are not usually considered as individuals with specific needs.

So we have two entities. On the one hand, we have the resources of the operation which have the capability to *supply* to customers, but as yet have not been given the instructions on how to do so. On the other hand, we have a set of both general and specific *demands* from the actual and potential customers for the operation's products or services. Planning and control activities provide the systems, procedures and decisions which bring these two entities together. It connects up the resources of the operation which are capable of supplying goods and services with the demand that it was designed to satisfy. All planning and control activities in some way are concerned with reconciling the supply capabilities of an operation with the demands placed upon it. Usually they do this through a set of systems, procedures and decision methods which operations managers can use in the ongoing running of the operation. This model of planning and control as the connecting activity between supply and demand is one that we shall use throughout this part of the book. Different aspects of supply and demand, and different circumstances under which supply and demand must be reconciled, will be treated in the various chapters. But in every case the purpose is the same – to make a connection between the two, which will trigger the operation into satisfying its customers.

Constraints on the planning and control task

In any operation the supply of resources is not infinite. The electrical work for the concert could be performed in a few hours if several hundred electricians all arrived and set about the task simultaneously, but this would be more expensive than using a smaller number over a longer time. There might also be a physical constraint on how many electricians are available in the time. Even with an infinite budget, if there are only ten electricians available to do the work within the time period, then that is the limit on the number which can be hired. There will also be constraints imposed by the quality of what is required by the concert promoters. For example, it might be possible, with a relatively small number of electricians and in a relatively short space of time, to set up some kind of basic sound system. However, the requirements of the performers and the promoter and the expectations of the customers will be for a higher standard of sound. Finally, the most evident constraint will be the timing of the concert. In this kind of event it is an absolute requirement that everything must be ready for the planned 'delivery date' of the concert. No concert promoter can put all the effort into advertising such an event only to ask the ticket holders to wait a couple of days because everything isn't finished.

The nature of the rock concert is that of a 'one-off' product. Nevertheless, all the characteristics used to plan and control the 'manufacture' of this product will hold true for other products and services. Similarly, the constraints within which the planning and control activity had to take place will also apply to most types of operation. Generally these are as follows.

- *Cost constraints* – products and services must be produced within an identified cost.
- *Capacity constraints* – products and services must be produced within the designed capacity limits of the operation.[1]
- *Timing constraints* – products and services must be produced within the time when they still have value for the customer.
- *Quality constraints* – products and services must conform to the designed tolerance limits of the product or service.

The difference between planning and control

In this text we have chosen to treat planning and control together. This is because the division between planning and control is not clear, either in theory or in practice. However, there are some general features that help to distinguish between the two.

A *plan* is a formalization of what is intended to happen at some time in the future. A plan does not guarantee that an event will actually happen; it is a *statement of intention* that it will happen. Plans are based on expectations, however, and expectations are only hopes concerning the future. When operations attempt to implement plans, things do not always happen as expected. Customers change their minds about what they want and when they want it. Suppliers may not always deliver on time, machines may fail, staff may be absent through illness. Any of these reasons may mean that the plan cannot be carried out. There are many different variables, any one of which could cause a plan to become unworkable. *Control* is the process of coping with changes in these variables. It may mean plans need to be redrawn in the short term. It may also mean that an 'intervention' will need to be made in the operation to bring it back 'on track'. For example, finding a new supplier who can deliver quickly, repairing the machine which failed, or moving staff from another part of the operation to cover for the absentees. Control makes the adjustments which allows the operation to achieve the objectives which the plan set, even when the assumptions which the plan made do not hold true.

We can define a plan as an intention and control as the driving through of the plan, monitoring what actually happens and making changes as necessary. For example, it may be intended in the plan that the rock concert takes place at a set time. A temperamental performer may try and delay that time; control is immediately exercised by someone persuading the performer to get ready more quickly, while at the same time other people are stepping up the complimentary services of music and entertainment for the waiting audience, concessions are increasing the amount of food and drinks they vend. The control is intended to reduce the potential of customer dissatisfaction that may arise because the plan is not being adhered to, as well as minimizing the disruption to the operation.

The balance of planning and control over time

When the rock concert is being planned as a date in the promoter's diary two years hence, the nature of the planning and control task is largely one of forward planning. As those two years go by, more plans have to be formulated and implemented. The closer the rock concert gets, the more difficult it becomes to change the plans. Once promotional activity has started and ticket sales have been made it is very difficult to change the date and venue of the concert. As the event date gets very close, replanning of the number of T-shirts for sale is not possible. It is also difficult to arrange for additional lighting at short notice because it has to work with the rest of the lighting set. The implications of changing some plans at short notice are just too disruptive to the whole event to be justifiable. In the short term, control is exercised to cope within the limits of those plans which cannot be changed. Adjustments are made to those parts of the plan which can be changed, but on the day of the concert relatively little replanning is possible. Any deviations from the plan at that point can only be treated by direct intervention in the process. Figure 10.2 shows how the control aspects of planning and control increase in significance closer to the date of the event.

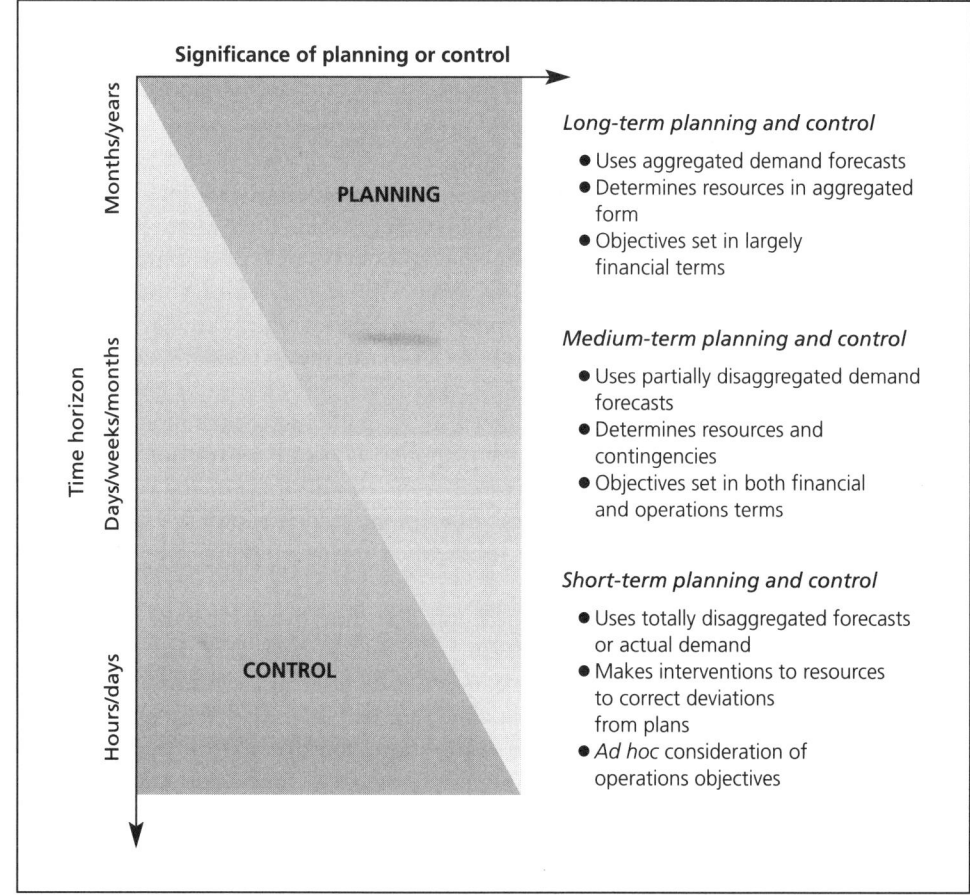

**Figure 10.2
The balance between planning and control activities changes in the long, medium and short terms**

Long-, medium- and short-term planning and control

All operations are similar to the rock concert described previously in the sense that the nature of planning and control changes over time. In the very long term, operations managers make plans concerning what they intend to do, what resources they need, and what objectives they hope to achieve. The emphasis is on planning rather than control because there is little to control as such. They will use forecasts of likely demand which are described in aggregated terms. For example, a hospital will make plans for '2000 patients' without necessarily going into the details of the individual needs of those 2000 patients. Similarly, the resources will be planned in an aggregated form. For example, the hospital might plan to have 100 nurses and 20 doctors but again without deciding on the specific attributes of the staff. In carrying out their planning activities the operations managers will be concerned mainly to achieve financial targets. Budgets will be put in place which identify the costs and revenue targets which it is intended to achieve.

Medium-term planning and control is concerned with both planning in more detail (and replanning if necessary). It looks ahead to assess the overall demand which the operation must meet in a partially disaggregated manner. By this time, for example, the hospital must distinguish between different types of demand. The number of patients coming as accident and emergency cases will need to be distinguished from those who are requiring routine operations. Similarly, resources will be set at a more disaggregated level. For example, different categories of staff will have been identified and broad staffing levels in each category set. Just as important, contingencies will have been put in place which allow for slight deviations from plans. These contingencies will act as 'reserve' resources and make planning and control easier in the short term.

In short-term planning and control many of the resources will have been set and it will be difficult to make large-scale changes in resourcing. However, short-term interventions are possible if things are not going to plan. By this time demand will be assessed on a totally disaggregated basis. For example, the hospital will be treating all types of surgical procedures as individual activities. More importantly, individual patients will have been identified by name and specific time slots booked for their treatment. In making short-term intervention and changes to plans, operations managers will be attempting to balance the quality, speed, dependability, flexibility, and costs of their operation on an *ad hoc* basis. It is unlikely that they will have the time to carry out detailed calculations of the effects of their short-term planning and control decisions on all these objectives, but a general understanding of priorities will form the background to their decision making.

NATURE OF DEMAND AND SUPPLY

If planning and control is the process of reconciling demand with supply then the nature of the decisions taken to plan and control an operation will depend both on the nature of demand and the nature of supply in that operation. In this next section we examine some differences in demand and supply which can affect the way in which operations managers plan and control their activities.

OPERATIONS CONTROL AT BRITISH AIRWAYS[2]

British Airways (BA) is the world's largest international airline operator, with 240 aircraft flying between 155 destinations in 72 different countries. A BA flight takes off somewhere around the world, on average, every 90 seconds. The difficulties in planning a schedule which involves the world-wide resources of British Airways and ensuring that every flight leaves on time must be one of the most complex planning and control tasks in any operation.

The BA headquarters at Heathrow Airport near London is its busiest hub. It is there that you will find a small, but vitally important department known as Operations Control, which handles the seven days prior to take-off for long-haul flights, and the three days prior to take-off for short-haul flights. It is a full-time operation because there are flights in the air around the clock all over the world. Initial flight schedules are produced up to two years in advance, and the route schedules are negotiated at a six-monthly global conference. The planning and scheduling group at BA will then manage the production of a flight timetable, taking account of the longer-term implications of allocating certain aircraft types to each route. Any new routes or timings agreed are passed to Operations Control for comment on the practicalities of what is being proposed.

Operations Control inherits this final flight schedule, and can only make minor changes in order to cope with unexpected situations arising during the period prior to take-off. It is responsible for coordinating the three main resources required to provide the flight services, which are the schedule, the aircraft and the crew. They also are responsible for managing the knock-on effects of any delays, shortages or disruption to any of these inputs. The Operations Control team is effectively still in charge of every flight until it lands, when departments such as Engineering and Station Control can take over. This handover is illustrated in Fig. 10.3.

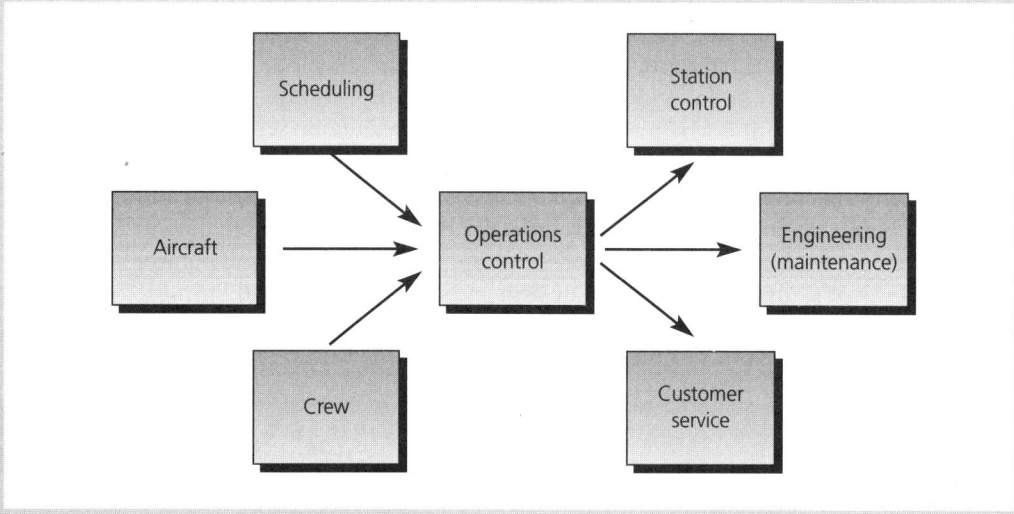

Figure 10.3 British Airways – Operations control centre

The performance of the Operations Control team is evaluated in terms of the *regularity* and subsequent *punctuality* of their flights. Regularity is defined as the percentage of flights actually taking off compared with the number scheduled. Passengers need to have total confidence that their flight will actually operate and current performance is almost 99 per cent (cancelling a flight is the very last resort for Operations Control). Punctuality is the measure of the timing of the take-offs. BA sets an internal standard whereby a flight is considered late if it does not take off at the time defined in the schedule. Thus a flight can only be early, dead-on-time, or late. Current performance standards are about 60 per cent punctuality. The IATA standards allow for a 15-minute buffer after the scheduled take-off time before a flight is defined as 'late'. Measured in this way, British Airways achieve a much higher punctuality figure.

Operations Control is organized such that staff work in teams of two. One focuses his or her efforts on continuous improvement, and the other takes control of the current activities. Peter Saxton, the Operations Control Manager, feels that the combination of these two perspectives ensures that both the day-to-day activities, and the longer-term thinking, are dealt with in equal proportions in a part of the business that has traditionally been viewed as reactive.

'Traditionally, the job in Operations Control has been about fire fighting and that is what the staff have grown up with and enjoy doing. Now we are trying to switch the emphasis more towards developing systems that are more flexible, looking for longer-term issues, using more information to make better informed decisions, and building better relationships with our service partners in the British Airports Authority and Air Traffic Control, as well as other internal BA departments.'

Other component parts of the Operations Control Centre are the Emergency Procedures Information Centre (EPIC) and the Operations Control Intelligence Centre (OCIC) back-up centres. These are unmanned areas, set up to deal with certain types of incident at the 'press of a button'. The staff who would operate the centres are nominated, and are well trained in advance, even down to having simulated exercises on a regular basis. The EPIC centre is activated should BA, or any other contracted airline (there are over 60 subscribers to the service) be involved in an accident or serious incident, and it acts as a contact point for the public, and as a focal point for information regarding those on board. The OCIC centre is used only when a serious global incident, such as war, is affecting the entire BA business. Again the centre is manned by specially trained staff and headed by a BA board director. The team will then be on 24-hour action stations until the crisis has been resolved. These two crisis centres have become well known, and EPIC is frequently used by other organizations.

The strategy of having independent crisis centres means that the day-to-day business units do not have to cater for every eventuality. They continue to work in the knowledge that an emergency situation will not be their responsibility, and they can thus focus more efficiently on the core operation. ∎

Uncertainty in supply

Some operations are reasonably predictable and usually run to plan. In these situations, the need for control is minimal. For example, cable TV services provide programmes to a schedule into subscribers' homes via reliable technology. It is rare that the programme schedule, or plan, is not adhered to. Conversely, local village carnivals rarely work to plan. Processions take longer to arrive than expected, some of the acts scheduled in the programme may be delayed *en route*, some traders do not turn up on the day. The event requires a good compère to keep the event rolling along and the crowd amused while they're waiting. The compère and his or her helpers are exercising much of the short-term control which is used to minimize customer dissatisfaction.

Uncertainty in demand

Demand can also be uncertain, but not in all operations; in some demand is fairly predictable. In a school, for example, once classes are fixed and the term, or semester, has started, a teacher knows how many pupils are in his or her class. When planning how many handouts are required, the demand is predictable. Any absentee can have his or her handouts on return so this variable does not affect demand. However, this is the medium and short term of the total planning and control of the school's operation. Prior to the start of the year, the head teacher may not know exactly how many new pupils will be joining the school and how many existing pupils will leave the area or move to another school. Therefore, in the long term, the head teacher has to predict this demand to determine resources such as staff, books, and computers, for which commitment must be made in advance.

In other operations, demand is unpredictable even in the short term. A fast-food outlet inside a shopping centre does not know how many people will arrive, when they will arrive and what they will order. It is possible to predict certain patterns, such as an increase in demand over the lunch and tea-time periods, but a sudden rain storm that drives shoppers indoors into the centre could significantly increase demand unpredictably in the very short term. Demand for fast moving consumer goods such as packets of biscuits varies enormously depending on television advertising campaigns – a successful campaign can have an impact the following day which can cause demand to soar to ten times its normal selling pattern. While some extra stocks could be provided to supermarkets in advance of the campaign, the size of the reaction is not easy to predict.

Dependent and independent demand

Some operations can look ahead and make forward provision because they have firm orders from customers into the future. In addition to these orders, the operation may have a reasonably good idea of what other customers will order. Other operations, however, can only make predictions, often based on history, and use this as their best indicator of what the future will hold. They have no absolute certainty on which to depend. In the first case the operation is said to be driven by *dependent demand* and in the second case, it is driven by *independent demand*. The difference between the two is easily described by the analogy of driving a car. We drive cars *dependent* on what the road ahead looks like. Driving the car *independently* would be done by having a 'prediction' of the road ahead (based partly on looking in the rear-view mirror). If the road ahead (future demand) is very similar to the road the driver has just travelled on (previous demand) it may be possible to drive for a short time without crashing. Also, if the driver has taken the route many times before and there is no other traffic (competitors) the curves in the road may be predicted. However, if the driver is on a country road with many twists and turns (an uncertain future demand) the operation has a good chance of 'going off the road'.

Dependent demand, then, is demand which is relatively predictable because it is dependent upon some factor which is known. For example, the manager who is in charge of ensuring that there are sufficient tyres in an automobile factory will not treat the demand for tyres as a totally random variable. He or she will not be totally surprised by the exact quantity of tyres which are required by the plant every day. The process of demand forecasting is relatively straightforward. It will consist of examining the manufacturing schedules in the car plant and deriving the demand for tyres from these. If 200 cars are to be manufactured on a particular day, then it is simple to calculate that 1000 tyres will be demanded by the car plant on that day (each car has five tyres). Demand is dependent on a known factor – the number of cars to be manufactured. Because of this, the tyres can be ordered from the tyre manufacturer to a delivery schedule which is closely in line with the demand for tyres from the plant. In fact the demand for every part of the car plant will be derived from the assembly schedule for the finished cars. Manufacturing instructions and purchasing requests will all be dependent upon this figure. Other operations will act in a dependent demand manner because of the nature of the service or product which they provide. For example, a jobbing dressmaker will not buy fabric and patterns and make up dresses in many different sizes just in case someone comes along and wants to buy one. Nor will a high-class restaurant begin to cook food just in case a customer arrives and requests it. In both these cases a combination of *risk* and the *perishability* of the product or service prevents the operation from starting to create the goods or services until it has a firm order.

Dependent demand planning and control concentrates on the consequences of the demand within the operation. Materials requirements planning, which is treated in Chapter 14, is one such dependent demand approach.

Some operations have little choice but to take decisions on how they will supply demand without having any firm forward visibility of customer orders. For example, customers do not have to inform a supermarket when they are arriving and what they will buy. The supermarket takes its planning and control decisions based on its experience and understanding of the market, independent of what may actually happen. They run the risk of being out of stock of items when demand does not match their expectations. For example, the Ace Tyre Company, which operates a drive-in tyre replacement service, will need to manage a stock of tyres. In that sense it is exactly the same task as faced the manager of tyre stocks in the car plant. However, demand is very different for Ace Tyres. They cannot predict either the volume or specific needs of customers. They must make decisions on how many and what type of tyres to stock, based on demand forecasts and in the light of the risks they are prepared to run of being out of stock. This is the nature of *independent demand planning and control*. It makes 'best guesses' concerning future demand, attempts to put the resources in place which can satisfy this demand, and attempts to respond quickly if actual demand does not meet forecast. Inventory planning and control, treated in Chapter 12, is typical of independent demand planning and control.

Responding to demand

Dependent and independent demand concepts are closely related to how the operation chooses to respond to demand. In conditions of dependent demand an operation will only start the process of producing goods or services when it needs to. Each order triggers the planning and control activities to organize their production. For example, a specialist house builder might only start the process of planning and controlling the construction of a house when requested to do so by the customer. The builder might not even have the resources to start building before the order is received. The material which will be necessary to build the house will be purchased only when the timing and nature of the house are certain. The staff and the construction equipment might also be 'purchased' only when the nature of demand is clear. In a similar way, a specialist conference organizer will start planning for an event only when specifically requested to do so by the clients. A venue will be booked, speakers organized, meals arranged, and the delegates contacted only when the nature of the service is clear. The planning and control necessary for this kind of operation can be called *resource-to-order* planning and control.[3]

Other operations might be sufficiently confident of the nature of demand, if not its volume and timing, to keep 'in stock' most of the resources it requires to satisfy its customers. Certainly it will keep its transforming resources if not its transformed resources. However, it would still make the actual product or service only to a firm customer order. For example, a house builder who has standard designs might choose to build each house only when a customer places a firm order. Because the design of the house is relatively standard, suppliers of materials will have been identified, even if the building operation does not keep the items in stock itself. The equivalent in the conference business would be a conference centre which has its own 'stored' permanent resources (the building, staff, etc.) but only starts planning a conference when it has a firm booking. In both cases the operations would need *make-to-order* planning and control.

Some operations produce goods or services ahead of any firm orders 'to stock'. For example, some builders will construct pre-designed standard houses or apartments ahead of any firm demand for them. This will be done either because it is less expensive to do so or because it is difficult to create the goods or services on a one-off basis (it is difficult to make each apartment only when a customer chooses to buy one). If demand is high, customers may place requests for houses before they are started or during their construction. In this case the customer will form a backlog of demand and must wait. The builder is also taking the risk, however, of holding a stock of unsold houses if buyers do not come along before they are finished. In fact it is difficult for small builders to operate this way, but less so for (say) a bottled cola manufacturer or other mass producer. The equivalent in the conference market would be a conference centre which schedules a series of events and conferences, programmed in advance and open to individual customers to book into or even turn up on the day. Cinemas and theatres usually work in this manner. Their performances are produced and supplied irrespective of the level of actual demand. Operations of this type will require *make-to-stock* planning and control.

P:D ratios[4]

Another way of characterizing the graduation between resource-to-order planning and control and make-to-stock planning and control is by contrasting the total length of time customers have to wait between asking for the product or service and receiving it, demand time, *D,* and the total throughput time, *P.* Throughput time is how long the operation takes to obtain the resources, produce and deliver the product or service.

P and *D* times depend on the operation

In a typical make-to-stock operation, such as those making consumer durables, demand time, *D,* is the sum of the times for transmitting the order to the company's warehouse or stock point, picking and packing the order and physically transporting it to the customer – the 'deliver' cycle. Behind this visible order cycle, however, lie other cycles. Reduction in the finished goods stock will eventually trigger the decision to manufacture a replenishment batch. This cycle – the 'make' cycle – involves scheduling work to the various stages in the manufacturing process. Physically this involves withdrawing materials and parts from input inventories and processing them through the various stages of the manufacturing route. Behind the 'make' cycle lies the 'purchase' cycle – the time for replenishment of the input stocks – involving transmitting the order to suppliers and awaiting their delivery.

So, for this type of manufacturing, the 'demand' time which the customer sees is very short compared with the total 'throughput' cycle. Contrast this with a resource-to-order operation. Here *D* is the same as *P.* Both include the 'purchase', 'make' and 'delivery' cycles. The make-to-order operation lies in between the two (*see* Fig. 10.4).

Some operations are hybrids. Take, for example, a manufacturer of industrial couplings whose product range is far wider than the range of components it makes because it can configure components in many different ways. Given its wide range of finished products, the company does not hold them as inventories. Instead it makes most of its components 'to stock' and then assembles its products (a relatively short process) 'to order'. This is shown in Fig. 10.5. Not all the company's products are made in this way, however. Some are demanded so infrequently that it makes them entirely to order as 'specials'. Most operations will operate with different *P:D* ratios for different classes of product or service.

P:D ratios indicate the degree of speculation

In the company described above, reducing total throughput time *P* will have varying effects on the time the customer has to wait for demand to be filled. For many of its 'specials', *P* and *D* are virtually the same thing – the customer waits from the material being ordered, through all stages in the production process and for delivery. Speeding up any part of *P* will reduce the customer's waiting time, *D.* On the other hand, the customers purchasing standard 'assemble-to-order' products would only see reduced *D* time if the 'assemble' and 'deliver' parts of *P* were reduced and savings in times were passed on to the customer.

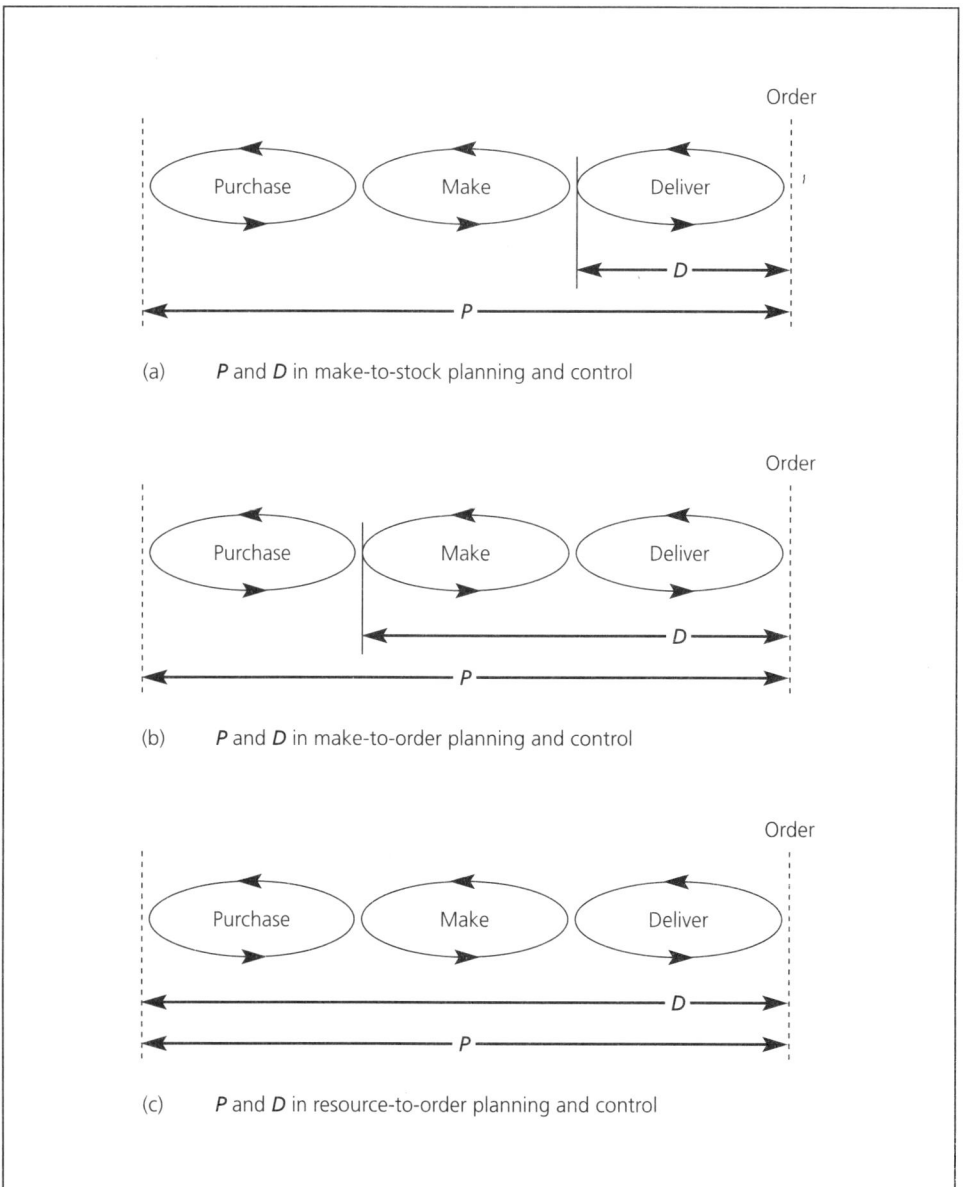

Figure 10.4
P and D for the different types of planning and control

In Fig. 10.4, *D* is always shown as being smaller than *P*, which is the case for most companies. How much smaller *D* is than *P* is important because it indicates the proportion of the operation's activities which are speculative: that is, carried out on the expectation of eventually receiving a firm order for the work. The larger *P* is compared with *D*, the higher the proportion of speculative activity in the operation and the greater the risk the operation carries. The speculative element in the operation is not there only because *P* is greater than *D*, however; it is there because *P* is

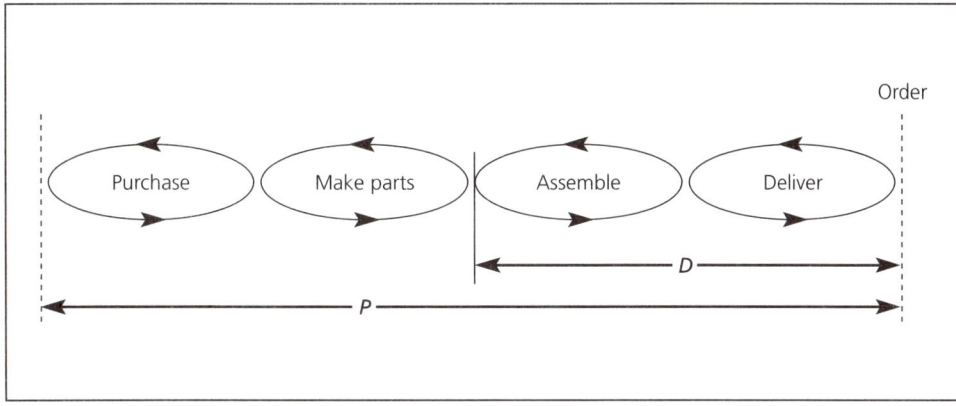

Figure 10.5
P and D in make-to-stock, assemble-to-order planning and control

greater than *D and* demand cannot be forecast perfectly. With exact or close to exact forecasts, risk would be non-existent or very low no matter how much bigger *P* was than *D*. Expressed another way: when *P* and *D* are equal, then no matter how inaccurate the forecasts are, speculation is eliminated because everything is made to a firm order (although bad forecasting will lead to other problems). Reducing the *P*:*D* ratio becomes, in effect, a way of taking some of the risk out of operations planning and control.

THE PLANNING AND CONTROL TASK

Planning and control requires the reconciliation of supply and demand in terms of *volumes*, in terms of *timing*, and in terms of *quality*. In this chapter we will focus on volume and timing because most of this part of the book is concerned with these issues. Chapter 17 will deal with quality planning and control. To reconcile volume and timing, three distinct, though integrated, activities are performed:

- *loading* – determining the volume that an operation can cope with;
- *sequencing* – determining the priority of tasks to be performed;
- *scheduling* – deciding on a start and finish time for each task.

Loading

Loading is the amount of work that is allocated to a work centre. For example, a machine on the shop floor of a manufacturing business is available, in theory, 168 hours a week. However, this does not necessarily mean that 168 hours of work can be loaded on to that machine. Figure 10.6 shows what erodes this available time. For some periods the machine cannot be worked; for example, it may not be available on statutory holidays and weekends. Therefore, the load put on to the machine must take this into account. Of the time that the machine is available for work, some tasks other

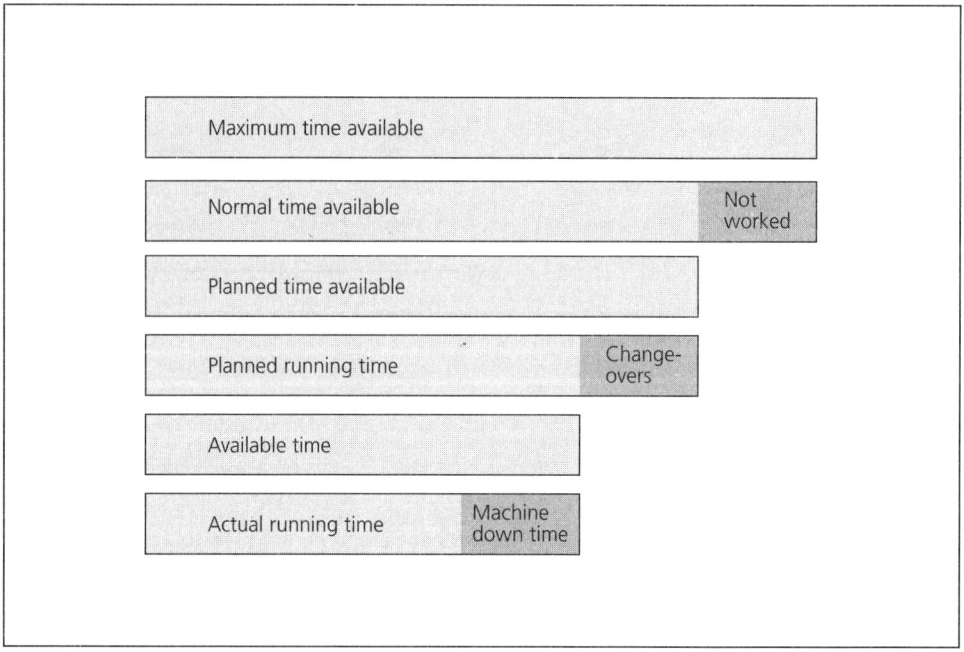

**Figure 10.6
The reduction in
the time available
for loading work
on to a machine**

than producing output must be performed, which further reduces available time. For example, time may be lost while changing over from making one component to another. In addition, the machine may need cleaning between operations before another can be started. These lost times must also be taken into account when a plan is formed of how much work can be loaded on to the machine. If the machine breaks down, it will not be available. If there is machine reliability data available, this must also be taken into account.

There are two main approaches to loading operations – *finite* and *infinite loading*.

Finite loading

Finite loading is an approach which only allocates work to a work centre (a person, a machine, or maybe a group of people or machines) up to a set limit. This limit is the estimate of capacity for the work centre (based on the times available for loading). Work over and above this capacity is not accepted. Figure 10.7 shows that the load on the work centre is not allowed to exceed the capacity limit.

Finite loading is particularly relevant for operations where:

● *it is possible to limit the load*. For example, it is possible to run an appointment system for a general medical practice or a hairdresser.
● *it is necessary to limit the load*. For example, for safety reasons a finite number of people and weight of luggage is allowed on aircraft.
● *the cost of limiting the load is not prohibitive*. For example, the cost of maintaining a finite order book at a specialist sports car manufacturer does not adversely affect demand, and may even enhance it.

Infinite loading

Infinite loading is an approach to loading work which does not limit accepting work, but instead tries to cope with it. Figure 10.8 illustrates a loading pattern where capacity constraints have not been used to limit loading.

Infinite loading is relevant for operations where:

● *it is not possible to limit the load.* For example, an accident and emergency department in a hospital should not turn away arrivals needing attention.
● *it is not necessary to limit the load.* For example, fast-food outlets are designed to flex capacity up and down to cope with varying arrival rates of customers. During busy periods, customers may accept that they must queue for some time before being served. Unless this is extreme, the customers may not go elsewhere.
● *the cost of limiting the load is prohibitive.* For example, if a retail bank turned away customers at the door because a set amount were inside, customers would feel less than happy with the service.

In complex planning and control activities where there are multiple stages, each with different capacities and with a varying mix arriving at the facilities, such as a machine shop in an engineering company, the constraints imposed by finite loading make loading calculations complex and not worth the considerable computational power which would be needed.

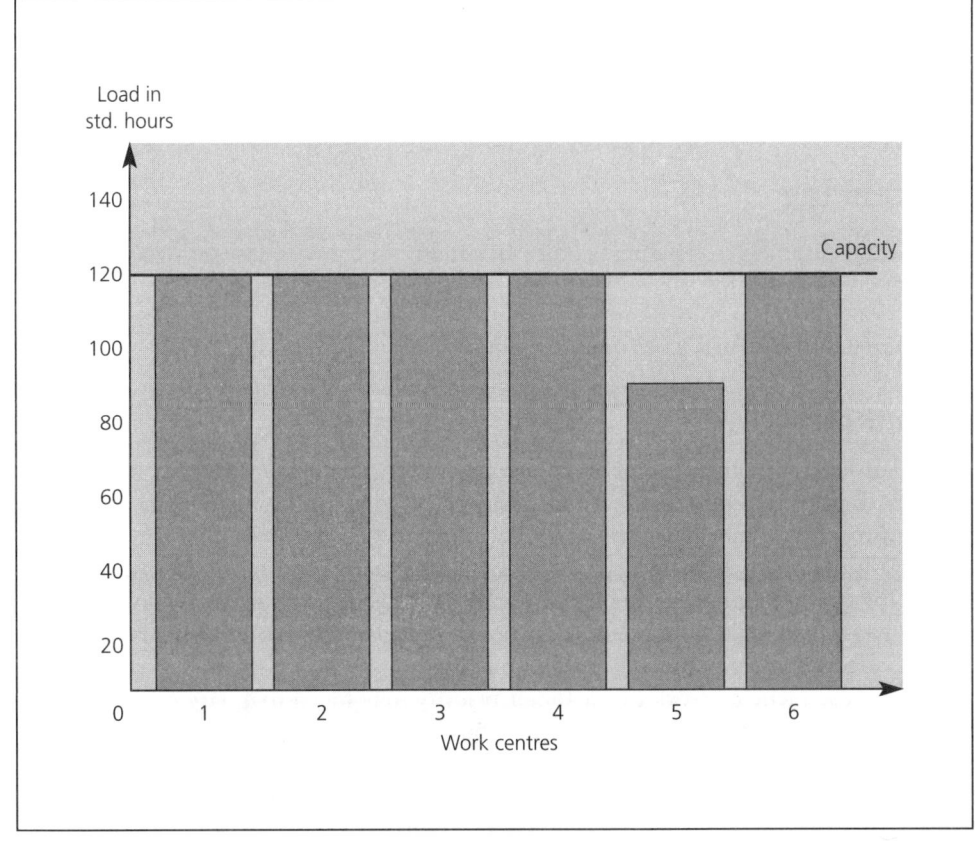

Figure 10.7
Finite loading

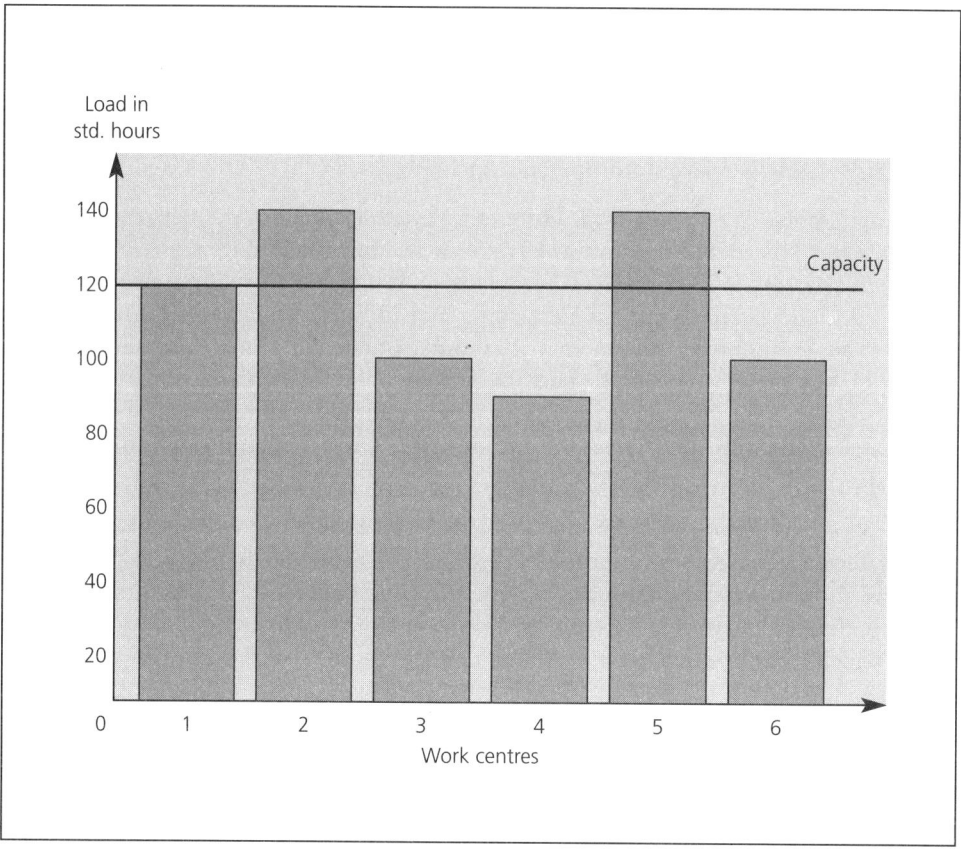

Figure 10.8
Infinite loading

Sequencing

Whether the approach to loading is finite or infinite, when work arrives, decisions must be taken on the *order* that the work will be tackled. This activity is termed *sequencing*.

The priorities given to work in an operation are often set by some predefined set of rules. Some of these rules are summarized below.

Customer priority

Operations will sometimes allow an important or aggrieved customer, or item, to be 'processed' prior to others, irrespective of the order of arrival of the customer or item. This approach is typically used by operations whose customer base is skewed, containing a mass of small customers and a few large, very important customers. Some banks, for example, give priority to important customers. Similarly, in hotels, complaining customers will be treated as a priority because their complaint may have an adverse affect on the perceptions of other customers.

However, sequencing work by customer priority may mean that 'large-volume' customers receive a very high-level service, but service to many other customers is eroded. This may lower the average performance of the operation if existing work flows are disrupted for important customers. It can also erode the quality and productivity of the operation, making it less efficient overall.

Due date

Prioritizing by due date means that work is sequenced according to when it is 'due' for delivery, irrespective of the size of each job or the importance of each customer. For example, a support service in an office block, such as a reprographic unit, will often ask when photocopies are required, then sequence the work according to that due date. Due date sequencing usually improves the delivery reliability of an operation and improves average delivery speed. However, it may not provide optimal productivity as a more efficient sequencing of work may reduce total costs. However, it can be flexible when new, urgent work arrives at the work centre.

LIFO

Last-In-First-Out (LIFO) is a method of sequencing usually selected for practical reasons. For example, unloading an elevator is more convenient on a LIFO basis as there is only one entrance and exit. However, it is not an equitable approach. Patients at hospital clinics may be infuriated if they see medical records added to a pile in the sequence of arriving patients, if the doctor takes the records from the top of the pile first, therefore serving the patients in reverse order of when they arrived. LIFO has a very adverse effect on delivery speed and reliability. The sequence is not determined for reasons of quality, flexibility or cost, therefore none of these performance objectives are well served by this method.

FIFO

Some operations serve customers in exactly the sequence they arrive in, on a First-In-First-Out (FIFO) basis. For example, the UK passport offices receive post and put it in a pile according to the day on which it arrived. They work through the post, opening it in sequence, then processing the passport applications as they come to them. Queues in theme parks may be designed so that one long queue snakes around the lobby area until the row of counters is reached. When customers reach the front of the queue they are served at the next free counter.

In high-contact operations, arrival time may be viewed by customers in the system as a fair way of sequencing, thereby minimizing customer complaints and enhancing service performance. However, because there is no consideration of urgency or due date, some customers' needs may not be served as well as others. Delivery speed and delivery reliability, therefore, may not be at their highest. It is also difficult to be flexible in a system where this prioritization is visible to customers. If the 'queue' is not physically visible, it may be more possible to exercise some flexibility, allowing some work to queue jump without other customers being aware of it happening.

Longest operation/longest total job time first

Under certain circumstances operations may feel obliged to sequence their longest jobs first. This has the advantage of occupying the work centres within the operation for long periods. Relatively small jobs progressing through an operation will take up time at each work centre which will need to change over from one job to the next. Especially where staff are under some incentive to keep utilization high, such a sequencing rule might seem attractive. However, although utilization may be high (and therefore cost relatively low) this rule does not take into account delivery speed, delivery reliability or flexibility. Indeed it may work directly against these performance objectives.

Shortest operation/shortest total job time first

Most operations at some stage become cash constrained. In these situations, the sequencing rules may be adjusted to tackle short jobs first. These jobs can then be invoiced and payment received to ease cashflow problems. Larger jobs that take more time will not enable the business to invoice as quickly. This has an effect of improving delivery performance, if the unit of measurement of delivery is jobs. However, it may adversely affect total productivity and can damage larger customers.

Scheduling

Having determined the sequence in which work is to be tackled, some operations require a detailed timetable showing at what time or date jobs should start and when they should end. This is a schedule. Schedules are familiar statements of volume and timing in many consumer environments. For example, a bus schedule shows that more buses are put on routes at more frequent intervals during rush-hour periods. The bus schedule shows the time each bus is due to arrive at each stage of the route.

Gantt charts

The most commonly used method of scheduling is by use of the Gantt chart. A Gantt chart is a simple device (first devised by H.L. Gantt in 1917) which represents time as a bar, or channel, on a chart. Often the charts themselves are made up of long plastic channels into which coloured pieces of paper can be slotted to indicate what is happening with a job or a work centre. The start and finish times for activities can be indicated on the chart and sometimes the actual progress of the job is also indicated on the same chart. Figures 10.9 and 10.10 illustrate two Gantt

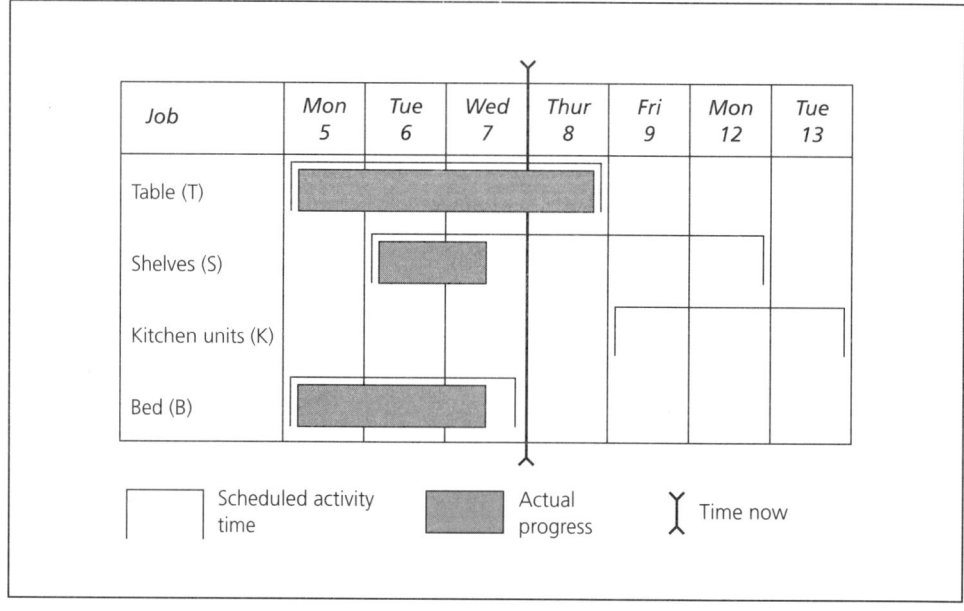

**Figure 10.9
Gantt chart for
job progress**

charts for a small specialist furniture manufacturer. Figure 10.9 is a *job progress* Gantt chart. This indicates when each job is scheduled to start and finish as well as the degree of completion of the job. Also indicated on the chart is the current time. In this case the table has been completed already, even though it was not scheduled to be completed until the end of the next day. On the other hand, both the shelves and the bed are behind schedule. The manufacturer of the kitchen units is not scheduled to start for another day. Figure 10.10 illustrates another Gantt chart which may be used by this company. This time it indicates the activities which are taking place at each work centre. Here we can see that the shelves seem to be held up in the wood preparation work centre, while the bed has yet to complete its scheduled painting operations.

The advantages of Gantt charts are that they provide a simple visual representation of what should be happening and what actually is happening in the operation. Furthermore, they can be used to 'test out' alternative schedules. Especially when using moveable pieces of paper, it is a simple task to represent alternative schedules (even if it is a far from simple task to find a schedule which fits all the resources satisfactorily). Of course the Gantt chart is in no way an optimizing tool. It merely facilitates the development of alternative schedules by communicating them effectively.

The complexity of scheduling[5]

The scheduling activity is one of the most complex tasks in operations management. First, schedulers must deal with several different types of resource simultaneously. Machines will have different capabilities and capacities; staff will have different skills. More importantly the number of possible schedules increases rapidly as the number of activities and processes increases. For example, suppose one machine has

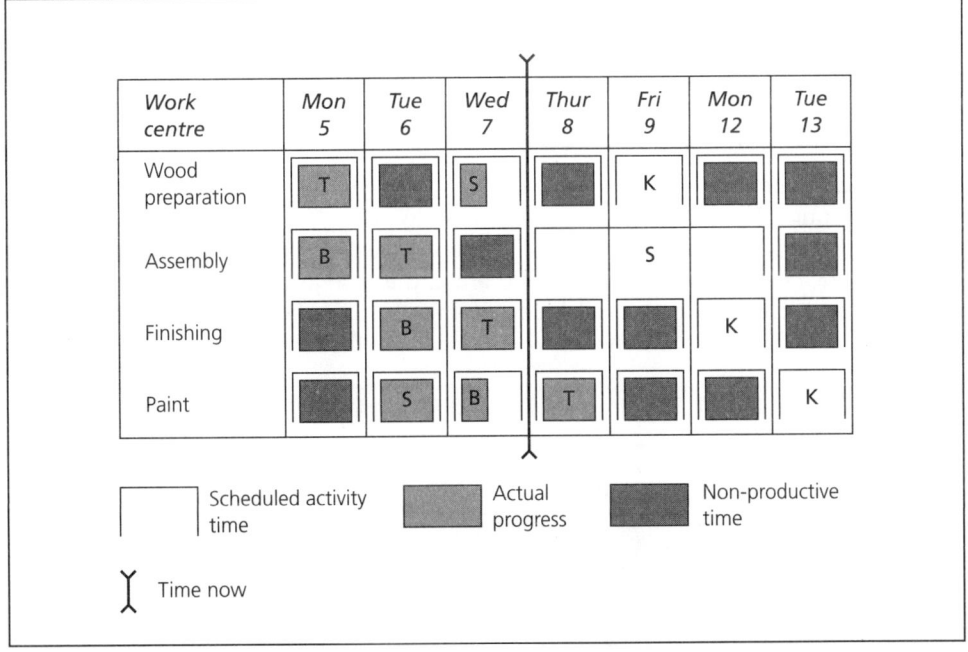

Figure 10.10 Gantt chart for work centres

five different jobs to process. Any of the five jobs could be processed first and following that any one of the remaining four jobs, and so on. This means that there are

$5 \times 4 \times 3 \times 2 = 120$ different schedules possible.

Or, more generally, for *n* jobs there are *n!* (factorial n) different ways of scheduling the jobs through a single process.

We can now consider what impact there would be if, in the same situation, there was more than one type of machine. If we were trying to minimize the number of set-ups on two machines, there is no reason why the sequence on Machine 1 would be the same as the sequence on Machine 2. If we consider the two sequencing tasks to be independent of each other, for two machines there would be:

$120 \times 120 = 14\ 400$ possible schedules of the two machines and five jobs.

A general formula can be devised to calculate the possible number of schedules in any given situation. This is:

Number of possible schedules $= (n!)^m$
where   *n* is the number of jobs
             m is the number of machines.

If we relate this to a real situation, where there may be 100 jobs going through 30 machines, in a route which takes each individual job through five different machines, then we can see that the scheduling task rapidly becomes very complicated. Within this vast number of schedules there are many acceptable options as to which are appropriate routes and sequences for any set of jobs. Even where a product is manufactured repeatedly there may be a number of different routes which that product could take. However, most of the schedules which are possible in theory will not be workable in practice and these can be rapidly eliminated.

The scheduling task has to be repeated on a very frequent basis to allow for market variations and product mix changes. Remember that even minor product mix changes may cause the capacity constraints within the facility to change very dramatically over a comparatively short period of time, hence bottle-neck operations may move about the factory quite quickly.

Forward and backward scheduling

Forward scheduling involves starting work as soon as it arrives. Backward scheduling involves starting jobs at the last possible moment to prevent them being late. For example, assume that it takes six hours for a contract laundry to wash, dry and press a batch of overalls. If the work is collected at 8.00 am and is due to be picked up at 4.00 pm, there are more than six hours available to do the work. Table 10.1 shows the different start times of each job, depending on whether they are forward or backward scheduled.

Table 10.1 The effects of forward and backward scheduling

Task	Duration	Start time (backwards)	Start time (forwards)
Press	1 hour	3.00 pm	1.00 pm
Dry	2 hours	1.00 pm	11.00 am
Wash	3 hours	10.00 am	8.00 am

The choice of backward or forward scheduling depends largely upon the circumstances. Table 10.2 lists some advantages and disadvantages of the two approaches. In theory, both materials requirements planning (MRP) (*see* Chapter 14) and just-in-time (JIT) (*see* Chapter 15) both use backwards scheduling, only starting work when it is required. In practice, however, users of materials requirements planning have tended to allow too long for each task to be completed, therefore each task is not started at the last possible time. In comparison, just-in-time is started, as the name suggests, just-in-time.

Table 10.2 Advantages of forward and backward scheduling

Advantages of forward scheduling	*Advantages of backward scheduling*
High labour utilization – workers always start work to keep busy	Lower material costs – materials are not used until they have to be, therefore delaying added value until the last moment
Flexible – the time slack in the system allows unexpected work to be loaded	Less exposed to risk in case of schedule change by the customer
	Tends to focus the operation on customer due dates

Push and pull scheduling

In a *push system* of planning and control, activities are scheduled by means of a central system, and completed in line with central instructions, such as an MRP system. Each work centre pushes out work without considering whether the succeeding work centre can make use of it. Work centres are coordinated by means of the central operations planning and control system. In practice, however, there are many reasons why actual conditions differ from planned. As a consequence, idle time, inventory and queues often characterize push systems.

In a *pull system* of planning and control the pace and specification of what is done is set by the 'customer' workstation, who 'pulls' work from the preceding (supplier) workstation. The customer acts as the only 'trigger' for movement. If a request is not passed back from the customer to the supplier, the supplier cannot produce anything or move any materials. A request from a customer not only triggers production at the supplying stage, it will also prompt the supplying stage to request a further delivery from its own suppliers. In this way demand is transmitted back through the stages from the original point of demand by the original customer.

The inventory consequences of push and pull

Understanding the differing principles of push and pull is important because they have different effects in terms of their propensities to accumulate inventory in the operation. Pull systems are far less likely to result in inventory build-up and are therefore favoured by JIT operations (*see* Chapter 15). To understand why this is so consider two analogies. The 'gravity' analogy is illustrated in Fig. 10.11. Here a push system is represented by an operation, each stage of which is on a lower level than the

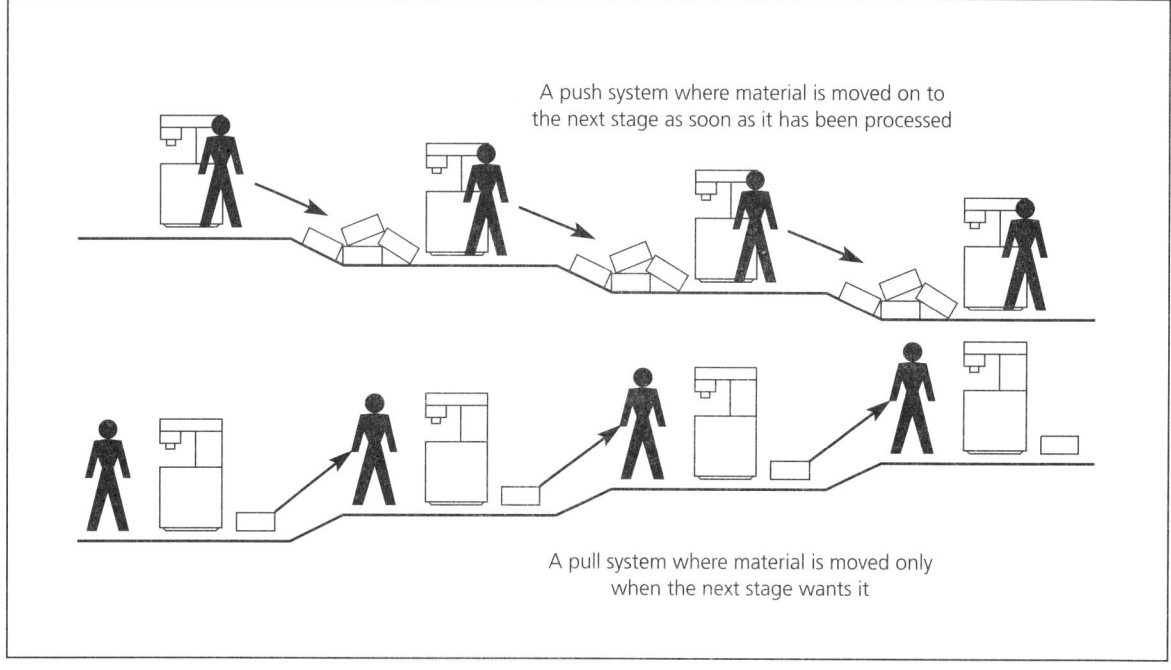

A push system where material is moved on to the next stage as soon as it has been processed

A pull system where material is moved only when the next stage wants it

Figure 10.11 Push versus pull: the gravity analogy

THE HOSPITAL TRIAGE SYSTEM[6]

One of the most difficult-to-schedule environments in a hospital is the Accident and Emergency Department, where patients arrive at random, without any prior warning, throughout the day. It is up to the hospital's reception, and the medical staff, to devise very rapidly a schedule which meets most of the necessary criteria. In particular, patients who arrive having had very serious accidents, or presenting symptoms of a serious illness, need to be attended to urgently. Therefore, the hospital will schedule these cases first. Less urgent cases – perhaps where patients are in some discomfort, but their injuries or illnesses are not life-threatening – will have to wait until the urgent cases are treated. Routine non-urgent cases will have the lowest priority of all. In many circumstances these patients will have to wait for the longest time, which may be many hours, especially if the hospital is busy. Sometimes these non-urgent cases may even be turned away if the hospital is too busy with more important cases.

In situations where hospitals expect sudden influxes of patients, they have developed what is known as a *triage system*, whereby medical staff hurriedly sort through the patients who have arrived to determine which category of urgency each patient fits into. In this way a suitable schedule for the various treatments can be devised in a short period of time. ■

previous stage. When parts are processed by each stage it pushes them down the slope to the next stage. Any delay or problem at that stage will result in the parts accumulating as inventory. In the pull system, parts cannot naturally flow up hill, so they can only progress if the next stage along deliberately pulls them forward. Under these circumstances inventory cannot accumulate as easily.

Johnson's Rule[7]

In many operations scheduling is still more of an art than a science. Although mathematically optimizing approaches have been developed in certain specialist applications, true optimizing models can usually be used only on the simplest of applications. One such optimizing rule is 'Johnson's Rule'. This applies to the scheduling of n jobs through two work centres. Figure 10.12 illustrates the use of Johnson's Rule. In this case a printer has to print and bind six jobs. The times for processing each job through the first work centre (printing) and the second work centre (binding) are shown in the figure. The rule is simple. First look for the smallest processing time. If that time is associated with the first work centre (printing in this case) then schedule that job first, or as near first as possible. If the next smallest time is associated with the second work centre then schedule that job last or as near last as possible. Once a job has been scheduled delete it from the list. Carry on allocating jobs until the list is complete. In this particular case the smallest processing time is 35 minutes for printing job B. Because

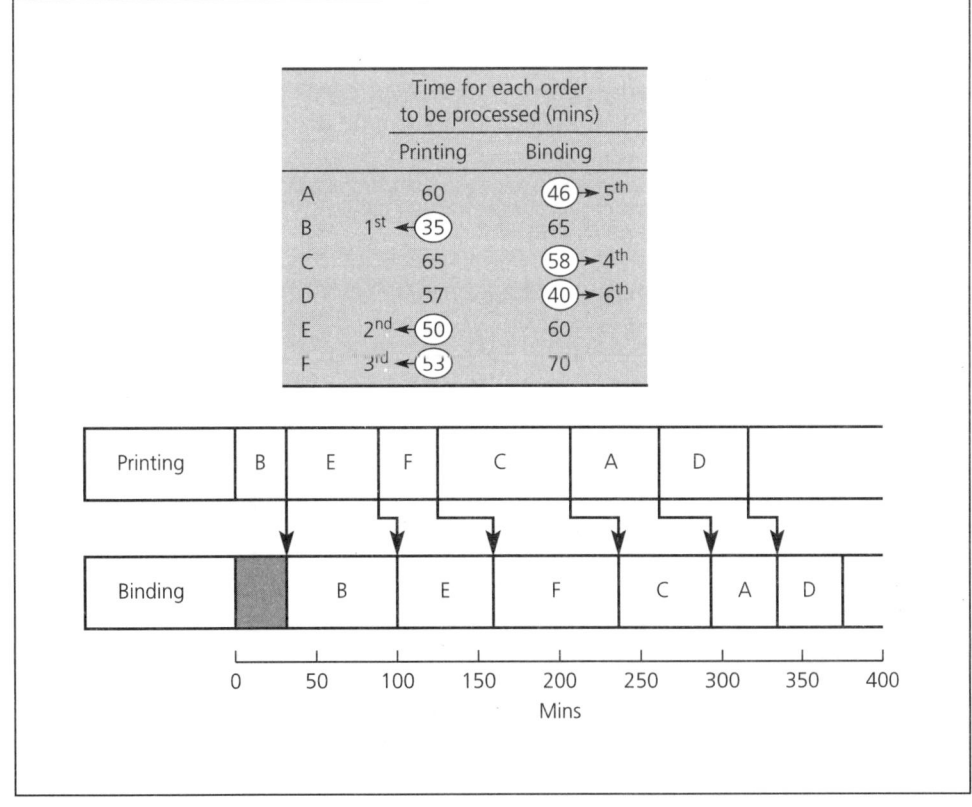

Figure 10.12
The application of Johnson's Rule for scheduling n jobs through two work centres

this is at the first process (printing), job B is assigned first position in the schedule. The next smallest processing time is 40 minutes for binding – job D. Because this is at the second process (binding), it is scheduled last. The next lowest processing time after jobs B and D have been struck off the list is 46 minutes for binding job A. Because this is at the second work centre it is scheduled as near last as possible, which in this case is fifth. This process continues until all the jobs have been scheduled. It results in a schedule for the two processes which is also shown in Fig. 10.12.

THE VOLUME–VARIETY EFFECT ON PLANNING AND CONTROL

In Chapter 4 we identified that many of the detailed design decisions in operations management were significantly affected by the volume–variety position of an operation. This is also true of the planning and control activities. Operations which produce a high variety of products or services in relatively low volume will clearly have customers who require a different set of factors and use processes which have a different set of needs to those operations which create standardized products or services in high volume (*see* Table 10.3).

Again, let us take the two operations which were discussed in Chapter 4 which occupy the two extremes of the volume–variety spectrum – an architects' practice and an electricity utility. The architects' high variety means that their services will have little or no standardization. This means that they cannot produce their designs in advance of customers requesting them. Because of this the time it will take to respond to customers' requests will be relatively slow. Indeed their customers will understand this and expect to be consulted extensively as to their needs. Because of this the $P{:}D$ ratio of the operation will be 1 or very close to 1. The details and requirements of

Table 10.3 The volume–variety effects on planning and control

Volume	Variety	Customer responsiveness	Planning horizon	Major planning decision	Control decisions	Robustness
Low	High	Slow	Short	Timing	Detailed	High
↓	↓	↓	↓	↓	↓	↓
High	Low	Fast	Long	Volume	Aggregated	Low

each job will emerge only as each individual building is designed to the client's requirements. This means that planning occurs on a relatively short-term basis. The architects are unlikely to be able to plan several years ahead because they do not know what jobs they will be doing at that time. The individual decisions which are taken in the planning process will usually concern the timing of activities and events: for example, when a design is to be delivered, when building should start, when each individual architect will be needed to work on the design and so on. Most of the control decisions will be at a relatively detailed level. A small delay in calculating one part of the design could have very significant implications in many other parts of the job. In general, the planning and control of the operation cannot be totally routinized, rather it will need managing on an individual project basis. Finally, the robustness of the operation (that is its vulnerability to serious disruption if one part of the operation breaks down) will be relatively high. There are probably plenty of other things to get on with if an architect is prevented from progressing one part of the job.

The electricity utility, on the other hand, will exhibit very different planning and control characteristics. Volume is high, production continuous, and variety is virtually non-existent. Customers expect extremely fast response to their request for the product. In effect they expect instant 'delivery' whenever they plug in an appliance. The planning horizon in electricity generation can be very long. Major decisions regarding the capacity of power stations are made many years in advance. Even the fluctuations in demand over a typical day can be forecast to a certain extent in advance. Popular television programmes can affect minute-by-minute demand and these are scheduled weeks or months ahead. The weather, which also affects demand, is less prone to being forecast, but can to some extent be predicted. The individual planning decisions made by the electricity utility will centre not around the timing of output, but rather the volume of output. Control decisions will not be concerned with the detailed intricacies of the operation's output because the product is more or less homogeneous. Rather, control will concern aggregated measures of output such as the total kilowatts of electricity generated. Finally, the robustness of the operation is very low insomuch as, if the generator fails, the operation's capability of supplying electricity from that part of the operation also fails (*see* Table 10.3).

Scheduling work patterns

Where the dominant resource in an operation is its staff, then the schedule of work times effectively determines the capacity of the operation itself. The main task of scheduling, therefore, is to make sure that sufficient numbers of people are working at any point in time to provide a capacity appropriate for the level of demand at that point in time. Operations such as postal delivery services, telephone operators, policing services, holiday couriers, shop workers, and hospital staff, will all need to schedule the working hours of their staff with demand in mind. This is a direct consequence of these operations having relatively high customer contact (we introduced the idea of high customer contact in Chapter 1). Such operations cannot store their outputs in inventories and so must respond directly to customer demand.

For example, Fig. 10.13 shows the scheduling of shifts for one part of a home-banking enquiry service. This particular department gives advice to customers on home loans and insurance. It advertises a 24-hour service and, indeed, some customers do make use of the enquiry service throughout the night. However, during this period demand is relatively low. It builds up during the morning to peak half-way through the day. There is another small peak in the early evening, but demand then falls away during the later part of the evening. The scheduling task here is to allocate start and finish times to staff such that:

- capacity matches demand;
- the length of each shift is neither excessively long nor too short to be attractive to staff;
- working at unsocial hours is minimized.

THE WIZARD SYSTEM AT AVIS

It is possible to rent cars at almost every major airport and city centre in the world, and there is invariably intense competition to attract and keep customers. Since the hire companies all offer similar ranges of relatively new vehicles, and the reliability of these cars is taken for granted by most customers, competition is generally on service and/or price. The most critical service factor is the availability of the desired category (size and specification) of car, and the speed with which all the hire contract paperwork can be completed, so that the customer is not unnecessarily delayed. This depends on the effectiveness of the hire company's planning and control system. One of the most important Avis sites in Belgium is the operation at Brussels National Airport at Zaventem, which deals predominantly with business customers, and hires out up to 200 cars on a busy day. Avis's advertisement, targeted at the business market, emphasizes its ability to process customers quickly and efficiently. The objective is to complete the transaction in less than two minutes, and this is facilitated by Avis's well developed computer system known as WIZARD which handles all reservations, preparation of hire contracts at the service desks, inventory management and invoicing systems. WIZARD is a globally integrated system, with over 15 000 terminals in Avis branches world-wide, allowing international reservations to be made with accuracy and certainty, and helping to maximize the utilization of vehicles throughout the network.

Regular customer surveys and analyses of actual demand patterns are carried out to determine the customers' preferences in terms of type and category of vehicles, providing a guide to the Belgian fleet composition, which is managed from the central 'clearing house' at Machelen. Because each of the Belgian branch offices has access to a pool of cars held at Machelen, their local buffer stock requirements can be minimized. The requirements for the movement of car inventory between branches and between countries is centralized in this way, allowing the branches to concentrate on the task of providing good customer service. Each regular business customer has a unique reference number in WIZARD, allowing reservations to be made and rental contracts to be completed quickly, with only three pieces of information: the customer's number, the type of car required, and the duration of the hire. This type of transaction is usually completed in under two minutes, after which the customer goes directly to the car park and collects the car. ■

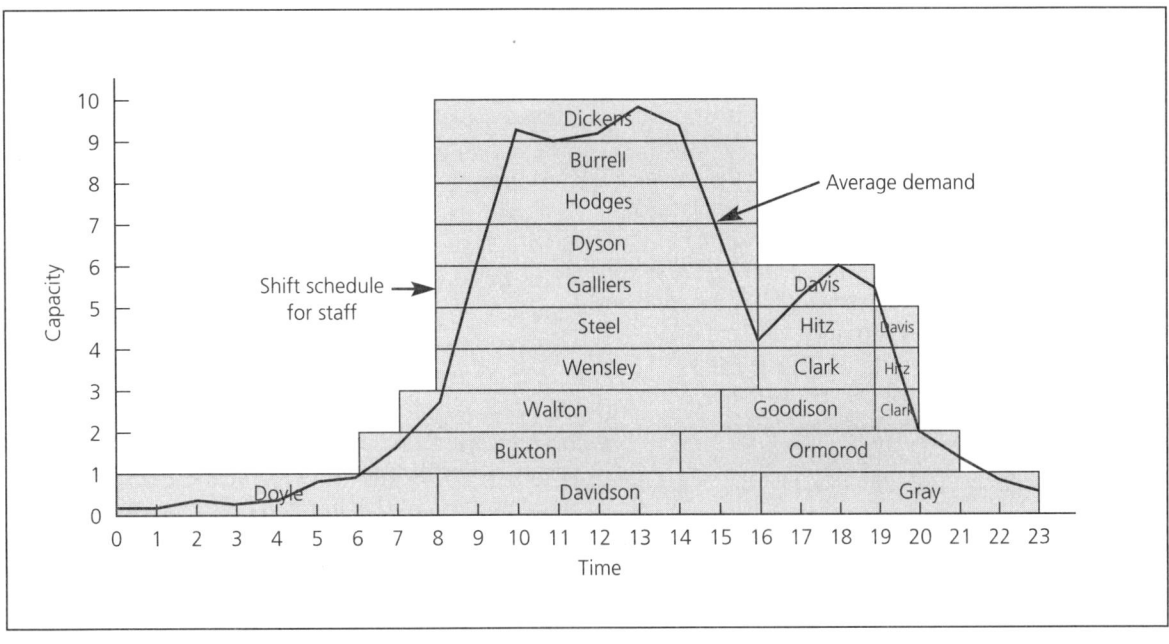

Figure 10.13 Shift scheduling on a home-banking enquiry service

Paola Petré, Brussels Airport Terminal Company SA

BATC is the recently privatized operating company responsible for the passenger- and baggage-handling processes at Brussels National Airport at Zavantem, on the outskirts of Europe's busy administrative capital.

Paola studied business administration at the Université Libre de Bruxelles, and then joined a large bank, working in a department responsible for improving operating systems, mainly in back-office administrative processes.

'The broad experience that I gained in the analysis and development of systems and procedures has been invaluable in my career development, and has been a good foundation for my work in operations planning at the airport. My current position as Allocation Controller involves analysis of the utilization of key resources in the terminal; particularly the check-in desks, baggage-handling systems, and the gates or stands where the aircraft park.

'Most of the airlines operating here would prefer to be able to occupy more check-in desks than they really need, and these would stand idle for most of the time except at the peak periods in the morning and evening. As with almost all operations at the airport, space is limited, and with the growth in traffic it is not possible to satisfy all this demand. It is my responsibility to allocate what we have on a fair and equitable basis, based on a thorough understanding and analysis of schedules and passenger numbers for the different types of service. Check-in procedures are very fast for charter flights, and passengers tend to arrive long before departure, and are queue (line) tolerant. On the other hand, European scheduled flights are predominantly business people; many arrive at the last moment possible, and if they are not processed quickly, will become very upset. Long-haul flights usually involve much larger numbers of passengers, longer check-in ▶

times, and much more baggage handling. To complicate the analysis further, until recently, there were different check-in computer systems for each of the three handlers: American Airlines, Sabena and Belgavia, so allocations became fixed by the system incompatibility. I was closely involved in the planning of the new terminal, which will give us 120 new desks, all using a common computer system, allowing me the flexibility to allocate on a more logical basis. I held many briefing meetings with the handlers to ensure that they "bought-in" to the analysis.

'Each check-in desk has a baggage conveyor that connects it to the new baggage hall below. Each item carries a bar code, and drops into a tray which is then automatically sorted into its correct loading "chute". These are rather like the spiral slides found at funfairs: there are only 132 of them, which might sound a lot, but really is another bottle-neck for me to deal with. The handlers like to keep different classes of baggage separate (First, Club, Business, Economy, and Transfer) and on long-haul, several chutes will be needed to cope with the large volumes of items. Different schedules are needed every day to cope with the changing mix of traffic, so this is a very complex operation to plan. It is vital for me to ensure that the schedule meets the needs of all the users, without wasted capacity, and yet avoid bottle-necks building up that could delay loading of the aircraft. Our top priority is to ensure that the baggage systems

resource at Brussels allows the handlers to achieve faster throughput than comparable airports in Europe. This will be one of our "competitive edges" in the quest for more business.

'Another of my responsibilities is to allocate gates and stands for aircraft. During the middle of the day there are lots of empty gates, allowing access for all suitably sized aircraft to link up to air bridges. At peak times, however, it is necessary to tightly schedule the requirements of the airlines, both to ensure that large planes and long-haul flights always get a space, and to be seen to be fair to all the operators, and minimize the use of buses to remote stands. The allocation of the gates is a similar problem to that of the chutes; demand equals or exceeds capacity, and optimization/ prioritization decisions must be made.

'This has been a fantastic period to work for BATC. I have been closely involved with the planning of the enormous new facility, which has more than doubled capacity, and I have worked with the airlines and handlers to analyse and agree our planning and control systems. Now we can also have the satisfaction of monitoring the improvements we have made in throughput speed and quality. It is fascinating to watch the smooth flow of passengers which is the result of all our years of detailed work in the back office.' ■

Source: By kind permission of Paola Petré

SUMMARY

■ The purpose of planning and control is to ensure that the operation runs effectively and produces products and services as it should do.

■ One way of characterizing all planning and control decisions is as a reconciliation of the potential of the operation to supply products and services, and the demand of its customers on the operation.

■ All planning and control situations take place under resource constraints. These resource constraints are usually:
  cost constraints
  capacity constraints
  timing constraints
  quality constraints.

■ Although planning and control are theoretically separable, these are usually treated together. Planning is the act of setting down expectations of what should happen. Control is the process of coping with changes when they occur.

■ The balance between planning and control changes over time. In long-term planning and control the emphasis is on the aggregated planning and budgeting of activities. At the other extreme, short-term planning and control usually operates within the resource constraints of the operation but makes interventions into the operation in order to cope with short-term changes in circumstances.

■ Uncertainty, both in supply and demand, will affect the complexity of the planning and control task.

■ Demand can be treated either as dependent demand or independent demand. Dependent demand is relatively predictable because it is dependent on some known factor. Independent demand is less predictable because it depends on the chances of the market.

■ Operations can respond to demand by:
  resourcing to order;
  making to order; or
  making to stock.

■ These different ways of responding to demand can be characterized by differences in the $P{:}D$ ratio of the operation. The $P{:}D$ ratio is the ratio of total throughput time to demand time.

■ In planning and controlling the volume and timing of activity in operations three distinct activities are necessary:
  loading
  sequencing
  scheduling.

■ Loading dictates the amount of work which is allocated to each part of the operation. This may be performed on a finite or infinite basis.

■ Sequencing decides the order in which work is tackled within the operation. There are many different priority decision rules which can help operations to make this decision.

■ Scheduling determines the detailed timetable of activity and determines when activities are started and finished.

■ Scheduling can be performed either on a backward scheduling or forward scheduling basis.

■ Scheduling can also be classified as push or pull scheduling. Push scheduling is a centralized system whereby planning and control decisions are issued to work centres who are required to perform their task and send their parts to the next workstation. Pull scheduling is a system whereby demand is triggered by requests from a work centre's (internal) customer.

■ Pull schedules generally have far lower inventory levels than push schedules.

■ The volume and variety position of an operation has an effect on the nature of its planning and control. Customer responsiveness, planning horizon, the major planning decisions, the control decision, and the robustness of planning and control are especially affected by volume and variety.

Rosslyn Safaris – service with a difference

Rosslyn Safaris is a 90 000-hectare ranch near Victoria Falls in the north-west of Zimbabwe, and caters for rifle hunting, bird shooting and game viewing. It is supplemented by two other ranches – one in the Gwaai area and one just outside Bulawayo – and various other shared concessions around the country. Running a smooth service operation without the benefits of a good telephone system or direct use of a fax, nearby quality grocery shops or full-time electricity is a challenge that has been well met by Peter and Carole Johnstone over the last 30 years.

Booking the safari

Safaris are usually booked a year in advance through an agent in the USA, Germany or Spain. Many prospective clients hear of Rosslyn Safaris through word of mouth, or remember seeing their booth at the annual safari convention held in Reno, USA. While the latter does not necessarily cover costs in the hunts generated by this visit, the public relations exercise offered is invaluable. Adverts in hunting magazines also expose the business to prospective clients.

Preferred safari dates are conveyed to Peter Johnstone, who has a schedule of calendar months for each guide. Some clients have preferences about who they hunt with, either because of the guide's reputation, or because the client has hunted with him before. Fitting clients into particular dates means juggling hunting areas as well as guides. This is due to quotas followed in each area, worked out each year to maintain the optimum level of various species. Rosslyn Safaris also has a policy of limiting hunters in an area at one time, particularly if they are hunting the same species. Peter recalls a particular incident where a rather loud American shot a trophy leopard that had been feeding on a Spaniard's leopard bait. If a guide is unavailable, Peter will suggest other guides.

The hunt dates are confirmed when a deposit of 50 per cent of the daily rate has been received. The client stipulates which animals he is interested in, and these are confirmed according to the quota. For example, only seven buffalo a year may be shot on the concession, despite their being one of the most popular hunting animals. Each client receives an information pack on clothes to bring, malaria pills to take and travel options.

Past clients are kept in contact through the annual newsletter and Christmas cards. Many become old friends, and come back time and again. Each client is put on a reference list that is given to prospective clients. Quality of service offered is important to Rosslyn, and is necessary for the successful hunting operation.

The hunt

- Guides can hunt with a maximum of two clients each, but usually prefer to have just one hunter at a time. Each client is accompanied in an allocated land cruiser by the guide and two trackers. These trackers usually hunt with one particular guide, simply because a relationship is built up between the men over years of working together. Their prime goal is to ensure that the hunt is done in a professional manner, with no wounded animals.

- Cats (lion and leopard) can be pre-baited if requested by the client. Non-trophy animals, usually impala for leopard and buffalo for lion, are used for bait and are paid for by the client. The bait is set up in a position usually known to be frequented by the cats and a grass blind is usually built for each cat hunt. Shooting the bait before the client arrives can be done by a learner hunter, for the experience. During the off-season, heavy duty maintenance and fixing of vehicles, pumps, roads and buildings takes place.

- The price of each hunt differs according to the length of the hunt and the different animals being taken on that hunt. Usually, there are certain criteria that need to be met for the more popular animals, such as a longer hunt. The basic price for a hunt is calculated on the type of hunt: for example, an 18-day lion and leopard hunt with supporting quota, or a 15-day elephant only hunt, which the client pays for regardless of getting that particular animal. 50 per cent of the daily rate is put down as a deposit before the hunt is confirmed. 15 per cent of the total daily rate is given to the agent as commission. The cost of each animal shot, plus packing and documentation, is added onto the final cost of the hunt and the bill is settled accordingly on the last day. Each client receives an itemized bill, which lists each animal shot and its tag number for easy reference. These costs are inclusive of pick-up from the airport, meals, drinks and transfers. Once the payment has been made at the beginning and end of the hunt, the money is sent to the bank. The deposit slip is kept with the 'NP9' book as proof of all foreign currencies received being banked. This book has to be stamped by the bank before export permits are finalized.

- A small aeroplane may be used to pick up clients on arrival. However, the client is usually picked up by the guide, in his land cruiser. This allows the client to spend the day in Victoria Falls, if so desired. The client usually arrives the day before the hunt begins, to give time to recover from jet lag and to sight rifles. If the client is transferred to another hunting area, he will be driven there by his guide, although in some cases the tracker will drive the equipment there, and the client will be flown in to the camp.
- Non-hunters are welcome, and are merely charged a lower non-hunting daily rate. They spend their time at camp, or shopping in Victoria Falls, or out on the jeep with their hunting partner. Children are usually not recommended, although there have been exceptions.

The trophies

As Rosslyn is a concessionaire, law requires permits before the hunt may begin. All rifle hunting permits are applied for from the National Parks Board about a month before the hunt starts. Without this permit, the hunt is illegal, and the safari operator will face criminal charges. After the animals have been shot, the skins and horns are cured, and then taken to the National Parks Board to be measured and recorded. While the client may keep the skins and horns, the meat is kept by the safari operator. It is used in a number of different ways: for feeding the clients and staff, or to sell in the form of meat packs, biltong or as an entire carcass to a butcher.

Trophies, once cured and recorded, are ready to be shipped to taxidermists, which are chosen by the client. Before they may be shipped, however, a great deal of paperwork needs to be completed. The hunting permits, the NP9 for proof and detail of payment, the pre-hunt form, the CITES form (for leopard or elephant) from the client's country of origin if it is a signatory to the CITES convention, the CD1 Form to show what money has been paid and vet permits to prove trophies have been treated correctly. Each of the client's trophies is packed into a strong, wooden-framed cardboard box.

Spain requires incoming trophies to be sealed in a thick, transparent plastic. This may be a problem in the summer if the skins or horns have not been cured properly.

The home ground

This is probably where the challenge is greatest – how to provide delicious meals three times a day, with the nearest shop over 100km away on bad roads? An added problem is that there are different camps feeding interchanging clients. Electricity at each camp is provided by a small generator, so fridges and freezers are run on paraffin. An inverter that uses solar power may be used for a limited time to run computers or small appliances.

Every Friday, the foreman drives into Hwange, the nearest town, to do chores and pick up needed supplies. The grocery order is telephoned through to a supermarket in Bulawayo on Thursday, giving them time to put the groceries on the overnight 'Swift' carrier to reach Hwange on Friday. A large vegetable garden and an almost unlimited supply of meat does help the situation. Before the hunt starts, a menu is devised, using seasonal ingredients. If possible, a client is not fed the same dish twice on a hunt, which can become difficult on a 31-day hunt! These menus are kept for reference when the client returns for another hunt. While the menus are constantly revised during the hunt, it becomes a complicated juggling act when two hunting parties share the same camp for some nights. There is a core team of cooks, proficient in cooking the dishes on the menu, who are sent off to the different camps as needed.

On booking the hunt, the client is asked to provide details of any allergies or food preferences, to facilitate catering. Diets have ranged from the sensible to the ludicrous, but each has to be catered for. While the clients usually eat a 'scoff-box' breakfast and lunch, and only come home in time for dinner, there are the non-hunters to consider. Fresh bread is made every day and meals are provided for those customers left back at the camp. ■

Questions

1 What resource constraints exist in this business?

2 What resource management techniques are applicable?

3 Describe the planning activities and the control activities that are appropriate for success in this service operation.

4 How would you schedule the meals for customers in this case?

DISCUSSION QUESTIONS

1 Identify the ways in which planning and control activity could reconcile supply and demand in the following operations:

    an ambulance service
    a medical centre
    a pizza-manufacturing company
    a national rail service
    a psychotherapy clinic
    a bespoke tailor.

2 What is the difference between dependent and independent demand?

3 To what extent is demand dependent or independent in the following types of operation:

    a manufacturer of nuclear-powered submarines
    a specialist catering company
    a fast-food hamburger restaurant
    a specialist packaging manufacturer who supplies
    a computer manufacturer
    a television production company?

4 How does scheduling affect the five performance objectives of operations management?

5 How might a police force schedule its officers so as to match its capacity to demand?

6 If you were a tutor at a local university which sequencing rule would you use to determine the order in which you saw your students? What do you think are the advantages and disadvantages of each sequencing rule in this particular situation?

7 A painter of fake masterpieces has been commissioned to paint and frame five different paintings.

Each of the paintings requires a different, but ornate, frame. The painter wishes to execute this commission as quickly as possible and has estimated the times for painting and framing the paintings as follows:

Van Gogh	painting 2 hours	framing $4\frac{1}{2}$ hours
Monet	painting 3 hours	framing $3\frac{1}{2}$ hours
Polock	painting 10 minutes	framing 1 hour
Renoir	painting 4 hours	framing 2 hours
Picasso	painting $1\frac{1}{2}$ hours	framing $4\frac{1}{2}$ hours

The painter has employed a specialist framer to join him on this enterprise. In what order should the pair tackle the paintings?

8 In the chapter a description was given of the planning and control of a rock concert. How do you think these planning and control activities would change if the organization promoting the concerts gave the same concert every week of the year?

9 Visit a local automotive service centre which carries out servicing and repairs on cars and find out the following:
(a) What is their approach to prioritizing jobs?
(b) What is the typical utilization of some of their equipment?
(c) How do they cope when a job takes longer than they expect?

10 What is the main difference between planning and controlling a hospital where the majority of surgical procedures are routine operations and planning and controlling a hospital which has a very high level of accident and emergency work?

NOTES ON CHAPTER

1 Some specialist planning and control approaches are designed to organize operations around capacity bottle-necks. See the discussion on OPT in Chapter 14.
2 Source: Discussions with company staff.
3 For an interesting discussion of how these categories of planning and control can be modelled, *see* Wild, R. (1988) *Production and Operations Management*, Cassell.
4 The concept of *P:D* ratios comes originally from Shingo, S. (1981) 'Study of Toyota Production Systems', Japan Management Association, and was

extended by Mather, K. (1988) *Competitive Manufacturing*, Prentice Hall.
5 We are grateful to Paul Walley of Loughborough University for this section.
6 Source: Walley, P. and Slack, N. (1994) MBA Course Notes, Warwick University, UK.
7 Johnson, S.M. (1954) 'Optimal Two-stage and Three-stage Production Schedules', *Naval Logistics Quarterly*, Vol 1, No 1.
8 By kind permission of Rosslyn Safaris.

SELECTED FURTHER READINGS

Baker, K.R. (1984) *Introduction to Sequencing and Scheduling*, John Wiley.

Browne, J.J. (1979) 'Simplified Scheduling of Routine Work Hours and Day Off', *Industrial Engineering*, Dec.

Conway, R.W. (1965) 'Priority Despatching and Job Lateness in a Job Shop', *Journal of Industrial Engineering*, Vol 16, No 4.

Fry, T.D. and Philipoom, P.R. (1989) 'A Despatching Rule for Allowing Trade-offs Between Inventory and Customer Satisfaction', *International Journal of Operations and Production Management*, Vol 9, No 7.

Goldratt, E.Y. and Cox, J. (1984) *The Goal*, North River Press.

Kanet, J.K. and Hayya, J.C. (1982) 'Priority Despatching with Operation Due Dates in a Job Shop', *Journal of Operations Management*, Vol 2, No 3.

CAPACITY PLANNING AND CONTROL

INTRODUCTION

Providing the capability to satisfy current and future demand is a fundamental responsibility of operations management. An appropriate balance between capacity and demand can generate high profits and satisfied customers, whereas getting the balance 'wrong' can be potentially disastrous. Yet although planning for, and controlling, capacity is a major responsibility of operations managers, it should also involve other functional managers. There are three reasons for this. The first is that capacity decisions have a company-wide impact. The second is that all the other functions provide vital inputs to the planning process. The third is that each business function will usually have to plan and control the capacity of its own 'micro operations' to match that of the main operations function.

What we have called here *capacity planning and control* is also sometimes referred to as *aggregate planning and control*. This is because, at the 'highest level' of the planning and control process, demand and capacity calculations are usually performed on an aggregated basis which does not discriminate between the different products and services which an operation might produce. The essence of the task is to reconcile, at a general and aggregated level, the supply of capacity with the level of demand which it must satisfy (*see* Fig. 11.1).

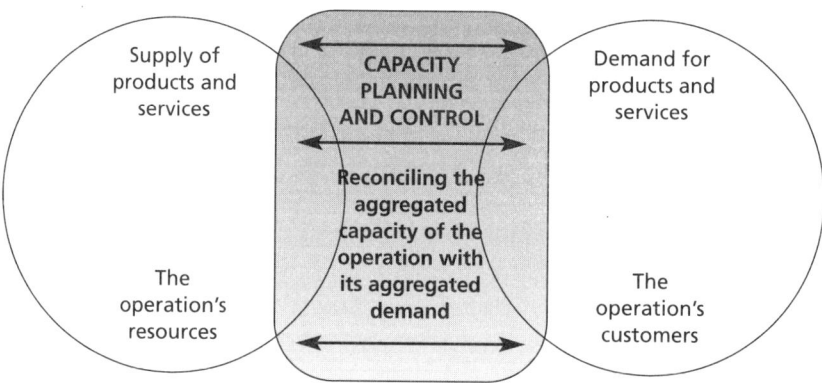

Figure 11.1 A definition of capacity planning and control

WHAT IS CAPACITY?

The most common use of the word 'capacity' is in the static, physical sense of the fixed *volume* of a container, or the space in a building. This meaning of the word is also sometimes used by operations managers. For example, a pharmaceutical manufacturer may invest in new 1000-litre capacity reactor vessels; a property company purchases a 500-vehicle capacity city-centre car park; and a 'multiplex' cinema is built with ten screens and a total capacity of 2500 seats. While these capacity measures describe the *scale* of these operations, they do not reflect the processing capacities of these investments. To do this we must incorporate a *time* dimension appropriate to the use of assets. So the operations manager of the pharmaceutical company will be concerned with the level of output that can be achieved using the 1000-litre reactor vessel. If a batch of standard products can be produced every hour, the planned processing capacity could be as high as 24 000 litres per day. If the reaction takes four hours, and two hours are used for cleaning between batches, the vessel may only produce 4000 litres per day. Similarly, the car park may be fully occupied by office workers during the working day, 'processing' only 500 cars per day. Alternatively it may be used for shoppers staying on average only one hour, and theatre-goers occupying spaces for three hours in the evening. The processing capacity would then be up to 5000 cars per day. Thus the definition of the capacity of an operation is the *maximum level of value-added activity over a period of time* that the process can achieve under normal operating conditions.

Capacity constraints

Many organizations operate at below their maximum processing capacity, either because there is insufficient demand to 'fill' their capacity completely, or as a deliberate policy, so that the operation can respond quickly to every new order. Often though, organizations find themselves with some parts of their operation operating below their capacity while other parts are at their capacity 'ceiling'. It is the parts of the operation which are operating at their capacity 'ceiling' which are the *capacity constraint* for the whole operation.

The concept of one micro operation acting as the 'bottle-neck' constraint on capacity was introduced in Chapter 6. Depending on the nature of demand, different parts of an operation might be pushed to their capacity ceiling and act as a constraint on the total operation. For example, a retail superstore might offer a gift-wrapping service which at normal times can cope with all requests for its services without delaying customers unduly. At Christmas, however, the demand for gift wrapping might increase proportionally far more than the overall increase in custom for the store as a whole. Unless extra resources are provided to increase the capacity of this micro operation it could constrain the capacity of the whole store.

PLANNING AND CONTROLLING CAPACITY

Capacity planning and control is the task of setting the effective capacity of the operation so that it can respond to the demands placed upon it. This usually means deciding how the operation should react to fluctuations in demand. We have faced this issue before in Chapter 6 where we examined long-term changes in demand and the alternative capacity strategies for dealing with the changes. These strategies were concerned with introducing (or deleting) major increments of physical capacity. We called this task *long-term capacity strategy*. In this chapter we are treating the shorter time-scale where capacity decisions are being made largely within the constraints of the physical capacity limits set by the operation's long-term capacity strategy.

Medium- and short-term capacity

Having established long-term capacity, operations managers must decide how to adjust the capacity of the operation in the *medium term*. This usually involves an assessment of the demand forecasts over a period of 2 to 18 months ahead, during which time planned output can be varied, for example, by changing the number of hours the equipment is used. In practice, however, few forecasts are accurate, and most operations also need to respond to changes in demand which occur over a shorter time-scale. Hotels and restaurants have unexpected and apparently random changes in demand from night to night, but also know from experience that certain days are on average busier than others. So operations managers also have to make *short-term capacity adjustments*, which enable them to flex output for a short period, either on a predicted basis (for example, bank check-outs are always busy at lunchtimes) or at short notice (for example, a sunny warm day at a theme park).

Aggregate demand and capacity

The important characteristic of capacity planning and control, as we are treating it here, is that it is concerned with setting capacity levels over the medium and short terms in aggregated terms. That is, it is making overall, broad capacity decisions, but is not concerned with all of the detail of the individual products and services offered. Thus aggregate plans assume that the mix of different products and services will remain relatively constant during the planning period. Figure 11.2 shows how four operations might aggregate their capacity and demand levels.

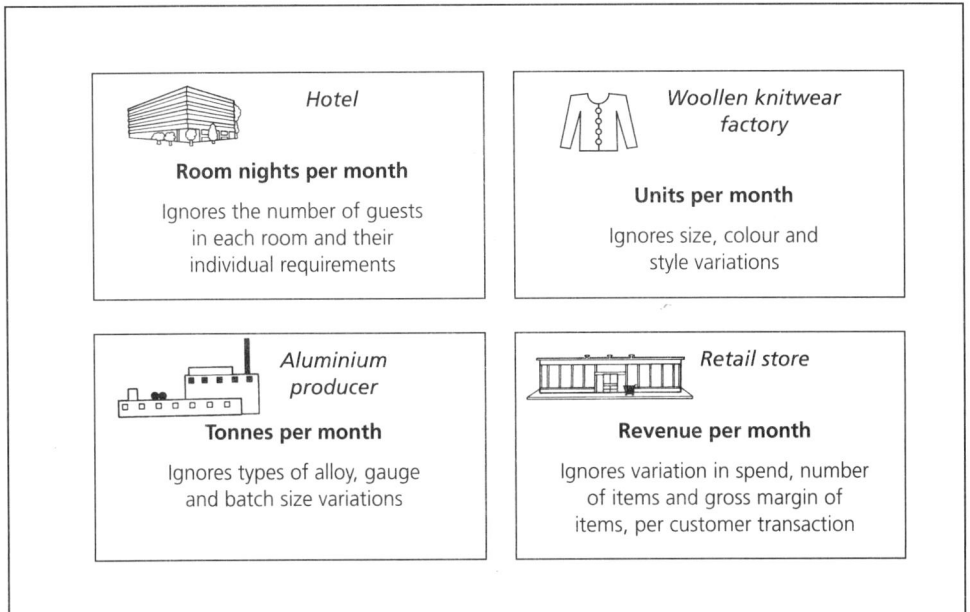

Figure 11.2 Examples of aggregation in capacity and demand measurement

The objectives of capacity planning and control

The decisions taken by operations managers in devising their capacity plans will affect several different aspects of performance.

● *Costs* will be affected by the balance between capacity and demand (or output level if that is different). Capacity levels in excess of demand could mean under-utilization of capacity and therefore high unit cost.

● *Revenues* will also be affected by the balance between capacity and demand, but in the opposite way. Capacity levels equal to or higher than demand at any point in time will ensure that all demand is satisfied and no revenue lost.

● *Working capital* will be affected if an operation decides to build up finished goods inventory prior to demand. This might allow demand to be satisfied but the organization will have to fund the inventory until it can be sold.

● *Quality* of goods or services might be affected by a capacity plan which involved large fluctuations in capacity levels, by hiring temporary staff for example. The new staff and the disruption to the routine working of the operation could increase the probability of errors being made. (*See* box on Eurocamp.)

● *Speed* of response to customer demand could be enhanced, either by the build-up of inventories (allowing customers to be satisfied directly from the inventory rather than having to wait for items to be manufactured) or by the deliberate provision of surplus capacity to avoid queueing.

● *Dependability* of supply will also be affected by how close demand levels are to capacity. The closer demand gets to the operation's capacity ceiling, the less able it is to cope with any unexpected disruptions and the less dependable its deliveries of goods and services could be.

● *Flexibility*, especially volume flexibility, will be enhanced by surplus capacity. If demand and capacity are in balance, the operation will not be able to respond to any unexpected increase in demand.

The steps of capacity planning and control

The sequence of capacity planning and control decisions which need to be taken by operations managers is illustrated in Fig. 11.3. Typically operations management is faced with a forecast of demand which is unlikely to be either certain or constant. They will also have some idea of their own ability to meet this demand. Nevertheless, before any further decisions are taken they must have quantitative data on both capacity and demand. So the first step will be to *measure the aggregate demand and capacity* levels for the planning period. The second step will be to *identify the alternative capacity plans* which could be adopted in response to the demand fluctuations. The third step will be to *choose the most appropriate capacity plan* for their circumstances.

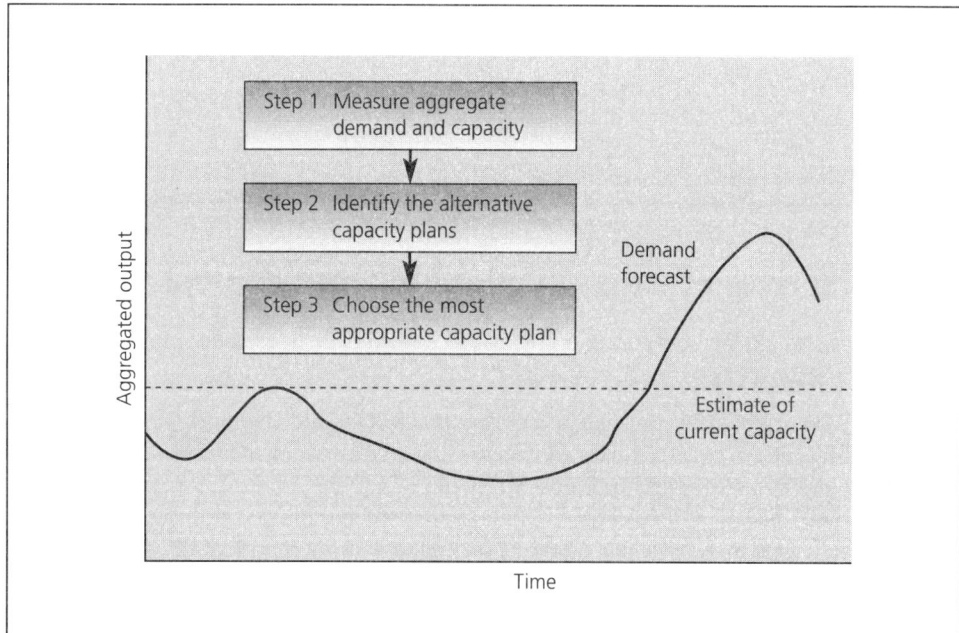

**Figure 11.3
The steps in
capacity planning
and control**

MEASURING DEMAND AND CAPACITY

Forecasting demand fluctuations

In most organizations, demand forecasting is the responsibility of the sales and/or the marketing departments. However, it is a major input into the capacity planning and control decision which is usually an operations management responsibility. After all, without an estimate of future demand it is not possible to plan effectively for future events, only to react to them. It is therefore important for operations managers to understand the basis and rationale for these demand forecasts. Appendix 1 at the end of the book describes forecasting techniques. As far as capacity planning and control is concerned there are three requirements from a demand forecast.

It is expressed in terms which are useful for capacity planning and control

If forecasts are expressed only in money terms and give no indication of the demands that will be placed on an operation's capacity, they will need to be translated into realistic expectations of demand, expressed in the same units as the capacity (e.g. machine hours per year, operatives required, space, etc.).

It is as accurate as possible

In capacity planning and control the accuracy of a forecast is important because whereas demand can change instantaneously, there is a lag between deciding to change capacity and the change taking effect. Thus many operations managers are faced with a dilemma. In order to attempt to meet demand they must often decide output in advance, based on a forecast which might change before the demand occurs, or worse prove not to reflect actual demand at all.

It gives an indication of relative uncertainty

Decisions to operate extra hours and recruit extra staff are usually based on forecast levels of demand, which could in practice differ considerably from actual demand, leading to unnecessary costs or unsatisfactory customer service. For example, Fig. 11.4 shows the average demand levels of a supermarket throughout one day in terms of the number of customers entering the store. Demand is initially slow but then builds up to a lunchtime rush. After this, demand slows only to build up again for the early evening rush and finally falls again at the end of trading. The supermarket manager can use this forecast to adjust (say) check-out capacity throughout the day. But

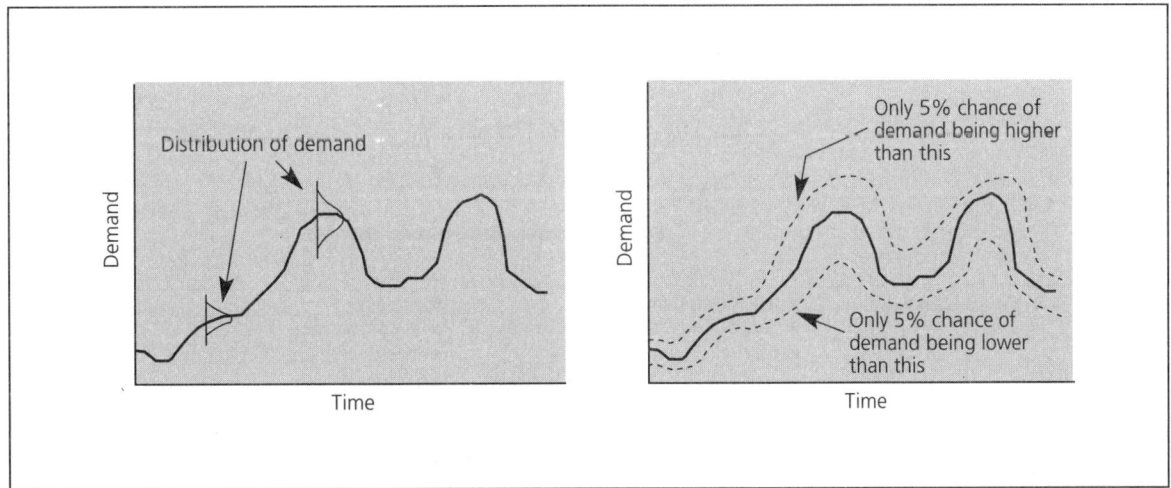

Figure 11.4 Good forecasts are essential for effective capacity planning but so is an understanding of demand uncertainty because it allows the operation to judge the risks to service level

although this may be an accurate average demand forecast, no single day will exactly conform to this pattern. Of equal importance is an estimate of how much actual demand could differ from the average. This can be found by examining demand statistics to build up a distribution of demand at each point in the day. The importance of this is that the manager now has an understanding of when it will be important to have reserve staff, perhaps filling shelves while on call to staff the check-outs should demand warrant it. Generally the advantage of probabilistic forecasts such as this is that they allow operations managers to make a judgement between possible plans that would virtually guarantee the operation's ability to meet actual demand, and plans that minimize costs. Ideally, this judgement should be influenced by the nature of the way the business wins orders: price-sensitive markets may require a risk-avoiding cost minimization plan that does not always satisfy peak demand, whereas markets that value responsiveness and service quality may justify a more generous provision of operational capacity.

Seasonality of demand

In many organizations capacity planning and control is concerned largely with coping with seasonal demand fluctuations. Almost all products and services have some *seasonality of demand* and some also have *seasonality of supply*, usually where the inputs are seasonal agricultural product: for example, processing frozen vegetables. These fluctuations in demand, or in supply, may be reasonably forecastable, but some are usually also affected by unexpected variations in the weather, and by changing economic conditions. Figure 11.5 gives some examples of seasonality.

Consider the four organizations previously referred to in Fig. 11.2. Their demand patterns are shown in Fig. 11.6. The woollen knitwear business and the city hotel both have seasonal sales demand patterns, but for different reasons: the woollen knitwear

Figure 11.5 Many types of operation have to cope with seasonal demand

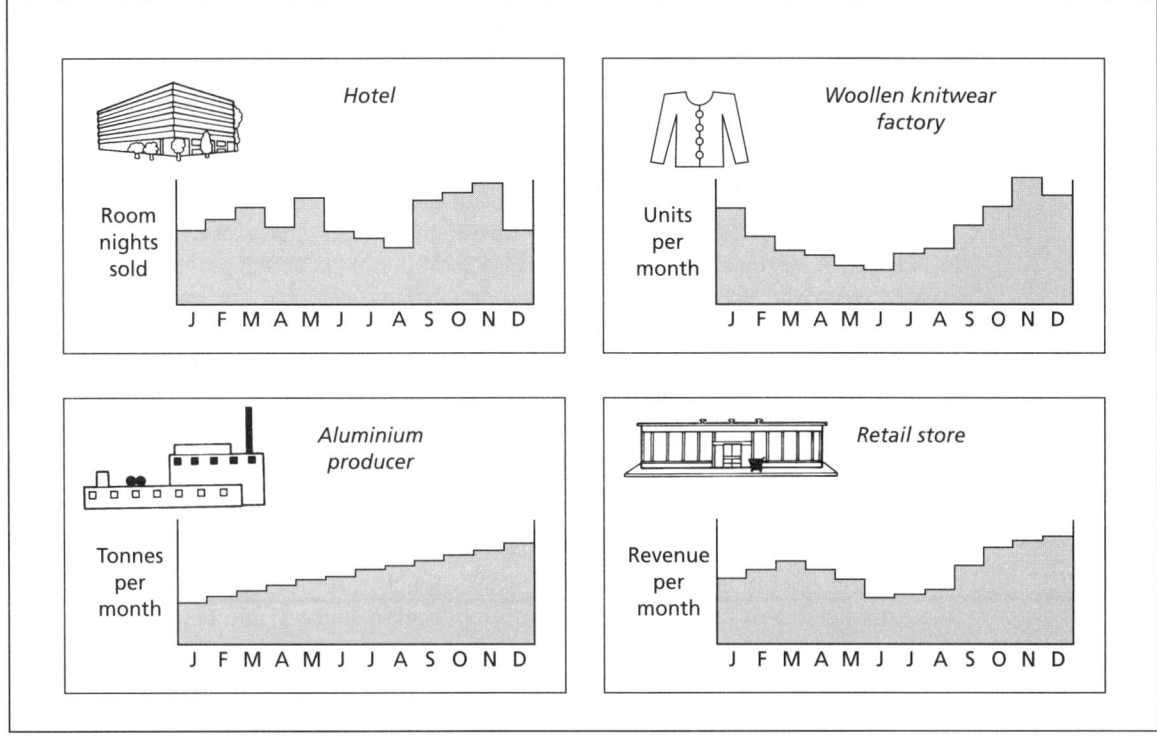

Figure 11.6 Aggregate demand fluctuations for four organizations

because of climatic patterns (cold winters, warm summers) and the hotel because of demand from business people, who take vacations from work at Christmas and in the summer. The retail supermarket is a little less seasonal, but is affected by pre-vacation peaks, and reduced sales during vacation periods. The aluminium producer shows virtually no seasonality, but is showing a steady growth in sales over the forecast period.

Weekly and daily demand fluctuations

Seasonality of demand occurs over a year, but similar predictable variations in demand can also occur for some products and services on a shorter cycle. We have already illustrated the daily demand pattern of a supermarket in Fig. 11.4, and it will also be subjected to predictable demand fluctuations over a week. Demand might be low on Monday and Tuesday, build up during the latter part of the week and reach a peak on Friday and Saturday. Banks, public offices, telephone sales organizations and electricity utilities all have weekly and daily or even hourly demand patterns which require capacity adjustment. The extent to which an operation will have to cope with very short-term demand fluctuations is partly determined by how long its customers are prepared to wait for their products or services. An operation whose customers are incapable of, or unwilling to, wait will have to plan for very short-term demand fluctuations. Emergency services, for example, will need to understand the hourly variation in the demand for their services and plan capacity accordingly. Similarly, the order-taking department of a catalogue retailer must be able to answer customers' telephone enquiries within a few rings of the telephone. If they cannot, the probability of the customer hanging up increases significantly.

Measuring capacity

Measuring demand provides part of the basic information for capacity planning. The main problem in obtaining this information is that demand is intrinsically uncertain. The main problem with measuring capacity is less its uncertainty but rather its complexity. Only when the operation is highly standardized and repetitive is capacity easy to define unambiguously. Thus if a television factory produces only one basic model, the weekly capacity could be described as 2000 Model A televisions. A government office may have the capacity to print and post 500 000 tax forms per week. A fast ride at a theme park might be designed to process batches of 60 people every 3 minutes – a capacity to transform 1200 people per hour. In each case, the *output* is the most appropriate measure of capacity because the output from the operation does not vary in its nature. For many operations, however, the definition of capacity is not so obvious. Especially when a much wider range of outputs places varying demands on the process, output measures of capacity are less useful. Here *input* measures are frequently used to define capacity.

Almost every type of operation could use a mixture of both input or output measures, but in practice, most choose to use one or the other. In high-volume, repetitive, low-variety operations, output measures of capacity are often preferred, because of their predictable relationships to the required input resources, and because actual and forecast sales are usually defined in terms of quantity of outputs (for example, cars per month). In complex operations producing a wide variety of outputs, each requiring different inputs, measures of capacity based on inputs are usually considered to be most appropriate (for example, beds in a hospital). *See* Table 11.1.

Table 11.1 Input and output capacity measures for different operations

Operation	Input measure of capacity	Output measure of capacity
Air conditioner plant	Machine hours available	**Number of units per week**
Hospital	**Beds available**	Number of patients treated per week
Theatre	**Number of seats**	Number of customers entertained per week
University	**Number of students**	Students graduated per year
Retail store	**Sales floor area**	Number of items sold per day
Airline	**Number of seats available on the sector**	Number of passengers per week
Electricity company	Generator size	**Megawatts of electricity generated**
Brewery	Volume of fermentation tanks	**Litres per week**

(Note: The most commonly used measure is shown in bold.)

Creating input measures from output measures (and *vice versa*)

Although input measures of capacity are the preferred capacity measurement for many operatives, they are of little value *per se* when capacity has to be planned against a changing forecast of demand stated in output terms, such as units or value. However, it is usually possible, with certain assumptions, to convert from one measure to another. In a retail store, for example, if an average experienced check-out operative can maintain a scanning rate of 1000 items per hour, the manager could determine the required capacity (in check-out operative hours) from the forecast output sales in units over the same period. Similarly, a brewery, knowing the capacity of the fermentation vessels and the standard fermentation times, could calculate the output capacity in litres per week. In turn, this could be converted to a quantity of 500 ml bottles, which would define the bottling capacity required in machine hours. Almost all organizations have to make these types of calculations to plan and control the relationship between capacity and expected demand. Note again though that the capacity of the transforming resources is usually defined by a time-based measure: for example, operations managers calculate the capacity *per hour*, *per day*, or *per year*. Brussels Airport has a capacity of 10 million passengers *per year*; the Morgan Car Company can produce nine of its specialist cars *a week*; a check-out operator in a supermarket may be able to 'scan' 20 items *a minute*.

Capacity depends on activity mix

The hospital measures its capacity in terms of its resources, partly because there is not a clear relationship between the number of beds it has and the number of patients which it treats. If all its patients required relatively minor treatment with only short stays in hospital, it could treat many people per week. Alternatively, if most of its patients require long periods of observation or recuperation it will treat far fewer. Output depends on the mix of activities in which the hospital is engaged, and because most hospitals perform many different types of activities output is difficult to predict. Certainly it is difficult to compare directly the capacity of hospitals which have very different activities.

Example

Suppose an air conditioner factory produces three different models of air conditioner unit: the deluxe, the standard and the economy. The deluxe model can be assembled in 1.5 hours, the standard in 1 hour and the economy in 0.75 hour. The assembly area in the factory has 800 staff hours of assembly time available each week.

If demand for deluxe, standard and economy units is in the ratio 2:3:2, the time needed to assemble $2 + 3 + 2 = 7$ units is:

$(2 \times 1.5) + (3 \times 1) + (2 \times 0.75) = 7.5$ hours

The number of units produced per week is:

$$\frac{800}{7.5} \times 7 = 746.7 \text{ units}$$

If demand changes to a ratio of deluxe, economy, standard units of 1:2:4, the time needed to assemble $1 + 2 + 4 = 7$ units is:

$(1 \times 1.5) + (2 \times 1) + (4 \times 0.75) = 6.5$ hours

Now the number of units produced per week is:

$$\frac{800}{6.5} \times 7 = 861.5 \text{ units}$$

Design capacity and effective capacity

The theoretical capacity of an operation – the capacity which its technical designers had in mind when they commissioned the operation – cannot always be achieved in practice. For example, a company coating photographic paper will have several coating lines which deposit thin layers of chemicals on to rolls of paper at high speed. Each line will be capable of running at a particular speed. Multiplying the maximum coating speed by the operating time of the plant gives the *theoretical design capacity* of the line. But in reality the line cannot be run continuously at its maximum rate. Different products will have different coating requirements, so the line will need to be stopped while it is changed over. Maintenance will need to be performed on the line, which will take out further productive time. Technical scheduling difficulties might mean further lost time. Not all of these losses are the operations manager's fault; they have occurred because of the market and technical demands on the operation. The actual capacity which remains, after such losses are accounted for, is called the *effective capacity* of operation. Not that these causes of reduction in capacity will be the only losses in the operation. Such factors as quality problems, machine breakdowns, absenteeism and other avoidable problems will all take their toll. This means that the *actual output* of the line will be even lower than the effective capacity. The ratios of the output actually achieved by an operation to design capacity and to effective capacity are called respectively the *utilization* and the *efficiency* of the plant.

$$\text{Utilization} = \frac{\text{Actual output}}{\text{Design capacity}}$$

$$\text{Efficiency} = \frac{\text{Actual output}}{\text{Effective capacity}}$$

Example

Suppose the photographic paper manufacturer has a coating line whose design capacity is 200 square metres per minute and the line is operated on a 24-hour day, 7 days per week (168 hours per week) basis.

Design capacity is $200 \times 60 \times 24 \times 7 = 2.016$ million square metres per week. The records for a week's production show the following lost production time:

1	Product change-overs (set-ups)	20 hrs
2	Regular preventative maintenance	16 hrs
3	No work scheduled	8 hrs
4	Quality sampling checks	8 hrs
5	Shift change times	7 hrs
6	Maintenance breakdown	18 hrs
7	Quality failure investigation	20 hrs
8	Coating material stockouts	8 hrs
9	Labour shortages	6 hrs
10	Waiting for paper rolls	6 hrs

During this week the actual output was only 582 000 square metres.

The company categorizes each type of lost production as either planned or unplanned. The first five categories of lost production occur as a consequence of reasonably unavoidable, planned occurrences and amount to a total of 59 hours. The last five categories are unplanned, and avoidable, losses and amount to 58 hours.

Measured in hours of production, and illustrated in Fig. 11.7:

Design capacity   = 168 hours per week

Effective capacity = 168 − 59   = 109 hrs

Actual output   = 168 − 59 − 58 = 51 hrs

$$\text{Utilization} = \frac{\text{Actual output}}{\text{Design capacity}} = \frac{51 \text{ hrs}}{168 \text{ hrs}} = 0.304$$

$$\text{Efficiency} = \frac{\text{Actual output}}{\text{Effective capacity}} = \frac{51 \text{ hrs}}{109 \text{ hrs}} = 0.468$$

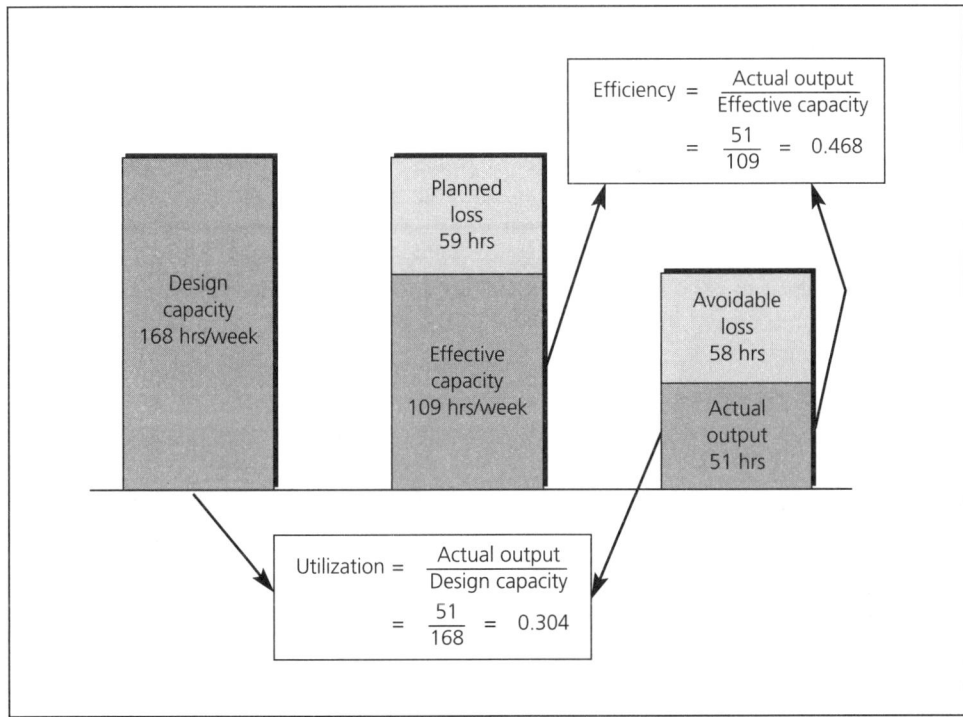

Figure 11.7
Utilization and efficiency

Utilization as a measure of operations performance

For many businesses, utilization is used as one of the key measures of the performance of the operation. It is an indication of the proportion of the designed capacity that has been used to produce value-added goods or services. The justification for placing such importance on utilization is usually that any lost production time could have been used to produce more outputs which would generate more profit (this is called the 'opportunity cost' argument). Many organizations require high utilization levels before they will authorize investment in additional capacity, arguing that this maximizes the return on capital employed in the business. Utilization can be measured against any agreed level of time-based design capacity (for example, 40 hours, 80 hours, 120 hours or 168 hours per week). It can be used to measure single pieces or groups of equipment, individuals or teams of employees, and even whole operations. Utilization may also be known by different names in different industries. For example:

- the 'room occupancy levels' in hotels;
- the 'load factor' for aircraft seats;
- 'uptime' in some factories.

Unfortunately, as a measure of an operation's performance, it can be misleading. Low utilization could result either from low demand, or because the plant is frequently breaking down, or running out of materials, or suffering labour unrest. Hence, it is measuring the performance of many parts of the business (sales, maintenance, purchasing, human resources management) yet is frequently used only as an operations performance indicator. Nor is seeking high utilization always desirable. Particularly in batch-type operations, an emphasis on high utilization can result in the build-up of in-process inventories, creating weeks or months of work held up in queues, tying up valuable materials and delaying completion of orders. This occupies valuable space, and increases the management costs of planning and controlling the operation. This is discussed further in Chapter 15 on just-in-time planning and control. High utilization can also adversely affect the customer if it reduces the speed and volume flexibility of the overall operation. Popular, high utilization ATMs at banks will frequently be accompanied by long queues. High runway utilization at airports during the morning and evening commuter rush results in aircraft 'stacking' which wastes fuel and delays passengers. High utilization of assistants in shops can be off-putting to busy shoppers, who may decide to go elsewhere. Occasionally, however, high utilization is seen favourably by customers: live rock music events and charity concerts, for example, are enhanced by a full crowd, perhaps because of the psychological impact of attending a 'successful' event.

THE ALTERNATIVE CAPACITY PLANS

With an understanding of both demand and capacity, the next step is to consider the alternative methods of responding to demand fluctuations. There are three 'pure' options for coping with such variation which are available.

- Ignore the fluctuations and keep activity levels constant (*level capacity plan*).
- Adjust capacity to reflect the fluctuations in demand (*chase demand plan*).
- Attempt to change demand to fit capacity availability (*demand management*).

In practice most organizations will use a mixture of all of these 'pure' plans, although often one plan might dominate.

Level capacity plan

In a level capacity plan, the processing capacity is set at a uniform level throughout the planning period, regardless of the fluctuations in forecast demand. This means that the same number of staff operate the same processes and should therefore be capable of producing the same aggregate output in each period. Where non-perishable materials are processed, but not immediately sold, they can be transferred to finished goods inventory in anticipation of sales at a later time period. Thus this plan is feasible (but not necessarily desirable) for our examples of the woollen knitwear company and the aluminium producer (*see* Fig. 11.8).

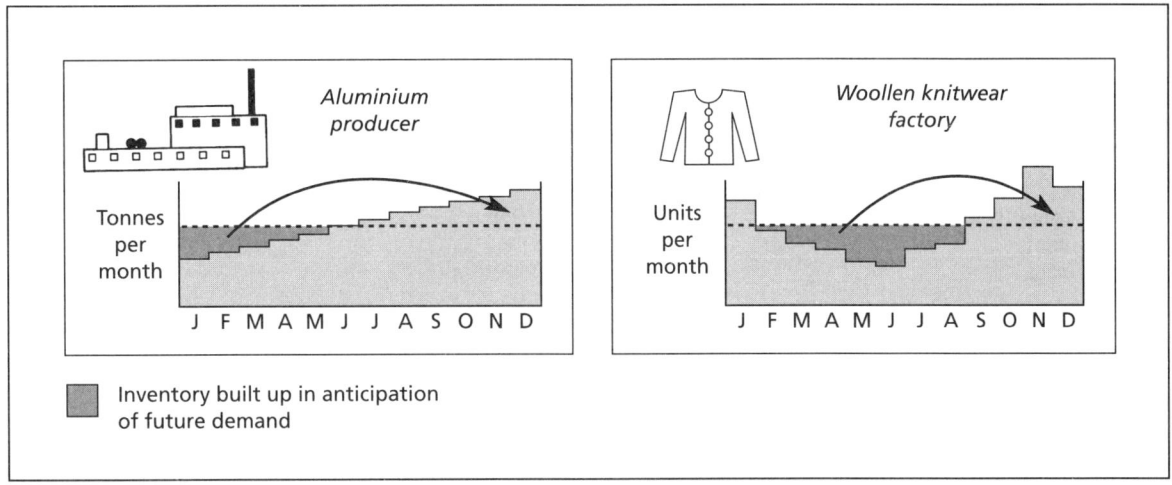

Figure 11.8 Level capacity plans which use anticipation inventory to supply future demand

Level capacity plans of this type can achieve the objectives of stable employment patterns, high process utilization, and usually also high productivity with low unit costs. Unfortunately, they can also create considerable inventory which has to be financed and stored. Perhaps the biggest problem, however, is that decisions have to be taken as to what to produce for inventory rather than for immediate sale. Will green woollen sweaters knitted in July still be fashionable in October? Could a particular aluminium alloy in a specific sectional shape still be sold months after it has been produced? Most firms operating this plan, therefore, give priority to only creating inventory where future sales are relatively certain and unlikely to be affected by changes in fashion or design. Clearly, such plans are not suitable for 'perishable' products such as foods, some pharmaceuticals, and for products where fashion changes rapidly and unpredictably (for example, popular music CDs, young people's clothing), or where products are tailor-made against specific customer requirements.

A level capacity plan could also be used by the hotel and supermarket, although this would not be the usual approach of such organizations, because it usually results in a waste of staff resources, reflected in low productivity. Because service cannot be stored as inventory, a level capacity plan would involve running the operation at a uniformly high level of capacity availability. The hotel would employ sufficient staff to service all the rooms, to run a full restaurant, and to staff the reception even in months when demand was expected to be well below capacity. Similarly, the supermarket would plan to staff all the check-outs, warehousing operations, and so on, even in quiet periods (*see* Fig. 11.9).

Very high under-utilization levels can make level capacity plans prohibitively expensive in many service operations, but may be considered appropriate where the opportunity costs of individual lost sales are very high: for example, in the high-margin retailing of jewellery and in (real) estate agents. It is also possible to set the capacity somewhat below the forecast peak demand level in order to reduce the degree of under-utilization. However, in the periods where demand is expected to exceed planned capacity, customer service may deteriorate. (*See* box on Eurocamp.) Customers may have to queue for long periods or may be 'processed' faster and less sensitively. While this is obviously far from ideal, the benefits to the organization of stability and productivity may outweigh the disadvantages of upsetting some customers.

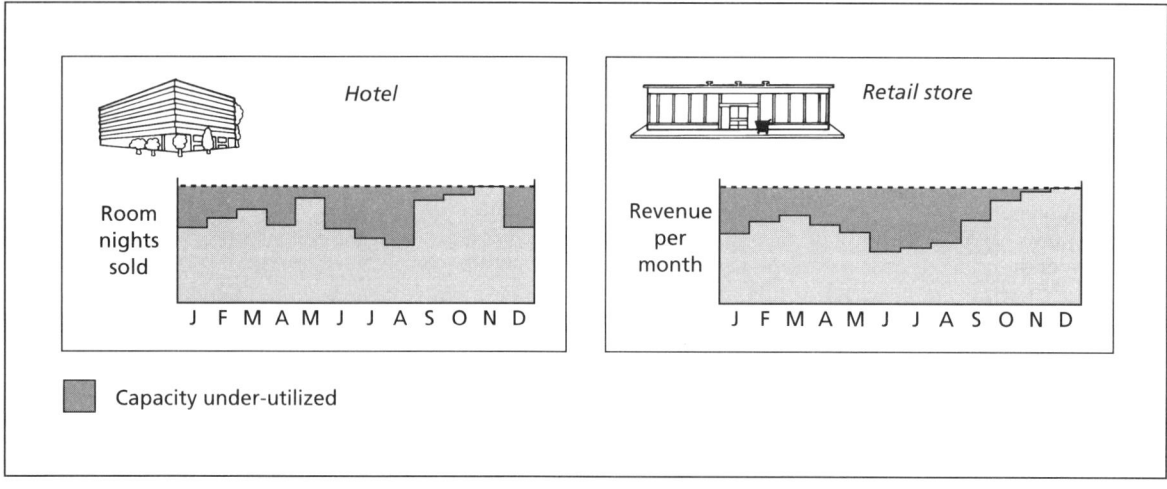

Figure 11.9 Level capacity plans with under-utilization of capacity

Chase demand plan

The opposite of a level capacity plan is one which attempts to match capacity closely to the varying levels of forecast demand. This is much more difficult to achieve than a level capacity plan, as different numbers of staff, different working hours, and even different amounts of equipment may be necessary in each period. For this reason pure chase demand plans are unlikely to appeal to operations which manufacture standard, non-perishable products. Also where manufacturing operations are particularly capital-intensive, the chase demand policy would require a level of physical capacity, all of which would only be used occasionally. It is for this reason that such a plan is less likely to be appropriate for the aluminium producer than for the woollen garment manufacturer (*see* Fig. 11.10). A pure chase demand plan is more usually adopted by operations which cannot store their output, such as customer-

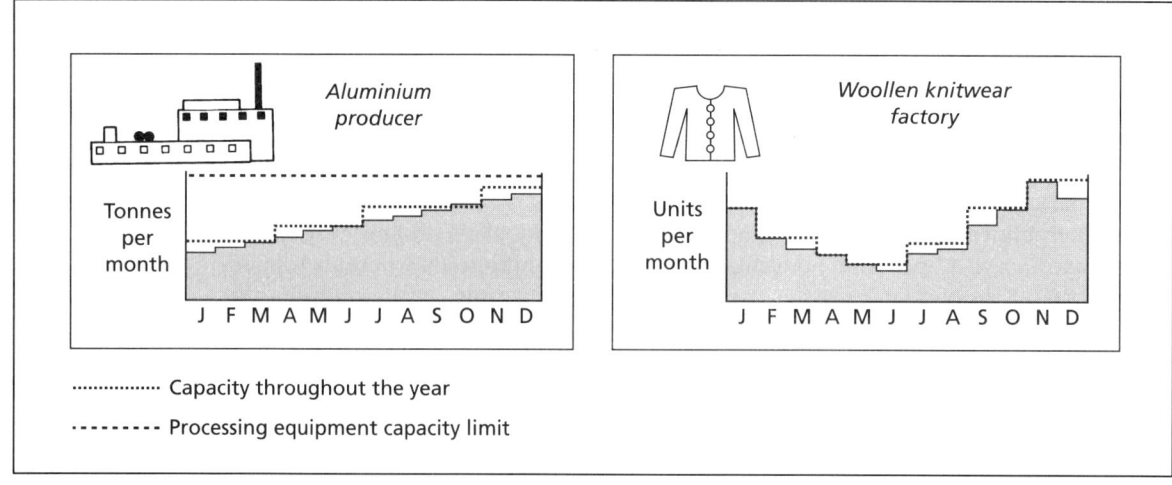

Figure 11.10 Chase demand capacity plans with changes in capacity which reflect demand change

CAPACITY MANAGEMENT AT EUROCAMP[1]

Eurocamp Travel Limited is a leading holiday company which, as its name suggests, provides camping holidays on three hundred sites throughout Europe in fully equipped, company-owned, pre-erected, luxury tents and mobile homes. A Eurocamp holiday normally comprises a package of services which may also include cross-Channel travel (for UK customers), overnight accommodation on the journey, motor-rail transport for their car, insurance, and air travel or car hire if required. Both the promotion of Eurocamp's holidays, which takes place from their headquarters, and the delivery of the holiday service itself are highly seasonal.

Area supervisors manage groups of camp sites and on each site there is a small team of couriers who take care of customers and the equipment. Most of these couriers are students or graduates who are available to work from June to September, although some are seasonal employees who return every year. Couriers clean and prepare the tents and mobile homes (referred to as units) at the change-overs between different families using them. They also greet new arrivals and help them settle in and sort out any problems that might arise. Some of the large sites also employ specialist couriers to entertain children.

Promotion activities start with the distribution of catalogues in September, when over 130 000 mailings are sent to existing customers. Catalogues are also sent out in response to new enquiries throughout the year and demand reaches its peak between December and March, with low levels of demand during the summer. These activities require a large number of computer-based telesales staff between November and March. These operate from the sales offices in the UK, Netherlands and Germany. Temporary staff, who only wish to work during this period of the year, are used to supplement other trained permanent staff who are moved on to telesales for this period. Major peaks in telephone reservations occur in the weekday evenings when the operation is staffed until 8 pm. Also during this period large numbers of part-time staff are employed on Saturdays and Sundays, alongside permanent employees working overtime.

Couriers, who are recruited during the winter, undertake their initial training course just before the beginning of the season. The first intake of 1000 couriers must complete their three-day course before travelling to their sites. A second wave of recruits is then trained to provide the extra courier capacity which is needed during the peak period of July and August. In this way courier capacity is adjusted to follow approximate patterns of demand. However, the balance of capacity and demand is more difficult to achieve in small sites, where only one or two couriers are needed. Unit utilization is usually 100 per cent for most of the peak period and couriers work long hours to ensure that their tasks are completed and customers are well served. However, inevitably, service levels are more difficult to maintain during very busy periods. The change-over cleaning task takes about 30 minutes per unit so the number of couriers required is also related to the average stay. Certain sites which are *en route* from the Channel ports and tunnel to the south of Europe have very short average stays, so these require an above average number of couriers to cope with the change-overs. ■

processing operations or manufacturers of perishable products. It avoids the wasteful provision of excess staff that occurs with a level capacity plan, and yet should satisfy customer demand throughout the planned period. Where output can be stored, the chase demand policy might be adopted in order to minimize or eliminate finished goods inventory.

Sometimes it is difficult to achieve very large variations in capacity from period to period. If the changes in forecast demand are as large as those in the hotel example (*see* Fig. 11.11), significantly different levels of staffing will be required throughout the year. This would mean employing part-time and temporary staff, requiring permanent employees to work longer hours, or even bringing in contract labour. The operations managers will then have the difficult task of ensuring that quality standards and safety procedures are still adhered to, and that the customer service levels are maintained. Both in the hotel and the supermarket, forecast demand is lower than average during vacation periods. This could assist the operations manager, as employees would be encouraged to take their vacations at that time. Unfortunately, many services are busiest during the summer, and managers must try to ensure that experienced, permanent staff take their vacations at other times.

Methods of adjusting capacity

The chase demand approach requires that capacity is adjusted by some means. There are a number of different methods of achieving this, although all may not be feasible for all types of operation. Some of these methods are listed below.

Overtime and idle time

Often the quickest and most convenient method of adjusting capacity is by varying the number of productive hours worked by the staff in the operation. When demand is higher than nominal capacity, the working day may be extended, and when demand is lower than nominal capacity the amount of time spent by staff on productive work can be reduced. In the latter case it may be possible for staff to engage in some other activity such as cleaning or maintenance. This method is only useful if the timing of the extra productive capacity matches that of the demand. For example, there is little to be gained in asking a retail operation's staff to work extra hours in the evening if all the extra demand is occurring during their normal working period. The costs associated with this method are either the extra payment which is normally necessary to secure the agreement of staff to working overtime, or in the case of idle time, the costs

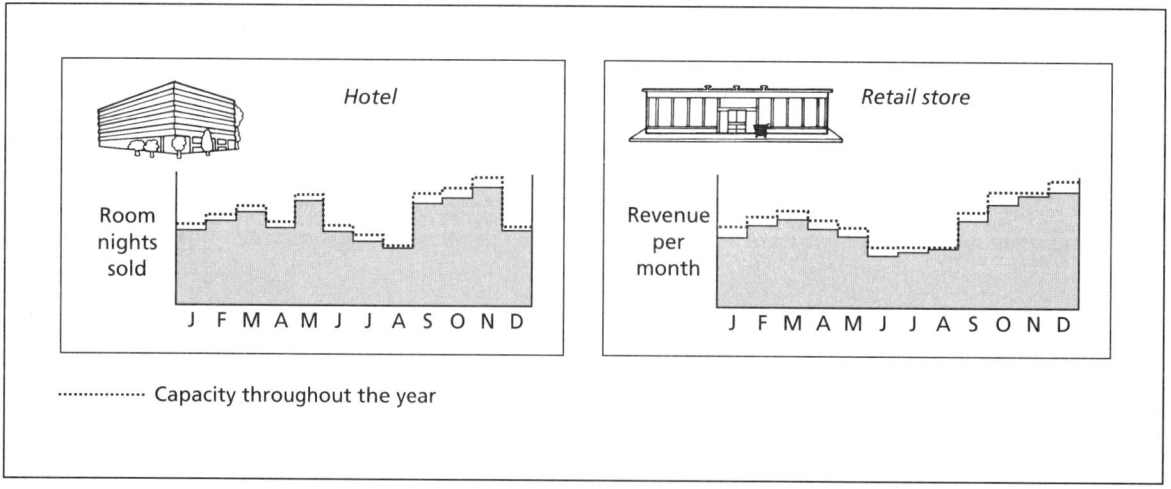

Figure 11.11 Chase demand capacity plans with changes in capacity which reflect demand change

of paying staff who are not engaged in direct productive work. Further, there might be costs associated with the fixed costs of keeping the operation heated, lit and secure over the extra period staff are working. There is also a limit to the amount of extra working time which any workforce can deliver before productivity levels decrease.

Varying the size of the workforce

If capacity is largely governed by workforce size, one way to adjust capacity is to adjust the size of the workforce. This is done by hiring extra staff during periods of high demand and laying them off as demand falls. However, there are cost implications, and possibly also ethical ones, to be taken into account before adopting such a method. The costs of hiring extra staff include those associated with recruitment, as well as the costs of low productivity while new staff go through the learning curve. The costs of lay-off may include possible severance payments, but might also include the loss of morale in the operation and loss of goodwill in the local labour market.

Using part-time staff

A variation on the previous strategy is to recruit staff on a part-time basis, that is for less than the normal working day. This method is extensively used in service operations such as supermarkets and fast-food restaurants but is also used by some manufacturers to staff an evening shift after the normal working day. However, if the fixed costs of employment for each employee, irrespective of how long they work, are high then using this method may not be worthwhile.

Sub-contracting

In periods of high demand an operation might buy capacity from other organizations. This might enable the operation to meet its own demand without the extra expense of investing in capacity which will not be needed after the peak in demand has passed. Again, there are costs associated with this method. The most obvious one is that sub-contracting can be very expensive. The sub-contractor will also want to make sufficient margin out of the business. A sub-contractor may not be as motivated to deliver on time or to the desired levels of quality. Finally, there is the risk that the sub-contractors might themselves decide to enter the same market.

Manage demand

Although most operations try to plan for forecast variations in demand, stable and uniform demand could allow an organization to reduce costs *and* improve service; capacity could be better utilized, and profit potential could be enhanced. Many organizations have recognized these benefits, and attempt to 'manage demand' in various ways. The objective is to transfer customer demand from peak periods to quiet periods. This is usually beyond the immediate responsibility of operations managers, being the responsibility of marketing and/or sales functions. The primary role of the operations manager is, therefore, to identify and evaluate the benefits of demand management, and to ensure that the resulting changes in demand can be satisfactorily met by the operations system. One method of managing demand is to *change demand* by altering part of the 'marketing mix', such as by changing prices or promotional activities, and sometimes by small changes to the product or service to make it more attractive in off-peak periods. More radical policies may create *alternative products or services* to fill capacity in quiet periods.

Change demand

The most obvious mechanism to change demand is through price. Although this is probably the most widely applied approach in demand management, it is less common for products than services. For example, some city hotels offer low-cost 'city break' vacation packages in the months when fewer business visitors are expected. Skiing and camping holidays are cheapest at the beginning and end of the season and are particularly expensive during school vacations. Discounts are given by photo-processing firms during winter periods, but never around summer holidays. Ice-cream is 'on offer' in many supermarkets during the winter. Examples of seasonal pricing vary from country to country, but the objective is invariably to stimulate off-peak demand and to constrain peak demand, in order to smooth demand as much as possible.

Organizations can also attempt to increase demand in low periods by appropriate advertising. This could suggest that the quality of service could be better at that time (because there will be less crowds) or could simply arouse a greater interest in the product or service. This approach is often combined with offers of bargain prices and modified products. For example, turkey growers in the UK and the USA make vigorous attempts to promote their products at times other than Christmas and Thanksgiving.

Mixed plans

Each of the three 'pure' plans are applied only where their advantages strongly outweigh their disadvantages. For many organizations, however, these 'pure' approaches do not match their required combination of competitive and operational objectives. Most operations managers are required to balance the many, often conflicting, performance objectives identified earlier. They are expected simultaneously to reduce costs

GETTING THE MESSAGE[2]

Companies which traditionally operate in seasonal markets can demonstrate some considerable ingenuity in their attempts to develop counter-seasonal products. One of the most successful industries in this respect has been the greetings card industry. Mother's Day, Father's Day, Hallowe'en, Valentine's Day, and other occasions have all been promoted as times to send (and buy) appropriately designed cards. Now, having run out of occasions to promote, greetings card manufacturers have moved on to 'non-occasion' cards, which can be sent at any time. These have the considerable advantage of being less seasonal, thus making the companies' seasonality less marked.

Hallmark Cards, the market leader in North America, has been the pioneer in developing non-occasion cards. Their cards include those intended to be sent from parent to child with messages such as, 'Would a hug help?', or 'Sorry I made you feel bad', and 'You're perfectly wonderful – it's your room that's a mess'. Other cards deal with more serious adult themes such as friendship ('You're more than a friend, you're just like family') or even alcoholism ('This is hard to say, but I think you're a much neater person when you're not drinking'). Whatever else these products may be, they are not seasonal! ■

and inventory, to minimize capital investment, and yet to provide a responsive and customer-oriented approach at all times. For this reason, most organizations choose to follow a mixture of the three approaches. This can be best illustrated by the woollen knitwear company example in Fig. 11.12. Here, some of the peak demand has been brought forward by the company offering discounts to selected retail customers (manage demand plan). Capacity has also been adjusted at two points in the year to reflect the broad changes in demand (chase demand plan). Yet the adjustment in capacity is not sufficient to avoid totally the build-up of inventories (the level capacity plan).

Yield management

In operations which have relatively fixed capacities, such as airlines and hotels, it is important to use the capacity of the operation for generating revenue to its full potential. One approach used by such operations is called *yield management*.[3] This is really a collecting of methods, some of which we have already discussed, which can be used to ensure that an operation maximizes its potential to generate profit. Yield management is especially useful where:

- capacity is relatively fixed;
- the market can be fairly clearly segmented;
- the service cannot be stored in any way;
- the services are sold in advance;
- the marginal cost of making a sale is relatively low.

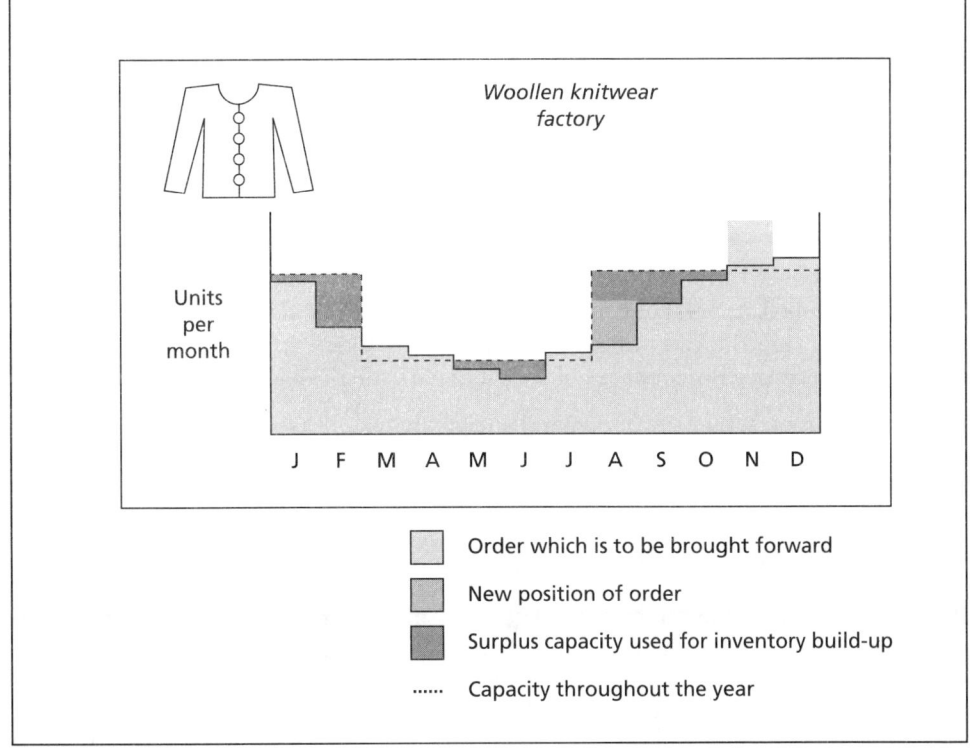

Order which is to be brought forward

New position of order

Surplus capacity used for inventory build-up

...... Capacity throughout the year

**Figure 11.12
A mixed capacity plan for the woollen knitwear factory**

Airlines, for example, fit all these criteria. They adopt a collection of methods to try to maximize the yield (i.e. profit) from their capacity. These include the following:

● *Over-booking capacity.* Not every passenger who has booked a place on a flight will actually show up for the flight. If the airline did not fill this seat it would lose the revenue from it. Because of this, airlines regularly book more passengers on to flights than the capacity of the aircraft can cope with. If they over-book by the exact number of passengers who fail to show up, they have maximized their revenue under the circumstances. Of course, if more passengers show up than they expect, the airline will have a number of upset passengers to deal with (although they may be able to offer financial inducements for the passengers to take another flight). If they fail to over-book sufficiently they will have empty seats. By studying past data on flight demand, airlines try to balance the risks of over-booking and under-booking.
● *Price discounting.* At quiet times, when demand is unlikely to fill capacity, airlines will also sell heavily discounted tickets to agents who then themselves take the risk of finding customers for them. In effect this is using the price mechanism to affect demand.
● *Varying service types.* Discounting and other methods of affecting demand are also adjusted depending on the demand for particular types of service. For example, the relative demand for first-, business-, and economy-class seats varies throughout the year. There is no point discounting tickets in a class for which demand will be high. Yield management also tries to adjust the availability of the different classes of seat to reflect their demand. They will also vary the number of seats available in each class through upgrading or even changing the configuration of airline seats (*see* box in Chapter 4 on the new Boeing 777).

CHOOSING A CAPACITY PLANNING AND CONTROL APPROACH

Before an operation can decide which of the capacity plans to adopt, it must be aware of the consequences of adopting each plan on its own set of circumstances. For example, a manufacturer, given an idea of its current capacity and given a demand forecast, must calculate the effect of setting its output rate at a particular level. Similarly, a supermarket must understand the likely consequences of staffing only 20 of its 30 check-outs during the busy lunch period. Two methods are particularly useful in helping to assess the consequences of adapting particular capacity plans:

● cumulative representations of demand and capacity;
● queueing theory.

Cumulative representations

Figure 11.13 shows the forecast aggregated demand for a chocolate factory which makes confectionery products. Demand for its products in the shops is greatest at Christmas. To meet this demand and allow time for the products to work their way through the distribution system, the factory must supply a demand which peaks in

September, as shown. One method of assessing whether a particular level of capacity can satisfy the demand would be to calculate the degree of over-capacity below the graph which represents the capacity levels (areas A and C) and the degree of under-capacity above the graph (area B). If the total over-capacity is greater than the total under-capacity for a particular level of capacity, then that capacity could be regarded as adequate to satisfy demand fully, the assumption being that inventory has been accumulated in the periods of over-capacity.

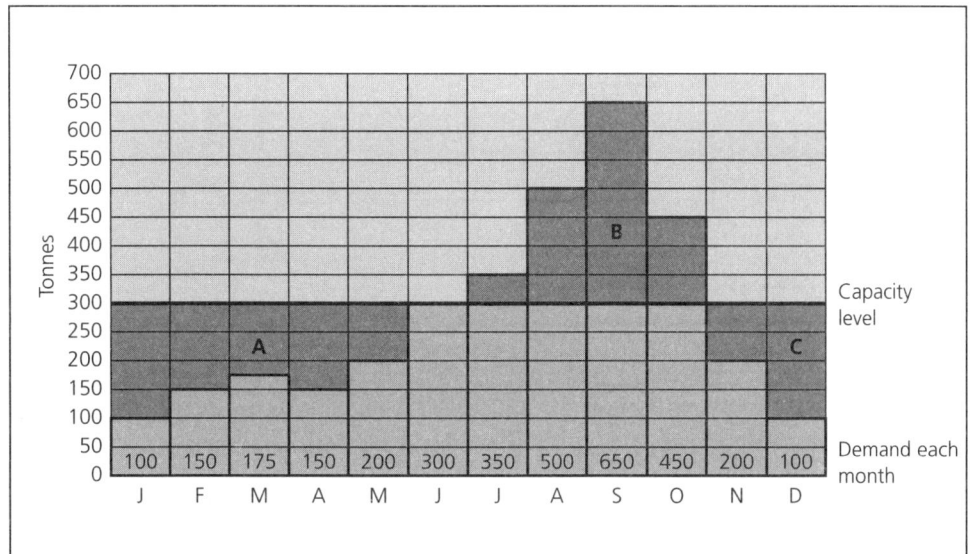

**Figure 11.13
If the over-capacity areas (A+C) are greater than the under-capacity area (B), the capacity level seems adequate to meet demand. This may not necessarily be the case, however**

However, there are two problems with this approach. The first is that each month shown in Fig. 11.13 may not have the same amount of productive time. Some months (August, for example) may contain vacation periods which reduce the availability of capacity. The second problem is that, even if each month period is drawn with its width proportional to its productive days, a capacity level which seems adequate may only be able to supply products *after* the demand for them has occurred. For example, if the period of under-capacity occurs at the beginning of the year, no inventory could have accumulated to meet demand. A far superior way of assessing capacity plans is first to plot demand on a *cumulative* basis. This is shown in Fig. 11.14.

The cumulative representation of demand immediately reveals more information. First, it shows that although total demand peaks in September, because of the restricted number of available productive days, the peak demand per productive day occurs a month earlier in August. Second, it shows that the fluctuation in demand over the year is even greater than it seemed. The ratio of monthly peak demand to monthly lowest demand is 6.5:1, but the ratio of peak to lowest demand per productive day is 10:1. Demand per productive day is more relevant to operations managers because productive days represent the time element of capacity.

The most useful consequence of plotting demand on a cumulative basis is that, by plotting capacity on the same graph, the feasibility and consequences of a capacity plan can be assessed. Figure 11.15 shows a level capacity plan which produces at a rate of 14.03 tonnes per productive day. This meets cumulative demand by the end of the year. It would also pass our earlier test of total over-capacity being the same or greater than under-capacity.

However, if one of the aims of the plan is to supply demand when it occurs, the plan is inadequate. Up to around day 168 the line representing cumulative production is above that representing cumulative demand. This means that at any time during this period more product has been produced by the factory than has been demanded from it. In fact the vertical distance between the two lines is the level of inventory at

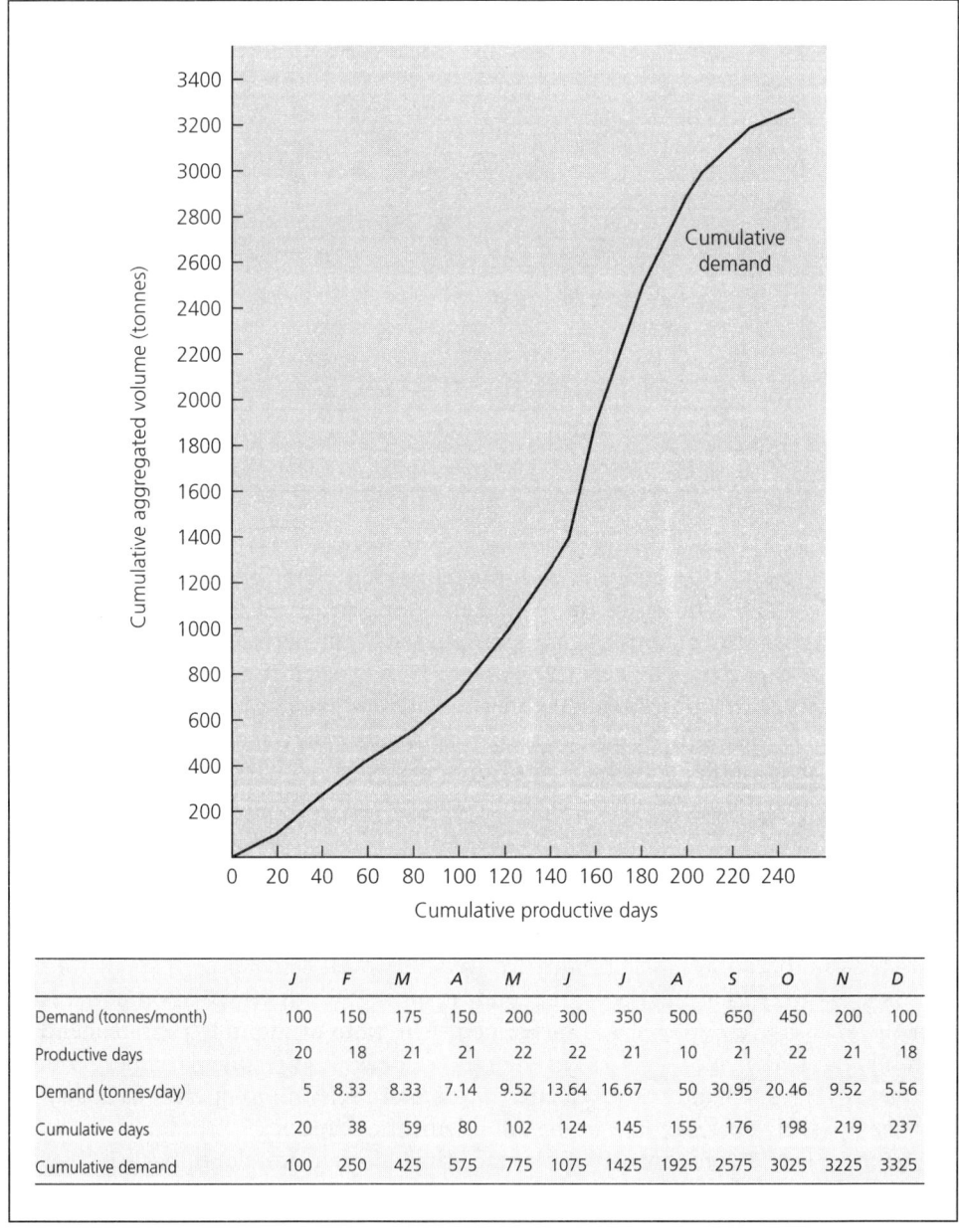

	J	F	M	A	M	J	J	A	S	O	N	D
Demand (tonnes/month)	100	150	175	150	200	300	350	500	650	450	200	100
Productive days	20	18	21	21	22	22	21	10	21	22	21	18
Demand (tonnes/day)	5	8.33	8.33	7.14	9.52	13.64	16.67	50	30.95	20.46	9.52	5.56
Cumulative days	20	38	59	80	102	124	145	155	176	198	219	237
Cumulative demand	100	250	425	575	775	1075	1425	1925	2575	3025	3225	3325

Figure 11.14
Demand calculated on a cumulative basis

that point in time. So by day 80, 1122 tonnes have been produced but only 575 tonnes demanded. The surplus of production over demand, or inventory, is therefore 547 tonnes. When the cumulative demand line lies above the cumulative production line the reverse is true. The vertical distance between the two lines now indicates the shortage, or lack of supply. So by day 198, 3025 tonnes have been demanded but only 2778 tonnes produced. The shortage is therefore 247 tonnes.

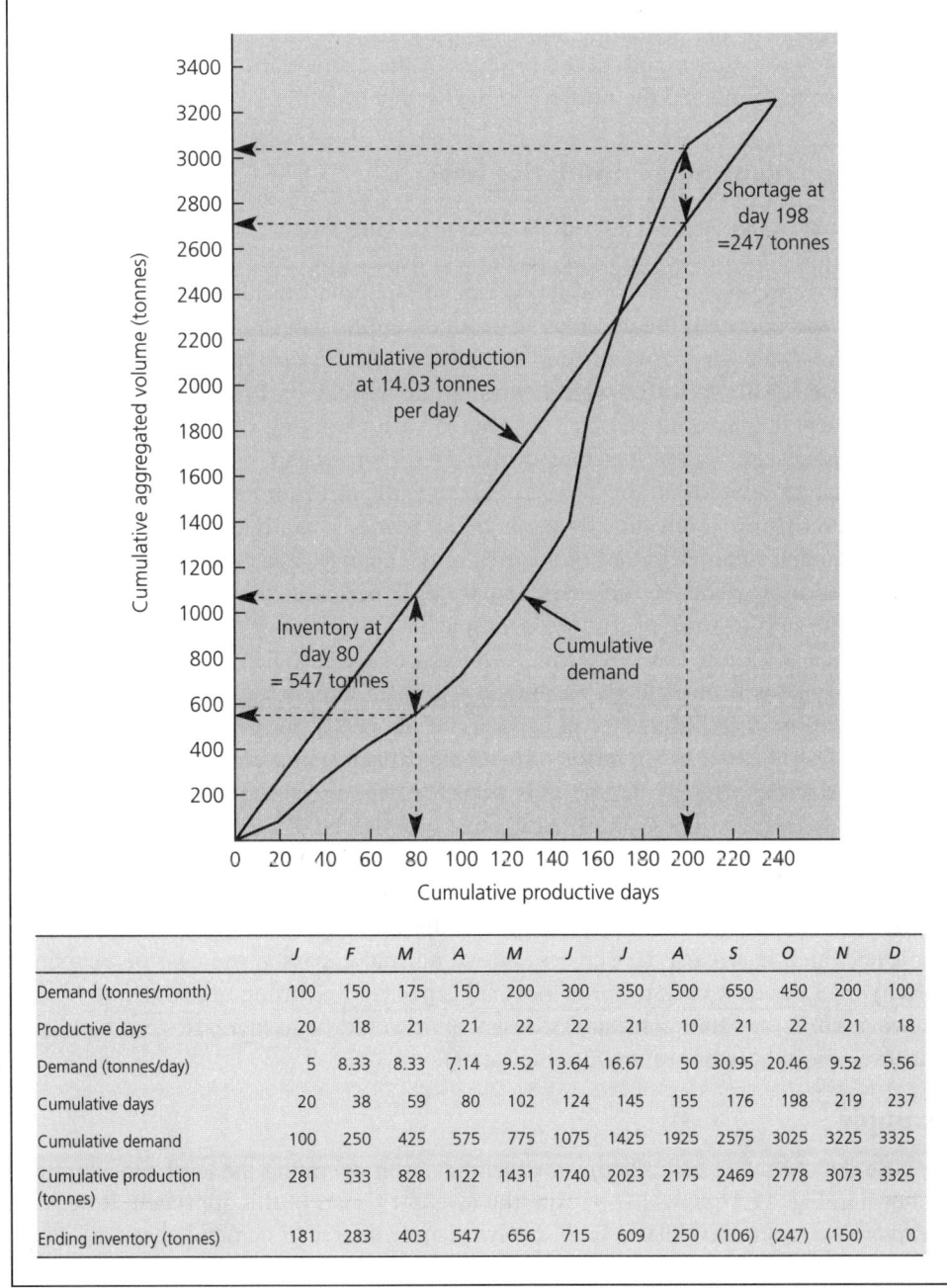

	J	F	M	A	M	J	J	A	S	O	N	D
Demand (tonnes/month)	100	150	175	150	200	300	350	500	650	450	200	100
Productive days	20	18	21	21	22	22	21	10	21	22	21	18
Demand (tonnes/day)	5	8.33	8.33	7.14	9.52	13.64	16.67	50	30.95	20.46	9.52	5.56
Cumulative days	20	38	59	80	102	124	145	155	176	198	219	237
Cumulative demand	100	250	425	575	775	1075	1425	1925	2575	3025	3225	3325
Cumulative production (tonnes)	281	533	828	1122	1431	1740	2023	2175	2469	2778	3073	3325
Ending inventory (tonnes)	181	283	403	547	656	715	609	250	(106)	(247)	(150)	0

Figure 11.15
A level capacity plan which produces shortages in spite of meeting demand at the end of the year

For any capacity plan to meet demand as it occurs, its cumulative production line must always lie above the cumulative demand line. This makes it a straightforward task to judge the adequacy of a plan, simply by looking at its cumulative representation. An impression of the inventory implications can also be gained from a cumulative representation by judging the area between the cumulative production and demand curves. This represents the amount of inventory carried over the period. Figure 11.16 illustrates an adequate level capacity plan for the chocolate manufacturer, together with the costs of carrying inventory. It is assumed that inventory costs R2 per tonne per day to keep in storage. The average inventory each month is taken to be the average of the beginning and end-of-month inventory levels, and the inventory carrying cost each month is the product of the average inventory, the inventory cost per day per tonne and the number of days in the month.

Comparing plans on a cumulative basis

Chase demand plans can also be illustrated on a cumulative representation. Rather than the cumulative production line having a constant gradient, it would have a varying gradient representing the production rate at any point in time. If a pure demand chase plan was adopted, the cumulative production line would match the cumulative demand line. The gap between the two lines would be zero and hence inventory would be zero. Although this would eliminate inventory carrying costs, as we discussed earlier, there would be costs associated with changing capacity levels. These *capacity change costs* are sometimes drawn as shown in Fig. 11.17. The cost of a capacity change depends on the degree of change, the direction of the change, and the capacity level from which the change is being made. Usually the marginal cost of making a capacity change increases the greater the change. For example, if the chocolate manufacturer wishes to increase capacity by 5 per cent, this can be achieved by requesting its staff to work overtime – a simple, fast and relatively inexpensive option. If the change is 15 per cent, overtime cannot provide sufficient extra capacity and temporary staff will need to be employed – a more expensive solution which also would take more time. Increases in capacity of above 15 per cent might exceed the factory's physical capacity (in terms of machine capacity) and could only be achieved by sub-contracting some work out. This would be even more expensive as well as taking longer to arrange. The cost of the change will also be affected by the point from which the change is being made as well as the direction of the change. Usually it is less expensive to change capacity towards what is regarded as the 'normal' capacity level than it is further away from it. For example, if the chocolate manufacturer is operating at a level which is already 10 per cent above normal capacity, the cost of 'relaxing' capacity by 5 per cent back towards 'normal' capacity (by cutting overtime and by not renewing temporary staff contracts) is less than it would be to increase a further 5 per cent (even more overtime and temporary staff).

Example

Suppose the chocolate manufacturer, which has been operating the level capacity plan as shown in Fig. 11.16, is unhappy with the inventory costs of this approach. It decides to explore two alternative plans, both involving some degree of demand chasing.

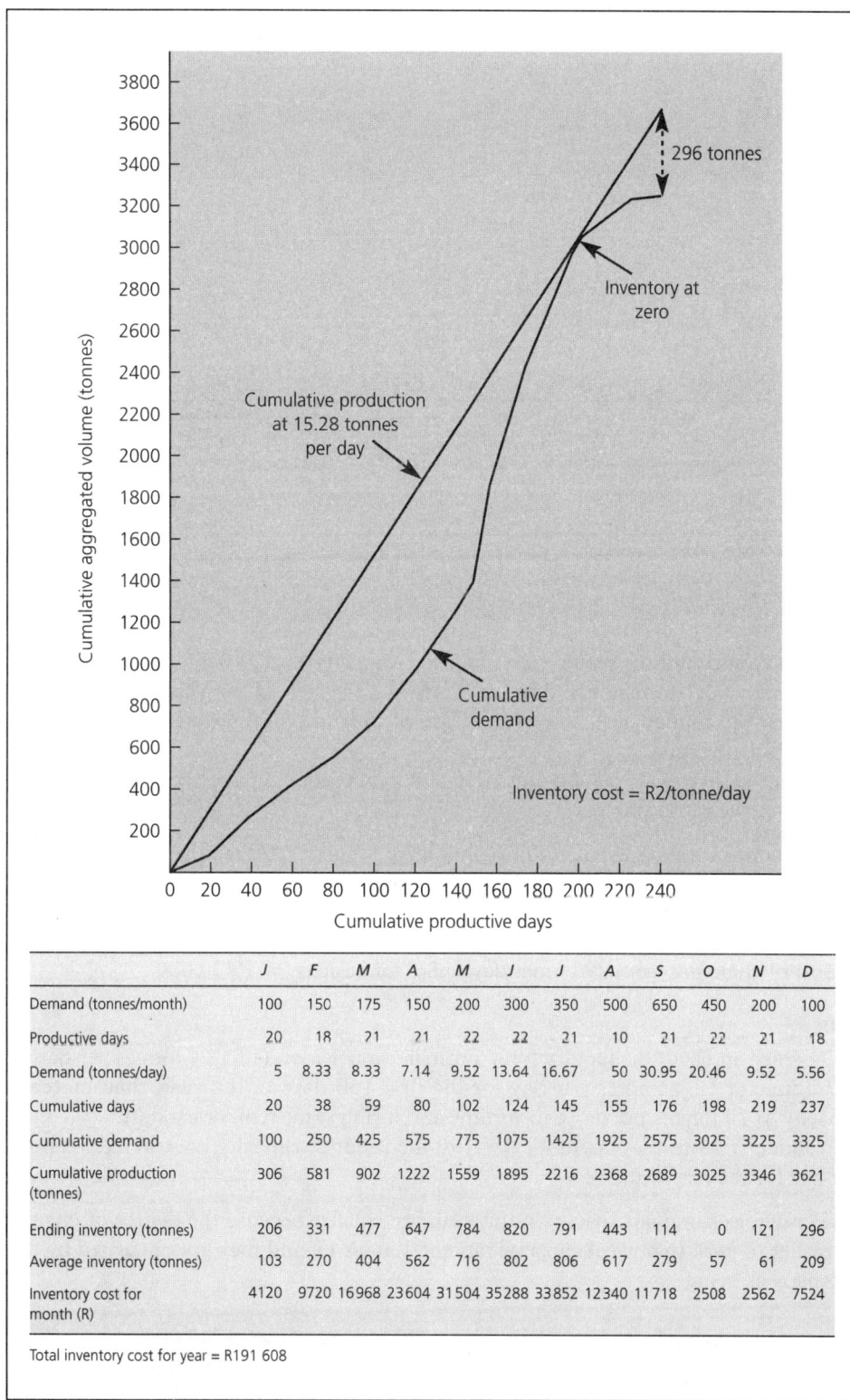

	J	F	M	A	M	J	J	A	S	O	N	D
Demand (tonnes/month)	100	150	175	150	200	300	350	500	650	450	200	100
Productive days	20	18	21	21	22	22	21	10	21	22	21	18
Demand (tonnes/day)	5	8.33	8.33	7.14	9.52	13.64	16.67	50	30.95	20.46	9.52	5.56
Cumulative days	20	38	59	80	102	124	145	155	176	198	219	237
Cumulative demand	100	250	425	575	775	1075	1425	1925	2575	3025	3225	3325
Cumulative production (tonnes)	306	581	902	1222	1559	1895	2216	2368	2689	3025	3346	3621
Ending inventory (tonnes)	206	331	477	647	784	820	791	443	114	0	121	296
Average inventory (tonnes)	103	270	404	562	716	802	806	617	279	57	61	209
Inventory cost for month (R)	4120	9720	16968	23604	31504	35288	33852	12340	11718	2508	2562	7524

Total inventory cost for year = R191 608

**Figure 11.16
A level capacity
plan which meets
demand at all
times during the
year**

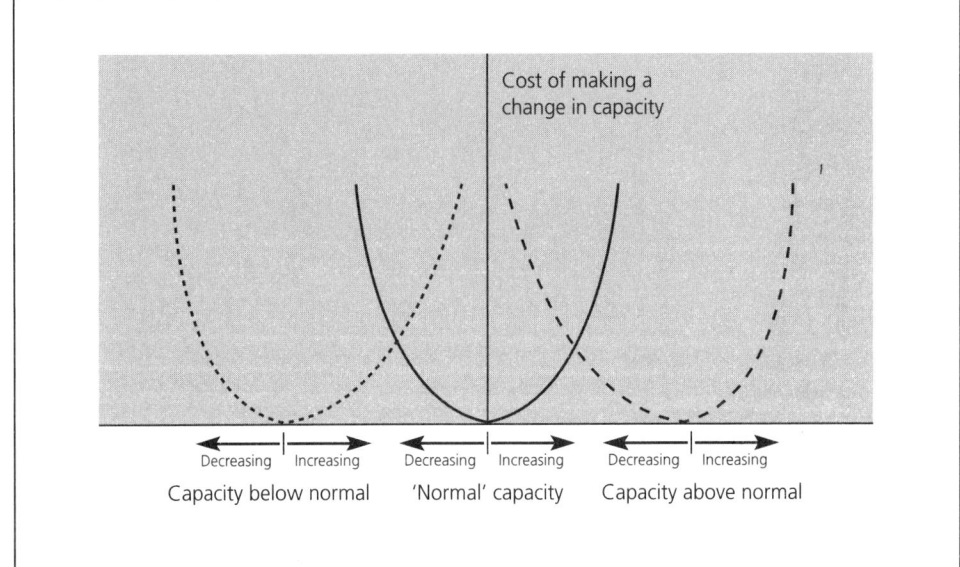

Figure 11.17
The costs of
changing capacity
will depend on the
point from which
the change is
made, the degree
of change and the
direction of the
change

Plan 1

● Organize and staff the factory for a 'normal' capacity level of 8.7 tonnes per day.
● Produce at 8.7 tonnes per day for the first 124 days of the year, then increase capacity to 29 tonnes per day by heavy use of overtime, hiring temporary staff and some sub-contracting.
● Produce at 29 tonnes per day until day 194 then reduce capacity back to 8.7 tonnes per day for the rest of the year.

The costs of changing capacity by such a large amount (the ratio of peak to normal capacity is 3.33 to 1) are calculated by the company as being:

Cost of changing from 8.7 tonnes/day to 29 tonnes/day = R770 000
Cost of changing from 29 tonnes/day to 8.7 tonnes/day = R420 000

Plan 2

● Organize and staff the factory for a 'normal' capacity level of 12.4 tonnes per day.
● Produce at 12.4 tonnes per day for the first 150 days of the year, then increase capacity to 29 tonnes per day by overtime and hiring some temporary staff.
● Produce at 29 tonnes/day until day 190 then reduce capacity back to 12.4 tonnes per day for the rest of the year.

The costs of changing capacity in this plan are smaller because the degree of change is smaller (a peak to normal capacity ratio of 2.34 to 1), and they are calculated by the company as being:

Cost of changing from 12.4 tonnes/day to 29 tonnes/day = R245 000
Cost of changing from 29 tonnes/day to 12.4 tonnes/day = R105 000

Figure 11.18 illustrates both plans on a cumulative basis. Plan 1 which envisaged two drastic changes in capacity has high capacity change costs but, because its production levels are close to demand levels, it has low inventory carrying costs. Plan 2 sacrifices some of the inventory cost advantage of Plan 1 but saves more in terms of capacity change costs.

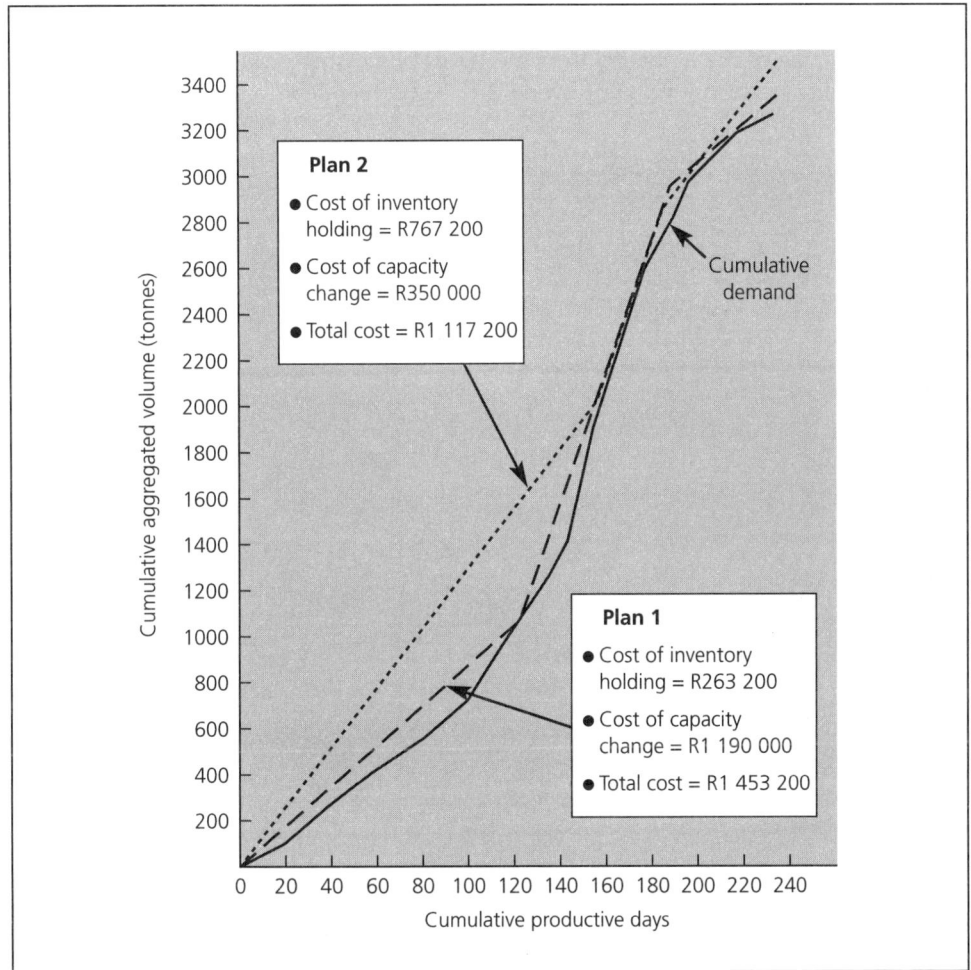

**Figure 11.18
Comparing two
alternative capacity
plans**

Queueing theory

Cumulative representations of capacity plans are useful where the operation has the ability to store its finished goods as inventory. For operations which, by their nature, cannot store their output, such as most service operations, capacity planning and control presents a different set of problems.

Although service operations do, of course, make forecasts of their expected average level of demand, they cannot usually predict exactly when each individual customer or order will arrive. A distribution which describes the probability of customers arriving might be known, but not each individual arrival. This makes providing adequate capacity particularly difficult. Furthermore, as well as the arrival of customers being uncertain, the time which each customer will need in the operation might also be uncertain. Figure 11.19 shows the general form of this capacity issue. Customers arrive according to some probability distribution, wait to be processed (unless part of the operation is idle), when they have reached the front of the queue they are processed by one of the n parallel 'servers' (their processing time also being described by a probability distribution), after which they leave the operation.

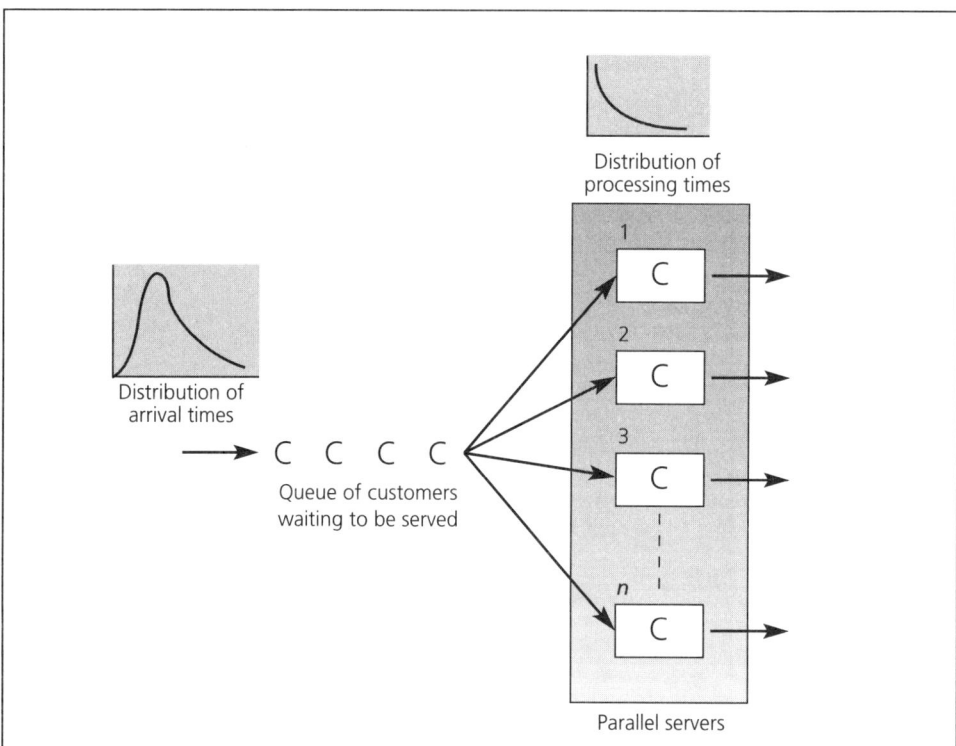

**Figure 11.19
The general form of the capacity decision in queueing systems**

The capacity planning and control problem here is how many parallel servers to have available for service at any point in time. Because of the probabilistic arrival and processing times, only rarely will the arrival of customers match the ability of the operation to cope with them. Sometimes, if several customers arrive in quick succession and require longer than average processing times, queues will build up in front of the operation. At other times, when customers arrive less frequently than average and also require lower than average processing times, some of the servers in the system will be idle. So even when the average capacity (processing capability) of the operation matches the average demand (arrival rate) on the system, both queues and idle time will occur. There are many examples of this kind of system. Table 11.2 illustrates some of these.

Table 11.2 Examples of operations which have parallel processors

Operation	Arrivals	Processing capacity
Bank	Customers	Tellers
Supermarket	Shoppers	Check-outs
Hospital clinic	Patients	Doctors
Graphic artist	Commissions	Artists
Custom cake decorators	Orders	Cake decorators
Ambulance service	Emergencies	Ambulances with crews
Telephone switchboard	Calls	Telephonists
Maintenance department	Breakdowns	Maintenance staff

If the operation has too few servers (that is, capacity is set at too low a level) queues will build up to a level where customers become dissatisfied with the time they are having to wait, although the utilization level of the servers will be high. If too many servers are in place (that is, capacity is set at too high a level) the time which customers can expect to wait will not be long but the utilization of the servers will be low. This is why the capacity planning and control problem for this type of operation is often presented as a trade-off between customer waiting time and system utilization. What is certainly important in making capacity decisions is being able to predict both of these factors for a given queueing system.

Analytical queueing models

Management scientists have developed formulae which can predict the steady-state behaviour of different types of queueing system. The type of system which we illustrated in Fig. 11.19 is the most useful for capacity management purposes, but it is only one of several types of queueing system. Unfortunately, these formulae can be extremely complicated, especially for all but the most simple assumptions, and are beyond the scope of this book. In fact computer programs are almost always now used to predict the behaviour of queueing systems. However, Fig. 11.20 shows some curves, derived from queueing formulae, which give the relationship between the mean number of customers in the system (either queueing or being served) and the 'utilization factor' (which indicates the average proportion of their time which the servers are processing customers) for various values of n, the number of parallel servers.

The curves in Fig. 11.20 are calculated on the assumption that customers arrive in a random fashion. That is, the arrival of each customer is independent of that of the other customers. The number of arrivals per unit of time is assumed to be described by a Poisson distribution. Processing times are assumed to be described by a negative exponential distribution. Both these assumptions are made largely for mathematical convenience, but are usually quite appropriate for actual arrival and processing rates in many real systems. The final assumptions are that customers are sufficiently patient to stay in the queue once they have joined it, and are processed on a 'first come, first served' basis.

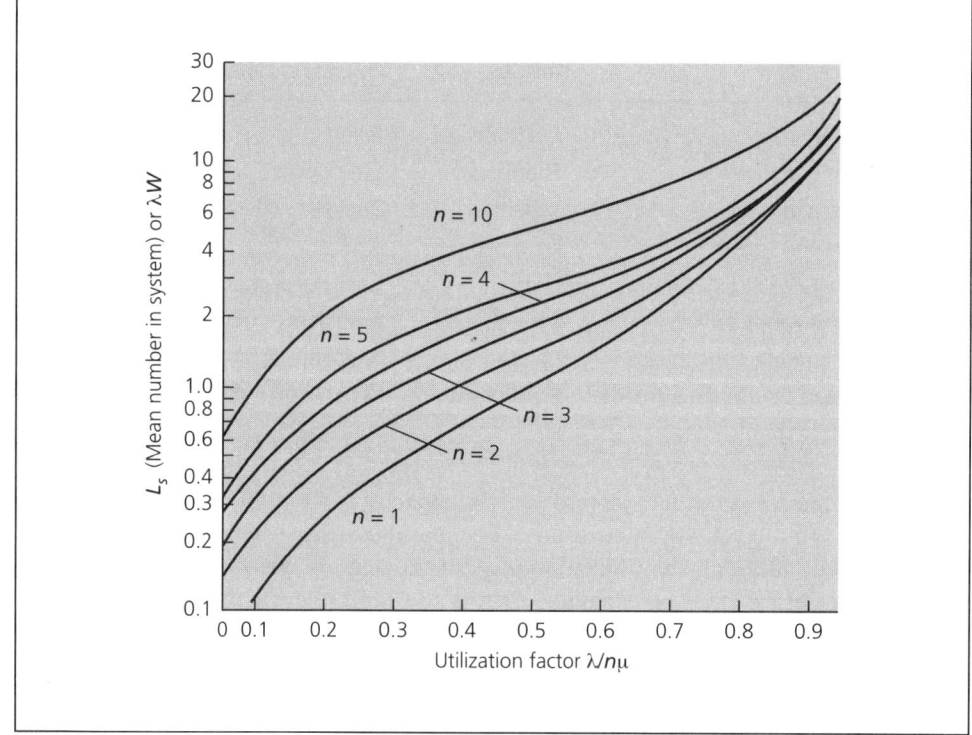

**Figure 11.20
Queueing curves
for a system with *n*
parallel servers**
Source: Adapted from
Fitzsimmons, J.A. and
Fitzsimmons, M.J.
(1994) *Service
Management for
Competitive Advantage,*
McGraw-Hill, copyright
McGraw-Hill, with
permission

We shall use the following notation:

λ = mean arrival rate (customer arrivals per hour)

μ = mean service rate per busy server (capacity, in customers per hour)

ρ = traffic intensity (λ/μ)

n = number of servers

L_s = mean number of customers in the system

L_q = mean number of customers in queue = $L_s - \rho$

W_s = mean time customer spends in the system $= \dfrac{L_q}{\lambda} + \dfrac{1}{\mu}$

W_q = mean time customer spends in the queue $= \dfrac{L_q}{\lambda}$

Example

A bank wishes to decide how many enquiry staff to schedule during the busy lunch
period. Their investigations have revealed that, during this period, customers arrive at
a rate of nine per hour and the enquiries which customers have during this period
(checking on accounts, opening new accounts, arranging loans, etc.) take, on average,
15 minutes. The bank manager feels that four staff should be on duty during this
period but wants to make sure that customers do not wait more than three minutes on
average before they are served.

λ = arrival rate = 9 per hour

μ = service rate = $\dfrac{1}{0.25}$ = 4 per hour

n = 4 servers

Utilization factor = $\dfrac{\lambda}{n\mu}$ = $\dfrac{9}{4 \times 4}$

$\qquad\qquad\qquad = 0.5625$

From Fig. 11.20, for a utilization factor of 0.5626 and $n = 4$,

L_s = mean number of customers in the system = 2.56
L_q = mean number of customers in the queue = $L_s - \rho$

$\qquad = 2.56 - \dfrac{9}{4} = 0.31$

W_q = mean queueing time = $\dfrac{L_q}{\lambda}$

$\qquad = \dfrac{0.31}{9} = 0.0344$ hrs

$\qquad = 2.07$ minutes

So the manager can be assured that with a capacity of four enquiry staff during the lunch period, the average time a customer will wait is less than three minutes.

The dynamics of capacity planning and control

Our emphasis so far has been on the planning aspects of capacity management. We have discussed how, given demand forecasts, operations managers can plan to provide a particular level of capacity at points of time in the future. This is an important task, and all operations managers need to have made these kinds of plan. However, in practice, the management of capacity is a far more dynamic process which involves controlling and reacting to *actual* demand and *actual* capacity as it occurs. The capacity control process can be seen as a sequence of partially reactive capacity decision processes, as shown in Fig. 11.21. At the beginning of each period, operations management considers its forecasts of demand, its understanding of current capacity and (if appropriate) how much inventory has been carried forward from the previous period. Based on all this information it makes plans for the following period's capacity. During the next period demand might, or might not, be as forecast and the actual capacity of the operation might, or might not, turn out as planned. But whatever the actual conditions during that period, at the beginning of the next period the same type of decision must be made, but in the light of the new circumstances.

The outlook matrix[4]

One of the main influences on operations managers, when they are making period-by-period capacity decisions, is their confidence in future demand matching their future capacity. If they are confident that, in the long term, demand is likely to exceed current capacity then, irrespective of the current level of demand, they will be more likely to be tolerant of policies which could lead to short-term over-capacity. Conversely, if

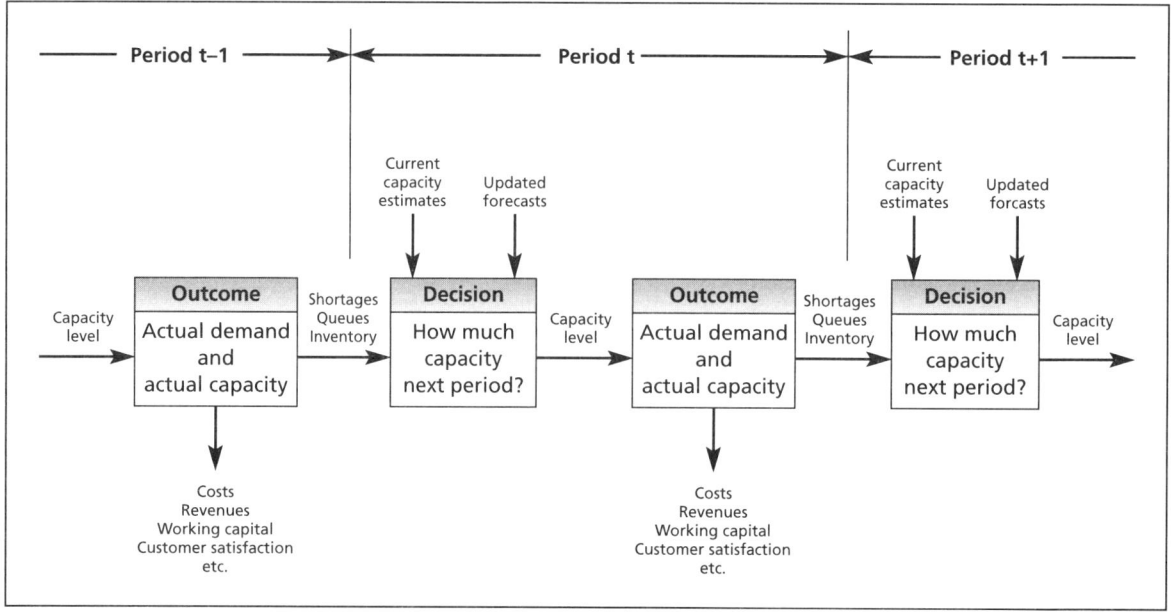

Figure 11.21 Capacity planning and control as a dynamic sequence of decisions

long-term demand looks poor it will be necessary to start implementing policies which will reduce long-term capacity. Overlaying this are the needs of current demand. Even if long-term demand looks poor it might be necessary to increase capacity if there is a

THREE-PHASE PRODUCTION AT BOOTS[5]

In the United Kingdom, when your sales rely on the weather, demand forecasting is understandably problematic. An extreme example of this is the manufacture of sun tan cream. A good summer can leave the shelves empty while poor weather could mean a warehouse full of unwanted product. Boots, the UK manufacturer and retailer, which manufactures the Soltan range of sun preparation products, attempts to reduce the uncertainty in its sun tan product factory by phasing its production in three stages. This allows the company to compensate for weather patterns early in the season by increasing or decreasing its production rate in the final phase of production. About 70 per cent of all its sales are made between the beginning of May and the end of August. The peak production time is somewhat earlier (to allow for distribution) and runs between October and April. Because of the lag between manufacture and demand in the shops, Boots has to commit itself to the first two phases. The results of the weather come too late to affect production. However, it can use the third phase to react to sales early in the season. If the weather has been poor, no product may be needed in the third phase, whereas good weather will mean production continuing throughout the summer. Nevertheless, a decision must be made by the end of May. Decisions after that would come too late to affect that year's sales. ■

short-term requirement. Figure 11.22 gives examples of the type of methods which might be adopted for different combinations of long-term and short-term outlook. Here outlook is defined as:

$$\text{Outlook} = \frac{\text{Forecast demand}}{\text{Forecast capacity}}$$

Three broad states of outlook are identified both for the long and short term. 'Poor' is when the ratio of forecast demand to forecast capacity is less than 1. 'Normal' is when the ratio is approximately equal to 1. 'Good' is when the ratio is greater than 1.

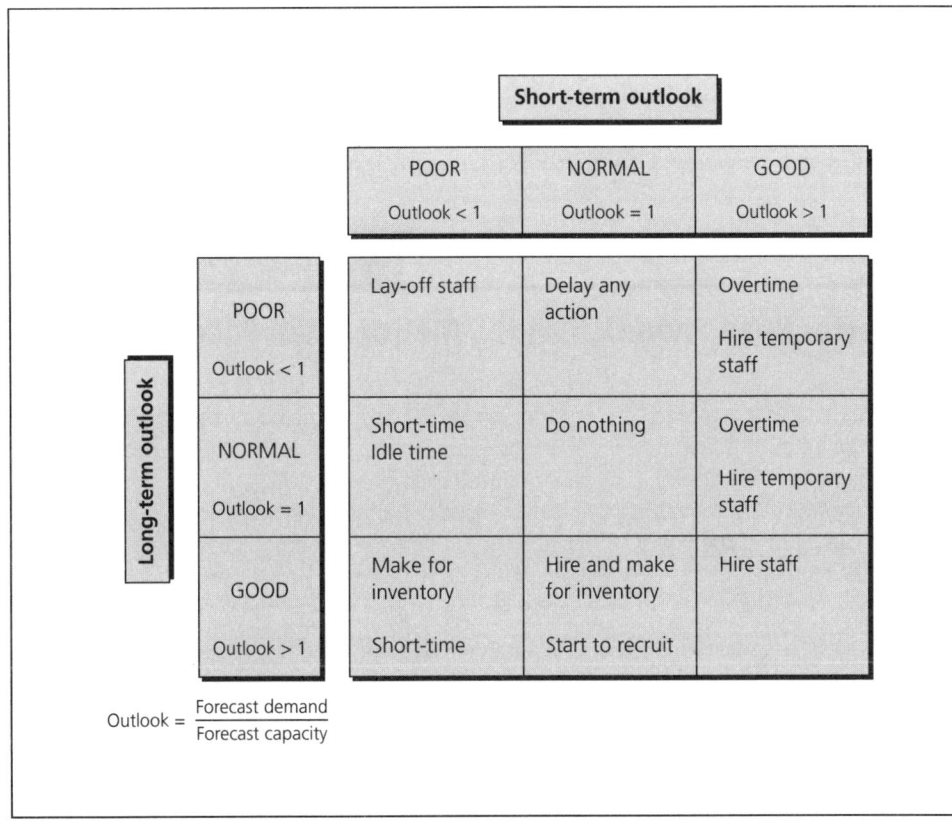

Figure 11.22 The dynamics of capacity planning are governed partly by the combination of long-term and short-term outlook

When both long- and short-term outlook is poor there is relatively little choice but to reduce the capacity of the operation; capacity is not needed now nor is it likely to be in the future. Staff lay-offs might be the only method of achieving this. When short-term outlook is normal, but long-term outlook is poor, current capacity needs to be maintained though certainly not increased. Under these circumstances the operation is most likely to delay any decisions. Certainly it would not commit investments into capacity which are unlikely to be needed in the future. When short-term outlook is good in spite of long-term outlook being poor, the operation faces a dilemma. It does not want to make any permanent commitments to increase capacity because the extra capacity will not be needed in the future. However, it does need to meet current levels of demand. Under these circumstances the use of overtime or the recruitment of temporary staff might be the least permanent methods of achieving short-term capacity requirements.

When long-term outlook is normal and short-term outlook is poor, capacity needs to be temporarily reduced but not in such a way as to compromise longer-term requirements. The operation here is likely to tolerate a certain amount of unproductive or idle time, or might perhaps reduce the working hours of its staff temporarily. When both long-term and short-term outlook are normal no action is required. However, when short-term outlook is good, capacity will need to be increased but not in any permanent manner. Again, overtime and the use of temporary staff are likely to be appropriate methods.

When the long-term outlook is good there will be a requirement to build up capacity in some way, irrespective of short-term circumstances. So, when the short-term outlook is poor the operation will not want to do anything which compromises long-term capacity. It may even, if possible, use any short-term surplus capacity to build up inventory. It is also likely to do this when long-term outlook is good and the short-term outlook is normal. Here though it will need to start recruiting extra staff or working overtime if it wants to make products for inventory. Finally, when both long-term and short-term outlook is good, capacity will need to be increased relatively quickly and probably in a permanent manner through hiring extra staff.

Chief Inspector Brian Paddick, London Metropolitan Police

Brian has overall policing responsibility for the Brixton Division, one of London's largest inner-city areas, which employs many hundreds of police officers. Around two-thirds are uniformed; these officers interact directly with the public, and are seen 'on the beat', at the front-office desks of the police stations, and at the scenes of disturbances, crimes, accidents, and so on. The Division is, of course, required to provide its services at all times, so Brian has to ensure that there is sufficient 'officer coverage' in his capacity management plan.

'The level of demand for policing can never be accurately predicted in advance because of the random – and often intangible – nature of demand, but there are actually some significant factors which we can take into account. For example, when it rains there is usually a significantly lower level of street crimes and disturbances, but the frequency of accidents increases, so the mix of our work changes. Thursday, Friday, and Saturday evenings are usually busy, particularly in the summer, because many people in the area spend their free time socializing on the streets. There is potential for small disturbances to escalate and with large numbers of naturally inquisitive people on the scene of an incident, there may be a small minority who will join in, or who will take advantage of the opportunity to commit a separate crime. We also anticipate a peak on Monday mornings, when businesses discover burglaries that have occurred over the weekend.

'In our capacity planning and workforce scheduling, the safety of our officers must be given high priority, so we always try to ensure that there is support and back-up to provide a minimum safety level of staffing. We operate using "core teams" to provide twenty-four hour cover for the whole Division and "sector teams" for the town centre shopping areas and housing estates. The sector teams are scheduled with different starting times throughout the day, so that we can have maximum capacity when indicated by crime trend analysis. These officers work a five-shift rota that enables us to provide a relatively level capacity coverage on the normal four-shift basis, as well as scheduling other small teams from the fifth shift to coincide with the anticipated peaks. We like these officers to be very visible to the public, particularly in those areas that are likely to attract crowds; partly as a deterrent, but equally to support the public's need for a feeling of security on the street. The deployment of these teams is highly targeted on specific problems which have been highlighted by detailed crime analysis.

'Frequently our officers are required to attend court, and this is invariably during weekdays, in daytime. Officers attending court deplete our scheduled availability for teams, and so we have to use overtime to provide cover. Sometimes the high level of activity on the Brixton streets on warm summer evenings has led us to call in help from neighbouring police stations to provide the extra needed capacity. Until recently, policy had prevented us from using any part-time staff, but this is now permitted: for example, we now have a part-time Sergeant. She is responsible for the process of submitting papers to the Crown Prosecution. I am sure that the use of part-time staff will give us better scope to cover duties that have relatively predictable levels of fluctuating demand.

'Some special events give us particular capacity management problems. For example, Europe's largest street carnival is held annually in the nearby area of Notting Hill, on a holiday weekend in late August, and this has been attracting ever larger crowds; well over one million spectators attend. It is a very colourful and enjoyable event but from a policing perspective, it is a major task, both for crowd safety and for crime prevention. Our Division is required to provide large numbers of officers to help in this task, so our rota is designed to require everyone to be on duty on the busiest day. The careful planning for this event has brought dividends – the level of serious crime that marred the event in its early years has been almost eliminated, and the huge numbers of spectators seem to be having a safe, happy and crime-free day out. Good policing requires attention to detail, not least in the planning of capacity to match the needs, and it is my responsibility to ensure that we can provide acceptable cover, while not wasting our resources, at all times. This is a difficult balance to achieve, but critically important for us and our customers!' ∎

SUMMARY

∎ The capacity of an operation is the maximum level of value-added activity which it can achieve under normal operating conditions over a period of time.

∎ Operations managers must make capacity decisions in the long, medium and short terms. This chapter has dealt with medium- and short-term capacity management where the capacity level of the organization is adjusted within the fixed physical limits which are set by long-term capacity decisions. But even in the short term, capacity is treated at an aggregated level.

∎ Decisions made in capacity planning and control affect costs, revenues, working capital, quality, speed, dependability and flexibility performance.

∎ The first step in the capacity planning and control task is to understand and measure the likely fluctuations in demand and the extent of available capacity in the organization. Neither of these is a straightforward task. Forecasting demand is char-acterized by high levels of uncertainty, whereas measuring capacity is characterized by high levels of complexity.

∎ The most common type of demand fluctuation which operations have to cope with is that due to seasonality. Seasonality affects many different types of operation and can be caused by climatic, economic, social, political and festive factors. Some operations also have shorter-cycle seasonality-type fluctuations in demand over a month, week or even on an hourly basis.

∎ There are many ways in which capacity can be measured but most organizations adopt a measure of capacity which is based either on inputs to the operation, such as the number of beds available at a hospital, or on the outputs from the operation, such as the number of litres of beer brewed per week by a brewery.

∎ The second step of capacity planning and control is to identify the plans for coping with demand fluctuation. There are three pure plans:

411

– ignoring fluctuations and keeping activity levels constant (the level capacity plan);
– adjusting capacity to reflect the fluctuations in demand (the chase demand plan);
– attempting to change demand to fit capacity availability (demand management).

■ All these pure plans have costs associated with them. Most organizations adopt a mixture of all three to achieve an appropriate balance between costs and customer service.

■ The third step in capacity planning and control is deciding which of the approaches to capacity planning are appropriate. Two techniques are useful in this task. These are:

– cumulative representations, which allow demand and capacity to be compared for feasibility;
– queueing theory, which is able to evaluate the consequences of capacity decisions in many queueing-type service operations.

Fine Country Fruit Cakes

1992 was a year to remember for Mary and Dave DuPlessis. Their twin sons, Michael and Alan, now five years old, started school, and in the same year, Dave, a 29-year-old master baker at a large bakery, was made redundant. Mary, who had a part-time secretarial job with a local builder, saw this misfortune to be an unrepeatable opportunity. They had always wanted to work together, and it seemed to be a good chance to set up a small speciality business, based on Dave's skills and financed by his redundancy payments plus a small loan.

Traditionally, small local baking and confectionery businesses produce a wide range of breads, cakes, biscuits, etc., many on a daily basis. This involves a very early start (4 am), high complexity and considerable risk. Dave wanted a 'simpler' business that would involve relatively normal hours of work, for both himself and his wife. Neither wanted to be employers; the business would be run by just the two of them. Dave felt that his greatest satisfaction came from producing high-quality decorated fruit cakes, so together they decided that there was an opportunity to specialize in this product. Using an old family recipe, samples were made and packaged. 'Market research' was confined to taking these samples to various retail outlets in the area; the reaction was so enthusiastic, and the potential margin seemed so high, that by January 1993 they were in business. They rented a small modern factory near home, modestly equipped with weighing and preparation equipment, a large 15 kg food mixer, two small catering ovens, a small coolroom, and sundry utensils. Talking to a friend early in 1995, Dave recalled:

'At the beginning of 1993 we only made one size: beautiful 2 kg cakes, symmetrically decorated on top with a pattern of almonds, cherries, walnuts and ginger. We sold most to cafés and restaurants; their customers loved portions of them with their teas/coffees. Demand ran at about 150–200 cakes a month, which wasn't enough to make much of a living, but we had time to visit our customers and to try new outlets. Although sales were growing it gradually became clear that we should be selling a smaller cake to retail shops for family purchasers – one which could be bought as a treat, or as a gift for friends. We introduced the 1kg cake (with the same recipe) in July 1993. We had no problems selling these, and demand soon exceeded all our expectations. The delicatessens in the area heard about our products and soon sales of the 1kg cake overtook those of the original 2 kg cake. Somehow, however,

it's not been so easy running the business since then; we can only just cope every day making the cakes. Mary can go to get the children from school at about 3.30 pm (a neighbour takes them in the morning) but I rarely get back before 7.00 pm in the week; and we usually do our selling and prospecting for new customers on Saturdays. We certainly don't want to start production at weekends; we couldn't cope with that! Anyway, although we're making a reasonable profit now, I feel we could do a better job somehow. There were times last year (1994) when we had over-produced, and we had to sell off some stock at a discount because of its age. Tests have shown that this recipe of rich fruit cakes lasts for up to 12 months, but for best flavour and texture, it should really be eaten within six months. The retailers demand at least three months of this, so I can't keep stock more than three months here at the factory. Anyway, I only have space for about 3000 kg in the coolroom, allowing for stock rotation.'

Mary's view of the business was somewhat different:

'I think we are chasing the wrong markets! The delicatessens demand big discounts and are always expecting us to deliver at short notice, particularly around Easter (March/April) and at Christmas (November/December) when the cakes are apparently popular gifts. I have found that craft shops and visitor centres of local tourist spots can also sell our 1kg cakes and, moreover, they don't expect much discount! We were really pleased with the level of orders from these outlets last summer. I really should go and take some more samples! I also feel we should open a factory shop where regular users could come and buy directly, but I am sure we would need to provide a bigger range of cakes. We could develop lots of different types in the two sizes – then we would get a lot more repeat business!'

Production

PREPARATION

In order to simplify weighing, mixing, and baking, all production is done in nominal 10 kg batches of one size at a time. Thus a batch is either ten 1 kg cakes or five 2 kg cakes. For each batch, dried fruits (raisins, sultanas, currants, cherries, crystallized ginger, etc.) are weighed and cleaned as necessary, other ingredients are prepared and measured, and a cake mixture is made in the mixer. Tins are greased, and the mixture is weighed into each; the top surface is then decorated with carefully selected specimen dried fruits and nuts,

▶

413

Table 11.3 Company records of sales 1993/94 and forecast sales for 1995

	1993	1994														1995
		Jan	Feb	Mar	Apr	May	Jun	Jul	Aug	Sep	Oct	Nov	Dec	Total	(Forecast)
1 kg cakes	900	80	200	600	320	120	80	120	80	240	480	800	1 600	4 720	6 000
2 kg cakes	1 950	160	340	300	240	140	160	240	160	180	260	300	400	2 880	3 500
Total (kg)	4 800	400	880	1 200	800	400	400	600	400	600	1 000	1 400	2 400	10 480	13 000

and brushed with a glaze. This complete preparation stage takes almost exactly 30 minutes per batch for Dave and Mary working as a team, for either size of cake. Each batch is prepared just before the oven is ready to accept it, to avoid contamination, and to maintain consistency of method, and hence of texture.

BAKING

The ovens are turned on at 8.00 am and are ready by 8.30 when the first batch is loaded (which only takes a few minutes). A 10 kg batch of cakes fills one oven; baking time is three hours for the 1 kg cakes, four and a half hours for 2 kg cakes. When ready, the cakes are removed from the hot oven, which is ready for a further batch in a quarter of an hour. For convenience, Dave has always baked the 1kg cakes in the oldest oven (Oven 1) to avoid having to carry 10 tins to Oven 2 which is further from the workbench. Each oven normally bakes only two batches per day. Dave thinks that Oven 1 temperature control is inaccurate which would be a particular problem for the larger size cakes!

PACKING

Cakes are turned out on to racks to cool overnight. The next day, once the first batches are into the oven, the previous day's cakes are then inspected, packed in a film, a decorative ribbon and an outer-wrap, and are then labelled and dated. Packed cakes are then carried to the coolroom and stacked according to size. These processes take two people six minutes per cake (either size). The couple take one hour for lunch from 12.30 to 1.30 (when Oven 2 is ready to unload).

PLANNING

'The only times in 1994 that we changed production were in March, April and November and December when we increased 2kg output only by 50 per cent (one extra batch per day). I had to bake the 2 kg cakes in Oven 1 and the quality wasn't really so good, but none of our regular customers noticed! Even so, I had to work into the evenings all those months; it was a lot of work. All other months we have kept to the plan of two batches of each size each day (1 kg, followed by 2 kg, 1 kg, 2 kg) which helps us keep to a rhythm.'

SALES

Records were kept of monthly sales of each size during 1994 (Table 11.3). On 1st January 1994 there was an opening stock of 100 of each size of cake. Dave commented:

'I am worried that we won't be able to cope with demand in 1995, and that we will start giving bad service. Perhaps we should drop the idea of selling to the tourist spots, although the margins are very attractive. Clearly, we musn't upset the retailers who give us so much business.' ■

Questions

1 With the current method of working, what is the monthly and annual capacity of the business? Is the total weight (kg) of product a useful aggregate measure of capacity for this business? How does capacity compare with demand in 1994 and forecast demand in 1995?

2 Why did Dave have to sell stock at reduced prices in 1994? In which months do you think that happened, and explain clearly the reasons. Justify your answer with simple calculations.

3 Mary believed that they should try to get more business from craft shops and tourist centres. What advantages/disadvantages would this market have compared with the existing retail outlets?

4 What are the main differences in operations tasks of running the proposed retail shop? What are the implications of this for the owners?

5 What are the operational implications of making ten varieties of cake, each in two sizes?

1 Explain what is meant by capacity planning and control and describe the implications of a capacity constraint in one of the micro operations of an organization of your own choice.

2 Discuss the implications of having too much or too little capacity for the following operations:
- a national train network
- a lecture room
- a vineyard's grape-pressing equipment.

3 Discuss with an operations manager the demand trends for the organization's products or services, covering the long, medium and short terms. Find out the periods over which the manager makes or uses forecasts and the problems resulting from any inaccuracies in those forecasts.

4 Identify several ways in which the following organizations might measure their capacity (discuss the relative merits of each and suggest the one you think each organization will use):
- a city bus company
- a dentist
- a lift (elevator) maintenance company
- a jobbing plumber.

5 A car battery manufacturer makes four types of car battery: compact, compact-heavy duty, standard and standard-heavy duty. Table 11.4 shows the number of batteries of each type currently produced to order for existing customers and the amount of time each battery spends with the acid-filling machine. The machine is capable of working up to 24 hours a day and needs no adjusting between battery types. The operations manager is under pressure to increase the utilization of the plant. The company has been approached by two new customers to supply batteries. Company A requires someone to supply them with between 80 and 100 batteries per day of various types. Company B requires 10 compact and 70 standard batteries a day, all heavy duty; however, delivery must be assured.

Assuming the acid-filling machine is the only capacity constraint, review the merits of each order.

6 Explain how utilization might be measured in the operations below and discuss the relative merits of

Table 11.4

	Number produced per day	Time with acid filler (mins)
Compact	80	3
Compact HD	50	5
Standard	90	4
Standard HD	20	6

using utilization and efficiency as measures of operations performance:
- a doctor's surgery
- a university lecture
- an ice-cream manufacturer.

7 Discuss with an operations manager how capacity is managed. Identify the different plans used and how they are implemented.

8 Which do you think will be the main capacity plans, and how might they be implemented, for the following organizations:
- a university
- an accident and emergency ward at a hospital
- a compact disc producer
- a taxi service?

(Explain the reasons for your choice.)

9 The management of an hotel on a popular Greek holiday island is concerned that its hotel is full between March and September, is about 80 per cent occupied in February, March and December and about 30 per cent occupied during the other months. Discuss ways in which they might try to move towards 100 per cent occupancy all the year round.

10 A computer bureau's telephone help desk is staffed by ten people throughout the day. It is known that the bureau handles about 15 customers an hour and the average time it takes to deal with a problem is ten minutes. The operations manager believes that customers will be aggrieved if they have to wait for more than two minutes for their calls to be answered. Comment on the situation.

11 The Speedy Cleaning Company operates a drive-in car valeting service. This comprises a number of cleaning bays where customers can drive in and use special cleaning equipment to valet their cars. On Saturday mornings the arrival rate averages five customers per hour. The arrival rate appears to conform to a Poisson distribution. The average time to clean a car is ten minutes, with times being distributed according to a negative exponential distribution. How many bays should the company open to ensure that customers wait no longer than three minutes before being able to enter a bay?

12 The Johannesburg Express Pizza Company has a demand forecast for the next 12 months which is shown in Table 11.5.

The current workforce of 100 staff can produce 1000 cases of pizzas per month.

(a) Prepare a production plan which keeps the output level. How much warehouse space would the company need for this plan?

(b) Prepare a demand chase plan. What implications would this have for staffing levels, assuming that the maximum amount of overtime would result in production levels of only ten per cent greater than normal working hours?

Table 11.5

Months	Demand (cases per month)
January	600
February	800
March	1000
April	1500
May	2000
June	1700
July	1200
August	1100
September	900
October	2500
November	3200
December	900

NOTES ON CHAPTER

1 Source: Interviews with company staff.
2 Source: *The Economist*, 10 Aug 1991.
3 Kimes, S. (1989) 'Yield Management: A Tool for Capacity-constrained Service Firms', *Journal of Operations Management*, Vol 8, No 4.
4 Based on Colley, J.L., Landell, R.D. and Fair, R.R. (1978) *Operations Planning and Control*, Holden Day.
5 Source: Gabb, A. (1991) 'Braving the Elements', *Management Today*, Jan.

SELECTED FURTHER READINGS

Adendorff, S.A., de Wit, P.W.C., Botes, P.S., van Loggerenberg, B.J., Steenkamp, R.J. (1997) *Production and Operations Management: A South African Perspective* (2nd edn), ITP (Southern Africa).

Bleuel, W.H. (1975) 'Management Science's Impact on Service Strategy', *Interfaces*, Vol 6, No 1.

Buxey, G. (1993) 'Production Planning and Scheduling for Seasonal Demand', *International Journal of Operations and Production Management*, Vol 13, No 7.

Chaiken, J.M. and Larson, R.C. (1972) 'Methods for Allocating Urban Emergency Units Survey', *Management Science*, Vol 19, No 4.

Coker, J.L. (1985) 'Analysing Production Switching Heuristics for Aggregate Planning Models via an Application', *Production and Inventory Management*, 4th Quarter.

Fitzsimmons, J.A. and Fitzsimmons, M.J. (1994) *Service Management for Competitive Advantage*, McGraw-Hill.

Gallagher, G.R. (1980) 'How to Develop a Realistic Master Schedule', *Management Review*, Apr.

Grassman, W.K. (1988) 'Finding the Right Number of Servers in Real-World Queueing Systems', *Interfaces*, Vol 8, No 2.

Holt, C., Modigliani, C.F. and Simon, H. (1955) 'A Linear Decision Rule for Production and

Employment Scheduling', *Management Science*, Vol 2, No 2.

Lee, S.M. and Moore, L.J. (1974) 'A Practical Approach to Production Scheduling', *Production and Inventory Management*, Quarter 1.

Lee, W.B. and Khumwala, B.M. (1974) 'Simulation Testing of Aggregate Production Planning Models in an Implementation Methodology', *Management Science*, Vol 20, No 6.

Mangiameli, P. and Krajewski, L. (1983) 'The Effects of Work Force Strategies on Manufacturing Operations', *Journal of Operations Management*, Vol 3, No 4.

Mapes, J. (1993) 'The Effect of Capacity Limitations on Safety Stock', *International Journal of Operations and Production Management*, Vol 13, No 10.

Northcraft, G.B. and Chase, R.B. (1985) 'Managing Service Demand at the Point of Delivery', *Academy of Management Review*, Vol 10, Jan.

Rothstein, M. (1985) 'Operations Research and the Airline Overbooking Problem', *Operations Research*, Vol 33.

Sasser, W.E. (1976) 'Match Supply and Demand in Service Industries', *Harvard Business Review*, Vol 54, No 6.

Vollmann, T.E., Berry, W.L. and Whybark, D.C. (1988) *Manufacturing Planning and Control Systems*, Irwin.

CHAPTER 12

INVENTORY PLANNING
AND CONTROL

INTRODUCTION

Operations managers usually have an ambivalent attitude towards inventories. On the one hand they are costly, tying up sometimes considerable amounts of working capital. On the other hand, they provide some security in a complex and uncertain environment. Certainly when a customer goes elsewhere because just one item is out of stock, or when a major project is waiting for just one small part, the value of inventories seems indisputable. This is the dilemma of inventory management: in spite of the cost and the other disadvantages associated with holding stocks, they do facilitate the smoothing of supply and demand. In fact they only exist because supply and demand are not in harmony with each other (*see* Fig. 12.1).

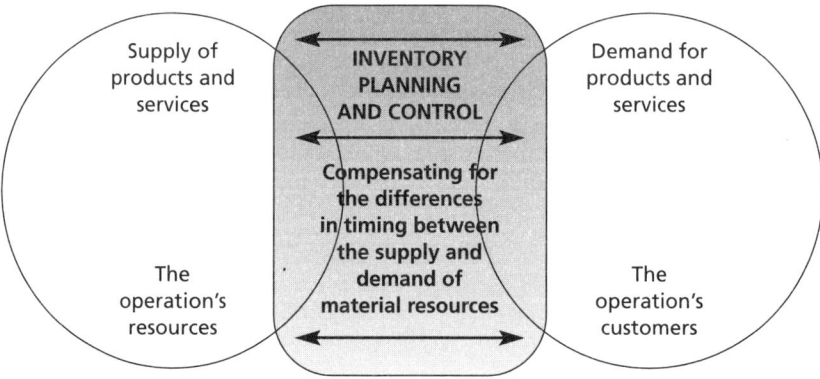

Figure 12.1 A definition of inventory planning and control

OBJECTIVES

This chapter will examine:

- the role, position and types of inventories in operations;

- the order quantity decision and inventory costs;

- economic order quantity (EOQ) type approaches and the criticisms of EOQ;

- the replenishment order timing decision for continuous and periodic review systems;

- inventory control decisions, inventory classifications, measures of inventory and inventory control systems.

WHAT IS INVENTORY?

Inventory, or 'stock' as it is more commonly called in some countries, is defined here as *the stored accumulation of material resources in a transformation system*. Usually we use the term to refer to *transformed input resources*. So a manufacturing company will hold stocks of materials, a tax office will hold stocks of information and a theme park will hold stocks of customers (when it is customers which are being processed we normally refer to the 'stocks' of them as 'queues').

In this chapter we will deal particularly with inventories of material. Inventories of customers are referred to elsewhere in Chapter 11.

All operations keep inventories

If you walk around any operation you will see several types of stored material. Table 12.1 gives some examples for several operations. However, there are differences between the examples of inventory given in Table 12.1. Some are relatively trivial to the operation in question: for example, the cleaning materials which are stored in the television factory are far less important than the stocks of steel, plastic and components which it also holds. The value of the cleaning materials held by the factory will be considerably less than the value of its steel, plastic and components. More importantly, the television plant would not stop if it ran out of cleaning materials, whereas if it ran out of any of its component parts, its activities would be severely disrupted. However, cleaning materials would be a far more important item of inventory for an industrial cleaning company, not only because it uses far more of this input, but also because its operation would stop if it ever ran out of them.

There is also a difference between how often the operations stock the items. Some of the examples of inventory are items which are stored just once within the operation. For example, food in an hotel is delivered to the hotel, stored and then used. Similarly, in the retail store items are delivered to the shop, held until they are requested by the customer, and then taken away by the customer. In some operations most items are stored twice as inventory. For example, the automotive parts distributor will receive deliveries of the parts from its various suppliers, store them in a central depot (inventory 1), transport them to the various local distribution points (inventory 2) where they are either collected by or sent to the customers. So inventories occur both before and after the operation's major process of distribution. In some operations, items are stored several times. For example, in the television factory a single piece of material is likely to progress through many different stages before it eventually leaves the operation as part of the finished television. Between each stage it has probably been stored as inventory.

Table 12.1 Examples of inventory held in operations

Operation	Examples of inventory held in operations
Hotel	Food items, drinks, toilet items, cleaning materials
Hospital	Wound dressings, disposable instruments, whole blood, food, drugs, cleaning materials
Retail store	Goods to be sold, wrapping materials
Warehouse	Goods being stored, packaging materials
Automotive parts distributor	Automotive parts in main depot, automotive parts at local distribution points
Television manufacturer	Components, raw materials, part-finished sub-assemblies, finished televisions, cleaning materials
Precious metal	Material (gold, platinum, etc.) waiting to be processed, material partly processed, fully refined material

The value of inventories

Perhaps the most obvious difference between the operations in Table 12.1 is in the value of the inventories which they hold. In some, the value of inventory is relatively small compared to the costs of the total inputs to the operation. In others, it will be far higher, especially where storage is the prime purpose of the operation. For example, the value of the goods held in the warehouse is likely to be very high compared to its day-to-day expenditure on such things as labour, rent and running costs. Sometimes the value of the inventories can be so high that it is not even included in the organization's general financial accounts; this would be true for example of the precious metals refiner.

The difference in the value of stocks in various organizations is illustrated in Table 12.2.[1]

Table 12.2 Inventory (stocks) and sales in selected companies

Company	Country	Business	Stock	Sales	Stock/Sales
Atlas Copco	Sweden	Construction and mining	SEK 4 425 million	SEK 16 007 million	0.28
British Gas	UK	Natural gas	£593 million	£10 254 million	0.058
Sandoz	Switzerland	Pharmaceuticals	SFr. 3 027 million	SFr. 14 416 million	0.21
Essilor	France	Opthalmics	US$ 281 million	US$ 1 018 million	0.27
BP	UK	Petroleum	£3 379 million	£33 250 million	0.1
Elf	France	Chemicals	FFr. 22 107 million	FFr. 36 288 million	0.61
Reebok	USA	Sportswear	US$ 434 million	US$ 3 022 million	0.14
BMW	Germany	Auto	DM 3 140 million	DM 31 241 million	0.1
Carnaud Metalbox	France	Metal packaging	FFr. 3 534 million	FFr. 24 830 million	0.14
Stena Line	Sweden	Shipping	SEK 152 million	SEK 7 979 million	0.019
Carlsberg	Denmark	Brewing	DKK 1 646 million	DKK 14 957 million	0.11
PSA Peugeot–Citroën	France	Auto	FFr. 27 000 million	FFr. 155 431 million	0.17
Eurocoptor	France	Helicopters	FFr. 10 210 million	FFr. 11 600 million	0.88

Why inventory exists

No matter what is being stored as inventory, or where it is positioned in the operation, it will exist because there is a difference in the timing or rate of supply and demand. If the supply of any item occurred exactly when it was demanded the item would never be stored. A common analogy is the water tank shown in Fig. 12.2. If, over time, the rate of supply of water to the tank differs from the rate at which it is demanded, a tank of water (inventory) will be needed if supply is to be maintained. (More generally we use the process charting symbols (from Appendix 3 at the end of the book) which are also shown in Fig. 12.2.) When the rate of supply exceeds the rate of demand inventory increases; when the rate of demand exceeds the rate of supply inventory decreases. The obvious point to make is that if an operation can make efforts to match supply and demand rates it will also succeed in reducing its inventory levels. This important point is the basis of the just-in-time approach to inventory which we shall explore in more detail in Chapter 15.

Types of inventory[2]

The various reasons for an imbalance between the rate of supply and demand at different points in any operation lead to the different types of inventory. There are four types of inventory: buffer inventory, cycle inventory, anticipation inventory and pipeline inventory.

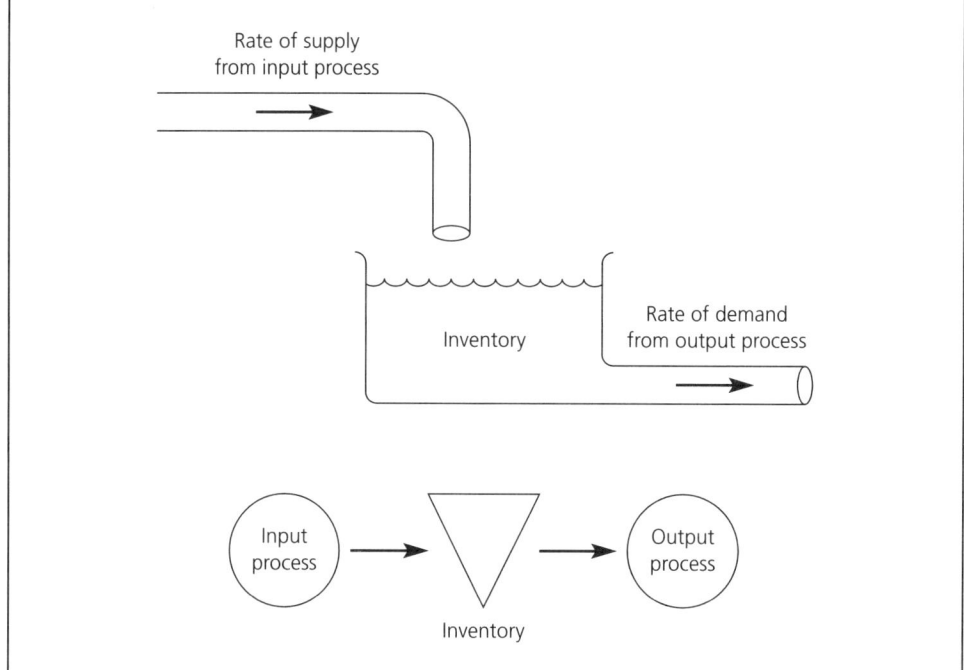

**Figure 12.2
Inventory is
created to
compensate for the
differences in
timing between
supply and
demand**

Buffer inventory

Buffer inventory is also called safety inventory. Its purpose is to compensate for the uncertainties inherent in supply and demand. For example, a retail operation can never forecast demand perfectly, even when it has a good idea of the most likely demand level. It will order goods from its suppliers such that there is always a certain amount of most items in stock. This minimum level of inventory is there to cover against the possibility that demand will be greater than expected during the time taken to deliver the goods. This is *buffer*, or *safety*, *inventory*. It compensates for the uncertainties in the process of the supply of goods into the store and that of the demand of goods from the store.

Cycle inventory

Cycle inventory occurs because one or more stages in the operation cannot supply all the items it produces simultaneously. For example, suppose a baker makes three types of bread, each of which are equally popular with customers. Because of the nature of the mixing and baking process, only one kind of bread can be produced at any time. The baker would have to produce each type of bread in batches (or 'lots' as they are sometimes known) as shown in Fig. 12.3. The batches must be large enough to satisfy the demand for each kind of bread between the times when each batch is ready for sale. Thus, even when demand is both steady and predictable as in Fig. 12.3, there will always be some inventory to compensate for the irregular supply of each type of bread.

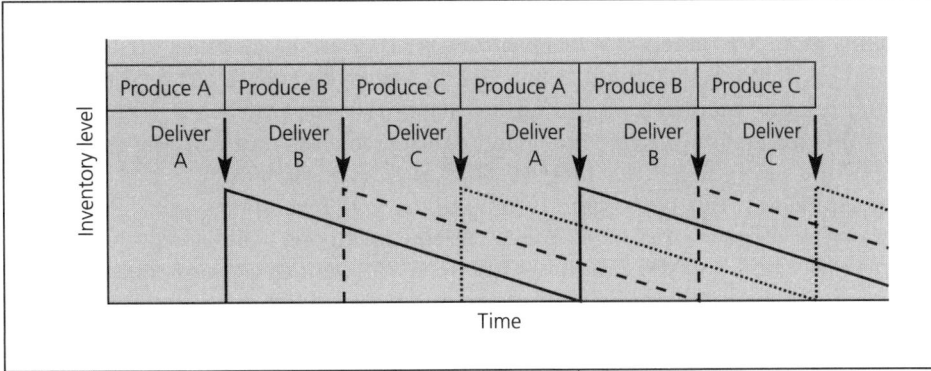

Figure 12.3
Cycle inventory in a bakery

Anticipation inventory

We have already seen how anticipation inventory can be used in Chapter 11. Again it was used to compensate for differences in the timing of supply and demand. In one of the examples from Chapter 11, rather than make chocolate only when it was needed, it was produced throughout the year ahead of demand and put into inventory until it was needed. *Anticipatory inventory* is most commonly used when demand fluctuations are significant but relatively predictable. It might also be used when supply variations are significant, such as in the canning of seasonal foods. Similarly, a company may take the opportunity to buy in inventories on an opportunistic or speculative basis if they are only available spasmodically, or if they believe there might be disruptions to supply. These inventories are being stored in anticipation of changes in supply.

Pipeline inventory

Pipeline inventory exists because material cannot be transported instantaneously between the point of supply and the point of demand. If a retail store orders a consignment of items from one of its suppliers, the supplier will allocate the stock to the retail store in its own warehouse, pack it, load it on to its truck, transport it to its destination, and unload it into the retailer's inventory. From the time that stock is allocated (and therefore it is unavailable to any other customer) to the time it becomes available for the retail store, it is said to be *in the pipeline*. All stock thus in transit is pipeline inventory.

The position of inventory

Not only are there several reasons for supply–demand imbalance, there could also be several points where such imbalance could exist between different stages in the operation. Figure 12.4 illustrates different levels of complexity of inventory relationships within an operation. Perhaps the simplest level is the single-stage inventory system, such as a retail store, which will have only one stock of goods to manage. The automotive parts distribution operation mentioned previously will have a central depot containing inventory and various local distribution points which also contain inventories of the same items. In the television plant, like many manufacturers of standard items, there are three types of inventory. The *raw material and components store inventories* (sometimes called input inventories) receive goods from the operation's suppliers; the raw materials and components work their way through the various stages of the production process but spend considerable amounts of time as *work-in-progress* (WIP) before finally reaching the *finished goods inventory*.

A development of this last system is the *multi-echelon* inventory system. This maps the relationship of inventories between the various operations within a supply network. Chapter 6 discussed how the relationship between different operations could be modelled as a supply network. In the illustration in Fig. 12.4 there are five interconnected sets of inventory systems. The second-tier supplier's (yarn producer's) inventories will feed the first-tier supplier's (cloth producer's) inventories, who will in turn supply the main operation. After the products have been manufactured they are distributed to local warehouses from where they are shipped to the final customers. We will discuss the behaviour and management of such multi-echelon systems in the next chapter.

Inventory decisions

At each point in the inventory system (of any type: single-stage, two-stage, or multi-stage) operations managers need to manage the day-to-day tasks of running the system. Orders will be received from internal or external customers; these will be dispatched and demand will gradually deplete the inventory. Orders will need to be placed for replenishment of the stocks, deliveries will arrive and require storing. In managing the system, operations managers are involved in three major types of decision:

● *How much to order.* Every time a replenishment order is placed, how big should it be (sometimes called the *volume decision*)?
● *When to order.* At what point in time, or at what level of stock, should the replenishment order be placed (sometimes called the *timing decision*)?
● *How to control the system.* What procedures and routines should be installed to help make these decisions? Should different priorities be allocated to different stock items? How should stock information be stored?

THE VOLUME DECISION – HOW MUCH TO ORDER

Inventory costs

In making a decision on how much to purchase, operations managers first try to identify the costs which will be affected by their decision. A number of costs are relevant.

1 *Cost of placing the order.* Every time an order is placed to replenish stock a number of transactions are needed which incur costs to the company. These include the clerical tasks of preparing the order and all the documentation associated with it, arranging for the delivery to be made, arranging to pay the supplier for the delivery, and the general costs of keeping all the information which allows us to do this. If we are placing an order on part of our own operation, there are still likely to be the same types of transaction concerned with internal record-keeping, but also there could be a 'change-

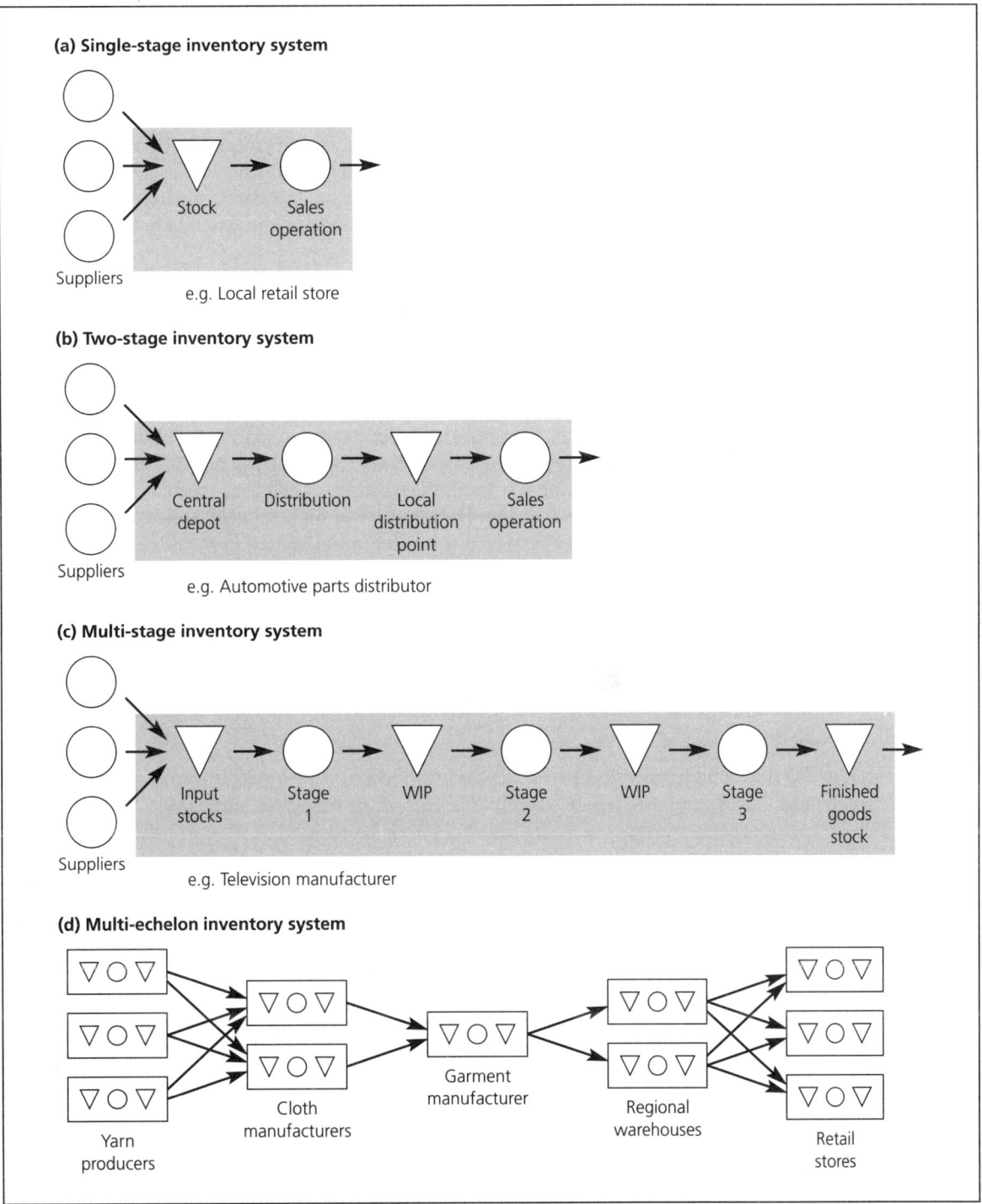

Figure 12.4 (a) Single-stage, (b) two-stage and (c) multi-stage inventory systems and (d) a multi-echelon inventory system

over' cost incurred by the part of the operation which is to supply the items and caused by the need to change from producing one type of item to another.

2 *Price discount costs.* In many industries suppliers offer discounts on the normal purchase price for large quantities; alternatively they might impose extra costs for small orders.

3 *Stock-out costs.* If we misjudge the order quantity decision and our inventory runs out of stock there will be costs to us incurred by failing to supply our customers. If the customers are external they may take their business elsewhere; if internal, stock-outs could lead to idle time at the next process, inefficiencies and eventually again, dissatisfied external customers.

4 *Working capital costs.* Soon after we place a replenishment order suppliers will demand payment for their goods. Eventually, when we supply our own customers, we in turn will receive payment. However, there will probably be a lag between paying our suppliers and receiving payment from our customers. During this time we will have to fund the costs of however much we have in stock. This is called the *working capital* which we need to run the inventory. The costs associated with it are the interest we pay the bank for borrowing it, or the opportunity costs of not investing it elsewhere.

5 *Storage costs.* These are the costs associated with physically storing the goods. Renting, heating and lighting the warehouse can be expensive, especially when special conditions are required such as low-temperature or high-security storage.

6 *Obsolescence costs.* If we choose an ordering policy which involves very large order quantities, which will mean that stocked items spend a long time stored in inventory, there is a risk that the items might either become obsolete (in the case of a change in fashion, for example) or deteriorate with age (in the case of most foodstuffs, for example).

7 *Production inefficiency costs.* According to just-in-time philosophies, high inventory levels prevent us seeing the full extent of problems within the operation. This argument is fully explored in Chapter 15.

We can divide all these inventory-associated costs into two groups. The first three categories are costs which usually decrease as order size is increased. The other categories of cost usually increase as order size is increased.

Inventory profiles

An inventory profile is a visual representation of the inventory level over time. Figure 12.5 shows a simplified inventory profile for one particular stock item in a retail operation. Every time an order is placed, Q items are ordered. The replenishment order arrives in one batch instantaneously. Demand for the item is then steady and perfectly predictable at a rate of D units per month. When demand has depleted the stock of the items entirely, another order of Q items instantaneously arrives and so on. Under these circumstances:

The average inventory $= \dfrac{Q}{2}$ (because the two shaded areas in Fig. 12.5 are equal)

The time interval between deliveries $= \dfrac{Q}{D}$

The frequency of deliveries $=$ the reciprocal of the time interval $= \dfrac{D}{Q}$

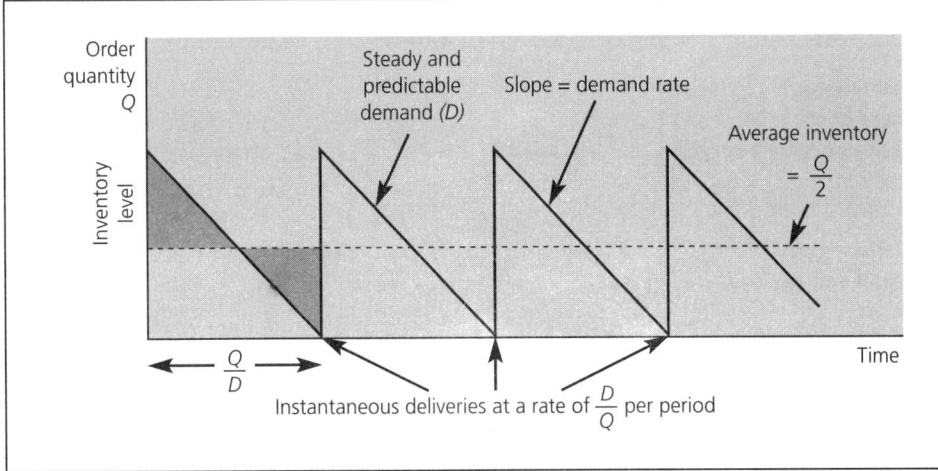

Figure 12.5
Inventory profiles
chart the variation
in inventory level

The economic order quantity (EOQ) formula

The most common approach to deciding how much of any particular item to order when stock needs replenishing is called the economic order quantity (EOQ) approach. Essentially this approach attempts to find the best balance between the advantages and the disadvantages of holding stock. For example, Fig. 12.6 shows two alternative order quantity policies for an item. Plan A, represented by the unbroken line, involves ordering in quantities of 400 at a time. Demand in this case is running at 1000 units per year. Plan B, represented by the dotted line, envisages smaller but more frequent replenishment orders. This time only 100 are ordered at a time with orders being placed four times as often. However, the average inventory for plan B is one quarter of that in plan A.

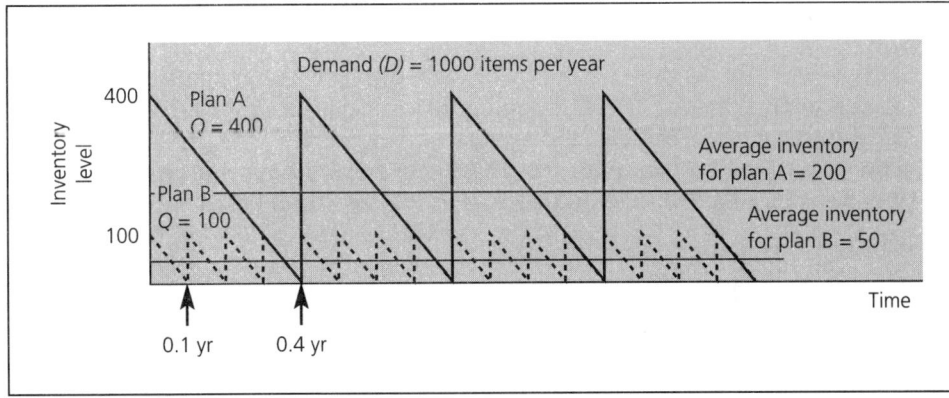

Figure 12.6
Two alternative
inventory plans
with different
order quantities (Q)

To find out whether either of these plans, or some other plan, minimizes the total cost of stocking the item we need some further information, namely the total cost of holding one unit in stock for a period of time (C_h) and the total costs of placing an order (C_o). Generally, holding costs are taken into account by including:

HOLDING
COSTS

- working capital costs
- storage costs
- obsolescence risk costs.

Order costs are calculated by taking into account:

- cost of placing the order (including transportation of items from suppliers if relevant);
- price discount costs.

In this case the cost of holding stocks is calculated at R1 per item per year and the cost of placing an order is calculated at R20 per order.

We can now calculate total holding costs and ordering costs for any particular ordering plan as follows:

Holding costs $\quad$ = Holding cost/unit × average inventory

$$= C_h \times \frac{Q}{2}$$

Ordering costs $\quad$ = Ordering cost × number of orders per period

$$= C_o \times \frac{D}{Q}$$

So, total cost, $C_t \quad = \dfrac{C_h Q}{2} + \dfrac{C_o D}{Q}$

We can now calculate the costs of adopting plans with different order quantities. These are illustrated in Table 12.3. As we would expect with low values of Q, holding costs are low but the costs of placing orders are high because orders have to be placed very frequently. As Q increases the holding costs increase but the costs of placing orders decrease. Initially the decrease in ordering costs are greater than the increases in holding costs and the total cost falls. After a point, however, the decrease in ordering costs slows, whereas the increase in holding costs remains constant and the total cost starts to increase. In this case the order quantity Q, which minimizes the sum of holding and order costs, is 200. This 'optimum' order quantity is called the *economic order quantity (EOQ)*. Graphically, this is illustrated in Fig. 12.7.

A more elegant method of finding the EOQ is to derive its general expression. This can be done using simple differential calculus as follows. From before:

Total cost $\quad$ = Holding cost + Order cost

$$C_t \quad = \frac{C_h Q}{2} + \frac{C_o D}{Q}$$

The rate of change of total cost is given by the first differential of C_t with respect to Q

$$\frac{dC_t}{dQ} = \frac{C_h}{2} - \frac{C_o D}{Q^2}$$

The lowest cost will occur when $\dfrac{dC_t}{dQ} = 0$.

Table 12.3 Costs of adoption of plans with different order quantities

Demand (D) = 1000 units per year   Holding costs (C_h) = R1 per item per year   Order costs (C_o) = R20 per order

Order quantity (Q)	Holding costs (0.5Q × C_h) — I	+	Order costs ((D/Q) × C_o) — R20	=	Total costs
50	25		$\frac{1000}{50}$ 20 × 20 = 400		425
100	50		$\frac{1000}{100}$ 10 × 20 = 200		250
150	75		6.7 × 20 = 134		209
200	100		5 × 20 = 100		200*
250	125		4 × 20 = 80		205
300	150		3.3 × 20 = 66		216
350	175		2.9 × 20 = 58		233
400	200		2.5 × 20 = 50		250

* Minimum total cost

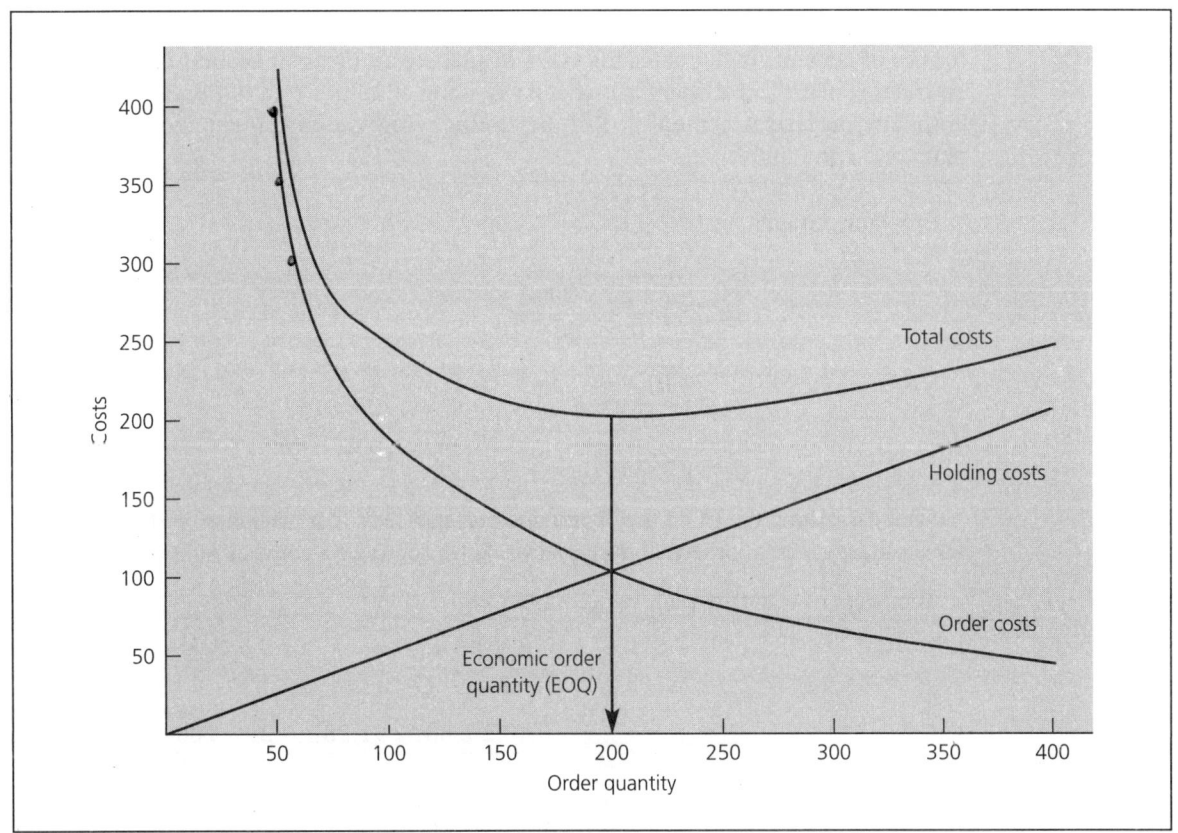

Figure 12.7 Graphical representation of the economic order quantity

That is:

$$0 = \frac{C_h}{2} - \frac{C_o D}{Q_o^2}$$

where $Q_o =$ the EOQ

Rearranging this expression gives:

$$Q_o = EOQ = \sqrt{\frac{2C_o D}{C_h}}$$

When using the EOQ:

$$\text{Time between orders } = \frac{EOQ}{D}$$

$$\text{Order frequency } = \frac{D}{EOQ} \text{ per period}$$

Example

A building materials stockist obtains its cement from a single supplier. Demand for cement is reasonably constant throughout the year. Last year the company sold 2000 tonnes of cement. It estimates the costs of placing an order at around R25 each time an order is placed, and charges inventory holding at 20 per cent of purchase cost. The company purchases cement at R60 per tonne. How much cement should the company order at a time?

$$EOQ \text{ for cement } = \sqrt{\frac{2C_o D}{C_h}}$$

$$= \sqrt{\frac{2 \times 25 \times 2000}{0.2 \times 60}}$$

$$= \sqrt{\frac{100\,000}{12}}$$

$$= 91.287 \text{ tonnes}$$

After calculating the EOQ the operations manager feels that placing an order for 91.287 tonnes *exactly* seems somewhat over-precise. Why not order a convenient 100 tonnes?

$$\text{Total cost of ordering plan for } Q = 91.287$$

$$= \frac{C_h Q}{2} + \frac{C_o D}{Q}$$

$$= \frac{(0.2 \times 60) \times 91.287}{2} + \frac{25 \times 2000}{91.287}$$

$$= \text{R1095.454}$$

Total cost of ordering plan for $Q = 100$

$$= \frac{(0.2 \times 60) \times 100}{2} + \frac{25 \times 2000}{100}$$

$$= R1100$$

The extra cost of ordering 100 tonnes at a time is R1100 – R1095.45 = R4.55. The operations manager therefore should feel confident in using the more convenient order quantity.

Gradual replacement – the economic batch quantity (EBQ) model

Although the simple inventory profile shown in Fig. 12.5 made some simplifying assumptions, it is broadly applicable in most situations where each replacement order arrives as a single delivery to the inventory point. In many cases, however, a replenishment order arrives over a time period rather than in one lot. A typical example of this is where an order is placed within the operation for a batch of parts to be produced on a machine. The machine will start to produce the parts and ship them in a more or less continuous stream into the inventory point. During the time that these units are being added to the inventory, demand is continuing to take place. Provided the rate at which parts are being made and put into the inventory (P) is higher than the rate at which demand is depleting the inventory (D) then the size of the inventory will increase. After the batch has been completed the machine will go on to produce some other part and demand will continue to deplete the inventory level. The resulting profile is shown in Fig. 12.8. Such an inventory profile is typical of the inventories supplied by batches or 'lots' of items produced internally. For this reason the minimum-cost order quantity for this profile is called the *economic batch quantity (EBQ)*. It is also sometimes known as the economic manufacturing quantity (EMQ) or the production order quantity (POQ). It is derived as follows:

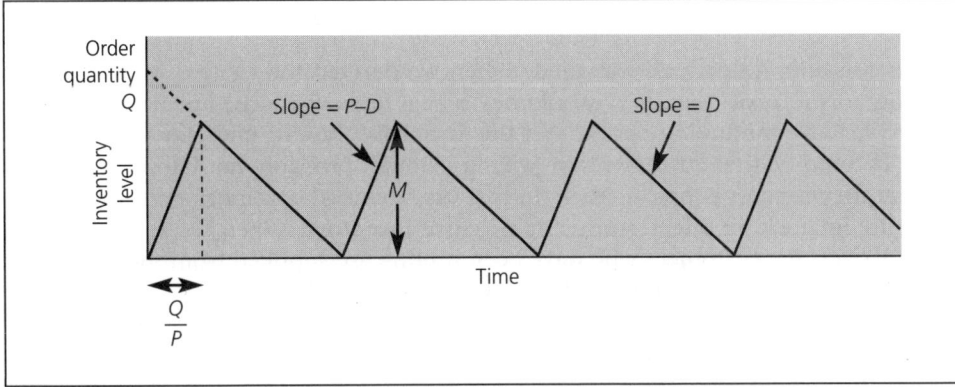

Figure 12.8 Inventory profile for gradual replacement of inventory

$$\text{Maximum stock level} = M$$
$$\text{Slope of inventory build-up} = P - D$$

Also:

$$\text{Slope of inventory build-up} = M \div \frac{Q}{P}$$
$$= \frac{MP}{Q}$$

So,

$$\frac{MP}{Q} = P - D$$
$$M = \frac{Q(P-D)}{P}$$

$$\text{Average inventory level} = \frac{M}{2}$$
$$= \frac{Q(P-D)}{2P}$$

As before:

$$\text{Total cost} = \text{Holding cost} + \text{Order cost}$$
$$C_t = \frac{C_h Q(P-D)}{2P} + \frac{C_o D}{Q}$$
$$\frac{dC_t}{dQ} = \frac{C_h(P-D)}{2P} - \frac{C_o D}{Q^2}$$

Again, equating to zero and solving Q gives the minimum cost order quantity EBQ:

$$EBQ = \sqrt{\frac{2C_o D}{C_h(1-(D/P))}}$$

The economic batch quantity with shortages

Another assumption which was made when we derived the basic economic batch quantity formula was that there would never be a time where the inventory level fell to zero for any continuing period. Yet this is not the case in many inventory situations. It could be that customers are willing (though probably not happy) to wait if an item they request is not in stock. In this case demand continues even though no items are in stock, in effect producing negative inventory. When the replenishment order arrives, the customers who have been waiting are supplied from the replenishment order before it is counted into the stock levels. This results in a profile as shown in Fig. 12.9.

Deriving an expression for the EBQ in a similar manner gives:

$$EBQ = \sqrt{\frac{2DC_o}{C_h}} \sqrt{\frac{C_h + C_s}{C_s}}$$

where C_s = cost per unit of shortage per time period.

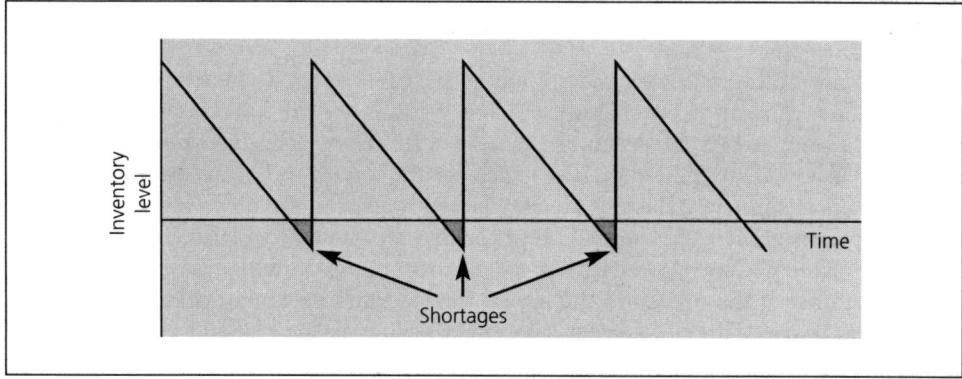

Figure 12.9
Inventory plans
allowing for
shortages

Example

Super Soups manufactures specialist gourmet frozen soups for the restaurant trade. All its soups used to sell at a reasonably steady rate of 700 litres per day. Recently the company adopted a policy of reducing the price by R1 per litre for every day a customer had to wait for delivery. Normally orders are delivered on the same day as ordering but if the soup is not in stock, customers have to wait until it is next manufactured. Keeping soup frozen is expensive and the company charges itself for storage at a rate of R0.16 per litre per day. It has also calculated that the cost of changing its production processes to make a different flavour costs R100. The new policy was a success and increased demand for all its soups to 1000 litres per day. What effect should these changes have on the company's stock-ordering policy?

Previously:

$$D = 700 \text{ litres/day}$$

$$C_o = R100$$

$$C_h = R0.16 \text{ per day}$$

$$EOQ = \sqrt{\frac{2 \times 700 \times 100}{0.16}} = 935 \text{ litres}$$

Now:

$$C_s = R1 \text{ per litre per day}$$

From formula allowing shortages:

$$EOQ = \sqrt{\frac{2 \times 1000 \times 100}{0.16}} \times \sqrt{\frac{0.16 + 1}{1}}$$

$$= 1207$$

The economic order quantity needs to be increased from 935 litres per day to 1207 litres per day.

If customers won't wait – the news-seller problem

A special case of the inventory order quantity decision refers to the situation where an order quantity of items is purchased for a specific event or time period, after which the items are unlikely to be sold. A simple example of this is the decision taken by a newspaper seller of how many newspapers to stock for the day. If the news-seller should run out of papers customers will either go elsewhere or decide not to buy a paper that day. If any newspapers are left over at the end of the day the value of yesterday's news is zero. Demand for the newspapers varies day by day depending on who happens to be passing, the weather at the time, and the appeal of that day's news. In deciding how many newspapers to carry the news-seller is in effect balancing the risk and consequence of running out of newspapers against that of having newspapers left over at the end of the day. The method for determining the optimum order quantity is best illustrated through an example.

Example

A concert promoter needs to decide how many concert T-shirts to order emblazoned with the logo of the main act. The profit on each T-shirt sold at the concert is R5 and any unsold T-shirts are returned to the company who supplies them, but at a loss to the promoter of R3 per T-shirt. Demand is uncertain but is estimated to be between 200 and 1000. The probabilities of different demand levels are as follows:

Demand level	200	400	600	800
Probability	0.2	0.3	0.4	0.1

How many T-shirts should the promoter order? Table 12.4 shows the profit which the promoter would make for different order quantities and different levels of demand.

Table 12.4 Pay-off matrix for T-shirt order quantity (profit or loss in rands)

Demand level	200	400	600	800
Probability	0.2	0.3	0.4	0.1
Promoter orders 200	1000	1000	1000	1000
Promoter orders 400	400	2000	2000	2000
Promoter orders 600	−200	1400	3000	3000
Promoter orders 800	−800	800	2400	4000

We can now calculate the *expected* profit which the promoter will make for each order quantity by weighting the outcomes by their probability of occurring.

If promoter orders 200 T-shirts:

$$\text{Expected profit} = 1000 \times 0.2 + 1000 \times 0.3 + 1000 \times 0.4 + 1000 \times 0.1$$

$$= \text{R}1000$$

If promoter orders 400 T-shirts:

$$\text{Expected profit} = 400 \times 0.2 + 2000 \times 0.3 + 2000 \times 0.4 + 2000 \times 0.1$$

$$= \text{R1680}$$

If promoter orders 600 T-shirts:

$$\text{Expected profit} = -200 \times 0.2 + 1400 \times 0.3 + 3000 \times 0.4 + 3000 \times 0.1$$

$$= \text{R1880}$$

If promoter orders 800 T-shirts:

$$\text{Expected profit} = -800 \times 0.2 + 800 \times 0.3 + 2400 \times 0.4 + 4000 \times 0.1$$

$$= \text{R1440}$$

The order quantity which gives the maximum profit is 600 T-shirts, which results in a profit of R1880.

Criticism of the EOQ approach[3]

The approach to determining order quantity which involves optimizing costs of holding stock against costs of ordering stock, typified by the EOQ and EBQ models, has always been subject to criticisms. Originally these concerned the validity of some of the assumptions of the model; more recently they have involved the underlying rationale of the approach itself. We shall examine three classes of criticism concerning:

- the assumptions included in the models;
- the real costs of stock in operations;
- the use of the models as prescriptive devices.

Model assumptions

In order to keep EOQ-type models relatively straightforward it was necessary to make assumptions concerning such things as the stability of demand, the existence of a fixed and identifiable ordering cost, the cost of stock holding which can be expressed by a linear function, shortage costs which were identifiable, and so on. For example, the assumption of steady demand (or even demand which conforms to some known probability distribution) is untrue for a wide range of the operation's inventory problems. For example, a book seller might be very happy to adopt an EOQ-type ordering policy for some of its products such as dictionaries and other reference books. However, estimating demand for some books is far more difficult. For some novels the probability distribution which describes likely demand is bi-modal. If the book does not catch the public's imagination it will sell a reasonable number to customers who are familiar with the author; however, if it is well reviewed or other publicity surrounds it the demand could be many times what it would otherwise be. An EOQ approach has difficulty in coping with such wild fluctuations in demand.

Other questions surround some of the assumptions made on the nature of stock-related costs. For example, placing an order with a supplier as part of a regular and multi-item order might be relatively inexpensive, whereas asking for a special one-off delivery of one item could prove far more costly. Similarly with stock-holding costs, although many companies make a standard percentage charge on the purchase price of stock items, this might not be appropriate over a wide range of stock-holding levels. The marginal costs of increasing stock-holding levels might be merely the cost of the working capital involved. On the other hand, it might necessitate the construction or lease of a whole new stock-holding facility such as a warehouse. Operations managers using an EOQ-type approach must check that the decisions implied by the use of the formulae do not exceed the limits within which the cost assumptions apply.

How costly is stock?

It is useful at this stage to examine the effect on an EOQ approach of regarding stock as being more costly. Increasing the slope of the holding cost line increases the level of total costs of any order quantity, but more significantly, shifts the minimum cost's optimum point substantially to the left, in favour of a lower economic order quantity. In other words, the less sanguine an operation is about holding stock, the more it should move towards smaller, more frequent ordering.

Using EOQ models as prescriptions

Perhaps the most fundamental criticism of the EOQ approach again comes from the Japanese-inspired JIT philosophies. The emphasis of EOQ is on trying to determine representative costs of ordering and stock holding and then optimizing order decisions in the light of these costs. Implicitly the costs are taken as fixed, in the sense that the task of operations managers is to find out what are the true costs rather than to change them in any way. EOQ is essentially a reactive approach. Some critics would argue that it fails to ask the right question. Rather than asking the EOQ question of 'What is the optimum order quantity?', operations managers should really be asking, 'How can I change the operation in some way so as to reduce the overall level of stocks it is necessary to hold in the operation?'.

For example, many organizations have made considerable efforts to reduce the effective cost of placing an order. Often they have done this by working to reduce change-over times on machines. This means that less time is taken changing over from one product to the other and therefore less operating capacity is lost, which in turn reduces the cost of the change-over. Under these circumstances, the order cost curve in the EOQ formula reduces and, in turn, reduces the effective economic order quantity. Figure 12.10 shows the EOQ formula represented graphically with increased holding costs (see the previous discussion). Figure 12.10 also shows the further effects of reduced order costs, the net effect of which is to shift the value of the EOQ even further to the left.

THE TIMING DECISION – WHEN TO PLACE AN ORDER

When we assumed that orders arrived instantaneously and demand was steady and predictable, the decision on when to place a replenishment order was self-evident. An order would be placed as soon as the stock level reached zero. This would arrive

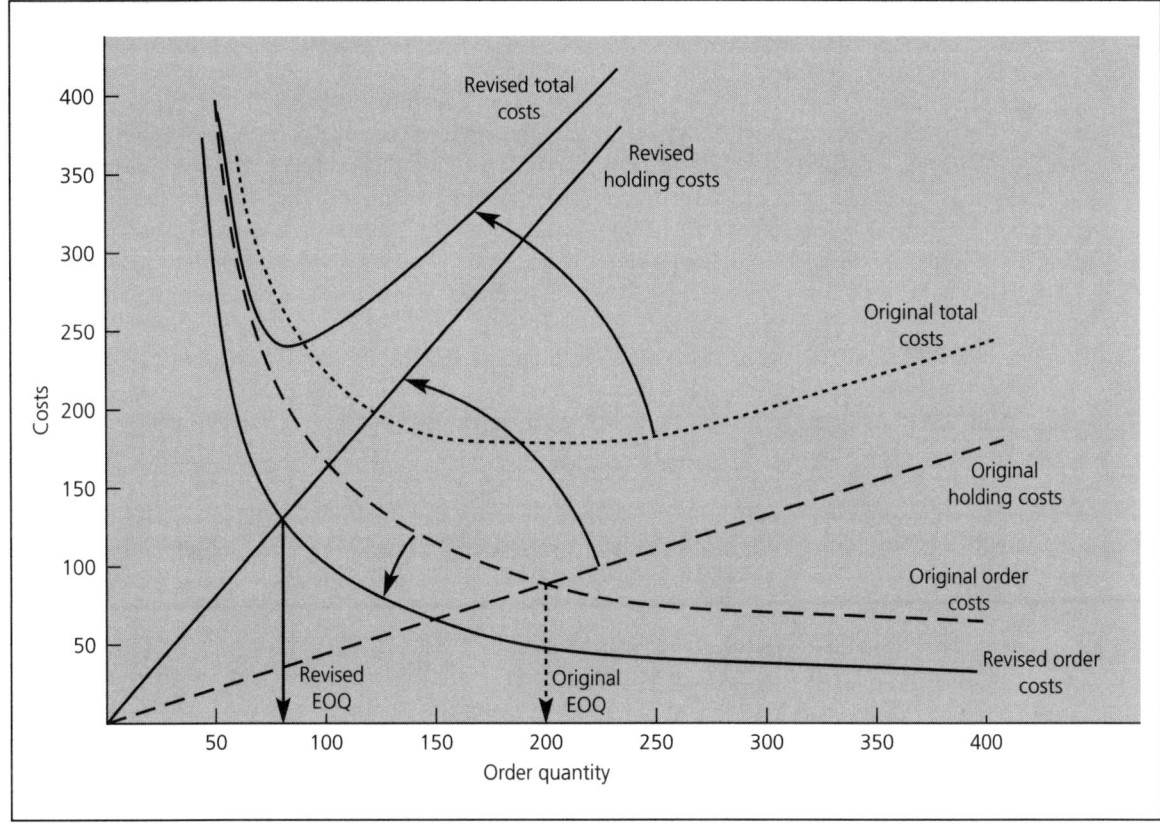

Figure 12.10 Reducing the cost of ordering (or change-over) can reduce the EOQ further

instantaneously and prevent any stock-out occurring. If replenishment orders do not arrive instantaneously but have a lag between the order being placed and it arriving in the inventory, we can calculate the timing of a replacement order as shown in Fig. 12.11. The lead time for an order to arrive is in this case two weeks, so the re-order point (ROP) is the point at which stock will fall to zero minus the order lead time. Alternatively, we can define the point in terms of the level which the inventory will have reached when a replenishment order needs to be placed. In this case this occurs at a re-order level (ROL) of 200 items.

However, this assumes that both the demand and the order lead time are perfectly predictable. In most cases of course this is not so. Both demand and the order lead time are likely to vary to produce a profile which looks something like Fig. 12.12. In these circumstances it is necessary to make the replenishment order somewhat earlier than would be the case in a purely deterministic situation. This will result in, on average, some stock still being in the inventory when the replenishment order arrives. This is buffer or safety stock (s). The earlier the replenishment order is placed, the higher will be the expected level of safety stock (s) when the replenishment order arrives. But because of the variability both of lead time (t) and demand rate (d), there will sometimes be a higher than average level of safety stock and sometimes lower. The main consideration in setting safety stock is not so much the average level of stock when a replenishment order arrives but rather the probability that the stock will not have run out before the replenishment order arrives.

437

SHOULD WE RE-ORDER? – THE MARKS & SPENCER APPROACH[4]

A special case of the 'How much to order?' decision in inventory control is the 'Should we order any more at all?' decision. Retailers especially need continually to review the stocked lines they keep on the shelves. One company known for its ruthless approach to the restocking decision is Marks & Spencer (M & S), which is one of the most successful large retailers in Europe in terms of the profitability of its operations. M & S has a simple philosophy: if it sells, restock it quickly and avoid stock-outs; if it doesn't sell, get it off the shelves quickly and replace it with something which *will* sell. The M & S approach is purely pragmatic, based on trial-and-error, and very unsentimental. This often means putting a new line on the shelves of a pilot store and watching customer reaction very closely. The store most often used for these trials is the company's Marble Arch store in London – said to have the fastest stock turnover of any store in the world. Sometimes it is possible to make a restocking decision within a few hours – not surprising when the time frame for stock rotation can be as little as a week.

For more routine stock control decisions the company uses an automatic stock-ordering system which it calls ASR (Assisted Stock Replenishment – *see also* box in Chapter 13, page 476). This helps it always to have the right stock of textile products in the store at the right time. The system, which is now installed in its flag-ship Marble Arch store, takes into account all goods bought at the till through the electronic point-of-sale (EPOS) system and automatically generates an order to replenish that item. The system anticipates orders for each item based on the previous week's sales and delivers in advance. The current day's sales are continually reviewed and any extra items required are delivered the next day. Orders arrive at the store from the local distribution centre at Neasden in North London. New orders are usually placed before 8.30 am and 85 per cent of these will arrive before close of business that day. The remainder arrives the following morning before opening time. The number of deliveries each day varies between 14 and 24 depending on the level of business.

On the sales floor the main stock control tasks are to ensure that all the clothing rails are fully stocked, that the stock tickets reflect the sales information on display and that everything is neatly and correctly arranged. During the day the area supervisor watches the stock levels and the flow of customers around the displays in case any changes to stock location need to be made. The store has a policy of not bringing stock out on to the floor during opening hours; but in the case of fast moving items, this can be unavoidable at times. ∎

The key statistic in calculating how much safety stock to allow is the probability distribution which shows the *lead time usage*. The lead time usage distribution is a combination of the distributions which describe lead time variation and the demand rate during the lead time. If safety stock is set below the lower limit of this distribution then there will be shortages every single replenishment cycle. If safety stock is set above the upper limit of the distribution there is no chance of stock-outs occurring. Usually safety stock is set to give a predetermined likelihood that stock-outs will not occur. Figure 12.12 shows that, in this case, the first replenishment order arrived after t_1 resulting in a lead time usage of d_1. The second replenishment order took longer, t_2, and demand rate was also higher, resulting in a lead time usage of d_2. The third order cycle shows several possible inventory profiles for different conditions of lead time usage and demand rate.

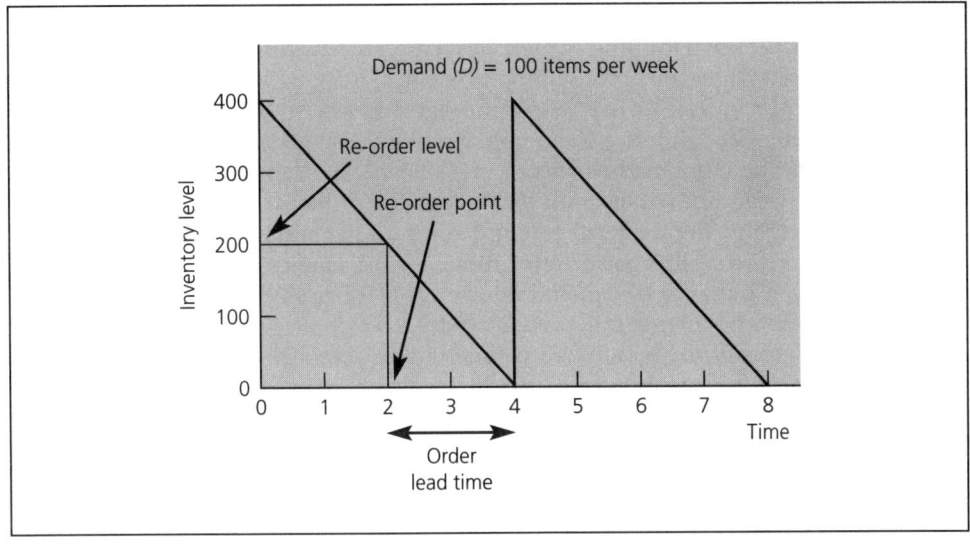

**Figure 12.11
Re-order level
(ROL) and re-order
point (ROP) are
derived from the
order lead time
and demand rate**

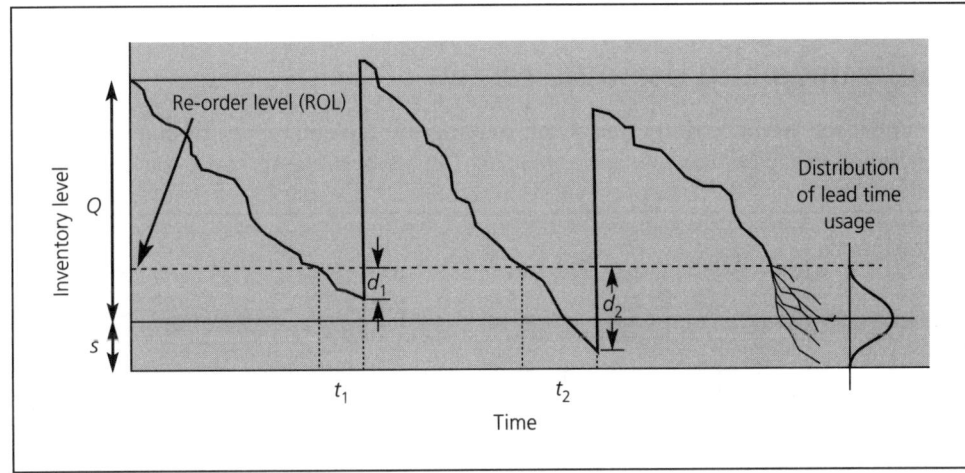

**Figure 12.12
Safety stock (s)
helps to avoid
stock-outs when
demand and/or
order lead time is
uncertain**

Example

A company which imports running shoes for sale in its sports shops can never be certain of how long, after placing an order, the delivery will take. Examination of previous orders reveals that out of ten orders one took one week, two took two weeks, four took three weeks, two took four weeks and one took five weeks. The rate of demand for the shoes also varies between 110 pairs per week to 140 pairs per week. There is a 0.2 probability of the demand rate being either 110 or 140 pairs per week and a 0.3 chance of demand being either 120 or 130 pairs per week. The company needs to decide when it should place replenishment orders if the probability of a stock-out is to be less than 10 per cent.

Both lead time and the demand rate during the lead time will contribute to the lead time usage. So the distributions which describe each will need to be combined. Figure 12.13 and Table 12.5 show how this can be done. Taking lead time to be either one, two, three, four or five weeks and demand rate to be either 110, 120, 130 or 140 pairs per week, and also assuming the two variables to be independent, the distributions can be combined as shown in Table 12.5. Each element in the matrix shows a possible lead time usage with the probability of its occurrence. So if the lead time is one week and the demand rate is 110 pairs per week, the actual lead time usage will be 1 × 110 = 110 pairs. Since there is a 0.1 chance of the lead time being one week, and a 0.2 chance of demand rate being 110 pairs per week, the probability of both these events occurring is 0.1 × 0.2 = 0.02.

We can now classify the possible lead time usages into a histogram form. For example, summing the probabilities of all the lead time usages which fall within the range 100–199 (all the first column) gives a combined probability of 0.1. Repeating this for subsequent intervals results in Table 12.6.

This shows the probability of each possible range of lead time usage occurring, but it is the cumulative probabilities which are needed to predict the likelihood of stock-out (*see* Table 12.7).

Setting the re-order level at 600 would mean that there is only a 0.08 chance of usage being greater than available inventory during the lead time, i.e. there is a less than 10 per cent chance of a stock-out occurring.

Continuous and periodic review

The approach we have described when making the replenishment timing decision is often called the *continuous review approach*. This is because to make the decision in

**Figure 12.13
The probability
distributions for
order lead time
and demand rate
combine to give
the 'lead time
usage' distribution**

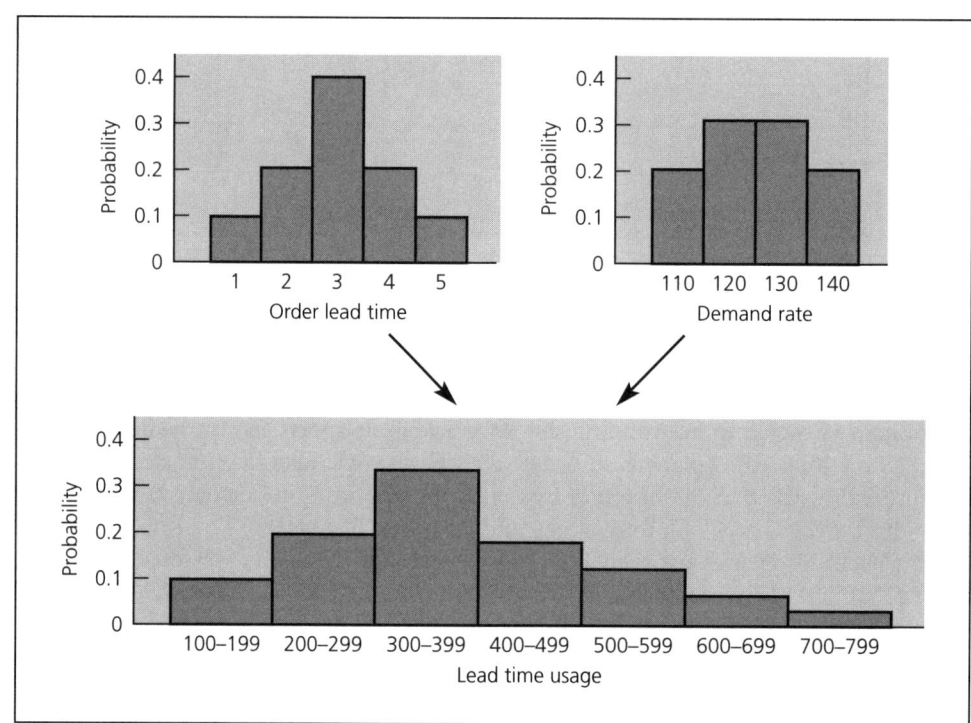

Table 12.5 Matrix of lead time and demand rate probabilities

			Lead time probabilities				
			1	*2*	*3*	*4*	*5*
			0.1	*0.2*	*0.4*	*0.2*	*0.1*
Demand rate probabilities	*110*	*0.2*	110 (0.02)	220 (0.04)	330 (0.08)	440 (0.04)	550 (0.02)
	120	*0.3*	120 (0.03)	240 (0.06)	360 (0.12)	480 (0.06)	600 (0.03)
	130	*0.3*	130 (0.03)	260 (0.06)	390 (0.12)	520 (0.06)	650 (0.03)
	140	*0.2*	140 (0.02)	280 (0.04)	420 (0.08)	560 (0.04)	700 (0.02)

Table 12.6 Combined probabilities

Lead time usage	100–199	200–299	300–399	400–499	500–599	600–699	700–799
Probability	0.1	0.2	0.32	0.18	0.12	0.06	0.02

Table 12.7 Combined probabilities

Lead time usage X	100	200	300	400	500	600	700	800
Probability of usage being greater than X	1.0	0.9	0.7	0.38	0.2	0.08	0.02	0

this way operations managers need continuously to review the stock level of each item and then place an order when the stock level reaches its re-order level. The virtue of this approach is that, although the timing of orders may be irregular (depending on the variation in demand rate), the order size (Q) is constant and can be set at the optimum economic order quantity. However, continually checking on inventory levels can be time consuming, especially when there are many stock withdrawals compared to the average level of stock.

An alternative and far simpler approach, but one which sacrifices the use of a fixed (and therefore possibly optimum) order quantity, is called the *periodic review* approach. Here, rather than ordering at a predetermined re-order level, the periodic approach orders at a fixed and regular time interval. So the stock level of an item could be checked, for example, at the end of every month and a replenishment order placed to bring the stock level up to a predetermined level. This level is calculated to cover demand between the replenishment order being placed and the following replenishment order arriving. Figure 12.14 illustrates the parameters for the periodic review approach.

At time T_1 in Fig. 12.14 the inventory manager would examine the stock level and order sufficient to bring the stock level up to some maximum stock level Q_m. However, that order of Q_1 items will not arrive until a further time of t_1 has passed, during which demand continues to deplete the stocks. Again both demand and lead time are uncertain. The Q_1 items will arrive and bring the stock level up to some level lower than Q_m (unless there has been no demand in t_1). Demand then continues until T_2 when again an order Q_2 is placed which is the difference between the current stock at T_2 and Q_m. This order arrives after t_2 by which time demand has depleted the stocks further. Thus the replenishment order placed at T_1 must be able to cover for the demand which occurs until T_2 and t_2. Safety stocks will need to be calculated, in a similar manner to before, based on the distribution of usage over this period.

The time interval

The interval between placing orders, t_1, is usually calculated on a deterministic basis, and derived from the EOQ. So, for example, if the demand for an item is 2000 per year, the cost of placing an order R25, and the cost of holding stock R0.5 per item per year:

$$EOQ = \sqrt{\frac{2C_oD}{C_h}} = \sqrt{\frac{2 \times 2000 \times 25}{0.5}} = 447$$

The optimum time interval between orders t_f is therefore:

$$t_f = \frac{EOQ}{D} = \frac{447}{2000} \text{ years}$$

$$= 2.68 \text{ months}$$

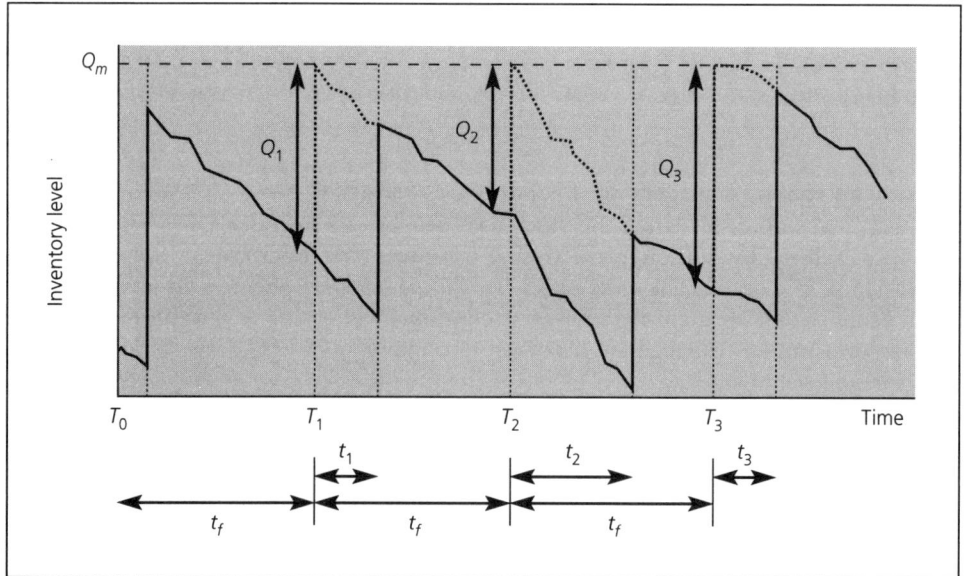

Figure 12.14
A periodic review approach to order timing with probabilistic demand and lead time

It may seem paradoxical to calculate the time interval assuming constant demand when demand is, in fact, uncertain. However, uncertainties both of demand and lead time can be allowed for by setting Q_m to allow for the desired probability of stock-out based on usage during the period t_f + lead time.

INVENTORY ANALYSIS AND CONTROL SYSTEMS

The models we have described so far, even the ones which take a probabilistic view of demand and lead time, are still simplified compared to the complexity of real stock management. Coping with many thousands of stocked items, supplied by many hundreds of different suppliers, with possibly tens of thousands of individual customers, makes for a complex and dynamic operations task. In order to control such complexity, operations managers have to do two things. First, they have to discriminate between different stocked items, so that they can apply a degree of control to each item which is appropriate to its importance. Second, they need to invest in an information processing system which can cope with their particular set of inventory control circumstances.

Inventory priorities – the ABC system

In any inventory which contains more than one stocked item, some items will be more important to the organization than others. Some items, for example, might have a very high usage rate so if they ran out many customers would be disappointed. Other items might be of particularly high value so excessively high inventory levels would be particularly expensive. One common way of discriminating between different stock items is to rank them by the *value of their usage* (their usage rate multiplied by their individual value). Items with a particularly high value of usage are deemed to warrant careful control whereas those with low usage values need not be controlled quite so rigorously. Generally a relatively small proportion of the total items contained in an inventory will account for a large proportion of the total inventory value. This phenomenon is known as the *Pareto law* (after the person who described it), sometimes referred to as the 80/20 rule. It is called this because, typically, 80 per cent of an operation's inventory value is accounted for by only 20 per cent of all stocked item types. Here the relationship can be used to classify the different types of items kept in an inventory by their usage value. This allows inventory managers to concentrate their efforts on controlling the more significant items of stock.

● *Class A items* are those 20 per cent or so of high-value items which account for around 80 per cent of the total stock value.
● *Class B items* are those of medium value, usually the next 30 per cent of items which account for around 10 per cent of the total value.
● *Class C items* are those low-value items which, although comprising around 50 per cent of the total types of items stocked, probably only account for around 10 per cent of the total value of stocked items.

443

INVENTORY MANAGEMENT AT FLAME ELECTRICAL[5]

Inventory management in some operations is more than just a part of their responsibility; it is their very reason for being in business. Flame Electrical, South Africa's largest independent supplier and distributor of lamps, is such a business. It stocks over 2900 different types of lamp which vary in value from 25 cents to over R5000. The lamps, which are sourced from 14 countries including South Africa, are stored in a 5000 square metre warehouse, and distributed to customers throughout the country.

'In effect our customers are using us to manage their stocks of lighting sources for them', says Jeff Schaffer, the Managing Director of Flame Electrical. *'They could, if they wanted to, hold their own stock but might not want to devote the time, space, money or effort to doing so. Using us they get the widest range of products to choose from, and an accurate, fast and dependable service.'*

Central to the company's ability to provide the service which its customers expect is its computerized stock management system. The system holds information on all of Flame's customers, the type of lamps they may order, the quality and brand of lamps they prefer, the price to be charged, the internal product codes which Flame uses to identify each item it stocks and the location of each item in the warehouse. When a customer phones in to order, the computer system immediately accesses all this information, which is confirmed to the customer. This only leaves the quantity of each lamp required by the customer to be keyed in. The system then generates an instruction to the warehouse to pick and dispatch the order. This instruction includes the shelf location of each item. The system even calculates the location of each item in the warehouse which will minimize the movement of stock for warehouse staff.

Orders for the replenishment of stocks in the warehouse are triggered by a re-order point system. The re-order point is set for each stocked item depending on the likely demand for the product during the order lead time (forecast from the equivalent period's orders the previous year), the order lead time for the item (which varies from 24 hours to 4 months) and the variability of the lead time (from previous experience). The size of the replenishment order depends on the lamp being ordered. Flame prefers most orders to be for a whole number of container loads (the shipping costs for part-container loads being more expensive). However, lower order quantities of small or expensive lamps may be used. The order quantity for each lamp is based on its demand, its value and the cost of transportation from the suppliers. However, all this can be overridden in an emergency. If a customer, such as a hospital, urgently needs a particular lamp which is not in stock, the company will even use a fast courier to fly the item in from overseas – all for the sake of maintaining its reputation for high service levels.

'We have to get the balance right', says Jeff Schaffer. *'Excellent service is the foundation of our success. But we could not survive if we did not control stocks tightly. After all we are carrying the cost of every lamp in our warehouse until the customer eventually pays for it. If stock levels were too high we just could not operate profitably. It is for that reason that we go as far as to pay incentives to the relevant staff based on how well they keep our working capital and stocks under control.'* ∎

Example

Table 12.8 shows all the parts stored by an electrical wholesaler. The 20 different items stored vary both in terms of their usage per year and cost per item, as shown. However, the wholesaler has ranked the stock items by their usage value per year. The total usage value per year is R5 569 000. From this it is possible to calculate the usage value per year of each item as a percentage of the total usage value, and from that a running cumulative total of the usage value, as shown. The wholesaler can then plot the cumulative percentage of all stocked items against the cumulative percentage of their value. So, for example, the part with stock number A/703 is the highest value part and accounts for 25.14 per cent of the total inventory value. As a part, however, it is only one-twentieth or 5 per cent of the total number of items stocked. This item, together with the next highest value item (D/012), account for only 10 per cent of the total number of items stocked, yet account for 47.37 per cent of the value of the stock, and so on.

This is shown graphically in Fig. 12.15. Here the wholesaler has classified the first four part numbers as class A items and will monitor the usage and ordering of these items very closely. A few improvements in order quantities or safety stocks for these items could bring significant savings. Part number A/500 through to A/138 are to be treated as class B items with slightly less effort devoted to their control. All other items are classed as class C items whose stocking policy is reviewed only occasionally.

Although annual usage and value are the two criteria most commonly used to determine a stock classification system, other criteria might also contribute towards classifying each item.

● *Consequence of stock-out.* High priority might be given to those items which would seriously delay or disrupt other operations if they were not in stock.
● *Uncertainty of supply.* Some items, although of low value, might warrant more attention if their supply is erratic or uncertain.
● *High obsolescence or deterioration risk.* Items which lose their value through obsolescence or deterioration might need extra attention and monitoring.

Some more complex stock classification systems might include these criteria by classifying on an A, B, C basis for each. For example, a part might be classed as A/B/A meaning it is an A category item by value, a class B item by consequence of stock-out and a class A item by obsolescence risk.

Measuring inventory

In our example of ABC classifications we used the monetary value of the annual usage of each item as a measure of inventory usage. Monetary value can also be used to measure the absolute level of inventory at any point in time. This would involve taking the number of each item in stock, multiplying it by its value (usually the cost of purchasing the item) and summing the value of all the individual items stored. This is a useful measure of the investment which an operation has in its inventories but gives no indication of how large that investment is relative to the total throughput of the operation. To do this we must compare the total number of items in stock against their rate of usage. There are two ways of doing this. The first is to calculate the amount of time the inventory would last, subject to normal demand, if it were not replenished. This is sometimes

Table 12.8 Warehouse items ranked by usage value

Stock no.	Usage (items/year)	Cost (R/item)	Usage value (R/yr) (R000s)	% of total value	Cumulative % of total value
A/703	700	20.00	1400	25.14	25.14
D/012	450	2.75	1238	22.23	47.37
A/135	1000	0.90	900	16.16	63.53
C/732	95	8.50	808	14.51	78.04
C/375	520	0.54	281	5.05	83.09
A/500	73	2.30	168	3.02	86.11
D/111	520	0.22	114	2.05	88.16
D/231	170	0.65	111	1.99	90.15
E/781	250	0.34	85	1.53	91.68
A/138	250	0.30	75	1.34	93.02
D/175	400	0.14	56	1.01	94.03
E/001	80	0.63	50	0.89	94.92
C/150	230	0.21	48	0.86	95.78
F/030	400	0.12	48	0.86	96.64
D/703	500	0.09	45	0.81	97.45
D/535	50	0.88	44	0.79	98.24
C/541	70	0.57	40	0.71	98.95
A/260	50	0.64	32	0.57	99.52
B/141	50	0.32	16	0.28	99.80
D/021	20	0.50	10	0.20	100.00
Total			5569	100.00	

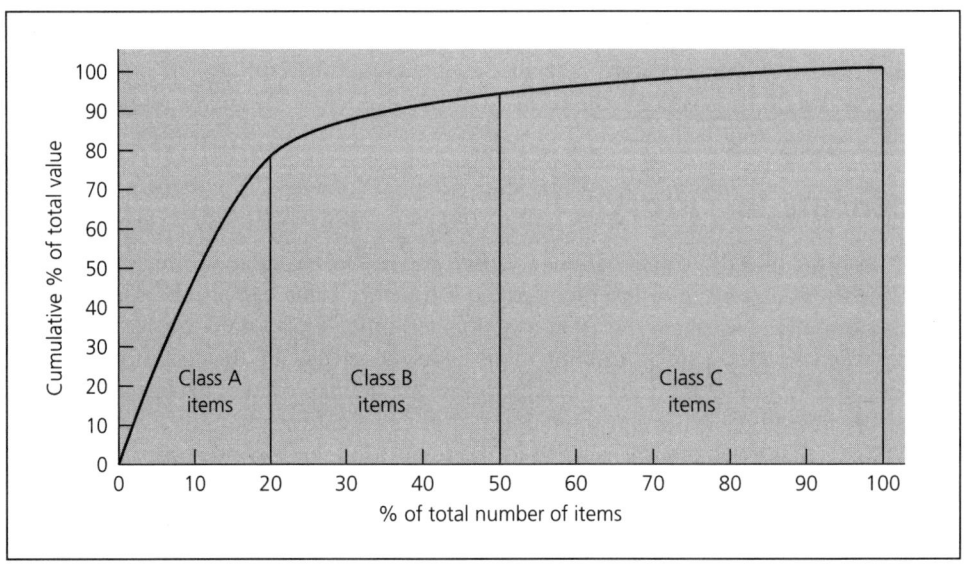

Figure 12.15 Pareto curve for items in a warehouse

called the number of weeks' (days', months', years', etc.) *cover* of the stock. The second method is to calculate how often the stock is used up in a period. This is called the *stock turn* or *turnover of stock* and is the reciprocal of the stock-cover figure mentioned earlier.

Inventory information systems

Most inventories of any significant size are managed by computerized systems. The large number of relatively routine calculations involved in stock control lend themselves to computerized support. This is especially so since data capture has been made more convenient through the use of bar-code readers and the point-of-sale recording of sales transactions. Many commercial systems of stock control are available, although they tend to share certain common functions. These include the following:

Updating stock records

Every time a transaction takes place (such as the sale of an item, or the movement of an item from a warehouse into a truck, or the delivery of an item into a warehouse) the position, status, and possibly value of the stock will have changed. This information needs recording so that operations managers can determine their current inventory status at any time.

Generating orders

The two major decisions we have described previously, namely how much to order and when to order, can both be made by a computerized stock control system. The first decision, setting the value of how much to order (Q), is likely to be taken only at relatively infrequent intervals. The system will hold all the information which goes into the economic order quantity formula but might periodically check to see if demand or order lead times, or any of the other parameters, have changed significantly, and recalculate Q accordingly. The decision on when to order, on the other hand, is a far more routine affair which computer systems make according to whatever decision rules operations managers have chosen to adopt: either continuous review or periodic review. Furthermore the systems can automatically generate whatever documentation is required, or even transmit the re-ordering information electronically through an electronic data interchange (EDI) system. Chapter 8 explained how EDI systems worked.

Generating inventory reports

Inventory control systems can generate regular reports of stock value for the different items stored which can help management monitor their inventory control performance. Similarly, customer service performance, such as the number of stock-outs, or the number of incomplete orders, can be regularly monitored. Some reports may be generated on an exception basis. That is, the report is only generated if some performance measure deviates from acceptable limits.

Forecasting

All inventory decisions are based on forecast future demand. The inventory control system can compare actual demand against forecast and adjust the forecast in the light of actual levels of demand.

Control systems of this type are treated in more detail in Chapter 14.

THE NATIONAL BLOOD SERVICE

In September 1994 a plea was transmitted on the national news in South Africa for blood donors to give blood urgently. The empty racks in the blood storage bank on the television screens graphically portrayed the urgency of the request. Momentarily the National Blood Transfusion Service had lost its continuing battle to balance the supply of blood with demand.

The National Blood Transfusion Service has one of the most difficult inventory control tasks to perform of any operation. Its regional centres are responsible for collecting blood from donors, testing it, processing it into different by-products, storing them and distributing them to hospitals. In addition they perform other services including tissue typing to match donor organs with potential recipients and testing 150 000 antenatal samples every year. Their inventory control task is complicated by the high variety of blood types and of by-products which they are expected to stock, the uncertainty in both demand and supply for blood, and the perishability of their 'products'.

Blood and by-products need to be stored under a variety of conditions. Red blood cells, used for surgical procedures and to correct anaemia, have to be stored at 4°C and have a shelf life of 35 days. Platelets, extracted from donated blood and used to treat leukaemia and bone marrow transplants, have to be stored at 20–24°C and have a shelf life of only five days, during which time they have to be constantly agitated. Frozen fresh plasma is used for liver transplants and for massive transfusion operations. It has to be stored at –30–40°C and has a shelf life of six months. Other by-products also need different storage conditions and have different shelf lives. In addition, blood can be categorized by two main systems or groups. The ABO group includes A, B, AB, and O. The rhesus group includes Rh-positive and Rh-negative. In addition there are many less common and more complex types of blood, often relating to ethnic groups. Blood has to be matched with the recipient's blood type. Giving a patient the wrong type of blood can be fatal. However, group O negative can be given to emergency patients before blood tests have been made. It is therefore a flexible type of blood. Because of this hospitals like to stock O negative. However, O negative represents only 8 per cent of the population, whereas 12 per cent of blood issued is of this type.

Neither demand nor supply is constant. Demand is affected significantly by accidents. One serious accident involving a cyclist used 750 units of blood, which completely exhausted the available supply (miraculously, he survived). Large-scale accidents usually generate a surge of offers from donors wishing to make immediate donations. There is also a more predictable seasonality to the donating of blood, however, with a low period during the summer vacation period.

Controlling the inventory levels of blood has also a financial aspect. Unless blood is controlled carefully it can easily go past its 'use-by date' and be wasted. Even though the blood has been donated free of charge, the cost of collection, testing, storage and distribution is still significant, so money is wasted if blood is wasted. For some patients the control of the age of stored blood is more critical than this. For example, new-born babies, the elderly, and patients whose immune systems have been suppressed so that they do not reject transplanted organs, are all prone to infection. Very fresh blood is therefore kept 'on hold' for these patients. Very rare blood types also pose a problem. It is generally not feasible to store all types of blood, so some donors become 'walking inventories' of blood to be called in at short notice if they are required to donate. ■

Gerrit Kruger, ADTrans

Gerrit Kruger is the CEO of ADTrans, a firm involved in the traction or railway equipment industry. Gerrit has over 25 years' experience in the electrical engineering industry and did his MBL thesis on the subject of inventory control in this industry. He has, at various times, been MD of AEG SA Pty Ltd as well as of GEC Electrical Machines.

'The electrical engineering industry in South Africa generates high levels of demand for electrical components. This industry, with an annual size in excess of R300 million, is served by over 40 competitors, each of whom strives to offer a full range of components to the local market. These have quite a wide range of component types, ranging from relays and air circuit breakers to overloads and miniature circuit breakers. Each broad component type is available in a number of options and each of these options requires a further number of accessories. A typical supplier of components into this industry could easily have as many as 10 000 different items in stock, being the number of likely permutations that may be ordered. The difficulties are compounded by the fact that the vast majority of materials are imported. The supply lead times vary from a week for air freight to over ten weeks for sea freight. The price penalty between these two freight options is 15 per cent of cost price for the former and 7 per cent for the latter.

'Demand for these items typically falls into two broad categories: project-based demand and routine demand. The first category is typified by a longer delivery lead time and a client propensity to wait as long as the promised delivery period is met. The primary demand behind this category is long-term capital projects. This demand category is therefore easy to plan for as long as the project delivery lead time is longer than the material delivery lead time.

This category of demand is fairly lumpy in nature because it involves irregular peaks. The second category is typified by less predictable demand and a lower propensity to wait. The number of clients is higher, with a lower volume of demand from each. This demand is driven by a variety of primary demands, ranging from maintenance of plant to sales of associated new capital equipment such as motors. This category of demand is fairly smooth and predictable due to the regular nature of purchases.

'The stocking policies for these supplies is quite a sensitive one given the high rate of new product introduction and the associated risks of obsolescence. This is further emphasized by the price penalty associated with the two freight options. A final problem is the high level of South African interest rates, which raises the opportunity costs associated with the holding of stock. The margins available in this industry do not permit the support of vast levels of stocks and for this reason the main driver of profitability in this industry is optimum stock management.

'Logistic issues are clearly a nightmare and take on strategic and not just operational proportions. The stock strategy favoured in this industry is a two pronged one:

'For project demand we ship out directly from the overseas principal on receipt of order. The choice of freight medium is determined by the project lead time. Only the exact quantity is ordered.

'For routine demand we maintain stocks of material on the basis of a replenishment model linked to historical trends. The choice of shipment method is primarily by sea, although this can vary depending on how well designed the individual company's inventory model is and the demand fluctuations within its particular market niche.' ■

Source: By kind permission of Gerrit Kruger/ADTrans

449

SUMMARY

■ Inventory occurs in operations because the timings of supply and demand do not always match. Inventories (or stocks as they are often called) are used to smooth the differences between supply and demand.

■ All operations keep inventories of some sort. (In this chapter we have used inventory to mean the storage of material resources.) The items kept in stock in different operations will vary considerably in value. Some types of operation, such as professional services, will hold relatively low levels of inventories, while others, such as retail operations or warehouses, will hold very large amounts of inventory.

■ There are four main reasons for keeping inventory and, therefore, four types of inventory. These are:

buffer inventory
cycle inventory
anticipation inventory
pipeline inventory.

■ Inventory can occur in several points within an operation. In some operations, such as a retail shop, there is one major store of goods, while at the other extreme, in a complex manufacturing system, for example, there are many points at which inventory can occur.

■ There are three major types of decision which operations managers need to make regarding the planning and control of their inventory. These are:
– how much to order each time a replenishment order is placed;
– when to order the replenishment of stocks;
– how to control the system of inventory planning and control.

■ The decision of how much to order involves balancing the costs associated with holding stocks against the costs associated with placing an order. The main stock-holding costs are usually related to working capital, whereas the main order costs are usually associated with the transactions necessary to generate the information to place the order.

■ The most common approach to determining the amount of an order is the economic order quantity (EOQ) formula. The EOQ formula can be adapted to different types of inventory profile using different stock behaviour assumptions. It gives the optimum (lowest cost) order quantity but the function which describes the total cost associated with an ordering policy is relatively insensitive to small errors in the estimation of costs.

■ The EOQ approach to determining order quantity has been subject to a number of criticisms. These criticisms fall into three main categories:
– that the assumptions regarding demand and cost used in the EOQ models are sometimes unrealistic;
– that the real cost of stock, in terms of its effect within an operation, is far higher than is assumed;
– that the use of EOQ-type models as prescriptive devices seems to emphasize an approach which takes many of the costs associated with ordering as fixed rather than encouraging an approach which tries to reduce or improve costs.

■ The decision of when to place an order becomes important when demand is treated as probabilistic. Orders are usually timed to leave a certain level of average safety stock when the order arrives. The level of safety stock is influenced by the variability both of demand and lead time. These two variabilities are usually combined into lead time usage variations.

■ Using re-order level as the trigger for placing a replenishment order necessitates the continual review of inventory levels. This can be time consuming and expensive. An alternative approach is to make a replenishment order of varying size at fixed time periods.

■ Managers must discriminate in the level of control which they apply to different stock items. The most common way of doing this is by what is known as the ABC classification of stock. This uses the Pareto principle to distinguish between class A items, class B items and class C items.

■ Inventory can be measured in several different ways but the three most common are:

total value of the stock
the stock cover provided by the average stock
the stock turn.

■ Inventory is usually managed through sophisticated computer-based information systems which have a number of functions: most importantly the updating of stock records, the generation of orders, the generation of inventory status reports, forecasting demand.

CASE EXERCISE

Plastix (Pty) Ltd

Plastix (Pty) Ltd is one of Africa's largest and most profitable manufacturers of plastic household durables. The factory makes a range of 300 products which are sold to wholesalers and large retailers throughout Africa. The company offers ex-stock delivery of all items, and dispatch within 24 hours of receipt of orders by a reputable international haulier; on this basis, customers expect to receive all their requirements within one week.

Concerned about the declining delivery reliability, increased levels of finished goods inventory, and falling productivity (apparently resulting from 'split-batches' where only part of a planned production batch is produced to overcome immediate shortages), the Managing Director, Daniel Tshabalala, employed consultants to undertake a complete review of operations. On 1 September 1993, a full physical inventory check was

Table 12.9 Details of a representative sample of 20 Plastix products

Product reference number*	Description	Unit manufg variable cost (R)	Last 12 mths' sales (000s)	Physical inventory 1 Sept 93 (000s)	Re-order quantity (000s)	Standard moulding rate** (items/hour)
016GH	Storage bin large	1.60	10	0	2	240
033KN	Bread bin + lid	2.40	60	8	2	200
041GH	10 litre bucket	0.50	2200	360	600	300
062GD	Grecian pot	3.00	40	15	5	180
080BR	Bathroom mirror	5.00	5	6	5	260
101KN	1 litre jug	0.60	100	20	10	600
126KN	Pack (10) bag clips	0.30	200	80	50	2000
143BB	Baby bath	2.50	50	1	2	120
169BB	Baby potty	1.50	60	0	2	180
188BQ	Barbecue table	10.80	10	8	5	120
232GD	Garden bird bath	2.00	2	6	2	200
261GH	Broom head	0.80	60	22	8	400
288LY	Pack (10) clothes pegs	1.00	10	17	50	1000
302BQ	Barbecue salad fork	0.20	5	12	2	400
351GH	Storage bin small	1.00	25	2	2	300
382KN	Round mixing bowl	0.50	800	25	80	650
421KN	Pasta jar	2.00	1	3	5	220
444GH	Wall hook	0.05	200	86	50	3000
472GH	Dustbin + lid	6.00	300	3	10	180
506BR	Soap holder	0.80	10	9	20	400

* The reference number uses the following codes for ranges:

    BB = Babycare   BQ = Barbecue   BR = Bathroom
    GD = Garden   GH = General household   KN = Kitchen
    LY = Laundry

** Moulding rate is for the product as described (e.g. includes lids, or pack quantities).

taken; a representative sample of 20 products is shown in Table 12.9.

Plastix uses batch-production, injection-moulding processes; typical set-ups (change-overs) take four hours, costing approximately R400. Because of current high demand for Plastix products, the backlog of work for planned stock replenishment currently averages eight weeks, and so all factory orders must be planned at least eight weeks in advance. Actual re-order quantities (*see* Table 12.9) are always established by the Estimating Department when each new product is designed and the manufacturing costs are established, based on Marketing's estimates of likely demand. However, in order to minimize the cost of set-ups, and to maximize capacity utilization, all products are now planned for a *minimum* production run of 20 hours, with re-order levels based on the previous 13 weeks' average sales. About 20 per cent of the products (e.g. Barbecue Range and Garden Range) are very seasonal, with peak demand August–April.

Storage bins sell particularly well from October to December. Monthly forecasts of sales value are prepared annually a nd reviewed quarterly; this analysis is by product range (e.g. Babycare, Gardenware) for budgeting, cashflow forecasting, and for aggregate capacity planning. The Marketing Manager sum-marized the current position thus:

'Our coverage of the market has never been so comprehensive; we are able to offer a full range of household plastics in fashionable colours, which appeals to most tastes. But we will not retain our newly developed markets unless we can give distributors confidence that we will supply all their orders within one week. Unfortunately, at the moment, many receive several deliveries for each order, spread over many weeks. This certainly increases their administrative and handling costs, and our haulage costs. And sometimes the shortfall is only some small low-value items like clothes pegs!'

The factory operates on three shifts, Monday to Friday: 120 hours per week. Regular overtime, typically 16 hours on a Saturday, has been worked most of the last year. Sunday is never used for production, allowing access to machines for routine and major overhauls. Machines are laid out in groups so that each operator can be kept highly utilized, attending to at least four machines. Although the moulding processes run automatically, the operators are needed to ensure that inputs of raw materials and outputs of products continue to flow without problems. They are encouraged by an output-based bonus scheme which directly rewards the productivity of each operator. All machines are the same size to allow full interchangeability of the tooling, so any product can be made on any machine.

Riaan Eksteen, the Manufacturing Director, gave more details about production:

'Because of the fast output rates of all the moulding machines, it is very easy to produce slightly faulty products at a very fast rate! Typical problems could be damaged or worn tooling causing poor surface finish (marks and scratches); or perhaps slightly bent or twisted products caused by incorrect adjustment of temperatures or pressures. The real problem is that our operators' perception of a fault may be different to that of the inspectors, particularly just after we have had a few customer complaints! The Quality Control Manager, Cilla Rose, reports directly to the MD. Her 14 inspectors (four per shift, two on Saturday mornings) are fully occupied taking random samples from each of our 30 moulding machines, checking them in the laboratory for critical variables and attributes. Recently the reject rate has increased, yet we are also getting higher levels of complaints from the trade ... but that is probably to be expected as our products become more up-market and complicated. Fortunately, all faulty products can be ground up and made into garden pots, so we don't lose any of the expensive material. Cilla has recently persuaded the MD to employ another inspector on each shift to try to reduce the quality problems, and I am sure that will help. I am worried, however, that the effect may be to make our delivery problems worse as even more batches are rejected or delayed while problems are rectified. Also further valuable factory and warehouse space are being allocated to Quality Control for their working and storage needs, which I really cannot afford to give up!

'At the moment our warehouse is full, with products stacked on the floor in every available corner, which makes it vulnerable to damage from passing forklifts and from double-handling. We have finally agreed to approve a R1 million warehouse extension to be constructed January–May 1994, which will give good payback, as it will replace contract warehousing and associated transport which is costing us about five per cent of the manufacturing costs of the stored capital. The return on investment is well above our current ten per cent cost of capital. There is no viable alternative, because if we run out of space, production will have to stop for a time. Some of our products occupy very large volumes of rack space!

▶

'We all work hard to keep down manufacturing costs. Our Group Central Purchasing Department sources all our raw materials, and because of their purchasing power, we are able to get the lowest prices for all types of plastics. Recently they contracted a Hungarian company to supply polyethylene granules for the Industrial Products Division, and we are able to get this material at a saving of about five per cent. We will have to sample this material carefully, as it is likely to be more variable than African-sourced material. Cilla, the Quality Control Manager, is a polymer chemist, so she has agreed to do the tests herself every morning to save the cost and time involved in using an outside laboratory.' ■

Questions

1 Why is Plastix unable to deliver all its products within the target of one week, and what effects might that have on the distributors?
2 What internal problems result from the current planning and control policies? Categorize these broadly into categories of scheduling, capacity management, and inventory management. Do these policies interact?
3 What recommendations would you make to Daniel Tshabalala?
4 How does the company's inventory management impact on its quality performance?

DISCUSSION QUESTIONS

1 Describe and categorize the types of material inventories that might be found in the following organizations:

a theatre
a furniture retailer
a brewery
a city bus company.

2 Talk to an operations manager about the different types of inventory that the organization holds. Find out if there are different ways of planning and controlling some of the different types of inventory.

3 Get hold of the last few years' Annual Report and Accounts for a material processing organization of your choice. Calculate the organization's stock–turnover ratio and the proportion of inventory to current assets over the last few years. Try to explain what you think are the reasons for any trends you can identify and discuss the likely advantages and disadvantages for the organization concerned.

4 The Shocking Electricity Company uses 3000 metres of wire every month. The cost of placing an order for the wire has been calculated at R40 and the cost of stocking the wire is 5c per metre per year. In what quantities should the company order the wire? If it adopts an EOQ approach to ordering, what would be its annual inventory cost?

5 A university's printing department uses paper at the rate of 86 packets per day. A pack of paper costs R20 and the annual stock-holding cost is calculated at 10 per cent of the cost of the paper. If it costs R250 every time an order is placed and the department works 250 days in the year, what is the EOQ for the paper? If it takes three days between placing an order and receiving it, what is the re-order point at which an order should be placed?

6 The Pride of Scotland Butchers Limited has a haggis machine which can produce at a rate of 1000 haggises per day. Traditionally the company produces a day's worth of haggises which fully satisfies the demand for one week. The company sells its haggises throughout 50 weeks of the year. Each time the haggis machine is set up to produce a batch of haggises it costs R100. The haggises have to be kept in particularly cool and hygienic conditions and therefore it costs the company R0.5 per haggis per day to store stock. How much money is the company losing by producing 1000 haggises per week in one batch rather than adopting an EBQ policy (make any assumptions you believe reasonable)?

7 A company which has been using the EOQ formula to determine its order quantities has now found that demand has increased by 50 per cent since it last calculated the optimum order quantity. What adjustment will it have to make to its order quantity? What further adjustment will it have to make to its ordering quantity if its stock-holding costs increase by 50 per cent?

8 A university MBA programme keeps sweatshirts in stock for its students with the university's logo emblazoned on the front. On average it sells 200 of these sweatshirts every year. There is a fixed postage and packing charge of R5 every time it places an order. The cost of the sweatshirts is R15 and inventory is charged by the university at 30 per cent per year. How many sweatshirts should the university order at a time? The new programme director has responded to complaints from the students that the sweatshirts were out of stock last year by offering to pay R20 into the students' entertainment fund every time there is a stock-out. How would this affect the economic order quantity?

9 An ice-cream seller is required to purchase the ice-creams which are then kept in a cold box at the beginning of a sales day. The seller pays R1 for every ice-cream. Ice-creams are sold at R5 each but any ice-creams left at the end of the day cannot be returned and go to waste. The ice-cream seller classifies demand as either low, medium or high. Low demand is between 40 and 80 ice-creams, medium demand is between 80 and 120 ice-creams, and high demand is between 120 and 160 ice-creams. The probability of demand being low is 0.2, the probability of demand being medium is 0.5, and the probability of demand being high is 0.3. Approximately how many ice-

creams would you advise the ice-cream seller to purchase every morning? If competition forces the price which the ice-cream seller can charge down to R4 does this change the decision?

10 A furniture store sells tables which it obtains from a local furniture factory. Each time it places an order on the factory there is a delivery charge and general transaction cost of R60 per order. The stock-holding cost is estimated to be R10 per table per year. Both demand and lead time vary according to the distribution in Table 12.10. Devise a re-order level policy for the furniture store if it is to have less than a five per cent probability of being out of stock each order cycle.

Table 12.10

Lead time usage	Probability
600–650	0.2
650–700	0.2
700–750	0.3
750–800	0.2
800–850	0.05
850–900	0.05

NOTES ON CHAPTER

1 Sources: Company accounts (1992/93).
2 There are several different ways of classifying inventory. This is probably the most straightforward.
3 For further discussion on the limitations of the EOQ, *see* Schonberger, R.J. and Knod, E.M. (1994) *Operations Management: Continuous Improvement* (5th edn), Irwin.
4 Sources: *The Economist*, 26 June 1993, and Horovitz, J. and Jurgens Panak, M. (1992) *Total Customer Satisfaction*, FT/Pitman Publishing, and discussion with company staff.
5 We thank Jeff Schaffer for his help in supplying the information for this box.

SELECTED FURTHER READINGS

Adendorff, S. A., de Wit, P. W. C., Botes, P. S., van Loggerenberg, B. J. and Steenkamp, R. J. (1997) *Production and Operations Management: A South African Perspective* (2nd edn), ITP (Southern Africa).

Adkins, A.C. Jr. (1984) 'EOQ in the Real World', *Production and Inventory Management*, Vol 25, No 4.

Austin, L.M. (1977) 'Project EOQ: A Success Story in Implementing Academic Research', *Interfaces*, Vol 7, Aug.

Hall, R. (1983) *Zero Inventories*, Dow Jones–Irwin.

Jessop, D. and Morrison, A. (1991) *Storage and Control of Stock*, Pitman Publishing.

Jinchiro, N. and Hall, R. (1983) 'Management Specs for Stockless Production', *Harvard Business Review*, Vol 61, No 3.

Lockyer, K.G. and Wynne, R.M. (1989) 'The Life Profile of Stock as a Control Measure', *International Journal of Operations and Production Management*, Vol 9, No 1.

Mapes, J. (1993) 'The Effect of Capacity Limitations on Safety Stock', *International Journal of Operations and Production Management*, Vol 13, No 10.

Newell, S., Swan, J. and Clarke, P. (1993) 'The Importance of User Design in the Adoption of New Information Technologies: The Example of Production and Inventory Control Systems', *International Journal of Operations and Production Management*, Vol 13, No 2.

Primrose, P.L. (1992) 'The Value of Inventory Savings', *International Journal of Operations and Production Management*, Vol 12, No 5.

Ronen, D. (1983) 'Inventory Service Measures – A Comparison of Measures', *International Journal of Operations and Production Management*, Vol 3, No 2.

Schonberger, R.J. and Schniederjans, M.J. (1984) 'Reinventing Inventory Control', *Interfaces*, Vol 14, No 3.

Silver, E.A. and Peterson, R. (1985) *Decision Systems for Inventory Management and Production Planning*, John Wiley.

Snyder, R.D. (1993) 'A Computerized System for Forecasting Spare Parts Sales: A Case Study', *International Journal of Operations and Production Management*, Vol 13, No 7.

Tersine, R.J. (1987) *Principles of Inventory and Materials Management* (2nd edn), North Holland.

Williams, K., Williams, J. and Haslam, C. (1989) 'Why Take the Stocks Out? Britain *versus* Japan', *International Journal of Operations and Production Management*, Vol 9, No 8.

CHAPTER 13

SUPPLY CHAIN PLANNING AND CONTROL

INTRODUCTION

Historically, operations managers have seen their main responsibility lying within their own operation. However, increasingly they now have to look beyond this traditional internal view to be able to manage their function. As operations become more focused on a tightly defined set of tasks and consequently buy in more of their materials and services from specialist suppliers, the contribution of purchasing and supply to the business increases in importance. At the demand side of the business it is being claimed that up to 25 per cent of total costs can lie in the distribution chain which transports goods and services to customers. This flow of materials and information through a business from the purchasing activity, through the operation and out to customers, by way of a distribution or service delivery activity, is what we described in Chapter 6 as the 'immediate' supply network or supply chain. When operations managers have sought to control this flow they have found that they can obtain speed, dependability, flexibility, cost and quality benefits compared with just managing the flow within the operation itself. Even beyond the immediate supply chain, there are often strategic benefits to be gained from managing the flow between customers' customers and suppliers' suppliers. Inter-company operations management of this nature is now more commonly termed supply chain management. In Chapter 6 we raised the strat-egic and structural issues of designing supply networks. In this chapter we are going to consider the more 'infrastructural' issues of planning and controlling the 'strands' in the supply network. These are called supply 'chains'. Figure 13.1 illustrates the supply–demand linkage treated in this chapter.

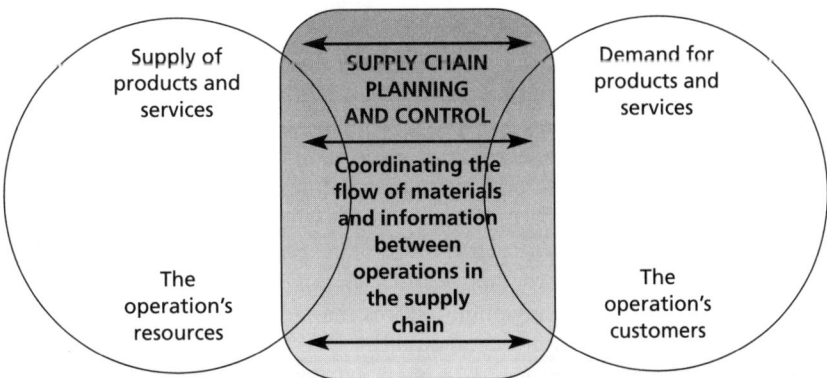

Figure 13.1 Supply chain management is concerned with managing the flow of materials and information between the operations which form the strands or 'chains' of a supply network

---

OBJECTIVES

This chapter will examine:

● definitions of purchasing, physical distribution management, logistics, materials management, and supply chain management;

● purchasing and supplier development;

● physical distribution management;

● integration of the internal operations functions by the concepts of logistics and materials management;

● integration of organizations by the concept of supply chain management.

WHAT IS SUPPLY CHAIN PLANNING AND CONTROL?

In Chapter 6 we used the term 'supply network' to refer to all the operations which were linked to provide the supply of goods and services to an operation and the demand for its goods and services through to the end customers. In this chapter we are dealing with the flow of goods and services through this network along individual channels or strands of the network. In large organizations there can be many hundreds of strands of linked operations through which goods and services flow into and out of the operation. These strands are more commonly referred to as *supply chains*. Many of the topics covered in this chapter on supply chain planning and control are relatively new. This means that some of the terms used to describe them are not universally applied. Furthermore, some of the concepts behind the terminology overlap in the sense that they refer to common parts of the total supply network. This is why it is useful first of all to distinguish between the different terms we shall use in this chapter. These are illustrated in Fig. 13.2.

● *Purchasing and supply management* is a well accepted term in business practice for the function that deals with the operation's interface with its supply markets.
● *Physical distribution management* is again a well accepted term for managing the operation of supplying immediate customers.
● *Logistics* is an extension of physical distribution management and usually refers to the management of materials and information flow from a business, down through a distribution channel, to end customers (although sometimes the concept is extended to include more of the supply chain, as we will discuss later).
● *Materials management* refers to the management of the flow of materials and information through the immediate supply chain. This has been defined as including purchasing, inventory management, stores management, operations planning and control and physical distribution management.[1]
● *Supply chain management* has been developed into a concept with a much broader span of concern and an holistic approach to managing across company boundaries. It is recognized that there are substantial benefits to be gained from strategically trying to drive a whole chain in the direction of satisfying end customers.[2]

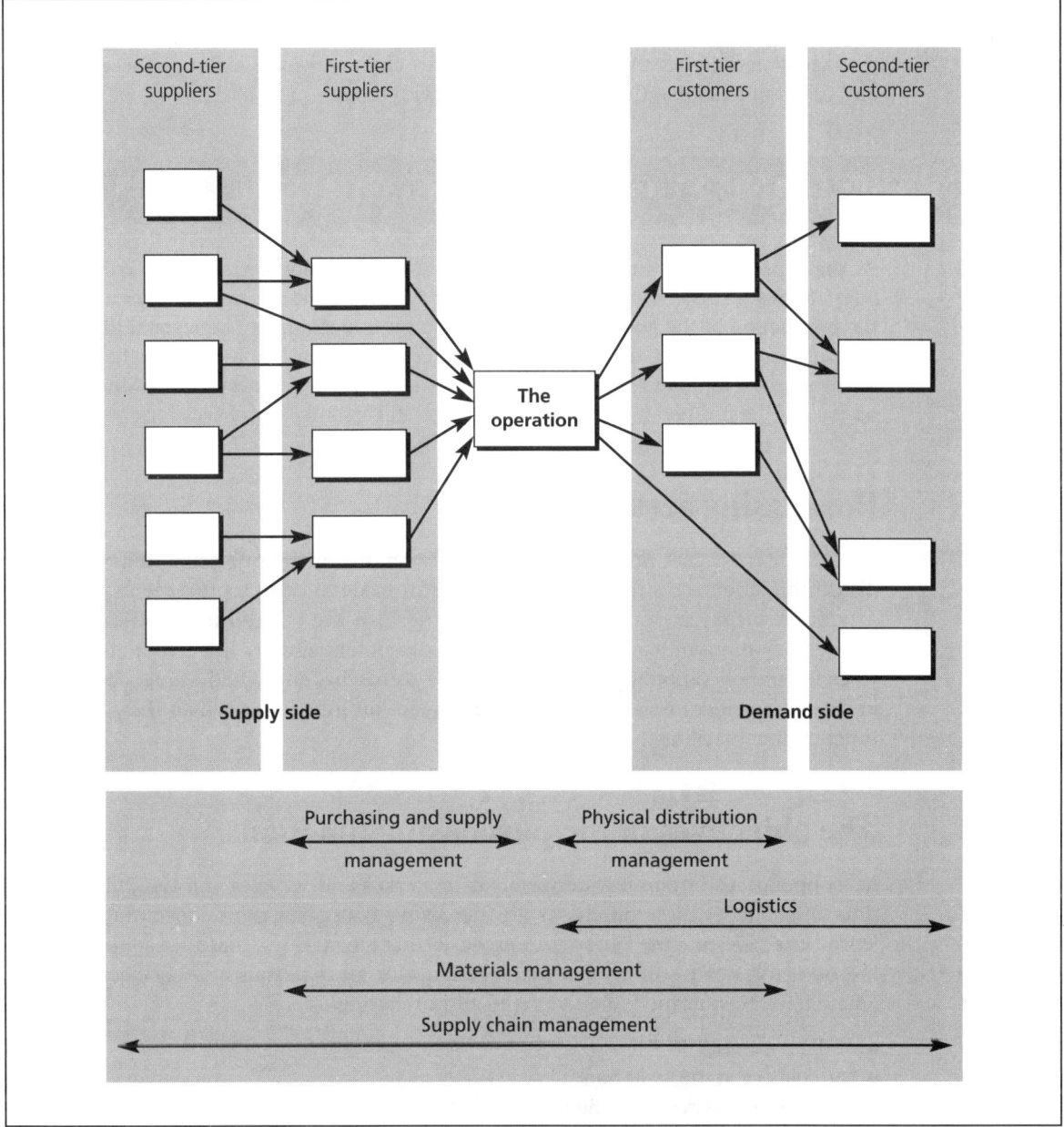

Figure 13.2 Some of the terms used to describe the management of different parts of the supply chain

A supply chain as a whole can be viewed as the flow of water in a river: organizations located closer to the original source of supply are described as being 'upstream', while those located closer to the end customer are 'downstream'. (However, whether an individual operation is regarded as upstream or downstream depends on the exact position of the operation in the stream.) The terms which we have defined above represent an increasing degree of integration – being concerned with the flow of the whole river. Purchasing and supply, and physical distribution relate to only one part of the whole supply chain, upstream and downstream respectively. Logistics and materials management take in larger parts of the supply chain, while supply chain management includes the whole chain. In this chapter we will examine these concepts and the organizational functions associated with them.

PURCHASING AND SUPPLIER DEVELOPMENT

At the supply end of the business, the purchasing function forms contracts with suppliers to buy in materials and services. Some of these materials and services are used in the production of the goods and services sold on to customers (we termed these transformed resources, *see* Chapter 1). Other materials and services are used to help run the business: for example, staff catering services or oil for machinery. These do not make up part of the finished good or service but are still essential purchases for operations.

Purchasing activities

Purchasing managers provide a vital link between the operation itself and its suppliers. To do this effectively they must understand, in detail, the requirements of all the processes within the operation it serves and also the capabilities of the suppliers (sometimes thousands in numbers) who could potentially provide products and services for the operation. Figure 13.3 shows a somewhat simplified sequence of events in the management of a typical supplier–operation interaction which the purchasing function must facilitate.

The objectives of the purchasing function

Most operations buy-in a wide variety of materials and services and typically the volume and value of these purchases are increasing as organizations concentrate on their 'core tasks'. Despite the variety of purchases that a firm buys, there are some underlying objectives of purchasing which are true for all materials and services bought. These have been termed 'the five rights of purchasing':[3]

- at the *right price*
- for delivery at the *right time*
- of goods and services to the *right quality*
- in the *right quantity*
- from the *right source*.

Purchasing at the right price

The most obvious benefit of purchasing at the right price is that it can provide an operation with a *cost advantage*. Historically, this objective of purchasing has been emphasized in purchasing theory and practice. Much of the skill of professional purchasing staff was concerned traditionally with negotiation with suppliers to secure the best overall price deal. The performance of purchasing staff was even judged using

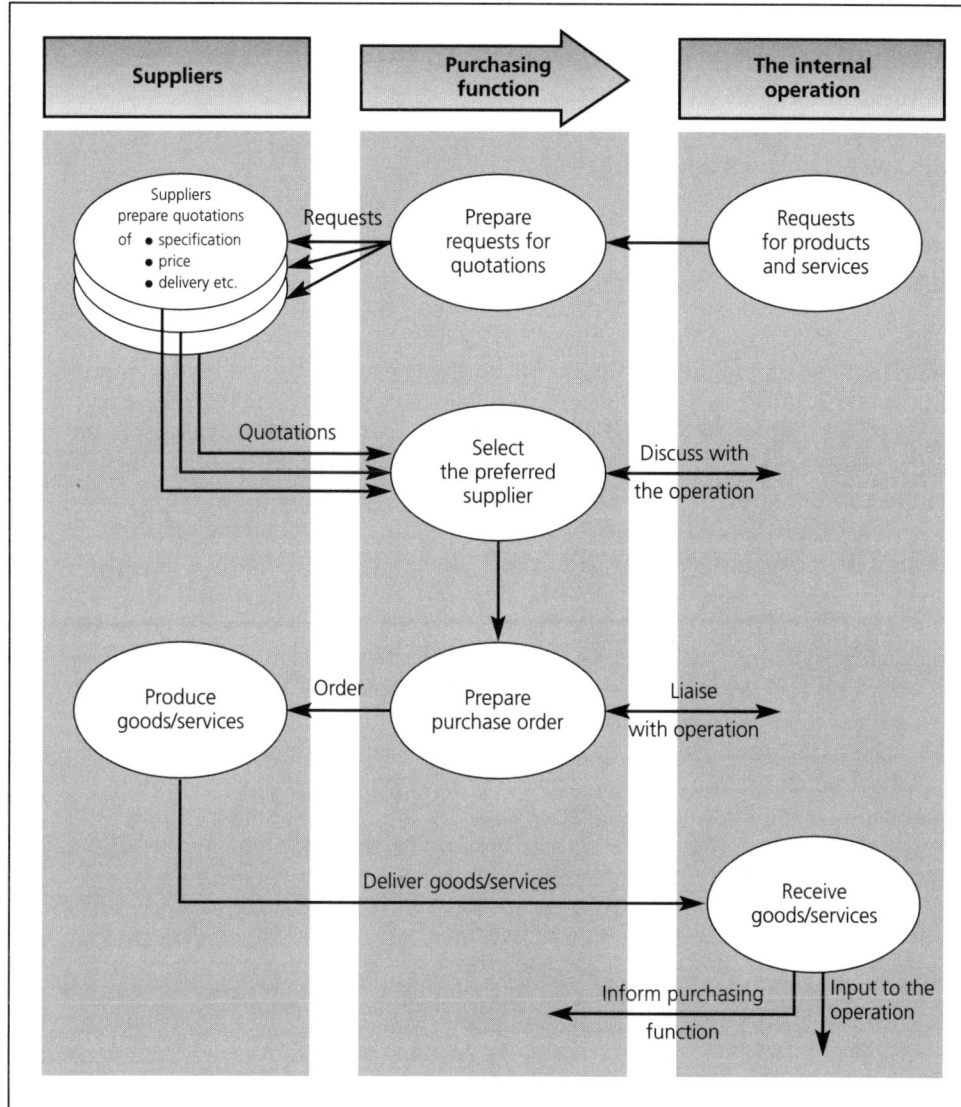

Figure 13.3
The purchasing function brings together the operation with its suppliers

cost savings as the main measure. The reason for this emphasis on 'the right cost' is understandable because purchasing can have a very significant impact on any operation's costs. This in turn will have an impact on the organization's profits.

To illustrate the impact which price-conscious purchasing can have on profits, consider a simple manufacturing operation with the following financial details:

$$
\begin{aligned}
\text{Total sales} &= \text{R10 000 000} \\
\text{Purchased services and materials} &= \text{R7 000 000} \\
\text{Salaries} &= \text{R2 000 000} \\
\text{Overheads} &= \text{R500 000} \\
\text{Therefore, profit} &= \text{R500 000}
\end{aligned}
$$

Profits could be doubled to R1 million by any of the following:

- increase sales revenue by 100 per cent
- decrease salaries by 25 per cent
- decrease overheads by 100 per cent
- decrease purchase costs by 7.1 per cent.

FRESH FROM THE POD[4]

If you are travelling in the vicinity of Grimsby (in the UK) one summer, you could hardly fail to notice large numbers of trucks loaded with green, freshly harvested and podded peas, on their way to Ross Young's processing plant, where they are cleaned, fast-frozen, and packed. An extremely seasonal operation, the peas must be picked and processed at their peak condition. If the peas are harvested too early, they do not meet the company's stringent size requirements; too late and they are over-ripe and too tough. But another constraint is that the factory has the capacity to process only up to 30 tonnes per hour, so it would be a disaster if all the harvest of around 20 000 tonnes was ready on the same day.

Because of these constraints, Ross Young's has to work very closely with its suppliers – the farmers who grow the peas and their haulage companies who transport them. Farmers are treated as partners, and given the best technical advice on varieties, planting times and location of fields. This ensures that the harvest is spread out over as long a period as possible. For example, in south-facing fields with light soils, farmers are advised to plant early varieties to get the first crops. North-facing fields with heavy soils are sown with late-maturing varieties. This advice is of direct benefit to the farmers, since their own knowledge and skills in growing the crop are enhanced, and their own harvesting capacity problems minimized. The Ross Young's purchasing team's knowledge of the terrain within a 50 km radius of the factory is vital. In a normal year it is possible to spread the harvest over 60 days, but sometimes exceptionally hot and dry weather can compress this to 40 days. This creates capacity problems both in the harvesting operations and at the factory. The factory must then work day and night without any breaks.

As well as the purchasing team 'designing' the plan for an extended harvest season, it must also control the precise time of the harvesting on a load-by-load basis. Harvested peas deteriorate very quickly, so to ensure consistent high quality, Ross Young's specification limits the time between the first pea in a batch being picked, and the last being blanched to 145 minutes. Thus, only farmers who have the capability to conform to this stringent specification are selected. They must have a track record of reliability and integrity, be willing to conform to start times notified to them by radio from the factory planners, and be able to complete the picking reliably using dependable equipment of the right capacity. Similar characteristics are required for road hauliers, who must be able to guarantee availability to match the harvest times.

The development of working partnerships with preferred suppliers has ensured that the right types and quality of peas, from carefully selected growing locations, are harvested at the right time, are delivered reliably to the factory at precisely agreed times, and are available in the right quantities so that processing can continue as an uninterrupted flow into the freezers. This partnership ensures that waste is minimized, that productivity is high, and that the growers have a guaranteed market, with full technical support from Ross Young's. ■

Doubling sales revenue does sometimes occur in very fast growing markets, but would be regarded by most sales and marketing managers as an exceedingly ambitious target. Decreasing the salaries bill by a quarter is unlikely to be well received by staff even if, over the long term, it were possible. Similarly, reducing overheads by 100 per cent is unlikely to be possible over the short to medium term without compromising the business. However, reducing purchase costs by 7.1 per cent, although a challenging objective, is usually far more of a realistic option than the other actions.

The reason for the dramatic impact which purchase price savings can have on total profitability is that purchase costs are such a large proportion of total costs. Relatively small changes in purchase costs will therefore be large compared with profits. The higher are purchase costs as a proportion of total costs, the more profitability can be improved in this way. This is why retail operations such as supermarkets devote such efforts to reducing the costs of their bought-in goods. Figure 13.4 illustrates this.

Purchasing for delivery at the right time and in the right quantity

Purchasing at the right time and in the right quantity can impact on the operation's performance in terms of delivery speed, delivery reliability and flexibility. Chapter 12 on inventory management describes how order volumes and times are calculated based on current stock levels and historical demand. Chapter 14 describes how these volume and timing decisions for purchases are determined by looking forward at what will be required to satisfy future demand. However, purchasing must also deal with some characteristics of an operation's supply market which can affect the volume and timing decisions. For example, international purchasing that involves deep-sea transportation may mean that purchases must be made two months earlier than if they were bought locally. This allows the time for the purchases to be transported to the docks, loaded, shipped over, unloaded and transported to their

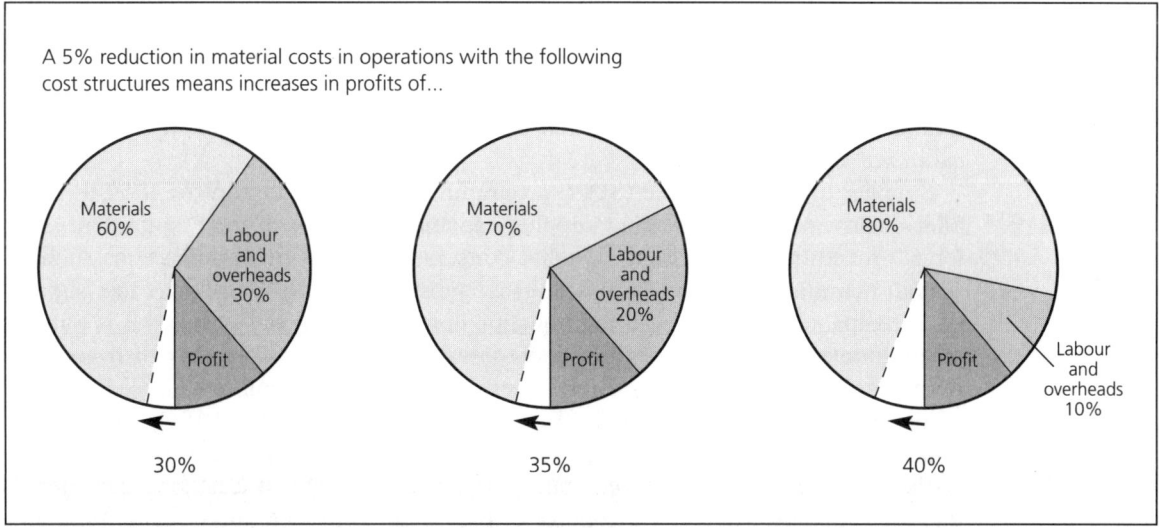

Figure 13.4 The larger the level of material costs as a proportion of total costs, the greater the effect on profitability of a reduction in material costs

destination. There may also be characteristics of the products or services themselves which determine the timing of the purchase. For example, many food crops have to be purchased and picked at exactly the right time when they become ripe (*see* box on pea purchasing).

But whether the volume and timing of purchases are determined through forecasting ahead, through evaluating economic order quantities or through special product or market characteristics, the purchasing function will be involved: usually by originating the orders which authorize suppliers to supply at the required time and in the required volume. Sometimes the job of ensuring that purchase orders and contracts are adhered to is performed by an 'expediting' function whose responsibility is to track or 'progress' orders with suppliers until the goods and services are delivered. In this situation purchasing staff form the contract with the supplier and the expediter 'chases' it. This chasing function adds no value to the transaction. Indeed, if all suppliers kept to their end of the bargain, it would be redundant. In recent years, suppliers have been encouraged to be more reliable and so the role of expediting in most organizations has been either substantially reduced or removed completely. In South Africa this trend will require more time and effort to take hold.

Purchasing at the right quality

Buying the right quality of products and services will have a significant effect on whether the operation itself can provide a quality advantage. In addition, quality will also affect delivery speed and reliability. Poor quality components or services can delay delivery of the finished product or service. Similarly, quality failures of bought-in products or services will also increase costs. Traditionally, suppliers were not trusted to provide goods and services of the right quality. When goods were supplied or when services were provided they were inspected to ensure that they conformed to the required specification. More recently suppliers have been encouraged to ensure that they take responsibility themselves to provide a 'right-first-time' level of quality. Furthermore, they are required to certify to the purchasing company that quality levels are met. This self-certification is based on a level of trust and confidence which has come about partly because purchasing organizations have invested time, money and effort into helping their suppliers reach the required quality levels. This effort has often been through investment in *supplier quality assurance* programmes.

Supplier quality assurance (SQA) programmes monitor and improve levels of supplier quality, partly by assessing supplier capability in terms of their equipment, systems, procedures and training. Quality-conscious purchasing organizations such as aircraft manufacturers have always invested substantial effort in ensuring that suppliers are capable of meeting the right quality. For many other businesses this is a more recent innovation in their purchasing process. Suppliers can self-certify their capability by having their systems and processes certified as conforming to internationally recognized standards such as the British Standard BS5750 and ISO 9000 or the South African standard SABS 0157 (these are discussed in Chapter 20). In becoming accredited to a set of recognized standards, purchasers can at least gain confidence that the suppliers' systems are capable of providing them with good quality products and services. However, these standards of accreditation only indicate the *capability* of achieving good quality – they do not *guarantee* good quality of output from suppliers.

Purchasing from the right source

On first examination it might seem important to consider the source of products or services only as far as they influence price, quality and delivery. However, purchasing staff might sometimes choose to buy from a particular source because of the current or future *potential* from that source rather than its immediate and direct benefits. For example, a purchasing department might be comparing two suppliers A and B. Supplier A has submitted a quotation which is superior on price and delivery and, as far as they can tell, on quality also. However, the purchasing department might suspect that supplier A might be inflexible in terms of changing the terms of the supply arrangement. They might also judge that supplier A does not have the capability to develop new products or services which they might require in the future. Supplier B, on the other hand, although its initial quotation might not match that of supplier A, might be judged to have more potential for improvement, or might possess the core capabilities of meeting future requirements. It might even be that the purchasing department judges supplier B to have a 'better attitude' in terms of its willingness to improve the service which it provides.

Single- and multi-sourcing

The decision of what constitutes the 'right source' also includes, by implication, the decision of whether to source each individual product or service from one or more than one supplier. This is known as *single-sourcing* and *multi-sourcing*. Some of the advantages and disadvantages of single- and multi-sourcing are shown in Table 13.1.

It may seem as though companies who multi-source do so exclusively for their own short-term benefit. However, this is not always the case: multi-sourcing can have an altruistic motive or at least one which brings benefits to both supplier and purchaser in the long term. For example, Robert Bosch GmbH, the German automotive components manufacturer and distributor, at one time required that sub-contractors do no more than 20 per cent of their total business with them.[5] This was to prevent suppliers becoming too dependent on them. The purchasing organization could then change volumes up and down without pushing the supplier into bankruptcy. However, despite these perceived advantages, there has been a trend for purchasing functions to reduce their supplier base in terms of numbers of companies supplying any one part or service. For example, Rank Xerox, the copier and document company, reduced its supply base from 5000 suppliers to a little more than 300 over a six-year period.[6] Some Japanese automotive manufacturers involve fewer than 300 suppliers in new product development projects (often their Western equivalents may deal with 1000 to 2500).[7] This trend of supply base reduction has come about because of the realization of far greater benefits of developing long-term co-operative relationships with suppliers rather than trading with them at arm's length in an adversarial, hostile way.

Make-or-buy decisions

When an operation decides to purchase products or services from a supplier it is implicitly making the decision not to create those products or services itself. This may not always be a straightforward decision. In some cases the operation may be able to produce parts or services in-house at a lower cost or at a higher quality than can

Table 13.1 Advantages and disadvantages of single- and multi-sourcing

	Single-sourcing	Multi-sourcing
Advantages	• Potentially better quality because more SQA possibilities • Strong relationships which are more durable • Greater dependency encourages more commitment and effort • Better communication • Easier to co-operate on new product/service development • More scale economies • Higher confidentiality	• Purchaser can drive price down by competitive tendering • Can switch sources in case of supply failure • Wide sources of knowledge and expertise to tap
Disadvantages	• More vulnerable to disruption if a failure to supply occurs • Individual supplier more affected by volume fluctuations • Supplier might exert upward pressure on prices if no alternative supplier is available	• Difficult to encourage commitment by supply • Less easy to develop effective SQA • More effort needed to communicate • Suppliers less likely to invest in new processes • More difficult to obtain scale economies

suppliers. Yet in other cases suppliers may be able to specialize in the production of certain parts or services and produce them more cheaply or at higher quality than the operation can itself. It is part of the responsibility of the purchasing function to investigate whether the operation is better served buying in products or services, or choosing to create them itself. This is called the *'make-or-buy' decision*.

Often the major criterion used to decide whether to make or buy is financial. If a company can make a part or service in-house more cheaply than it can buy it, it is likely to do so unless there are other overriding reasons for not doing. However, the financial analysis involved is not always straightforward. The decision often needs to be based on the *marginal* cost of producing something in-house. The marginal cost is the *extra* cost which is incurred by the operation in creating the product or service. For example, if an operation already has the equipment and staff in place to make a particular product and there is spare capacity within the part of the operation which could make that product, then the extra, or marginal, cost of making the products in-house will be the variable costs associated with their manufacture. In other cases, an operation might decide on grounds other than cost. An increasingly popular rationale for buying in services, for example, is that they are not 'core' to the operation's main activity. Many companies are increasingly 'out-sourcing' such services as transportation, cleaning, computing, catering and maintenance. Putting these services out to specialists allows an operation to concentrate on what directly wins it business in the market place (*see* box on Wimpy SA).

WIMPY FAST-FOOD RESTAURANTS[8]

Wimpy, part of the Pleasure Foods group, won the South African franchiser of the year award in 1995. A number of years ago Wimpy owned and ran its restaurants. Now, it is the individual franchise holder that owns and runs the restaurant. Wimpy, as a core operation, has delegated much of the business to the individual entrepreneurs that take up the challenge of making money this way. The head office of Wimpy is responsible for the selection of these entrepreneurs and it is very careful about who it chooses. A lot of experience has been gained in how to choose such business champions and the right choice brings great rewards for both parties.

The individual businesses take responsibility for hiring their own staff, for the quality of their service and food, for purchasing and for the maintenance of facilities. Local decisions are taken on how to increase the number of customers. However, the head office retains some very important functions at its core. First, the ability to negotiate good raw food prices on a national basis brings competitive benefits. Second, the aggregation of food consumption forecasts from all the restaurants allows head office to coordinate deliveries by suppliers. Third, head office controls the brand name, its advertising and all prices. The design of all menus is kept uniform and in line with the market requirements. A strict watch is kept on the implementation of these menu designs, down to the way in which food is laid out on the plate.

Wimpy's growth and success in South Africa, and now internationally, is due to its attention to detailed customer requirements. It controls only what it has to maintain the brand. The rest is up to the entrepreneur. The question of what to keep at the core of a business and what to allow out, as a responsibility or as a sub-contract, is important for all organizations, not just the franchising business. ■

PHYSICAL DISTRIBUTION MANAGEMENT

On the demand side of the organization, products and services need to be 'communicated' or moved to the customer. In the case of manufacturing operations, this involves the physical transportation of the goods from the manufacturing operation to the customer. In the case of high customer contact services, the service is created in the presence of the customer. Here we limit ourselves to manufacturing operations who need physically to distribute their products to customers (and implicitly to those transportation operations, such as trucking companies, whose primary concern is physical distribution).

Multi-echelon inventory systems

In Chapter 12 we identified some inventory systems as 'multi-echelon' systems. By this we meant that materials flowing through a system would be stored at different points, including points outside the operation, before reaching the customer. Figure 13.5 illustrates the demand-side part of the multi-echelon system we described in Chapter 12. In this case the garment manufacturer, after manufacturing the products,

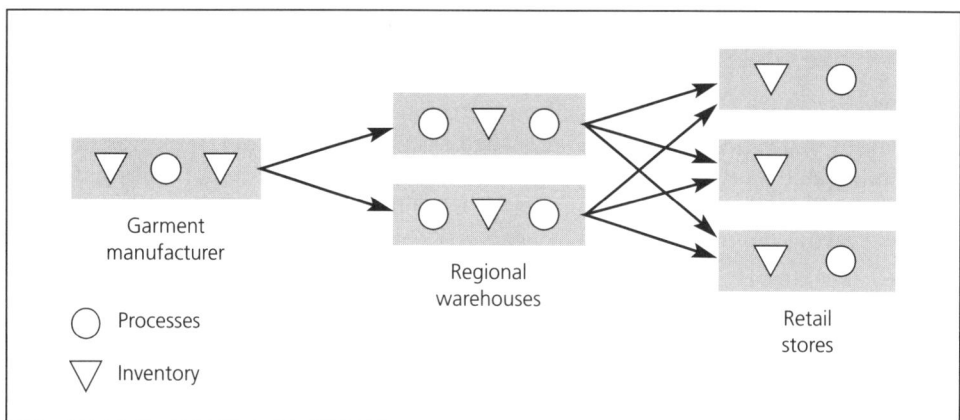

**Figure 13.5
Multi-echelon
inventory system**

will store them in its own finished goods warehouse. From there they are transported to regional warehouses whose function is to serve as a distribution point for retail stores. When the retail stores require deliveries of garments they will request them from their local warehouse who will arrange for the transportation of these garments to the retail store. The function of the warehouse is to provide an intermediate stage in the distribution system so that the manufacturer does not have to deal with every single customer. From the customers' point of view it also means that they do not have to deal with a whole range of suppliers.

Warehouses can simplify routes and communications

To understand how warehouses can simplify physical distribution, consider Fig. 13.6. Here a manufacturing operation which has three factories is supplying six customers. In the arrangement in Fig. 13.6(a) each factory supplies each customer. This means in total there are 18 routes (one between each pair of factory and customer). Each factory must have separate lines of communication with all six customers and each customer will need to communicate directly with each of three factories. Now consider the bottom arrangement in Fig 13.6(b). Two regional warehouses have been imposed between the factories and the customers. The three factories now distribute their products to the two regional warehouses from which their local customers are supplied. The total number of routes has been reduced from 18 to 12. Probably more significantly each factory now has only to deal directly with two sources for its products instead of the previous six. Similarly, each customer now only has to deal with one supplier (its local warehouse) instead of six as previously.

The mode of transport in physical distribution

As well as the arrangement of the distribution system, physical distribution managers must decide on which mode of transport is best to distribute their products to their customers. By mode of transport we mean the technology which is used to move goods.

The modes of transport available to the physical distribution manager are:

- road
- rail
- water
- air
- pipeline.

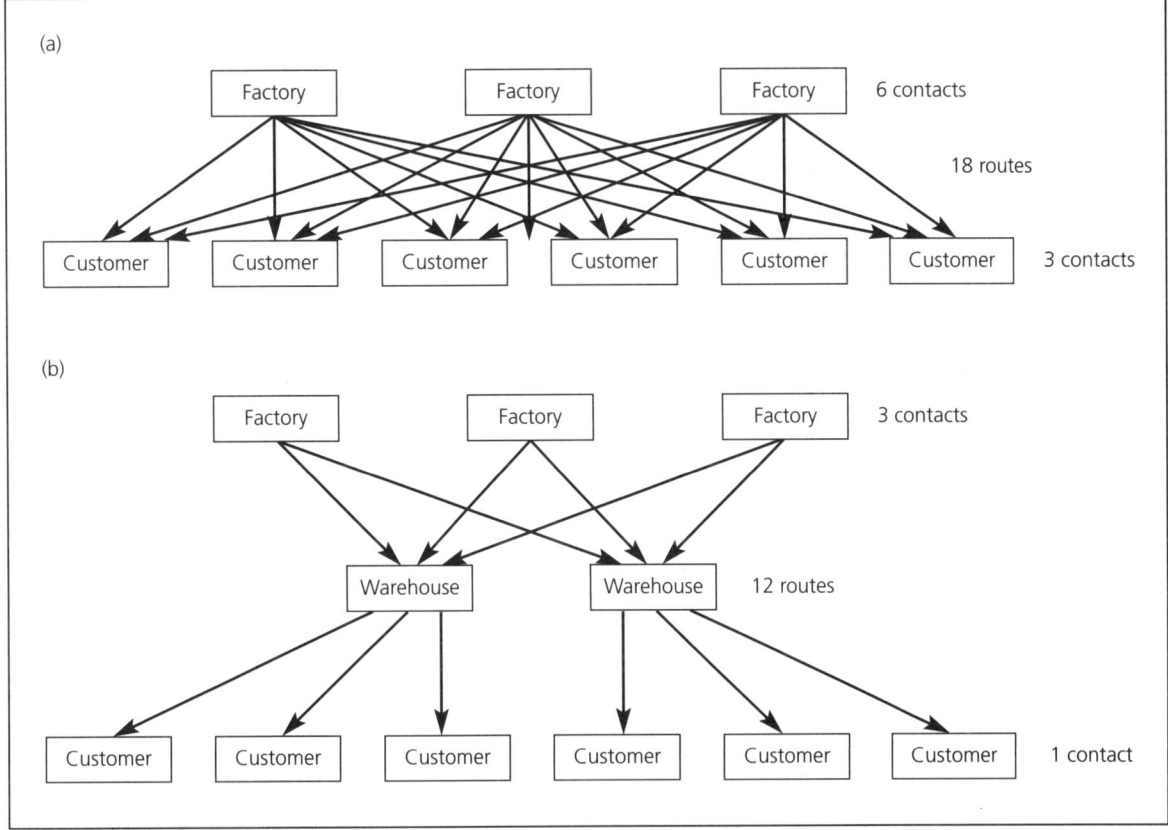

Figure 13.6 The introduction of a warehouse stage in a multi-echelon physical distribution system can simplify routes and communications

Each of these modes has different characteristics which affect its suitability for the transportation of particular products. For example, air transport is very expensive and limited in the space available (to the size of the aircraft). It is therefore typically used for low-volume, high-value goods which require rapid delivery. Conversely, bulk raw materials such as coal or iron ore lend themselves to carriage by slower, cheaper forms of transport such as water or rail. Figure 13.7 illustrates the volume–value characteristics of the different modes of transport.

Not all modes of transport will be suitable for all types of products. The physical characteristics of the product could limit the choice available to distribution managers. For example, only gases and liquids can be conveniently transported by pipeline; or physically large products such as building sections would not fit within the confines of most aircraft. However, the mode of transport is usually chosen with reference to the relative importance of:

- delivery speed
- delivery dependability
- possible quality deterioration
- transportation costs
- route flexibility.

Table 13.2 gives an approximate ranking of each mode of transport under these headings.

469

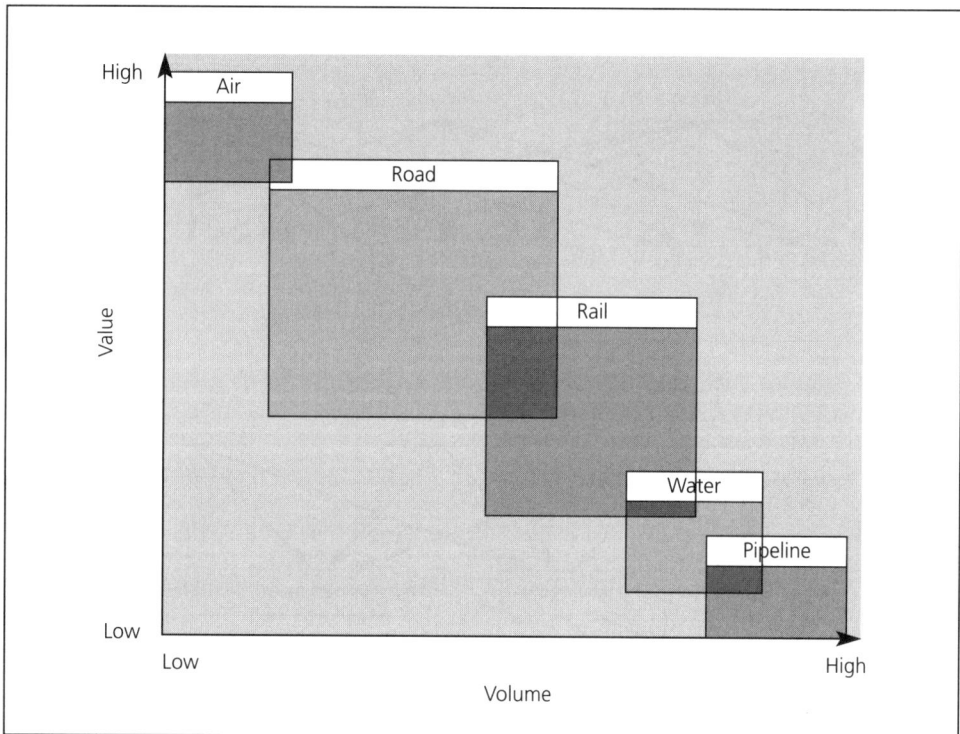

**Figure 13.7
Volume–value
determinants of
transport mode**

Table 13.2 The relative performance of each mode of transport

Operation's performance objective	Mode of transport				
	Road	Rail	Air	Water	Pipeline
Delivery speed	2	3	1	5	4
Delivery dependability	2	3	4	5	1
Quality	2	3	4	5	1
Cost	3	4	5	2	1
Route flexibility	1	2	3	4	5

Key: 1 = Best performance, 5 = Worst performance

The mode of transport chosen will also have an effect on other decisions made by the operation. For example, firms may choose to locate their operations near to ports, airports, railway sidings, or close to junctions of motorways, depending on the mode of transport chosen. At a more day-to-day level, the decision on batch sizes and order quantities will be affected by the carrying capacity of each mode of transport.

Contract terms

In any supply transaction the buyer and the supplier have to agree on who takes responsibility for the risk and who pays for the transportation. This is a particular specialism in international trade where knowledge of international trade agreements, legislation and documentation are critical to purchasing successfully from other countries. Internationally recognized shipping terms are now in operation which are applied to international transportation by sea or air. There are many variations on these terms but the main categories and definitions are as follows:

Ex-works

In an ex-works contract the purchaser accepts full responsibility for arranging transportation from the supplier's location. This involves arranging transportation, insurance and documentation to move the goods to the required port (air or sea), have them loaded on to the mode of transport, transported, unloaded at the destination port, cleared through customs and transported to the purchaser's location. This type of contract may be used if the supplier has little experience of international trade or the purchaser has a transportation network already in place which can group purchases together and ship them in bulk. More recently, purchasers and suppliers have sub-contracted this transportation function to specialists such as Federal Express. (*See* the case exercise at the end of this chapter.)

Free alongside (FAS)

In this arrangement the supplier agrees to deliver to the port specified by the purchaser and is responsible for the transportation and insurance of the goods to that point. However, the purchaser has to arrange and pay for loading on to the vessel and all onward transportation, insurance and documentation.

Free on board (FOB)

Here the supplier pays for and arranges loading on to the outward bound transportation and thereafter the purchaser becomes responsible.

Cost and freight (C&F)

This is a split responsibility arrangement in that the supplier arranges and pays for transportation to an agreed point but the purchaser has to pay insurance from when the goods are loaded on board. The purchaser has to acquire any documentation required by the country of origin. Once the goods have been unloaded at the port of entry, the purchaser is responsible for all ongoing transportation and insurance to its site.

Cost, insurance and freight (CIF)

This is similar to C&F except here the insurance during transportation is the responsibility of the supplier.

Delivered

This is the opposite of ex-works in that the supplier has total responsibility for the goods, their transportation, insurance and all documentation until they are delivered and accepted by the purchaser.

Cost and lead time of the international pipeline

In addition to the contract arrangements, international purchasing and supply has a significant impact on the planning and control within the operation. While goods are in transit they are not yielding any benefit to the buyer who may have had to pay with letter of credit for some or all of the load prior to it departing. If goods are being moved across 'deep sea' over the major oceans, this may take one to three months, depending on the journey and the efficiency of the documentation arrangers. During this time, all the costs of inventory apply: namely the opportunity cost of capital tied up in the inventory, obsolescence, pilferage (a major problem with lower-security forms of transportation), spoilage and the costs of storage, such as refrigeration costs.

The risks of international trade

In addition to the costs of international transportation, there is the risk, albeit a slight one, of the entire load being lost through accident or piracy: the more valuable and more easily saleable the load, the higher this risk becomes. Interestingly, some exporters have different difficulties when transporting to some countries where wooden packing crates, which can be used for making shanty housing, etc., are valued more highly than the goods inside them. Particular care is required where security is poor. It is often preferred practice in these situations to use local freight forwarders who are familiar with the local conditions and can plan accordingly.

INTEGRATED CONCEPTS

So far we have discussed the linkage between a purchaser in one operation and a supplier in another. Purchasing and supplier development considered the flow of information from purchaser to supplier. Physical distribution considered the physical movement of goods from the supplier to the purchaser. Together they form the links in the supply chain. Any supply chain will consist of a sequence of these purchaser–supplier linkages. In this part of the chapter we move on to consider ways in which more than one of these linkages can be considered as an integrated whole. *See* Fig. 13.8.

There are many different ways in which the linkages involved in the flow of materials and services can be integrated or grouped together. Four main concepts will be discussed here. These have focused attention on managing *across* the traditional functional areas of purchasing operations and physical distribution. These are *materials management, merchandising* and *logistics* and *supply chain management*. This latter concept is by far the most comprehensive, which is why we have used it as the title of this chapter. Nevertheless, it is important to understand the progressively more integrative concepts which lead up to the development of supply chain management.

Materials management

This concept originated from purchasing functions who understood the importance of integrating materials flow and its supporting functions, both throughout the business and out to immediate customers. It includes the functions of purchasing, expediting, inventory management, stores management, production planning and control and physical distribution management. Figure 13.9 illustrates the extent of the materials management concept.

At the time of its inception during the 1970s, materials management was seen as a means of reducing 'total costs associated with the acquisition and management of materials'.[9] Different stages in the movement of materials through a multi-echelon system are typically buffered by inventory, as shown in Fig. 13.9. Where materials management is not in place as an integrating concept, these different stages are often managed by different people, reporting to different senior managers within the organization. For example, a production director or vice-president will probably have responsibility for the factory, a procurement director for purchasing, with a marketing or sales director controlling the physical distribution function. These different functions are managed separately, each with its own targets, each optimizing its own small part of the total materials flow system.

The result of this separate functional management of the materials flow is often high inventory levels. The lead time to move materials through the system is long because of the wasted time while materials are held in inventory. Because of the long lead time, materials have to be purchased much earlier to ensure they are available at the start of production. This makes the system inflexible to change because commitment to design and volumes is made much earlier. The whole materials movement is difficult to control. It is difficult to keep track of materials because they could be in so many different places, and organizational effort is needed just to track the whereabouts of materials. Materials management means giving responsibility for the whole materials and information flow to one part of the organization. It then becomes possible to make improvements which allow the coordination, reduction and even removal of some intermediate inventories. This speeds up the operation, which reduces lead times, which in turn means less commitment has to be made so far in advance for purchases, thereby reducing the horizon for forecasting in the business. With reduced forecasting, greater accuracy of schedules is possible, bringing about greater planning stability. All this leads to reduced costs, which was the original intention of the concept.

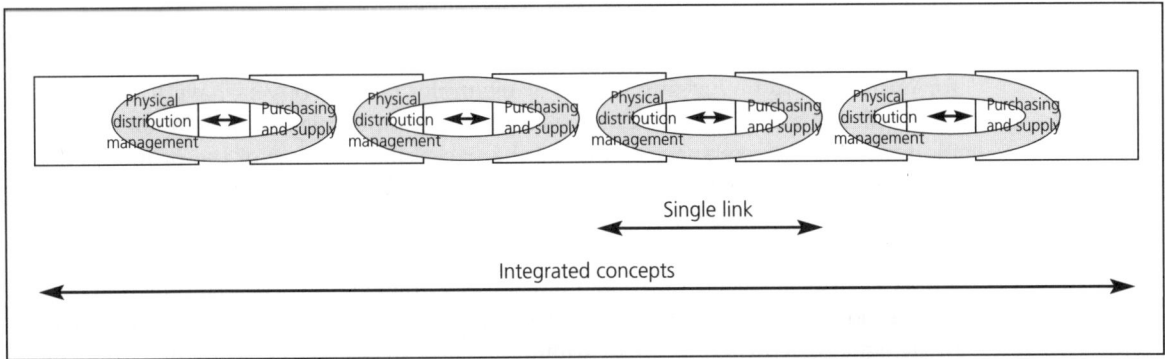

Figure 13.8 The next part of this chapter discusses concepts which integrate more than one link in the supply chain

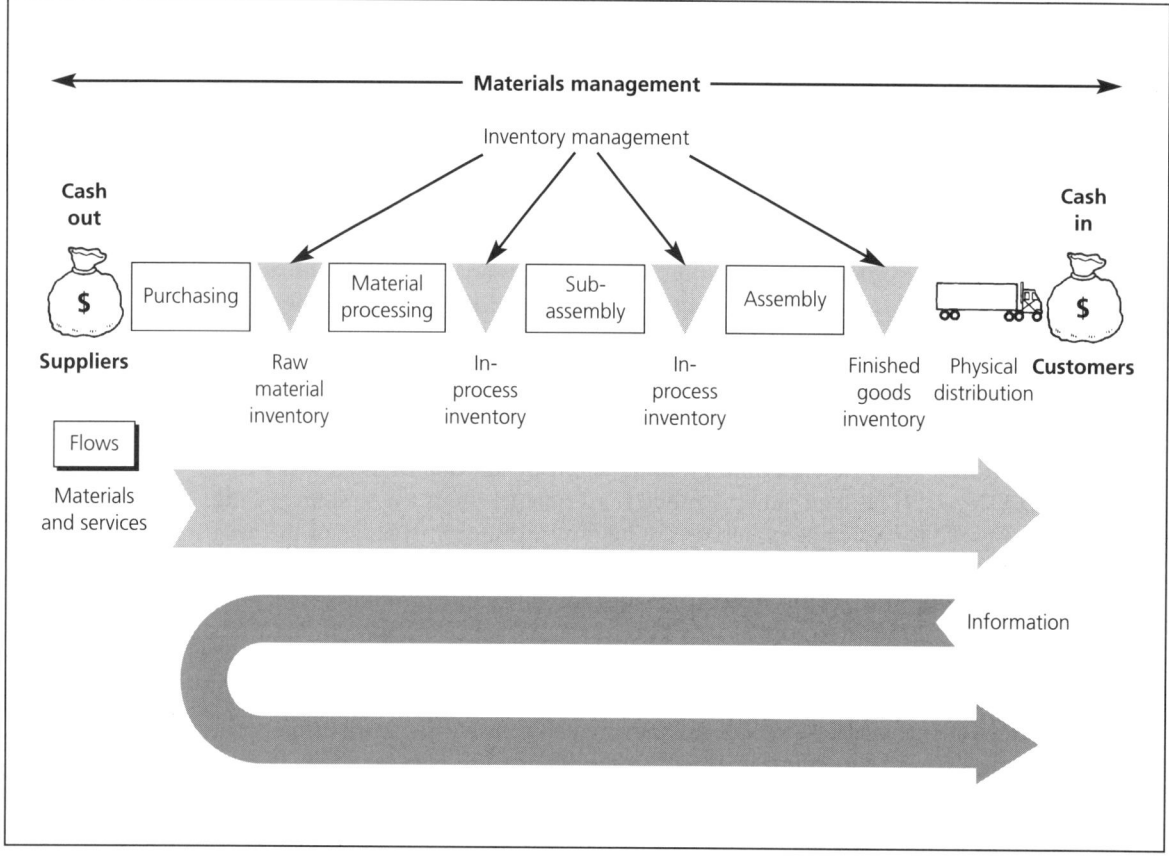

Figure 13.9 The materials management concept

Merchandising

In retail operations the purchasing task is frequently combined with the sales and physical distribution task into a role termed *merchandising*. A merchandiser typically has responsibility for organizing sales to retail customers, the layout of the shop floor, inventory management and purchasing. This is because retail purchase operations have to be so closely linked to daily sales to ensure the right mix of goods is available for customers to buy at any time. For example, fashion buyers have to understand what will sell and how garments will look when on display in their retail outlets. In food retailing, buyers specify in detail the packaging in terms of the printing process and materials, to ensure the product looks appealing when displayed in their stores. Daily trends of sales in some retail situations (typically food and fashion) can vary enormously. Replenishment of regularly stocked items has to be very quick to avoid empty shelves or rails. Electronic point-of-sale systems help the planning and control of fast moving consumer goods: as items are registered as sold at the till, a replenishment signal is returned to the distribution centre to deliver replacements. To facilitate this link, many retail operations use bar coding to update the inventory situation and replenish shelves and rails.

Logistics

Logistics originated during the Second World War when it related to the movement and coordination of troops, armaments and munitions to the required location. When adopted by the business world as a concept, it referred to the movement and coordination of finished products. There are many organizations who have a logistics function which manages the total flow of finished goods downstream from the plant to the customers. Here the term logistics is being used as analogous to what we called earlier 'physical distribution management'. However, logistics has more recently been extended to include more of the total flow of materials and information. Some authorities adopt a definition of logistics which is identical to that of materials management. For example, this strategic view of logistics is adopted by Professor Martin Christopher at Cranfield University, who includes 'procurement, movement of materials, their storage and inventory management and their distribution through marketing channels' in his definition of logistics.[10] There are some differences between materials management and this extended view of logistics, however. Materials management does not concentrate on the physical distribution of finished product, but focuses more on the planning and control of the processes inside an operation (including MRP and JIT, *see* Chapters 14 and 15). Logistics, on the other hand, tends to treat manufacturing as a 'black box', but does provide an emphasis on physical distribution management. These differences, though not great, are present because of the backgrounds of the two groups who have originated the concepts. The logisticians tend to come from marketing; the materials managers from operations management, particularly purchasing. Students should be aware of these differences to appreciate the content and focus of discussion of different authors, but should recognize that the common underlying theme is one of benefit through integrated control of the flow of materials and information.

During the last ten years an even broader, more ambitious and strategically significant concept has emerged – *supply chain management*.

Supply chain management

While logisticians have devoted relatively little attention to managing the chain of supply upstream of the purchasing function into suppliers' operations, and materials managers have more or less ignored the management of the flow of finished goods and services downstream through distribution channels, supply chain management views the entire chain as a system to be managed. Supply chain management can be defined as 'managing the entire chain of raw material supply, manufacture, assembly and distribution to the end customer'.[11]

Objectives of supply chain management

To focus on satisfying end customers

Because supply chain management includes all stages in the total flow of materials and information, it must eventually include consideration of the final customer. The final customer has the only 'real' currency in the supply chain. When a customer decides to make a purchase, he or she triggers action along the whole chain. All the businesses in the supply chain pass on portions of that end customer's money to each other, each retaining a margin for the value it has added.

THE LOGISTICS SUPPLY CHAIN AT MARKS & SPENCER[12]

In Chapter 12, a box described part of the Marks & Spencer approach to controlling in-store inventory. Behind each store the company also operates a huge logistics operation. It has to: Marks & Spencer operates over 600 stores throughout the world and employs 62 000 people. The business is split between General Merchandise, which includes Home Furnishings, and Foods on a 60:40 basis with approximately 80 per cent of the goods sold being produced in the UK. Fifteen million people a week shop in their 300 UK stores, selecting millions of items or stock-keeping units (SKUs) – all of which adds up to a formidable logistics task.

For General Merchandise, Marks & Spencer works with suppliers up to a year in advance of the selling season, discussing styles, designs and colours. These are then consolidated into ranges and eventually contracts are placed for the production of merchandise. These products are manufactured to very strict M&S specifications. Some garments are manufactured pre-season but a significant proportion is now manufactured within the season itself. This gives M&S the ability to control the total volume and flow of production in line with sales. Stock is pulled through the system into distribution centres (DCs), each servicing 30 to 40 stores. It is these DCs which respond to store orders on a daily basis, as was described in Chapter 12.

The system which is used to operate the distribution centres is called the 'User Warehouse System' and was designed and programmed within Marks & Spencer as a special development project over a two-year period at a total cost of £30 million. Through daily transmission of stock availability and on-orders, sales assistants are able to order merchandise from the distribution centre where picking instructions are generated and the merchandise is delivered into the store within 24 hours.

The system has been a great success, with a reduction in storage space, greater transport efficiency and enhanced productivity in stores. The logistics chain alone saw a 20 per cent reduction in the percentage costs to sales, and a substantial number of stockrooms were converted into sales floor space as lower stock levels were achieved. As an additional benefit, goods were moving much faster through the chain and the average period of time from supplier 'call-off' to arriving on the sales floor moved from around two weeks to less than one week.

Recent developments with the use of radio frequency technology are producing a 'paperless environment' within the distribution centres. These developments will complete the paperless chain which commenced in 1987 when Marks & Spencer became the first UK retailer to implement EDI (see Chapter 8) connecting all of its clothing suppliers. This implementation was financially justified purely on the basis of the removal of paper and the elimination of couriers who took the printed reports from the computer centre to all their suppliers throughout the country. There were many other benefits, however, including speedier operations and improved dependability of service.

After the system took over the transmission of orders to the suppliers, it was further developed to allow the transmission to Marks & Spencer of supplier product availability information which is used to update the central database directly. On General Merchandise, the system has now moved on to the position where suppliers declare electronically the availability of their merchandise daily, which then automatically triggers the ordering and allocation process. As part of this paperless interface, Marks & Spencer has also moved to a system of 'positive proof of delivery'. This means the supplier does not issue an invoice but is paid based on the merchandise that is received into Marks & Spencer distribution centres. ∎

To formulate and implement strategies based on capturing and retaining end-customer business

The key operation in a chain is the strongest business which is in a position to influence and direct the others, so that they work together in the common cause of capturing and retaining the end customer's business. In retail chains, particularly food retailing, the key operation may be the retail operation which sets the direction for the rest of the chain to follow. Some of the food manufacturers further up the chain may be far bigger companies in terms of world-wide sales but may still follow the lead taken by the retailer. In automotive manufacture, the key operation is usually the vehicle assembler, even though it is located several links upstream in the supply chain. It sets the standards and often determines the design of the infrastructure, such as the information systems used, which the downstream dealer network complies with. (*See* also Chapter 6 for some strategic design considerations when managing supply chains.)

To manage the chain effectively and efficiently

Taking a holistic approach to managing an entire supply chain opens up many opportunities for analysis and improvement. For example, in a supply chain for innovative products or services the time for new products to come to market may be critical. Analysing the chain as a whole to find out where most of the time delays currently occur allows the supply chain manager to focus attention on those 'bottle-neck' businesses in order to shorten time to market. In end-customer markets which are very price competitive, performing a cost and value analysis on the entire supply chain can reveal the sources of cost and the potential cost savings.

DELL COMPUTERS SHAPES ITS SUPPLY CHAIN[13]

As the personal computer industry matured, and competition increasingly focused on the cost of its products, some companies decided to cut out a tier of their network and sell directly to customers rather than through retail outlets. This move into mail-order selling was prompted originally by the need to trim costs. With most manufacturers buying their components from the same group of suppliers, the potential for cost cutting on the supply side of the network was limited. Furthermore, the nature of customers was changing. The growing number of sophisticated second- or third-time customers no longer needed quite the same degree of technical support from dealers. Cutting them out seemed a good move to Dell Computers, who initially became the most successful of the computer companies to bypass its demand-side supply chain and deal directly with its ultimate customers.

Yet Dell also found that reshaping its supply chain yielded benefits other than lower costs. Its (now direct) contact with customers meant that it could learn more about their needs and preferences ahead of rival manufacturers. Realizing that this new found potential needed to be exploited, Dell built computer-based information systems which could track every contact with customers, from their first enquiry through to details of every service and repair, thus building a service history for every machine. As well as helping to sell and service computers more effectively in the short term, this information base also let sales and support staff pass better information back to product development teams. ■

Barriers to supply chain management

The concept of strategically coordinating supply chains made up of businesses owned and run by different people, each with his or her own business objectives, sounds attractive, if somewhat daunting. In long supply chains, involving many businesses, it is not easy to coordinate the whole chain. This is especially true when part of the supply chain serves two sets of end customers.

For example, many manufacturers of automotive components serve two distinctly different groups of end customers. One group (the vehicle market) buys cars which contain their components; the other group (the spares market) buys spare parts for the repair of cars already in service. The latter group of customers is known as the 'aftermarket' for components. These two groups are shown in Fig. 13.10.

The operations management implications of managing supply chains which 'branch' to more than one end customer, such as these, are significant. In this case the competitive factors of importance to vehicle manufacturers are focused heavily towards achievement of quality and price. The volumes required by these customers are high and efforts are made by vehicle manufacturers to stabilize planning and control schedules so as to give some stability to the component manufacturers. This is a very different business to the other branch of the chain: the 'aftermarket'. The demands from here are for a much greater variety of parts as they have to support vehicles up to 20 years old which are still on the roads. Delivery speed is also very important. Repair and service of vehicles usually have to be carried out on the same

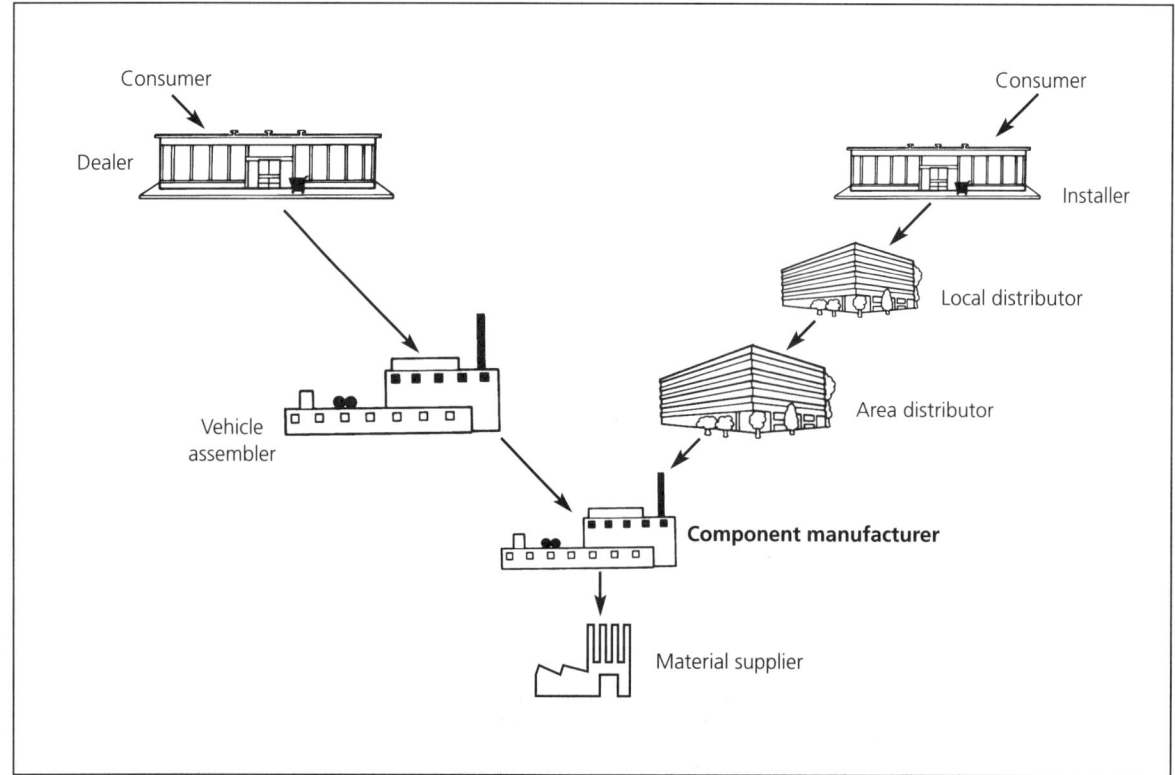

Figure 13.10 Two main groups of end customers served by an auto components manufacturer

day and, in most cases, the garage carrying out the repair does not know which parts are required until the vehicle is up on the ramp. Technical support and service from component manufacturers is high on the agenda of businesses in the aftermarket supply chains because they may not have the expertise to solve all of the repair problems they encounter.

This gives the component manufacturers who are trying to manage their supply chains some problems. In effect they have two quite different supply chains which value different competitive factors. The way each link in the two supply chains is managed, the role of inventory, the planning and control priorities and price negotiations will all be different for each chain. Unfortunately, the components for both chains are probably made in the same operation. Unless this is carefully managed, or the operation split between the two chains, this can lead to considerable confusion.

Supply chain dynamics

It was demonstrated in the 1960s by Jay Forrester[14] that certain dynamics exist between firms in supply chains that cause errors, inaccuracies and volatility, and that these increase for operations further upstream in the supply chain. This effect (also known as the Forrester Effect) is analogous to the children's game of Chinese Whispers. The first child whispers a message to the next child who, whether he or she has heard it clearly or not, whispers an interpretation to the next child, and so on. The more children the message passes between, the more distorted it tends to become. When the game finishes and the last child says out loud what the message is, the first child and all the intervening children are amused by the distortion of the original message.

The Forrester Effect is caused not only by errors and distortions. In fact the main cause is a perfectly understandable and rational desire by the different links in the supply chain to manage their production rates and inventory levels sensibly.

TYPES OF RELATIONSHIPS IN SUPPLY CHAINS

One of the main decisions of interest in supply chain management is how much of the supply chain should be owned by each business. This is called the extent of *vertical integration* and was described in Chapter 6. The alternative to vertical integration is some other form of relationship, not necessarily involving ownership. The relationship between the links of the supply chain will be examined in more detail in terms of the flows between the operations involved. These flows may be of transformed resources such as materials or of transforming resources such as people or equipment. The term used to include all the different types of flow is *exchange*.

The different relationship types which we will describe are as follows:

- integrated hierarchy
- semi-hierarchy
- co-contracting
- coordinated contracting
- coordinated revenue links
- medium-/ long-term trading commitment
- short-term trading commitment.

THE BENETTON SUPPLY CHAIN[15]

One of the best known examples of how an organization can use its supply chain to achieve a competitive advantage is the Benetton Group. Founded by the Benetton family in the 1960s, the company is now one of the largest garment retailers, with stores which bear its name located in almost all parts of the world. Part of the reason for its success has been the way it has organized both the supply side and the demand side of its supply chain.

Although Benetton does manufacture much of its production itself, on its supply side the company relies heavily on 'contractors'. Contractors are companies (many of which are owned, or part-owned, by Benetton employees) who provide service to the Benetton factories by knitting and assembling Benetton's garments. These contractors, in turn, use the services of sub-contractors to perform some of the manufacturing tasks. Benetton's manufacturing operations gain two advantages from this. First, its production costs for woollen items are significantly below some of its competitors because the small supply companies have lower costs themselves. Second, the arrangement allows Benetton to absorb fluctuation in demand by adjusting its supply arrangements, without itself feeling the full effect of demand fluctuations.

On the demand side of the chain Benetton operates through a number of agents, each of whom are responsible for their own geographical area. These agents are responsible for developing the stores in their area. Indeed many of the agents actually own some stores in their area. Products are shipped from Italy to the individual stores where they are often put directly on to the shelves. Benetton stores have always been designed with relatively limited storage space so that the garments (which, typically, are brightly coloured) can be stored in the shop itself, adding colour and ambience to the appearance of the store. Because there is such limited space for inventory in the stores, store owners require that deliveries of garments are fast and dependable. Benetton factories achieve this partly through their famous policy of manufacturing garments, where possible, *in greggio*, or in grey, and then dying them only when demand for particular colours is evident. This is a slightly more expensive process than knitting directly from coloured yarn but their supply-side economies allow them to absorb the cost of this extra flexibility, which in turn allows them to achieve relatively fast deliveries to the stores. ■

Integrated hierarchy

What is known as an integrated hierarchy is a fully vertically integrated firm which houses all activities in the supply chain from raw material source to dispatch to end customer, as well as all its support activities on one site. This is shown in Fig. 13.11. In an integrated hierarchy there is no inter-company exchange of orders, information and materials because the entire supply chain is 'under one roof'. Examples of such a totally vertically integrated chain are rare. One example is a small vegetarian restaurant where the owners grow their own vegetables in the back garden, pick them, prepare them, cook them and serve them in the restaurant.

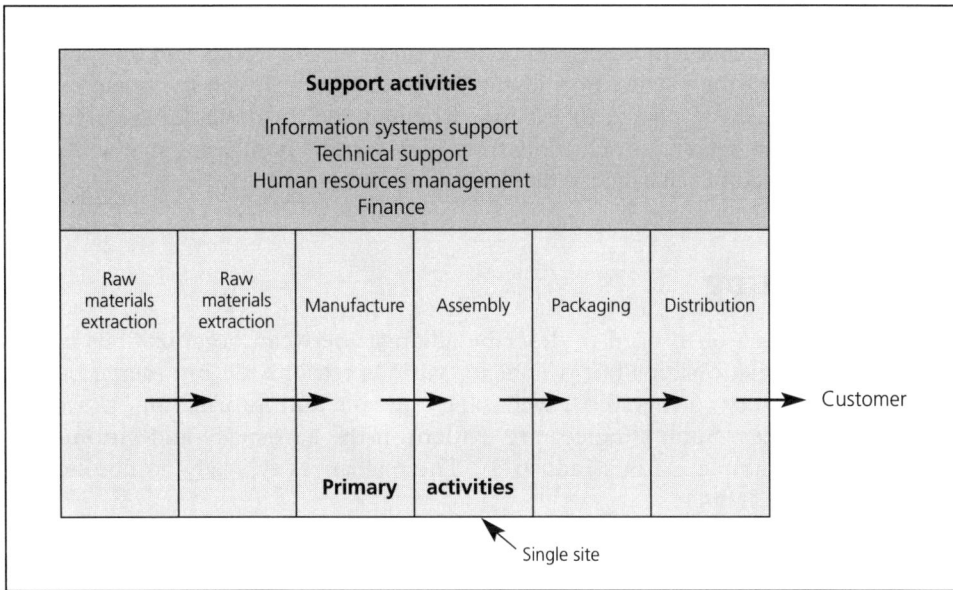

Figure 13.11
Integrated hierarchy organizational form

Semi-hierarchy

In a semi-hierarchy organization, the firms in the supply chain are owned by the same holding company or are part of the same group, but they operate as separate business units, as shown in Fig. 13.12. Oil companies who extract, refine, distribute and retail their products are an example of this type of arrangement.

Both integrated hierarchy and semi-hierarchy are examples of vertical integration, as in both cases ownership is by the same firm. In a semi-hierarchy, however, there is an exchange process between different organizations where materials, services and

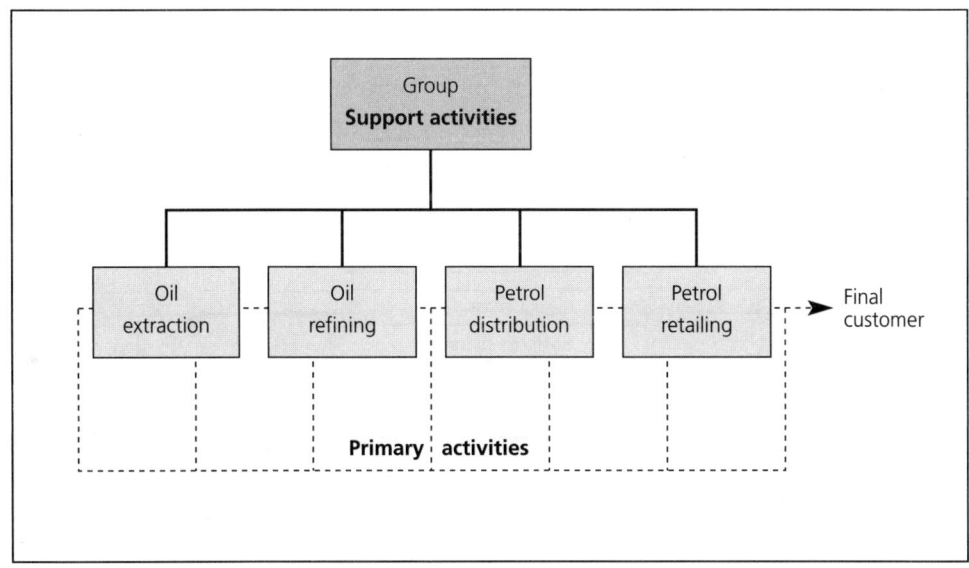

Figure 13.12
Semi-hierarchy organizational form

481

money changes hands between the separate business units. In addition to material and information exchange, there is likely to be a common set of systems and technologies exchanged between the parties. People may be exchanged between the organizations for particular projects or on a regular basis, depending on the design of the organization structure. The benefits which come from high-volume purchasing may exchange if there is centralized purchasing for the corporation.

Co-contracting

Co-contracting is a term used to describe alliances between organizations which have long-term relationships but which, for various reasons, do not merge but do transfer some equity (ownership), technology, people and information, as well as goods and services. Such alliances are evident in the aerospace and automotive industries (for example, Airbus Industrie). These alliances typically do not include the whole supply chain.

The elements of exchange in co-contracting are shown in Fig. 13.13.

A type of co-contracting receiving significant attention is what is called a 'partnership'.[16] This is, '*the sharing of risks and rewards, of technology and innovation leading to a reduction in costs, improvements in delivery and quality and the creation of sustainable competitive advantage*'.

In both partnership and lean relationships, boundaries may become 'blurred' which can create close connections between the two parties involved. However, the partners do not lose their own legal identity, as happens in merger or acquisition. They also retain their own culture, structure and pursue their own strategies. Inevitably, however, they reduce their freedom of action to some extent by strengthening their ties with the other organizations.

Coordinated contracting

Coordinated contracting involves a prime contractor, such as a jobbing builder, who employs a set of sub-contractors, such as carpenters, bricklayers and electricians, with whom a long-standing relationship exists over several contracts. They are used on a contract basis for each specific job but in between jobs there is no continuing

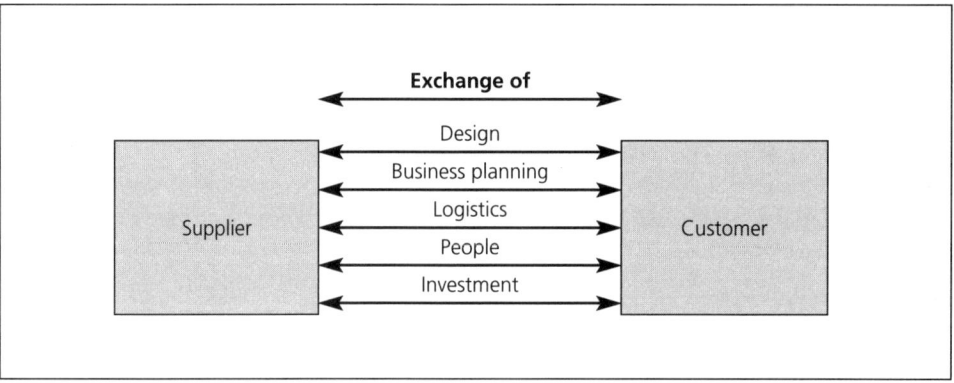

Figure 13.13
Co-contracting

WOOLWORTHS' LOGISTICS MANAGEMENT[17]

Woolworths is a South African retail chain offering a selected range of clothing, foods and homeware under its own brand name. According to Woolworths, its aim is to exceed its customers' expectations by giving them exceptional quality merchandise at reasonable prices, thereby offering excellent value for money. They are committed to providing a higher standard of knowledgeable and friendly service by offering a pleasant shopping experience, which enhances the trust and loyalty that their customers have for them. Woolworths is part of the Wooltru Group, which includes other retail stores like Topics, Truworths, Dion and Makro. Woolworths has its headquarters in Cape Town and three geographically dispersed divisions: the South Division, which includes the areas from Durban to Cape Town; the North Division, which comprises areas in the Northern Province and the Free state; and the Transvaal Division. Each division has various regions. The divisional headquarters of the Transvaal are at Centurion Park in Pretoria and comprise ten regions. It is at regional level that autonomous operational standards are set. However, Woolworths has further decentralized its operations to individual stores where there is healthy inter-store competition for excellence of service. There are 109 stores country-wide and four depots, which are distribution centres. Included in these stores are 14 franchise stores that are dispersed in neighbouring states like Botswana, Swaziland, Lesotho, Namibia and Zimbabwe.

Contrary to the trend of sub-contracting all but your core competencies, Woolworths has its own value-adding 'meat factory'. The meat factory is quite unique, in that it is owned and operated by a retail organization and forms part of the logistics and operations systems of the group. The reasons for the building of this factory are, first, to move away from in-store butcheries because of the inconvenience to the customer and, second, to reduce the building up of inventories that end up in losses through waste.

Woolworths does not buy its stock from the open market. Instead it buys from selected suppliers who prepare their products specifically for Woolworths under the Woolworths brand name. This has ensured the establishment of a long-term relationship between Woolworths and its suppliers. Woolworths' management believes that these long-term relationships with suppliers guarantee stable supplies, reduce costs, improve flexibility and reliability and, most importantly, provide high-quality products. Woolworths' cooperation goes beyond existing contracts. It works closely with suppliers, providing them with training and staff (quality inspectors) who help to support the supplier in the production of high-quality goods. Woolworths sees quality as its competitive advantage over other retailers and has embedded this concept in both the attitudes of its employees and its organizational practices. It has dedicated suppliers (farms) for cattle, sheep and chickens. Its own quality inspectors work within various suppliers' factories. Quality checks on textile merchandise take place in the stockroom during unpacking. This ensures that poor quality merchandise does not get through to the sales floor. Merchandise that does not match the quality standard of Woolworths is returned to suppliers.

The entire Woolworths supply chain is monitored, controlled and measured at every interval by various functions of management. The just-in-time practices they employ ensure reliability and responsiveness. Logistics is an information-intensive business function. Woolworths has long recognized that information technology is a key enabler of an integrated logistics process. Woolworths' 'SASTEK system' assists in developing a sustained competitive advantage. Its IT system not only enables internal integration but also enables the company to manage logistics throughout the supply chain on a real-time basis. This understanding of entire supply chains and the part that each player in the chain plays, is crucial for the cooperation that is required to meet ever higher customer demands. ■

relationship. In coordinated contracting the contractor usually provides the specification and instructions for the production of goods and services to be exchanged. It may provide materials and will usually take responsibility for the planning and control of all the sub-contractors. The sub-contractors will often provide the necessary tools and equipment required for their trade or profession. As this example indicates, this type of relationship is often found in project-type operations (*see* Chapter 16). The elements of exchange in coordinated contracting are shown in Fig. 13.14.

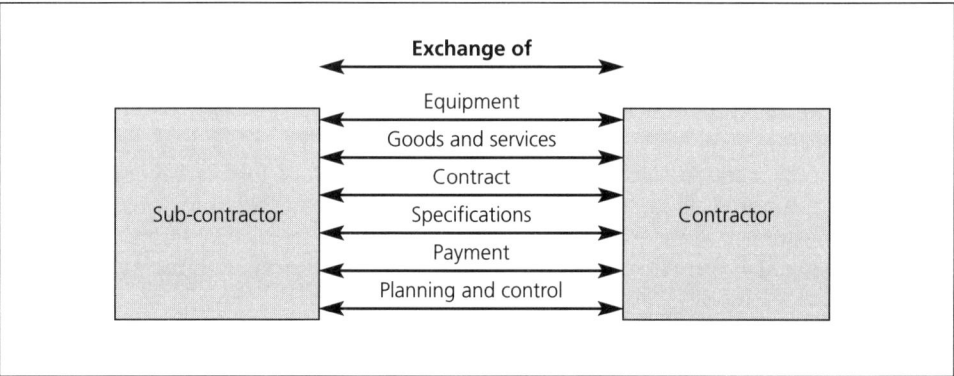

Figure 13.14
Coordinated
contracting

Coordinated revenue links

This category is used primarily for licensing and franchising and is a form of relationship which transfers ownership to other, usually smaller, firms while still retaining a guaranteed income for the licensor or franchiser.

One of the most significant things to pass between parties in this type of relationship is the contract, which often specifies such things as the following:

● property rights to the product or service, which usually remain with the licensor/franchiser;
● the territory within which the licensee or franchisee can operate;
● the product and service specification;
● the process specification to be used within the operation;
● the process of monitoring of performance, and any action that could result from poor performance.

This type of relationship is common in many services, especially those with very high customer contact. These operations need many small local sites which can be located for the convenience of their customers. Rather than manage all the sites themselves, the original owners of the service concept will licence out each individual operation to separate owners. Instant-printing operations, fast-food outlets and dry-cleaning operations are often organized on this basis. Figure 13.15 illustrates the exchange relationship in the 'coordinated revenue link' arrangement.

Medium- / long-term trading commitment

It is not uncommon for businesses to trade with each other for 20 years or more but never to exchange formal long-term contracts that legally tie them together. However, where this medium- to long-term trading takes place, some commitment beyond each delivery of a different type can be made. One example is what is called a 'blanket order'. This is an agreement for the purchasing organization to buy a total volume over a period of time at a price determined by the total, rather than the individual, daily, weekly or monthly purchased quantity. For example, in the purchase of materials and components there may be a delivery schedule specifying how many items are required each week but also a yearly agreement, on which the price is based. In a service environment there may be a service contract, such as for the regular upkeep of gardens as part of a tenancy agreement, specifying the amount of time that should be spent or the standard to which the gardens should be maintained.

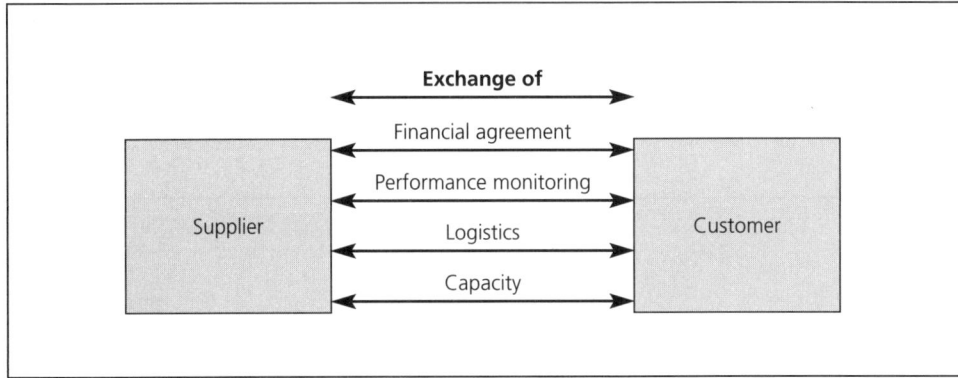

Figure 13.15 Coordinated revenue links

The elements of exchange in these medium- to long-term trading relationships are shown in Fig. 13.16.

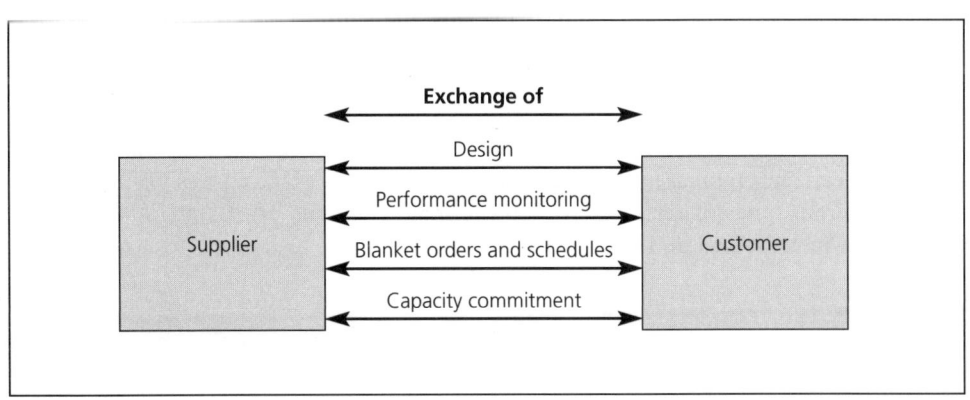

Figure 13.16 Medium- and long-term trading relations

485

Short-term trading commitment

In situations where there is no interdependence beyond one order, all that is transferred between the parties to the transaction are the order one way and goods and services the other. The agreement is reached after a market search, sometimes competitive tendering and often price negotiation. Once the goods or services are delivered and payment is made, there may be no further trading between the parties. The transfer made in this short-term relationship is shown in Fig. 13.17.

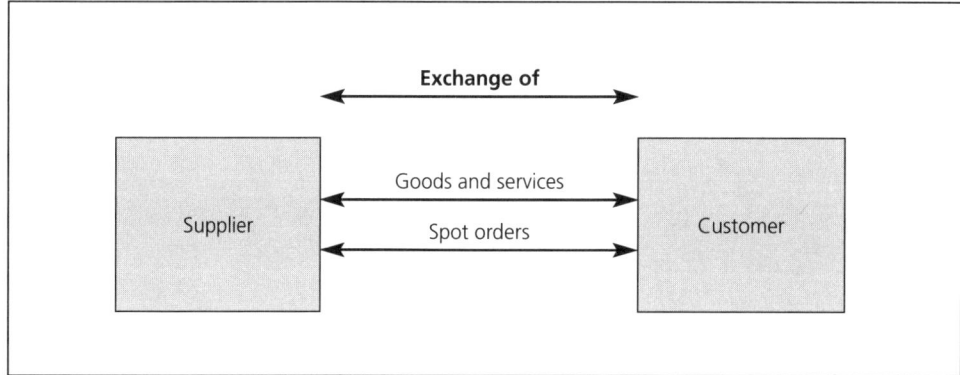

Figure 13.17
Short-term or spot
transactions

Short-term relationships like this may be used when new companies are being considered as more regular suppliers. Many purchases made by all operations are one-off or very irregular. For example, the replacement of all the windows in an office block would typically involve this type of competitive-tendering relationship, whereas it might form a longer-term relationship with its supplier of cleaning services.

Some public sector purchasing of goods and services is still based on short-term contracts such as these. This is mainly because of the need to prove that public money is being spent as judiciously as possible. However, this short-term, price-oriented type of relationship can have a downside in terms of ongoing support and reliability. This may mean that a 'least cost' purchase decision actually involves a higher total cost to the purchasing organization over time. For example, a higher education institution purchased a room full of microcomputers on a lowest cost spot-order basis, only to find that the computer agent who sold them was a small business whose main income was as a bicycle supplier. The ongoing technical support the university received was problematic.

The different types of relationship and the main elements of exchange in the relationship are summarized in Table 13.3.

Table 13.3 Exchange in different types of relationships

Relationship type	Exchange elements	Examples
Integrated hierarchy	People, materials, goods and services, technologies, information, money, equity	Single product firm, e.g. paper, aluminium
Semi-hierarchy	People, materials, goods and services, technologies, information, money, equity, centralized control, divisional reporting	Multi-divisional firm, holding company, e.g. chemicals, food
Co-contracting	Medium-/long-term contract, technologies, people, specifications, materials, goods, services, knowledge	Co-makership, joint venture, e.g. automotive
Coordinated contracting	Specification, payment, planning and control information, materials	Projects, e.g. construction
Coordinated review links	Contract, performance measures, specification of processes and products/ services, brand package, facilities, training	Licensing, franchising, e.g. fast-food chains
Long-term trading commitment	Reservation of future capacity, goods and services, payments, demand information	Single and dual source, blanket order, e.g. electronics
Medium-term trading commitment	Partial commitment to future work, reservation of capacity, goods and services, specifications	Preferred supplier, e.g. defence
Short term trading commitment	Goods and services, payment, order documentation	Spot orders, e.g. stationery purchases

Julia Dawson, Rover Group

The Rover Group is the UK's largest vehicle manufacturer. Julia Dawson joined the company after graduating in European Business. She is now Logistics Manager, planning component delivery for new models.

'A placement at Fiat in Italy, during my degree course in European Business, convinced me that I wanted to work in manufacturing industry, where there was a clear need for people with a combination of engineering, business and interpersonal skills. Logistics was first explained in the final year of my course. We were shown how it can have a significant effect on the efficiency and success of a business, by improving product flows and by building better customer–supplier relationships, and thereby reducing the levels of raw material and work-in-progress.

'The idea of working in logistics at Rover appealed, and I joined as a graduate on completion of my course. The training in the Logistics Department was very "hands on" and emphasized the need to be able to handle an ever-changing environment. Initially my job involved managing the scheduling, storage, transport, and movement of the Rover Cabriolet hood (soft top) from a supplier in Italy, which is the most expensive single component delivered to the factory. To do the job properly required intimate knowledge of the build strategy and related processes, both of the supplier and of Rover itself. I had to understand the component scheduling methods used in the manufacturing area and to ensure that the suppliers understood and complied with those systems. I had to have a detailed knowledge of component lead times, and of the scheduling of vehicles on the production line. The production plan can be liable to change at short notice and any component delivery planning had to incorporate some flexibility as a key objective.

'Logistics also plays a key role in the planning of new models by ensuring that the supplies will be continuous and cost-effective, involving the development of relationships with the major suppliers allied to the manufacturing strategy within Rover Group.

'I normally enjoy the job tremendously, but I have to admit that there are obviously some frustrating times when seemingly insignificant details are holding up the negotiation process. On the whole, I find that I am always in the thick of things, and need to be up to date with our current position in order to communicate confidently with suppliers. I also have to liaise with a range of internal customers and suppliers such as manufacturing and facilities engineering to ensure that our plans can be realistically fulfilled. Logistics is about being in the middle – being an effective link in the supply chain ...' ∎

SUMMARY

■ A supply chain is a strand, or chain, of operations within an organization's supply network which passes through the organization.

■ There are many different terms, some of which overlap, which are used to describe various parts of the supply chain. The terms (and the concepts described by them) which we have described are purchasing and supply management, physical distribution management, logistics, merchandising, materials management, and supply chain management. These represent an increasing degree of integration between the linkages of the supply chain.

■ Purchasing and supply development is concerned with the supply-side activities of an organization. Purchasing activities include the formal preparation of requests to suppliers for a quotation, the evaluation of suppliers, the issuing of formal purchase orders, and the monitoring of delivery.

■ The purchasing function attempts to obtain goods or services:
– at the right price,
– for delivery at the right time,
– in the right quality,
– in the right quantity,
– from the right source.

■ The effect of savings on the bought-in materials bill of most organizations has a disproportionate effect on their profitability. The greater the proportion of their total costs which are devoted to bought-in materials, the greater the saving for a given reduction in bought-in material costs.

■ One of the major decisions which purchasing managers have to take is whether to buy from a single source or several sources. Recent trends have moved many organizations towards single-sourcing.

■ Physical distribution management is the management of the (often multi-echelon) inventory and transportation systems which link the operation with its customers. Decisions taken within physical distribution include the number and position of warehouses in the system, and the mode of physical transport to adopt.

■ Materials management is an integrated concept which includes both purchasing and supply activities, as well as physical distribution activities. More importantly it also includes the flow of materials and information within the operation.

■ Logistics includes the demand-side physical distribution of goods, often beyond the immediate customers, through the supply chain to the end customer.

■ Supply chain management is a broader and strategically more significant concept which includes the entire supply chain from the supply of raw materials, through manufacture, assembly and distribution to the end customer. It includes the strategic and long-term consideration of supply chain management issues, as well as the shorter-term control of flow throughout the supply chain.

■ The Forrester Effect is the amplification of demand changes as they affect upstream operations within the supply chain.

■ The exact nature of the relationship between the different linkages within the supply chain can be viewed on a continuum which goes from highly integrated at one extreme through to temporary and short-term trading commitments at the other.

CASE EXERCISE

Laura Ashley's strategic alliance with Federal Express[18]

Laura Ashley (LA) is a global manufacturer and retailer with its headquarters in a small village in Wales. It must be the benchmark for almost every aspiring entrepreneur's dreams; it has blossomed from Laura and Bernard Ashley's experiments in printing textiles on their kitchen table in 1953, to a business with over 6000 staff and 540 shops in 28 countries. Laura Ashley is famous throughout the world for its unique brand of women's garments, curtain and upholstery fabric and wallpapers, mostly designed with a pastoral, nostalgic and distinctly 'English' style. It uses only natural fabrics including cotton, silk and linen, printed in a wide and constantly evolving range of styles and patterns.

Unfortunately, however, Laura Ashley's spectacular success in product development and design, and in bringing products to market, was not matched in its operations. The company, which had been so profitable throughout the '80s, reported major losses in 1990 and for the following few years. The problem seemed to be that while the business had grown, it had also become very complex, and its logistics operations had failed to adapt, with the resulting symptoms being extremely long lead times for orders, huge inventories, high levels of stock-outs, inventory shortages, and enormous write-offs of obsolete products. The company operated eight major warehouses, contracted eight principal carriers, and ten unconnected management systems. The 1990 and 1991 accounts showed £6.7m and £4.8m exceptional items covering 'restructuring, systems costs, inventory writedowns and other one-time events'. From the external customers' perspective, Laura Ashley's service had deteriorated badly, but the internal customers both at the factories and at the shops also suffered from the inadequacies of the system.

In September 1991 Dr Jim Maxmin was appointed Chief Executive, and set about a strategic and operational review aimed at building the brand and restoring the company to profitability. Maxmin's objectives were for LA to become 'strategically led, competitively focused, market oriented, employee driven, and operationally excellent'. He described the existing warehousing, distribution, and delivery operations as 'a disaster, out of control', and formed a global team, headed up by Phil Baker, Special Projects Director in Global Finance, to evaluate

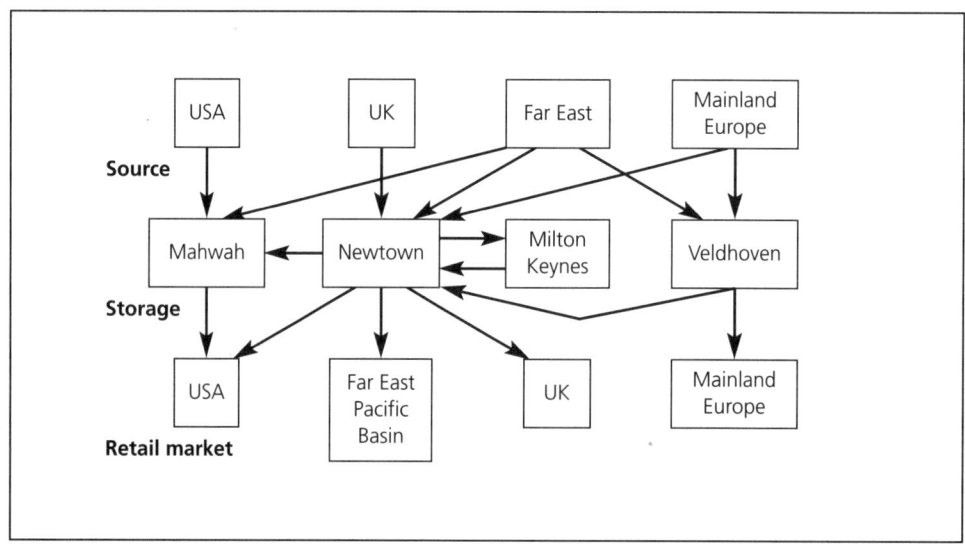

Figure 13.18 Laura Ashley: before

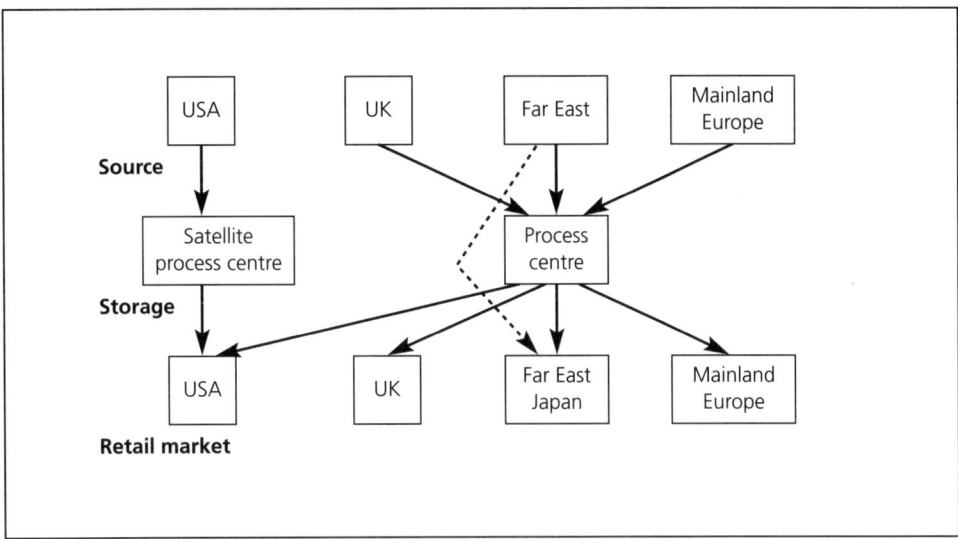

Figure 13.19 Laura Ashley: after

options for solving the problems. They were tasked with creating a system which would increase availability from 80 per cent to 99 per cent, allow all deliveries to be made to stores anywhere in the world within 24 or 48 hours, and reduce inventory by 50 per cent. The existing supply chain held up to 18 months' inventory from product design to point of sale, and inventory turns averaged less than two! During the review, Baker visited an LA store in Germany. A fast-selling item was out of stock, and new supplies would not be available for four months; on his return to Wales, he found that the warehouse had five hundred in unallocated stock.

'Right now, we're the very opposite of service maximization and cost minimization',

he commented. Fig. 13.18 shows LA's logistics structure before the later changes.

After extensive review, the team concluded that the necessary logistic resources and skills could never be developed quickly enough within LA to meet the objectives, and supported Jim Maxmin's proposals for a strategic partnership with Federal Express Business Logistics Service (BLS). Maxmin had previous experience with Federal Express, and the company was already an important supplier of shipping services. The idea of an alliance was very controversial, as many executives felt that it was dangerous to depend on a single supplier, which would be taking over the Welsh warehouses and all of LA's distribution activities world-

wide. The strategic alliance between Federal Express and Laura Ashley commenced in March 1992. It was based on a minimum ten-year term to facilitate an extensive programme of developments, although both parties talked of a 'life-time' partnership. Figure 13.19 shows the new logistics structure.

Several of the warehouses around the world were phased out, and the Welsh facility at Newtown became the 'processing centre', forming the single hub of global distribution, much of it by air on the Federal Express fleet. Consolidating inventory at one site reduces the magnitude of random demand variations experienced at the smaller, local warehouses, so total inventory can be reduced while service level is improved. Direct shipment from the warehouse to the stores has eliminated double handling and, surprisingly perhaps, some of the transportation costs involved in the dual shipments. Integration and updating of inventory, point-of-sale and logistics information systems were begun immediately. These and other systems are being continually developed. The specific details of the financial arrangements between the companies have not been made public.

Above all, however, the deal was conceived to provide new opportunities for both partners. Phil Baker summarized his view of the partnership:

'We really can't find any downsides. This is a fantastic opportunity for both companies ... The way things had become, there was little else we could have done!'

▶

Laura Ashley's goals for its agreement with Federal Express Business Logistics Services were:

- reduce inventory held in the supply chain at any time by 50 per cent;
- cut logistics operating costs by 10–12 per cent, based on like-for-like services;
- eliminate the need to hold out-of-stock lines in stores (currently at 16 per cent);
- develop the capability for a global mail-order operation by September 1993;
- integrate and improve all service levels. ■

Questions

1 What arguments against the agreement might have been made by LA managers and why? How could Maxmin and Baker get their staff to 'buy-in' to this deal, and what approach could have been taken with those who resisted?

2 Do you agree with Phil Baker that there was no alternative to this scheme? If not, what should have been done to transform LA's logistics performance?

3 What risks were taken by Federal Express in reaching this agreement?

4 How could the last objective (integrate and improve all service levels) be evaluated? What performance measures, if any, should be used?

DISCUSSION QUESTIONS

1 If you were the owner of a small, local retail shop, what criteria would you use to select suppliers for the goods which you wish to stock in your shop? Visit three shops which are local to you and ask the owners how they select their suppliers. In what ways were their answers different to what you thought they might be?

2 What do you understand by the terms logistics, merchandising, materials management and supply chain management?

3 If you were drawing up a document to be sent out to potential suppliers of a new photocopying machine for your local library, what would you ask them to specify in their quotation?

4 How is vertical integration different from partnership purchasing?

5 A company is considering buying in leaflets to be included with the packaging of its products. Its own in-house printing department could produce the leaflets but not at the same level of quality which a specialist printer could supply. Nevertheless, the in-house printing department is keen to be given the job of printing the leaflets. The costs of printing the leaflets in-house are R100 per 1000 leaflets. This cost includes the cost of the paper and inks (R70), the cost of the energy used by the printing machines (R5) and a standard overhead charge cal-culated according to the time the job would take (R25). The in-house printing department has suffi-cient capacity to print all the leaflets which will be required without any extra staff or machines. The company's purchasing department has several quo-tations from local printers, the cheapest of which is R85 per 1000 leaflets, although the printer had made it clear that delivery times would be at least two weeks for each order because they have so much other business currently. How would you advise the company if it asked you whether it should buy in the leaflets or allow its own in-house printing unit to do the job?

6 If you were designing a system to evaluate the performance of a company's purchasing function what criteria would you use?

7 Why do you think the use of expediters is less common than it once was? Do you think expediters could still play a useful role?

8 How is logistics different from materials manage-ment?

9 What do you think should be the main informa-tion which is exchanged between the purchasing function and other parts of the organization?

10 Under what circumstances do you think multi-sourcing would be advantageous?

NOTES ON CHAPTER

1 Coyle, R.G. (1982) 'Assessing the Controllability of a Production Raw Material System', *IEEE Transactions*, SMC–12, Vol 6.

2 Harland, C. (1993) Unpublished PhD thesis.

3 Baily, P., Farmer, D., Jessop, D. and Jones, D. (1994) *Purchasing Principles and Management*, Pitman Publishing.

4 Source: Interviews with company staff.

5 Sable, C., Herrigel, G., Kazis, R. and Deeg, R. (1987) 'How to Keep Mature Industries Innovative', *Technology Review*, Vol 90, No 3.

6 Morgan, I. (1987) *The Purchasing Revolution*, McKinsey Quarterly, Spring.

7 Lamming, R. (1993) *Beyond Partnership: Strategies for Innovation and Lean Supply*, Prentice Hall.

8 Source: Discussions with Keith Tindale, MD of Wimpy SA.

9 Lee, L. and Dobler, D.W. (1977) *Purchasing and Materials Management*, McGraw-Hill.

10 Christopher, M.G. (1992) *Logistics and Supply Chain Management*, Pitman Publishing.

11 Jones, C. (1989) 'Supply Chain Management – The Key Issues', *BPICS Control*, Oct/Nov.

12 Source: Company staff.

13 Source: 'It's in the Mail', *The Economist*, 2 March 1991.

14 Forrester, J.W. (1961) *Industrial Dynamics*, MIT Press.

15 Benetton, A. (1984), Harvard Business School Case Study 6-985-014, and company literature.

16 Lamming, R., *op. cit.*

17 Source: By kind permission of Woolworths Pty Ltd.

18 Source: Discussion with company staff.

SELECTED FURTHER READINGS

Bailey, P. and Farmer, D. (1994) *Purchasing Principles and Management* (7th edn), Pitman Publishing.

Blumenfeld, D.E., Burns, L.D., Daganzo, C.F., Frick, M.C. and Hall, R.W. (1987) 'Reducing Logistics Costs at General Motors', *Interfaces*, Vol 17, Jan–Feb.

Bund, J.B. (1985) 'Build Customer Relationships That Last', *Harvard Business Review*, Vol 63, No 6.

Burt, D.N. (1984) *Proactive Purchasing*, Prentice Hall.

Burt, D.N. (1989) 'Managing Suppliers Up to Speed', *Harvard Business Review*, Vol 67, No 4.

Burt, D.N. and Soukup, W.R. (1985) 'Purchasing's Role in New Product Development', *Harvard Business Review*, Vol 63, No 5.

Carr, C.H. and Truesdale, T.A. (1992) 'Lessons From Nissan's British Suppliers', *International Journal of Operations and Production Management*, Vol 12, No 2.

Carter, J.R. and Narasimhan, R. (1990) 'Purchasing in the International Market Place: Implications for Operations', *Journal of Purchasing and Materials Management*, Summer.

Cousins, P. (1992) 'Choosing the Right Partner', *Purchasing and Supply Management Journal*, Mar.

Cousins, P.D. (1992) 'Purchasing: The Professional Approach', *Purchasing and Supply Management*, Sept.

Harrison, A. and Voss, C. (1990) 'Issues in Setting up JIT Supply', *International Journal of Operations and Production Management*, Vol 10, No 2.

Lamming, R. (1993) *Beyond Partnership: Strategies for Innovation and Lean Supply*, Prentice Hall.

Lee L. and Dobler D.W. (1977) *Purchasing and Materials Management*, McGraw-Hill.

Macbeth, D.K., Baxter, L.F., Ferguson, N. and Neil, G.C. (1989) 'Not Purchasing but Supply Chain Management', *Purchasing and Supply Management Journal*, Nov.

Ramsay, J. and Wilson, I. (1990) 'Sourcing/Contracting Strategy Selection', *International Journal of Operations and Production Management*, Vol 10, No 8.

Schneider, L.M. (1985) 'A New Era in Transportation Strategy', *Harvard Business Review*, Vol 63, No 2.

Sharman G (1984) 'The Rediscovery of Logistics', *Harvard Business Review*, Vol 62, No 5.

Walleigh, R.C. (1986) 'Getting Things Done: What's Your Excuse for Not Using JIT?', *Harvard Business Review*, Vol 64, No 2.

Womack, J.P., Jones, D.T. and Roos, D. (1990) *The Machine that Changed the World*, Rawson Associates.

MRP

INTRODUCTION

There are two different but related definitions of MRP. Both, however, share the same underlying theme – they help businesses plan and control their resource requirements with the aid of computer-based information systems. MRP can stand for both materials requirements planning or manufacturing resource planning. Over time, the concept of MRP has developed from an operations-management focused concept, which helped in planning and controlling materials requirements, to become, in recent years, a business system which helps plan all business resource requirements. Typically, MRP is used in manufacturing businesses, though there are some examples of its application in non-manufacturing environments. Figure 14.1 shows the purpose of MRP in reconciling the supply and demand of resources.

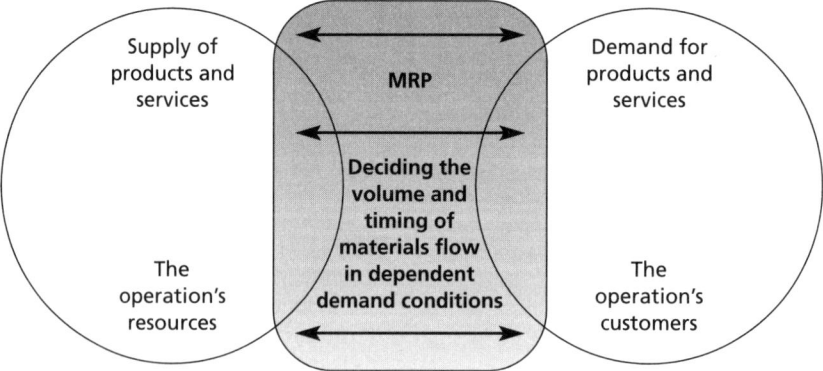

Figure 14.1 A definition of MRP

OBJECTIVES

This chapter will examine:

- the meaning of MRP, both MRP I and MRP II;

- the concept of MRP;

- the process of MRP I;

- the main elements or modules of MRP I systems;

- closed-loop MRP;

- the concept of MRP II.

WHAT IS MRP?

The original MRP dates back to the 1960s, when the letters stood for *Materials Requirements Planning* (now called MRP One or MRP I). MRP I enables companies to calculate how many materials of particular types are required, and at what times they are required. To do this it uses a sales order book which records known future orders and also a forecast of what sales orders the business is reasonably confident might be won. MRP then checks all the ingredients or components which are required to make these future orders and ensures they are ordered in time.

MRP is a system that helps companies make *volume* and *timing* calculations. Prior to the 1960s companies had always had to do these types of calculations manually to ensure that they had the right materials available in their business at the right time. However, with the advent of computers and their more widespread use in business from the 1960s onwards, this provided the opportunity to perform these time-consuming, detailed calculations by computer quickly and relatively easily.

During the 1980s and 1990s the system and the concept of materials requirements planning has expanded and been integrated with other parts of the business. This enlarged version of MRP is now known as *Manufacturing Resource Planning*, or MRP II. MRP II enables companies to examine the engineering and financial implications of future demand on the business, as well as examining the materials requirements implications. Oliver Wight,[1] who with Joseph Orlicky[2] is considered to be the founder of modern MRP, described manufacturing resource planning as a 'total game plan' for a business.

Manufacturing businesses may make and sell several thousand different variations of end products to a customer base of several hundred regular customers as well as many hundreds of customers who order only irregularly. Many of these customers are also likely to vary their demand for the products.

Materials requirements planning is still the heart of any MRP system (I or II) and therefore the majority of this chapter will be concerned with establishing the basic purpose and principles of MRP I.

WHAT IS REQUIRED TO RUN MRP I?

In order to perform the volume and timing calculations of the type just described, materials requirements planning systems (MRP I) typically require an operation to keep certain data records in computer files which, when the MRP I program is run, can be checked and updated.

Figure 14.2 shows the information required to perform MRP I and some of the outputs from it.

Starting at the top of Fig. 14.2, the first inputs to material requirements planning are customer orders and forecast demand. The first are firm orders scheduled for some identified date in the future while the second are realistic estimates of the quantity and timing of future orders. MRP performs its calculations based on the combination of these two parts of future demand. All other requirements calculated within the MRP process are derived from, and dependent on, these demands. Because of this, MRP is what we described in Chapter 10 as a *dependent demand system*. As a reminder, dependent demand is demand which is derived from some other decision taken within the operation, whereas independent demand systems are designed to operate where demand is outside the control of the operation.

Demand management

Taken together, the management of customer orders and sales forecasts is termed *demand management*. Demand management encompasses a set of processes which interface with the customer market. Depending on the business, these processes may include sales order entry, demand forecasting, order promising, customer service and physical distribution. For example, if you place an order with a mail-order catalogue and ring up a week later to check why your purchase has not arrived, you will frequently be dealt with by a telesales customer service operator. This operator, looking at a computer screen, can access the details of your particular order, and advise why there might have been a hold-up in delivery. In addition he or she may be able to provide you with a delivery promise of when you should receive the item, and inform you

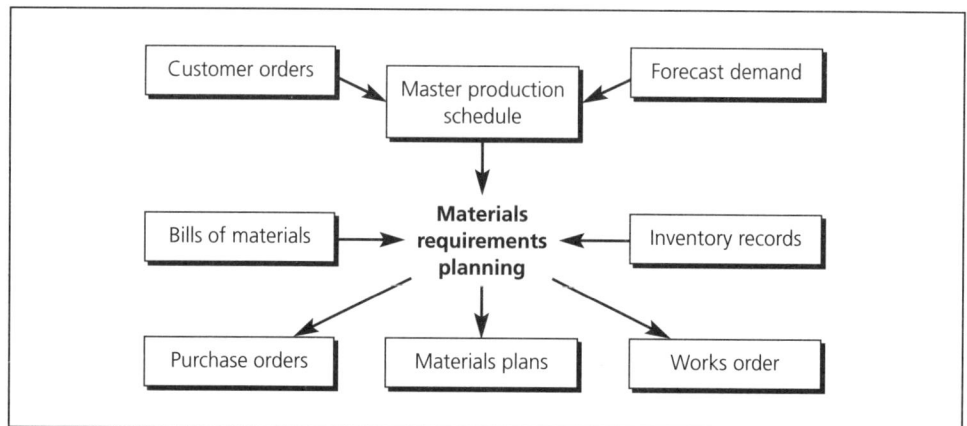

Figure 14.2 Materials requirements planning (MRP I) schematic

what mode of delivery will be used (for example, if a courier will deliver it). The interaction with customers and the resulting requirements from that interaction trigger a chain reaction of operations requirements. To satisfy the customer, the item has to be picked from a warehouse; a stores operator must therefore be provided with the appropriate information to do that. A courier must also be booked for a particular time.

We now consider customer orders and forecast demand, as shown in Fig. 14.3.

Customer orders (Fig. 14.3)

Sales functions in most businesses typically manage a dynamic, changing, order book made up of confirmed orders from customers. Of particular interest to the MRP I process of calculating materials requirements are the records of exactly what each customer has ordered, how many they have ordered and when they require delivery.

Variation of sales orders

Sales orders usually represent some contractual commitment on behalf of the customer. However, depending on what business a company is in, this may not be as fixed as it may at first seem. Customers can change their minds about what they require, after having placed their orders. They may require a smaller or larger number of a particular item or they may change the date they want their order to be delivered. Because customer service and flexibility are increasingly important competitive factors, having to change requirements is becoming a more common feature in most operations. Indeed, if customers are purchasing industrial goods such as components from a company, it may be that their own customers are the cause of the changing requirements (this aspect of managing the supply chain was discussed in Chapter 13). Considering that each of several hundred customers may make changes to their sales orders, not once, but possibly several times after the order has been placed, it is evident that managing the sales order book is a complex and dynamic process.

Organizations have to make decisions about how much flexibility they will afford to customers and at what stage their customers have to accept liability for the implications of their changes. For example, many cinemas that take credit card bookings will not allow these 'orders' to be changed; the nature of their booking operation is such

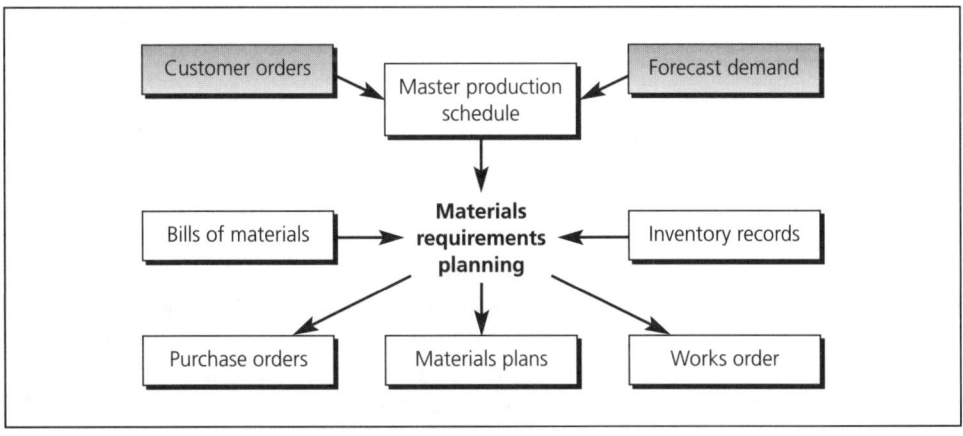

Figure 14.3 The demand management inputs to the MRP process

that this type of flexibility would make their management of capacity and seat allocation process more complicated if changes were allowed. However, cross-channel ferry-crossing operators allow changes in bookings right up to the time of the crossing – passengers arriving early may be allowed on an earlier crossing than they were booked on, if there is space available. These decisions about how much flexibility is allowed to customers have an enormous impact on the operations of the business as a whole and on the calculation of detailed materials and resource requirements.

Not all operations have the same degree of forward 'visibility' in terms of known customer orders. Customers of supermarkets do not have to give advance notice of their arrival or their likely purchases prior to the time they shop. Some train seats can be pre-booked but many, particularly on local services, are purchased by passengers arriving at the station with a desire to travel as soon as possible. Similarly within manufacturing businesses, because competitive environments change so frequently, customers are becoming more reluctant to make firm commitments in advance in the form of detailed orders for specific parts. Furthermore, as delivery speed becomes increasingly important because of just-in-time supply (*see* Chapter 15), when firm orders are received there may be insufficient time to buy the required materials, perform the required manufacturing processes on those materials and then deliver the product to the customer. Therefore, for all these reasons, many businesses have to *forecast* their likely future requirements to ensure they have raw materials available to start their own processes once a sales order is received.

The techniques involved in forecasting are discussed in Appendix 1.

Forecast demand

Driving a business using forecasts based on history has been compared to driving a car by looking only at the rear view mirror.[3] To satisfy customers' demands for delivery speed, automotive manufacturers, for example, at the time a customer places an order, have already made estimates of the models, the engines and the colours they think will be sold. When a customer places the order, one of the models in the chosen colour with the right-size engine is already in production and is allocated to him or her. The customer can, at the time of ordering, choose from a wide range of options in terms of trim (such as upholstery and interior colours), audio systems and glass tinting, etc., all of which can be added to the main assembly, effectively giving the impression of customization. The manufacturer has to predict ahead the likely required mix of models and colours to manufacture and the likely mix of options to purchase and have available in inventory.

Combining orders and forecasts

A combination of known orders and forecasted orders are used to represent demand in many businesses. It is important that the forecast which is used for operations planning is not a sales *target*, which might be set optimistically high to give incentives to the sales force. While many businesses use targets, a forecast is something different. It should be the best estimate at any time of what reasonably could be expected to happen.

In Fig. 14.4 one of the most important features of demand management is evident: that is, the further ahead you look into the future, the less certainty there is about demand. Most businesses have knowledge in the short term about demand in terms of individual orders. However, few customers place orders well into the future. Based on history and on market information gained from field sales operatives, a forecast is put together to reflect likely demand. As orders come in, the forecast element of the demand profile should be reduced, giving the impression of the forecast being 'consumed' over time by firm orders.

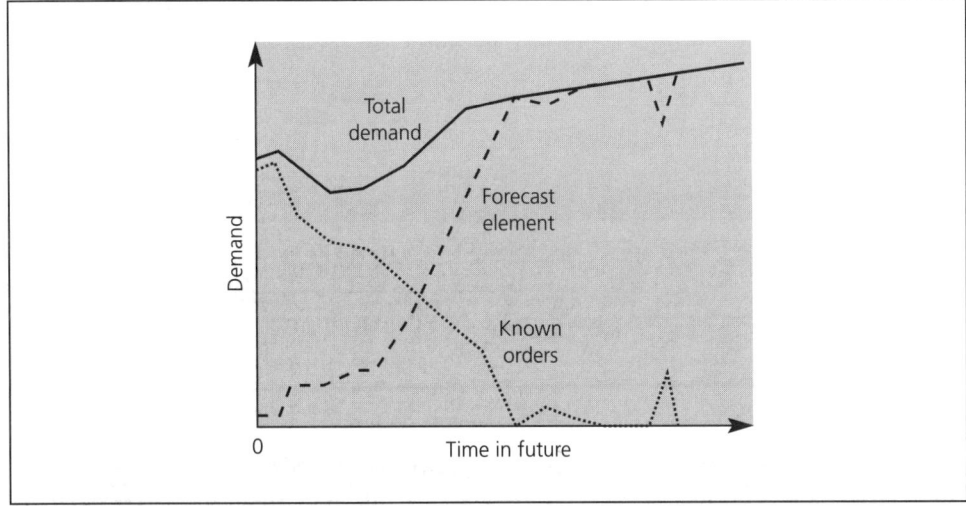

Figure 14.4
Combining known orders and forecast orders

Different types of operations have different profiles in terms of the mix of known orders and forecast orders. A make-to-order business, such as a jobbing printer, tends to have greater visibility of known orders over time than does a make-for-stock business, such as a consumer durable manufacturer. 'Purchase-to-order' businesses do not order most of their raw materials until they receive a confirmed customer order. For example, a jobbing dressmaker would not order fabrics until they were sure that they had been awarded a contract. Other businesses not only cannot risk ordering materials, they also cannot place contracts for labour or equipment. These can be termed 'resource-to-order' businesses. For example, a civil engineering project manager would not order most of the materials for building a bridge until the tender had been won, but also would not be committed to labour and plant hire. At the opposite end of the spectrum, there are some operations who have very little order certainty at the time they take most of their decisions. For example, newspaper publishers distribute newspapers to retail outlets on a sale-or-return basis: that is, real demand is only evident to them after each day's trading has finished and they calculate how many papers were actually sold. (*See* Fig. 14.5.)

Many businesses have to operate with a varying combination of known orders and forecasts. For example, the week before Mothers' Day, small local florists receive a large volume of orders for bouquets and flower arrangements. At other times of the year, a greater amount of their business is passing trade which is affected by the weather and shopping patterns. From a planning and control perspective, the output from demand management is a prediction ahead over time of what customers will purchase. This information, be it known sales orders, forecast, or a combination of both, is the major input to the master production schedule.

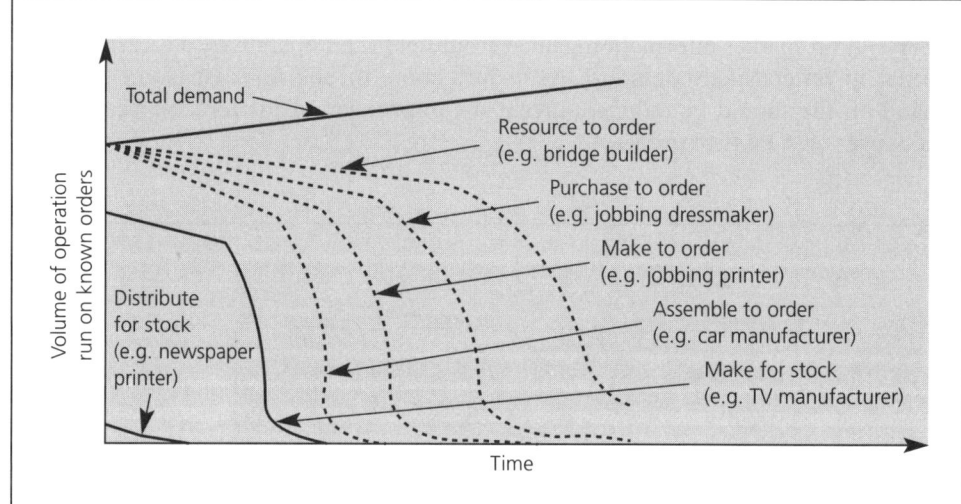

**Figure 14.5
Significance of
forecasting to
different types of
operation**

OVERCOMING FORECAST PROBLEMS AT RACAL RECORDERS[4]

Racal Recorders manufactures recording systems which are used in a wide variety of applications, from recording emergency telephone conversations through to recording automobile performance on the test track for later analysis. The technology of these products is sophisticated and the task of controlling their manufacture complex. Racal Recorders, through a combination of product superiority and manufacturing professionalism, are the market leaders with a turnover of around R250 million per annum.

One of its major production planning and control problems is how to coordinate the production and movement of all the parts which go into its product when virtually all products and systems are configured to meet the requirements of individual customers. An MRP system is needed to translate orders and forecasts into works instructions for purchasing and manufacturing parts, sub-assemblies and finished products. Its main problem was that after running the MRP process, the finished goods were put into stock to await customer orders. Yet the orders when they came never exactly matched what had been manufactured based on the forecast of demand. Some products remained in storage while others had to go back to the workshops to be re-manufactured to form the configurations which customers really did want.

Racal's solution to this was to analyse the common elements within its systems and manufacture 'modules' which could be built up to make whole systems. Forecasts were prepared for the modules which, when manufactured, were kept on the shop floor until orders were firm. On the receipt of a confirmed order the modules could be assembled to form the finished system as specified by the customer. ■

Master production schedule

The master production schedule (MPS) is the most important planning and control schedule in a business, and forms the main input to materials requirements planning (*see* Fig. 14.6).

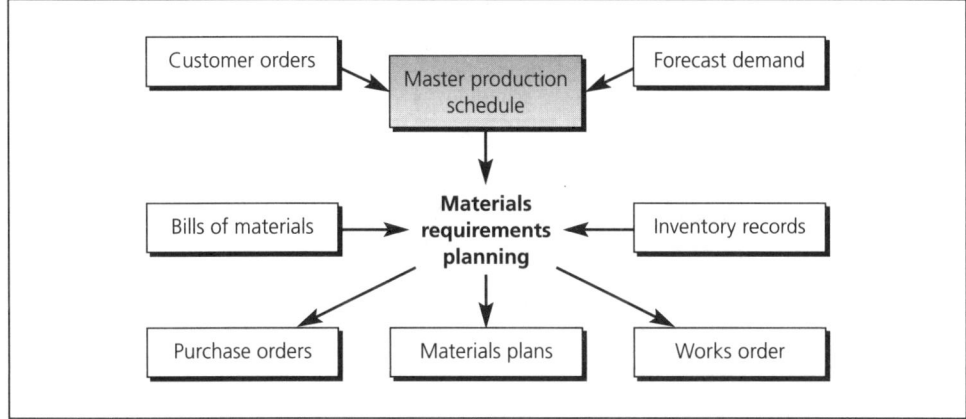

Figure 14.6 The master production schedule in the MRP I schematic

MPS in manufacturing

In manufacturing the MPS contains a statement of the volume and timing of the end products to be made; this schedule drives the whole operation in terms of what is assembled, what is manufactured and what is bought. It is the basis of planning the utilization of labour and equipment and it determines the provisioning of materials and cash.

MPS in services

MPS also can be used in service organizations. For example, in a hospital theatre there is a master schedule which contains a statement of which operations are planned and when. This drives the provisioning of materials for the operations, such as the sterile instruments, blood and dressings. It also governs the scheduling of staff for operations, including anaesthetists, nurses and surgeons.

Sources of information for the MPS

It is important that all sources of demand are considered when the master production schedule is created. It is often the 'odds and ends' of requirements in a business that disrupt the entire planning system. For example, if a manufacturer of earth excavators plans an exhibition of its products and allows a project team to raid the stores so that it can build two pristine examples to be exhibited, this is likely to leave the factory short of parts. Figure 14.7 shows the inputs that may be taken into account in the creation of a master production schedule.

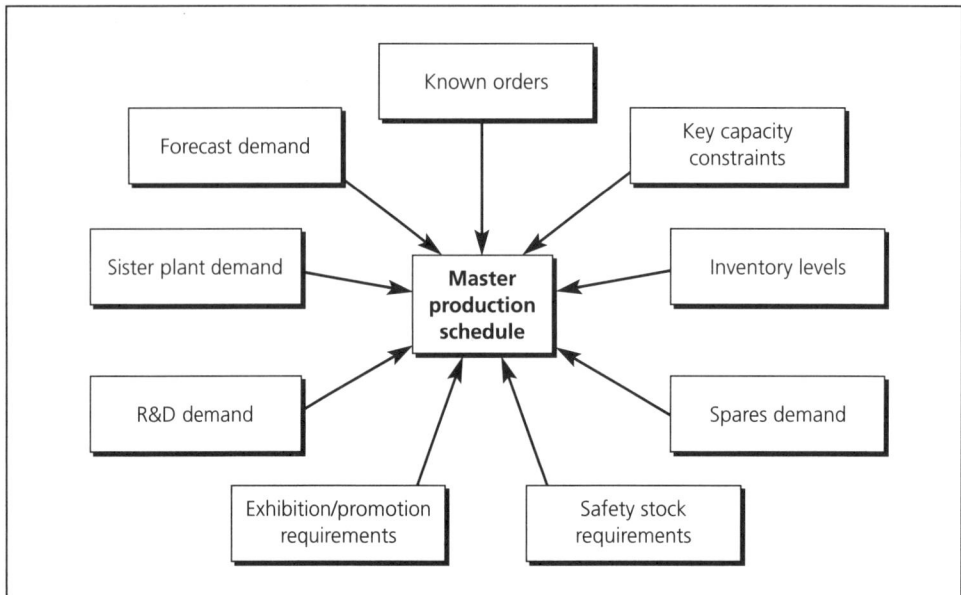

**Figure 14.7
Inputs into the
master production
schedule**

The master production schedule record

Master production schedules are time-phased records of each end product, which contain a statement of demand and currently available stock of each finished item. Using this information, the available inventory is projected ahead in time. When there is insufficient inventory to satisfy forward demand, order quantities are entered on the master schedule line.

Table 14.1 is a simplified example of part of a master production schedule for one item. The known sales orders and any forecast are combined to form 'Demand'. This is shown in the first row and can be seen to be gradually increasing. The second row, 'Available', shows how much inventory is expected to be in stock of this item at the end of each weekly period. The opening inventory balance, 'On hand', is shown separately at the bottom of the record. Here 30 of this part are currently in stock in week 0. The available figure of 20 in the first week is calculated by taking demand of 10 away from the on-hand inventory of 30. The third row is the master production schedule, or MPS; this shows how many finished items need to be completed and available in each week to satisfy demand. As there is adequate inventory already

Table 14.1 Example of a master production schedule

		Week number								
		1	2	3	4	5	6	7	8	9
Demand		10	10	10	10	15	15	15	20	20
Available		20	10	0	0	0	0	0	0	0
MPS		0	0	10	10	15	15	15	20	20
On hand	30									

available in weeks 1 and 2, no plans are made to complete more in those weeks. However, in week 3, it is necessary for production to complete ten of these items to satisfy projected demand; if production cannot complete ten at this time, there is the possibility that customers will be put on back order (that is, they will be made to queue).

Chase or level master production schedules

In the example in Table 14.1, the MPS increases as demand increases and aims to keep available inventory at 0 – the master production schedule is 'chasing' demand. As we discussed in Chapter 11 on capacity planning and control, chasing demand involves adjusting the provision of resources, which may not always be desirable. An alternative level MPS for this situation is shown in Table 14.2.

Level scheduling involves averaging the amount required to be completed to smooth out peaks and troughs. Table 14.2 shows how this level schedule generates more inventory than the previous MPS. In this case the average projected inventory of finished items over the nine-week period is 25 per week (that is, more than any one month's demand during this period). In the previous table the average inventory was only 3.

Table 14.2 Example of a 'level' master production schedule

		Week number								
		1	2	3	4	5	6	7	8	9
Demand		10	10	10	10	15	15	15	20	20
Available		31	32	33	34	30	26	22	13	4
MPS		11	11	11	11	11	11	11	11	11
On hand	30									

Available to promise (ATP)

The master production schedule provides the information to the sales function on what can be promised to customers and when delivery can be promised. The sales function can load known sales orders against the master production schedule and keep track of what is *available to promise (ATP)* (*see* Table 14.3).

The available to promise (ATP) line in the master production schedule shows the maximum in any one week that is still available, against which sales orders can be loaded. If the sales function promises above that figure, it will not be able to keep its promise and the business will be viewed as unreliable by its customers. If sales orders are possible over and above this ATP figure, negotiation should take place with the master production scheduler to see if there is any possibility of satisfying these increased orders by adjusting the MPS. However, this must be run through the MRP process to see the resulting effects on resource requirements.

Examples of poor practice in master scheduling

Unfortunately, many companies accept all sales orders and then try to cope. There are two possibilities here. The first is that the operation fails to cope, cannot manufacture the products, and lets down its customer. The second is that the company somehow always seems to manage. This indicates that its planning system is carrying excess capacity, or slack, in the system, which is not known within the MRP process. Both of these scenarios represent common bad practice in running MRP systems.

Table 14.3 Example of a level master production schedule including available to promise

		Week number								
		1	*2*	*3*	*4*	*5*	*6*	*7*	*8*	*9*
Demand		10	10	10	10	15	15	15	20	20
Sales orders		10	10	10	8	4				
Available		31	32	33	34	30	26	22	13	4
ATP		31	1	1	3	7	11	11	11	11
MPS		11	11	11	11	11	11	11	11	11
On hand	30									

The bill of materials

The master schedule drives the rest of the MRP process. Having established this top-level schedule, MRP performs calculations to work out the volume and timing of assemblies, sub-assemblies and materials required to meet this master schedule. To explain the process, an example product – a board game called 'Treasure Hunt' – will be used. This fictitious product is a boxed game which involves two to eight players tackling certain quests to find where treasure is buried on a board. To do this, adventure characters use a horse, an air balloon, a cart and other modes of transport to move around the board. Players take turns using two dice to determine their move. A set of instructions is provided with the game.

To be able to manufacture this game, Warwick Operations Inc. needs to understand what parts are required to go into each boxed game. If it wishes to use an MRP system to perform this task, it requires computer records of the ingredients or components that go into each item, much the same as a cook requires a list of ingredients required to prepare a dish. These records are called *bills of materials*. The position of the bill of materials in the MRP schema is shown in Fig. 14.8.

Materials requirements planning programmes need to check the components or ingredients for each item that is to be made. In Chapter 5 we discussed design and introduced the idea of product structures. A bill of materials shows which parts and how many of them are required to go into which other parts. It is simplest to think about these as a product structure initially (*see* Fig. 14.9). The product structure in Fig. 14.9 is a simplified structure showing the parts required to make the game. It shows that to make one game you require the components of the game – board, dice, characters and quest cards – a set of rules and the packaging. The packaging comprises a printed cardboard box and inside the base is an injection-moulded plastic inner tray. Since the game was launched, finance was provided for television advertising, so an additional sticker stating 'As advertised on TV' is now stuck on the plastic inner tray and on the front of the complete box.

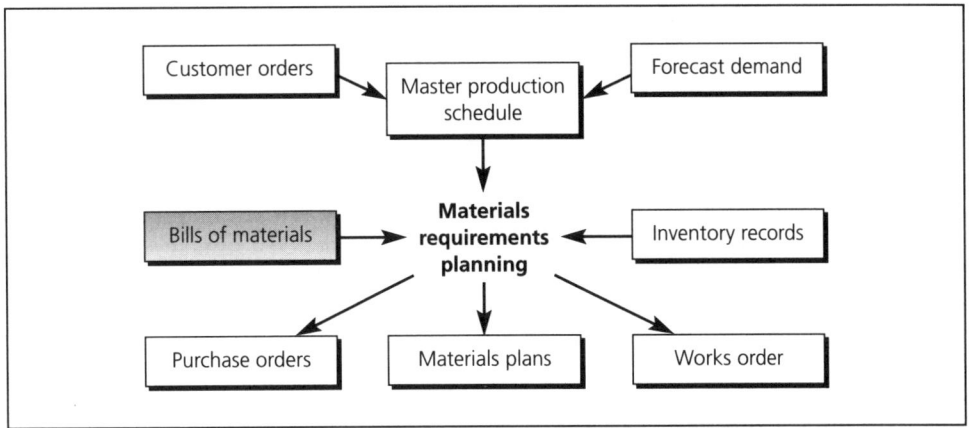

**Figure 14.8
Bills of materials in
the MRP schematic**

Levels of assembly

The product structure shows that some parts go into others which, in turn, go into others. In MRP we term these *levels of assembly*. The finished product – the boxed game – is said to be at level 0. The parts and sub-assemblies that go into the boxed game are at level 1, the parts that go into the sub-assemblies are at level 2, and so on.

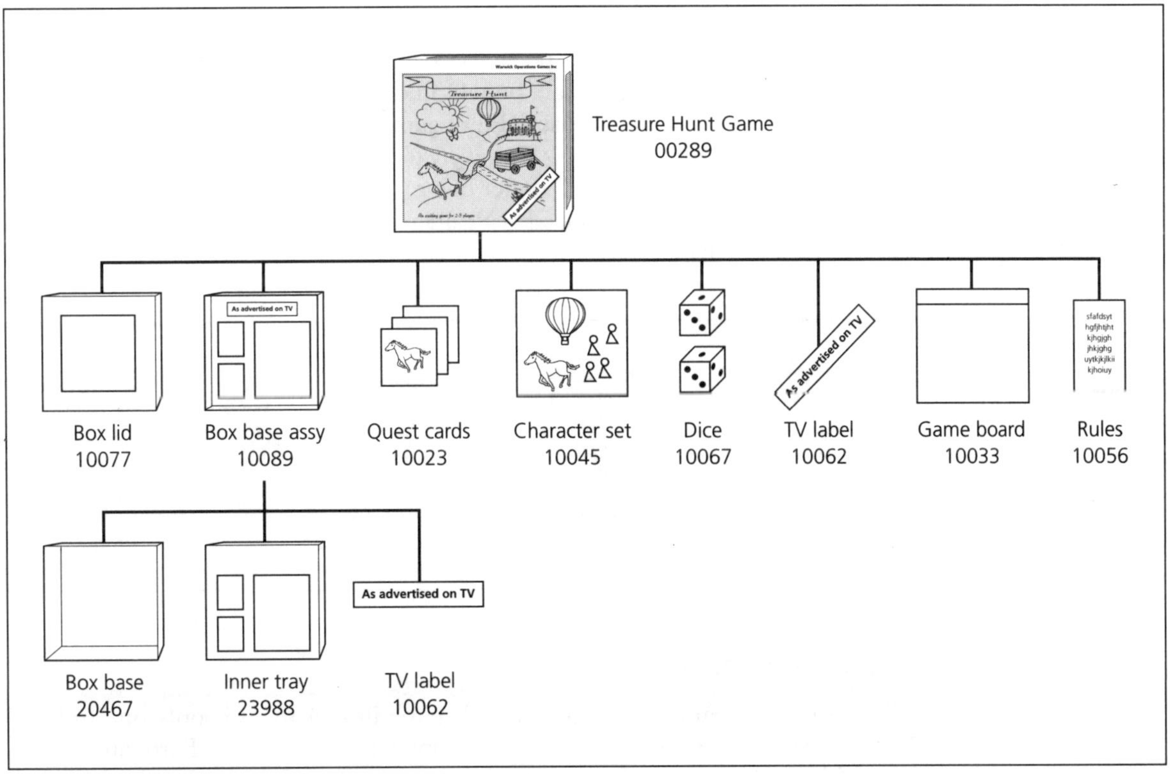

Figure 14.9 Product structure for the Treasure Hunt game

Features of MRP to note

There are several features of this product structure and of MRP generally that should be noted at this time.

● *Multiples* of some parts are required; this means that MRP has to know the required number of each part to be able to multiply up the requirements.
● The same part (the TV label, part number 10062) may be used in different parts of the product structure. In this example, the label is needed to make the box base assembly and also to complete the Treasure Hunt game. This means that MRP has to cope with this commonality of parts and, at some stage, aggregate the requirements to check how many labels in total are required.
● The product structure stops when it gets down to parts that are not made by this business; for example, another operation makes and supplies the plastic inner trays. This supplier needs to know the product structure for the trays – the weight of plastic granules and the colour of plastic which is required – but the game manufacturer's MRP system treats the plastic tray as a single, bought-in item. Its product structure is not relevant to the in-house MRP.

The 'shape' of the product structure

The nature of the product structure is closely related to the design of the product. This is reflected in the 'shape' of the product structure. The shape is partly determined by the number of components and parts used at each level – the more used, the wider the shape. Therefore, standardizing components to reduce variety slims the shape of the product structure. Shape is also determined by the amount of the item made in house. If most of the parts are bought in complete, with only assembly occurring in house, such as with the Treasure Hunt game, then the resulting product structure is very shallow, with few levels. However, if all the components are made from raw materials and then assembled all under one roof, the resulting product structure is very deep. There are some recognized typical shapes of product structure – 'A', 'T', 'V' and 'X' (*see* Fig. 14.10).

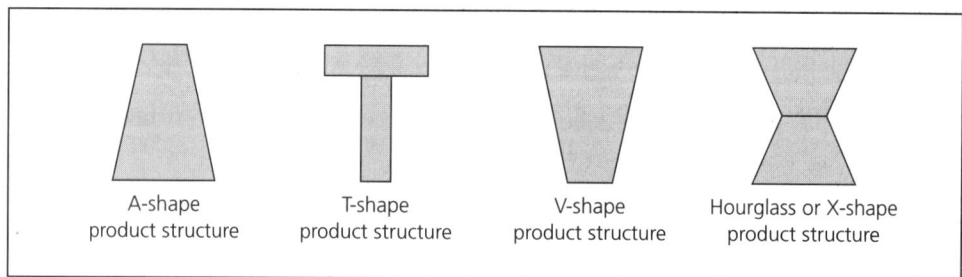

Figure 14.10 Different shapes of product structure

| A-shape product structure | T-shape product structure | V-shape product structure | Hourglass or X-shape product structure |

'A'-shape product structures

The Treasure Hunt game has a shallow 'A' shape in that there is only one finished product into which go a greater number of components. The Henry Ford 'any colour, so long as it's black' approach to automotive manufacture offered a standard product with no customization. This standard product was made from a wide range of materials but resulted in a very small number of finished products. The product structure for this would therefore have been an 'A' shape. The implications of an 'A'-shape structure are that the business only has a limited product range to offer the customer. However, because there is little variety, the volumes of standardized production can give some economies of scale. Such products can also be made for stock, therefore the operation can be planned smoothly, rather than having to chase demand.

'T'-shape product structures

A 'T'-shape product structure is typical of operations that have a small number of raw materials and a relatively standard process but they produce a very wide range of highly customized end products: an example of this is a label manufacturer producing personal name and address labels. Because the final part of the process is highly customized, it must therefore be performed to order. The earlier processes, however, are standard and can provide some economies of scale. The operations difficulties facing a company operating with 'T' structures often relate to product flow. The part of the operation which makes to order is supplied by a continuous process. This can be difficult to manage because very different styles of operations management are required. The high-volume, low-variety part of the business is aiming for cost reduction and high utilization whereas the high-variety, customized part of the business is aiming for delivery speed and service performance.

'V'-shape product structures

Similar to a 'T' shape, but with less standardization of process, the 'V'-shape product structure is typical of the petro-chemical industry. Here a small number of raw materials are used to create a wide range of products and by-products, depending on slight changes of mix of the input materials. Operations which have these types of products are driven by customer orders. Because of their reliance on a small number of raw materials, it is critical that these are reliably supplied. Failure of supply on one material can cause disruption of service to much of the customer base.

'X'-shape product structures

Some manufacturers have standardized their designs to consist of a small number of standard modules. For example, kitchen unit manufacturers make standardized bodies to which a wide range of doors and fittings can be attached. These standard modules are represented by the cross of the X. They are combined with a customized selection of features and options, giving a wide range of finished products.

An automotive manufacturer is typical of this 'X'-shape product structure. The same chassis assemblies, transmission assemblies, braking systems and engines are now used on a wide range of vehicles. To some extent the 'X' shape provides the best of both worlds – customization and the impression of making to order at the final assembly stage, combined with the economies and stability of large-volume production in module manufacture. Companies with product structures of this shape tend to master schedule at the intersection of the X, rather than at the level of the ultimate finished product. The intersection represents a manageable number of items to plan and control.

Single-level and indented bills of materials

Referring back to the simple product structure for the board game given earlier, it clearly would not be possible to represent bills of materials in full graphical form. They would simply be too unwieldy. In sophisticated engineering environments, there may be 15 levels of assembly and 5000 different parts within a finished product. MRP systems cope with this by using *single-level bills of materials* and *indented bills of materials*.

In single-level bills of materials, the details of the relationships between parts and sub-assemblies is stored as one single level at a time. For example, the single-level bills for the board game in the example provided previously are shown in Table 14.4. Each single-level bill of materials shows only the parts that immediately go into it.

Table 14.4 Single-level bills for board game

Part number: 00289
Description: Board game
Level: 0

Level	Part number	Description	Quantity
1	10089	Box base assy	1
1	10077	Box lid	1
1	10023	Quest card set	1
1	10062	TV label	1
1	10045	Character set	1
1	10067	Die	2
1	10033	Game board	1
1	10056	Rules booklet	1

Part number: 10089
Description: Box base assy
Level: 1

Level	Part number	Description	Quantity
2	20467	Box base	1
2	10062	TV label	1
2	23988	Inner tray	1

Most MRP systems store the relationships of parts to particular assemblies in this way but they also usually have the capability of presenting them in the form of an *indented bill of materials* to show several levels at the same time. Table 14.5 shows the whole indented bill of materials for the board game. The term 'indented' refers to the indentation of the level of assembly, shown in the left-hand column.

Table 14.5 Indented bill of materials for board game

Part number: 00289
Description: Board game
Level: 0

Level	Part number	Description	Quantity
0	00289	Board game	1
.1	10077	Box lid	1
.1	10089	Box base assy	1
..2	20467	Box base	1
..2	10062	TV label	1
..2	23988	Inner tray	1
.1	10023	Quest cards set	1
.1	10045	Character set	1
.1	10067	Die	2
.1	10062	TV label	1
.1	10033	Game board	1
.1	10056	Rules	1

STAEDTLER: MANUFACTURING AND THE USE OF MRP[5]

Staedtler is one of the world's premier manufacturers and suppliers of writing instruments with an annual turnover in the region of over R1,5 billion, and employing almost 4000 people. The Staedtler range extends from standard, high-volume consumer products such as pens, pencils, crayons and erasers, to highly specialized items designed for specific technical applications and for professional users. As the range has expanded, Staedtler has found that it can achieve very high-quality production by careful selection of raw materials, and by using the latest precision manufacturing techniques. The technologies employed include wood and graphite processing, injection moulding and extrusion of plastics, and the fine engineering of metals. Modern automated assembly machines allow the low-cost mass-production of volume products such as ball-point pens.

In managing the production of its complex range of over 6000 products, Staedtler has been aided by the use of a well-tried MRP system. While some items, such as standard pencils, have a bill of materials with only a few levels, some of the more involved products require a breakdown of up to seven levels.

An example of a typical Staedtler bill of materials is shown in Table 14.6. This illustrates the different levels of production involved in manufacturing a '110-HB Tradition Pencil in Dozen Box' (level 0). The top level on the bill (shown as .1) gives all the items involved in the final packaging, including the finished pencil itself – coded FTRAD. The next levels in the bill are all required in the production of pencils themselves, with level 2 being the materials required to label the pencils with the Staedtler name and the paint for the dipping to give the ▶

Table 14.6 The bill of materials for Staedtler's 'Tradition Pencil in Dozen Box'

Indented explosion		Sales unit	Parent/Sales number	Parent description
		GS	110-HB	Tradition pencil in dozen box

Production level	Component quantity	Component unit	Component number	Component description
.1	12.000000	PC	V12TI	Tradition inners
.1	0.000600	PC	V12TF	Tradition shrinkwrap
.1	0.050000	PC	V12C	Tradition carton
.1	1.000000	GS	FTRAD	Pre-packing tradition pencils
..2	0.007000	KG	DLW	White dip lacquer
..2	0.020000	KG	DLB	Black dip lacquer
..2	0.023000	PC	GFT	Tradition gold foil
..2	1.000000	GS	PTRAD	Pre-finishing tradition pencils
...3	0.100000	KG	PLR	Red polishing lacquer
...3	0.030000	KG	SLB	Black stripe lacquer
...3	1.000000	GS	RTRAD	Pre-polishing tradition pencils
....4	0.050000	PC	CCP2	Wood slats – CCP
....4	0.000600	KG	RASKG	Wood glue
....4	1.000000	GS	STRAD	Tradition pencil slips

Units: PC = Suppliers' unit
KG = Kilogram
GS = Gross of pencils

Source: Reproduced by kind permission of Staedtler (UK) Ltd

traditional 'dipped end' on the end of the pencil. At level 3 are the lacquers and paints required to coat the basic pencil and finally level 4 details the raw materials, slats of wood, pencil lead slips, and glue which are used in the initial production of the pencil.

The bills of materials for every end product are stored on the MRP system, as well as routing and standard times for the products through each manufacturing and assembly process. An inventory file is kept for every end item, at every level. The master production schedule is initially analysed to ensure that the weekly loadings on each work centre are realistic, and then the full MRP output is created, which schedules all the production requirements at each level. Once a production order has been completed and booked back on to the system, the inventory levels of all items mentioned on the bill of materials are deducted accordingly. The production control staff at Staedtler have recognized that the key to running a successful MRP operation is to have simple, user-friendly systems. This will be their highest priority when they come to design and specify improvements to the system in order that the operations remain efficient, and the data accurate. ∎

Planning bills of materials

Because each end product has its own, often large and detailed, bill of materials, it can become unwieldy to use these detailed bills for planning in the medium to long term. Instead, a smaller number of bills that represent an average product are used. For example, a particular model of car might have two-, three-, four- or five-door choices available. When planning across all models of cars made, the master production scheduler may use a 'super-bill' – a type of planning bill of materials – which lists the average numbers of components across a family of products. The average number of doors may be 3.5; obviously, no car of any model is made with 3.5 doors. However, the purpose of the planning bill is to allow longer-term forward planning to give a rough idea of how many doors (and other items) may be required in the future.

Inventory records

The bill of materials file therefore provides MRP with the base data on the ingredients or structure of products. Rather than simply take these ingredients and multiply them up in line with demand to determine the total materials requirements, MRP recognizes that some of the required items may already be in stock. This stock may be in the form of finished goods, work-in-progress or raw materials. It is necessary, starting at level 0 of each bill, to check how much inventory is available of each finished product, sub-assembly and component, then to calculate what is termed the 'net' requirements – the extra requirements needed to supplement the inventory so that demand can be met. To do this, MRP requires that inventory records are kept (*see* Fig. 14.11).

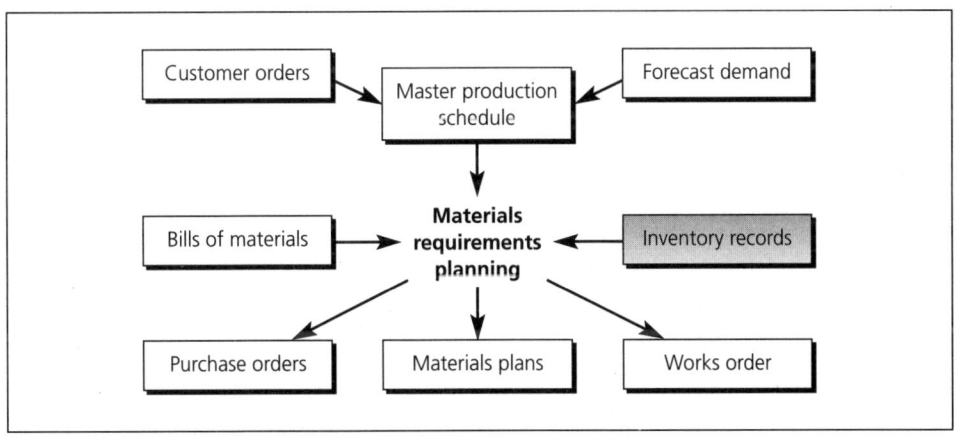

Figure 14.11 Inventory records in the MRP schematic

There are three main files kept in MRP systems that help to manage inventory. These are:

- the item master file
- the transaction file
- the location file.

The item master file

The key to all inventory records is usually a part number. Each part used in a manufacturing business has to be recognizable by one standard identification so that there is no confusion between people buying and supplying the part or using the part in the manufacturing process. Most manufacturers therefore assign a number to each part. Part numbers might be totally numeric or may be an alphanumeric combination of letters and numbers.

In addition to a part number, the item master file contains all the stable data on a part; this is often a computer screen of fields including the part description, the unit of measure (flour may be recorded in tonnes, washers in 1000s and engines in single discrete units) and a standard cost. Interestingly, the lead time to buy or make the part is often treated as fixed data by virtue of the fact that it is located in the item master file. Many firms fail to monitor adequately the lead time of an item. This may vary between suppliers and change at different times of the year and according to supply market conditions. Instead, many companies still err on the side of caution, entering the maximum lead time that is likely ever to occur. This means that the gap between real lead times and planned lead times in many manufacturing businesses can be quite large.

The transaction file

In order to take inventory levels into account, MRP needs to know the level of inventory of each part. The transaction file keeps a record of receipts into stock, issues from stock and a running balance. In the past, these transactions were entered on to the computer overnight or at periodic intervals; this caused problems in that the information was always lagging behind reality. MRP systems today run their inventory in real time. This means the transaction file is updated at the time a receipt or issue occurs. This has implications for the number of computer terminals required by the operation, their location and the number of people trained to use them. The benefits of real-time processing, however, far outweigh any increased cost of equipment and training.

The location file

The stores, or inventory points in the operation, need to be managed. Some stores operate a fixed location system so that a particular part can always be found at a particular location. However, companies that operate with a wide and changing range of inventory items find this system inefficient. Instead they operate a random location system where parts are located in the nearest available place. A random location system requires careful control as the same item may be kept in several different locations at any one time. In addition to being more efficient on space utilization, a random location system can make it easier to ensure that stock physically 'turns over' by making a first-in-first-out principle easy to implement. When the computer generates picking lists instructing store operators (mechanical or human) to pick items from stock, it can ensure that the oldest stock is picked by sending the picker to the longest standing location for an item.

Accuracy of the inventory files

As with the management of bills of materials, it is critical to an MRP system that inventory records are accurate and up to date. Mistakes do occur and inventory is pilfered or perishes, so inventory records will never reflect exactly what is physically in stock in a business. Because of this, *perpetual physical inventory* checking (PPI) is performed in many companies.

PPI involves checking that the physical inventory level and location of a part matches the computer record. Where a difference is confirmed, the computer record is updated to reflect reality. Before the PPI process was well established in companies, stock was only checked annually to comply with end-of-year accounting procedures. This meant that, particularly towards the end of the year, there were frequent examples of stores pickers finding empty stores containers while the computer was instructing them to pick items for production. The implications of inaccuracy of inventory records are shortages which lead to the rescheduling of production with resulting inefficiencies and, possibly, failure to satisfy a customer order.

MRP CALCULATIONS

So far we have examined all the information which is needed for operations to start the planning process. Although this information is a necessary prerequisite to MRP, it is not the 'heart' of the procedure. At its core MRP is a systematic process of taking this planning information and calculating the volume and timing requirements which will satisfy demand. This next part of the chapter examines the way these calculations are performed, starting with what is probably the most important step, the *netting process*.

The MRP netting process

Figure 14.12 shows simplistically the process that MRP performs to calculate the *volumes* of materials required. MRP takes the master production schedule (the planned production schedule for each end item) and 'explodes', or examines the implications of, this schedule through the single-level bill of materials, checking how many sub-assemblies and parts are required. Before moving down the product structure to the next level, MRP checks how many of the required parts are already available in stock. It then generates 'works orders', or requests, for the net requirements of items that are made in house. These net requirements then form the schedule which is exploded through the single-level bill of materials at the next level down. Again, available inventory of those items is checked; works orders are generated for the net requirements that are made in house, as are purchase orders for the net requirements of items that are bought from suppliers. This process continues until the bottom of the product structure is reached.

Figure 14.13 uses our example of the board game to describe this part of the MRP process. Just considering the volume requirements at this moment, a top-level requirement for ten board games does not automatically generate a works order to build ten.

First the available inventory is checked. Because three board games are in stock, a works order to build seven board games is issued. MRP then checks the top, single-level bill for the board game and finds, among other parts, that one box base assembly – 10089 – is required per board game. MRP then checks how many box base assemblies are in stock and, finding two, generates a works order for the net requirement of five. Next the single-level bill of materials for the box base assembly is checked. This shows that one box base (20467), one inner tray (23988) and one TV

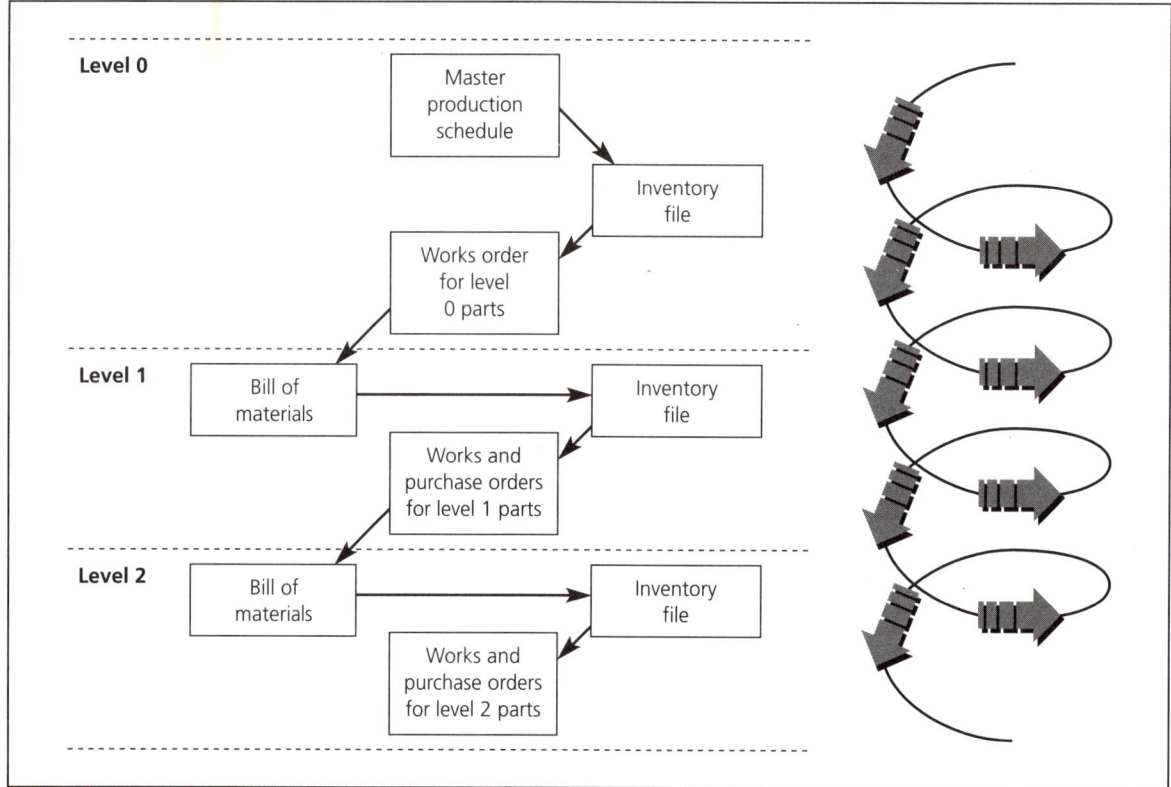

Figure 14.12 The MRP netting process

label (10062) are required for each box base assembly. Again, the inventory is checked and, as there is one box base in stock, an order to purchase four more is generated. As there are more than enough TV labels in stock, there is no need to raise a replenishment instruction.

Back scheduling

In addition to calculating the volume of materials required, MRP also considers *when* each of these parts is required, that is the timing and scheduling of materials. It does this by a process called *back-scheduling* which takes into account the *lead time* at each level of assembly. Again, using the example of the board game, assume that ten board games are required to be finished by a notional planning day we will term day 35. To determine when we need to start work on all the parts that make up the game, we need to know how much time to allow for each part of the process. These times are called lead times and are stored in MRP files for each part (*see* Table 14.7).

Now examine the Gantt chart shown in Fig. 14.14 which includes the lead time information. If it takes two days to carry out the final assembly, the sub-assemblies must be complete and available on the shop floor at the beginning of day 33. In this way the programme is worked backwards to determine the tasks which have to be performed and the purchase orders which have to be placed. It can be seen in the

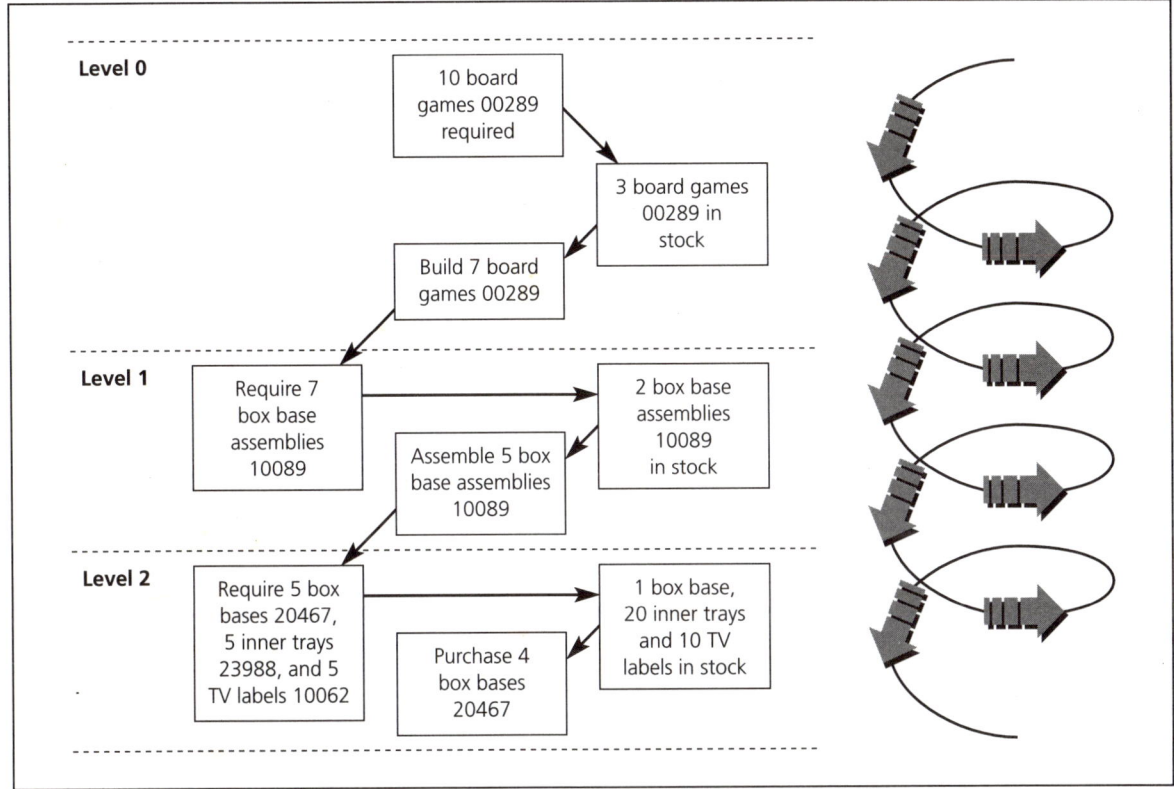

Figure 14.13 Example of MRP netting process

example that to deliver the required board games on time, the inner trays must be purchased now.

Given the lead times in Table 14.7 and the inventory levels shown in Table 14.8, the MRP records shown in Fig. 14.15 can be derived.

The gross requirements of each part at level 1 can be derived directly from the planned order release of the whole game. So at day 33, seven box lids, box base assemblies, TV labels, etc. are needed. Back scheduling by the lead times for each level-1 item gives their planned order release time. Similarly, the level-2 items which are needed to produce the box base assembly are subject to the same procedure. Note that the TV label is both a level-1 and a level-2 item and has gross requirements originating from the planned order releases of both the game and the box base assembly.

In reality, some items can only be acquired in minimum size batches. Because of the time taken and costs involved to set up a machine, it may be seen to be efficient to run it for a reasonable size batch. Similarly, some purchased items are bought in pack sizes or in order quantities of a size large enough to gain a volume discount, even though this means that more are brought than are needed. Another reason why some operations make or buy more than they immediately need is to give them a margin of safety in the event of unplanned variations in either demand or supply. All these issues of batch sizes and safety stocks were dealt with in Chapter 12.

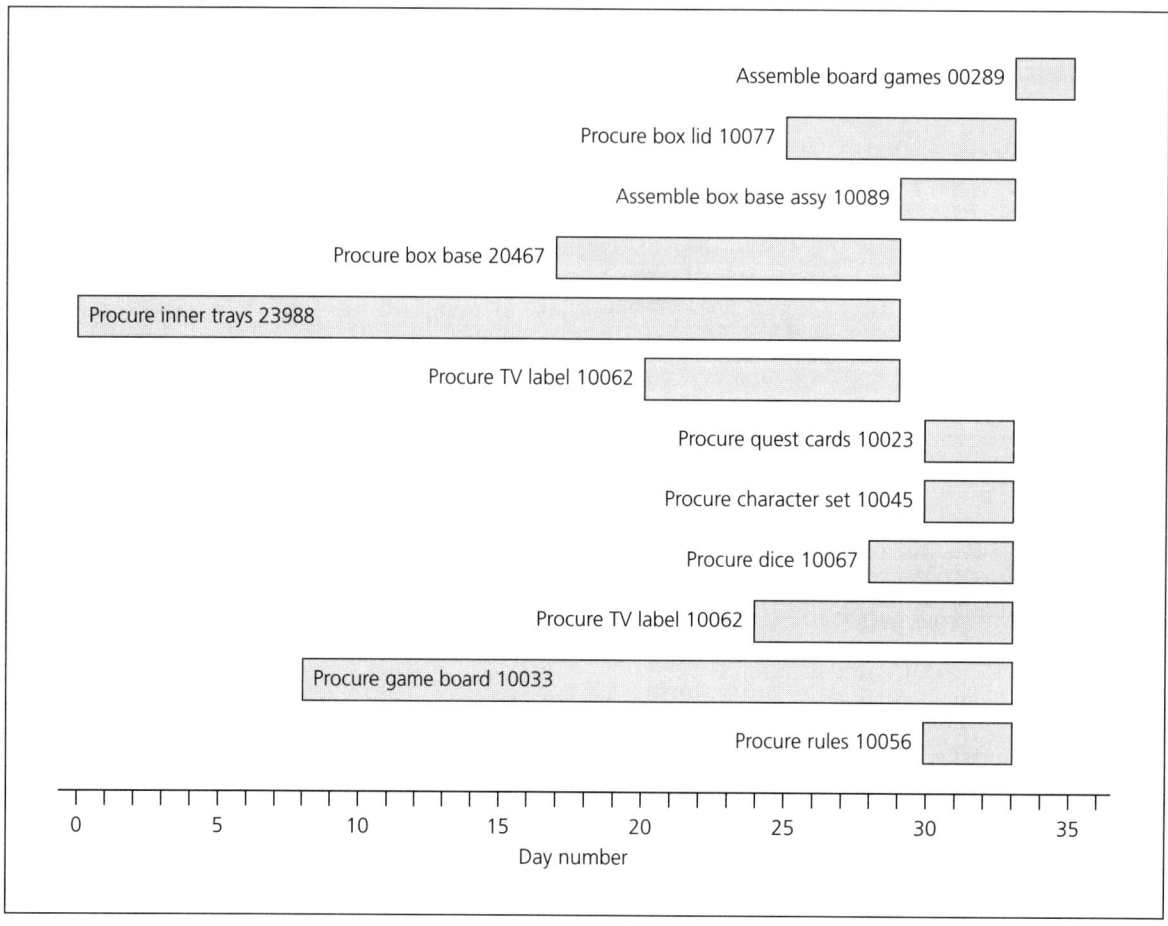

Figure 14.14 Back-scheduling of requirements in MRP: back-scheduled Gantt chart for board game manufacture

Table 14.7 Back-scheduling of requirements in MRP

Part no.	Description	Lead time (in days)
00289	Board game	2
10077	Box lid	8
10089	Box base assy	4
20467	Box base	12
23988	Inner tray	29
10062	TV label	8
10023	Quest cards set	3
10045	Character set	3
10067	Die	5
10033	Game board	25
10056	Rules	3

Table 14.8 Inventory of parts for board game

Part no.	Description	Inventory
00289	Board game	3
10077	Box lid	4
10089	Box base assy	2
20467	Box base	1
23988	Inner tray	20
10062	TV label	10
10023	Quest cards set	0
10045	Character set	0
10067	Die	0
10033	Game board	0
10056	Rules	0

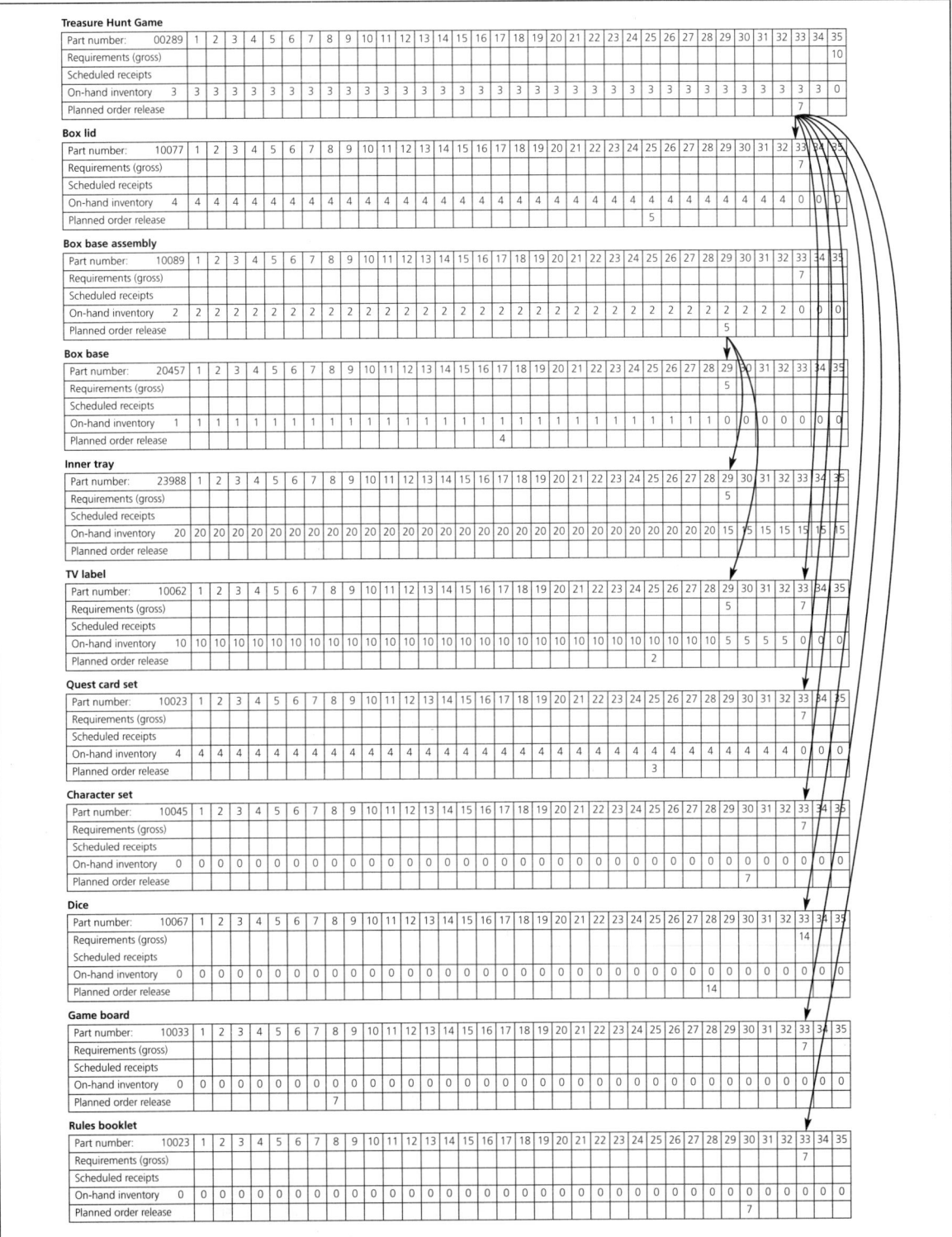

Figure 14.15 Extract of the MRP records for the board game

Closed-loop MRP

When MRP was originally used in manufacturing, materials plans were launched at the beginning of the week, then a complete replanning exercise took place the following week, launching a new set of plans. This process was repeated weekly but there was no feedback loop to say whether a plan was achievable and whether it had actually been achieved. MRP systems which started to include feedback loops became known as 'closed-loop MRP'.

Closing the planning loop in MRP systems involves checking production plans against available resources. Therefore capacity is checked throughout the process and if the proposed plans are not achievable at any level they are revised (*see* Fig. 14.16). All but the simplest MRP systems are now closed-loop systems. They use three planning routines to check production plans against the operation's resources:

- resource requirements plans
- rough-cut capacity plans
- capacity requirements plans.

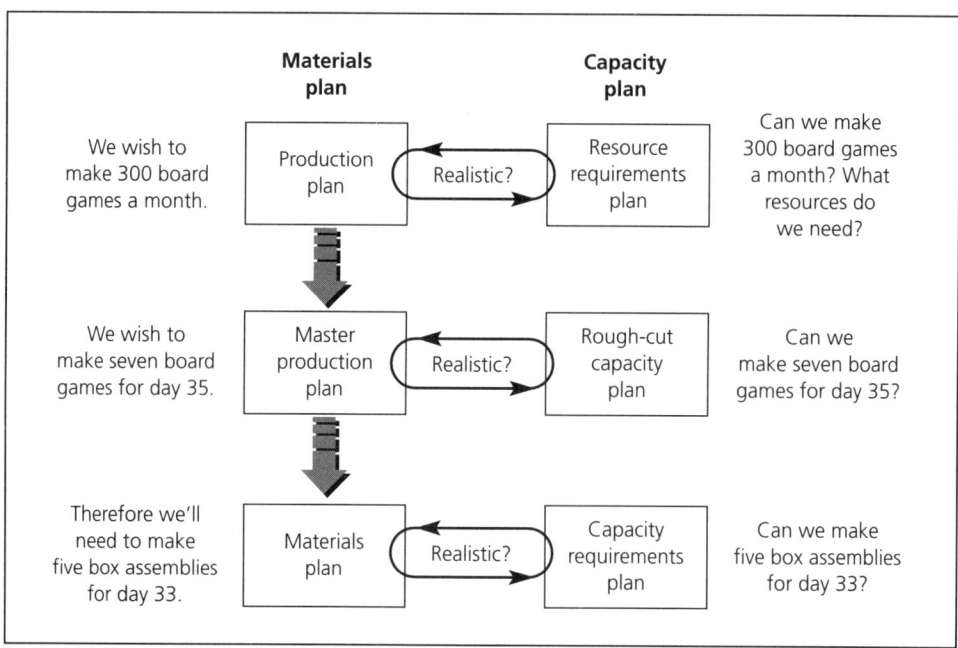

Figure 14.16
Closed-loop MRP

Resource requirements plans (RRP)

Resource requirements plans are static level plans which involve looking forward in the long term to predict the requirements for large structural parts of the operation, such as the numbers of, locations of, and sizes of new plants. Because they are attempts at facilitating the long-term production plan by making arrangements to have the required resources available, they are sometimes termed 'infinite capacity plans' as they assume an almost infinite ability to step up production if demand warrants it.

Rough-cut capacity plans (RCCP)

In the medium to short term, master production schedules have to use capacity which is available. The feedback loop at this level checks the MPS against known capacity bottle-necks and key resources only. If the MPS is not achievable, it should be adjusted. So, unlike the RRP, rough-cut capacity plans are 'finite capacity plans' because they have to operate within certain constraints.

Capacity requirements plans (CRP)

On a day-to-day basis, works orders intended to be issued from the MRP will often have a variable effect on the loading of particular machines or individual workers. Capacity requirements plans (CRP) project this load ahead. They are 'infinite capacity plans' insomuch as they do not take the capacity constraints of each machine or work area into account. If this load is lumpy it may be smoothed by replanning to a finite capacity, or by allocating temporary resources to the area.

The closed-loop system of MRP can be further developed to drive very short-term plans, as is shown in Fig. 14.17.

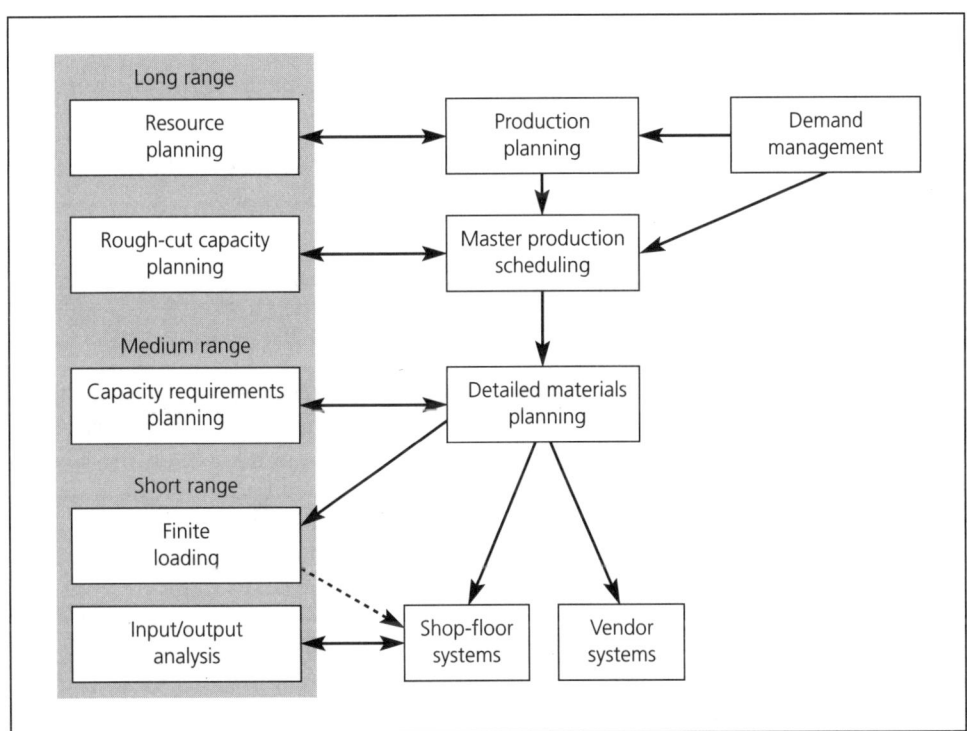

Figure 14.17 Closed-loop MRP
Source: Vollmann, T.E., Berry W.L. and Whybark, D.C. (1992) Manufacturing Planning and Control Systems (3rd edn), Irwin, p 122

Manufacturing resource planning (MRP II)

MRP I was essentially aimed at the planning and control of production and inventory in manufacturing businesses. However, the concepts have been extended to other areas of the business. This extended concept was termed MRP II by Oliver Wight, one of the founders of MRP. Wight[6] defined MRP II as:

'a game plan for planning and monitoring all the resources of a manufacturing company: manufacturing, marketing, finance and engineering. Technically it involves using the closed-loop MRP system to generate the financial figures.'

Without MRP II integrated systems, separate databases are held by different functions. For example, a product structure or bill of materials is held in engineering and also in materials management. If engineering changes are made to the design of products, both databases have to be updated. It is difficult to keep both databases entirely identical and discrepancies between them cause problems, which often are not apparent until a member of staff is supplied with the wrong parts to manufacture the product. Similarly, cost information from finance and accounting, which is used to perform management accounting tasks such as variance analysis against standard costs, needs to be reconciled with changes made elsewhere in the operation, such as changes in inventory holding or process methods.

MRP II is based on one integrated system containing a database which is accessed and used by the whole company according to individual functional requirements. However, despite its dependence on the information technologies which allow such integration, MRP II still depends on people-based decision making. Levy[7] described this well:

'Until we can provide genuine Artificial Intelligence there is no way in which a computer can optimize the myriad variables in manufacturing and substitute for the intelligence, intuition and local knowledge of committed factory personnel.'

In other words, the closing of the loop in MRP systems is still largely down to people taking decisions and corrective action on a minute-by-minute basis.

OPTIMIZED PRODUCTION TECHNOLOGY (OPT)

Other concepts and systems have been developed which also recognize the importance of planning to known capacity constraints, rather than overloading part of the production system and failing to meet the plan. Perhaps the best known is the Theory of Constraints (TOC) which has been developed to focus attention on the capacity constraint or bottle-neck parts of the operation. By identifying the location of constraints, working to remove them, then looking for the next constraint, an operation is always focusing on the part that critically determines the pace of output.

The approach which uses this idea is called *optimized production technology* (OPT). Its development and the marketing of it as a proprietary software product was originated by Eliyahu Goldratt.[8]

OPT is a computer-based technique and tool which helps to schedule production systems to the pace dictated by the most heavily loaded resources, i.e. bottle-necks. If the rate of activity in any part of the system exceeds that of the bottle-neck, then items are being produced that cannot be used. If the rate of working falls below the pace at the bottle-neck, then the entire system is under-utilized.

There are principles underlying optimized production technology which demonstrate this focus on bottle-necks.

OPT principles

1 Balance flow, not capacity.
2 The level of utilization of a non bottle-neck is determined by some other constraint in the system, not by its own capacity.
3 Utilization and activation of a resource are not the same.
4 An hour lost at a bottle-neck is an hour lost for ever out of the entire system.
5 An hour saved at a non bottle-neck is a mirage.
6 Bottle-necks govern both throughput and inventory in the system.
7 The transfer batch may not, and many times should not, equal the process batch.
8 The process batch should be variable, not fixed.
9 Lead times are the result of a schedule and cannot be predetermined.
10 Schedules should be established by looking at all constraints simultaneously.

OPT should not be viewed as a replacement to MRP; nor is it impossible to run both together. However, the philosophical underpinnings of OPT outlined above do show that it could conflict with the way that many businesses run their MRP systems in practice. While MRP as a concept does not prescribe fixed lead times or fixed batch sizes, many operations run MRP with these elements fixed for simplicity. However, as demand, supply, and the process within a manufacturing operation all present unplanned variations on a dynamic basis, bottle-necks therefore are dynamic, changing their location and their severity. For this reason, lead times are rarely constant over time. Similarly, if bottle-necks determine schedules, batch sizes may alter throughout the plant depending on whether a work centre is a bottle-neck or not.

OPT uses the terminology of 'drum, buffer, rope' to explain its planning and control approach. Using OPT the bottle-neck work centre becomes a '*drum*', beating the pace for the rest of the factory. This 'drum beat' determines the schedules in non bottle-neck areas, pulling through work (the *rope*) in line with the bottle-neck capacity, not the capacity of the work centre. A bottle-neck should never be allowed to be working at less than full capacity; therefore, inventory *buffers* should be placed before it to ensure it never runs out of work.

Some of the arguments for using OPT in MRP environments are that it helps to focus on critical constraints and that it reduces the need for very detailed planning of non bottle-neck areas, therefore cutting down computational time in MRP.

available and an annual production output in excess of 50 000 fittings. Each fitting comprises an average of 50 components. A further problem is that order quantities per each discrete model are quite small, thus leading to works orders of typically less than 100 per order, with very little predictability of demand. The company has therefore chosen to operate in an assemble-to-order manner, given its inability to   forecast demand.

'The production process is quite simple because, given an existing design, we only assemble the finished product before testing and then packing the product for shipment. All component manufacture is done by the, over 100, suppliers contracted to our firm. Since we cannot test and therefore cannot ship an order if even one component is short, a great deal of emphasis has to be placed on getting the right material, in the exact quantities required, into our plant at exactly the right time.

'A great deal of disruption has arisen in the past because work would have to halt on a particular works order due to component shortages. The assembly line would then have to be changed over to replace the original works order with some other order for which, hopefully, material is available. Stock-outs have generally lengthened lead times, increased work-in-progress and lowered labour efficiencies. Maintaining high stock levels has not been an option open to us, due to the low profit margins associated with this business, the high South African interest rates and the high degree of obsolescence.

'An MRP system is now used for resource scheduling in order to optimize this rather complex, batch assembly environment. The MRP system, operating on a midi-computer, has been set up with only two levels on the bills of materials. These levels are 'bought-out components' and 'complete assemblies'. This is done because the assembly time is so low that it is measured in minutes per fitting.

Work-in-progress is therefore rarely more than half a day's output, so no effort is made to attain fine control over it.

'The master production schedule is based on actual customer orders and on an ex-works delivery lead time of four to six weeks. The first two weeks (working back from the delivery date) are fixed, in other words no changes are permitted. The next two weeks are flexible in terms of mix but not volume. The remaining two weeks of the plan are flexible on both mix and volume. Components are purchased based on an explosion of the bills of materials and an aggregation of dependent demand at component level. We are now able to provide our suppliers with a four-week window on what our requirements are likely to be. Material purchases are timed to arrive a week before they are needed, to facilitate our pre-kitting process.

'MRP is run once a week to print a list of the components for the next week's assembly line work. A key part of our strategy is a pre-kitting process that is based on this component list. We physically pick all components per works order and palletize them in works order priority sequence per the MPS. This permits us to identify and expedite any shortages before they have an impact on the line. It also allows us to make back-up plans and to test their suitability in advance. The kits are issued to the assembly line every Monday for the entire week's production.

'This has allowed us to achieve a 30 per cent reduction in stock, a 25 per cent improvement in labour productivity and a 40 per cent reduction in lead time. Our hit rate on meeting the promised order delivery date has also improved to over 90 per cent. We would not have been able to achieve this without the use of the MRP system. These results were recognized externally when the firm received the TOMA Award from the Engineering Association of South Africa in 1996, after having been nominated as a finalist in 1995.' ■

SUMMARY

■ Materials requirements planning (MRP I) systems are dependent demand systems which calculate materials requirements and production plans to satisfy known and forecasted sales orders.

■ The logic of MRP I systems has been extended to manufacturing resource planning (MRP II) which incorporates engineering, financial and marketing information in an integrated business system for manufacturing businesses.

■ Different types of businesses rely to differing extents on forecast sales, as opposed to firm orders.

■ While it is desirable that operations reduce or remove the need for forecasting, many have no alternative. Therefore, their planning and control systems depend heavily on the ability and knowledge of the forecasters.

■ The master production schedule drives any MRP system and should be a realistic, achievable plan of which end products will be made and when.

■ Bills of materials contain the ingredients or parts lists which indicate the amount and type of materials required to manufacture any part.

■ Different businesses have different shapes of product structures.

■ Inventory files contain data vital to running MRP, including a unique identification for each part, where it is located, how many are in stock and what issue and receipt transactions have occurred against any part.

■ The process of MRP explodes top-level requirements down through bills of materials, taking into account inventory and lead times at each level. MRP effectively back-schedules from due date to generate its materials plans and orders.

■ Closed-loop MRP systems contain feedback loops which ensure that checks are made against capacity to see if plans are feasible.

■ MRP II systems are a development of MRP I which integrate many processes which are related to MRP, but located outside the operations function, with the MRP system.

■ OPT systems concentrate on scheduling around bottle-necks in the manufacturing system.

Psycho Sports Ltd

Peter Townsend knew that he would have to make some decisions pretty soon. His sports goods manufacturing business, Psycho Sports, had grown so rapidly over the last two years that he would soon have to install some systematic procedures and routines to manage the business. His biggest problem was in manufacturing control. He had started making specialist high-quality table tennis bats but now made a wide range of sports products including tennis balls, darts and protective equipment for various games. Furthermore, his customers, once limited to specialist sports shops, now included some of the major sports retail chains.

'We really do have to get control of our manufacturing. I keep getting told that we need what seems to be called an MRP system. I wasn't sure what this meant and so I have bought a specialist production control book from our local bookshop and read all about MRP principles. I must admit, these academics seem to delight in making simple things complicated. And there is so much jargon associated with the technique, I feel more confused now than I did before.

'Perhaps the best way forward is for me to take a very simple example from my own production unit and see whether I can work things out manually. If I can follow the

process through on paper then I will be far better equipped to decide what kind of computer-based system we should get, if any!'

Peter decided to take as his example one of his new products: a table tennis bat marketed under the name of the 'high-resolution' bat, but known within the manufacturing unit more prosaically as Part Number 5654. Figure 14.18 shows the product structure for table tennis bat Part Number 5654.

As can be seen from Fig. 14.18, the table tennis bat is made up of two main assemblies: a handle assembly and a face assembly. In order to assemble the two main assemblies together to form the finished bat, various fixings are required, such as nails, connectors, etc.

The gross requirements for this particular bat are shown below. The bat is not due to be launched until Week 13 (it is now Week 1), and sales forecasts have been made for the first 23 weeks of sales:

Weeks 13–21 inclusive, 100 per week
Weeks 22–29 inclusive, 150 per week
Weeks 30–35 inclusive, 200 per week.

Peter also managed to obtain information on the current inventory levels of each of the parts which made up the finished bat, together with cost data and lead times.

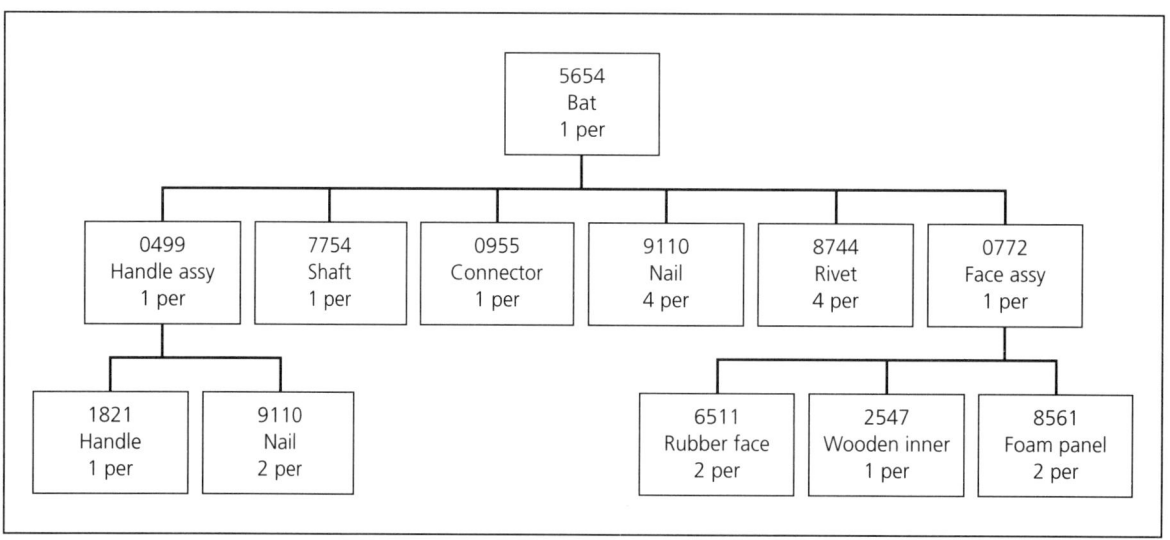

Figure 14.18 Product structure for bat 5654

Table 14.9

Part no.	Description	Inventory	EQ	LT	Std. cost
5645	Bat	0	500	2	12.00
0499	Handle assy	0	400	3	4.00
7754	Shaft	15	1000	5	1.00
0955	Connector	350	5000	4	0.02
9110	Nail	120	5000	4	0.01
8744	Rivet	3540	5000	4	0.01
0772	Face assy	0	250	4	5.00
1821	Handle	0	500	4	2.00
6511	Rubber face	0	2000	10	0.50
2547	Wooden inner	10	300	7	1.50
8561	Foam panel	0	1000	8	0.50

LT = Lead time for ordering (in weeks), EQ = Economic quantity for ordering, Std. cost = Standard cost in R.

He was surprised, however, how long it took him to obtain this information.

'It has taken me nearly two days to get hold of all the information I need. Different people held it, nowhere was it conveniently put together and sometimes not even written down. To get the inventory data I actually had to go down to the stores and count how many parts were in the boxes.'

The data Peter collected was as shown in Table 14.9.

Peter set himself six exercises which he knew he would have to master if he was to understand fully the basics of MRP.

Exercise 1

Draw up:
(a) the single-level bills of materials for each level of assembly;
(b) a complete indented bill of materials for all levels of assembly.

Exercise 2

(a) Create the materials requirements planning records for each part and sub-assembly in the bat.
(b) List any problems that the completed MRP records identify.
(c) What alternatives are there that the company could take to solve any problems? What are their relative merits?

Exercise 3

Based on the first two exercises, create another set of MRP records, this time allowing one week's safety lead time for each item: that is, ensuring the items are in stock the week prior to when they are required.

Exercise 4

Over the time period of the exercise, what effect would the imposition of a safety lead time have on average inventory value?

Exercise 5

If we decided that our first task was to reduce inventory costs by 15 per cent, what action would we recommend? What are the implications of our action?

Exercise 6

How might production in our business be smoothed? ■

Questions

1 Why did Peter have such problems getting to the relevant information?
2 Perform all the exercises which Peter set for himself. Do you think he should now fully understand MRP?

DISCUSSION QUESTIONS

1 What is the difference between MRP I and MRP II?

2 A manufacturer of defence electronic equipment uses an MRP system to control its production. At any time it has regular orders for its standard products as well as specific orders for its specially adapted products. Occasionally also, one-off orders of standard products are received from foreign customers. Part of the company's competitive strategy is to offer a service which includes a full repair, spare-parts supply, and remanufacturing service to its customers. What elements will constitute the sources of demand which it must feed into its MRP system?

3 A company makes two types of mirror. The super-mirror has a golden frame, while the basic mirror has a plain black frame. Both mirrors are the same size. As well as the frame, the standard mirror piece and a backing piece is needed to manufacture each product. Both these last two items are exactly the same for both products. The lead time to manufacture either product is two weeks, while the lead time for the frame material is one week, for the mirror material (cut to size) is three weeks, and for the backs (again cut to size) is two weeks. Each mirror needs two and a half metres of frame material. Neither product will be needed for ten weeks when there will be an order to be filled for 200 of each type of mirror. In 11 weeks a further 100 of these standard mirrors will be needed and in 12 weeks 300 of the gold-framed mirrors will be needed. The next order will be in Week 14 when, again, 200 of each mirror will be needed. Currently, there is no inventory of any of the materials on hand. Using MRP procedures derive a schedule which will meet the demand.

4 Draw up a product structure and indented bill of materials for a product described as follows. The main product A consists of one sub-assembly B and two sub-assemblies C. Sub-assembly B consists of one part D and two part Es. Sub-assembly C consists of one part E, one part F and two part Gs.

5 What different methods are there for a company to decide on how many of its parts to order at any time? What are the advantages and disadvantages of ordering whatever is required every single period?

6 What is meant by a closed-loop MRP system?

7 A company manufactures product A which is made up of one unit of B, and half a unit of C. Each unit of B is made up of one unit of D, two units of E, and one unit of F. Each unit of C needs half a unit of G and three units of H. The lead times to manufacture all these components are as follows:

A 2 weeks	E 3 weeks
B 1 week	F 1 week
C 2 weeks	G 2 weeks
D 2 weeks	H 1 week

All these parts have 20 units in stock. It is required to make 100 units of A for delivery in seven weeks' time.

(a) Draw up a product structure and indented bill of materials for the product.
(b) Draw up a gross materials requirements plan for the manufacturer of the product.
(c) Construct a net materials requirements plan for the manufacturer of the product.

NOTES ON CHAPTER

1 Wight, O. (1984) *Manufacturing Resource Planning: MRP II*, Oliver Wight Ltd.
2 Orlicky, J. (1975) *Materials Requirements Planning*, McGraw-Hill.
3 Kotler, P. (1991) *Marketing Management*, Prentice Hall.
4 Source: 'A Matter of Life and Death', *Manufacturing Today* (1993) Published by MSPL, an ICL company which installed Racal Recorders' MRP II system.
5 Source: Discussions with company staff at Staedtler.
6 Wight, O. (1984), *op. cit.*
7 Levy (1986).
8 Goldratt, E.M. and Cox, J. (1986) *The Goal*, North River Press.

SELECTED FURTHER READINGS

Berry, W.L. (1972) 'Lots Sizing Procedures for Requirements Planning Systems: A Framework for Analysis', *Production and Inventory Management*, Vol 13, 2nd quarter.

Berry, W.L. and Mabert, V.A. (1992) 'ITEC: An Integrated Manufacturing Instructional Exercise', *International Journal of Operations and Production Management*, Vol 12, No 6.

Burns, O.M., Turnipseed, D. and Riggs, W.E. (1991) 'Critical Success Factors in Manufacturing Resource Planning Implementation', *International Journal of Operations and Production Management*, Vol 11, No 4.

Buxey, G. (1993) 'Production Planning and Scheduling for Seasonal Demand', *International Journal of Operations and Production Management*, Vol 13, No 7.

Miller, J.G. and Sprague, L.G. (1975) 'Behind the Growth in Materials Requirements Planning', *Harvard Business Review*, Vol 53, No 5.

Orlicky, J. (1975) *Material Requirements Planning*, McGraw-Hill.

Primrose, P.L. (1990) 'Selecting and Evaluating Cost Effective MRP and MRP II', *International Journal of Operations and Production Management*, Vol 10, No 1.

Shah, S. (1991) 'Optimum Order Cycles in MRP Form a Geometric Progression', *International Journal of Operations and Production Management*, Vol 11, No 5.

Steinberg, E.E., Khumawala, B. and Scamell, R. (1982) 'Requirements Planning Systems in the Health Care Environment', *Journal of Operations Management*, Vol 2, No 4.

Vollmann, T.E., Berry, L. and Whybark, D.C. (1989) *Manufacturing Planning and Control Systems* (3rd edn), Irwin.

White, E.M., Anderson, J.C., Schroeder, R.G. and Tupy, S.E. (1982) 'A Study of the MRP Implementation Process', *Journal of Operations Management*, Vol 2, No 3.

Wight, O.W. (1982) *The Executive's Guide to Successful MRP II*, Prentice Hall.

JUST-IN-TIME PLANNING AND CONTROL

INTRODUCTION

In this chapter, we will examine just-in-time (JIT) both as a philosophy, and as a method of operations planning and control. This means that, for much of the chapter, we will take a relatively focused view of JIT, concentrating on its planning and control aspects, although in practice it has much wider implications for improving operations performance. In fact many of the wider implications of JIT underlie much of the material presented in this book. The JIT principles which were a radical departure from traditional operations practice in the early 1980s have now themselves become the accepted wisdom in operations management. In effect the chapter addresses the question: 'What is JIT, and how does it impact on operations planning and control?' Figure 15.1 illustrates the concept of JIT planning and control.

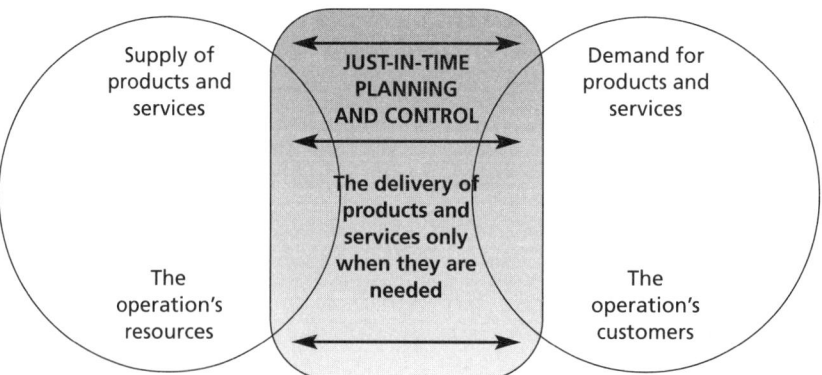

Figure 15.1 Just-in-time planning and control aims to meet demand instantaneously, with perfect quality and no waste

WHAT IS JUST-IN-TIME?

At its most basic, JIT can be taken literally – JIT means producing goods and services exactly when they are needed – not before they are needed so that they wait as inventory, nor after they are needed so that it is the customers who have to wait. In addition to this 'time-based' element of JIT we can add the requirements of quality and efficiency. A definition of JIT can then be taken as follows:

JIT aims to meet demand instantaneously, with perfect quality and no waste.[1]

Alternatively, for those who prefer a fuller definition:

Just-in-time (JIT) is a disciplined approach to improving overall productivity and eliminating waste. It provides for the cost-effective production and delivery of only the necessary quantity of parts at the right quality, at the right time and place, while using a minimum amount of facilities, equipment, materials and human resources. JIT is dependent on the balance between the supplier's flexibility and the user's flexibility. It is accomplished through the application of elements which require total employee involvement and teamwork. A key philosophy of JIT is simplification.[2]

Remember though that the first definition is a statement of *aims*, it does not imply that, by adopting a JIT approach to organizing operations, these aims will be achieved immediately. Rather, it describes a state which a JIT approach helps to work towards. No definition of JIT fully conveys its full implications for operations practice, however. This is why so many different phrases and terms exist to describe JIT-type approaches. For example:

- continuous flow manufacture
- high value-added manufacture
- stockless production
- low-inventory production

529

● fast-throughput manufacturing
● lean manufacturing
● enforced problem solving
● short cycle time manufacturing.

The best way to understand how a JIT approach differs from more traditional approaches to manufacturing is to contrast the two simple manufacturing systems in Fig. 15.2. The traditional approach assumes that each stage in the manufacturing process will place the parts it produces in an inventory which 'buffers' that stage from the next one downstream in the total process. The next stage down will then (eventually) take the part from the inventory, process it, and pass it through to the next buffer inventory. These buffers are not there accidentally; they are there to insulate each stage from its neighbours. The buffers make each stage relatively independent so that if, for example, stage A stops producing for some reason (say a machine breakdown or parts shortage), stage B can continue working, at least for a time. Stage C can continue working for even longer because it has the contents of two buffers to get through before it runs out of work. The larger is the buffer inventory, the greater is the degree of insulation between the stages, and therefore the less is the disruption caused when a problem occurs. This insulation has to be paid for in terms of inventory (working capital) and slow throughput times (slow customer response) but it does allow each stage to operate in an uninterrupted, and therefore efficient, manner.

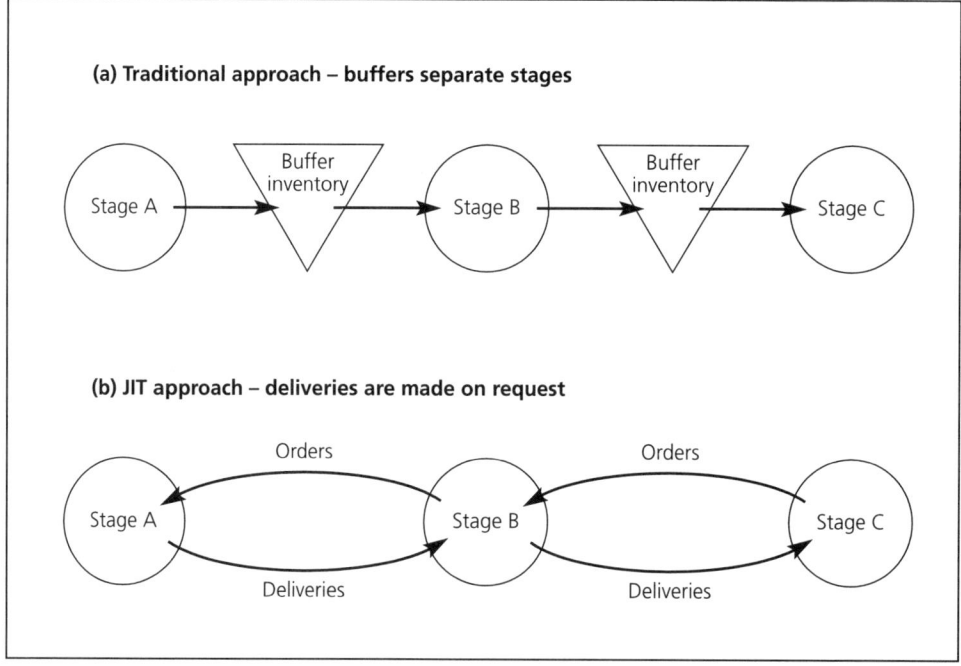

**Figure 15.2
(a) Traditional and
(b) JIT flow
between stages**

The main argument against this traditional approach lies in the very conditions it seeks to promote, namely the insulation of the stages from one another. When a problem occurs at one stage, the problem will not immediately be apparent elsewhere in the system. The responsibility for solving the problem will be centred largely on the staff within that stage and the consequences of the problem will be prevented from spreading to the whole system. However, contrast this position with that illustrated in the bottom system in Fig. 15.2, which is an extreme form of JIT. Here parts are produced and then passed directly to the next stage 'just-in-time' for them to be processed. Problems at any stage have a very different effect in such a system. For example, now if stage A stops production, stage B will notice immediately and stage C very soon after. Stage A's problem is now quickly exposed to all the system and all the system is affected by the problem. One result of this is that the responsibility for solving the problem is no longer confined to the staff at stage A but is now shared by everyone. This considerably improves the chances of the problem being solved, if only because it is now too important to be ignored. In other words, by preventing inventory from accumulating between stages, the operation has increased the chances of the intrinsic efficiency of the plant being improved.

Although simplified, this highlights the differences between a traditional and a JIT approach. Although they both seek to encourage high efficiency in the operation, they take different routes to doing so. Traditional approaches seek to encourage efficiency by protecting each part of the operation from disruption. Long uninterrupted production runs are its ideal state. The JIT approach takes the opposite view. Exposure of the system (although not suddenly as in our simplified example) to problems can both make them more evident and change the 'motivation structure' of the whole system towards solving the problems. JIT sees inventory as a 'blanket of obscurity' which lies over the production system and prevents problems being noticed. The idea of obscuring effects of inventory is often illustrated diagrammatically as in Fig. 15.3. The many problems of the operation are shown as rocks in a river bed which cannot be seen because of the depth of the water. The water in this analogy represents the inventory in the operation. Yet even though the rocks cannot be seen, they slow the progress of the river's flow and cause turbulence. Gradually reducing the depth of the water (inventory) exposes the worst of the problems which can be resolved, after which the water is lowered further, exposing more problems and so on.

The same argument can be used to characterize the relationship between the stages of production on a larger scale, where each stage is a 'macro' operation. Here stages A, B and C could be a supplier operation, a manufacturer and a customer's operation respectively. At this level the two approaches are traditional 'mass-production' operations and the JIT operation.

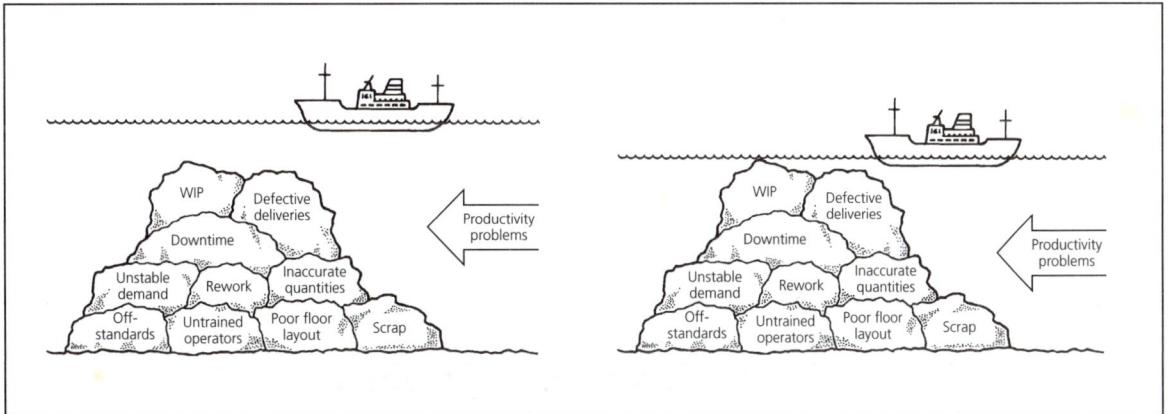

Figure 15.3 Reducing the level of inventory (water) allows operations management (the ship) to see the problems in the operation (the rocks) and work to reduce them

What JIT requires

This JIT approach places important new demands on the operations function. In fact, ideally, JIT requires a high standard in all an operation's performance objectives.

● *Quality* must be high because disruption in production due to quality errors will slow down the throughput of materials, reduce the internal dependability of supply, and possibly cause inventory to build up if errors slow the production rate at any point in the operation.

● *Speed,* in terms of fast throughput of materials, is essential if customer demand is to be met directly from production rather than from inventory.

● *Dependability* is a prerequisite for fast throughput, or put the opposite way, it is difficult to achieve fast throughput if the supply of parts or the reliability of equipment is not dependable.

● *Flexibility* is especially important in order to achieve small batch sizes and therefore fast throughput and short delivery lead times. We are referring here primarily to the mix and volume flexibilities described in Chapter 2.

JIT and capacity utilization

In JIT the main sacrifice is capacity utilization. Return to the production system shown in Fig. 15.2. In the JIT system any stoppage will affect the rest of the system, causing stoppages throughout the operation. This will necessarily lead to lower capacity utilization, at least in the short term. However, JIT proponents would argue that there is no point in producing output just for its own sake. Unless the output is useful and causes the operation as a whole to produce saleable production, there is no point in producing it anyway. In fact producing just to keep utilization high is not only pointless it is counterproductive because the extra inventory produced merely serves to make improvements less likely. Figure 15.4 illustrates the two approaches to capacity utilization.

JIT – a philosophy and a set of techniques

To understand JIT it must be viewed on two levels. At its most general, JIT is often called a *philosophy* of manufacturing: that is, JIT gives a clear view which can be used to guide the actions of operations managers in many different activities and many different contexts. At the same time, JIT is a collection of several *tools and techniques* which promote the operational conditions which support its philosophy. This chapter summarizes JIT philosophy, draws together some of the techniques described elsewhere, and treats in more detail the planning and control aspects of JIT (*see* Fig. 15.5).

THE PHILOSOPHY OF JUST-IN-TIME

Just-in-time philosophy and Japanese practice

JIT is the Western embodiment of a philosophy and series of techniques developed by the Japanese. The philosophy is founded on doing the simple things well, on gradually doing them better and on squeezing out waste every step of the way. Leading the

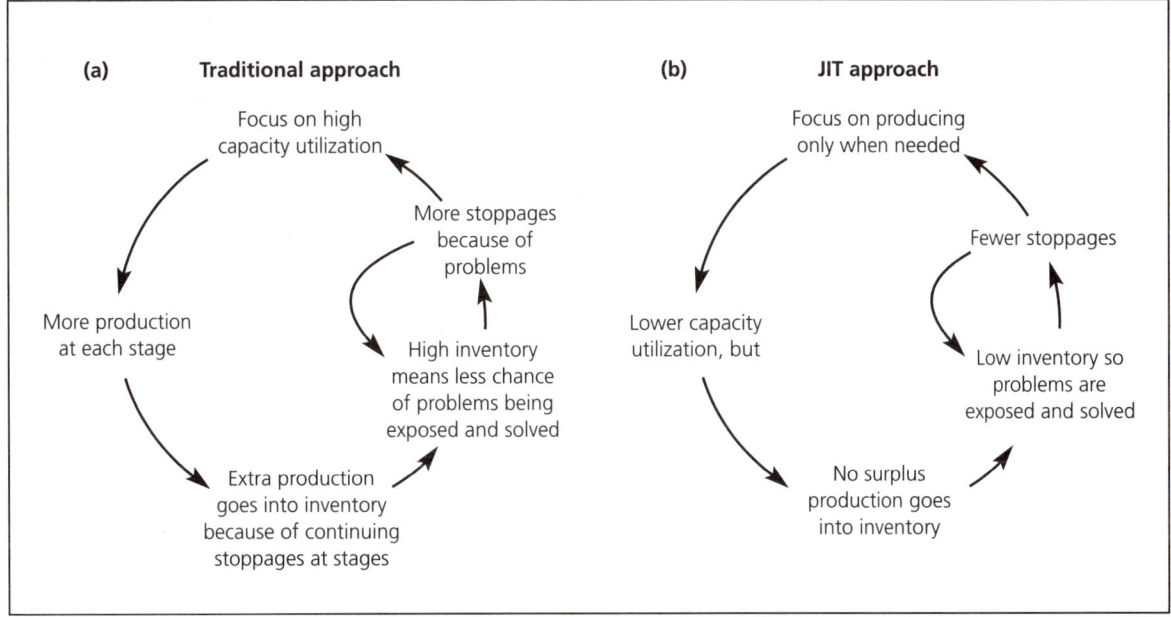

Figure 15.4 The different views of capacity utilization in (a) traditional and (b) JIT approaches to operations

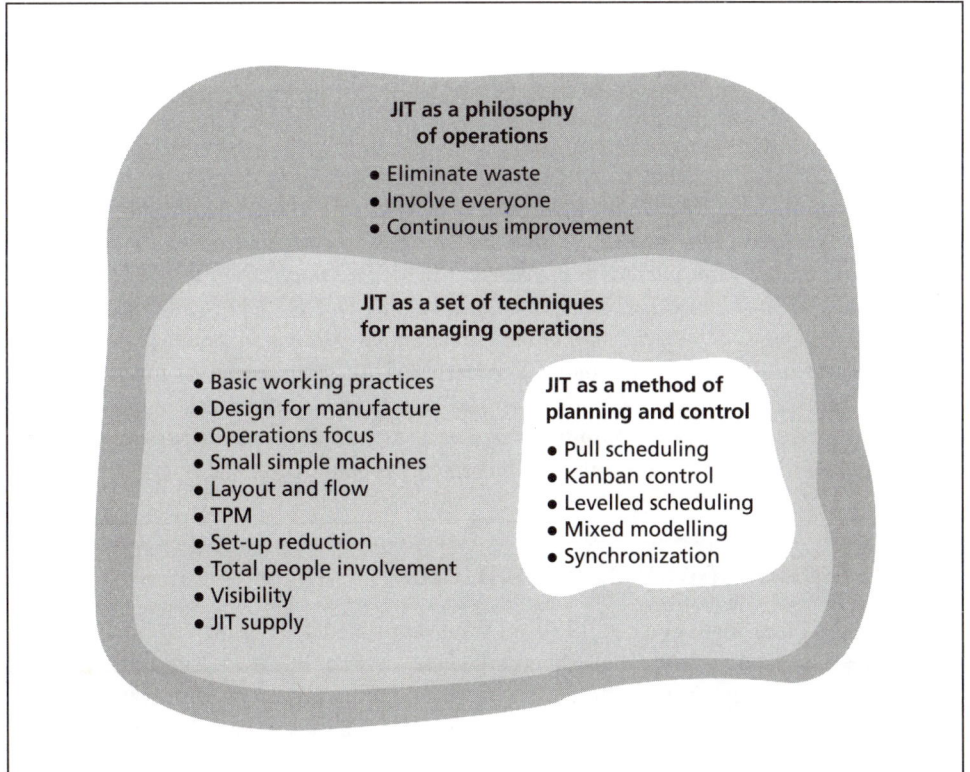

**Figure 15.5
JIT is a philosophy, a set of techniques and a method of planning and control**

development of JIT in Japan has been the Toyota Motor Company. (*See* box on Toyota later in this chapter.) Toyota's strategy in Japan has been progressively to interface manufacturing more closely with its customers and its suppliers. It has done this by developing a set of practices which have largely shaped what we now call JIT. Indeed some would argue that the origins of JIT lie within Toyota's reaction to the 'oil shock' of rising oil prices in the early 1970s.[3] The need for improved manufacturing efficiencies which this provoked spurred Toyota to accelerate its JIT ideas which were already forming. These developments by Toyota, and other Japanese manufacturers, were undoubtedly encouraged by the national cultural and economic circumstances. Japan's attitude towards waste ('make every grain of rice count'), together with its position as a crowded and virtually natural resourceless country, were ideal conditions in which to devise a manufacturing philosophy which emphasizes low waste and high added value.[4]

The high dependency theory

One explanation of the JIT approach to operations management is called the high dependency theory.[5] It derives partly from the logic which we used earlier to describe the benefits of low buffer inventories. With high inventories insulating each stage in the production process, the dependency of the stages on one another was low. Take away the inventory and their mutual dependency increases. This is not the only example of high dependency in JIT (and Japanese practice generally). The JIT practice of empowering 'shop-floor' staff makes the organization dependent on their actions. The use of the internal customer concept (mentioned in Chapter 1 but explained further in Chapter 20) formalizes the dependence between all parts of the operation. The use of Total Productive Maintenance (TPM) (explained in Chapter 19) and the JIT-influenced supplier development policies (from Chapter 13) are also examples of dependency. Professors Nick Oliver and Barry Wilkinson sum up the dependency theory in this way:

'Japanese systems of production, particularly JIT and total quality control, heighten the dependency of the organization on its agencies, or 'constituents', especially employees and supplying companies. This means . . . that the ability of the organization's constituents to exert leverage in their own interests is increased. The obvious implication is that it is imperative that such organizations take steps to counterbalance this by averting the possibility of such power being used . . . In the light of the vulnerability of Japanese production systems to disruption and in the light of the high dependencies of the organization on its constituents, we suggest that such a system will only work successfully in a situation where organizations have either actively taken the appropriate measures to guard against disruption, or where social, economic and political conditions automatically provide safeguards.'[6]

The JIT philosophy of operations

What is it then that distinguishes JIT from other approaches to improved business performance? Three key reasons have been suggested which, in effect, define the core of JIT philosophy.[7] They are the elimination of waste, the involvement of staff in the operation, and the drive for continuous improvement. We will look at each briefly in turn.

Eliminate waste

Waste can be defined as any activity which does not add value. For example, when Cummins Engineering, the engine manufacturer in the United Kingdom, began its JIT work, it carried out a study of how long it took for a number of products to work through the factory.[8] The study used the simple process charting symbols (*see* Appendix 3) to classify each activity which an engine went through during the course of manufacture. These symbols are shown again in Fig. 15.6.

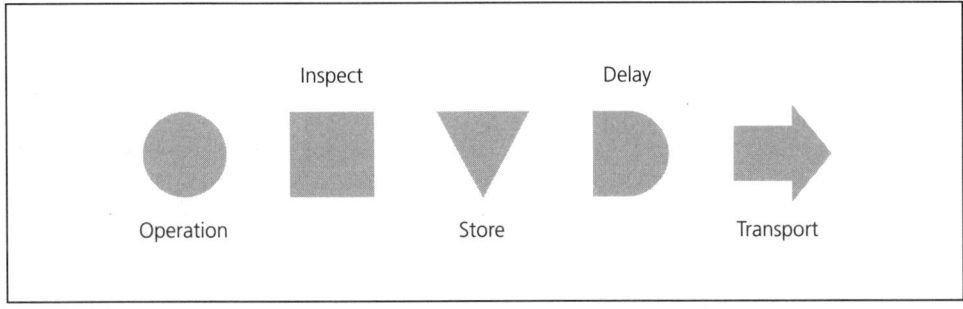

Inspect

Delay

Operation   Store   Transport

Figure 15.6
Not all these
process charting
symbols add value
in an operation

Of the symbols, only the one representing an *operation* is adding value, the rest are one type of waste or another. The Cummins study showed that, at best, an engine was only being worked on for 15 per cent of the time it was in the factory. At worst, this fell to 9 per cent, which meant that for 91 per cent of its time, the operation was adding cost to the engine, not adding value. Although already a relatively efficient manufacturer in Western terms, the results alerted Cummins to the enormous waste which still lay dormant in its operations, and which no performance measure then in use had exposed. Cummins shifted its objectives to reducing the non-value-added activities and to enriching the value added.[9]

Toyota identified seven wastes, which have been found to apply in many different types of operations – both service and production.

Over-production

Producing more than is immediately needed by the next process in the operation is the greatest source of waste according to Toyota. This source of waste builds on our initial JIT definition, where we referred to 'producing instantaneously', that is at the moment when the customer requires the product.

Waiting time

Machine efficiency and labour efficiency are two popular measures which are widely used to measure machine and labour waiting time respectively. Less obvious is the real amount of waiting time disguised by operators who are kept busy producing WIP which is not needed at the time.

Transport

Although transport clearly does not add value to the product, operations often built it into their process as a 'given'. For example, Raleigh Industries, the bicycle manufacturer, found at the start of its improvement programme that a cycle frame travelled a total flow distance of 6.5 miles. Layout changes which bring processes closer together, improvements in transport methods and workplace organization, all became important in the reduction of waste.

Process

The process itself may be a source of waste. Some operations may only exist because of poor component design, or poor maintenance, and so could be eliminated. Some processes are themselves waste. In one factory operators had to bend the offcuts from the guillotine so that they would fit into a pallet. The pallet was redesigned so that it could take long strips, thus eliminating the need for the operation.[10]

Inventory

Under a JIT philosophy all inventory becomes a target for elimination.

Motion

An operator may look busy because he or she is looking for a missing box of parts, or going to the supervisor's office to collect another job card. The value added is actually non-existent. Simplification of work by improving jigs and fixtures is a rich source of reduction in the waste of motion.

Defective goods

Quality waste is often very significant in operations even if actual measures of quality are limited. Scrap figures indicate the material and maybe part of the labour cost involved in poor quality. Disruption to the production control system, expediting actions, and the failure to deliver as promised are less visible, however. Total costs of quality are much greater than traditionally has been considered, and it is therefore more important to attack the causes of such costs. This is discussed further in Chapter 20.

The involvement of everyone

JIT philosophy is often put forward as a 'total' system. Its aim is to provide guidelines which embrace everyone and every process in the organization. An organization's culture is seen as being important in supporting these objectives through an emphasis on involving all of the organization's staff. This new culture is sometimes seen as synonymous with 'total quality', and is discussed in detail in Chapter 20. In fact JIT and Total Quality Management have many aspects in common, and they are sometimes referred to together as 'JIT/TQM'.

This JIT approach to people management has also been called the 'respect-for-humans' system. It encourages (and often requires) team-based problem solving, job enrichment (by including maintenance and set-up tasks in operators' jobs), job rotation and multi-skilling. The intention is to encourage a high degree of personal responsibility, engagement and 'ownership' of the job.

Continuous improvement

JIT objectives are often expressed as ideals, such as our previous definition . . . 'to meet demand instantaneously with perfect quality and no waste'. While any organization's performance may be far removed from such ideals, a fundamental belief of JIT is that it is possible to get closer to them over time. Without such beliefs to drive progress, JIT proponents claim improvement is more likely to be transitory than continuous. If the aims of JIT are set in terms of ideals which individual organizations may never fully achieve, then the emphasis must be on the way in which an organization moves closer to the ideal state. The Japanese word for continuous improvement is *kaizen,* and it is a key part of JIT philosophy. It is explained fully in Chapter 18.

JIT TECHNIQUES

There are many techniques which could be termed 'JIT techniques' and they follow on naturally and logically from the overall JIT philosophy. We will, for the sake of completeness, refer to some here which are treated elsewhere in this book and cross-reference accordingly.

Basic working practices[11]

'Basic working practices' according to JIT principles are summarized in Fig. 15.7.

1 *Discipline.* Work standards which are critical for the safety of company members and the environment, and for the quality of the product, must be followed by everyone all the time.

2 *Flexibility.* It should be possible to expand responsibilities to the extent of people's capabilities. This applies equally to managers as it does to shop-floor personnel. Barriers to flexibility, such as grading structures and restrictive practices, should be removed.

3 *Equality.* Unfair and divisive personnel policies should be discarded. Many traditional organizations have divisive 'perks' for different grades of personnel: 'staff car parks' and dining rooms, for example. Japanese companies, even outside Japan, are taking the egalitarian message further – to company uniforms, consistent pay structures which do not differentiate between full-time staff and hourly-rated staff, and open-plan offices.

4 *Autonomy.* Another principle is to delegate increasing responsibility to people involved in direct activities of the business, so that management's task becomes one of supporting the shop floor. Such autonomy is manifest in a JIT operation in activities such as the following:

● *Line stop authority*: if a quality problem arises, an assembly line operative has the authority to stop the line.

● *Material scheduling*: parts are made to well-known rules (for example, do not produce more unless the customer needs more). Many routine aspects of material scheduling can thereby be delegated away from the central production control system.

● *Data gathering*: data relevant to shop-floor performance monitoring is gathered and used by shop-floor personnel.

● *Problem solving*: shop-floor personnel get first chance at solving problems which affect the work they do. Only if they need help from experts should that help be sought and provided.

5 *Development of personnel.* Over time, the aim is to create more company members who can support the rigours of being competitive. This ensures a richer mix of people

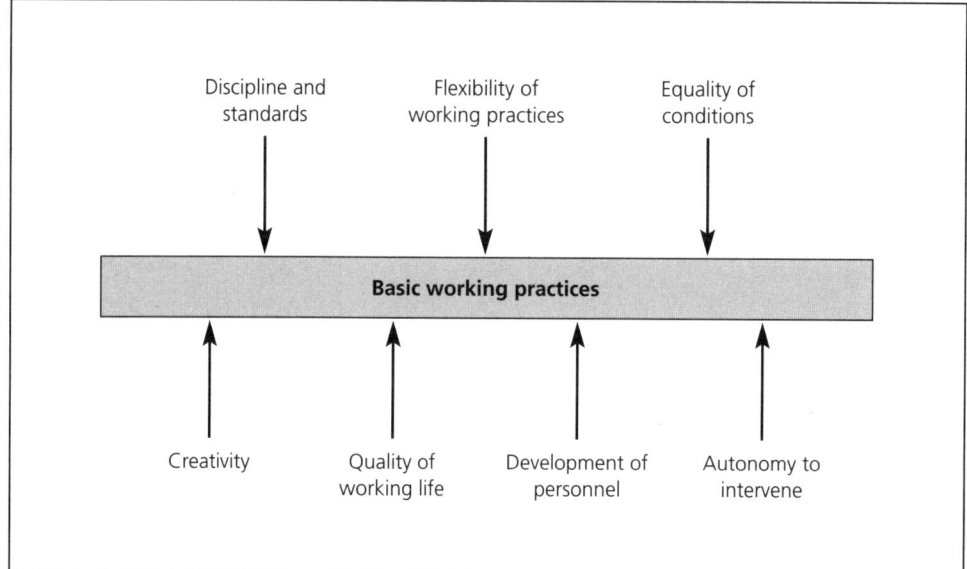

Figure 15.7
The basic working practices of JIT

working on improvement activities than in the average company. Partly, this is achieved by long-term personal development of company members.

6 *Quality of working life (QWL)*. Many JIT concepts fall into this category. For example:
● involvement in decision making
● security of employment
● enjoyment
● working area facilities.

7 *Creativity*. Most of us enjoy not just doing the job successfully, but also improving it for the next time.

Design for manufacture

Studies in automotive and aerospace companies have shown that design determines 70 to 80 per cent of production costs.[12] Design improvements can dramatically reduce product cost through changes in the number of components and sub-assemblies, and better use of materials and processing techniques. Often improvements of this magnitude would not be remotely possible by manufacturing efficiency improvements alone.

Operations focus

The concept behind operations focus is that simplicity, repetition, and experience breed competence.[13] Focus within manufacturing is:

● learning to focus each plant on limited, manageable sets of products, technologies, volumes, and markets;
● learning to structure basic manufacturing policies and supporting services so that they focus on one explicit manufacturing task instead of many implicit, inconsistent, conflicting tasks.

Small simple machines

The principle behind this technique is that several small machines are used instead of one large machine. Also 'home-grown', inexpensive equipment can be used to modify general-purpose machines so that they perform more reliably, are easy to maintain, and produce better quality over time. This demands that in-house engineering skills are available, and can be utilized to modify the machines so that new models can be introduced inexpensively. Small machines are also easily moved, so that layout flexibility is enhanced, and the risks of making errors in investment decisions are reduced because small machines usually need lower investment.

Layout and flow

Layout techniques can be used to promote the smooth flow of materials, of data, of people in the operation. Flow is an important concept in JIT. Long process routes around a factory provide opportunities for inventory build-up, add no value to the products, and slow down the throughput time of products, all of which are contrary to JIT principles. Considerations for layout and flow were described in Chapter 7. The principles of layout which JIT particularly recommends are:

● placing workstations close together so that inventory cannot build up;
● placing workstations so that the whole set of workstations which make a particular part are in sight of each other, making flow transparent to all parts of the line;
● using U-shaped lines so that staff can move between workstations to balance capacity;
● adopting cell-based layout (*see* Chapter 7).

Total productive maintenance (TPM)

TPM aims to eliminate the variability in operations processes which is caused by the effect of unplanned breakdowns. This is achieved by involving all staff in the search for maintenance improvements. Process owners are encouraged to assume ownership of their machines and to undertake routine maintenance and simple repair tasks. By so doing, maintenance specialists can then be freed to develop higher order skills for improved maintenance systems. TPM is treated in more detail in Chapter 19.

Set-up reduction (SUR)

Set-up time is defined as the time taken to change over the process from the previous batch to the first good piece of the next batch. Compare the time it takes you to change the tyre on your car with the time taken by a Formula 1 team. In SUR, set-up times can be reduced by a variety of methods such as cutting out time taken to search for tools and equipment, the pre-preparation of tasks which delay change-overs, and the constant practice of set-up routines. Often relatively simple mechanical changes can reduce set-up times considerably.

The other common approach to SUR is to convert work which was previously performed while the machine was stopped (called internal work) to be performed while the machine is running (called external work). There are three major methods of achieving the transfer of internal set-up work to external work.[14]

1 Pre-set tools so that a complete unit is fixed to the machine instead of having to be built up while the machine is stopped. Preferably, all adjustment should be carried out externally, so that the internal set-up is an assembly operation only.

2 Attach the different tools or dyes to a standard fixture or jig. Again, this enables the internal set-up to consist of a simple and standardized assembly operation.

3 Make the loading and unloading of new tools and dyes easy. Using improved material handling devices such as roller conveyor, ball-mounted surface tables can greatly help.

SUR is the means by which Cummins Engineering at Daventry in the UK first convinced itself of the power of JIT. Set-up time on the head face drill (a CNC machine tool on the block line) was 17 minutes. The operator team reduced this time to just 8 seconds, and spent less than R100 in doing so. Within a few months all set-up times on the block line were down to less than five minutes. Batch sizes were cut from about 80 (two weeks' production) to 1.[15]

Total people involvement

Total people involvement[17] can be seen as an extension of 'basic working practices'. However, it sees staff taking on much more responsibility to use their abilities to the

FLEXIBILITY HELPS JIT AT L'ORÉAL[16]

L'Oréal cosmetics is now the world's largest toiletries and cosmetics group, with a presence in over 140 different countries. In the UK the 45 000 square metre purpose-built facility in mid-Wales produces 1300 product lines in a spotlessly clean environment which is akin to a pharmaceutical plant in terms of hygiene, safety and quality. The plant has 55 production lines and 45 different production processes, and the manufacturing systems employed are of a flexibility that allows them to run each of the 1300 product lines every two months. That means over 150 different lines each week. But the plant was not always as flexible as this. It has been forced to enhance its flexibility by the requirement to ship over 80 million items each year. The sheer logistics involved in purchasing, producing, storing and distributing the volume and variety of goods has led to its current focus on introducing JIT principles into the manufacturing process.

To help achieve its drive for flexibility and for just-in-time production, L'Oréal organized the site into three production centres, each autonomous and focused within technical families of products. Their processes and production lines are then further focused within product sub-divisions. Responsible for all the activities from pre-weighing to dispatch within his area is the Production Centre Manager and his role also encompasses staff development, training and motivation. Within the focused production centres, improvement groups have been working on improving shop-floor flexibility, quality and efficiency. One of the projects reduced the set-up times on the line which produces hair colourants from 2.5 hours to only 8 minutes. These new change-over times mean that the company can now justify even smaller batches and it gives them the flexibility to meet market needs just-in-time. Prior to the change in set-up time, batch size was 30 000 units; now batches as small as 2000 to 3000 units can be produced cost effectively. ∎

benefit of the company as a whole. They are trained, capable and motivated to take full responsibility for all aspects of the work they do. In turn, they are trusted to carry out these responsibilities with autonomy for their own work area. Staff are expected to participate in such activities as the following:

- the selection of new recruits;
- dealing directly with suppliers over schedules, quality issues and delivery information;
- the self-measurement of performance and improvement trends;
- spending improvement budgets (for example, SP Tyres at Washington in the UK delegates 25 per cent of capital budgets to sections in the factory to spend as they see fit);[18]
- planning and reviewing work done each day through communication meetings;
- dealing directly with customer problems and requirements.

Visibility

Problems, quality projects and operations checklists are made visible by displaying them so that they can be easily seen and understood by all staff. Visibility measures include:

- displayed performance measures in the workplace;
- coloured lights indicating stoppages;
- displayed SPC control charts (*see* Chapter 17);
- visible improvement techniques and checklists;
- a separate area displaying samples of products and competitors' products together with samples of good and defective products;
- visual control systems such as kanbans;
- open-plan workplace layouts.

JIT supply

Just-in-time supply epitomizes the popular meaning of the term 'JIT', and conjures up the vision of parts arriving at the assembly process 'just-in-time'. Indeed, a misinterpretation of this view was first seized upon by some non-Japanese manufacturers, who often forced their suppliers to deliver just-in-time while contributing little or nothing to improved logistics themselves. In Chapter 13 we described 'partnerships' and 'lean' relationships which are both based on JIT supply principles.

JIT planning and control techniques

Also classed as JIT techniques are those which deal specifically with the planning and control of operations. These techniques are treated under a separate heading because they relate directly to the planning and control theme of this part of the book.

The techniques and approaches described are as follows:

- kanban control
- levelled scheduling
- mixed modelling
- synchronization.

JUST-IN-TIME PLANNING AND CONTROL

One of the sources of waste identified earlier was that caused by inventory timing. Poor inventory timing (parts arriving too early or too late) causes unpredictability in an operation. Inventory timing is governed by the two schools of thought which were described in Chapter 10 – 'push' planning and control and 'pull' planning and control. JIT planning and control is based on the principle of a 'pull system', while the MRP approach to planning and control which was described in the previous chapter is a 'push system'.

Kanban control

The term *kanban* was sometimes used as being equivalent to 'JIT planning and control' (which it is not) or even to the whole of JIT (which it most certainly is not). However, kanban control is one method of operationalizing a pull-based planning and control system. Kanban is the Japanese for 'card' or 'signal'. It is sometimes called the 'invisible conveyor' which controls the transfer of materials between the stages of an operation. In its simplest form, it is a card used by a customer stage to instruct its supplier stage to send more materials. Kanbans can also take other forms. In some Japanese companies they are solid plastic markers or even coloured ping-pong balls, the different colours representing different parts. There are also different types of kanban.

● *The conveyance kanban.* A conveyance kanban is used to signal to a previous stage that material can be withdrawn from inventory and transferred to a specific destination. This type of kanban would normally have details of the particular part's name and number, the place where it should be taken from, and the destination to where it is being delivered.

● *The production kanban.* A production kanban is a signal to a production process that it can start producing a part or item to be placed in an inventory. The information contained on this type of kanban usually includes the particular part's name and number, a description of the process itself, the materials required for the production of the part, and the destination to which the part or parts need to be sent when they are produced.

● *The vendor kanban.* Vendor kanbans are used to signal to a supplier to send material or parts to a stage. In this way it is similar to a conveyance kanban but it is usually used with external suppliers.

Whichever kind of kanban is being used, the principle is always the same; that is, that the receipt of a kanban triggers the conveyance, production or supply of one unit or a standard container of units. If two kanbans are received it triggers the conveyance, production or supply of two units or standard containers of units, and so on. The kanbans are the *only* means by which conveyance, or production or supply can be authorized. This is true even when the kanban is not a card or object. Some companies use 'kanban squares'. These are marked spaces on the shop floor or bench which are drawn to fit one or more containers. The existence of an empty square triggers production at the stage which supplies the square.

There are two procedures which can govern the use of kanbans. These are known as the single-card system and the dual-card system. The single-card system is most often used because it is by far the simplest system to operate. It uses only conveyance kanbans (or vendor kanbans when receiving supply of material from an outside source). The dual-card system uses both conveyance and production kanbans. Each procedure is explained below.

The single-card system

Figure 15.8 shows the operation of a single-card kanban system. At each stage (only two stages are shown, stage A and stage B) there is a work centre and an area for holding inventory. All production and inventory is contained in standard containers, all of which contain exactly the same number of parts. When stage B requires some more parts to work on, it withdraws a standard container from the output stock point of stage A. After work centre B has used the parts in the container it places the conveyance kanban in a holding area and sends the empty container to the work centre at stage A. The arrival of the empty containers at stage A's work centre is the signal for production to take place at work centre A. The conveyance kanban is moved from the holding box back to the output stock point of stage A. This acts as authorization for the collection of a further full container to be moved from the output stock of stage A through to the work centre at stage B. Two closed loops effectively control the flow of materials between the stages. The conveyance kanban loop (illustrated by the thin arrows) keeps materials circulating between the stages, and the container loop (illustrated by the thicker arrows) connects the work centres with the stock point between them and circulates the containers, full from A to B and empty back from B to A.

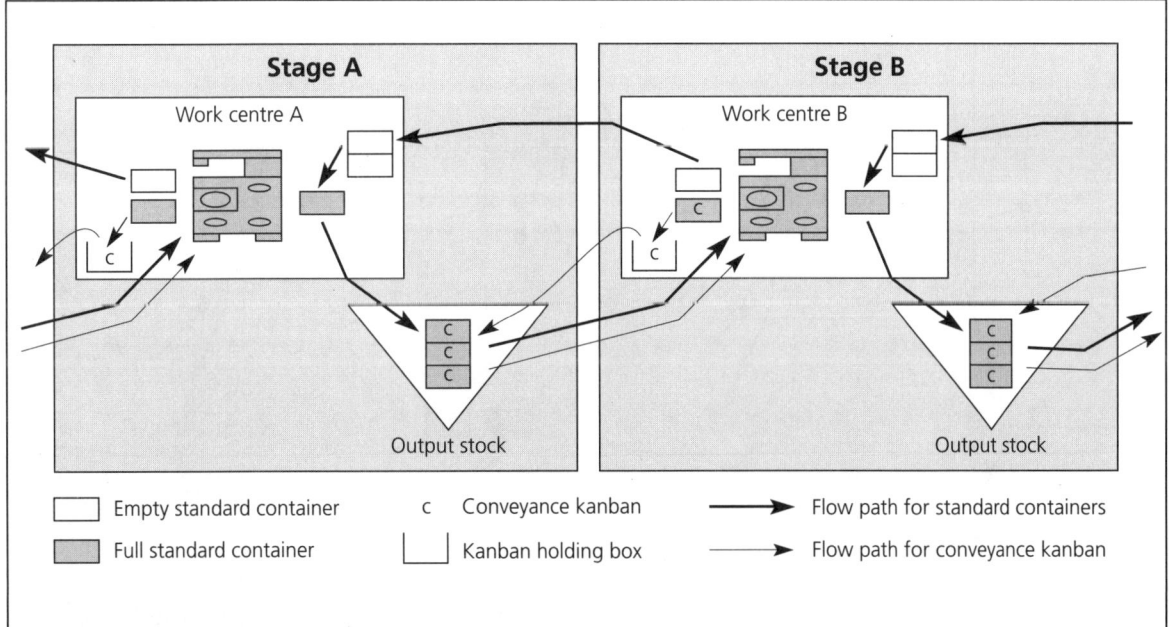

Figure 15.8 The operation of the single-card kanban system of pull control

The dual-card kanban system

Somewhat more complicated, and used by the Toyota Motor Company, is the dual-card kanban system. This is illustrated in Fig. 15.9. It uses two types of kanban: the *conveyance kanban* and the *production kanban*. It is also more adept at controlling flow between stages where the number of different parts produced by each stage is relatively high. Consider again the flow between stage A and stage B. This time each stage has two stock points: one handling incoming containers and parts and the other handling outgoing containers and parts. The conveyance kanban loop is similar to that used in the single-card system. Working from the input stock point of stage B, when work centre B requires parts to work on, it collects them from its input stock point and places the conveyance kanban in the holding box. When work centre B has finished working on all the parts in the container and it is empty, it is put with the conveyance kanban from input stock point B and they are both transported back to output stock point A. The conveyance kanban authorizes the release of a full container from stock point A and is placed in the container which is then shipped to the input stock point at stage B. This completes the conveyance kanban loop. The empty container, meanwhile, waits in stock point A until it is needed in work centre A to hold processed parts. The movement of containers between each work centre and its output stock point is controlled by a loop of production kanbans. When the empty container, which has been moved from output stock point A to work centre A, is eventually filled, a production kanban is attached to it from the holding box at work centre A and the, now full, container is moved to the output stock point at stage A. Before this container is withdrawn (on the authority of a conveyance kanban from stage B) its production kanban is placed in a holding box at output stock point A. This is moved up to the holding box at work centre A where it is eventually attached to a full container and moved back to stock point A, thus completing the loop.

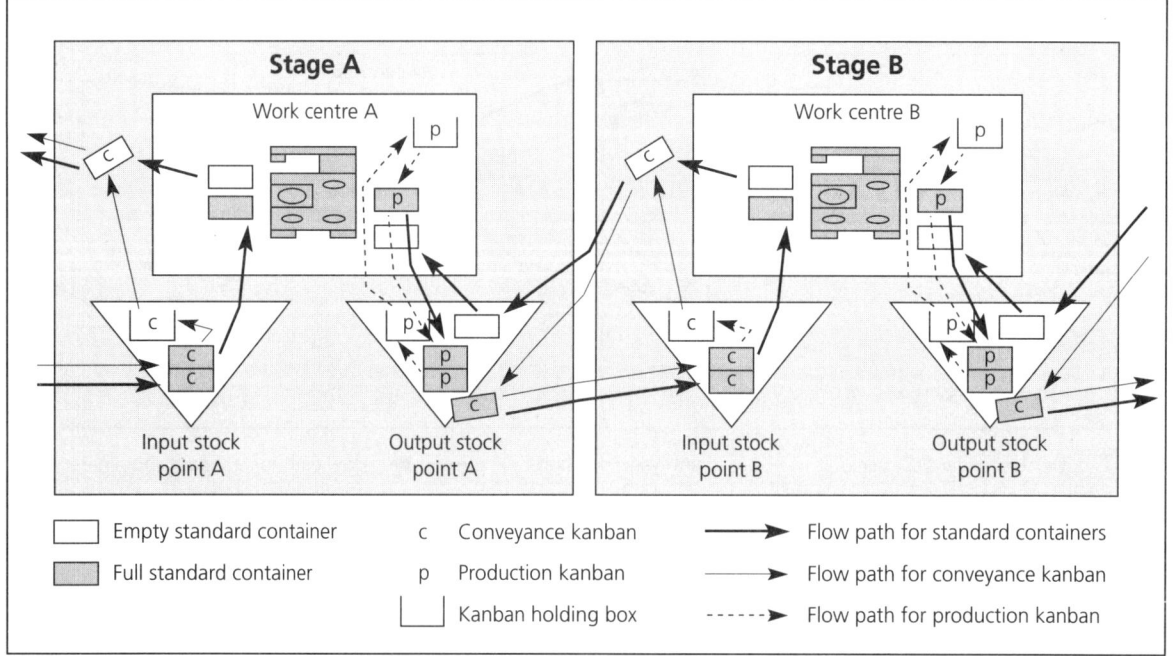

Figure 15.9 The operation of the dual-card kanban system of pull control

The number of kanbans which are put into the loops between the stages or between the stock points and the work centres equals the number of containers in the system and therefore the inventory which can accumulate. Taking a kanban out of the loop has the effect of reducing the inventory.

The number of kanbans

In any system other than a very simple sequential flow the number of kanbans at each stage will vary depending on the nature of the work being performed. Production rates, set-up times and the number of parts per container can all vary. The formula to calculate the number of kanbans which are required at each stage is given as follows:

$$n = \frac{d \times t \times (1 + e)}{c}$$

where n = the number of kanbans (either conveyance or production)

d = planned average daily production for the stage (in units)

t = the average time either to set up the machine (for production kanbans) or transport the container (for conveyance kanbans) expressed as a proportion of the day

e = a value which lies between 0 and 1 and represents either the efficiency of the workstation (for production kanbans) or the level of safety stock (for conveyance kanbans)

c = the unit capacity of the container.

Levelled scheduling

Heijunka is the Japanese word for overall levelling of the production schedule so that mix and volume are even over time. For example, instead of producing 500 parts in one batch which would cover the needs for the next three months, levelled scheduling would require the operation to only make one piece per hour regularly. The principle of levelled scheduling is straightforward but the requirements to put it into practice are quite severe, though the benefits resulting from it can be substantial. The move from conventional to levelled scheduling is illustrated in Fig. 15.10. Conventionally, if a mix of products were required in a time period (usually a month), the economic batch quantity (EBQ) would be calculated for each product (*see* Chapter 12 for a discussion of EBQ) and the batches produced in some sequence. The Fig. 15.10 (a) shows three products which are produced in a 20-day time period in a production unit.

Quantity of product A required = 3000
Quantity of product B required = 1000
Quantity of product C required = 1000

EBQ of product A   =   600
EBQ of product B   =   200
EBQ of product C   =   200

Starting at day 1 the unit commences producing product A. During day 3 the batch of 600 As are finished and dispatched to the next stage. The batch of Bs is started but

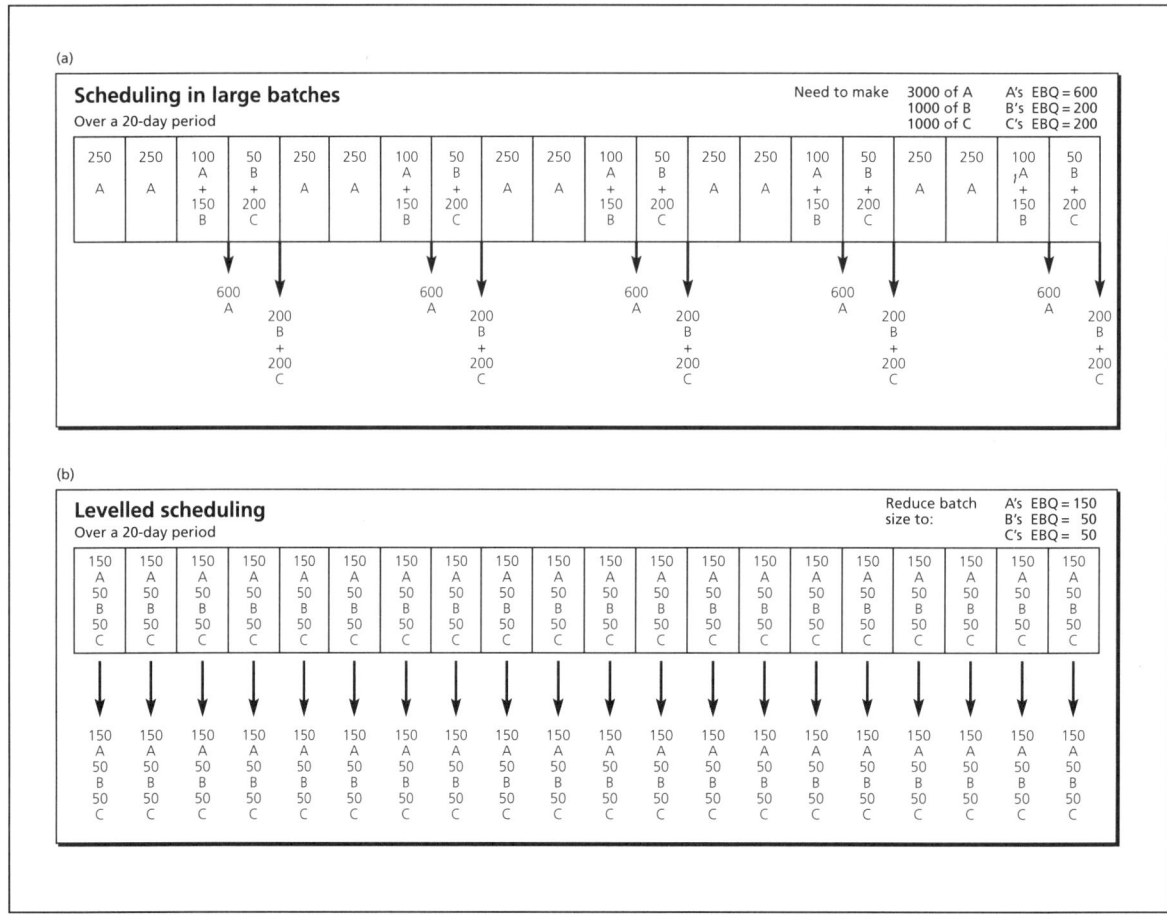

Figure 15.10 Levelled scheduling equalizes the mix of products made each day

is not finished until day 4. The remainder of day 4 is spent making the batch of Cs and both batches are dispatched at the end of that day. The cycle then repeats itself. The consequences of using large batches are first that relatively large amounts of inventory accumulate within and between the units, and second that most days are different from one another in terms of what they are expected to produce (in more complex circumstances no two days would be the same).

Now suppose that the flexibility of the unit could be increased to the point where the EBQs for the products were reduced to a quarter of their previous levels (*see* Fig. 15.10 (b)).

$$\text{EBQ of product A} = 150$$
$$\text{EBQ of product B} = 50$$
$$\text{EBQ of product C} = 50$$

A batch of each product can now be completed in a single day, at the end of which the three batches are dispatched to their next stage. Smaller batches of inventory are

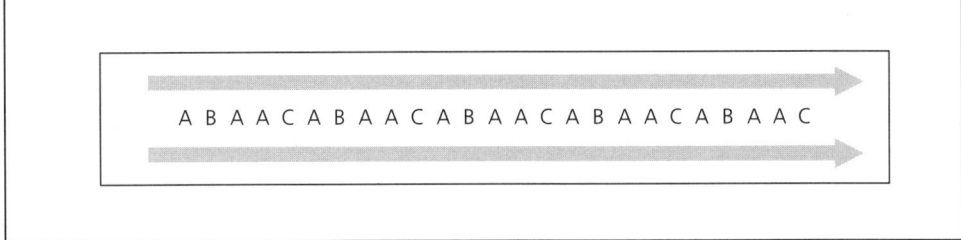

A B A A C A B A A C A B A A C A B A A C A B A A C

Figure 15.11
The sequence of products delivered by the operation with fully levelled scheduling with an EBQ = 1

moving between each stage which will reduce the overall level of work-in-progress in the operation. Just as significant, however, is the effect on the regularity and rhythm of production at the unit. Now every day in the month is the same in terms of what needs to be produced. This makes planning and control of each stage in the operation much easier. For example, if on day 1 of the month the daily batch of As were finished by 11.00 am, and all the batches were successfully completed in the day, the next day the unit knows that if it again has completed all the As by 11.00 am, it is on schedule. When every day is different, the simple question, 'Are we on schedule to complete our production today?' requires some investigation before it can be answered. However, when every day is the same, everyone in the unit can tell whether production is on target by looking at the clock. Control becomes visible and transparent to all.

Mixed modelling

The principle of levelled scheduling can be taken further to give a repeated mix of parts. Suppose that the machines in the production unit can be made so flexible that they achieve the JIT ideal of an EBQ of one. The sequence of individual products emerging from the unit would be as illustrated in Fig. 15.11. This would produce a steady stream of each product flowing continuously from the unit.

However, the sequence of products does not always fall as conveniently as in Fig. 15.11. The unit production times for each product are not usually identical and the ratios of required volumes are less convenient.

Example

Suppose the number of products required in the 20-day period are:

Product A = 1920
Product B = 1200
Product C = 960

Assuming an eight-hour day, the cycle time for each product – that is, the interval between the production of each of the same type of product (*see* Chapter 7 for a full explanation of cycle time) – is as follows:

$$\text{Product A, cycle time} = \frac{20 \times 8 \times 60}{1920} = 5 \text{ mins}$$

$$\text{Product B, cycle time} = \frac{20 \times 8 \times 60}{1200} = 8 \text{ mins}$$

$$\text{Product C, cycle time} = \frac{20 \times 8 \times 60}{960} = 10 \text{ mins}$$

So, the production unit must produce:

1 unit of A every 5 minutes
1 unit of B every 8 minutes
1 unit of C every 10 minutes

Put another way, by finding the common factor of 5, 8 and 10:

8 units of A every 40 minutes
5 units of B every 40 minutes
4 units of C every 40 minutes

This means that a sequence, which mixes eight units of A, five of B and four of C, and repeats itself every 40 minutes, will produce the required output. There will be many different ways of sequencing the products to achieve this mix. For example:

. . . BACABACABACABACAB . . . repeated . . . repeated

This sequence repeats itself every 40 minutes and produces the correct mix of products to satisfy the monthly requirements.

Synchronization

Many companies make a wide variety of parts and products, not all of them with sufficient regularity to warrant the full levelled scheduling treatment. Synchronization means the pacing of output at each stage in the production process to ensure the same flow characteristics for each part or product as they progress through each stage. To do this, parts need to be classified according to the frequency with which they are demanded. One method of doing this, which was devised by Lucas, the UK-based manufacturing company, distinguishes between what it terms *runners, repeaters,* and *strangers.*[19]

- *Runners* are products or parts which are produced frequently, such as every week.
- *Repeaters* are products or parts which are produced regularly, but at longer time intervals.
- *Strangers* are products or parts which are produced at irregular and possibly unpredictable time intervals.

There are advantages in trying to reduce the variability of timing intervals for producing runners and repeaters. The aim is to synchronize processes concerned with parts and sub-assemblies for such products so that they appear to take place on a 'drumbeat' pulse which governs material movements. It might even be better to slow down faster operations than to have them produce more than can be handled in the same time by the next process. In this way output is made regular and predictable.

TOYOTA'S PRODUCTION SYSTEM

Toyota's version of JIT, which it calls the Toyota Production System (TPS), has been the driving force behind its advance into what has been called a 'truly great manufacturing company'. The 'two pillars' of TPS are (and have always been):

- *JIT pull scheduling.* The production and conveyance of what is needed, when it is needed in the amount that is needed.
- *Jidoka.* Stopping the operations process in the event of problems, either by the staff who are process owners (who use a 'line-stop' button), or by the machines themselves (which sense abnormalities automatically). In this way, defects cannot be passed on to the next process and inspection is eliminated.

To Toyota the key control tool is their kanban system. The kanban is seen as serving three purposes:

- It is an instruction for the preceding process to send more.
- It is a visual control tool to show up areas of over-production and lack of synchronization.
- It is a tool for *kaizen* (continuous improvement). Toyota's rules state that 'the number of kanbans should be reduced over time'.

Toyota uses two of the basic types of kanban to support JIT pull scheduling: the 'production' kanban and the 'move' kanban (what we called the conveyance kanban).

The number of parts per container is governed by factors such as part size and commonality between processes. Toyota believes that it is usually best that the number is divisible by 8 to facilitate hourly synchronization. This also means that the number of parts per container should be standardized where possible. The number of containers (hence the number of kanbans) is influenced by demand per hour, the lead time for the part and the number of parts per container. This is increased by a factor to allow for disruptions like breakdowns and absenteeism. The number of kanbans should of course never be fixed, but subject to *kaizen*.

Major sub-assemblies like engines are not controlled by kanban. There are numerous different end options for such major sub-assemblies, and inventory would simply be generated if separate kanbans were used for each one. Engines are therefore controlled by a different method. They are sequenced by *assembly line broadcasting*. In this approach, the exact customer requirements for a vehicle are broken down to major components and communicated ('broadcast') to the relevant production section. The procedure, therefore, is to sequence control major sub-assemblies, and to use kanbans for components and smaller sub-assemblies. ■

JIT IN SERVICE OPERATIONS

Many of the principles and techniques of just-in-time, although they have been described in the context of manufacturing operations, are also applicable to service settings. In fact some of the philosophical underpinning to just-in-time can also be seen as having its equivalent in the service sector. The comparison between manu-

Table 15.1 Inventory and queues have similar characteristics

	Inventory (Queues of material)	Queues (Queues of people)
Cost	Ties up capital	Waste time
Space	Needs warehouse	Need waiting areas
Quality	Defects are hidden	Give negative impression
Decoupling	Makes stages independent	Promote division of labour and specialization
Utilization	Stages kept busy by work-in-progress	Servers kept busy by waiting customers
Coordination	Avoids having to synchronize flow	Avoid having to match supply and demand

Source: Adapted from Fitzsimmons, J.A. (1990) 'Making Continual Improvement: A Competitive Strategy for Service Firms' *in* Bowen, D.E., Chase, R.B., Cummings, T.G. and Associates, *Service Management Effectiveness*, Jossey-Bass

facturing systems which held large stocks of inventory between stages and those which did not, centred on the effect which inventory had on improvement and problem solving. Exactly the same argument could be applied when, instead of queues of material (inventory), an operation has to deal with queues of customers. Table 15.1 shows how certain aspects of inventory are analogous to certain aspects of queues.

In this part of the chapter we describe two service organizations who have benefited from applying some of the principles of just-in-time. The first is the Little Chef restaurant chain and the second is a hospital. You might also like to read the case exercise at the end of this chapter which gives a further example of just-in-time in a hospital setting.

Little Chef

Most drivers in the UK are familiar with the Little Chef roadside restaurant chain, which has over 350 sites located on busy roads around the UK. Growth has been particularly rapid in the last ten years. Success has come through offering consistency and reliability of service throughout its network. Little Chef customers have come to expect four main service qualities:

● good food, freshly cooked
● value for money
● clean, pleasant surroundings
● prompt, friendly service.

Of Little Chef's 35 million customers a year, most are on journeys of over two hours. While time is important to them, they also need to relax. Week-day users are mostly business travellers, while leisure travellers take over at weekends and during school holidays. All restaurants trade from 7.00 am to 10.00 pm, 364 days a year and offer an all-day menu, supplemented by part-day menus and various seasonal promotions.

Customers receive a table service of cooked-to-order meals. Target times are 30 minutes for a starter plus main course with an extra ten minutes for a dessert. Each restaurant is run as a profit centre with an average management team of four staff. With a simple, standardized service package, many aspects of JIT-style operations can be seen in the Little Chef operation. Here we review operations planning and control issues at a typical Little Chef restaurant which is located at Towcester East (in the central part of the UK).

Operations planning

Figure 15.12 shows that demand levels fluctuate by season, by day of the week and throughout the day. To achieve a high standard of customer service, it is necessary to forecast demand as accurately as possible, and then to provide for sufficient resources (staff, food, etc.) to meet that demand. In practice, an all-year-round core of regular staff is maintained, supplemented by seasonal staff at peak periods. Staff planning is undertaken at three levels:

● *The quarterly manpower plan.* The main input to this plan is the forecast number of customers for each of the 12 weeks of the forecast period. The forecast is based on a mix of historical data and trends, adjusted by the personal view of the manager.
● *The weekly forecast.* The sales forecast from the quarterly plan is updated and broken down into daily sales. The forecast 'covers' (number of customers) and the average spend per head (a key productivity measure) are multiplied together to give forecast sales. Actual figures are added to this document as the week progresses. The document therefore starts as a planning tool, becomes a monitoring tool, and is later used again as a planning tool for the same week next year.
● *The daily plans.* The duty manager draws up a shift planner to plan the allocation of duties between staff. This is a working tool, and is updated during the day.

All materials (food, cleaning items and crockery) are supplied from a single supplier. This helps to ensure that goods are up to a consistent standard. Each restaurant has three deliveries a week, typically Monday, Wednesday and Friday, with orders being placed the same morning. A weekly stock-take provides consumption of each item. The manager uses a locally determined re-order level combined with forecast daily sales to compute material orders. Most foods are delivered and stored frozen. Only salads and cured meats arrive date coded, usually with four to five days' shelf life after delivery. Bread and milk are delivered daily by local suppliers. Stockholding amounts to about seven days at any one time.

Operations control

Each restaurant has a 'menu manual', which specifies the ingredients, cooking procedures and presentation standards for every item on the menu. Orders are added to the cook's-order pad, including the time when the waitress took the order. Orders are marked once cooking has started, and marked again when cooking has finished. The cooking process is simple, and does not require special qualifications. Most restaurants have a 'cook skills sharer', who has undergone special training in order to teach others to cook. The cooking equipment is also simple – griddles, fryers and pre-programmed microwave ovens. Similarly, a housekeeping board is maintained as both a planning and control tool, enabling 'at a glance' an assessment of jobs which need to be done. Standard cleaning products and methods are used throughout the company, and each cleaning task is broken down into 'how, what, when' elements. To help

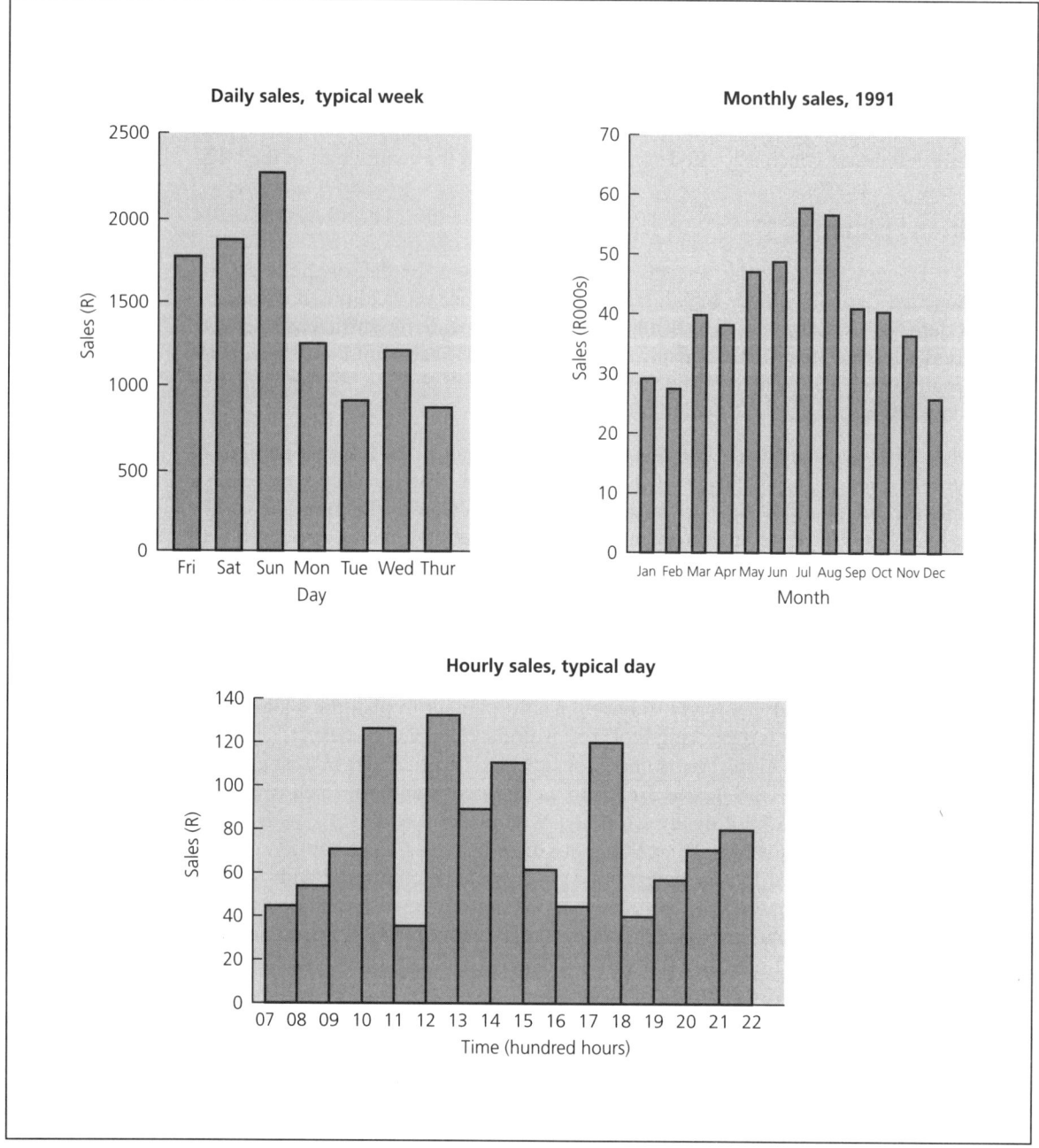

Figure 15.12 Demand variation at Little Chef restaurant at Towcester East

ensure that standards are maintained across the network, quality audits are conducted every three months by the local training officer.

Tasks fall into eight categories; there is usually enough flexibility to react on a daily basis to changing needs, however:

- reception/cashier
- cooking/production
- beverage production
- sweet/salad production
- serving to tables
- re-laying tables
- washing up
- cleaning/toilet checks.

Staff are cross-trained for greater flexibility. Fifty per cent of staff can cook, for example. At busy times, each function is staffed, but at quieter times, one person may perform more than one task. To support staff flexibility, Little Chef provides a computer-based training package which provides details of all tasks to be performed, tests understanding and records training. Facility flexibility is assisted by moveable tables and chairs so that parties of varying sizes can be accommodated.

Although different from a manufacturing company, some of the principles which apply in the Little Chef case are similar to those used in a JIT manufacturer.

- *Limited product range* – this helps to simplify the material control task. The operation only produces 'runners' and 'repeaters'.
- *Simple products* – which only require basic production equipment.
- *Pull scheduling* – known customer orders are used to pull meals from the kitchen to the restaurant according to actual demand. There are no buffer stocks. The signal to make more is the order from the waitress. The routine is simple but strict: order one, make one, supply one in response to specific customer demand.
- *A batch size of one* – orders are not held up (or batched) until a sufficient number have been accumulated, nor are they produced in advance; they are made on receipt of the order.
- *Flexibility* – a standard time for serving a customer is aimed for irrespective of the demand level. This is done by flexing the number of staff on duty.
- *JIT supply* – replenishment stocks are ordered on a short (daily) cycle from Little Chef's sole supplier.
- *Visibility* – recipes, preparation methods, pictures of ideal finished products and cleaning checklists are all examples of how key data can be made visible to all staff, both for control and audit purposes.

Temple University Hospital, Pennsylvania

The Temple University Hospital in Pennsylvania in the USA is a 500-bed acute-care, university-affiliated teaching hospital. The array of services provided covers 11 surgical areas, including cardio-thoracic, neurology, and orthopaedics. It uses the latest surgical technology and carries out 11 000 procedures per year in a new building housing 14 operating rooms. A layout for this building is shown in Fig. 15.13.

Before changing its methods, Temple Hospital held high inventories of materials. Eleven charge nurses staffed the 14 operating rooms (ORs), each nurse dedicated to a surgical speciality. Their prime task was to ensure that the materials which were needed for operations by the physicians were always available. Physicians used different supply sources for the same operation, and each nurse had an individual system for controlling materials. Case carts which hold the materials ready for the operations

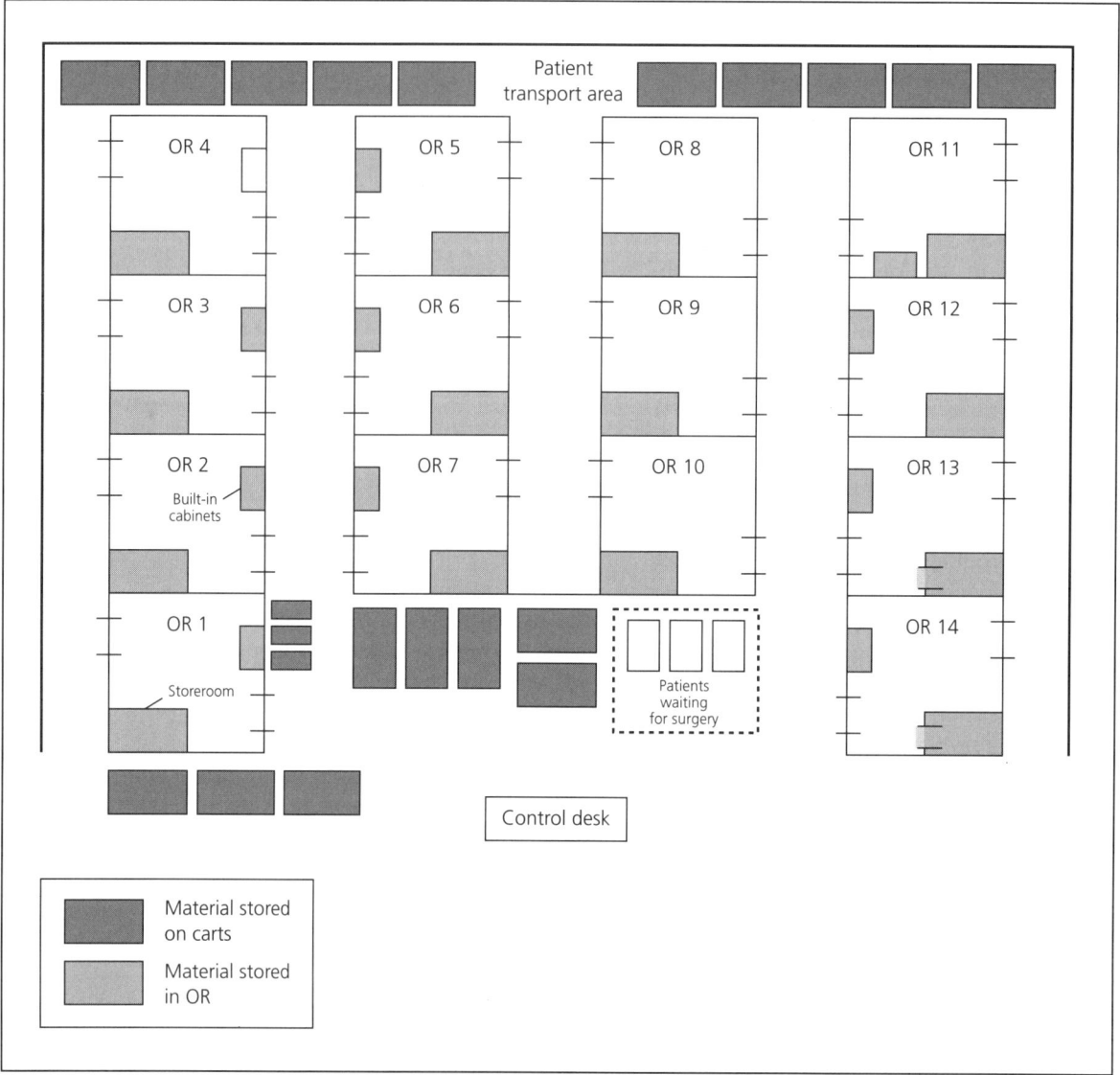

Figure 15.13 The layout of operating rooms (ORs) at Temple Hospital prior to use of exchange-cart and case-cart systems

were located along the rear corridor of the building. Stocks of materials were held in cabinets and storage rooms in the operating rooms and elsewhere. A further buffer stock was held in a central store, which is not shown in the figure. Cabinets and storage rooms were kept full. The goal for charge nurses was to provide a 100 per cent service to the physicians. It was important never to run out of anything which might be needed. As a result, numerous parts were kept as 'squirrel stocks', including expensive items like artificial joints. The material inventory was estimated at $750 000, of which $80 000 was estimated to be obsolete. In effect the hospital was a good example of a 'just-in-case' stock policy.

In the USA, the government pays for the treatment of about 40 per cent of patients through the Medical Aid (Medicaid) system. In order to control costs, 460

'Diagnostic-Related Groups' (DRGs) were defined. DRGs limit the amount that a hospital can charge for a defined operation, and lead to hospitals being paid on a 'cost-to-deliver' basis. The DRG specifies standard materials which must be used in the operation in order to encourage tighter control. In effect, DRGs define the bill of materials for a given operation. Once hospitals had accepted the concept of DRGs, the insurance companies followed suit. This encouraged the standardization of methods by the physicians themselves. It also provided an attractive opportunity. If surgery could be predicted in advance, a master schedule could be defined and material requirements could be forecast.

The planning and control breakthrough at Temple was to recognize the value of the operating room controller, who had hitherto been an under-utilized resource. He or she was in a position to schedule operations up to two weeks ahead, which was well above the lead time for most materials (average three days). It was possible, therefore, to arrive at a master schedule, and to input this into the materials procurement system. This enabled operation-specific materials to be scheduled by means of DRGs.

The material management system at Temple University hospital was implemented at three levels, as follows:

- *An exchange cart system*. This is used for general-purpose materials such as bandages and sutures. These are supplied on a 'pull' basis by Central Supply & Distribution (CSD), who maintain stocks on a real-time computer system. Bar coding and computer terminals at the receiving areas are used to check receipt of carts. Availability of these materials is assured by flow of a few fully stocked exchange carts from CSD to the operating rooms several times a day. The carts themselves act as a kanban between CSD and the theatres.
- *A case-cart system*. This is used for materials associated with specific surgical procedures. By scheduling operations through the planning and control system, the relevant materials are called up for the given procedure and surgeon. Purchasing personnel order materials called up for all operations. CSD personnel then make up case carts containing all such intermediate value materials. These are delivered on a JIT basis to the operating rooms.
- *The high-value speciality item*. The bill of materials has been designed to identify special delivery requirements for these parts. Suppliers bypass the normal delivery to CSD, and instead deliver directly to the given operating room, also on a JIT basis.

The implementation of the new low-stock JIT system required that surgeons needed to be convinced that the system's reliability would be at least as good as the previous method. Communication between material suppliers and the operating areas needed to be such that there was confidence to operate with low stocks. After implementation it was accepted that the JIT system had actually *improved* communication links. Eliminating buffer stocks had the effect of forcing improved integration between the surgeons, the nurses, CSD, purchasing and finance.

JIT AND MRP

The wide acceptance of the JIT principles and techniques outlined in this chapter came in the 1980s, after many manufacturing operations had made use of the MRP-based systems which were described in Chapter 14. Furthermore, the operating philosophies of MRP and JIT do seem to be fundamentally opposed. JIT encourages a 'pull' system of planning and control, while MRP is a 'push' system. JIT has aims which are wider than the operations planning and control activity, while MRP is essentially a planning and control 'calculation mechanism'. Yet the two approaches can co-exist in the same operation, provided their respective advantages are preserved. This part of this chapter will address two important questions for operations managers:

● How can JIT and MRP be combined in the same operation?
● How do we choose whether to use an MRP-based or a JIT-based or a combined approach to planning and control?

JIT and MRP similarities and differences

Examining some of the assumptions and advantages of each approach gives an indication of how they can be used together. For example, there is the irony that the ultimate aim of MRP is really to deliver products just-in-time for when they are needed. Its objectives are to make sure that the plant produces goods just as they are needed by the market. MRP starts by looking forward and asking what end items need to be shipped at what time *in the future*. This is an important point: MRP can plan production when we want to anticipate future output requirements. It uses the bill of materials to calculate how many of which parts need to be ordered from the upstream parts of the operation, and from this how many parts and materials to order from suppliers. By doing this it connects customer demand with the supply network. MRP can also deal with complexity. It can handle detailed parts requirements, even for products which are made infrequently and in low volumes.

JIT, on the other hand, is not comfortable with great complexity. It performs best with relatively simple product structures, relatively predictable (and preferably level) demand and clearly defined material flows in the operation. Furthermore, the paradox of JIT is that there are circumstances where it is less capable than MRP of achieving literally 'just-in-time' delivery. This is because pure JIT is a *reactive* idea – it responds to changes in demand only with difficulty. It is not of itself a system which anticipates demand – that is both its virtue and its limitation. The very system which protects upstream parts of the operation from fluctuations in demand makes it less capable of reacting flexibly to changes, especially where complexity of the product structure is already straining JIT's need for simplicity. Yet in spite of this, JIT ideals are attractive to a whole variety of operations, not just those with stable, high-volume production. This is because of the direct and powerful impact JIT principles have at the 'shop-floor' level of almost any operation. The simple and transparent principles of pull control, together with its continuous improvement imperative, provide the discipline which makes efficient day-to-day control feasible.

Putting the relative advantages and disadvantages of JIT and MRP together suggests how the two approaches can be blended. Two blends are briefly described.

Separate systems for different products

Using the runners, repeaters, strangers terminology described earlier, pull scheduling using kanban can be used for 'runners' and 'repeaters'. MRP control can then be used for strangers in which works orders are issued to explain what must be done at each stage and then the work itself is monitored to push materials through manufacturing stages.[20] The advantage of this is that by increasing responsiveness and reducing inventories it makes it worthwhile to increase their number by design simplification.

MRP for overall control and JIT for internal control

MRP planning of supplier materials aims to ensure that sufficient parts are in the pipeline to enable them to be called up 'just-in-time'.[21] Figure 15.14 illustrates a simplified version of what may be achieved by the use of pull scheduling in manufacture supported by MRP material procurement. The master production schedule (*see* Chapter 14) is broken down by means of MRP for supplier schedules (forecast future demand). Actual material requirements for suppliers are signalled by means of kanban to facilitate JIT delivery. Within the factory, all material movements are governed by kanban loops between operations. The 'drum beat' for the factory is set by the factory assembly schedule.

A number of advantages over conventional MRP are claimed by combining the two systems in this way:

- There is no need for internal inter-stage works orders.
- In-process inventory need only be monitored between cells rather than for each activity.
- The bill of materials has fewer levels than in a conventional MRP system.
- Process-route information is simplified.
- Work-centre planning and control is simplified.
- Lead times and WIP are reduced.

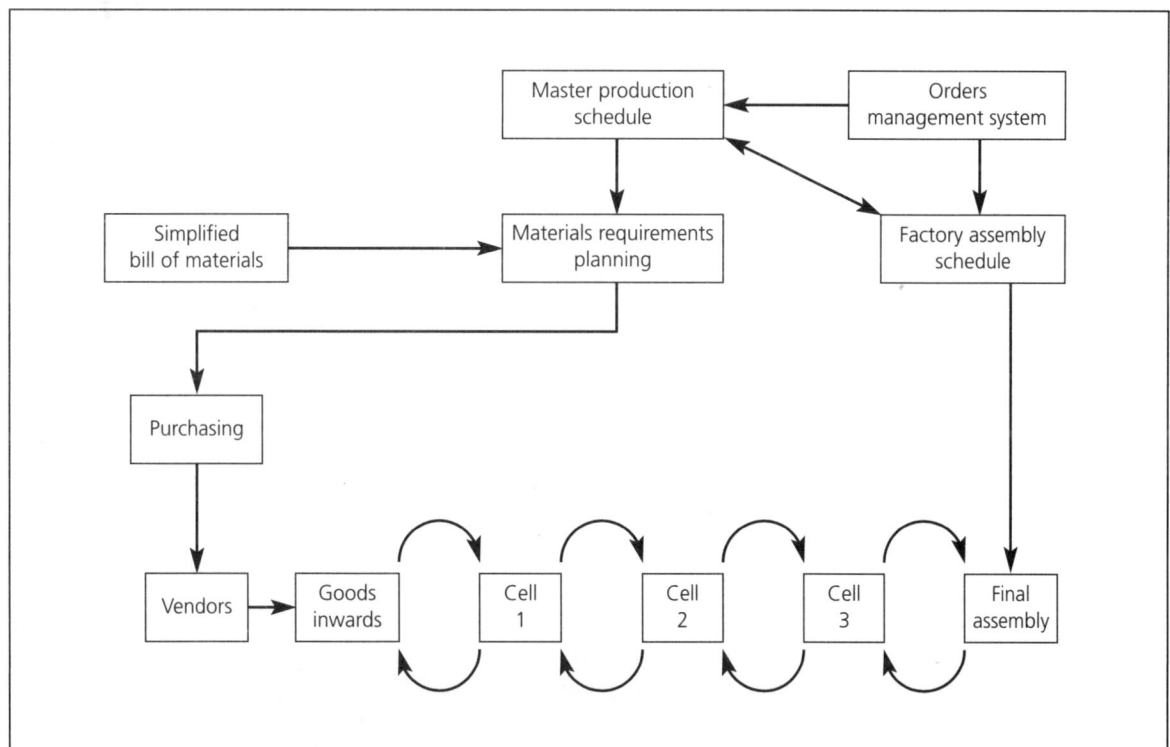

Figure 15.14 Using MRP to control the final assembly schedule and purchasing while kanbans control flow internally

When to use JIT, MRP and combined systems

Again it is the advantages and disadvantages of JIT and MRP which guide when to use 'pure' versions of the two, or one of the combined options. There are two ways of looking at this: one uses the system's ability to handle complexity as the main determinant of the decision, the other combines the volume and variety characteristics of the operation and the level of control required in order to make the choice.

The complexity determinant

Figure 15.15 distinguishes between the complexity of product structures and the complexity of the flow-path routings through which they must pass.[22] Simple product structures which have routings with high repeatability are prime candidates for pull control. JIT can easily cope with their relatively straightforward requirements. As structures and routings become more complex, so the power of the computer is needed in order to break down product structures and so to assign orders to suppliers.

In many environments, it is possible to use pull scheduling for the control of most internal materials. Again, prime candidates for pull control are materials which are used regularly each week or each month. Their number can be increased by design standardization, as indicated by the direction of the arrow in Fig. 15.15.

As structures and routings become even more complex, and parts usages become more irregular, so the opportunities for using pull scheduling decrease. Very complex structures require networking methods like PERT (program evaluation and review technique – *see* Chapter 16 on project planning and control) for planning and control. Such structures provide few opportunities for pull scheduling. However, even in this environment, a possible use for JIT is to limit the build-up of inventory, for example by means of kanban squares painted on the floor, so work cannot move to the next operation until a square is free.

The volume–variety and level of control determinants

Figure 15.16 again uses a matrix to determine the relative suitability of planning and control approaches. This time the dimensions are the type of production process and the level for which the control system is being designed.[23]

The *type of production* uses the volume–variety characteristics we have used before. Taken together they indicate the complexity of manufacturing. Variation in processing lead times, the number of alternative product routes, the complexity of product structures, and the variety of product types, can all be related to volume and variety.

The *level of control* indicates which set of production control tasks are being considered. High-level control involves broadly coordinating the flow of materials to the various parts of the plant as well as giving an indication of what level of output they will be expected to achieve in future periods. Medium-level control is the detailed allocation of production orders to each part of the plant. Low-level control is the detailed monitoring and re-adjustment of day-to-day shop-floor activities.

Two of the areas in Fig. 15.16 need some explanation. Area A indicates that, in some high-volume automated-type manufacturing, the shop-floor level of control may be incorporated into the technology itself. For example, the integrated technologies of some food-processing plants automatically transfer materials from one part of the plant to another. It usually requires intervention on the part of operations management to prevent transfer occurring. Area B represents the detailed shop-floor

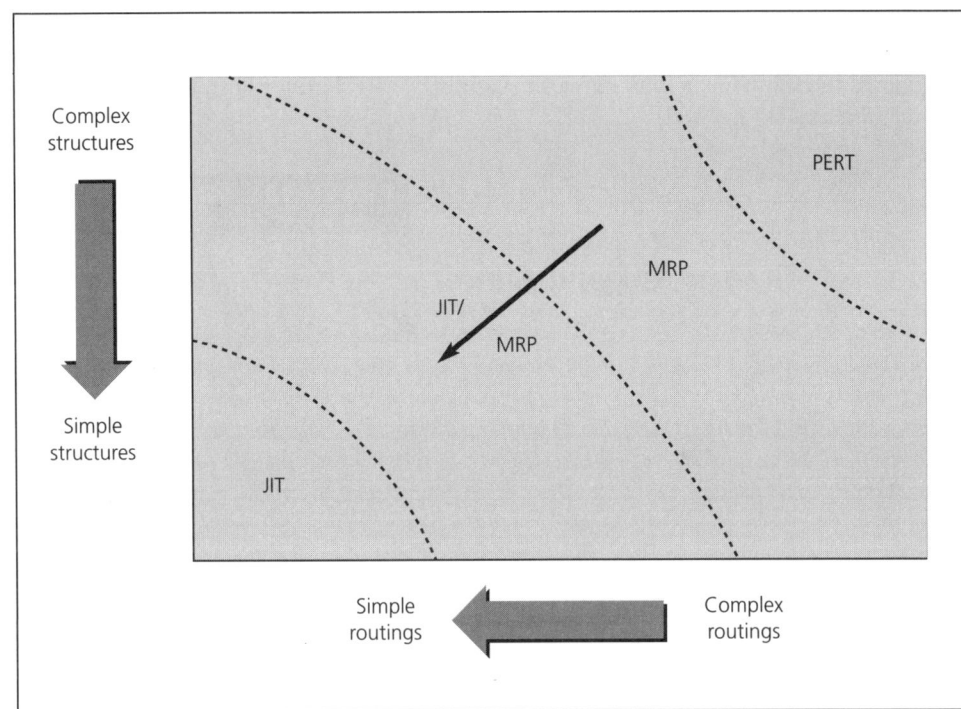

**Figure 15.15
Complexity as a
determinant of an
appropriate
planning and
control system**
Source: from Voss,
C.A. and Harrison, A.[22]

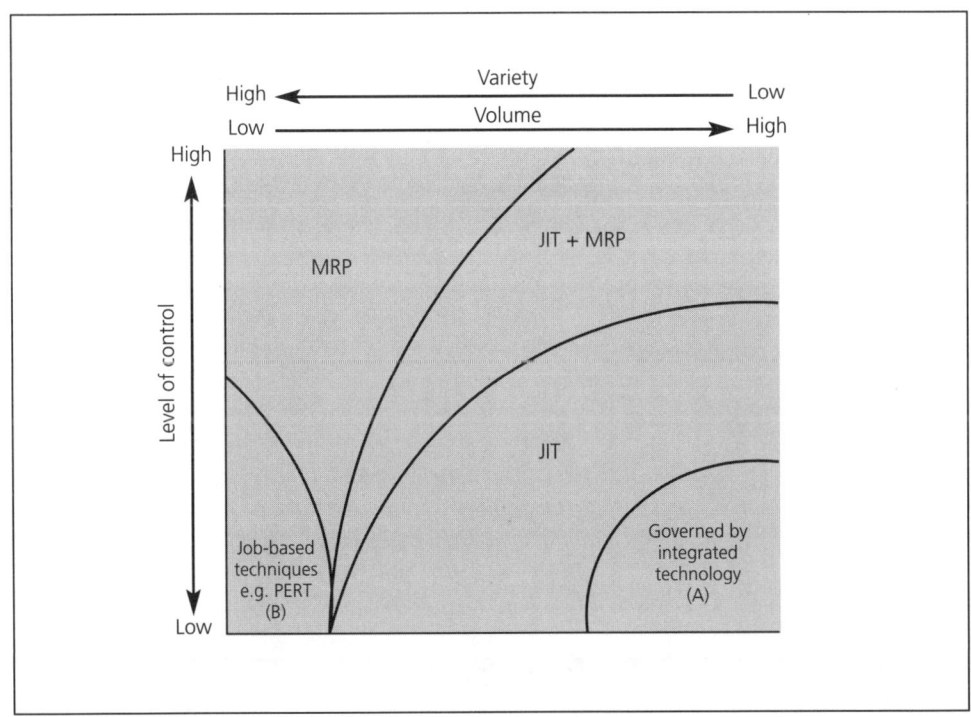

**Figure 15.16
Volume–variety
and the level of
control as
determinants of
the appropriate
planning and
control system**

scheduling and control in very complex, high-variety customized manufacture. Here it is the nature of each individual job which dominates the production control task. Specialized techniques such as network planning (PERT, for example – *see* the next chapter) are usually needed.

Graham Kirkland, Suncorp

Graham Kirkland is the Managing Director of Suncorp Manufacturing. This company is a Black Economic Empowerment venture involved in the local production of photo-voltaic modules for use in remote area power supplies. The objective of this firm has been to provide product to be used in rural electrification projects to uplift the quality of life of the 60 per cent (24 million) of South Africans who currently have no access to electricity.

The company has implemented a rather lean internal resource management system that epitomizes the concept of JIT in action. Graham takes up the story.

'The production of solar modules is a rather delicate and detailed process that requires ongoing quality testing and batch control due to the rather rigorous product application and the guarantee offered of 10–20 years. The firm exists in an industry in which demand fluctuates quite widely and where the supply lines are rather long. It is a paradox that JIT has been able to operate this well in an industry with these characteristics. The mystery is explained by the fact that we decided at the inception of the firm to run the plant with a balanced assembly schedule using buffers at the supply and demand end. This allowed us to gain all of the advantages of JIT internally while buffering the plant from the dramatic swings in demand and the excessive supply lead times.

'The production process involves a sophisticated assembly operation with specialized equipment in a clean environment. It starts with a soldering process to string the solar cells together, after which four strings of cells are joined to form the final array. The array is then placed onto the glass substrate and a series of layers of fibreglass, insulation and aluminium sheets are applied in a lay-up to create the laminate that is then bonded together in a Laminator. On conclusion of the lamination cycle, the hot bonded laminate is allowed to cool down before it is subjected to a High Voltage test. The application of the diodes, terminals and junction boxes is performed in a batch process before the final "flashing" of each module in the Sun-Simulator. Each module is then boxed and the batch is palletized for dispatch.

'The solar cells constitute the lion's share of the material cost of the module, over 70 per cent, and are also rather light. They are therefore air-freighted in on a weekly basis. The delivery lead time on the balance of the basic raw material, about 30 items, is six weeks ex-works in America followed by consolidation and sea freight of five weeks. Customs clearance in Durban and trucking up to the factory in Gauteng consume a further two weeks. The total replenishment lead time on the balance of the module material is hence over three months! For this reason we chose to bring in a shipment once every two months. All finished product is shipped weekly to our distributor.

'Typically, the total inventory in the plant is made up of a week's worth of cells, four to eight weeks' worth of the balance of module materials and half a week's worth of completed modules. This equates by value to less than three weeks' worth of stocks. The actual inventory in the production area, however, is less than two to three days' stocks. This is because of perfect line balance and daily replenishment from our raw materials store. The design of the line has also been optimized to allow for the movement of material easily between workstations sequentially through the plant.

'Some key operational points are:

- The plant is managed on the basis of output rate per day both as a whole and at each station;
- The employees are multi-skilled;
- We do not permit volume fluctuations of more than about 10 per cent;
- The equipment has been optimized for the product, to minimize adjustments;
- The layout has avoided areas in the plant where inventory can build up, with the exception of the batch processes;
- The standard time for a module, about 2.5 hours, is almost equal to the average time that a module takes through the plant. In other words, the plant produces a complete module every two hours that the plant works.

'The plant has also been set up to make full use of the complete ambit of JIT and Total Quality Management techniques:

- SPC at all stages with visibility charts at each workstation;
- 100 per cent inspection;
- self-inspection by the individual workers (we do not employ inspectors!);
- the monitoring of all scrap;
- the use of root-cause analysis techniques;
- the implementation of Total Productive Maintenance;
- the use of fool-proofing techniques.

'The ultimate result of this is a production facility that:

- produces with a reject level of less than one in 1000;
- has a labour productivity rate that is better than that in equivalent plants in Europe and America;
- is the lowest cost producer in the country;
- exceeds the normal prescribed levels of technical performance laid down by regulatory authorities in the industry;
- has a negative working capital brought about by the combination of tight operations control and attractive payment terms such that the business only pays for raw materials after it has sold the finished product.

'The plant has been modelled on a supermarket. Components stay the least amount of time on the assembly line and profits are possible from judicious management of working capital. This is made possible by the use of JIT resource scheduling techniques. A further novel innovation is that all employees are shareholders in the plant. This has acted to support the high levels of motivation and teamwork required in an environment such as this.'

Source: By kind permission of Suncorp

SUMMARY

■ The overall aim of just-in-time operations is to meet demand instantaneously with perfect quality and no waste. It must be stressed, however, that this is an aim rather than a short-term realistic target. Nevertheless, JIT does aim to produce parts and products just-in-time for them to be needed by customers – not earlier than they need them nor later than they need them.

■ The central justification for just-in-time delivery is that the low inventory levels it produces not only save working capital but also have a significant impact on the ability of an operation to improve its intrinsic efficiency. This leads to a broader definition of JIT which can be seen as an operation's philosophy which attacks all kinds of waste in the operation.

■ JIT can be seen as an overall philosophy of operations but also as a collection of tools and methods which support its aims. Many of these tools and techniques in fact appear in other parts of this book.

■ There is no clear consensus of the origins of JIT apart from the agreement that it developed in Japan after the Second World War. However, the cultural and economic environment of Japan at this time is thought also to have been very significant in the development of JIT. The origins of JIT can be seen in the way it can be characterized as a high-dependency model of operations practice.

■ As a philosophy, JIT can be summarized as concerning three overlapping elements. These are the elimination of waste in all its forms, the inclusion of all staff in the operation in its improvement, and the idea that all improvement should be on a continuous basis.

■ Many JIT techniques directly concern the planning and control activity in operations. The specific techniques which JIT uses to plan and control are:
– Pull scheduling which puts the onus on customer operations to request delivery rather than supply operations sending deliveries.
– Kanban control which is sometimes erroneously seen as the equivalent to JIT. Kanbans are simple control objects such as cards which govern the movement of materials between stages and the production of items into stock. Single-card kanban routines and dual-card kanban routines can be used to govern the movement of kanbans.
– Levelled scheduling attempts to smooth the flow of goods out of a production area by shortening the period within which the production sequence of goods is repeated.
– Mixed modelling carries this process further and suggests a sequence of products which assume an EBQ of 1 and therefore give a smooth stream of the mix of products required.
– Synchronization is the process by which the rhythm, or 'drum beat', of production is regularized for higher volume products.

■ Although JIT and MRP might seem to be very different approaches to planning and control, they can be combined to form a hybrid system. There are several ways in which they can be combined but they each try to exploit the relative advantages of MRP and JIT.

■ A number of determinants can be identified which govern the choice of which type of planning control approach to use. The complexity of product structures and routing can influence which approach is used, as can the volume–variety position of the operation and the level of control required.

CASE EXERCISE

Just-in-time at Jimmy's [24]

St. James's Hospital, affectionately known as 'Jimmy's', is Europe's largest teaching hospital. It employs around 4500 people to support the 90 000 in-patient treatments per year and over 450 000 total admissions. Under increasing pressure to reduce costs, to contain inventory and to improve service, the Supplies Department undertook a major analysis of its activities, helped by the consultancy division of Lucas Industries, the UK-based manufacturing company.

The initial review highlighted that Jimmy's had approximately 1500 suppliers of 15 000 different products at a total cost of £15 million. Traditionally, the Supplies Department ordered what the doctors asked for, with many cases of similar items supplied by six or more firms. Under a cross-functional task force, comprising both medical and supply staff, a major programme of supplier and product rationalization was undertaken, which also revealed many sources of waste. For example, the team found that wards used as many as 20 different types of gloves, some of which were expensive surgeons' gloves costing around £1 per pair, yet in almost all cases these could be replaced by fewer and cheaper (20 pence) alternatives. Similarly, anaesthetic items, which were previously bought from six suppliers, were single-sourced. The savings in purchasing costs, inventory costs, and general administration were enormous in themselves, but the higher order volumes also helped the hospital negotiate for lower prices. Suppliers are also much more willing to deliver frequently in smaller quantities when they know that they are the sole supplier. Peter Beeston, the Supplies Manager said,

'We've been driven by suppliers for years . . . they would insist that we could only purchase in thousands, that we would have to wait weeks, or that they would only deliver on Wednesdays! Now, our selected suppliers know that if they perform well, we will assure them of a long-term commitment. I prefer to buy 80 per cent of our requirements from 20 or 30 suppliers, whereas previously, it involved over a hundred.'

The streamlining of the admissions process also proved fertile ground for improvement along JIT principles. For example, in the Urology Department, one third of patients for non-urgent surgery found their appointments were being cancelled. One reason for this was that in the time between the consultant saying that an operation was required and the patient arriving at the operating theatre, there were 59 changes in responsibility for the process. The hospital reorganized the process to form a 'cell' of four people who were given complete responsibility for admissions for Urology. The cell was located next to the ward and made responsible for all record keeping, planning all operations, ensuring that beds were available as needed, and telling the patient when to arrive. As a result, the 59 handovers are now down to 13 and the process is faster, cheaper and more reliable.

Jimmy's also introduced a simple kanban system for some of its local inventory. In Ward Nine storeroom, for example, there are just two boxes of 10 mm syringes on the shelf. When the first is empty, the other is moved forward and the Ward Sister then orders another. The next stage will be to simplify the re-ordering: empty boxes will be posted outside the store, where codes will be periodically read by the Supplies Department, using a mobile data recorder.

The hospital's management are convinced of the benefits of their changes.

'Value for money, not cost cutting, is what this is all about. We are standardizing on buying quality products and now also have more influence on the buying decision . . . from being previously functionally oriented with a number of buyers, we now concentrate on materials management for complete product ranges. The project has been an unmitigated success and although we are only just starting to see the benefits, I would expect savings in cost and in excess inventory to spiral! The report on Sterile Wound Care Packs shows the potential that our team has identified.

'The "old" pack consisted of:

— four pairs of plastic forceps
— cotton wool balls
— a plastic pot

which were used with or without additional gloves. This pack cost approximately 60 pence excluding the gloves.

▶

The "new" pack consists of:

— *a plastic pot*
— *swabs, etc.*
— *one pair of latex gloves only.*

This pack costs approximately 33 pence including gloves. Total target saving is approximately £20 000.' ■

Questions

1 List the elements in St. James's new approach which could be seen as deriving from JIT principles of manufacturing.

2 What further ideas from JIT manufacturing do you think could be applied in a hospital setting such as St. James's?

DISCUSSION QUESTIONS

1 Explain your views on whether you think that JIT is a philosophy, a strategy or a selection of techniques.

2 Why does continuous improvement require a long-term view of the business? Discuss what is meant by an 'enabling company culture' in which continuous improvement can flourish?

3 How do make-to-order businesses avoid waste?

4 Why are work-in-progress and lead time related? How does this relationship affect a building society on a Saturday morning?

5 If you were aiming to develop your company into a JIT company, what would you look for in your suppliers?

6 Simplicity is often a theme associated with JIT companies. How does Little Chef incorporate this theme into its management of operations?

7 What are the deficiencies of the Economic Order Quantity (EOQ) from a JIT point of view?

8 Explain how mixed modelling is used to develop a detailed operations schedule. How does this differ from a master schedule?

9 How can new technology be used to supply kanbans in a JIT operation?

10 Explain how JIT techniques can be used to support volume and mix flexibility in operations management.

11 Why is Jidoka (line-stop authority) described as a 'cornerstone of the Toyota Production System'?

12 Referring to the Temple Hospital case described in the text, explain the advantages of ordering materials at 'three different levels'. How did this lead to more accurate material provisioning to the physicians

while stocks were actually reduced?

13 Explain the key differences between a 'traditional' approach and a JIT approach to manufacturing. Do these differences occur in service organizations?

14 Discuss the advantages and disadvantages of working just-in-time.

15 The elimination of waste is a core philosophy of JIT. What is meant by 'waste' and explain the origins and intentions of this approach?

16 Discuss the benefits of set-up time reduction on each of the five operations' performance objectives: cost, flexibility, quality, dependability and speed.

17 Explain the difference between 'push' and 'pull' planning and control. Why might different organizations choose such approaches?

18 Discuss how kanbans might be applied, and the form they might take, in a fast-food restaurant.

19 A manufacturer of printed circuit boards (PCBs) is currently producing them at a rate of one every three minutes from a four-part container. The overall efficiency of the system has been estimated to be 90 per cent and the existing set-up times are 180 minutes per day. The management would like to develop a JIT system but with no more than three kanbans. To what level will set-up times need to be reduced to achieve this?

20 Discuss the benefits of reducing batch quantities.

21 What do you think might be the advantages and disadvantages of employing 'jidoka' in service organizations? Illustrate your answer using an organization of your choice.

NOTES ON CHAPTER

1 Bicheno, J. (1991) *Implementing Just-in-time*, IFS.
2 Voss, C.A. (1987) *in* Voss, C.A. (ed) *Just-in-time Manufacture*, IFS/Springer-Verlag.
3 Voss, C.A., *op. cit.*
4 Schonberger, R. (1982) *Japanese Manufacturing Techniques*, Free Press.
5 Oliver, N. and Wilkinson, B. (1988) *The Japanization of British Industry*, Basil Blackwell.
6 Oliver, N. and Wilkinson, B., *op. cit.*
7 Harrison, A. (1992) *Just-in-time in Perspective*, Prentice Hall.
8 Lee, D.C. (1987) 'Set-up Time Reduction: Making JIT Work' *in* Voss, C.A. (ed), *Just-in-time Manufacture*, IFS/Springer-Verlag.
9 Quoted in Harrison, A., *op. cit.*
10 Quoted in Harrison, A., *op. cit.*
11 Harrison, A., *op. cit.*
12 Whitney, D.E. (1990) 'Manufacturing by Design', *Harvard Business Review*, Vol 68, No 4.
13 Skinner, W. (1978) *Manufacturing in the Corporate Strategy*, John Wiley.
14 Yamashina, H. 'Reducing Set-up Times Makes your Company Flexible and More Competitive', unpublished, quoted in Harrison A., *op. cit.*
15 Harrison, A., *op. cit.*
16 Source: 'Behind the Face of Beauty – Manufacturing Flexibility for the Mass Market', *Europlus*, Jan 1994.
17 Hall, R. (1987) *Attaining Manufacturing Excellence*, Dow Jones/Irwin.
18 Harrison, A., *op. cit.*
19 Parnaby, J. (1988) 'A Systems Approach to the Implementation of JIT Methodologies in Lucas Industries', *International Journal of Production Research*, Vol 26, No 3.
20 Parnaby, J., *op. cit.*
21 Parnaby, J., *op. cit.*
22 Voss, C.A. and Harrison, A. (1987) 'Strategies for Implementing JIT' *in* Voss, C.A. (ed) *Just-in-time Manufacture*, IFS/Springer-Verlag.
23 Slack, N. (1991) *The Manufacturing Advantage*, Mercury Books.
24 Sources: *The Independent on Sunday*, 4 July 1993, *Update*, Issue 18, Aug 1993.

SELECTED FURTHER READINGS

Bennett, D.J. and Rajput, S.K. (1989) 'Design and Implementation of Production Systems for High Variety Electronics Assembly', *International Journal of Operations and Production Management*, Vol 9, No 5.

Bicheno, J. (1991) *Implementing JIT*, IFS Publications.

Faull, N.H.B. (1990) 'Lessons Learned from MRP and JIT', *South African Mining World*, Vol 9, No 7, pp 37–42.

Fiedler, K., Galletly, J.E. and Bicheno, J. (1993) 'Expert Advice for JIT Implementation', *International Journal of Operations and Production Management*, Vol 13, No 6.

Goyal, S.K. and Deshmukh, S.G. (1992) 'A Critique of the Literature on Just-in-time Manufacturing', *International Journal of Operations and Production Management*, Vol 12, No 1.

Harrison, A. and Voss, C. (1990) 'Issues in Setting up JIT Supply', *International Journal of Operations and Production Management*, Vol 10, No 2.

Harrison, A.S. (1992) *Just-in-Time Manufacturing in Perspective*, Prentice Hall.

Jordan, H.H. (1988) 'Inventory Management in the JIT Age', *Production and Inventory Management Journal*, Vol 29, No 13.

Marisako, S. (1992) *Prices, Quality and Trust*, Cambridge University Press.

Murata, K. with Harrison, A.S. (1991) *How to Make Japanese Management Methods Work in the West*, Gower.

Oliver, N. and Wilkinson, B. (1992) *The Japanisation of British Industry* (2nd edn), Blackwell.

Oliver, N. (1990) 'Human Factors in the Implementation of Just-in-time Production', *International Journal of Operations and Production Management*, Vol 10, No 4.

Schniederjans, M.J. (1993) *Topics in Just-in-Time Management*, Allyn & Bacon.

Schonberger, R.J. (1982) *Japanese Manufacturing Techniques: Nine Hidden Lessons in Simplicity*, Free Press.

Schonberger, R.J. (1986) *World Class Manufacturing: The Lessons of Simplicity Applied*, Free Press.

Schonberger, R.J. and Schniederjans, M.J. (1983) 'Reinventing Inventory Control', *Interfaces*, Vol 13, No 3.

Sohal, A.S., Keller, A.Z. and Fouad, R.H. (1988) 'A Review of Literature Relating to JIT', *International Journal of Operations and Production Management*, Vol 8, No 3.

Sohal, A.S., Ramsey, L. and Samson, D. (1993) 'JIT Manufacturing Industry: Analysis and a Method for Implementation', *International Journal of Operations and Production Management*, Vol 13, No 7.

Vollmann, T., Berry, L. and Whybarck, D.C. (1992) *Manufacturing Planning and Control Systems* (3rd edn), Irwin.

Womack, J. P., Jones, D.T. and Roos, D. (1990) *The Machine that Changed the World*, Rawson Associates.

PROJECT PLANNING AND CONTROL

INTRODUCTION

This chapter is concerned with the planning and control of operations which occupy the low volume–high variety end of the continuum which we introduced in Chapter 4. These 'project' operations are engaged in complex, often large-scale, activities with a defined beginning and end. The pioneers of planning and controlling project operations were the engineers and planners who worked on complex defence and construction projects. More recently, the methods they developed have been applied to projects as diverse as new product launches, education projects in the Third World and theatrical productions. Project planning and control is important because all managers will, at some point, get involved with managing projects. Many of these projects may be relatively small – a human resources manager planning a training course, for example. Some will be far larger, for example where the manager is part of a project team – such as an accountant providing cost information for a new marketing promotion. Whether large or small, however, the planning and control aspects of managing projects follow similar principles. *See* Fig. 16.1.

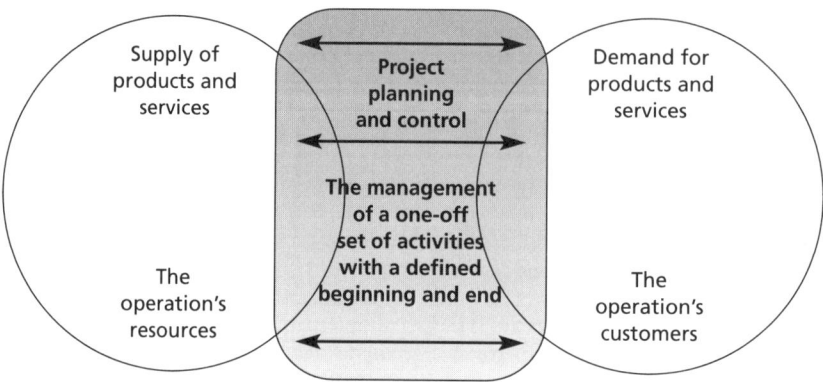

Figure 16.1 A definition of project planning and control

OBJECTIVES

This chapter will examine:

- the nature of projects and of project management;

- the environment in which projects take place;

- how projects can be defined in terms of their objectives, their scope and the strategy for their completion;

- how projects are planned;

- how projects are controlled;

- how network analysis can be used for planning and controlling projects.

WHAT IS A PROJECT?

A project is a set of activities which have a defined start point and a defined end state, pursue a defined goal and use a defined set of resources. Although many small-scale operations management endeavours conform to this definition of a project, we will devote the majority of this chapter to examining the management of larger-scale projects. The management of small projects can be treated as a special case of what is normally just referred to as 'project management'. The assumption of 'large projects' when we discuss project management provides us with the opportunity to explore some of the special characteristics which come with large-scale activities. Large-scale (and therefore complex) undertakings consume a relatively large amount of resources, take a long time to complete and typically involve interactions between different parts of an organization. To plan and control a project, a company needs to devise a model which describes the project's complexity and project it forward in time to make sure that the project will achieve its goals. The model of the project (its plan) can then be used to check progress as the real project proceeds (control of the project).

The first project to be managed in a way which we would today recognize as project management was the Manhattan project which created the first atom bomb. However, the enterprises undertaken by the ancient civilizations were of a scale and complexity (even if the resources which they used were less constrained) to imply some form of organization. It is difficult to imagine the construction of the great pyramids of Egypt being achieved without an ordered and systematic planning and control effort. Today projects come in many and various forms, including the following:

- The Apollo moon programme
- Cleaning the exterior of the Houses of Parliament
- An AIDS information campaign
- Producing a television programme
- Constructing the Channel Tunnel
- Designing the Airbus
- Putting on a one-week course in project management

- Relocating a factory
- Buying and moving into a new house
- Refurbishing an hotel
- Installing a new information system
- Conducting the first universal elections in South Africa
- Cleaning up after an oil tanker spillage.

The elements of a project

To a greater or lesser extent all these projects have some elements in common. These common elements form the characteristics which will help us to understand the nature of projects and therefore project planning and control.

- *An objective.* A definable end result, output, or product, which is typically defined in terms of the cost, the quality and timing of the output from the project activities.
- *Complexity.* Many different tasks are required to be undertaken to achieve a project's objectives. The relationship between all these tasks can be complex, especially when the number of separate tasks in the project is large.
- *Uniqueness.* A project is usually a 'one-off', not a repetitive undertaking. Even 'repeat' projects, such as the construction of another chemical plant to the same specification, will have distinctive differences in terms of resources used and the actual environment in which the project takes place.
- *Uncertainty.* All projects are planned before they are executed and therefore carry an element of risk. A 'blue sky' research project carries the risk that expensive, high technology resources will be committed with no worthwhile outcome.
- *Temporary nature.* Projects have a defined beginning and end, so a temporary concentration of resources is needed to carry out the undertaking. Once their contribution to the project objectives has been completed, the resources are usually redeployed.
- *Life cycle.* The resource needs for a project change during the course of its life cycle. The typical pattern of resource needs for a project follow a predictable path. From a planning and control perspective, it is therefore necessary to divide up the life cycle of a project into *project phases*.

These elements serve to distinguish projects from other types of operation. They also serve to distinguish *projects* from *programmes*. A *programme,* such as a continuous improvement programme (*see* Chapter 18), has no defined end point. Rather it is an ongoing process of change. Programmes often share some project characteristics such as complexity and uncertainty, and as a result can benefit from the use of selected project planning and control methods.

Although the management of projects is associated with operations of the low volume–high variety type, this does not mean that only these types of operation will ever be concerned with projects. High-volume and continuous production operations, such as a bulk chemical producer, will be a customer for projects. The chemical company's new plant will be constructed as a 'one-off' project, the plant will be maintained according to a project plan, its staff will be trained by services organized on a project basis, and so on. However, the operations which create these projects for the bulk chemical producer are likely to be of the low volume–high variety type (a construction company, maintenance contractors and the training department respectively). It is necessary therefore for managers in all types of operation to understand the nature of project planning and control. Even if their prime operations rationale is not to create projects, they are likely to be either customers for them or suppliers to them at some time.

A typology of projects

Selecting two of the above elements of projects, Fig. 16.2 illustrates a typology for projects according to their *complexity* – in terms of size, value and the number of people involved in the project – and their *uncertainty* of achieving the project objectives of cost, time and quality.

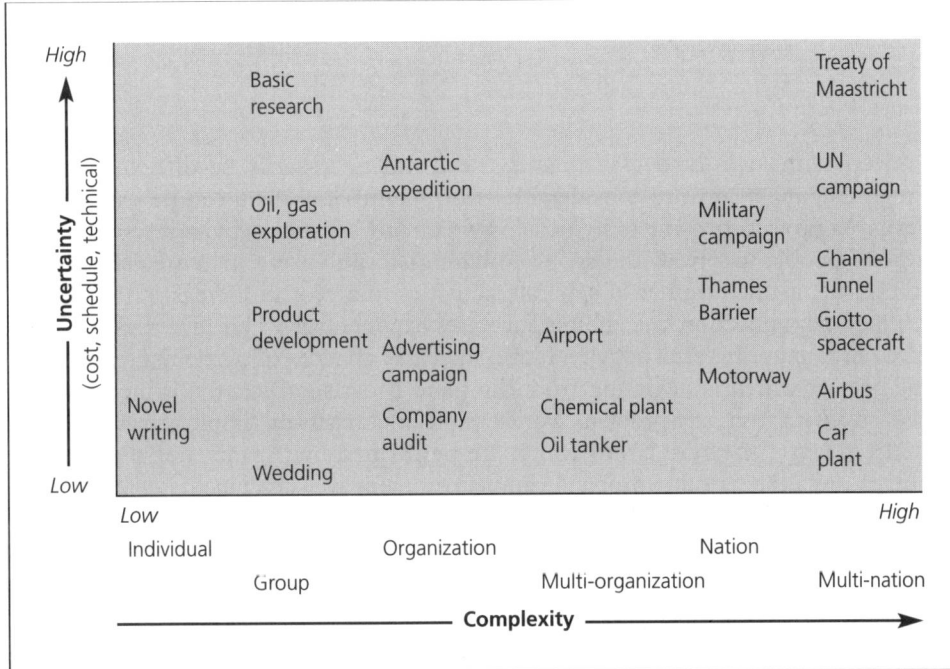

Figure 16.2
A typology of projects
Source: Adapted from Nicholas, J. M. (1990)[1]

The typology helps to give a rational presentation of the vast range of undertakings where project management principles can be applied.[1] It also gives a clue to the nature of the projects and the difficulties of managing them. Uncertainty particularly affects project planning and complexity particularly affects project control.

Projects with *high uncertainty* are likely to be especially difficult to define and set realistic objectives for. If the exact details of a project are subject to change during the course of its execution, the planning process is particularly difficult. Resources may be committed, times may be agreed but if the objectives of the project change or if the environmental conditions change, or if some activity is delayed, then all the plans which were made prior to the changes will need to be redrawn. Uncertainty is the enemy of stable planning. When uncertainty is high, the whole project planning process needs to be sufficiently flexible to cope with the consequences of change. For example, the implementation of a political treaty in the European Union is subject to the ratification of all the member governments. Politics being an uncertain business, any of the member countries might either fail to ratify the treaty or attempt to renegotiate it. The central planners at EU headquarters must therefore have contingency plans in place which indicate how they might have to change the 'project' to cope with any political changes. Table 16.1 illustrates the effects of uncertainty on project planning.

Table 16.1 The effects of uncertainty on project planning

Aspect of project planning	Uncertainty	
	High	Low
Planning objectives	Evolving	Determined
Extent of planning	Ill defined	Clear
Outline of plan	Fuzzy	Defined

Projects with *high levels of complexity* need not necessarily be difficult to plan, although they might involve considerable effort; controlling them can be problematic, however. As projects become more detailed with many separate activities, resources and groups of people involved, the scope for things to go wrong increases alarmingly. Furthermore, as the number of separate activities in a project increases, the ways in which they can impact on one another increases exponentially. This increases the effort involved in monitoring each activity. It also increases chances of overlooking some part of the project which is deviating from the plan. Most significantly, it increases the 'knock-on' effect from any problem. For example, in a relatively simple project with few activities (even if they are large) which are performed by organizationally separate resources, any delay or other problem can be reasonably well contained; it will not affect the other parts of the project. However, in a project with many separate activities with a high degree of dependency between them and involving shared resources, any delay in one part of the project will transmit its consequences to the rest of the project. Put both uncertainty and complexity together in a project and it tests even the most dedicated and skilled project manager.

SUCCESSFUL PROJECT MANAGEMENT

All projects are prone to different problems and fail for different reasons. There are some points of commonality in success and failure, however, which allow us to identify some general points which seem to minimize the chances of a project failing to meet its objectives. The following factors are particulary important:[2]

● *Clearly defined goals*: including the general project philosophy or general mission of the project, and a commitment to those goals on the part of the project team members.
● *Competent project manager*: a skilled project leader who has the necessary interpersonal, technical, and administrative skills.
● *Top-management support*: top-management commitment for the project that has been communicated to all concerned parties.

● *Competent project team members*: the selection of, and if necessary, the training of, project team members, who between them have the skills necessary to support the project technically.
● *Sufficient resource allocation*: resources, in the form of money, personnel, logistics, etc., which are available for the project in the required quantity.
● *Adequate communications channels*: sufficient information is available on project objectives, status, changes, organizational conditions, and client's needs.
● *Control mechanisms*: the mechanisms which are in place to monitor actual events and recognize deviations from the plan.
● *Feedback capabilities*: all parties concerned with the project are able to review the project's status, and make suggestions and corrections through formal feedback channels or review meetings.
● *Responsiveness to clients*: all potential users of the project are concerned with and are kept up to date on the project's status.
● *Trouble-shooting mechanisms*: a system or set of procedures which can tackle problems when they arise, can trace them back to their root cause and resolve them.
● *Project staff continuity*: the continued involvement of key project personnel over the project life cycle. Frequent turnover of staff can dissipate the learning which is acquired in the project team.

Project managers

In order to coordinate the efforts of many people in different parts of the organization (and often outside it as well), all projects need a project manager. Put simply, the role of the project manager is to achieve the project objectives. They do this by planning and controlling the project from initiation to conclusion, trying to bring order to complexity and reducing the level of uncertainty. Many of a project manager's activities are concerned with managing human resources. The people working in the project team need to work effectively with a clear understanding of their roles in the, usually, temporary organization. They must take responsibility for effective communication. Controlling an uncertain project environment requires the rapid exchange of relevant information with the project stakeholders, both within and outside the organization. They also need to procure all the resources for the project. People, equipment and other resources must be identified and allocated to the various tasks. Finally, they are concerned with controlling uncertainty by forecasting, planning for, and resolving problems. Undertaking these tasks successfully makes the management of a project a particularly challenging operations management activity. Both 'technical' and personal qualities are needed. Five characteristics in particular are seen as important in an effective project manager:[3]

● background and experience which are consistent with the needs of the project;
● leadership and strategic expertise, in order to maintain an understanding of the overall project and its environment, while at the same time working on the details of the project;
● technical expertise in the area of the project in order to make sound technical decisions;
● interpersonal competence and the people skills to take on such roles as project champion, motivator, communicator, facilitator and politician;
● proven managerial ability in terms of a track record of getting things done.

PROJECT FAILURE AT THE LONDON AMBULANCE SERVICE[4]

An ambulance service deals in life and death. Its fast and accurate response to emergency calls and its paramedic skills can dictate the survival of any of us when we are at our most vulnerable.

On 26 October 1992 the ambulance service in the UK's capital city was thrown into utter disarray. The computer system which logged emergency calls to the service, traced and dispatched ambulances and monitored the status of each emergency had malfunctioned under the strain of trying to cope with only a slightly higher than average number of emergency calls. On a normal day the service could expect to deal with around 2300 calls. On that day the number had risen to 2900 but it broke the system. Calls were left unanswered, whole banks of logged calls were wiped off the system and the service's target response time of 14 minutes extended into the distance. The whole of the service was paralysed. The failure had caused incalculable pain, suffering, and perhaps death, and the root cause of it was bad project management.

The three-person team of enquiry which later investigated the failure put the blame directly on the recently installed computer system. The project management team which had designed, commissioned and installed the system had, according to the inquiry team, '. . . *made virtually every mistake in the book*'.

● The project was always a 'high-uncertainty' investment in a new technology. This was never fully appreciated. It was an over-ambitious project which had an unrealistic total project time of two years. Five years might have been a better estimate.

● Procurement rules for buying in services concentrated on quantitative criteria to the detriment of qualitative criteria.

● The budget for the project of £1.5 million was too low. Around £4 million would have been more realistic.

● The whole culture of the project revolved around a fear of failure and, despite early signs of problems, the management team had pressed on.

● The project manager's qualifications and motivation were questioned.

● One part of the software development was sub-contracted to a small software house who had little experience of handling projects of this complexity or scope.

● The installation team at the contract company had failed to meet the initial programme schedule of January '92 and, under pressure to stay on track, had installed and tested the system on a piecemeal basis throughout the year.

● There was insufficient ownership of the system by its developers and mistrust by its users.

● There was insufficient training of the staff who eventually had to use the system. ■

THE PROJECT PLANNING AND CONTROL PROCESS

Figure 16.3 proposes a project management model which is used as a framework for this chapter. The model categorizes project management activities into five stages, four of which are relevant to project planning and control.

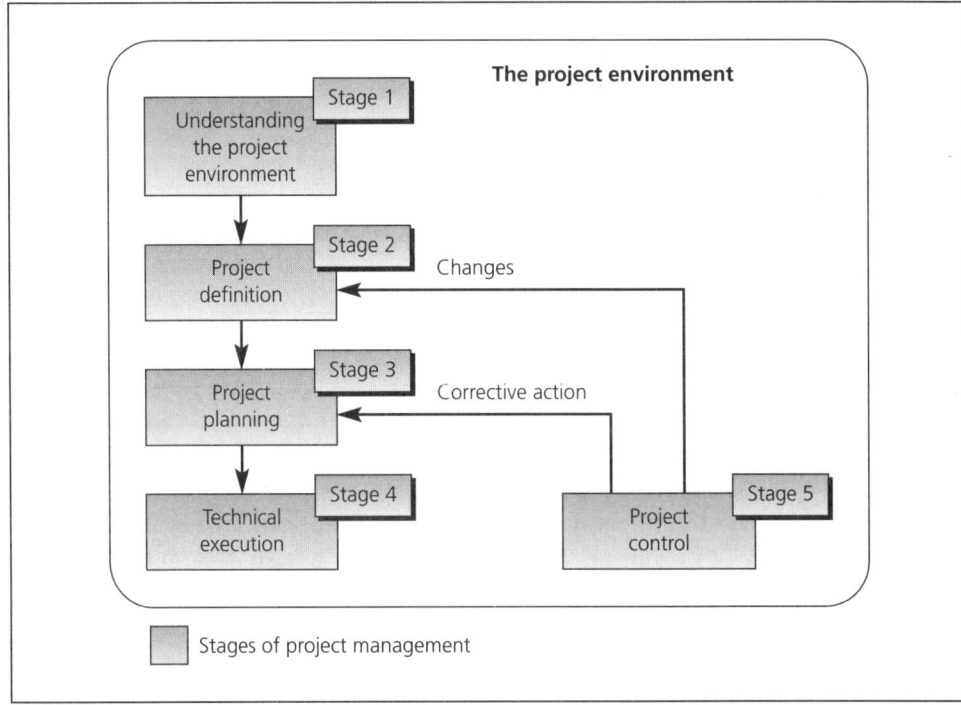

**Figure 16.3
The project
management
model**

Stage 1 Understanding the project environment – internal and external factors which
may influence the project.

Stage 2 Defining the project – setting the objectives, scope and strategy for the project.

Stage 3 Project planning – deciding how the project will be executed.

Stage 4 Technical execution – performing the technical aspects of the project.

Stage 5 Project control – ensuring that the project is carried out according to plan.

We shall examine project planning and control under the headings of Stages 1, 2, 3,
and 5 – project environment, project definition, project planning and project control.
(Stage 4, the technical execution of the project, is determined by the specific technicalities of individual projects.) However, it is important to understand that the stages
are not a simple sequential chain of steps; it is essentially an *iterative* process.
Problems or changes which become evident in the control stage may require replanning and may even cause modifications to the original project definition.

Stage 1 – Understanding the project environment

The project environment comprises all the factors which may affect the project during
its life. It determines the setting and circumstances in which the project is executed.
Examples of factors which may affect the environment are shown in Fig. 16.4.

Understanding the importance of the environment in which a project will be undertaken is essential for two reasons. First, the environment influences the way a project
is executed. For example, the scale, timing and nature of any other projects being

573

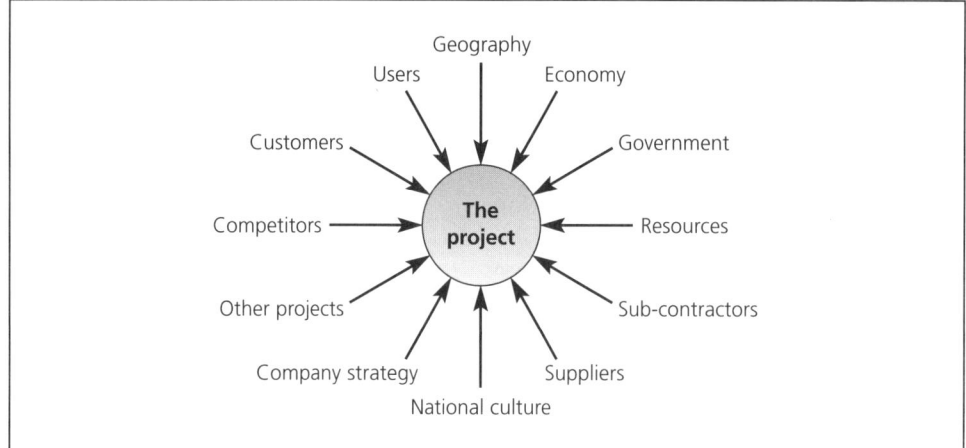

**Figure 16.4
The project
environment
consists of all the
factors which can
affect the project**

carried out by an organization could affect the plans which are drawn up for a new project. The history of previous projects carried out for a customer might influence how a current project is managed. Second, the environment of the project is the main determinant of the uncertainty which will be inherent in it. For example, the state of a supplier's financial security will influence a project management's willingness to use it. The political uncertainty in a country might influence the timing and resourcing of the separate activities of the project, and so on.

Stage 2 – Project definition

Before starting the complex task of planning and executing a project, it is necessary to be as clear as possible about what is going to be done. This is not always straightforward. Some projects are simpler to define than others. Projects where all the major tasks have been done before – such as the construction of a repeat coal-fired power station, where methods and equipment have already been proven – can be defined reasonably well in advance. Completely new projects – such as a major one-off aerospace project like the Giotto satellite construction and launch (*see* box) – will be much more difficult to define. Three different elements are needed to define a project:

- *its objectives*: the end state which project management is trying to achieve;
- *its scope*: the exact range of the responsibilities taken on by project management;
- *its strategy*: how project management is going to meet its objectives.

Project objectives

A project's objectives provide the overall direction for the project and help staff to focus on the rationale of the project and its expected results. Paradoxically, objective setting requires the project manager to start at the end of the project, that is to decide what end state must be achieved before the project could be deemed a success. The better the idea about what end point needs to be achieved, the easier is the process of planning how to get to that point. Objectives help to provide a definition of the end point which can be used to monitor progress and to identify when success has been achieved. This is not always uncontentious. The judgement on the success of a project can depend on who is asked. For example, a project to design and install a new production planning and control information system in a factory might be regarded as successful by the customer who commissioned the project (the Information Systems Department) but less so by the people who use the new system (the production controllers). This is why it is useful to phrase the objectives of a project in *user terms*.

The hierarchy of objectives

The objectives of each part of the project must be related to its overall objective or goal. The goal to '. . . place an American on the moon this decade and to return him safely to earth . . .' dictated the objectives of all the projects which contributed to achieving it. Within those projects (each of them major in their own right) the objectives of each sub-project will have been related to the project's objectives, and so on. In other words, any project can be disaggregated into a set of sub-projects whose objectives form an hierarchy (*see* Fig. 16.5).

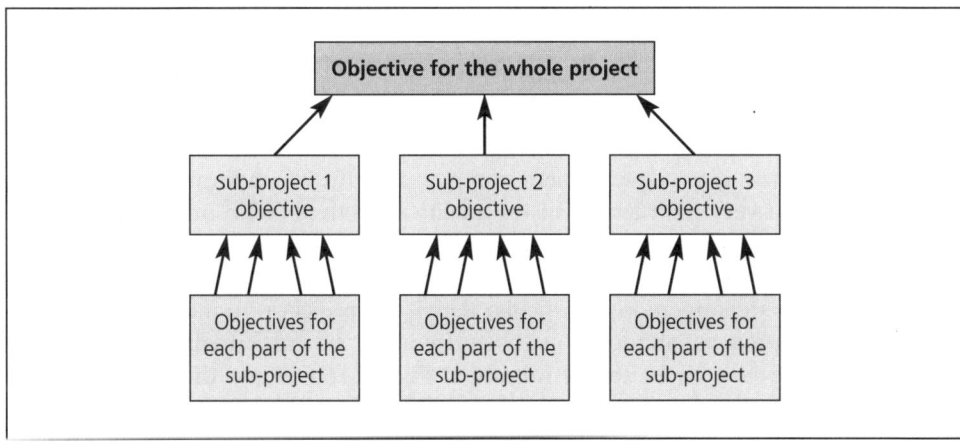

Figure 16.5
The hierarchy of project objectives

Objectives must be clear

Good objectives are those which are clear, measurable and, preferably, quantifiable. If they are not clear it is difficult to assess whether the project has been successful. One method of clarifying objectives which has been found helpful is to break down project objectives into three categories – the purpose, the end results, and the success criteria. For example, a project which is expressed in general terms as 'improve process X' could be broken down into:

● *Purpose* – to prevent production from failing to meet output targets as forecast.
● *End result* – a report which identifies the causes of lost production, and which recommends how the target output can be met.
● *Success criteria* – the report should be completed by 30 June. The recommendation should enable output to reach at least 70 tonnes per year. Cost of the recommendations should not exceed R700 000.

Performance objectives in project management

Projects, like any other operations, can be judged in terms of the five performance objectives we outlined in Chapter 2 – quality, speed, dependability, flexibility and cost. However, the convention in project management is slightly different. First, flexibility is regarded as a 'given' in most projects which, by definition, are to some extent one-offs. Second, speed and dependability are compressed to one composite objective – 'time'. This results in what are known as the 'three objectives of project management' – cost, time and quality.

● *Cost.* Although money is a 'flexible' resource within the project, the project's overall cost is set at the outset. A key project management task is to control resources so that the planned cost is not exceeded. This consideration applies equally whether the project is commercial in nature or whether it is 'not-for-profit'.

● *Time.* Time is a totally inflexible resource: once a day has passed, nothing can bring it back. Although activities can be shortened, the time to complete a project can only be changed through a redefinition of its objectives.

● *Quality.* The output from a project undertaking must be fit for its intended purpose; that is, it must work as it is supposed to. (The various aspects of quality will be explored fully in Chapter 17.) Project quality is here taken to include both the conformance of the finished project to its original specification and the appropriateness of the specification itself.

The relative importance of each objective will differ for different projects. Some aerospace projects, such as the development of a new aircraft, which impact on passenger safety will place a very high emphasis on quality objectives. With other projects, for example those which are being performed within a fixed price, cost might predominate. Other projects emphasize time, for example the organization of an open-air music festival has to happen on a particular date if the project is to meet its objectives. In each of these projects, although one objective might be particularly important, the other objectives can never be totally forgotten. Figure 16.6 shows the 'project objectives triangle' with these three types of project marked.[5]

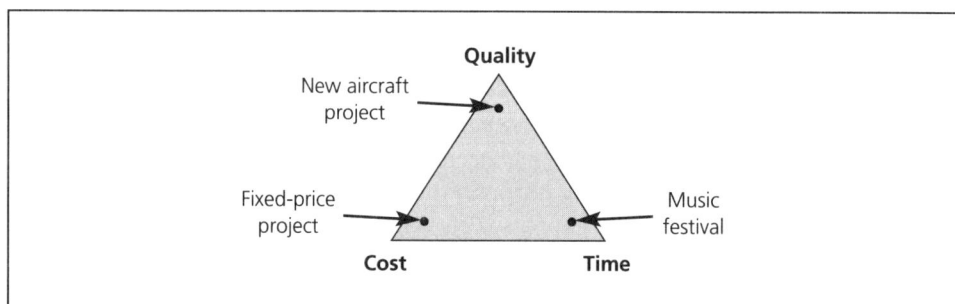

**Figure 16.6
The project
objectives triangle**

Project scope

The second part of a project's definition is the project scope. The scope of a project identifies its work content and its products or outcomes. It is essentially a boundary-setting exercise which attempts to define the dividing line between what each part of the project will do and what it won't do. Such identification helps in project definition by ensuring that the project is neither too complex nor unmanageable. It also helps clarify the responsibilities of all the parties who are involved in the project. Typically, a statement of the scope of the work to be done is needed for all the parts of a project, including those parts done by external 'contractors'. Defining scope is particularly important for managing contractors because of the commercial and legal aspects of their relationship with the organization which is managing the project. A contractor's *scope of supply* will identify the boundaries within which the work must be done. For example, a contractor commissioned to install an automated guided vehicle system would have the scope of the work defined to include timing, costs, conditions of work, contract with the main customer, and accompanying civil works, lighting and heating.

In general, defining the scope of a project or work package is helped by defining the following:

- *The parts of the organization which are affected*: for example, 'designing and installing an automated guided vehicle system in the warehouse up to the receiving bay'.
- *The time period involved*: for example, 'installation to begin no earlier than 15 January and be completed no later than 2 March'.
- *The business processes involved*: for example, 'to interface with the current order retrieval system and stock location system'.
- *The resources to be used*: for example, 'to provide own power supply and limit the number of staff working on the installation to five at any time'.
- *The contractor's responsibilities*: for example, 'to include all ancillary power and information supply systems, full maintenance schedules and initial training'.

The project specification

The scope of the project is formalized in the *project specification*, which is the written, pictorial and graphical information used to define the output, and the accompanying terms and conditions. Although written before the project starts, changes may have to be made to the scope which was originally specified, especially in managing high uncertainty projects. In such projects, better ways of doing things are often recognized only after work has begun. This is illustrated by the larger feedback loop in Fig. 16.3. There are two broad categories of change which need to be considered: internal and external changes. *Internal changes* result from decisions by the project management to do things differently from the original specification. For example, a chemical plant construction company might decide to use a different type of storage vessel for a part of the plant because it was not available at the time the project specification was agreed, yet it can do the same job as the originally specified vessel but is less expensive. If an internal change might affect some other part of the specification of the project it will need to be agreed with the customer. *External changes* occur when a customer has decided to change the specification. This can often occur in long projects where the environment is prone to change. For example, in a defence project a European air force may need to change the specification of the communication equipment in an aircraft if the agreed standards change within NATO. The difference between these two types of change in a commercial project can be very important. Often the company managing the project can demand payment for external changes, but not for internal changes. Companies managing large projects find it particularly important to have accounting systems which rigorously distinguish between the two types of change. Failure to do so can significantly affect the profitability of the project.

Project strategy

The third part of a project's definition is the project strategy. The project strategy defines, in a general rather than specific way, how the organization is going to achieve its project objectives and meet the related measures of performance. It does this in two ways. First, the project strategy should define the *phases* of the project. Phases break the project down into time-based sections. The phases may be very simple, for example the beginning, the middle and the end phases, or more detailed. While there may be considerable overlap and iteration between phases, they are a valuable way of conceiving the project and simplifying the process of project definition. In the case of a software development project, the phases might be as follows:

● *Specification phase*: where customer requirements are specified, and a systems specification is drawn up.
● *Design phase*: where systems design and sub-system specifications are determined.
● *Implementation phase*: where modules are specified.
● *Module-testing phase*: where each module is tested separately.
● *Integration-testing phase*: where sub-systems and finally the complete system are tested.
● *Delivery phase:* where the system is handed over to the customer.

Second, the project strategy should set milestones. Milestones are important events during the project life at which specific reviews for time, cost and quality are made. They are the significant points in the project which indicate whether a project is on schedule. At this stage the actual dates for each milestone are not necessarily determined – that will probably come later in the planning stage. It is useful, however, to at least identify the significant milestones, either to define the boundary between phases or to help in discussions with the customer. Indeed the formal contract between the project manager and a customer will often gear payments or penalties to milestones.

For example, the milestones which are defined for the production of a television commercial campaign might be as follows:

Milestone 1	Overall concept agreed with client
Milestone 2	Story board outline prepared and agreed
Milestone 3	Shooting fully planned and organized
Milestone 4	First portfolio presented to client
Milestone 5	Final cut agreed with client.

Although we have divided the project definition stage into setting objectives, defining scope and devising strategy, all three are clearly related (*see* Fig. 16.7).

Stage 3 – Project planning

The planning process fulfils four distinct purposes:

● It determines the cost and duration of the project. This enables major decisions to be made – such as the decision whether to go ahead with the project at the start.
● It determines the level of resources which will be needed.
● It helps to allocate work and to monitor progress. Planning must include the identification of who is responsible for what.
● It helps to assess the impact of any changes to the project.

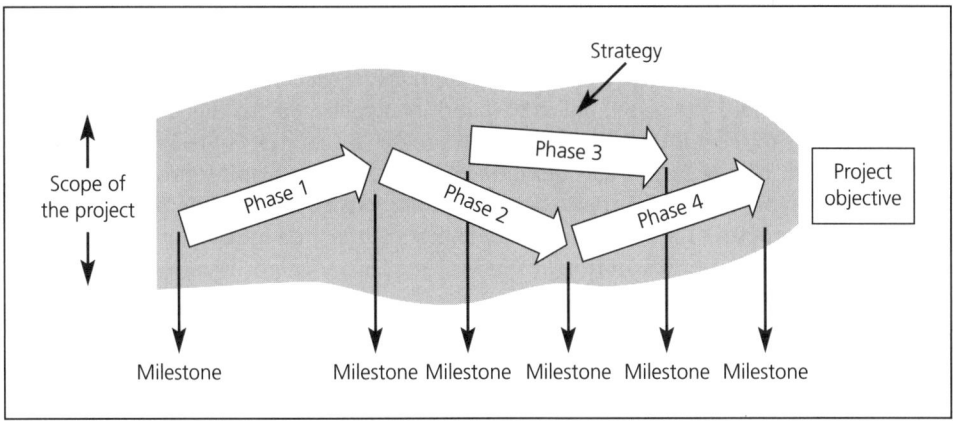

Figure 16.7 Relationship between the objectives, scope and strategy in a project definition

Planning is not a one-off process. It may be repeated several times during the project's life as circumstances change. Nor is replanning a sign of project failure or misman-agement. In uncertain projects especially, it is a normal occurrence. In fact later stage plans typically mean that more information is available, and that the project is becom-ing less uncertain. The process of project planning, whether carried out for the first time or as a re-plan, involves five steps (*see* Fig. 16.8). Each of these processes is now described, followed by an illustration of its application to a simple 'project'.

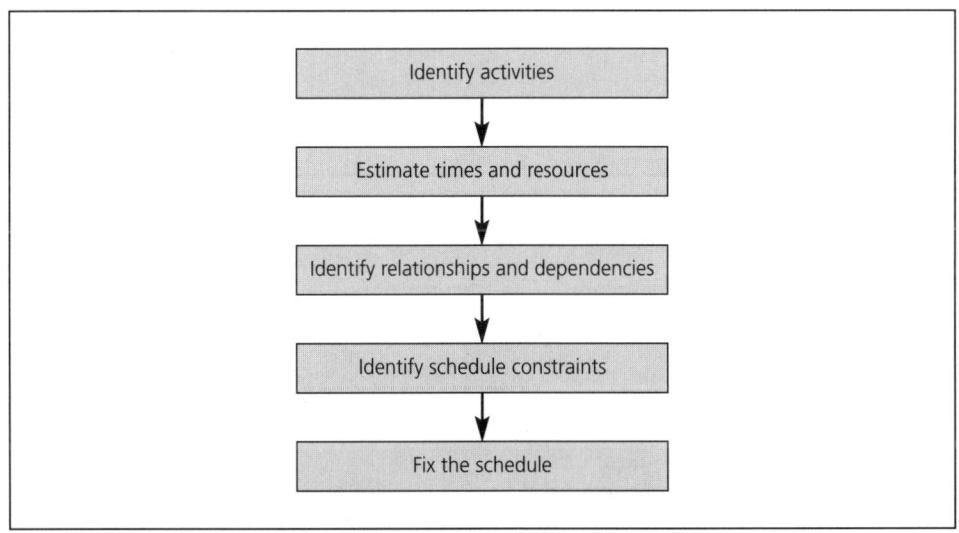

Figure 16.8 The process of project planning

Identify activities – the work breakdown structure

Most projects are too complex to be planned and controlled effectively unless they are first broken down into manageable portions. This is achieved by structuring the project into a 'family tree', along similar lines to the bill of materials (Chapter 14). But unlike the bill of materials, which specifies items, this specifies the major tasks or sub-projects.

579

These in turn are divided up into smaller tasks until a defined, manageable series of tasks called a *work package* is arrived at. Each work package can be allocated its own objectives in terms of time, cost and quality. The output from this is called the *work breakdown structure* (WBS). It should be carried out in a logical, systematic way so that each level of the structure relates to the one above and to the one below. A hierarchy of tasks is thus generated. The WBS brings clarity and definition to the project planning process. It shows 'how the jigsaw fits together'.[6] It also provides a framework for building up information for reporting purposes. The WBS is one of the first planning documents to be produced.

Example project

As a simple example to illustrate the application of each stage of the planning process, let us examine the following domestic project.

The project definition is:

● *purpose:* to make breakfast in bed;
● *end result:* breakfast in bed of boiled egg, toast and orange juice;
● *success criteria:* plan uses minimum staff resources and time, and product is high quality (egg freshly boiled, warm toast, etc.);
● *scope:* project starts in kitchen at 6.00 am, and finishes in bedroom; needs one operator and normal kitchen equipment.

The work breakdown structure is based on the above definition and can be constructed as shown in Fig. 16.9.

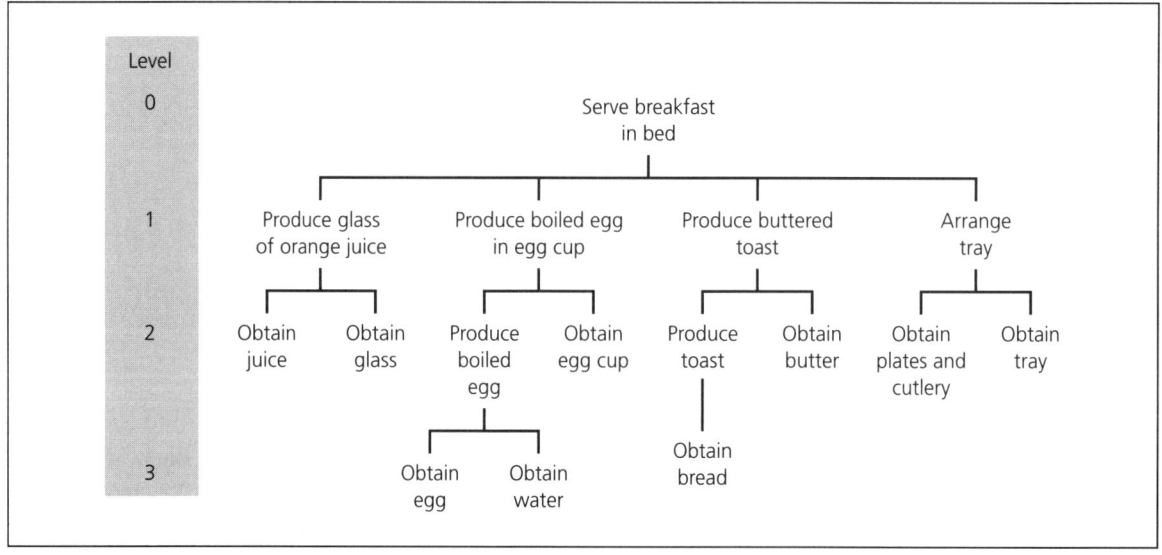

Figure 16.9 A work breakdown structure for a simple domestic project

Estimate times and resources

The next stage in planning is to identify the time and resource requirements of the work packages. Time and resource estimates are fundamental to decision making in project management. Without some idea of how long each part of a project will take and how many resources it will need, it is impossible to define what should be happening at any time during the execution of the project. Estimates are just that, however – a systematic best guess, not a perfect forecast of reality. Estimates may never be perfect but they can be made with some idea of how accurate they might be. The more effort is put into making an estimate, the better it should be. To some extent, therefore, the accuracy of a forecast reflects the willingness of project managers to spend time and money on obtaining it. This will depend on what use is going to be made of the estimate. Figure 16.10 illustrates how estimates which are to be used for different purposes are likely to have different degrees of accuracy. The degree of accuracy of an estimate is strongly related to the stage of the project's life when it is used. At the start of a project when a rough 'ball park' estimate is needed, the actual figure only has an 'illustrative' value, whereas during the detailed execution of the project, final 'definitive' estimates are needed to control on a day-to-day basis.

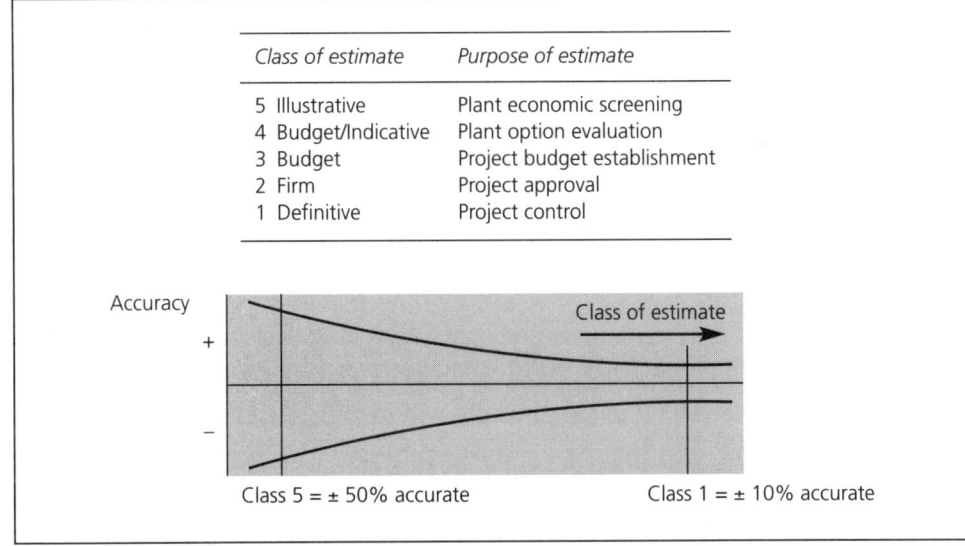

Figure 16.10
Estimates need to be progressively more accurate as the project proceeds

Example project

Returning to our very simple example 'breakfast-in-bed' project, the activities were identified and times estimated as in Table 16.2.

While some of the estimates may appear generous, they take into account the time of day and the state of the operator.

Probabilistic estimates

The amount of uncertainty in a project has a major bearing on the level of confidence which can be placed on an estimate. The impact of uncertainty on estimating times leads some project managers to use a probability curve to describe the estimate. In practice, this is usually a positively skewed distribution, as in Fig. 16.11. The greater the risk, the greater the range of the distribution. The natural tendency of

Table 16.2 Time and resources estimates for a 'breakfast-in-bed' project

Activity	Effort (person-min)	Duration (min)
Butter toast	1	1
Pour orange juice	1	1
Boil egg	0	4
Slice bread	1	1
Fill pan with water	1	1
Bring water to boil	0	3
Toast bread	0	2
Take loaded tray to bedroom	1	1
Fetch tray, plates, cutlery	1	1

some people is to produce *optimistic* estimates, but this will have a relatively low probability of being correct because it represents the time which would be taken if *everything* went well. *Most likely* estimates have the highest probability of proving correct. Finally, *pessimistic* estimates assume that almost everything which could go wrong does go wrong. Because of the skewed nature of the distribution the expected time for the activity will not be the same as the most likely time.

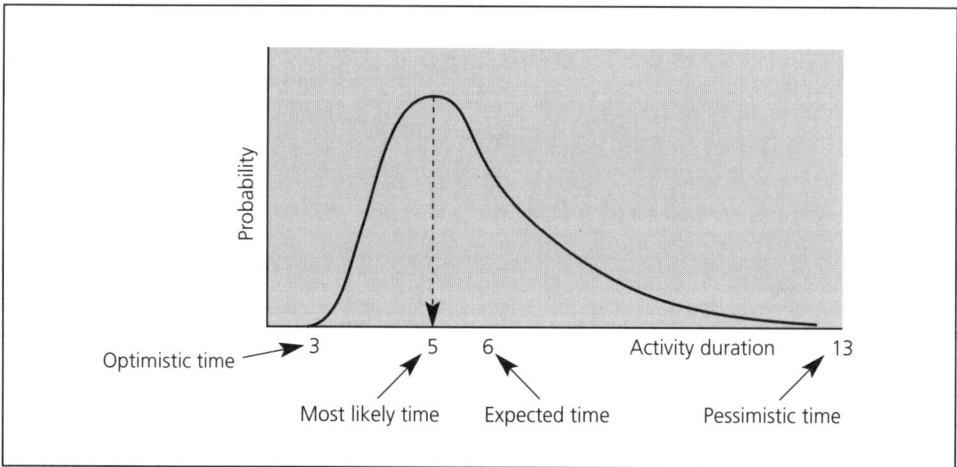

Figure 16.11 Probability distribution of time estimates

Identify relationships and dependencies

All the activities which are identified as comprising a project will have some relationship with one another which will depend on the logic of the project. Some activities will by necessity need to be executed in a particular order. For example, in the construction of a house, the foundations must be prepared before the walls are built, which in turn must be completed before the roof is put in place. These activities have a *dependent* or

THE CHANNEL TUNNEL[7]

The Channel Tunnel project was the largest construction project ever undertaken in Europe and the biggest single investment in transport anywhere in the world. For years there had been talk of linking the UK and France with a tunnel and it was only in 1986 that the two governments came to an agreement which allowed the project to get underway. The project, which was funded by the private sector, made provision for a 55-year concession for the owners to design, build and run the operation. The Eurotunnel Group (technically two holding companies, one French and one in the UK) awarded the contract to design and build the tunnel to TML (Trans-Manche Link), a consortium of ten French and British construction companies. The plan was for about half the capacity of the tunnel to be given to the national rail networks of the UK and France and the other half to be devoted to the local rail service 'Le Shuttle', to be run by Eurotunnel themselves. The finished operation was planned to be the busiest railway line in the world.

For the project managers it was a formidable undertaking. The sheer scale of the project was daunting in itself. Two main railway tunnels, split by a service/access tunnel, each 7.6 metres in diameter, run 40 metres below the sea bed. In total there are in excess of 150 kilometres of tunnel in the total project. The project was also subject to various types of uncertainty. During the early negotiations, political uncertainty surrounded the commitment of both governments. In the planning phase geological uncertainty had to be reduced by a complex series of tests. The financing of the project, which required investment by over 200 banks and finance houses, as well as over half a million shareholders, resulted in periodic financial uncertainty. Finally, the technical problems, both in the drilling itself and, more importantly, in the commissioning of the tracks and systems within the tunnel, needed to be overcome in order to reduce technical uncertainty.

The historic breakthrough came on 1 December 1990 when the French and English teams working on the service tunnel met at a point 22.3 kilometres from the UK and 15.6 kilometres from France. The real breakthrough came in 1994, however, when first freight, and then passenger services started to connect two countries through perhaps the greatest civil engineering project management achievement of all time. ■

---

series relationship. Other activities do not have any such dependence on one another. The rear garden of the house could probably be prepared totally independently of the garage being built. These two activities have an *independent* or *parallel* relationship.

Example project

Table 16.2 identified the activities for the breakfast preparation project. The list shows that some of the activities must necessarily follow others. For example, 'boil egg' cannot be carried out until 'fill pan with water' and 'bring water to boil' have been completed. Further logical analysis of the activities in the list shows that there are two major 'chains', where activities must be carried out in a definite sequence:

Slice bread – Toast bread – Butter toast
Fill pan with water – Bring water to boil – Boil egg

Both of these sequences must be completed before the activity 'take loaded tray to bedroom'. The remaining activities ('pour orange juice' and 'fetch tray, plates, cutlery') can be done at any time provided that they are completed before 'take loaded tray to bedroom'. An initial project plan might be as shown in Fig. 16.12. Here, the activities have been represented as blocks of time in proportion to their estimated durations. From this, we can see that the 'project' can be completed in nine minutes. Some of the activities have spare time (called float) indicated by the dotted line. The sequence 'Fill pan – Boil water – Boil egg – Bedroom' has no slack, and is called the *critical path* of the project. By implication, any activity which runs late in this sequence would cause the whole project to be delayed accordingly. We shall discuss this further later in the chapter.

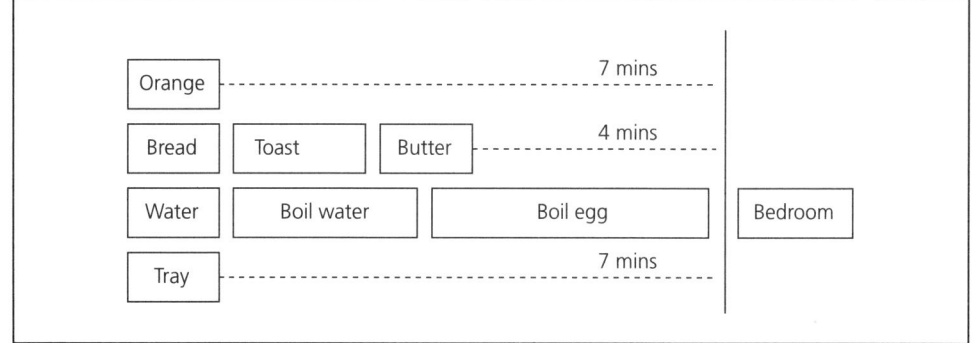

**Figure 16.12
Initial project plan
for a simple project**
Source: Courtesy of Neil
Anderson, DCE

Identify schedule constraints

Once estimates have been made of the time and effort involved in each activity, and their dependencies identified, it is possible to compare project requirements with the available resources. The finite nature of critical resources – such as special skills – means that they should be taken into account in the planning process. This often has the effect of highlighting the need for more detailed replanning, or for alternative approaches such as sub-contracting. There are essentially two fundamental approaches:[8]

● *Resource constrained.* Only the available resource levels are used in resource scheduling, and are never exceeded. As a result, the project completion may slip. Resource-limited scheduling is used, for example, when a project company has its own highly specialized assembly and test facilities.
● *Time constrained.* The overriding priority is to complete the project within a given time. Once normally available resources have been used up, alternative ('threshold') resources are scheduled.

Example project

Returning to the breakfast-in-bed project, we can now consider the resource implications of the plan in Fig. 16.12. Each of the four activities scheduled at the start (pour orange, cut bread, fill pan, fetch tray) consume staff resources. Charting the required resources will give a resource profile as in Fig. 16.13. There is clearly a resource-loading problem, because the project definition states that only one person is available. This is not an insuperable difficulty, however, because there is sufficient slack to move some of the activities. A plan with levelled resources can be produced which is shown in Fig. 16.14. All that has been necessary is to delay the toast preparation by one minute, and to use the elapsed time during the toasting and water boiling processes to pour orange and fetch the tray.

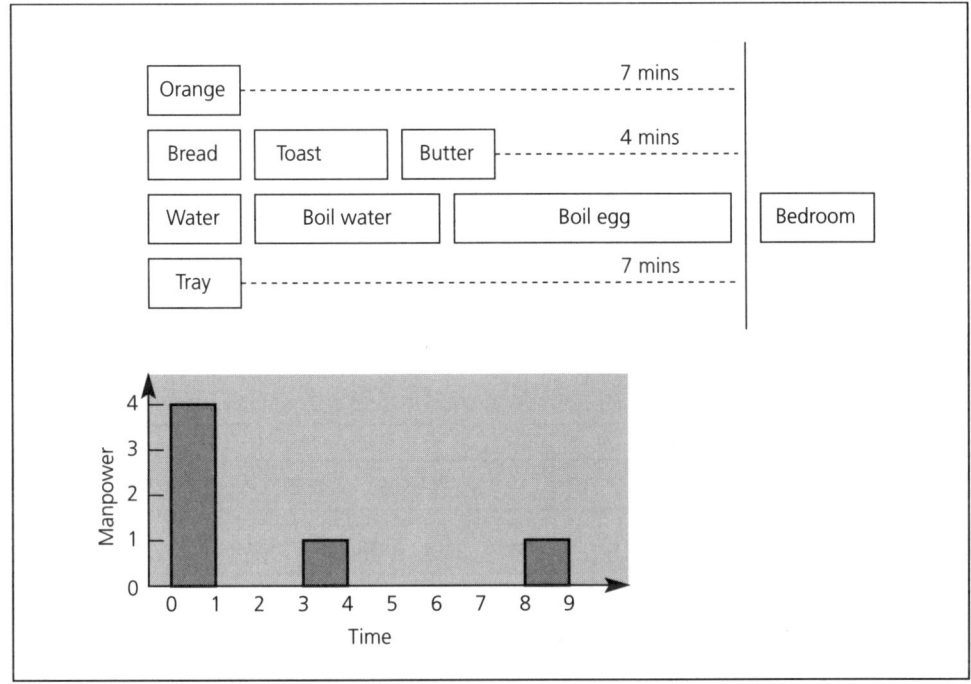

Figure 16.13
Plan with resource allocation

Fix the schedule

Project planners should ideally have a number of alternatives to choose from. The one which best fits project objectives can then be chosen or developed. For example, it may be appropriate to examine both resource-limited and time-limited options. However, it is not always possible to examine several alternative schedules. Especially in very large or very uncertain projects, the computation could be prohibitive. However, modern computer-based project management software is making the search for the best schedule more feasible.

Example project

A further improvement to the plan can yet be made. Looking again at the project definition, the success criteria state that the product should be 'high quality'. In the plan shown in Fig. 16.14, while the egg is freshly boiled, the toast might be cold. An 'optimized' plan which would provide hot toast would be to prepare the toast during the 'boil egg' activity. This plan is shown in Fig. 16.15.

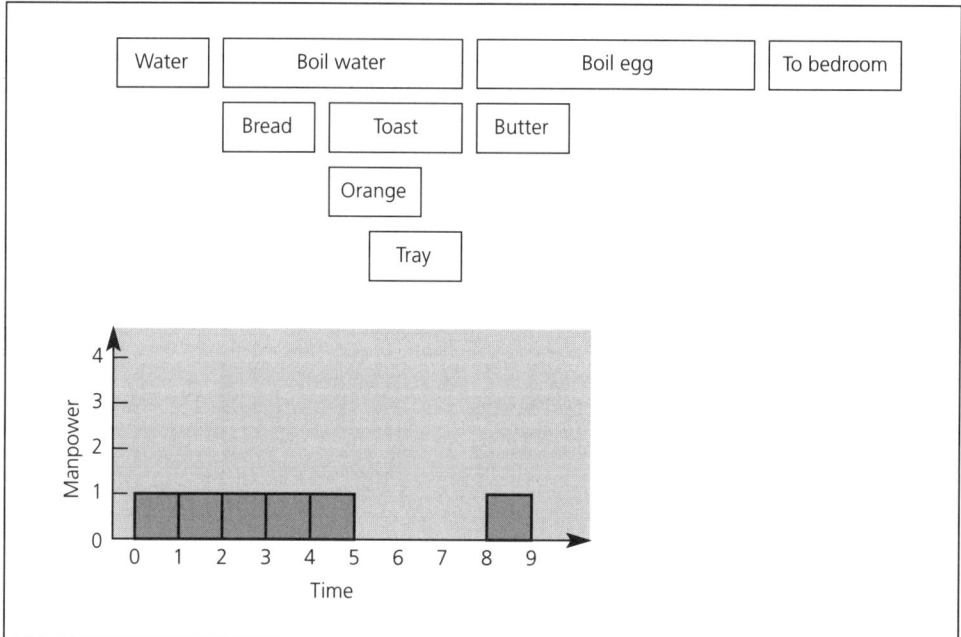

**Figure 16.14
Revised plan with
resource allocation**

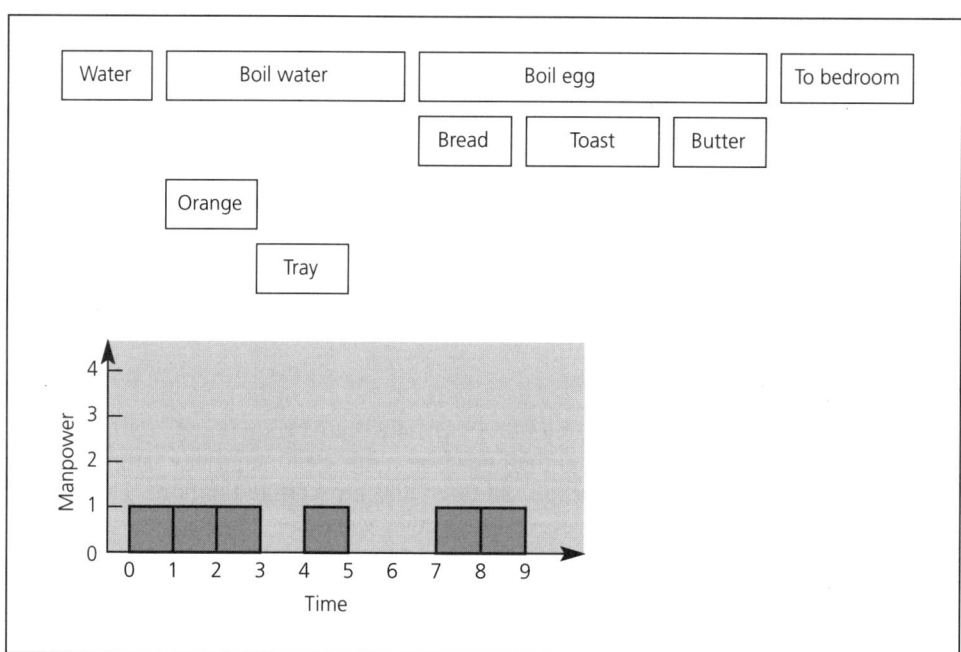

**Figure 16.15
Plan with levelled
resources and
warm toast**

Stage 5 – Project control

The stages in project planning and control have so far all taken place before the actual project takes place. This stage deals with the management activities which take place during the execution of the project. Project control is the essential link between planning and doing.

The process of project control involves three sets of decisions:

● how to *monitor* the project in order to check on its progress;
● how to *assess the performance* of the project by comparing monitored observations of the project with the project plan;
● how to *intervene* in the project in order to make the changes which will bring it back to plan.

Project monitoring

The first decision of project managers as they attempt to control an ongoing project is, 'What should we be looking out for?' The project objective triangle in Fig. 16.6 gives some answers. If the main objectives of project management are cost, quality and time, then that is what should be monitored. Usually a variety of measures are monitored, some of which relate directly to one of the performance objectives and some of which indicate problems with two or all three of them. Table 16.3 illustrates some typical monitored measures and the main performance objectives which they affect.

Note how some monitored measures in Table 16.3 affect mainly cost, some mainly time, but when something affects the quality of the project there are also time and cost implications. This is because quality problems in project planning and control usually have to be solved in a limited amount of time.

Assessing project performance

The monitored measures of project performance at any point in time need to be assessed so that project management can make a judgement concerning overall per-

Table 16.3 Monitored measures and their effect on project performance objectives

Monitored measure	Main performance objectives affected
Costs exceeding budget	Cost
Cash running low	Cost
Supplier price changes	Cost
Excessive overtime	Cost
Changes in project scope	Cost, Quality, Time
Technical performance poor	Quality, Time, Cost
Inspection failures	Quality, Time, Cost
Errors in information	Quality, Time, Cost
Waiting for resource delays	Time, Cost
Supplier delays	Time, Cost
Customer changes delivery date	Time, Cost
Activities not started on time	Time
Activities not finished on time	Time
Missed milestones	Time

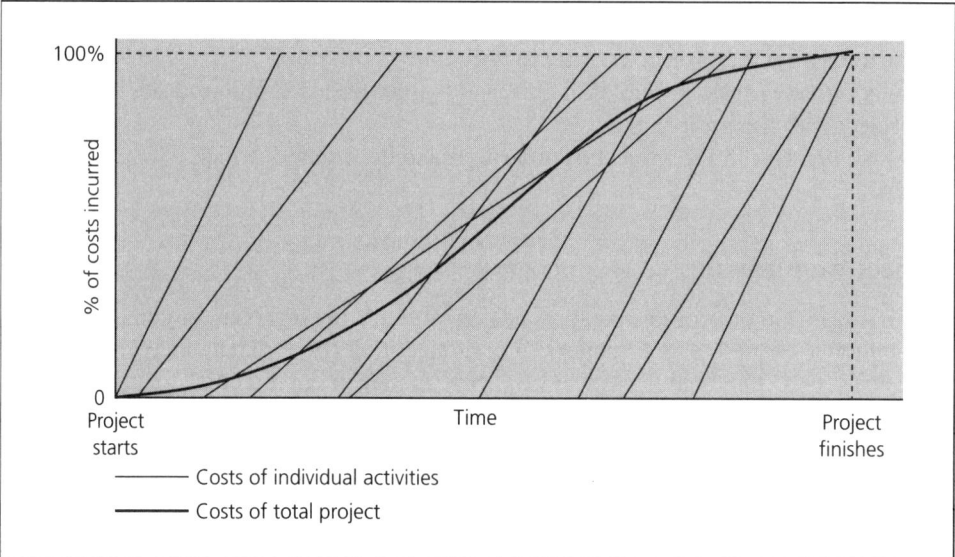

Figure 16.16
Typical S-shaped
cost curve for the
total project

formance. Again this is done for all three project performance objectives: cost, quality and time. Most detailed effort often goes into assessing cost and time, however. Quality problems will show up (as we noted earlier) as cost and time problems eventually. The first step in this process is to return to the planning stage in order to see what state the project should be in at any point in time. The planned times for each activity's start and finish can be taken from the schedule of our activities, such as that shown in Fig. 16.15. The planned costs expended at any time can also be derived from the project schedule of activities.

A typical planned cost profile of a project through its life is shown in Fig. 16.16. At the beginning of a project some activities can be started, but most activities will be dependent on others finishing. As more activities finish, therefore, even more can be started. Finally only a few activities remain to be completed. This pattern of a slow start followed by a faster pace with an eventual tail-off of activity holds true for almost all projects, which is why the rate of total expenditure follows an S-shaped pattern as shown in Fig. 16.16, even when the cost curves for the individual activities are linear. For any particular project a planned cost or expenditure curve can be drawn in this way, derived from the activity schedule. It is against this curve that actual costs can be compared in order to check whether the project's costs are being incurred to plan. Figure 16.17 shows the planned and actual cost figures compared in this way. It shows that the project is incurring costs, on a cumulative basis, ahead of what was planned. This would need to be investigated to see whether the cost over-run was likely to be sustained and make the whole project cost more than planned.

Earned value control

The 'earned-value' method of project control assesses performance of the project by combining cost and time together. Rather than measure the progress of the project in days, it measures it in the value of the work done. A project whose total value was R1 000 000, therefore, would be half complete when the value of the activities which had actually been

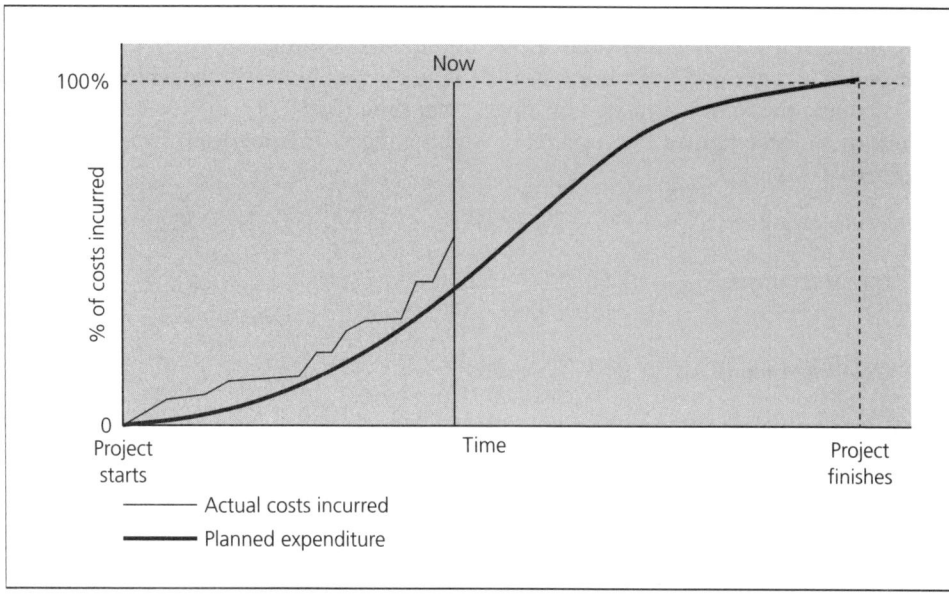

**Figure 16.17
Comparing
planned with
actual expenditure**

completed was R500 000. Figure 16.18 shows the progress of a project measured on an earned-value basis. It shows actual cost incurred against work completed. Because the work done is measured in monetary units, the line which represents the project plan will be at 45 degrees, that means that when R100 000 of work has been completed, the expenditure should have actually been R100 000, and so on. It actually shows that, at the end of three periods, this project has completed R500 000 worth of work when it should have completed R600 000 worth. Furthermore, the actual cost it has incurred is R650 000. These three figures each have terms to describe them:

● *The budgeted cost of work scheduled* (BCWS) is the amount of work which should have been completed by a particular time (R600 000 in our example).

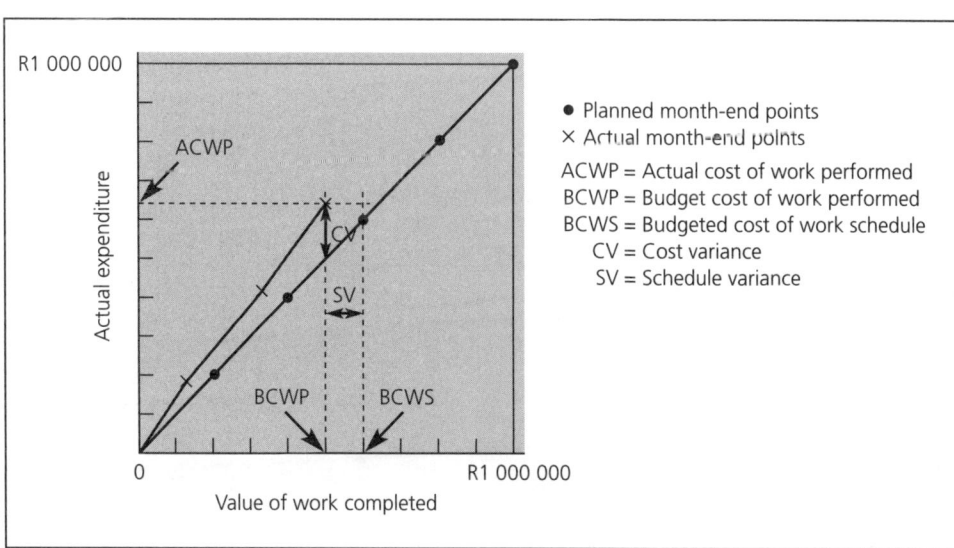

**Figure 16.18
Comparing the
planned and actual
values of work
completed in order
to calculate cost
and schedule
variances**

● *The budgeted cost of work performed* (BCWP) is the actual amount of work which has been completed by a particular time (R500 000 in our example).
● *The actual cost of work performed* (ACWP) is the actual expenditure which has been spent on doing the work completed by a particular time (R650 000 in our example).

From these three figures two *variances*, which indicate the deviation from plan, can be derived:

$$\text{Schedule variance (SV)} = \text{BCWP} - \text{BCWS}$$

$$\begin{aligned}\text{In our example: SV} &= \text{R500 000} - \text{R600 000} \\ &= -\text{R100 000}\end{aligned}$$

$$\text{Cost variance (CV)} = \text{BCWP} - \text{ACWP}$$

$$\begin{aligned}\text{In our example: CV} &= \text{R500 000} - \text{R650 000} \\ &= -\text{R150 000}\end{aligned}$$

Intervening to change the project

Once a judgement has been made concerning the current performance of a project, a decision is needed as to whether project managers need to intervene in the project activity. If the project is obviously out of control in the sense that its costs, quality levels or times are significantly different from those planned, then some kind of intervention is almost certainly likely to be required. The exact nature of the intervention will depend on the technical characteristics of the project, but it is likely to need the advice of all the people who would be affected. Given the interconnected nature of projects – a change to one part of the project will have knock-on effects elsewhere – this means that interventions often require wide consultation.

Sometimes intervention is needed even if the project looks to be proceeding according to plan. For example, Fig. 16.19 shows the schedule and cost variances for a project, together with the 'allowable range' of variance. These are the tolerance

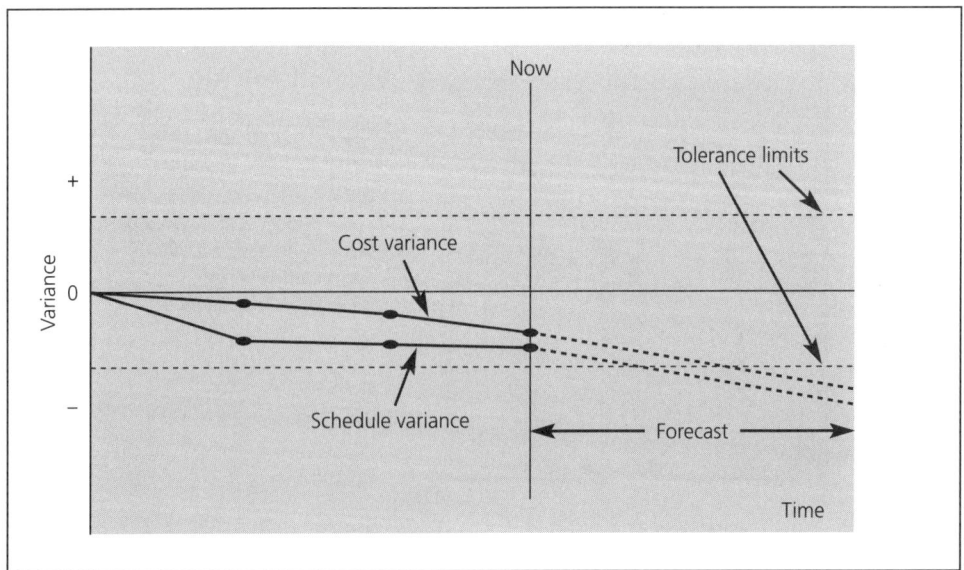

**Figure 16.19
Plotting cost and schedule variance over time and forecasting from the trend**

limits between which the variance can move without it indicating that there is necessarily a problem. The project appears to be on target. When the project managers look forward and project activities and cost into the future, however, they see that problems are very likely to arise. In this case it is the *trend* of performance which is being used to trigger intervention.

ONCE IN A LIFETIME[9]

The opportunity to carry out some projects comes just once in a lifetime. Such projects cannot be late. The Giotto project was of this type. Giotto was the name given to the spacecraft designed to intercept Halley's Comet when it was 100 million miles away from Earth on 2 July 1985. The project was funded and managed by the European Space Agency and contracted out in the main part to British Aerospace. The accepted payload consisted of ten experiments which were designed to establish, in more detail than ever before, the exact characteristics and composition of the comet. If the project missed the launch date significantly the whole project would have been judged a massive waste of millions of ECU.

The ten experiments on board were contributed by various groups in 11 different member countries. Although this enhanced the international image of the project, it also added to the complexity of a project which was dominated by a demanding and inflexible completion requirement. Leading up to the delivery of the spacecraft, the project moved through four phases which were termed (1) concept, (2) sub-system definition and bids, (3) project definition and formal bid for delivery and (4) procurement and assembly. During the project, emphasis was placed by all parties on co-operation between the management team from the ESA and its international partners. The cost management involved initial capital proposals and then a re-assessment of the costs after the first two phases of the project. All the activities which made up the programme of work were planned in fine detail and all planning information placed on a central computer system which was visible to all involved. Any modifications were dealt with very quickly. The policy was never to have more than three or four outstanding modifications over any three-week period, so as to reduce the amount of uncertainty in the project. This relied on the team paying particular attention to ensuring visible and efficient client contact or relationships. The team made considerable use of network planning methods such as PERT (*see* later section) which were particularly useful in keeping all information on the current state of, and the future plans for, the project fully visible.

Like many large scientific organizations, the European Space Agency has an intricate hierarchy of standards and approval procedures, all of which are time consuming. The project could never have been completed to schedule if the agency had not adopted a 'fast-track' procedure for getting approval through its various committees. It screened, in principle, aspects of technical compliance, feasibility and the financial resources backing any proposal.

The spacecraft was eventually shipped, on time, to the launch site on 29 April 1985 for trials and the final count-down to launch on 30 June 1985. The project itself was very successful, intercepting the comet as planned and contributing enormously to scientific knowledge and analysis of such phenomena. The final cost of developing and constructing the craft did overshoot its budget by about 10 per cent, which at the time was a relatively small amount for a project of this type. Good project planning and control, a clear project definition and disciplined project management had all played their part. ■

NETWORK PLANNING

The process of project planning and control, which we have described in this chapter, is greatly aided by the use of techniques which help project managers to handle its complexity and time-based nature. The simplest of these techniques is the Gantt chart (or bar chart) which we introduced in Chapter 10. This spawned later techniques, most of which go under the collective name of *network analysis*. It is these which are now used, almost universally, to help plan and control all significant projects but can also prove helpful in smaller ventures. The two network analysis methods we will examine are *critical path method* (CPM) or *analysis* (CPA) and *programme evaluation and review technique* (PERT).

Example

An example of a Gantt chart used to plan a project is shown in Fig. 16.20. The chart is being used to plan and monitor the implementation of a new logistics operation. The new operation will involve the purchase of a fleet of trucks, the design of new routes and the building of a new distribution centre and associated handling equipment. The following major activities are planned:

1 *Design logistics solution.* Approximately three months' duration, given good data and direction from customer. (Key task is getting information from people who are not directly involved with the project.)

2 *Refine logistics solution.* An ongoing process which must be kept on track once an outline has been selected. (It must be completed before suppliers can be briefed.)

3 *Prepare planning application.* Needs four weeks. (Building specification must be ready first.)

4 *System requirements.* An ongoing process of integrating information systems. (All systems are available, but they must be integrated into overall project objectives.)

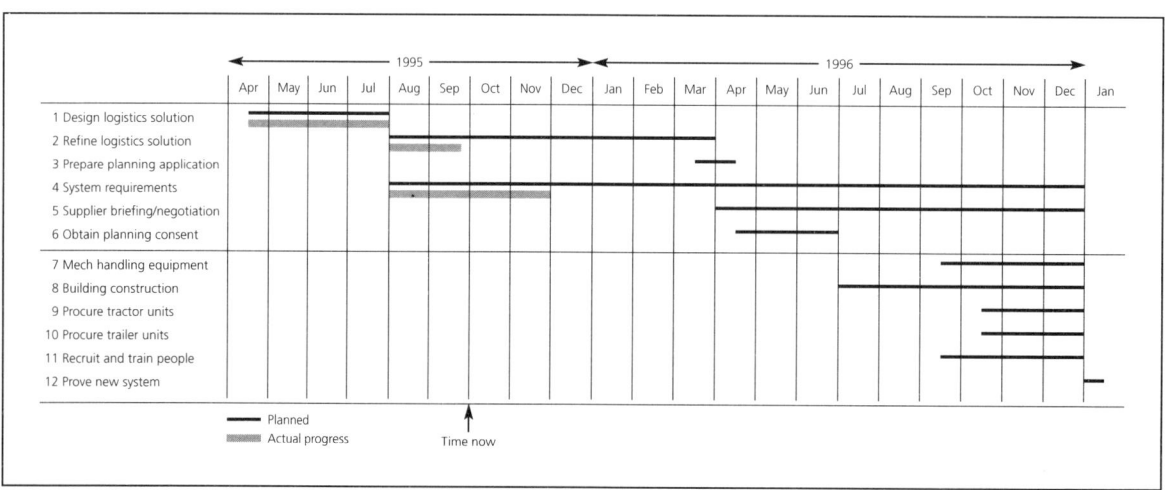

Figure 16.20 Implementing new logistics operation: Gantt chart
Source: Courtesy of Exel Logistics

5 *Supplier briefing/negotiation.* New procedures need to be explained on an ongoing basis to all suppliers by the central coordination team.

6 *Obtain planning consent.* Statutory time is eight weeks, but experience suggests that 12 weeks is the norm.

7 *Mechanical handling equipment.* Lead time is currently 12 weeks for standard equipment, up to 16 weeks for specialist. (Have assumed standard. This activity includes design and layout of racking.)

8 *Building construction.* This would be six months for a 100 000 square foot building. (Weather can have a major impact.)

9 *Tractor procurement.* Currently 10 to 12 weeks' lead time.

10 *Trailer procurement.* Eight weeks standard to 12 weeks for special requirements.

11 *Recruit and train.* Need to start recruitment of 100 staff three months before start-up. (Training to start two weeks before start-up.)

12 *Prove new system.* Two weeks are needed for system trials, proving and final training.

The length of the bar for each activity is directly proportional to the calendar time, and so indicates the relative duration of each activity. Progress against each activity is shown by the lower strips. The arrow which shows 'time now' indicates that all activities to the left should by now have been completed. Gantt charts are the simplest way to exhibit an overall project plan, because they have excellent visual impact and are easy to understand. They are also useful for communicating project plans and status to senior managers as well as for day-to-day project control. However, Gantt charts are limited in the number of activities which they can handle before they become too 'busy'.

Critical path method (CPM)

As project complexity increases, so it becomes necessary to identify the relationships between activities. It becomes increasingly important to show the logical sequence in which activities must take place. The two fundamental relationships which we described earlier were:

- *activities in series:* where activity A must be completed before activity B can start;
- *activities in parallel:* where activity B can proceed while activity A is still proceeding.

Critical path method (CPM) models the project by clarifying the relationships between activities diagrammatically. The first way we can illustrate this is by using arrows to represent each activity in a project. For example, examine the simple project in Fig. 16.21 which involves the decoration of an apartment. Six activities are identified together with their relationships. The first activity, *a*, 'remove furniture', does not require any of the other activities to be completed before it can be started. However, activity *b*, 'prepare bedroom', cannot be started until activity *a*, 'remove furniture', has been completed. The same applies to activity *d*, 'prepare the kitchen'. Similarly activity *c*, 'paint bedroom', cannot be started until activity *b* has been completed. Nor can activity *e*, 'paint the kitchen', be started until the kitchen has been prepared. Only when both the bedroom and the kitchen have been painted can the apartment be furnished again. The logic of these relationships is shown as an arrow diagram, where each activity is represented by an arrow (the lengths of the arrows are not proportional to the duration of the activities).

Activity	Immediate predecessors	Activity duration (in days)
a Remove furniture	None	1
b Prepare bedroom	a	2
c Paint bedroom	b	3
d Prepare kitchen	a	1
e Paint kitchen	d	2
f Replace furniture	c, e	1

Figure 16.21
The activities, relationships, durations and arrow diagram for the project 'decorate apartment'

Remove furniture → Prepare bedroom → Paint bedroom → Replace furniture

Prepare kitchen → Paint kitchen

This arrow diagram can be developed into a network diagram as shown in Fig. 16.22. At the tail (start) and head (finish) of each *activity* (represented by an arrow) is a circle which represents an *event*. Events are moments in time which occur at the start or finish of an activity. They have no duration and are of a definite recognizable nature. Networks of this type are composed only of activities and events.

The rules for drawing this type of network diagram are fairly straightforward.

Rule 1 An event cannot be reached until all activities leading to it are complete. Event 5 in Fig. 16.22 is not reached until activities *c* and *e* are complete.

Rule 2 No activity can start until its tail event is reached. In Fig. 16.22 activity *f* cannot start until event 5 is reached.

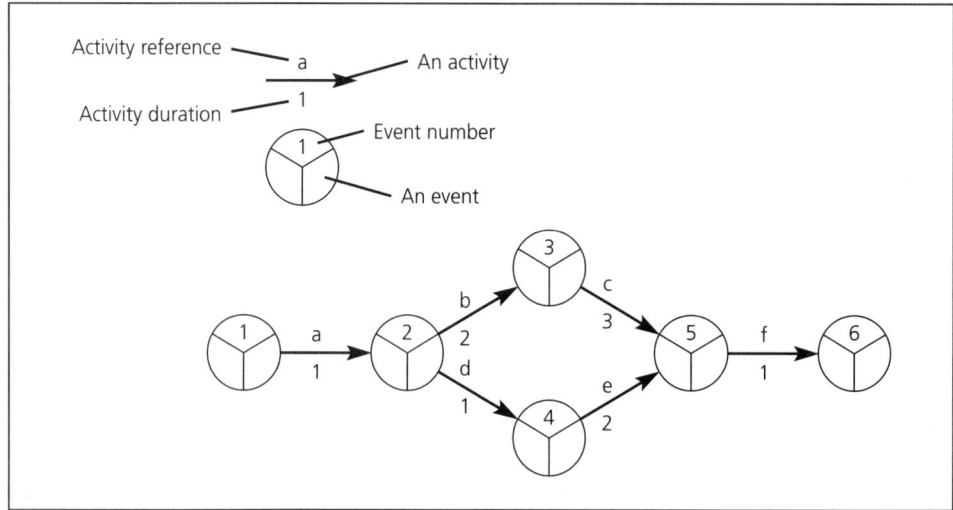

Figure 16.22
A network diagram for the project 'decorate apartment'

Rule 3 No two activities can have the same head and tail events. In Fig. 16.23 activities *x* and *y* cannot be drawn as first shown; they must be drawn using a *dummy activity*.

Dummy activities have no duration and are usually shown as a dotted line arrow. They are used either for clarity of drawing or to keep the logic of the diagram consistent with that of the project.

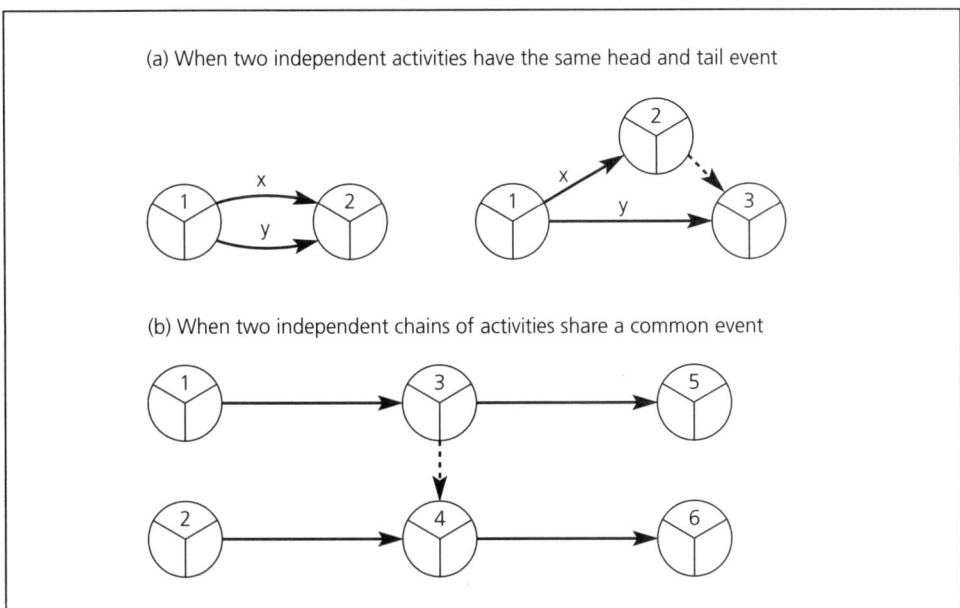

(a) When two independent activities have the same head and tail event

(b) When two independent chains of activities share a common event

Figure 16.23
When dummy activities are necessary

The critical path

In all network diagrams where the activities have some parallel relationships there will be more than one sequence of activities which will lead from the start to the end of the project. These sequences of activities are called *paths* through the network. Each path will have a total duration which is the sum of all its activities. The path which has the longest sequence of activities is called the *critical path* of the network (note that it is possible to have more than one critical path if they share the same joint longest time). It is called the critical path because any delay in any of the activities on this path will delay the whole project. Delays on activities not on the critical path will not necessarily delay the whole project.

Activity or node networks

The network we have described so far uses arrows to represent activities and circles at the junctions or nodes of the arrows to represent events. This method is called the *activity on arrow* (AoA) method. An alternative method of drawing networks is the *activity on node* (AoN) method. In the AoN representation activities are drawn as boxes and arrows are used to define the relationships between them. There are three advantages to the AoN method:

● It is often easier to move from the basic logic of a project's relationships to a network diagram using AoN than using the AoA method.
● AoN diagrams do not need dummy activities to maintain the logic of relationships.
● Most of the computer packages which are used in project planning and control use an AoN format.

Example

Returning to the 'new logistics' operation described previously, an AoN network diagram is shown in Fig. 16.24. In this example (as in most realistic examples) relationships are not always clear cut. For example, 'Refine logistics' has been shown as impacting only on 'Supplier negotiation'. In practice, it would also impact on 'System requirements', and probably also on the design issues in activities 7 through 11. Such relationships could be shown on a lower-level network, which goes into more detail on such issues. The activity on system requirements is a sub-project in itself, and would require its own bar charts and logic diagrams for planning and monitoring.

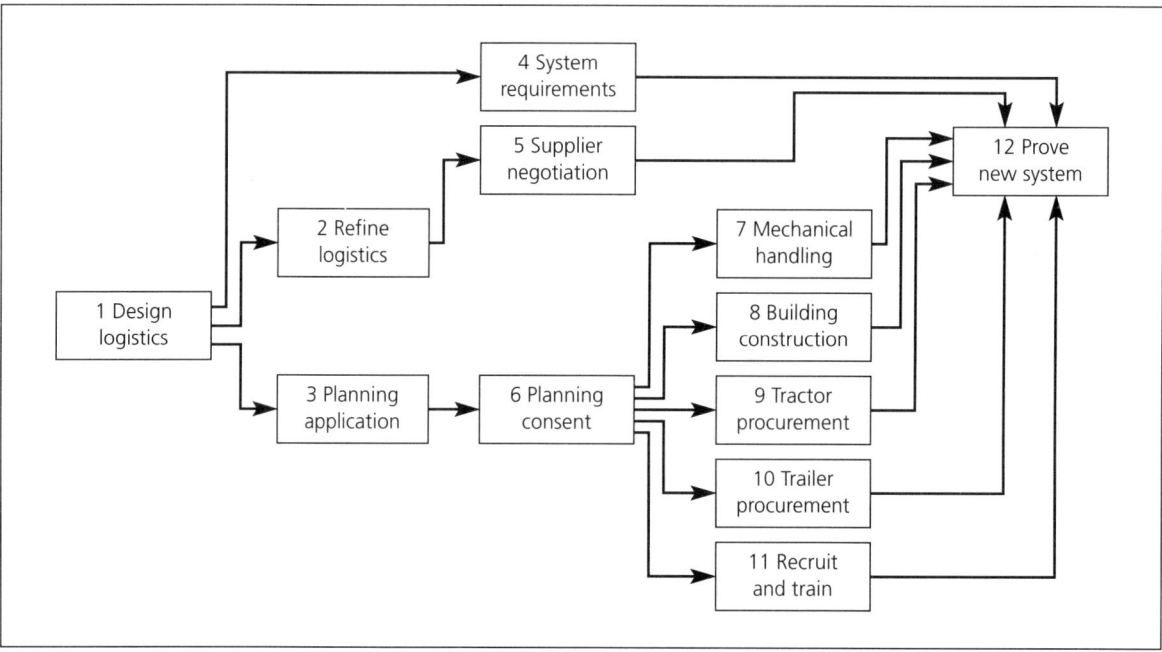

Figure 16.24 New logistics operation: logic diagram

Time analysis

Figure 16.25 provides a full AoN network for the simple diagram in Fig. 16.24. Activity numbers and abbreviated descriptions are as before. Each is now surrounded by a set of six numbers which signify information as shown in Fig. 16.26.

The *earliest start times* for each activity are found by working from left to right across the network. Each start event can begin at $t=0$. At a 'merge' event (two or more activities come together, as at event 12), use the latest completion date of the various

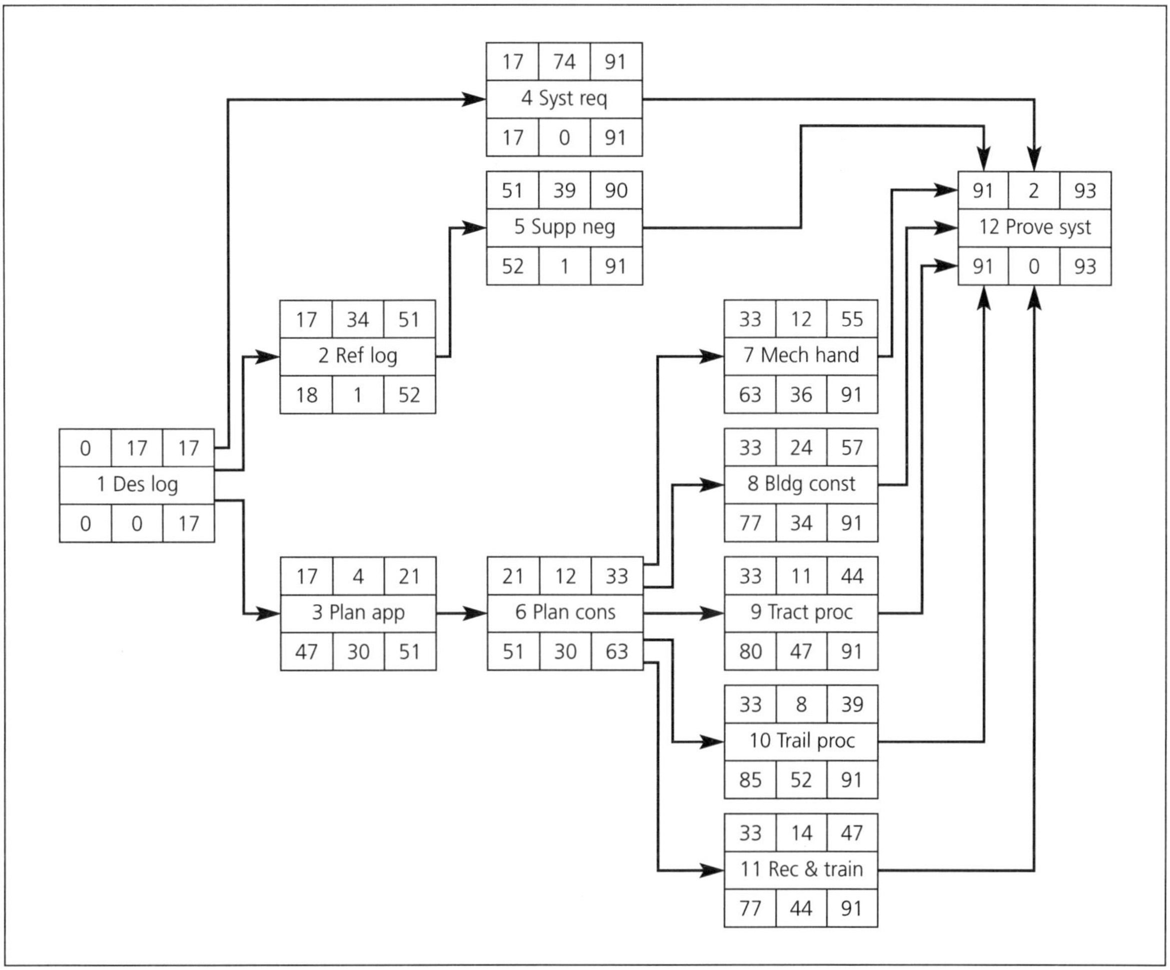

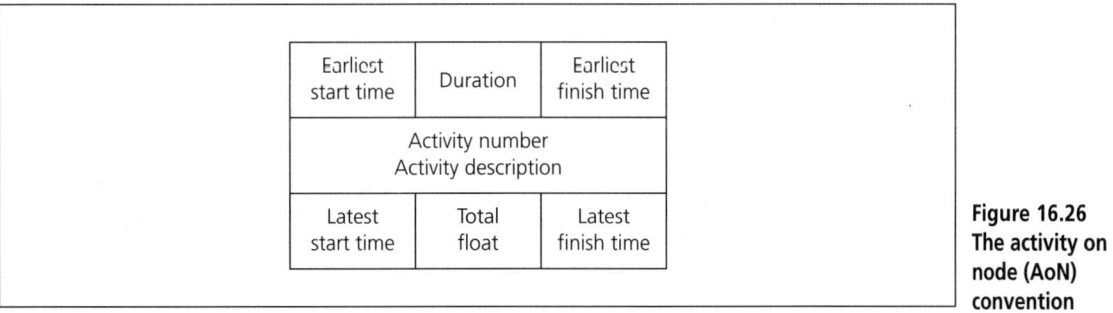

Figure 16.25   New logistics operation: precedence network

Earliest start time	Duration	Earliest finish time
Activity number Activity description		
Latest start time	Total float	Latest finish time

Figure 16.26 The activity on node (AoN) convention

activities which lead into it. Earliest finish times of a 'burst' activity (such as activity 6, where five succeeding activities literally 'burst' out) are carried forward to form the earliest start dates of the succeeding activities (7 through 11).

The *latest start times* for each activity are found by working back from right to left across the network. The earliest start time for the final event on the network is often used as the latest start time for that event as well. At a 'merge' event (such as event 6), use the earliest completion date of the various activities.

First, we carry out a *forward pass* of the network (i.e. proceed from left to right). Activity 1 is given a start date of week 0. The earliest finish is then week 17, because the duration is 17 weeks. Earliest start date for activity 2 must then also be week 17. Activity 5 starts at 17 + 34, the duration for activity 2. Activity 4 is in parallel with activity 2, and can start at the same time. The rest of the forward pass is straightforward until we reach activity 12. Here, seven activities merge, so we must use the highest earliest finish of the activities which lead into it as the earliest start time for activity 12. This is 91 (the earliest finish time for activity 4). Since the duration of activity 12 is two weeks, the earliest finish time for the whole network is 93 weeks.

Now we can carry out a *backward pass* by assuming that the latest finish time is also 93 weeks (the bottom right-hand box on activity 12). This means that there is no 'float', i.e. the difference between the earliest and latest start dates for this activity is zero. Hence, the latest start time is also week 91. This gets downdated into activities 7 through 11, which have week 91 as the latest finish time. The difference between week 91 and the various earliest finish times for these activities means that there is a lot of float on each one, that is that they can start much later than indicated by the earliest start dates. On the backward pass, activity 6 forms a merge event for activities 7 through 11. Take the lowest latest start time from these activities, i.e. week 63, as the latest finish time for activity 6. If all goes well, and the analysis is correct, there should also be zero float for activity 1.

The *critical path* for the network is then the line which joins the activities with minimum float, i.e. activities 1, 4 and 12. Note that the path 1-2-5-12 is a close second, with only one week of float. Both pathways through the network will merit special attention during the project because slippage on any of these activities will cause the whole project to overrun unless time can be saved elsewhere on the critical path. As yet, there is no indication that this is possible. It should never be assumed that time will be caught up later unless a specific action plan as to how this will be achieved has been made.

Going back to the progress reported on the Gantt chart in Fig. 16.20, the project manager will be relieved to see that activity 1 was completed on time, and that progress on activity 4 is ahead of schedule. Although progress on activity 2 is behind schedule, this does not appear to be critical at present. However, it may affect other activities in a way not shown on the network, and the prudent project manager will be taking action on this activity to make sure that it does not.

Programme evaluation and review technique (PERT)

The programme evaluation and review technique, or PERT as it is universally known, had its origins in planning and controlling major defence projects in the US Navy. The first reported success was the completion of the Polaris missile programme two years ahead of schedule in 1958. PERT had its most spectacular gains in the highly uncertain environment of space and defence projects. The technique recognizes that activity durations and costs in project management are not deterministic (fixed), and that probability theory can be applied to estimates, as was shown in Fig. 16.11.

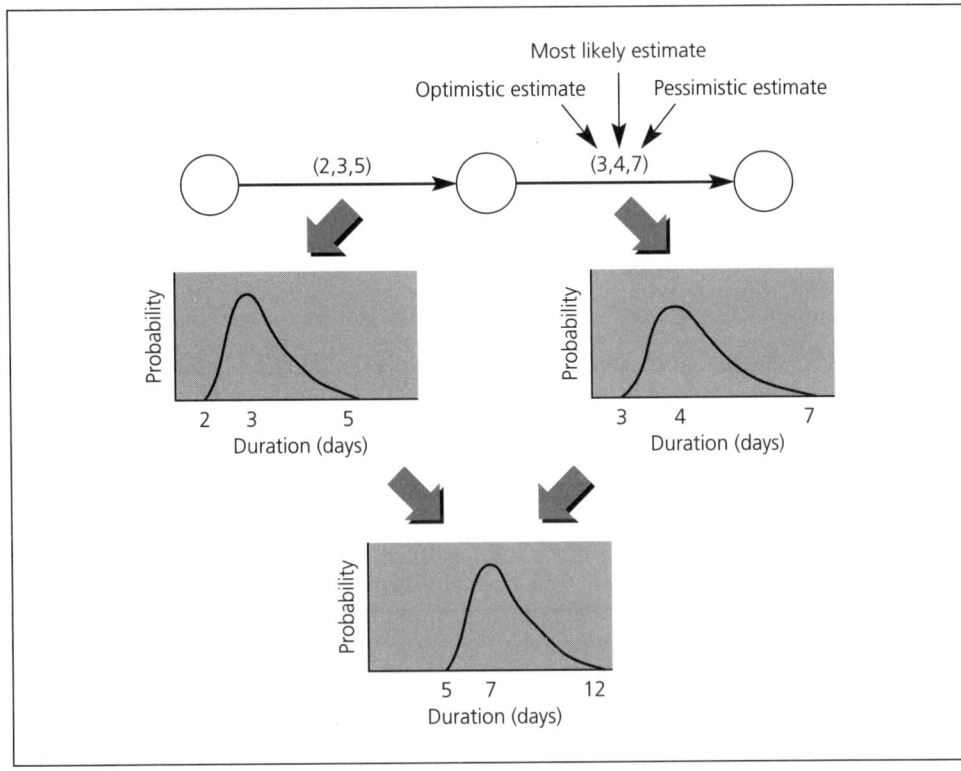

Figure 16.27
Probabilistic time estimates can be summed to give a probabilistic estimate for the whole project

In this type of network each activity duration is estimated on an optimistic, most likely and pessimistic basis, as shown in Fig. 16.27. If it is assumed that these time estimates are consistent with a beta probability distribution, the mean and variance of the distribution can be estimated as follows:

$$t_e = \frac{t_o + 4t_l + t_p}{6}$$

where

t_e = the expected time for the activity
t_o = the optimistic time for the activity
t_l = the most likely time for the activity
t_p = the pessimistic time for the activity

The variance of the distribution (V) can be calculated as follows:

$$V = \frac{(t_p - t_o)^2}{6^2} = \frac{(t_p - t_o)^2}{36}$$

The time distribution of any path through a network will have a mean which is the sum of the means of the activities which make up the path, and a variance which is a sum of their variances. In Fig. 16.27:

$$\text{The mean of the first activity} = \frac{2 + (4 \times 3) + 5}{6} = 3.17$$

599

$$\text{The variance of the first activity} = \frac{(5-2)^2}{36} = 0.25$$

$$\text{The mean of the second activity} = \frac{3 + (4 \times 4) + 7}{6} = 4.33$$

$$\text{The variance of the second activity} = \frac{(7-3)^2}{36} = 0.44$$

$$\text{The mean of the network distribution} = 3.17 + 4.33 = 7.5$$

$$\text{The variance of the network distribution} = 0.25 + 0.44 = 0.69$$

It is generally assumed that the distribution for the whole path will be normally distributed.

The advantage of this extra information is that we can examine the 'riskiness' of each path through a network as well as its duration. For example, Fig. 16.28 shows a simple two-path network. The top path is the critical one, the distribution of its duration is 10.5 with a variance of 0.06 (therefore a standard deviation of 0.245). The distribution of the non-critical path has a mean of 9.67 and a variance of 0.66 (therefore a standard deviation of 0.812). The implication of this is that there is a chance that the non-critical path could in reality be critical. Although we will not discuss the probability calculations here, it is possible to determine the probability of any sub-critical path turning out to be critical when the project actually takes place. However, on a practical level, even if the probability calculations are judged not to be worth the effort involved, it is useful to be able to make an approximate assessment of the riskiness of each part of a network.

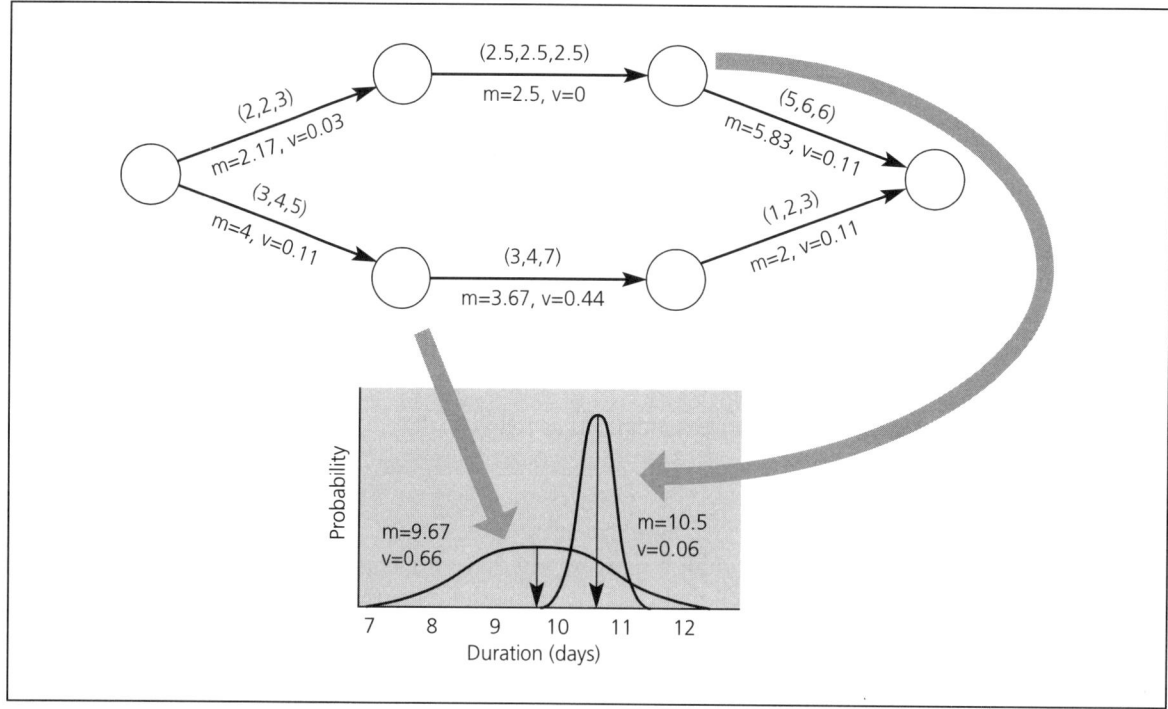

Figure 16.28 **One path in the network can have the longest expected duration while another path has the greater variance**

Introducing resource constraints

The logic which governs network relationships is primarily derived from the technical details of the project as we have described. However, the availability of resources may impose its own constraints which can materially affect the relationships between activities. Figure 16.29 shows a simple two-path network with details of both the duration of each activity as well as the number of staff required to perform each activity. The total resource schedule is also shown. The three activities on the critical path, a, c, and e, have been programmed into the resource schedule first. The remaining activities all have some float and therefore have flexibility as to when they are performed.

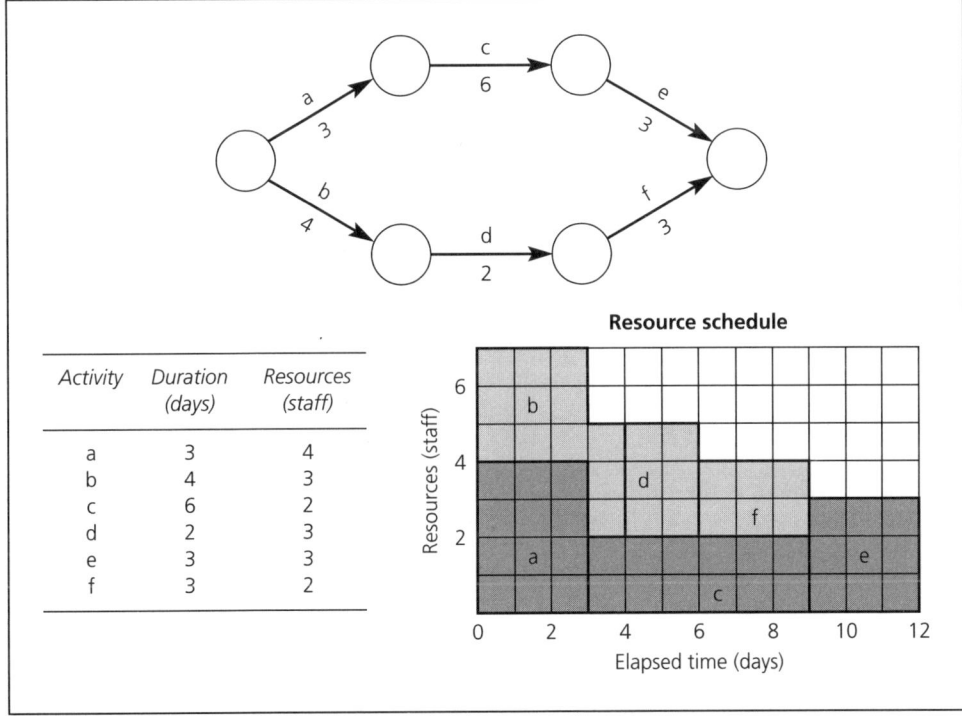

Activity	Duration (days)	Resources (staff)
a	3	4
b	4	3
c	6	2
d	2	3
e	3	3
f	3	2

Figure 16.29 Resource profile of a network assuming that all activities are started as soon as possible

The resource schedule in Fig. 16.29 has the non-critical activities starting as soon as is possible. This results in a resource profile which varies from seven staff down to three. Even if seven staff are available, the project manager might want to even out the loading for organizational convenience. If the total number of staff available is less than seven, however, the project will need rescheduling. Suppose only five staff are available. It is still possible to complete the project in the same time, as shown in Fig. 16.30. Activity b has been delayed until after activity a has finished. This results in a resource profile which varies only between four and five staff and is within the resourcing limit of five staff.

However, in order to achieve this it is necessary to *require* activity b to start only when activity a is completed. This is a logic constraint which, if it were included in the network, would change it as shown in Fig. 16.30. In this network all activities are critical, as indeed one can see from the resource schedule.

601

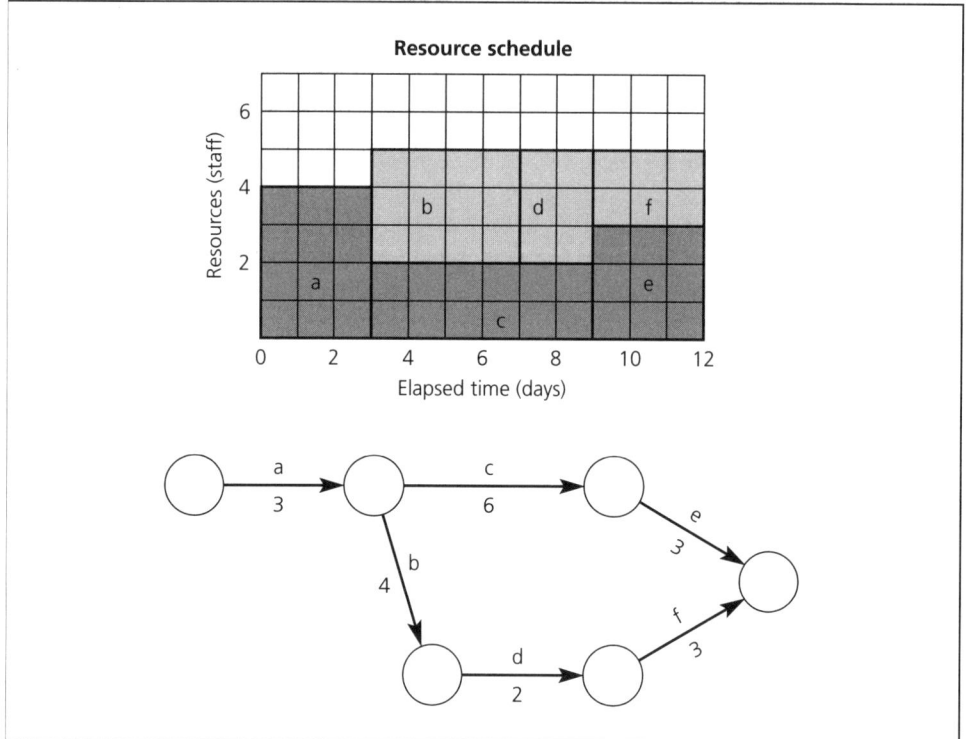

Figure 16.30
Resource profile of a network with non-critical activities delayed to fit resource constraints; in this case this effectively changes the network logic to make all activities critical

Crashing networks

Crashing networks is the process of reducing time spans on critical path activities so that the project is completed in less time. Usually, crashing activities incurs extra cost. This can be as a result of:

- overtime working;
- additional resources, such as manpower;
- sub-contracting.

Figure 16.31 shows an example of crashing a simple network. For each activity the duration and normal cost are specified together with the (reduced) duration and (increased) cost of crashing them. Not all activities are capable of being crashed; here activity *e* cannot be crashed. The critical path is the sequence of activities *a, b, c, e*. If the total project time is to be reduced, one of the activities on the critical path must be crashed. In order to decide which activity to crash, the 'cost slope' of each is calculated. This is the cost per time period of reducing durations. The most cost-effective way of shortening the whole project then is to crash the activity on the critical path which has the lowest cost slope. This is activity *a*, the crashing of which will cost an extra R2000 and will shorten the project by one week. After this, activity *c* can be crashed, saving a further two weeks and costing an extra R5000. At this point all the activities have become critical and further time savings can only be achieved by crashing two activities in parallel.

The shape of the time-cost curve in Fig. 16.31 is entirely typical. Initial savings come relatively inexpensively if the activities with the lowest cost slope are chosen.

Later in the crashing sequence the more expensive activities need to be crashed, and eventually two and more paths become jointly critical. Inevitably by that point savings in time can only come from crashing two or more activities on parallel paths.

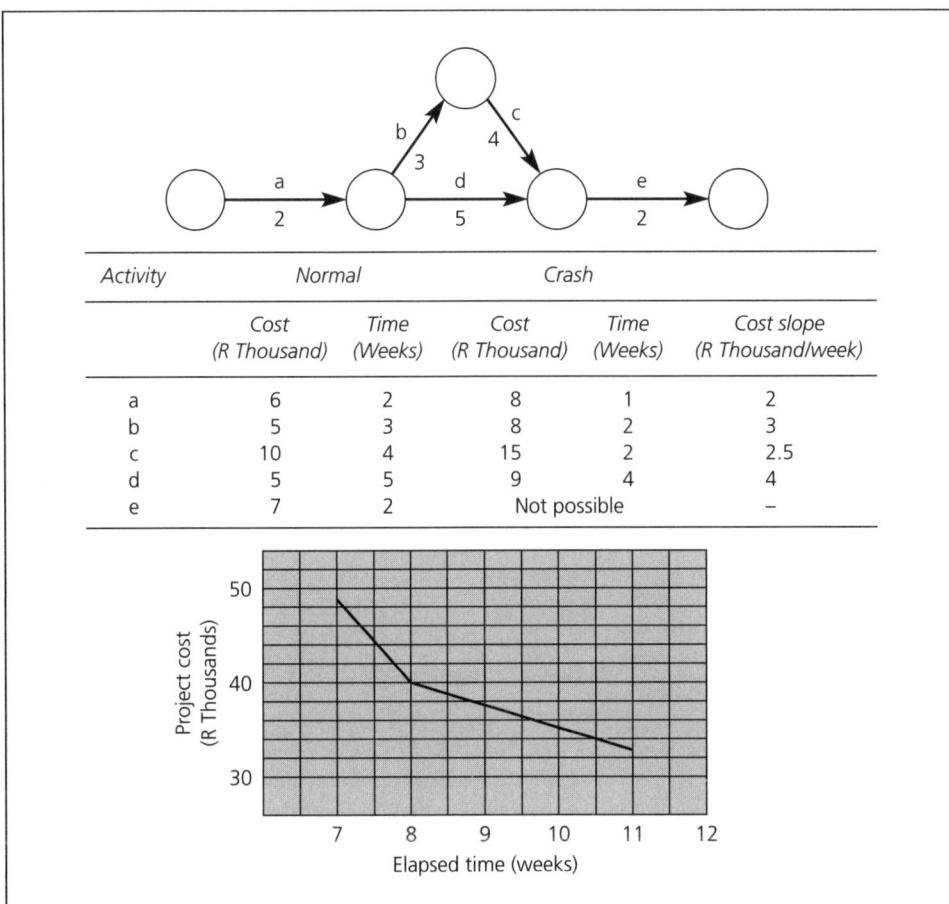

| Activity | Normal | | Crash | | Cost slope |
	Cost (R Thousand)	Time (Weeks)	Cost (R Thousand)	Time (Weeks)	(R Thousand/week)
a	6	2	8	1	2
b	5	3	8	2	3
c	10	4	15	2	2.5
d	5	5	9	4	4
e	7	2	Not possible		–

Figure 16.31 Crashing activities to shorten project time becomes progessively more expensive

PERSONAL PROFILE

Gerry Moolman, Sentech (Pty) Ltd

In 1984, Sentech (Pty) Ltd, the technical division of the South African Broadcasting Corporation (SABC), embarked on a major expansion of the, then, TV service in South Africa. Phase I of the project was to bring 84 new transmitter stations on-air. The capital expenditure involved was in the region of R1.4 billion.

This project was one of the biggest undertaken by Sentech at that time and it was acknowledged that a well coordinated approach was required if the project was to be a success.

Gerry Moolman, Head of Operations, was charged with the task of setting up a project management ▶

system that would ensure the project was completed successfully – on budget, on time and in accordance with required specifications and standards. The timing of this project was of paramount importance, as in the broadcasting business timing and deadlines are not negotiable!

Key in the initial set-up of this new project management system was the question of how the projects would be managed. Individual projects were allocated to multi-disciplinary teams and were headed up by a *dedicated project manager*. This approach, of integrating the functions, was chosen because it would enable the project manager to plan effectively and control efficiently a project toward its chosen objectives. The project manager would have both the responsibility and the authority regarding a particular project.

Although project management systems are now becoming the norm, rather than the exception, the implementation of the 'Project Commitment System' (PCS) at Sentech, in 1984, was unusual at the time. What made the PCS a success?

Gerry identifies the following success criteria:

'The Project Manager had sole accountability for the success of the project. Because of the support and resources given by the top-management structure, the Project Managers were empowered and tended to run projects as though they were running their own businesses.

Project Managers stayed with their projects until completion. This encouraged a consistency that promoted better learning within the project team.

Due to the make-up of the cross-functional teams, a project tended to be well thought through with relevant input from all team members and therefore all disciplines.

For the first time ever, financial and budgetary control for each project was a responsibility of the Project Manager. This was significant, as project teams became aware of the implications of going over budget and how this would impact on their team's success. To encourage further commitment to the meeting of budgets, the Project Manager

allocated the budget, appropriately, to the various functional heads. This pushed down the philosophy of individual responsibility and accountability.

The Project Manager encouraged a philosophy of critical cost evaluation. The objective was not to save costs at the expense of standards. However, linked to these cost savings was a bonus scheme that the Project Manager had the discretion to grant to the appropriate team members. In order to maintain the required objectivity, the Project Manager was not eligible for any part of this bonus.

Feedback mechanisms are critically important in successful project management. A formal reporting system was implemented, whereby functional leaders fed back written reports every month-end to the Project Manager. The Project Manager, in turn, issued both a status and budget reconciliation report to top management within two days of month-end. Where queries or problems required management feedback and/or support, management was expected to respond within 24 hours. This fast feedback system prevented problems from either escalating or forming a backlog.

Variance analysis reporting was instituted. These reports identified positive and negative outcomes throughout the project. The reason for this reporting was to establish a culture of learning that would help prevent mistakes being repeated and make widely known actions that brought success.'

The success of the PCS resulted in Sentech's transmitter expansion being completed in two years and four months, compared to a world benchmark of ten years. The entire project was completed on time and on budget, despite a massive depreciation of the rand against the Japanese yen. Much of Sentech's communications equipment is purchased from Japan.

'One could argue that the PCS is a very document-oriented system, but it is perhaps because of this that the PCS has been a remarkable success at Sentech.' ■

Source: By kind permission of Sentech (Pty) Ltd

SUMMARY

■ A project is a set of activities which have a defined start point and a defined end state, that pursue a defined goal and that use a defined set of resources.

■ Projects come in many shapes and sizes. Many projects that managers have to plan and control are relatively small, although large projects have an added dimension of complexity which gives particular problems.

■ All projects are characterized by having an objective, a certain degree of complexity, frequently uniqueness, uncertainty, are of a temporary nature, and go through a number of phases.

■ Projects can be characterized on two dimensions: complexity and uncertainty. Projects with high uncertainty are difficult to define and plan, whereas those with high complexity are particularly difficult to control.

■ Successful project management depends on the project having clearly defined goals, competent project management, the support of top management, competent team members, sufficient resources available, adequate channels of communication, satisfactory control mechanisms, the ability to encourage feedback, responsiveness to clients' needs, mechanisms for sorting out problems, and continuity among project staff.

■ Project management has five stages, four of which are relevant to project planning and control. These are:

Stage 1 – understanding the project environment;
Stage 2 – defining the project;
Stage 3 – project planning;
Stage 4 – technical execution (not part of the
        planning and control process);
Stage 5 – project control.

■ Understanding the project environment is important for two reasons. First, the environment influences the way a project is carried out. Second, the nature of the environment in which a good project takes place is the main determinant of the uncertainty surrounding it.

■ Defining a project is necessary in order that the project management has clear goals and objectives.

■ Project planning is necessary because it exposes the cost and duration of the project, as well as determining the level of resources which will be needed. It also helps to allocate work and monitor progress, and to assess the impact of any changes on the project.

■ Project planning is usually seen as involving five stages:
– identifying the activities within a project;
– estimating times and resources for the activities;
– identifying the relationships and dependencies between the activities;
– identifying the schedule constraints;
– fixing the schedule.

■ Project control consists of monitoring how the project is progressing, assessing the performance of the project by comparing monitored observations to the project plan, and intervening in the project if required in order to bring it back to plan. A particularly important part of project control is earned value control which puts both time and resources into monetary units in order to monitor progress.

■ Network diagrams can be drawn in either network on arrow or network on node formats. In both forms they are particularly useful in assessing the total duration of a project and the degree of flexibility or float of the individual activities within the project.

■ The most common method of network planning is called the critical path method (CPM). This uses single-point estimates for time. An alternative approach of estimating time is offered by the programme evaluation and review technique (PERT). This uses three estimates of time (optimistic, most likely and pessimistic) in order to take a probabilistic approach to time estimation.

■ The logic inherent in a network diagram can be changed by resource constraints. Even if two activities could be scheduled independently with infinite resources, the limited availability of resources might require them to be scheduled successively.

■ Network planning models can also be used to assess the total cost of shortening a project where individual activities can be 'crashed'.

Bushveld Television

Bushveld Television (BTV) is a television production company which specializes in making outside broadcast (OB) 'specials' for a South African television network. It was recently commissioned to make a series of 'summer roadshow' programmes which would be shot at locations around South Africa during the spring and early summer and broadcast by the customer (a satellite broadcasting network) during the summer. The programmes would involve circus acts, displays, events and computer-graphic displays to entertain the crowds and popular entertainment acts and interviews which would be interspersed with contestant games. Managing the preparation for the series was the responsibility of the show's producer, Rachel Cohen. Rachel, who had recently graduated with distinction from her MBA course, knew that she would need to keep a tight grip on the arrangements for the roadshow series. The shooting would start at the end of Novemeber and the final show would be recorded at the end of January. The shows would be broadcast between early January and late February, so any delay either in recording the material or in editing the programmes would cause considerable complications.

The company had known that it would be commissioned to make the programmes since June, but Rachel had only been allocated the job in early July! Her first act was to list the various jobs which would have to be done before shooting could start. She then discussed each job with the part of the company who would carry it out, to try to understand what decisions would need to be made before they could start on their jobs. The jobs which needed to be done prior to the start of the shooting are listed below, together with some details.

The producer's responsibility (as well as managing the whole project) was:

● *Scheduling the venues:* would take about two weeks to finalize and could be started straight away.
● *Defining the design concept:* would need discussions with the chief designer and would take about four weeks of considering alternative designs before finalizing the concept, but could be started straight away.
● *Specifying computer-graphic displays:* again in consultation with the chief designer, it would take about a week but could not be started until all the detailed planning had been finalized.

The design department's responsibility was:

● *Producing artwork for printed materials:* would take about three weeks but could be started only after completion of the detailed planning.

The programme planning department's responsibility was:

● *Booking the venues:* a one-week job which could be started as soon as the venues had been decided by Rachel.
● *Detailed planning:* the preparation of detailed plans and schedules, a two-week task which could be started once the design concept had been finalized and the venues booked.
● *Printing the brochures:* an outside printer could be given this job as soon as the artwork for the printed materials had been prepared by the design department. The printer usually quoted a four-week delivery from receipt of the artwork.
● *Printing the display posters:* again depended on the preparation of the artwork but could be delivered within two weeks of the artwork being ready.
● *Ordering the roadshow vehicles:* several trailer trucks and ancillary vehicles were needed which could be ordered on completion of the detailed planning. Delivery of the vehicles would take about six weeks.
● *Writing the graphic display software:* contracted out to a software house, it would take about four weeks but could only be started after the computer graphics had been specified by the producer and chief designer.
● *Final testing and rehearsals:* the programme planning department were finally responsible for getting the 'whole act together' immediately prior to shooting. Testing and rehearsals could only start once the brochures had been printed, the vehicles fully fitted out and customized and the promotion staff trained. Final tests and rehearsals should take around a week but, if things went wrong at any stage, could take longer.

The workshop's responsibility was:

● *Customizing and fitting out the vehicles:* after the vehicles were delivered and the artwork agreed and the computer-graphics software finished, the vehicles could be fitted out and customized for the shows. This would normally take around two weeks.

The personnel department's responsibility was:

● *Recruiting the promotion (promo) staff:* these were the staff (often 'resting' actors) who staffed the exhibits and entertained the crowds; they could be recruited as soon as the detailed planning was completed. Usually it took two weeks to recruit all the promo staff.

● *Training the promo staff:* once all promo staff had been recruited they would need training – a one-week task. ∎

Questions

1 Can Rachel get the project together in time to start shooting on schedule?

2 Which are the jobs which she will have to manage particularly closely?

3 What general advice would you give her which would help her to manage this project?

DISCUSSION QUESTIONS

1 Would professional services, such as a management consultancy project, benefit from the application of project management principles in the same way as would the manufacturer of a turbine generator set for a power station?

2 (a) Why is the concept of earliest and latest start times of value in project planning?
(b) Draw up cumulative cost/time curves for the new logistics operation shown in Fig. 16.20 and developed later in the chapter. Assume the total costs for each activity are as follows:

Activity 1   R34 000   Activity 7   R120 000
Activity 2   R68 000   Activity 8   R480 000
Activity 3   R12 000   Activity 9   R1.1m
Activity 4   R370 000   Activity 10   R400 000
Activity 5   R39 000   Activity 11   R42 000
Activity 6   nil cost   Activity 12   R20 000

Money is consumed in a linear manner over time: that is if one week has elapsed in a four-week activity, then one quarter of the cost has been incurred.
(c) Show cumulative cost curves assuming that:
all work starts at the earliest start times;
all work starts at the latest start times.

3 Why is the critical path a helpful concept in project planning and control?

4 (a) If the network shown in Fig. 16.25 had to be crashed to achieve a completion at week 80, which activities would need to have reduced durations?
(b) What would be the implications for activity 4?
(c) What would the cumulative time/cost curve now look like?

5 Identify possible differences between internal and external project performance reports.

6 Evaluate the job of the project manager.
(a) Does it tend to make people value short-term expediency in order to get the job done?
(b) Why does the project manager tend to resist changes?
(c) Is it good training for general management?

7 Identify a number of projects with which you have been involved, for example 'project work' as part of the university course, moving house, preparing a large meal, organizing a foreign trip for several people, etc. Assess each of them in terms of their project elements and the complexity–uncertainty typology.

8 Using the list of projects identified in question 7, assess the success of each of them. Did any fail or not succeed as well as planned and what do you think were the reasons for this? Compare your findings with the project management success factors.

9 Discuss the problems of managing a large-scale famine relief project.

10 Identify the key project planning phases for a major rock concert.

11 What criteria might you use to monitor a theatrical production?

12 The activities, their durations and precedences for designing, writing and installing a bespoke computer database are shown in Table 16.4. Draw a Gantt chart for the operation and calculate the fastest time in which the operation might be completed.

13 Construct a network diagram which satisfies the following relationships:

A, B and C are the first activities of the project and can start simultaneously.

A and B precede D.

B precedes E, F and H.

F and C precede G.

E and H precede I and J.

C, D, F and J precede K.

K precedes L.

I, G and L are the terminal activities of the project.

Table 16.4

Activity	Duration (weeks)	Activities that must be completed before it can start
1 Contract negotiation	1	–
2 Discussions with main users	2	1
3 Review of current documentation	5	1
4 Review of current systems	6	2
5 Systems analysis (a)	4	3, 4
6 Systems analysis (b)	7	5
7 Programming	12	5
8 Testing (prelim)	2	7
9 Existing system review report	1	3, 4
10 System proposal report	2	5, 9
11 Documentation preparation	19	5, 8
12 Implementation	7	7, 11
13 System test	3	12
14 Debugging	4	12
15 Manual preparation	5	11

14 A catering manager has been asked to organize a banquet for 100 guests. Table 16.5 shows the key activities, their durations and precedences. Identify the critical activities and prepare a Gantt chart showing all the activities and the float available for the non-critical activities.

Table 16.5

Activity	Duration	Preceding activities
A Prepare ingredients	30	–
B Clear/clean room	20	–
C Prepare room and lay tables	20	B
D Prepare dressings and cold dishes	20	A
E Prepare meat, to oven	30	A
F Meet and seat guests	50	C,D,E
G Plate, dress and serve starter	70	C,D,E
H Cook vegetables	30	C,E
I Plate up puddings	20	C,E
J Clear starter, serve main course	15	G,H
K Clear main, serve pudding and coffee	15	J
L Clear tables	20	K

Table 16.6

Activity	Duration (weeks)			Preceding activities
	Optimistic	Most likely	Pessimistic	
A	1	2	3	–
B	3	5	11	A
C	5	7	9	A
D	5	7	12	B
E	1	2	3	C
F	7	9	11	C
G	2	3	4	D, E

15 Given the information in Table 16.6:
(a) What is the shortest time in which the project can be completed?
(b) What are the critical activities?
(c) What is the standard deviation of the critical path?
(d) What is the probability that the project will be completed in 20 weeks?

16 The chief surveyor of a firm that moves earth in preparation for the construction of roads has identified the activities, their durations and the number of mechanical diggers required for each stage of an operation to prepare a difficult stretch of motorway (Table 16.7). The surveyor needs to know the minimum number of mechanical diggers required during the project.

Table 16.7

Activity	Duration (days)	Preceding activities	No. of mechanical diggers required
A	5	–	3
B	10	–	5
C	1	–	4
D	8	B	2
E	10	B	3
F	9	B	1
G	3	A, D	5
H	7	A, D	4
I	4	F	9
J	3	F	7
K	5	C, J	1
L	8	H, E, I, K	2
M	4	C, J	10

NOTES ON CHAPTER

1 Based on an idea by Nicholas, J.M. (1990) *Managing Business and Engineering Projects: Concepts and Implementation*, Prentice Hall.
2 Based on Pinto, J.K. and Slevin, D.P. (1987) 'Critical Success Factors in Successful Project Implementation', *IEEE Transactions on Engineering Management*, Vol 34, No 1.
3 Weiss, J.W. and Wysocki, R.K. (1992) *5-Phase Project Management: A Practical Planning and Implementation Guide*, Addison-Wesley.
4 Source: *Computer Weekly*, Mar 1993.
5 Barnes, M. (1985) 'Project Management Framework', *International Project Management Yearbook*, Butterworth Scientific.
6 Lock, D. (1993) *Project Management* (5th edn), Gower.
7 Source: Discussions with company staff.
8 Lock, D., *op. cit.*
9 Sources: ESA press releases.

SELECTED FURTHER READINGS

Baker, B.N. and Wileman, D.L. (1981) 'A Summary of Major Research Findings Regarding the Human Element in Project Management', *IEEE Engineering Management Review*, Vol 9, No 3.

Davis, E.W. (1973) 'Project Scheduling Under Resource Constraints – A Historical Review', *AIEE Transactions*, Vol 5, No 4.

Gilbreath, R.D. (1986) *Winning at Project Management*, John Wiley.

Harrison, F.L. (1981) *Advanced Project Management*, Gower.

Icmeli, O., Erenguc, S.S. and Zappe, C.J. (1993) 'Project Scheduling Problems: A Survey', *International Journal of Operations and Production Management*, Vol 13, No 11.

Kruger, L.P. and Steyn, P.G. (1995) 'The Success Factors in the Implementation of Project Management in Public Sector Work Departments', *Bestuursdinamika*, Vol 4, No 4, pp 49–68.

Littlefield, T.K. and Randolph, P.H. (1991) 'PERT Duration Times: Mathematical or MBO', *Interfaces*, Vol 21, No 6.

Lockyer, K. and Gordon, J. (1996) *Project Management and Project Network Techniques* (6th edn), Pitman Publishing.

Meredith, J.R. and Mantel, S. (1989) *Project Management: A Managerial Approach* (2nd edn), John Wiley.

Miller, R.W. (1962) 'How To Plan and Control With PERT', *Harvard Business Review*, Vol 40, No 2.

Morris, P.W. and Hough, G.H. (1987) '*The Anatomy of Major Projects*', John Wiley.

O'Neal, K. (1987) 'Project Management Computer Software Buyers Guide', *Industrial Engineering*, Vol 9, No 1.

Randolph, W.A. and Posner, B.Z. (1988) 'What Every Project Manager Needs to Know About Project Management', *Sloan Management Review*, Vol 29, No 4.

Reinertson, D.G. and Smith, P.G. (1991) *Developing Products in Half the Time*, Van Nostrand Reinhold.

QUALITY PLANNING AND CONTROL

INTRODUCTION

Quality is the only one of the five 'operations performance criteria' to have its own dedicated chapter in this book (or two chapters if you include Total Quality Management which is covered in Chapter 20). There are two reasons for this. First, in many organizations there is a separate and identifiable part of the operations function which is devoted exclusively to the management of quality. It is necessary, therefore, to examine the issues which concern staff in this area. Second, it is a current and key concern of many organizations. Business newspapers and management journals are dominated by articles on quality. It would appear that we have undergone a 'quality revolution'. Certainly there is a growing realization that high-quality goods and services can give an organization a considerable competitive edge. Good quality reduces costs of rework, scrap and returns and, most importantly, good quality generates satisfied customers. Some operations managers believe that, in the long run, quality is the most important single factor affecting an organization's performance relative to its competitors. Figure 17.1 illustrates the supply–demand relationship covered in the chapter.

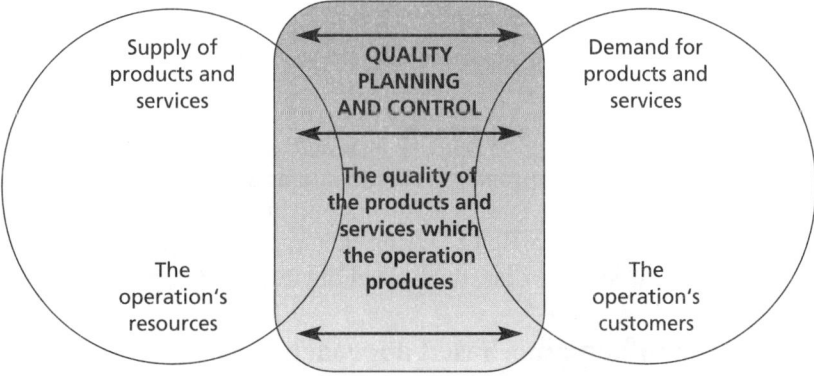

Figure 17.1 Quality planning and control is concerned with the systems and procedures which govern the quality of the products and services supplied by the operation

> **OBJECTIVES**
>
> This chapter will examine:
>
> - the various definitions of quality;
>
> - the perception–expectation gap theory of quality in operations;
>
> - quality characteristics of goods and services;
>
> - 'attribute' and 'variable' measures of quality and quality standards;
>
> - the use of statistical process control (SPC) in quality planning and control;
>
> - the use of acceptance sampling plans (ASP) in quality planning and control.

WHAT IS QUALITY AND WHY IS IT SO IMPORTANT?

It is worth revisiting some of the arguments which were presented in Chapter 2 regarding the benefits of high quality. This will explain why quality is seen as being so important by most operations. Both contributors to profitability can be improved by higher quality. Revenues can be increased by better sales and enhanced prices in the market. At the same time, costs can be brought down by improved efficiencies, productivity and the use of capital.

If quality is indeed so important to any organization's performance then a key task of the operations function must be to ensure that it provides quality goods and services to its internal and external customers. This is not necessarily straightforward. For example, despite the 'quality revolution', there is no clear or agreed definition of what 'quality' means. Indeed there seem to be nearly as many definitions of the word 'quality' as there are people writing about it.

Professor David Garvin[1] has categorized many of the various definitions into 'five approaches' to quality: *the transcendent approach, the manufacturing-based approach, the user-based approach, the product-based approach* and *the value-based approach*.

The transcendent approach

The transcendent approach views quality as synonymous with *innate excellence*. A 'quality' car is a Rolls Royce. A 'quality' flight is one provided by Singapore Airlines. A 'quality' watch is a Rolex. Using this approach, quality is being defined as the absolute – the best possible, in terms of the product's or service's *specification*.

The manufacturing-based approach

The manufacturing-based approach is concerned with making products or providing services that are *free of errors* and that conform precisely to their design specification. A car which is less expensive than a Rolls Royce, or a Swatch watch or an economy flight, although not necessarily the 'best' available, is defined as a 'quality' product provided it has been built or delivered precisely to its design specification.

The user-based approach

The user-based approach is about making sure that the product or service is *fit for its purpose*. This definition demonstrates concern not only for its adherence to specification but also with the appropriateness of that specification for the customer. A watch that is manufactured precisely to its design specification yet falls to pieces after two days is clearly not 'fit for its purpose'. The cabin service on a nightime flight from Sydney to Stockholm may be designed to provide passengers with drinks every 15 minutes, meals every four hours and frequent announcements about the position of the plane. This quality specification may not be appropriate, however, for the customer whose main need is a good sleep.

The product-based approach

The product-based approach views quality as a precise and *measurable set of characteristics* that are required to satisfy the customer. A watch, for example, may be designed to run, without the need for servicing, for at least five years while keeping time correct to within five seconds.

The value-based approach

Finally, the value-based approach takes the manufacturing definition a stage further and defines quality in terms of *cost and price*. This approach contends that quality should be perceived in relation to price. A customer may well be willing to accept something of a lower specification quality, if the price is low. A simple and inexpensive watch may give good value by performing quite satisfactorily for a reasonable period of time. A passenger may be willing to fly from Singapore to Johannesburg with a four-hour wait in Bangkok and endure cramped seating and mediocre meals in order to save hundreds of rands over the cost of a direct flight.

Quality – the operation's view

Here we try to reconcile some of these different views in our definition of quality:

> *Quality is consistent conformance to customers' expectations.*

The use of the word 'conformance' implies that there is a need to meet a clear specification (the manufacturing approach); ensuring a product or service conforms to specification is a key operations task. 'Consistent' implies that conformance to specification is not an *ad hoc* event but that the materials, facilities and processes have been designed and then controlled to ensure that the product or service meets the specification using a set of measurable product or service characteristics (the product-based approach). The use of 'customers' expectations' attempts to combine the user- and value-based approaches.[2] It recognizes that the product or service must meet the expectations of customers, who may indeed be influenced by price.

The use of the word 'expectations' in this definition, rather than needs or wants, is important. 'Wants' would imply that anything the customer desires should be provided by the organization. 'Needs' implies only the meeting of a basic requirement. Take the example of a car. Our *need* might be for a mobile box that gets us from A to

B. We might *want* a car that has the looks and acceleration of a sports car, with the carrying capacity of an estate, the ruggedness of a cross-country vehicle, and which comes to us at no cost. Our *expectation*, however, is that which we believe to be likely. We know that it is difficult to get sports performance with a large carrying capacity, and certainly not at zero cost.

Quality – the customer's view

One problem with basing our definition of quality on customer expectations is that individual customers' expectations may be different. Past experiences, individual knowledge and history will all shape their expectations. Furthermore, customers, on receiving the product or service, may each *perceive* it in different ways. One person may perceive a long-haul flight as an exciting part of a holiday; the person on the next seat may see it as a necessary chore to get to a business meeting. One person may perceive a car as a status symbol; another may see it merely as an expensive means of getting from home to work. Quality needs to be understood from a customer's point of view because, to the customer, the quality of a particular product or service is whatever he or she perceives it to be. If the passengers on a skiing charter flight perceive it to be of good quality, despite long queues at check-in or cramped seating and poor meals, then the flight really *is* of good, perceived quality. If customers believe that expensive German cars are of good quality despite short service intervals, expensive parts and poor fuel consumption, then the car really *is* of high perceived quality. Quality is in the eye of the beholder and customers' *perception* of quality is all important.[3]

Furthermore, in some situations, customers may be unable to judge the 'technical' operational specification of the service or product. They may then use surrogate measures as a basis for their perception of quality.[4] For example, after a visit to a dentist it might be difficult for a customer to judge the technical quality of the repair of a tooth except insofar as it does not give any more trouble. The customer may in reality judge, and therefore perceive, the quality of the repair in terms of such things as the dress and demeanour of the dentist and technician, the information that was provided, or the way in which it was provided.

Diagnosing quality problems[5]

Perceived quality is shown in Fig. 17.2. We can use it to diagnose quality problems. If the perceived quality gap is such that customer perceptions of the product or service fail to match the expectations of it, then the reason (or reasons) must lie in other gaps elsewhere in the model. The four other gaps could explain a perceived quality gap between customer perception and expectations in Fig 17.2.

Gap 1 The customer's specification–operation's specification gap

Perceived quality could be poor because there may be a mismatch between the organization's own internal quality specification and the specification which is expected by the customer. For example, a car may be designed to need servicing every 10 000 kilometres but the customer may expect 15 000 kilometre service intervals. An airline may have a policy of charging for drinks during the flight whereas the customer's expectation may be that the drinks would be free.

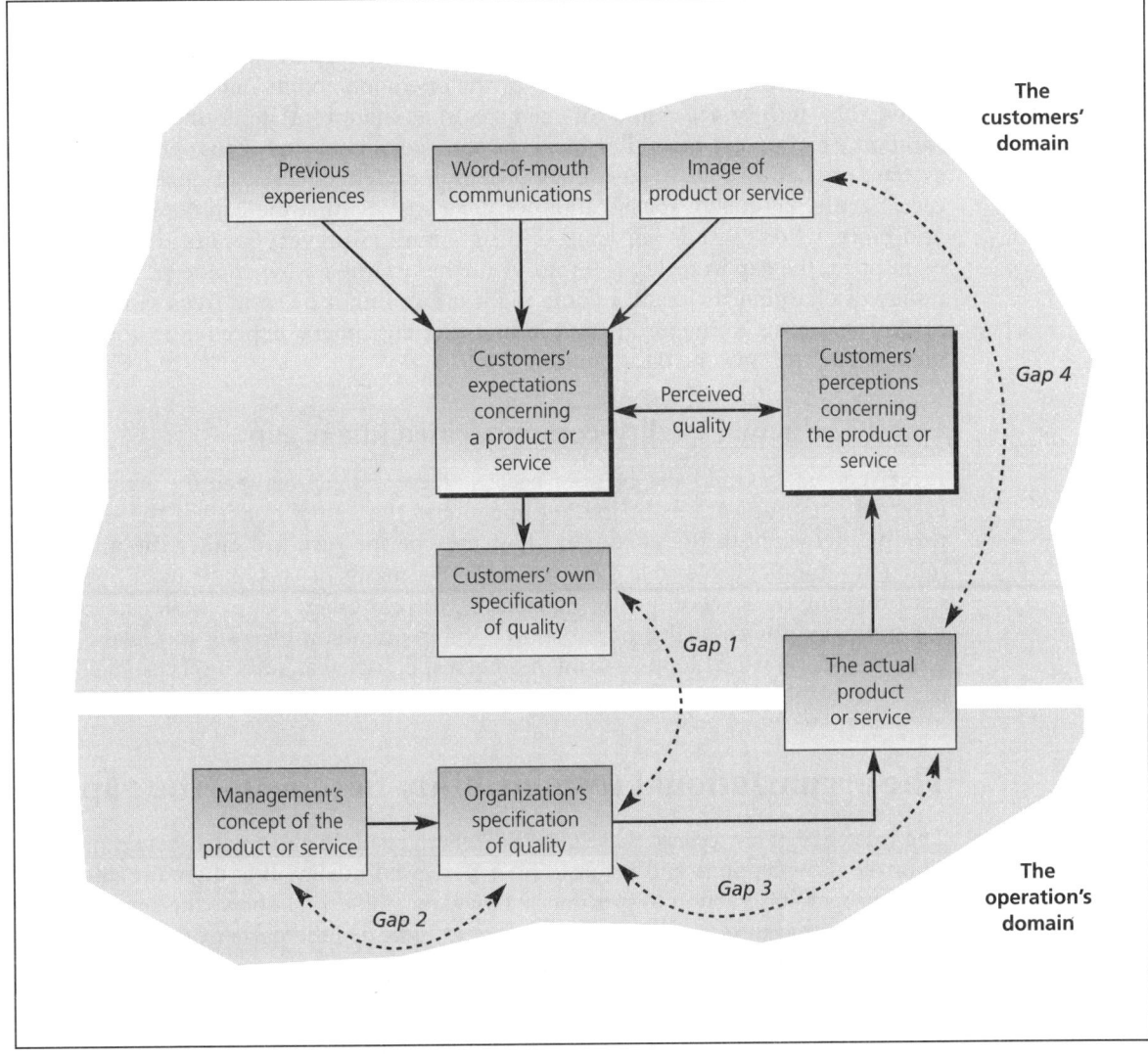

Figure 17.2 A gap between customers' expectations and their perception of a product or service could be explained by one or more gaps elsewhere in the model
Source: Adapted from Parasuraman, A. *et al.* (1985)

Gap 2 The concept–specification gap

Perceived quality could be poor because there is a mismatch between the product or service concept (*see* Chapter 5) and the way the organization has specified the quality of the product or service internally. For example, the concept of a car might have been for an inexpensive, energy-efficient means of transportation, but the inclusion of a catalytic converter may have both added to its cost and made it less energy efficient.

Gap 3 The quality specification–actual quality gap

Perceived quality could be poor because there is a mismatch between the actual quality of the service or product provided by the operation and its internal quality specification. This may be the result, for example, of an inappropriate or unachievable specification, or of poorly trained or inexperienced personnel, or because effective control systems are not in place to ensure the provision of defined levels of quality. For example, the internal quality specification for a car may be that the gap between its doors and body, when closed, must not exceed 7 mm. However, because of inadequate equipment, the gap in reality is 9 mm. A further example is where, despite an airline's policy of charging for drinks, some flight crews might provide free drinks, adding unexpected costs to the airline and influencing customers' expectations for the next flight where they may be disappointed.

Gap 4 The actual quality–communicated image gap

Perceived quality could also be poor because there is a gap between the organization's external communications or market image and the actual quality of the service or product delivered to the customer. This may be the result of either the marketing function setting unachievable expectations in the minds of customers or of operations not providing the level of quality expected by the customer. For example, an advertising campaign for an airline might show a cabin attendant offering to replace a customer's shirt on which food or drink has been spilt, whereas such a service may not in fact be available should this happen.

The organizational responsibility for closing the gaps

The existence of any one of these gaps is likely to result in a mismatch between expectations and perceptions and result in poor perceived quality. It is therefore important that managers take action to prevent quality gaps. Table 17.1 shows the actions which will be required to close each of the gaps and indicates the parts of the organization which bear the main responsibility for doing so.

Table 17.1 The organizational responsibility for closing quality gaps

Gap	Action required to ensure high perceived quality	Main organizational responsibility
Gap 1	Ensure that there is consistency between the internal quality specification of the product or service and the expectations of customers	Marketing Operations Product/service development
Gap 2	Ensure that the internal specification of the product or service meets its intended concept or design	Marketing Operations Product/service development
Gap 3	Ensure that the actual product or service conforms to its internally specified quality level	Operations
Gap 4	Ensure that the promises made to customers concerning the product or service can in reality be delivered by the operation	Marketing

Closing gaps 1 and 2 is the joint responsibility of marketing, operations and product/service development. (These issues were discussed in Chapter 5.) Gap 4 is a key task for marketing who are responsible for communicating with the market. The task for which operations bears most responsibility is to ensure that the product or service conforms to its required specification (gap 3). In other words, to make sure that gap 3 does not exist. This gap is called the 'conformance to specification' gap and the remainder of this chapter discusses how operations managers can try to ensure conformance to specification.

CONFORMANCE TO SPECIFICATION

Conformance to specification means producing a product or providing a service to its design specification. During the design of any product or service, its overall concept, purpose, package of components and the connection between the components will have been specified (*see* Chapter 5). This process should have involved not only the operations function but also the marketing and product/service design functions. The model used to describe this activity in Chapter 5 was shown in Fig. 5.2. We can extend this model to include the activities of ensuring that products and services are indeed made to conform with their specifications. This is the quality planning and control activity (*see* Fig. 17.3). Quality planning and control can be divided into six sequential steps:

Step 1   Define the quality characteristics of the product or service.
Step 2   Decide how to measure each quality characteristic.
Step 3   Set quality standards for each quality characteristic.
Step 4   Control quality against those standards.
Step 5   Find and correct causes of poor quality.
Step 6   Continue to make improvements.

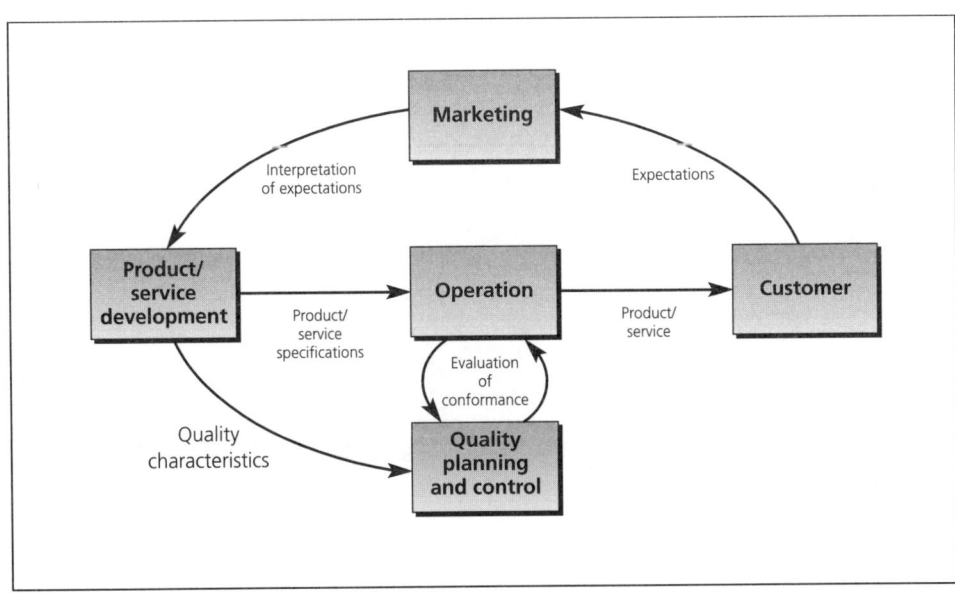

Figure 17.3
The product/service design cycle including quality planning and control

This chapter will deal with steps 1 to 4. Steps 5 and 6 are dealt with in Chapters 18, 19 and 20.

ENTREPRENEURIAL QUALITY[6]

In December 1995, Mr and Mrs Essay received some bad news. One of their very profitable businesses had to be closed down as the owner of the property was going to demolish it within a short period of time. Mr Essay, an optimist by nature, saw this as an opportunity rather than a hurdle. Within no time he began scouting around for an alternative business.

After considering a number of options, he heard through the business network that a franchise was for sale. Crown Pies, as the name suggests, was a manufacturer of a variety of pies, based in the Carlton Centre in central Johannesburg. The existing owner was willing to sell the franchise for a reasonable amount. Considering that it was a going concern, Mr Essay immediately knew that with a little creativity and a lot of hard work, the business could be successful. Since he took over, in January 1996, his business has been prosperous. Initially, due to a shortage of manpower, he had to assist with production, baking and delivering of pies. However, due to efficient organization, and trial and error, many of his problems have been overcome.

Crown Pies now employs a workforce of ten people. Each day they begin their work at 8.00 am and end at 5.00 pm. Mr Essay, however, since he is the owner of the business, has to put in additional hours in order to make his business a success, and, on average, he works 11 hours per day. During busy periods, casual labourers are called in to help meet demand.

Since a pie is a consumable product, quality is a very important aspect of production. As a result, it is vital that each pie fulfils the function of satisfying a customer's hunger. Mr Essay ensures that each pie is large enough and provides sufficient filling to meet the customer's expectation. In terms of their appearance, the pies look exceptionally appetizing, and if customers are still not convinced, one whiff and all resistance crumbles. Since each pie is made to a standard, the product is exceptionally reliable. Customers are aware that the same standard of quality will be obtained each time a purchase is made. In addition, each pie is reasonably durable for such a product. Baked pies can last for approximately three days and can be reheated to obtain a fresh-baked taste just prior to consumption. Frozen pies, which are delivered to wholesalers, last for up to three months in the refrigerator.

Crown Pies is a high-contact operation insofar as the majority of its 'value-adding' activities take place with the customer present. Customers in this type of operation have a relatively short waiting period. They are hungry people and will walk out if they are not served within a reasonable period of time. Quick service is vital and Crown Pies ensures that customers are seen to within a minute or less. Accordingly, Mr Essay emphasizes to his staff that *the customer is always right*. He believes that a satisfied customer is a regular customer – and a great advert. If the customers perceive that a member of staff is discourteous to them, they are likely to be dissatisfied. Given this, Mr Essay makes it his duty to train his staff to acquire good customer skills. Crown Pies has to ensure that it produces a high-quality, satisfying and inexpensive product.

Mr Essay is constantly filled with new and creative ideas. He realizes that if he can expand his business by focusing more on the wholesale area, he could find his business being more profitable in the long run. In order for him to do this, however, additional premises will have to be acquired for the sole purposes of preparation, baking and storage. From here, pies can be dispatched. In the meantime, Mr Essay aims to concentrate entirely on his current procedures. He constantly seeks customer suggestions and almost always implements beneficial improvements accordingly. After all, says Mr Essay, *'To make customers happy takes a lifetime, but to lose them takes just one day!'* ■

Step 1 – Define the quality characteristics

Much of what defines the 'quality' of a product or service will have been specified, at least implicitly, in its design. But not all the design details of a product or service are useful, however, in controlling the quality of its production. For example, the design of a television may specify that its outer cabinet is made with a particular veneer and that each electronic component must have particular characteristics. Each television is not checked, however, to make sure that the cabinet is indeed made from that particular veneer or that each component has its specified characteristics. Rather it is the *consequences* of the design specification which are examined – the appearance of the cabinet and the clarity of the picture, for example.

These consequences for quality planning and control of the design are called the *quality characteristics* of the product or service. Table 17.2 shows a list of the quality characteristics which are generally useful for planning and controlling the quality of both products and services. The terms in Table 17.2 need a little further explanation. *Functionality* means how well the product or service does the job for which it is intended. This includes its performance and the features or 'knobs and whistles' inherent in the product or service. *Appearance* refers to the sensory characteristics of the product or service: its aesthetic appeal, look, feel, sound and smell. *Reliability* is the consistency of the product's or service's performance over time, or the average time for which it performs within its tolerated band of performance. *Durability* means the total useful life of the product or service, assuming occasional repair or modification. *Recovery* means the ease with which problems with the product or service can be rectified or resolved. *Contact* refers to the nature of the person-to-person contact which might take place. For example, it could include the courtesy, empathy, sensitivity and knowledge of contact staff.

Table 17.2 Quality characteristics for a motor car and an air journey

Quality characteristic	Car	Air journey
Functionality	Speed, acceleration, fuel consumption, ride quality, road-holding, etc.	Safety and duration of journey, on-board meals and drinks, car and hotel booking services
Appearance	Aesthetics, shape, finish, door gaps, etc.	Decor and cleanliness of aircraft, lounges and crew
Reliability	Mean time to failure	Keeping to the published flight times
Durability	Useful life (with repair)	Keeping up with trends in the industry
Recovery	Ease of repair	Resolution of service failures
Contact	Knowledge and courtesy of sales staff	Knowledge, courtesy and sensitivity of airline staff

Step 2 – Decide how to measure each characteristic

For any particular product or service these characteristics must be defined in such a way that they can be measured and then controlled. This involves taking a very general quality characteristic such as the 'appearance' of a car and breaking it down, as far as one can, into its constituent elements. For example 'appearance' is difficult to measure as such, but 'colour match', 'surface finish', and 'number of visible scratches' are all capable of being described in a more objective manner. They may even be quantifiable. If so, the organization can measure changes in quality levels over time.

The process of disaggregating quality characteristics into their measurable sub-components, however, can result in the characteristics losing some of their meaning. For example, a quantified list of colour match, the 'roughness' or 'smoothness' of the surface finish and the number of visible scratches do not convey everything about the appearance of a product. Customers will react to more factors than these: the shape and character of the car, for example, the amount of chrome and so on. Many of the factors lost by disaggregating 'appearance' into its measurable parts, however, are those which are embedded in the design of the car rather than the way it is produced.

Some of the quality characteristics of a product or service cannot themselves be measured at all. The 'courtesy' of airline staff, for example, has no, even approximate, objective quantified measure. Operations with high customer contact, such as airlines, however, place a great deal of importance on the need to ensure courtesy in their staff. In cases like this the operation will have to attempt to measure customer *perceptions* of courtesy.

Variables and attributes

The measures used by operations to describe quality characteristics are of two types: *variables* and *attributes*. Variable measures are those that can be measured on a continuously variable scale (for example, length, diameter, weight or time). Attributes are those which are assessed by judgement and are dichotomous, i.e. have two states (for example right or wrong, works or does not work, looks OK or not OK). Table 17.3 categorizes some of the measures which might be used for the quality characteristics of the car and the airline journey.

Step 3 – Set quality standards

When operations managers have identified how any quality characteristic can be measured they need a quality standard against which it can be checked, otherwise they will not know whether it indicates good or bad performance. For example, suppose that, on average, one passenger out of every 10 000 complains about the food. Should the airline regard that as good because it seems that 9999 passengers out of 10 000 are satisfied? Or should it regard it as bad because, if one passenger complains, there must be others who, although dissatisfied, did not bother to complain? Or, if that level of complaint is broadly similar to other airlines, should it regard its quality as just about satisfactory? While it might seem to be appropriate to have an absolute standard – that is perfection – and indeed strive for it, to use perfection as an operational standard could be both demoralizing and expensive. Most manufactured products

Table 17.3 Variable and attribute measures for quality characteristics

Quality Characteristic	Car		Airline journey	
	Variable	Attribute	Variable	Attribute
Functionality	Acceleration and breaking characteristics from test bed	Is the ride quality satisfactory?	Number of journeys which actually arrived at the destination (i.e. didn't crash!)	Was the food acceptable?
Appearance	Number of blemishes visible on car	Is the colour to specification?	Number of seats not cleaned satisfactorily	Are the crew dressed smartly?
Reliability	Average time between faults	Is the reliability satisfactory?	Proportion of journeys which arrived on time	Were there any complaints?
Durability	Life of the car	Is the useful life as predicted?	Number of times service innovations lagged competitors	Generally, is the airline updating its services in a satisfactory manner?
Recovery	Time from fault discovered to fault repaired	Is the serviceability of the car acceptable?	Proportion of service failures resolved satisfactorily	Do customers feel that staff deal satisfactorily with complaints?
Contact	Level of help provided by sales staff (1 to 5 scale)	Did customers feel well served? (Yes or no)	The extent to which customers feel well treated by staff (1 to 5 scale)	Did customers feel that the staff were helpful? (Yes or no)

and delivered services are not 'perfect'. No car will last for ever. No airline could guarantee that there will always be seats available on its aircraft. Every aircraft will emit some noise.

If a car is meant to survive for a reasonable length of time, the critical question for operations is how long is reasonable? If cabin attendants have to respond to requests, how long may they take before it is unacceptable? How quickly should a car accelerate from 0 to 100 kph? What should be the mean time between failures for a product? What should be the acceptable noise level in an aircraft? The quality standard is that level of quality which defines the boundary between acceptable and unacceptable. Such standards may well be constrained by operational factors such as the state of technology in the factory, the number of staff on the pay-roll and the cost limits of making the product. At the same time, however, they need to be appropriate to the expectations of customers. The quality standard for the reliability of a watch might be ten maintenance-free years, for the availability of airline seats might be that seats should be available 95 per cent of the time, for the internal noise level of an aircraft might be 40 decibels, or for a car might be that it is expected to accelerate from 0 to 100 kph in six seconds, and so on.

Step 4 – Control quality against those standards

After setting up appropriate standards that are capable of being met by the operation and that will meet customers' expectations, the operation will then need to check that the products or services conform to those standards. In all operations there may well be times when products or services are produced which do not conform to those standards. When making manufactured goods, tools may wear or there may be variation in the materials used, or there may be variability in staff's behaviour. Similarly in service operations there may be technical breakdown and variability in staff behaviour. Changes in the mood and attitude of customer contact staff could lead to different customers being treated in different ways. Chapter 19 deals with the question of what operations can do when things do go wrong. Here we concern ourselves with how operations can try to ensure that the operation does things right, first time, every time. As far as operations managers are concerned this involves three decisions.

1 Where in the operation should they check that it is conforming to standards?
2 Should they check every product or service or take a sample?
3 How should the checks be performed?

Where should the checks take place?

The key task for operations managers is to identify the critical control points at which the service, products or processes need to be checked to ensure that the product or services will conform to specification. There are three main places where checks may be carried out: at the start of the process, during the process and after the process.

At *the start of the process* the incoming transformed resources could be inspected to make sure that they are to the correct specification. For example, a car manufacturer may wish to check that the car headlights which are supplied to its production line are of the right specification. An airline might check that incoming food is satisfactory. A night club may wish to check that its incoming guests are dressed appropriately. A university will wish to screen applicants to try to ensure that they have a high chance of not only getting through the programme but that they also have the right attitude to group work and are prepared to make a contribution in class.

During the process checks may take place at any stage, or indeed all stages, but there are a number of particularly critical points in the process where inspection might be important:[7]

- before a particularly costly part of the process;
- before a series of processes during which checking might be difficult;
- immediately after part of the process with a high defective rate or a fail point;
- before a part of the process that might conceal previous defects or problems;
- before a 'point of no return', after which rectification and recovery might be impossible;
- before potential damage or distress might be caused;
- before a change in functional responsibility.

Checks may also take place *after the process* itself to ensure that the product or service conforms to its specification or that customers are satisfied with the service they have received.

Check every product and service or take a sample?

Having decided the points at which the goods or services will be checked, the next decision is how many of the products or services to check. While it might seem ideal to check every single product being produced or every service being delivered there are many good reasons why this might not be sensible.

● It might be dangerous to inspect the whole item or every constituent part. A doctor, for example, checks just a small sample of blood rather than taking all of a patient's blood because this would be life-threatening. The characteristics of this sample are taken to represent those of the rest of the patient's blood.

● The checking of every single product or every customer might destroy the product or interfere with the service. It would be inappropriate for a light bulb manufacturer to check the length of life of every single light bulb leaving the factory, as this would entail the destructive testing of each bulb. Likewise, it would not be appropriate for a head waiter or tour courier to check whether his or her customers are enjoying the meal or having a good time every 30 seconds.

● Checking every product or service will be very time consuming and therefore very costly. For example, it just might not be feasible to check every single item from a high-volume plastic moulding machine, or it might be prohibitively expensive to check the feelings of every single bus commuter in a major city every day.

The use of 100 per cent checking, moreover, does not guarantee that all defects or problems will be identified, for a number of reasons:

● Making the checks may be inherently difficult. For example, although a doctor may undertake all the correct testing procedures to check for a particular disease, he or she may not necessarily be certain to diagnose it.

● Staff may become fatigued over a period of time, when inspecting repetitive items where it is easy to make mistakes. (For example, try counting the number of 'e's on this page. Count them again and see if you get the same score!)

● Quality measures may be unclear and staff making the checks may not know precisely what to look for. For example, how can an interviewer, making offers for university places, really tell whether a student will actually have the right attitude to group work or will be diligent?

● Wrong information may be given. For example, although all the customers in a restaurant may tell the head waiter, when asked, that 'everything is all right', they may actually have serious reservations about the food or their treatment.

Type I and Type II errors

Using a sample to make a decision about the quality of products or services, although requiring less time than 100 per cent checking, does have its own inherent problems. Like any decision activity, we may get the decision wrong. Take the example of a pedestrian waiting to cross a street. He or she has two main decisions: whether to continue waiting or to cross. If there is a satisfactory break in the traffic and the pedestrian crosses, then a correct decision has been made. Similarly, if that person continues to wait because the traffic is too dense then he or she has again made a correct decision. There are two types of incorrect decisions or errors, however. One incorrect decision would be if he or she decides to cross when there is not an adequate break in the traffic, resulting in an accident – this is referred to as a *Type I error*. Another incorrect decision would occur if he or she decides not to cross even though there was an adequate gap in the traffic – this is called a *Type II error*. In crossing the road, therefore, there are four outcomes which are summarized in Table 17.4.

Table 17.4 Type I and Type II errors for a pedestrian crossing the road

	Road conditions	
Decision	*Unsafe*	*Safe*
Cross	Type I error	Correct decision
Wait	Correct decision	Type II error

Type I errors are those which occur when a decision was made to do something and the situation did not warrant it. Type II errors are those which occur when nothing was done, yet a decision to do something should have been taken as the situation did indeed warrant it. For example, if a school's inspector checks the work of a sample of 20 out of 1000 pupils and all 20 of the pupils in the sample have failed, the inspector might draw the conclusion that all the pupils have failed. In fact the sample just happened to contain 20 out of the 50 students who had failed the course. The inspector, by assuming a high fail rate would be making a Type I error. Alternatively, if the inspector checked 20 pieces of work all of which were of a high standard, he or she might conclude that all the pupils' work was good despite having been given, or having chosen, the only pieces of good work in the whole school. This would be a Type II error. Although these situations are not likely, they are possible. Therefore any sampling procedure has to be aware of these risks.

How should the checks be performed?

In practice most operations will use some form of sampling to check the quality of their products or services. The decision then is what kind of sample procedure to adopt. There are two different methods in common use for checking the quality of a sample product or service so as to make inferences about all the output from an operation. Both methods take into account the statistical risks involved in sampling.

The first, and by far the best known, is the procedure called *statistical process control* (SPC). SPC is concerned with sampling the process during the production of the goods or the delivery of the service. Based on this sample, decisions are made as to whether the process is 'in control', that is operating as it should be. The second method is called *acceptance sampling* and is more concerned with whether to regard an incoming or outgoing batch of materials or customers as acceptable or not. The rest of this chapter is concerned with these two quality planning and control methods.

STATISTICAL PROCESS CONTROL (SPC)

Statistical process control (SPC) is concerned with checking a product or service during its creation. If there is reason to believe that there is a problem with the process then it can be stopped (where this is possible and appropriate) and the problem can be identified and rectified. For example, an international airport regularly may ask a sample of customers if the cleanliness of its restaurants is satisfactory. If an unacceptable number of customers in one sample is found to be unhappy, airport managers may have to consider improving the procedures in place for cleaning tables. Similarly, a car manufacturer periodically will check whether a sample of door panels conforms to its standards so as to know whether the machinery which produces them is performing correctly. Again, if a sample suggests that there may be problems, then the machines may have to be stopped and the process checked.

Control charts

The significant value of SPC, however, is not just to make checks of a single sample but to monitor the results of many samples over a period of time. It does this by using *control charts*, to see if the process looks as though it is performing as it should, or alternatively is going out of control. If the process does seem to be going out of control, then steps can be taken *before* there is a problem.

Looking for trends is an important use of control charts. If the trend suggests the process is getting steadily worse then it will be worth investigating the process. If the trend is steadily improving, it may still be worthy of investigation to try to identify what is happening that is making the process better. This information might then be shared with other parts of the organization, or, on the other hand, the process might be stopped as the cause could be adding unnecessary expense to the operation.

Variation in process quality

Common causes

All processes vary to some extent. No machine will give precisely the same result each time it is used. All materials vary a little. The staff in the operation differ marginally in the way they perform each time they perform a task. Even the environment in which the processing takes place will vary. Given this, it is not surprising that the measure of quality (whether attribute or variable) will also vary. Variations which derive from these *common causes* can never be entirely eliminated (although they can be reduced).

For example, if a machine is filling boxes with rice, it will not place *exactly* the same weight of rice in every box it fills; there will be some variation around an average weight. When the filling machine is in a stable condition (that is, no exceptional factors are influencing its behaviour) each box could be weighed and a histogram of the weights could be built up. Figure 17.4 shows how the histogram might develop. The first boxes weighed could lie anywhere within the natural variation of the process but are more likely to be close to the average weight (*see* Fig. 17.4 (a)). As more boxes are weighed they clearly show the tendency to be close to the process average (*see* Fig. 17.4 (b) and (c). After many boxes have been weighed they form a smoother distribution (Fig. 17.4 (d)) which can be drawn as a histogram (Fig. 17.4 (e)) which will approximate to the underlying process variation distribution (Fig. 17.4 (f)).

Usually this type of variation can be described by a normal distribution with 99.7 per cent of the variation lying within ± 3 standard deviations.

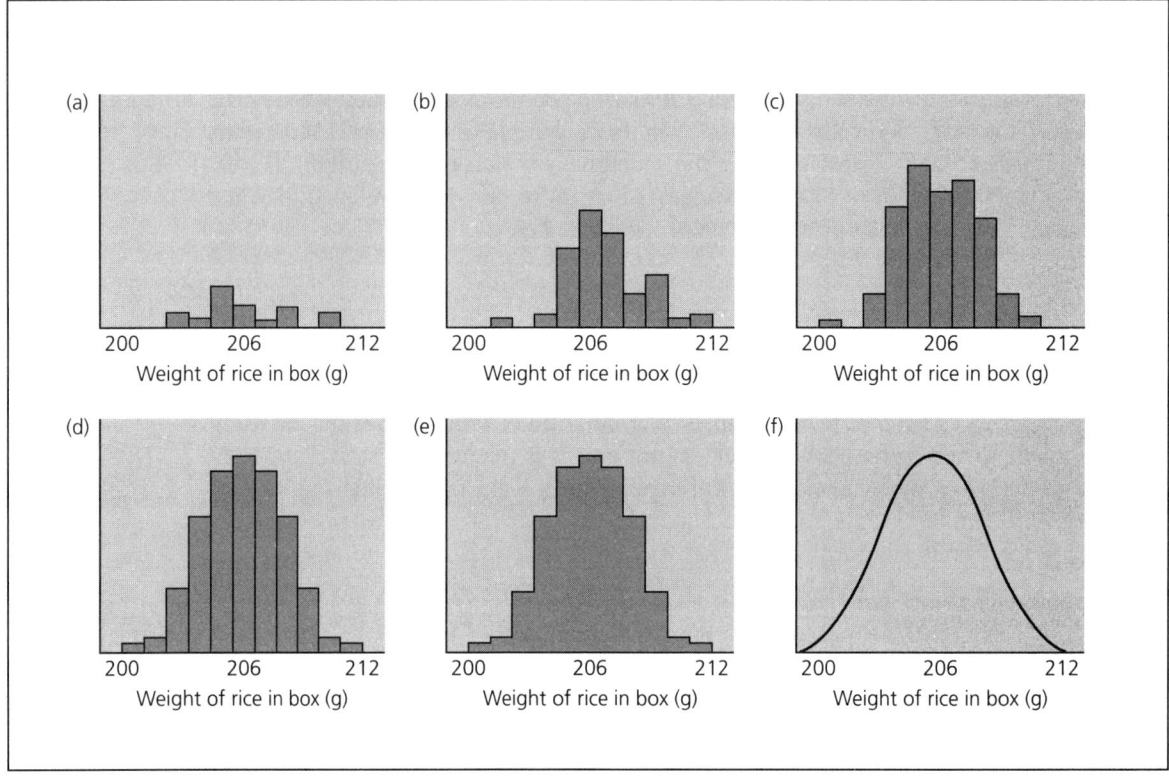

Figure 17.4 The natural variation in the filling process can be described by a normal distribution

In this case the weight of rice in the boxes is described by a distribution with a mean of 206 grams and a standard deviation of 2 grams. The obvious question for any operations manager would be 'Is this variation in the process performance acceptable?' The answer will depend on the acceptable range of weights which can be tolerated by the operation. This range is called the *tolerance range*, or *specification range*. If the weight of rice in the box is too small then the organization might infringe labelling regulations; if it is too large the organization is 'giving away' too much of its product for free. If, in this case, the specification range is 198 grams to 214 grams, the natural variation of the filling process (the process average ± 3 standard deviations) lies well within the specification.

$$\text{Specification range} = 214 - 198 = 16\,\text{g}$$
$$\text{Natural variation of process} = 6 \times \text{standard deviation}$$
$$= 6 \times 2 = 12\,\text{g}$$

Process capability

The *capability* of the process is a measure of the acceptability of the variation of the process. The simplest measure of capability (C_p) is given by the ratio of the specification range to the 'natural' variation of the process (i.e. ± 3 standard deviations).

$$C_p = \frac{UTL - LTL}{6s}$$

where UTL = the upper tolerance limit
   LTL = the lower tolerance limit
    s = the standard deviation of the process variability.

In the case of the filling process:

$$C_p = \frac{214 - 198}{6 \times 2} = \frac{16}{12} = 1.333$$

Generally, if the C_p of a process is greater than one it is taken to indicate that the process is 'capable', and a C_p of less than one to indicate that the process is not 'capable', assuming that the distribution is normal. (*See* Fig. 17.5 (a), (b) and (c).)

The simple C_p measure assumes that the average of the process variation is at the mid-point of the specification range. Often the process average is off-set from the specification range, however (*see* Fig. 17.5 (d)). In such cases *one-sided* capability indices are required to understand the capability of the process.

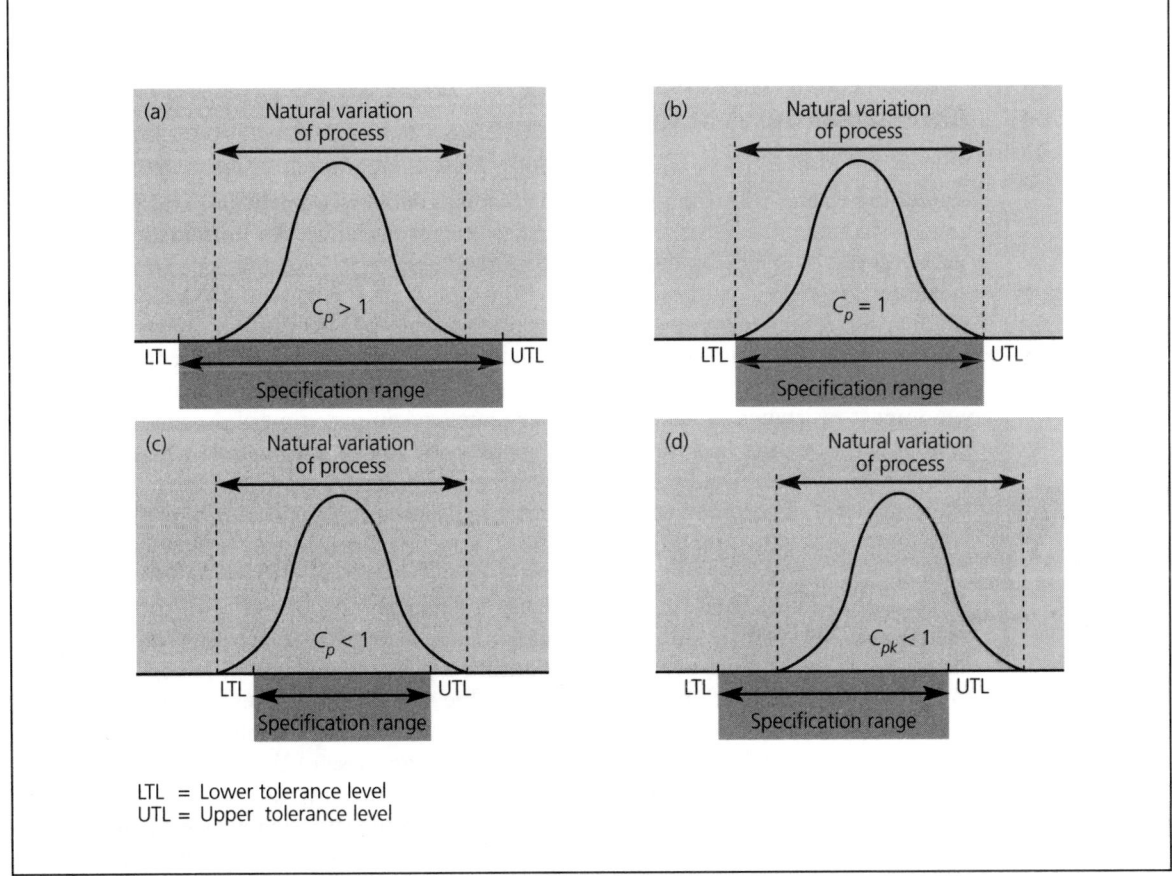

Figure 17.5 Process capability compares the natural variation of the process with the specification range which is required

$$\text{Upper one-sided index } C_{pu} = \frac{UTL - X}{3s}$$

$$\text{Lower one-sided index } C_{pl} = \frac{X - LTL}{3s}$$

where X = the process average.

Sometimes only the lower of the two one-sided indices for a process is used to indicate its capability (C_{pk}).

$$C_{pk} = \min (C_{pu}, C_{pl})$$

For example, if the natural variation of the filling process changed to have a process average of 210 grams but the standard deviation of the process remained at 2 grams:

$$C_{pu} = \frac{214 - 210}{3 \times 2} = \frac{4}{6} = 0.666$$

$$C_{pl} = \frac{210 - 198}{3 \times 2} = \frac{12}{6} = 2.0$$

$$C_{pk} = \min (0.666, 2.0)$$
$$= 0.666$$

Assignable causes of variation

Not all variation in processes is the result of common causes, however. There may be something wrong with the process which is assignable to a particular and preventable cause. Machinery may have worn or have been set up badly. An untrained member of staff may not be following the prescribed procedure for the process. The causes of such variation are called *assignable causes*. The question for operations management is whether the results from any particular sample, when plotted on the control chart, simply represent the variation due to common causes or due to some, specific and correctable, *assignable* cause. Figure 17.6, for example, shows the control chart for the average impact resistance of samples of door panels taken over time. Like any process the results vary, but the last three points seem to be lower than usual. The question is whether this is natural variation or the symptom of some more serious cause. Is the variation the result of common causes or does it indicate assignable causes in the process?

To help make this decision *control limits* can be added to the control chart which indicate the expected extent of 'common-cause' variation. If any points lie outside these control limits then the process can be deemed out of control in the sense that variation is likely to be due to assignable causes. These control limits could be set intuitively by examining past variation during a period when the process was thought to be free of any variation which could be due to assignable causes. For example, if the monthly survey of airport customers usually includes between three and four per cent of customers who are dissatisfied with the cleanliness of the airport's restaurants, an upper control limit could be set at four per cent complaints per month. If the actual proportion is over four per cent or more then the situation is investigated.

Control limits can be set in a more statistically revealing manner, however, based on the probability that the mean of a particular sample will differ by more than a set amount from the mean of the population from which it is taken. For example, if the

MOTOROLA'S SIX-SIGMA QUALITY[8]

It is not often that the technical details of process capability become synonymous with a company's total quality programme, but that is what has happened for Motorola. Motorola is one of the world's largest industrial corporations making electronic components, semiconductors and communication systems, among other things. It employs over 100 000 people throughout the world at in excess of 50 sites. All the people in all the sites and many outside the company have now heard of Motorola's six-sigma quality objectives.

The foundations for six-sigma quality were laid some years ago when the company decided on its aim of 'total customer satisfaction'. According to Motorola this is only achieved when the product is delivered when promised, with no defects, the product does not experience any early-life failures, and the product does not fail excessively in service. To achieve this, Motorola initially focused on removing manufacturing defects. It soon came to realize, however, that many problems were caused by latent defects, that is, defects hidden within the design of its products. They may not show initially but eventually will cause failures in the field. The only way to eliminate these defects would be to make sure that its design specifications were tight and its processes very capable indeed.

Motorola's six-sigma quality concept means that the natural variation of its processes (± 3 standard deviations) should be half their specification range. In other words, the specification range of any part of a product should be ± 6 times the standard deviation of the process. The Greek letter sigma (σ) is often used to indicate the standard deviation of a process, hence the six-sigma label. A process capability (C_p) of 1 is represented by '3 sigma' quality. This implies a defect rate of 2.7 defects per 1000. Six-sigma quality is considerably more ambitious. It implies a defect rate of only 3.4 defects per *million*. ∎

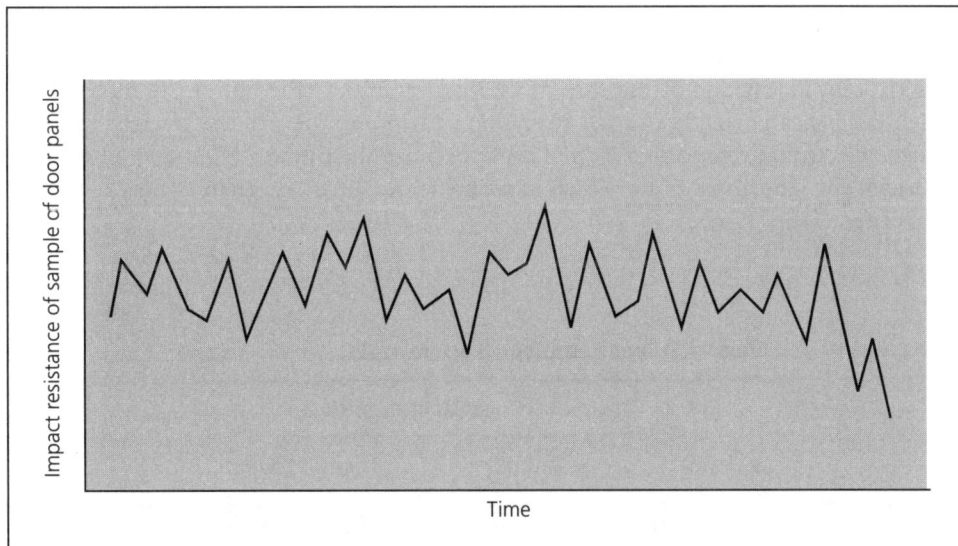

Figure 17.6 Control chart for the impact resistance of door panels

process which makes door panels had been measured to determine the normal distribution which represents its common-cause variation, then control limits can be based on this distribution. Figure 17.7 shows the same control chart as Fig. 17.6 with the addition of control limits put at ±3 standard deviations (of the population of sample means) away from the mean of sample averages. It shows that the probability of the final point on the chart being influenced by an assignable cause is very high indeed. When the process is exhibiting behaviour which is outside its normal 'common-cause' range, it is said to be 'out of control'.

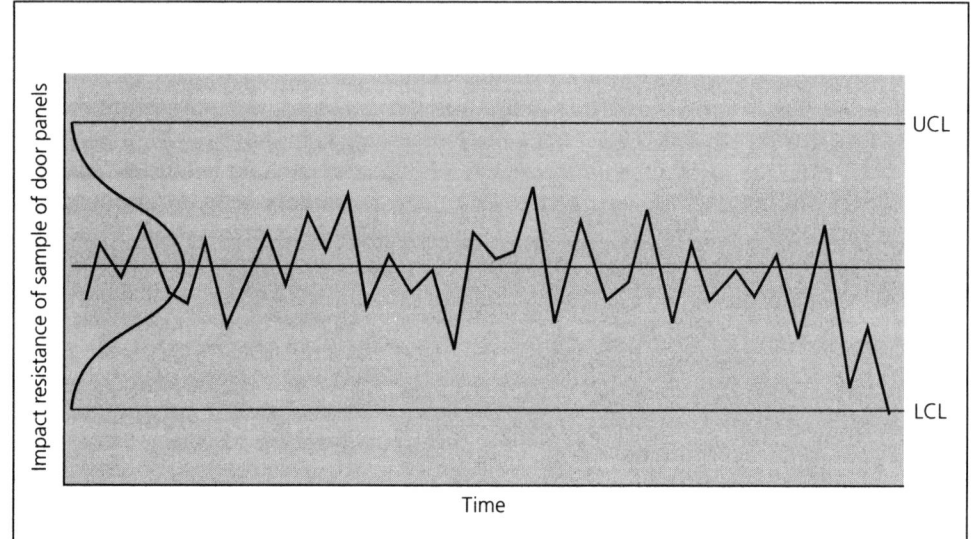

Figure 17.7 Control chart for the impact resistance of door panels with control limits added

From this evidence alone, however, we cannot be absolutely certain that the process is out of control. There is a small but finite chance that the (seemingly out of limits) point is just one of the rare but natural results at the tail of the distribution which describes perfectly normal behaviour. Stopping the process under these circumstances would represent a Type I error because the process is actually in control. Alternatively, ignoring a result which in reality is due to an assignable cause is a Type II error (*see* Table 17.5).

Table 17.5 Type I and Type II errors in SPC

	Actual process state	
Decision	In control	Out of control
Stop process	Type I error	Correct decision
Leave alone	Correct decision	Type II error

Control limits are usually set at three standard deviations either side of the population mean. This would mean that there is only a 0.3 per cent chance of any sample mean falling outside these limits by chance causes (that is, a chance of a Type I error of 0.3 per cent). The control limits may be set at any distance from the population mean, but the closer the limits are to the population mean, the higher the likelihood of investigating and trying to rectify a process which is actually problem-free. If the control limits are set at two standard deviations, the chance of a Type I error increases to about 5 per cent. If the limits are set at one standard deviation then the chance of a Type I error increases to 32 per cent. When the control limits are placed at ±3 standard deviations away from the mean of the distribution which describes 'normal' variation in the process, they are called the *upper control limit* (UCL) and *lower control limit* (LCL).

Control charts for attributes

Attributes have only two states ('right' or 'wrong', for example) so the statistic calculated is the proportion of wrongs (p) in a sample. (This statistic follows a binomial distribution.)

In calculating the limits, the population mean $(\bar{p})$ – the actual, normal or expected proportion of 'defectives' or wrongs to rights – may not be known. Who knows, for example, the actual number of city commuters that are dissatisfied with their journey time? In such cases the population mean can be estimated from the average of the proportion of 'defectives', $(\bar{p})$ from m samples each of n items, where m should be at least 30 and n should be at least 100:

$$p = \frac{p^1 + p^2 + p^3 \ldots p^n}{m}$$

One standard deviation can then be estimated from:

$$\sqrt{\frac{\bar{p}\,(1-\bar{p})}{n}}$$

The upper and lower control limits can then be set as:

UCL = $\bar{p}$ + 3 standard deviations

LCL = $\bar{p}$ – 3 standard deviations

Of course, the LCL cannot be negative, and when it is calculated to be so it should be rounded up to zero.

Example

A credit card company deals with many hundreds of thousands of transactions every week. One of its measures of the quality of service it gives its customers is the dependability with which it mails customers' monthly accounts. The quality standard it sets itself is that accounts should be mailed within two days of the 'nominal post date' which is specified to the customer. Every week the company samples 1000 customer accounts and records the percentage which were not mailed within the standard time. When the process is working normally, only 2 per cent of accounts are mailed outside the specified period; that is 2 per cent are 'defective'.

Control limits for the process can be calculated as follows:

Mean proportion defective, $\bar{p} = 0.02$

Sample size $n = 1000$

Standard deviation $s = \sqrt{\dfrac{\bar{p}\,(1-\bar{p})}{n}}$

$$= \sqrt{\dfrac{0.02\,(0.98)}{1000}}$$

$$= 0.0044$$

With the control limits at $\bar{p} \pm 3s$:

Upper control limit (UCL) $= 0.02 + 3(0.0044) = 0.0332$

$$= 3.32\%$$

and

Lower control limit (LCL) $= 0.02 - 3(0.0044) = 0.0068$

$$= 0.68\%$$

Figure 17.8 shows the company's control chart for this measure of quality over the last few weeks, together with the calculated control limits. It also shows that the process is in control.

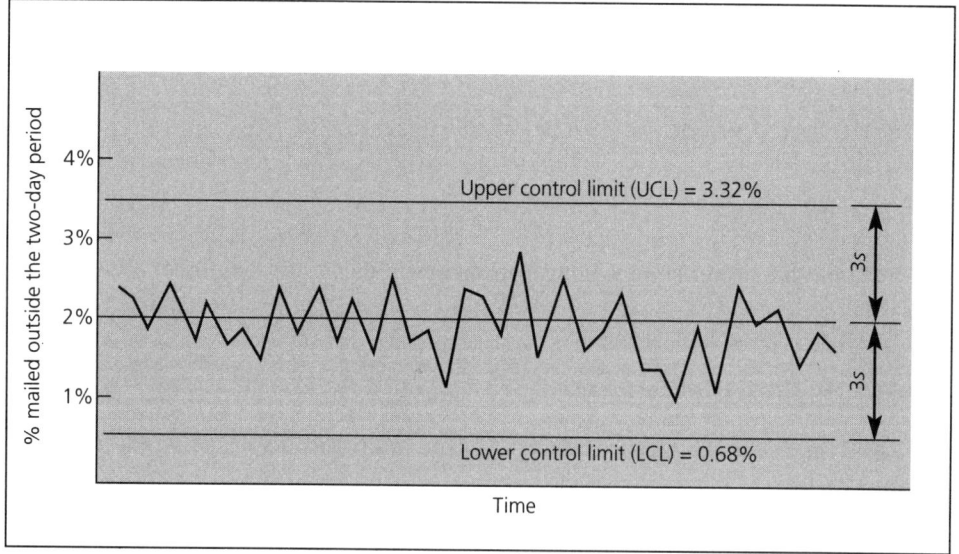

Figure 17.8 Control chart for the percentage of customer accounts which are mailed outside their two-day period

Control chart for variables

The most commonly used type of control chart employed to control variables is the $\overline{X}$-R *chart*. In fact this is really two charts in one. One chart is used to control the sample average or mean ($\overline{X}$). The other is used to control the variation within the sample by measuring the range (R). The range is used because it is simpler to calculate than the standard deviation of the sample.

The means ($\overline{X}$) chart can pick up changes in the average output from the process being charted. Changes in the means chart would suggest that the process is drifting generally away from its supposed process average, although the variability inherent in the process may not have changed (*see* Fig. 17.9).

The range (R) chart plots the range of each sample, that is the difference between the largest and the smallest measurement in the samples. Monitoring sample range gives an indication of whether the variability of the process is changing, even when the process average remains constant (*see* Fig. 17.10).

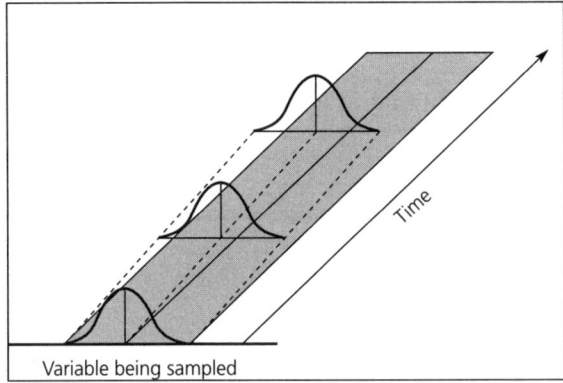

Figure 17.9 Process average changing over time with range constant

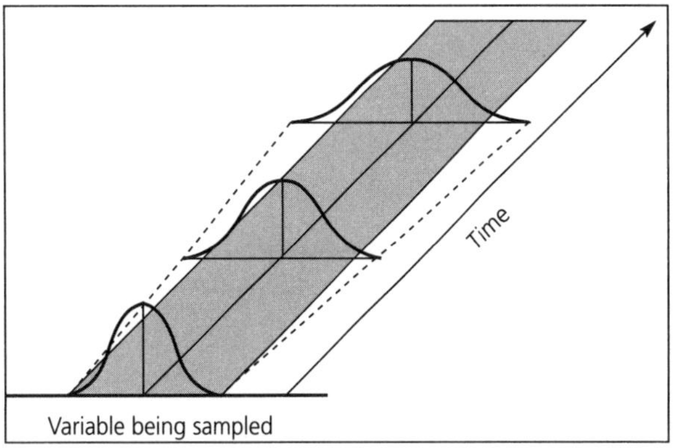

Figure 17.10 Range changing over time with process average constant

Control limits for variables control chart

As with attributes control charts, a statistical description of how the process operates under normal conditions (when there are no assignable causes) can be used to calculate control limits. The first task in calculating the control limits is to estimate the grand average or population mean ($\overline{\overline{X}}$) and average range ($\overline{R}$) using m samples each of sample size n.

The population mean is estimated from the average of a large number (m) of sample means:

$$\overline{\overline{X}} = \frac{\overline{X}_1 + \overline{X}_2 + \ldots \overline{X}_m}{m}$$

The average range is estimated from the ranges of the large number of samples:

$$\overline{R} = \frac{R_1 + R_2 + \ldots R_m}{m}$$

The control limits for the sample means chart are:

Upper control limit (UCL) = $\overline{\overline{X}} + A_2\overline{R}$

Lower control limit (LCL) = $\overline{\overline{X}} - A_2\overline{R}$

The control limits for the range charts are:

Upper control limit (UCL) = $D_4\overline{R}$

Lower control limit (LCL) = $D_3\overline{R}$

The factors A_2, D_3 and D_4 vary with sample size and are shown in Table 17.6.

The LCL for the means chart may be negative (for example, temperature or profit may be less than zero) but it may not be negative for a range chart (or the smallest measurement in the sample would be larger than the largest). If the calculation indicates a negative LCL for a range chart then the LCL should be set to zero.

Table 17.6 Factors for the calculation of control limits

Sample size n	A_2	D_3	D_4
2	1.880	0	3.267
3	1.023	0	2.575
4	0.729	0	2.282
5	0.577	0	2.115
6	0.483	0	2.004
7	0.419	0.076	1.924
8	0.373	0.136	1.864
9	0.337	0.184	1.816
10	0.308	0.223	1.777
12	0.266	0.284	1.716
14	0.235	0.329	1.671
16	0.212	0.364	1.636
18	0.194	0.392	1.608
20	0.180	0.414	1.586
22	0.167	0.434	1.566
24	0.157	0.452	1.548

Example

GAM (Groupe As Maquillage) is a contract cosmetics company, based in France but with plants around Europe, which manufactures and packs cosmetics and perfumes for other companies. One of its plants, in Ireland, operates a filling line which automatically fills plastic bottles with skin cream and seals the bottles with a screw-top cap. The tightness with which the screw-top cap is fixed is an important part of the quality of the filling line process. If the cap is screwed on too tightly there is a danger that it will crack; if screwed on too loosely it might come loose when packed. Either outcome could cause leakage of produce in its journey between the factory and the customer. The Irish plant had received some complaints of product leakage which it suspected was caused by inconsistent fixing of the screw-top caps on its filling line.

The 'tightness' of the screw tops could be measured by a simple test device which recorded the amount of turning force (torque) which was required to unfasten the tops. The company decided to take samples of the bottles coming out of the filling-line process, test them for their unfastening torque and plot the results on a control chart. Several samples of four bottles were taken during a period when the process was regarded as being in control. The following data were calculated from this exercise:

The grand average of all samples $\overline{\overline{X}}$ = 812 g/cm^3

The average range of the sample $\overline{R}$ = 6 g/cm^3

Control limits for the means $(\overline{X})$ chart were calculated as follows:

$$\begin{aligned} \text{UCL} &= \overline{\overline{X}} + A_2 \overline{R} \\ &= 812 + (A_2 \times 6) \end{aligned}$$

From Table 17.6, we know, for a sample size of four, $A_2 = 0.729$. Thus:

$$\begin{aligned} \text{UCL} &= 812 + (0.729 \times 6) \\ &= 816.37 \\ \text{LCL} &= \overline{\overline{X}} - (A_2 \overline{R}) \\ &= 812 - (0.729 \times 6) \\ &= 807.63 \end{aligned}$$

Control limits for the range chart (R) were calculated as follows:

$$\begin{aligned} \text{UCL} &= D_4 \times \overline{R} \\ &= 2.282 \times 6 \\ &= 13.69 \\ \text{LCL} &= D_3 \overline{R} \\ &= 0 \times 6 \\ &= 0 \end{aligned}$$

After calculating these averages and limits for the control chart, the company regularly took samples of four bottles during production, recorded the measurements and plotted them as shown in Fig. 17.11.

The control chart revealed that only with difficulty could the process average be kept in control. Occasional operator interventions were required. Also the process range was moving towards (and once breaking) the upper control limit. The process seemed to be becoming more variable. After investigation it was discovered that, because of faulty maintenance of the line, skin cream was occasionally contaminating the torque head (the part of the line which fitted the cap). This resulted in erratic tightening of the caps.

Interpreting control charts

Plots on a control chart which fall outside control limits are an obvious reason for believing that the process might be out of control, and therefore investigating the process. This is not the only clue which could be revealed by a control chart, however. Figure 17.12 shows some other patterns which could be interpreted as behaviour sufficiently unusual to warrant investigation.

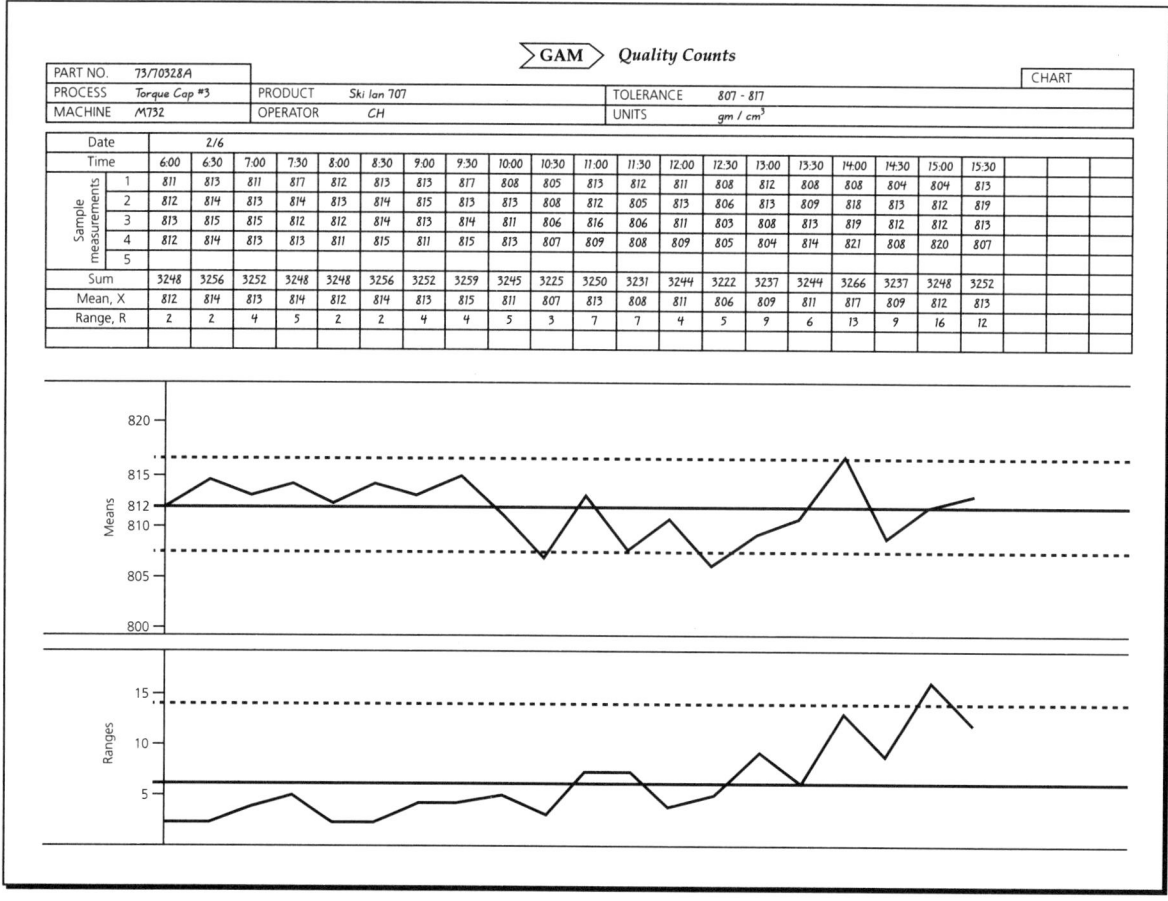

Figure 17.11 The completed control form for GAM's torque machine showing the mean ($\overline{X}$) and range (R) charts

ACCEPTANCE SAMPLING

Process control is usually the preferred method of controlling quality because quality is being 'built-in' to the process rather than being inspected afterwards. It is not always possible or practical, however. It may be necessary to inspect whole batches of products or services either before or after a process. The purpose of acceptance sampling is to decide whether, on the basis of a sample, to accept or reject the whole batch. Examples of when batches are judged on a basis of a sample include incoming component parts from a supplier, or a batch of finished products, or a large number of examination scripts from an internal examiner, or a batch of coded questionnaires from a market research company.

Acceptance sampling is usually carried out on attributes rather than variables. It uses the proportion of wrongs to rights, or defectives to acceptables. For example, one defective per thousand might be acceptable for incoming components or finished products; a 10 per cent failure rate might be normal for a particular examination.

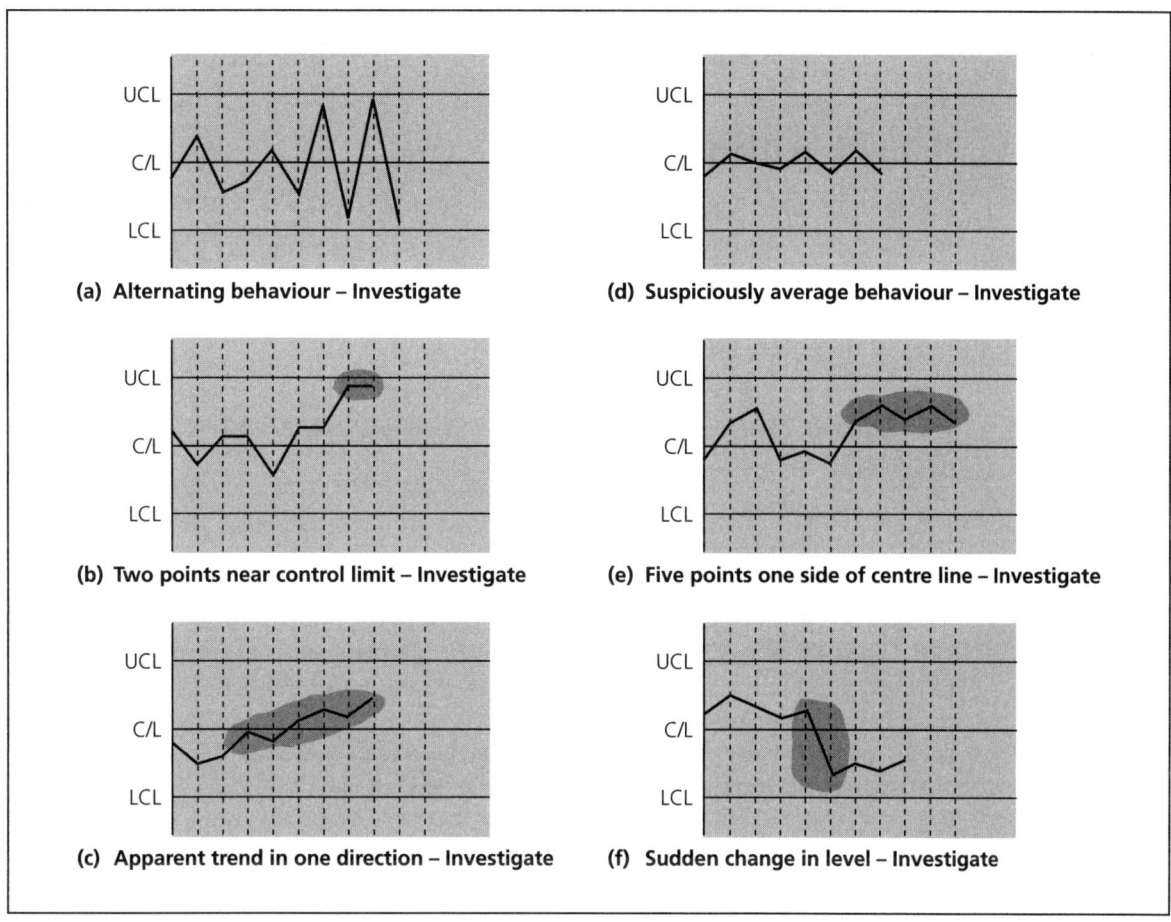

Figure 17.12 In addition to points falling outside the control limits other unlikely sequences of points should be investigated

Again in acceptance sampling, like process control, it is important to understand the risks inherent in using a sample to make a judgement about a far larger batch. Table 17.7 illustrates the risks of acceptance sampling in the form of Type I and Type II errors.

Table 17.7 The risks inherent in acceptance sampling

	The batch actually is	
Decision	OK	Not OK
Reject batch	Type I error	Correct decision
Accept batch	Correct decision	Type II error

In acceptance sampling the Type I risk is often referred to as the producer's risk because it is the risk that the operation rejects a batch that is actually of good quality.

The Type II risk is usually called the consumer's risk because it is the risk of accepting a batch that is actually poor and sending it to the consumer of the product or service.

Sampling plans

Acceptance sampling involves a sample being taken from a batch and a decision to accept or reject the batch being made by comparing the number of 'defects' found in the sample to a predetermined acceptable number. The sampling plan which describes this procedure is defined by two factors, n and c, where:

n = the sample size
c = the acceptance number of defects in the sample.

If x = number of defects actually found in the sample, a decision is made based on the following simple decision rule:

If $x \leq c$ then accept the whole batch.
If $x > c$ then reject the whole batch.

Unlike control charts it is not necessary for organizations to create their own acceptance plans. A set of tables called the Dodge-Romig Sampling Inspection Tables provide values for n and c for a given set of risks. The ability of this plan to discriminate between good batches and bad ones is based upon the binomial distribution and is described by an operating characteristic (OC) curve. The OC curve for a sampling plan shows the probability of accepting a batch as the actual percentage of defects varies.

An ideal operating characteristic curve would look like Fig. 17.13.

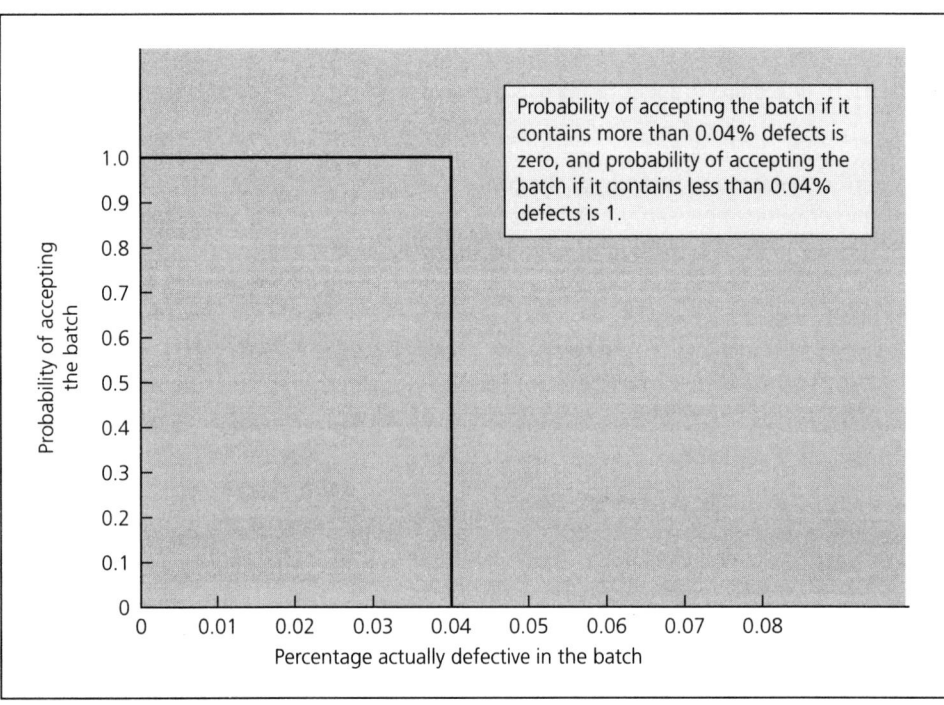

Figure 17.13
An ideal operating
characteristic curve

In this example the level of defects which is regarded as acceptable is 0.4 per cent and the sampling plan is perfect at discriminating between acceptable and unacceptable batches. The probability of accepting a batch whose actual level of defects is less than 0.4 per cent is 100 per cent and there is no chance of ever accepting a batch whose actual level of defects is more than 0.4 per cent. However, in practice, no procedure based on sampling, and therefore carrying risk, could ever deliver such an ideal curve. Only 100 per cent inspection using a perfect inspector could do so.

Any use of sampling will have to accept the existence of Type I and Type II errors. Figure 17.14 shows a sampling plan for sampling 250 items ($n=250$) and rejecting the batch if there is more than one defect ($c=1$) in the sample. A batch is acceptable if it contains 0.4 per cent or less defects ($1/250 = 0.04$ per cent).

What is not known is the actual percentage defective in any one batch, and because the procedure relies on a sample, there will always be a probability of rejecting a good batch because the number of defects in the sample is two or more despite the batch in fact being acceptable (Type I risk shown by the top shaded area). There is also a probability that in spite of accepting a batch (because the number of defects it contains is zero or one) the actual number of defects in the whole batch might be greater than 0.04 per cent (Type II risk shown in the lower shaded area of Fig. 17.14). If the sizes of these risks are felt to be too great, the sample size can be increased which will move the shape of the curve towards the ideal (*see* Fig. 17.15). However, this implies increased time and cost in inspecting the batch.

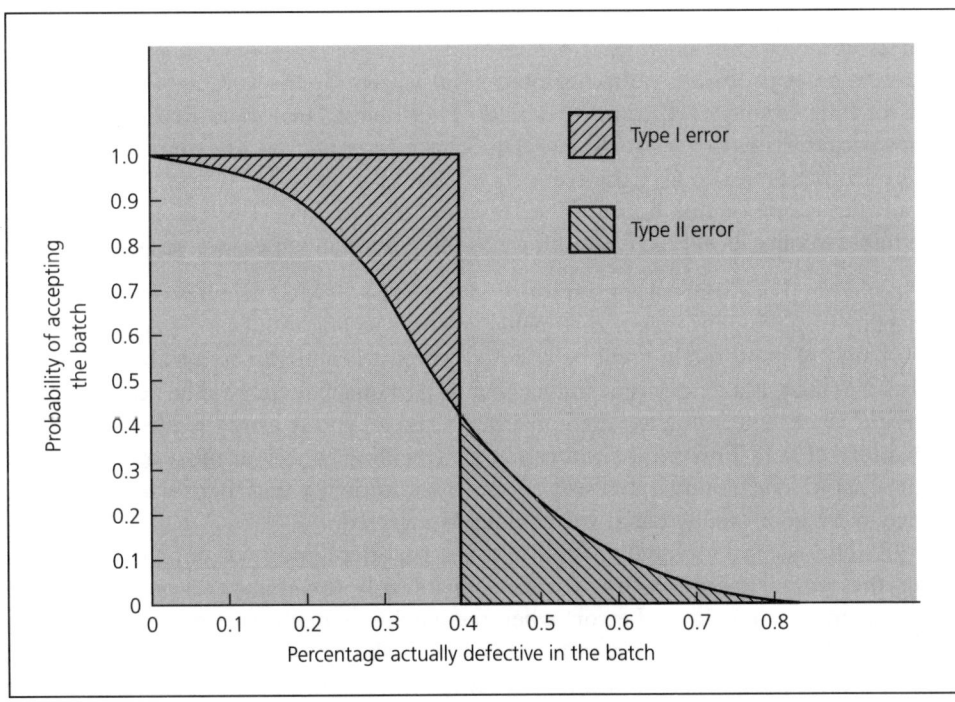

Figure 17.14
Type I and II errors in the operating characteristics of real sampling plans

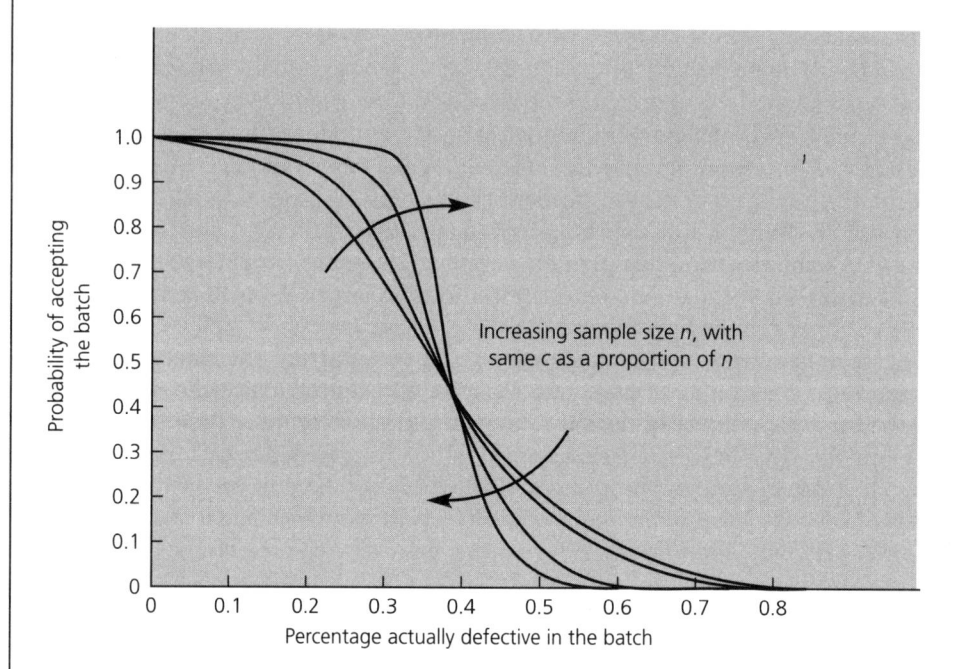

Figure 17.15
Even when the value of *c* as a proportion of the sample size *n* remains constant, the larger the sample size *n*, the closer the operating characteristic curve is to the ideal

Creating an acceptance sampling plan

To create an appropriate sampling plan (that is, decide the values of *n* and *c*) the levels of four factors need to be specified. These have been identified on the operating characteristic curve in Fig. 17.16. These four factors are then fed into the Dodge-Romig tables to give the respective values for *c* and *n*. (Using these tables is beyond the scope of this book.) The four factors are Type I error, Type II error, acceptable quality level (AQL) and lot tolerance percentage defective (LTPD).

● *Type I error.* The usual value used for producer's risk (Type I error) is often set with a probability of 0.05. This means that management is willing to take a 5 per cent chance that a batch of good quality will be rejected when it is actually acceptable. This also implies that there is a 95 per cent chance that a good quality batch will be accepted.

● *Type II error.* The value for the consumer's risk (Type II error) is often set with a probability of 0.1. This means management is willing to risk at most a 10 per cent chance that a poor quality batch will be accepted, implying that there is a 90 per cent chance that a poor quality batch will actually be rejected.

● *AQL.* The acceptable quality level is the actual percentage of defects in a batch which the organization is willing to reject mistakenly (by chance) 5 per cent of the time (assuming a 0.05 Type I error) when the batch is actually acceptable.

● *LTPD.* The lot tolerance percentage defective is the actual percentage of defects in a batch that management is willing to accept mistakenly 10 per cent of the time (assuming a 0.1 Type II error).

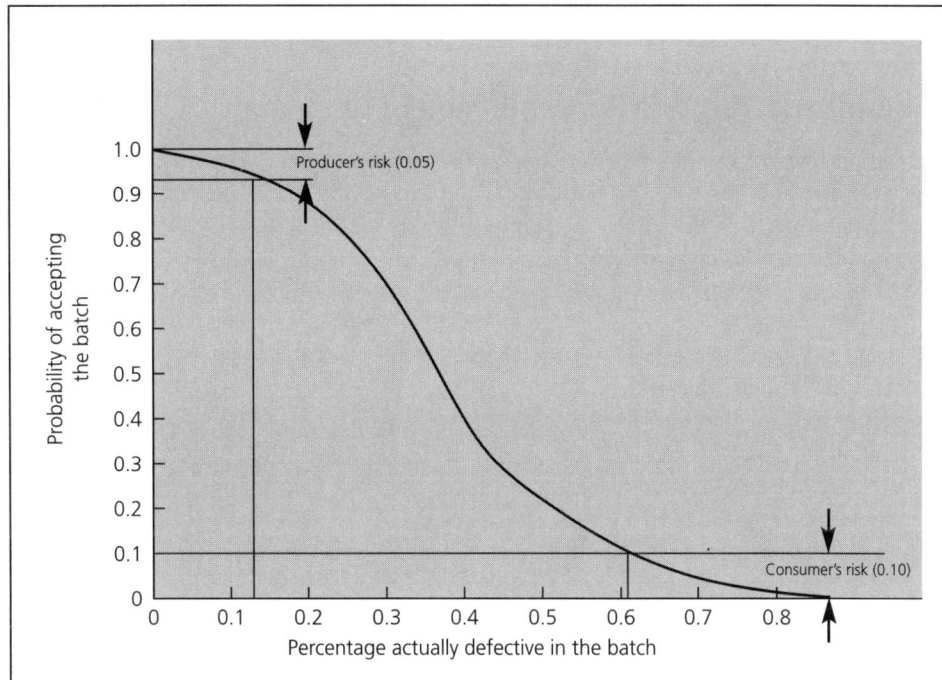

Figure 17.16 Operating characteristic showing average quality level (AQL), lot tolerance percentage defective (LTPD), producer's risk and consumer's risk

Criticisms of acceptance sampling

A frequently made criticism of acceptance sampling is that it assumes that some amount of defects and failure is acceptable to the organization, or its customers. By accepting the inevitability of failure and poor quality, it is argued, the operation will become 'lazy' at trying to eliminate the causes of bad quality. Rather than see quality as primarily something to be improved, acceptance sampling views it as being almost 'predetermined' by the characteristics of the process. The main task is to measure output and understand the risks involved, not to get to the root causes of poor quality. More recent approaches to quality management (such as TQM, *see* Chapter 20) suggest that 'right first time every time' is the only acceptable approach and that organizations should strive to produce zero defects rather than some 'acceptable quality level'.

Zak Limbada, Pretoria Portland Cement Company

After its country's first democratic elections South Africa's cement industry found itself at the centre of the new government's house building efforts. A typical 60 square metre house requires six tonnes of cement with, on average, another two tonnes required to provide roads and services. The Pretoria Portland Cement Company is the largest cement producer in the whole of Africa and provides 45 per cent of South Africa's requirements from its seven factories. Zak Limbada is a Production Superintendent at one of the plants. His job is to ensure the efficient and effective manufacture of the various cementitious products at the plant (but product quality is among his main concerns).

'Quality and consistency of quality is particularly important in cement manufacture because of the downstream implications in its application. Any deviations from the specified characteristics of the cement could affect its strength in use. This is why we put so much effort into quality control. First, the basic raw materials, limestone and iron ore, are milled to a powder form. This is where the factory's quality control starts. Samples of the milled output are automatically taken every hour. The samples are examined with an X-ray fluorescence spectrometer and the results fed into a process-control computer which automatically makes adjustments to the feeders which control the flow of input materials to the process. In this way we control the exact characteristics of the milled output.

'The next stage is the blending process where rotary distributors ensure that a consistent mixture of the milled materials is transferred to a storage silo. After blending, the material is sampled two hourly and fed to a kiln 148 metres long at a rate of 86 tonnes per hour and heated to 1400°C so that the lime and silica combine. The product from this process is called clinker. Quality checks here are made on an hourly basis. The clinker is now ready for the final milling process called 'cement milling'. Gypsum is added and the material crushed to a very fine powder. It is the fineness of this grinding process together with the chemical composition of the cement which determines the final strength of the cement. The best way to test for quality at this stage is to sample the output every hour for surface area and actually make a cube or prism of the daily composite of cement. This can be crushed in order to test its strength. The cement powder is then bagged and palletized, ready for sale to the market.'

The process which Zak manages is highly capital intensive. A typical factory costs R500 million to build and employs around 250 people. He sees people as the key factor in achieving a quality product, however.

'Although many of the quality improvements over the last few years have been made by improving the level of technology we use in the plant, it is our operating staff who release the potential of the technology. Vigilant staff can ensure good quality. Perfect vigilance means perfect quality. We rely on our staff to detect problems so that when necessary the "experts" can be called in to adjust the process. We work hard at equipping and motivating our staff to know how to make that judgement. Training can provide the skill but maintaining motivation in a fairly monotonous process is more of a challenge. We do this by communication and empowerment. Staff are responsible for quality testing and recording results on control charts. The statistical control limits on the charts trigger process adjustments. We also have what we call "green areas". These are special rooms, in the plant, where we meet every day to discuss quality and other work-related issues. We explain how production went yesterday, what problems were encountered, and through collective wisdom and input agree what we should do about them. It is a general forum for making sure that everyone knows what is going on, and that no quality problems are overlooked. More importantly, it demonstrates that everybody in the plant is involved in quality management. This is the key to the point. The paradox is that the advances in our process technology have made us even more dependent on our people.' ∎

SUMMARY

■ There are several approaches to defining quality. Among these are the transcendent approach, the manufacturing-based approach, the user-based approach, the product-based approach, and the value-based approach. In this book we put together several of these approaches to define quality as 'quality is consistent conformance to customers' expectations'.

■ Quality is regarded as a particularly important performance objective in operations because it so directly affects internal and external customers, and leads to both increased revenues and reduced costs.

■ Perceived quality is best modelled as the gap between customers' expectations concerning the product or service and their perceptions concerning the product or service. When expectations are greater than perceptions, perceived quality is poor. When expectations are lower than perceptions, perceived quality is good. When expectations and perceptions match, perceived quality is acceptable.

■ This perception–expectation gap approach can be used to model the factors which determine quality in the customers' domain and in the operation's domain. Such a model can be used as a diagnostic tool. If there is a gap between customers' expectations and their perceptions, it is likely to be caused by one or more gaps between the factors which influence expectations and perceptions. The gap which is of particular significance to operations managers is that between the actual product or service and its internally specified quality levels. This is the 'conformance to specification' approach to quality planning and control.

■ There are six steps involved in the production planning and control activity. These are:
1 Define quality characteristics.
2 Decide how to measure each of the quality characteristics.
3 Set quality standards for each characteristic.
4 Control quality against these standards.
5 Find the correct cause of the poor quality.

6 Continue to make improvements.
In this chapter we dealt with steps 1 to 4.

■ Quality characteristics can be seen as comprising functionality, appearance, reliability, durability, recovery, and contact.

■ Each quality characteristic can be measured either as a variable – which can be measured on a continuously variable scale – or an attribute – which has two states (for example, right or wrong).

■ Most quality planning and control involves sampling the operation's performance in some way. Sampling can give rise to erroneous judgements. These can be classed as either Type I or Type II errors. Type I errors involve making corrections where none were needed. Type II errors involve not making corrections where they are in fact needed.

■ Statistical process control (SPC) involves using control charts to track the performance of one or more quality characteristics of the operation. The power of control charting lies in its ability to set 'control limits' derived from the statistics of the natural variation of processes. These control limits are often set at ±3 standard deviations of the natural variation of the process samples.

■ Control charts can be used either for attributes or for variables. In the latter case both the sample mean and the sample range are usually plotted. This enables a judgement to be made as to whether the mean of the process variation or the standard deviation of the process deviation or both are changing over time.

■ The other major use of statistics in quality planning and control involves the use of acceptance sampling. Acceptance sampling involves making a judgement on a whole batch of products and services based on a sample taken from the batch. Inevitably this involves some risks, either of rejecting a good batch or of accepting a bad batch. The risks of any particular sampling plan are shown on its operating characteristic (OC) curve. The greater the number in the sample, the smaller are the risks involved in sampling.

Handles and Hinges Ltd (H&H)

H&H was established in Birmingham, England, in 1984 by two young entrepreneurs, Dave Philips and Chris Agnew, both experienced in the hardware trade. The business specialized in the 'designer' market for polished metal (brass or stainless-steel) door handles, cupboard knobs, furniture fittings (mostly used in shop/office furniture) and hinges. By 1994, sales had grown to about £5 million per year. This success was based on H&H's reputation for high-quality, unique designs of both traditional and modern products, many of which were selected and specified by architects for large and prestigious projects such as new office developments in London's Docklands. Dave, the Chief Executive Officer, with responsibility for sales, believed that most orders from construction companies were placed with H&H because they assumed they had no other choice once the H&H products had been specified. Larger companies would sometimes suggest to the architect that similar products were available at less than half the price. This advice was invariably ignored as the architect would be attracted by H&H's designs and quality, and would be reluctant to risk 'spoiling' multi-million-pound projects for the sake of saving a few thousand pounds. Dave outlines the characteristics of the changing market place.

'Because of the continuing recession in the construction industry, particularly in office building, we have, since 1990, expanded our direct sales to large UK hardware retail companies, which now account for about 40 per cent of our sales value, but only about 15 per cent of our gross profit. This segment is much more price-sensitive, so we must be able to manufacture good-quality, simple, standard products at low costs comparable to those of our competitors. Some of the reduced costs have been achieved by using thinner and cheaper materials similar to those used in our competitors' products. We have just received our first consignment of brass sheet from Poland with a saving of over 10 per cent in this case. We also had to re-organize to reduce our processing costs. Chris has done a great job of changing all production to modern batch methods (see Fig. 17.17). However, I am concerned that we are often late delivering to our UK retail customers, and this makes it difficult to keep good relationships, and to get repeat orders. Fast delivery of relatively small quantities is required in the 'retail segment'. Whereas the construction/contractors market allows very long production lead times, and dependable delivery is crucial to avoid completion delays, for which we have been held financially accountable on some occasions!

'When customers complain about delivery or about faulty products, we try to compensate them in some way to keep their business – for example, by credit notes or discounts on the next order. Our representatives each spend about one day a week dealing with the consequences of late deliveries, but on the positive side, a meeting with a client is an opportunity to get the next order. The hardware retail companies often require very quick delivery, which is often only achieved by switching production to the item which is required first.

'Really, I am more concerned about reports of quality problems; an increasing number of construction com-panies have complained to us about dented or scratched handles, but our production department assures us that they left the factory in good condition and must have been damaged on site; which is to be expected on a large construction site. The Quality Control Manager says, however, he cannot give an absolute guarantee that they were all OK, because we only do sampling of final production; if more than a few in a sample are found at final inspection to be sub-standard, the whole batch is rejected, re-inspected, sorted and re-worked. Using express courier transport and overtime in the factory, rework usually can be done in about a week, but invariably the contractors complain to the architect, perhaps because they dislike being told who to buy from. This can lead to lots of correspondence and meetings between H&H, the contractor and the architect, when we could be doing other things. This problem seems to have got worse in the last two years; often it's also difficult to agree if the product is sub-standard. It is frequently just a question of how shiny (or matt) the polish and lacquer finish is; at other times there are scratches in areas that really can't be seen in use. Often the customers are too fussy, anyway.'

Discussions with Chris (the Manufacturing Director) put a different perspective on the problem.

'The sales catalogue shows pictures of our products prepared for photography; special effects are used to give a bright polished finish but we actually use a matt finish. The samples used by Sales are specially made by experienced craftsmen to eliminate any scratching or minor faults; of course, we cannot always repeat that standard with the modern batch production methods.

'We were aware that the re-organization of production methods could lead to quality problems, so I introduced statistical control, a subject I studied extensively in a quantitative methods course at the local college. Our inspectors now take random samples of batches of components and

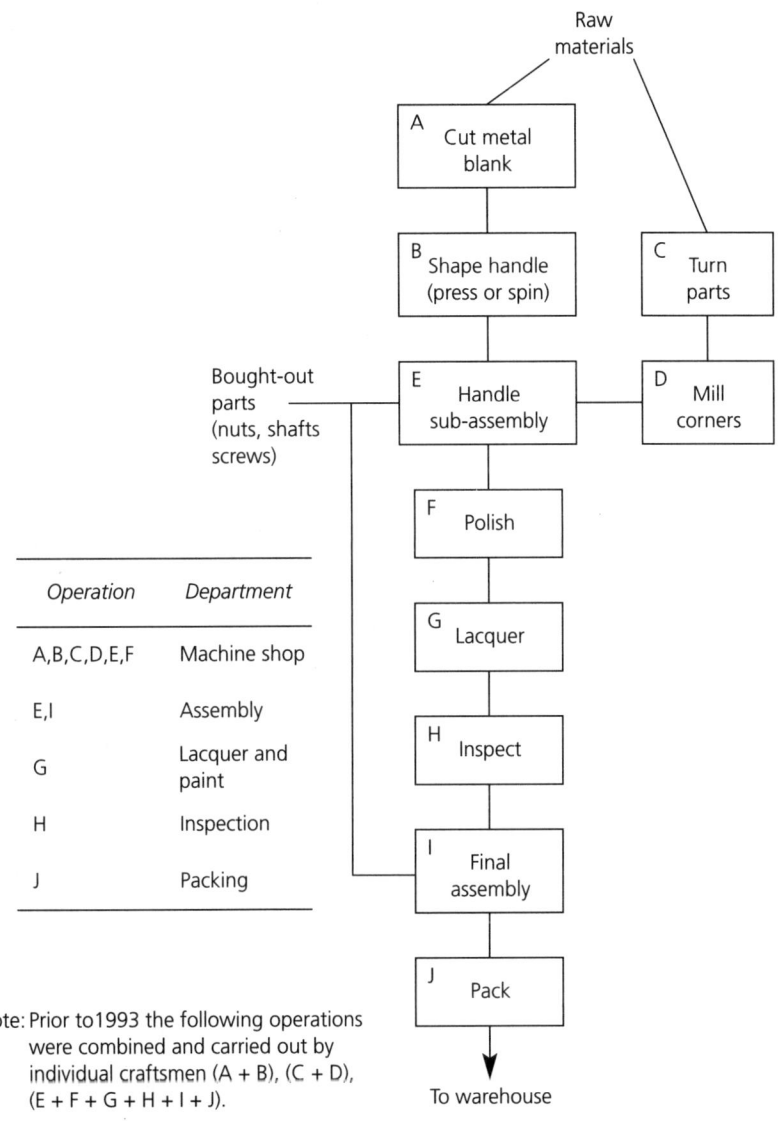

Raw materials

A	Cut metal blank
B	Shape handle (press or spin)
C	Turn parts
D	Mill corners
E	Handle sub-assembly
F	Polish
G	Lacquer
H	Inspect
I	Final assembly
J	Pack

Bought-out parts (nuts, shafts screws)

Operation	Department
A,B,C,D,E,F	Machine shop
E,I	Assembly
G	Lacquer and paint
H	Inspection
J	Packing

Note: Prior to 1993 the following operations were combined and carried out by individual craftsmen (A + B), (C + D), (E + F + G + H + I + J).

To warehouse

Figure 17.17 Typical production processes for batches of handles

measure important dimensions such as the diameter or length of brass handles, the thickness of the incoming materials, etc. Batches which fail are either rejected or reworked, and all material where we have identified any fault at all is returned to the supplier, and our buyers routinely threaten to place orders elsewhere. I instructed the supervisors to inspect press tooling just before the start of each production batch to ensure that there are no surface faults, so I think it is unlikely that the dents and blemishes are caused in production. I must make a point of checking that this is happening. Anyway, our final inspection sampling has been changed to give an acceptable quality level (AQL) of two per cent, whereas until recently it was only five per cent. We have had to increase the number of final inspectors by four at a cost of £15 000 each per annum, but all the management team agrees that with quality ▶

products we must be confident of the final quality before packing. We trained some of our best assemblers in SPC and made them full-time inspectors; the combination of their technical and statistical skills ensures that we have the right people for this job. We could not rely on our operators to do any dimensional checks; hardly any of them know how to measure using a metric rule, let alone a micrometer or vernier gauge. It is best to keep them concentrating on achieving correct output targets. I believe that most quality problems here must be caused by occasional operator carelessness.

'The batch method of production has given us much more control over operations. No longer do we have to rely on hard-to-recruit craftsmen who did everything slowly and unpredictably. Now we make the most of economic batches at each stage, benefiting from the economies of scale of longer runs and cheaper unskilled labour. With incentive

bonuses based on effective performance against agreed standard times, all our people are working faster to achieve the company's goal of higher productivity. There is no doubt that our operations are now more productive than they've ever been. With high quality and low costs, we are now set for a major assault on the competition. We expect our profit to rise dramatically from the currently inadequate one per cent return on sales.' ■

Questions

1 How does the company compete in its market place, and what is the role of 'quality' in its competitive strategy?
2 Do you think that the company's use of statistical quality control is sensible?
3 Apply the gap model of quality diagnostics (Fig. 17.2) to the company.

DISCUSSION QUESTIONS

1 Describe and explain the differences between needs, wants and expectations that a customer might have for:

> a tourist-class flight to America
> a talking doll
> an operations management course.

2 Define the quality characteristics for the following products and services and suggest ways in which each characteristic could be measured. Identify whether the characteristics are attributes or variables:

> a restaurant meal
> a washing machine
> a taxi service.

3 Discuss the advantages and disadvantages of 100 per cent inspection. Comment on the appropriateness of 100 per cent inspection, and how it might be carried out, in the following examples:

> the temperature of a restaurant meal
> the appropriateness of a student for a first-class honours degree
> the punctuality of a fleet of city buses
> the results to be obtained from a packet of garden seeds.

4 Explain why, when 100 per cent inspection takes place, errors in the product or service may still get through to the customer. Illustrate your answer with a product and service of your own choice. What might be done to try to minimize such errors occurring?

5 A factory uses two machines to slice plastic extrusions. The specification range for the output of machine 1 is 16.7 to 17.3 cm and is 22 to 26 cm for machine 2. The outputs of the machines are normally distributed around 17 and 24 cm respectively with standard deviations of 1.7 and 2.1 cm. The normal variation in the two machines is known to be 0.5 and 1.9 cm respectively. The operations manager has the budget to upgrade one of the two machines this year. Which one would you recommend is replaced on the basis of its ability to do the job?

6 A manufacturer of printed circuit boards (PCBs) is concerned that the process is becoming out of control. The usual proportion of defective boards is six per cent which is thought to be better than the industry average. The manager has taken one sample a day for the last ten days, with 100 boards in each sample. The results are shown below. Draw a control chart and comment on the process.

Sample no.	1	2	3	4	5	6	7	8	9	10
No. of defects	3	0	1	4	10	0	6	12	5	7

7 The regional manager of a national train network is considering giving guarantees to customers about the reliability of the trains arriving at the principal station in the region. The arrival times of 20 trains were checked each day over a period of several weeks when there were no known unusual circumstances. It was found that the trains were, on average, three minutes later than their scheduled time of arrival. The average range was 12 minutes. What advice would you give the manager?

8 Describe the advantages of using control charts to monitor processes. Discuss how appropriate they might be for the following activities:
- complaint monitoring for a package holiday company
- monitoring of marks for operations management examinations
- engine failure in aircraft
- supermarket check-out queues.

9 Once a day a company that specializes in ride-on lawnmowers undertakes a thorough check of a small sample of its products. There are five main checks covering the machine's appearance (measured in terms of the number of blemishes in the metalwork), its reliability (mean time between failures in hours), top speed (mph), fuel consumption (mpg) and noise levels (Db). Table 17.8 provides the UCLs, LCLs and averages for each factor and the results of the last ten checks. Comment on whether or not you think any parts of the process need investigating and explain your reasons.

10 Explain what is meant by acceptance sampling. Compare this approach to quality control with the total quality management (TQM) approach explained in Chapter 20.

Table 17.8

Factor	Appearance	Reliability	Speed	Fuel	Noise
UCL	5	190	10.5	45	3.4
Average	2	150	9	38	2.8
LCL	0	110	7.5	31	2.2
Sample					
1	2	112	8.6	41	3.0
2	1	161	8.4	38	2.9
3	2	120	8.7	43	2.6
4	2	182	8.8	35	2.8
5	1	115	9.0	32	2.9
6	2	173	9.6	41	2.7
7	4	143	9.1	34	3.0
8	4	180	9.2	33	2.3
9	4	119	9.8	33	2.3
10	4	175	9.5	32	2.5

NOTES ON CHAPTER

1 Garvin, D. (1984) 'What does "Product Quality" really mean?', *Sloan Management Review*, Fall.

2 Gummesson, E. (1993) 'Service Productivity, Service Quality and Profitability', *Proceedings of the 8th International Conference of the Operations Management Association*, Warwick, UK.

3 Parasuraman, A., Zeithaml, V.A. and Berry, L.L. (1985) 'A Conceptual Model of Service Quality and Implications for Future Research', *Journal of Marketing*, Vol 49, Fall, pp 41–50 and Gummesson, E. (1987) 'Lip Service: A Neglected Area in Services Marketing', *Journal of Services Marketing*, Vol 1, No 1, Summer, pp 19–23.

4 Haywood-Farmer, J. and Nollet, J. (1991) *Services Plus: Effective Service Management*, Morin.

5 Based on Parasuraman, A. *et al.* (1985), *op.cit.*

6 Source: By kind permission of Crown Pies.

7 Based on Wild, R. (1989) *Production and Operations Management*, Cassell.

8 Source: Discussions with company staff and company press releases.

SELECTED FURTHER READINGS

Bounds, G., Yorks, L., Adams, M. and Ranney, G. (1994) *Beyond Quality Management: Towards the Emerging Paradigm*, McGraw-Hill.

Dale, B.G. and Shaw, P. (1989) 'The Application of Statistical Process Control in UK Automative Manufacture: Some Research Findings', *Quality and Reliability Engineering International*, Vol 5, No 1.

Dale, B.G. and Shaw, P. (1991) 'Statistical Process Control: An Examination of Some Common Queries', *International Journal of Production Economics*, Vol 22, No 1.

Dale, B.G. (ed) (1994) *Managing Quality* (2nd edn), Prentice Hall.

Dodge, H.F. and Romig, G.H. (1959) *Sampling Inspection Tables – Single and Double Sampling* (2nd edn), John Wiley.

Duncan, A.J. (1974) *Quality Control and Industrial Statistics*, Irwin.

Evans, J.R. and Lindsay, W.M. (1993) *The Management and Control of Quality* (2nd edn), West.

Garrity, S.M. (1993) *Basic Quality Improvement*, Prentice Hall International.

Garvin, D.A. (1988) *Managing Quality*, The Free Press.

Gupta, V.K. and Sagar, R. (1993) 'Total Quality Control Using PCs in an Engineering Company', *International Journal of Production Research*, Vol 31, No 1.

Hostage, G.M. (1975) 'Quality Control in a Service Business', *Harvard Business Review*, Vol 53, No 4.

Montgomery, D.C. (1985) *Introduction to Statistical Quality Control*, John Wiley.

Montgomery, D.C. (1991) *Introduction to Statistical Quality Control* (2nd edn), John Wiley.

Mortimer, J. (ed) (1988) *Statistical Process Control – an ISF Executive Briefing*, IFS/Springer-Verlag.

Oakland, J.S. and Followell, R.F. (1990) *Statistical Process Control – A Practical Guide* (2nd edn), Heinemann.

Oakland, J.S. (1993) *Total Quality Management* (2nd edn), Butterworth-Heinemann.

Owen, M. (1993) *SPC and Business Improvement*, IFS.

Swenseth, S.R., Muralidhr, K. and Wilson, R.L. (1993) 'Planning for Continual Improvement in a Just-in-time Environment', *International Journal of Operations and Production Management*, Vol 13, No 6.

Zeithaml, V.A., Parasuraman, A. and Berry, L.L. (1990) *Delivering Quality Service: Balancing Customer Perceptions and Expectations*, Free Press.

PART FOUR

IMPROVEMENT

Even the best operation will need to improve because the operation's competitors will also be improving. This part of the book looks at how managers can make their operation perform better, how they can stop it failing, and how they can bring their improvement activities together.

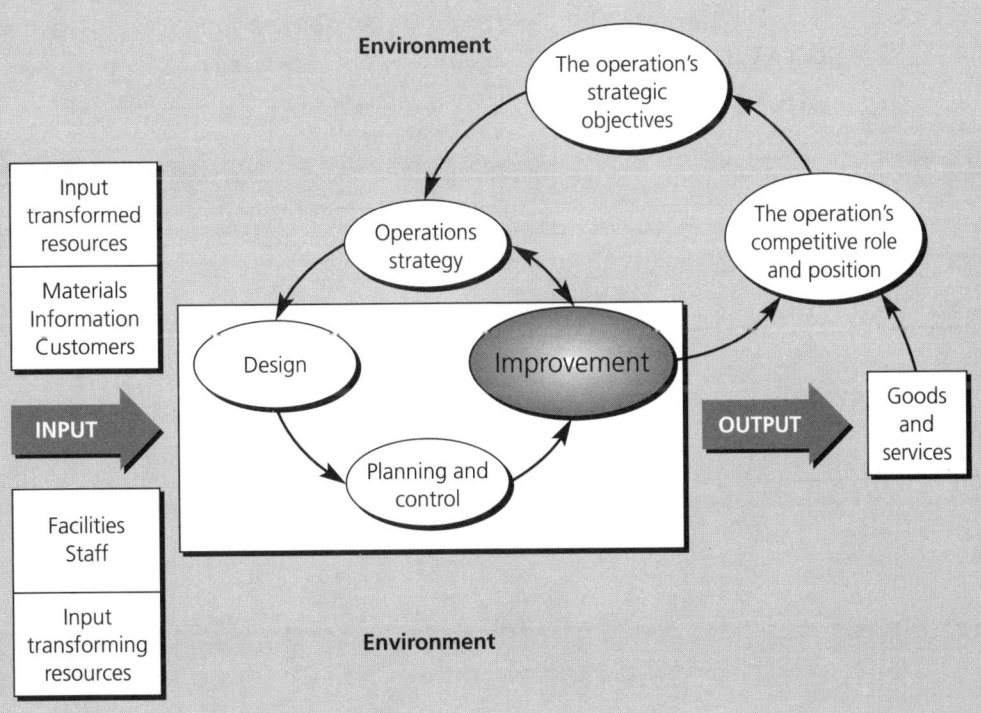

Chapter 18
OPERATIONS IMPROVEMENT

- *How should an operation decide how good it is?*
- *Where should operations managers start their improvement activities?*
- *Which techniques can operations managers use to help them improve their operations?*

Chapter 19
FAILURE PREVENTION AND RECOVERY

- *Why do operations fail?*
- *How can operations managers prevent failure occurring?*
- *What should operations managers do when failure does occur?*

Chapter 20
TOTAL QUALITY MANAGEMENT

- *How is TQM different from previous approaches to quality management?*
- *How can quality initiatives be managed through a TQM approach?*
- *What is the role of quality systems and quality awards in operations improvement?*

CHAPTER 18

OPERATIONS IMPROVEMENT

INTRODUCTION

Even when an operation is designed and its activities planned and controlled, the operations manager's task is not finished. All operations, no matter how well managed, are capable of improvement. In fact in recent years the emphasis has shifted markedly towards making improvement one of the main responsibilities of operations managers. In this part of the book we choose to treat the improvement process in three stages. The first, in this chapter, looks at the approaches and techniques which can be adopted to improve the operation. The second, in Chapter 19, looks at improvement from another perspective, that is how operations can prevent failure and how they can recover when they do suffer a failure. Finally, in Chapter 20, we look at how the whole improvement process can be supported through the total quality management (TQM) approach. These three stages are interrelated as shown in Fig. 18.1.

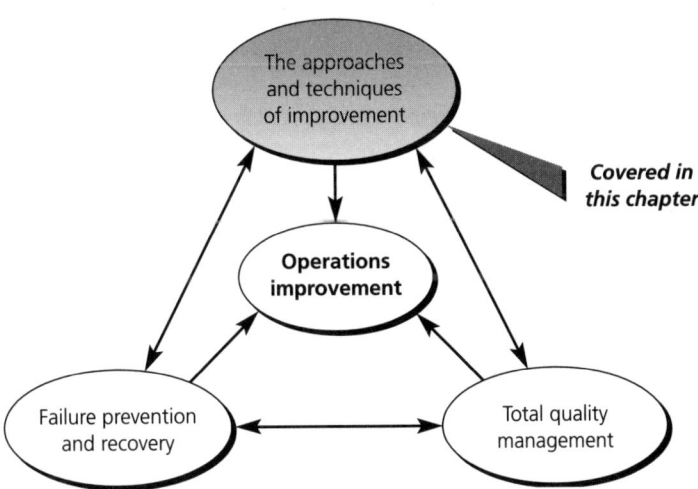

Figure 18.1 Model of operations improvement showing the issues covered in this chapter

> **OBJECTIVES**
>
> This chapter will examine:
>
> - how operations can measure their performance in terms of the five performance objectives;
>
> - the principles and stages of benchmarking;
>
> - the way in which operations managers can quantify the importance of their significant competitive factors and their achieved performance;
>
> - the prioritization process which brings importance and performance together in the importance–performance matrix;
>
> - the two contrasting improvement strategies of continuous and breakthrough improvement;
>
> - the business process re-engineering (BPR) approach to improvement;
>
> - some common techniques of operations improvement.

MEASURING AND IMPROVING PERFORMANCE

Before operations managers can devise their approach to the improvement of their operations, they need to know how good they are already. The urgency, direction and priorities of improvement will be determined partly by whether the current performance of an operation is judged to be good, bad or indifferent. All operations therefore need some kind of *performance measurement* as a prerequisite for improvement.

Performance measurement

Performance measurement is the process of *quantifying action*, where measurement means the process of quantification, and the performance of the operation is assumed to derive from actions taken by its management.[1] Performance here is defined as the degree to which an operation fulfils the five performance objectives at any point in time, in order to satisfy its customers.

The polar diagrams (which we introduced in Chapter 3) in Fig. 18.2 illustrate this concept. The five performance objectives which we have used throughout this book can be regarded as the dimensions of overall performance which satisfy customers. The market's needs and expectations of each performance objective will vary (as we also discussed in Chapter 3). The extent to which an operation meets its market's needs will also vary, possibly meeting them in some dimensions. In addition, market requirements and the operation's performance could also change over time. In Fig. 18.2 the operation is originally almost meeting the requirements of the market as far as quality and flexibility are concerned, but is underperforming on its speed, dependability and cost. After some time has elapsed the operation has improved its speed and

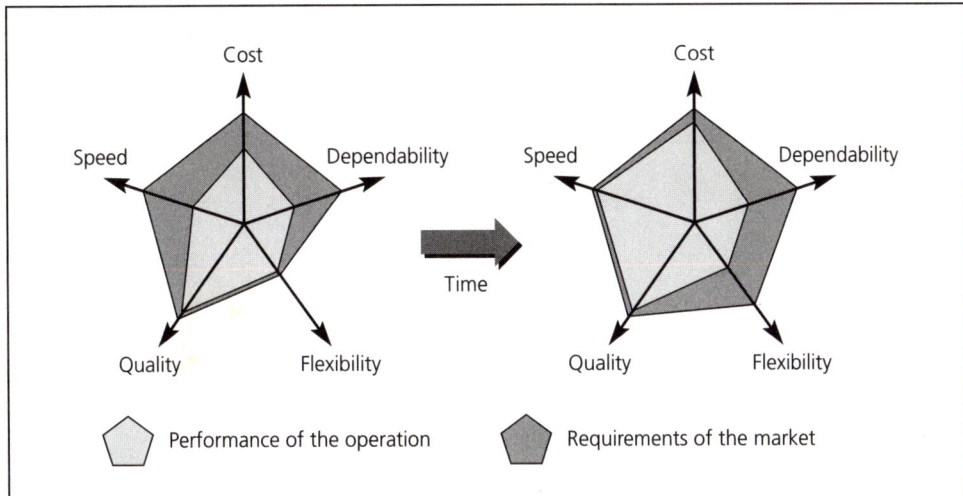

**Figure 18.2
Customers' needs
and the operation's
performance might
both change over
time**

cost to match market requirements but its flexibility no longer matches market requirements, not because it has deteriorated in an absolute sense but because the requirements of the market have changed.

Performance measures

The five performance objectives – quality, speed, dependability, flexibility and cost – are really composites of many smaller measures. For example, an operation's cost is derived from many factors which could include the purchasing efficiency of the operation, the efficiency with which it converts materials, the productivity of its staff, the ratio of direct to indirect staff and so on. All of these factors individually give a partial view of the operation's cost performance, and many of them overlap in terms of the information they include. Each of them does give a perspective on the cost performance of an operation, however, which could be useful either to identify areas for improvement or to monitor the extent of improvement. If an organization regards its 'cost' performance as unsatisfactory, therefore, disaggregating it into 'purchasing efficiency', 'operations efficiency', 'staff productivity', etc. might explain the root cause of the poor performance. If the significant causes of poor performance can be identified, they could be tracked over time to assess the degree of improvement.

Table 18.1 shows some of the partial measures which can be used to judge an operation's performance.

Performance standards

After an operation has measured its performance by using a 'bundle' of partial measures, it needs to make a judgement as to whether its performance is good, bad, or indifferent. There are several ways it can do this, each of which involves comparing the current achieved level of performance with some kind of standard. Four kinds of standard are commonly used.

Table 18.1 Some typical partial measures of performance

Performance objective	*Some typical measures*
Quality	Number of defects per unit Level of customer complaints Scrap level Warranty claims Mean time between failures Customer satisfaction score
Speed	Customer query time Order lead time Frequency of delivery Actual *versus* theoretical throughput time Cycle time
Dependability	Percentage of orders delivered late Average lateness of orders Proportion of products in stock Mean deviation from promised arrival Schedule adherence
Flexibility	Time needed to develop new products/services Range of products/services Machine change-over time Average batch size Time to increase activity rate Average capacity/maximum capacity Time to change schedules
Cost	Minimum delivery time/average delivery time Variance against budget Utilization of resources Labour productivity Added value Efficiency Cost per operation hour

Historical standards

Historical standards would mean comparing current performance against previous performance. For example, if an organization was delivering products to its customers four weeks after the customer initially requested them, its performance would be judged to be quite good if last year it was taking six weeks to deliver. Historical performance standards are effective when judging whether an operation is getting better or worse over time, but they give no indication as to whether performance should be regarded as satisfactory.

Target performance standards

Target performance standards are those which are set arbitrarily to reflect some level of performance which is regarded as appropriate or reasonable. For example, if, under the circumstances, it is regarded as reasonable for the previously mentioned operation to deliver within four weeks then the performance of an operation which actually did deliver in four weeks would be regarded as acceptable. The budgets which most large organizations prepare are examples of target performance standards.

Competitor performance standards

Competitor performance standards compare the achieved performance of the operation with that which is being achieved by one or more of the organization's competitors. For example, if the operation is delivering within four weeks but most of its competitors can deliver within three weeks then its performance would not be regarded as very good. The advantage of competitor-based performance standards is that they relate an operation's performance directly to its competitive ability in the market place. In terms of strategic performance improvement, competitive standards are the most useful. For some operations in the not-for-profit sector this type of performance standard needs to be modified. Comparison against competitors might not even be possible. A police department, for example, would find it difficult to identify its 'competitors' but could compare its performance to that of similar police departments elsewhere.

Absolute performance standards

An absolute performance standard is one which is taken to its theoretical limits. For example, the quality standard of 'zero defects' or the inventory standard of 'zero inventories' are both absolute standards. These standards are perhaps never achievable in practice but they do allow an operation to calibrate itself against a theoretical limit. In the previous example, the product which was in fact delivered in four weeks to the customer might take only four hours to be made within the factory and delivered to the customer. In practice the operation will probably never achieve a four-hour delivery time, but the standard has illustrated how much the operation could theoretically improve.

Benchmarking

One approach which some companies use to compare their operations with those of other companies is called *benchmarking*. Originally the term 'benchmark' derives from land surveying where a mark, cut in the rock, would act as a reference point. In 1979 the Xerox Corporation, the document and copying company, used the term 'competitive benchmarking' to describe a process:

'used by the manufacturing function to revitalize itself by comparing the features, assemblies and components of its products with those of competitors'.[2]

(*See* box on Rank Xerox's benchmarking process.) Since that time the term benchmarking has widened its meaning in a number of ways.[3]

● It is no longer restricted only to the manufacturing operations but is also seen as being applicable to other functional areas such as purchasing and marketing.
● It is no longer confined only to manufacturing organizations but has been used in services such as hospitals and banks.
● It is no longer practised only by experts and consultants but can involve all staff in the organization.
● The term 'competitive' has been widened to mean more than just the direct comparison with competitors. It is now taken to mean benchmarking to gain competitive advantage (perhaps by comparison with, and learning from, non-competitive organizations).

XEROX BENCHMARKING[4]

Possibly the best known pioneer of benchmarking in Europe is Rank Xerox, the document and imaging company, who created the original market for copiers. The virtual monopoly the company had in its sector almost became its undoing, however. By 1980 the threat to Rank Xerox from the emerging Japanese copier companies had become clear. An in-depth study within the company recognized that fundamental changes were needed. To understand how it should change, the company decided to evaluate itself externally – a process which became known as competitive benchmarking. The results of this study shocked the company. Its Japanese rivals were selling machines for about what it cost Xerox to make them. Nor could this be explained by differences in quality. The study found that, when compared with its Japanese rivals, the company had nine times more suppliers, was rejecting ten times as many machines on the production line and taking twice as long to get products to market. Benchmarking also showed that productivity would need to grow 18 per cent per year over five years if it was to catch up with its rivals.

Rank Xerox sees benchmarking as helping it achieve two objectives. At a strategic level it helps set standards of performance, while at an operational level it helps the company understand the best practices and operations methods which can help it achieve its performance objectives.

Its experience of using this approach has led Xerox to a number of conclusions:

● The first phase, planning, is crucial to the success of the whole process. A good plan will identify a realistic objective for the benchmarking study which is achievable and clearly aligned with business priorities.

● A prerequisite for benchmarking success is to understand thoroughly your own processes. Without this it is difficult to compare your processes against those of other companies.

● Look at what is already available. A lot of information is already in the public domain. Published accounts, journals, conferences and professional associations all can provide information which is useful for benchmarking purposes.

● Be sensitive in asking for information from other companies. The golden rule is 'Don't ask any questions that we would not like to be asked ourselves'. ■

Types of benchmarking

There are many different types of benchmarking (which are not necessarily mutually exclusive), some of which are listed below.

● *Internal benchmarking* is a comparison between operations or parts of operations which are within the same total organization. For example, a large motor vehicle manufacturer with several factories might choose to benchmark each factory against the others.

● *External benchmarking* is a comparison between an operation and other operations which are part of a different organization.

● *Non-competitive benchmarking* is benchmarking against external organizations which do not compete directly in the same markets.

● *Competitive benchmarking* is a comparison directly between competitors in the same, or similar, markets.

● *Performance benchmarking* is a comparison between the levels of achieved performance in different operations. For example, an operation might compare its own performance in terms of some or all of our performance objectives – quality, speed, dependability, flexibility and cost – against other organizations' performance on the same dimensions.

● *Practice benchmarking* is a comparison between an organization's operations practices, or ways of doing things, and those adopted by another operation. For example, a large retail store might compare its systems and procedures for controlling stock levels with those used by another department store. The objective is usually to see whether anything can be learned from the practices adopted by other organizations, which could then be transferred to the organization's own operational practices.

The objectives of benchmarking

Benchmarking is partly concerned with being able to judge how well an operation is doing. Many organizations find that it is the process itself of looking at different parts of their own company or looking at external companies which allows them to understand the connection between the external market needs which an operation is trying to satisfy and the internal operations practices it is using to try to satisfy them. In other words, benchmarking can help to reinforce the idea of the direct contribution which an operation has to the competitiveness of its organization. This link is represented by the thick arrows in Fig. 18.3.

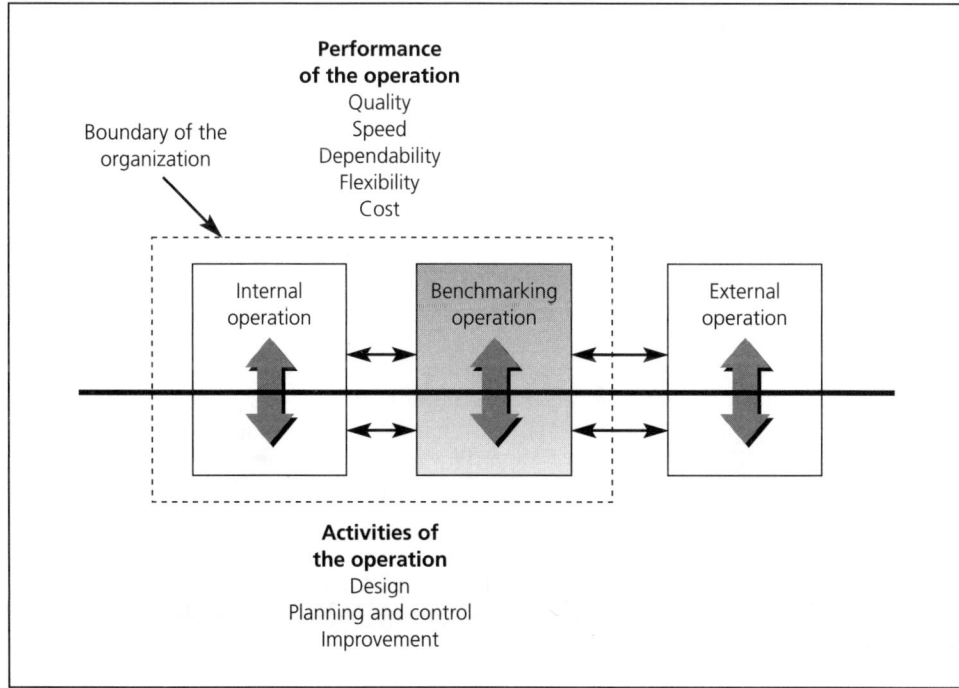

Figure 18.3 Benchmarking can involve internal and external comparisons and performance and activity comparisons

IMPROVEMENT PRIORITIES[5]

In Chapter 3 we identified two major influences on the way in which operations decide to which performance objectives they need to pay particular attention. These two influences were:

- the needs and preferences of customers, and
- the performance and activities of competitors.

The consideration of customers' needs has particular significance in shaping the objectives of all operations. The fundamental purpose of operations is to create goods and services in such a way as to meet the needs of their customers. What customers find important, therefore, the operation should also regard as important. If customers for a particular product or service prefer low prices to wide range, then the operation should devote more energy to reducing its costs than increasing the flexibility which enables it to provide a range of products or services. The needs and preferences of customers shape the *importance* within the operation.

The role of competitors is different to that of customers. Competitors are the points of comparison against which the operation can judge its performance. From a competitive viewpoint, as operations improve their performance, the improvement which matters most is that which takes the operation past the performance levels achieved by the competitors. The role of competitors then is in determining achieved *performance*.

Both importance and performance have to be brought together before any judgement can be made as to the relative priorities for improvement. Just because something is particularly important to its customers does not mean that an operation should necessarily give it immediate priority for improvement. It may be that the operation is already considerably better than its competitors at serving customers in this respect. Similarly, just because an operation is not very good at something when compared with its competitors' performance, it does not necessarily mean that it should be immediately improved. Customers may not particularly value this aspect of performance. Both importance and performance need to be viewed together to judge the prioritization of objectives.

CHOOSING BENCHMARKING TARGETS[6]

Any company which has decided to adopt the benchmarking approach will have to take the decision of who to benchmark themselves against. Some companies choose to benchmark themselves against directly comparable operations. For example, Rover halved the time it took to test its products after benchmarking itself against Honda.

Many organizations in South Africa employ benchmarking practices, particularly those that have international partners and the larger corporates such as Nampak. The benchmarking process is not yet understood by all, the greatest problem being the concept of benchmarking methods and ideas as opposed to mere targets. The National Productivity Institute has started a benchmarking facilitation body which hopes to promote useful local and international agreements on benchmarking between organizations. ■

Example: EXL Laboratories

EXL Laboratories is a subsidiary of a large defence electronics organization which carries out research and development contracts and technical problem-solving work for a wide range of companies. Although a large number of its customers are companies within the same group, it operates as a profit centre and charges full commercial rates for the investigations it undertakes. EXL is particularly keen to improve the level of service which it gives to its customers. As the first stage of this improvement process it had discussions with all of its most important customers and based on these discussions it devised a list of the most important aspects of its service.

● *The quality of its technical solutions*. This means the perceived appropriateness of the results of its research and development projects.
● *The quality of its communications with customers*. This means the frequency and usefulness of the information which it gives to customers while it is carrying out the investigations.
● *The quality of post-project documentation*. This means the appropriateness and usefulness of the instructions and documentations which it hands over to customers together with the final results of the investigation.
● *The delivery speed of its investigations*. This means the time between a customer requesting an investigation to be carried out and the final results of the investigation being delivered.
● *The delivery dependability of the investigations*. This means the ability of the laboratory to estimate the final project completion date accurately and deliver to that date.
● *The delivery flexibility with which it conducts the investigation*. This means the ability of the laboratory to speed up or slow down the investigation so as to deliver it to a revised delivery date.
● *The specification flexibility of the investigation*. This means the ability of the laboratory to change its investigation to cope with revised requirements from the customer.
● *The price of the investigation*. This means the total amount of money charged to the customer for carrying out the investigation.

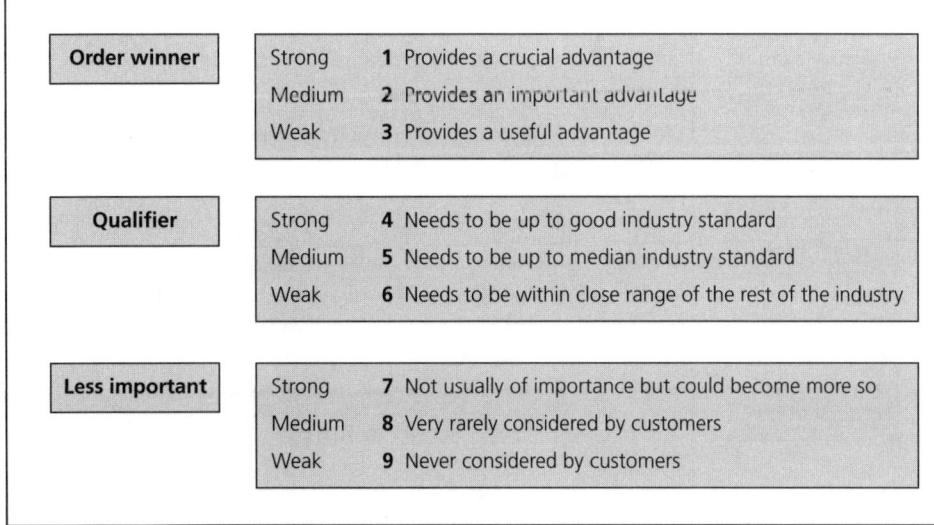

**Figure 18.4
A nine-point scale
of importance**

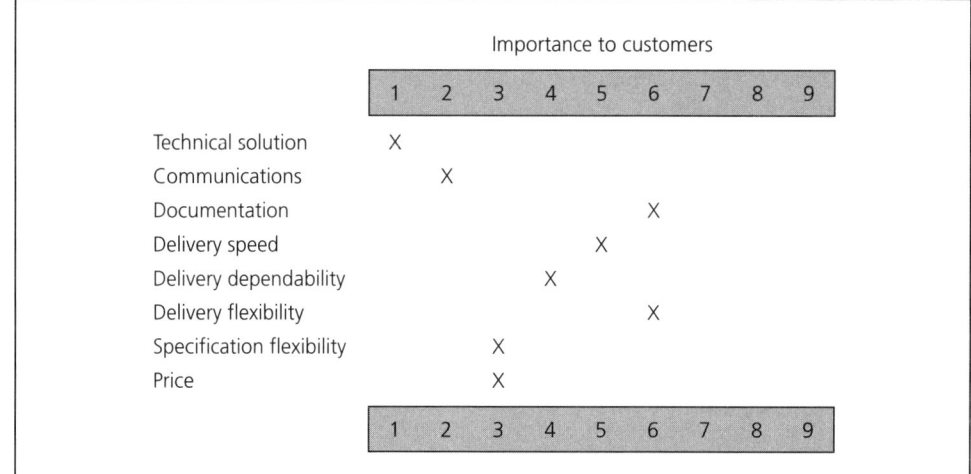

**Figure 18.5
Rating 'importance
to customers' on
the nine-point
scale**

Again, based on its discussions with customers, the laboratory manages to assign a score to each of these factors on the 1 to 9 scale, where 1 means that the factor is extremely important to customers and 9 means that it has no importance (*see* Fig. 18.4).

Figure 18.5 shows how the managers of the laboratory rated the factors. This represents the 'profile of importance' of the various factors as far as the customer is concerned (as perceived by EXL's managers).

Judging performance against competitors

At its simplest, a competitive performance standard would consist merely of judging whether the achieved performance of an operation is better than, the same, or worse than that of its competitors. However, in much the same way as the nine-point importance scale was derived, we can derive a more discriminating nine-point performance scale, as shown in Fig. 18.6.

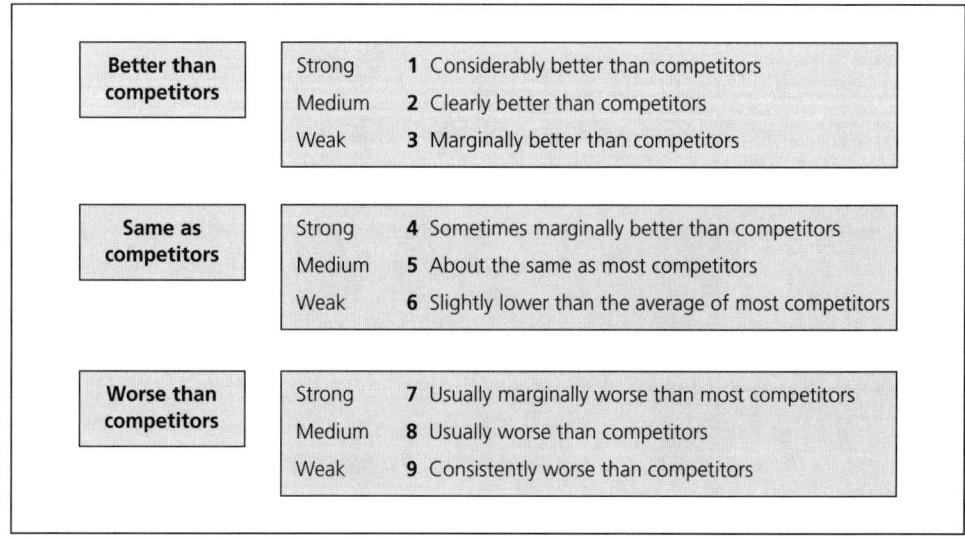

**Figure 18.6
A nine-point scale
of performance**

Example – EXL Laboratories (cont.)

The management of EXL turned their attention to judging the laboratories' performance using the same factors as they had identified as being of relevance to their customers. Although they could not exactly judge how good all their competitors were on every aspect of performance, they could make some initial estimates. These are shown in Fig. 18.7.

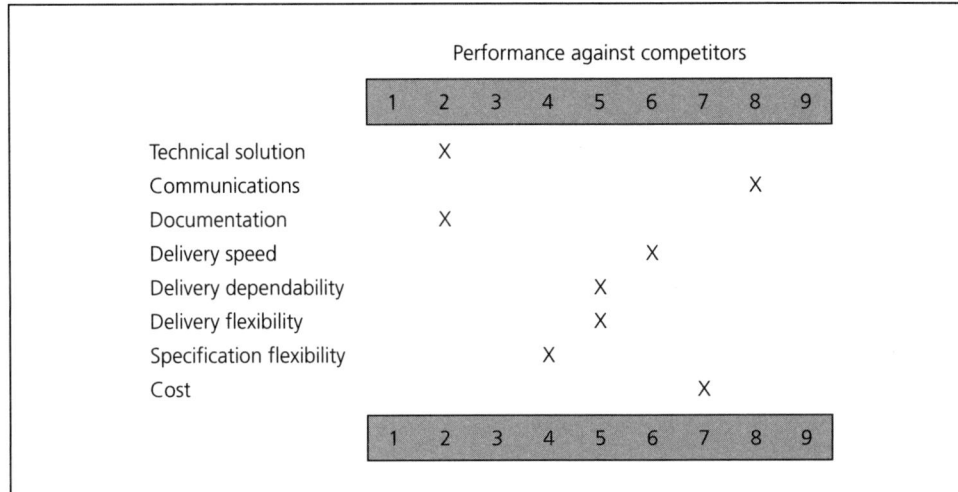

Figure 18.7 Rating 'performance against competitors' on the nine-point scale

The importance–performance matrix

The priority for improvement which each competitive factor should be given can be assessed from a comparison of their importance and performance. This can be shown on an importance–performance matrix which, as its name implies, positions each competitive factor according to its scores or ratings on these criteria. Figure 18.8 shows an importance–performance matrix divided into zones of improvement priority. The first zone boundary is the 'lower bound of acceptability' shown as line AB in Fig. 18.8. This is the boundary between acceptable and unacceptable performance. When a competitive factor is rated as relatively unimportant (8 or 9 on the importance scale) this boundary will in practice be low. Most operations are prepared to tolerate performance levels which are 'in the same ball-park' as their competitors (even at the bottom end of the rating) for unimportant competitive factors. They only become concerned when performance levels are clearly below those of their competitors. Conversely, when judging competitive factors which are rated highly (1 or 2 on the importance scale) they will be markedly less sanguine at poor or mediocre levels of performance. Minimum levels of acceptability for these competitive factors will usually be at the lower end of the 'better than competitors' class. Below this minimum bound of acceptability (AB) there is clearly a need for improvement, above this line there is no immediate urgency for any improvement. However, not all competitive factors falling below the minimum line will be seen as having the same degree of improvement priority. A boundary approximately represented by line CD represents a

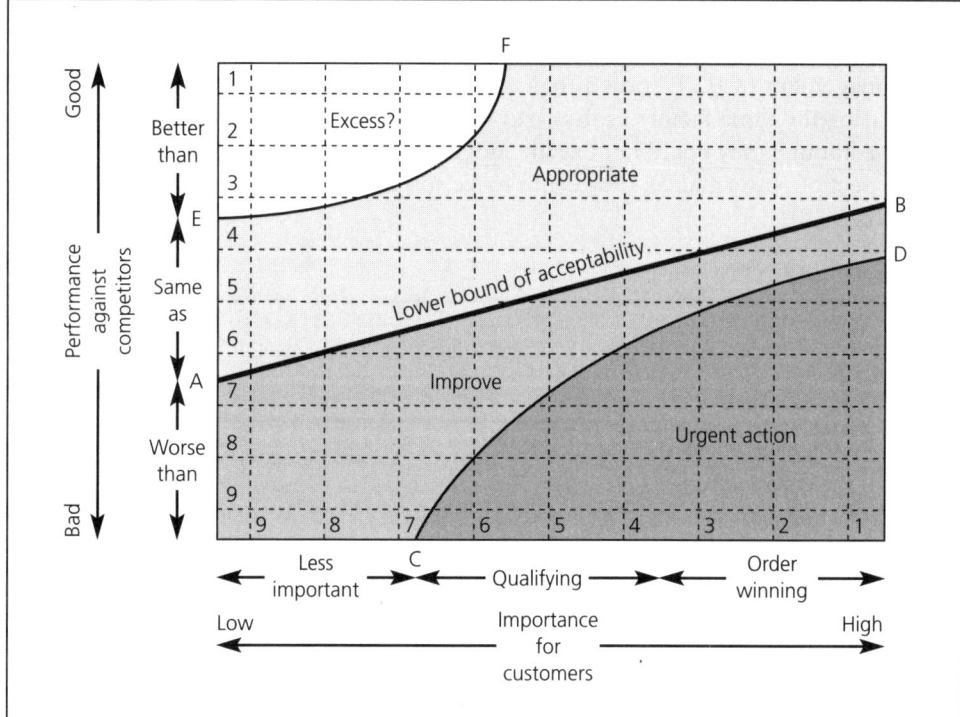

**Figure 18.8
Priority zones in
the importance–
performance
matrix**

distinction between an urgent priority zone and a less urgent improvement zone. Similarly, above the line AB, not all competitive factors are regarded as having the same priority. The line EF can be seen as the approximate boundary between performance levels which are regarded as 'good' or 'appropriate' on one hand and those regarded as 'too good' or 'excess' on the other. Segregating the matrix in this way results in four zones which imply very different priorities.

The 'appropriate' zone

This zone is bounded on its lower edge by the 'lower bound of acceptability', that is the level of performance which the company, in the medium term, would not wish the operation to fall below. Moving performance up to, or above, this boundary is likely to be the first-stage objective for any improvement programme. Competitive factors which fall in this area should be considered satisfactory, at least in the short to medium term. In the long term, however, most organizations will wish to edge performance towards the upper boundary of the zone.

The 'improve' zone

Any competitive factor which lies below the lower bound of the 'appropriate' zone will be a candidate for improvement. Those lying either just below the bound or in the bottom left-hand corner of the matrix (where performance is poor but it matters less) are likely to be viewed as non-urgent cases. Certainly they need improving, but probably not as a first priority.

The 'urgent-action' zone

More critical will be any competitive factor which lies in the 'urgent-action' zone. These are aspects of operations performance where achievement is so far below what it ought to be, given its importance to the customer, that business is probably being lost directly as a result. Short-term objectives must be, therefore, to raise the performance of any competitive factors lying in this zone at least up to the 'improve' zone. In the medium term they would need to be improved beyond the lower bound of the 'appropriate' zone.

The 'excess?' zone

The question mark is important. If any competitive factors lie in this area their achieved performance is far better than would seem to be warranted. This does not necessarily mean that too many resources are being used to achieve such a level, but it may do. It is only sensible therefore to check if any resources which have been used to achieve such a performance could be diverted to a more needy factor – anything which falls in the 'urgent-action' area, for example.

Example – EXL Laboratories (cont.)

The laboratory plotted the importance and performance ratings it had given to each of its competitive factors on an importance–performance matrix. This is shown in Fig. 18.9. It shows that the most important aspect of competitiveness – the ability to

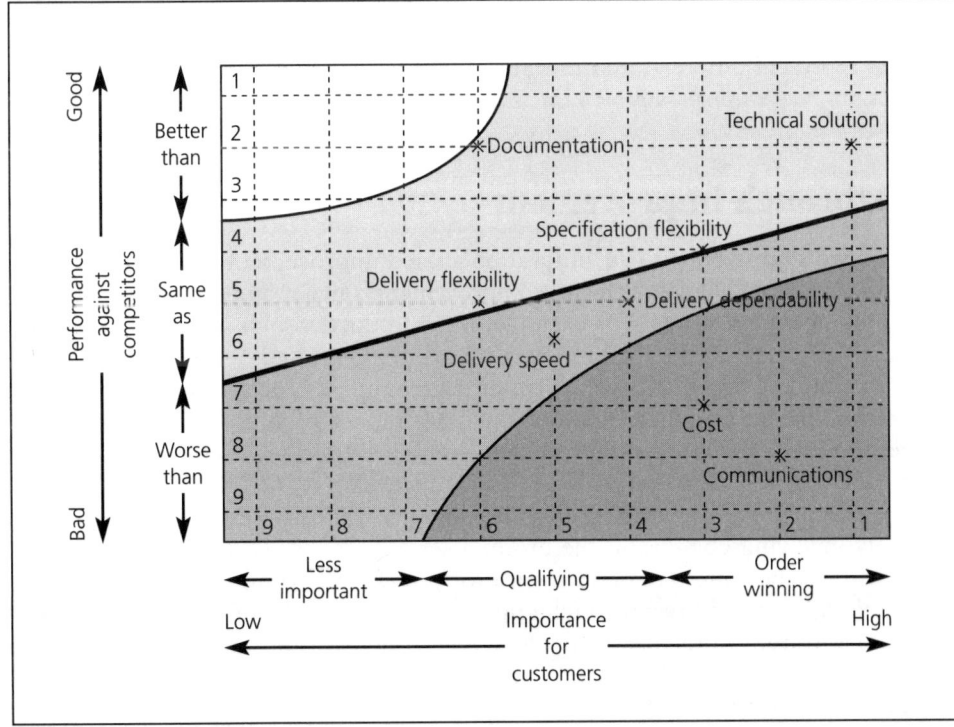

Figure 18.9 The importance–performance matrix for EXL Laboratories

deliver sound technical solutions to its customers – falls comfortably within the appropriate zone. Specification flexibility and delivery flexibility are also in the appropriate zone, although only just. Both delivery speed and delivery dependability seem to be in need of improvement as each is below the minimum level of acceptability for their respective importance positions. However, two competitive factors, communication and cost/price, are clearly in need of immediate improvement. If the manager's estimates of their importance and performance ratings are realistic, both could be losing business for the laboratory. These two factors should therefore be assigned the most urgent priority for improvement. The matrix also indicated that the company's documentation could be regarded as 'too good'.

The matrix did not reveal any total surprises to the laboratory staff as such. The competitive factors 'communication' and 'cost/price' were known to be in need of improvement. However, the exercise was regarded as useful for two reasons.

● It did help to discriminate between many factors which were in need of improvement. Prior to the exercise, the factors 'delivery dependability' and 'delivery speed' were also regarded as equally in need of improvement.

● The exercise gave a purpose and structure to a rather ill-defined debate on improvement priorities which had been ongoing for some time. It was the process of performing the exercise, as much as the results, which was regarded by the managers as being particularly useful.

APPROACHES TO IMPROVEMENT

Once the priority of improvement has been determined, an operation must consider the approach or strategy it wishes to take to the improvement process. Two particular strategies represent different, and to some extent opposing, philosophies. These two strategies are *breakthrough improvement* and *continuous improvement*.

Breakthrough improvement

Breakthrough improvement (or 'innovation'-based improvement as it is sometimes called) assumes that the main vehicle of improvement is major and dramatic change in the way the operation works. For example, the introduction of a new, more efficient machine in a factory, or the total redesign of a computer-based hotel reservation system, or the introduction of a new and better degree programme at a university, are all examples of breakthrough improvement. The impact of these improvements is relatively sudden, abrupt and represents a step change in practice (and hopefully performance). Such improvements are rarely inexpensive, usually calling for high investment of capital, often disrupting the ongoing workings of the operation, and frequently involving changes in the product/service or process technology. Figure 18.10 illustrates the pattern of performance with several breakthrough improvements.

One criticism of the breakthrough approach to improvement is that such major improvements are, in practice, difficult to realize quickly and impossible to realize instantly, as is implied by Fig. 18.10. The following experience reported by Professor Arnoud De Meyer is typical:[7]

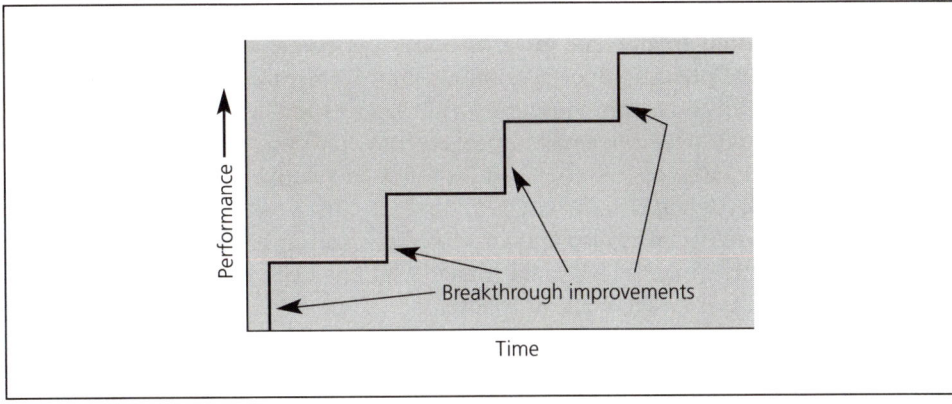

**Figure 18.10
The intended
pattern of
performance
improvement with
breakthrough
improvement**

'I was once involved in the start-up of a major green-field site petrochemical plant. That is obviously a major step. The first time that the plant was 'switched on' it ran for a fraction of a second. With much hard work, energy and dedication, the engineers and the workforce succeeded, after about six months, in reaching 99 per cent capacity utilization. Once the start-up period was over, however, dedication and energy went back to normal levels and capacity utilization slipped slightly.'

The improvement pattern illustrated in Fig. 18.11 is regarded by some as being more representative of what really occurs when operations rely on pure breakthrough improvement.

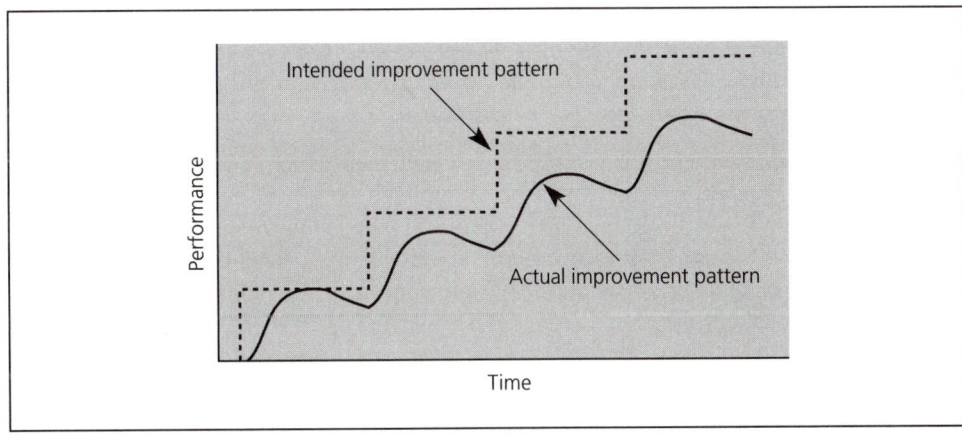

**Figure 18.11
The intended and
actual pattern of
performance
improvement with
breakthrough
improvement**

Continuous improvement

Continuous improvement, as the name implies, adopts an approach to improving performance which assumes more and smaller incremental improvement steps. For example, modifying the way a product is fixed to a machine to reduce change-over time, or simplifying the question sequence when taking a hotel reservation, or rescheduling the assignment completion dates on a university course so as to smooth the student's workload, are all examples of incremental improvements. While there is no guarantee that such small steps towards better performance will be followed by other steps, the whole philosophy of continuous improvement attempts to ensure that there will be. Continuous improvement is not concerned with promoting small improvements *per se*. It does see small improvements, however, as having one significant advantage over large ones – they can be followed relatively painlessly by other small improvements (*see* Fig. 18.12).

Continuous improvement is also known as *kaizen*. Kaizen is a Japanese word, the definition of which is given by Masaaki Imai[8] (who has been one of the main proponents of continuous improvement) as follows:

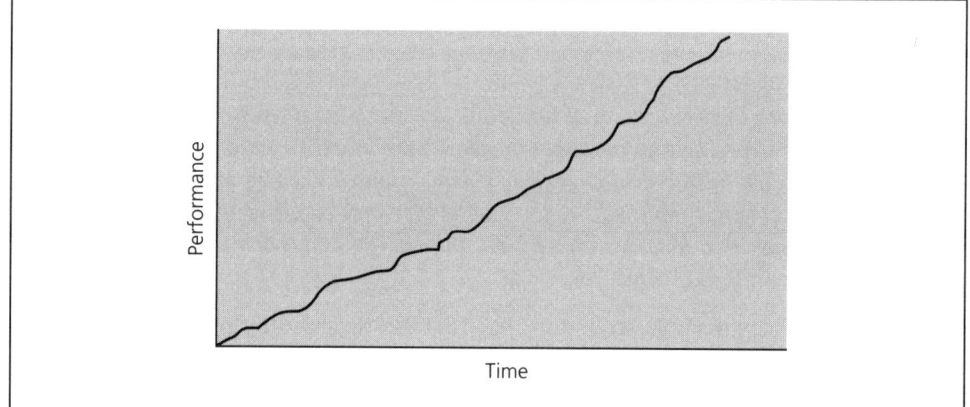

**Figure 18.12
The pattern of
performance
improvement with
continuous
improvement**

'*Kaizen means improvement. Moreover, it means improvement in personal life, home life, social life and work life. When applied to the workplace, kaizen means continuing improvement involving everyone – managers and workers alike.*'

In continuous improvement it is not the size of each step which is important. Rather it is the likelihood that improvement will be ongoing. It is not the *rate* of improvement which is important in continuous improvement; it is the *momentum* of improvement. It does not matter if successive improvements are small; what does matter is that every month (or week, or quarter, or whatever period is appropriate) some kind of improvement has actually taken place.

The differences between breakthrough and continuous improvement

Breakthrough improvement places a high value on creative solutions. It encourages free thinking and individualism. It is a radical philosophy insomuch as it fosters an approach to improvement which does not accept many constraints on what is possible. 'Starting with a clean sheet of paper', 'going back to first principles', and 'completely rethinking the system' are all typical breakthrough improvement principles. Continuous improvement, on the other hand, is less ambitious, at least in the short-term. It stresses adaptability, team work and attention to detail. It is not radical; rather it builds upon the wealth of accumulated experience within the operation itself, often relying primarily on the people who operate the system to improve it. One analogy which helps to understand the difference is the sprint and the marathon. Breakthrough improvement is a series of explosive and impressive sprints. Continuous improvement, like marathon running, does not require the expertise and prowess required for sprinting; but it does require that the runner (or operations manager) keeps on going. Table 18.2 lists some of the differences between the two approaches.

Notwithstanding the fundamental differences between the two approaches, it is possible to combine the two, albeit at different times. Large and dramatic improvements can be implemented as and when they seem to promise significant improvement steps, but between such occasions the operation can continue making its quiet and less spectacular kaizen improvements (*see* Fig. 18.13).

Table 18.2 Some features of breakthrough and continuous improvement (based on Imai[9])

	Breakthrough improvement	*Continuous improvement*
Effect	Short-term but dramatic	Long-term and long-lasting but undramatic
Pace	Big steps	Small steps
Time frame	Intermittent and non-incremental	Continuous and incremental
Change	Abrupt and volatile	Gradual and constant
Involvement	Select a few 'champions'	Everybody
Approach	Individualism, individual ideas and efforts	Collectivism, group efforts, systems approach
Stimulus	Technological breakthroughs, new inventions, new theories	Conventional know-how and state of the art
Risks	Concentrated – 'all eggs in one basket'	Spread – many projects simultaneously
Practical requirements	Requires large investment but little effort to maintain it	Requires little investment but great effort to maintain it
Effort orientation	Technology	People
Evaluation criteria	Results for profit	Process and efforts for better results

The PDCA cycle

The concept of continuous improvement implies a literally never-ending process of repeatedly questioning and re-questioning the detailed workings of an operation. The repeated and cyclical nature of continuous improvement is best summarized by what is called the PDCA cycle (or Deming wheel – named after the famous quality 'guru', W.E. Deming (*see* Chapter 20)). The PDCA cycle is the sequence of activities which are undertaken on a cyclical basis to improve activities (*see* Fig. 18.14).

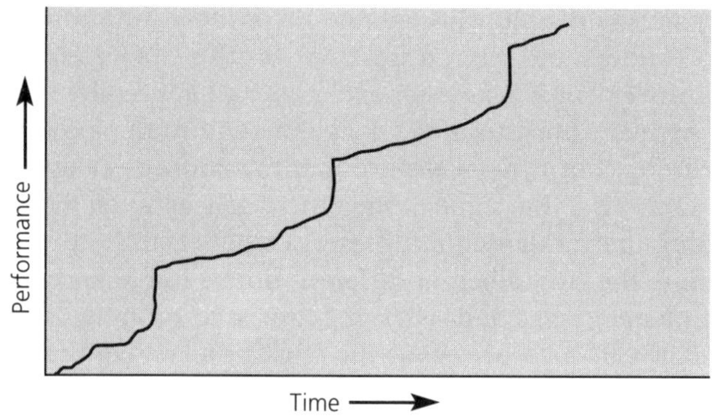

**Figure 18.13
The pattern of
performance
improvement with
continuous
improvement
superimposed on
to breakthrough
improvement**

The cycle starts with the P (for plan) stage, which involves an examination of the current method or the problem area being studied. This involves collecting and analysing data so as to formulate a plan of action which is intended to improve performance. (The next section of this chapter explains some of the techniques which can be used to collect and analyse data in this stage.) Once a plan for improvement has been agreed the next step is the D (for do) stage. This is the implementation stage during which the plan is tried out in the operation. This stage may itself involve a mini-PDCA cycle as the problems of implementation are resolved. Next comes the C (for check) stage where the new implemented solution is evaluated to see whether it has resulted in the expected performance improvement. Finally, at least for this cycle, comes the A (for act) stage. During this stage the change is consolidated or standardized if it has been successful. Alternatively, if the change has not been successful, the lessons learned from the 'trial' are formalized before the cycle starts again.

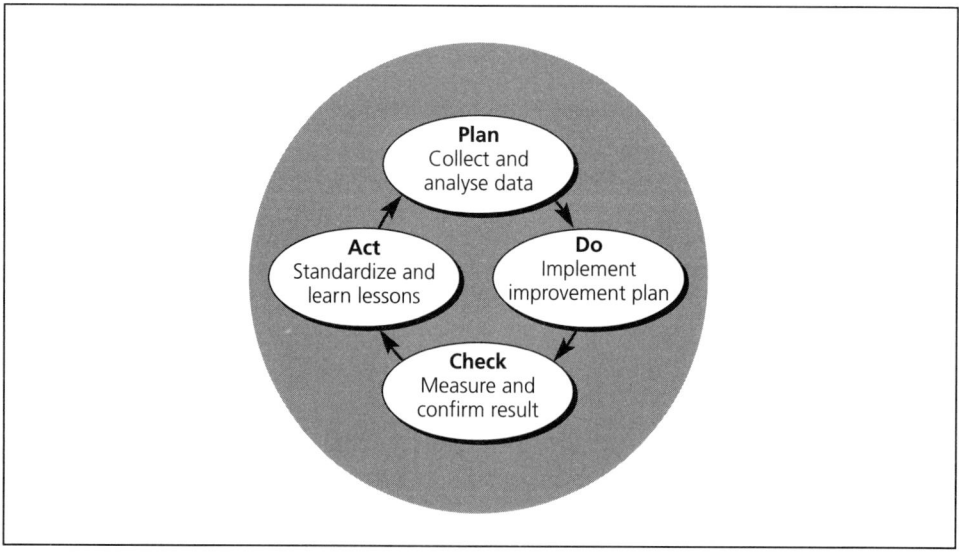

**Figure 18.14
The PDCA cycle**

NISSAN MOTORS (UK) LTD[10]

The first and most publicized of the Japanese motor company's European manufacturing 'implants', the Nissan Motor Manufacturing (UK) plant in the North-East of England is widely admired for its quality.

'They are the McDonald's of manufacturing,' said the Chief Executive of the local development corporation. *'Everyone was striving for quality before they arrived but no one had set their aspirations quite so high.'*[11]

Their arrival had a significant impact on competitors, who saw the new European plant as posing a considerable challenge.

Nissan's approach and commitment to improving its already excellent reputation for operations performance was not the least of the reasons for the competitors regarding it in this way. Quality improvement was quite explicitly put forward, along with team-working and flexibility, as part of its core philosophy. From the beginning the company's local management decided on three guiding principles for its quality and improvement policy.

● First, any programme had to be about more than quality. It needed to be integrated into the overall company activity instead of being a 'bolt-on'. Its purpose was partly instrumental, seen

'as a means of improving individual and team development and the participation of staff in the general day-to-day running of their work areas'.

● Second, it should be a natural extension of the way teams would normally operate. Team orientations, says Nissan, create the environment in which quality and improvement can prosper. For example, five minutes at the beginning of each shift is spent in the team meeting. Quality problems and potential solutions are discussed, along with the results of the product audit known as VES (vehicle evaluation system). This evaluates quantitatively the quality of several vehicles from each shift. Results are analysed and immediately fed back to the relevant teams.

● Third, quality should not be swamped by an external quality bureaucracy. There is a Quality Assistance Department at Nissan but its main objectives are to provide support and feedback to the rest of the company. Similarly the (unavoidable) steering committee operated with the minimum necessary formality and was firmly under the chairmanship of the Director of Production.

Choosing an overall approach and philosophy of improvement which would support these three principles was clearly an important decision for the company. Paradoxically, staff at the British plant chose the Japanese term 'kaizen' teams, rather than the better known 'Quality Circles', to describe their team-based activity. Kaizen conveys the idea that all improvement should be a continuous process which may involve the use of analytical techniques to solve problems and certainly does involve team-based problem solving. Teams even have access to 'kaizen workshops' – areas of the plant where manufacturing staff can go to make improvements.

Nissan South Africa has gone through some rather traumatic changes recently. The fiercely competitive car market in South Africa has brought its problems and as a result there is now much greater Japanese participation in the company. There have been many top management changes. It remains to be seen how improvement will be achieved at their manufacturing facility just outside Pretoria. ■

It is the last point about the PDCA cycle which is the most important – the cycle starts again. It is only by accepting that in a continuous improvement philosophy the PDCA cycle quite literally never stops, that improvement becomes part of every person's job (*see* Fig. 18.15).

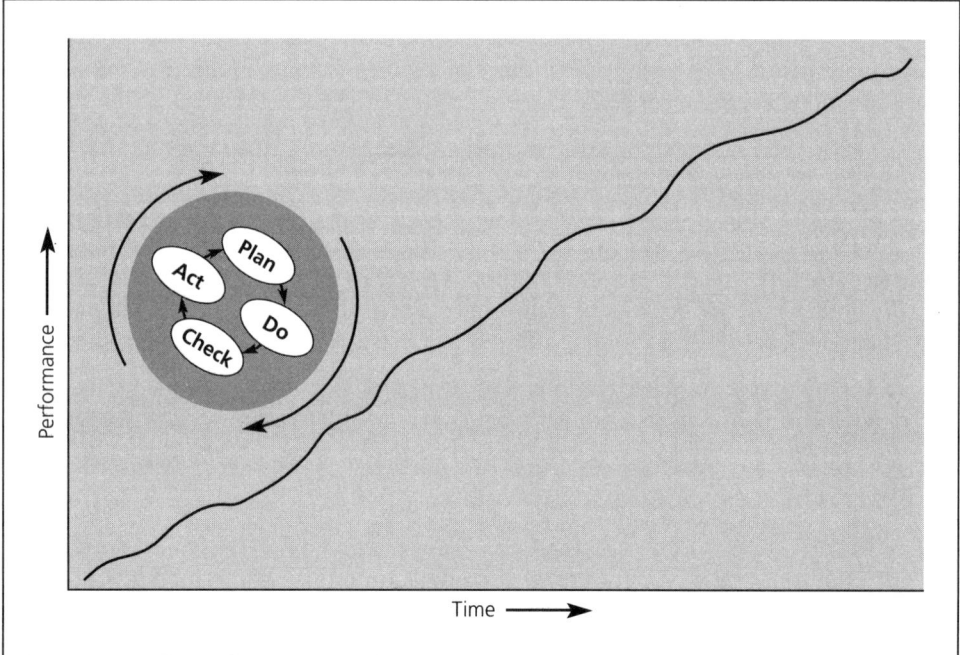

Figure 18.15
The PDCA cycle is the basis of continuous improvement

The business process re-engineering approach

Typical of the radical breakthrough way of tackling improvement is the 'business process re-engineering' (BPR) approach. BPR is a blend of a number of ideas which have been current in operations management for some time. Just-in-time concepts, process flow charting, critical examination in method study, operations network management and customer-focused operations, all contribute to the BPR concept. It was the potential of information technologies to enable the fundamental redesign of processes, however, which acted as the catalyst in bringing these ideas together. BPR has been defined as:

> '*the fundamental rethinking and radical redesign of business processes to achieve dramatic improvements in critical, contemporary measures of performance, such as cost, quality, service and speed.*'[12]

Process *versus* functions

Underlying the BPR approach is the belief that operations should be organized around the total process which adds value for customers, rather than the functions or activities which perform the various stages of the value-adding activity. Figure 18.16(a) shows

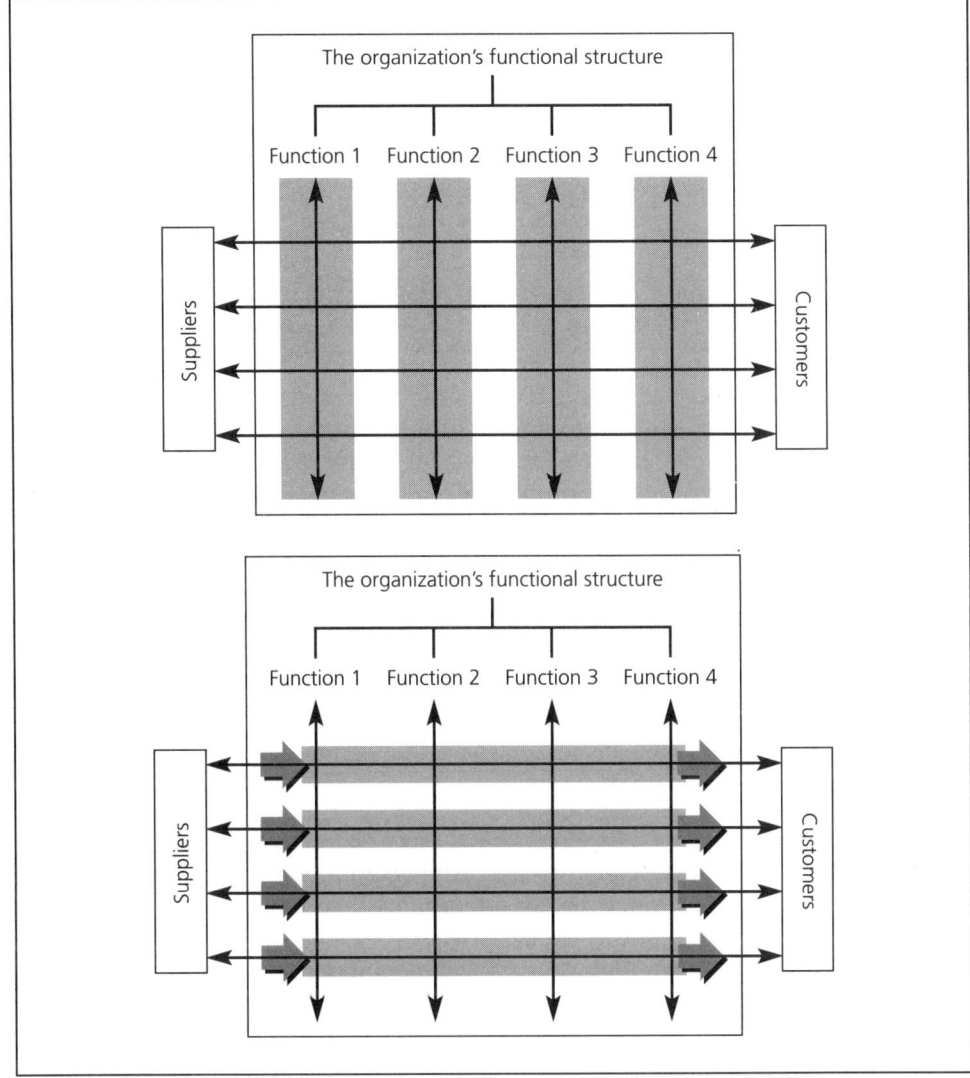

**Figure 18.16
(a) An organization organized by function, (b) an organization organized by process**

how organizations are traditionally organized around each specialist function. BPR advocates reorganization around the processes themselves, as in Fig. 18.16(b).

The principles of BPR

Even if BPR is not an entirely original idea, it can be seen as a useful collection of principles which embody the breakthrough approach. The main principles of BPR have been summarized as follows:[13]

● Rethink business processes in a cross-functional manner which organizes work around the natural flow of information (or materials or customers). This means organizing around outcomes of a process rather than the tasks which go into it.
● Strive for dramatic improvements in the performance by radically rethinking and redesigning the process.

671

- Have those who use the output from a process perform the process. Check to see if all internal customers can be their own supplier rather than depending on another function in the business to supply them (which takes longer and separates out the stages in the process).
- Put decision points where the work is performed. Do not separate those who do the work from those who control and manage the work. Control and action are just one more type of supplier–customer relationship which can be merged.

THE TECHNIQUES OF IMPROVEMENT[14]

All the techniques described in this book can be regarded as 'improvement' techniques insomuch as they attempt to improve some aspect of the performance of an operation. Some techniques are particularly useful for improving operations generally. For example, statistical process control (SPC) in Chapter 17 and failure mode and effect analysis (FMEA) in Chapter 19 could be used for almost any type of improvement project. In the remainder of this chapter we select some techniques which either have not been described elsewhere or need to be re-introduced in their role of helping operations improvement particularly. For example, flow charts were used in Chapter 5 as a design technique – later we will use essentially the same technique to generate improvements to existing operations.

Input–output analysis

From Chapter 1 onwards we have stressed that every department, section, site or division in any operation is involved in processing inputs to produce outputs. A prerequisite for understanding any improvement opportunity is to understand the context in which the input–process–output operation is set.

Three tasks are involved in formulating an input–output model:

1 identifying the inputs and outputs from the process;
2 identifying the source of the inputs and the destination of the outputs;
3 clarifying the requirements of the internal customers who are served by the outputs from the process, and clarifying what requirements the process has for the internal suppliers who provide inputs to the process.

Again we will illustrate techniques by using the same operation as the setting for their application.

Example: Kaston Pyral Services Ltd

Kaston Pyral Services Ltd (KPS) is the field service division of Kaston Pyral International, which manufactures and installs gas-fired heating systems. In the same group is KP Manufacturing, which makes the systems and spare parts, and KP Contracts, which installs the systems. The south-eastern region in the UK is the largest region in KPS. It serves a mixture of customers, large commercial office blocks, industrial buildings, schools, colleges and civic buildings. KPS was feeling under pressure from independent, often small, third-party service organizations who were undercutting KPS's prices. Partly as a response to this, KPS's south-eastern Regional Manager decided to initiate an improvement programme. He decided on a team approach which would include himself, all five service engineers in the unit, the accountant/administrator for the unit and occasionally a trainer from KP Group Personnel Department.

Identifying inputs and outputs

The team decided as a first step to draw an input–output diagram which would give them a common ground of shared understanding about their operation. The procedure here is to list all the inputs to the process. For example:

- information necessary for the process
- materials necessary for the process
- people who take part in the process
- plant and equipment used in the process.

Next the team should list all the outputs for the process. For example:

- physical, tangible products and goods
- information supplied
- anything which has changed as a result of the output.

They decided to include only the 'transformed' inputs rather than the permanent parts of their organization. The first category of inputs was information on the technical details of the products which they were servicing, information from customers on the way the system had been installed or modified in the customers' buildings, and requests from customers for service. The next class of input was the various types of material which came into the system. There were the spare parts, used to replace defective parts in the customers' systems, both new and reconditioned parts from their own workshops. There were also various small items of consumable materials. Also classed as an input were the advice and consultancy which the unit occasionally sought from the personnel of KP Contracts (the part of the group which was concerned with installing the boiler in the first place).

The outputs from the system were the regular preventative maintenance type of service and emergency servicing which involved responding quickly when a customer was having problems. After some discussion the team also decided to include advice and assistance as part of its outputs. Service engineers were often called upon to give advice and assistance to customers on the use of their boilers, to KPS Manufacturing when it found a particular problem with the design of boilers and to KPS Contracts when it found problems with the way in which the boilers had been installed. The team took the view that perhaps they had neglected this part of their output.

Identifying sources (suppliers) and destinations (customers)

Information on products and modifications to products usually came directly from KP, and from other heating manufacturers. Information on the individual customers' systems came from KP Contracts which had installed the systems and from service engineers and customers who also provided information. Customer requests for service came primarily through customers phoning up the unit. Occasionally, if the request was non-urgent, they would ask the service engineer performing regular maintenance to take back a particular request to the unit. New spare parts were delivered direct from the manufacturers, while reconditioned parts came mainly from the KPS workshop or, if the reconditioning was of a major nature, from the factory. Consumable materials came from a wide variety of suppliers, which delivered direct to the depot. On the output side, regular servicing, emergency servicing and advice on the use of the company's boilers were given to three types of customer – commercial, industrial and civic. Advice and information on design were sent to the manufacturing companies on an informal and irregular basis. Similarly, advice and information to the installation company was fed back to the company as the situation seemed to warrant.

Defining input and output requirements

On the input side, the requirement for all types of information input was that they must be accurate (error-free), comprehensive and arrive in time. The main requirements for spare parts, whether new or reconditioned, were primarily speed in making them available to the customer, dependability of delivery so that the maintenance visit to the company could be scheduled in advance, and high quality. The requirements for supply of advice from KP Contracts were that engineers should be made available as speedily as possible so as to give good service to the customer, that commitments made to supply a contract engineer should be honoured reliably, that the engineer should have sufficient flexibility in his or her own availability to enable visits to be scheduled when the customer wanted them, and finally that the engineer's diagnostic skills were high.

On the output side, the customers' requirements depended on which sector they came from. Commercial customers were primarily interested in the cost of the service, but also wanted high dependability, speed of response and technical advice. Industrial customers were interested in the ability of the company to schedule preventative maintenance outside of working hours, with speed of response, cost and technical advice also figuring. Civic customers were primarily interested in cost, and also valued the technical advice more highly than other customers; response and dependability could also be important to them.

The advice and information given to KP Manufacturing regarding the design of the boilers and to KP Contracts on installation procedures were more of a problem. In fact, KPS had never formally asked its sister companies what kind of information they would find useful and whether they wanted it at all. After discussion with both of these companies it was agreed that KP Manufacturing was particularly interested in the frequency with which problems occurred. KP Contracts, on the other hand, was keen to take advantage of the analysis of data on installation problems which KPS could perform.

Figure 18.17 shows an input–output diagram for KPS. The purpose is to reach an agreed understanding of the operational function of whichever part of the organization the problem is set in. It is not intended that input–output diagrams give any answers as such. They do, however, provide a useful 'way in' to the problem.

Flow charts

Input–output diagrams give a useful overview of the process context of improvement opportunities. A more detailed technique is the flow chart. Flow charts give a detailed understanding of parts of the process where some sort of flow occurs. They were briefly described in Chapter 5 in the context of new product and service design, but they have a far wider applicability. They record stages in the passage of information, products, labour or customers – in fact, anything which flows through the operation. They do this by requiring the decision makers to identify each stage in the flow process as either:

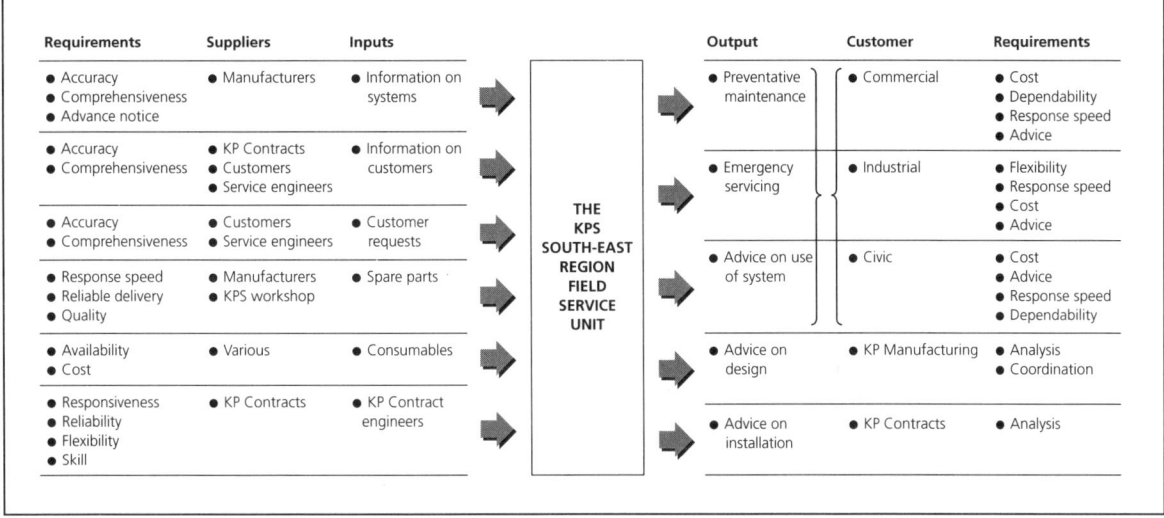

Figure 18.17 Full input–output diagram showing the suppliers and requirements of all inputs and the customers and requirements for all ouputs

- an *action* of some sort – recorded in a rectangular box – or
- a *question/decision* – recorded in a diamond-shaped box.

The purpose of this is to ensure that all the different stages in the flow processes are included in the improvement process, and that these stages are in some kind of logical sequence. The act of recording each stage in the process quickly shows up poorly organized flows. The technique can also clarify improvement opportunities and shed further light on the internal mechanics or workings of an operation. Finally, and probably most importantly, flow charts highlight problem areas where no procedure exists to cope with a particular set of circumstances.

Example: Kaston Pyral Services Ltd (cont.)

As part of their improvement programme the team at KPS are concerned that customers are not being served well when they phone in with minor queries over the operation of their heating systems. These queries are not usually concerned with serious problems, but often concern minor irritations which can be equally damaging to the customers' perception of KPS's service.

Figure 18.18 shows the flow diagram for this type of customer query. When a customer phones in, the telephonists listen to the nature of the customer query. If the telephonists understand the query, it will be diverted to the relevant engineer. If the telephonists cannot understand the nature of the customer's query, they divert the call through to the manager. If the manager does not understand the nature of the call, it is transferred to the relevant duty engineer. If the duty engineer cannot answer the query over the phone, he or she arranges for an engineer to visit the customer. If the engineer can answer the query over the phone but feels that it would be safer for the customer to receive a visit from a service engineer, this will be organized. If the duty engineer feels that no further visit is necessary, no further action takes place. If an engineer visits the customer site and can satisfactorily answer the customer query, again no further action takes place. If the customer is still not satisfied, he or she will report back to the manager. The manager then judges whether either the query or the customer is of sufficient importance for central engineering to be brought in. If so, he or she passes the customer query on to central engineering headquarters and the issue passes out of the regional unit. If the manager decides that the query is trivial, no further action takes place.

The team found the chart illuminating. The procedure had never been formally laid out in this way before, and it showed up three areas where information was not being recorded. These are the three points marked with question marks on the flow chart on Fig. 18.18. As a result of this investigation, it was decided to log all customer queries so that analysis could reveal further information on the nature of customer problems.

Scatter diagrams

Scatter diagrams are a quick and simple method of identifying whether there seems to be a connection between two sets of data: for example, the time at which you set off for work every morning and how long the journey to work takes. Plotting each journey on a graph which has departure time on one axis and journey time on the other could give an indication of whether departure time and journey time are related, and if so, how. Figure 18.19 shows the graph for one person's journeys. It would seem to show: (a) that there is a relationship between the two sets of data; (b) that the longest journeys were when departures were between 8.15 am and 8.22 am; and (c) that the journey is least predictable when departure is between 8.15 am and 8.30 am.

Scatter diagrams can be treated in a far more sophisticated manner by quantifying how strong is the relationship between the sets of data. But however sophisticated the approach, this type of graph only identifies the existence of a relationship, not necessarily the existence of a cause–effect relationship. If the scatter diagram shows a very strong connection between the sets of data, it is important evidence of a cause–effect relationship, but not proof positive. It could be coincidence!

Example: Kaston Pyral Services Ltd (cont.)

The KPS improvement team had completed its first customer satisfaction survey. The survey asked customers to score the service they received from KPS in several ways. For example, it asked customers to score services on a scale of one to ten on promptness, friendliness, level of advice, etc. Scores were then summed to give a 'total satisfaction score' for each customer – the higher the score, the greater the satisfaction.

The spread of satisfaction scores puzzled the team, and they considered what factors might be causing such differences in the way their customers viewed them. Two factors were put forward to explain the differences:

● the number of times in the past year the customer had received a preventive maintenance visit; and
● the number of times the customer had called for emergency service.

All this data was collected and plotted on scatter diagrams as shown in Fig. 18.20.

Figure 18.20(a) shows that there seems to be a clear relationship between a customer's satisfaction score and the number of times the customer was visited for regular servicing. The scatter diagram in Fig. 18.20(b) is less clear. While all customers

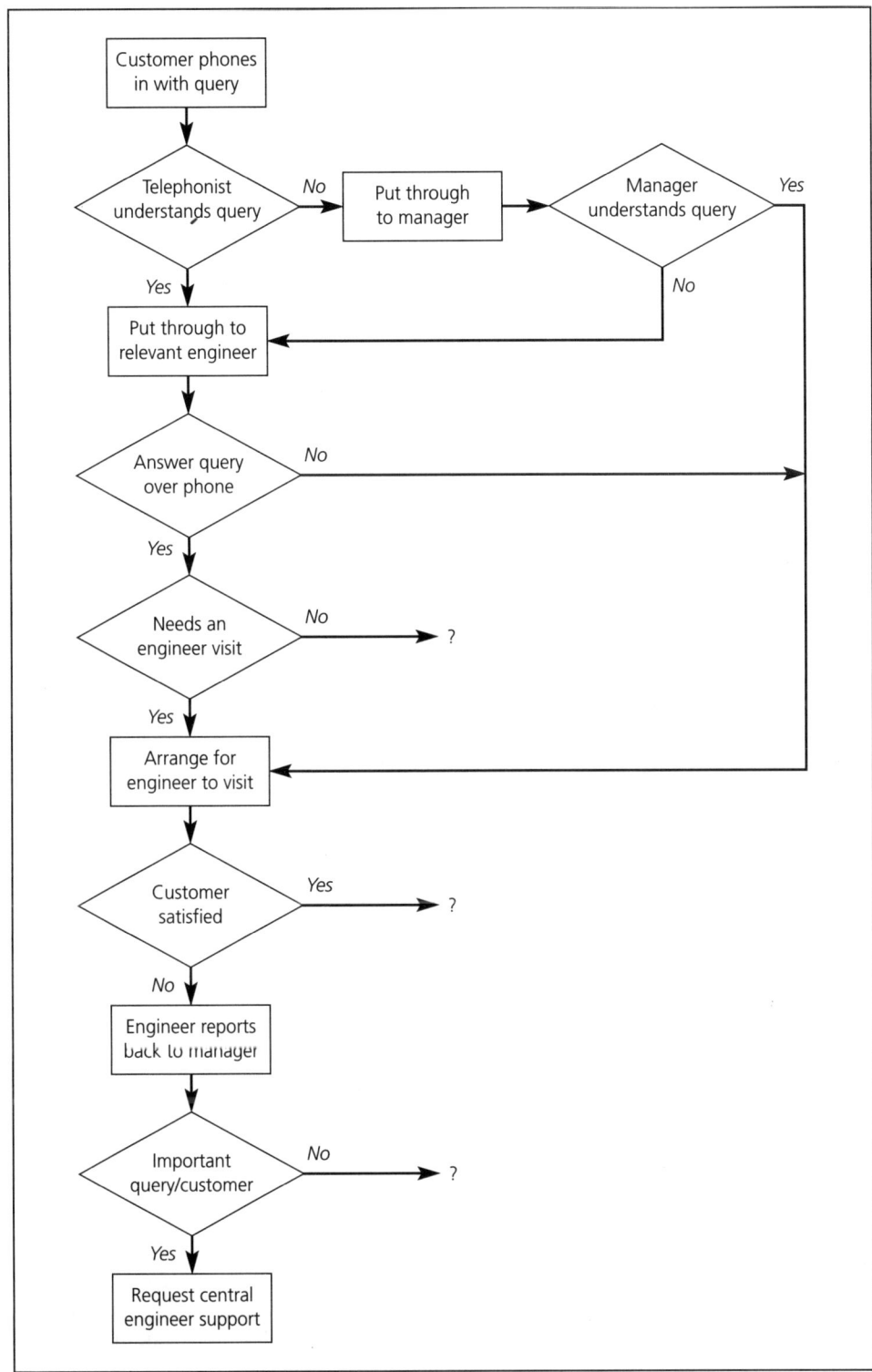

Figure 18.18
Flow chart for
customer query

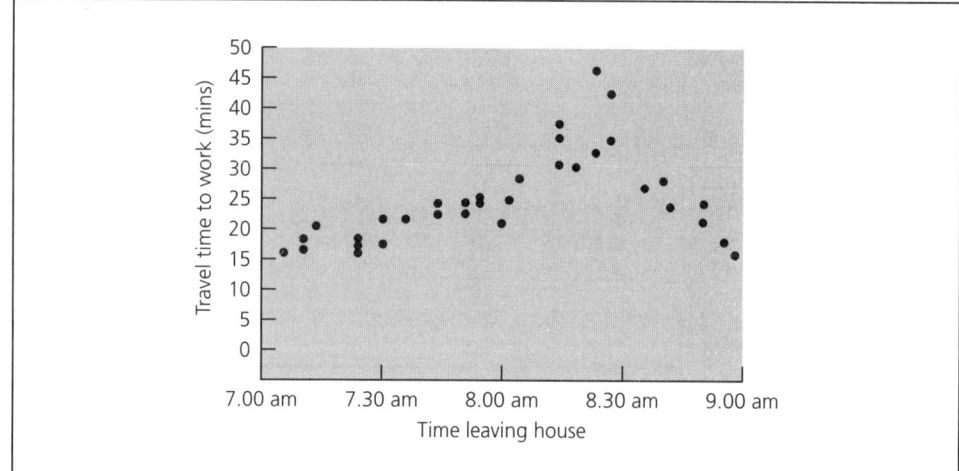

**Figure 18.19
Scatter diagram for
travel time against
departure time**

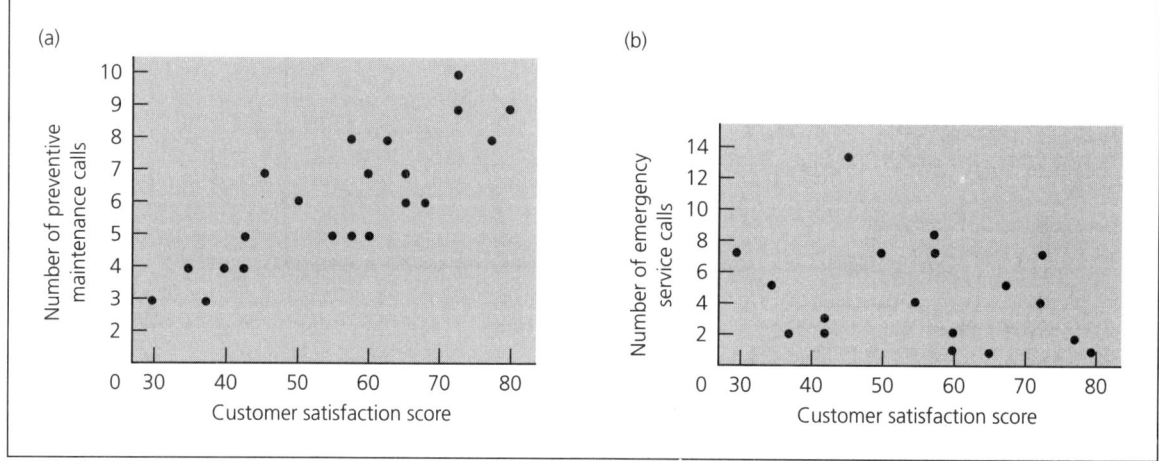

**Figure 18.20   Scatter diagrams for customer satisfaction *versus* (a) number of preventive maintenance calls and
(b) number of emergency service calls**

who had very high satisfaction scores had made very few emergency calls, so had
some customers with low satisfaction scores. As a result of this analysis, the team
decided to survey customers' views on its emergency service.

Cause–effect diagrams

Cause–effect diagrams are a particularly effective method of helping to search for the root
causes of problems. They do this by asking the what, when, where, how and why questions
as before, but this time adding some possible 'answers' in an explicit way. They can also be
used to identify areas where further data is needed. Cause–effect diagrams (which are also
known as 'fish-bone' and 'Ishikawa' diagrams) have become extensively used in improvement programmes. Figure 18.21 shows the general form of the cause–effect diagram.

The procedure for drawing a cause–effect diagram is as follows:

Step 1 State the problem in the 'effect' box.

Step 2 Identify the main categories for possible causes of the problem. Although any categorization can be used for the main branches of the diagram, there are five categories which are commonly used: machinery; manpower; materials; methods and procedures; money.

Step 3 Use systematic fact finding and group discussion to generate possible causes under these categories. Anything which may result in the effect which is being considered should be put down as a potential cause.

Step 4 Record all potential causes on the diagram under each category, and discuss each item in order to combine and clarify causes.

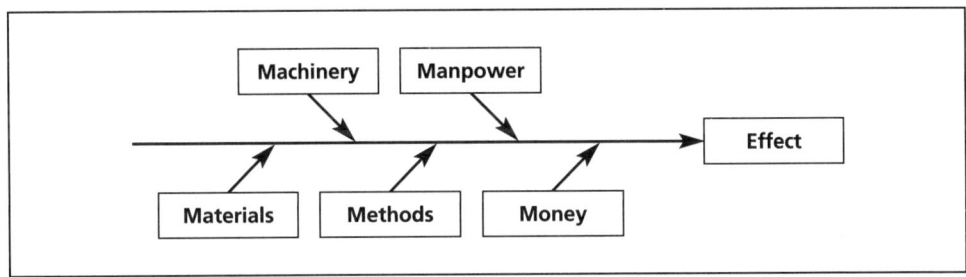

Figure 18.21
Cause–effect diagram

Some tips on using cause–effect diagrams

- Use separate diagrams for each problem. Do not confuse the issue by combining problems on a single diagram.
- Make sure diagrams are visible to everyone involved. Use large sheets of paper with plenty of space between items.
- Do not overload diagrams. Use separate diagrams for each major category on the cause–effect master diagram if necessary.
- Always be prepared to rework, take apart, refine and change categories.
- Take care not to use vague statements such as 'possible lack of'. Rather describe what is actually happening that demonstrates the issues: for example, 'people are not filling out forms properly'.
- Circle causes which seem to be particularly significant.

Example: Kaston Pyral Services Ltd (cont.)

The improvement team at KPS were working on a particular area which was proving a problem. Whenever service engineers were called out to perform emergency servicing for a customer, they took with them the spares and equipment which they thought would be necessary to repair the system. Although engineers could never be sure exactly what materials and equipment they would need for a job, they could guess what was likely to be needed and take a range of spares and equipment which would cover most eventualities. Too often, however, the engineers would find that they needed a spare or piece of equipment which they had not brought with them, and therefore they would have to return to the depot in order to collect it. Worse than that, very occasionally the required spare part would not be in stock, and so the

PROBLEM IDENTIFICATION AT HEWLETT-PACKARD[15]

Hewlett-Packard is proud of its reputation for high-quality products and services. Because of this it was especially concerned with the problems that it was having with its customers returning defective toner cartridges. About 2000 of these were being returned every month. The team suspected that not all the returns were actually the result of a faulty product, which is why the team decided to investigate the problem. The cause–effect diagram which they generated is shown in Fig. 18.22.

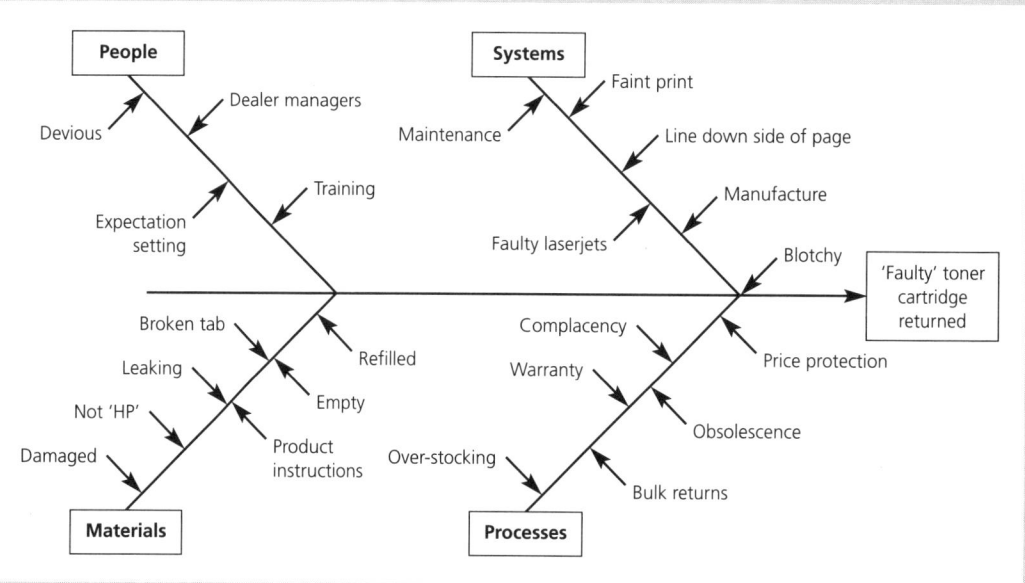

Figure 18.22   Cause–effect diagram for Hewlett Packard's toner analysis

Three major problems were identified. First, some users were not as familiar as they should have been with the correct method of loading the cartridge into the printer, or in being able to solve their own minor printing problems. Second, some of the dealers were also unaware of how to sort out minor problems. Third, there was clearly some abuse of Hewlett-Packard's 'no-questions-asked' returns policy. Empty toner cartridges were being sent to unauthorized refilling companies who would sell the refilled cartridges at reduced prices. Some cartridges were being refilled up to five times and were understandably wearing out. Furthermore, the toner in the refilled cartridges was not up to Hewlett-Packard's high-quality standards. The team went on to use the PDCA sequence of problem solving and made suggestions which tightened up their returns policy as well as improving the way in which customers were instructed on how to use the products. The results were impressive. Complaints in almost all areas shrank to a fraction of what they had been previously. ■

customer would have to wait until it was brought from another part of the country. The cause–effect diagram for this particular problem, as drawn by the team, is shown in Fig. 18.23.

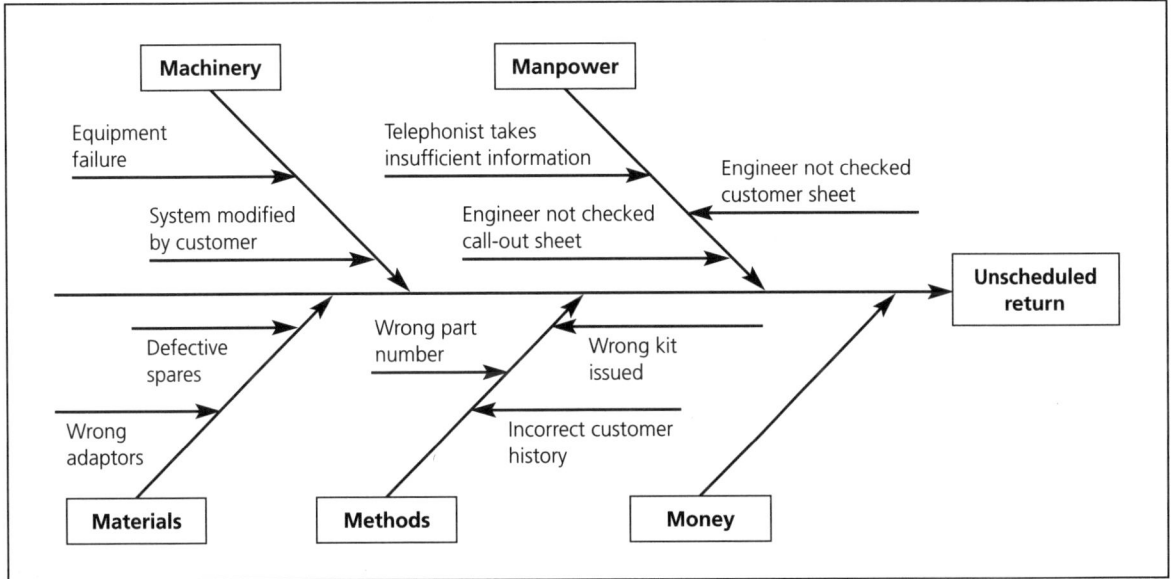

Figure 18.23   Cause–effect diagram of unscheduled returns at KPS

Pareto diagrams

In any improvement process, it is worthwhile distinguishing what is important and what is less so. The purpose of the Pareto analysis, which was introduced in Chapter 12, is to distinguish between the 'vital few' issues and the 'trivial many'. It is a relatively straightforward technique which involves arranging items of information on the types of problem or causes of problem into their order of importance. This can then be used to highlight areas where further decision making will be useful.

Pareto analysis is based on the frequently occurring phenomenon of relatively few causes explaining the majority of effects. For example, most revenue for any company is likely to come from relatively few of the company's customers. Similarly, relatively few of a doctor's patients will probably occupy most of his or her time.

Example: Kaston Pyral Services Ltd (cont.)

The KPS improvement team who were investigating unscheduled returns from emergency servicing (the issue which was described in the cause–effect diagram in Fig. 18.23) examined all occasions over the previous 12 months on which an unscheduled return had been made. They categorized the reasons for unscheduled returns as follows:

1 The wrong part had been taken to a job because, although the information which the engineer received was sound, he had incorrectly predicted the nature of the fault.

2 The wrong part had been taken to the job because there was insufficient information given when the call was taken.

3 The wrong part had been taken to the job because the system had been modified in some way not recorded on KPS's records.

4 The wrong part had been taken to the job because the part had been incorrectly issued to the engineer by stores.

5 No part had been taken because the relevant part was out of stock.

6 The wrong equipment had been taken for whatever reason.

7 Any other reason.

The relative frequency of occurrence of these causes is shown in Fig. 18.24. About a third of all unscheduled returns were due to the first category, and more than half the returns were accounted for by the first and second categories together. It was decided that the problem could best be tackled by concentrating on how to get more information to the engineer which would enable him to predict the causes of failure accurately.

Why–why analysis

We finish on another simple but effective technique for helping to understand the reasons for problems occurring. The technique starts by stating the problem and asking *why* that problem has occurred. Once the major reasons for the problem occurring have been identified, each of the major reasons is taken in turn and again the question is asked *why* those reasons have occurred, and so on. This procedure is continued until either a cause seems sufficiently self-contained to be addressed by itself or no more answers to the question 'Why?' can be generated.

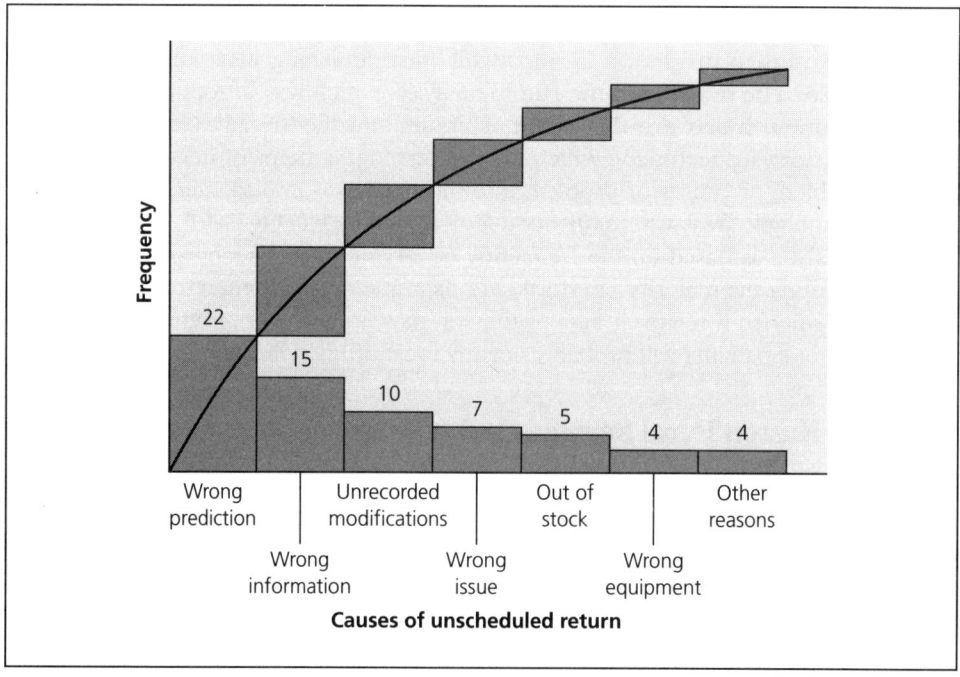

Figure 18.24 Pareto diagram for causes of unscheduled returns

USING PARETO CHARTS AT GOODYEAR[16]

An example of the use of Pareto charts to indicate the priority causes comes from the Goodyear Tyre and Rubber Company.

The manufacture of solvent-based adhesive involves mixing the product in batches. Each batch should contain (say) 30 per cent solids plus or minus a small percentage. The variation derives from 'deviations' in different parts of the process. The causes of deviations from specification are classified and their frequency of occurrence measured. The data are then put in a Pareto form as shown in Fig. 18.25. ■

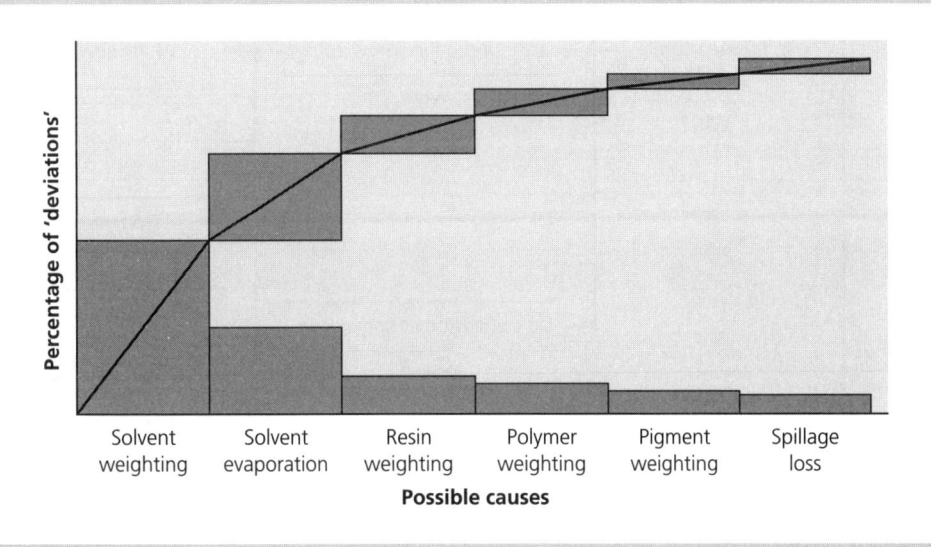

Figure 18.25   Pareto chart of reasons for deviation from required percentage of solids in solvent-based adhesives

Example: Kaston Pyral Services Ltd (cont.)

Figure 18.26 illustrates the general structure of the why–why analysis for the KPS example discussed previously. In this example the major cause of unscheduled returns was the incorrect prediction of reasons for the customer's system failure. This is stated as the problem in the why–why analysis. The question is then asked, why was the failure wrongly predicted? Three answers are proposed: first, that the engineers were not trained correctly; second, that they had insufficient knowledge of the particular product installed in the customer's location; and third, that they had insufficient knowledge of the customer's particular system with its modifications. Each of these three reasons is taken in turn, and the questions are asked, why is there a lack of training, why is there a lack of product knowledge, and why is there a lack of customer knowledge? And so on.

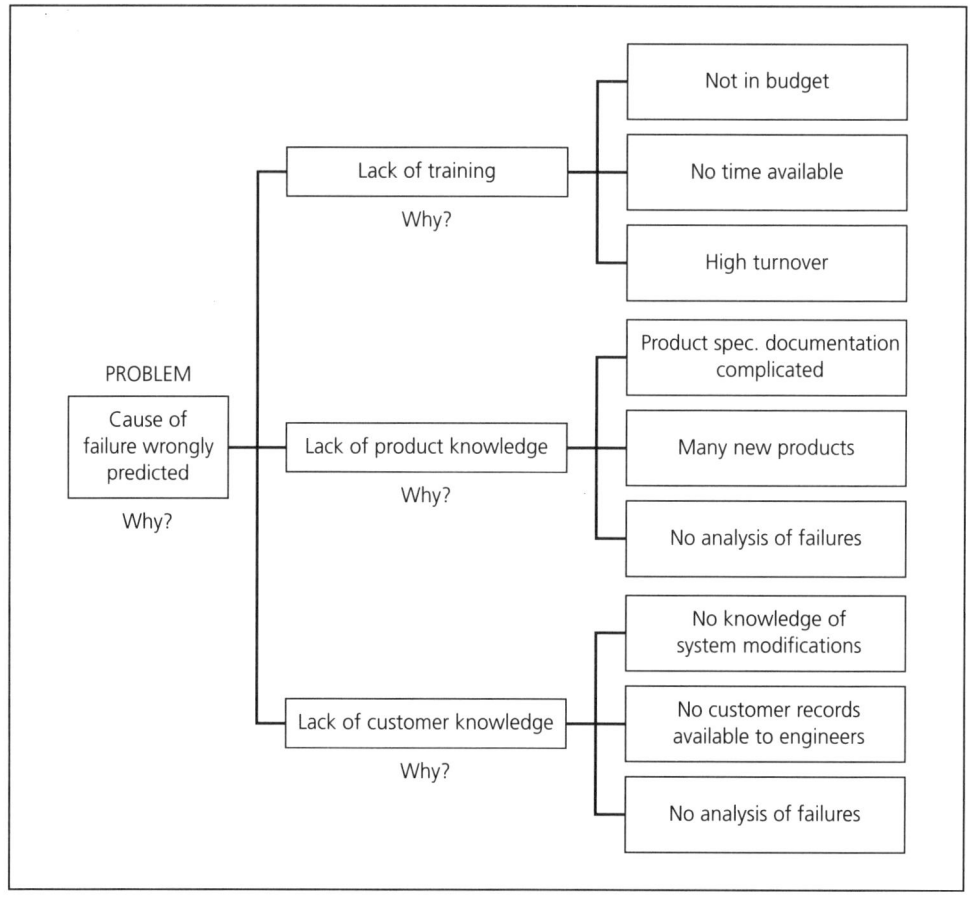

Figure 18.26
Why–why analysis

Charles Wilkins, Lever Pond's, Durban

Lever Pond's South Africa, part of the multinational consumer goods company Unilever, has undertaken a clear manufacturing strategy to improve dramatically operational performance and global manufacturing competitiveness. In order to prosper in today's world of demanding consumers and fierce competition, companies must create value that meets or exceeds the needs and expectations of customers.

'With the re-emergence of South Africa in the 1990s, we as manufacturers found ourselves competing with other manufacturers around the globe, as well as being able for the first time to access new export opportunities', says Lever Pond's Personal Wash Factory Manager, Charles Wilkins. 'We had a proud history of supplying the South African market with the bulk of its toilet and laundry soap needs and we remain market leaders, with well known brands such as Lux and Sunlight. With the socio-political changes in South Africa we naturally wanted to take advantage of new regional opportunities and maximize throughputs through our factory.

'We started with a manufacturing benchmarking process, where key factory management visited major global Unilever factories. We identified key success factors, best proven practices and performance levels required, to determine our improvement priorities. We then did an internal audit and found that, although we had invested in the best technology, our work practices and structures were outdated and skill levels did not match our technology.

'Following a two-year restructuring programme, new structures based on multi-disciplinary teams and fewer management levels were created. Improvement activities were introduced to change shop-floor practices in the areas of quality, continuous improvement, autonomous maintenance and machine maintenance. The idea behind autonomous maintenance is to encourage equipment operators to take responsibility, be accountable and take ownership for the equipment. To improve continually operational performance the international benchmarks were cascaded down each department team. Current performance was measured in terms of plant throughputs, reliability, product costs and annual targets agreed. Performance is continually monitored and visually

displayed at workplaces and then reviewed at weekly team meetings. Engineering and production staff are encouraged to solve problems through the meetings, fault tagging systems or continuous improvement suggestions schemes. They are also taught problem-solving techniques such as "the five whys" and "brainstorming" to get to the root-cause of problems. Technicians and mechanical and process improvement facilitators support the teams.

'Once a year the teams meet to review their performance and, where targets have been met, this is recognized by non-cash awards. New targets are then agreed in the light of the international benchmarks. Comparing ourselves with the best in the world is essential and I believe several of our operations are close to world standards.

'It is through this continual improvement in operational performance and the success of its overall manufacturing strategy, that the Lever Pond's South African soap factory will rank as one of the top-class soap manufacturers. Therefore job number one for everyone at Lever Pond's is to accelerate the improvement process in our factories.' ■

Source: By kind permission of Lever Pond's

SUMMARY

■ Before the performance of any operation can be improved it needs to be measured. This can be done under the headings of the five performance objectives of quality, speed, dependability, flexibility and cost. It is rare, however, for a single simple measure to be used for each performance objective. More usually a 'bundle' of measures, each of which is a partial representation of the performance objective, needs to be used.

■ In order to judge overall performance, each performance measure needs to be set against an appropriate performance standard. There are several ways in which a performance standard can be derived:
– Historical standards compare performance against previous performance.

– Target performance standards compare performance against some negotiated or arbitrary standard of what is considered reasonable.
– Competitor performance standards compare performance against that achieved by competitors.
– Absolute performance standards compare performance to its theoretical best achievable levels.

■ Improvement priorities can be determined by bringing together the relative importance of each competitive factor as judged by customers, with the performance which the operation achieves in each competitive factor, as judged against competitors. An operation's judgement about both importance and performance can be consolidated on to an 'importance–performance matrix'. Different areas on this matrix represent different relative degrees of importance.

■ An organization's approach to improving its operation can be characterized as adopting a position somewhere between the two extremes of 'pure' breakthrough improvement and 'pure' continuous improvement.

■ Breakthrough improvement, which is sometimes called innovation-based improvement, sees the rate of improvement as occurring in a few infrequent but major and dramatic changes. Although such changes can be abrupt and volatile, they often incorporate radical new concepts or technologies which can shift the performance of the operation significantly.

■ Continuous improvement assumes a series of never-ending but smaller incremental improvement steps. This type of improvement is sometimes called kaizen improvement. Continuous improvement is gradual and constant and often utilizes collective group-based problem solving. It does not focus on radical changes but rather attempts to develop an ingrained momentum of improvement.

■ Breakthrough and continuous improvement are not mutually exclusive. Organizations can improve by having occasional radical breakthroughs but utilizing a more incremental approach in between these major changes.

■ The most usual way of modelling continuous improvement is the plan, do, check, act cycle (PDCA cycle), by which the stages of problem solving are seen as forming a never-ending cycle.

■ A typical example of the radical approach to improvement is that of business process re-engineering (BPR) which attempts to redesign operations along a process rather than a functional basis by starting from first principles.

■ There are many techniques which can be used to help in the improvement process, including several which have been treated in other parts of this book.

Chamdor Brewery, South African Breweries

Chamdor Brewery is the fourth largest brewery of the eight breweries operated by South African Breweries. Thanks to systematic use of ultra-modern technology, SAB (now the fourth largest brewer in the world) ranks very high (or to be absolutely precise, very low) in the world listings for costs per hectolitre. Chamdor Brewery produces 200 million litres of beer per annum and produces the most diversified range of products in the SAB Beer Division in terms of brands and packaging. It is therefore characterized by short runs, flexible operations and frequent changes in its packaging units. It supplies four depots with generic beer products and a national supply network with speciality products.

In the early '90s the Chamdor Brewery embarked on a programme of continuous improvement in the packaging hall. More and more evidence is being presented to support the drive to spread a continuous improvement programme to other areas of the brewery. The three-year business plan contained the words, '...*our continuous improvement process has been a high priority for two years and remains so for the entire planning period ... this process is well known in packaging and is now being introduced in brewing and utilities ... the pace of implementation thus far has been slow...*'. Chamdor Brewery has been monitoring the effects over the years and Table 18.3 shows the extent of the improvements in the factory efficiencies of the units at this factory.

The first packaging line to introduce continuous improvement was Unit 2, the line where the greatest improvements have been seen. The internal audit feedback indicated that continuous improvement practices on this line were allowed to slip; it can be seen that the impact was felt on the factory efficiency. In subsequent years the other packaging line introduced improvement activities. Dr Ian Matheson, the Quality Assurance Manager and the person responsible for continuous improvement at Chamdor says, '*our continuous improvement process*

consists of three elements:

- *training and implementation ("where the rubber hits the road!")*
- *development work (job design, end-state analysis, preparation of training material, work instructions and workplace assessment schedules)*
- *conducive enironment (the formation of four levels of production teams – each with defined roles and team leaders; problem-solving at source and communication by means of shop-floor feedback sessions).*

'*One of the cornerstones of our continuous improvement initiative was to identify performance measures which reflect the correct world-class behaviours, which can be directly controlled by the shop-floor teams. One such measure was production reliability – absolute conformance to the production plan with no over- or under-production. This measure introduced at Chamdor has been a strong plus for our continuous improvement initiative.*

Our customers do not only demand reliable services from us; they expect value for money. Our maintenance must therefore not only be effective at reducing breakdowns, it must also be cost effective.'

Figure 18.27 shows the maintenance expenditure trends of the packaging area over the past few years. Included in these costs are all packaging lines, maintenance materials, building maintenance, workshop maintenance, non-scheduled maintenance and the general maintenance account. Unplanned maintenance results from equipment breakdowns, and a ratio of unplanned maintenance hours is a measure used to determine the effectiveness of Chamdor's preventive maintenance. Figure 18.28 traces the ratio, showing how the move from breakdown maintenance to reliability-centred maintenance (RCM) has led to a reduction in breakdowns. This is one of the key success factors of the continuous improvement initiative.

Table 18.3 Improvements in units

Unit \ Year	'91	'92	'93	'94	'95	'96	'97
Unit 2	60	64	73	76	79	77	82
Unit 3	67	68	77	77	79	81	84
Unit 4	60	64	67	68	67	69	72
Packaging hall	62	64	71	72	74	75	77

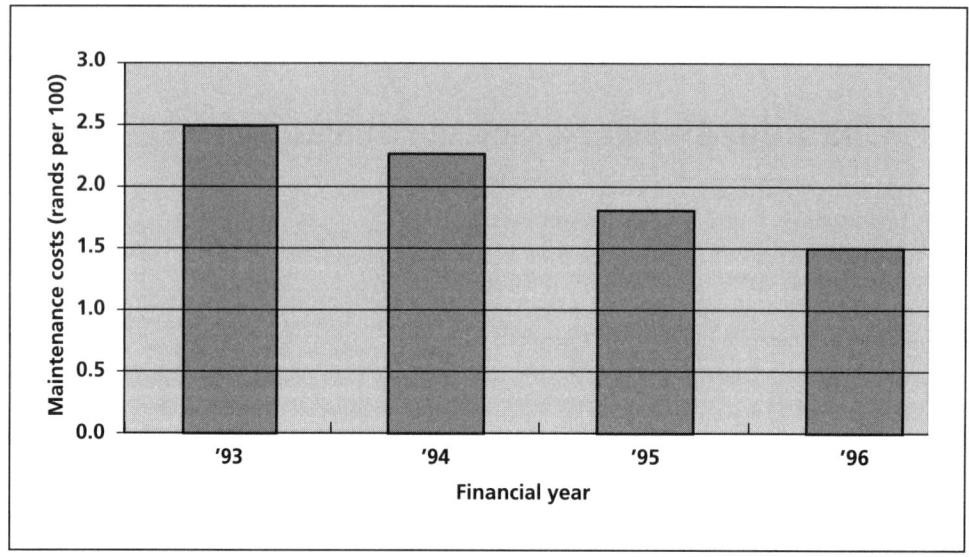

Figure 18.27 Total packaging maintenance costs

The third, and most important, demand placed on the brewery by its customers is for product quality. The end-of-line quality checks are combined into two indicators: product and outer packaging. The product quality has improved well over the last few years and the outer packaging quality has shown a similar improvement, boosted still further by the change from cardboard cartons to plastic crates in 1993. These improvements can be seen in Fig. 18.29. The major factor leading to Chamdor's quality improvement has been the focus on process control started by the improvement implementation programme. Of particular importance was the introduction of inherent process capability and statistical process control (SPC) through operator quality checks.

These were achieved by the introduction of team-based structures and team goals. Performance review was based on team output and collective responsibility. '*We have seen improvements in cost, quality and reliability that are directly attributable to continuous*

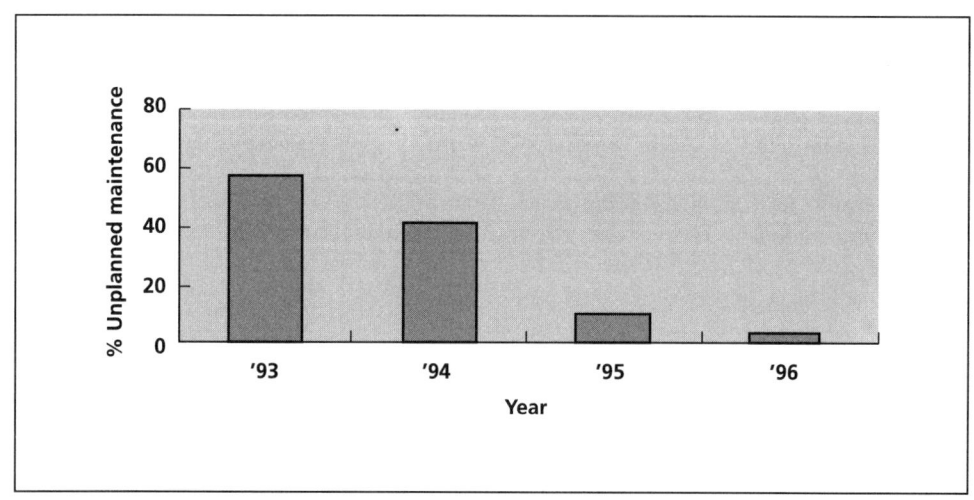

Figure 18.28 Unplanned maintenance as a percentage of total maintenance hours

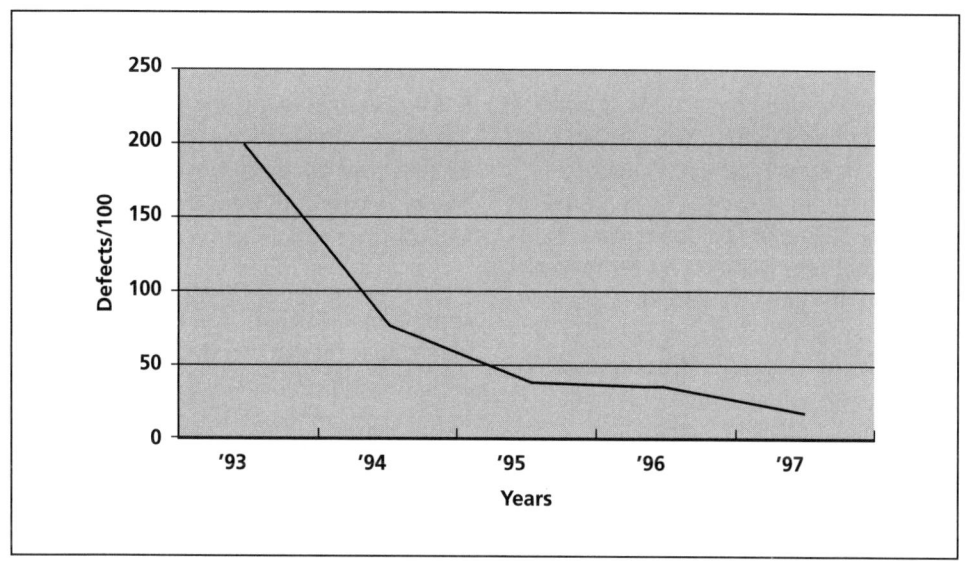

Figure 18.29 The downward trend in defects of outgoing products

improvement,' says Ian. He also asserts that '*These are exactly the elements our customers demand from a world-class manufacturer. Continuous improvement is more than getting the basics right. It involves the selection of the right performance measures to encourage the right behaviours, use of process control techniques on the shopfloor to improve quality, and the implementation of preventive maintenance techniques to prevent breakdowns and assure reliability.'* ■

Questions

1 On what competitive factors would you advise Ian to concentrate if he wished to improve further the competitive performance of his operation?

2 What do you suggest Ian does to sustain this level of improvement?

3 Demonstrate how Chamdor could identify its improvement priorities.

DISCUSSION QUESTIONS

1 A university library wishes to start a performance measurement programme which will enable it to judge the effectiveness with which it organizes its operations. The library loans books to students on both long-term and short-term loans, keeps an extensive stock of journals, will send off for specialist publications to specialist libraries, and has an extensive on-line database facility. What measures of performance do you think it would be appropriate to use in this kind of operation and what type of performance standards should the library adopt?

2 Assess the overall performance of an operation that is familiar to you using a polar diagram. Overlap the operation's performance with what you perceive to be the customers' needs and discuss any differences.

3 Using the five performance measures, list ways in which the performance of a university lecturer could be assessed.

4 Discuss with an operations manager how the performance of the operation is measured. Identify a range of measures and find out whether the targets used are based on historical, target performance, competitor performance or absolute performance standards.

5 List some of the micro operations of a humanitarian organization such as the International Red Cross, the Samaritans or United Nations High Commission for Refugees (UNHCR) and discuss the benefits of it benchmarking its operations. Which operations or micro operations might it be appropriate to benchmark against?

6 A university engineering department has chosen to benchmark itself against other university departments as the first step in an operations improvement process. What kinds of benchmarking do you think might be appropriate for the department, and on what performance objectives do you think it should be focusing?

7 Identify the order winners, qualifiers and less important criteria for an organization of your own choice. Ask a colleague to assess the same organization and compare and discuss your results.

8 Choose an organization and compare it with a competing organization in terms of whether it is better than, the same as, or worse than the competitor. Ask a colleague to undertake the same evaluation and compare and discuss your results.

9 A bank is conducting a survey of all the customer complaints which it has received in its personal loan department. This department deals with the authorization of loans requested by the bank's customers, processes all the information concerning the loans and then sends documents to the customers. Table 18.4 classifies the type of complaints made by customers together with their frequency of occurrence.

Table 18.4

Type of complaint	Frequency of occurrence
Authorization signature omitted	4%
Loan amount omitted	17%
Loan detail errors	12%
Arithmetic error	9%
One or more documents omitted	31%
Inappropriate documents included	2%
Payment details omitted	21%
Others	2%

Draw a Pareto diagram which describes the relative frequency of occurrence of different types of errors. Draw a cause–effect diagram which contains possible reasons for the most important category of error.

10 Explain the differences between breakthrough improvement and continuous improvement. Discuss the advantages and disadvantages of each.

11 List and describe ten modifications that could be made to your course. What breakthrough improvements could be made?

12 Apply the PDCA cycle to your method of preparing for lectures. Describe each part of the cycle and assess the outcome.

13 Briefly explain what is meant by business process re-engineering. Why do you think that BPR is seen as a radical and somewhat formidable approach to improvement by many managers, including many operations managers?

14 Develop cause–effect diagrams for the following types of problem:
– customers waiting too long for their calls to be answered when phoning to order from a mail-order catalogue store;
– poor food in the company restaurant;
– poor lecturing from teaching staff at a university;
– customer complaints that their free plastic toy in the breakfast cereal packet is missing;
– staff having to wait excessively long periods to gain access to the photocopier.

15 Construct a flow chart which identifies the different stages in a customer's complaint being processed in a large retail store. The chart should make sure the complaint is dealt with satisfactorily and the organization learns from this complaint to make sure it never happens again.

16 A computer systems field repair company is considering its operations strategy for its 'quickfit' service. This is a simple service which aims to respond to customer requests in less than two hours and repair or replace the defective part of the system within half an hour of the service engineer arriving at the customer's site. A survey of customers and competitors has given the results shown in Table 18.5.
(a) Demonstrate how the company could identify its improvement priorities for this service.
(b) How would you go about improving the company's performance at delivering this service?

Table 18.5

Performance objective	Importance to customers	Performance against main competitors
On-time arrival	Very important	Better than most competitors
Repair/replace in half-hour	Very important	Same as competitors
Helpfulness of service	Important	Same as competitors
Range of equipment covered by service	Very important	Narrower than most competitors
Helpfulness of HQ staff when making initial contact	Only moderately important	Very much better than competitors

NOTES ON CHAPTER

1 Based on Neely, A. (1993) *Performance Measurement System Design – Theory and Practice*, Manufacturing Engineering Group, Cambridge University, April.

2 Camp, C. (1989) 'Benchmarking: The Search for Best Practices Which Lead to Superior Performance – parts 1 to 5', *Quality Progress*, Jan–May.

3 Pickering, I.M. and Chambers, S. (1991) 'Competitive Benchmarking: Progress and Future Developments', *Computer Integrated Manufacturing Systems*, Vol 4, No 2.

4 Sources: Rogers, B. (1991) 'Benchmarking as a Tool in Rank Xerox's Quality Management Strategies', *Quality Link*, Nov–Dec, and Cross, R. and Leonard, P. (1994) 'Benchmarking: A Strategic and Tactical Perspective' *in* Dale, B. (ed) *Managing Quality* (2nd edn), Prentice Hall.

5 Based on Slack, N. (1994) 'The Importance–Performance Matrix as a Determinant of Improvement Priorities', *International Journal of Operations and Production Management*, Vol 14, No 5, pp 59–75.

6 Source: Houlder, V. (1994) 'Measuring Up to Success', The *Financial Times*, 1 August.

7 De Meyer, A. (1992) *Creating Product Value*, The *Financial Times*/Pitman Publishing.

8 Imai, M. (1986) *Kaizen – The Key to Japan's Competitive Success*, McGraw-Hill.

9 Imai, M., *op. cit.*

10 Based on Wickens, P. (1988) *The Road to Nissan*, Macmillan, and Harrison, A. (1992) *Just-in-time Management in Perspective*, Prentice Hall.

11 Griff, A. (1992) 'Hoping for the Fog on the Tyne to Lift', The *Daily Telegraph*, 23 Nov, quoted in Morrison, S.J. (1994) 'Managing Quality: A Historical Review' *in* Dale, B. (ed) (1994) *Managing Quality* (2nd edn), Prentice Hall.

12 Hammer, M. and Champy, J. (1993) *Re-engineering the Corporation*, Nicholas Brealey Publishing.

13 Hammer, M. (1990) 'Re-engineering Work: Don't Automate, Obliterate', *Harvard Business Review*, Vol 68, No 4.

14 All of this section of this chapter is adapted from Cooke, S. and Slack, N. (1991) *Making Management Decisions* (2nd edn), Prentice Hall.

15 Kowalski, E. and Walley, P. (1993) 'Employee Receptivity to Total Quality', *International Journal of Quality and Reliability Management*, Vol 10, No 1.

16 Miller, D.E. (1987) 'Statistical Process Control Emphasizes Zero Defects', *Adhesive Age*, July.

SELECTED FURTHER READINGS

Codling, S. (1992) *Best Practice Benchmarking*, Industrial Newsletter.

Dale, B.G. (ed) (1994) *Managing Quality* (2nd edn), Prentice Hall.

Evans, J.R. and Lindsay, W.M. (1993) *The Management and Control of Quality*, West.

Faull, N. (1990) 'How Can We Improve Productivity?', *Productivity SA*, Vol 16, No 1, pp 20–5.

Fitzgerald, L., Johnston, R., Brignall, S., Sylvestro, R. and Voss, C. (1991) *Performance Measurement in Service Businesses*, The Chartered Institute of Management Accountants.

Flood, R.L. (1993) *Beyond TQM*, John Wiley.

Oakland, J.S. (1993) *Total Quality Management* (2nd edn), Butterworth-Heinemann.

Phihlela, K.C. (1995) *Total Productive Maintenance: A Case for Autonomous Small Group Activities*, Navorsingsverslag/MBA Research Report, University of the Witwatersrand.

FAILURE PREVENTION AND RECOVERY

INTRODUCTION

Although no operation should be indifferent to failure, in some operations it is vital that products and services do not fail – aeroplanes in flight or electricity supplies to hospitals, for example. Other products and services should always be there when needed, such as car seat belts, the police service and other emergency services. In these situations dependability is not just desirable, it is essential. In less critical situations having dependable products and services is a way organizations can gain a competitive advantage. For example Japanese companies made great gains in market share in automobiles and electrical goods through their reputation for high product reliability.

Operations managers, who are almost always concerned with improving the dependability of their operations and the products and services which they produce, try to have strategies in place which attempt to minimize the likelihood of failure and learn from failure when it does occur. They also need to recognize, however, that failures will occur, in spite of all attempts to prevent them. What is then important is that they have plans in place which help them recover from the failures when they do occur. Figure 19.1 shows how this chapter fits into the operation's improvement activities.

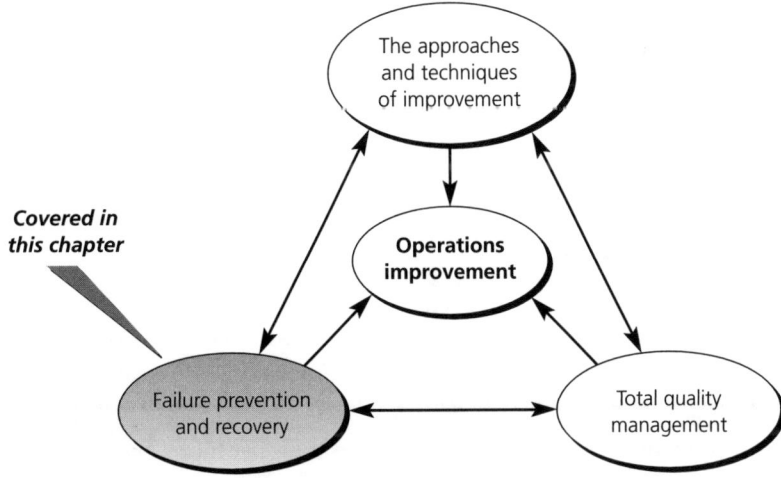

Figure 19.1 Model of operations improvement showing the issues covered in this chapter

---

OBJECTIVES

This chapter will examine:

● why systems fail;

● the various ways in which failure is measured;

● how failure and potential failure is detected and analysed to find its root cause;

● how operations improve their reliability to try to prevent failure – trying to engineer out failure and the maintenance of facilities;

● recovery strategies for dealing with failure – getting it *very* right the second time.

SYSTEM FAILURE

There is always a chance that in making a product or providing a service things might go wrong. Mistakes are inevitable and an intrinsic part of life; nothing is perfect. Accepting that failure will occur is not the same thing as ignoring it, however. Nor does it imply that operations cannot or should not attempt to minimize failure; yet not all failures are equally serious. Some failures are incidental and may not be noticed. In the finale of a concert performance a violinist may play a wrong note and the effect is unlikely to have any great impact. If he or she is giving a solo performance, however, then the error may sour the whole performance. The concert, like all systems, may be more tolerant of some types and some levels of failure than others. For example, if the cigarette lighter in a car or the pen used by a police officer to write a statement fails, the effect may be irritating but not necessarily serious. Conversely, the failure of one component of a system may jeopardize the whole system. For example, leaking hydraulics in a car or a prisoner not informed of his or her rights can put the whole of the process at risk.

Organizations therefore need to discriminate between failures and pay particular attention to those which are critical either in their own right or because they may jeopardize the rest of the operation (*see* box on Hoechst). To do this we need to understand why something fails and be able to measure the impact of the failure.

Why things fail

Failure in an operation can occur for many different reasons. Machines can break down, customers might make unexpected demands which the operation fails to meet, staff may make simple errors in their jobs which prevent normal working, materials from suppliers could be faulty, and so on. Here we classify failures as illustrated in Fig. 19.2:

● those which have their source inside the operation, because its overall design was faulty, or because its facilities (machines, equipment and buildings) or staff fail to operate as they should;

FAILURES PUNCTURE HOECHST'S REPUTATION[1]

The spring of 1993 was not a happy time for Hoechst, the giant German chemical company. For years it had been justly proud of its reputation for safety and environmental protection. The previous year it had spent DM1.3 billion on environmental protection. Then between 22 February and 2 April the company was hit by three serious accidents and 15 less serious safety failures. The first involved the company contaminating part of Frankfurt with 10 tonnes of toxic chemicals. A night-shift operator had neglected to switch on a stirrer in a reaction tank. This resulted in an uncontrollable build-up of pressure which caused the explosion and the resulting pollution. The second accident also involved an explosion and this time one worker was killed and another seriously injured. The final serious incident resulted in several hundred kilograms of fuming sulphuric acid leaking into the environment. All the accidents involved human failure of some sort, although, technically, they were all dissimilar. No single technology failure could be blamed for the trio of disasters. Human failure was also the root cause of the barrage of criticism which Hoechst faced during and after the accidents. Its response was seen by some as being arrogant, disorganized and defensive. Partly because of communication failures, the company's staff underestimated the seriousness, especially of the first accident. To compound the impression of aloofness, the Chairman of the company did not give a press conference or make any statement until ten days after the first accident. By the time of the third serious accident on 2 April the company had learnt some lessons. It immediately made all the board of the company jointly responsible for safety. Even so, a reputation built up over the years had been damaged in a few weeks. ■

- those which are caused by faults in the material or information inputs to the operation;
- those which are caused by the actions of customers.

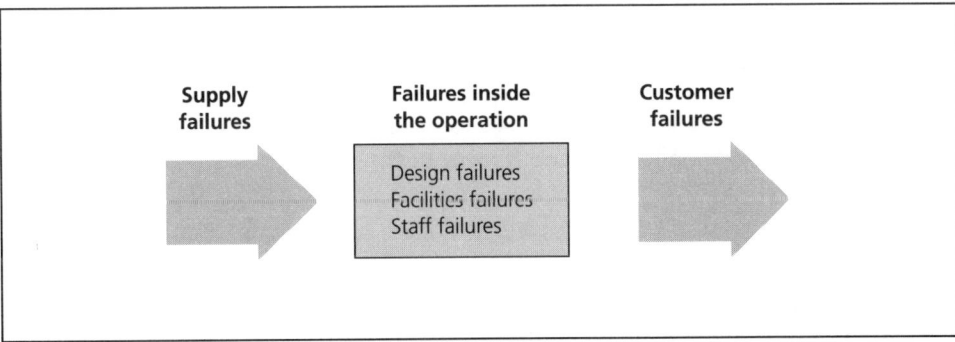

Figure 19.2 Types of failure which can occur in operations

Design failures

The overall design of an operation can prove to be the root cause of failure. In its design stage an operation might look fine on paper; only when it has to cope with real circumstances might inadequacies become evident. Some design failures occur because a characteristic of demand was overlooked or miscalculated. A production line might have been installed in a factory which in practice cannot cope with the demands placed upon it. Alternatively, a theatre front-of-house layout might cause confused and jumbled customer flow at peak times. In both examples there was no unexpected demand placed on the operations; it was straightforward errors in translating the requirements of demand into an adequate design which caused the problems. Other design-related failures occur because the circumstances under which the operation has to work are not as expected. For example, a biscuit production line might have been installed assuming a certain pack size but then the market demands a larger pack size which causes the machine to jam occasionally. The theatre's lighting controls might have been designed for simple lighting sequences, but because it now takes bookings for shows with complex lighting needs, the control system overloads and fails. In both cases the demands placed on the operation were unexpected at the point of design and cause some kind of failure. But they are still design failures (*see* box on the Socrates system). Adequate design includes identifying the range of circumstances under which the operation has to work and designing accordingly.

FAILED PHILOSOPHER[2]

Sleek, fast and smooth, the TGV trains of France's SNCF rail network look more like aircraft than the traditional train. They provide a service which speeds passengers throughout Europe at speeds in excess of 175 mph. Inside, too, the trains show the influence of air travel. Seats are wide and comfortable with space for leg-stretching relaxation. Descriptions in the French press described the TGV as being like 'an airbus on rails'. SNCF also decided to emulate the airlines by buying a high-tech seat reservation and ticketing system which they named after the Greek philosopher Socrates. That was when their problems began. Design flaws in the booking systems software, combined with inadequate training of SNCF staff, caused chaos for months after the system was introduced. Socrates refused to believe in the existence of some places. Suddenly it refused to issue tickets for Rouen or Barcelona, insisting that neither city existed. It also failed at times to recognize the existence of several of the trains which ran between Paris and Lyon. As a result the trains made the trip with only four passengers on board. However, these straightforward system design errors have been compounded by over-complexity of some parts of the system: the automatic ticket-vending machines often stand unused by passengers because they have given up trying to understand how to use them. The graffiti outside the Gare de Lyon station reads 'One hour from Lille to Paris ... one hour to buy a ticket!' Although the problems were eventually sorted out, the reputation of what was essentially a fast and efficient operation took longer to recover. ∎

Facilities failures

All the facilities (that is, the machines, equipment, buildings and fittings) of an operation are liable to break down. The 'breakdown' may only be partial, for example a worn or marked carpet in a hotel, or a machine which can only work at half its normal rate. Alternatively, it can be what we normally regard as a 'failure' – a total and sudden cessation of operation. Either way, it is the effects of a breakdown which are important. Some breakdowns can bring a large part of the operation to a halt. For example, a computer failure in a supermarket chain could paralyse several large stores until it is repaired. Other failures might only have a significant impact if they occur at the same time as other failures. For example, *see* box on air crashes.

TWO MILLION TO ONE[3]

As the number of people travelling by air has grown, the chances of suffering a fatal accident have fallen substantially. Air crashes still do happen, however. Predominantly, the reason for this is not mechanical failure but human failure such as pilot fatigue. Boeing, which dominates the commercial airline business, has calculated that over 60 per cent of all the accidents which have occurred in the past ten years had flight crew behaviour as their 'dominant cause'. In other words, the accidents probably would not have happened had there not been some error by the aircraft's crew.

The chances of an accident are still very small, however. One kind of accident which is known as 'controlled flight into terrain', where the aircraft appears to be under control and yet still flies into the ground, has a chance of happening only *once in two million flights*. For this type of failure to occur a whole chain of minor failures must happen. First, the pilot at the controls has to be flying at the wrong altitude – there is only one chance in a thousand of this. Second, the co-pilot would have to fail to cross-check the altitude – only one chance in a hundred of this. The air traffic controllers would have to miss the fact that the plane was at the wrong altitude (which is not strictly part of their job) – a one-in-ten chance. Finally, the pilot would have to ignore the ground proximity warning alarm in the aircraft (which can be prone to give false alarms) – a one-in-two chance.

Small though the chances of failure are, aircraft manufacturers and airlines are busy working on procedures which make it difficult for aircrew to make any of the mistakes which contribute to fatal crashes. For example, if the chances of the co-pilot failing to check the altitude are reduced to one in 200, and the chances of the pilot ignoring the ground proximity alarm are reduced to one in five, then the chances of this type of accident occurring fall dramatically to one in ten million. ■

Staff failures

People failures come in two types: *errors* and *violations*. 'Errors' are mistakes in judgement; with hindsight, a person should have done something different and the result is some significant deviation from normal operation. For example, if the manager of a sports shop fails to anticipate an increased demand for footballs during the World Cup, the shop will run out of stock and fail to supply its potential customers. This is an error of judgement. 'Violations' are acts which are clearly contrary to defined operating procedure. For example, if a machine operator fails to clean and lubricate his or her machine in the prescribed manner, it is eventually likely to fail. The operator has 'violated' a set procedure.

Supplier failures

Any failure in the delivery or quality of goods and services into an operation can cause failure within the operation. The failure of the band to turn up at a concert will cause the whole event to 'fail'. Similarly, if the band does show but proves to be of dubious talent, the concert could also be regarded as a failure. The more an operation relies on suppliers of materials or services, the more it is liable to failure which is caused by missing or sub-standard inputs.

Customer failures

Not all failures are (directly) caused by the operation or its suppliers. Customers can misuse the products and services which the operation has created. For example, a washing machine might have been manufactured in an efficient and fail-free manner, yet the customer who buys it could overload it or misuse it in some other way which causes it to fail. The customer is not 'always right'. Customers' inattention, incompetence or lack of common sense can be the cause of failure. However, merely complaining about customers is unlikely to reduce the chances of this type of failure occurring. Most organizations will accept that they have a responsibility to educate and train customers and to design their products and services so as to minimize the chances of failure. For example, the sequence of questions at automatic teller machines is designed by banks in such a way as to make their operation as 'fail-free' as possible.

Failure as an opportunity

Notwithstanding our categorization of failure, the origin of all failures is some kind of human failure. A machine failure might have been caused by someone's poor design or maintenance, a delivery failure by someone's errors in managing the supply schedules, and a customer mistake by someone's failure to provide adequate instructions. Failures are not the result of random chance; their root cause is usually human failure. The implications of this are, first, that failure can, to some extent, be controlled and, second, that organizations can learn from failure and modify their behaviour accordingly. The realization of this has led to what is sometimes called the *failure as an opportunity* concept. Rather than identifying a 'culprit' who is to be held responsible and blamed for the failure, failures are regarded as an opportunity to examine why they occurred, and to put in place procedures which eliminate or reduce the probability of them recurring. This is treated further, later in this chapter, when we examine 'failure planning'.

Measuring failure

There are three main ways of measuring failure:

● *failure rates* – how often a failure occurs;
● *reliability* – the chances of a failure occurring;
● *availability* – the amount of available useful operating time.

'Failure rate' and 'reliability' are different ways of measuring the same thing – the propensity of an operation, or part of an operation, to fail. 'Availability' is one measure of the consequences of failure in the operation.

Failure rate

Failure rate is calculated as the number of failures over a period of time. For example, the security of an airport can be measured by the number of security breaches per year, and the failure rate of an engine can be measured in terms of the number of failures divided by its operating time. Failure rate (FR) is usually calculated from examining actual operating or test data. It can be measured either as a percentage of the total number of products tested or as the number of failures over time:

$$FR = \frac{\text{number of failures}}{\text{total number of products tested}} \times 100$$

or

$$FR = \frac{\text{number of failures}}{\text{operating time}}$$

Example

A batch of 50 electronic components is tested for 2000 hours. Four of the components fail during the test as follows:

Failure 1	occurred at 1200 hours
Failure 2	occurred at 1450 hours
Failure 3	occurred at 1720 hours
Failure 4	occurred at 1905 hours

$$\text{Failure rate (as a percentage)} = \frac{\text{number of failures}}{\text{number tested}} \times 100 = \frac{4}{50} \times 100 = 8\%$$

The total time of the test $= 50 \times 2000 = 100\,000$ component hours

But

one component was not operating $2000 - 1200 = 800$ hours
one component was not operating $2000 - 1450 = 550$ hours
one component was not operating $2000 - 1720 = 280$ hours
one component was not operating $2000 - 1905 = 95$ hours

Thus:

Total non-operating time $= 1725$ hours

$$\begin{aligned}
\text{Operating time} &= \text{total time} - \text{non-operating time} \\
&= 100\,000 - 1725 \quad = 98\,275 \text{ hours}
\end{aligned}$$

$$\text{Failure rate (in time)} = \frac{\text{number of failures}}{\text{operating time}} = \frac{4}{98\,275}$$

$$= 0.000041$$

Failure over time – the 'bath-tub' curve

Failure, for most parts of an operation, is a function of time. At different stages during the life of anything the probability of it failing will be different. The probability of, for example, an electric lamp failing is relatively high when it is first plugged in. Any small defect in the material from which the filament is made or in the way the lamp was assembled could cause the lamp to fail. If the lamp survives this initial stage it could still fail at any point, but the longer it survives, the more likely its failure becomes. Most physical parts of an operation behave in a similar manner.

The curve which describes failure probability of this type is called the *bath-tub curve*. It comprises three distinct stages:

● the 'infant-mortality' or 'early-life' stage, where early failures occur caused by defective parts or improper use;

● the 'normal-life' stage, when the failure rate is usually low and reasonably constant, and caused by normal random factors;

● the 'wear-out' stage, when the failure rate increases as the part approaches the end of its working life and failure is caused by the ageing and deterioration of parts.

Figure 19.3 illustrates two bath-tub curves with slightly different characteristics. Curve A shows a part of the operation which has a high initial infant-mortality failure but then a long, low-failure, normal life followed by the gradually increasing likelihood of failure as it approaches wear-out. Curve B has roughly the same relative infant-mortality, normal-life and wear-out stages. It differs markedly, however, in the predictability with which failure occurs. Curve A shows a part with very predictable failure characteristics. If it survives infant mortality (that is past time x) it is very likely to survive at least until wear-out starts (at time y). However, after time y its chances of survival rapidly diminish. Curve B, on the other hand, shows a part which is far less predictable. The distinction between the three stages is less clear, with infant-mortality failure subsiding only slowly and a gradually increasing chance of wear-out failure.

Facilities with failure curves similar to that shown in curve B are far more difficult to maintain in a planned manner, as will be discussed later.

**Figure 19.3
Bath-tub curves for
two parts of an
operation. Curve A
represents a part
with relatively
predictable failure
and curve B repre-
sents a part with a
more random
failure pattern**

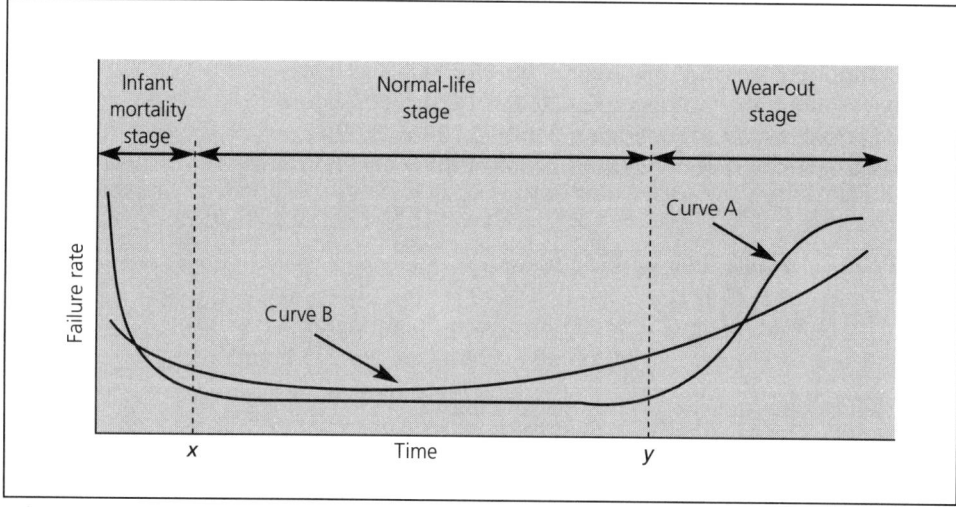

The failure of operations which rely more on human resources than on technology, such as some services, can follow a somewhat different curve. They may be less susceptible to component wear-out but more susceptible to staff complacency as the service, without review and regeneration, may become tedious and repetitive. In such a case there is an initial stage of failure reduction, equivalent to the infant-mortality stage, as problems in the service are ironed out. This may be followed by a long period of increasing failure (*see* Fig. 19.4).

Reliability

Reliability measures the ability of a system, product or service to perform as expected over time.

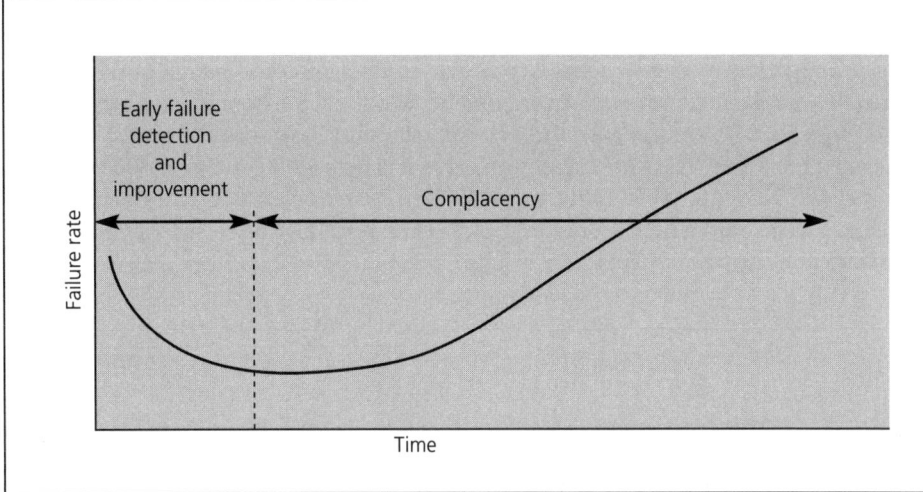

Figure 19.4
Service operations, after an early stage of failure detection and improvement, may suffer from steadily rising failure rates caused by increasing complacency

The importance of any particular failure is determined partly by the effect it has on the performance of the whole operation or system. This in turn depends on the way in which the parts of the system which are liable to failure are related. If components in a system are all interdependent, a failure in any individual component will cause the whole system to fail. For example, if an interdependent system has n components each with their own reliability R_1, R_2 ------ R_n, the reliability of the whole system, R_s, is given by:

$$R_s = R_1 \times R_2 \times R_2 \times \text{------} R_n$$

where

R_1 = reliability of component 1
R_2 = reliability of component 2
etc.

Example

An automated pizza-making machine in a food manufacturer's factory has five major components, with individual reliabilities (the probability of the component not failing) as follows:

Dough mixer	Reliability = 0.95
Dough roller and cutter	Reliability = 0.99
Tomato paste applicator	Reliability = 0.97
Cheese applicator	Reliability = 0.90
Oven	Reliability = 0.98

If one of these parts of the production system fails, the whole system will stop working. Thus the reliability of the whole system is:

$$R_s = 0.95 \times 0.99 \times 0.97 \times 0.90 \times 0.98$$
$$= 0.805$$

The number of components

In the example above, the reliability of the whole system was only 0.8, even though the reliability of the individual components was significantly higher. If the system had been made up of more components, then its reliability would have been even lower. The more interdependent components a system has, the lower its reliability will be. Figure 19.5 shows the reduction in system reliability as the number of components in the system increases. For a system composed of components which each have an individual reliability of 0.99, with 10 components the system reliability has shrunk to 0.9, with 50 components it is below 0.8, with 100 components it is below 0.4, and with 400 components it is down below 0.05. In other words, with a system with 400 components (not unusual in a large automated operation), even if the reliability of each individual component is 99 per cent, the whole system will be working for less than 5 per cent of its time.

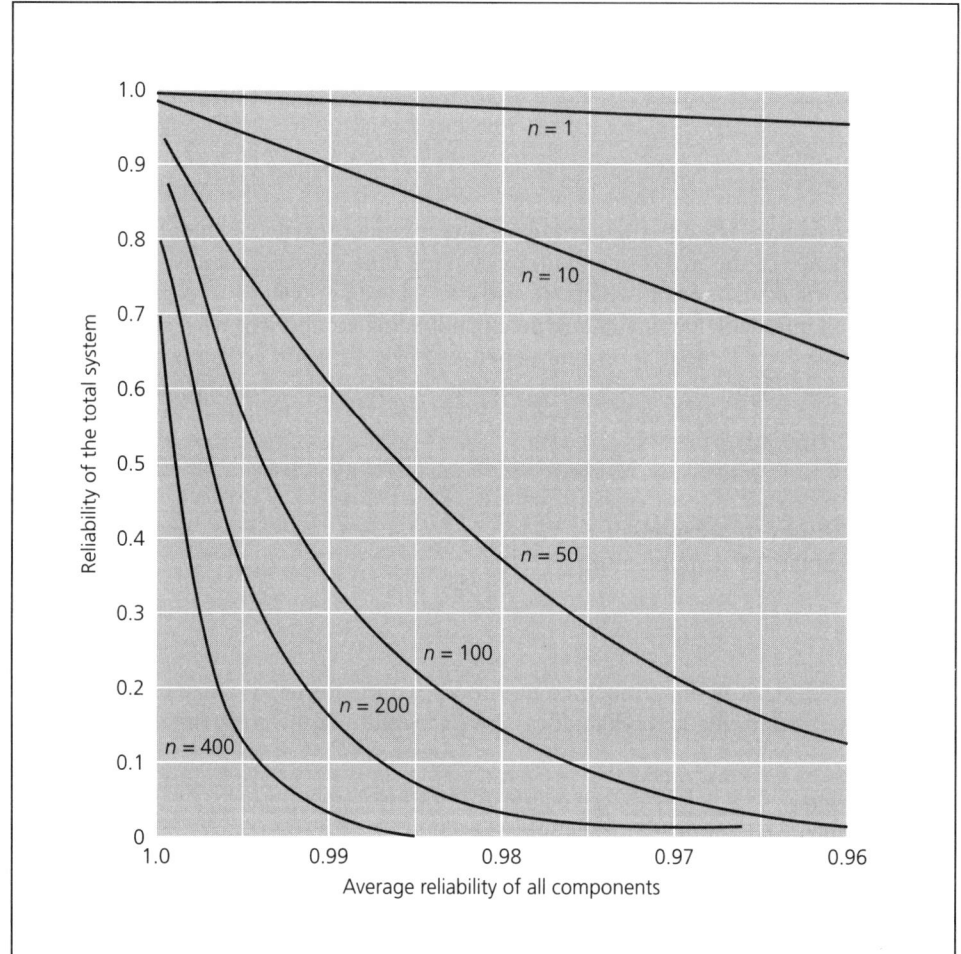

Figure 19.5
The effect of the number of components in a system (*n*) on the reliability of the total system

Mean time between failure

An alternative (and common) measure of failure is the *mean time between failure* (MTBF) of a component or system.

MTBF is the reciprocal of failure rate (in time). Thus:

$$\text{MTBF} = \frac{\text{operating hours}}{\text{number of failures}}$$

Example

In the previous example, which was concerned with electronic components, the failure rate (in time) of the electronic components was 0.000041. For that component:

$$\text{MTBF} = \frac{1}{0.000041} = 24\ 390.24 \text{ hours}$$

That is, a failure can be expected once every 24 390.24 hours on average.

Availability

Availability is the degree to which the operation is ready to work. An operation is not available if it has either failed or is being repaired following failure.

There are several different ways of measuring availability depending on how many of the reasons for not operating are included. Lack of availability because of planned maintenance or change-overs could be included, for example. However, when 'availability' is being used to indicate the operating time excluding the consequence of failure, it is calculated as follows:

$$\text{Availability (A)} = \frac{\text{MTBF}}{\text{MTBF} + \text{MTTR}}$$

where

MTBF = the mean time between failure of the operation
MTTR = the mean time to repair, which is the average time taken to repair the operation, from the time it fails to the time it is operational again.

Example

A company, which designs and produces display posters for exhibitions and sales promotion events, competes largely on the basis of its speedy delivery. One particular piece of equipment which the company uses is causing some problems. This is its large platform colour laser printer. Currently, the mean time between failures of the printer is 70 hours and its mean time to repair is six hours.

$$\text{Availability} = \frac{70}{70 + 6} = 0.92$$

The company has discussed its problem with the supplier of the printer who has offered two alternative service deals. One option would be to buy some preventive maintenance (*see* later for a full description of preventive maintenance) which would be carried out each weekend. This would raise the MTBF of the printer to 90 hours. The other option would be to subscribe to a faster repair service which would reduce the MTTR to four hours. Both options would cost the same amount. Which would give the company the higher availability?

With MTBF increased to 90 hours:

$$\text{Availability} = \frac{90}{90 + 6} = 0.938$$

With MTTR reduced to four hours:

$$\text{Availability} = \frac{70}{70 + 4} = 0.946$$

Availability would be greater if the company took the deal which offered the faster repair time.

Failure prevention and recovery

In practical terms, operations managers have three sets of activities which relate to failure. The first is concerned with understanding what failures are occurring in the operation and why they are occurring. Once the nature of any failures is understood, an operations manager's second task is to examine ways of either reducing the chances of failure or minimizing the consequences of failure. The third task is to devise plans and procedures which help the operation to recover from failures when they do occur. The first of these tasks is, in effect, a prerequisite for the other two (*see* Fig. 19.6). The remainder of this chapter deals with these three tasks.

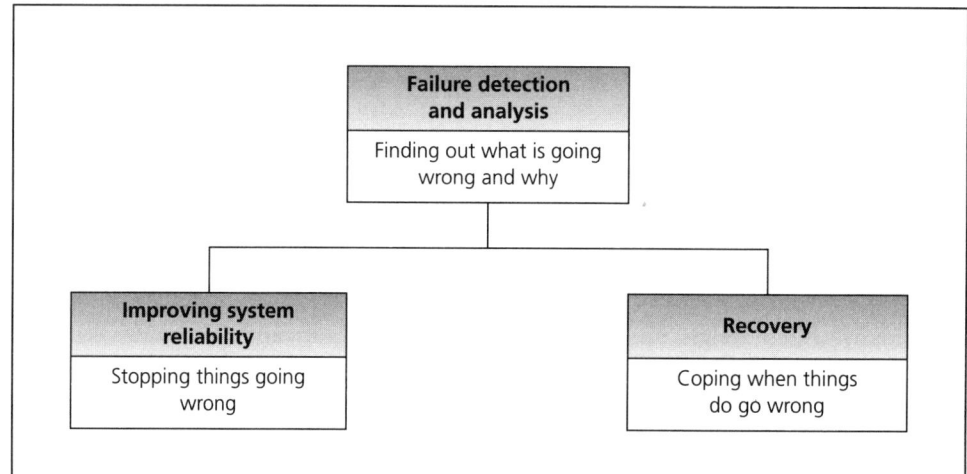

Figure 19.6
The three tasks of failure prevention and recovery

FAILURE DETECTION AND ANALYSIS

Given that failures will occur, operations managers must first have mechanisms in place which ensure that they are aware that a failure has occurred and, second, have procedures in place which analyse the failure to find out its root cause.

Mechanisms to detect failure

Organizations sometimes may not be aware that the system has failed and thereby lose the opportunity both to put things right for the customer and to learn from the experience. Customers dissatisfied with the food or the service at a restaurant are very likely to 'vote with their feet' and tell all their friends about the poor experience rather than complain to the management at the time. When customers do complain about a product or a service, the situation may be dealt with on the spot but the system may not be changed to prevent such problems occurring again. This may be due to staff fearing that drawing attention to a problem might be seen to be a sign of weakness or lack of ability, or because there are inadequate failure identification systems, or a lack of managerial support or interest in making improvements.

Many mechanisms are available to seek out failures in a proactive way.

- *In-process checks*. Employees check that the service is acceptable during the process itself. This is often undertaken in restaurants, for example ('Is everything alright with your meal, madam?'), although in some situations this form of failure detection can detract from the service itself.
- *Machine diagnostic checks*. A machine is tested by putting it through a prescribed sequence of activities designed to expose any failures or potential failures. Computer servicing procedures often include this type of check.
- *Point-of-departure interviews*. At the end of a service, staff may formally or informally check that the service has been satisfactory and try to solicit problems as well as compliments.
- *Phone surveys*. These can be used to solicit opinions about products or services. Television rental companies, for example, may check on the installation and servicing of equipment in this way.
- *Focus groups*. These are groups of customers who are asked together to focus on some aspects of a product or service. These can be used to discover either specific problems or more general attitudes towards the product or service.
- *Complaint cards or feedback sheets*. These are used by many organizations to solicit views about the products and services. The problem here is that very few people tend to complete them. It may be possible, however, to identify the respondents and so follow up on any individual problem.
- *Questionnaires*. These may generate a slightly higher response than complaint cards. They may only generate general information, however, from which it is difficult to identify specific individual complaints.

Failure analysis

One of the critical activities for an organization when failure has occurred is to understand why the failure occurred. This activity is called *failure analysis*. There are many different techniques and approaches which are used to uncover the root cause of failures. Some of these were described in the final part of the previous chapter. Some others are briefly described in this section.

Accident investigation

Large-scale national disasters like oil tanker spillages and aeroplane accidents are usually investigated by accident investigators specifically trained in the detailed analysis of the causes of the accident. Although the techniques they use have usually been developed to be appropriate for the particular type of accident being investigated, the common role of the accident investigators is to make recommendations to minimize or even eradicate the likelihood of any such failures occurring again.

Product liability

Many organizations (either by choice or more often because of a legal requirement) adopt 'product liability'. This ensures that all their products are traceable. Any failures can be traced back to the process which produced them, the components from which they were produced, or the suppliers who provided them. This means that any fault can be rectified and also that, if necessary, all other similar products can be recalled for checking. This is sometimes seen when car and electrical components or food items are recalled.

Complaint analysis

Complaints, just like errors, will always arise. They are increasingly seen to be a cheap and easily available source of information about errors. Complaints, and indeed compliments, need to be taken seriously as they are likely to represent only the 'tip of the iceberg' of customer attitudes. In some service operations it is believed that for every person who complains there are another 20 who have not. Two key advantages of complaints is that they come unsolicited and also they are often very timely pieces of information that can pin-point problems quickly within an organization. Complaint analysis also involves tracking the actual number of complaints over time, which can in itself be indicative of developing problems. The prime function of complaint analysis involves analysing the 'content' of the complaints to understand better the nature of the problem as it is perceived by the customer.

Critical incident analysis

Critical incident analysis simply requires customers to identify the elements of products or services that they found either particularly satisfying or not particularly satisfying. They are asked to write down incidents which gave them cause for dissatisfaction or satisfaction. The transcript of this anecdotal evidence is then analysed in detail for factors, traits and causes of the satisfaction and dissatisfaction. These causes can then be categorized and linked to possible causes of failure. It is a popular way of collecting information, especially in service operations. The critical incident technique (CIT) was originally developed during the Second World War by psychologist John Flanagan and was used to determine the reasons for the high rate of pilot failure during training. The analysis of his tests provided the basis for pilot selection tests that achieved a substantial reduction in failure rate. Flanagan[4] defined CIT as 'essentially a procedure for gathering certain important facts concerning behaviour in defined situations'. This technique has been applied to many different service industries, including hotels, banks and airlines.

Failure mode and effect analysis

The objective of failure mode and effect analysis (FMEA) is to identify the product or service features that are critical to various types of failure. It is a means of identifying failures before they happen by providing a 'checklist' procedure which is built round three key questions.

For each possible cause of failure:

- What is the likelihood that failure will occur?
- What would the consequence of the failure be?
- How likely is such a failure to be detected before it affects the customer?

Based on a quantitative evaluation of these three questions, a *risk priority number* (RPN) is calculated for each potential cause of failure. Corrective actions, aimed at preventing failure, are then applied to those causes whose RPN indicates that they warrant priority.

It is essentially a seven-step process:

Step 1 Identify all the component parts of the products or service.
Step 2 List all the possible ways in which the components could fail (the failure modes).
Step 3 Identify the possible effects of the failures (down-time, safety, repair requirements, effects on customers).
Step 4 Identify all the possible causes of failure for each failure mode.
Step 5 Assess the probability of failure, the severity of the effects of failure and the likelihood of detection.
Step 6 Calculate the RPN by multiplying all three ratings together.
Step 7 Instigate corrective action which will minimize failure on failure modes which show a high RPN.

Fault-tree analysis

This is a logical procedure that starts with a failure or a potential failure and works backwards to identify all the possible causes and therefore the origins of that failure. The *fault tree* is made up of branches connected by two types of nodes: *AND nodes* and *OR nodes*. The branches below an AND node all need to occur for the event above the node to occur. Only one of the branches below an OR node needs to occur for the event above the node to occur.

Figure 19.7 shows a simple tree identifying the possible reasons for a hot dish being served cold in a restaurant.

IMPROVING THE OPERATION'S RELIABILITY

Once a thorough understanding of the causes and effects of failure have been established, the next responsibility of operations managers is to try to prevent the failures occurring in the first place. They can do this in a number of ways:

- designing out the fail points in the operation;
- building redundancy into the operation;
- 'fail-safing' some of the activities in the operation;
- maintenance of the physical facilities in the operation.

We will examine each of these, but especially the maintenance of physical facilities (equipment, machines and buildings) which is an important activity in all operations.

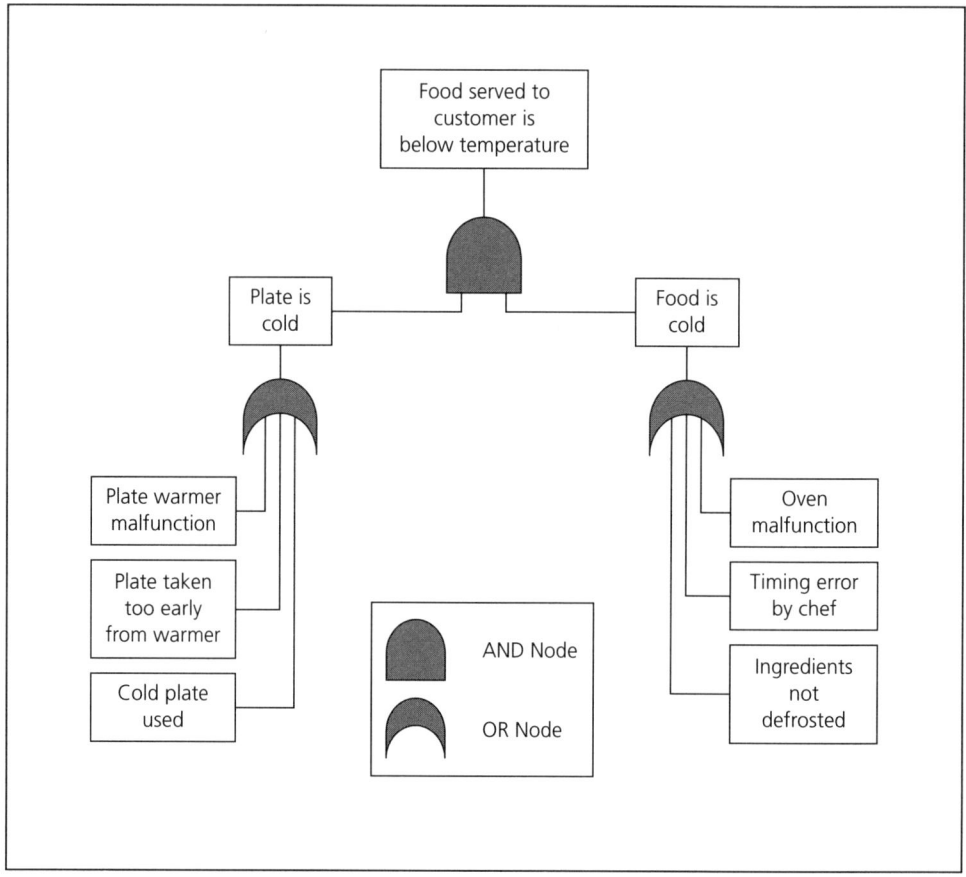

**Figure 19.7
Fault-tree analysis
for below
temperature food
being served to
customers**

Designing out fail points

Chapter 5 on product/service design and Chapter 17 on quality planning and control were concerned with identifying and then controlling product and service characteristics to try to prevent failures occurring. In particular, Chapter 17 described the use of process control charting to try to detect when a process was going out of control so that action could be taken before failures occurred.

All the process flow design methods described in Chapter 5 can be used to 'engineer out' the potential fail points in operations. For example, Fig. 19.8 shows a process flow chart for an automobile repair process. The stages in the process which are particularly prone to failure and the stages which are critical to the success of the service have been marked. This will have been done by the staff of this operation metaphorically 'walking themselves through' the process and discussing each stage in turn.

Redundancy

Building in redundancy to an operation means having back-up systems or components in case of failure. It can be an expensive solution to reduce the likelihood of failure and is generally used when the breakdown could have a critical impact. Redundancy means doubling

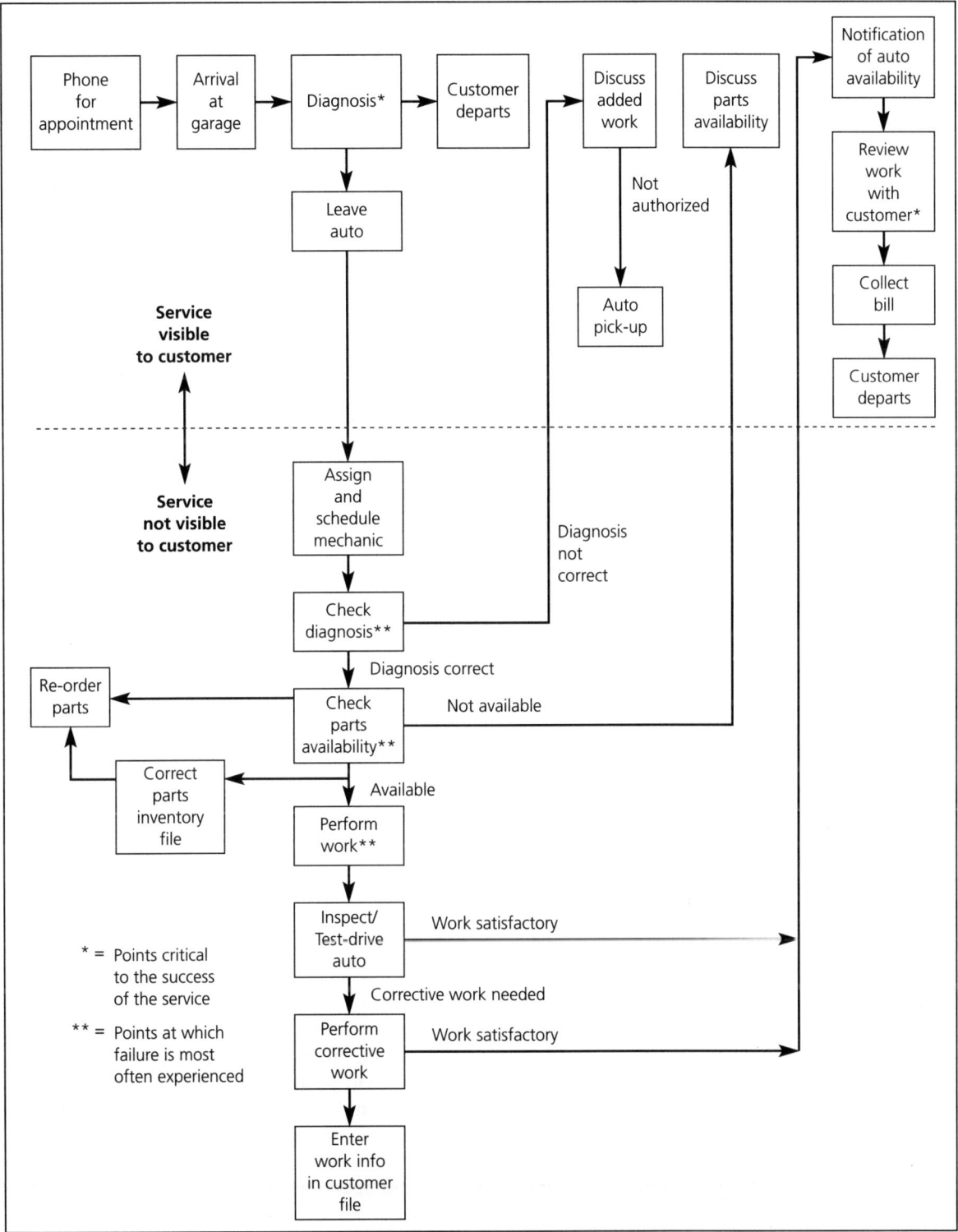

Figure 19.8 A process flow diagram for the auto repair process

or even tripling some of the components in a system so that these 'redundant' elements can come into action when one component fails. Nuclear power stations, hospitals and other public buildings have auxiliary or back-up electricity generators ready to operate in case the main electricity supply should fail. Some organizations also have 'back-up' staff held in reserve in case someone does not turn up for work or is held up on one job and is unable to move to the next. This is done by railways, theme parks and hospitals, for example.

Some 'redundant' components may be used all the time to reduce the likelihood of total failure. Spacecraft have several back-up computers on board that will not only monitor the main computer but will also act as a back-up in case of failure. Rear brake lighting sets built into the back of buses and lorries contain two bulbs to reduce the likelihood of showing no red light at the rear. Human bodies contain two of some organs – kidneys and eyes, for example – both of which are used in 'normal operation' but the body can cope with a failure in one of them.

The reliability of a component together with its back-up is given by the sum of the reliability of the original component and the likelihood that the back-up component will both be needed *and* be working.

$$R_{a+b} \quad = R_a + (R_b \times P \text{ (failure)})$$

where

R_{a+b} = reliability of component a with its back-up component b
R_a = reliability of a alone
R_b = reliability of back-up component b
P (failure) = the probability that component a will fail and therefore component b will be needed

Example

The food manufacturer in the earlier worked example has decided that the cheese depositor in the pizza-making machine is so unreliable that it needs a second cheese depositor to be fitted to the machine which will come into action if the first cheese depositor fails.

The two cheese depositors (each with reliability = 0.9) working together will have a reliability of:

$$0.9 + (0.9 \times (1 - 0.9)) = 0.99$$

The reliability of the whole machine is now:

$$0.95 \times 0.99 \times 0.97 \times 0.99 \times 0.98 = 0.885$$

Fail-safeing

The concept of fail-safeing has emerged since the introduction of Japanese methods of operations improvement. Called *poka-yoke* in Japan (from *yokeru* (to prevent) and *poka* (inadvertent errors)), the idea is based on the principle that human mistakes are to some extent inevitable. What is important is to prevent them becoming defects. Poka-yokes are simple (preferably inexpensive) devices or systems which are incorporated into a process to prevent inadvertent operator mistakes resulting in a defect.

Typical poka-yokes are such devices as:

● limit switches on machines which allow the machine to operate only if the part is positioned correctly;

- gauges placed on machines through which a part has to pass in order to be loaded on to, or taken off, the machine – an incorrect size or orientation stops the process;
- digital counters on machines to ensure that the correct number of cuts, passes or holes have been machined;
- checklists which have to be filled in, either in preparation for or on completion of an activity;
- light beams which activate an alarm if a part is positioned incorrectly.

More recently, the principle of fail-safeing has been applied to service operations. Professor Dick Chase and Douglas Stewart of the University of Southern California have collected examples of many service poka-yokes which they classify as those which 'fail-safe the server' (the creator of the service) and those which 'fail-safe the customer' (the receiver of the service).[5]

Examples of fail-safeing the server include:

- colour coding cash register keys to prevent incorrect entry in retail operations;
- the McDonald's french-fry scoop which picks up the right quantity of fries in the right orientation to be placed in the pack;
- trays used in hospitals with indentations shaped to each item needed for a surgical procedure – any item not back in place at the end of the procedure might have been left in the patient;
- the paper strips placed round clean towels in hotels, the removal of which helps housekeepers to tell whether a towel has been used and therefore needs replacing.

Examples of fail-safeing the customer include:

- the locks on aircraft lavatory doors, which must be turned to switch the light on;
- beepers on ATMs to ensure that customers remove their cards;
- height bars on amusement rides to ensure that customers do not exceed size limitations;
- outlines drawn on the walls of a child-care centre to indicate where toys should be replaced at the end of the play period;
- tray stands, strategically placed in fast-food restaurants to remind customers to clear their tables.

Maintenance

Maintenance is the term used to cover the way in which organizations try to avoid failure by taking care of their physical facilities. It is an important part of most operations' activities, especially those whose physical facilities play a central role in creating their goods and services. In such operations as power stations, hotels, airlines and petro-chemical refineries, maintenance activities will account for a significant proportion of operations management's time, attention and resources.

The benefits of maintenance

Before examining the various approaches to maintenance, it is worth considering why operations bother to care for their facilities in a systematic manner.

- *Enhanced safety*. Well maintained facilities are less likely to behave in an unpredictable or non-standard way, or fail outright, all of which could pose a hazard to staff.

- *Increased reliability.* This leads to less time lost while facilities are repaired, less disruption to the normal activities of the operation, less variation in output rates and more reliable service levels.
- *Higher quality.* Badly maintained equipment is more likely to perform below standard and cause quality errors.
- *Lower operating costs.* Many pieces of process technology run more efficiently when regularly serviced: motor vehicles, for example.
- *Longer life span.* Regular care, cleaning or lubrication can prolong the effective life of facilities by reducing the small problems in operation whose cumulative effect causes wear or deterioration.
- *Higher end value.* Well maintained facilities are generally easier to dispose of into the second-hand market.

The three basic approaches to maintenance

In practice an organization's maintenance activities will consist of some combination of the three basic approaches to the care of its physical facilities. These are *run to breakdown* (RTB), *preventive maintenance* (PM) and *condition-based maintenance* (CBM).

Run to breakdown (RTB)

As its name implies, this approach involves allowing the facilities to continue operating until they fail. Maintenance work is performed only after failure has taken place. For example, the televisions, bathroom equipment and telephones in a hotel's guest rooms will probably only be repaired when they fail. The hotel will keep some spare parts and the staff available to make any repairs when needed. Failure in these circumstances is neither catastrophic (although perhaps irritating to the guest) nor so frequent as to make regular checking of the facilities appropriate.

Preventive maintenance

Preventive maintenance attempts to eliminate or reduce the chances of failure by servicing (cleaning, lubricating, replacing and checking) the facilities at pre-planned intervals. For example, the engines of passenger aircraft are checked, cleaned and calibrated according to a regular schedule after a set number of flying hours. Taking aircraft away from their regular duties for preventive maintenance is clearly an expensive option for any airline. The consequences of failure while in service are considerably more serious, however. The principle is also applied to facilities with less catastrophic consequences of failure. The regular cleaning and lubricating of machines, even the periodic painting of a building, could be considered preventive maintenance.

Condition-based maintenance (CBM)

Condition-based maintenance attempts to perform maintenance only when the facilities require it. For example, continuous process equipment, such as that used in coating photographic paper, is run for long periods in order to achieve the high utilization necessary for cost-effective production. Stopping the machine to change, say, a bearing when it is not strictly necessary to do so would take it out of action for long periods and reduce its utilization. Here condition-based maintenance might involve continuously monitoring the vibrations, for example, or some other characteristic of the line. The results of this monitoring would then be used to decide whether the line should be stopped and the bearings replaced. Table 19.1 illustrates some of the characteristics which could be monitored to determine whether any maintenance intervention is required.

Table 19.1 Examples of the characteristics monitored and procedures for monitoring in condition-based maintenance

Characteristic	Monitoring procedure
Vibration (for example, bearings)	Quality and condition of a machine tool can be measured by vibration characteristics. Vibrations are measured near bearing positions and analysed by a computer program.
Composition (for example, the oil in a press machine)	Instead of replacing oil in presses every 2000 operating hours, samples are analysed regularly. Oil is tested chemically, spectrographically, and for particle contamination; an additional benefit is that oil impurities due to impending part failures can be detected.
Dimensions (for example, the thickness of assembly conveyor chains)	Thickness of chain elements is monitored. The elements of the conveyor are replaced only as necessary.
Temperature (for example, electric motors)	Constant load and operation leads to constant temperature; regular monitoring of the temperature leads to predictions about condition.
Quality of output (for example of manufactured products)	Dimensions of output parts can be an indication of machine condition. SPC can be linked to CBM (see Chapter 17).

Source: Adapted from Harrison, A. (1992) *Just-in-time Manufacturing in Perspective*, Prentice Hall

Mixed maintenance strategies

Each approach to maintaining facilities is appropriate for different circumstances. RTB is often used where repair is relatively straightforward (so the consequence of failure is small), where regular maintenance is very costly (making PM expensive), or where failure is not at all predictable (so there is no advantage in PM because failure is just as likely to occur after repair as before). PM is used where the cost of unplanned failure is high (because of disruption to normal operations) and where failure is not totally random (so the maintenance time can be scheduled before failure becomes very likely). CBM is used where the maintenance activity is expensive, either because of the cost of providing the maintenance itself, or because of the disruption which the maintenance activity causes to the operation.

Most operations adopt a mixture of these approaches because different elements of their facilities have different characteristics. Even a motor car uses all three approaches, (*see* Fig. 19.9). Some parts of the car are normally replaced only when they fail: light bulbs and fuses for example. A wise motorist might carry spares and some cars have warning systems to tell the driver when a light bulb has failed, so the failure can be identified and repaired immediately. More fundamental parts of the car should not be

SPACE-AGE MAINTENANCE

Repairing any kind of mechanical device, be it a washing machine or a motor car, can be expensive. When the device is orbiting the earth the cost is literally astronomical.

When the Hubble Space Telescope was launched in 1990, its makers had designed it to be accessible for maintenance and servicing during its expected life in space of 15 years. Their foresight proved wise sooner than expected. The first servicing mission was being planned almost as soon as the telescope settled into its orbit. The reason for the repair mission was a combination of failure and bad luck. The telescope was not in its ideal orbit; the solar arrays attached to the body of the telescope had distorted under the massive temperature gradients across the unit as it passed from daylight to darkness; and the craft was also susceptible to 'jitter' as it passed through these temperature changes. Most seriously, the primary mirror used to beam pictures back to earth had been manufactured to the wrong specification and the error, small though it was, resulted in the pictures being blurred on receipt.

The repair mission needed to correct the mirror error by using COSTAR – a corrective optics space telescope axial replacement – which included mirror lenses, the size of a finger nail, which would deflect the original beams of light prior to exposure to the primary mirror. The repair would also have to replace the solar arrays and incorporate the technology to reduce the 'jitter'. It was the most complex mission of its type attempted by NASA (the North American Space Agency). The solar arrays alone weighed in at 160 kilograms, measured 12 metres by 2.8 metres, and comprised over 50 000 solar cells which powered the telescope in orbit. The original objective was to remove the old arrays and bring them back to earth for analysis (to look at meteor and environmental damage). However, in practice, one of the old arrays was damaged to an extent that it could not be released safely and was jettisoned into space.

The main parties involved spent the majority of their time at Johnson Space Centre in the USA, liaising with the operations staff who would be responsible for the guidance and control of the shuttle once in space. The first year of the three which the project lasted was spent in specifying the modifications to be made and by seeking a payload to finance the flight. The remaining two years focused on staff training, on ensuring that the astronauts had been through the release and replace procedures time and time again, each time taking different failure possibilities into account. The mission plan had been set to last no more than 14 days and the project leaders had no wish to extend into the Christmas break. So, in working backwards, the return was to be no later than 23 December 1993, therefore the lift-off was set for no later than 9 December 1993. The test schedule was set to finish on 30 November 1993 and this left a minimal time span of nine days for lift-off (after an unsuccessful attempt, a gap of at least two days is required before the next try).

In fact the whole repair mission was a failure-free 'textbook' operation. The repairs were completed over five 'extra-vehicular-activity' (EVA) days. Each EVA is described as a maximum of six hours in outer space and the project team had then to plan the days so that the pattern of work fitted into these six-hour slots. The nature of the task also meant that the shuttle and the telescope would have to be left in safe condition at the end of each day in case the need arose to return urgently and abandon plans. For this purpose 25 minutes of checks were incorporated into the daily programme. On 13 December 1993, the space shuttle carrying the astronauts touched down safely after the most expensive repair mission in history. ■

run to breakdown, however. The engine oil would be subject to preventive mainten-ance at the car's regular service. At the service other parts of the car would also be checked and replaced as necessary. Finally, most drivers would also monitor the condi-tion of the car. Some monitoring would be done informally, by listening to the engine noise when driving. Other monitoring might be done regularly, such as measuring the amount of tread on the tyre. Either way, a repair (or replacement of the tyre) would be carried out only when the maintenance indicated that it was necessary.

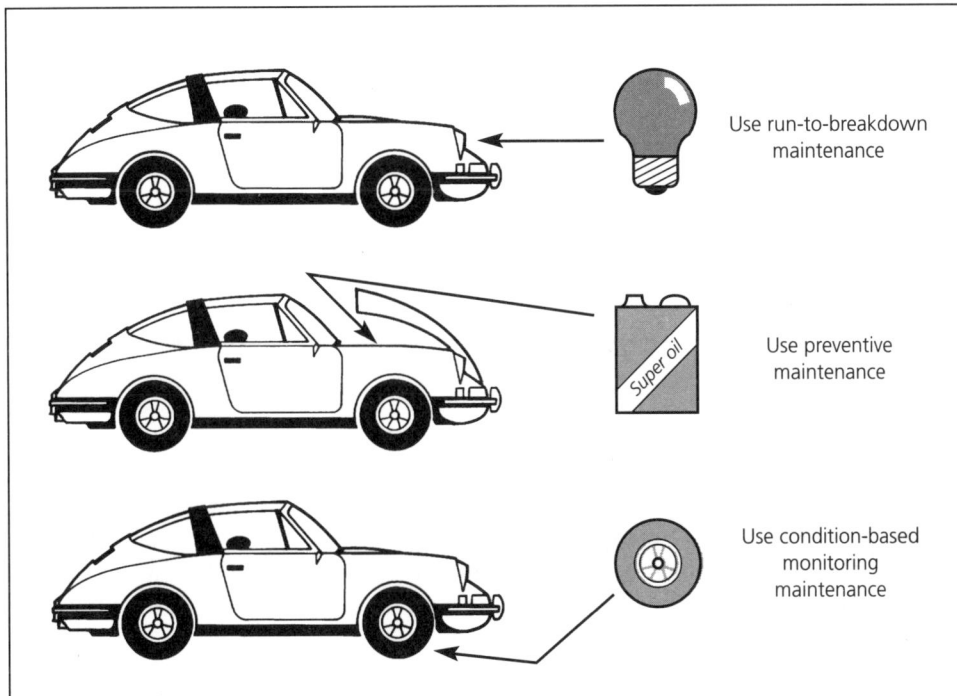

Use run-to-breakdown maintenance

Use preventive maintenance

Use condition-based monitoring maintenance

Figure 19.9
A mixture of maintenance approaches are often used (in a motor car for example)

Breakdown *versus* preventive maintenance

Most operations plan their maintenance to include a level of regular preventive mainten-ance which gives a reasonably low but finite chance of breakdown. Usually the more frequent the preventive maintenance episodes, the less are the chances of a breakdown. The balance between preventive and breakdown maintenance is set to minimize the total cost of breakdown. Infrequent preventive maintenance will cost little to provide but result in a high likelihood (and therefore cost) of breakdown maintenance. Conversely, very frequent preventive maintenance will be expensive to provide but will reduce the cost of having to provide breakdown maintenance (*see* Fig. 19.10). The total cost of maintenance appears to minimize at an 'optimum' level of preventive maintenance.

This representation of maintenance-related costs, however, although conceptually elegant, may not reflect reality in some operations. The cost of providing preventive maintenance may not increase quite so steeply as indicated in Fig. 19.10. The curve representing preventive-maintenance cost assumes that it is carried out by a separate set of people (skilled maintenance staff) whose time is scheduled and accounted for,

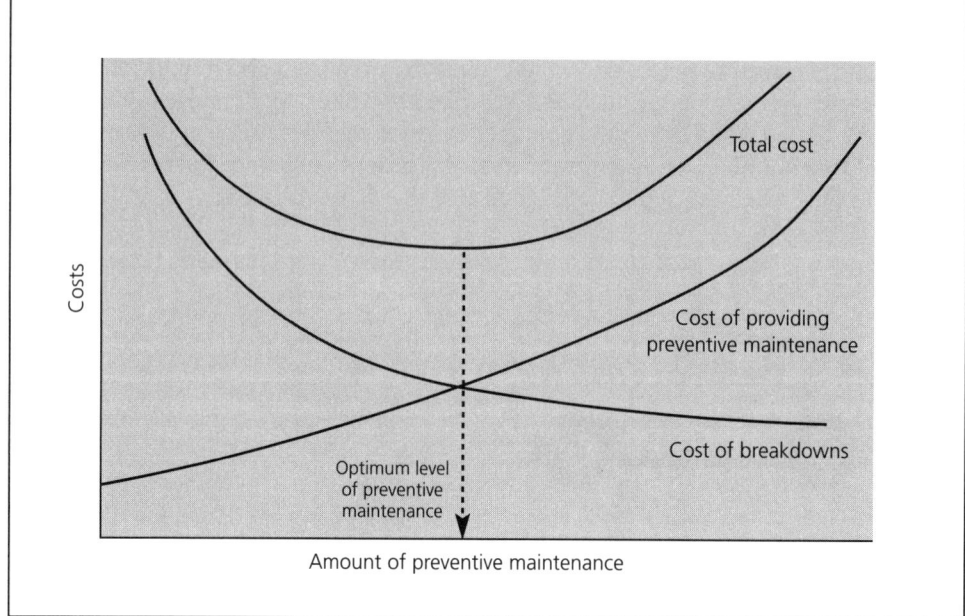

**Figure 19.10
One model of the
costs associated
with preventive
maintenance
shows an optimum
level of
maintenance effort**

separately from the 'operators' of the facilities. Furthermore, every time preventive maintenance takes place, the facilities cannot be used productively. This is why the slope of the curve increases, because the maintenance episodes start to interfere with the normal working of the operation. In many operations, however, at least some of the preventive maintenance can be performed by the operators themselves (which reduces the cost of providing it) and at times which is convenient for the operation (which minimizes the disruption to the operation). The cost of breakdowns could also be higher than is indicated in Fig. 19.10. Here the argument is similar to that which we used in Chapter 2 to describe dependability and in Chapter 12 to determine optimum stock levels (and will again in the next chapter when discussing the costs of quality). Unplanned breakdowns may do more than necessitate a repair and stop the operation; they can take away stability from the operation which prevents it being able to improve itself.

Put these two ideas together and the minimizing total curve and maintenance cost curve look more like Fig. 19.11. The emphasis is shifted more towards the use of preventive maintenance rather than run-to-breakdown maintenance.

Failure distributions

The shape of the failure probability distribution of a facility will also have an effect on the benefits of preventive maintenance. Figure 19.12 shows two probability curves for two machines, A and B. For machine A, the probability that it will break down before time x is relatively low. This machine will almost always break down between times x and y. If preventive maintenance was timed to occur just before point x it could reduce the chances of breakdown substantially. Machine B, on the other hand, has a relatively high probability of breaking down at any time, although again the probability of breakdown increases after time x. This means that applying preventive

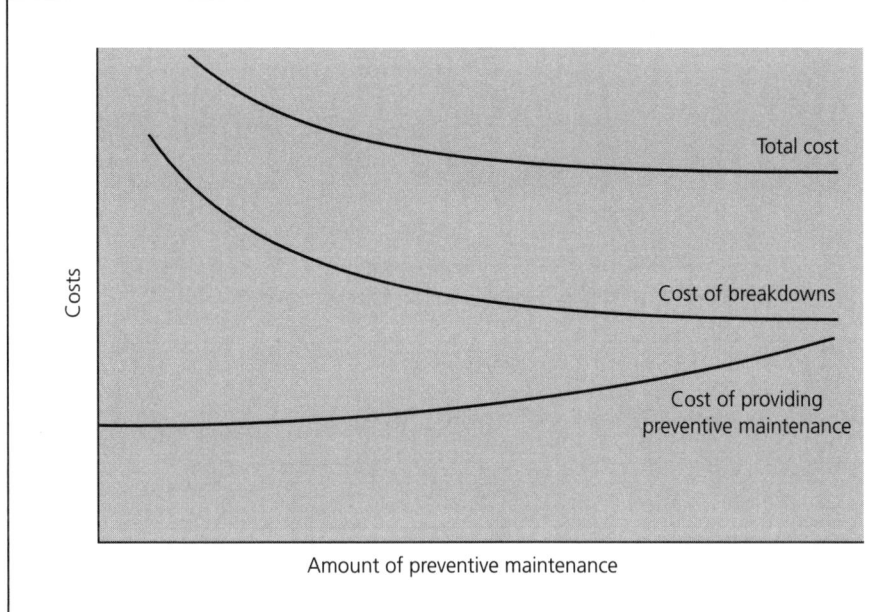

Figure 19.11
If routine preventive maintenance tasks are carried out by operators and if the real cost of breakdowns are considered, the 'optimum' level of preventive maintenance shifts towards higher levels

maintenance at point x (or any other time) cannot bring the dramatic reduction in breakdowns possible with machine A.

The implication of this is that preventive maintenance is more likely to lead to benefits when periods of high breakdown are reasonably predictable. When breakdown occurs in a relatively random manner there is less to gain from preventive maintenance because it has little effect on the chance of the machine breaking down in the future.

Total productive maintenance

Total productive maintenance (TPM) is defined as:

'...the productive maintenance carried out by all employees through small group activities'

where productive maintenance is:

'...maintenance management which recognizes the importance of reliability, maintenance and economic efficiency in plant design'.[6]

In Japan, where TPM originated, it is seen as a natural extension in the evolution from run-to-breakdown to preventive maintenance. TPM adopts some of the team-working and empowerment principles discussed in Chapter 9, as well as a continuous improvement approach to failure prevention as discussed in Chapter 18. It also sees maintenance as an organization-wide issue, to which staff can contribute in some way. It is analogous to the total quality management approach discussed in Chapter 20.

The five goals of TPM

TPM aims to establish good maintenance practice in operations through the pursuit of 'the five goals of TPM'.[7]

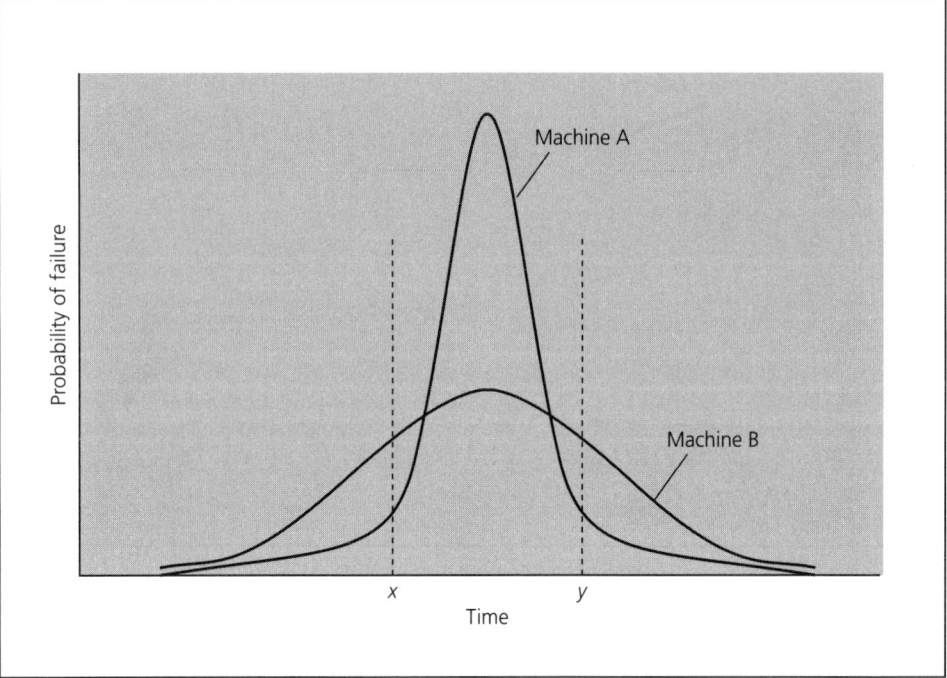

**Figure 19.12
Failure curves for
two machines, A
and B**

1 *Improve equipment effectiveness.* Examine how the facilities are contributing to the effectiveness of the operation by examining all the losses which occur. Loss of effectiveness can be the result of down-time losses, speed losses or defect losses (*see* Fig. 19.13).

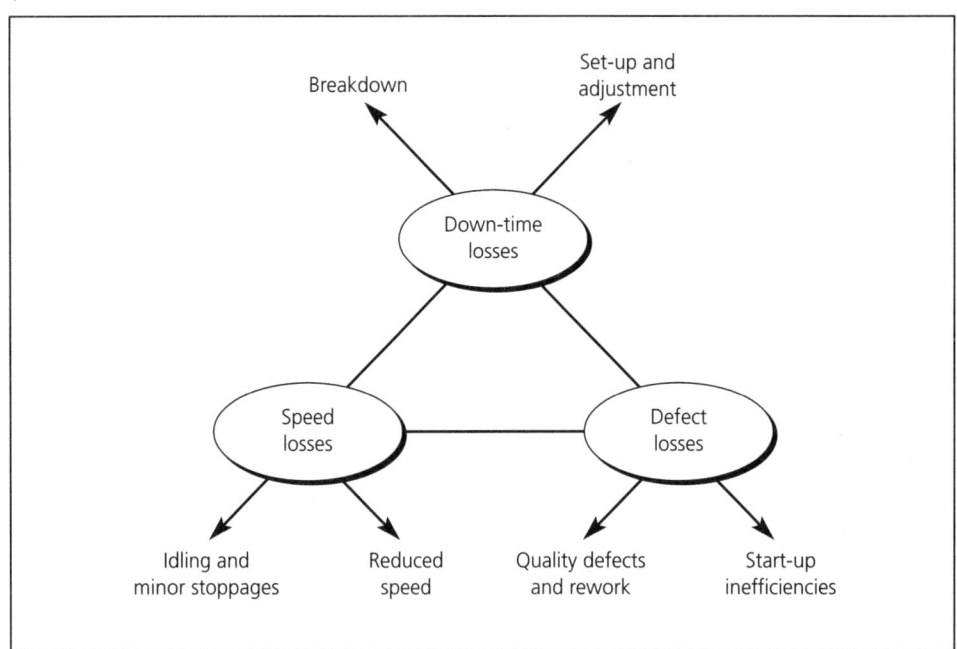

**Figure 19.13
Improving
equipment
effectiveness
requires that all
types of losses are
investigated**

2 *Achieve autonomous maintenance.* Allow the people who operate or use the operation's equipment to take responsibility for at least some of the maintenance tasks. Also encourage maintenance staff to take responsibility for the improvement of maintenance performance. Murata and Harrison, based on their work at Yuasa batteries, propose three levels at which staff take responsibility for maintenance:[8]

● Repair level. Staff carry out instructions, but do not predict the future, they simply react to problems.
● Prevention level. Staff can predict the future by foreseeing problems, and take corrective action.
● Improvement level. Staff can predict the future by foreseeing problems; they not only take corrective action but also propose improvements to prevent recurrence.

For example, suppose the screws on a machine become loose. Each week it jams up and is passed to maintenance to be fixed. A 'repair-level' maintenance engineer will simply repair it and hand it back to production. A 'prevention-level' maintenance engineer will spot the weekly pattern to the problem, and tighten the screws in advance of their loosening. An 'improvement-level' maintenance engineer will recognize that there is a design problem and modify the machine so that the problem cannot recur.

3 *Plan maintenance.* Have a fully worked out approach to all maintenance activities. This should include the level of preventive maintenance which is required for each piece of equipment, the standards for condition-based maintenance and the respective responsibilities of operating staff and maintenance staff. Table 19.2 illustrates the respective roles of 'operating' and 'maintenance' staff.

Table 19.2 The roles and responsibilities of operating staff and maintenance staff in TPM

	Maintenance staff	*Operating staff*
Roles	To develop ... ● preventive actions ● breakdown services	To take on ... ● ownership of facilities ● care of facilities
Responsibilities	Train operators Devise maintenance practice Problem solving Assess operating practice	Correct operation Routine preventive maintenance Routine condition-based maintenance Problem detection

4 *Train all staff in relevant maintenance skills.* The responsibilities listed in Table 19.2 require that both maintenance and operating staff have all the skills to carry out their roles. TPM places a heavy emphasis on appropriate and continuous training.

5 *Achieve early equipment management.* This goal is directed at going some way to avoiding maintenance altogether by 'maintenance prevention' (MP). MP involves considering failure causes and the maintainability of equipment during its design stage, its manufacture, its installation and its commissioning. In other words MP tries to trace all potential maintenance problems back to their root cause and then tries to eliminate them at that point.

THE PARLOUR FACTORY[9]

In many ways the striking difference between Japanese maintenance practice and that in other parts of the world is the emphasis put by the Japanese on caring for equipment as though it were a personal prized possession. Why, it is argued, should any of us accept standards of care and cleanliness in a factory that are different from what we would expect in our own homes? This argument can be taken literally. For example, the Nishio Pump factory of Aishin Seiki in Japan has been nicknamed the 'parlour' factory. In Japan one does not wear shoes in anyone's home. They would be left at the door before you entered. Within the Japanese home the zashiki or 'parlour' is the guest room where Japanese families would entertain. It is a matter of pride to the family that it is kept immaculately clean. The Nishio Pump factory is called a parlour factory because it is almost as clean as the parlour of any Japanese home. Although the factory is engaged in normally dirty processes, such as cutting metal and assembling parts together, it is spotlessly clean. There are no scrap parts lying about on the floor. There is not even metal-cutting waste on the floor, no oil splatters, no dust; the floor is clean and sparkling.

This may seem like taking things to extremes but the company would argue that it is the state of mind which is important. If the factory is clean and tidy, it encourages everyone to care for equipment as they would their own possessions in their own homes. Staff, it is argued, are more productive and less liable to make mistakes in a clean and orderly environment. Good housekeeping in the factory also allows staff to notice and correct process problems more quickly. Certainly at Aishin Seiki it seems to have been effective. Breakdowns, once running at more than 700 per month, now very rarely occur at all. Quality levels are even more impressive: only 11 defects in every one million pumps produced. ■

RECOVERY

In parallel with considering how to prevent failures occurring, operations managers need to decide what they will do when failures do occur. This activity is called *recovery* from failure. All types of operation can benefit from well planned recovery. For example, a construction company whose mechanical digger breaks down can have plans in place to arrange a replacement from a hire company. The breakdown might be disruptive but not as much as it might have been if the operations manager had not worked out what to do.

Recovery procedures will also shape customers' perceptions of failure. Even where the customer sees a failure it may not necessarily lead to dissatisfaction. Indeed, in many situations, customers may well accept that things do go wrong.[10] If a broken-down car is ten years old and badly in need of a service, or if there is a metre of snow on the train lines, or if the restaurant is particularly popular, we may accept that the product or service does not work or is not available. It is not necessarily the failure itself that leads to dissatisfaction but often the organization's response to the breakdown. The crucial point is that while mistakes may be inevitable, dissatisfied customers are not.

A failure may even be turned into a positive experience. If you are due to catch an aeroplane flight at midnight in a remote airport and are told that it is delayed by five hours, this is a potentially dissatisfying situation. Suppose, however, that then you are told that the aircraft was delayed taking off from its previous destination by a cyclone and that arrangements have been made for you to be taken to a local hotel for a complimentary meal with a room provided for a shower and rest, and that a telephone will be made available so that you can deal with any knock-on effects at the next destination. You might then feel that you have been dealt with well and even recommend that airline to others because you were so well looked after. A good recovery can turn angry, frustrated customers into loyal ones. An effective response to failure may have a high pay-off in terms of the long-term success of the organization. It can also send positive signals to customers and employees about the company's policy to encourage corrective action and to achieve high customer satisfaction.

Recovery in service operations

Recovery has been developed particularly in operating services. The word 'recovery' was said to have originated from British Airways' 'Putting the Customer First Campaign'.[11] Donald Porter, the consultant involved with BA, stated:

'It had never occurred to us before in any concrete way. "Recovery" was the term we coined to describe a very frequently repeated concern. If something goes wrong, as it often does, will anybody make special efforts to get it right? Will somebody go out of his or her way to make amends to the customer? Does anyone make an effort to offset the negative impact of a screw-up?'

It has also been suggested that service recovery does not just mean 'return to a normal state' but to a state of enhanced perception.

'All breakdowns require the deliverer to jump through a few hoops to get the customer back to neutral. More hoops are required for victims to recover.'[12]

Service operations managers need to recognize that all customers have recovery expectations that they want organizations to meet. Recovery needs to be a planned process. Organizations need to design appropriate responses to failure, therefore, linked to the cost and the inconvenience caused by the failure to the customer, that will meet the needs and expectations of the customer. Such recovery processes need to be carried out either by empowered front-line staff or trained personnel who are available to deal with recovery in a way which does not interfere with day-to-day service activities. (*See* the discussion of 'Empowerment' in Chapter 9.)

Failure planning

Identifying how organizations can recover from failure is of particular interest to service operations because they can turn failures around to minimize the effect on customers or even to turn failure into a positive experience. It is also of interest to other industries, however, especially those where the consequences of failure are particularly severe. Bulk chemical manufacturers and nuclear processors, for example, spend considerable resources in deciding how they will cope with failures. The activity of devising the procedures which allow the operation to recover from failure is called *failure planning*.

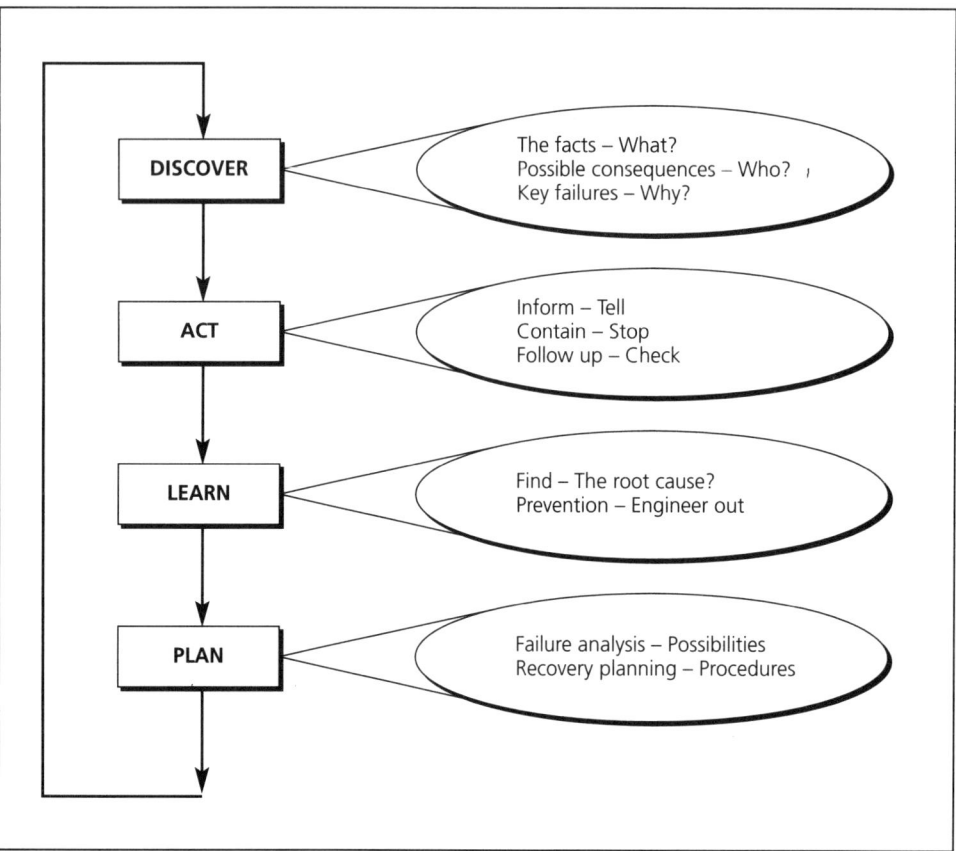

**Figure 19.14
The stages in
failure planning**

Failure planning is often represented by stage models showing the steps to be followed in the event of failure. These stage models all follow a similar pattern. One is represented in Fig. 19.14. We shall follow it through from the point where failure is recognized.

Discover

The first thing any manager needs to do when faced with a failure is to discover its exact nature. Three important pieces of information are needed. First of all, what exactly has happened, second, who will be affected by the failure, and, third, why did the failure occur? This last point is not intended to be a detailed inquest into the causes of failure (that comes later) but it is often necessary to know something of the causes of failure in case it is necessary to determine what action to take.

Act

The discover stage could only take minutes or even seconds, depending on the severity of the failure. Especially if the failure is a severe one with important consequences we need to move on to doing something about the failure quickly. This means carrying out three actions, the first two of which could be carried out in reverse order depending on the urgency of the situation. First, tell the significant people involved what you are proposing to do about the failure. In service operations this is especially important where the customers need to be kept informed both for their peace of mind and to demonstrate that something is being done. In all operations, however, it is important to communicate what action is going to happen so that everyone can set their own recovery plans in motion. Second, the effects of the failure need to be contained in order to stop the consequences spreading and causing further failures. The precise containment actions will depend on the nature of the failure. Third, there needs to be some kind of follow-up to make sure that the containment actions really have contained the failure.

Learn

As discussed earlier in this chapter, the benefits of failure in providing learning opportunities should not be underestimated. In failure planning learning involves re-visiting the failure to find out its root cause and then engineering out the causes of the failure so that it will not happen again.

Plan

Learning the lessons from a failure is not the end of the procedure. Operations managers need to incorporate formally the lessons into their future reactions to failures. This is often done by working through 'in theory' how they would react to failures in the future. Specifically, this involves first identifying all the possible failures which might occur (in a similar way to the FMEA approach). Second, it means formally defining the procedures which the organization should follow in the case of each type of identified failure.

PERSONAL PROFILE

Sifiso Dabengwa, Eskom

Eskom, 'The Power House of Africa', as the slogan goes, supplies more than half the total electricity consumed in Africa. It is actively involved in the establishment of a regional transmission grid to encourage and accelerate economic development in Southern Africa. Eskom currently exports electricity to Botswana, Zimbabwe, Mozambique, Namibia, Swaziland and Lesotho. The Eskom Electrification Programme adds approximately 800 new householders to its customer base every working day. Sifiso Ray Dabengwa is the executive director responsible for electrification and distribution. Part of Sifiso's responsibility is asset management which involves failure and risk management. Sifiso trained as an engineer and joined Eskom after graduating from Business School.

'Once it was agreed that little economic growth could occur without the widespread use of electricity, Eskom committed itself to the electrification of almost one million homes over the following five years, in areas where it had the right to supply. Eskom, with a total nominal capacity of 37 840 MW, has 75 years of experience as an electricity utility supplier. Availability, continuity/interruptions, restoration time, voltage fluctuations and service support from the supplier determine the quality of supply. A variety of power failures that affect the flow of electricity within an electric supply system are ▶

possible. Some of these failures can be damaging (lightning-induced high voltage spikes), whereas others are merely annoying (poor TV reception due to electrical "noise").

'Failure management is primarily a risk management issue. It is about finding a balance or compromise, usually based on the economic impact of the event. In a capital intensive industry like the electricity business, equipment failure results in costly equipment idling, loss of revenue, incremental operating costs due to repairs and, most of all, irate customers. Therefore the cost of outage (duration of non-supply of electricity) can be substantial, depending on the power-carrying capacity of the affected equipment.

'Minimizing equipment failure to acceptable levels thus becomes a key management strategy at Eskom. It may be accepted that at some stage equipment will fail, but it is the ability of management to antici-pate, detect and correct symptoms of the impending failure that can make a difference between disaster and satisfied customers. The amount of investment to avoid failure is a function of the impact and sus-ceptibility to failure. Large rotating machines at power stations are more prone to fail than static large power transformers at distribution points. Thus it would be expected that investment in failure avoiding systems, such as condition monitoring systems, would be higher on rotating equipment.

'The average customer suffers a power blackout less than once a year. And blackouts, when they do happen, usually emanate from the high voltage grid and, on average, last no more than an hour or two. Blackouts are only the tip of the iceberg of lesser supply disturbances. Industry's growing reliance on electrical equipment not only means that we are more at risk from supply but also that the equipment itself can exacerbate the failures by introducing disturbances in the system.

'Information, on all equipment with a notable impact if it does not perform, such as age, maintenance history, operating conditions and supplier service support, is critical to effective failure management. We store all asset information in a database that is accessible by all relevant personnel at Eskom. Our transmission and distribution engineers are looking at artificial intelligence to help us understand and operate power-generating systems. The neural-network-based solutions known as AdSPAR (adaptive single-pole auto-reclosure) developed by the University of Bath, UK, and Reyrolle Protection, currently under trial by Eskom, is proving to be successful.'

Sifiso maintains that his focus areas are on significant change in customer satisfaction, electrification and integrated energy planning. Additionally he wishes to reduce further the price of electricity by 15 per cent, so as to become the world's lowest cost supplier and to electrify an additional 1 750 000 homes, thus improving the lives of 11 million South Africans. ■

Source: By kind permission of Sifiso Dabengwa/Eskom

SUMMARY

■ Failure problems and mistakes are an inevitable and intrinsic part of operations life. Things are always going wrong. This is why operations managers need to be concerned with the causes and effects of failure, as well as being active in attempting to minimize failure. Not all failures are equally serious and attention is usually directed at those which have the most impact on the operation or its customers.

■ Failures occur in operations for several reasons. Some are as a direct result of goods or services which are supplied to the operation. Others happen within the operation, either because there is an overall failure in its design, because one or more of its physical facilities break down, or because there is human error. Customers can also cause failures through their incompetent handling of goods and services.

■ There are three ways of measuring failure. Failure rates indicate how often a failure is likely to occur; reliability measures the chances of a failure occurring; and availability is the amount of available and useful operating time left after taking account of failures.

■ The probability of anything failing over time can be described by a probability curve. The most common of these is the 'bath-tub' curve which has three stages – the infant-mortality or early-life stage, the normal operating life stage, the final wear-out stage.

■ Failure detection and analysis involves putting mechanisms in place which sense when some kind of failure has occurred and then analysing the failure to try to understand its root causes.

■ After detecting and understanding a failure, operations managers need to work on improving the reliability of operation. This can be done by trying to design out the fail points of the operation, by building redundancy into the operation, by fail-safing the operation so as to make failure and potential failures obvious. The most common method of improving the operation's reliability, however, is by maintaining the physical facilities in some planned and systematic manner.

■ There are three broad approaches to maintenance. The first is running all facilities until they break down and then repairing them; the second is regularly maintaining the facilities even if they have not broken down so as to prevent the possibility of future breakdown; the third is to monitor facilities closely to try to predict when breakdown might occur and pre-empt it by repairing the facility.

■ The total productive maintenance (TPM) concept is the latest in a development of maintenance ideas. It is analogous to TQM in that it proposes shifting the responsibility of maintenance and care throughout the organization.

■ In parallel with attempting to prevent failure, operations management must plan for what they do if failure does occur. This is important because recovering from failure can have a significant effect on shaping customers' perceptions of the organization. Failure planning provides a systematic framework which can be used to react to failures when they do occur.

CASE EXERCISE 1

Better late and happy than just late

Linda Langa sat and enjoyed her coffee at Harare airport. Returning home to South Africa after a week of energetic academic research, she was pondering her latest project – how service businesses have to be more aware of their customers' needs and how, in order to compete, they must be able to offer a high level of customer service, especially if the intended delivery package has been compromised in some way.

She knew that airlines, especially, had well developed recovery procedures. In the case of failure the airline could activate various levels of preconceived and *ad hoc* customer care.

Harare airport was busy with passengers waiting to board the afternoon South African Airways flight to Johannesburg International, the anticipation growing as they passed through the scanners and walked down the aisle on to the aircraft. Safely in their seats, the 200 travellers were soon dismayed to hear from the captain that there was a slight mechanical problem and that their take-off would be delayed by approximately half an hour. This delay did not merit having to disembark and complimentary drinks were soon on the way round.

Inevitably, the half-hour delay soon blossomed into a bigger problem and an apologetic captain announced that he felt that passengers would be better placed, waiting for the repair to be completed, back in the departure lounge and please could they take all of their hand baggage off the plane with them. A few grumbles and mutters about connections at Johannesburg International and other missed appointments – but generally the mood was fairly genial and the airline staff went out of their way to try to accommodate passenger queries. One representative escorted a worried passenger off to the airline office to allow her to phone home and advise her family of her late departure. She had spent all of her Zimbabwean 'holiday money' and couldn't use the standard phones in the departure area. After an hour in the departure lounge and with no definitive answer available on the estimated take-off time, the airline moved into the next stage of its 'customer-placating programme' by providing meal vouchers for everyone and directing them to the airport restaurant. As the mood quietened and passengers began to question further just how long they

were going to have to wait, the airline announced the departure time – some four hours behind schedule.

The flight itself went according to plan and the cabin crew walked up and down the aisles answering, where possible, queries on connecting flights and subsequent travel arrangements.

On arrival (finally) at Johannesburg International, the captain, who had been very apologetic throughout the whole process, bade the passengers farewell, expressing his concerns at the late arrival and hoping that it hadn't inconvenienced them too greatly. For some, though, the four-hour delay meant considerable problems in trying to reach their onward destinations that evening and the airline sales desk was soon busy with anxious passengers looking for help. Several were to be put up in a local hotel, courtesy of the airline, leaving them to recommence their travels, fresh, the next morning. Others did not have so far to go and to stay overnight in Johannesburg would actually mean more inconvenience the following day. Unperturbed, the airline's Customer Service Manager quickly took it upon himself to arrange chauffeur-driven transport for these people, ensuring that the inconvenience caused by the delay was effectively minimized. The priority wasn't necessarily to deal with each customer as quickly as possible, but to ensure that each person was given a solution that suited his or her needs. No awkward questions asked – only 'How can I help you?' (What can I possibly do to ensure that given the choice you will fly again with our airline?)

Linda was certainly impressed, and although very late back, glad to be safely home as planned. ∎

Questions

1 Is Linda a particularly tolerant person or was she right to be impressed by the way South African Airways reacted?

2 Draw up a 'failure plan' for delays of this type. How could it help the airline to improve its recovery procedures further?

3 When are failure and recovery particularly important to an operation?

The Chernobyl failure[13]

At 1.24 in the early hours of Saturday morning on 26 April 1986 the worst accident in the history of commercial nuclear power generation occurred. Two explosions in quick succession blew off the 1000-tonne concrete sealing cap of the Chernobyl–4 nuclear reactor. Molten core fragments showered down on the immediate area and fission products were released into the atmosphere. The accident cost probably hundreds of lives and contaminated vast areas of land in the Ukraine.

Many reasons probably contributed to the disaster. Certainly the design of the reactor was not new – around 30 years old at the time of the accident – and had been conceived before the days of sophisticated computer-controlled safety systems. Because of this, the reactor's emergency-handling procedures relied heavily on the skill of the operators. This type of reactor also had a tendency to run 'out of control' when operated at low power. For this reason the operating procedures for the reactor strictly prohibited it being operated below 20 per cent of its maximum power. It was mainly a combination of circumstance and human error which caused the failure, however. Ironically, the events which led up to the disaster were designed to make the reactor safer. Tests, devised by a specialist team of engineers, were being carried out to evaluate whether the emergency core cooling system (ECCS) could be operated during the 'free-wheeling' run-down of the turbine generator, should an off-site power failure occur. Although this safety device had been tested before, it had not worked satisfactorily and new tests of the modified device were to be carried out with the reactor operating at reduced power throughout the test period. The tests were scheduled for the afternoon of Friday, 25 April 1986 and the plant power reduction began at 1.00 pm. However, just after 2.00 pm, when the reactor was operating at about half its full power, the Kiev controller requested that the reactor should continue supplying the grid with electricity. In fact they were not released from the grid until 11.10 that night. The reactor was due to be shut down for its annual maintenance on the following Tuesday and the Kiev controller's request had in effect shrunk the 'window of opportunity' available for the tests.

The following is a chronological account of the hours up to the disaster together with an analysis by James Reason, which was published in the *Bulletin of the British Psychological Society* the following year. Significant operator actions are italicized. These are of two kinds: *errors* (indicated by an 'E') and *procedural violations* (marked with a 'V').

25 April 1986

1.00 pm Power reduction started with the intention of achieving 25 per cent power for test conditions.

2.00 pm ECCS disconnected from primary circuit. (This was part of the test plan.)

2.05 pm Kiev controller asked the unit to continue supplying grid. *The ECCS was not reconnected (V).* (This particular violation is not thought to have contributed materially to the disaster; but it is indicative of a lax attitude on the part of the operators toward the observance of safety procedures.)

11.10 pm The unit was released from the grid and continued power reduction to achieve the 25 per cent power level planned for the test programme.

26 April 1986

12.28 am *Operator seriously undershot the intended power setting (E).* The power dipped to a dangerous 1 per cent. (The operator had switched off the 'auto-pilot' and had tried to achieve the desired level by manual control.)

1.00 am After a long struggle, the reactor power was finally stabilized at 7 per cent – well below the intended level and well into the low-power danger zone. *At this point, the experiment should have been abandoned, but it was not (E).* This was the most serious mistake (as opposed to violation): it meant that all subsequent activity would be conducted within the reactor's zone of maximum instability. This was apparently not appreciated by the operators.

1.03 am *All eight pumps were started (V).* The safety regulations limited the maximum number of pumps in use at any one time to six. This showed a profound misunderstanding of the physics of the reactor. The consequence was that the increased water flow (and reduced steam fraction) absorbed more neutrons, causing more control rods to be withdrawn to sustain even this low level of power.

1.19 am *The feedwater flow was increased threefold (V).* The operators appear to have been attempting to cope ▶

with a falling steam-drum pressure and water level. The result of their actions, however, was to further reduce the amount of steam passing through the core, causing yet more control rods to be withdrawn. *They also overrode the steam-drum automatic shut-down (V).* The effect of this was to strip the reactor of one of its automatic safety systems.

1.22 am   The shift supervisor requested printout to establish how many control rods were actually in the core. The printout indicated only six to eight rods remaining. It was strictly forbidden to operate the reactor with fewer than 12 rods. *Yet the shift supervisor decided to continue with the tests (V).* This was a fatal decision: the reactor was thereafter without 'brakes'.

1.23 am   *The steam line valves to No. 8 turbine generator were closed (V).* The purpose of this was to establish the conditions necessary for repeated testing, but its consequence was to disconnect the automatic safety trips. This was perhaps the most serious violation of all.

1.24 am   An attempt was made to 'scram' the reactor by driving in the emergency shut-off rods, but they jammed within the now warped tubes.

1.24 am   Two explosions occurred in quick succession. The reactor roof was blown off and 30 fires started in the vicinity.

1.30 am   Duty firemen were called out. Other units were summoned from Pripyat and Chernobyl.

5.00 am   Exterior fires had been extinguished, but the graphite fire in the core continued for several days.

The subsequent investigation into the disaster highlighted a number of significant points which contributed to it.

● The test programme was poorly worked out and the section on safety measures was inadequate. Because the ECCS was shut off during the test period, the safety of the reactor was in effect substantially reduced.
● The test plan was put into effect before being approved by the design group who were responsible for the reactor.
● The operators and the technicians who were running the experiment had different and non-overlapping skills.
● The operators, although highly skilled, had probably been told that getting the test completed before the shut-down would enhance their reputation. They were proud of their ability to handle the reactor even in unusual conditions and were aware of the rapidly reducing window of opportunity within which they had to complete the test. They had also probably 'lost any feeling for the hazards involved' in operating the reactor.
● The technicians who had designed the test were electrical engineers from Moscow. Their objective was to solve a complex technical problem. In spite of having designed the test procedures, they probably would not know much about the operation of the nuclear power station itself.
● Again, in the words of James Reason:

'Together, they made a dangerous mixture: a group of single-minded but non-nuclear engineers directing a team of dedicated but over-confident operators. Each group probably assumed that the other knew what it was doing. And both parties had little or no understanding of the dangers they were courting, or of the system they were abusing.' ■

Questions

1 What were the root causes which contributed to the ultimate failure?
2 How could failure planning have helped prevent the disaster?

1 Briefly describe a time when a product you bought or a service you received failed. Identify all the different reasons why this happened and assess which you think was the most likely.

2 In what ways could customers 'fail' in their use of a bank? How might the bank's management use this information to improve its operations?

3 What do you think will be the best ways of measuring failure for:

a university course
a lift (elevator)
a security service
a home pregnancy-testing kit
a car.

4 A 24-hour ATM machine outside a bank was closed down between the following times during a seven-day period:

11.00 am Monday – 2.00 pm Monday
1.00 am Monday – 10.30 am Tuesday
4.00 am Tuesday – 10.00 am Wednesday
3.00 pm Friday – 10.00 am Saturday

Calculate the ATM's failure rate (in time), the mean time between failures, and its availability.

5 A manufacturer has four machines which are used in sequence: stripping, steaming, buffing and polishing. The reliabilities of the individual machines are 95 per cent, 78 per cent, 45 per cent and 56 per cent respectively. This year the Managing Director has agreed to buy one new machine to replace one of the old ones. The failure rates of the possible replacement machines are shown in Table 19.3. Which one would you recommend should be chosen to maximize the reliability of the whole process?

6 A catering company that provides catering services in people's homes for dinner parties, etc., has encountered a number of problems. From their past activities the managers have identified how many times these problems have occurred and have rated them for importance and the likelihood of detection by the customer, as shown in Table 19.4. The managers wish to try to improve their reputation for a quality service. Which area would you recommend them giving most attention to first?

Table 19.3

Possible replacement machines	Known failure rates
Superstripper	1/10
Stripper XXXX	7/30
Steadysteam	1/20
The Steam Machine	3/40
Buffer Mark2	1/10
Buffalot	4/25
Buffalotmore	3/25
Polishoff	6/70
Superfinish[*]	1/5
Finishkwik[*]	1/6

[*]Note the Superfinish and Finishkwik machines will replace both the buffing and polishing machines.

Table 19.4

Problems encountered	Times problem occurred	Severity of failure	Probability of customer finding out
Insufficient food	1/800	5	50%
Host/hostess wants to be involved	1/25	1	10%
Food damaged in transit	1/3	7	20%
Food kept at wrong temperatures	1/30	9	70%
Breaking customers' equipment	1/90	7	90%

7 Flow chart a service process you have recently encountered, identifying what you consider to be the key fail-points. Assess any poka-yokes in evidence and explain how you might design poka-yokes to overcome the fail-points you have identified.

8 Describe the difference between 'run-to-break-down', 'condition-based maintenance' and 'prevent-ive-maintenance' approaches to maintenance. Provide examples from your own experience to illustrate your answer.

9 Talk to an operations manager in a car repair garage or a catering operation, for example, and find out the different ways in which the organization maintains its equipment. Assess the organization's approach to maintenance.

10 Describe a recent equipment, product or service failure that involved you. Did the organization make any attempt to recover from the situation? If so, how? If not, what steps might have been taken to bring about a recovery?

NOTES ON CHAPTER

1 Source: Cookson, C. (1993) 'Years of Mishaps Ruins a Caring Reputation', the *Financial Times*, 18 June.

2 Sources: Ridding, J.(1994) 'Recession and Blunders Derail SNCF', the *Financial Times*, 28 January, and Jenkins, I. (1993) 'Socrates Derails French Travellers', *The Sunday Times*, 29 August.

3 Source: 'Air Crashes, But Surely ...', *The Economist*, 4 June.

4 Flanagan, J. (1954) 'The Critical Incident Technique', *Psychological Bulletin*, Vol 51, No 4.

5 Chase, R.B. and Stewart, D.M. (1994) 'Make Your Service Fail-safe', *Sloan Management Review*, Spring, Vol 35, No 3.

6 Nakajima, S. (1988) *Total Productive Maintenance*, Productivity Press.

7 Nakajima, S., *op. cit.*

8 Murata, K. and Harrison, A. (1991) *How To Make Japanese Management Methods Work In The West*, Gower.

9 Examples based on Nakajima, *op. cit.*, and Koelsch, J.R. (1991) 'Where's the Grease?', *Manufacturing Engineering*, Vol 107, No 3.

10 For a full discussion of this idea, *see* Hart, C.W.L., Heskett, J.L. and Sasser, W.E. (1990) 'The Profitable Art of Service Recovery', *Harvard Business Review*, Vol 68, No 4.

11 Zemke, R. and Schaaf, R. (1990) *The Service Edge: 101 Companies that Profit from Customer Care*, Plume Books.

12 Zemke, R. and Bell, C.R., *Service Wisdom: Creating and Maintaining the Customer Service Edge*, Lakewood Books.

13 Based on information from Read, P.P. (1994) *Ablaze: The Story of Chernobyl*, Secker and Warburg, and Reason, J. (1987) 'The Chernobyl Errors', *Bulletin of the British Psychological Society*, Vol 4, pp 201–6.

SELECTED FURTHER READINGS

Albrecht, K. and Bradford, L.J. (1990) *The Service Advantage*, Dow Jones Irwin.

Dale, B.G. (ed) (1994) *Managing Quality* (2nd edn), Prentice Hall.

Dhillon, B.S. and Reiche, H. (1985) *Reliability and Maintainability Management*, Van Nostrand Reinhold.

Evans, J.R. and Lindsay, W.M. (1993) *The Management and Control of Quality* (2nd edn), West.

Harrison A. (1992) *Just-in-Time Manufacturing in Perspective*, Prentice Hall.

Hayes, R.H. and Clark, K.B. (1986) 'Why Some Factories are More Productive Than Others', *Harvard Business Review*, Vol 64, No 5.

Heskett, J.L., Sasser, W.E. and Hart, C.W.L. (1990) *Service Breakthroughs: Changing the Rules of the Game*, Free Press.

Nakajima, S. (1988) *Total Productive Maintenance*, Productivity Press.

Raouf, A., Ali, Z. and Duffuaa, S.O. (1993) 'Evaluating a Computerized Maintenance Management System', *International Journal of Operations and Production Research*, Vol 13, No 3.

Robinson, C.J., Ginder, A.P. (1995) *Implementing TPM: The North American Experience*, Productivity Press.

Sherwin, D.J. (1990) 'Inspect or Monitor', *Engineering Costs and Production Economics*, Jan.

Total Productive Maintenance, Proceedings of the First International Conference 1992, Published by Industrial Newsletters.

Wilkinson, J.J. (1968) 'How to Manage Maintenance', *Harvard Business Review*, Vol 46, No 2.

CHAPTER 20

TOTAL QUALITY
MANAGEMENT

INTRODUCTION

Total quality management (TQM) is arguably the most significant of the new ideas which have swept across the operations management scene over the last few years. There can be few, if any, managers in any developed economy anywhere in the world who have not heard of TQM. It certainly has had an impact on most industries which goes beyond its recent fashionability. There are two reasons for this: first, the ideas of TQM have a great intuitive attraction for many people – most of us want to be 'high quality'. Second, a TQM approach to improvement can result in sometimes dramatic increases in operational effectiveness. In this book we have separated the treatment of general quality planning and control (in Chapter 17) from TQM because TQM is concerned with more than quality alone. It is concerned with the improvement of *all* aspects of operations performance and particularly how improvement should be managed.

This chapter looks at TQM both as a philosophy of improvement and also as an organizational process which can be used to manage the improvement effort (*see* Fig. 20.1).

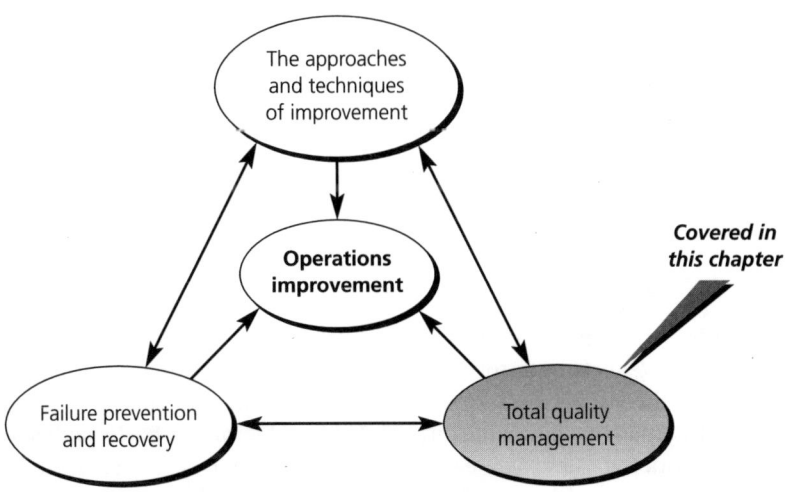

Figure 20.1 Model of operations improvement showing the issues covered in this chapter

THE ORIGINS OF TQM

The notion of total quality management was introduced by Feigenbaum in 1957. More recently, it has been developed through a number of widely recognized approaches put forward by several 'quality gurus' such as Deming, Juran, Ishikawa, Taguchi and Crosby. Therefore, to understand the origins of TQM, it is important to understand the contributions from these quality pioneers.

The quality gurus

Armand Feigenbaum

Armand Feigenbaum was a doctoral student at the Massachusetts Institute of Technology in the 1950s when he completed the first edition of his book *Total Quality Control*. He defines TQM as:

'an effective system for integrating the quality development, quality maintenance and quality improvement efforts of the various groups in an organization so as to enable production and service at the most economical levels which allow for full customer satisfaction'.[1]

Despite his early writings in America it was the Japanese who first made the concept work on a wide scale and subsequently popularized the approach and the term TQM.

W.E. Deming

W. Edwards Deming, considered in Japan to be the father of quality control, asserted that quality starts with top management and is a strategic activity.[2] It is claimed that much of the success in terms of quality in Japanese industry was the result of his lectures to Japanese companies in the 1950s.[3] Deming's basic philosophy is that quality and productivity increase as 'process variability' (the unpredictability of the process) decreases. In his *14 points for quality improvement*, he emphasizes the need for statistical control methods, participation, education, openness and purposeful improvement.

1 Create constancy of purpose.
2 Adopt new philosophy.
3 Cease dependence on inspection.
4 End awarding business on price.
5 Improve constantly the system of production and service.
6 Institute training on the job.
7 Institute leadership.
8 Drive out fear.
9 Break down barriers between departments.
10 Eliminate slogans and exhortations.
11 Eliminate quotas or work standards.
12 Give people pride in their job.
13 Institute education and a self-improvement programme.
14 Put everyone to work to accomplish it.

J.M. Juran

Joseph M. Juran was also a key educator of the Japanese in quality management. He tried to get organizations to move away from the traditional manufacturing-based view of quality as 'conformance to specification' to a more user-based approach, for which he coined the phrase 'fitness for use'. He pointed out that a dangerous product could conform to specification but would not be fit to use. Like Deming, Juran was concerned about management activities and the responsibility for quality, but he was also concerned about the impact of individual workers and involved himself to some extent with the motivation and involvement of the workforce in quality improvement activities.[4]

K. Ishikawa

Kaoru Ishikawa, basing his work on that of Deming, Juran and Feigenbaum, has been credited with originating the concept of quality circles and cause-and-effect diagrams (*see* Chapter 18). Ishikawa[5] claimed that there had been a period of over-emphasis on statistical quality control (in Japan), and as a result people disliked quality control. They saw it as something unpleasant because they were given complex and difficult tools rather than simple ones. Furthermore, the resulting standardization of products and processes and the creation of rigid specification of standards became a burden that not only made change difficult but made people feel bound by regulations. Ishikawa saw the worker participation as the key to the successful implementation of TQM. Quality circles, he believed, were an important vehicle to achieve this.

G. Taguchi

Genichi Taguchi (*see* also Chapter 5) was the director of the Japanese Academy of Quality and was concerned with engineering-in quality through the optimization of product design combined with statistical methods of quality control. He encouraged interactive team meetings between workers and managers to criticize and develop product design. Taguchi's definition of quality uses the concept of the loss which is imparted by the product or service to society from the time it is created. His quality loss function (QLF) includes such factors as warranty costs, customer complaints and loss of customer goodwill.[6]

P.B. Crosby

Phillip B. Crosby[7] is best known for his work on the cost of quality. He suggested that many organizations do not know how much they spend on quality, either in putting it right or getting it wrong. He claimed that organizations that have measured their costs say that they equate them to about 30 per cent of sales. (Juran estimated that total quality costs in manufacturing average 10 per cent of sales turnover and Feigenbaum suggested the ideas of a 'hidden plant' in every organization that uses, to no benefit, one tenth of productive capacity.) Crosby tried to highlight the costs and benefits of implementing quality programmes though his book *Quality is Free* in which he provided a *zero defects* programme which he believed would reduce the total cost of quality. This is summarized in his absolutes of quality management:[8]

1 Quality is conformance to requirements.
2 Prevention not appraisal.
3 The performance standard must be 'zero defects'.
4 Measure the 'price of non-conformance' (PONC).
5 There is no such thing as a quality problem.

and his 14 quality steps:[9]

1 Establish management commitment.
2 Form inter-departmental quality teams.
3 Establish quality measurement.
4 Evaluate the cost of quality.
5 Establish quality awareness.
6 Instigate corrective action.
7 *Ad hoc* committee for the zero defects programme.
8 Supervise employee training.
9 Hold a zero defects day.
10 Employee goal setting.
11 Error cause removal.
12 Recognition for meeting and exceeding goals.
13 Establish quality councils.
14 Do it over again.

While not an exhaustive catalogue of those who have contributed to TQM thinking, the above list does give the flavour of how TQM developed. Even from these brief summaries of their work, it is evident that each 'guru' stressed a different set of issues from which emerged the TQM approach to operations improvement. Each contributor, with hindsight, is seen as having made some particularly significant points, and as having perhaps neglected other issues, now seen as important. Table 20.1 summarizes the strengths and weaknesses of each guru's approach.

WHAT IS TQM?

On the face of it, it would appear that these gurus provide different solutions to bringing about improvement in organizations. However, Professor John Oakland, an authority on TQM, has suggested that 'they are all talking the same "language" but

Table 20.1 The relative strengths and weaknesses of some of the quality gurus[10]

Quality 'guru'	Strengths of approach	Weaknesses of approach
Feigenbaum	• Provides a total approach to quality control • Places the emphasis on the importance of management • Includes socio-technical systems thinking • Participation by all staff is promoted	• Does not discriminate between different kinds of quality context • Does not bring together the different management theories into one coherent whole
Deming	• Provides a systematic and functional logic which identifies stages in quality improvement • Stresses that management comes before technology • Leadership and motivation are recognized as important • Emphasizes role of statistical and quantitative methods • Recognizes the different contexts of Japan and North America	• Action plan and methodological principles are sometimes vague • The approach to leadership and motivation is seen by some as idiosyncratic • Does not treat situations which are political or coercive
Juran	• Emphasizes the need to move away from quality hype and slogans • Stresses the role of the customer, both internal and external • Management involvement and commitment are stressed	• Does not relate to other work on leadership and motivation • Seen by some as undervaluing the contribution of the worker by rejecting bottom-up initiatives. • Seen as being stronger on control systems than the human dimension in organizations
Ishikawa	• Strong emphasis on the importance of people and participation in the problem-solving process • A blend of statistical and people-oriented techniques • Introduces the idea of quality control circles	• Some of his problem-solving methods seen as simplistic • Does not deal adequately with moving quality circles from ideas to action
Taguchi	• Approach pulls quality back to the design stage • Recognizes quality as a societal issue as well as an organizational one • Methods are developed for practising engineers rather than theoretical statisticians • Strong on process control	• Difficult to apply where performance is difficult to measure (e.g. in the service sector) • Quality is seen as primarily controlled by specialists rather than managers and workers • Regarded as generally weak on motivation and people management issues
Crosby	• Provides clear methods which are easy to follow • Worker participation is recognized as important • Strong on explaining the realities of quality and motivating people to start the quality process	• Seen by some as implying that workers are to blame for quality problems • Seen by some as emphasizing slogans and platitudes rather than recognizing genuine difficulties • Zero defects sometimes seen as risk avoidance • Insufficient stress given to statistical methods

they use different dialects'.[11] TQM is a philosophy, a way of thinking and working, that is concerned with meeting the needs and expectations of customers. It attempts to move the focus of quality away from being a purely operations activity into a major concern for the whole organization. Through TQM, quality becomes the responsibility of all parts, departments and sections in the organization. Further, it is the responsibility of all people in an organization. It is concerned with reducing all of the costs of quality, in particular failure costs. TQM also espouses the process of continuous improvement which we discussed in Chapter 18.

TQM is an extension of quality control

TQM can be viewed as a logical extension of the way in which quality-related practice has progressed (*see* Fig. 20.2). Originally quality was achieved by inspection – screening out defects before they were noticed by customers. The quality control (QC) concept developed a more systematic approach to not only detecting, but also treating quality problems. Quality assurance (QA) widened the responsibility for quality to include functions other than direct operations. It also made increasing use of more sophisticated statistical quality techniques. TQM included much of what went before but developed its own distinctive themes. We will use some of these themes to describe how TQM represents a clear shift from traditional approaches to quality.

Specifically TQM can be seen as being concerned with the following:

- meeting the needs and expectations of customers;
- covering all parts of the organization;
- including every person in the organization;
- examining all costs which are related to quality;
- getting things 'right first time', i.e. designing in quality rather than inspecting it in;
- developing the systems and procedures which support quality and improvement;
- developing a continuous process of improvement (this was treated in Chapter 18).

TQM meets the needs and expectations of the customers

In Chapter 17 we defined quality as 'consistent conformance to customers' expectations'. There is little point in putting a quality system in place – calculating costs, training and motivating people and so on – unless it meets the requirements of the customers. In most organizations, defining customer expectations is a key task for marketing. Marketing, however, must also understand the ability of the operation so that it does not promise something that cannot be delivered. Chapter 17 explained a number of ways in which organizations can find out what customer expectations are. However, in the TQM approach, meeting the expectations of customers means more than this; it means seeing things *from a customer's point of view*. This involves the whole organization in understanding the central importance of customers to its success and even to its survival. Customers are seen not as being *external* to the organization but the most important *part* of it. Customers are also seen as human beings, rather than statistics, with individual needs and expectations and deserving of attentive and courteous treatment.

Often companies state their TQM aims in terms of how they manage to serve their customers (*see* Fig. 20.3).

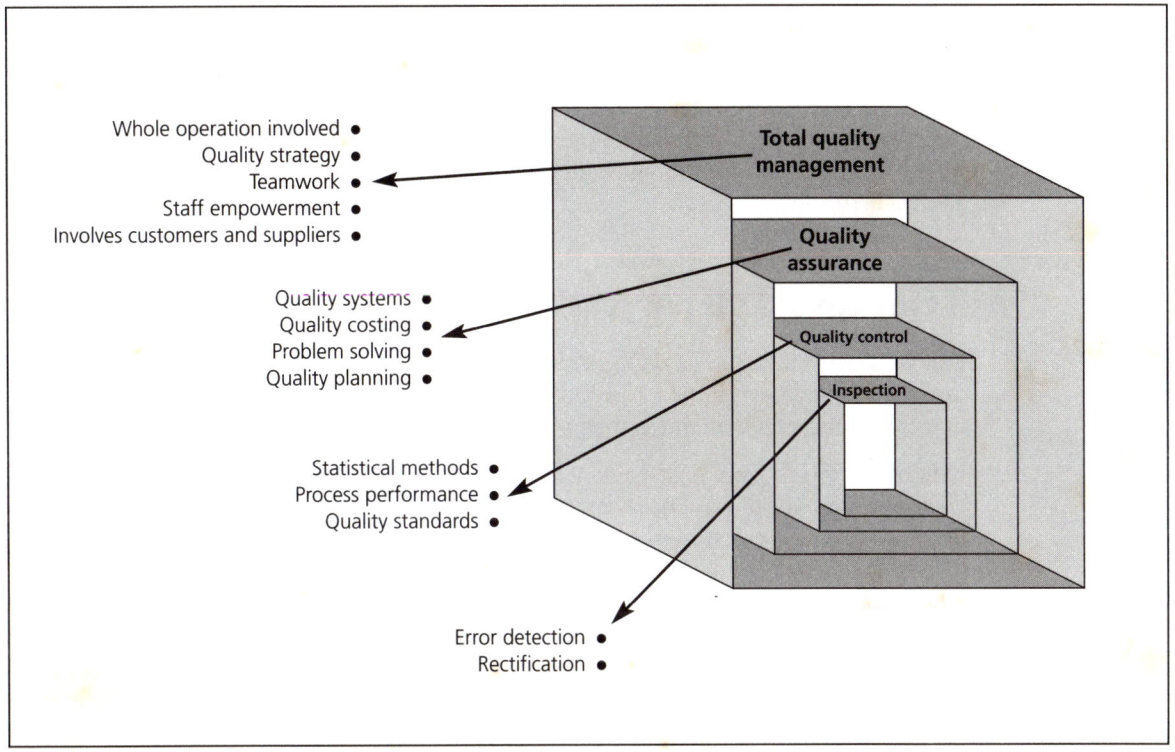

Whole operation involved ●
Quality strategy ●
Teamwork ●
Staff empowerment ●
Involves customers and suppliers ●

Quality systems ●
Quality costing ●
Problem solving ●
Quality planning ●

Statistical methods ●
Process performance ●
Quality standards ●

Error detection ●
Rectification ●

Total quality management

Quality assurance

Quality control

Inspection

Figure 20.2 Total quality management can be viewed as a natural extension of earlier approaches to quality management

Woolworths ... we offer our customers a select range of clothing, foods, and homeware under our own brand name. Our mechandise is of excellent quality, is reasonably priced and represents outstanding value for money.

Guardian National ... one of our corporate values is quality in everything we do.

TrustBank ... naturally, the degree of satisfaction varies from bank to bank, but where we believe TrustBank has the edge is in that quality service is part of our mission.

Dion ... We promise to refund or exchange your purchase in full if you are not entirely satisfied, within 14 days, no questions asked.

Ocean Harvest ... when it comes to providing quality food, there's only one choice that provides so many, Ocean Harvest.

Kolosus Leather Resources ... and we've designed our quality to meet the most stringent international demands of those who design for quality.

Figure 20.3 Extracts from the published accounts of selected South African companies emphasizing their commitment to the quality of their customer service (extracted from 1995/1996 company accounts)

TQM puts the customer at the forefront of decision making. It requires that the implications for the customer are considered at all stages in corporate decision making and that decisions are made and systems created that will not detract from the customer's experience. Not all companies succeed. For example, one South African packaging company used to deliver packaging material to a brewery according to a delivery schedule that suited the packaging company. The schedule was designed to be as efficient as possible, minimizing the distance travelled by the delivery vehicles and maximizing the number of deliveries made. This thinking was fine for the packaging company but did not take into account the needs of its customers. In fact it could make life very difficult for them. One brewery was located in the centre of a major industrial area and had its busiest times in the mornings. However, this was the time of the week when the packaging company scheduled its own deliveries, causing severe disruption.

TQM covers all parts of the organization

'For an organization to be truly effective, every single part of it, each department, each activity, and each person and each level, must work properly together, because every person and every activity affects and in turn is affected by others.'[12]

One of the most powerful aspects to emerge from TQM is the concept of the internal customer and supplier. This is a recognition that everyone is a customer within the organization and consumes goods or services provided by other internal suppliers, and is also an internal supplier of goods and services for other internal customers. The implication of this is that errors in the service provided within an organization will eventually affect the product or service which reaches the external customer. So one of the best ways to ensure that external customers are satisfied is to establish the idea that every part of the organization contributes to external customer satisfaction by satisfying its own internal customers. The idea of internal customer–supplier relationships was introduced in Chapter 1 when we discussed the hierarchy of operations and described how 'micro operations' form an interconnecting network of physical and information flows within the 'macro operation'.

TQM utilizes this concept by stressing that each 'micro operation' has a responsibility to manage these internal customer–supplier relationships. They do this primarily by defining as clearly as possible what their own and their customers' *requirements* are. In effect this means defining what constitutes 'error-free' service – the quality, speed, dependability and flexibility required by internal customers. The exercise replicates what should be going on for the whole operation and its external customers (*see* Fig. 20.4).

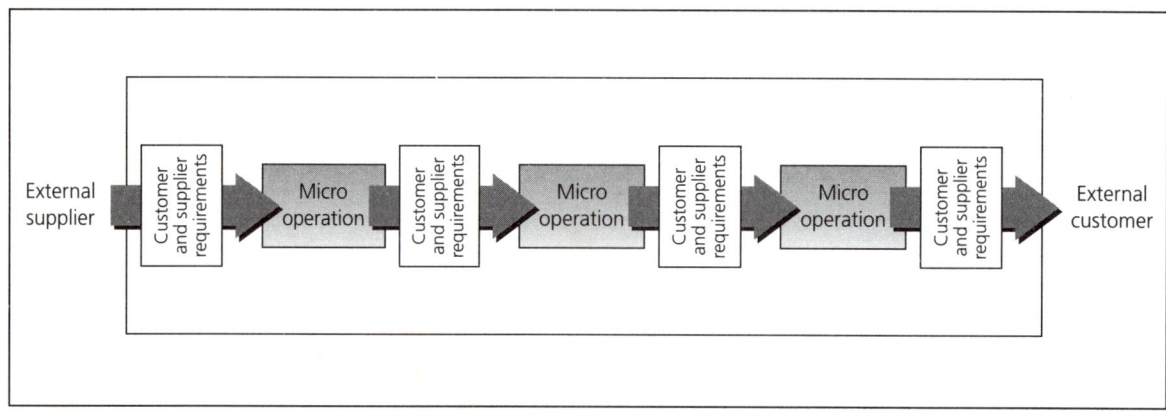

Figure 20.4 The internal customer–supplier relationship between micro operations

HEWLETT-PACKARD'S INTERNAL CUSTOMER CHECKLIST[13]

The computer industry has always been in the forefront of developing and utilizing quality concepts. Quality failures of hardware, software or service are both immediately obvious to customers and seriously damaging to their trust in the supplier. Hewlett-Packard, the world-wide information systems company, is no exception. It was one of the first companies to make a success of the internal-customer concept in its operations. One part of the way it used the concept was a short, but effective, checklist 'pocket guide' which came out of its South Queensferry plant in Scotland. The Pocket Guide which it developed was distributed throughout the company. It suggests each part of the organization should ask itself seven questions which it regards as fundamental to the operation:

- Who are my customers?
- What do they need?
- What is my product or service?
- What are my customers' expectations and measures?
- Does my product or service meet their expectations?
- What is the process for providing my product or service?
- What action is required to improve the process?

H-P then went on to devise a problem-solving methodology, based on its seven questions, the stages for which were as follows:

- Select the quality issue.
- Write an issue statement.
- Identify the process.
- Draw a flow chart.
- Select a process performance measure.
- Conduct a cause-and-effect analysis.

- Collect and analyse the data.
- Identify the major causes of the quality issue.
- Plan for improvements.
- Take the corrective action.
- Collect and analyse the data again.
- Are the objectives met?
- If yes, document and standardize the changes. ■

As well as helping to embed the quality imperative in every part of the operation, the internal-customer concept is useful because it impacts on the 'upstream' parts of the internal supply network. These parts of the organization, especially those who provide internal services, can be the origin of errors which do not always become evident until later in the process. Errors may show up further down the physical process route and have to be traced back to their source. In manufacturing operations the product design department is a good example of this. If an error is made in the basic design of a part, the error could have been transmitted through the detailed design, purchasing, production engineering, and early stages of manufacture before it becomes obvious, probably at the assembly stage.

This chain of customers and suppliers is a central concept of TQM but the picture in Fig. 20.4 belies its complexity. In the creation of final products and services there are usually a myriad of activities and functions which are related, but not normally so clearly as this simple diagram depicts. The relationships are complex, but the principle is clear – everyone has to 'do their bit right' in terms of meeting the expectations of *their* customers. Any one failure in any one place of the internal network of customer–supplier relationships, and there may be significant ramifications for the rest of the organization and its external customers.

Service-level agreements

Some organizations bring a degree of formality to the internal customer concept by encouraging (or requiring) different parts of the operation to agree 'service-level agreements' (SLAs) with each other. SLAs are formal definitions of the dimensions of service and the relationship between two parts of an organization. The type of issues which would be covered by such an agreement could include response times, the range of services, dependability of service supply and so on. Boundaries of responsibility and appropriate performance measures could also be agreed.

For example, an SLA between an information systems support unit and a research unit in the laboratories of a large company could define such performance measures as:

● the types of information network services which may be provided as 'standard';
● the range of special information services which may be available at different periods of the day;
● the minimum 'up-time', i.e. the proportion of time the system will be available at different periods of the day;
● the maximum response time and average response time to get the system fully operational should it fail;
● the maximum response time to provide 'special' services, and so on.

Every person in the organization contributes to quality

TQM is sometimes referred to as 'quality at source'. This notion stresses the impact that each individual staff member has on quality as well as the idea that it is each person's personal responsibility to get quality right. Every single person in an operation has the potential to impair seriously the quality of the products or services received by customers. Some staff can affect quality directly. The staff who physically make products, and the staff who, face-to-face, serve customers, all have the capability to make mistakes which will be immediately obvious to customers (although the effects will be noticed much sooner in high customer contact service operations). Other staff who may be less directly involved in producing goods and services can also generate problems, however – the keyboard operator who mis-keys data, the product designer who fails to investigate thoroughly the conditions under which products will be used in practice, the market forecaster who neglects to find out what information would really be useful to operations management, even the floor sweeper who fails to set proper standards of hygiene in a factory. Each of these people could set in motion a chain of events which customers will eventually see as poor quality products and services.

It follows then, that, if everyone has the ability to impair quality, they also have the ability to improve quality – if only by 'not making mistakes'. It is partly because of this that TQM philosophies place considerable emphasis on the contribution which the individual staff of the organization can make to quality. An understanding of their influence over quality and an acceptance of their responsibility to (at the very least) avoid errors can, it is argued, have a major effect on quality levels. In TQM, however, the contribution of all individuals in the organization is expected to go beyond under-standing their contribution and a commitment to 'not make mistakes'. Individuals are expected to bring something positive to the way they perform their jobs. Everyone is capable of improving the way in which they do their own jobs and practically every-one is capable of helping others in the organization to improve theirs. Therefore, neglecting this potential in staff is neglecting a powerful source of improvement. The principles of 'empowerment' (*see* Chapter 9) are frequently cited as supporting this aspect of TQM.

The shift in attitude which is needed to view employees as the most valuable intel-lectual and creative resource which the organization possesses can still prove difficult for some organizations. When TQM practices first began to migrate from Japan in the late 1970s the ideas seemed even more radical. Some Japanese industrialists even thought (mistakenly) that companies in Western economies would never manage to change. Take, for example, a statement by Konosuke Matsushito which attracted con-siderable publicity.

'We are going to win and the industrial West is going to lose out – there is nothing much you can do about it, because the reasons for your failure are within yourselves. For you, the essence of management is getting the ideas out of the heads of bosses into the hands of labour. For us, the core of management is precisely the art of mobilizing and pulling together the intellectual resources of all employees in the service of the firm. Only by drawing on the com-bined brainpower of all its employees can a firm face up to the turbulence and constraints of today's environment.

'That is why our large companies give their employees three to four times more training than yours. This is why they foster within the firm such intensive exchange and communica-tion. This is why they seek constantly everybody's suggestions and why they demand from the educational system increasing numbers of graduates as well as bright and well-educated generalists, because these people are the lifeblood of industry.'[14]

All of this has implications for the style of management employed within the org-anization generally. It is difficult to imagine the basic principles of total quality management fitting comfortably with any management style other than a relatively part-icipative one. In TQM, performance is centred on individuals who don't make mistakes, individuals who improve the way they do the job, and individuals who learn from their experience. It is not centred directly on procedures or techniques (although these may have a place). These are only the means to an end. They are the means to influence the individual's contribution to quality. The whole decision-making style of the operation, therefore, needs to reflect the inclusion and the contribution of its individuals.

All costs of quality are considered

Few, if any, operations managers would doubt that quality management is a good thing and needs to be done. The benefits have been discussed in Chapters 2 and 17. However, there is a price to pay. The costs of controlling quality may not be small, whether the responsibility lies with each individual or a dedicated quality control department. It is therefore necessary to examine all the costs and benefits associated with quality (in fact 'cost of quality' is usually taken to refer to both costs and benefits of quality). These costs of quality are usually categorized as *prevention costs*, *appraisal costs*, *internal failure costs* and *external failure costs*.

Prevention costs

Prevention costs are those costs incurred in trying to prevent problems, failures and errors from occurring in the first place. They include such things as:

● identifying potential problems and putting the process right before poor quality occurs;
● designing and improving the design of products and services and processes to reduce quality problems;
● training and development of personnel in the best way to perform their jobs.

Appraisal costs

Appraisal costs are those costs associated with controlling quality to check to see if problems or errors have occurred during and after the creation of the product or service. They might include such things as:

CLUB MED[15]

Back in 1950 a sports enthusiast named Gérard Blitz wanted to create some means for others to enjoy sporting holidays at an affordable price. His concept of the Club Med was intended to provide an opportunity for people to holiday together and share the costs and chores of the holiday among themselves. Today many of those principles which Gérard created can still be seen in the way Club Med delivers its services, even though there are now 120 Club Med holiday villages throughout 35 countries. Holiday-makers from more than 60 countries are greeted by Club Med's staff representing 67 nationalities. It is typical of the way Club Med thinks of its staff, however, that it doesn't call them staff, or employees, or agents. It calls them GOs (*Gentils Organisateurs*). Furthermore, it doesn't call its customers customers. It calls them GMs (*Gentils Membres*). Every one of the company's GOs is regarded as having an immediate and direct impact on the quality image of the company. Club Med has consistently refused to appoint a quality director. They are afraid that if they do appoint such a person then everyone would say 'Quality? We've got a director for that!' According to Jean-Louis Pello, Club Med's Director of Internal Communications, the company has over 20 000 quality directors – every member of its staff! All GOs are expected to know and understand Club Med's quality service standards. Over the years these quality service standards have been modified and improved by GOs of all nationalities, in direct response to the realities of everyday life in the Club's villages.

'The GM who spends two weeks in our village in Bali one year and a week in Columbus or anywhere else the next can rest assured of receiving the same levels of service, both tangible and intangible. The GOs and the village managers guarantee coherence, continuity and consistency of service. The values (inherent in the quality service standards) are universal values that everybody can identify with. They are based on respect, generosity, attention, charm and tolerance. Everybody is seen as a person; the village team stimulates individual happiness rather than happiness for everybody – an important distinction. Furthermore, following the simple and ancient principle of giving respect in order to receive it back later, every GO who arrives in a village for a season's work is welcomed as a VIP by a Personnel Service Supervisor and the village manager. In turn that GO will offer the same welcome to thousands of others throughout his or her stay.' ■

- the setting up of statistical process control programmes and acceptance sampling plans;
- the time and effort required to inspect inputs, processes and outputs;
- obtaining processing inspection and test data;
- investigating quality problems and providing quality reports;
- conducting customer surveys and quality audits.

Internal failure costs

Internal failure costs are failure costs associated with errors which are dealt with inside the operation. These costs might include such things as:

- the cost of scrapped parts and material;
- reworked parts and materials;
- the lost production time as a result of coping with errors;
- lack of concentration due to time spent trouble-shooting rather than improvement.

External failure costs

External failure costs are those which are associated with an error going out of the operation to a customer. These costs include such things as:

- loss of customer goodwill affecting future business;
- aggrieved customers who may take up time;
- litigation (or payments to avoid litigation);
- guarantee and warranty costs;
- the cost to the company of providing excessive capability (too much coffee in the pack or too much information to a client).

The relationship between quality costs

In traditional quality management it was assumed that failure costs will decrease as the money spent on appraisal and prevention increases. Furthermore, it was assumed that there is an *optimum* amount of quality effort to be applied in any situation which minimizes the total costs of quality. The argument is that there must be a point beyond which diminishing returns set in – that is, the cost of improving quality gets larger than the benefits which it brings. Figure 20.5 sums up this idea. As quality effort is increased, the costs of providing the effort – through extra quality controllers, inspection procedures and so on – increases proportionally. At the same time, however, the cost of errors, faulty products and so on, decreases because there are fewer of them.

Criticisms of the traditional quality cost model

A 'pure' TQM approach would be to assert that this logic is flawed in a number of important respects.

1 This compromise position implies that failure and poor quality are acceptable. It recognizes that the 'optimum' point is one where there will be errors and failures. TQM challenges the whole concept of the acceptable quality level (AQL) which was outlined in Chapter 17. Why, it is argued, should any operation accept the *inevitability* of errors? Some occupations seem to be able to accept a zero-defect standard (even if they do not always achieve it). No one accepts that it is inevitable that pilots will crash

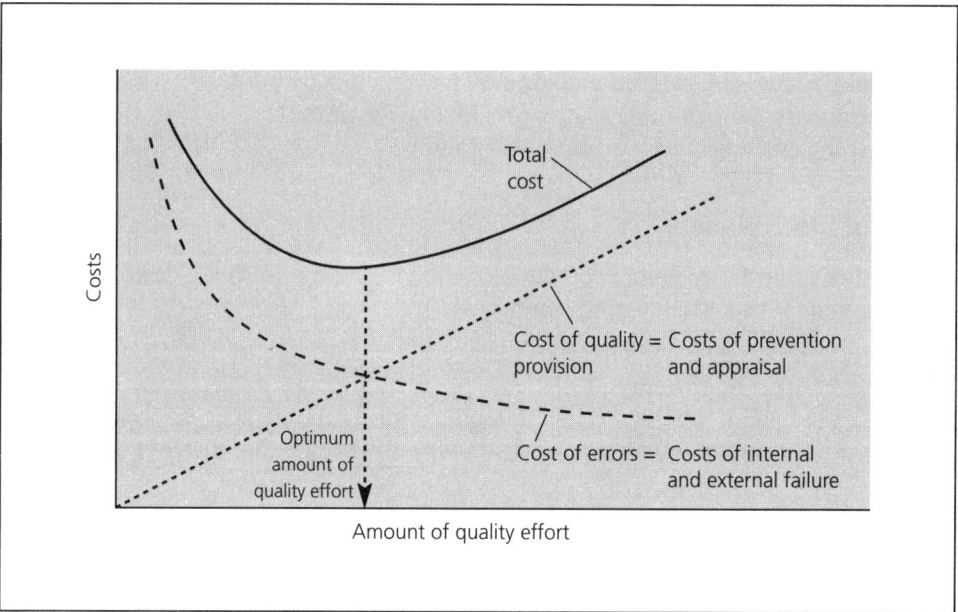

**Figure 20.5
The traditional cost
of quality model**

a certain proportion of their aircraft, or that nurses will drop a certain proportion of the babies which they deliver.

2 It assumes that the costs are known and measurable. Obtaining precise costs of quality is not straightforward, however. Putting realistic figures to the quality cost categories of prevention, appraisal and failure is not a straightforward matter. One study exposes a number of difficulties, including the following:[16]

● It is not easy to separate quality-related costs from those which are an integral part of the manufacturing operation anyway.
● The categorization of costs into prevention, appraisal and failure is more meaningful to quality managers than operations managers.
● Costs of activities which are part-time activities of indirect staff are particularly difficult to derive.

DELIBERATE DEFECTIVES

A story which illustrates the difference in attitude between a TQM and a non-TQM company has become almost a legend among TQM proponents. It concerns a plant in Ontario, Canada, of IBM, the computer company. It ordered a batch of components from a Japanese manufacturer and specified that the batch should have an AQL of three defective parts for every 1000. When the parts arrived in Ontario they were accompanied by a letter which expressed the supplier's bewilderment at being asked to supply defective parts as well as good ones. The letter also explained that they had found it difficult to make parts which were defective, but had indeed managed it. These three defective parts per thousand had been included and were wrapped separately for the convenience of the customer. ■

● Accounting systems are not designed to yield quality-related costs and different accounting practices can distort the results in different ways.

● The significance of warranty costs is difficult to gauge because they relate to earlier manufacture.

3 Failure costs in the traditional model are greatly underestimated. In practice, the failure cost is usually taken to include the cost of 'reworking' defective products, 're-serving' customers, the cost of scrapping parts and materials and the loss of goodwill or even warranty costs if the defective part gets out to the customer. All these are real and important elements of the cost of poor quality, but one of the most important costs is that associated with the disruption which errors cause. The real cost of not having quality should include all the management time wasted in organizing rework and rectification. Even more important, it should take into account the loss of concentration, the erosion of confidence between parts of the operation, and the general disruption which quality problems cause. If we include these, even though they are difficult costs to measure, it becomes clear that error costs can be considerably higher than traditionally thought.

4 It implies that prevention costs, the cost of getting towards zero defects, is inevitably costly. The TQM approach, by stressing the importance of quality to every individual, makes quality an integral part of everyone's work. The traditional assumption is that more quality is primarily achieved by using more inspectors, and therefore means more cost. For example, it is assumed that doubling the effort put into quality means, if not doubling the resources devoted to it, certainly a considerable increase in costs. This need not necessarily be so, however. At the very heart of TQM is the idea that each of us has a responsibility for his or her own quality and is capable of 'doing it right'. This may incur some costs – training, gauges, anything which helps to prevent errors occurring in the first place – but not such a steeply inclined cost curve as the 'optimum-quality' theory.

5 The 'optimum-quality level' approach, by accepting compromise, does little to challenge operations managers and staff to find ways of improving quality.

Put these corrections into the optimum-quality effort calculation and the picture looks very different (*see* Fig. 20.6). If there is an 'optimum', it is a lot further to the right, in the direction of putting more effort (but not necessarily cost) into quality. We used a similar argument to this when describing the 'optimum' degree of preventive maintenance in Chapter 19.

The TQM quality cost model

TQM rejects the optimum-quality-level concept and strives to reduce all known and unknown failure costs by preventing errors and failure taking place. Rather than looking for 'optimum' levels of quality effort it is more usual for TQM proponents to stress the relative balance between different types of quality cost. Of the four cost categories, two – costs of prevention and costs of appraisal – are open to managerial influence, while the other two – internal costs of failure and external costs of failure – show the consequences of changes in the other two. Of the two categories open to direct managerial influence, rather than placing most emphasis on appraisal (so that 'bad products and service don't get through to the customer') TQM emphasizes prevention (to stop errors happening in the first place).

What seems to happen is that when more effort is put into defect prevention it has a significant, positive effect on internal failure costs, followed by reductions both in

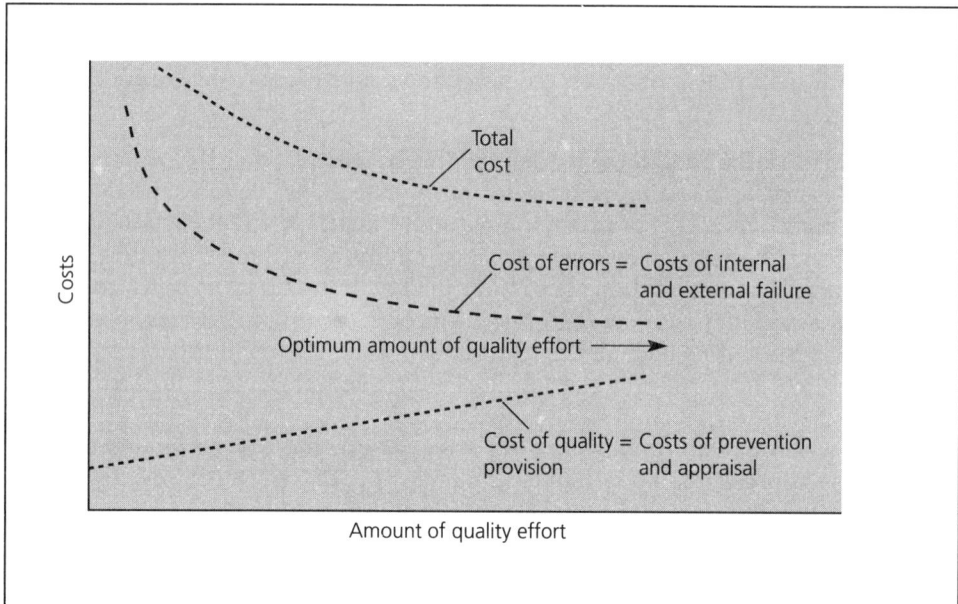

**Figure 20.6
The traditional cost
of quality model
with adjustments
to reflect TQM
criticisms**

external failure costs and, once confidence has been firmly established, in appraisal costs. Eventually even prevention costs can be stepped down in absolute terms, though prevention remains a significant cost in relative terms. Figure 20.7 illustrates this idea. Initially total quality costs may rise as investment in some aspects of prevention – mainly training – is increased. However, some reduction in total costs can quickly follow.

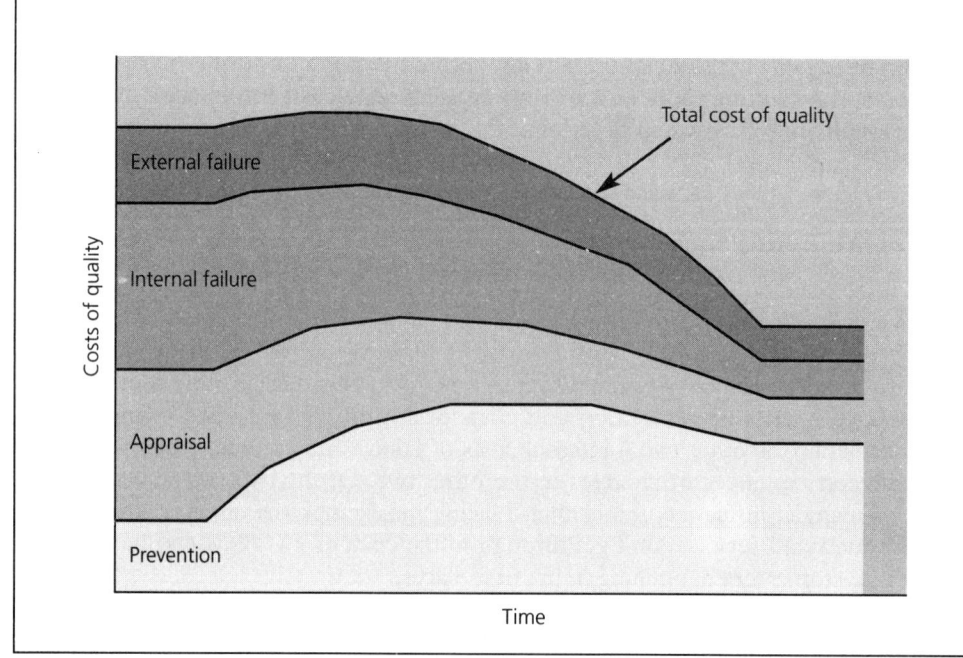

**Figure 20.7
Increasing the
effort into
preventing errors
occurring in the
first place brings
a more than
equivalent
reduction in other
cost categories**

Getting things 'right first time'

Accepting the relationships between categories of quality cost as illustrated in Fig. 20.7 has a particularly important implication for how quality is managed. It shifts the emphasis from *reactive* (waiting for something to happen) to *proactive* (doing something before anything happens). This change in the view of quality costs has come about with a movement from an inspect-in (appraisal-driven) approach, to a design-in (getting it right first time) approach.

Quality systems and procedures

Improving quality is not something that happens simply by getting everyone in an organization to 'think quality'. Very often people are prevented from making improvements by the organization's systems and procedures. Indeed there is a belief that direct operators can only correct, at the moment, 15 per cent of quality problems; the other 85 per cent are management's responsibility because they are due to 'the system' or the lack of one.

A quality system is defined as:

'the organizational structure, responsibilities, procedures, processes and resources for implementing quality management.'[17]

According to Barrie Dale of the University of Manchester Institute of Science and Technology:

'The quality system should define and cover all facets of an organization's operation, from identifying and meeting the needs and requirements of customers, design, planning, purchasing, manufacturing, packaging, storage, delivery and service, together with all relevant activities carried out within these functions. It deals with organization, responsibilities, procedures and processes. Put simply, a quality system is good management practice.'[18]

The documentation which is used in a quality system can be defined at three levels.

Level 1 *Company quality manual.* This is the fundamental document and provides a concise summary of the quality management policy and quality system along with the company objectives and its organization.

Level 2 *Procedures manual.* Describes the system functions, structure and responsibilities in each department.

Level 3 *Work instructions, specifications and detailed methods for performing work activities.*

There can also be a database (Level 4) which contains all other reference documents (forms, standards, drawings, reference information, etc.).

The ISO 9000 and SABS 0157 quality systems

The ISO 9000 series is a set of world-wide standards that establishes requirements for companies' quality management systems. ISO 9000 is being used world-wide to provide a framework for quality assurance. Most countries have their own quality system standards which are equivalent (usually identical) to the ISO 9000 series. Australia has AS3900, Belgium NBN X50, Denmark DS/EN 29000, Malaysia MS985,

Netherlands NEN-9000, South Africa SABS 0157, Sweden SS-ISO 9000, the UK BS5750, and Germany DIN ISO 9000.

ISO 9000 registration requires a third-party assessment of a company's quality standards and procedures and regular audits are made to ensure that the systems do not deteriorate.

The ISO series provides detailed recommendations for setting up quality systems.

ISO 9000 Deals with ... 'quality management and quality assurance standards and guidelines for selection and use'.

ISO 9001 Deals with ... 'quality systems model for quality assurance in design/development, production, installation and servicing'.

ISO 9002 Deals with ... 'quality systems model for quality assurance in production and installation'.

ISO 9003 Deals with ... 'quality systems model for quality assurance in final inspection and test'.

ISO 9004 Deals with ... 'quality management and quality system elements: guidelines'.

The purpose of ISO 9000 is to provide an assurance to the purchasers of products or services that they have been produced in such a way that they meet their requirements. The best way to do this, it is argued, is to define the procedures, standards, and characteristics of the management control system which governs the operation. Such a system will then help to ensure that quality is 'built into' the operation's transformation processes. This is why ISO 9000 is seen as providing benefits both to the organizations adopting it (because it gives them detailed guidance on how to design their control procedures) but most especially to customers (who have the assurance of knowing that the products and services they purchase are produced by an operation working to a defined standard). However, the adoption of ISO 9000 is not seen as beneficial by all authorities, and has been subject to some criticism. The following are just some of the advantages and disadvantages associated with ISO 9000.[19]

Advantages

● Many operations do find that it provides a useful discipline to stick to 'sensible' procedures.

● Many operations have benefited in terms of error reduction, reduced customer complaints and reduced costs of quality.

● The ISO 9000 audit (when an organization is inspected to see if it warrants the award of the ISO, or local country, accreditation) is generally accepted and takes the place of other audits such as customer audits.

● Adopting ISO 9000 procedures can identify existing procedures which are not necessary and can be eliminated.

● Gaining the certificate demonstrates to actual and potential customers that the company takes quality seriously; it therefore has a marketing benefit.

Disadvantages

● The emphasis on standards and procedures encourages 'management by manual' and over-systematized decision making.

● Choosing which of the various ISO 9000 series of standards to apply for is not always easy.

● The standards are too much geared to the engineering industries and some of the terms used are unfamiliar in other industries.

● The whole process of writing procedures, training staff and conducting internal audits is expensive and time consuming.

● Similarly, the time and cost of achieving and maintaining ISO 9000 registration is excessive.

● There is little encouragement or guidance in ISO 9000 on such important issues as continuous improvement and statistical quality control.

ISO 9000 AT SASOL SYNTHETIC FUELS[20]

Although ISO 9002 certification was a competitive advantage for those who had it five years ago, it is now a competitive disadvantage for those who do not have it. This is one of the reasons why Sasol Synthetic Fuels decided to seek ISO 9000 certification. Sasol Synthetic Fuels in Secunda started the ISO 9002 journey with those production units and supporting functions that produce, handle, test and dispatch high-volume, high-value, mostly export products. It was decided that all new plants would be included in the programme. A large number of support functions are centralized which means that Sasol had to include the relevant ones in the programme. They are now certified for the production and delivery of chemical solvents, anode and green coke as well as hydrogen-rich and methane gas.

Sasol Synthetic Fuels has 60 000 drawings, kept, copied and distributed from a central point away from the plant. Three microfilms, one hard copy master and a further 18 additional copies are made for approval of all new and revised drawings. An average of 39 000 copies are made per month. Anybody that wants a drawing has to fill in a request, wait at least three hours, and more likely drive there by car, pick-up or motor cycle. It is, therefore, not surprising that people in the plant did not destroy their drawings after use, but hung on to them for future use. Small modifications were marked up on these private drawings, but were not fed back to the drawing office. Before implementing ISO 9000 people used to spend hours driving up and down in search of relevant documents in order to do their job. Sasol had 250 procedure libraries when Sasol Two and Sasol Three were still managed as two separate plants. This was reduced to 190 when they were combined into Sasol Synthetic Fuels (Pty) Ltd. Sasol developed and implemented a computerized indexing system to control and manage documentation, equipment and records and the changes thereto.

'It has become evident to Sasol,' says Jan Hatting, Total Quality Manager, *'that you cannot become a world-class producer if you do not, among other things, have proper control over and trust in the accuracy of your documentation, data and records. Complying with the ISO 9000 standard requirements has helped Sasol Synthetic Fuels achieve that goal. We believe that ISO 9002 is a good minimum standard foundation on which to build a total quality management programme. The same applies for the compilation and continuous improvement of our manufacturing policy, strategy, procedures and work instructions.'* ■

IMPLEMENTING TQM IMPROVEMENT PROGRAMMES

Not all of the TQM initiatives which are launched by organizations, often with high expectations, will go on to fulfil their potential of having a major impact on performance improvement. *The Economist* magazine, reporting on some companies' disillusionment with their TQM experiences, quoted from several surveys.[21] For example:

'Of 500 US manufacturing and service companies, only a third felt their TQ programmes had significant impact on their competitiveness.'

'Only a fifth of the 100 British firms surveyed believed their quality programmes had achieved tangible results.'

'Of those quality programmes that have been in place for more than two years, two thirds simply grind to a halt because of their failure to produce hoped-for results.'

There are two broad types of failure which affect TQM implementation:

● the TQM initiative is not introduced and implemented effectively,
and
● after the TQM has been introduced successfully its effectiveness fades over time.

TQM implementation

A number of factors appear to influence the eventual success of performance improvement programmes such as TQM. These are as follows:

A quality strategy

Without thinking through the overall purpose and long-term goals of a TQM programme it is difficult for any organization to know where it is going. A quality strategy is necessary to provide the goals and guidelines which help to keep the TQM programme heading in a direction which is appropriate for the organization's other strategic aims. Specifically, the quality strategy should have something to say about the following:

● the competitive priorities of the organization, and how the TQM programme is expected to contribute to achieving increased competitiveness;
● the roles and responsibilities of the various parts of the organization in the quality improvement;
● the resources which will be available for quality improvement;
● the general approach to, and philosophy of, quality improvement in the organization.

Top management support

The full understanding, support and leadership of an organization's top management emerges as a crucial factor in almost all the studies of TQM implementation. For example, Table 20.2 shows one such study.

The importance of top management support goes far beyond the allocation of resources to the programme; it sets the priorities for the whole organization. If the organ-

Table 20.2 Quality barriers ranked in order of 'very significant' replies[22]

Top management commitment	92%
Too narrow an understanding of quality	38%
Horizontal boundaries: functions and specialisms	31%
Vested interests	29%
Organizational politics	28%
Cynicism	28%
Organizational structure	27%
Customer expectations	26%
Speed of corporate action	24%

ization's senior managers do not understand and show commitment to the programme, it is only understandable that the rest of the organization will ask why they should do so. By 'top management support' TQM proponents usually mean that senior personnel must put in a lot more effort at an operational level. It means that they must:

● understand and believe in the link between 'doing things right' and the company's overall business;
● understand the practicalities of quality and be able to get over the principles and techniques (for example, statistical process control) to the rest of the organization;
● be able to participate in the total problem-solving process to eliminate errors;
● formulate and maintain a clear idea of what quality means for the organization.

A steering group

The task of a steering group is to plan the implementation of the programme. It could be argued that it also has a second task, that is to make sure that, even if it does not work itself totally out of a job, its role diminishes over time. The first of these tasks involves planning the overall direction of the programme in terms of what it should achieve as it gathers pace. It also involves deciding where to start the programme and who initially to involve. Further, the group is responsible for monitoring the programme and making sure that all the learning and experience, which is accumulated as the programme progresses, is not lost. The second task is achieved at least partly by establishing self-supporting improvement groups.

Group-based improvement

No one can really know a process quite like the people who operate it. The staff who work in the operation are often the ones who know best, for example, how to stop the machines malfunctioning, or who can predict that most adjustments will be needed after a product change. People inside the system have access to the informal as well as the formal information networks. Furthermore, they not only have the experience of the process, they are most affected by changes to it. However, working as individuals staff cannot pool their experience nor learn from one another. This is why successful TQM programmes are almost always based on teams.

The nature and composition of the team will depend on the circumstances. *Quality circles* are much used in Japan but have encountered mixed success in the west. These

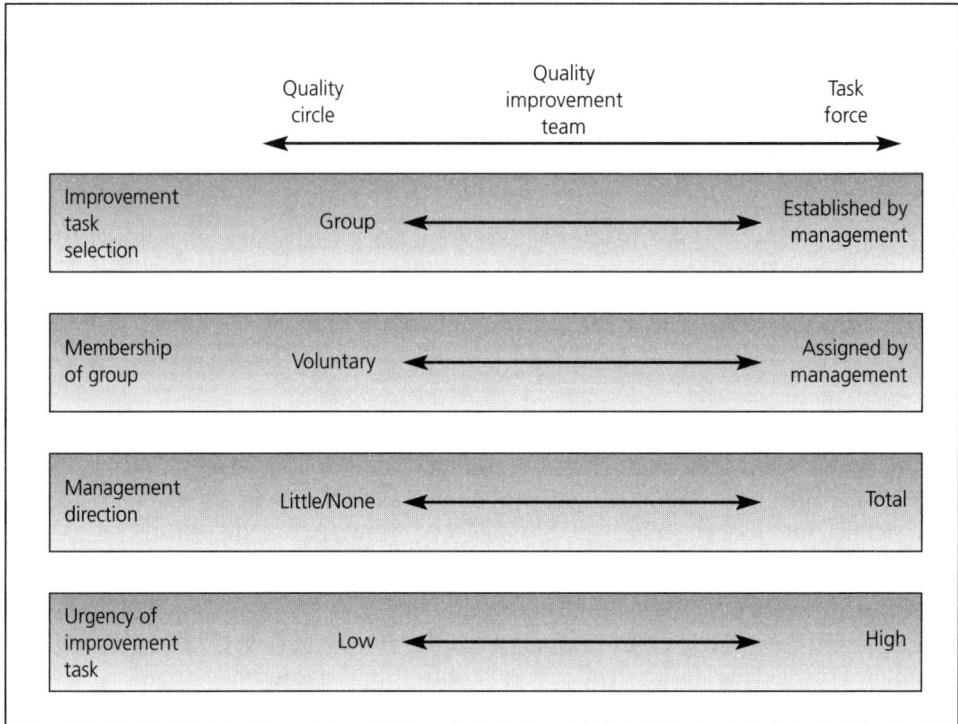

**Figure 20.8
Different types of
improvement
group have
different
characteristics**

are usually voluntary groups who work on the improvement issues which they them-selves see as worth studying. A very different type of team is the '*task force*', or what some US companies call a 'tiger team'. Compared with quality circles, this type of group is far more management directed and focused. Most quality improvement teams are between these two extremes (*see* Fig. 20.8).

Improvement groups cannot be formed, then left to fend for themselves. They need support – technical, managerial and emotional. In some types of operations this is particularly important. For example, if a manufacturing process is large, integrated and technically complex, many (although, it should be stressed, not all) of the technical sources of errors are possibly beyond the control of the immediate staff. The more straightforward the process technology, or labour intensive the processes, then generally the more scope an improvement group has. Even where technology makes self-generated improvement difficult, however, the group can usefully influence and guide the specialists called in to deal with the problem.

Success is recognized

Any TQM implementation needs to consider how it should respond to the efforts of the improvement teams. If quality improvement is so important, then success should be marked in some way. Recognizing success formally stresses the importance of the qual-ity improvement process as well as rewarding effort and initiative. Participating in the development process itself (a part of their job which most managers take for granted) is also sometimes seen as rewarding by many in the organization. For example, a company making lighting products in KwaZulu-Natal has several manufacturing sites. At one site an improvement team had developed, together with some manufacturing systems engineering help, a whole new cell layout with in-process gauging devices and quality charting methods. The company's management decided to launch a similar series of quality improvement initiatives at one of its other sites. The improvement group of seven operatives together with their supervisor, production management and quality supervisor were asked to give a presentation at the other site. To quote one of the operators:

'We had a rehearsal a few days before we went and we were all nervous – remember we aren't used to doing this kind of thing. But we took photographs of the cell and generally got our act together before the visit. The presentation took place in the works canteen, and I think that we were all daunted by the sea of faces, but it seemed to go well. When they started asking us questions it was surprising how interested they were in our answers; no one has taken that much notice of me before! At the end they all applauded! That was the best reward of all.'

Training is the heart of quality improvement

It is no coincidence that so many successful programmes have a training manager as one of their prime movers. TQM is, partly at least, an attitudinal change, so the development task is fundamental to it. There are techniques for staff to learn as well, of course, but the purpose of the techniques is solely to work towards the basic objective – the elimination of errors.

TQM loses its effectiveness

Even TQM programmes which are successfully implemented are not necessarily guaranteed to continue to bring long-term improvement. They may lose their impetus over time. This phenomenon has been variously described as *quality disillusionment*[23] and *quality droop*.[24] Figure 20.9 illustrates this loss of effectiveness.

Various researchers and consultants who have experienced quality disillusionment have put forward prescriptions which are intended to reduce the risk of it occurring. Typically, these prescriptions include the following:[25]

● Do not define 'quality' in TQM narrowly; it includes all aspects of performance (what we have called the performance objectives of operations management).
● Make all quality improvement relate to the performance objectives of the operation. TQM is not an end in itself; it is a means of improving performance.
● TQM is not a substitute for the responsibilities of normal managerial leadership. Ineffective managers are not made better simply by adopting TQM.
● TQM is not a 'bolt-on' attachment to the company – an activity which is separate from the other activities of the organization. It should be integrated with and indistinguishable from everyday activities.
● Avoid the hype. TQM has a considerable intuitive attraction for many. It is sometimes tempting to exploit the motivational 'pull' of TQM through slogans and exhortations rather than thoroughly thought-out plans.
● Adapt TQM to the circumstances of the organization. Different organizations will have different needs depending on their circumstances. This means that different aspects of TQM might become more or less important.

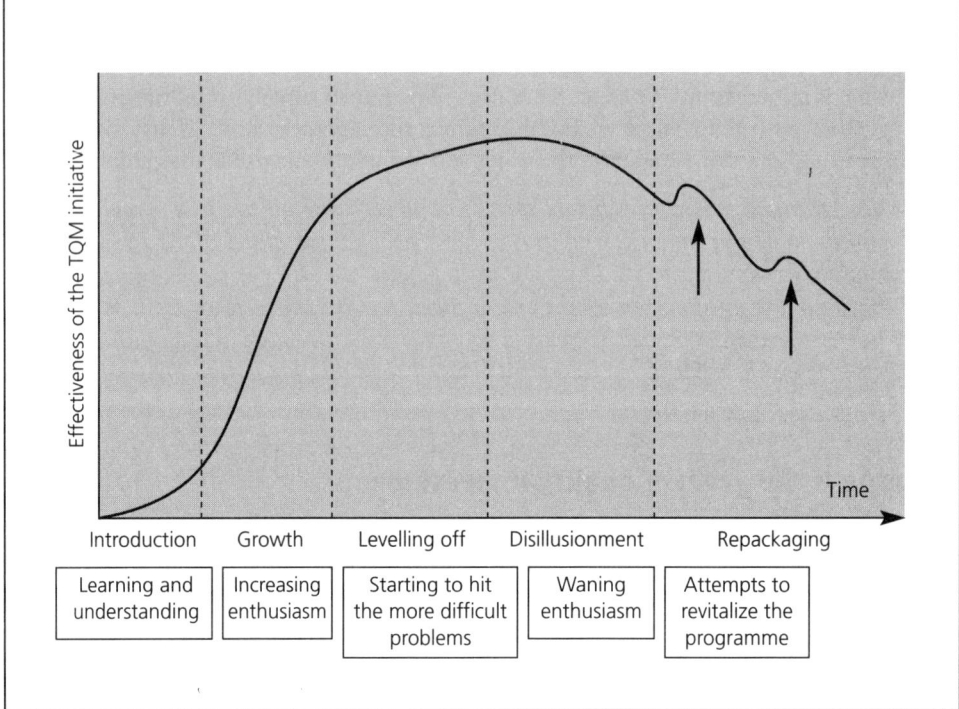

**Figure 20.9
The pattern of
some TQM
programmes which
run out of
enthusiasm**

QUALITY AWARDS

The importance of quality, and especially of TQM, has been recognized world-wide as an important integrator of many aspects of operations improvement. Following this recognition, various bodies have sought to stimulate quality improvement through establishing quality awards.

A number of quality award schemes have been developed since the 1950s to recognize leaders in the improvement of quality and as a spur for many other organizations. The three best known awards are The Deming Prize, The Malcolm Baldridge National Quality Award and the European Quality Award.

The Deming Prize

The Deming Prize was instituted by the Union of Japanese Scientists and Engineers in 1951 and is awarded to those companies, initially in Japan, but more recently opened to overseas companies, which have successfully applied 'company-wide quality control' based upon statistical quality control. There are several categories of winners including individuals, factories and divisions. There are also ten major assessment categories:

policy and objectives, organization and its operation, education and its extension, assembling and disseminating of information, analysis, standardization, control, quality assurance, effects and future plans.

Hundreds of applications are made for the prize each year. The applicants are required to submit a detailed description of quality practices. This is a significant activity in itself and many companies claim a great deal of benefit from having done so. A shortlist is then created and site visits are made by inspectors to the organizations on the shortlist. The site visits include company presentations, in-depth questioning by examiners, top management meetings and the opportunity for examiners to see any parts of the plant and question any worker.

The Malcolm Baldridge National Quality Award

In the early 1980s the American Productivity and Quality Center recommended that an annual prize, similar to the Deming Prize, should be awarded in America. The award was named after the Secretary of Commerce, Malcolm Baldridge, who was killed in an accident shortly before the legislation for the award became law in 1987.

The purpose of the awards was to stimulate American companies to improve quality and productivity, to recognize achievements, to establish criteria for a wider quality effort and to provide guidance on quality improvement.

The main examination categories are: leadership, information and analysis, strategic quality planning, human resource utilization, quality assurance of products and services, quality results and customer satisfaction.

The process, like that of the Deming Prize, includes a detailed application and site visits.

European Quality Award

In 1988 14 leading Western European companies formed the European Foundation for Quality Management (EFQM). By July 1993 there were more than 300 members from most Western European countries and most business sectors. An important objective of the EFQM is to recognize quality achievement. Because of this, in 1992, it launched the European Quality Award (EQA). The European Quality Award is awarded to the most successful exponent of total quality management in Western Europe each year. European quality prizes are awarded to a number of companies that demonstrate excellence in the management of quality as their fundamental process for continuous improvement. To receive a prize, companies must demonstrate that their approach to total quality management has contributed significantly to satisfying the expectations of customers, employees and others with an interest in the company for the past few years. Prize-winning companies are intended to be a model of excellence through quality, against which all companies can measure their own quality achievements and their own drive for continuous improvement.

As yet, there is no official, national quality award in South Africa. A number of organizations are working on the concept of such an award, including the South African Quality Institute. It is anticipated that there will be an award format announced soon.

Cyril Gamede, Umgeni Water

Umgeni Water is the largest agent for bulk storage, treatment and distribution of potable water in the KwaZulu-Natal servicing area of more than 24 000 km². The main infrastructure consists of 12 dams, 13 waterworks, 10 waste-waterworks, a number of pumpstations and an extensive network of tunnels, aqueducts and pipelines. Cyril Gamede is the director responsible for operations at Umgeni Water. He says,

'Caring for the environment and the millions of people living in KwaZulu-Natal, the Umgeni Water's environmental thrust has been largely targeted at improving the quality of life of the people while enabling them to conserve their natural resources – both land and water. The constant rise in the number of people who live in informal settlements around streams and other water resources has placed an increasing pressure on this scarce resource. Farmers spraying their crops with chemical pesticides and hormonal chemicals, littering, oil/chemicals/ medicines and industrial effluent in general also affect water quality. These chemicals can seep into the ground water and eventually flow into streams and rivers. Umgeni Water in association with the Department of Water Affairs and Forestry, has embarked on a Water Quality Management programme that involves the public in a drive to 'clean up' the river basin and prevent further pollution of our scarce resources. Umgeni has obtained the services of a full-time consultant who is under contract to implement the Water Quality Management system throughout the organization. The programme involves the identification of areas where environmental impacts can be improved and the implementation of changes to the systems and practices which, at present, do not contribute to the improvement of the environment.

'One of the fundamental principles underpinning Umgeni Water's Quality Management system is that of considering environmental impacts from "cradle to grave". Umgeni Water is committed to applying the principles of Quality Management to all projects. In order to ensure that this occurs in practice, a number of measures have been implemented:

- *Environmental specifications are now a standard feature of all civil, mechanical, electrical and building contract documents;*
- *Environmental impact mitigation measures are collated into quality management plans during preliminary design;*
- *The environmental, health and safety risks associated with construction and operational activities are assessed by performing a Hazards and Operability Study (HAZOPS) during detailed design;*
- *Quality awareness programmes in Zulu and English were instituted at construction sites for contractors and consultants;*
- *An environmental officer is appointed to each major project to conduct quality audits and provide professional guidance.*

'Monitoring procedures and regular audits will be developed to check operational compliance with accepted environmental standards. During the year only three complaints were received from members of the public and our next step is to place public complaints registers at all major sites and to report these matters in the Quality Officer's audit reports.

'Monitoring of "bugs" in rivers, dams and wastewater effluents continues to provide us with an early warning system for possible health hazards in raw water supplies, especially to those people who rely on the rivers as their source of water.

'All these efforts have earned us ISO 9002 certification from the SABS and this has significantly contributed towards the management of our water resources.' ∎

Source: By kind permission of Cyril Gamede/Umgeni Water

SUMMARY

■ Although the origins of total quality management go back to the 1940s and '50s, the term was first used formally in 1957 by Feigenbaum. Many authorities have contributed to the development of the ideas, however. These authorities include Feigenbaum, Deming, Juran, Ishikawa, Taguchi and Crosby. The emphasis placed on various aspects of total quality management varies among the authorities, but the general thrust of their arguments are similar.

■ Total quality management can be seen as being an extension of the traditional approach to quality. Quality control was replaced by the concept of quality assurance which in turn has been superseded by TQM.

■ TQM puts customers at the forefront of quality decision making. Customers' needs and expectations are always considered first in measuring achieved quality.

■ TQM is a philosophy which applies to all parts of the organization. If everybody in the organization can detract from the company's effectiveness, then everyone also has the potential to make a positive contribution. A central concept of TQM is its use of internal customers and suppliers to enable each part of the organization to identify its contribution to overall quality.

■ TQM places considerable emphasis on the role and responsibilities of every member of staff within an organization to influence quality. It often encourages the idea of empowering individuals to improve their own part of the operation.

■ The cost model implied by TQM is very different from that used in the more traditional approach to quality. Whereas traditionally the emphasis was usually placed on finding an 'optimum' amount of quality effort which minimized the costs of providing quality effort and the benefits in terms of reduction in errors, TQM emphasizes the balance between different types of quality costs. It classifies quality costs into prevention costs, appraisal costs, internal failure costs and external failure costs. TQM argues that by increasing the amount of cost and effort placed on prevention there will be a more than equivalent reduction in the other cost categories.

■ TQM assumes that organizations will need to put in place management control systems which facilitate quality improvements. Such systems help to formalize what is good management practice anyway.

■ The most universal set of systems and procedures relating to quality are those influenced by the ISO 9000 standards. These standards are intended to assure purchasers of products and services that they have been produced in a way which meets customer requirements. However, ISO 9000 base standards have received some criticism as being inflexible.

■ A number of factors appear to be influential in ensuring the success of TQM initiatives. These are:
– the existence of a fully worked-out quality strategy;
– top management support;
– a steering group to guide the initiative;
– group-based improvements;
– success in quality being recognized;
– an emphasis on appropriate training.

■ A number of organizations have attempted to encourage TQM by the award of prizes and certificates. The best known of these are the Deming Prize, the Malcolm Baldridge National Quality Award, and, in Europe, the European Quality Award (EQA).

The Waterlander Hotel[26]

The previous evening's banquet for Plastix International had been a complete disaster, and Walter Hollestelle, the hotel General Manager, was still recovering from the series of telephone conversations of that morning.

First, with the Vice-President of Global Marketing, Plastix International Plc:

'I had hoped that by having our annual sales conference at your renowned hotel in Amsterdam we would be treated to an even better level of service than last year, when we were at Rotterdam; but we were to be deeply disappointed. After all the problems you have caused us over the last two days, from faulty video projection to shortages of cups at coffee breaks, I had hoped that at least the final conference dinner would run smoothly, but you let us down badly. The cocktail reception was a farce: the choice of non-alcoholic drinks that we specially ordered didn't appear until the last minute, and as the President's wife is teetotal, you can imagine the embarrassment that caused! A spilt tray of snacks was not cleared up quickly and several guests got food all over their shoes and dresses. And why did the reception drag on for so long?

'When we were finally asked into the dining room, it clearly wasn't properly prepared. Some of the tables (including ours) were without flowers, which upset my wife, who had been involved with the selection of arrangements. Even the flowers that were there were the wrong variety and looked as if they had been on the tables since yesterday.

'The meal was the worst I have ever seen! I never expect banquet food to be as good as à la carte, but this was awful! The starter was dried up and chewy, and the sweet soufflés were flat and rubbery. And we couldn't believe that anyone could mess up a simple entrée. We were served the cutlets and potatoes, but the sauce and vegetables didn't appear until I'd nearly finished mine.

'And what happened to the microphones on the top table? The photographer didn't turn up either, which is perhaps a blessing, as the tables weren't cleared completely after the sweet, and I'm sure that everyone would have looked in a bad mood after all the mess-up! I can tell you straight – we won't be paying all your exorbitant charges for this banquet and I expect a written apology for all the upset we have been caused. The President must think I am an idiot to have chosen this hotel, and I think he has a point ...'

Next, with the Manager of Aalsmeer Electronics:

'... I was told that the public address system had to be set up by 7.00 pm. We often do jobs of this type, and two hours is more than enough, so we allowed an extra half-hour and started at 4.30 pm. Your staff wouldn't let us get to the tables to wire them, and we had to wait until they cleared them off for us ...'

Then, with his own Hotel Services Manager:

'... it has always been agreed that we must wait until the cutlery has been laid before we set out the flowers, and yesterday we simply weren't given enough time to see to all the tables. As for the types of flowers, we were never told that the client wanted red and pink arrangements. I would have recommended other colours anyway, as reds would not look good against the dining room decor. Unfortunately, the electricians moved our arrangements out of the way against a heating outlet, so by the time we got to them, the flowers looked a bit beyond their best condition. I suppose that's what happens if you allow contractors to interfere with our operation.'

And, with the Conference Manager:

'We were never told that the client wanted to use the video equipment, which was scheduled for repairs next weekend. Had I known, we could have hired in another projector, but we never got the conference check-list back from the client. If we had got that, it would also have indicated that there were an extra ten delegates here just for the morning to make some sort of presentation to the conference. These problems are all down to the client: if they don't follow our system, it's their fault if things go wrong.'

From the Head Chef:

'... I always get a detailed schedule from the head waiter. I get the fish, the sauces, the vegetables and the desserts ready according to that schedule – if things run as late as they did last night, you can expect a few problems. Cooking is an art. All the chefs know how to cook to perfection every time, but if we can't serve the food when it's ready, it will be messed up. I can tell you that if you think the customer was angry, you should have come into the kitchen. Some of the conference delegates were rude to the waiters, who came back into the kitchen and told the chefs. All the staff were really upset and Pierre, our sauce chef, refused to start on the cutlet sauce until the fish course was cleared.'

From the Head Waiter:

'... we weren't told that the electricians would have to wire the tables. They worked setting up the loudspeakers and amplifiers while we were setting the table cloths and laying the place settings. Their foreman then told us that the tables *would have to be cleared for them, so you can imagine the problems that caused. I think we did very well to put everything right in under half an hour.'*

Finally, with the photographer:

'... we were booked for 10.00 pm and the Conference Manager told us that, according to the customer, we would only be needed for half an hour during the speeches. When we arrived they were still in the middle of the meal, and so I waited a bit, but we had another booking at the Concert Hall at the end of a performance at 11.00 pm, so I had to rush off. If we'd known earlier I could have arranged for a partner to come along ...' ■

Questions

1 Why did things go wrong at the banquet?
2 How could a TQM approach to the hotel's operations help to prevent such disasters occurring in the future?
3 How could ISO 9000 help the hotel?

DISCUSSION QUESTIONS

1 Find out more about one of the 'quality gurus'. Describe his background, his approach to quality and his key contributions to the subject.

2 Talk to an operations manager about TQM. Try to assess what TQM means for that organization and the benefits and problems that have resulted.

3 Identify some of the micro operations that might be found in a high-class restaurant operation. Describe some of the things that might go wrong in each of them and assess the impact of them on the final, external customer.

4 A university is considering creating service-level agreements for its lecturing staff. Explain what is meant by a service-level agreement and suggest some performance measures that might be used.

5 What resistance might there be in an organization to Matsushito's assertion that 'the core of management is precisely the art of mobilizing and pulling together the intellectual resources of all employees in the service of the firm'?

6 Identify the main costs of quality for the following organizations:
    a university library
    a washing machine manufacturer
    a nuclear electricity generating plant
    a church.

7 Discuss the differences between the 'traditional' and the TQM views on the cost of quality.

8 Get hold of a copy of ISO 9000 or an equivalent and assess its potential impact on quality.

9 Ask an operations manager to describe *how* quality has been improved in the organization over the last few years. Compare and contrast your findings with the section in this chapter on TQM implementation.

10 Discuss the advantages and disadvantages for an organization considering applying to be assessed for a major quality award.

NOTES ON CHAPTER

1 Feigenbaum, A.V. (1986) *Total Quality Control*, McGraw-Hill.

2 Deming, W.E. (1982) *Quality, Productivity and Competitive Position*, MIT Center for Advanced Engineering Study.
Deming, W.E. (1986) *Out of Crisis*, MIT Center for Advanced Engineering Study.

3 Oakland, J.S. (1992) *Total Quality Management* (2nd edn), Butterworth-Heinemann.

4 Juran, J.M. (1989) *Juran on Leadership for Quality, and Executive Handbook*, Free Press.
Juran, J.M. and Gryna, F.M. (1980) *Quality Planning and Analysis*, McGraw-Hill.
Juran, J.M., Gryna, F.M. and Bingham, R.S. (eds) (1988) *Quality Control Handbook* (4th edn), McGraw-Hill.

5 Ishikawa, K. (1972) *Guide to Quality Control*, Asian Productivity Organization.
Ishikawa, K. (1985) *What is Total Quality Control? – The Japanese Way*, Prentice Hall.

6 Taguchi, G. and Clausing, D. (1990) 'Robust Quality', *Harvard Business Review*, Vol 68, No 1, pp 65–75.

7 Crosby, P.B. (1979) *Quality is Free*, McGraw-Hill.

8 Crosby, P.B., *op. cit.*

9 Crosby, P.B., *op. cit.*

10 Based on the analysis by Flood, R.L. (1993) *Beyond TQM*, John Wiley.

11 Oakland, J.S., *op. cit.*

12 Muhlemann, A., Oakland, J. and Lockyer, K. (1992) *Production and Operations Management* (6th edn), Pitman Publishing.

13 Source: Rees, J. and Rigby, P. (1988) 'Total Quality Control – The Hewlett-Packard Way' *in* Chase, R.L. (ed) (1988) *Total Quality Management*, IFS.

14 Matsushito, K. (1985) 'Why the West will Lose', *Industrial Participation*, Spring.

15 Source: Pello, J-L. and Prioriol, M. (1993) 'What's Good for GMs is Good for Club Med', *European Quality*, June.

16 Source: Plunkett, J.J. and Dale, B.S. (1987) 'A Review of the Literature in Quality-Related Costs', *The International Journal of Quality and Reliability Management*, Vol 4, No 1.

17 International Standards Organization, ISO 8402, 1986.

18 Dale, B.G. (1994) 'Quality Management Systems' *in* Dale B.G. (ed), *Managing Quality*, Prentice Hall.

19 Dale, B.G. *in* Dale, B.G. (ed), *op. cit.*

20 Source: Discussions with Sasol staff.

21 Quoted in Smith, S., Tranfield, D., Foster, M. and Whittle, S. (1994) 'Strategies for Managing the TQ Agenda', *International Journal of Operations and Production Management*, Vol 14, No 1.

22 Binney, G. (1992) 'Making Quality Work: Lessons from Europe's Leading Companies', The Economist Intelligence Unit, *Special Report*, No. P655.

23 Oakland, J.S. (1992), *op. cit.*

24 Slack, N. (1991) *The Manufacturing Advantage*, Mercury Business Books.

25 Slack, N., *op. cit.*

26 Based on an idea originally used by Professor Keith Lockyer.

SELECTED FURTHER READINGS

Albrecht, K. and Bradford, L.J. (1990) *The Service Advantage*, Dow Jones Irwin.

Armistead, C.G. (ed) (1994) *The Future of Services Management*, Kogan Page.

Berry, L.L. and Parasuraman, A. (1991) *Marketing Services: Competing Through Quality*, Free Press.

Boaden, R.J., Dale, B.G. and Polding, E. (1991) 'A State-of-the-Art Survey of Total Quality Management in the Construction Industry', *a Research Report to the European Construction Institute*, Loughborough.

Bounds, G., Yorks, L., Adams, M. and Ranney, G. (1994) *Beyond Total Quality Management: Towards the Emerging Paradigm*, McGraw-Hill.

Brown, S.W., Gummesson, E., Edvardsson, B. and Gustavsson, B. (eds) (1991) *Service Quality: Multidisciplinary and Multinational Perspectives*, Lexington Books.

Collier, D.A. (1994) *The Service/Quality Solution: Using Service Management to Gain Competitive Advantage*, Irwin and ASQC Quality Press.

Crosby, P.B. (1979) *Quality is Free*, McGraw-Hill.

Cullen, J.M. (1991) 'Conditions for Success', *Total Quality Management*, June.

Dale, B.G. (1991) 'Starting on the Road to Success', *TQM Magazine*, Vol 3, No 2.

Dale, B.G. (1994) *Managing Quality* (2nd edn), Prentice Hall.

Dale, B.G. and van der Wiele, T. (1993) *Total Quality Management Directory*, The University Press, Rotterdam.

Deming, W.E. (1986) *Out of the Crisis*, MIT Press.

Desatnick, R.L. (1987) *Managing to Keep the Customer*, Jossey-Bass.

Feigenbaum, A.V. (1986) *Total Quality Control*, McGraw-Hill.

Garvin, D.A. (1983) 'Quality on the Line', *Harvard Business Review*, Vol 61, No 5, pp 65–75.

Garvin, D.A. (1984) 'What Does "Product Quality" Really Mean?', *Sloan Management Review*, Fall, pp 25–43.

Garvin, D.A. (1987) 'Competing on the Eight Dimensions of Quality', *Harvard Business Review*, Vol 65, No 6, pp 101–9.

Garvin, D.A. (1988) *Managing Quality: The Strategic and Competitive Edge*, The Free Press.

Garvin, D.A. (1991) 'How the Baldridge Award Really Works', *Harvard Business Review*, Vol 69, No 6.

Harari, O. (1993) 'Ten Reasons Why TQM Doesn't Work', *Management Review*, Jan.

Knowles, R. (1992) 'Building Quality People', *Quality Forum*, Vol 18, No 1.

Lockyer, K.G., Oakland, J.S. and Duprey, C.H. (1982) 'Quality Control in British Manufacturing Industry', *Quality Assurance*, Vol 8, No 2.

Oakland, J.S. (1992) *Total Quality Management* (2nd edn), Butterworth-Heinemann.

Øvretveit, J. (1992) *Health Service Quality*, Blackwell.

Parmee, J.L. (1995) 'Quality Assurance in the Management of Water Supply', *SABS Bulletin*, Vol 14, No 6, pp 7–8.

Taguchi, G. (1986) *Introduction to Quality Engineering: Designing Quality into Products and Process*, Asian Productivity Organization.

Teboul, J. (1991) *Managing Quality Dynamics*, Prentice Hall.

THE OPERATIONS CHALLENGE

The ultimate test for any operations manager is whether he or she can develop an operation which meets the challenges which lie ahead for the organization. This final part of the book identifies a number of key challenges which all operations managers will eventually face.

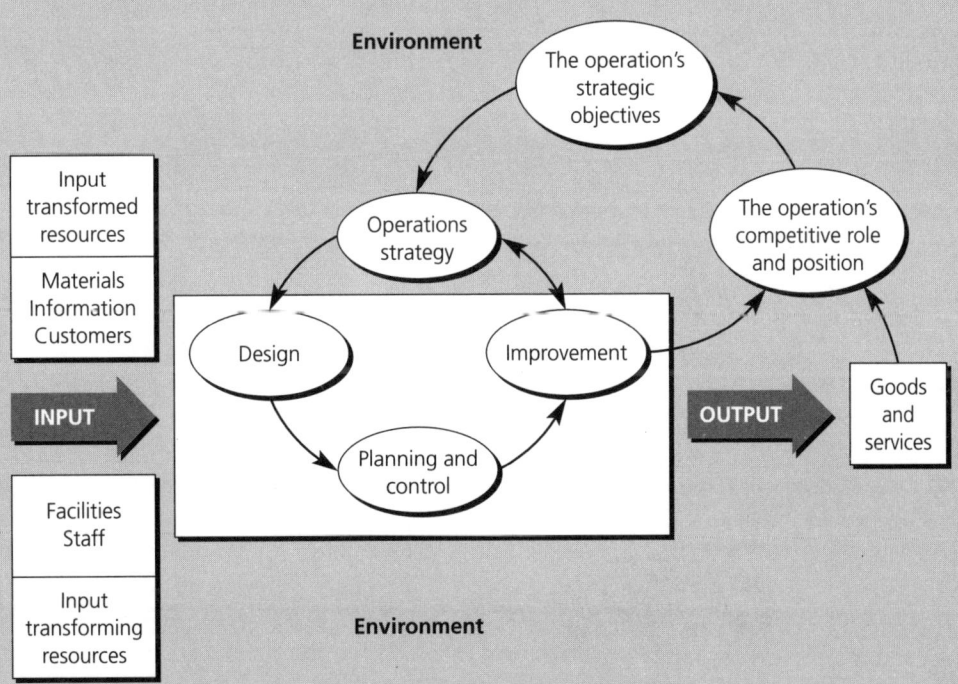

Chapter 21
THE OPERATIONS CHALLENGE

- *How are operations strategies formulated?*
- *What ethical issues do operations managers encounter?*
- *How should operations managers develop their international perspective?*
- *How creative do operations managers have to be in putting strategies into practice?*

THE OPERATIONS CHALLENGE

INTRODUCTION

In the preceding 20 chapters we have outlined the nature, purpose and decisions of operations management, and we are now in a position to pull together some of the threads which have run through our treatment of the subject. We have chosen to do this in two ways. First, we return to the strategic view of operations and discuss the *process* of operations strategy – that is the way in which operations strategies are formulated. Second, we identify some of the challenges which face all operations managers in their continuing attempts to cut through the complexity which characterizes most operations and develop their own operations strategies appropriate for the modern world. Of course this list of strategic 'challenges' could be very long, but we have identified four in particular for attention – the moral imperative to develop *ethical* operations strategies, the necessity to consider the *international* dimension of operations strategies, the need for *creativity* in devising operations strategies and finally the ultimate challenge of *implementing* the chosen strategies. Figure 21.1 illustrates these issues.

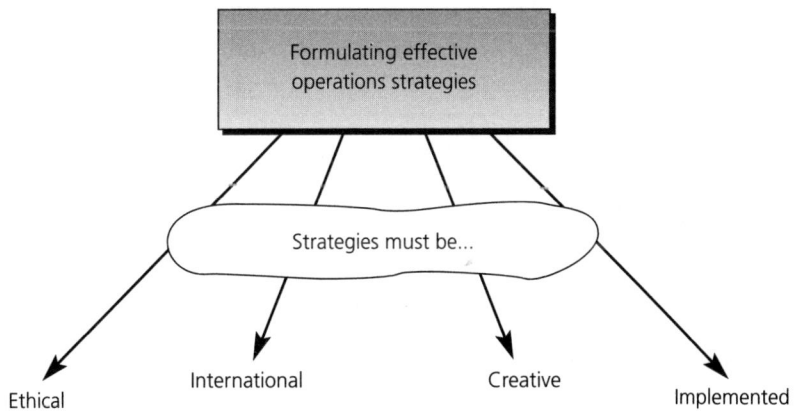

Figure 21.1 Issues covered in this chapter

OBJECTIVES

This chapter will examine:

- why and how operations strategies are put together;

- the way in which the decisions resulting from operations strategies have an ethical dimension;

- how operations managers need to consider their operations strategies from an international perspective;

- why achieving creative operations strategies involves challenging the trade-off paradigm of operations;

- how operations managers need to set an 'implementation agenda' to put their strategies into practice.

THE STRATEGY CHALLENGE

In Chapter 3 we distinguished between the *content* of operations strategy (the priorities and decisions which would determine the overall direction of the operation) and the *process* of operations strategy (the way in which these decisions are made). Content is the output from operations strategy; process is the act of creating the strategy. This is where the challenge lies. The acid test for operations managers is not just their understanding and command of the detailed complexity of all the operations decisions which we have outlined in this book (important though these are). Rather it is whether they can make enough sense of the operation to fit it into a strategic context, reshape and improve it, and then make sure that its contribution to competitiveness is both clear and ongoing.

All operations should have a strategy

So why should operations go to the bother of putting a strategy together? It requires considerable effort and time. All the operation's senior management need to be involved for at least part of their time over a period which has been variously estimated at between four to 18 months.[1] The obvious answer is that an effective operations strategy helps the organization to compete more effectively. There is some empirical evidence to support this. For example, an organization's technology strategy, among other things, shapes the integration between different parts of its processes. Its planning and control strategy has to work within the constraints imposed by the technology. A shared strategy allows not only both areas to measure their own decisions against the common purpose, but also allows the implications of each other's strategy areas to be explored. In this way a formally constructed operations strategy gives the basic structure which ensures that the many individual decisions taken around the organization all point in the same direction.

Difficulties in formulating operations strategy

Even a cursory study of the previous 20 chapters of this book should have made the point that operations management is a complex business, so trying to make strategic sense of any operation will always be a difficult task. Four particular difficulties affect most attempts at the formulation process. The first is the dispersal problem. Operations managers are central to the strategy formulation process, yet they, more than most, are likely to be geographically dispersed among the company's sites. As one operations director of a food-processing company put it,

'My marketing colleague has her senior people all within a few steps of her office. By contrast, my senior people are spread around Europe. The effort of getting them together is not something we can go through every week.'

Second, operations managers operate in 'real time'. They can only allow their attention to drift from the running of the operation for relatively short periods. This responsibility for the day-to-day running of the operation means that they operate under a 'need to deliver' from which only the most important strategic pressures can divert them. Third, the inertia of operational resources imposes a certain amount of conservatism on whoever manages them. With the majority of the organization's resources under their control, no operations manager will, or can, change operational direction without very good reason. Understandable though such caution might be, it does, at times, retard imaginative strategic change.

Generic operations strategies

Before looking at the process by which operations strategies can be formulated, it is worthwhile examining what some people have called 'generic operations strategies'. These are common approaches to organizing the operations function which have been observed to be adopted by different types of organization. So, if the operations strategies of many different organizations were reviewed (as they have been in some research studies) it becomes evident that the strategies of the individual organizations can be clustered into groups within which the strategies are similar, or possess common elements. So, for example, the Hayes and Wheelwright four-stage model which we described in Chapter 2 could be considered to be a generic operations strategy classification. All operations could be placed in one of the four categories which they identified.

A more useful and somewhat broader categorization is provided by Mike Sweeney of Cranfield University.[2] This is shown in Fig. 21.2. Based on his own and several other researchers' investigations, he categorizes operations (more strictly, manufacturing operations) on two dimensions. The first dimension concerns the approach the company takes to process design. Some organizations take a traditional approach to designing their processes which do not include many of the innovations in technology, layout, job design, organization, and so on, which we have described elsewhere in this book. Others have developed a more enhanced approach to process design which includes such innovations as business process re-engineering, cellular manufacture, JIT organization, etc. The other dimension relates to the approach which the organization takes towards providing service to its customers. The resulting four-way classification results in generic operations strategies which are termed caretaker, marketeer, reorganizer, and innovator strategies.

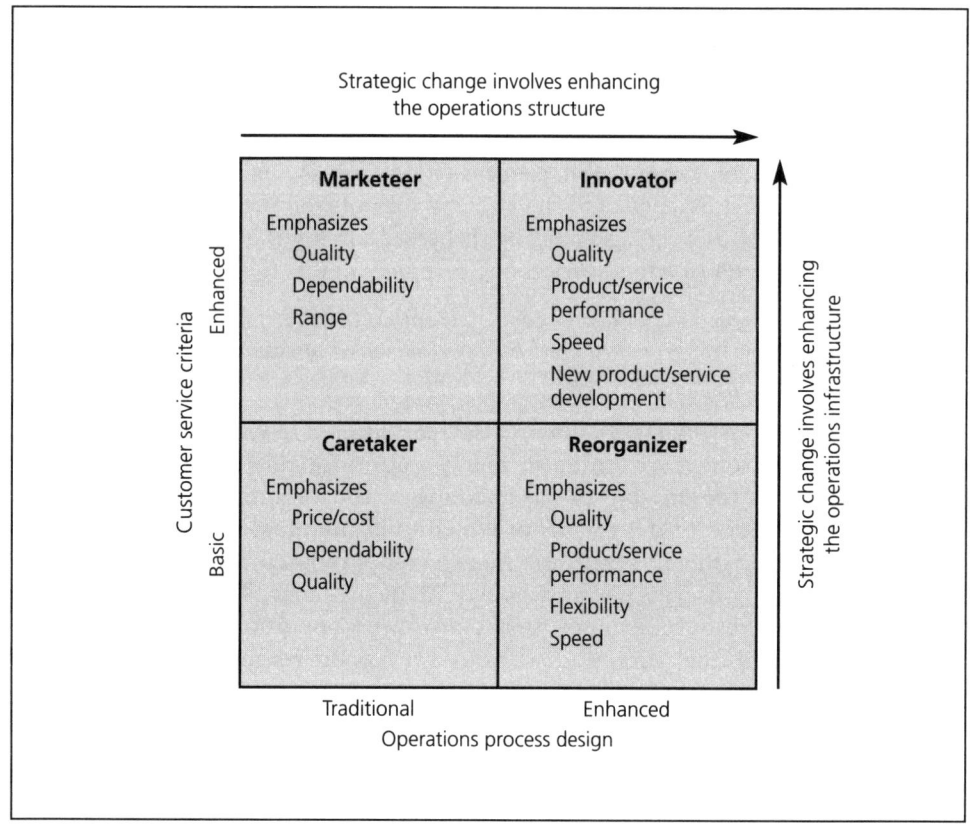

**Figure 21.2
Sweeney's generic
strategies**

The caretaker strategy

This strategy is often employed when an organization believes that there is little competitive advantage to be gained by differentiating itself from its competitors. The operations function is expected to provide as efficient and reliable a service to the rest of the organization as possible without much investment, change or disruption. Operations managers are expected to make sure things do not go wrong, rather than provide much in the way of innovation or creativity.

The marketeer strategy

Marketeer strategies are often used by organizations which experience increased competition and respond by enhancing or extending the level of customer service which they offer. This might include such things as broadening the range of their products or services, increasing quality levels or giving delivery guarantees. No fundamental change has been made to the physical design and organization of the operation itself but it is expected to respond to marketing-led changes in competitive stance. The operations function tries to do this by developing its infrastructural resources such as planning and control systems, working practices, or quality management methods.

The reorganizer strategy

This strategy implies a change in the way an organization designs and manages its processes. This could mean investment in new technology and (more significantly) a different way of organizing its methods of producing goods and services. Companies adopting JIT and cellular manufacturing principles are typical of organizations adopting this strategy. The new processes often give the enhanced flexibility which allows the operation to respond quickly and effectively to changes in marketing strategy.

The innovator strategy

The innovator strategy is a combination of the marketeer and the reorganizer strategies. Not only has the organization adopted an enhanced approach to designing its operations, it also expects enhanced customer service from its operations function. In other words, it has enhanced not only its structure but also its infrastructure. Usually this means a very high degree of integration between product or service design, operations, and marketing in order not only to be flexible in the short term in response to competitive pressure, but also to introduce new products and services faster and more effectively than competitors.

Those organizations adopting either a caretaker or a marketeer strategy are recommended first to enhance their operations structure to achieve a reorganizer strategy, after which they can undertake the more difficult infrastructural changes towards an innovator strategy.

Formulation procedures

Most organizations, even if they finish up adopting one of the generic strategies described above, will want to formulate their own operations strategy to cope with what they see as their individual competitive circumstances. There are several alternative procedures which have been suggested as providing the outline framework for developing an operations strategy. Most consultancy companies have developed their own frameworks, as have several academics. Two well-known procedures are briefly described here to give the flavour of how operations strategies are formulated in practice. These are the *Hill methodology* and the *Platts–Gregory procedure*.

The Hill methodology[3]

One of the first, and certainly most influential, approaches to operations strategy formulation (although once again its development is largely connected with manufacturing operations) is that devised by Professor Terry Hill of London Business School. The so-called 'Hill methodology' is illustrated in Fig. 21.3. Hill's model, which is here adapted to the terminology used in this book, follows the well-tried approach of providing a connection between different levels of strategy making. It is essentially a five-step procedure. Step one involves understanding the long-term corporate objectives of the organization so that the eventual operations strategy can be seen in terms of its contribution to these corporate objectives. Step two involves understanding how the marketing strategy of the organization has been developed to achieve corporate objectives. This step, in effect, identifies the products/service markets which the operations strategy must satisfy, as well as identifying the product or service characteristics such as range, mix and volume which the operation will be required to provide. Step three translates marketing strategy into what we have called in Chapter 3 'competitive factors'. These are the things which are important to the operation in terms of winning business or satisfying customers. Hill goes on to divide the factors which win business into order-winners and qualifiers (again we have explained this distinction of Hill's in Chapter 3). Step four is what Hill calls 'process choice'. This is similar to the volume–variety analysis which we carried out in Chapter 4. Its purpose is to define a set of structural characteristics of the operation which are consistent with each other and appropriate for the way the company wishes to compete. Step five involves a similar process but this time with the 'non-process' infrastructural features of the operation.

Hill's methodology is not intended to imply a simple sequential movement from step one to step five, although during the formulation process the emphasis does move in this direction. Rather, Hill sees the process as an iterative one, whereby operations managers cycle between an understanding of the long-term strategic requirements of the operation and the specific resource developments which are required to support strategy. In this iterative process the identification of competitive factors in step three is seen as critical. It is at this stage where any mismatches between what the organization's strategy *requires* and what its operation can *provide*, become evident.

Step 1	Step 2	Step 3	Step 4	Step 5
Corporate objectives	Marketing strategy	How do products or services win orders?	Operations strategy	
			Process choice	Infrastructure
• Growth • Profit • ROI • Other 'financial' measures	• Product/service markets and segments • Range • Mix • Volumes • Standardization or customization • Innovation • Leader or follower	• Price • Quality • Delivery speed • Delivery dependability • Product/service range • Product/service design • Brand image • Technical service	• Process technology • Trade-offs embodied in process • Role of inventory • Capacity, size, timing, location	• Functional support • Operations planning and control systems • Work structuring • Payment systems • Organizational structure

Figure 21.3 The Hill methodology of operations strategy formulation
Source: Adaped from Hill, T. (1993) *Manufacturing Strategy* (2nd edn), Macmillan

The Platts–Gregory procedure[4]

Another influential process is that developed by Ken Platts and Professor Mike Gregory of Cambridge University. The framework for their approach is shown in Fig. 21.4. The procedure has three stages. Stage one involves developing an understanding of the market position of the organization. This is done by assessing the opportunities and threats within the competitive environment. More specifically it also involves identifying the factors which are required by the market and compares these to the level of achieved performance (in terms of the operation being able to satisfy the market). This is an important part of the Platts–Gregory procedure and is different in emphasis from the Hill methodology described previously. Whereas the Hill methodology places its main emphasis on an operations strategy being developed from the customers' view of competitive factors, this procedure explicitly makes the comparison between what the market wants and how the operation performs. In this way it is similar to the importance–performance matrix described in Chapter 18. Instead of a matrix the procedure uses 'profiles' of market requirements and achieved performance to show up the gaps which the operation strategy must address.[5] Figure 21.5 illustrates the use of these profiles.

Stage two of the procedure involves assessing the capabilities of the operation. Its purpose is to identify current operations practice and assess the extent to which this practice helps to achieve the type of performance which was indicated as being important in stage one.

Stage three concerns the development of new operations strategies. This stage involves reviewing the various options which are available to the organization and selecting those which best satisfy the criteria identified in the two previous stages.

Common elements of operations strategy procedures

The two formulation procedures described here are broadly representative of those available. Yet neither includes all the various points and issues which, taken together, operations strategy formulation procedures address. Typically many of the formulation processes include the following elements:

● a process which formally links the total organization strategic objectives (usually a business strategy) to resource level objectives;
● the use of competitive factors (called various things such as order winners, critical success factors, etc.) as the translation device between business strategy and operations strategy;
● a step which involves judging the relative importance of the various competitive factors in terms of customers' preference;
● a step which includes assessing current achieved performance, usually as compared against competitor performance levels;
● an emphasis on operations strategy formulation as an iterative process;
● the concept of an 'ideal' or 'green field' operation against which to compare current operations. Very often the question asked is

'If you were starting from scratch on a green field site how, ideally, would you design your operation to meet the needs of the market?'

This can then be used to identify the differences between current operations and this ideal state;

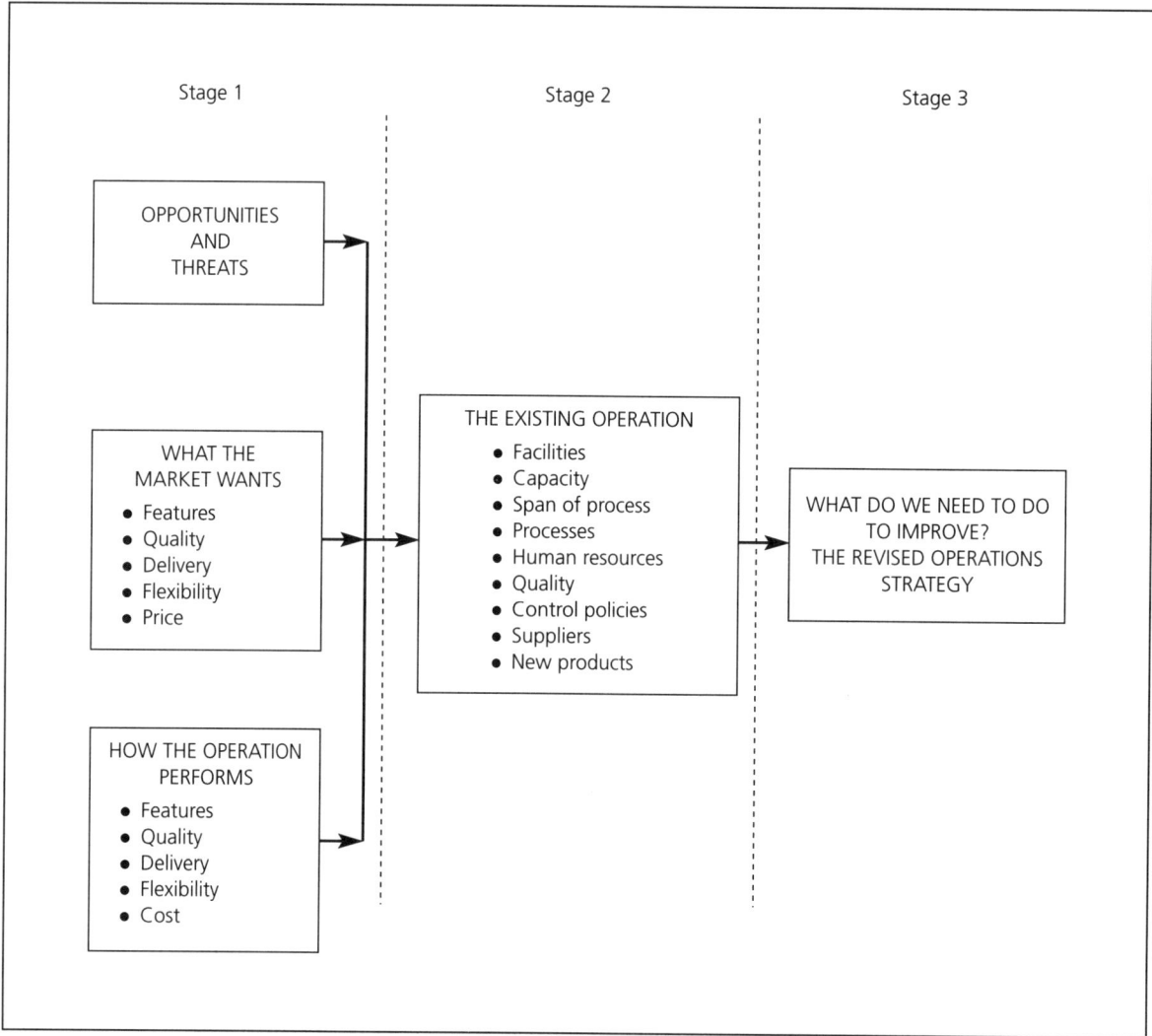

Figure 21.4 The Platts–Gregory procedure

● A 'gap based' approach. This is a well-tried approach in all strategy formulation which involves comparing what is required of the operation by the market place against the levels of performance which the operation is currently achieving.

Judging the effectiveness of operations strategy

An effective operations strategy should clarify the links between overall competitive strategy and the development of the company's operations resources. It should be able to answer the important 'so what' questions. For example,

'We intend to compete through aggressive pricing – so what does that imply for the way we develop process technology?' Or 'We have customers with different requirements for different

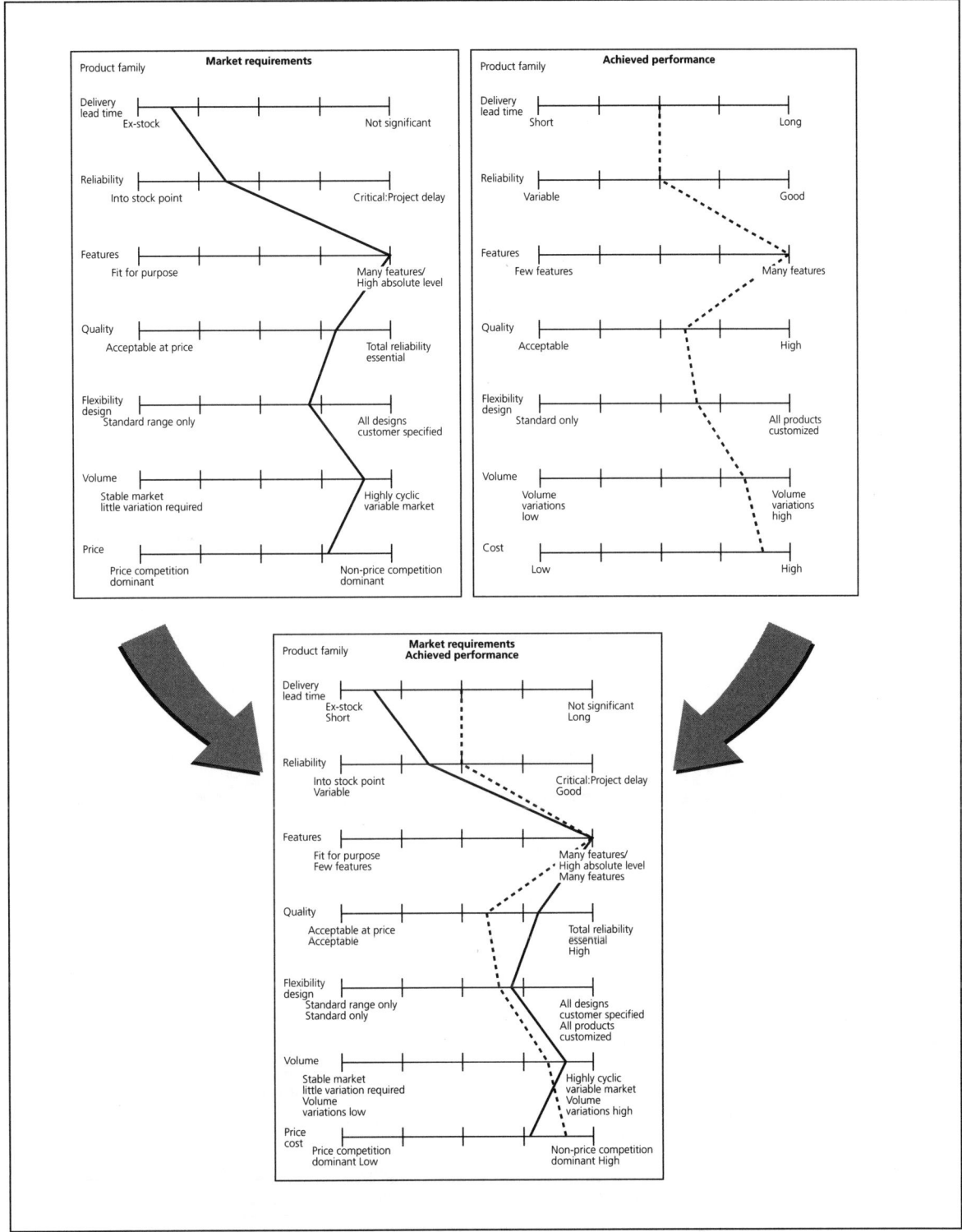

Figure 21.5 Uses of profiling in the Platts–Gregory procedure

product groups – so what does that imply for the way in which we set performance targets?' Or *'We operate in a turbulent market with frequent product changes – so what does that mean for the way we organize the production, service design–operations interface?'*

More specifically, an operations strategy should be:

● *Appropriate*. If the formulation process is to connect operations to the organization's concept of competitiveness then above all it must provide appropriate improvements. In other words, the strategy should direct operations change in a direction which on balance is the most likely to provide the performance which best supports the company's competitive strategy.

● *Comprehensive*. An operations strategy cannot define every minor operational decision but it does have to indicate how all parts of the operations function are expected to perform. No part of the operations function is without influence on performance, therefore no part should be left without guidance.

● *Coherent*. Including all parts of the operation in the strategy is a necessary but not sufficient condition for effectiveness. The policies recommended for each part of the function must all point roughly in the same direction. Potential conflicts between the various areas will need addressing directly.

● *Consistent over time*. While no organization benefits from an overly rigid strategy, the lead time of operations improvement means that consistency must be maintained over a reasonable time period. Failing to provide consistency confuses the organization, but worse it leads to cynicism ...

'Last year was the year of quality, this year it's flexibility, what will be in fashion next year?'

● *Credible*. A strategy which is not regarded as achievable by the organization will not be supported. Its subsequent failure could merely reinforce the perceived futility of the whole process, therefore strategic change should be seen as feasible.

STRATEGIES MUST BE ETHICAL

The concept of ethical decision making permeates operations management. There are ethical implications in almost every decision area described in this book. Table 21.1 identifies just some of these ethical considerations.

Table 21.1 Some ethical considerations of operations management decisions

Decision area	Some ethical issues
Product/Service design	● Customer safety ● Recyclability of materials ● Energy consumption
Network design	● Employment implications of location ● Employment implications of plant closure ● Employment implications of vertical integration ● Environmental impact of location
Layout of facilities	● Staff safety ● Disabled customer access ● Energy efficiency

Table 21.1 (cont.)

Decision area	Some ethical issues
Process technology	<ul><li>Staff safety</li><li>Waste and product disposal</li><li>Noise pollution</li><li>Fume and emission pollution</li><li>Repetitive/alienating work</li><li>Energy efficiency</li></ul>
Job design	<ul><li>Staff safety</li><li>Workplace stress</li><li>Repetitive/alienating work</li><li>Unsocial working hours</li><li>Customer safety (in high contact operations)</li></ul>
Planning and control (including MRP, JIT and project planning and control)	<ul><li>What priority to give customers waiting to be served</li><li>Materials utilization and wastage</li><li>Unsocial staff working hours</li><li>Workplace stress</li><li>Restrictive organizational cultures</li></ul>
Capacity planning and control	<ul><li>'Hire and fire' employment policies</li><li>Working hours fluctuations</li><li>Unsocial working hours</li><li>Service cover in emergencies</li><li>Relationships with sub-contractors</li><li>'Dumping' of products below cost</li></ul>
Inventory planning and control	<ul><li>Price manipulation in restricted markets</li><li>Energy management</li><li>Warehouse safety</li><li>Obsolescence and wastage</li></ul>
Supply chain planning and control	<ul><li>Honesty in supplier relationships</li><li>Transparency of cost data</li><li>Non-exploitation of developing country suppliers</li><li>Prompt payment to suppliers</li><li>Minimizing energy consumption in distribution</li><li>Using recycled materials</li></ul>
Quality planning and control and TQM	<ul><li>Customer safety</li><li>Staff safety</li><li>Workplace stress</li><li>Scrap and wastage of materials</li></ul>
Failure prevention and recovery	<ul><li>Environmental impact of process failures</li><li>Customer safety</li><li>Staff safety</li></ul>

For our purposes ethics can be considered as the framework of moral behaviour which determines whether we judge a particular decision as either being right or wrong.[6] In operations management, as in other areas of management, ethical judgements are not straightforward. What might be unremarkable in one country's or company's ethical framework could be regarded as highly dubious in another's.

THE DOWN-TO-EARTH COLLECTIVE[7]

The ethical stance of an organization will affect its approach to operations management decisions, especially when its ethical principles are part of its raison d'être. Even so it may choose to compromise its ethical stance when forced.

Down-to-Earth was a retail collective which sold wholefoods to the general public. As well as rice, beans, cereals, dried fruit, etc., it also retailed a limited variety of organically grown vegetables. The collective had been set up some years earlier by three students of the local university. They had provided the capital to start the business and were paid interest on the capital, but had no rights of ownership of the business. Decision-making rights were shared by all members of the collective, who numbered five. As to the objectives of the collective, one member described her perception as follows:

'The original three people, who set up the shop, saw it as means of providing themselves with an occupation which would not be too taxing and would be socially useful at the same time. More importantly, though, it was a means of supporting themselves financially without having to work for an organization in an employer/employee relationship. I guess that we see the business in more or less the same way. It is a pleasant thing to do for a few years after you leave college, and it provides just enough money for us to live on. We all believe in eating the type of food we sell, and we know we are providing a service to other people who want to buy it. I guess there is something evangelical in the way we operate, but not to the point that we constantly preach at customers. Nevertheless, our beliefs do influence all the decisions we take about the business.'

The effect of the members' ethical stance can be illustrated by describing one of its operations decisions.

The location decision. Four years after the founding of the business, the lease on the shop expired, and the members of the collective at the time had to decide on a suitable new location. Their four years' experience had taught them that the location of a retail business is one of the major factors in determining its success. Ideally, all the members of the collective would have preferred a shop location in one of the poorer districts of the city – it was, after all, the poorer people who were most in need of wholesome basic foods which the shop could provide. If the business saw one of its objectives as educating people into a simpler but better diet, then surely it should go where it could do the most good? The members of the collective were aware, however, that the vast majority of their clientele was middle-class. It was the younger, educated, relatively more affluent citizens who were more attracted to the types of food the shop sold.

Here, then, was the ethical dilemma. If the objective of the decision was 'choose a location where there is the most need', then a poorer area of the city was almost certain to be selected. If, on the other hand, the objective was to 'choose a location where there is the most business', then one of the affluent areas of the city would be selected. The 'go to the greatest need' option was ethically more attractive to the members of the collective than the 'go to the greatest business' option. However, as one member of the collective put it:

'The prime objective of this organization is to provide a pleasant and socially useful job for us. We therefore would put survival as our main objective. While we don't want survival at any price, there is no point in going to an area of the city where we know that we just could not survive in the short term.'

The decision was eventually taken to move into an area on the edge of an affluent part of the city where they could retain their old customers and attract new ones relatively easily. This was justified on the grounds that it was better to survive, and do some good, than fail gloriously. ■

Customers' welfare is directly affected by many of the decisions made by operations managers. The first and most obvious effect is that their safety might be compromised by poor operations management decisions. If a product is badly assembled or if the equipment used in a service (such as a rail transport system) is not maintained, customers can come to harm. But customer safety is influenced by more than good manufacturing or maintenance practice, it could also be affected by the degree to which an operation discloses the details of its activities. When should an airline admit that it has received bomb threats? Should all the components or ingredients in a product be fully disclosed? For example, one company used very small amounts of grated peanuts in a pie topping in order to make it look brown and attractive. The company failed however to disclose this ingredient on the package. Subsequently, one of its customers, who was allergic to peanuts, died through eating what she regarded as a safe product. At a less serious level, the ethical framework of operations decisions can affect the equity and fairness with which customers are treated. For example, should a bank discriminate between different customers in order to give priority to those from whom they can make more profit?

Staff are constantly exposed to the ethical framework of the organization throughout their working lives. Organizations have a duty to their staff to prevent their exposure to hazards at work. This means more than preventing catastrophic physical injuries; it means that organizations must take into account the longer-term threat to staff health from, say, repetitive strain injury (RSI) due to short cycle, repetitive work motions.

Suppliers are always a source of an ethical dilemma for the operation. Is it legitimate to put suppliers under pressure not to trade with other organizations, either to ensure that you get focused service from them, or to deny competitors this source of supply? Also do you have any right to impose your own ethical standards on your suppliers, for example, because you would not wish to exploit workers in developing countries? How much effort should you put in to making sure that your suppliers are operating as you would? More significantly, would you be prepared to pay a higher price for their product or service if it meant them abandoning what you regard as unethical practice? The recent increase in the transparency expected from suppliers also poses ethical dilemmas. If you are expecting your supplier to be totally honest and transparent in opening up their costing calculations to you, should you be equally transparent in revealing to them your own internal costings?

The *community* also has a right to expect its organizations to adopt a responsible attitude. At its most obvious level, organizations have a direct impact on levels of environmental pollution in the community. All manufacturing processes have waste emissions of some sort. What then should be the balance between an operation's responsibility to minimize its pollution-causing activities on one hand, and the cost of doing this on the other? Most countries have legislation which sets minimum standards for such decisions, but should an organization try to achieve a better standard if it is technically possible to do so? The ethical dilemma is similar for a company's products after they have been sold. To what extent should an organization ensure that its products are easily disposed of, or recycled, or perhaps even made so durable that they do not need replacing for a long time? Clearly this last option could have a negative effect on a company's revenues. The responsibility to the community means more than pollution and recycling. It also means sharing responsibility for other groups and organizations within the community such as schools, hospitals, groups representing special interests and so on. To what extent should an operation fund or take part in projects with these groups within the community?

Finally, *shareholders* and owners are also due some ethical duties, even though it may be obvious to state them. They are entitled to a reasonable return on their investments, although what constitutes 'reasonable', and whether the return should be judged in the short-term or long-term, are both open to interpretation.

Company values

Some decisions take on greater ethical implications, in particular in operations. For example, deciding on staffing levels in a television manufacturing operation is largely a matter of economics, whereas in a hospital, staffing levels can have life and death implications. Of course, staffing level decisions are also a matter of economics in the hospital; that is exactly what makes the staffing level decision difficult for the operations managers in the hospital. Indeed, very few of the ethical dilemmas described above are straightforward, but no operation can afford to ignore them. Those organizations which understand the importance of the ethical dimension to operations decisions tend to take a proactive approach to their own ethical stance. This involves deciding the principles upon which they will make ethically-sensitive decisions by developing an explicit set of principles which allow organizations to avoid ethically ambiguous activities and gradually build up an ethical framework which becomes accepted within the organizational culture of the operation. Typically such organizations adopt an explicit and public set of values. Table 21.2 shows the mission statement for the University of Port Elizabeth, a regionally based university in the Eastern Cape. The mission statement consists of a long-term statement of the university's vision and various 'statements of strategy'. Some of these statements of strategy have quite clear ethical undertones, for example 'afford all members of staff, as the University's most important resource for the persuance of its mission, irrespective of creed, race or sex, opportunities for personal growth in a stable, challenging and congenial working environment'. However the core values which the university sees itself as promoting are identified separately.[8]

STRATEGIES MUST BE INTERNATIONAL

Few organizations can afford to limit their operations strategies to within their national boundaries. Only the smallest organizations do not buy any of their supplies from abroad, or do not sell any of their products and services abroad, or should not be, at least, considering doing so. For operations managers the 'environment' within which they make their decisions is, increasingly, a global one. This is especially true for large multinational organizations, who have four types of strategic operations decisions to make:

1 Where should their operations facilities be located?
2 How should their operations network be managed across national boundaries?
3 Should operations in different countries be allowed to develop their own way of doing business?
4 Should an operations practice which has been successful in one part of the world be transferred to another?

Table 21.2 The mission statement of the University of Port Elizabeth

The mission of the University of Port Elizabeth is to provide tertiary education at the highest level for the community, with admission on an equitable basis, taking into account existing educational inequalities. All students, irrespective of creed, race or sex, are afforded the opportunity of developing themselves to their full intellectual and personal potential.

To realize this mission the University strives:

♦ To provide teaching with appropriate support services that take into account the needs of all students;
♦ To provide a stable and supportive learning environment that encourages study and academic achievement;
♦ To provide continuing education for personal growth;
♦ To achieve excellence in research;
♦ To generate and disseminate knowledge relevant to community needs;
♦ To involve staff and students, in collaboration with the Eastern Cape community, in service programmes based on the University's teaching and research resources;
♦ To employ the expertise and innovative ability of staff and students in addressing issues confronting society;
♦ To promote the development of students by the fostering of leadership and critical thinking skills;
♦ To encourage freedom of thought, expression and association and the recognition of freedom of religion;
♦ To provide support structures for subject societies' cultural, sporting and social life;
♦ To afford all members of staff, as the University's most important resource for the pursuance of its mission, irrespective of creed, race or sex, opportunities for personal growth in a stable, challenging and congenial working environment;
♦ To create structures and/or opportunities, where appropriate, for consultation with students, staff and the community in the determination of university policy.

Corporate values

Academic excellence
♦ Teaching and research of high quality through the maintenance of a balanced integration of scientific excellence, social relevance and the personal growth of students and staff.

Academic freedom
♦ Learning and working, without fear of any harm, in an open, empowering and creative organizational culture.

Equity
♦ Equity through the maintenance of the principle of equality and through affirmative action aimed at the equalization of opportunities and outcomes.

Democracy
♦ Representative and meaningful participation in decision making.

Institutional integrity
♦ Pursuing the full realization of the institution's potential in dynamic interaction with its environment.

Accountability
♦ Demonstration of public and internal responsibility through openness in decisions and processes, as well as responsible action by the Council, staff and students.

Development
♦ The democratic enablement and empowerment of staff, students and community, as well as the conservation of the natural environment.

Organizational effectiveness
♦ The efficient achievement of appropriate objectives.

International location

The location decision has been discussed in general terms in Chapter 6 as part of the design of the overall network. Networks of operations can spread across several geographic regions. Large global companies such as Mercedes, the vehicle manufacturer, or Kodak, the photographic materials company, have operations all over the world. However, not all organizations will choose to design their international networks to the same pattern. Different configurations of operations will be appropriate for different organizations. Four configuration strategies have been identified in the location behaviour of international companies.[9]

Strategy 1 – Home country configuration

The simplest strategy for an organization trading around the world is not to locate plants outside its home country and to export its products to foreign markets. In effect any organization adopting this strategy is avoiding the necessity of locating any part of the network over which it has direct control outside its own home country. The reason for adopting this strategy might be, for example, that the technology employed in the product is so novel that it needs to be manufactured close to its Research and Development headquarters. Alternatively, the home location of the company might be part of the attraction of a product such as high fashion garments from Paris.

Strategy 2 – Regional configuration

An alternative strategy is to divide the company's international markets into a small number of regions: for example, the European region, the Pacific region, the American region. Any company adopting this strategy might then try to make each region as self-contained as possible. So for example, the European region's market would be served by an operation or operations in the European region. This can only be achieved if each region has the full range of operations capabilities needed to make the full range of products marketed in the region. Companies adopting this strategy usually do so because their (often industrial) customers demand speedy delivery and prompt after-sales service. If products or services were created outside the region it would be difficult to provide such a level of service, although regional warehouses and service centres could go some way to achieving the required customer service.

Strategy 3 – Global coordinated configuration

The converse of the regional strategy, for companies with world-wide locations, is termed the global coordinated configuration. Here the various operations concentrate on a narrow set of activities and products and then distribute their products to the markets around the world. So, for instance, a company might take advantage of low labour costs in one region and allocate products with a high labour content to its operations in that region. Another region might have a well developed technical support infrastructure and so is allocated products which have higher technological requirements. This strategy therefore seeks to exploit the particular advantages of each site or region, but by doing so it does place a coordination requirement on the headquarters of the company. All product allocations, operations capacities and movement of products need to be planned centrally.

Strategy 4 – Combined regional and global coordinated configuration

The regional strategy has the advantage of organizational simplicity and clarity, the global coordinated strategy of well exploited regional advantages. Firms often attempt to seek the advantages of both by adopting a compromise between them. Under such a strategy, regions might be reasonably autonomous but certain products could still be moved between regions to take advantage of particular regional circumstances. This is the strategy which many companies such as Mercedes and Kodak adopt in practice. Many of their products are made in more than one location around the world but each regional market is served by more than the plants in that region. Figure 21.6 illustrates in diagrammatic form the broad shape of each of the four configurations.

Managing across national boundaries

Once the international network of facilities has been configured there comes the, in some ways more difficult, task of managing the network on a day-to-day basis. This is not always easy. Operations managers in different plants, located in different parts of the world, are likely to face different problems and probably speak different languages. How then can a company exploit the particular advantages of having geographically disparate sites while at the same time getting them to work together in a coordinated manner? How does the company prevent the national interests of one part of the network over-riding the good of the whole network while at the same time encouraging constructive internal competition within the network?

Kodak, for example, maintains a global operations performance measurement system which allows all Kodak plants to assess their own performance against other Kodak plants around the world. So if one plant was dissatisfied with its own performance in (say) delivery reliability, it could consult the international database to find the Kodak plants who were performing particularly well in this area and then seek advice from them. The plants which have the best performance in each performance measure (called 'Kodak class' plants) are expected to be cooperative in terms of helping other Kodak plants to emulate their own success. Of course, such a system is not without its costs. The amount of effort and coordination which goes into running the performance database and the expertise necessary to interpret it in a sensible manner is available only to relatively large and sophisticated organizations. The ability to compare plants around the world can be a major asset for multinational companies. It enables them continually to keep abreast of good operations practice and it prevents their individual plants from becoming either parochial or complacent.

It is the ability of multinationals to compare the performance of plants in different parts of the world that helps them develop a global and multi-cultural perspective. Multi-culturalism is the goal to which many multinational firms aspire. It means that the company sees itself as being a part of all the communities in which it is involved rather than as being primarily associated with its original country of origin. Asea Brown Boveri (ABB), the Swedish–Swiss electrical engineering company, is one such example. The company has a board of eight directors from four different nationalities and an executive committee of eight senior managers from five different countries who run its day-to-day business. With a headquarters in Zurich, English is its corporate language while its financial results are reported in US dollars. It also moves its business around the world in response to global changes. In the first half of 1994 its workforce in the

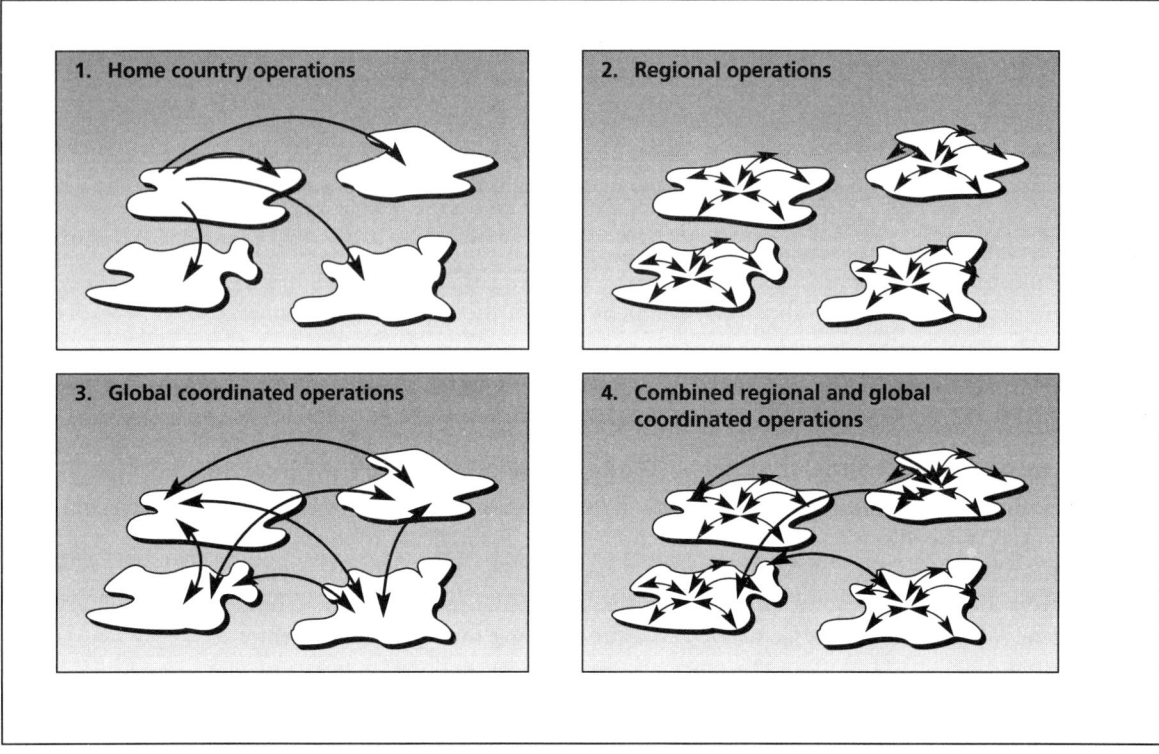

Figure 21.6 Four broad types of international operations network configurations

Asian region increased by 8500 while its workforce in Western Europe decreased by 4000. Partly this was a response to high labour costs in its European operations but also it was because of forecast market growth in Asia.[10]

Different regions – different practices

Different parts of the world, because of their differing cultures, economic conditions, history, market needs, demography and so on, are likely to develop different operations practices. The most obvious example is the way just-in-time and 'lean manufacturing' practice grew up in Japan in the aftermath of the Second World War (*see* Chapter 15). The question, therefore, which multinationals have to face is,

'Should we allow our facilities in different parts of the world to develop their own operations strategies to suit their own conditions, or should we encourage a uniformity of practice which reflects our corporate values?'

For example, linking this back to our discussion of ethics in the earlier part of this chapter, should an organization which originates in a culture where any kind of gift or bribe is highly unethical, prevent its operations from giving small gifts to potential suppliers or customers in a country where this is culturally acceptable? Similarly, should an organization which has built up a strong world-wide brand image allow this to be adapted in different regions? For example, McDonald's, the fast-food chain, developed a rigorous and highly standardized way of organizing its operations, which was one of the main reasons for its world-wide success. Yet eventually it had to allow a certain amount of discretion to local managers to adapt for local tastes (for example, serving Teriyaki burgers in Japan, or serving wine in Lyons).

Transferring operations practices

Different parts of the world, because of their different conditions, develop their own approach to operations management, so can the practices which grew up under one set of conditions transfer successfully to parts of the world where conditions might be very different? Again Japanese manufacturing industry provides us with an example. When just-in-time manufacturing began to be noticed by the rest of the world it was common to hear the view expressed that although it was fine for Japan it would never work 'over here'. North American, European and South African cultures especially were considered to be unsuitable for Japanese methods of manufacture. With hindsight this view was flawed in two ways. First, it failed to distinguish between the 'technical' aspects of just-in-time (such as kanban control, or set-up time reduction) which were relatively easily transferable, and the way in which just-in-time was implemented by harnessing certain 'cultural' factors of Japanese life (such as the emphasis on consensus decision making). While just-in-time manufacture has now spread throughout the world it is not always applied in exactly the same way in North America or South Africa, for example, as it is in Japan. Some of the technical aspects may be identical but the way it is put into practice has often been tailored to suit national culture. Second, it is an over-simplification to assume that all countries within one region of the world have the same work culture.

Yet sometimes an operational practice which is wildly successful in one part of the world does not transfer easily. For example, the Federal Express Corporation in America practically invented the overnight express delivery service. Its 'hub-and-spoke' operations structure in the United States enables it to guarantee overnight delivery from any part of the country to any other part by routing all packages through a single hub in Memphis, Tennessee. Influenced partly by the moves towards greater European integration, Federal Express attempted to duplicate its US operation in Europe. However, Europe is far from being a single integrated economic entity in the same way as is the US. Differences in language, currency, culture, tax rates and so on, posed problems which were not experienced in the US. After some years of struggling to develop the overnight express business it gave up the struggle and closed this part of its business.

Long-term transfers of operations practice

In the long term one can trace the movement and development of operations management practice as it responds to conditions in one part of the world and then is adopted by other parts. Let us return to the example of just-in-time or 'lean' manufacturing. In fact lean manufacturing is just one stage in what might be an ongoing process of development. Figure 21.7 illustrates this for the case of automobile assembly. Automobiles were originally made by craft-based processes. Each car would be built individually (as horse-drawn coaches had been prior to the development of the internal combustion engine). This was also true in the early years of automobile manufacture in the United States. It was only when demand grew to the point that warranted the development of mass production methods by Henry Ford and others, that the 'standard' way of producing motor cars moved to the assembly-line based mass production system. So effective was this method of manufacture that it spread from the USA to Europe and later to Japan. As we have already mentioned, the conditions and culture of Japan led to the further development of manufacturing with the adoption of just-in-time methods and continual improvement on to the basic framework of mass production. Again the appropriateness of this new method of manufacturing to late twentieth-century conditions led to its transferring both back to the USA and to Europe. However, in some parts of Europe some elements of the original craft-based production had survived, either in the luxury end of the motor car business, or where some of the negative factors of mass production were less acceptable. Most notably Scandinavian manufacturers, both of motor cars and trucks, had adopted what has been termed a 'dock' system of manufacture (which we described in Chapter 7 as a 'short fat' layout). There are now some attempts to combine the economic efficiency of lean manufacturing with the more acceptable social ideals of dock manufacturing. This has been termed 'reflective manufacturing'.

STRATEGIES MUST BE CREATIVE

The operations strategy formulation procedures which we described earlier in this chapter provide a structure and a logical process which help operations managers to move in a sensible direction. However, they will not provide the single best strategic solution. They tell operations managers how to go about developing a strategy; they do not tell them what to do. Different sets of operations managers faced with exactly the same set of circumstances will probably come out with very different strategic solutions. Some might follow fairly conventional and orthodox routes (which may well provide adequate solutions), while others might be more imaginative and creative in coming up with their own original strategic solutions, or at least developing ones which embody some original idea. Many successful operations are successful because they thought of an original way of creating their products and services. Federal Express, the parcel delivery company which we described earlier in this chapter, is a good example of this. It was the first to use the 'hub and spoke' principle, whereby all parcels are routed through a central hub, to provide overnight parcel delivery. It is now an 'obvious' solution which is used throughout the world. But it only became obvious after Federal Express thought of it.

The issue which marks the boundary between orthodox and pedestrian operations strategies on one hand, and original, creative and imaginative strategies on the other, is that of how operations managers view the relationship between performance objectives. One way of characterizing this relationship is called the trade-off paradigm. We shall describe this and put forward the hypothesis that only by overcoming the trade-off paradigm will operations strategies be sufficiently creative to provide a significant competitive advantage.

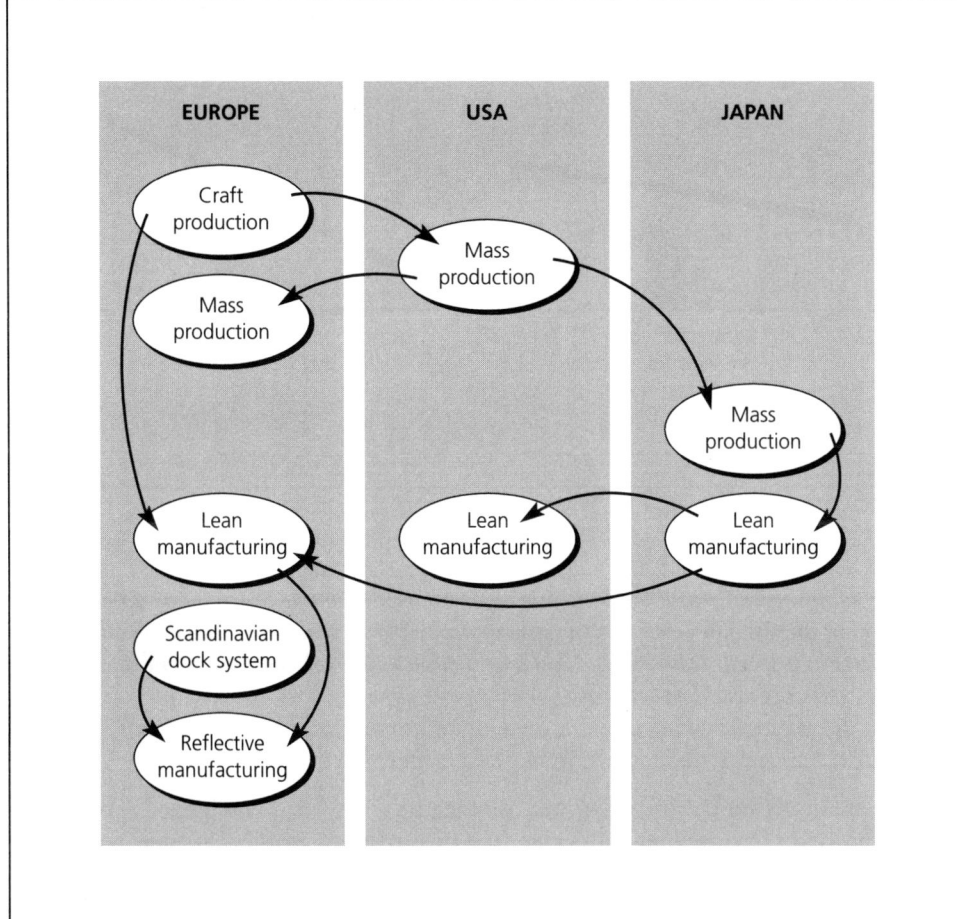

**Figure 21.7
The transfer of
operations practice
in the automotive
industry**

Do performance objectives trade-off?

One of the important questions which any operation has to decide is the relative priority of its performance objectives. To do this it must consider the possibility that one way in which it can improve its performance in one objective is to sacrifice some performance in another. Put another way, it must consider trading-off one aspect of performance with another. This idea is called the *trade-off paradigm* of operations, and, taken to its extreme, it implies that improvement in one aspect of an operation's performance can only be gained at the expense of performance in another. 'There is no such thing as a free lunch' could be taken as a summary of the trade-off theory (*see* Fig. 21.8).

Probably the best known summary of the trade-off idea comes from Professor Wickham Skinner, the most influential of the originators of the strategic approach to operations. He said:

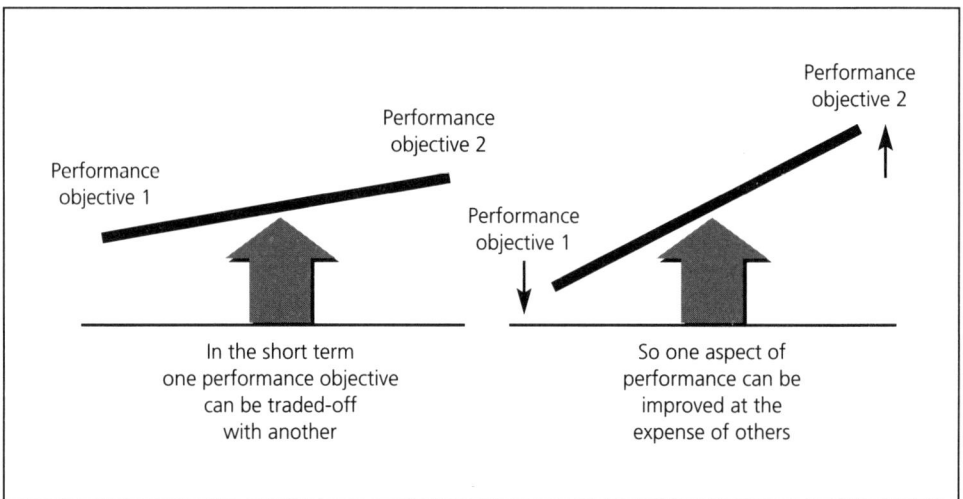

**Figure 21.8
The trade-off
paradigm**

*'... most managers will readily admit that there are compromises or trade-offs to be made in
designing an airplane or truck. In the case of an airplane, trade-offs would involve matters
such as cruising speed, take-off and landing distances, initial cost, maintenance, fuel consumption, passenger comfort and cargo or passenger capacity. For instance, no one today can
design a 500 passenger plane that can land on an aircraft carrier and also break the sound
barrier. Much the same thing is true in manufacturing.'*[11]

Yet this trade-off model of performance objectives has been challenged – mainly by
companies who have managed to give 'the best of both worlds' to their customers.
Perhaps the most dramatic example is how the supposed 'trade-off' between quality
and cost was challenged and overcome by many types of operation. At one time a
high-quality, reliable and error-free automobile was inevitably an expensive automobile. Now, with few exceptions, we expect even budget priced automobiles to
be reliable and almost free of any defects.

It is mainly the attitude of operations managers which has changed. Taking their lead
from pioneering Japanese manufacturers, most manufacturers found that not only
could they reduce the number of defects on their vehicles without necessarily incurring
extra costs, but they could actually reduce costs by reducing errors in manufacture.
They changed their view of quality from one of 'screening the bad products out', to
one of 'stopping the mistakes being made in the first place'. Put in terms of the 'lever'
model in Fig. 21.8, there are two ways to improve the position of one end of the lever.
One is to depress the other end – in other words improving one aspect of performance
at the expense of another. But the other way is to raise the pivot of the lever. This
would raise one end of the lever without depressing the other end. Alternatively it
could raise both ends. The 'pivot' in a real operation is the set of constraints which prevent both aspects of performance being improved simultaneously. Sometimes the
constraints are technical, sometimes attitudinal. But the 'pivot' is stopping one aspect
of performance improving without it reducing the performance of another. It should
therefore be the prime target for any improvement process and the basis for developing
creative strategic solutions in the operation. Figure 21.9 illustrates this.

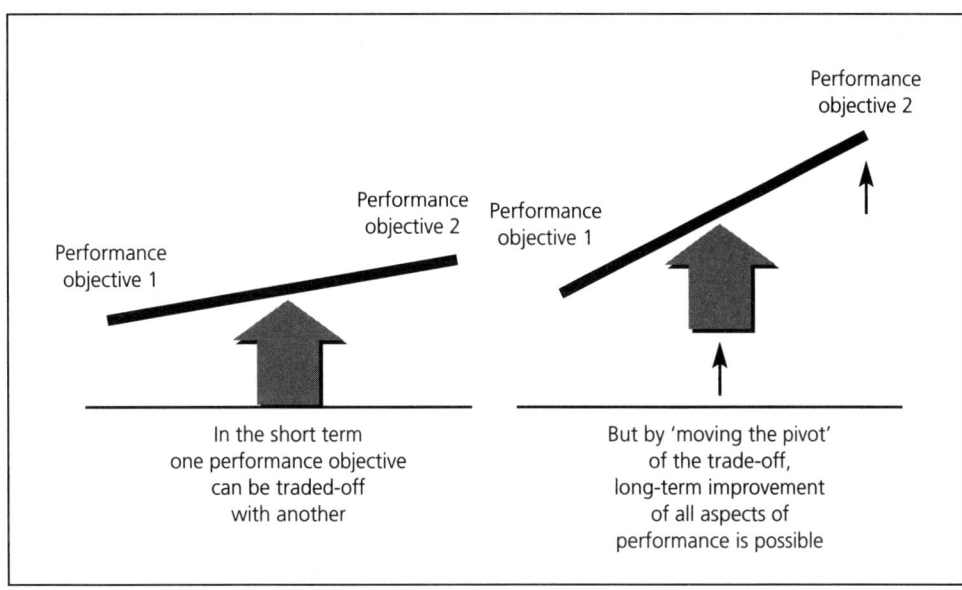

Figure 21.9 Challenging the trade-off paradigm by 'raising the pivot'

The approach which has been generally adopted in this book is that, although there are some situations where (especially in the short term) trade-offs between performance objectives have to be made, one of the main jobs of operations managers is to change whatever in the operation is causing one performance objective to deteriorate as the other improves. In fact the 'pivot' of the trade-off is the main target of continuous improvement in operations.

Reducing the trade-off

Even what seem to be inevitable trade-offs can be reduced to some extent. For example, one of the decisions that any supermarket manager has to make is how many check-out positions to open at any time. If too many check-outs are opened there will be times when the check-out staff do not have any customers to serve and will be idle. The customers however will have excellent service in terms of little or no waiting time. Conversely, if too few check-outs are opened the staff will be working all the time but customers will have to wait in long queues. There seems to be a direct trade-off between staff utilization (and therefore cost) and customer waiting time (speed of service). Yet even the supermarket manager deciding how many check-outs to open can go some way to affecting their trade-off between customer waiting time and staff utilization. The manager might, for example, allocate a number of 'core' staff to operate the check-outs but also arrange for those other staff who are not performing other jobs in the supermarket to be trained and 'on-call' should demand suddenly increase. If the manager on duty sees a build-up of customers at the check-outs these other staff could quickly be used to staff check-outs. By devising a flexible system of staff allocation they can both improve customer service while keeping staff utilization high. Chapter 11 examined other ways of dealing with demand fluctuations.

Blocks to creativity

Although creativity in operations strategy is seen to be a desirable condition, one can, without too much effort, identify a variety of factors which either block creativity or create a climate in which there is little encouragement for staff to demonstrate their creative abilities. These blocks to creativity range from the way in which staff jobs are structured to the way in which we, as individuals, all respond to each other's ideas. The factors which inhibit creativity include the following:

● Developing operations control systems which emphasize efficiency over creativity.
● Dividing jobs into those who are expected to be creative and those who are not.
● Expecting certain functions in the organization (such as research and development or marketing) to be creative while other functions (such as operations and finance) are not expected to be creative.
● Expecting only staff above a certain organizational level to contribute new ideas.
● Not recognizing or rewarding those staff who do generate creative solutions to operations strategy.

Socialization into non-creativity

Many staff, especially in large organizations, do not often take part in decision-making activities where they are called upon to exercise some degree of discretion. They are often engaged in carrying out activities that depend on decisions which have already been made by other staff elsewhere in the organization. Even when they do exercise choice it may be with little or no discretion. The alternative courses of action between which they choose may have already been identified and the decision process may merely consist of following a pre-set rule. Under these circumstances individual staff may become *socialized* into an attitude towards their work in which creativity plays little or no part. They just do not see their jobs as being, in any way, creative. This makes the task of harnessing the potential of all staff in the creative process particularly difficult for operations managers. They must themselves then be creative in encouraging creativity.

STRATEGIES MUST BE IMPLEMENTED

Too often operations strategies fail at the implementation stage. A strategy may set the direction of the operation but implementation defines how it gets there, which is a more difficult task. Operations managers need to start the task by addressing their implementation agenda – the list of general questions, the answers to which set the basic plan for implementation. The questions are:

● When to start?
● Where to start?
● How fast to proceed?
● How to coordinate the implementation programme?

When to start?

There is probably only one absolute rule here, which is not to start until all the issues on the implementation agenda have been addressed. Starting off without a reasonably clear idea of how the strategy is to be implemented is a sure way to reduce the chances of success. The implementation agenda in effect charts how progress is supposed to be made. Nevertheless, some start times are better than others. Implementation should ideally be started when one can be sure of resourcing it adequately (for example, when the operation's engineers and managers can devote enough time to the project).

Where to start?

There are two schools of thought here. The first recommends starting where the operation will get most direct benefit, by being rational and putting effort and resources where the likely return, in terms of improved performance, will be maximized. This could be either where performance is so poor that relatively small improvement gives a disproportionate benefit, or where the potential for dramatic improvement is high. The second favours starting where the operations managers believe there is the best chance of succeeding, preferably in a relatively calm backwater of the operation where any problems will not set back the whole strategy. By doing this, managers can start small and build up experience, learn as they go, keep mistakes small scale and, above all, maintain credibility in the organization. By the time the really important parts of the operation are being tackled, the implementation team will have both the authority and the experience, if not to guarantee success, to make it far more likely. Both approaches are perfectly legitimate, though the second has much to commend it when the improvement programme is inherently risky or when the implementation team has little experience of the type of change being made.

How fast to go?

Managing the speed of improvement means understanding (and often combining) the two modes of improvement – breakthrough improvement and continuous improvement, which are described in Chapter 18.

How to coordinate the programme?

An operations strategy implementation is like any other project in that it needs managing using the principles which are described in Chapter 16. The organizational environment in which the programme will have to fight for attention and resources needs to be predicted. Operations managers must answer questions such as, what conditions will the programme have to cope with during its implementation? For example, are there product/service modifications or new product/service launches planned for the period? If so, how will they interfere with the programme? Are there organizational or system changes planned by any other functions which could affect the programme?

Jeff Max Bloch, Nando's International

Jeff Max Bloch, Nando's Head of International Operations, says, *'What I enjoy about my job are the synergies that I have to identify in different countries and heterogeneous markets, in order to introduce successfully the Nando's culture.'*

Nando's was conceived in 1984 as a corner café in Rosenttenville, East of Johannesburg, and has to date built itself an empire of 107 franchises world-wide. Nando's main objective is to fight for client 'share of stomach' and establish fast-food outlets with a lifestyle of their own. In order to expand globally Nando's is dependent on the success of national approaches and procedures.

'Each country in which we operate is reliant on the broad South African operational infrastructures which include management of quality, service, flexibility, staffing levels and equipment. Nando's operations operate on central kitchen structures, which supply all "reachable" outlets on a "just-in-time" basis. Food is purchased and prepared centrally and then delivered.'

Nando's operational strategy is to ensure that an international partner can fund the entire expansion in the chosen country at the expected growth rate. Therefore, before Nando's can consider a potential partner it is important that a market test is performed in the following order:

1 For each new country set-up it is necessary to determine whether there is a market in that country that can be adapted to Nando's ingredients and cooking style.
2 An initial interview is set up with a potential franchisee to test for the existence of similar personalities and synergies.
3 A business plan is constructed to ensure that the investor understands the direction and the objectives of the expansion.
4 The supply-side influences specific to each

country are analysed: the labour relations, skills level, health regulations, wages and salaries, etc.

'To run the global operation effectively we have established ten points to which every franchisee in each global market has to adhere,' says Bloch. The broad outline of Nando's international operations consists of establishing store designs, day-to-day management procedures, and monitoring systems. Flexibility is an operational objective and is designed to give customers a 'taste of Portugal' anywhere in the world (including Portugal) and ensure that customers' needs are fully met.

'For example, in Australia we introduced a Nando's chicken burger with bacon and egg, as this is a standard meal there. Our store also takes into account the culture of the community our customers come from. For example, in India our store is divided into smaller cubicles where families can sit together to enjoy a meal. This was so designed because in India women are not allowed to be in the company of men other than their husbands.'

Monitoring is on a two-tier basis: internal and external. Internally, Nando's has inventory control monitoring systems that are highly advanced. Nando's computer system captures stock turns 24 hours a day from all franchises. Till systems enable daily downloading of data which reflect turnover, daily activity patterns, margins and inventories levels. From an external perspective, store decor, cleanliness, service standards and procedures are reported and checked regularly. A 24-hour hot-line for monitoring customer complaints is in place.

Design for both store and kitchen layout is standard. Store contents are made in South Africa and shipped to stores around the world. As the Nando's saying goes:

'Whatever Nando's does, wherever in the world, it must encapsulate the Nando's experiperience [sic].' ■

Source: By kind permission of Nando's International

Successful implementation – the key elements

In the several studies of operations strategy implementation, both successful and unsuccessful, a number of key elements recur regularly, either as important prerequisites of success or as omissions which seriously harmed implementation success.[12]

Top management support

This always comes out as being important, especially at times of 'breakthrough' improvement where the 'champion' role requires top management to allocate and coordinate resources. Continuous improvement requires a different kind of support, emphasizing a long-term continuing expectation of improvement.

Business driven

All operations strategy change is only a means to an end – improved competitiveness. The organization's overall competitive imperatives must be clearly linked to every part of the operations strategy programme throughout its life.

Strategy drives technology

Not the other way round. Competitiveness should drive operations strategy, so in turn, operations strategy determines the way technology is developed.

Change strategies are integrated

Successful operations strategy programmes involve change over several fronts, technological, organizational, cultural. Only considering one aspect is too limiting a view. Integrating improvement strategies so that they support each other gets the operation 'firing on all cylinders'.

Invest in people as well as technology

Some organizations are reluctant to invest in their human resources even a fraction of the cash they do in technology. Yet changes in methods, organization or technology must be supported by changes in attitude by all employees – especially the managerial structure. Technological 'retooling' must be accompanied by 'social retooling'.

Manage technology as well as people

Conversely, organizations often seem reluctant to 'manage' technology after the investment decision has been made. Technology needs integrating into the operation on strictly managerial criteria.

Everybody on board

Any effective operations strategy must be understood and supported throughout the organization, particularly the management structure. Without this, changes are implemented into 'unreformed' traditional structures, attitudes and work practices.

Clear explicit objectives

If staff know what is expected of them it is easier to succeed. An obvious point maybe, but since operations strategy usually involves cross-functional change, the need for explicit communication of overall purpose becomes vital.

Time-framed project management

Keeping control is a prerequisite for maintaining support. Objective setting, schedules, resource plans, and milestones are as important here as for any other project.

SUMMARY

■ The process of operations strategy is concerned with the act of creating the strategy, whereas the content of operations strategy (treated in Chapter 3) is concerned with the output from the operations strategy formulation process. Although not all operations have operations strategy, there is some evidence to suggest that those who do are more likely to be successful, and those operations managers who take part in the strategy, formulation process should have obtained a better understanding of the organization's overall strategy.

■ There are a number of difficulties in formulating operations strategies. In particular operations managers tend to be geographically dispersed; they also operate in 'real time' and so therefore need to manage the operation at the same time as they are formulating its strategy; they cannot easily change resources which have consumed considerable investment; and finally, they are often not in the habit of contributing to strategic change.

■ Operations strategies can be classified into categories of generic strategies. One such classification distinguishes between caretaker strategies, marketeer strategies, reorganizer strategies, and innovator strategies.

■ The Hill methodology uses a five-step procedure which progressively establishes a strategic logic between the long-term corporate objectives of the organization, the marketing strategy of the organization, its competitive factors for each product or service group, the structural process choice decisions of operations and the infrastructural decisions of operations.

■ The Platts–Gregory procedure places a greater emphasis on comparing the needs of markets with the achieved performance of operations. It uses profiling methods to determine the gaps between the importance of competitive factors and the operation's performance at delivering them.

■ Operations strategies can be judged on the following criteria:
Are they appropriate?
Are they comprehensive?
Are they coherent?
Are they consistent over time?
Are they credible?

■ Nearly all decisions made by operations managers have some kind of ethical dimension. These ethical considerations affect one or more of the following groups:
the operation's customers
the operation's staff
the operation's suppliers
the community in which the operation exists
the operation's shareholders and owners.

■ Some companies make their ethical stance explicit through a statement of mission and values.

■ When locating operations internationally organizations can adopt four configurations. These are:
home country configuration
regional configuration
global coordinated configuration
combined regional and global coordinated configuration.

■ International operations need to address the problems of managing their operations across national boundaries.

■ Different regions in the world often develop different operations practices depending on the economic, social and political circumstances in which they operate. However some of these practices developed in one part of the world can be transferred (albeit in a modified form) to other parts of the world.

■ One of the most sought after behaviours in the process of devising new operations strategies is that of creativity. Creativity often involves breaking the implicit trade-off paradigm which is seen by some as governing the relationship between performance objectives. Creativity is needed to devise ways in which the 'pivot' of the trade-off can be shifted. This means overcoming some of the blocks to creativity present in most organizations.

■ Successfully implementing operations strategies is partly a matter of identifying an implementation agenda for any change. The questions answered by the implementation agenda are:

When to start an implementation?

Where to start an implementation?

How fast to proceed with the implementation?

How to coordinate the implementation programme?

Banco Evora do Sul

'You can never tell what is going to happen after deregulation. We certainly do not want a Scandinavian type situation here. Yet some of Portugal's largest banks have responded to deregulation by some very aggressive lending policies, and all this despite signs that the economy is starting to slow down.'

Alexandere Vaz Pinto, Chairman of the Bankers' Association in Portugal, was commenting on the frenetic activity in the retail banking sector which had built up in his country. He was likening it to the unhealthy loan boom which had occurred after the deregulation of the Scandinavian banking industry. Some banks had been more adventurous than others. Assets at Banco Portugues do Atlantico (BPA) and Banco Commercial Portugues (BCP), two of the largest, recently leapt by 29.4 per cent and 37.5 per cent respectively. This rapid increase in banking activity had been building up since the mid-1980s when banking regulations had been relaxed. Furthermore, several of Portugal's biggest banks had been privatized.

One of those to be privatized was the Banco Evora do Sul (BES). Although not one of the more aggressive lenders, it had nevertheless made quite an impact on the market.

'We must make up for lost time. For years we have been weakened by the state meddling in our affairs. Now we need to get close to our customers and compete on service and innovation. We are already developing a network of alliances with financial institutions throughout Europe, as well as exploring the options for cross-selling our financial services in Portugal.' (Customer Services Manager at BES.)

The development of retail banking services

BES had always been strong in retail banking, especially in the provision of small loans to private customers, for example for the purchase of cars and domestic equipment. It had also invested in both information technology and in refurbishing its branches. So it was generally regarded as being the most innovative in the retail banking area in Portugal. For example, most large branches had interactive computing facilities which allowed customers to model their own mortgages or loan repayments. Also 80 per cent of branches had been refurbished in the previous two years. This investment in computing facilities and in bricks and mortar had, the

Bank felt, brought it closer to its customers. Yet it knew it was not alone in following this direction. Its competitor banks were pursuing more or less the same strategy. For example, in the last year Portuguese banks opened over 500 new branches. Even so, with roughly one branch for every 4000 people, Portugal was still less heavily banked than most other European countries.

To pay for all this investment BES knew it needed to increase its revenues, partly by improving the market share of its loan products.

The personal loan product

BES had decided to form a special working group to look at the potential of its personal loan product. This product, known as 'Besloan' was not very dissimilar from its rivals' products. It was a relatively standardized product on which loans were advanced for relatively small sums (up to the equivalent of around US$50 000) and for which all banks charged more or less the same interest rate.

Because of its standardization the product could be operated relatively profitably. For example, it did not require any special senior management involvement to authorize loans. When the customer had filled in an application form, it was sent to the regional office where a decision was taken at a relatively low level by utilizing a simple 'scoring' process. Also the procedures for issuing the loans and collection of repayments were well-tried and standardized. In fact it consumed relatively little overhead in the bank.

The task party decided to trawl through the bank for any information it could gather on how the loan product was viewed by customers and how other banks operated their equivalent products.

One of the first facts that emerged was that an independent academic study had revealed that Portugal's banks varied somewhat in the proportion of their current account customers who also held personal loans with the same bank. This 'current account penetration' figure varied between 9 per cent and 15 per cent with an average for the larger banks of 12.5 per cent. BES's current account penetration varied between regions but averaged 10.7 per cent.

The working group consolidated the information it had gathered thus far. Exhibit 1 shows a summary of the main points to emerge from a retail banking seminar held in London which two of the working group members had attended. Probably the most important pieces of information though were the results of two surveys carried out by two different parts of the bank two years before. The first was a customer survey which had been carried out by the bank's Marketing Department. In fact the Department had been conducting this survey regularly for a period of about five years. This is included in Exhibit 2.

The Working Group also unearthed a survey of the bank's competitors which had been carried out almost simultaneously with the customer survey but independently of it. This had been carried out by the Business Development part of the bank as part of a larger study and unfortunately was not fully compatible with the customer survey insomuch as it examined personal loans on slightly different criteria. This information is contained in Exhibit 3.

The problem which faced the working group was how to make sense of this information, at least up to the point where they could determine the strategy for the 'Besloan' product.

'It is a matter of getting our strategy right in the way we serve customers in our branches. Personal loans are particularly profitable for us since customers do not seem to realize how much interest they are paying. Nevertheless, we need to keep our costs down in order to maintain our profitability, yet at the same time we must improve our quality of service. But where do we start, that is the dilemma.' (BES Customer Service Manager.) ■

Exhibit 1 Excerpts from Retail Banking Services Seminar – April 1994

Retail banking sector
• The threat from foreign owned banks which seemed imminent two or three years ago has probably diminished in the short term but could still be important in the longer term.
• Alliances between main European banks could be aimed at providing 'European wide' business, travel and vacation cover with 'look-alike services' in the next five to six years.
• All main banks believe that quality of service is likely to be an important differentiator in the near future.

Retail products
• Most banks recognize their errors in 'product proliferation' over the last ten years.
• The absolute number of products will grow little (if at all) in the next five years.
• Innovation is likely to become important, both in product replacement and at the 'general branch service' level.
• Clearer boundaries are likely to be set between standard and non-standard products.
• More guidance is likely to be given to branch management on the rules for customizing selected products.

• There is still considerable evidence that all banks have problems with their staff's product familiarity.

Retail operation and organization
• Location of branches – in some countries (notably the UK) there will be a combination of rationalization (i.e. in the number of branches, probably fewer) and relocation of some branches to more prominent 'high street' locations. In other countries (such as Portugal) branch expansion is likely to continue.
• The quality of service is still a problem for all banks in spite of service initiatives.
• Moves towards 'open environment', high contact design of branches will continue.
• There will be less 'back-office' activity at branches for several reasons:
   – a move towards separating-out back office activity into separate regional/national administration centres;
   – the increased sophistication of distributed information access systems, primarily for customer related information;
   – more computer-based expert systems to give guidance for routine decisions;
   – the possible out-sourcing (sub-contracting) of back-office functions to specialist companies.

Exhibit 2 Customer Survey No 90/32

Date: 30th June 1994

SUMMARY

Subject – Factors influencing customers'[1] choice of product	Score[2]	Spread[3]	Relative to last survey[4]
C/A inertia[5]	4.3	0.3	−0.4
Price	3.9	0.7	+0.1
Advertising	4.0	0.2	same
Trust in 'honesty' of advice	4.7	0.1	+0.2
Trust in technical competence	3.1	0.3	−0.1
Response time	4.5	0.3	same
Response reliability	3.6	0.5	+0.1
Property factors[6]	2.8	0.1	same
Quality of previous service	3.7	0.6	+0.3
Branch advice	4.6	0.5	+0.3
Branch 'atmosphere'[7]	3.6	0.1	+0.1
Branch queuing	3.7	0.2	same
Location convenience	4.0	0.1	−0.2

This data has been modified and codified, it should not be taken as in any way representing policy.

Notes to Exhibit 2

1 The survey includes far more factors than are shown here. Some factors listed are composites.
2 A five-point scale where 1 = very unimportant and 5 = very important is used as standard.
3 Spread is an indication of the degree of consensus expressed by customers surveyed.
4 Compared with previous survey (14 months previously) a positive sign means that the factor's importance rating has increased, a negative means that it is less important.
5 Current account inertia – the propensity of customers to take automatically a personal loan at the bank where they hold their current account.
6 Property factors – decor and layout of branch.
7 Composite of several factors relating to 'friendliness' and quality of customer contact.

Exhibit 3 Survey of Competitors[1]

Date: 4th June 1994

SUMMARY

Product – Personal Loan

Factors	BES	Bank No 2	Bank No 3	Bank No 4	Bank No 5
Image retention[2]	3.2	4.2	3.7	3.0	2.9
Image gap[3]	3.0	3.5	3.0	3.1	3.0
Branch expertise[4]	4.5	4.0	4.3	3.8	3.0
Branch attractiveness	4.1	3.3	3.5	3.9	3.9
Contact skills	4.2	4.0	3.9	4.3	3.8
Availability of info	4.0	4.2	4.0	4.0	4.2
Form design	3.3	4.2	3.8	3.5	3.0
Document errors					
• set up	2.5	3.1	3.3	3.2	4.0
• operation	3.8	3.5	3.3	3.9	3.8
Response time					
• for advice	3.0	2.9	2.8	3.3	3.5
• for decision	2.5	3.0	2.8	3.0	3.2
Response reliability	3.0	3.5	3.7	3.6	3.6
Location site score	4.1	4.2	4.1	4.0	4.7
Opening hours	4.0	4.0	3.5	3.5	4.7

Notes to Exhibit 3
1 Conducted by sampling competitors and own branches without prior notice. Also uses data from public published surveys. 1 = very poor, 5 = very good.
2 Degree to which advertising 'image' is retained by customers.
3 Gap between customers' reported experiences and product image as advertised. 1 = large gap, 5 = small gap.
4 Estimate of quality banking expertise available at branch level.

Questions

1 Describe the retail operation of BES (especially relating to the Besloan product) from an operations management perspective. Do this by identifying the issues which the bank's managers would be concerned with under the chapter headings used in this book.

2 How would you advise the bank to formulate its operations strategy?

3 Use either the Hill methodology or the Platts–Gregory procedure (or the importance–performance matrix described in Chapter 18) to identify the competitive factors which the bank should improve if it is to make personal loan product more competitive.

4 What should the bank do to improve these competitive factors?

5 What ethical considerations do you think are important for a retail bank like BES?

6 How relevant is the 'internationalization of operations' to retail banks?

DISCUSSION QUESTIONS

1 If a busy operations manager said to you, *'Why should I spend time and effort on putting an operations strategy together? I already have enough to do as it is, if I devote any time to such luxuries I would fail to satisfy our customers' immediate needs. This would put us out of business and no operations strategy is going to help us then!',* how would you make a case to the operations manager which convinced him that operations strategies formulation was worthwhile?

2 What do you think the difficulties in operations strategy formulation might be in:
(a) a small manufacturer of cellular telephone communication stations whose business was growing at a rate of over 100 per cent a year, and
(b) an international luxury hotel group with hotels around the world?

3 Do you think that operations which have an 'innovator' generic operations strategy will always outperform those which adopt a 'caretaker' operations strategy?

4 Visit a local service operation such as a theatre, a library, a fast-food outlet, a retail store, or a public transportation company, and by interviewing management (where possible) and by observation perform a brief operations strategy review using both the Hill methodology and the Platts–Gregory procedure.

5 What do you see as being the major differences between the Hill methodology and the Platts–Gregory procedure?

6 What purpose do you think the concept of a 'green field' operation has in developing an operations strategy for an existing organization which cannot afford to move to a new site?

7 List all the operations management decisions which you think will have an impact on the following:
the safety of the operation's staff
the safety of the operation's customers
environmental pollution
energy efficiency.

8 A wholefood cooperative similar to that described in the Down-to-Earth case study has decided to offer a ten per cent discount to senior citizens on Mondays. It has decided to do this because it wishes to aid this section of society, while at the same time moving demand from busy Saturday mornings to quiet Mondays. Do you think such a move compromises the implicit ethical stance of such an operation?

9 If organizations were charged directly through the tax system for all the direct or indirect pollution for which they are responsible, what effect do you think this would have on the daily working lives of operations managers?

10 Draw up a statement of values which you think would be appropriate for a university.

11 Choose any organization with which you are familiar (either as a member of staff or as a customer) and list the operations trade-offs which may be assumed by the management of the operation. For each of these trade-offs identify ways in which the performance of both factors may be improved.

12 A university wishes to implement a strategy which involves the systematic counselling of all its students twice a year on their progress and general study skills. What options should the university's operations managers be considering when putting together their implementation agenda?

NOTES ON CHAPTER

1 *See,* for example, Voss, C. (1990) 'The Process of Manufacturing Strategy Implementation', *Proceedings of the OMA Conference,* Warwick University, or Gunn, T.A. (1987) *Manufacturing Strategy for Competitive Advantage,* Ballinger, Cambridge, Mass.

2 Sweeney, M.T. (1991) 'Towards a Unified Theory of Manufacturing Management', *International Journal of Operations and Production Management,* Vol 11, No 8.

3 Hill, T. (1993) *Manufacturing Strategy* (2nd edn), Macmillan.

4 Platts, K.W. and Gregory, M.J. (1990) 'Manufacturing Audit in the Process of Strategy Formulation', *International Journal of Operations and Production Management,* Vol 10, No 9. Also for a very full explanation of all the steps in this procedure see *Competitive Manufacturing,* The Department of Trade and Industry and IFS Publications, Kempston, UK (1988).

5 This profiling method is based on New, C.C. (1987) *UK Manufacturing: The Challenge of Transformation,* Cranfield School of Management.

6 Thompson, A. and Strickland, A.J. (1992) *Strategic Management, Concepts and Cases* (6th edn), Irwin, Homewood, Ill.

7 Based on Scholes, H.K. 'Down to Earth', held in the European Case Clearing House, Cranfield University, UK. Part of this example appeared in Cooke, S. and Slack, N. (1991) *Making Management Decisions* (2nd edn), Prentice Hall.

8 From Stocks, N., Davies, R. and Bland, J. (1993) 'Sparked by Initiative', *Managing Service Quality,* May.

9 Du Bois, F.C. and Oliff, M.D. (1992) 'International Manufacturing Configuration and Competitive Priorities' *in* Voss, C.A. *Manufacturing Strategy: Process and Content,* Chapman and Hall.

10 Sources – Narborough, C. (1994) 'Switch to Low-cost Countries Aids ABB', *The Times,* 18 August, and 'The Discrete Charm of the Multinational', *The Economist,* 30 July 1994.

11 Skinner, W. (1969) 'Manufacturing the Missing Link in Corporate Strategy', *Harvard Business Review,* Vol 47, No 3.

12 Based on Tranfield, D. and Smith, S. (1987) 'A Strategic Methodology for Implementing Technical Change in Manufacturing', *BAM Conference.*

SELECTED FURTHER READINGS

Adam, E.E. and Swamidass, P.M. (1989) 'Assessing Operations Management from a Strategic Perspective', *Journal of Management*, Vol 15, No 2.

Adams, J.L. (1988) *The Care and Feeding of Ideas*, Penguin.

Anderson, J.C., Cleveland, G. and Schroeder, R.G. (1989) 'Operations Strategy: A Literature Review', *Journal of Operations Management*, Vol 8, No 2.

Bennett, D. and Forrester, P. (1993) *Market Focussed Production Systems*, Prentice Hall.

De Bono, E. (1982) *Lateral Thinking for Management*, Penguin.

Fine, C.H. and Hax, A.C. (1985) 'Manufacturing Strategy: A Methodology and an Illustration', *Interfaces*, Vol 15, No 6.

Guth, W.D. and Tagruri, R. (1965) 'Personal Values and Corporate Strategy', *Harvard Business Review*, Vol 43, No 5.

Harrison, M. (1993) *Operations Management Strategy*, Pitman Publishing.

Hayes, R.H. and Wheelwright, S.C. (1984) *Restoring Our Competitive Edge*, John Wiley, New York.

Hayes, R.H., Wheelwright, S.C. and Clark, K.B. (1988) *Dynamic Manufacturing*, Free Press.

Hill, T. (1993) *Manufacturing Strategy* (2nd edn), Macmillan.

Mather, H. (1988) *Competitive Manufacturing*, Prentice Hall International.

Mintzberg, H. (1978) 'Patterns in Strategy Formulation', *Management Science*, Vol 24, No 9.

Platts, K.W. and Gregory, M.J. (1990) 'Manufacturing Audit in the Process of Strategy Formulation', *International Journal of Operations and Production Management*, Vol 10, No 9.

Roth, A.V. and Giffi, C.A. (1991) 'Manufacturing's Secret Arsenal for the 1990s', *Duke University Working Paper*.

Skinner, W. (1985) *Manufacturing: The Formidable Competitive Weapon*, John Wiley, New York.

Slack, N. (1991) *The Manufacturing Advantage*, Mercury Books.

Stonebreaker, P.W. and Leong, G.K. (1994) *Operations Strategy: Focussing Competitive Excellence*, Allyn and Bacon, Boston.

Swamidass, P.M. and Newell, W.T. (1987) 'Manufacturing Strategy, Environmental Uncertainty, and Performance: A Path Analytic Model', *Management Science*, Vol 33, No 4.

Thompson, A.A. and Strickland, A.J. (1992) *Strategic Management: Concepts and cases* (6th edn), Irwin.

Vancil, R.F. (1986) 'Strategy Formulation in Complex Organisations', *Sloan Management Review*, Vol 17, No 2.

Voss, C.A. (1992) *Manufacturing Strategy*, Chapman and Hall.

APPENDIX 1
FORECASTING THE VOLUME OF DEMAND

Any model which describes some aspect of the behaviour of any system or phenomenon can be used to predict its future behaviour. Here, however, we are specifically concerned with some of the more common models or techniques which are used largely for the prediction of demand levels. Demand is the main determinant of volume, and volume has significant impact on design in operations.

There are several ways in which forecasting models and techniques can be classified. One classification divides techniques into:

- subjective and objective, and
- non-causal and causal.

Subjective forecasting techniques are those which involve judgement and intuition from one or more individuals, whose approach to the forecasting task is unlikely to be explicit, but will be based on experience.

Objective techniques are those which have specified and systematic procedures. This means that results produced by these methods are reproducible no matter who uses them.

Non-causal techniques are those which use the past values of a variable to predict its future values. They assume that the underlying causes of events, which have pertained in the past, will continue to shape events in exactly the same way in the future.

Causal techniques attempt to make predictions on the basis of causal relationship. If the cause–effect relationship between variables can be modelled, then predictions of the factors which influence whatever we are trying to forecast will enable a forecast to be made. The assumption of such methods is that these causal variables can be mea-

sured and projected more accurately than actual demand itself.

Some of the more common forecasting methods which we shall briefly describe are classified in Fig. A1.1.

Time series analysis

Time series techniques examine the pattern of past behaviour of a phenomenon over time, and use the analysis to forecast the phenomenon's future behaviour. For example, suppose a company is attempting to predict the future sales of a product. The past three years' sales, quarter by quarter, are shown in Fig. A1.2(a). This series of past sales may be analysed to indicate future sales. For instance, underlying the series might be a linear upward trend in sales. If this is taken out of the data, as in Fig. A1.2(b), we are left with a cyclical seasonal variation. The mean deviation of each quarter from the trend line can now be taken out, to give the average seasonality deviation. What remains is the random variation about the trends and seasonality lines, Fig. A1.2(c). Future sales may now be predicted as lying within a band about a projection of the trend, plus the seasonality. The width of the band will be a function of the degree of random variation.

Forecasting unassignable variations

The random variations which remain after taking out trend and seasonal effects are without any known or assignable cause. This does not mean

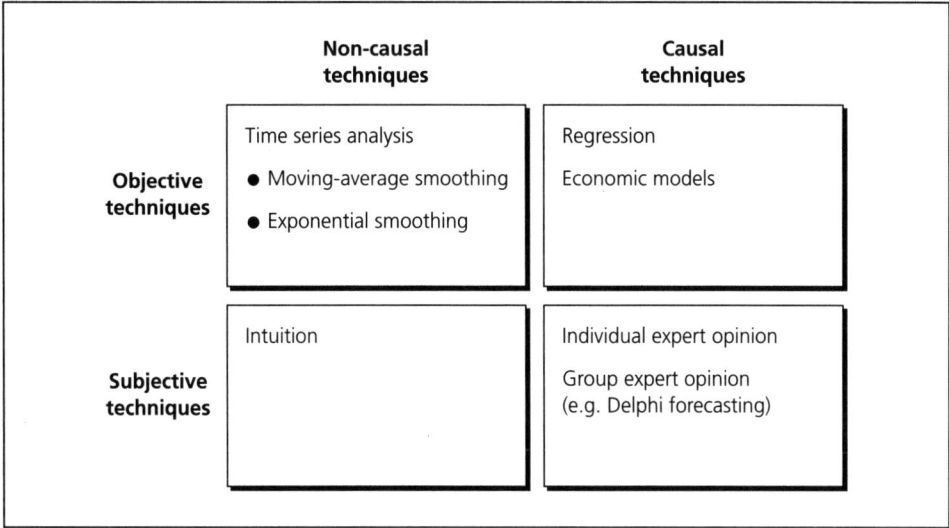

Figure A1.1 Some common forecasting techniques

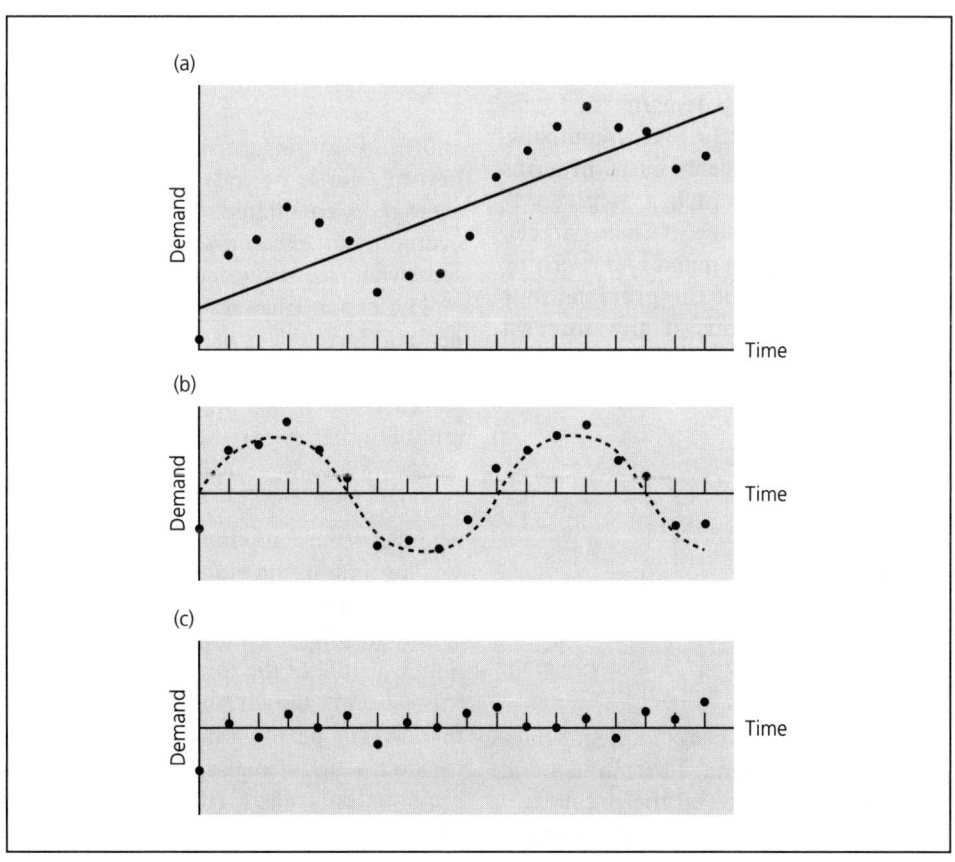

Figure A1.2 Time series analysis with (a) trend, (b) seasonality and (c) random variation

that they do not have a cause, however, just that we do not know what it is. Nevertheless, some attempt can be made to forecast it, if only on the basis that future events will, in some way, be based on past events. We will examine two of the more common approaches to forecasting which are based on projecting forward from past behaviour. These are:

- moving-average based forecasting;
- exponentially smoothed forecasting.

Moving-average based forecasting

The moving-average approach to forecasting takes the previous n periods' actual demand figures, calculates the average demand over the n periods, and uses this average as a forecast for the next period's demand. Any data older than the n periods plays no part in the next period's forecast. The value of n can be set at any level, but is usually in the range 4 to 7.

Example – Eurospeed parcels

Table A1.1 shows the weekly demand for Eurospeed, a European-wide parcel delivery company. It measures demand, on a weekly basis, in terms of the number of parcels which it is given to deliver (irrespective of the size of each parcel). Each week, the next week's demand is forecast by taking the moving average of the previous four weeks' actual demand. Thus if the forecast demand for week t is F_t and the actual demand for week t is A_t, then:

$$F_t = \frac{A_{t-1} + A_{t-2} + A_{t-3} + A_{t-4}}{4}$$

For example, the forecast for week 35:

$$F_{35} = (72.5 + 66.7 + 68.3 + 67.0)/4$$
$$= 68.8$$

Exponential smoothing

There are two significant drawbacks to the moving-average approach to forecasting. First, in its basic form, it gives equal weight to all the previous n periods which are used in the calculations (although this can be overcome by assigning different weights to each of the n periods). Second,

Table A1.1 Moving-average forecast calculated over a four-week period

Week	Actual demand (thousands)	Forecast
20	63.3	
21	62.5	
22	67.8	
23	66.0	
24	67.2	64.9
25	69.9	65.9
26	65.6	67.7
27	71.1	66.3
28	68.8	67.3
29	68.4	68.9
30	70.3	68.5
31	72.5	69.7
32	66.7	70.0
33	68.3	69.5
34	67.0	69.5
35		68.6

and more important, it does not use data from beyond the n periods over which the moving average is calculated. Both these problems are overcome by *exponential smoothing*, which is also somewhat easier to calculate.

The exponential-smoothing approach forecasts demand in the next period by taking into account the actual demand in the current period and the forecast which was previously made for the current period. It does so according to the formula:

$$F_t = \alpha A_{t-1} + (1 - x) F_{t-1}$$

where α = the smoothing constant.

The smoothing constant α is, in effect, the weight which is given to the last (and therefore assumed to be most important) piece of information available to the forecaster. However the other expression in the formula includes the forecast for the current period which included the previous period's actual demand, and so on. In this way all previous data has a (diminishing) effect on the next forecast.

Table A1.2 shows the data for Eurospeed's parcels forecasts using this exponential-smoothing method, where $\alpha = 0.2$. For example, the forecast for week 35 is:

$$F_{35} = 0.2 \times 67.0 + 0.8 \times 68.3 = 68.04$$

The value of α governs the balance between the *responsiveness* of the forecasts to changes in demand, and the *stability* of the forecasts. The closer α is to 0, the more forecasts will be dampened by previous forecasts (not very sensitive but stable). Figure A1.3 shows the Eurospeed volume data plotted for a four-week moving average, exponential smoothing with $\alpha = 0.2$ and exponential smoothing with $\alpha = 0.3$.

Regression models

Regression models use statistical techniques to determine the 'best fit' expression which describes the relationship between the variable being forecast and other variables. For example, suppose an ice-cream company is trying to forecast its future sales. After examining previous demand, it figures that the main influence on demand at the factory is the average temperature of the previous week. To understand this relationship, the company plots

Table A1.2 Exponentially smoothed forecast calculated with smoothing constant $\alpha = 0.2$

Week (t)	Actual demand (thousands) (A)	Forecast ($F_t = \alpha A_{t-1} + (1-\alpha) F_{t-1}$) ($\alpha = 0.2$)
20	63.3	60.00
21	62.5	60.66
22	67.8	60.03
23	66.0	61.58
24	67.2	62.83
25	69.9	63.70
26	65.6	64.94
27	71.1	65.07
28	68.8	66.28
29	68.4	66.78
30	70.3	67.12
31	72.5	67.75
32	66.7	68.70
33	68.3	68.30
34	67.0	68.30
35		68.04

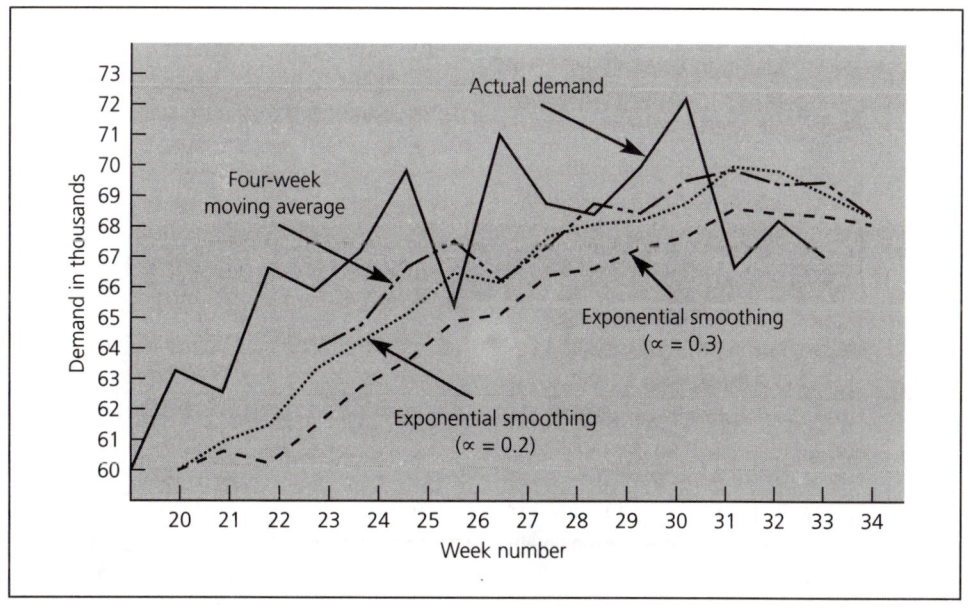

Figure A1.3 A comparison of a moving-average forecast and exponential smoothing with the smoothing constant $\alpha = 0.2$ and 0.3

demand against the previous week's temperatures. This is shown in Fig. A1.4. Using this graph, the company can make a reasonable prediction of demand, once the average temperature is known, provided that the other conditions prevailing in the market are reasonably stable. If they are not, then these other factors which have an influence on demand will need to be included in the regression model, which becomes increasingly complex.

Econometric models

At very high levels of demand forecasting, examining growth rates for a whole industry sector for example, complex regression approaches are called *econometric modelling*. Econometric models consist of a set of regression equations which describe complex cause–effect relationships. These equations are solved simultaneously, which allows a more realistic representation of the relationships within the decision. However, the cost of developing such models is usually very high.

Individual expert judgement

Some events which we may wish to forecast cannot be expressed in a manner which allows the use of quantative objective models. The rate of technological change in an industry, for example, might be particularly important to a company forecasting demand for its products which are bought as 'add-ons' to other manufacturers' products. The rate of technical change is not a factor which can be predicted by any objective method. Under such circumstances, decision makers have to rely on the opinions of people who, through their experience of similar situations or familiarity with the current problem, are deemed to be 'experts'.

Sometimes, using expert judgement is partially a substitute for some more rigorous but expensive method. For example, a company wishing to predict how its sales will stand up to a well publicized rival product, due to be launched shortly, may ask all its sales people for their opinions. The sales people will probably base their opinions partly on their perceptions of, and 'feel' for the market, and

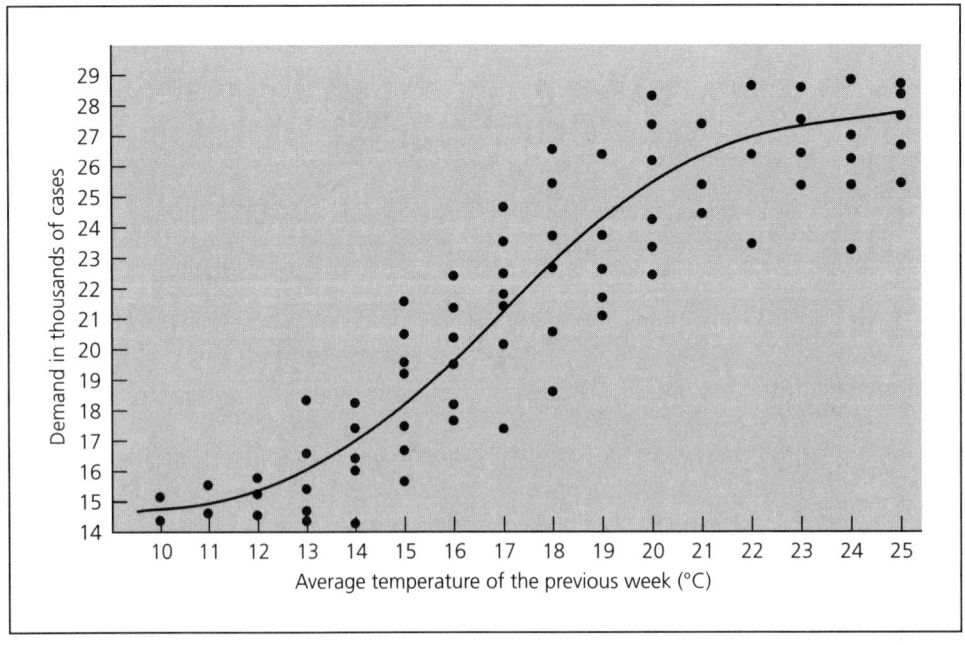

Figure A1.4 Regression line showing the relationship between the previous week's average temperature in degrees centigrade and demand in thousands of cases

partly on the comments made to them by the customers with whom they are in everyday contact. This latter element of expert judgement could well be performed with greater accuracy by a customer survey. However, a customer survey would be more costly, would take time, and might inadvertently publicize the rival product.

Delphi group forecasts

This technique is one of several used to bring together the opinions and forecasts of a group of experts. It has been defined as 'a method of structuring a group or communication process, so that the process is effective in allowing a group of individuals, as a whole, to deal with a complex problem'.[1] The technique seeks to obtain a group opinion through an anonymous process of controlled iterative feedback. The usual method is for a panel of experts (who are not allowed to communicate about the problem) to be interrogated through questionnaires. The information from the group is then collected together, summarized, aggregated and presented anonymously as feedback to the group. Each member of the group can then compare his or her own prediction with the group 'average'. The individual may then modify (or not as the case may be) his or her first-round prediction, and the process is repeated. Eventually it becomes clear whether a consensus is emerging from the group.

The performance of forecasting models

Forecasting models are widely used in management decision making, and indeed most decisions require a forecast of some kind, yet the performance of this type of model is far from impressive. Hogarth and Makridakis[2], in a comprehensive review of the applied management and finance literature, show that the record of forecasters using both judgement and sophisticated mathematical methods is not good. What they do suggest, however, is that certain forecasting techniques perform better under certain circumstances. In short-term forecasting there is:

'. . . considerable inertia in most economic and natural phenomena. Thus the present states of any variables are predictive of the short-term future (i.e. three months or less). Rather simple mechanistic methods, such as those used in time series forecasts, can often make accurate short-term forecasts and even outperform more theoretically elegant and elaborate approaches used in econometric forecasting.'[3]

Long-term forecasting methods, although difficult to judge because of the time lapse between the forecast and the event, do seem to be more amenable to an objective causal approach. In a comparative study of long-term market forecasting methods, Armstrong and Grohman[4] conclude that econometric methods offer more accurate long-range forecasts than do expert opinion or time series analysis, and that the superiority of objective causal methods improves as the time horizon increases.

Notes

1 Linstone, H.A. and Turoof, M. (1975) *The Delphi Method: Techniques and Applications*, Addison-Wesley.
2 Hogarth, R.M. and Makridakis, S. (1981) 'Forecasting and Planning: An Evaluation', *Management Science*, Vol 27, pp 115–38.
3 Hogarth, R.M. and Makridakis, S., *op. cit.*
4 Armstrong, J.S. and Grohman, M.C. (1972) 'A Comparative Study of Methods for Long-Range Market Forecasting', *Management Science*, Vol 19, No 2, pp 211–21.

APPENDIX 2
TIME ESTIMATION–WORK MEASUREMENT

Time estimation

One of the most important pieces of information in the design activity of any organization is how long particular tasks will take to complete. Some estimate of a task's duration is an essential prerequisite for many key design decisions. The following list identifies some applications for time data:

Designing products, services and processes (Chapter 5)

● Evaluating alternative product designs which have different methods of assembling or manufacturing products.
● Evaluating alternative ways of designing the serving of customers in high customer contact services.

Designing the operations network (Chapter 6)

● Evaluating transportation times in location decisions.
● Evaluating whether to perform a task in-house.
● Evaluating the amount of capacity which will be needed in the operation.

Layout and flow (Chapter 7)

● Evaluating the times to perform tasks at each stage of a process.
● Evaluating alternative routings through an operation.
● Balancing the work allocated to each stage of an operation (identifying bottle-necks).

Process technology (Chapter 8)

● Evaluating alternative types of technologies.
● Evaluating alternative sizes of machines and equipment.

Job design (Chapter 9)

● Evaluating alternative work methods.
● Evaluating safety allowances.
● Evaluating remuneration schemes and 'allowed-time' schemes.
● Evaluating the performance of individuals, or groups of staff.

It is because of this wide variety of uses for time estimates that all organizations need to make some kind of estimate of the length of time which will be needed for each of the tasks which are performed. In order to get such an estimate all organizations have three options:

● they can guess;
● they can assume that the time which *is* taken to do a job is in fact the *correct time* to do it;
● they can use a measuring technique which is systematic and has reasonably predictable limits of accuracy.

It is the latter approach which we will examine in this Appendix. It involves applying systematic techniques to tasks and work-time estimation, and it is known as *work measurement*.

Work measurement

'Work measurement is the application of techniques designed to establish the time for a qualified worker to carry out a specified job at a defined level of performance.'

This statement of what work measurement sets out to achieve poses three important questions:

- What is a qualified worker?
- What is a specified job?
- What is a defined level of performance?

None of these questions can be defined with much degree of precision, but generally it is agreed that a *specified job* is one for which specifications have been established to define most aspects of the job. For example:

- the quality standard required;
- the method to be followed by the person performing the job;
- the equipment and materials to be used;
- the working conditions under which the job is performed.

A *qualified worker* is one who is accepted as having the necessary physical attributes, intelligence, skill, education and knowledge to perform the task to satisfactory standards of safety, quality and quantity.

The term *performance* means a rate of working, or alternatively a rate of output, expressed as an average of the working day or shift. In fact, traditionally, there are two basic conceptions of what the level of performance should be:

- that it should be set at the level of performance which can be reasonably expected under 'motivation' conditions; and
- that it should be set at the level of performance which can be reasonably expected under 'non-motivation' conditions.

The various bodies round the world who recommended standards of practice for work measurement recommend that performance should be pitched at the 'motivation' level. The term used to describe this level of performance is *standard performance*, and is defined as:

'The rate of output which qualified workers will achieve without over-exertion as an average over the working day provided they are motivated to apply themselves to their work.'

Basic times

Terminology is important in work measurement. The terms which are used for time estimates of various types are all different, and using the wrong term can lead to confusion. When a *qualified worker* is working on a *specified job* at *standard performance*, the time he or she takes to perform the job is called the *basic time* for the job.

Basic times are useful because they are the 'building blocks' of time estimation. With the basic times for a range of different tasks, an operations manager can construct a time estimate for any longer activity which is made up of the tasks. For example, suppose an operations manager of a company which erects temporary buildings needs to estimate the time which should be taken to erect a particular building. The time could be estimated by adding together the basic times for each part of the total job. This is the idea behind 'synthetic' time estimating which will be explained later.

Standard times

The *standard time* for a job is an extension of the basic time and has a different use. Whereas the basic time for a job is a piece of information which can be used as the first step in estimating the time to perform a job under a wide range of conditions, standard time refers to the time *allowed* for the job under specific circumstances. This is because standard time includes *allowances* which reflect the rest and relaxation which is to be allowed because of the conditions under which the job is performed.

So the standard time for each element consists principally of two parts (although in some cases extra allowances may be applicable):

- *Basic time:* the time taken by a qualified worker, doing a specified job at standard performance;
- *Relaxation allowance:* the allowances which are added to the basic time to allow for rest, relaxation and personal needs.

Most of the techniques of work measurement involve the breaking down of the job to be studied into *elements*. For each of these elements, separate *standard times* are then determined. The standard time of the job as a whole is then the sum of all the standard times of its constituent elements (*see* Fig. A2.1).

Example

Suppose a task has four elements, each of which warrants a different allowance as shown in Table A2.1.

This is shown diagrammatically in Fig. A2.2.

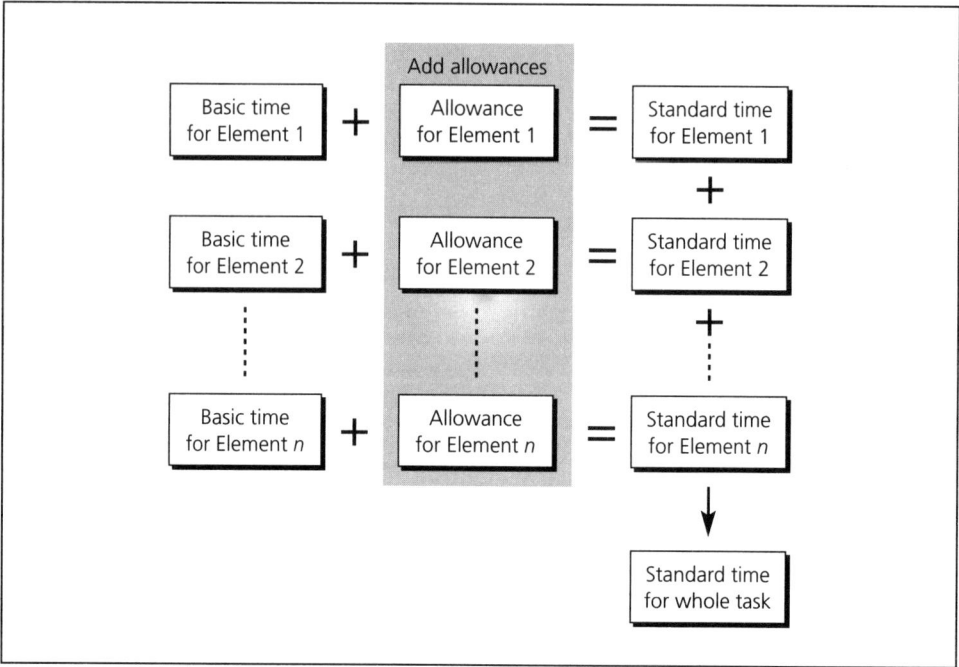

Figure A2.1 The standard time for a whole job is made up of the basic times for all its elements with the addition of the allowances for each element

Table A2.1

Element	Basic time (mins)	Relaxation allowance (%)	Relaxation allowance (mins)	Standard time (mins)
a	0.67	18	0.12	0.79
b	0.43	14	0.06	0.49
c	0.85	12	0.10	0.95
d	0.30	17	0.05	0.35
Total	2.25		0.33	2.58

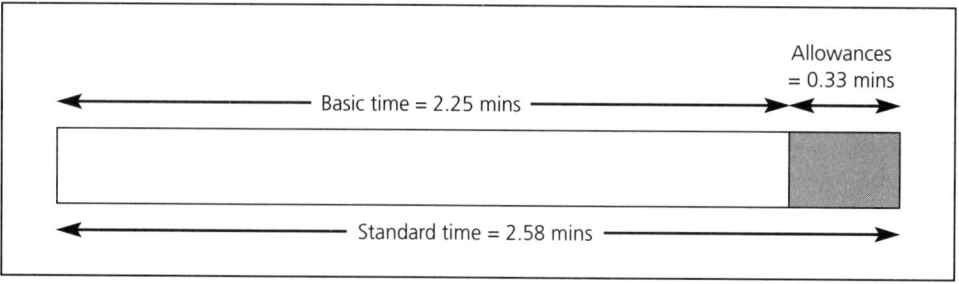

Figure A2.2 Standard time calculation for the example

The advantages of standard time

The standard time for any task is not necessarily the time which will be taken actually to perform it in reality. That is not a disadvantage, however, provided the operations managers who work with the information know how it has been derived. In fact the 'basic time', which is the time which a 'qualified worker, working at standard performance' would take is often a more useful piece of information at the micro level of design. Nevertheless, the standard time for a task, because it is both *normalized* to the performance of someone working at standard performance and also contains the *allowances* which staff should be taking, can be particularly useful.

The standard time for a task is, in effect, an estimate of the total amount of *work* which is needed to perform the task. It enables all types of work to be expressed in terms of a common unit – the 'standard minute' or 'standard hour' (SMs or SHs). For different tasks the proportion of the standard minute or hour spent actually working and the proportion spent resting will vary, but the two parts together always add up to the common unit. Figure A2.3 illustrates this idea.

Allowances

There are several allowances which may be applied to the basic time depending on the circumstances. The main one is *relaxation allowance*. Special allowances may also be applied, such as:

- contingency allowances
- interfaces or synchronization allowances

- introductory allowances
- unusual condition allowances
- unoccupied time allowances.

Relaxation allowance is defined as,

'. . . *an addition to the basic time intended to provide the worker with the opportunity to recover from the physiological and psychological effects of carrying out specified work under specified conditions and to allow attention to personal needs. The amount of the allowance will depend on the nature of the job.*'

The way in which relaxation allowance is calculated, and the exact allowances given for each of the factors which determine the extent of the allowance, varies considerably between different organizations. Table A2.2 illustrates the allowance table used by one company which manufactures domestic appliances. The table shows the percentage allowance to be applied to each element of the job. All allowances are additive and a personal needs allowance of ten per cent is added to all elements.

The techniques of work measurement

The method of moving from the basic times for each element of a task to the standard time for the whole task is more or less the same no matter how the basic time is derived. The basic time itself can be measured or estimated by a number of techniques, however. The work measurement approach uses five techniques:

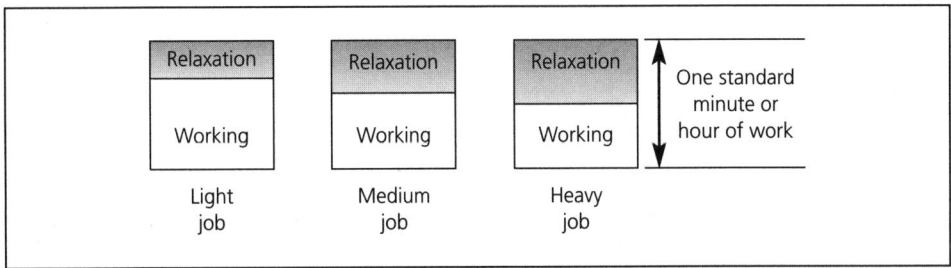

Figure A2.3 Using the standard time approach to work measurement, the standard unit of work remains the same, only the proportions of relaxation and working time vary

1 Time study
2 Synthesis from elemental data
3 Predetermined motion-time systems
4 Analytical estimating
5 Activity sampling.

A brief description of each technique follows.

Time study

'A work measurement technique for recording the times and rate of working for the elements of a specified job, carried out under specified conditions, and for analysing the data so as to obtain the time necessary for the carrying out of the job at a defined level of performance.'

The times for the job are recorded using one or more stopwatches on the shop floor which is why time study has met, and still does encounter, opposition. The use of direct timing can be seen as intrusive. Nevertheless, even though time study is now used far less for generating standards which are used in payment schemes (the major source of the technique's unpopularity), it is still used extensively. The technique takes three steps to deriving the basic time for the elements of the job:

Table A2.2 An allowances table used by a domestic appliance manufacturer

Allowance factors	Example	Allowance (%)
Energy needed		
Negligible	none	0
Very light	0–3 kg	3
Light	3–10 kg	5
Medium	10–20 kg	10
Heavy	20–30 kg	15
Very heavy	Above 30 kg	15–30
Posture required		
Normal	Sitting	0
Erect	Standing	2
Continuously erect	Standing for long periods	3
Lying	On side, face or back	4
Difficult	Crouching, etc.	4–10
Visual fatigue		
Nearly continuous attention		2
Continuous attention with varying focus		3
Continuous attention with fixed focus		5
Temperature		
Very low	Below 0°C	over 10
Low	0–12°C	0–10
Normal	12–23°C	0
High	23–30°C	0–10
Very high	Above 30°C	over 10
Atmospheric conditions		
Good	Well ventilated	0
Fair	Stuffy/smelly	2
Poor	Dusty/needs filter	2–7
Bad	Needs respirator	7–12

- observing and measuring the time taken to perform each element of the job through several cycles of the job, while at the same time rating the performance of the person doing the job;
- adjusting, or 'normalizing', each observed time in the light of the rating of performance observed while the element was being timed;
- averaging the adjusted times to derive the basic time for the element.

Step 1 – observing, measuring and rating

After analysing the job to be studied in order to divide the whole job into its constituent elements, the job is observed through several cycles. Each time an element is performed it is timed using a stopwatch. There are procedures for using one or more stopwatches which allow the observer to time consecutive elements while minimizing observation error. Simultaneously with the observation of time, a rating of the perceived performance of the person doing the job is recorded.

The *rating* of observed times is probably the most controversial part of time study. It is defined as:

'the process of assessing the worker's rate of working relative to the observer's concept of the rate corresponding to standard performance. The observer may take into account, separately or in combination, one or more factors necessary to carrying out the job, such as speed of movement, effort, dexterity, consistency, etc.'

At the most charitable it is a subjective, and at times arbitrary, procedure. Rating does perform a necessary function, however. All individuals have different skills, motivations, and standards of what constitutes a reasonable pace of working. Unless the observer is to measure a large number of people, all performing the same job, then there is little alternative but to 'normalize' the observed times. This normalization adjustment is intended to bring the time to that which a qualified worker, working at standard performance, would have taken.

There are several ways of recording the observer's rating. The most common is on a scale which uses a rating of 100 to represent standard performance. If an observer rates a particular observation of the time to perform an element at 100, the time observed is the actual time which anyone working at standard performance would take. If the rating was lower than 100, a person working at standard performance would have taken less time, and if the rating was higher than 100, the person working at standard performance would have taken more time.

Figure A2.4 shows the results of a simple study. Ten observations of a four-element task were taken and each observed time rated.

Step 2 – adjusting the observed times

The adjustment to normalize the observed time is:

$$\frac{\text{observed rating}}{\text{standard rating}}$$

where standard rating is 100 on the common rating scale we are using here.

For example if:

The observed time = 130 mins
The observed rating = 90

$$\text{The basic time} = 1.30 \times \frac{90}{100} = 1.17 \text{ mins}$$

Figure A2.5 shows the data from the previous study but with the observed times adjusted to derive individual basic times.

Step 3 – average the basic times

In spite of the adjustments made to the observed times through the rating mechanism, each separately calculated basic time will not be the same. This is not necessarily a function of inaccurate rating, or even the vagueness of the rating procedure itself; it is a natural phenomenon of the time taken to perform tasks. Any human activity cannot be repeated in *exactly* the same time on every occasion. There will be some 'natural' variation in the time taken which is caused by minor variations in the speed or manner in which the job is performed. Usually this variation is positively skewed (*see* Fig. A2.6).

Element		Observation										Average basic time	Allowances	Element standard time
		1	2	3	4	5	6	7	8	9	10			
Make box	Observed time	0.71	0.71	0.71	0.69	0.75	0.68	0.70	0.72	0.70	0.68			
	Rating	90	90	90	90	80	90	90	90	90	90			
	Basic time													
Pack x 20	Observed time	1.30	1.32	1.25	1.33	1.33	1.28	1.32	1.32	1.30	1.30			
	Rating	90	90	100	90	90	90	90	90	90	90			
	Basic time													
Seal and secure	Observed time	0.53	0.55	0.55	0.56	0.53	0.53	0.60	0.55	0.49	0.51			
	Rating	90	90	90	90	90	90	85	90	100	100			
	Basic time													
Assemble outer,	Observed time	1.12	1.21	1.20	1.25	1.41	1.27	1.11	1.15	1.20	1.23			
fix and label	Rating	100	90	90	90	90	90	100	100	90	90			
	Basic time													

Job _Pack 20 x pt # 73/2A_____   Location _Packing Dept._____   Observer _FWT_____

Raw standard time

Allowances for total job [%]

Standard time for job [SM]

Figure A2.4 Time study on a packing task – raw data

The positive skewing of the variation is intuitively explained by the fact that while there is a theoretical lower limit to the time necessary to perform any task (a time faster than which it is not feasible to go), there is theoretically no upper limit to how long a task can take.

Figure A2.7 shows how the data from the study described previously can be further manipulated to give average basic times for each element in the job. These are the basic times which are used to derive the standard time for the job. Figure A2.7 also shows how the standard time is calculated by including the allowances (low in this example) for each element.

Synthesis from elemental data

'A work measurement technique for building up the time for a job at a defined level of performance by totalling element times obtained previously from the studies in other jobs containing the elements concerned or from synthetic data.'

Predetermined motion-time systems (PMTS)

'A work measurement technique whereby times established for basic human motions (classified according to the nature of the motion and the conditions under which it is made) are used to build up the time for a job at a defined level of performance.'

Analytical estimating

'A work measurement technique, being a development of estimating whereby the time required to carry out the elements of a job at a defined level of performance is estimated from knowledge and experience of the elements concerned.'

Job _Pack 20 x pt.# 73/2A_____   Location _Packing Dept._____   Observer _FWT_____

Element		Observation										Average basic time	Allowances	Element standard time
		1	2	3	4	5	6	7	8	9	10			
Make box	Observed time	0.71	0.71	0.71	0.69	0.75	0.68	0.70	0.72	0.70	0.68			
	Rating	90	90	90	90	80	90	90	90	90	90			
	Basic time	0.64	0.64	0.63	0.62	0.60	0.61	0.63	0.65	0.63	0.61			
Pack x 20	Observed time	1.30	1.32	1.25	1.33	1.33	1.28	1.32	1.32	1.30	1.30			
	Rating	90	90	100	90	90	90	90	90	90	90			
	Basic time	1.17	1.19	1.25	1.20	1.20	1.15	1.19	1.19	1.17	1.17			
Seal and secure	Observed time	0.53	0.55	0.55	0.56	0.53	0.53	0.60	0.55	0.49	0.51			
	Rating	90	90	90	90	90	90	85	90	100	100			
	Basic time	0.48	0.5	0.5	0.50	0.48	0.48	0.51	0.5	0.49	0.51			
Assemble outer,	Observed time	1.12	1.21	1.20	1.25	1.41	1.27	1.11	1.15	1.20	1.23			
fix and label	Rating	100	90	90	90	90	90	100	100	90	90			
	Basic time	1.12	1.09	1.08	1.13	1.27	1.14	1.11	1.15	1.08	1.21			

Raw standard time [ ]

Allowances for total job [%] [ ]

Standard time for job [SM]

Figure A2.5 Time study on a packing task with basic times calculated at each observation

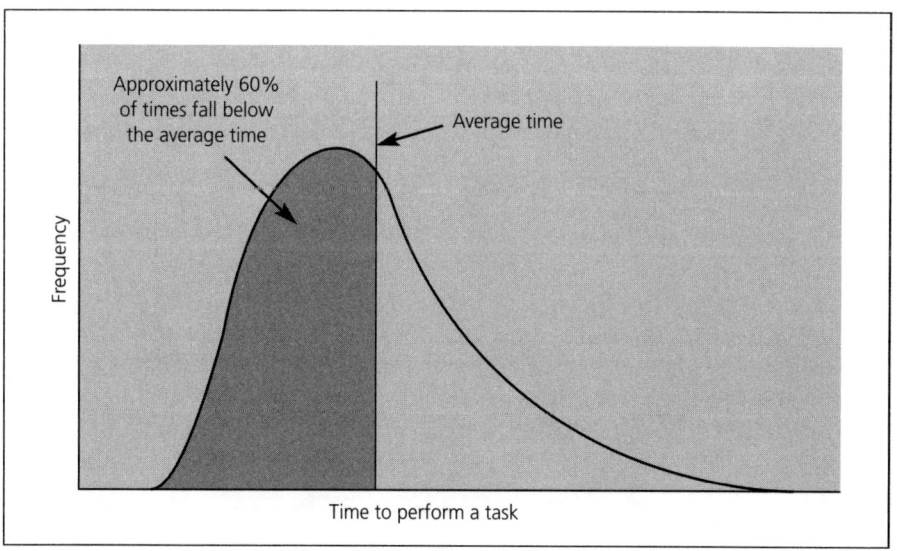

Figure A2.6 The distribution of the time taken to perform most human-influenced tasks is positively skewed

Job _Pack 20 x pt # 73/2A_ ......   Location _Packing Dept._ ....   Observer _FWT_ ....

Element		Observation										Average basic time	Allowances	Element standard time
		1	2	3	4	5	6	7	8	9	10			
Make box	Observed time	0.71	0.71	0.71	0.69	0.75	0.68	0.70	0.72	0.70	0.68			
	Rating	90	90	90	90	80	90	90	90	90	90			
	Basic time	0.64	0.64	0.63	0.62	0.60	0.61	0.63	0.65	0.63	0.61	0.626	10%	0.689
Pack x 20	Observed time	1.30	1.32	1.25	1.33	1.33	1.28	1.32	1.32	1.30	1.30			
	Rating	90	90	100	90	90	90	90	90	90	90			
	Basic time	1.17	1.19	1.25	1.20	1.20	1.15	1.19	1.19	1.17	1.17	1.168	12%	1.308
Seal and secure	Observed time	0.53	0.55	0.55	0.56	0.53	0.53	0.60	0.55	0.49	0.51			
	Rating	90	90	90	90	90	90	85	90	100	100			
	Basic time	0.48	0.5	0.5	0.50	0.48	0.48	0.51	0.5	0.49	0.51	0.495	10%	0.545
Assemble outer,	Observed time	1.12	1.21	1.20	1.25	1.41	1.27	1.11	1.15	1.20	1.23			
fix and label	Rating	100	90	90	90	90	90	100	100	90	90			
	Basic time	1.12	1.09	1.08	1.13	1.27	1.14	1.11	1.15	1.08	1.21	1.138	12%	1.275

Raw standard time		3.817
Allowances for total job	5%	
Standard time for job		4.01 SM

Figure A2.7 Time study of packing task – standard time for the whole task calculated

Activity sampling

'A technique in which a large number of instantaneous observations are made over a period of time of a group of machines, processes or workers. Each observation records what is happening at that instant and the percentage of observations recorded for a particular activity or delay is a measure of the percentage of time during which that activity or delay occurs.'

APPENDIX 3
THE RECORDING TECHNIQUES OF METHOD STUDY

In Chapter 9 a flow process chart was used as an illustration of one of the many techniques of work study which can be used to record the present method of doing a job. The flow process chart was chosen because it is probably the best known and most used of these techniques. Nevertheless, there are others which deserve at least a mention. Most of these techniques can be used for several purposes but tend to focus on one particular purpose – namely recording the sequence of tasks, recording the time relationships between different parts of a job, and recording the movement of staff, information or materials within the job.

Those techniques which focus primarily on determining the sequence of tasks include:

- outline process charts
- flow process charts
- two-handed process charts.

Those which concentrate primarily on the time relationships between parts of a job include:

- multiple-activity charts
- simo charts.

Those which concentrate on the movement of elements within the job include:

- micro-motion analysis
- memo-motion analysis
- flow diagrams.

Process charts

The flow process chart described in Chapter 9 used the five symbols to describe the sequence of tasks as either operations, inspections, transportations, delays or storages. In fact there are three types of process chart – outline process charts, flow process charts, and two-handed process charts. The symbols may have marginally different meanings, depending on which of these charts is being used. Process charts can be applied either to the flow of materials or information through a job, or alternatively can be used to chart the sequence of activities done by the member of staff. Table A3.1 gives the meanings of each symbol for each kind of process chart.

For example, a job might need both a material (or information) flow process chart and a staff flow process chart to describe it completely. Figure A3.1 gives an example of this for the job of adjusting and packing a test meter where each meter is adjusted to a customer's particular requirements.

Outline process charts

Sometimes as a precursor to a full flow process chart a job might be described by means of an outline process chart. An outline process chart adopts the same principles as the flow process chart but uses only the operation and inspection symbols and often aggregates several small tasks into one overall operation. Figure A3.2 shows an outline process chart for the assembling and packing operation described previously.

Two-handed process charts

The two-handed process chart again adopts the same principles but this time on a more micro

Table A3.1 The symbols used in process charts

Symbol	Outline process chart	Flow process chart (for staff)	Flow process chart (for materials)	Two-handed process chart
●	Operation	Operation	Operation	Operation
➡	Not used	Transportation	Transportation	Transportation
◗	Not used	Delay	Delay	Delay
■	Inspection	Inspection	Inspection	Not used
▼	Not used	Not used	Storage	Hold

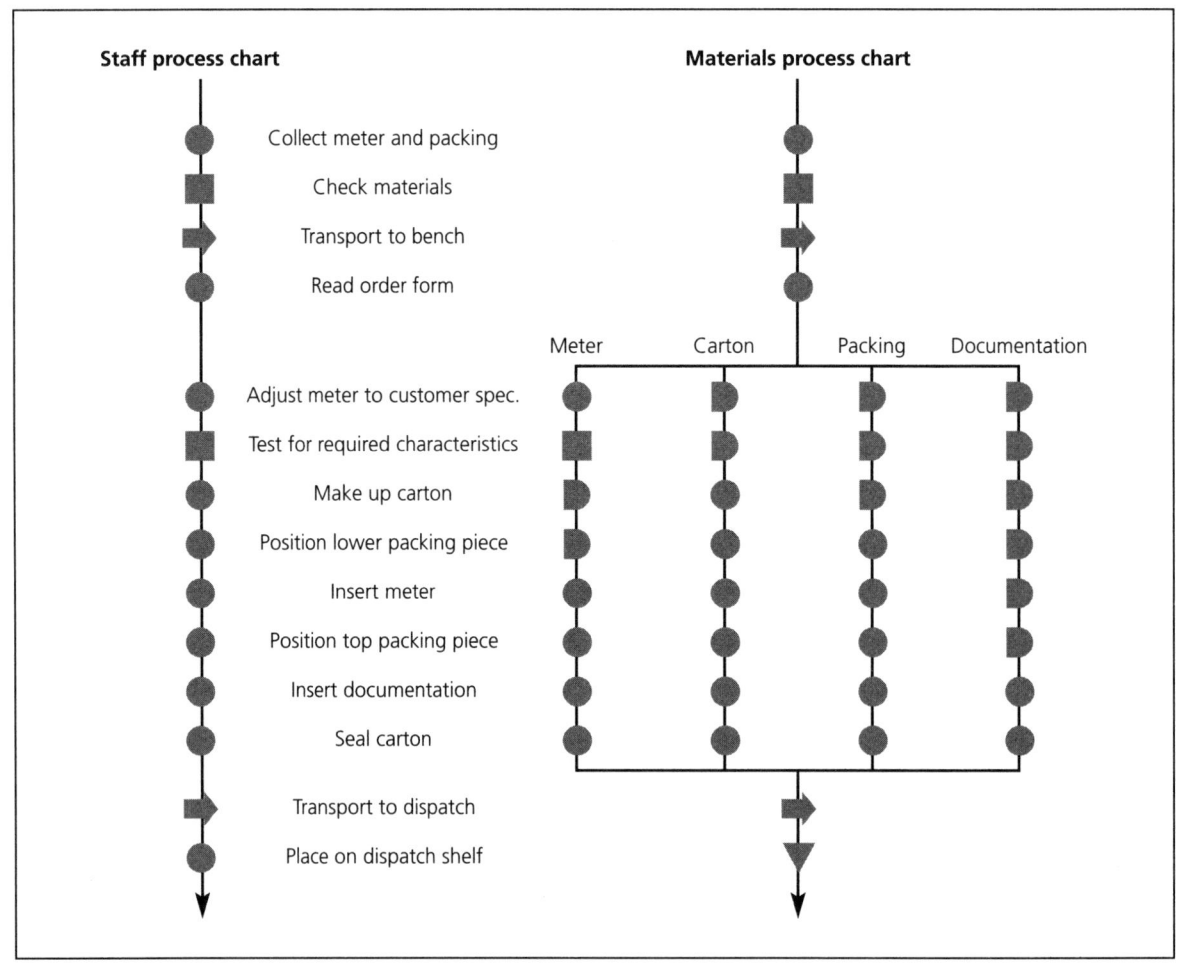

Figure A3.1 Staff and materials flow process charts for an adjustment and packing task

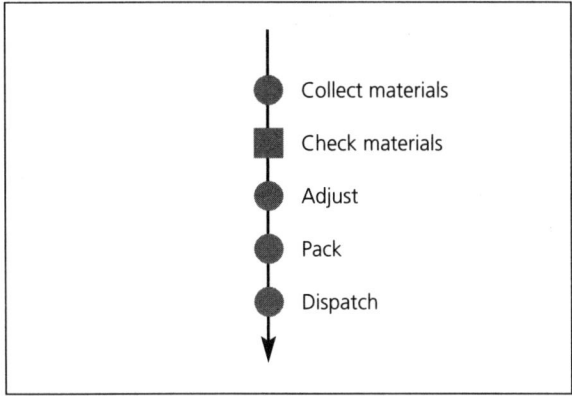

Figure A3.2 Outline process chart for adjustment and packing task

scale. The sequence of motion of each hand is charted using the same symbols as before. There are slight changes to the meaning of the symbols, however. The delay symbol is used to indicate that the hand is waiting to carry out its next task. The storage symbol is used to indicate that the hand is holding on to a piece of material or a document. Usually two-handed process charts are shown on a pre-formatted diagram similar to that shown in Fig. A3.3. Here a particular assembly job is described by recording the activities of each hand during the total job. The advantage of using a pre-formatted diagram such as this is that the analysis also gives an indication of the relationship of the activities performed by each hand.

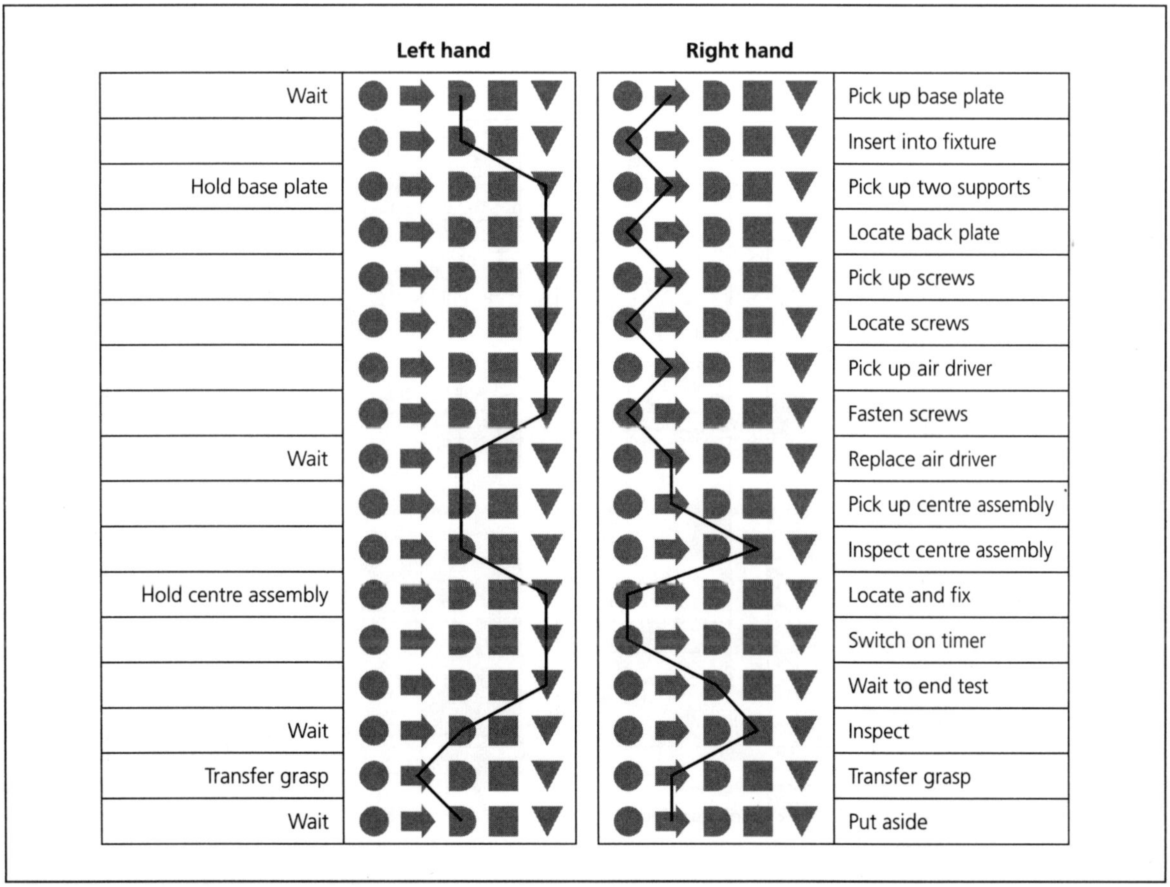

Left hand		Right hand
Wait		Pick up base plate
		Insert into fixture
Hold base plate		Pick up two supports
		Locate back plate
		Pick up screws
		Locate screws
		Pick up air driver
		Fasten screws
Wait		Replace air driver
		Pick up centre assembly
		Inspect centre assembly
Hold centre assembly		Locate and fix
		Switch on timer
		Wait to end test
Wait		Inspect
Transfer grasp		Transfer grasp
Wait		Put aside

Figure A3.3 Two-handed process chart

Time relationship techniques

This idea of describing the time relationship between parts of the job is carried further with techniques such as multiple-activity charts and micro-motion analysis.

Multiple-activity charts

Often jobs involve either more than one member of staff and/or machines. It is sometimes necessary to record and understand the interrelationships between these different resources in the job. To do this multiple-activity charts are used to record activities against the same time scale, placing the 'time map' for each resource against each other to make comparison easy. For example, Fig. A3.4 shows a multiple-activity chart for two people changing and adjusting a machine used to slit paper reels into smaller reels.

The simo chart

The principles behind the multiple-activity chart and the two-handed process chart may be combined in a simo chart. Whereas the two-handed process chart has a separate line for each element in the job, the simo chart is drawn on a time-based scale. This allows the job designer to see the relative time taken by each part of the job. Figure A3.5 shows a simo chart for the same job that was described in Fig. A3.3.

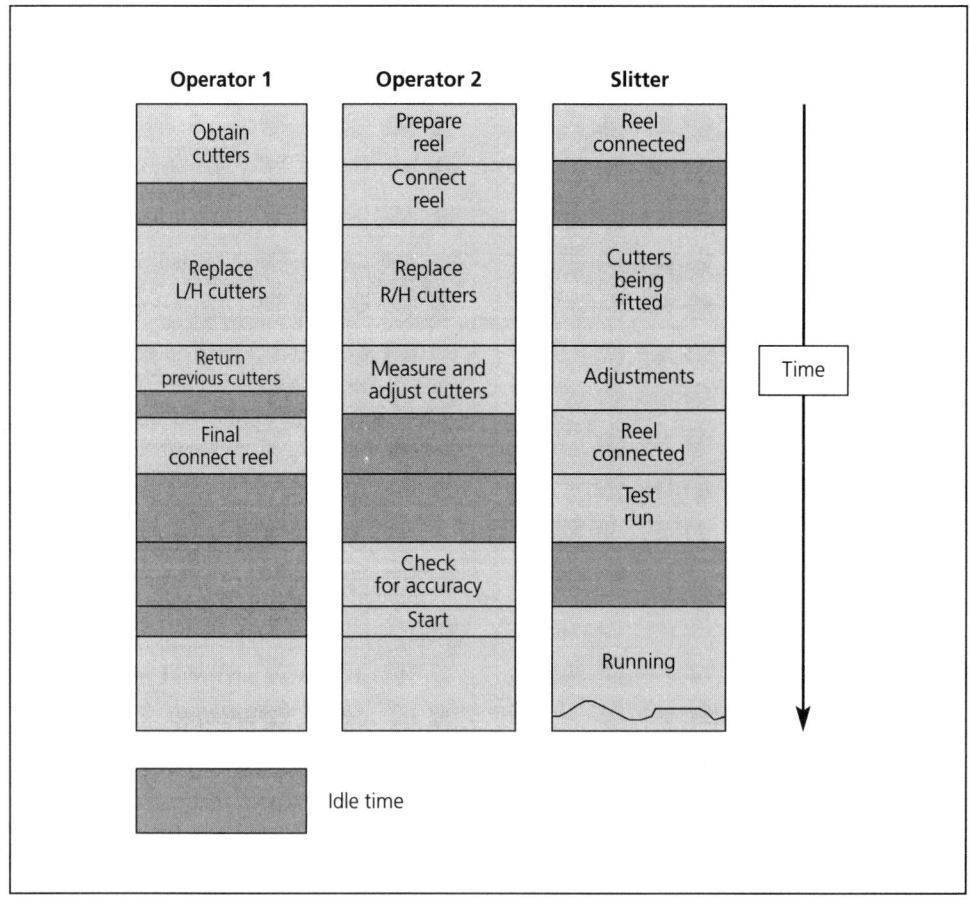

Figure A3.4 Multiple-activity chart for a two-person crew changing a slitting machine

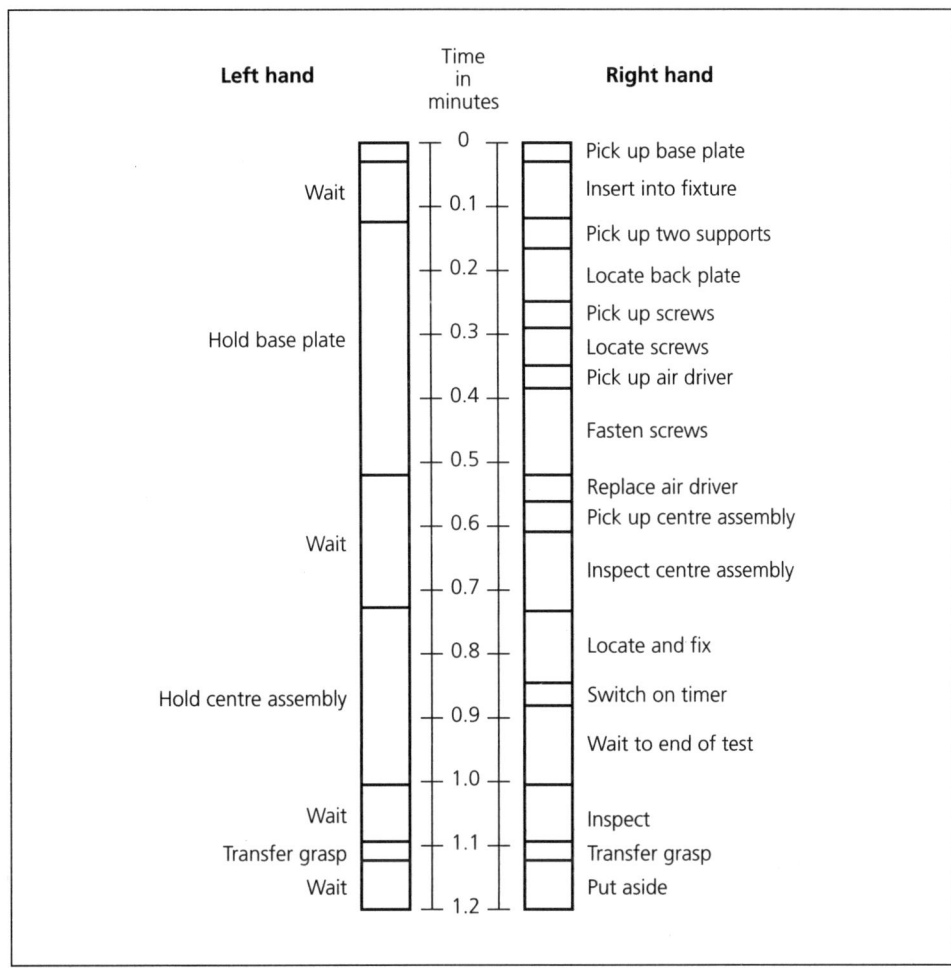

Figure A3.5 Simo chart

Path of movement techniques

In some jobs the path of movement of either material, information or staff is the major concern of the job designer. Work study provides a number of techniques which can be used to track the movement of resources.

Memo-motion video recording

One of the most convenient ways to record the path of movement of any aspect of a job is to record long periods of the job using video cameras. A speeded up play-back of the recording can then compress hours of activity into a few min-utes. More importantly the path of movement within the job can be recorded on charts or plans of the area of work.

Micro-motion analysis

The same principle can be used in the opposite way. For the examination of every detail of fast work (for example, the hand movements in a complicated routine assembly task) video recording of the task can be slowed down to allow the job designer to trace the exact path of movement of the hands during the job. Again this path can be superimposed on a diagram or picture of the workplace.

INDEX

A-shape product structures 506–7
ABC inventory system 443–7
absolute performance
        standards 655
acceptable quality levels (AQL)
        640, 642
acceptance sampling 636–41, 642
accident investigation 705–6
activity mix 385
activity on arrow (AoA) network
        method 595–6
activity on node (AoN) network
        method 595–6
activity sampling 814
actual cost of work performed
        (ACWP) 590
ADTrans 449
Aerotek South Africa 97
air travel 89, 697
Aishin Seiki 720
Alcan 182
analytical estimating 814
anticipation inventories 423
appraisal costs 742–3
Asea Brown Boveri (ABB)
        Robotics 267, 781–2
assembly lines 308
automated guided vehicles (AGVs)
        266–8
automation 292–3, 308
autonomy 306, 537
available to promise (ATP) 503
Avis 368

BA (British Airways) 348–9
back-office technology 285
backward scheduling 362–3,
        514–17
balancing loss 246, 250
banks 114
bar-code scanner technology 288
basic working practices 537–8

BATC (Brussels Airport Terminal
        Company SA) 369–70
batch access systems 277, 278
batch processes 127
'bath-tub' curve 699–700
behavioural approach to job design
        327–30, 332
benchmarking 95, 655–7, 658
Benetton 480
Bessant, Professor John 272
bill of materials (BOM) 150, 151,
        504, 508–11
blanket orders 485
Bloch, Jeff Max 790
Body Shop 22
Boeing 109
Boots 408
Braun AG 140–1
break-even analysis 205–6
breakthrough improvement
        664–5, 666–7
British Airways (BA) 348–9
British Standard BS5750 464
Brussels Airport Terminal
        Company SA (BATC)
        369–70
budgeted cost of work performed
        (BCWP) 590
budgeted cost of work scheduled
        (BCWS) 589
buffer inventories 422, 530
buffering operations 21–2
business process re-engineering
        (BPR) 670–2

CAD (computer-aided design)
        162–4
capacity
    adjusting 392–3
    break-even analysis 205–6
    capacity requirement plans
        (CRP) 519

constraints 377–8
costs of change 400, 402
definition 377
design capacity 386–7
measuring 384–8
optimum levels 198–200
outlook matrix 407–10
over-booking 396
planning and control 378–80
    chase demand plan 390–3,
        400, 503
    level capacity plans 388–90,
        399, 401
    mixed plans 394–5
and product/service life cycle
        204–5
    queueing theory 403–7
    strategies 198–206, 378
    timing of changes 202–4
    utilization 386, 387–8, 532
    vertical integration 180–4
    yield management 395–6
    see also demand; location of
        capacity
caretaker strategy 768
Carmichael, Colin 207–8
cause–effect diagrams 678–9
CBM (condition-based
        maintenance) 712–13
cell layout 219–23, 240–4
centralized information processing
        277
centre-of-gravity capacity location
        method 195–7
change demand 393–4
Channel Tunnel 583
chase demand planning 390–3,
        400, 503
China 189–90
Christopher, Martin 475
CIM (computer-integrated
        manufacturing) 274–7

CIT (critical incident analysis) 706
closed-loop MRP systems 518–19
Club Med 742
co-contracting 482
Colgate–Palmolive 282
commitment 332–3
community cost factors 188, 191
community responsibility 777
company values 778, 779
competitive-tendering 486
competitiveness 77, 139–40, 179
competitors
  and concept generation 146
  and improvement priorities 658
  judging performance against 660
  performance influences 79–82,
    655
complaint analysis 706
complaint cards 705
computer-aided design (CAD)
  162–4
computer-integrated
  manufacturing (CIM) 274–7
concept generation 145–8
concept screening 149–50
condition-based maintenance
  (CBM) 712–13
configuration strategy 780–1
conflict resolution 167–9
conformance to specification
  617–24
continuous improvement 536–7,
  665–7
continuous processes 128
continuous review re-stocking
  440–1
control 32, 332–3, 345
  see also planning and control
control charts 625
  for attributes 631–2
  interpreting 635–6
  for variables 632–5
control limits 628, 629–31, 633–5
conveyance kanban 542, 544
coordinated contracting 482–4
coordinated revenue links 484
corporate strategy 71, 73
corporate values 778, 779
cost, insurance and freight (CIF)
  contracts 471

cost & freight (C&F) contracts
  471
cost-to-function analyses 161
costs
  of appraisal 742–3
  of capacity change 400, 402
  of capacity location 186–91
  and demand-capacity balance
    379
  of distribution 457
  of energy 188
  of failures 743
  of inventories 424–6, 436
  of obsolescence 426
  and performance objectives 50,
    61–5
  in project management 576, 588
  and purchasing 460–3
  of quality 734, 741–6
  of transportation 188, 200, 472
  and vertical integration 184
  and volume–variety 124
CPM (critical path network
  planning) 593–8
crashing networks 602–3
creativity 538, 784–8
critical incident analysis (CIT)
  706
critical path method (CPM)
  593–8
Crosby, P.B. 734, 735
Crown Pies 618
culture
  different regional practices
    782–3
  multi-culturalism 781
  organizational culture 304, 536
Cumming, Neil 333–4
customer contact 17, 26–9
customer processing 15, 154–5,
  284–92
customers
  and capacity location 193
  and concept generation 145–6
  customer–staff technology
    interaction 286
  and ethical decision making 777
  influences on performance
    77–8, 79
  and input–output analysis 673–4

needs/expectations 107, 736–8
priority sequencing 358
and product failure 698
and supply chain management
  475, 477
training in technology use 290–2
view of quality 614
cycle inventories 422
cycle time of product layouts
  244–5

Dabengwa, Sifiso 723–4
data gathering 537
Dawson, Julia 488
De Meyer, Arnoud 664–5
decentralized information
  processing 278–80
defective goods 536
delivered contracts 471
delivery flexibility 58–9
Dell Computers 477
Delphi group forecasts 805
demand 347–55
  aggregate demand and capacity
    378–9
  changing demand 393–4
  cumulative representations
    396–403
  demand-capacity balance
    200–1, 379
  dependent and independent
    350–1, 496
  distribution of 382
  forecasting 380–3, 498–500,
    800–5
  management 393–4, 496–7
  networks 177
  queueing theory 403–7
  reconciling with supply 344
  responding to 352
  seasonality of 382–3
  uncertainty in 350
Deming, W.E. 667, 732–3, 735
Deming Prize 754–5
dependability 50, 53–6, 61, 124,
  184, 380, 532, 693
dependent demand 350–1, 496
design activities
  and competitive advantage
    139–40

concept to specification 113–18, 143–4
and customer needs 107
definition 106–7
environmental issues 121
evaluation and improvement 155–62
four Cs of design 119–20
interactive design 165–71
network decisions 180
objectives 108, 112
preliminary design 150–5
and products 31–2, 108–11, 143, 619
prototyping 162–4
simulation 118–19
and the transformation model 111–12
volume–variety effect 122–5
see also job design
design failure 695–6
design for manufacture 538
design teams 331
diagnostic checks 705
discipline 537
discounts 396, 426
Disney World 261–2
distributed processing 279
distribution, see physical distribution management; transportation
division of labour 308–10, 332
Down-to-Earth 776
dual-card kanban system 544–5
due date sequencing 359

earned-value project control 588–9
Ecco 267–8
econometric models 805
economic batch quantity (EBQ) model 431–3
economic order quantity (EOQ) formula 427–31, 435–6
efficiency 386, 387
electronic data interchange (EDI) 280–1, 282
electronic point-of-sale (EPOS) system 438, 474
empowerment 330–2
energy costs 188

environmental design 306, 324–6
environmental issues 121
equality in personnel policies 537
equipment
    failure 310
    positioning 306
ergonomics 306, 321–7, 332
Eskom 723
ethical decision making 774–8
Eurocamp 391
European Quality Award 755
ex-works contracts 471
EXL Laboratories 659–60, 661, 663–4
exponential smoothing 803–4
external failure costs 743

facilities failures 696
fail-safeing 710–11
failure
    as an opportunity 698
    analysis 705–7
    costs 743
    detection 704–5
    measuring 698–704
    planning 721–3
    prevention 704, 742
    probability distributions 716–17
    reasons for 694–8
    recovery procedures 704, 720–3
    see also reliability
failure mode and effect analysis (FMEA) 706–7
fault-tree analysis 707
Federal Express Corporation 783, 784
feedback 329, 705
Feigenbaum, Armand 732, 735
finance departments 150
finished goods inventory 424
finite loading 356
First-In-First-Out (FIFO) sequencing 359
fixed position layout 216–17, 218–19, 230–5
Flame Electrical 444
flexibility 56–61, 124, 184, 310, 380, 497–8, 532, 537
flexible manufacturing systems (FMS) 268–72, 293

flexible transfer lines (FTLs) 274
flow charts 152–3, 154, 156, 318–20, 674–6
focus groups 145–6, 705
Ford Motor Company 168
forecasting demand 380–3, 498–500, 800–5
Formule 1 29
Forrester Effect 479
forward scheduling 362–3
free alongside (FAS) contracts 471
free on board (FOB) contracts 471
front-office technology 285
functional activities 7–10
    see also operations function
functional strategy 72
Fyodorov, Svyatoslav 24

Gainsford, Tony 64
Gamede, Cyril 756
Gantt charts 360–1, 592–3
Garvin, David 612
GEC Alsthom 218–19
General Motors (GM) 314–15
Gilbreth, Frank 311
Giotto project 591
global coordinated configuration 780, 781
globalization 778–84
Godiva Chocolatier 59–60
Goldratt, Eliyahu 520
goods, see products
Goodyear 683
greeting cards industry 394
group-based improvement 751–3

Hackman, R.J. 328, 329
Hallmark Cards 394
Hayes, R.H. 44–5, 767
health & safety 307, 310, 537
heijunka, see level scheduling
Hewlett-Packard 680, 739
hierarchy of operations 18–20
high dependency theory 534
high involvement 332
Hill methodology 769–70
historical performance standards 654

Hoffmann-la-Roche 147
home country configuration 780
Hubble Space Telescope 714
human factors, *see* ergonomics

IBM 744
ICL 158–60
idea generation 145–8
idle time 392–3
IKEA 4–5
illumination levels 325
immediate supply networks 177
Imperial Car Rental 83
importance–performance matrix
    661–3
improvement groups 751–3
in-process checks 705
indented bill of materials 508–9
independent demand 350–1
infinite loading 357
information–processing 15,
    277–84, 447
infrastructural strategies 70–1
innovation 263–4, 664–5, 769
input inventories 424
input–output analysis 672–4
integrated hierarchy supply chains
    480–1
integrated services digital networks
    (ISDN) 280
integrated technology 275–6, 295
Intel Corporation 318–20
interactive design 165–71
internal customer/supplier concept
    20–1, 738–40
internal failure costs 743
international trade 472
inventories
    ABC system 443–7
    anticipation inventories 423
    buffer inventories 422, 530
    costs 424–6, 436
    cycle inventories 422
    definition 419
    information systems 447
    need for 421
    perpetual physical inventory
        (PPI) checking 513
    pipeline inventories 423
    profiles 426

record files 447, 511–13
and speed of response 52
systems development 423–4,
    425
types of stored material 419–20
value 420–1, 443–7
see also ordering
ISDN (integrated services digital
    networks) 280
Ishikawa, K. 733, 735
ISO 9000 747–9
item master files 512

Japanese companies 191–2, 720,
    783
JIT, *see* just-in-time (JIT)
job design
    behavioural approach 327–30,
        332
    division of labour 308–10, 332
    elements of 304–6
    empowerment 330–2
    ergonomics 321–6, 332
    neurological aspects 322
    objectives 307–8
    scientific management 310–20,
        332
job enlargement 330
job enrichment 330
job involvement 330–2
job rotation 329–30
jobbing processes 127
Johannesburg International Airport
    228
Johnson's Rule 365–6
Juran, J.M. 733, 735
just-in-time (JIT)
    and capacity utilization 532
    combined with MRP 556–60
    compared to MRP 555–6
    compared to traditional
        approaches 530–1
    definition 529
    eliminating waste 535–6
    high dependency theory 534
    and layout 539
    philosophy of 532–7
    planning and control 542–8,
        558, 560
    requirements 532

in service operations 549–55
techniques 537–41

kaizen 536–7, 665–7
kanban 542–5
Kaston Pyral Services Ltd (KPS)
    672–4, 675–6, 678, 679,
    680, 681–2, 683
Kirkland, Graham 560
Kneen, Mark 296
Kodak 781
Kotler, P. 84
Kruger, Gerrit 449

labour
    costs 186–8
    skills 192, 306
    workforce size 393
    see also staff
land costs 188
LANs (local area networks)
    279–80
Last-In-First-Out (LIFO)
    sequencing 359
layout
    basic procedure 214–16
    cell 219–23, 240–4
    detailed designs 216, 228–53
    fixed position 216–17, 218–19,
        230–5
    and just-in-time 539
    objectives of a good layout
        229–30
    process layout 217, 219, 235–40
    product layout 223, 244–53
    selection of 227–8
    types of 215–25
    and volume–variety 225–7
lead time usage 438
level capacity plans 388–90, 399,
    401
level scheduling 503, 545–7
levels of assembly 505
Lever Pond's 685
life cycles 121, 204–5, 262–3, 568
lighting 325
Limbada, Zak 641–2
line stop authority 537
line-balancing 244, 246
Little Chef 550–3

loading 355–7
local area networks (LANs) 279–80
location of capacity 185–97
  costs 186–91
  decision process 185–6
    centre-of-gravity method 195–7
    objectives of 186
    weighted scoring method 194–5
  demand-side influences 192–7
  international networks 780–1
  resource location analysis 230–5
  site suitability 192
  supply-side influences 186–92
location files 512
location of jobs 306
logistics 458, 460, 475, 483, 592–3
London Ambulance Service 572
longest operation sequencing 359
L'Oreal 540
lot tolerance percentage defective (LTPD) 640
Lundberg, Debbie 170

McDonald's 783
machine tools 264–5
maintenance 711–19
  mixed strategies 713–15
  preventive maintenance 712, 715–16
  Total Productive Maintenance (TPM) 717–19
make-or-buy decisions 465–6
make-to-order 353–5
make-to-stock 353–5
Malcolm Baldridge National Quality Award 755
Malcomess, Bob 253
management information systems (MIS), see information processing
managers 6, 30–3, 571
manufacturing
  master production schedules 501
  operations 110
  process types 126–8

quality approach 612
technologies 272–7
Manufacturing Resource Planning (MRP II) 494, 495, 519–20
marketing 145, 149, 768
marketing mix 393
Marks & Spencer 438, 476
mass processes 127
mass production 784
mass services 128
master production schedules 501–4
material scheduling 537
materials management 458, 472–3
materials processing 14, 264–77
Materials Requirements Planning, see MRP I
memo-motion video recording 819
merchandising 474
method study 311, 313–20
micro-motion analysis 819
mix flexibility 57–8
mixed layouts 224–5
mixed modelling 547–8
Molex SA 64
monotony of tasks 309
Moolman, Gerry 603–4
motion economy 318
motivation 328
Motorola 629
moving-average based forecasting 802
MRP I (Materials Requirements Planning)
  back scheduling 514–17
  bill of materials 504, 508–11
  closed-loop systems 518–19
  customer orders 497–8
  definition 494, 495
  demand management 496–7
  forecast demand 498–500
  information requirements 496
  inventory records 511–13
  levels of assembly 505
  master production schedules 501–4
  netting process 513–14
  product structure shapes 506–7
MRP II (Manufacturing Resource

Planning) 494, 495, 519–20
multi-culturalism 781
multi-echelon inventory system 424, 467–8
multi-sourcing 465, 466
multinational companies 781
multiple-activity charts 818

Nampak Polyfoil 333
Nando's International 790
National Blood Service 448
netting process 513–14
network planning 592–603
  crashing networks 602–3
  critical path method (CPM) 593–8
  operations networks 177–80
  programme evaluation and review technique (PERT) 598–600
  resource constraints 601–2
News International 269
Nine O'Clock News 57
Nishio Pump 720
Nissan Motors 669
noise levels 325–6
non-productive work 309
Northern Telecom 52
numerically controlled (NC) machine tools 264–5
NUMMI plant 314–15

Oakland, John 734, 736
objectives
  of design activities 108, 112
  of job design 307–8
  of layout 229–30
  order-winning objectives 78–9
  in project planning and control 574–6
  see also performance objectives
obsolescence costs 426
office ergonomics 326, 327
Oldham, G. 328, 329
operations focus 538
operations function 6, 7–10
  concept screening 150
  Four-Stage Model 45–7
  hierarchies 18–20
  role of 42–4

types of operations 23–9
operations management
    definition 6
    model 33–5
operations managers 6, 30–3
operations networks 177–80
operations strategy 70–5
    content and process 74–5
    definition 71
    and design activities 91, 92
    effectiveness 772–4
    ethical considerations 774–8
    formulation procedures 767,
        769–72
    generic strategies 767–9
    globalization 778–84
    hierarchical model 71–3
    improvement activities 93, 94–5
    need for 766
    and performance objectives
        95–6
    and planning and control 91–3
    purpose of 94
    structural and infrastructural
        strategies 70–1
    see also strategy
optimized production technology
    (OPT) 520–1
order lead times 437–8
order-winning objectives 78–9
ordering
    economic batch quantity (EBQ)
        model 431–3
    economic order quantity (EOQ)
        formula 427–31, 435–6
    information system 447
    for a specific event 434–5
    timing of orders 436–43
    see also sales orders
organizational culture 304, 536
organizational structure 169–71
Ouma's Koeksisters (OK) 248–9
outlook matrix 407–10
over-booking 396
over-production 535
overtime 392–3

P:D ratios 353–5
Paddick, Chief Inspector 410–11
Pareto charts 681, 683

Pareto law 443
part-time staff 393
path of movement techniques 819
PDCA cycle 667–70
performance measurement 652–7
    benchmarking 655–7, 658
    importance–performance matrix
        661–3
    judging performance against
        competitors 660
    setting standards 653–5
performance objectives 48–65,
    76–90
    competitor influences 79–82
    costs 50, 62–5
    customer influences 77–8, 79
    dependability 50, 53–6, 61
    of design activities 108
    flexibility 56–61
    and operations strategy 95–6
    order-winning and qualifying
        objectives 78–9
    polar representation 90
    product/service life cycle
        influence 84–9
    and products 80
    quality 49–50
    in services 81
    speed of response 51–3
    trade-off paradigm 785–7
periodic review re-stocking 441–2
perpetual physical inventory (PPI)
    checking 513
personal computers (PCs) 262–3
personnel, see staff
Petré, Paola 369–70
Phillips, Alan 34–5
phone surveys 705
physical distribution management
    467–72
    contract terms 471
    costs 457
    multi-echelon inventory system
        424, 467–8
    warehouses 468
    see also transportation
pipeline inventories 423
planning 32, 345
    failure planning 721–3
    see also network planning

planning bills of materials 511
planning and control
    constraints on 344–5
    definition 343–4
    independent and dependent
        demand 350–1
    loading 355–7
    make-to-order 353–5
    make-to-stock 353–5
    resource-to-order 352
    scheduling 360–6, 367–8
    sequencing 358–60
    timescales 346–7
    volume–variety effect 366–9,
        558–9
Platts–Gregory procedure 771,
    773
point-of-departure interviews 705
poka-yoke, see fail-safeing
polar representation of
    performance objectives 90
precedence diagrams 247, 249
predetermined motion-time
    systems (PMTS) 814
Pretoria Portland Cement
    Company 641–2
prevention of failure 704, 742
preventive maintenance 712,
    715–16
pricing 394, 396
problem diagnosis 614–17
problem identification 680
problem solving 537
process capability 626–8
process charts 815–17
process definition 152–5
process technology
    innovation in 263–4
    life cycle effects 262–3
    management 263
    and product/service technology
        261–2
processes
    design 108–11, 143
    flow charts 152–3, 154, 156,
        318–20, 674–6
    layout 217, 219, 235–40
    in manufacturing 126–8
    selecting process type 125–30,
        215

in services 128–9
waste 536
product–process matrix 129–30
product/service technology
    innovation in 263–4
    life cycle effects 262–3
    and process technology 261–2
production flow analysis (PFA)
    243–4
production inefficiency costs 426
production kanban 542, 544
products
    concept aspect 142–3
    concept generation 145–8
    concept screening 149–50
    defective goods 536
    design activities 31–2, 108–11,
        143, 619
    and layout 223, 244–53
    liability 706
    life cycle 84–9, 204–5
    performance objectives 80
    product/service flexibility 57
    quality approaches 613
    structure shapes 506–7
    time content 112
professional services 128
programme evaluation and review
    technique (PERT) 598–600
programmes 568
project managers 571
project processes 126–7
project-based organization
    structures 169–71
projects
    complexity of 569, 570
    control process 586–91
    costs 576, 588
    definition of the project 574–8
    effects of uncertainty on 569–70
    elements of 568–9
    intervening to change 590–1
    management 570–2
    monitoring 587
    performance assessment 587–90
    planning process 578–86
    relationships and dependencies
        582–4
    schedules 584–6
    scope of 576–7

specification 577
strategy 578
time and resource estimates
    580–2
understanding the environment
    573–4
prototyping 162–4
public sector purchasing 486
pull scheduling 363–5, 558
purchasing 460–7
    and costs 460–3
    international trade 472
    make-or-buy decisions 465–6
    public sector 486
    and quality 464
    quantity 463–4
    sourcing decisions 465
    timing of delivery 463–4
push scheduling 363–5

qualifying factors 78–9
quality
    acceptance sampling 636–41,
        642
    approaches to 612–13
    awards 754–5
    checking products/services
        622–4
    conformance to specification
        617–24
    costs 734, 741–6
    customer's view 614
    definition 612
    and flexible manufacturing
        systems (FMS) 272
    importance of 611, 612
    measurement of characteristics
        620, 621
    operation's view 613–14
    as a performance objective
        49–50
    problem diagnosis 614–17
    product design 17, 619
    and purchasing 464
    in services 17
    standards 464, 620–4, 747–9
    Type I and II errors 623, 624,
        630, 639–40
    and vertical integration 183–4
    volume–variety influences 122–3

see also statistical process control
    (SPC); Total Quality
    Management (TQM)
quality circles 733, 751–2
quality function deployment
    (QFD) 157–60
quality loss function (QLF) 733
quality of working life (QWL)
    307, 328, 538
Quasar 291
'questioning technique' 316–17
questionnaires 705
queueing theory 403–7

Racal Recorders 500
Raj Siriram 132–3
Rank Xerox 465, 656
recovery procedures 704, 720–3,
    721
redundancy 708–10
Reeks, Mary 97
regional configuration 780, 781
regression models 803–4
reliability 700–1, 707–20
    designing out fail points 708
    fail-safeing 710–11
    maintenance 711–19
        mixed strategies 713–15
        preventive maintenance 712,
            715–16
        Total Productive Maintenance
            (TPM) 717–19
    redundancy 708–10
reorganizer strategy 768–9
repetitive strain injury (RSI) 310
research & development (R&D)
    146, 147
resource-to-order 352
resources
    allocating to cells 242–3
    constraints 601–2
    location analysis 230–5
    requirement plans (RRP) 518
    transformation model 11–14
revenues 379
reverse engineering 146–7
risk management 53
Robeco Group 287
Robert Bosch GmbH 465
robotics 265–6

Ross Young 462
Rotterdam Educational Group
    (REG) 238–40
rough-cut capacity plans (RCCP)
    519
routing sheets 154
Rover 94–5
run to breakdown (RTB) 712

SABS 0157 464, 747–9
sales orders
    forecasting 498–500
    variation in 497–8
sampling
    acceptance sampling 636–41,
        642
    activity sampling 814
    see also statistical process control
        (SPC)
sampling plans 638–41
Sasol Synthetic Fuels 749
scale of technology 294
Scania 268
scatter diagrams 676
scheduling 360–6, 367–8
scientific management of job
    design 310–20, 332
seasonality of demand 382–3
seasonality of supply 382
semi-hierarchy supply chains
    481–2
Sentech (Pty) Ltd 603–4
sequencing 358–60
service level agreements 740
service shops 129
services
    design activities 111
    just-in-time (JIT) activities
        549–55
    master production schedules
        501
    performance objectives 81
    process types 128–9
    quality 17
    recovery procedures 721
    see also products
set-up reduction (SUR) 539–40
Shandon Scientific Ltd 224
shareholders 778
shortest operation sequencing 360

Siemens 164
simo chart 819–20
simulation 118–19
simultaneous development 166–7
single-card kanban system 543
single-level bill of materials 508
single-sourcing 465, 466
site suitability 192
skills and capabilities 192, 306
Skinner, Wickham 785–6
small simple machines technique
    539
SNCF rail network 696
sourcing decisions 465
Spar Group 221
speed of response 51–3, 123, 184,
    379, 532
Staedtler 509–10
staff
    and concept generation 146
    customer–staff technology
        interaction 286
    development 537–8
    and ethical decision making 777
    failures 697
    part-time 393
    skills and capabilities 192, 306
    socialized into non-creativity
        788
statistical process control (SPC)
    624–36
    control charts 625, 631–6
    control limits 628, 629–31,
        633–5
    variation in process quality
        625–31
stock, see inventories
stock-out costs 426
storage costs 426
strategy
    capacity strategies 198–206, 378
    configuration strategy 780–1
    corporate 71, 73
    and creativity 784–8
    functional 72
    implementing 788–92
    management responsibilities 31
    of projects 578
    structural 70–1
    trade-off paradigm 784–7

see also operations strategy
structural strategies 70–1
sub-contracting 393
suggestion involvement 330
supplier quality assurance (SQA)
    programmes 464
suppliers 426, 673–4, 697, 777
supply chains
    coordinating the chain 478–9
    definition 458–60
    dependability of supply 380
    Forrester Effect 479
    immediate supply networks 177
    logistics 458, 460, 475, 483,
        592–3
    management 458, 475–9
    materials management 458,
        472–3
    merchandising 474
    reconciling supply and demand
        344
    relationship types 479–87
    seasonality of supply 382
    total supply networks 177–8
    uncertainty of supply 350
    see also physical distribution
        management; purchasing
surveys 705
Swatch 7
Sweeney, Mike 767
Synchro Signals and Control
    (SSC) 74, 86–7, 88
synchronization 548–9
system failure, see failure

T-shape product structures 507
Tabane, Andreas 521–2
Taguchi, G. 733, 735
Taguchi methods 161–2
targets 498, 654–5
task allocation 305
task sequence 305
task-rotation 306
task-time variation 245–6
Taylorism 310–11
teams 331, 752
technology
    customer processing 284–92
    degrees of automation 292–3
    degrees of integration 275–6, 295

information processing 277–84
manufacturing 272–7
materials processing 264–77
process technology 261–4
product/service technology 261–4
scale of 294
telecommunications 280–1
teleprocessing 277, 278
temperature at work 324–5
Temple University Hospital 553–5
Tesco 282
TGV trains 696
theoretical design capacity 386–7
Theory of Constraints (TOC) 520
tiger teams 752
time analysis of activities 596–8
time estimation 806–14
time relationship techniques 818
time series analysis 800–3
time-to-market (TTM) 165
timescales in planning and control 346–7
timing of orders 436–43
TML (Trans-Manche Link) 583
total people involvement 540–1
Total Productive Maintenance (TPM) 534, 539, 717–19
Total Quality Management (TQM)
    contribution of individuals 740–1
    costs of quality 741–6
    and customer needs/expectations 736–8
    definition 734, 736
    implementation 750–3
    internal customer/supplier concept 738–40
    loss of effectiveness 753–4
    origins 732–4
    and quality control 736
    systems and procedures 747–9

total supply networks 177–8
Toyota 314, 534, 549
trade-off paradigm 784–7, 785–7
trading commitments 485–6
training 308, 753
    customers in technology use 290–2
transaction files 512
transcendent approach to quality 612
transferring operations practices 783–4
transformation model 10–17, 33, 111–12
transportation 468–70, 535–6
    costs 188, 200, 472
triage system 364
Type I errors 623, 624, 630, 639–40
Type II errors 624, 630, 639–40

Umgeni Water 756
University of Port Elizabeth 779
user-based approach to quality 613
utilization of capacity 386, 387–8, 532

V-shape product structures 507
value engineering 160–1
value-based approach to quality 613
variation dimension 26
variation in process quality 625–31
    assignable causes 628–31
    common causes 625–6
    process capability 626–8
variety, see volume–variety
VBA (Verenigde Bloemenveilingen Aalsmeer) 283–4
vendor kanban 542
vertical integration 180–4
vertical loading 329

virtual reality 120
visibility measures 541
volume flexibility 58
volume–variety
    characteristics 273–4
    costs 124
    and design activities 122–5
    and layout type 225–7
    and planning and control 366–9, 558–9
    and quality 122–3
    variety dimension 25
    volume dimension 23–5, 112
Volvo 120
Voss, Professor Chris 272

waiting times 535
warehouses 468
weighted scoring capacity location method 194–5
Wheelwright, S.C. 44–5, 767
why–why analysis 682, 684
Wight, Oliver 519–20
Wilkins, Charles 685
Wimpy 467
WIZARD system 368
Woolworths 483
work breakdown structures (WBS) 579–80
work measurement 311, 807–15
work patterns scheduling 367–8
work study 311
work-in-progress (WIP) 424
workforce size 393
working capital 379, 426
working temperature 324–5
workplace design 322

$\overline{X}$-$\overline{R}$ charts 632–3
X-shape product structures 507
Xerox 465, 656

Yamazaki Mazak 270–1
yield management 395–6